HP-UX 11i System Administration Handbook and Toolkit

ISBN 0-13-060081-4

90000

9 780130 600813

Hewlett-Packard® Professional Books

OPERATING SYSTEMS

Fernandez	Configuring CDE: The Common Desktop Environment
Lund	Integrating UNIX and PC Network Operating Systems
Madell	Disk and File Management Tasks on HP-UX
Poniatowski	HP-UX 11i System Administration Handbook and Toolkit
Poniatowski	HP-UX 11.x System Administration Handbook and Toolkit
Poniatowski	HP-UX 11.x System Administration "How To" Book
Poniatowski	HP-UX System Administration Handbook and Toolkit
Poniatowski	Learning the HP-UX Operating System
Poniatowski	UNIX User's Handbook
Rehman	HP Certified, HP-UX System Administration
Sauers, Weygant	HP-UX Tuning and Performance
Stone, Symons	UNIX Fault Management
Weygant	Clusters for High Availability: A Primer of HP Solutions, Second Edition

ONLINE/INTERNET

Amor	The E-business (R)evolution: Living and Working in an Interconnected World
Greenberg, Lakeland	A Methodology for Developing and Deploying Internet and Intranet Solutions
Greenberg, Lakeland	Building Professional Web Sites with the Right Tools
Ketkar	Working with Netscape Server on HP-UX
Klein	Building Enhanced HTML Help with DHTML and CSS
Werry, Mowbray	Online Communities: Commerce, Community Action, and the Virtual University

NETWORKING/COMMUNICATIONS

Blommers	OpenView Network Node Manager: Designing and Implementing an Enterprise Solution
Blommers	Practical Planning for Network Growth
Bruce, Dempsey	Security in Distributed Computing: Did You Lock the Door?
Lucke	Designing and Implementing Computer Workgroups

ENTERPRISE

Blommers	Architecting Enterprise Solutions with UNIX Networking
Cook	Building Enterprise Information Architectures
Missbach/Hoffmann	SAP Hardware Solutions: Servers, Storage, and Networks for mySAP.com
Pipkin	Halting the Hacker: A Practical Guide to Computer Security
Pipkin	Information Security: Protecting the Global Enterprise
Sperley	The Enterprise Data Warehouse, Volume 1: Planning, Building, and Implementation
Thornburgh	Fibre Channel for Mass Storage
Thornburgh, Schoenborn	Storage Area Networks: Designing and Implementing a Mass Storage System
Todman	Designing a Data Warehouse: Supporting Customer Relationship Management

PROGRAMMING

IMAGE PROCESSING

OTHER TITLES OF INTEREST

Hewlett-Packard Professional Books

MORE BOOKS FROM MARTY PONIATOWSKI

HP-UX 11i System Administration Handbook and Toolkit

◆

HP-UX 11.x System Administration Handbook and Toolkit

◆

HP-UX 11.x System Administration "How To" Book, Second Edition

◆

HP-UX System Administration Handbook and Toolkit

◆

HP-UX 10.x System Administration "How To" Book

◆

Learning the HP-UX Operating System

HP-UX 11i System Administration
Handbook and Toolkit

Marty Poniatowski

Hewlett-Packard Company

www.hp.com/hpbooks

Prentice Hall PTR
Upper Saddle River, New Jersey 07458
www.phptr.com

Library of Congress Cataloging-in-Publication Data

Poniatowski, Marty.
    HP-UX 11i system administration Handbook and toolkit / Marty Poniatowski.
      p. cm. -- (Hewlett-Packard professional books)
    Includes index.
    ISBN 0-13-060081-4
    1. HP-UX.   2. Operating systems (Computers)   I. Title.   II. Series.

    QA76.76.O63 P6475 2001
    005.4'4769--dc21   2001018549

Editorial/production supervision: *Patti Guerrieri*
Cover design director: *Jerry Votta*
Cover design: *Talar Agasyan*
Manufacturing manager: *Alexis Heydt*
Acquisitions editor: *Jill Pisoni*
Editorial assistant: *Justin Somma*
Marketing manager: *Dan DePasquale*

Manager, Hewlett-Packard Retail Book Publishing: *Patricia Pekary*
Editor, Hewlett-Packard Professional Books: *Susan Wright*

Published by Prentice Hall PTR
Prentice-Hall, Inc.
Upper Saddle River, New Jersey 07458

Prentice Hall books are widely used by corporations and government agencies for training, marketing, and resale.

The publisher offers discounts on this book when ordered in bulk quantities. For more information, contact Corporate Sales Department, Phone: 800-382-3419; FAX: 201-236-7141;
E-mail: corpsales@prenhall.com
Or write: Prentice Hall PTR, Corporate Sales Dept., One Lake Street, Upper Saddle River, NJ 07458.

All products or company names mentioned herein are the trademarks or registered trademarks of their respective owners.

Printed in the United States of America
10 9 8 7 6 5 4 3 2

ISBN 0-13-060081-4

Prentice-Hall International (UK) Limited, *London*
Prentice-Hall of Australia Pty. Limited, *Sydney*
Prentice-Hall Canada Inc., *Toronto*
Prentice-Hall Hispanoamericana, S.A., *Mexico*
Prentice-Hall of India Private Limited, *New Delhi*
Prentice-Hall of Japan, Inc., *Tokyo*
Pearson Education Asia Pte. Ltd.
Editora Prentice-Hall do Brasil, Ltda., *Rio de Janeiro*

UNIX Section

CHAPTER 23   Introduction to Shell Programming   1487

HP-UX and Windows Interoperability Section

PREFACE

About The Book

The change in name from HP-UX 11 to HP-UX 11i (i for Internet) reflects the intense focus of HP-UX on the Internet. Whether your HP-UX-based application is directly connected to the Internet or not, chances are the the Internet has made it more critical. Some of the most "traditional" applications that are many layers deep within companies have still been affected by the Internet. For example, it used to be that human resources information was kept under lock and key and was totally inaccessible from the outside world - now we're posting job openings on-line. Pricing information was shared only between sales people and their valued customers - now we have Internet-based auctions. I'm sure you've seen the impact the Internet has had on your HP-UX applications, making them more critical to the success of your business and making your knowledge as an HP-UX system administrator more valuable as well.

The paradox of the Internet age is that you need printed books more than ever to get your system administration job done. Athough system administrators use the Internet to obtain a lot of useful information, books are more essential than ever to keeping up with advancements in operating systems. The *HP-UX 11i System Administration Handbook and Toolkit* is here to give you the information you need to get your HP-UX systems up and running quickly.

As in all of my books, I cover what my customers tell me are the most critical aspects of HP-UX system administration. You can cover a lot in 1500 pages - but not everything. I carefully decided what material to cover in this book. Most of the material in the book is new or updated information from previous books. There are many advancements in the area of system administration that are new in HP-UX 11i.

One of the requests I received since my last book was published was to cover more on system setup before booting the HP-UX operating system. I now cover the boot process (PDC, ISL, hpux), Secure Web Console setup, Guardian Service Processor (GSP) setup, and other important setup topics in the first chapter.

As with my other books, this book includes a blueprint from which you can work. Many tips and recommendations are included in the book from my experience of working with HP-UX, as well as what I have learned working with many HP-UX system administrators over the years.

No matter how detailed a training course or manual, it always leaves out some of the specific tasks you'll need to perform. Instead of getting mired down in excruciating detail, I'll provide the common denominator of information every HP-UX system administrator needs to know. I'll provide you with all the essential information you'll need so that you'll be able to take on new and unforeseen system administration challenges with a good knowledge base.

You may very well find that you need additional resources as your system administration challenges increase. No matter what anyone tells you, no single resource can answer everything you need to know about HP-UX system administration. Just when you think you know everything there is to know about HP-UX system administration, you'll be asked to do something you've never dreamed of before. That's why I'm not trying to be all things to all people with this book. I cover what everyone needs to know and leave topics in specific areas to other people. You may need training courses, manuals, other books, or consulting services to complete some projects. In any case, I'll bet that every topic in this book would be worthwhile to know for every HP-UX system administrator. *HP-UX 11i System Administration Handbook and Toolkit* covers tasks all system administrators need to perform: It shows you how to perform each task, tells why you are doing it, and explains how it is affecting your system. Much of the knowledge I have gained has come from the fine HP-UX manual set and the concise on-line manual pages. Some of the procedures in the book are based on those in the HP-UX manual set and some of the command summaries in the book are based on the on-line manual pages. I am grateful for all of the hard work my HP associates have put into both the manual set and the on-line manual pages.

Speaking of examples, there have been many new HP 9000 hardware advancements made since my last book was published. Most of the examples have been updated to include new hardware, however, there are hundreds of thousands of existing systems that will be upgraded to HP-UX 11i so you will see examples on some older systems as well. There are also many system administration aspects of HP-UX that haven't changed since HP-UX 10.x, so the examples would apply on any hardware.

I hope you enjoy reading the book and learning the material as much as I did writing it.

Marty Poniatowski

marty_poniatowski@hp.com

Organization of The Book

The HP-UX 11i System Administration Handbook and Toolkit is composed of the chapters shown in the Table of Contents and on the inside cover of the book. This book is divided into the following three sections:

- Section 1 - HP-UX
- Section 2 - UNIX®
- Section 3 -   Windows® and HP-UX Interoperability

I have Section 2 due to the many requests I received to provide UNIX background for those readers with limited exposure to UNIX. Thus, this is a complete HP-UX system administration book, including this UNIX background.

Relevant URLs

There are many Web sites that can assist you in your HP-UX system administration endeavors. I have listed some of the more prominent HP-UX-related Web sites below as they existed at the time of this writing:

IT Resource Center
(This is essential for every HP-UX administrator):
http://www.itrc.com

Technical documentation, including most all HP-UX documents:
http://www.docs.hp.com

Software depot home page:
http://www.software.hp.com

vPar product information:
http://www.hp.com/go/servicecontrol

vPar User's Guide:
http://docs.hp.com/hpux/

Instant Capacity on Demand (iCOD):
http://www.hp.com/go/icod

The International Association of HP Computing Professionals:
http://www.interex.org

Configurable kernel parameters:

http://docs.hp.com/hpux/onlinedocs/os/KCparams.OverviewAll.html

Index of HP-UX online documents:

http://docs.hp.com/hpux/onlinedocs/os

Register name servers at:

http://www.icann.org/registrars/accredited-list.html.

Excellent unsupported system administration scripts at:

ftp://contrib:9unsupp8@hprc.external.hp.com/sysadmin/

Software used for UNIX and Windows interoperability at:

http://www.hummingbird.com/products/evals/index.html

Manual Pages Supplied with this Book

I am most grateful to Hewlett Packard Company for having allowed me to include select HP-UX manual pages in this book. I have received a great deal of positive feedback on the inclusion of manual pages in my previous books. Many readers find it helpful to have the manual pages in the book to refer to when reading it when there is no system available to check on a command (apparently a lot of people are reading my books while not at the office).

The manual pages included in the book are for HP-UX 10.x. This is done only for formatting reasons - the 10.x manual pages looked much better when inserted into the book. There are minimal differences between the manual pages of 10.x and 11i for the commands I have included in this book.

When a command is used for which there is an online manual page included in the book, the following information appears in the margin:

This is a "man page" block, which includes the man page icon, the command name, in this case **isl**, and the chapter number in which the online manual page appears, in this case Chapter 1.

The Table of Contents contains a complete list of the man pages appearing at the end of each chapter. The man pages for a command appear in the chapter to which the command is most applicable, even if it is not the first chapter in which the command is used. Commands pertaining to performance, for instance, have their man pages in the performance chapter, even if those commands are mentioned in an earlier chapter.

Acknowledgments

There were too many people involved in helping me with this book to list each and every one. I have, therefore, decided to formally thank those who wrote sections of the book and those who took time to review it. I'm still not sure whether it takes more time to write something or review something that has been written to ensure it is correct.

Duane Zitzner

Duane Zitzner is President Computing Systems and Vice President Hewlett-Packard Company. Duane acted as the executive champion and sponsor of this book. His support was invaluable in helping get the resources necessary to complete this book.

The Author - Marty Poniatowski

Marty has been a Technical consultant with Hewlett-Packard Company for fourteen years in the New York area. He has worked with hundreds of Hewlett Packard customers in many industries, including Internet startups, financial services, and manufacturing.

Marty has been widely published in computer industry trade publications. He has published over 50 articles on various computer-related topics. In addition to this book, he is the author of nine other Prentice Hall books: Marty holds an M.S. in Information Systems from Polytechnic University (Brooklyn, NY), an M.S. in Management Engineering from the University of Bridgeport (Bridgeport, CT), and a B.S. in Electrical Engineering from Roger Williams University (Bristol, RI).

Donna Kelly

Donna wrote the "Common Desktop Environment (CDE)" chapter of this book and reviewed almost every chapter in the book. Donna and I have collaborated on a number of projects together. Donna has painstakingly reviewed many of my books for both technical accuracy and readability.

Donna is both a technical expert in many operating systems and an excellent evaluator of the usefulness of a topic and the way it is covered. She not only ensures that the material is technically accurate, but she also makes certain that each topic is covered in a useful manner and that it is easy to read and comprehend.

Donna has been responsible for a number of computing environments of Hewlett Packard in Roseville, CA. She has experience with several operating systems, including HP-UX, MPE, and AS/400. Donna is also a Microsoft Certified Systems Engineer (MCSE).

Elizabeth Zinkann

Elizabeth reviewed all of the chapters in the UNIX section of the book.

Elizabeth is a Contributing Editor and Review Columnist for *Sys Admin Magazine*, The Journal for UNIX System Administrators. Her articles have also appeared in Performance Computing, Linux Magazine, and Network Administrator. As an independent computer consultant, she has built Linux servers, maintained computers utilizing Linux, Solaris, Macintosh, and Windows environments, and taught UNIX, shell programming, and Internet essentials. In a former life, she also programmed communications features for both domestic and international databases at AT&T Network Systems.

Brian Hackley

Brian supplied material on DNS and BIND (along with Corey Dow), NFS Performance Assessment (along with Pat Kilfoyle), and NIS background used in various sections throughout the book. Brian is a member of the Hewlett Packard North American Response Center UNIX Network Team (NETUX.)

Brian came to Hewlett Packard as a result of the HP-Apollo merger in 1989. Until 1993, he was an Offline Technical Marketing Support Engineer, responsible for NPI (New Product Introduction) for Apollo Domain network products, and later part of the HP-UX 9.0x and 10.0 project teams. Brian moved into the Chelmsford Response Center in 1993, where he worked first as a NETUX-Foreground, and then an NETUX-Background, Engineer. During this time, Brian began telecommuting full-time for HP.

Brian worked for Sun Microsystems in 1995 and 1996, and returned to HP and re-joined the HP Response Center NETUX Team in early 1997. Assignments since his return include HP-UX Network Response Center Engineer for High Availability and Strategic Enterprise (HASE) customers, HP-UX Network Product Competency Center RCE, and most recently, a Network Business Recovery Specialist for Mission Critical Support.

Brian lives and works in Lexington Massachusetts, is married to Wendy Carter, Registered Pharmacist. They have a son, Steve who is a Computer Science Major at Lawrence Technological College in Southfield, Michigan.

Corey Dow

Corey supplied material on DNS and BIND, collaborating with Brian Hackley. Corey is a Senior Engineer working for the North American Response Center UNIX Network Team (NETUX) out of Roseville, California.

Corey began his career with HP in 1998, starting as a UNIX Networking Engineer in Atlanta, responding to customer calls regarding Internet Services and Lan Link protocols, before moving to the Roseville facility in early 1999. He has provided DNS consulting services to Fortune 500 companies such as Motorola, assisting in the migration of their nameservers to newer releases, and has attended classes taught by Cricket Lui, former HP hostmaster and author of several DNS books.

Corey enjoys spending free time with his girlfriend, Valerie, living each day to the fullest.

Pat Kilfoyle

Pat (along with Brain Hackley) supplied material on DNS and BIND, NFS Performance Assessment, and NIS background used in various sections throughout the book.

Pat received a BSEE from the University of Alaska in 1983. He came to work for HP as a Customer Engineer in the Bellevue, WA office immediately afterwards.

Pat then moved into a network support position, where he became involved in all aspects of network support including: NFS; X.25; interconnect devices such as bridges, routers, LANs, and WAN; and even worked as a project manager on cabling and ifrastructure projects.

In 1991, Pat joined the HP Escalation Center supporting the full range of networking products that included hardware and software for the HP 9000, HP 3000, and Intel servers.

In 1994 Pat became involved in the support of networking software and support tools development. He specialized in socket programming, NFS, kernel transport, LAN driver code areas, and kernel performance support.

Pat is currently a Senior Systems Support Engineerg on HP's Crisis Management Team. He is assigned to specific customers with HP's Business Continuity Support (BCS.)

Permissions

There is a wealth of information inside of HP in various forms that I was generously given permission to include in this book. In addition to the afore mentioned man pages, I would like to thank the following HP representatives for the permission they granted for material to be used in the book: Aparna Das Caro and Wade Satterfield for the detailed kernel parameter information that is part of the System Administration Manager (SAM); Scott Eldridge for the technical "cheat sheets" included on the CD-ROM; Dimitris Dovas for the N-Class Hardware/Firmware document information that is used in Chapter 1 on the boot process as well as on the CD-ROM; Ute Albert for the Virtual Partitions white paper on which Appendix A is based and that appears on the CD-ROM; and Dionne Morgan for the IT Resource Center information on the CD-ROM. Although much of this information is available either on various HP Web sites or on your system itself, it is valuable to have all of this information as part of this book.

Reviewers

In all there were about 25 reviewers of this book. I'm not sure what makes
someone agree to review a book. You don't get the glory of a contributing
author, but it is just as much work. I would like to thank the many people
who devoted a substantial amount of time to reviewing this book to ensure
that I included topics important to new system administrators and covered
those topics accurately.

Conventions Used in this Book

I don't use a lot of complex notations in the book. Here are a few simple conventions I've used to make the examples clear and the text easy to follow:

$ and #	The HP-UX command prompt. Every command issued in the book is preceded by a command prompt. Either one of these two will be used or a system name are usually used as prompts.
italics	Italics are used for variable values and when referring to functional areas and menu picks in the System Administration Manager (SAM).
bold and " "	Bold text is the information you would type, such as the command you issue after a prompt or the information you type when running a script. Sometimes information you would type is also referred to in the text explaining it, and the typed information may appear in quotes.
<----	When selections have to be made, this convention indicates the one chosen for the purposes of the example.
[ ]	Brackets indicate optional items and command descriptions.
{ }	Curly braces indicate a list from which you must choose.
I	A vertical bar separates items in a list of choices.
<Enter>	Indicates the "Enter" key has been pressed on the keyboard. Sometimes <Return> is used to indicate the return key has been pressed.

One additional convention is that used for command formats. I don't use command formats more than I have to because I could never do as thorough a job describing commands as the HP-UX manual pages. The manual pages go into detail on all HP-UX commands. Here is the format I use when I cover commands:

```
form 1      command [option(s)] [arg(s)]
form 2      command [option(s)] [arg(s)]
form n      command [option(s)] [arg(s)]
```

I try not to get carried away with detail when covering a command, but there are sometimes many components that must be covered in order to understand a command. Here is a brief description of the components listed above:

form # -There are sometimes many forms of a command. If there is more than one form of a command that requires explanation, then I will show more than one form.

command - The name of the executable.

option(s) - Several options may appear across a command line.

cmd_arg(s) - Command arguments such as path name.

CHAPTER 1

Booting (PDC, ISL, hpux), Secure Web Console, GSP Configuration

Background

In the first few sections of this chapter, I want to give you an overview of the low-level boot and configuration of an HP 9000, setting up HP Secure Web Console, and then configuring the Guardian Service Processor (GSP). You might perform these in the opposite order in which I present them. I chose to cover boot first, however, because it is an area of much confusion for new system administrators. Not everyone has a Secure Web Console, so I decided to cover this second. Securing your Guardian Service Processor can be done after the system boots, so I cover this third.

The system used In the examples in this chapter is an L-Class system. I intentionally used a simple system so we could concentrate on the boot process with a minimum amount of hardware-related messages. Reviewing the boot process in this chapter won't make you an HP Customer Engineer (CE) or take the place of any formal training; however, knowing a little of what is going on "pre-operating system" may be helpful. In addition, if you are an experienced UNIX system administrator but haven't before used an HP 9000, these sections will

1

serve as a introduction to booting a system. Since booting varies from system to system, even within the HP 9000 family, this is not a comprehensive study, but rather an overview.

Boot Process Overview

The boot process on an HP 9000 system can be reduced in its simplist form to three steps. I'll provide a quick description of the three steps and then we'll take a look at some example boot processes so we can see these three steps in action. The following is a description of the three steps:

PDC   HP 9000 systems come with firmware installed called Processor Dependent Code (PDC - man page pdc). After the system is powered on or the processor is RESET, the PDC runs self test operations and initializes the processor. PDC also identifies the console path so it can provide messages and accept input. PDC would then begin the "autoboot" process unless you were to interrupt it during the 10-second interval that is supplied. If you interrupt the "autoboot" process, you can issue a variety of commands. The interface to PDC commands is called the Boot Console Handler (BCH.) This is sometimes a point of confusion; that is, are we issuing PDC commands or BCH commands? The commands are normally described as PDC commands and the interface through which you execute them is the BCH.

ISL   The Initial System Loader (ISL - man page isl) is run after PDC. You would normally just run an "autoboot" sequence from ISL; however, there are a number of commands you could run from the ISL prompt.

man page

isl - 1

man page

hpux - 1

hpux   The hpux utility manages loading the HP-UX kernel and gives control to the kernel. ISL can have hpux run an "autoexecute" file or commands can be given interactively. In most situations, you would just want to automatically boot the system; however, we'll take a look at some of the hpux commands you can execute. This is sometimes called the Secondary System Loader (SSL.)

I find there is a lot of confusion related to the boot process for new system administrators. To begin with, there is not much documentation that comes with new systems related to HP 9000 boot. Secondly, without any background on the boot process, it is difficult to determine at which phase of the boot your system is at any given time. Table 1-1 shows some system states and the corresponding prompts you can expect for each state in roughly the order you might see them at the time of system boot:

TABLE 1-1   **/sbin/set_parms** Arguments

Boot State of System	Prompt
Boot Console Handler (BCH) Seen when you discontinue boot within 10 seconds. Used to perform PDC-related work.	`Main Menu: Enter command or menu >`
Initial System Loader (ISL) Seen after PDC-related work.	`ISL> ?`

Boot State of System	Prompt
hpux Prompt varies. You usually issue **hpux** command at ISL prompt to boot. This is sometimes called the Secondary System Loader (SSL).	Varies depending on the state of the system.
Guardian Service Processor (GSP) Seen when you type ^b (control b) to get access to GSP.	GSP>

man page

boot - 1

There is only one way to describe the boot process and that is through example. The boot of a system with minimal hardware will be covered in the upcoming sections. I choose the boot of a system with minimal hardware so as not to get bogged down in hardware-related details, but to instead focus on the boot process. The messages supplied as a result of booting this modest system will allow us to focus on the boot process rather than on the many hardware components. The boot process consists of mostly the same steps for any HP 9000, so you can apply this information to your system. It may be, however, that you have a much larger system with more components that will produce more lengthy boot messages.

Boot Console Handler (BCH) & Processor Dependent Code (PDC)

man page

pdc - 1

As mentioned earlier, HP 9000 systems come with firmware installed called Processor Dependent Code (PDC.) After the system is powered on or the processor is RESET, the PDC runs self test operations and initializes the processor. PDC also identifies the console path so it can provide messages and accept input. PDC would then begin the "auto-boot" process, unless you were to interrupt it during the 10-second interval that is supplied. If you interrupt the "autoboot" process, you can issue a variety of commands.

The following example shows booting an L-Class system and the PDC-related messages we receive on the system. The first messages you see are a variety of self-test-related messages. The processor, memory, I/O and other components are run through a variety of tests. I abbreviated the list of messages in the example, wherever you see three dots, because the complete list of test results was too long to include in this book:

man page

pdc - 1

```
Value of TERM has been set to "vt100".
WARNING:  YOU ARE SUPERUSER !!1.00] (see /etc/issue)
Console Login: root
# reboot -h...checking for disk quotas
Shutdown at 17:41 (in 0 minutes) ckard Co.,  All Rights Reserved.
(c)Copyright 1979, 1980, 1983, 1985-1993 The Regents of the Univ. of California
(c)C*** FINAL System shutdown message from root@hp.serviceengine.com ***
(c)Copyright 1986-1992 Sun Microsystems, Inc.
System going down IMMEDIATELY Massachusetts Institute of Technology
(c)Copyright 1989-1993  The Open Software Foundation, Inc.
System shutdown time has arrivedent Corp.
(c)Copyright 1990 Motorola, Inc.
(c)Copyright 1990, 1991, 1992 Cornell University
(c)Copyright 1989-1991 The University of Maryland
Console reset done.arnegie Mellon University
(c)Copyright 1991-1997 Mentat, Inc.
Boot device reset done.ng Star Technologies, Inc.
(c)Copyright 1996 Progressive Systems, Inc.
(c)Copyright 1997 Isogon Corporation

System has halted
OK to turn off power or reset systemD RIGHTS LEGEND
UNLESS "WAIT for UPS to turn off power" message was printed above to
restrictions as set forth in sub-paragraph (c)(1)(ii) of the Rights in
********** VIRTUAL FRONT PANEL **********se in DFARS 252.227-7013.
System Boot detected
*****************************************
LEDs:  RUN          ATTENTION      FAULT      REMOTE      POWER
       ON           FLASH          OFF        OFF         ON
                          Palo Alto, CA 94304 U.S.A.
platform                 config              626F
processor                slave rendezvous    1C17ies are as set
processor                test                1142
processor                test                1100
processor                test                1100
processor                test                1100
processor                test                1100
processor                test                1100
processor                test                1100
processor                test                1100
processor                test                1100
processor                test                1100
PDH                      config              322F
PDH                      test                3149
PDH                      test                3160
platform                 test                616A
processor                test                1146
processor                INIT                1701
processor                INIT                1701
processor                test                1110
.
```

```
    .
    .
processor                    test                    111C
processor                    test                    111D
processor                    test                    111D
processor  cache             test                    2111
processor  cache             test                    2111
processor  cache             test                    2112
processor  cache             test                    2112
processor  cache             test                    2113
processor  cache             test                    2113
processor  cache             test                    2121
processor  cache             test                    2121
    .
    .
    .
memory                       test                    71A4
memory                       test                    71A5
memory                       test                    71A5
memory                       test                    71A6
memory                       test                    71A6
memory                       config                  7210
I/O                          INIT                    8701
I/O                          test                    8118
I/O                          test                    8118
I/O                          INIT                    8701
I/O                          INIT                    8701
I/O                          INIT                    8701
I/O                          INIT                    8701
I/O                          INIT                    8701
I/O                          INIT                    8701
I/O                          INIT                    8701
I/O                          INIT                    8701
I/O                          INIT                    8701
memory                       config                  7240
memory                       INIT                    7702
memory                       config                  7241
memory                       config                  7243
memory                       config                  72A0
memory                       test                    71A1
memory                       test                    71A2
    .
    .
    .
processor                    test          /         1120
processor                    slave rendezvous        1C40
processor                    test                    1142
processor                    test                    113B
platform                     test                    612A
I/O                          config                  8238


*****************************************

************ EARLY BOOT VFP *************
End of early boot detected
*****************************************

Firmware Version  39.46

Duplex Console IO Dependent Code (IODC) revision 1

--------------------------------------------------------------------------
```

```
--------------------------------------------------------------------------

   Processor   Speed           State          CoProcessor State  Cache Size
   Number                                      State              Inst    Data
   ---------   --------   --------------------  ----------------  -----------
       0       440  MHz   Active                Functional        512 KB   1 MB
       3       440  MHz   Idle                  Functional        512 KB   1 MB

   Central Bus Speed (in MHz)  :        82
   Available Memory            :   2097152  KB
   Good Memory Required        :     11468  KB
```

```
    Primary boot path:     0/0/1/1.2
    Alternate boot path:   0/0/2/0.2
    Console path:          0/0/4/0.0
    Keyboard path:         0/0/4/0.0


Processor is booting from first available device.

To discontinue, press any key within 10 seconds.
```

After the "early" boot is complete, we get a brief system summary, including the firmware revision on our system, and are then given the option to automatically boot off of the primary path or press any key to stop the boot process. Under normal system operation, you would autoboot; however, in our case, we'll interrupt the boot process to see what commands are available in the PDC. When we interrupt the boot process, the following menu appears:

man page

pdc - 1

```
Boot terminated.

---- Main Menu --------------------------------------------------------------

      Command                          Description
      -------                          -----------
      BOot [PRI|ALT|<path>]            Boot from specified path
      PAth [PRI|ALT] [<path>]          Display or modify a path
      SEArch [DIsplay|IPL] [<path>]    Search for boot devices

      COnfiguration menu               Displays or sets boot values
      INformation menu                 Displays hardware information
      SERvice menu                     Displays service commands

      DIsplay                          Redisplay the current menu
      HElp [<menu>|<command>]          Display help for menu or command
      RESET                            Restart the system
----
Main Menu: Enter command or menu >
```

The interface to the PDC is called the Boot Console Handler (BCH.) In our discussion the commands we are issuing are PDC commands and the interface through which we issue them is the BCH. Many of the commands in this menu are helpful to system administrators, but are sometimes ignored because they are pre-operating system and therefore usually overlooked.

We'll skip the first three commands for the time being and start by looking at the *COnfiguration* menu command by typing *co*. The uppercase *"CO"* in *COnfiguration* means you could type just *co* as an abbeviation for configuration:

```
Main Menu: Enter command or menu > co

---- Configuration Menu ----------------------------------------------------

       Command                        Description
       -------                        -----------
       AUto [BOot|SEArch|STart] [ON|OFF] Display or set specified flag
       BootID [<proc>] [<bootid>]     Display or set Boot Identifier
       BootINfo                       Display boot-related information
       BootTimer [0 - 200]            Seconds allowed for boot attempt
       CPUconfig [<proc>] [ON|OFF]    Config/Deconfig processor
       DEfault                        Set the system to predefined values
       FAn [HI|NORmal]                Display or change fan speed
       FastBoot [ON|OFF]              Display or set boot tests execution
       PAth [PRI|ALT] [<path>]        Display or modify a path
       SEArch [DIsplay|IPL] [<path>]  Search for boot devices
       TIme [c:y:m:d:h:m:[s]]         Read or set the real time clock in GMT

       BOot [PRI|ALT|<path>]          Boot from specified path
       DIsplay                        Redisplay the current menu
       HElp [<command>]               Display help for specified command
       RESET                          Restart the system
       MAin                           Return to Main Menu
----
Configuration Menu: Enter command >
```

Under the *COnfiguration* menu are several useful commands. You can, for example, enable *FastBoot* which gives control over tests run at boot time. We'll issue the **FastBoot** command to see how our system is currently set but not change the value of *FastBoot*:

```
Configuration Menu: Enter command > FastBoot

    Fastboot:              OFF

Configuration Menu: Enter command >
```

Our system has *FastBoot off*, meaning we'll run all available tests at boot time. If you would like to reduce system boot time and are willing to bypass boot tests then you would turn *on* FastBoot.

There are a variety of other commands under the *COnfiguration* menu that you may want to issue, depending on your needs, such as *CPUconfig* to configure and deconfigure processors.

Let's now issue the *Main* command to get back to the *Main* menu and then *IN* to get access to the *INformation* menu:

```
Configuration Menu: Enter command > main

---- Main Menu -------------------------------------------------------------

     Command                        Description
     -------                        -----------
     BOot [PRI|ALT|<path>]          Boot from specified path
     PAth [PRI|ALT] [<path>]        Display or modify a path
     SEArch [DIsplay|IPL] [<path>]  Search for boot devices

     COnfiguration menu             Displays or sets boot values
     INformation menu               Displays hardware information
     SERvice menu                   Displays service commands

     DIsplay                        Redisplay the current menu
     HElp [<menu>|<command>]        Display help for menu or command
     RESET                          Restart the system
----
Main Menu: Enter command or menu > IN

---- Information Menu ------------------------------------------------------

     Command                        Description
     -------                        -----------
     ALL                            Display all system information
     BootINfo                       Display boot-related information
     CAche                          Display cache information
     ChipRevisions                  Display revisions of major VLSI
     COprocessor                    Display coprocessor information
     FRU                            Display FRU information
     FwrVersion                     Display firmware version
     IO                             Display I/O interface information
     LanAddress                     Display Core LAN station address
     MEmory                         Display memory information
     PRocessor                      Display processor information
     WArnings                       Display selftest warning messages

     BOot [PRI|ALT|<path>]          Boot from specified path
     DIsplay                        Redisplay the current menu
     HElp [<command>]               Display help for specified command
     RESET                          Restart the system
     MAin                           Return to Main Menu
----
Information Menu: Enter command >
```

The *INformation* menu is a hidden gem for system administrators. Among the menu selections is one to display *ALL* system information, which produces the following report for our L-Class system. I abbreviated this report at the point where you see the three dots near the end of the report:

```
Information Menu: Enter command > all

  Model:                   9000/800/L2000-44

PROCESSOR INFORMATION

                     HVERSION  SVERSION
   Processor  Speed    Model   Model/Op   CVERSION     State
   ---------  -------  -------- ---------  --------  -------------
       0      440 MHz  0x05c4   0x0491     2.  4     Active
       3      440 MHz  0x05c4   0x0491     2.  4     Idle

   Central Bus Speed (in MHz) :        82
   Software ID (dec)          :   143901527
   Software ID (hex)          :  0x0893c357
   Software Capability        :  0x01f0


COPROCESSOR INFORMATION

               Coprocessor   Coprocessor      Coprocessor
   Processor      Model        Revision          State
   ---------   -----------   -----------   -----------------
       0      0x00000010           1       Functional
       3      0x00000010           1       Functional

CACHE INFORMATION

   Processor   Instruction Cache Size   Data Cache Size
   ---------   ----------------------   ---------------
       0              512 KB                 1 MB
       3              512 KB                 1 MB

MEMORY INFORMATION

   MEMORY STATUS TABLE (MB) (Current Boot Status)

Slot 0a   512M   Active
Slot 0b   512M   Active
Slot 1a   512M   Active
Slot 1b   512M   Active

Slot 2a    -
Slot 2b    -
Slot 3a    -
Slot 3b    -

Slot 4a    -
Slot 4b    -
Slot 5a    -
Slot 5b    -

Slot 6a    -
Slot 6b    -
Slot 7a    -
Slot 7b    -

Subtotal 2048M

   TOTAL =  2048 MB
            ---------


                   Memory Installation Guidelines
                   ------------------------------

- For DIMMs to work, both DIMMs in a slot pair (a/b) must be the same type.
   (Same part number = same type)
```

```
  - For proper cooling, install DIMMs in the following order:
     0a/b 1a/b 2a/b 3a/b 4a/b 5a/b 6a/b 7a/b.


     Active, Installed Memory       :       2048  MB of SDRAM
     Deallocated Pages              :          0  Pages
                                           -----------
     Available Memory               :       2048  MB

     Good Memory Required by OS     :         12  MB

           Memory
     HVERSION  SVERSION
     --------  ----------
      0x0950  0x00000900
```

I/O MODULE INFORMATION

Type	Path (dec)	Slot Number	HVERSION	SVERSION	IODC Vers
System bus adapter	0		0x5820	0xb10	0x0
Local bus adapter	0/0	1	0x7820	0xa00	0x0
Local bus adapter	0/1	6	0x7820	0xa00	0x0
Local bus adapter	0/2	8	0x7820	0xa00	0x0
Local bus adapter	0/3	10	0x7820	0xa00	0x0
Local bus adapter	0/4	12	0x7820	0xa00	0x0
Local bus adapter	0/5	7	0x7820	0xa00	0x0
Local bus adapter	0/6	9	0x7820	0xa00	0x0
Local bus adapter	0/7	11	0x7820	0xa00	0x0

PCI DEVICE INFORMATION

Description	Path (dec)	Vendor Id	Device Id	Bus #	Slot #
Ethernet cntlr	0/0/0/0	0x1011	0x19	0	1
SCSI bus cntlr	0/0/1/0	0x1000	0xb	0	1
SCSI bus cntlr	0/0/1/1	0x1000	0xb	0	1
SCSI bus cntlr	0/0/2/0	0x1000	0xf	0	1
SCSI bus cntlr	0/0/2/1	0x1000	0xf	0	1
Comp. ser cntlr	0/0/4/0	0x103c	0x1048	0	2
Comp. ser cntlr	0/0/5/0	0x103c	0x1048	0	2
Ethernet cntlr	0/3/0/0	0x1011	0x19	24	10
SCSI bus cntlr	0/4/0/0	0x1000	0xf	32	12
SCSI bus cntlr	0/4/0/1	0x1000	0xf	32	12
SCSI bus cntlr	0/7/0/0	0x1000	0xf	56	11
SCSI bus cntlr	0/7/0/1	0x1000	0xf	56	11

BOOT INFORMATION

```
     Processor            Boot ID
     ---------            -------
         0                   2
         3                   2

     Autoboot:            ON
     Autosearch:          ON
     Autostart:           ON
     Fastboot:            OFF

     Primary boot path:   intscsib.2
                          0/0/1/1.2
                          0/0/01/01.2     (hex)
     Alternate boot path: intscsia.2
                          0/0/2/0.2
                          0/0/02/0.2      (hex)
     Console path:        0/0/4/0.0
                          0/0/04/0.0      (hex)
     Keyboard path:       0/0/4/0.0
                          0/0/04/0.0      (hex)

     LAN Station Address: 001083-fc9288

     Wed Apr  19 22:02:46 GMT 2000    (20:00:04:19:22:02:46)
```

```
FIRMWARE INFORMATION

    Firmware Version:           39.46

        Module                  Revision
        ------                  --------
        System Board            A443938
        PA 8500 CPU Module      2.4
        PA 8500 CPU Module      2.4

FRU INFORMATION

FRU Name:                   SYS_BD
Part Number:                A5191-60001
Serial Number:              A56405282277
Physical Location:          00ffff0001ffff69
Engineering Date Code: 3938
Art Work Revision:          A4
Scan Revision:
FRU Specific Info:          USS40130E3

FRU Name:                   IO_BP
Part Number:                A5191-60002
Serial Number:              52SCFK23WX
Physical Location:          00ffff0002ffff69
Engineering Date Code: 3942
Art Work Revision:          A2
Scan Revision:
FRU Specific Info:

FRU Name:           LAN_SCSI_CORE_IO
Part Number:                A5191-60011
Serial Number:              52SCFK28DE
Physical Location:          000000ffff01ff85
Engineering Date Code: 3933
Art Work Revision:          A5
Scan Revision:
FRU Specific Info:

    .
    .
    .

FRU Name:                   DIMM_512
Part Number:                A5798-60001
Serial Number:              A56E02093896
Physical Location:          0000ff00001bff74
Engineering Date Code: 3938
Art Work Revision:          A4
Scan Revision:
FRU Specific Info:

Information Menu: Enter command >
```

This report would be an excellent addition to a system administration notebook. Knowing such information as the firmware revision levels and the settings of the boot flags is valuable.

In the previous example, we used the BCH to issue the PDC commands *INformation* and then *ALL*. Both *INformation* and *ALL* are PDC commands issued through the BCH interface. Sometimes PDC and BCH are used interchangeably in documentation, however, knowing that BCH is the interface through which PDC commands are issued will usually serve you well when looking for information on specific commands.

Let's now go back to the *Main* menu and then look at the *SERvice* menu:

```
Service Menu: Enter command > main

---- Main Menu --------------------------------------------------------

     Command                          Description
     -------                          -----------
     BOot [PRI|ALT|<path>]            Boot from specified path
     PAth [PRI|ALT] [<path>]          Display or modify a path
     SEArch [DIsplay|IPL] [<path>]    Search for boot devices

     COnfiguration menu               Displays or sets boot values
     INformation menu                 Displays hardware information
     SERvice menu                     Displays service commands

     DIsplay                          Redisplay the current menu
     HElp [<menu>|<command>]          Display help for menu or command
     RESET                            Restart the system
----
Main Menu: Enter command or menu > ser

---- Service Menu -----------------------------------------------------

     Command                          Description
     -------                          -----------
     CLEARPIM                         Clear (zero) the contents of PIM
     SCSI [option] [<path>] [<val>]   Display or set SCSI controller values
     MemRead <address> [<len>]        Read memory and I/O locations
     PDT [CLEAR]                      Display or clear the PDT
     PIM [<proc>] [HPMC|LPMC|TOC]     Display PIM information
     ProductNum <O|C> [<number>]      Display or set Product Number
     SELftests [ON|OFF]               Enable/disable self test execution

     BOot [PRI|ALT|<path>]            Boot from specified path
     DIsplay                          Redisplay the current menu
     HElp [<command>]                 Display help for specified command
     RESET                            Restart the system
     MAin                             Return to Main Menu
----
Service Menu: Enter command >
```

Among the options you have in *SERvice* menu is to manipulate the Processor Internal Memory, display SCSI controller values, and enable and disable self tests. In the following example, we run *SCSI* to get information on our SCSI interfaces and then return to the *Main* menu:

```
Service Menu: Enter command > SCSI

Path (dec)      Initiator ID    SCSI Rate    Auto Term
-----------     -------------   ----------   ---------------
0/0/1/0         7               Fast         Unknown
0/0/1/1         7               Ultra        Unknown
0/0/2/0         7               Ultra        Unknown
0/0/2/1         7               Ultra        Unknown

Service Menu: Enter command > main

---- Main Menu ------------------------------------------------------

    Command                         Description
    -------                         -----------
    BOot [PRI|ALT|<path>]           Boot from specified path
    PAth [PRI|ALT] [<path>]         Display or modify a path
    SEArch [DIsplay|IPL] [<path>]   Search for boot devices

    COnfiguration menu              Displays or sets boot values
    INformation menu                Displays hardware information
    SERvice menu                    Displays service commands

    DIsplay                         Redisplay the current menu
    HElp [<menu>|<command>]         Display help for menu or command
    RESET                           Restart the system
----
Main Menu: Enter command or menu >
```

man page

pdc - 1

Now that we've looked at some of the PDC commands let's get back to the process of booting by looking at the first three commands under *Main* menu.

BOot allows you to specify the path from which you'll boot your system. *PAth* allows you to display or modify the boot paths. *SEArch* will display boot paths. In the following example, we'll *SEArch* to show all potential boot devices on our L-Class system, run *PAth* to display our existing boot path, and then specify the device from which we want to boot our system:

```
Service Menu: Enter command > main

---- Main Menu ------------------------------------------------------

    Command                         Description
    -------                         -----------
    BOot [PRI|ALT|<path>]           Boot from specified path
    PAth [PRI|ALT] [<path>]         Display or modify a path
    SEArch [DIsplay|IPL] [<path>]   Search for boot devices

    COnfiguration menu              Displays or sets boot values
    INformation menu                Displays hardware information
    SERvice menu                    Displays service commands

    DIsplay                         Redisplay the current menu
    HElp [<menu>|<command>]         Display help for menu or command
    RESET                           Restart the system
```

```
----
Main Menu: Enter command or menu >
Main Menu: Enter command or menu > sea

Searching for potential boot device(s)
This may take several minutes.

To discontinue search, press any key (termination may not be immediate).


    Path#  Device Path (dec)   Device Path (mnem)  Device Type
    -----  -----------------   ------------------  -----------
    P0     0/0/1/1.2           intscsib.2          Random access media
    P1     0/0/2/0.2           intscsia.2          Random access media


Main Menu: Enter command or menu > pa

    Primary boot path:      intscsib.2
                            0/0/1/1.2
                            0/0/01/01.2    (hex)

    Alternate boot path:    intscsia.2
                            0/0/2/0.2
                            0/0/02/0.2     (hex)

    Console path:           0/0/4/0.0
                            0/0/04/0.0     (hex)

    Keyboard path:          0/0/4/0.0
                            0/0/04/0.0     (hex)

Main Menu: Enter command or menu > bo p0
Interact with IPL (Y, N, or Cancel)?> y
```

The *SEArch* command shows two potential boot devices; in this case, our two internal disks on two different SCSI buses. The path of the two boot devices is composed of numbers separated by slashes (/), which indicate bus converters, and dots (.), which indicate cards, slot numbers, and addresses. You sometimes end up decoding these paths to figure out what boot devices map to what hardware devices on your system. In our case we have only the two internal disks, one on bus 1 and the other on bus 2.

The *PAth* command shows that the primary boot device is the disk on internal bus 1 and the alternate boot device is the disk on internal bus 2.

When I issued the *BOot* command in the previous example, I specified a device of *p0,* which corresponds to the disk on internal bus1 shown in the *SEArch* command results. I responded that I did indeed want to interact with IPL, which would normally not be the case when booting the system; however, I want to look briefly at IPL in the upcoming IPL section.

man page

pdc - 1

PDC commands issued through BCH are a mystery to many new system administrators. I covered enough in this section to get you comfortable enough on your system to look at the non-intrusive commands, that is, those that supply useful information without changing the settings on your system. Please be careful if you issue commands that change your configuration. Under

MAIN-CON-CPU

for instance you can configure and reconfigure processors. You would not want to experiment with this command unless your system unused.

PDC Commands

The following is a list of PDC commands available on an N-Class system at the time of this writing. Although an L-Class system was used in the examples in this chapter, the PDC for the L-Class and N-Class are similar. Keep in mind that the PDC commands for your system may be somewhat different than those listed. The PDC is updated occassionally, so the list for the N-Class may also be somewhat different than what is shown in Table 1-2.

TABLE 1-2　List of PDC Commands for N-Class

Command	Explanation
ALL	Display the collection of all information provided by other display commands typically resident in INFORMATION menu.
AUTO	Used to display or set status of AUTOBOOT, AUTOSEARCH, or AUTOSTART flags.
BOOT	Initiate boot sequence.
BOOTID	Display or modify boot *id* for the processors present.
BOOTINFO	Display PDC-level information about the configured parameters used for system boot.

Command	Explanation
BOOTTIMER	Sets a delay value in the system to wait for external mass storage devices to come on-line.
CACHE	Displays information about the cache memory portion of all installed processors.
CHASSISCODES	Displays a queue of the most recent chassis codes.
CHIPREVISIONS	Used to display the revisions of major Very Large Scale Integration (VLSI) in the system.
CLEARPIM	Used to clear (zero) the contents of the Processor Internal Memory (PIM).
CONFIGURATION	Used to enter the Configuration sub-menu.
COPROCESSOR	Displays information about all installed coprocessors.
CPUCONFIG	Allows the user to configure or deconfigure processors in the system.
DEFAULT	Used to set the system to pre-defined defaults.
DISPLAY	Used to redisplay the current menu.
FAN	Used to display or set the speed of system internal fans.
FASTBOOT	Used to display or set the fastboot flag.
FWRVERSION	Displays the revision of currently installed firmware.
HELP	Returns help information for the specified command, menu, or the system itself.
INFORMATION	Used to acess the Information menu.
IO	Displays I/O interface on all I/O modules in the system.
LANADDRESS	Allows the user to display station address.
LANCONFIG	Used to configure the LAN card.
MAIN	User interface for PDC.
MEMORY	Displays memory information for total amount of physical memory as well as configured memory in a system.
MEMREAD	Used to read memory locations.
MONITOR	Allows the user to view and change the monitor type for graphic cards.
PATH	Used to set and/or display the system paths from Stable Storage.
PDT	Display or clear the Page Deallocation Table (PDT).
PIM	Displays Processor Internal Memory (PIM) Information.
PROCESSOR	Displays information about the processor(s) in the system.
RESET	Resets the machine state.
SEARCH	Search for boot devices in the system.

Command	Explanation
SECURE	Used to display or set the secure mode flag.
SERVICE	Allows the user to go to the Service menu.
TIME	Read or set the real time clock in GMT.
WARNINGS	Display any warning messages that may have resulted from the previous PDC selftest execution.

Initial System Load

man page

isl - 1

As mentioned earlier, the Initial System Loader (ISL) is run after the PDC. You would normally just run an "autoboot" sequence from ISL, however, there are a number of commands you could run from the ISL prompt.

Picking up where we left off in the previous example, we have chosen to *BOot* off of device *p0* and interact with IPL as shown in the following example:

```
Main Menu: Enter command or menu > bo p0
Interact with IPL (Y, N, or Cancel)?> y

Booting...
Boot IO Dependent Code (IODC) revision 1


HARD Booted.

ISL Revision A.00.38  OCT 26, 1994

ISL> ?
        HELP        Help Facility
        LS          List ISL utilities
        AUTOBOOT    Set or clear autoboot flag in stable storage
        AUTOSEARCH  Set or clear autosearch flag in stable storage
        PRIMPATH    Modify primary boot path in stable storage
        ALTPATH     Modify alternate boot path in stable storage
        CONSPATH    Modify system console path in stable storage
        DISPLAY     Display boot and console paths in stable storage
        LSAUTOFL    List contents of autoboot file
        FASTSIZE    Sets or displays FASTSIZE
        800SUPPORT  Boots the s800 Support Kernel from the boot device
        700SUPPORT  Boot the s700 Support Kernel from the boot device
        READNVM     Displays contents of one word of NVM
        READSS      Displays contents of one word of stable storage
```

```
         LSBATCH          List contents of batch file
         BATCH            Execute commands in batch file
         LSEST            List contents of EST (Extended Self Test) file
         EST              Execute commands in EST (Extended Self Test) file

Enter 'LS' to see a list of the ISL utilities.

ISL>
```

man page

isl - 1

Issuing a *?* produces a list of ISL commands that we could issue. Issuing the *DISPLAY* command shows the boot and console paths and *LS* lists the ISL utilities available as shown in the following example:

```
ISL> display

     Fastsize value is 0000000F

     Autoboot is ON (enabled)

     Autosearch is ON (enabled)

     Primary boot path is 0/0/1/1.2.0.0.0.0.0
     Primary boot path is (hex) 0/0/1/1.2.0.0.0.0.0

     Alternate boot path is 0/0/2/0.2.0.0.0.0.0
     Alternate boot path is (hex) 0/0/2/0.2.0.0.0.0.0

     System console path is 0/0/4/0.0.0.0.0.0.0
     System console path is (hex) 0/0/4/0.0.0.0.0.0.0

ISL> ls

     Utilities on this system are:

filename    type    start    size     created
===================================================
ODE         -12960  584      1216     00/01/21 16:45:48
HPUX        -12928  3480     800      99/10/28 15:23:53

ISL>
```

DISPLAY produced the information we expected based on what we had seen in the previous section produced by PDC. *LS* produced two utilities available to us: *ODE* and *HPUX*. *ODE* is the Offline Diagnostics Environment. The following example shows listing the *ODE* utilities available on the system by running *ODE*, the *HELP* command to see what commands are available, and *LS* to list the *ODE* utilities:

```
ISL> ode


*************************************************************************
******                                                           ******
******               Offline Diagnostic Environment              ******
******                                                           ******
******    (C) Copyright Hewlett-Packard Co 1993-2000             ******
******                 All Rights Reserved                       ******
******                                                           ******
******    HP shall not be liable for any damages resulting from the ******
******    use of this program.                                   ******
******                                                           ******
******                 TC  Version A.02.20                       ******
******                 SysLib Version A.00.74                    ******
******                 Loader Version A.00.59                    ******
******                 Mapfile Version A.01.23                   ******
******                                                           ******
*************************************************************************

Type HELP for command information.
ODE> help

ODE Help

    Basic Commands
    --------------
    HELP -- Prints detailed information to the screen, when "help <command>"
            or "help <var>" is typed
    LS -- List modules available on boot medium
    <Module_Name> -- Load and initialize a module by typing its name
                    (For more help, type "help module_name")
    MENU -- Launch ODE's ease-of-use interface
    RUN -- Run a module (after setting desired environment variables)
    Control-Y|Control-C -- Abort an ODE command; pause a module run
    RESUME -- Restart a paused module
    DISPLOG -- After running a module, display contents of a log
    EXIT -- Return to next higher level prompt

    Environmental Variables
    -----------------------
    SHOWSTATE -- Display the value of the following environment variables:
        LOOP -- Run a test this many times
        ERRPRINT [ON|OFF] -- Print low-level error messages to console
                            (primarily for manufacturing use)
        ERRNUM [ON|OFF] -- Print one-line, numbered errors to the console

Continue ([y]/n)? y

        ERRPAUSE [ON|OFF] -- Pause module upon error detection
        ERRONLY [ON|OFF] -- Print ONLY error messages; disable non-error
                            and isolation message printing
        INFOPRINT [ON|OFF] -- Print informational messages to the console
        ISOPRINT [ON|OFF] -- Print fault isolation messages to the console
        ISOPAUSE [ON|OFF] -- Pause module when isolation message is generated
    LOGSIZE -- Set the size of a message log
    DEFAULT -- Reset environment variables to default state

ODE> ls

        Modules on this boot media are:

filename    type    size    created    description
-------------------------------------------------------------------------
MAPPER2     TM      126     00/01/21   64 bit version of the system mapping ut
IOTEST2     TM      88      00/01/21   64 bit version that runs ROM-based self
PERFVER2    TM      124     00/01/21   64 bit version that runs ROM-based self

ODE>
```

When we ran *ODE* in this example and issued *LS* the three utilities at the end of the example were listed. I always load *ODE* as a part of system installations to help in the event of a possible system hardware problem an HP CE may need to diagnose.

Next we'll proceed with the boot process by running the *HPUX* utility:

HPUX Secondary System Loader (hpux)

man page

hpux - 1

man page

isl - 1

As mentioned earlier, the *hpux* utility manages loading the HP-UX kernel and gives control to the kernel. ISL can have hpux run an "autoexecute" file or commands can be given interactively. In most situations, you would just want to automatically boot the system, however, in our example so far, we have decided to interact with IPL in the interest of looking at some of the functionality in ISL. We proceed with the boot process by simply issuing the *HPUX* utility name as shown in the following example:

```
ISL> hpux

Boot
: disk(0/0/1/1.2.0.0.0.0.0;0)/stand/vmunix
7094272 + 849200 + 724128 start 0x241068


alloc_pdc_pages: Relocating PDC from 0xf0f0000000 to 0x7f9ab000.
gate64: sysvec_vaddr = 0xc0002000 for 1 pages
NOTICE: nfs3_link(): File system was registered at index 4.
NOTICE: autofs_link(): File system was registered at index 6.

    System Console is on the Built-In Serial Interface
Entering cifs_init...
Initialization finished successfully... slot is 8
Logical volume 64, 0x3 configured as ROOT
Logical volume 64, 0x2 configured as SWAP
Logical volume 64, 0x2 configured as DUMP
    Swap device table:  (start & size given in 512-byte blocks)
        entry 0 - major is 64, minor is 0x2; start = 0, size = 2097152
Starting the STREAMS daemons-phase 1
Checking root file system.
file system is clean - log replay is not required
Root check done.
```

```
Create STCP device files
Starting the STREAMS daemons-phase 2
    B2352B/9245XB HP-UX (B.11.00) #1: Wed Nov  5 22:38:19 PST 1997

Memory Information:
    physical page size = 4096 bytes, logical page size = 4096 bytes
    Physical: 2097152 Kbytes, lockable: 1574352 Kbytes, available: 1815496 Kbytes

/sbin/ioinitrc:

/sbin/bcheckrc:
Checking for LVM volume groups and Activating (if any exist)
Volume group "/dev/vg00" has been successfully changed.
vxfs fsck: sanity check: root file system OK (mounted read/write)
Checking hfs file systems
/sbin/fsclean: /dev/vg00/lvol1 (mounted) ok
HFS file systems are OK, not running fsck
Checking vxfs file systems
/dev/vg00/lvol8 :
vxfs fsck: sanity check: /dev/vg00/lvol8 OK
/dev/vg00/lvol3 :
vxfs fsck: sanity check: root file system OK (mounted read/write)
/dev/vg00/lvol4 :
vxfs fsck: sanity check: /dev/vg00/lvol4 OK
/dev/vg00/lvol5 :
vxfs fsck: sanity check: /dev/vg00/lvol5 OK
/dev/vg00/lvol6 :
vxfs fsck: sanity check: /dev/vg00/lvol6 OK
/dev/vg00/lvol7 :
vxfs fsck: sanity check: /dev/vg00/lvol7 OK


(c)Copyright 1983-1997 Hewlett-Packard Co.,   All Rights Reserved.
(c)Copyright 1979, 1980, 1983, 1985-1993 The Regents of the Univ. of California
(c)Copyright 1980, 1984, 1986 Novell, Inc.
(c)Copyright 1986-1992 Sun Microsystems, Inc.
(c)Copyright 1985, 1986, 1988 Massachusetts Institute of Technology
(c)Copyright 1989-1993  The Open Software Foundation, Inc.
(c)Copyright 1986 Digital Equipment Corp.
(c)Copyright 1990 Motorola, Inc.
(c)Copyright 1990, 1991, 1992 Cornell University
(c)Copyright 1989-1991 The University of Maryland
(c)Copyright 1988 Carnegie Mellon University
(c)Copyright 1991-1997 Mentat, Inc.
(c)Copyright 1996 Morning Star Technologies, Inc.
(c)Copyright 1996 Progressive Systems, Inc.
(c)Copyright 1997 Isogon Corporation


                     RESTRICTED RIGHTS LEGEND
Use, duplication, or disclosure by the U.S. Government is subject to
restrictions as set forth in sub-paragraph (c)(1)(ii) of the Rights in
Technical Data and Computer Software clause in DFARS 252.227-7013.


                 Hewlett-Packard Company
                 3000 Hanover Street
                 Palo Alto, CA 94304 U.S.A.

Rights for non-DOD U.S. Government Departments and Agencies are as set
forth in FAR 52.227-19(c)(1,2).

   .
   .
   .
Console Login:
```

I abbreviated this listing where the three dots appear before the
Console Login: prompt.

We have a number of options we can issue with the *HPUX* utility. The manual page at the end of this chapter describes several options in detail. Table 1-3 is a list of examples of some common *HPUX* utility booting options, some of which are from the man page:

man page

hpux - 1

TABLE 1-1   hpux Examples

Command (all at *ISL>* prompt)	Comments
Automatic Boot	No interaction - autoboot sequence.
hpux -is	Bring up system at run level *s* for single user mode.
hpux	Default boot sequence from **autoexecute** normally object file is **/stand/vmuinx**.
hpux vmunix.test	Boot object file **vmunix.test**.
hpux (52.5.0.0) /stand/vmunix	Boot from **/stand/vmunix** on the disk at the path *52.5.0.0*.
hpux lan(32) /stand/vmunix	Boot from LAN.
hpux -v	Get HP-UX version numbers..
hp-ux ll /stand	List contents of **/stand** on root disk.

The part of the boot that takes place after the **hpux** command is issued is in the four following parts:

1. HP-UX initializes the system hardware and devices - The HP-UX kernel locates and initializes system hardware such as memory, I/O busses and devices, and so on. Kernel device drivers are associated with I/O devices at this time. You see many messages fly-by on the system console as this process is taking place.

2. HP-UX kernel data structures are created and initialized - There are many tables for system processes and memory, file systems, and so on that are created. You also see the status of this part of the boot on the system console.

3. HP-UX searches for the root file system - The base file system contains critical system files and is usually found on the disk from which HP-UX boots. Many commands are run as part of this process.

4. HP-UX starts the init process called **/sbin/init** - The init process, which has an ID of one, starts all other processes on the system. The init process reads **/etc/inittab** for direction. There is a detailed description of the contents of **/etc/inittab** in Chapter 7.

I encourage you to issue some of the PDC, ISL, and hpux utility commands covered earlier, especially those that do not modify your system in any way but only provide information about the system.

The next section covers configuring the Secure Web Console.

Secure Web Console

You have a choice concerning the type of console to use with your HP 9000. You can connect a terminal to the console port or use a browser and the Secure Web Console (there is also a LAN console port available on systems as another alternative). There is also a console consolidation solution that supports up to 224 consoles that I won't cover here. The Secure Web Console is a device that connects to the HP 9000 console port that has a built-in Web server that allows you to use your browser as a console. This means that from one system running a browser, you can open up several windows that are the console screens for different HP 9000 systems. This obviates the need to walk from console to console when you want to perform system administration functions - you can sit at one system running a browser and adminstrate many systems.

In this section, I'll cover configuring a Secure Web Console and include several screen shots so you can decide whether you prefer the Secure Web Console or a dedicated terminal as a console.

\

You can download the document that describes the procedure of installing and configuring the Secure Web Console from http://docs.hp.com/hpux/content/swc_inst/config.html at the time of this writing. I'll provide an example of a configuration in this section.

Connecting and Configuring the Secure Web Console

The Secure Web Console is a device that is connected to the console port on your HP 9000 and to your LAN. On an L-Class system, for instance, slot 2 has in it a Core I/O card that includes a LAN console port and a connector for the UPS and console - the serial port on the Secure Web Console is plugged into this console cable. There is also a networking port on the Secure Web Console so you can connect it to your LAN. Figure 1-1 depicts the general setup of the Secure Web Console:

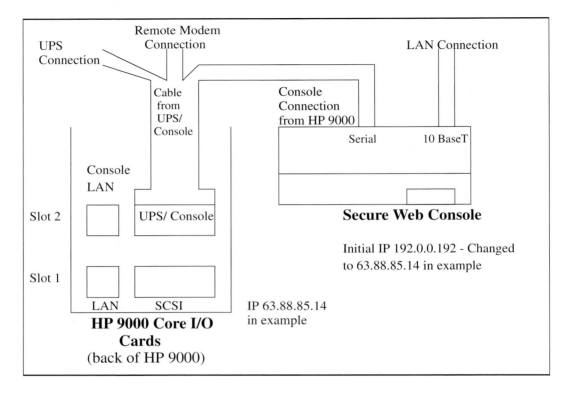

Figure 1-1 Secure Web Console Connectivity on L-Class Used in Upcoming Example

Keep in mind that the HP 9000 connections on your system may differ from what is shown in the figure. The cable connected to the UPS/Console port turns into the three connections shown in Figure 1-1. The Secure Web Console connects to the right-most of the three connectors when facing the back of the computer on my system. Its other connection is a networking connection to the LAN. The Secure Web Console also has its own power source so you can connect to it from your browser even when the computer is powered off.

The Secure Web Console has a default IP address of 192.0.0.192. This address is assigned so that you can connect to the Secure Web Console upon installation and reconfigure it.

With the hardware connections complete, we'll proceed to setup the system running a browser and connect to the Secure Web Console using the following steps:

Disable Proxies   Assuming you are running a supported version of a browser, you want to "Disable Proxies" or use "No Proxies" until the Secure Web Console configuration is complete.

Add a Route   Use the following command to add a route from the computer where your browser is running to the Secure Web console:

route add 192.0.0.192 63.88.95.15

In this example the computer on which I'm running my browser has an IP address of 63.88.95.15

Check connection Use the **ping** command to check the connection between the computer running the browser and the default IP address of the Secure Web Console:

ping 192.0.0.192

Use **arp**   If you did not receive a response using **ping** you may have to use **arp** as shown below for a PC and UNIX system:

PC: **arp -s 192.0.0.192 00-10-83-fa-3f-11**

UNIX: **arp -s 192.0.0.192 00: 10: 83: fa: 3f: 11**

I have not had to use the **arp** command in my configurations, however, the document at

man page

ping - 12

the URL earlier mentioned recommends the **arp** command if indeed your **ping** fails. Re-issue the **ping** command after using **arp** to check your connection. The *-s* option is for a static **arp**.

Web Browser   With a successful **ping** you can now access the Secure Web Console through your browser.

man page

route - 12

Figure 1-2 shows the steps I performed. You can see **route** and **ping** on my PC at the command line to get access to the Secure Web Console:

```
Command Prompt                                              _ □ ×
Microsoft(R) Windows NT(TM)
(C) Copyright 1985-1996 Microsoft Corp.

D:\>ping 192.0.0.192

Pinging 192.0.0.192 with 32 bytes of data:

Destination host unreachable.
Destination host unreachable.
Destination host unreachable.
Destination host unreachable.

D:\>route add 192.0.0.192 63.88.85.15

D:\>ping 192.0.0.192

Pinging 192.0.0.192 with 32 bytes of data:

Reply from 192.0.0.192: bytes=32 time=10ms TTL=255
Reply from 192.0.0.192: bytes=32 time<10ms TTL=255
Reply from 192.0.0.192: bytes=32 time<10ms TTL=255
Reply from 192.0.0.192: bytes=32 time<10ms TTL=255

D:\>
```

Figure 1-2 **route** and **ping** with Secure Web Console

This screen shot does not show the "disable proxies" step I performed prior to the commands issued at the prompt.

> Note: I sometimes configure the Secure Web Console by connecting a crossover LAN cable from the Secure Web Console directly to my laptop computer. After I have completed the initial configuration steps I then connect the Secure Web Console to the LAN and use a desktop system to access it with a browser. The connection to my portable is only a temporary connection in order to configure the Secure Web Console with its final IP address.

With a connection having been established and the browser properly configured on my computer (proxy server was earlier disabled), I can use the browser to connect to the Web server on the Secure Web Console. You must be on the same subnet for this to work in most situations. Figure 1-3 is a screen shot showing that I specified the pre-configured IP address of the Secure Web Console with http:// 192.0.0.192:

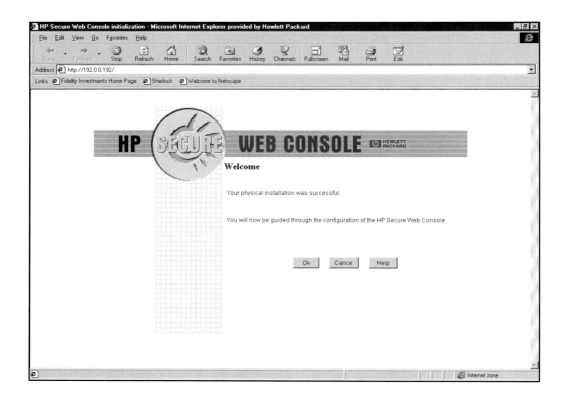

Figure 1-3   Initial Secure Web Console Screen

The "Welcome" screen confirms that we performed the necessary configuration to make our initial connection to the Secure Web Console. After you select "OK" on this screen, you can proceed with the configuration of the Secure Web Console.

The next screen in Figure 1-4 shows the initial information related to the Secure Web Console for which you will be prompted when you select "OK". This information is for an administrator of the Secure Web Console, not for the HP 9000. In the upcoming examples, I zoom in so you can see the Secure Web Console information more clearly. The browser information is not shown in the figures, but it is insignificant as far as the Secure Web Console configuration is concerned from this point foward.

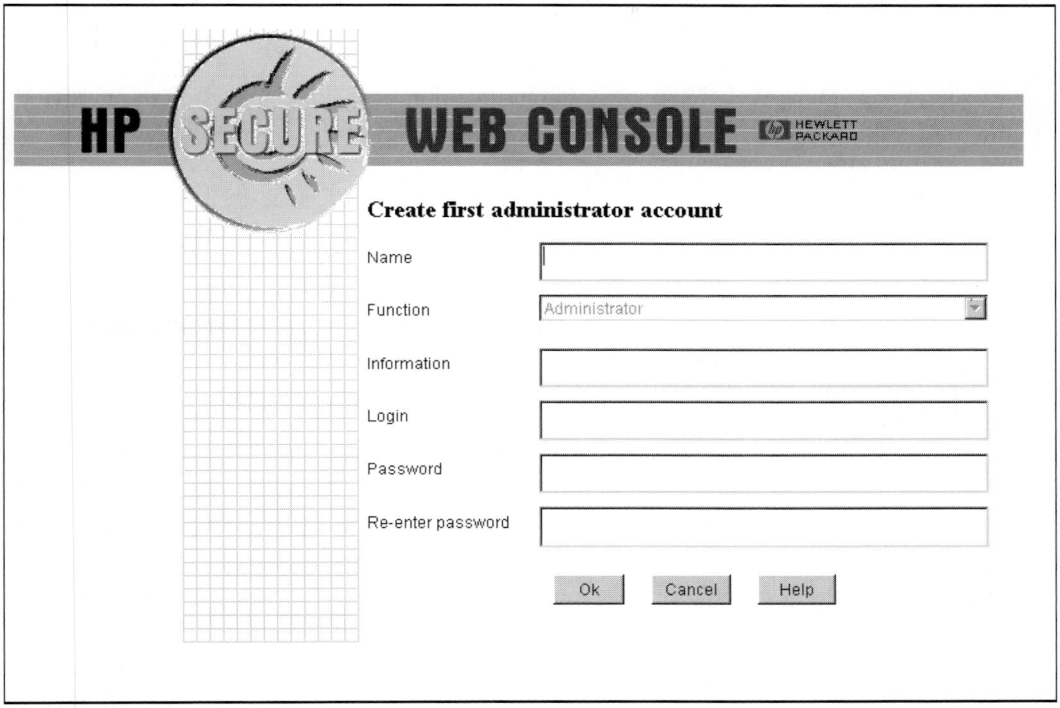

Figure 1-4 Secure Web Console Screen for First Administrator Account

After adding all of this information, you have configured the initial administrator account. As we'll see later, you can add subsequent administrator and operator accounts to the Secure Web Console.

The next screen, in Figure 1-5, shows the network-related configuration we'll make to the Secure Web Console. Since it came with a pre-configured IP address, we'll now assign the dedicated IP address for the device.

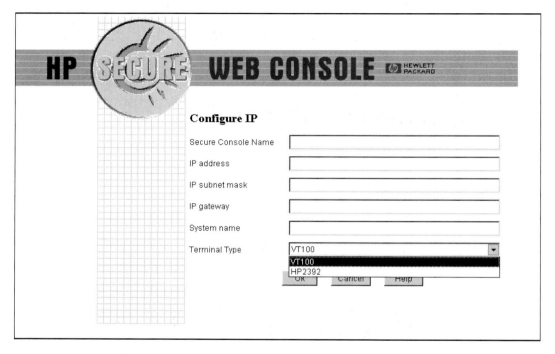

Figure 1-5   Secure Web Console Screen to Configure Final IP Address

In Figure 1-5 I show the two types of terminals that you can select. In this "Configure IP" screen, you'll enter both a name for the Secure Web Console and the computer to which it is connected. All of the IP-related information is entered in this screen as well. The Secure Web Console requires a dedicated IP address because you connect directly to it to make a console connection to the HP 9000.

When all of the information has been added, we select "OK" on this screen and are shown the following message in Figure 1-6:

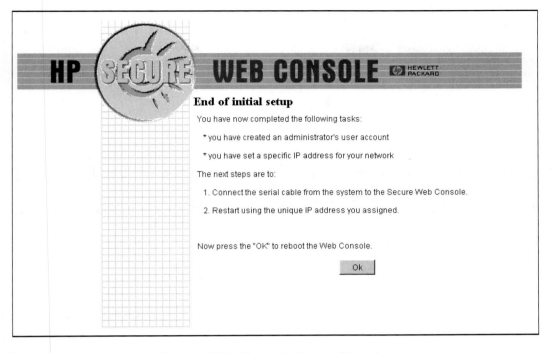

Figure 1-6 Initial Secure Web Console Setup Complete

After we select "OK" in Figure 1-6, we can reconnect to the Secure Web Console using the IP address we assigned to it during the configuration. In our case, we would use http://15.88.85.14 to reconnect as shown in Figure 1-7:

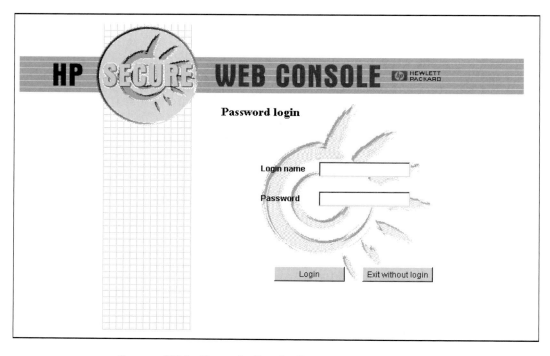

Figure 1-7   Secure Web Console Login Screen

We log in with the name and password we earlier defined for the Secure Web Console administrator and are then connected as shown in Figure 1-8:

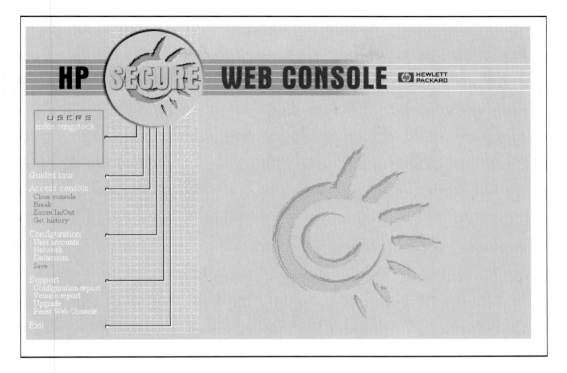

Figure 1-8 Secure Web Console Menu

At this point, you can select from a number of Secure Web Console-related functions to perform, such as configuring additional users, or you can access the console on your HP 9000 which is the purpose of connecting the device. The *Access console* selection gives us the console of the HP 9000 as shown in Figure 1-9:

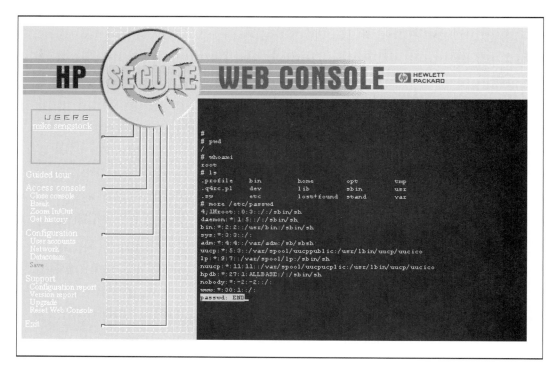

Figure 1-9   Initial Secure Web Console Screen

Notice that we are logged in as root when we select *Access console*. You could use the Secure Web Console menu to configure additional administrators and operators (we configured only one administrator in our example and no operators) to give multiple users access to your HP 9000 through the Secure Web Console.

The Secure Web Console can be a good alternative to using a dedicated console on each HP 9000. I wanted to provide you with the basic information for configuring the Secure Web Console, the URL for the configuration document, and an overview of the product to help you determine if it is right for your environment.

Configuring the Guardian Service Processor (GSP)

The Guardian Service Processor (GSP) is a built-in processor on most HP 9000 systems, such as the L-Class and N-Class, that can be used for either local or remote system administration functions. I won't cover the use of the GSP, but I will cover its initial configuration. The initial configuration is important because the first person to gain access to the GSP before it has been configured is a GSP administrator by default.

You gain access to the GSP with ^b (control b). If the GSP has not been configured, anyone who gets access to the console can type ^b and gain access to the system. I recommend you perform GSP configuration as soon as possible after installing your system.

The following example shows issuing a ^b, which results in the *GSP>* prompt, and issuing **he** for help:

```
Service Processor login:
Service Processor password:



        Hewlett-Packard Guardian Service Processor

        9000/800/L2000-44 System Name: uninitialized

GSP Host Name:  uninitialized
GSP>



GSP Host Name:  uninitialized
GSP> he


HE
        Hardware Revision 8  Firmware Revision  A.01.06  Aug  2 1999,11:38:47
AC : Alert Display Configuration      PC : Remote Power Control
AR : Config. Automatic System Restart PS : Power Management Module status
CA : Configure serial port parameters RP : Reset password configuration
CE : Log repair info in history buffer RS : System reset through RST signal
CL : Display console history           SDM: Set Display Mode (hex or text)
CO : Return to Console Mode            SE : Activate a system session
DC : Default configuration             SL : Display SPU status logs
```

```
DI : Disconnect remote or LAN console   SO : Security options & access control
DR : Disable remote or LAN console      SS : System's processor status
ER : Enable remote or LAN console       TC : System reset through INIT signal
HE : Display the available commands      TE : Sends a message to other terminals
IT : Modify GSP inactivity timeouts     VFP: Activates Alert Log Display
LC : Configure LAN console              WHO: Display list of GSP connected users
LS : Display LAN console status         XD : GSP Diagnostics and Reset
MR : Modem Reset                        XU : Upgrade the GSP Firmware
MS : Display the status of the Modem

GSP Host Name:  uninitialized
GSP>
```

You can see that in order to login after the ^b was issued neither a login name or password were required. This is because GSP users have not yet been configured, so anyone can get access to this menu with ^b at the system console.

There are several commands here to which you don't want unauthorized users to have access, so the first step we'll take is to setup security with **SO**:

```
GSP> so

SO

This command allow you to modify the security options and access control.

GSP wide parameters are:
  . Login Timeout: 1  minutes.
  . Number of Password Faults allowed: 3
  . Flow Control Timeout: 5  minutes.
Do you want to modify the GSP wide parameters? (Y/[N])

User number 1 parameters are:
  . User's Name:
  . User's Login:
  . Organization's Name:
  . Dial-back configuration: Disabled
  . Access Level: Operator
  . Mode: Single
  . User's state: Disabled
```
Do you want to modify the user number 1 parameters? (Y/[N]/Q to quit) :

From this menu, you can change GSP-wide parameters and establish GSP users. The first user added the first time you enter this screen will be the GSP system administrator. This is the user you want to set initially so your system is secure. You can add one administrator and 19 users. This is an important step since users will now have to add a username and password to gain access to GSP. The user information you add is shown in the previous listing and is self-explanatory.

In addition to configuring users, there are many useful features of GSP so I encourage you to experiment with it. One feature I often use is to issue **CL** to display a console history as shown in the following listing for the L-Class system used throughout the examples in this chapter:

```
GSP> cl

CL



Firmware Version  39.46

Duplex Console IO Dependent Code (IODC) revision 1

------------------------------------------------------------------------------
   (c) Copyright 1995-1998, Hewlett-Packard Company, All rights reserved
------------------------------------------------------------------------------

   Processor   Speed           State         CoProcessor State  Cache Size
   Number                                    State              Inst      Data
   ---------   --------   -------------------- ----------------- ----------------
        0      440  MHz   Active               Functional       512 KB    1 MB
        3      440  MHz   Idle                 Functional       512 KB    1 MB

   Central Bus Speed (in MHz)  :        82
   Available Memory            :   2097152  KB
   Good Memory Required        :     11468  KB

Press Q/q to quit, Enter to continue:

   Primary boot path:     0/0/1/1.2
   Alternate boot path:   0/0/2/0.2
   Console path:          0/0/4/0.0
   Keyboard path:         0/0/4/0.0

 WARNING:  The non-destructive test bit was set, so memory was not tested
           destructively.  Information only, no action required.


Processor is booting from first available device.

To discontinue, press any key within 10 seconds.

10 seconds expired.
Proceeding...

Trying Primary Boot Path
------------------------
Booting...
Boot IO Dependent Code (IODC) revision 1


Press Q/q to quit, Enter to continue:

HARD Booted.

ISL Revision A.00.38  OCT 26, 1994
```

```
ISL booting  hpux

Boot
: disk(0/0/1/1.2.0.0.0.0.0;0)/stand/vmunix
6340608 + 821576 + 695024 start 0x210ce8


alloc_pdc_pages: Relocating PDC from 0xf0f0000000 to 0x7f9ab000.
gate64: sysvec_vaddr = 0xc0002000 for 1 pages
Unexpected interrupt on EIRR bit 32
NOTICE: autofs_link(): File system was registered at index 3.
NOTICE: nfs3_link(): File system was registered at index 5.


     System Console is on the Built-In Serial Interface
Logical volume 64, 0x3 configured as ROOT
Logical volume 64, 0x2 configured as SWAP
Logical volume 64, 0x2 configured as DUMP
     Swap device table:  (start & size given in 512-byte blocks)
          entry 0 - major is 64, minor is 0x2; start = 0, size = 2097152
Starting the STREAMS daemons-phase 1
Checking root file system.
log replay in progress
replay complete - marking super-block as CLEAN
Root check done.
Create STCP device files
Starting the STREAMS daemons-phase 2
     B2352B/9245XB HP-UX (B.11.00) #1: Wed Nov  5 22:38:19 PST 1997

Memory Information:
     physical page size = 4096 bytes, logical page size = 4096 bytes

     Physical: 2097152 Kbytes, lockable: 1575156 Kbytes, available: 1816368 Kbyts

/sbin/ioinitrc:
/dev/vg00/lvol1: 34 files, 0 icont, 25716 used, 173665 free (81 frags, 21698 bl)

/sbin/bcheckrc:
Checking for LVM volume groups and Activating (if any exist)
Volume group "/dev/vg00" has been successfully changed.
Activated volume group
Volume group "/dev/vg01" has been successfully changed.
Resynchronized volume group /dev/vg00
Resynchronized volume group /dev/vg01
vxfs fsck: sanity check: root file system OK (mounted read/write)
Checking hfs file systems
/sbin/fsclean: /dev/vg00/lvol1 (mounted) ok
HFS file systems are OK, not running fsck

Checking vxfs file systems
/dev/vg00/lvol8 :
vxfs fsck: sanity check: /dev/vg00/lvol8 needs checking
log replay in progress
replay complete - marking super-block as CLEAN
/dev/vg01/lvol09 :
vxfs fsck: sanity check: /dev/vg01/lvol09 needs checking
log replay in progress
replay complete - marking super-block as CLEAN
/dev/vg00/lvol3 :
vxfs fsck: sanity check: root file system OK (mounted read/write)
/dev/vg00/lvol4 :
vxfs fsck: sanity check: /dev/vg00/lvol4 needs checking
log replay in progress
replay complete - marking super-block as CLEAN
/dev/vg00/lvol5 :
vxfs fsck: sanity check: /dev/vg00/lvol5 needs checking
log replay in progress
replay complete - marking super-block as CLEAN
/dev/vg00/lvol6 :
vxfs fsck: sanity check: /dev/vg00/lvol6 needs checking
log replay in progress
replay complete - marking super-block as CLEAN
/dev/vg00/lvol7 :
vxfs fsck: sanity check: /dev/vg00/lvol7 needs checking
```

```
log replay in progress
replay complete - marking super-block as CLEAN
```

```
/sbin/auto_parms: DHCP access is disabled (see /etc/auto_parms.log)

/sbin/rc: failed to read row and column info from screen

        HP-UX Start-up in progress
        ─────────────────────────

        Configure system crash dumps ............................. OK
        Mount file systems ....................................... OK
        Update kernel and loadable modules ....................... N/A
        Initialize loadable modules .............................. N/A
        Setting hostname ......................................... OK
        Set privilege group ...................................... N/A
        Display date ............................................. N/A
        Save system crash dump if needed ......................... N/A
        Enable auxiliary swap space .............................. OK
        Start syncer daemon ...................................... OK
        Configure HP Fibre Channel interfaces .................... OK
        Configure Loopback interfaces (lo0) ...................... OK
        Start Software Distributor agent daemon .................. OK
        Configuring all unconfigured software filesets ........... OK
        Recover editor crash files ............................... OK
        Clean UUCP ............................................... OK
        List and/or clear temporary files ........................ N/A
        Clean up old log files ................................... OK
        Start system message logging daemon ...................... OK
        Start pty allocator daemon ............................... OK
        Start network tracing and logging daemon ................. OK
        Configure HP Ethernet interfaces ......................... OK
        Configure HP 100BT interfaces ............................ OK
        Configure HP SPP 100BT interfaces ........................ N/A
        Configure LAN interfaces ................................. OK
        Start name server daemon ................................. N/A
        Start NFS core subsystem ................................. OK
        Start NIS+ server subsystem .............................. OK
        Start NIS+ client subsystem .............................. OK
        Start NIS server subsystem ............................... OK
        Start NIS client subsystem ............................... OK
        Start NFS client subsystem ............................... OK
        Start the Trusted Mode with Nis+ subsystem ............... N/A
        Configure pseudo devices for MAC/LLA access .............. OK
        Start multicast routing daemon ........................... N/A
```

```
Start Internet services daemon .......................... OK
Start dynamic routing daemon ............................ N/A
Start router discover protocol daemon ................... N/A
Configuring PPP Interface ............................... OK
Start RARP protocol daemon .............................. N/A
Start remote system status daemon ....................... N/A
Configuring man pages for Internet Services ............. OK
Starting mail daemon .................................... OK
Starting outbound connection daemons for DDFA software .... N/A
Start SNMP Master Network Management daemon .............. OK
Start OSPF MIB Network Management subAgent ............... N/A
Start SNMP HP-UNIX Network Management subAgent ........... OK
Start SNMP MIB-2 Network Management subAgent ............. OK
Start SNMP Trap Dest Network Management subAgent ......... OK
Start DCE daemons ....................................... N/A
Start RPC daemon if needed .............................. OK
Start the Isogon License Server daemon .................. N/A
Start remote boot daemon ................................ OK
Starting X Font Server at TCP port 7000 ................. OK
Start vt daemon ......................................... OK
Start time synchronization .............................. N/A
Start accounting ........................................ N/A
Starting the password/group assist subsystem ............ OK
Starting HP Disk Array Manager daemons. ................. OK
Starting disk array monitor daemons. .................... OK
Start print spooler ..................................... N/A
Starting HP Distributed Print Service ................... OK
Start clock daemon ...................................... OK
Support Tools Informational Fileset ..................... OK
Start environment monitoring daemon ..................... OK
Start auditing subsystem ................................ N/A
Start audio server daemon ............................... N/A
Start Distributed Single Logical Screen daemon .......... OK
SAM System administration configuration ................. OK
Reinitialize Software Distributor agent daemon .......... OK
Configure HP Fibre Channel Mass Storage interfaces ...... OK
Start NFS server subsystem .............................. OK
Start X print server(s) ................................. N/A
Starting ColdFusion Application Server .................. OK
Start CDE login server .................................. OK


The system is ready.

GenericSysName [HP Release B.11.00] (see /etc/issue)
Console Login:
***********************10/100 Mb/s LAN/9000 Networking*******************@#%
Fri May 26 EDT 2000 15:43:26.401827  DISASTER    Subsys:BASE100    Loc:00000
<6001> HPCORE 10/100BASE-T driver detected bad cable connection between
       the adapter in slot 0 and the hub or switch.
~~~~~~~~~~~~~~~~~~~~~~~~~~~~~~~~~~~~~~~~~~~~~~~~~~~~~~~~~~~~~~~~~~~~~~~~~~~~~

***********************10/100 Mb/s LAN/9000 Networking*******************@#%
Fri May 26 EDT 2000 17:18:31.401884  DISASTER    Subsys:BASE100    Loc:00000
<6001> HPCORE 10/100BASE-T driver detected bad cable connection between
       the adapter in slot 0 and the hub or switch.
~~~~~~~~~~~~~~~~~~~~~~~~~~~~~~~~~~~~~~~~~~~~~~~~~~~~~~~~~~~~~~~~~~~~~~~~~~~~~

GenericSysName [HP Release B.11.00] (see /etc/issue)
Console Login: root
Password:
```

This listing shows a smooth boot; however, there are often boot-related problems you may encounter and you can produce this listing with ^b anytime to review the sequence of events that took place at the time of boot.

You can obtain the status of power modules with **ps** as shown in the following listing:

```
GSP> ps


PS

Power Monitor Status:
Temperature      : Normal     Over temperature: Enable
Power Switch     : ON         Soft power      : Disable
Global fan state: Normal      System power state: On

          Power supplies          | Fan
  #   State           Type        | States
---------------------------------------------------------
0   Normal          1220 Watt     | Normal
1   Normal          1220 Watt     | Normal
2   Not Installed       -         | Normal
3   -                   -         | Normal
4   -                   -         | Normal
5   -                   -         | Normal
6   -                   -         | Normal
7   -                   -         | Normal


GSP Host Name:  uninitialized
GSP>
```

This shows that we have two power supplies installed and a third is not installed.

You can view processor status with **ss** as shown in the following listing:

```
GSP> ss


SS

System Processor Status:

   Monarch Processor: 0

   Processor 0 is : Installed and Configured
   Processor 1 is : Not Installed
   Processor 2 is : Not Installed
   Processor 3 is : Installed and Configured


GSP Host Name:  uninitialized
GSP>
```

After you have completed your GSP-related work you can return to console mode from the GSP prompt simply by issuing **co** as shown in the following listing:

```
GSP> co


CO

Leaving Guardian Service Processor Command Interface and entering
Console mode. Type Ctrl-B to reactivate the GSP Command Interface.



GenericSysName [HP Release B.11.00] (see /etc/issue)
Console Login:
```

Anytime you are on the console, you can issue ^b and get access to GSP to issue any GSP commands and then get back to console mode with **co**.

The following is a list of GSP commands available on an N-Class system at the time of this writing. Although an L-Class system was used in the examples in this chapter, the GSP for the L-Class and N-Class are similar. Keep in mind the GSP commands for your system may be somewhat different than those listed. GSP is updated occasionally, so the list for the N-Class may also be somewhat different than what is shown in the Table 1-4.

TABLE 1-4   List of GSP Commands for N-Class

Command (Function)	Explanation
AR (Config)	Configure the Automatic System Restart.
CA (Config)	Configure Asynchronous and Modem parameters.

Command (Function)	Explanation
CE (Chassis Codes)	Log a chassis code in the SAS chassis code history.
CL (Console)	Display console history.
CO (Console)	Return to console mode.
DC (Config)	Default configuration.
DI (Remote)	Disconnect remote or LAN console.
DR (Remote)	Disable remote or LAN console access.
ER (Remote)	Enable remote or LAN console access.
HE (Help)	Display the list of available commands.
IT (Admin)	Modify SAS inactivity timeouts.
LC (Config)	Configure LAN connected and PPP console.
LR (Paging)	Reserve modem for paging.
LS (Console)	Display LAN connected and PPP console status.
MR (Remote)	Modem Reset.
MS (Remote)	Display the status of the modem.
PC (Remote)	Remote power control.
PG (Paging)	Configure Paging.
PS (Status)	Display the status of the power.
RP (Reset)	System reset through RST signal.
SE (Session)	Activate a system session on local or remote port. (One session/remote and local console.)

Command (Function)	Explanation
SL (Status)	Display SPU status logs.
SO (Admin)	Configure security options and access control.
SS (Reset)	Display the status of the system processors.
TC (Session)	System reset through INIT signal.
TE (Admin)	Sends a message to other terminals.
TN (Session)	Start a Telnet session on local or remote port.
UR (Remote)	Unlock remote support modern access.
VSC (Config)	Configure the Virtual Front Panel display.
VFD (Chassis Codes)	Activates the immediate display of the Virtual Front Panel.
WHO (Admin)	Display a list of SAS connected users.
XD	SAS Diagnostics and Reset.
XU	Upgrade the GSP firmware.
ZTOGCCD (Chassis Codes)	DEBUG feature: Change the way the chassis codes are displayed by SL command and VFPD.

Manual Pages for Commands Used in Chapter 1

The following section contains copies of the manual pages for commands used in Chapter 1. This makes a quick reference for you to use when issuing the commands commonly used during your system administration day. The manual pages, more commonly referred to as man pages, are listed in full detail.

boot

boot - Bootstrap process overview.

```
boot(1M)                    Series 700/800 Only                    boot(1M)

NAME
     boot - bootstrap process

DESCRIPTION

     The Series 700 and 800 bootstrap process involves the execution of
     three software components:

         -  pdc (see pdc(1M),

         -  isl (see isl(1M), and

         -  hpux (see hpux_800(1M)).

     After the processor is RESET, pdc, the processor-dependent code
     (firmware), performs a self-test and initializes the processor.  It
     then loads and transfers control to isl, the operating-system-
     independent initial system loader.  isl, in turn, loads and transfers
     control to the hpux utility, the HP-UX-specific bootstrap loader.
     hpux then downloads the HP-UX kernel object file from an HP-UX file
     system and transfers control to the loaded kernel image.

SEE ALSO
     hpux(1M), hpux_800(1M), isl(1M), pdc(1M).
```

hpux

hpux - Boot HP-UX operating system.

```
hpux(1M)                                                                hpux(1M)


NAME
     hpux - HP-UX bootstrap

SYNOPSIS

     hpux [-F] [-lm] [-a[C|R|S|D] devicefile] [-fnumber] [-istring] [boot]
     [devicefile]
     hpux ll [devicefile] (same as hpux ls -aFln)
     hpux ls [-aFiln] [devicefile]
     hpux set autofile devicefile string
     hpux show autofile [devicefile]
     hpux -v
     hpux restore devicefile (Series 700 only; see DEPENDENCIES.)

DESCRIPTION
     hpux is the HP-UX specific secondary system loader (SSL) utility for
     bootstrap (see isl(1M) for the initial system loader).  It supports
     the operations summarized below, as shown in the SYNOPSIS and detailed
     later in this DESCRIPTION.

          boot               Loads an object file from an HP-UX file
                             system or raw device and transfers control
                             to the loaded image.  (Note, the boot
                             operation is position dependent).

          ll                 Lists the contents of HP-UX directories in
                             a format similar to ls -aFln.  (See ls(1);
                             ls only works on a local disk with a HFS
                             file system).

          ls                 Lists the contents of HP-UX directories.
                             (See ls(1); ls only works on a local disk
                             with a HFS file system).

          show autofile      Displays the contents of the autoexecute
                             file.

          set autofile       Changes the contents of the autoexecute
                             file to that specified by string.

          -v                 Displays the release and version numbers of
                             the hpux utility.

          restore            Recovers the system from a properly
                             formatted bootable tape.  (Series 700
                             specific; see DEPENDENCIES.)

     hpux commands can be given interactively from the keyboard, or
     provided in an isl autoexecute file.

     hpux is limited to operations on the interface initialized by pdc(1M).
     In most cases, operations are limited to the boot device interface.
```

Notation
hpux accepts numbers (numeric constants) in many of its options.
Numbers follow the C language notation for decimal, octal, and
hexadecimal constants. A leading 0 (zero) implies octal and a leading
0x or 0X implies hexadecimal. For example, 037, 0x1F, 0X1f, and 31
all represent the same number, decimal 31.

hpux boot, ll, ls, set autofile, show autofile, and restore operations
accept devicefile specifications, which have the following format:

    manager(w/x.y.z;n)filename

The devicefiles specification is comprised of a device name and a file
name. The device name (manager(w/x.y.z;n)), consists of a generic
name of an I/O system manager (device or interface driver) such as
disc, a hardware path to the device, and minor number. The manager
name can be omitted entirely if the default is used. w/x.y.z is the
physical hardware path to the device, identifying bus converters, slot
numbers, and hardware addresses. For Series 700 machines, there are a
set of mnemonics that can be used instead of the hardware paths. The
n is the minor number that controls manager-dependent functionality.
The file name part, filename, is a standard HP-UX path name. Some
hpux operations have defaults for particular components. A devicefile
specification containing a device part only specifies a raw device. A
devicefile specification containing a file name implies that the
device contains an HP-UX file system, and that the filename resides in
that file system.

A typical boot devicefile specification is

    disc(2/4.0.0;0)/stand/vmunix

The manager is disc, the hardware path to the disk device is 2/4.0.0,
the minor number shown as 0 by default, and the /stand/vmunix is the
filename for the boot device.

hpux now supports a consolidated list of managers: disc, tape, and
lan. The manager disc manages all CS/80 disks connected via HP-IB
(formerly disc0); CS/80 disks connected via the HP27111 interface
(formerly disc2); CS/80 disks connected via NIO HP-IB (formerly
disc1); all disks connected via SCSI, (formerly disc3), and all
autochanger disk devices (formerly disc30). The manager lan manages
remote boot through the HP28652A NIO based LAN interface (formerly
lan1). Remote boot is currently supported on this card only and not
on any CIO-based LAN card. The manager tape manages the HP7974,
HP7978, and HP7980 tape drives via HP-IB (formerly tape1) and tape
drives via SCSI (formerly tape2).

The hardware path in a devicefile specification is a string of
numbers, each suffixed by slash, (/), followed by a string of numbers
separated by dots (.), each number identifying a hardware component
notated sequentially from the bus address to the device address. A
hardware component suffixed by a slash indicates a bus converter and
may not be necessary on your machine. For example, in w/x.y.z w is
the address of the bus converter, x is the address of the MID-BUS
module, y is the CIO slot number, and z is the HP-IB address or
HP27111 bus address.

The minor number, n, in a devicefile specification controls driver-
dependent functionality. (See the manual, Configuring HP-UX for
Peripherals, for minor-number bit assignments of specific drivers).

File names are standard HP-UX path names. No preceding slash (/) is
necessary and specifying one will not cause problems.

Defaults

Default values chosen by hpux to complete a command are obtained
through a sequence of steps. First, any components of the command
specified explicitly are used. If the command is not complete, hpux
attempts to construct defaults from information maintained by pdc (see
pdc(1M)). If sufficient information to complete the command is
unavailable, the autoexecute file is searched. If the search fails,
any remaining unresolved components of the command are satisfied by
hard-coded defaults.

There is no hard-coded default choice for a manager; if none can be
chosen, hpux reports an error.

When the hardware path to the boot device is not specified, hpux
defaults to information maintained by pdc. The hardware path element
has no hard-coded default.

If the minor number element is not supplied, hpux takes its default
from the autoexecute file. Failing that, the hard-coded default of 0
is used.

For the boot command, a devicefile specification without a file name
indicates that the boot device does not contain an HP-UX file system.
hpux interprets this as a NULL (instead of missing) file name and does
not search for a default. If the entire devicefile specification is
missing, hpux searches for a default; either the autoexecute file
contents or the hard-coded default is chosen.

There are two possible hard-coded default devicefile specifications.
One hard-coded default devicefile specification is /vmunix. The other
hard-coded default devicefile specification is /stand/vmunix.

If you have a LVM system where the boot volume and the root volume are
on different logical volumes, the kernel would be /vmunix. This is
because the boot volume will be mounted under /stand when the system
is up.

For all other configurations, the kernel would be /stand/vmunix.

The search order for the hard-coded defaults is /stand/vmunix and then
/vmunix.

boot Operation

The boot operation loads an object file from an HP-UX file system or
raw device as specified by the optional devicefile. It then transfers
control to the loaded image.

Any missing components in a specified devicefile are supplied with a
default. For example, a devicefile of vmunix.new would actually
yield:

        disc(8.0.0;0)vmunix.new

and a devicefile of (8.0.1)/stand/vmunix, for booting from the disk at
HP-IB address 1, would yield

        disc(8.0.1;0)/stand/vmunix

Regardless of how incomplete the specified devicefile may be, boot
announces the complete devicefile specification used to find the
object file. Along with this information, boot gives the sizes of the
TEXT, DATA, and BSS, segments and the entry offset of the loaded
image, before transferring control to it.

The boot operation accepts several options. Note that boot options
must be specified positionally as shown in the syntax statement in the

SYNOPSIS.   Options for the boot operations are as follows:

-a[C|R|S|D] devicefile   Accept a new location (as specified by
                             devicefile) and pass it to the loaded
                             image. If that image is an HP-UX
                             kernel, the kernel will erase its
                             predefined I/O configuration, and
                             configure in the specified devicefile.
                             If the C, R, S, or D option is
                             specified, the kernel configures the
                             devicefile as the console, root, swap,
                             or dump device, respectively. Note
                             that -a can be repeated multiple times.

-fnumber   Use the number and pass it as the flags
                             word to the loaded image.

-istring   Set the initial run-level for init (see
                             init(1M)) when booting the system. The
                             run-level specified will override any
                             run-level specified in an initdefault
                             entry in /etc/inittab (see inittab(4)).

-lm   Boot the system in LVM maintenance
                             mode, configure only the root volume,
                             and then initiate single user mode.

-F   Use with SwitchOver/UX software.
                             Ignore any locks on the boot disk. The
                             -F option should be used only when it
                             is known that the processor holding the
                             lock is no longer running. (If this
                             option is not specified and a disk is
                             locked by another processor, the kernel
                             will not boot from it, to avoid the
                             corruption that would result if the
                             other processor were still using the
                             disk).

boot places some restrictions on object files it can load. It accepts
only the HP-UX magic numbers EXECMAGIC (0407), SHAREMAGIC (0410), and
DEMANDMAGIC (0413). See magic(4). The object file must contain an
Auxiliary Header of the HPUX_AUX_ID type and it must be the first
Auxiliary Header (see a.out(4)).

ll and ls Operations
    The ll and ls operations list the contents of the HP-UX directory
    specified by the optional devicefile. The output is similar to that
    of ls -aFl command, except the date information is not printed.

    The default devicefile is generated just as for boot, defaulting to
    the current directory.

set autofile Operation
    The set autofile operation overwrites the contents of the autoexecute
    file, autofile, with the string specified (see autoexecute in the
    EXAMPLES section).

show autofile Operation
    The show autofile operation displays the contents of the autoexecute
    file, autofile (see autoexecute in the EXAMPLES section).

DIAGNOSTICS
    If an error is encountered, hpux prints diagnostic messages to

indicate the cause of the error. These messages fall into the
General, Boot, Copy, Configuration, and System Call categories.
System Call error messages are described in errno(2). The remaining
messages are listed below.

General
  bad minor number in devicefile spec
        The minor number in the devicefile specification is not
        recognized.

  bad path in devicefile spec
        The hardware path in the devicefile specification is not
        recognized.

  command too complex for parsing
        The command line contains too many arguments.

  no path in devicefile spec
        The devicefile specification requires (but does not contain) a
        hardware path component.

  panic (in hpuxboot): (display==number, flags==number) string
        A severe internal hpux error has occurred. Report to your
        nearest HP Field Representative.

Boot
  bad magic
        The specified object file does not have a recognizable magic
        number.

  bad number in flags spec
        The flags specification in the -f option is not recognized.

  Exec failed: Cannot find /stand/vmunix or /vmunix.
        Neither /stand/vmunix or /vmunix could be found.

  booting from raw character device
        In booting from a raw device, the manager specified only has a
        character interface, which might cause problems if the block size
        is incorrect.

  isl not present, please hit system RESET button to continue
        An unsuccessful boot operation has overlaid isl in memory. It is
        impossible to return control to isl.

  short read
        The specified object file is internally inconsistent; it is not
        long enough.

  would overlay
        Loading the specified object file would overlay hpux.

Configuration
  cannot add path, error number
        An unknown error has occurred in adding the hardware path to the
        I/O tree. The internal error number is given. Contact your HP
        Field Representative.

  driver does not exist
        The manager specified is not configured into hpux.

  driver is not a logical device manager
        The manager named is not that of a logical device manager and
        cannot be used for direct I/O operations.

  error rewinding device"

> An error was encountered attempting to rewind a device.

error skipping file
> An error was encountered attempting to forward-space a tape
> device.

negative skip count
> The skip count, if specified, must be greater than or equal to
> zero.

no major number
> The specified manager has no entry in the block or character
> device switch tables.

path incompatible with another path
> Multiple incompatible hardware paths have been specified.

path long
> The hardware path specified contains too many components for the
> specified manager.

path short
> The hardware path specified contains too few components for the
> specified manager.

table full
> Too many devices have been specified to hpux.

EXAMPLES
> As a preface to the examples which follow, here is a brief overview of
> HP-UX system boot-up sequences.

Automatic Boot
> Automatic boot processes on various HP-UX systems follow similar
> general sequences. When power is applied to the HP-UX system
> processor, or the system Reset button is pressed, processor-dependent
> code (firmware) is executed to verify hardware and general system
> integrity (see pdc(1M)). After checking the hardware, pdc gives the
> user the option to override the autoboot sequence by pressing the Esc
> key. At that point, a message resembling the following usually
> appears on the console.

> > (c) Copyright. Hewlett-Packard Company. 1994.
> > All rights reserved.
> >
> > PDC ROM rev. 130.0
> > 32 MB of memory configured and tested.
> >
> > Selecting a system to boot.
> > To stop selection process, press and hold the ESCAPE key...

> If no keyboard activity is detected, pdc commences the autoboot
> sequence by loading isl (see isl(1M)) and transferring control to it.
> Since an autoboot sequence is occurring, isl finds and executes the
> autoexecute file which, on an HP-UX system, requests that hpux be run
> with appropriate arguments. Messages similar to the following are
> displayed by isl on the console:

> > Booting from: scsi.6 HP 2213A
> > Hard booted.
> > ISL Revision A.00.09 March 27, 1990
> > ISL booting hpux boot disk(;0)/stand/vmunix

> hpux, the secondary system loader, then announces the operation it is
> performing, in this case boot, the devicefile from which the load
> image comes, and the TEXT size, DATA size, BSS size, and start address

of the load image, as shown below, before control is passed to the image.

```
Booting disk(scsi.6;0)/stand/vmunix
966616+397312+409688 start 0x6c50
```

The loaded image then displays numerous configuration and status messages.

Interactive Boot

To use hpux interactively, isl must be brought up in interactive mode by pressing the Esc key during the interval allowed by pdc. pdc then searches for and displays all bootable devices and presents a set of boot options. If the appropriate option is chosen, pdc loads isl and isl interactively prompts for commands. Information similar to the following is displayed:

```
Selection process stopped.

Searching for Potential Boot Devices.
To terminate search, press and hold the ESCAPE key.

Device Selection    Device Path                  Device Type
-----------------------------------------------------------
P0                  scsi.6.0                     QUANTUM PD210S
P1                  scsi.1.0                     HP      2213A
p2                  lan.ffffff-ffffff.f.f        hpfoobar

b)  Boot from specified device
s)  Search for bootable devices
a)  Enter Boot Administration mode
x)  Exit and continue boot sequence

Select from menu: b p0 isl

Trying scsi.6.0
Boot path initialized.
Attempting to load IPL.

Hard booted.
ISL Revision A.00.2G  Mar  27, 1994
ISL>
```

Although all of the operations and options of hpux can be used from isl interactively, they can also be executed from an autoexecute file. In the examples below, user input is the remainder of the line after each ISL> prompt shown. The remainder of each example is text displayed by the system. Before going over specific examples of the various options and operations of hpux, here is an outline of the steps taken in the automatic boot process. Although the hardware configuration and boot paths shown are for a single Series 800 machine, the user interfaces are consistent across all models. When the system Reset button is depressed, pdc executes self-test, and assuming the hardware tests pass, pdc announces itself, sends a BELL character to the controlling terminal, and gives the user 10 seconds to override the autoboot sequence by entering any character. Text resembling the following is displayed on the console:

```
Processor Dependent Code (PDC) revision 1.2
Duplex Console IO Dependent Code (IODC) revision 3

Console path       = 56.0.0.0.0.0.0    (dec)
                     38.0.0.0.0.0.0.0   (hex)

Primary boot path  = 44.3.0.0.0.0.0    (dec)
                     2c.00000003.0.0.0.0.0.0   (hex)
```

```
Alternate boot path = 52.0.0.0.0.0.0   (dec)
                      34.0.0.0.0.0.0    (hex)
```

```
32 MB of memory configured and tested.
```

```
Autosearch for boot path enabled
```

```
To override, press any key within 10 seconds.
```

If no keyboard character is pressed within 10 seconds, pdc commences the autoboot sequence by loading isl and transferring control to it. Because an autoboot sequence is occurring, isl merely announces itself, finds and executes the autoexecute file which, on an HP-UX system, requests that hpux be run with appropriate arguments. The following is displayed on the console.

```
10 seconds expired.
Proceeding with autoboot.

Trying Primary Boot Path
------------------------
Booting...
Boot IO Dependent Code (IODC) revision 2

HARD Booted.

ISL Revision A.00.2G Mar  20, 1994

ISL booting  hpux
```

hpux then announces the operation it is performing, in this case boot, the devicefile from which the load image comes, and the TEXT size, DATA size, BSS size, and start address of the load image. The following is displayed before control is passed to the image.

```
Boot
: disc3(44.3.0;0)/stand/vmunix
3288076 + 323584 + 405312 start 0x11f3e8
```

Finally, the loaded image displays numerous configuration and status messages, then proceeds to init run-level 2 for multiuser mode of operation.

isl must be brought up in interactive mode to use the operations and options of hpux. To do this, simply enter a character during the 10 second interval allowed by pdc. pdc then asks if the primary boot path is acceptable. Answering yes (Y) is usually appropriate. pdc then loads isl and isl interactively prompts for commands. The following lines show the boot prompt, the Y response, subsequent boot messages, and finally the Initial System Loader (ISL) prompt that are sent to the display terminal:

```
Boot from primary boot path (Y or N)?> y
Interact with IPL (Y or N)?> y

Booting...
Boot IO Dependent Code (IODC) revision 2

HARD Booted.

ISL Revision A.00.2G Mar  20, 1994

ISL>
```

Although all of the operations and options of hpux can be used from

isl interactively, they can also be executed from an autoexecute file.
In the examples below, all user input follows the ISL> prompt on the
same line. Subsequent text is resultant messages from the ISL.

Default Boot
   Entering hpux initiates the default boot sequence. The boot path read
   from pdc is 8.0.0, the manager associated with the device at that path
   is disc, the minor number, in this case derived from the autoexecute
   file, is 4 specifying section 4 of the disk, and the object file name
   is /stand/vmunix.

       ISL> hpux

       Boot
       : disc3(44.3.0;0)/stand/vmunix
       3288076 + 323584 + 405312 start 0x11f3e8

Booting Another Kernel
   In this example, hpux initiates a boot operation where the name of the
   object file is vmunix.new.

       ISL> hpux vmunix.new

       Boot
       : disc3(44.3.0;0)/stand/vmunix.new
       3288076 + 323584 + 405312 start 0x11f3e8

Booting From Another Section
   In this example (shown for backward compatibility), a kernel is booted
   from another section of the root disk. For example, suppose kernel
   development takes place under /mnt/azure/root.port which happens to
   reside in its own section, section 3 of the root disk. By specifying
   a minor number of 3 in the above example, the object file
   sys.azure/S800/vmunix is loaded from /mnt/azure/root.port.

       ISL> hpux (;3)sys.azure/S800/vmunix

       Boot
       : disc(8.0.0;0x3)sys.azure/S800/vmunix
       966616+397312+409688 start 0x6c50

Booting From Another Disk
   Only the hardware path and file name are specified in this example.
   All other values are boot defaults. The object file comes from the
   file system on another disk.

       ISL> hpux (52.5.0.0)/stand/vmunix

       Boot
       : disc(52.5.0.0)/stand/vmunix
       966616+397312+409688 start 0x6c50

Booting From LAN
   This example shows how to boot a cluster client from the LAN. Though
   this example specifies a devicefile, you can also use default boot, as
   shown in a previous example. For a boot operation other than default
   boot, the file name must be specified and can be no longer than 11
   characters. Booting to isl from a local disk then requesting an image
   to be loaded from the LAN is not supported.

       ISL> hpux lan(32)/stand/vmunix

       Boot
       : lan(32;0x0)/stand/vmunix
       966616+397312+409688 start 0x6c50

Booting To Single User Mode
In this example, the -i option is used to make the system come up in
run-level s, for single user mode of operation.

```
ISL> hpux -is

Boot
: disc(8.0.0;0x0)/stand/vmunix
966616+397312+409688 start 0x6c50

    Kernel Startup Messages Omitted

INIT: Overriding default level with level 's'

INIT: SINGLE USER MODE
WARNING:  YOU ARE SUPERUSER !!
#
```

Booting With A Modified I/O Configuration
Here, a tape driver is configured in at CIO slot 2, HP-IB address 0.
Regardless of what was present in the kernel's original I/O
configuration, the driver tape is now configured at that hardware
path. Similarly, mux0 is configured in at CIO slot 1 which is to be
the console. The only other devices configured are the console and
root device, which boot derived from pdc.

```
ISL> hpux -aC mux0(8.1) -a tape(8.2.0)

Boot
: disc(8.0.0;0x0)/stand/vmunix
: Adding mux0(8.1;0x0)...
: Adding tape(8.2.0;0x0)...
966616+397312+409688 start 0x6c50
Beginning I/O System Configuration.
cio_ca0 address = 8
   hpib0 address = 0
      disc0 lu = 0 address = 0
   mux0 lu = 0 address = 1
   hpib0 address = 2
      tape1 lu = 0 address = 0
I/O System Configuration complete.

    Additional Kernel Startup Messages Omitted
```

Booting From A Raw Device
This example shows booting from a raw device (that is, a device
containing no file system). Note that no file name is specified in
the devicefile. The device is an HP7974 tape drive, and therefore
tape is the manager used. The tape drive is at CIO slot 2, HP-IB
address 3. The first file on the tape will be skipped. The minor
number specifies a tape density of 1600 BPI with no rewind on close.
Depending on the minor number, tape requires the tape be written with
512 or 1024 byte blocks.

```
ISL> hpux tape(8.2.3;0xa0000)

Boot
: tape(8.2.3;0xa0000)
966616+397312+409688 start 0x6c50
```

Displaying The Autoexecute File
In this example, show autofile is used to print the contents of the
autoexecute file residing in the boot LIF, on the device from which
hpux was booted. Optionally, a devicefile can be specified in order
to read the autoexecute file from the boot LIF of another boot device.

```
ISL> hpux show autofile
Show autofile
: AUTO file contains (hpux)
```

Changing The Autoexecute File
This example shows how to change the contents of the autoexecute file.
Once done, the system can be reset, and the new command will be used
during any unattended boot.

```
ISL> hpux set autofile "hpux /stand/vmunix.std"
Set autofile
: disk(2/0/1.3.0.0.0.0.0;0)
: AUTO file now contains "(hpux /stand/vmunix.std)"
```

Listing Directory Contents
The contents of the directory (/stand) on the root disk are listed.
The format shows the file protections, number of links, user id, group
id, and size in bytes for each file in the directory. There are three
available kernels to boot: vmunix, vmunix.test, and vmunix.prev.
Listing the files over the LAN is not supported.

```
ISL> hpux ll /stand

Ls
: disk(2/0/1.3.0.0.0.0.0;0)/stand
dr-xr-xr-x    3 2        2            1024 ./
drwxr-xr-x   17 0        0            1024 ../
-rw-r--r--    1 0        3             191 bootconf
drwxr-xr-x    2 0        0            1024 build/
-rw-r--r--    1 0        0             632 ioconfig
-rw-r--r--    1 0        3              82 kernrel
-r--r--r--    1 0        3             426 system
-rw-r--r--    1 0        3             437 system.prev
-rwxr-xr-x    1 0        3         7771408 vmunix*
-rwxr-xr-x    1 0        3         7771408 vmunix.prev*
```

Getting The Version
The -v option is used to get the version numbers of hpux.

```
ISL> hpux -v

Release: 10.00
Release Version:
@(#) X10.20.B HP-UX() #1: Dec  4 1995 16:55:08
```

DEPENDENCIES
Series 700 Only
The restore operation is provided as a recovery mechanism in the event
that a disk becomes totally corrupted. It copies data from a properly
formatted bootable tape to disk. When this tape contains a backup
image of the disk, the entire disk is restored. To create a properly
formatted tape (DDS ONLY), the following commands should be executed:

```
dd if=/usr/lib/uxbootlf of=/dev/rmt/0mn bs=2k
dd if=/dev/rdsk/1ss of=/dev/rmt/0m bs=64k
```

The first dd puts a boot area on the tape, making it a bootable image
(see dd(1)). Once the boot image is on tape, the tape is not rewound.
The next dd appends an image of the disk to the tape. The entire
process takes about one hour for a 660 MB HP2213 disk. To avoid later
problems with fsck after the disk is restored, bring the system to
single user mode and type sync a few times before doing the second dd
(see fsck(1M)). Once created, the tape can be used to completely
restore the disk:

1. Insert the tape into the tape drive.

2. Instruct the machine to boot to ISL from the tape. This is usually done by specifying scsi.3 as the boot path.

3. Enter the following in response to the ISL prompt:

    ISL> hpux restore disk(scsi.1;0)

This restores the disk image from the tape to the actual disk at scsi.1. Any existing data on the disk will be lost. This command destroys the contents of the device specified by devicefile. The restoration process takes about one hour for a 660 MB drive.

NOTE: There is a 2 GB limit on the amount of data that can be restored. The tape and disk must be on the boot device interface.

Also, this command may be replaced in the future by superior installation and recovery mechanisms. At that time, this command will be removed.

SEE ALSO
    boot(1M), fsck(1M), init(1M), isl(1M), pdc(1M), errno(2), a.out(4), inittab(4), magic(4).

isl

isl - Initial System Loader (isl) overview.

```
isl(1M)                        Series 800 Only                      isl(1M)

NAME
        isl - initial system loader

DESCRIPTION

        isl implements the operating system independent portion of the
        bootstrap process.  It is loaded and executed after self-test and
        initialization have completed successfully.

        The processor contains special purpose memory for maintaining critical
        configuration related parameters (e.g. Primary Boot, Alternate Boot,
        and Console Paths).  Two forms of memory are supported: Stable Storage
        and Non-Volatile Memory (NVM).

        Typically, when control is transferred to isl, an autoboot sequence
        takes place.  An autoboot sequence allows a complete bootstrap
        operation to occur with no intervention from an operator.  isl
        executes commands from the autoexecute file in a script-like fashion.
        autoboot is enabled by a flag in Stable Storage.

        autosearch is a mechanism that automatically locates the boot and
        console devices.  For further information, see pdc(1M).

        During an autoboot sequence, isl displays its revision and the name of
        any utility it executes.  However, if autoboot is disabled, after isl
        displays its revision, it then prompts for input from the console
        device.  Acceptable input is any isl command name or the name of any
        utility available on the system.  If a non-fatal error occurs or the
        executed utility returns, isl again prompts for input.

    Commands
        There are several commands available in isl. The following is a list
        with a short description.  Parameters may be entered on the command
        line following the command name.  They must be separated by spaces.
        isl prompts for any necessary parameters that are not entered on the
        command line.

                ?
                help           Help - List commands and available utilities

                listf
                ls             List available utilities

                autoboot       Enable or disable the autoboot sequence
                               Parameter - on or off

                autosearch     Enable or disable the autosearch sequence
                               Parameter - on or off

                primpath       Modify the Primary Boot Path
                               Parameter - Primary Boot Path in decimal
```

altpath	Modify the Alternate Boot Path	
	Parameter - Alternate Boot Path in decimal	
conspath	Modify the Console Path	
	Parameter - Console Path in decimal	
lsautofl		
listautofl	List contents of the autoexecute file	
display	Display the Primary Boot, Alternate Boot, and Console Paths	
readnvm	Display the contents of one word of NVM in hexadecimal	
	Parameter - NVM address in decimal or standard hexadecimal notation	
readss	Display the contents of one word of Stable Storage in hexadecimal	
	Parameter - Stable Storage address in decimal or standard hexadecimal notation	

DIAGNOSTICS

isl displays diagnostic information through error messages written on the console and display codes on the LED display.

For the display codes, CE0x are informative only. CE1x and CE2x indicate errors, some of which are fatal and cause the system to halt. Other errors merely cause isl to display a message.

Non-fatal errors during an autoboot sequence cause the autoboot sequence to be aborted and isl to prompt for input. After non-fatal errors during an interactive isl session, isl merely prompts for input.

Fatal errors cause the system to halt. The problem must be corrected and the system RESET to recover.

```
CE00    isl is executing.
CE01    isl is autobooting from the autoexecute file.
CE02    Cannot find an autoexecute file.  autoboot aborted.
CE03    No console found, isl can only autoboot.
CE05    Directory of utilities is too big, isl reads only 2K bytes.
CE06    autoexecute file is inconsistent.  autoboot aborted.
CE07    Utility file header inconsistent: SOM values invalid.
 CE08     autoexecute file input string exceeds 2048 characters.    autoboot
aborted.
CE09    isl command or utility name exceeds 10 characters.
CE0F    isl has transferred control to the utility.
CE10    Internal inconsistency: Volume label - FATAL.
CE11    Internal inconsistency: Directory - FATAL.
CE12    Error reading autoexecute file.
CE13    Error reading from console - FATAL.
CE14    Error writing to console - FATAL.
CE15    Not an isl command or utility.
CE16    Utility file header inconsistent: Invalid System ID.
CE17    Error reading utility file header.
CE18    Utility file header inconsistent: Bad magic number.
CE19    Utility would overlay isl in memory.
CE1A    Utility requires more memory than is configured.
CE1B    Error reading utility into memory.
CE1C    Incorrect checksum: Reading utility into memory.
CE1D    Console needed - FATAL.
CE1E    Internal inconsistency: Boot device class - FATAL.
CE21    Destination memory address of utility is invalid.
```

        CE22   Utility file header inconsistent: pdc_cache entry.
        CE23   Internal inconsistency: iodc_entry_init - FATAL.
        CE24   Internal inconsistency: iodc_entry_init - console - FATAL.
        CE25   Internal inconsistency: iodc_entry_init - boot device - FATAL.
        CE26   Utility file header inconsistent: Bad aux_id.
        CE27   Bad utility file type.

SEE ALSO
        boot(1M), hpux_800(1M), pdc(1M).

pdc

man page

pdc - 1

pdc - Processor Dependent Code (pdc) overview.

```
pdc(1M)                                                              pdc(1M)

NAME
     pdc - processor-dependent code (firmware)

DESCRIPTION
     pdc is the firmware that implements all processor-dependent
     functionality, including initialization and self-test of the
     processor.  Upon completion, it loads and transfers control to the
     initial system loader (isl(1M)).  Firmware behavior varies somewhat,
     depending on the hardware series as described below.

   Series 800 Behavior
     To load isl from an external medium, pdc must know the particular
     device on which isl resides.  Typically the device is identified by
     the Primary Boot Path that is maintained by pdc in Stable Storage.  A
     path specification is a series of decimal numbers each suffixed by
     '/', indicating bus converters, followed by a series of decimal
     numbers separated by '.', indicating the various card and slot numbers
     and addresses.  The first number, not specifying a bus converter, is
     the MID-BUS module number (that is, slot number times four) and
     followed by the CIO slot number.  If the CIO slot contains an HP-IB
     card, the next number is the HP-IB address, followed by the unit
     number of the device if the device supports units.  If the CIO slot
     contains a terminal card, the next number is the port number, which
     must be zero for the console.

     When the processor is reset after initialization and self-test
     complete, pdc reads the Console Path from Stable Storage, and attempts
     to initialize the console device.  If the initialization fails, pdc
     attempts to find and initialize a console device.  Algorithms used to
     find a console device are model-dependent.  pdc then announces the
     Primary Boot, Alternate Boot, and Console Paths.

     If autoboot (see isl(1M)) is enabled, pdc provides a 10-second delay,
     during which time the operator can override the autoboot sequence by
     typing any character on the console.  If the operator does not
     interrupt this process, pdc initializes and reads isl from the Primary
     Boot Path.  On models that support autosearch, if this path is not
     valid and autosearch (see isl(1M)) is enabled, pdc then searches
     through the MID-BUS modules and CIO slots to find a bootable medium.
     Currently, autosearch is only implemented on the model 825.

     If the autoboot sequence is unsuccessful, overridden by the operator,
     or not enabled in the first place, pdc interactively prompts the
     operator for the Boot Path to use.  Any required path components that
     are not supplied default to zero.

     The Primary Boot, Alternate Boot, and Console Paths as well as
     autoboot and autosearch enable can be modified via isl.

   Series 700 Behavior
     To load isl from an external medium, pdc must know the particular
```

device on which isl resides. Typically the device is identified by
the Primary Boot Path that is maintained by pdc in Stable Storage. A
path specification is an I/O subsystem mnemonic that varies according
to hardware model.

When the processor is reset after initialization and self-test
complete, pdc reads the Console Path from Stable Storage, and attempts
to initialize the console device. If the initialization fails, pdc
attempts to find and initialize a console device. Algorithms used to
find a console device vary according to hardware model.

If autoboot and autosearch (see isl(1M)) are enabled, pdc waits for
approximately 10 seconds during which time the operator can override
the autoboot sequence pressing and holding the ESC (escape) key on the
console.

The system then begins a search for potentially bootable devices. If
allowed to complete, a list of potentially bootable devices is
displayed, labeled with abbreviated path identifiers (P0, P1, etc). A
simple menu is then displayed where the user can:

- Boot a specific device, using the abbreviated path identifier,
  or the full mnenomic.

- Start a device search where the contents are searched for IPL
  images (note the first search only identified devices and did
  not check the contents).

- Enter the boot administration level.

- Exit the menu and return to autobooting

- Get help on choices

The search of potentially bootable devices can be aborted by pressing
and holding the escape key. The search for device contents can also
be aborted by pressing and holding the escape key.

If the operator does not interrupt the search process, pdc initializes
and reads isl from the Primary Boot Path.

If the autoboot sequence is unsuccessful, overridden by the operator,
or not enabled in the first place, pdc executes the device search and
enters the menu described above.

The Primary Boot, Alternate Boot, and Console Paths as well as
autoboot and autosearch enable can be modified via isl or at the pdc
boot administration level.

SEE ALSO
    boot(1M), hpuxboot(1M), isl(1M).

CHAPTER 2

Installing HP-UX

Topics Covered in this Chapter

We'll cover several topics related to installing HP-UX in this chapter. These topics are covered in the order in which you would install the software when initially loading your system:

- Installing the HP-UX 11i *Operating Environment*.
- Setting system parameters at time of first boot after loading HP-UX 11i with **set_parms**.
- Installing application software with Software Distributor.
- Download and install select patches on your system.
- Software Distributor background.

You would typically load software in the order shown above: install the base *Operating Environment*; boot your system and use **set_parms**; load application software; and finally download and install select patches.

Install HP-UX 11i Operating Environment

Installing HP-UX means installing one of the 11i *Operating Environments* and later building your complete fully functional HP-UX system by installing both HP and non-HP applications. The initial system is loaded from the 11i media, or from another system on the network using Ignite-UX. This chapter covers installing from media. The Ignite-UX chapter covers installing from a server.

You can have your system delivered with instant ignition, which means that HP-UX has been loaded on your system and you'll only have to add to it the application software you'll need. I cover the complete installation process from media so you can see the process from start to finish. If you have instant ignition on your system, you may need to install additional software on your system in the future and can, therefore, use some of the techniques described in this section to load that software.

One of the features of moving any version of the 11.x operating system (including 11i) is the option of taking advantage of 64-bit computing. Whereas previous versions of HP-UX supported only the 32-bit processor, with 11.x, you have the option of running either the 32-bit or the 64-bit version. Which version of the operating system you choose is dependent on two things: what hardware you are using and your application requirements. The 64-bit version is not supported on some Series 700 workstations and many of the low-end Series 800s, but it is required for the L-Class, N-Class, V-Class, and Superdome servers. With other Series 800s, most notably the K Class and T Class servers, you have the option to install either the 32-bit or the 64-bit version. But don't worry too much if you are unsure whether your hardware supports 64-bit or not. If your hardware doesn't support the 64-bit version, you won't be prompted as to which version to install. The 32-bit version will be installed automatically. If you have the option to install the 32-bit or 64-bit version, then your hardware supports either.

Your application requirements will also help determine whether you will install the 32-bit or 64-bit operating system. If your applications are 32-bit, then you really have no reason to run the 64-bit version. If, however, you will be running a 64-bit application, then you obviously will need to install the 64-bit operating system. The good news is that if you install the 32-bit operating system and then find that an application you want to install is 64-bit, you can upgrade to the 64-bit operating system, assuming, of course, that your hardware also supports it.

Boot System and "Advanced Installation"

In order to install HP-UX software, place the core operating system media for HP-UX 11i into the DVD-ROM or CD-ROM drive. At the time of this writing, the CD-ROM was labeled *HP-UX Release 11.11.* There were two CD-ROMs as part of the core operating system I was working with because I was loading the *Mission Critical Operating Environment* which was on two CD-ROMs (more about the *Operating Environments later.)* Be sure to insert the CD-ROM Install media before you begin the installation. As your HP 9000 unit boots, you will see a variety of messages fly by, including information about your processors, busses, boot paths, and so on. See Chapter 1, which covered the boot process, to get more information about booting.

The following example shows several steps that were taken. The example begins at the end of early boot. The early boot is the first part of the load process from media. There were many early boot-related messages that appeared before the point where our example begins. We discontinued the boot process by pressing a key. After discontinuing the boot we run *SEArch* to find bootable devices. Among the devices shown is the DVD-ROM drive containing our operating system media. We select *p0* to boot off of with the **bo p0** command. We then choose not to interact with IPL.

```
************ EARLY BOOT VFP *************
End of early boot detected
*******************************************

Firmware Version  39.46

Duplex Console IO Dependent Code (IODC) revision 1

---------------------------------------------------------------------------
   (c) Copyright 1995-1998, Hewlett-Packard Company, All rights reserved
```

```
--------------------------------------------------------------------------

    Processor    Speed              State          CoProcessor State  Cache Size
    Number                                         State              Inst    Data
    ---------    --------    --------------------   -----------------  ------------
         0       440  MHz    Active                 Functional         512 KB   1 MB
         3       440  MHz    Idle                   Functional         512 KB   1 MB

    Central Bus Speed (in MHz)  :        82
    Available Memory            :    2097152  KB
    Good Memory Required        :      16908  KB

     Primary boot path:      0/0/1/1.2
     Alternate boot path:    0/0/2/0.2
     Console path:           0/0/4/0.0
     Keyboard path:          0/0/4/0.0

    WARNING:  The non-destructive test bit was set, so memory was not tested
              destructively.  Information only, no action required.


  Processor is booting from first available device.

  To discontinue, press any key within 10 seconds.

  Boot terminated.


  ---- Main Menu ----------------------------------------------------------

        Command                           Description
        -------                           -----------
        BOot [PRI|ALT|<path>]             Boot from specified path
        PAth [PRI|ALT] [<path>]           Display or modify a path
        SEArch [DIsplay|IPL] [<path>]     Search for boot devices

        COnfiguration menu                Displays or sets boot values
        INformation menu                  Displays hardware information
        SERvice menu                      Displays service commands

        DIsplay                           Redisplay the current menu
        HElp [<menu>|<command>]           Display help for menu or command
        RESET                             Restart the system
  ----
  Main Menu: Enter command or menu > search

  Searching for potential boot device(s)
  This may take several minutes.

  To discontinue search, press any key (termination may not be immediate).


    Path#  Device Path (dec)   Device Path (mnem)   Device Type
    -----  -----------------   ------------------   -----------
    P0     0/0/1/0.3           extscsi.3            Random access media
    P1     0/0/1/1.2           intscsib.2           Random access media
    P2     0/0/2/0.2           intscsia.2           Random access media


  Main Menu: Enter command or menu > bo P0
  Interact with IPL (Y, N, or Cancel)?> n

  Booting...
```

The *SEArch* command in the previous listing showed us the bootable devices. There are three possible boot devices. The second two

are in the internal disks, one of which would normally be the primary boot device and the other which is normally the alternate boot device. These two disks are on two different SCSI busses internal to the L-Class. The first device was the external DVD-ROM that contains the HP-UX 11i CD-ROM, which is operating system media off of which we want to boot.

In order to boot off of the media and not interact with IPL (for more information on IPL, see Chapter 1), we issued the following command:

```
Main Menu: Enter command or menu > bo p0
Interact with IPL (Y or N)?> N
```

After booting off of *P0*, we are given the *Welcome to the HP-UX installation/recovery process!* menu shown in the following example:

```
             Welcome to the HP-UX installation/recovery process!

      Use the <tab> key to navigate between fields, and the arrow keys
      within fields.  Use the <return/enter> key to select an item.
      Use the <return> or <space-bar> to pop-up a choices list.  If the
      menus are not clear, select the "Help" item for more information.

      Hardware Summary:      System Model: 9000/800/L2000-44
      +--------------------+----------------+--------------------+ [ Scan Again  ]
      | Disks: 2  ( 33.9GB) | Floppies: 0    | LAN cards:    2    |
      | CD/DVDs:         1   | Tapes:    0    | Memory:   2048Mb  |
      | Graphics Ports: 0    | IO Buses: 8    | CPUs:         2    | [ H/W Details ]
      +--------------------+----------------+--------------------+

                          [    Install HP-UX        ]

                          [  Run a Recovery Shell   ]

                          [   Advanced Options       ]


          [ Reboot  ]                              [ Help  ]
```

The *Welcome to the HP-UX installation/recovery process!* menu is the first menu displayed. It gives a summary of the hardware on your system. If you want to see more detail, select the *H/W Details* option on the right side of the screen. This takes you to a detailed listing of your hardware. It includes items such as hardware paths, disk drive capacities, and LAN addresses. We won't perform any other functions in this example other than our selection of *Install HP-UX*.

When we select *Install HP-UX*, we get the *User Interface and Media Options* menu shown in the following example:

```
                     User Interface and Media Options

     This screen lets you pick from options that will determine if an
     Ignite-UX server is used, and your user interface preference.

   Source Location Options:
     [ * ]   Media only installation
     [   ]   Media with Network enabled (allows use of SD depots)
     [   ]   Ignite-UX server based installation

   User Interface Options:
     [   ]   Guided Installation    (recommended for basic installs)
     [ * ]   Advanced Installation (recommended for disk and filesystem management)
     [   ]   No user interface - use all the defaults and go


    Hint: If you need to make LVM size changes, or want to set the
          final networking parameters during the install, you will
          need to use the Advanced mode (or remote graphical interface).



   [   OK   ]                      [ Cancel ]                    [  Help  ]
```

This menu gives you the option of installing from the media only, installing from the media combined with the software depots on your network, or the Ignite-UX product. We'll be installing from the media only in our example.

We next select *Advanced Installation* because this gives us the greatest level of flexibility when installing. *Guided Installation* leads you through a basic system configuration setup. It allows for only a few system-specific options. *Advanced Installation* is much more flexible and allows for extensive system-specific parameters to be set. We'll walk through the *Advanced Installation* steps.

The display that now appears is similar to that used by Ignite-UX. In fact, it is the same except that Ignite-UX uses a graphical user interface (GUI) versus the terminal user interface (TUI). Figure 2-1 shows this display.

```
/--------------------------------------------------------------------\
|                      /opt/ignite/bin/itool                         |
|                                                                    |
| /-------\/----------\/---------\/-------------\/----------\        |
| | Basic || Software|| System || File System || Advanced |        |
| \        \-----------------------------------------------/        |
|  Configurations:  [ HP-UX B.11.11 Default    ->] [ Description... ]|
|                                                                    |
|  Environments:     [ Mission Critical OE-64bit  ->] (HP-UX B.11.11)|
|                                                                    |
|  [ Root Disk... ] SEAGATE ST318203LC, 0/0/1/1.2.0, 17366 M        |
|                                                                    |
|  File System:     [ Logical Volume Manager (LVM) with VxFS  ->]   |
|                                                                    |
|  [ Root Swap (MB)... ] 1024   Physical Memory (RAM) =  2048 MB    |
|        [ Languages... ] English  [ Keyboards... ] [ Additional... ]|
|                                                                    |
|  ----------------------------------------------------------------- |
|  [ Show Summary... ]                         [ Reset Configuration ]|
|  ----------------------------------------------------------------- |
|      [ Go! ]              [ Cancel ]              [Help]           |
|                                                                    |
\--------------------------------------------------------------------/
```

Figure 2-1 Ignite/UX Display *Basic* Tab Area Using TUI

The *Advanced Installation* menu lets you choose from among the menu tab areas with the ability of going back and forth among them until you are satisfied with your choices.

Across the top of the menu display are five tab areas: *Basic*, *Software*, *System*, *File System*, and *Advanced*. By pressing the tab key, each Tab area can be highlighted. To select the highlighted tab area, press the Enter/Return key. This will cause that tab area's screen to be displayed. Within each of these areas are several parameters that can be modified for your specific system. Listed below are the main features of each tab area:

- *Basic* - configuration and environment information.
- *Software* - ability to choose optional software to be installed. Mostly the same options that appear under *Guided Installation*.
- *System* - networking parameters. Also configurable via the **set_parms** command.
- *File System* - disk space allocation.
- *Advanced* - advanced disk, file system, logical volume, and volume group parameters.

We configure our system beginning with the *Basic* screen as shown in Figure 2-1.

Items of particular importance are discussed below:

- Configuration - we use *HP-UX B.11.11 Default.* HP-UX 11i is called by its original name, 11.11, in some cases.
- Environments - there are four 11i environments to select from at the time of this writing. This is a major change in the software distribution method for HP-UX 11i. The *Operating Environments* are bundles of software that make installing 11i easier. We'll select the first of the four, which is the top level, or most elaborate, of the *Operating Environments* as shown in the following example:

```
Mission Critical OE-64bit .>] (HP-UX B.11.11)
                 Enterprise OE-64bit
                 HP-UX 11i OE-64bit
                 HP-UX 11i Base OS-64bit
```

- Root Disk - the default selection for the root disk is the first internal disk drive, which is the disk with a path of 0/0/1/1.2.0 in our example.

- File System - we are given the option of choosing wholedisk (not LVM) with HFS, Logical Volume Manager with HFS, or Logical Volume Manager with VxFS. If you have not reviewed the Logical Volume Manager section of this chapter, you will want to do so before you make this selection (LVM is Logical Volume Manager). I am a strong advocate of using Logical Volume Manager with VxFS whenever possible.

- Root Swap - the system automatically selects an amount twice the size of your main memory, or a maximum of 1024 MB. You will want to consider your primary swap space very carefully. The L-Class system in our example has 2GBytes of memory and we'll go with the default of 1 GByte of swap as shown.

- Languages - We'll install English on our system; however, there are many languages available for 11i systems.

- Additional - this is the pick at the bottom right corner of the screen, not the tab area. Here is where you can configure such things as a second swap area, adding a second disk drive to the root volume, and disabling DHCP. With 11i, DHCP, Dynamic Host Configuration Protocol, works with an Ignite-UX server that automatically assigns system name, IP address, etc.

The major difference between the selections just discussed for 11i and earlier releases of 11.x are the *Operating Environments.* 11i is the first HP-UX release for which *Operating Environments* are available.

Moving to the *Software* tab area, we find software on the installation CD-ROM for 11i that has been marked for installation. Since we have selected the *Mission Critical Operating Environment* there is a lot of software automatically selected as part of this installation.

Figure 2-2 shows some of the software we have selected in the *Software* tab area. We have selected *All* so that we can see all of the software that has been selected as part of the *Mission Critical Operating Environment*. We could scroll down to see additional software.

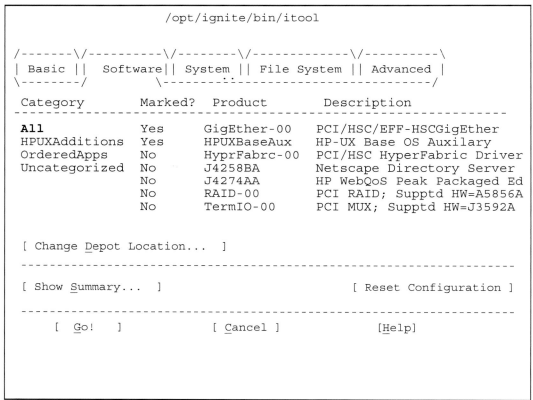

Figure 2-2 *Software* Tab Area

Other software you may want to install can be selected from the installation CD. In the example the first two items have automaticallly been selected as part of the *Mission Critical Operating Environment*.

At this point, we could select additional software such as *Hyperfabric* and *Netscape Directory Server* in this window. Keep in mind the software shown in this window is on the core operating system CD-ROM for 11i. You may later want to install application software from the HP-UX Applications CD set. This is done using Software Distributor. An overview of the Software Distributor product used for installing all HP-UX 11i software appears later in this chapter. You may want to take a look at this overview to get a feel for the type of functionality Software Distributor offers. The **swinstall** program is the Software Distributor program used to install software. If you have application software to be installed, you will interact with **swinstall,** and possibly be asked for codeword information for some of the software to be installed. If your software is protected, you will have to enter the codeword information. If you need a codeword, it should be printed on the CD-ROM certificate you received with your software. This codeword is tied to the ID number of a hardware device in your system.

With the software we wish to load on our system having been selected we can move on to the next area.

The *System* tab area, shown in Figure 2-3, is where system identification-related configuration information can be found. Since we want to configure networking and other related information after the installation is complete, we have changed only the first item on this screen. The options for the first item are:

Final system parameters: [Set parameters now]

[Ask at first boot]

We selected *Ask at first boot.*

```
                            /opt/ignite/bin/itool


/-------\/-----------\/--------\/-------------\/----------\
| Basic || Software|| System || File System || Advanced |
\-------------------/'         \------------------------/

     Final System Parameters:  [ Ask at first boot     ->]


  All of the system parameters will be collected interactively.
  during the initial boot of the system.

  If you wish to specify these parameters now, please select
  "Set parameters now".



  -------------------------------------------------------------------
[ Show Summary... ]                           [ Reset Configuration ]
  -------------------------------------------------------------------

    [ Go!   ]                [ Cancel ]             [Help]
```

Figure 2-3 *System* Tab Area

When the system first boots, we'll be asked to enter system identification-related information.

The *File System* tab area, shown in Figure 2-4, is of particular importance. Here is where you can change file system sizes. You will not normally be satisfied with the default sizes of some of the logical volumes. I normally spend some time in this tab area increasing the sizes of some of the logical volumes. Figure 2-4 also shows the layout of the *File System* screen and the values of three of the logical volumes with their updated sizes. Root is highlighted in this example so the paramenters related to it appear under *Usage, Size,* and so on.

```
                        /opt/ignite/bin/itool

/--------\/----------\/--------\/------------\/----------\
| Basic || Software|| System || File System || Advanced |
\-----------------------::--------/          \----------/

Mount Dir      Usage    Size(MB)   % Used  Group    S

/stand         HFS      300        7       vg00     F ^ [ Add      ]
primary        SWAP+D   1024       0       vg00     R   [ Modify   ]
/              VxFS     400        9       vg00     F v [ Remove   ]

Usage:  [ VxFS       ->]   Group:  [ vg ->]   Mount Dir:  /_____

Size:  [ Fixed MB     ->]   400      Avail: 13360 MB

[ Add/Remove Disks... ]    [ ---- Additional Tasks ----    ->]


-----------------------------------------------------------------

[ Show Summary... ]                        ' [ Reset Configuration ]

-----------------------------------------------------------------

   [  Go!  ]              [ Cancel ]              [Help]
```

Figure 2-4 *File System* Tab Area

    To make logical volume size changes, you select the mount directory of the logical volume, tab down to *Size,* and enter the desired new size. In addition to *Size,* there are several other parameters related to the logical volume that you can change.

    You will notice that *Avail* shows you how much disk space is left to be allocated on your disk drive. It is perfectly all right to leave some disk space unallocated. This will give you a cushion for when you need to increase disk space down the road.

    After making all the volume size-related modifications, we are ready to go ahead and install the system. However, first we want to choose the *Show Summary* option towards the bottom of the screen.

This option will show us a summary of all the changes we made. This gives us a chance to make sure that we didn't forget something. Figure 2-5 shows the *General Summary* screen.

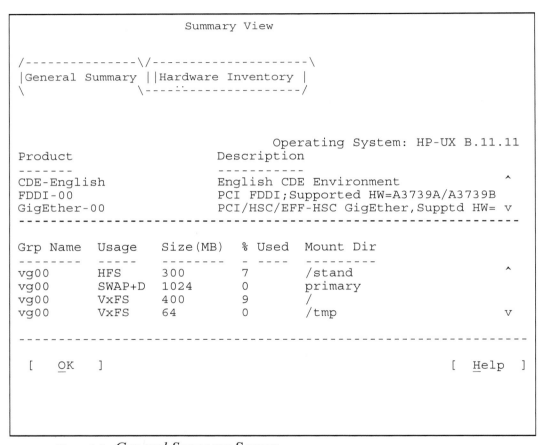

Figure 2-5 *General Summary* Screen

This screen provides information on the software we have selected to load and informatoin on our logical volumes.

Figure 2-6 shows the *Hardware Inventory* summary screen.

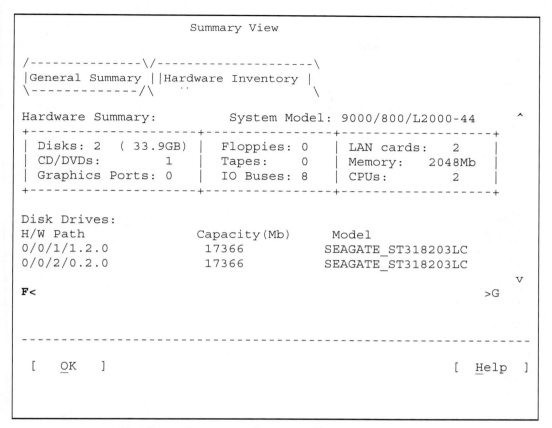

Figure 2-6 *Hardware Inventory Summary* Screen

The *Hardware Inventory Summary* Screen information provides a short summary of system hardware.

Since we are satisfied with all of the modifications we have made we are ready to load the operating system. We choose *Go!* which appears at the bottom of all the tab area screens and the screen in Figure 2-7 appears:

```
                        itool Confirmation

All data will be destroyed on the following disks:

Addr           Disk Size(MB)   Description
----           -------------   -----------
0/0/1/1.2.0    17366 MB        SEAGATE_ST318203LC




The results of the pre-install analysis are:


WARNING: The disk at: 0/0/1/1.2.0 (SEAGATE_ST318203LC)
appears to contain a file system and boot area.  Continuing
the installation will destroy any existing data on this
disk.



-----------------------------------------------------------------
    [  Go!   ]              [ Cancel ]              [Help]
```

Figure 2-7 *Go!* Screen

       This screen warns us that there is an operating system already
present on our target disk, but we want to proceed with the installation
anyway and select *Go!*. The load of the HP-UX is automatic at this
point and you can come back in an hour or so to check the log file and
see if loading the operating system completed successfully.

       It may be that your HP-UX 11i *Operating Environment* requires
a second CD-ROM to complete the installation as is the case with our
Mission Critical Operating Environment. As shown in the upcoming
listing you'll be prompted to load the second CD-ROM:

```
=======================================================================
                    USER INTERACTION REQUIRED:
To complete the installation you must now insert the
"MC_OE" CD.

Once this is done, press the <Return> key to continue:

        * Starting swinstall of the source (MC_OE).
        * Running command: "/usr/sbin/swinstall -s/tmp/ign_configure/SD_CDROM
          -f/tmp/ign_configure/software_file  -x os_release=B.11.11 -x
          os_name=HP-UX:64 "
```

When the operating system load is complete we're asked for the system identification-related information we did not earlier enter. The following listing shows the first of these screens:

```
                        Welcome to HP-UX!

Before using your system, you will need to answer a few questions.

The first question is whether you plan to use this system on a network.

Answer "yes" if you have connected the system to a network and are ready
to link with a network.

Answer "no" if you:

        * Plan to set up this system as a standalone (no networking).

        * Want to use the system now as a standalone and connect to a
          network later.
```

```
Are you ready to link this system to a network?

Press [y] for yes or [n] for no, then press [Enter]
```

If you choose to connect your system network, you'll be asked a variety of questions about the networking configuration. You don't have to enter this information now because there is a command called **set_parms** that we'll cover in the next section which is an alternative way of entering system identification-related information. We'll cover this command in the next section.

Now that our *Mission Critical Operating Environment* installation is complete, we'll check the operating system revision with

uname -a and software bundles that have been loaded on the system
with **swlist** in the upcoming listing:

```
# uname -a
HP-UX l3 B.11.11 U 9000/800 143901527 unlimited-user license
# swlist
# Initializing...
# Contacting target "l3"...
#
# Target:  l3:/
#

#
# Bundle(s):
#

  CDE-English          B.11.11.%20A   English CDE Environment
  FDDI-00              B.11.11.%20    PCI FDDI;Supported HW=A3739A/A3739B;SW=J3 626AA
  GigEther-00          B.11.11.11.08  PCI/HSC/EFF-HSC GigEther,Supptd HW=A4926A
                                      ,A4929A,A4924A,A4925A;SW=J1642AA
  HPUX11i-OE-MC        B.11.11.%20A   HP-UX Mission Critical Operating
                                      Environment Component
  HPUXBase64           B.11.11.%20A   HP-UX 64-bit Base OS
  HPUXBaseAux          B.11.11.%20A   HP-UX Base OS Auxilary
     #
```

This listing shows that HP-UX 11i has indeed been loaded, shown as
11.11 in the listing, and that several software bundles have been loaded as
well, inluding the *Mission Critical Operating Environment.*

Let's now move to the next section in which we'll specify the system-
related information we have put off during our installation.

Set System Parameters after Boot

When the system comes up after installation, a series of windows appear that allow you to configure your system name, time zone, root password, Internet Protocol (IP) address, subnet mask, and other networking settings (IP address and subnet mask background is provided in the Networking chapter). One of the first questions you will be asked is whether or not you wish to use DHCP to obtain networking information. Dynamic host configuration protocol works with an Ignite-UX server that automatically assigns system name, IP address, and so on. Since our installation does not use this, I answered "no" which means we'll have to enter all of our information manually.

The system-specific information to be entered next can also be entered, after your system boots, by running **/sbin/set_parms**. This program can be used to set an individual system parameter or all the system parameters that would be set at boot time. **/sbin/set_parms** uses one of the arguments in Table 2-1, depending on what you would like to configure.

TABLE 2-1 /sbin/set_parms Arguments

set_parms Argument	Comments
hostname	Set hostname.
timezone	Set time zone.
date_time	Set date and time.
root_passwd	Set root password.
ip_address	Set Internet Protocol address (see Chapter 2 for networking background).
addl_network	Configure subnet mask, Domain Name System, and Network Information Service.
initial	Go through the entire question-and-answer session you would experience at boot time.

If you use the **initial** argument, you'll interact with a variety of dialog boxes asking you for information. The System Hostname dialog box is shown in Figure 2-8.

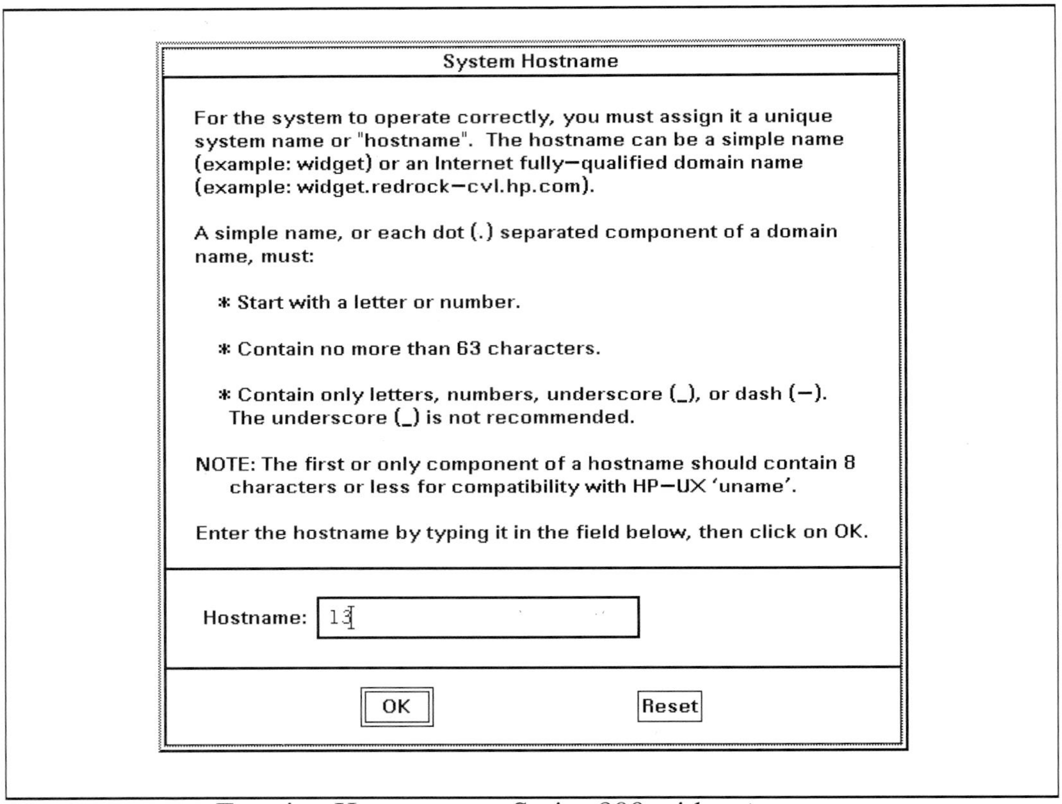

System Hostname

For the system to operate correctly, you must assign it a unique system name or "hostname". The hostname can be a simple name (example: widget) or an Internet fully-qualified domain name (example: widget.redrock-cvl.hp.com).

A simple name, or each dot (.) separated component of a domain name, must:

    * Start with a letter or number.

    * Contain no more than 63 characters.

    * Contain only letters, numbers, underscore (_), or dash (−).
      The underscore (_) is not recommended.

NOTE: The first or only component of a hostname should contain 8 characters or less for compatibility with HP−UX 'uname'.

Enter the hostname by typing it in the field below, then click on OK.

Hostname: | 13 |

| OK | | Reset |

Figure 2-8 Entering Hostname on Series 800 with **set_parms**

You'll then be asked for your time zone and root password. Figure 2-9 shows the dialog box for entering your IP address:

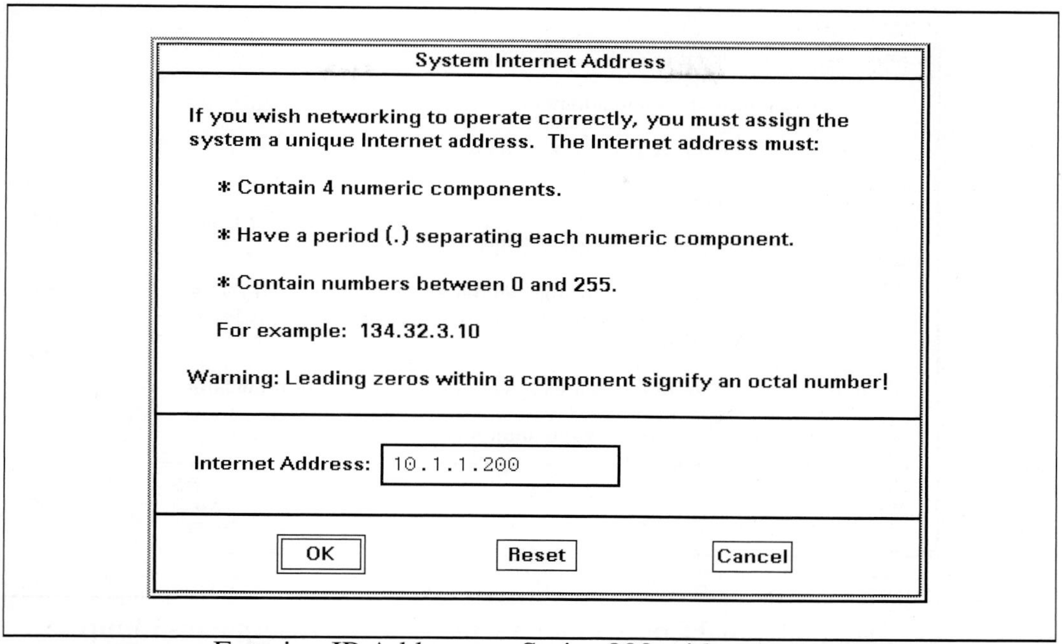

```
┌─────────────────────────────────────────────────────────────┐
│  ┌───────────────────────────────────────────────────────┐  │
│  │                System Internet Address                │  │
│  │                                                       │  │
│  │  If you wish networking to operate correctly, you must assign the  │  │
│  │  system a unique Internet address.  The Internet address must:     │  │
│  │                                                       │  │
│  │      * Contain 4 numeric components.                  │  │
│  │                                                       │  │
│  │      * Have a period (.) separating each numeric component.        │  │
│  │                                                       │  │
│  │      * Contain numbers between 0 and 255.             │  │
│  │                                                       │  │
│  │      For example:  134.32.3.10                        │  │
│  │                                                       │  │
│  │  Warning: Leading zeros within a component signify an octal number! │  │
│  │                                                       │  │
│  │                                      ┌──────────────┐  │  │
│  │  Internet Address:                   │ 10.1.1.200   │  │  │
│  │                                      └──────────────┘  │  │
│  │                                                       │  │
│  │    ┌────────┐        ┌─────────┐       ┌─────────┐    │  │
│  │    │   OK   │        │  Reset  │       │ Cancel  │    │  │
│  │    └────────┘        └─────────┘       └─────────┘    │  │
│  └───────────────────────────────────────────────────────┘  │
└─────────────────────────────────────────────────────────────┘
```

Figure 2-9 Entering IP Address on Series 800 with **set_parms**

You can then configure your subnet mask and other networking parameters.

Configuration includes the items shown in Figure 2-10:

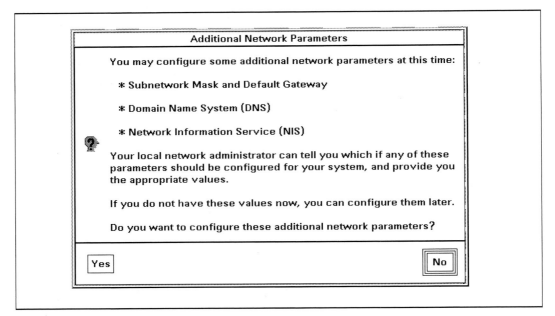

Figure 2-10   Additional Configuration with **set_parms setparms3.bmp**

Running **set_parms initial** or **set_parms** with other options allows you to specify all of the initial information related to your system setup. This saves you the trouble of finding all of the relevant files in which you'd have to place the information you provide to **set_parms**.

Software Distributor Example

Software Distributor-HP-UX (I'll call this Software Distributor throughout the book; HP documentation typically uses SD-UX) is the program used in HP-UX 11i to perform all tasks related to software management. Software Distributor will be used in an example to install software on the same system we loaded our operating system on earlier in this chapter. Software Distributor is a standards-based way to perform software management. It conforms to the Portable Operating System Interface (POSIX) standard for packaging software and utilities related to software managment. The Software Distributor product described in this section comes with your HP-UX system. Additional functionality can be obtained by buying the OpenView Software Distributor (SD-OV) product. SD-OV provides support for additional platforms, allows you to push software out to target systems, features centralized monitoring, and provides a job browser to assist in managing software on target systems. In this section, I won't cover SD-OV, but will make some comments about SD-OV functionality where appropriate.

man page
"sw" - 2

Software Distributor can be invoked using the commands described in this section, by using SAM (covered in Chapter 10), or by installing software for the first time as described earlier in this chapter.

The following are the four phases of software installation performed with Software Distributor:

- Selection(1) - You can select the source and software you wish to load during this phase. In the upcoming example, the graphical user interface of Software Distributor is used and you'll see how easily you can select these.

- Analysis(2) - All kinds of checks are performed for you, including free disk space; dependencies; compatibility; mounted volumes; and others. One of the very useful outputs of this phase is the amount of space the software you wish to load will consume on each logical volume. This will be shown in the example.

• Load(3) - After you are satisfied with the analysis, you may proceed with loading the software.

• Configuration(4) - The software you load may require kernel rebuilding and a system reboot. Startup and shutdown scripts may also need to be modified.

man page

"sw" - 2

There is some terminology associated with Software Distributor that I tend to use somewhat loosely. I have nothing but good things to say about Software Distributor, but I don't tend to conform to the official Software Distributor terminology as much as I should. I tend, for instance, to use the word *"system"* a lot, which could mean many different things in the Software Distributor world. For instance, Software Distributor uses *"local host"* (a system on which Software Distributor is running or software is to be installed or managed by Software Distributor), *"distribution depot"* (a directory that is used as a place for software products), and *"development system"* (a place where software is prepared for distribution). I will use the word *system* to mean the system on which we are working in the examples, because software is loaded onto the system from media.

The example of Software Distributor in this section describes the process of loading software from CD-ROM or DVD to the local system. What I show here only begins to scratch the surface of functionality you have with Software Distributor, but since I want to get you up and running quickly, this overview should be helpful. You can load software from a variety of media as well as across the network. You can run **swinstall** through the graphical interface used throughout this section, the character user interface, or the command line. You can use the **swinstall** command from the command line specifying source, options, target, etc. I would recommend using the character or graphical user interface because they are so much easier. If, however, you like to do things the "traditional UNIX" way, you can issue the **swinstall** command with arguments. You can look at the manual page for **swinstall** to understand its arguments and options and use this command from the command line. The graphical user interface of Software Distributor works with the **sd** (this is an SD-OV command and may also be invoked with **swjob -i**), **swcopy**, **swremove, swlist**, and **swinstall** commands. There is also an interactive terminal user interface for these commands if you don't have a graphics display.

man page

"sw" - 2

On the L-Class system used in the upcoming example, there wasn't much to do in order to load software from a CD-ROM. I just physically put the CD-ROM in the DVD drive and typed **swinstall** at the command line. To mount the DVD-ROM device manually, I issued the command **mount /dev/dsk/c0t3d0 /cdrom**. To find the disk devices on your system, including DVD-ROMs and CD-ROMs you issue the command **ioscan -funC disk**. I was given the screen shown in the Figure 2-11 after invoking **swinstall** which shows the source for the software installation:

```
┌──────────────────────────────────────────────────────────────┐
│ ─── │             Specify Source (I3)                    │ □ │
├──────────────────────────────────────────────────────────────┤
│                                                                │
│ Specify the source type, then host name, then path on that host. │
│                                                                │
│ Source Depot Type:  ┌────────────────────────┐  ┌─────────────┐ │
│                     │ Network Directory/CDROM □│  │ Find Local CD│ │
│                     └────────────────────────┘  └─────────────┘ │
│                                                                │
│  ┌─────────────────────┐  ┌──────────────────────────────────┐ │
│  │  Source Host Name...│  │ I3                                │ │
│  └─────────────────────┘  └──────────────────────────────────┘ │
│                                                                │
│  ┌─────────────────────┐  ┌──────────────────────────────────┐ │
│  │  Source Depot Path...│  │ /cdrom                           │ │
│  └─────────────────────┘  └──────────────────────────────────┘ │
│                                                                │
├──────────────────────────────────────────────────────────────┤
│  ┌────────┐         ┌──────────┐              ┌────────┐       │
│  │   OK   │         │  Cancel  │              │  Help  │       │
│  └────────┘         └──────────┘              └────────┘       │
└──────────────────────────────────────────────────────────────┘
```

Figure 2-11 *Specify Source* Software Distributor Screen

swinstall filled in the information shown in the dialog box. I did not have to create the directory **/cdrom** or issue the **mount** command

man page

"sw" - 2

at the command line as I often had to do in past releases of HP-UX. **swinstall** filled in all of the information shown in Figure 2-12. The applications CD-ROM from which we'll be loading applications in this example was labeled *HP-UX Release 11.11 and Application Products*.

After accepting the information shown in the figure, I proceeded to select (Step 1 - Selection) the software from the list that I wanted to load by "marking" it.

When selecting software to load you may receive a "Yes" in the "Marked?" column or a "Partial." "Yes" means all of the filesets associated with your selection will be loaded and "Partial" means only some will be loaded. Figure 2-12 shows "Yes" in the "Marked?" column for software that has been selected.

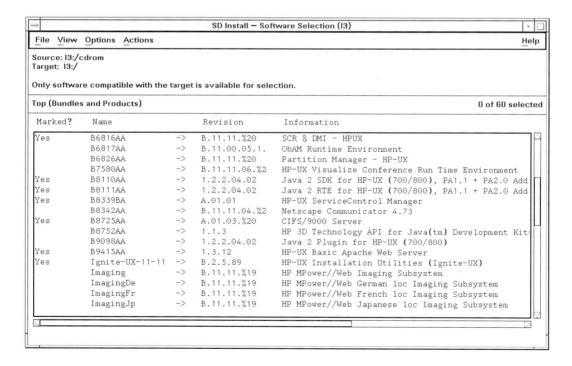

Figure 2-12 *Software Selection* Software Distributor Screen

A bundle of software you select to install may be composed of products, subproducts, and filesets. You can select any item you have "Marked" for loading to see of what filesets it is comprised. I have done this for a Java products for 11i. I selected this *bundle* to see the software of which it is comprised in the Figure 2-13:

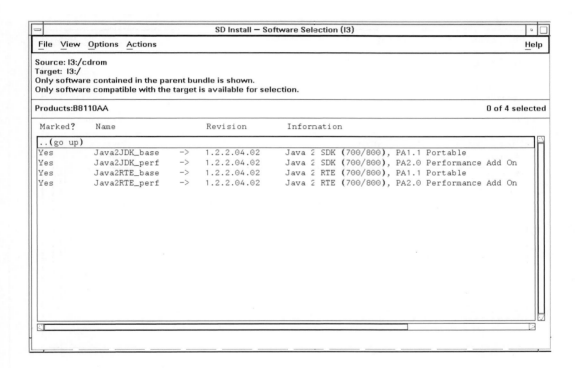

Figure 2-13 Components of a Software Product

Figure 2-13 shows that the Java software is indeed composed of many components. To go back to the top , we select *(go up)*.

Selecting *Install* runs analysis (Step 2 - Analysis) on the software you have selected to load. After the analysis has been completed, you can take a look at the logfile, view the disk space analysis, and perform other tasks. I normally take a look at the disk space analysis just to see the impact the software I am loading is having on free disk space as shown in Figure 2-14:

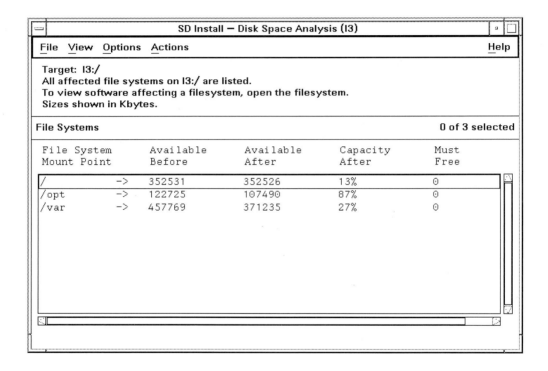

Figure 2-14 *Disk Space Analysis* Software Distributor Screen

I also look at the products to ensure I'm loading the software I expect to load as shown in Figure 2-15 for the products earlier marked for installation:

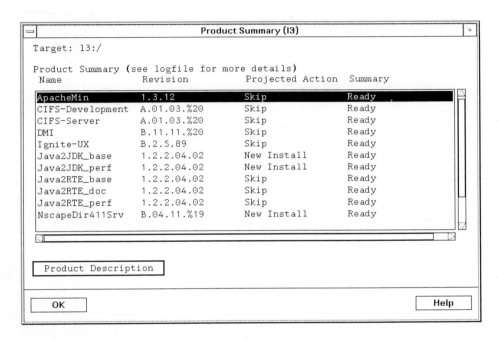

Figure 2-15 *Product Summary* Software Distributor Screen

After you are satisfied with the analysis, you can proceed with the installation (Step 3 - Load.) Figure 2-16 shows the type of status you are provided as software is loaded on the system:

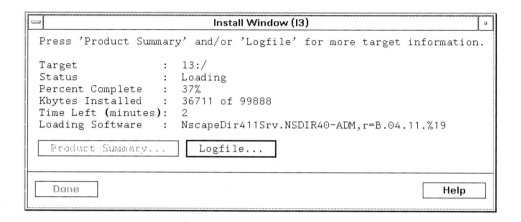

Figure 2-16 *Install Window* Software Distributor Screen Showing Status

In this case, we have loaded about *37%* of the total software we have selected. The software currently being loaded is *Netscape Directory Server.* We could view the logfile to see the status of what has been loaded thus far.

After the load of your software is complete, you can either exit the session or you will be given a message indicating that a reboot will be required to complete the configuration (Step 4 - Configuration). Not all software requires a reboot in order for configuration to take place. Most software will run configuration routines after the software is loaded without the need for a reboot. If a reboot is required you will be asked if you wish to reboot; but it could be a bad time to reboot so you may want to wait, or delay the reboot.

The process of loading software from media using Software Distributor is easy and thorough. The user interface to Software Distributor makes it easy to select and load software from media.

Loading Patches

HP-UX patches can be obtained from a variety of sources. Most people start at *IT Resource Center (us-support.external.hp.com)* because a variety of useful HP-UX information can be found there using your browser.

When you set up your account with *IT Resource Center* initially, you will want to enter your system handle, and the serial number of one of your systems if you have it to get full access to all of the information on the site.

The process of viewing individual patches on *IT Resource Center* is self-explanatory when you log in to the site. Selecting *Individual Patches* and *HP-UX Patches* will allow you to select a specific release of HP-UX, such as 11.11 for HP-UX 11i, and select the patch(es) you wish to load on your system. You can then add the patches to your *Shopping Cart* and download them.

When you search *IT Resource Center* for a patch, you will be told if the patch has been replaced by a more recent patch. After selecting the patch you wish to view, a lot of useful information related to the patch will be available, including:

Patch Files
Dependencies
Supersedes
Size
Critical
Symptoms
Defect Description
Installation Instructions

I always view the installation instructions for a patch while on the web site to see if any special work is required to load the patch. The following are the installation instructions for installing a patch we'll download and install in our example

```
1. Back up your system before installing a patch.

                        2. Login as root.

                        3. Copy the patch to the /tmp directory.

                        4. Move to the /tmp directory and unshar the patch:

                        cd /tmp
                        sh PHCO_21187

                        5. Run swinstall to install the patch:

                        swinstall -x autoreboot=true -x patch_match_target=true \
                          -s /tmp/PHCO_21187.depot

                        By default swinstall will archive the original software in
                        /var/adm/sw/save/PHCO_21187.  If you do not wish to retain a
                        copy of the original software, use the patch_save_files option:

                        swinstall -x autoreboot=true -x patch_match_target=true \
                          -x patch_save_files=false -s /tmp/PHCO_21187.depot

                        WARNING: If patch_save_files is false when a patch is installed,
                          the patch cannot be deinstalled.  Please be careful
                          when using this feature.

                        For future reference, the contents of the PHCO_21187.text file is
                        available in the product readme:

                        swlist -l product -a readme -d @ /tmp/PHCO_21187.depot

                        To put this patch on a magnetic tape and install from the
                        tape drive, use the command:

                        dd if=/tmp/PHCO_21187.depot of=/dev/rmt/0m bs=2k

Special Installation Instructions: None
```

In the installation procedure for many patches, a reboot is required. This patch has the *autoreboot* option equal to *true,* meaning that a reboot will automatically take place if indeed a reboot is required. With HP-UX 11i, there are many more *Dynamic Patches* being introduced, which means that a reboot is not required when the patch is installed. You will see more and more patches for which a reboot is not required. Combined with *Dynamically Loadable Kernel Modules* and *Dynamically Tunable Kernel Parameters,* there will be fewer and fewer reboots required of 11i systems.

After reviewing the information related to the patch, we'll download it using a browser by selecting the patch and *Add to Cart*. Figure

2-17 shows a patch that has been placed in the *Shopping Cart* and is ready for download:

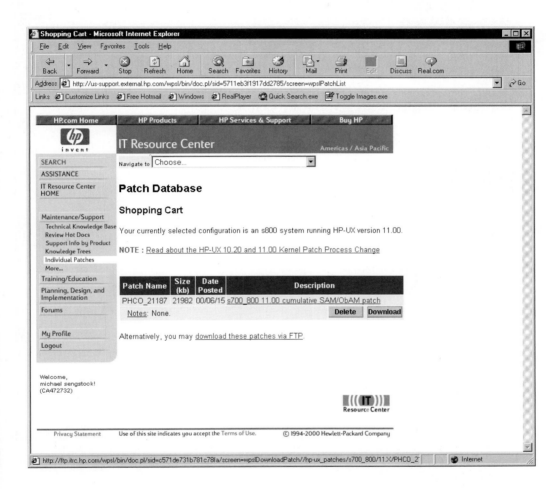

Figure 2-17 Patch in *Shopping Cart* Ready to Download

Note at the bottom of the figure that you can select to download the patch(es) with FTP instead of through the browser.

Figure 2-18 shows a patch that is in the process of being downloaded through the browser:

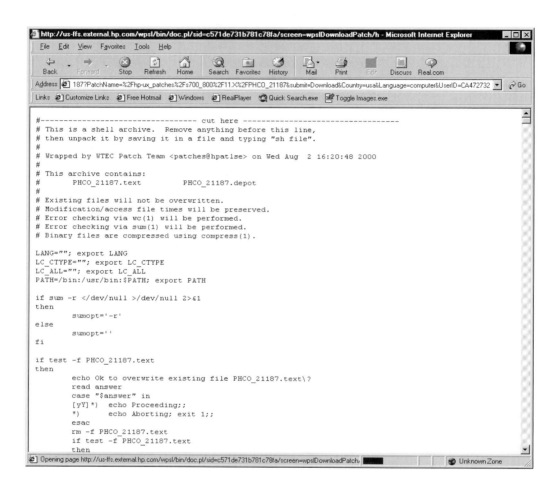

Figure 2-18   Patch Download

Once the patch is downloaded, you simply follow the instructions for installing the patch, such as those that were shown earlier for
the patch in our example. You normally download a patch into the
/tmp directory and run **sh** against the downloaded file, which pro-

duces *patchname*.**depot**. You can then run *Software Distributor* commands on the command line as shown in the instructions.

For the patch in our example, I've run **sh** against the file downloaded which produced a **.depot** file. We'll run **swinstall** to invoke the user interface. Figure 2-19 shows specifying the source as a *Local Directory* rather than a *Network Directory/CDROM,* as in the earlier example in this chapter, and the *Source Depot Path* of our **.depot** file in the **/tmp** directory:

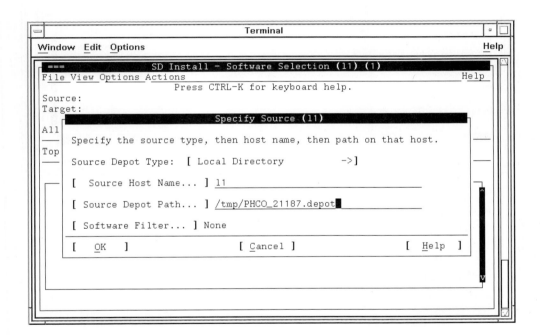

Figure 2-19 *Specify Source* of Patch

We would then mark the patch for installation as shown in Figure 2-20:

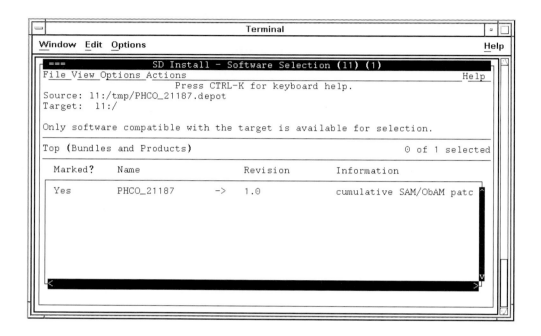

Figure 2-20 Patch Marked for Installation

You can load patches using **swinstall** interactively as I have done
in this example, or following the instructions embedded in the patch
and running **swinstall** from the command line.

Software Distributor Background

You need to have some background on the way software is organized in Software Distributor. There are the four following types of objects into which software is grouped in Software Distributor; bundle, product, subproduct, and fileset. Figure 2-21 shows the hierarchy of Software Distributor objects.

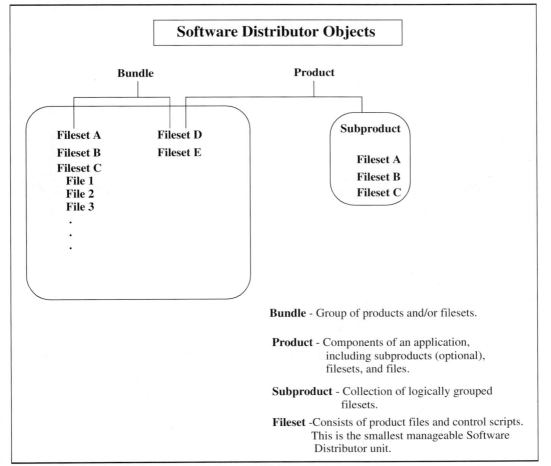

Figure 2-21   Software Distributor Objects

You can look at the bundle in Figure 2-22 as a group of software. This can be products, subproducts, and filesets, as shown in the diagram. The concept here is to organize software in such a way that it is easy to manage. The diagram shows that some filesets are shared between different bundles and products. This hierarchical organization and sharing makes managing software with Software Distributor flexible.

Here are some of the common software management-related tasks you can perform with Software Distributor.

Installing and Updating Software (Command Line or GUI)

man page

"sw" - 2

The **swinstall** command is used to install and update software. The source of the software you are loading can come from a variety of places, including, CD-ROM, magnetic tape, or a "depot" directory from which software can be distributed. Using the depot, you can load software into a directory and then install and update software on other nodes from this directory. Software loaded from CD-ROM with Software Distributor must be loaded onto the local system; this technique is used in the upcoming example. You have a lot of flexibility with SD-OV when selecting the target system onto which you want to load software and the source from which you will load the software. You can, for instance, load software from a depot that is on another system on your network. This command can be run at the command line or with the graphical user interface.

Copying Software to a Depot (Command Line or GUI)

The **swcopy** command is used to copy software from one depot to another. The depot used in the upcoming examples is a CD-ROM. By setting up depots, you can quickly install or update software to other nodes simultaneously with SD-OV. This command can be run at the command line or with the graphical user interface.

Removing Software from a System (Command Line or GUI)

The **swremove** command is used to remove software from a system that has had software loaded with Software Distributor. This includes removing installed and configured software from a system or removing software from a depot. This command can be run at the command line or with the graphical user interface.

man page

"sw" - 2

List Information about Installation Software

The **swlist** command provides information about the depots that exist on a system, the contents of a depot, or information about installed software. Examples of using this command are provided shortly. This command can be run at the command line or with the graphical user interface.

Configure Installed Software

The **swconfig** command configures or unconfigures installed software. Configuration of software normally takes place as part of **swinstall,** but configuration can be deferred until a later time.

Verify Software

The **swverify** command confirms the integrity of installed software or software stored in a depot.

Package Software That Can Later Be Installed (Local Sys Only)

You may want to produce "packages" of software that you can later put on tape or in a depot with the **swpackage** command. This packaged software can then be used as a source for **swinstall** and be managed by other Software Distributor commands.

Control Access to Software Distributor Objects

You may want to apply restricted access to Software Distributor objects such as packaged software. Using the **swacl** command, you can view and change the Access Control List (ACL) for objects.

Modify Information about Loaded Software (Local System Only)

The Installed Products Database (IPD) and associated files are used to maintain information about software products you have loaded. **swmodify** can be run at the command line to modify these files.

Register or Unregister a Depot

A software depot can be registered or unregistered with **swreg**. This means you don't have to remove a depot; if you temporarily don't want it used, you can unregister it.

Manage Jobs (Command Line or GUI, this is SD-OV only)

Software Distributor jobs can be viewed and removed with **swjob.** The graphical user interface version of this command can be invoked with **sd** or **swjob -i**.

man page

"sw" - 2

Listing Software

Although I like the graphical user interface of **swinstall,** you can also issue Software Distributor commands at the command line. One example is the **swlist** command. The **swlist** command is useful for viewing the software you have loaded on your system, viewing the software you have loaded in a depot, or producing a list of depots. A graphical user interface to the **swlist** command can be invoked with the *-i* option and is also available in SAM. With the **swlist** command, you perform many functions, including the following:

- List the software you have at the specified level with the **-l** option. I will show several examples shortly. The levels you can specify are:

  root
  depot
  bundle
  product
  subproduct
  fileset
  file

Levels are delineated by "." so you will see *bundle.[product].[subproduct].[fileset].* You can get all kinds of useful information out of **swlist** and use this for other purposes. Some of the things you can do with **swlist** are:

- Display the table of contents from a software source.

- Specify which attributes you wish to see for a level of software such as name, size, revision, etc.

- Create a list of products that can be used as input to other Software Distributor commands such as **swinstall** and **swremove**.

When you run **swlist** with no options, you get a list of the software products installed on your system. Let's try a few **swlist** commands with the **-l** option to view software installed on a system (by default, **swlist** will list installed products; you can use the **-s** option to specify a software depot or other source). The following example shows listing software at the *bundle* level.

```
$ swlist -l bundle

# various header information
#             .
B2491BA       B.11.00 MirrorDisk/UX
B3701AA_TRY   B 11.00.31 Trial HP GlancePlus/UX Pak s800
B3929BA       B11.00   HP   OnLineJFS (Advanced VxFS)
B3947BA       B.11.00 HP Process Resource Manager
B5725AA       B.1.4    HP-UX Installation Utilities (Ignite-UX)
HPUXEng32RT   B 11.00 English HP-UX 32-bit Runtime Environment
```

This system has the HP-UX runtime environment, GlancePlus/UX trial software, HP OnLineJFS, and MirrorDisk/UX.

If we run **swlist** at the product level, the following is produced for GlancePlus/UX trial software:

```
$ swlist -l product B3701AA_TRY

# various header information
#             .
#             .
#             .
B3701AA_TRY                   B.11.00.31  Trial HP GlancePlus/UX Pak for s800 11.00
B3701AA_TRY.MeasurementInt    B.11.00.31 HP-UX Measurement Interface for 11.00
B3701AA_TRY.MeasureWare       B.11.00.31  MeasureWare Software/UX
B3701AA_TRY.Glance            B.11.00.31  HP GlancePlus/UX

  (bundle)  (product)
```

GlancePlus/UX is comprised of the two products shown in this example. Are there any subproducts of which GlancePlus/UX is comprised? The following example will help us determine the answer.

```
$ swlist -l subproduct B3701AA_TRY

# various header information
#          .
#          .
#          .
B3701AA_TRY                B.11.00.31  Trial HP GlancePlus/UX Pak for s800 11.00
B3701AA_TRY.MeasurementInt B.11.00.31 HP-UX Measurement Interface for 11.00
B3701AA_TRY.MeasureWare    B.11.00.31 MeasureWare Software/UX
B3701AA_TRY.Glance         B.11.00.31 HP GlancePlus/UX

(bundle)   (product)
```

The output of the products and subproducts levels is the same; therefore, there are no subproducts in GlancePlus/UX. We can go one step further and take this to the fileset level, as shown in the following example:

```
$ swlist -l fileset B3701AA_TRY

# various header information
#          .
#          .
#          .
B3701AA_TRY                       B.11.00.31  Trial HP GlancePlus/UX Pak for s800 11.00
B3701AA_TRY.MeasurementInt        B.11.00.31  HP-UX Measurement Interface for 11.00
B3701AA_TRY.MeasurementInt.ARM    B.11.00.31  HP-UX Application Response Measurement
for 11.00
B3701AA_TRY.MeasurementInt.MI     B.11.00.31 HP-UX Measurement Interface for 11.00
B3701AA_TRY.MeasureWare           B.11.00.31 MeasureWare Software/UX
B3701AA_TRY.MeasureWare.MWA       B.11.00.31 MeasureWare Software files
B3701AA_TRY.MeasureWare.MWANO     B.11.00.31 MeasureWare NOS Connectivity Module
Software files
B3701AA_TRY.MeasureWare.PERFDSI   B.11.00.31 HP PCS Data Source Integration
B3701AA_TRY.Glance                B.11.00.31 HP GlancePlus/UX
B3701AA_TRY.Glance.GLANC          B.11.00.31 HP GlancePlus files
B3701AA_TRY.Glance.GPM            B.11.00.31    HP GlancePlus Motif interface files

(bundle)   (product) (fileset)
```

man page

"sw" - 2

With the **swlist** command and the *-l* option, we have worked our way down the hierarchy of HP GlancePlus/UX. Going down to the file level with the *-l file* option produces a long list of files associated with this product.

Table 2-2 shows some of the *-l* options to **swlist** that I use:

TABLE 2-2   List of Some swlist -l Options

Command	Explanation
swlist -l root	Shows the root level.
swlist -l shroot	Shows the shared roots.
swlist -l prroot	Shows the private roots.
swlist -l bundle	Shows bundles only.
swlist -l product	Shows products only.
swlist -l subproduct	Shows both products and subproducts.
swlist -l fileset	Shows products, subproducts, and filesets.
swlist -l file	Shows products, subproducts, filesets, files and numbers.
swlist -l category	Shows all categories of available patches if they have category in their definition.
swlist -l patch	Shows all applied patches.
swlist -l depot	Shows all depots on the local host.
swlist -l depot @ sys	Shows all depots on *sys*.

man page

"sw" - 2

I also like to use the *-a* option with **swlist.** *-a* specifies that you would like see a specific attribute associated with the software you are listing. You can look at the **sd** manual page on your HP-UX system to get a complete list of attributes. One attribute I often look at is *size.* To get a list of the *subproducts* in *NETWORKING* and their *size* in KBytes you would issue the following command:

```
$ swlist -l subproduct -a size NETWORKING
```

Another attribute I often view is *revision,* which you can view with the following command:

```
$ swlist -l subproduct -a revision NETWORKING
```

Sometimes, the brief descriptions of filesets that are given are insufficient to really understand the fileset. The *title* attribute provides a descriptive title, which you can see with the following command for the fileset level:

```
$ swlist -l fileset -a title NETWORKING
```

Table 2-3 is a list of some attributes that you may find of interest.

TABLE 2-3   List of Some Attributes of Interest

Attribute	Explanation
architecture	Shows the target systems supported by the software.
category	Shows the type of software.
description	Shows more detailed description of sofware.
title	Shows the official name of the software.
owner	Shows the owner of the file.
path	Shows the full pathname of the file.
revision	Shows the revision number of the software object.
size	Shows the size of all filesets.
state	Shows the state of the fileset.

The other Software Distributor commands listed earlier can also be issued at the command line. You may want to look at the manual pages for these commands as you prepare to do more advanced Software Distributor work than loading software from DVD, CD-ROM, or tape.

To system administrators familiar with HP-UX 9.x, there is a different organization of software in HP-UX 10.x and 11.x, but the graphical user interface of **swinstall** combined with the better organization of Software Distributor makes this an advantage of HP-UX 11.x.

man page

"sw" - 2

Manual Pages for Commands Used in Chapter 2

The following section contains copies of the manual pages for commands used in Chapter 2. This makes a quick reference for you to use when issuing the commands commonly used throughout your system administration day. The manual pages, more commonly referred to as man pages, are listed in detail with the exception of the Software Distributor (SD-UX). Because Software Distributor is commonly used from the GUI, only a summary of the command-line version of these commands is given. These commands are listed under "sw command summaries."

"sw" command summaries

"sw" commands - Command summaries related to software distribution.

man page

"sw" - 2

```
swacl(1M)                   Hewlett-Packard Company            swacl(1M)

NAME
     swacl - View or modify the Access Control Lists (ACLs) which protect
     software products

SYNOPSIS

     swacl -l level [-M acl_entry| -D acl_entry| -F acl_file] [-x
     option=value]
     [-X option_file] [-f software_file] [-t target_file]
     [software_selections] [@ target_selections]




swagentd(1M)                Hewlett-Packard Company          swagentd(1M)
swagent(1M)                                                   swagent(1M)

NAME
     swagentd - Serve local or remote SD software management tasks,
     including invoking a swagent command.

     swagent - Perform SD software management tasks as the agent of an SD
     command.

     SWAGENTD.EXE - Perform HP OpenView Software Distributor PC software
     management tasks, or serve local PC software for distribution. See
     "Remarks:" below.

SYNOPSIS

     swagentd [-k] [-n] [-r] [-x option=value] [-X option_file]

     SWAGENTD.EXE (HP OpenView Software Distributor only)




swcluster(1M)                                               swcluster(1M)

NAME
     swcluster - install or remove software from diskless server

SYNOPSIS

     swcluster [XToolkit Options] [-v][v] [-i] [-p] [-f] [-r] [-b] [-l
     list_class] [-n] [-s source]
     [-C session_file] [-S session_file] [-x option=value] [-X option_file]
     [software_selections] [@ target_selections]
```

```
swconfig(1M)              Hewlett-Packard Company    .       swconfig(1M)
```

NAME
     swconfig - Configure, unconfigure, or reconfigure installed software

SYNOPSIS
     swconfig [-p] [-v] [-u] [-x option=value] [-X option_file] [-f
     software_file] [-t target_file]
     [-C session_file] [-S session_file] [-Q date] [-J jobid]
     [software_selections] [@ target_selections]


```
swgettools(1M)            Hewlett-Packard Company        swgettools(1M)
```

NAME
     swgettools - Utility for retrieving the SD product from new SD media

SYNOPSIS
     swgettools -s <source_media_location> [-t <temp_dir_location>]


```
swinstall(1M)             Hewlett-Packard Company         swinstall(1M)
swcopy(1M)                                                   swcopy(1M)
```

NAME
     swinstall - Install and configure software products

     swcopy - Copy software products for subsequent installation or
     distribution

SYNOPSIS
     swinstall [XToolkit Options] [-i] [-p] [-v] [-r] [-s source] [-x
     option=value] [-X option_file]
     [-f software_file] [-t target_file] [-C session_file] [-S session_file]
     [-Q date] [-J jobid]
     [software_selections] [@ target_selections]

     swcopy [XToolkit Options] [-i] [-p] [-v] [-s source] [-x option=value]
     [-X option_file]
     [-f software_file] [-t target_file] [-C session_file] [-S session_file]
     [-Q date] [-J jobid]
     [software_selections] [@ target_selections]


```
swjob(1M)                 Hewlett-Packard Company            swjob(1M)
sd(1M)                                                         sd(1M)
```

NAME
     swjob - Display job information and remove jobs.

     sd - Interactive interface for creating and monitoring jobs.

     For a description of the HP OpenView Software Distributor objects,

attributes and data formats, see the sd(4) manual page by typing:
        man 4 sd

For an overview of all HP OpenView Software Distributor commands, see
the sd(5) manual page by typing:
        man 5 sd

SYNOPSIS

        swjob [-i] [-u] [-v] [-R] [-a attribute] [-x option=value] [-X
        option_file] [-f jobid_file]
        [-t target_file] [-C session_file] [-S session_file] [jobid(s)] [
        @ target_selections]

        sd [-x option=value] [-X option_file]

swlist(1M)   Hewlett-Packard Company   swlist(1M)

NAME
        swlist - Display information about software products

SYNOPSIS

        swlist [-d|-r] [-l level] [-v] [-a attribute] [-R] [-s source] [-x
        option=value] [-X option_file]
        [-f software_file] [-t target_file] [-C session_file] [-S session_file]
        [software_selections] [@ target_selections]

swmodify(1M)   Hewlett-Packard Company   swmodify(1M)

NAME
        swmodify - Modify software products in a target root or depot

SYNOPSIS

        swmodify [-d|-r] [-p] [-P pathname_file] [-v[v]] [-V] [-u]
        [-s product_specification_file| -a attribute=[value]] [-x option=value]
        [-X option_file]
        [-f software_file] [-C session_file] [-S session_file]
        [software_selections] [@ target_selection]

swpackage(1M)   Hewlett-Packard Company   swpackage(1M)

NAME
        swpackage - Package software products into a target depot or tape

        For a description of the Product Specification File used as input to
        the swpackage command, see the swpackage(4) manual page by typing:
                man 4 swpackage

SYNOPSIS

        swpackage [-p] [-v[v]] [-V] [-s product_specification_file|directory]

```
[-d directory|device]
[-x option=value] [-X option_file] [-f software_file] [-C session_file]
[-S session_file]
[software_selections] [@ target_selection]
```

swreg(1M)   Hewlett-Packard Company   swreg(1M)

NAME
     swreg - Register or unregister depots and roots

SYNOPSIS

```
swreg -l level [-u] [-v] [-x option=value] [-X option_file] [-f
object_file] [-t target_file]
[-C session_file] [-S session_file] [objects_to_(un)register] [
@ target_selections]
```

swremove(1M)   Hewlett-Packard Company   swremove(1M)

NAME
     swremove - Unconfigure and remove software products

SYNOPSIS

```
swremove [XToolkit Options] [-i] [-p] [-v] [-d|-r] [-x option=value]
[-X option_file] [-f software_file] [-t target_file] [-C session_file]
[-S session_file] [-Q date] [-J jobid] [software_selections] [
@ target_selections]
```

swverify(1M)   Hewlett-Packard Company   swverify(1M)

NAME
     swverify - Verify software products

SYNOPSIS

```
swverify [-v] [-d|-r] [-x option=value] [-X option_file] [-f
software_file] [-t target_file]
[-C session_file] [-S session_file] [-Q date] [-J jobid]
[software_selections] [@ target_selections]
```

CHAPTER 3

Building an HP-UX Kernel

Modify and Build an HP-UX Kernel

You may need to modify your HP-UX 11i kernel in some way, such as changing a kernel parameter, and then rebuild your kernel. You may need to create a new HP-UX kernel in order to add device drivers or subsystems, to tune the kernel to get improved performance, to alter configurable parameters, or to change the dump and swap devices. If you update or modify a dynamic element of your kernel, as shown in the example in this chapter, a reboot is not required. Updating or modifying a static element requires a reboot and may also require some additional steps.

With HP-UX 11i it is not necessary to rebuild your kernel for all changes that take place to it. In 11i, there are many *Dynamically Tunable Kernel Parameters* and *Dynamically Loadable Kernel Modules* that will modify your kernel but not require a reboot. Combined with many *Dynamic Patches* that are available in 11i, you will need to reboot your system less often.

In the next section, we'll modify a *Dynamically Tunable Kernel Parameter*, thereby modifying the kernel, and not have to reboot the system in order for the change to take place. We'll then make a change to the kernel and fully rebuild it so you can see the process of a complete rebuild, including a reboot. I normally use the System Administration Manager (SAM) covered in Chapter 10 to make kernel modifications. There is, however, no substitute for understanding the process by which you would manually build an HP-UX kernel and, therefore, be more informed when you have SAM do this for you in the future. In this chapter, I discuss various commands related to kernel generation and cover the process by which you would manually create a kernel.

Dynamically Loadable Kernel Modules

New with 11.0 was the introduction of dynamically loadable kernel modules. In 11.x, the infrastructure for this feature was put into place, providing a separate system file for each module. With 11.0 is provided the ability of specially created modules to be loaded or unloaded into the kernel without having to reboot the system as long as the module is not being used. HP-UX 11i continues to support all of this dynamic functionality. This new mechanism provides great flexibility and improved system uptime. Detailed information about this advanced feature can be reviewed in the *HP-UX 11.x Release Notes*. Most of the dynamically loadable kernel modules available at the time of this writing are third party. The *IT Resource Center* Web site (*itrc.hp.com*) contains information on this topic, including a developer's guide.

Building a Kernel

man page

sysdef - 3

To begin, let's take a look at an existing kernel running on an HP-UX 11i L-Class system used in many of the examples throughout this book. The **sysdef** command is used to analyze and report tunable parameters of a currently running system. You can specify a particular file to analyze if you don't wish to use the currently running system.

The following is a *partial* listing of having run **sysdef** on an 11i L-Class system:

```
# /usr/sbin/sysdef
NAME                    VALUE       BOOT        MIN-MAX         UNITS     FLAGS
acctresume              4           -           -100-100        -
acctsuspend             2           -           -100-100        -
allocate_fs_swapmap     0           -           -               -
bufpages                32074       -           0-              Pages     -
create_fastlinks        0           -           -               -
dbc_max_pct             50          -           -               -
dbc_min_pct             5           -           -               -
default_disk_ir         0           -           -               -
dskless_node            0           -           0-1             -
eisa_io_estimate        768         -           -               -
eqmemsize               23          -           -               -
file_pad                10          -           0-              -
fs_async                0           -           0-1             -
hpux_aes_override       0           -           -               -
maxdsiz                 2           -           0-655360        Pages     -
maxdsiz_64bit           16384       -           256-1048576     Pages     -
maxfiles                60          -           30-2048         -
maxfiles_lim            1024        -           30-2048         -
maxssiz                 65536       -           0-655360        Pages     -
maxssiz_64bit           262144      -           256-1048576     Pages     -
maxswapchunks           512         -           1-16384         -
maxtsiz                 2048        -           0-655360        Pages     -
maxtsiz_64bit           2048        -           256-1048576     Pages     -
maxuprc                 75          -           3-                        -
maxvgs                  10          -           -               -
msgmap                  2555904     -           3-              -
nbuf                    18720       -           0-              -
ncallout                515         -           6-              -
ncdnode                 150         -           -               -
ndilbuffers             30          -           1-              -
netisr_priority         -1          -           -1-127          -
netmemmax               0           -           -               -
nfile                   920         -           14-             -
nflocks                 200         -           2-              -
ninode                  476         -           14-             -
no_lvm_disks            0           -           -               -
nproc                   400         -           10-             -
npty                    60          -           1-              -
nstrpty                 60          -           -               -
nswapdev                10          -           1-25            -
nswapfs                 10          -           1-25            -
public_shlibs           1           -           -               -
remote_nfs_swap         0           -           -               -
rtsched_numpri          32          -           -               -
sema                    0           -           0-1             -
semmap                  4128768     -           4-              -
shmem                   0           -           0-1             -
shmmni                  200         -           3-1024          -
streampipes             0           -           0-              -
swapmem_on              1           -           -               -
swchunk                 2048        -           2048-16384      kBytes    -
timeslice               10          -           -1-2147483648   Ticks     -
unlockable_mem          1800        -           0-              Pages     -
#
```

man page

sysdef - 3

man page

ioscan - 4

In addition to the tunable parameters, you may want to see a report of all the hardware found on your system. The **ioscan** command does this for you. Using **sysdef** and **ioscan,** you can see what your tunable parameters are set to and what hardware exists on your system. You will then know how your system is set up and can then make changes to your kernel. The following is an **ioscan** output of the same HP-UX 11i L-Class system for which **sysdef** was run:

```
# /usr/sbin/ioscan -f
Class      I  H/W Path    Driver   S/W State  H/W Type    Description
==============================================================================
root       0              root     CLAIMED    BUS_NEXUS
ioa        0  0           sba      CLAIMED    BUS_NEXUS   System Bus Adapter (582)
ba         0  0/0         lba      CLAIMED    BUS_NEXUS   Local PCI Bus Adapter (782)
lan        0  0/0/0/0     btlan    CLAIMED    INTERFACE   HP PCI 10/100Base-TX Core
ext_bus    0  0/0/1/0     c720     CLAIMED    INTERFACE   SCSI C896 Fast Wide LVD
target     0  0/0/1/0.7   tgt      CLAIMED    DEVICE
ctl        0  0/0/1/0.7.0 sctl     CLAIMED    DEVICE      Initiator
ext_bus    1  0/0/1/1     c720     CLAIMED    INTERFACE
                                                          SCSI C896 Ultra Wide Single-Ended
target     1  0/0/1/1.2   tgt      CLAIMED    DEVICE
disk       1  0/0/1/1.2.0 sdisk    CLAIMED    DEVICE      SEAGATE ST318203LC
target     2  0/0/1/1.7   tgt      CLAIMED    DEVICE
ctl        1  0/0/1/1.7.0 sctl     CLAIMED    DEVICE      Initiator
ext_bus    2  0/0/2/0     c720     CLAIMED    INTERFACE   SCSI C875 Ultra Wide
Single-Ended
target     3  0/0/2/0.2   tgt      CLAIMED    DEVICE
disk       2  0/0/2/0.2.0 sdisk    CLAIMED    DEVICE      SEAGATE ST318203LC
target     4  0/0/2/0.7   tgt      CLAIMED    DEVICE
ctl        2  0/0/2/0.7.0 sctl     CLAIMED    DEVICE      Initiator
ext_bus    3  0/0/2/1     c720     CLAIMED    INTERFACE
                                                          SCSI C875 Ultra Wide Single-Ended
target     5  0/0/2/1.4   tgt      CLAIMED    DEVICE
disk       3  0/0/2/1.4.0 sdisk    CLAIMED    DEVICE      TOSHIBA CD-ROM XM-6201TA
target     6  0/0/2/1.7   tgt      CLAIMED    DEVICE
ctl        3  0/0/2/1.7.0 sctl     CLAIMED    DEVICE      Initiator
tty        0  0/0/4/0     asio0    CLAIMED    INTERFACE   PCI Serial (103c1048)
tty        1  0/0/5/0     asio0    CLAIMED    INTERFACE   PCI Serial (103c1048)
ba         1  0/1         lba      CLAIMED    BUS_NEXUS   Local PCI Bus Adapter (782)
ba         2  0/2         lba      CLAIMED    BUS_NEXUS   Local PCI Bus Adapter (782)
ba         3  0/3         lba      CLAIMED    BUS_NEXUS   Local PCI Bus Adapter (782)
lan        1  0/3/0/0     btlan    CLAIMED    INTERFACE
                                              HP A5230A/B5509BA PCI 10/100Base-TX Addon
ba         4  0/4         lba      CLAIMED    BUS_NEXUS   Local PCI Bus Adapter (782)
ext_bus    4  0/4/0/0     c720     CLAIMED    INTERFACE
                                                          C875 Fast Wide Differential
target     7  0/4/0/0.7   tgt      CLAIMED    DEVICE
ctl        4  0/4/0/0.7.0 sctl     CLAIMED    DEVICE      Initiator
ext_bus    5  0/4/0/1     c720     CLAIMED    INTERFACE   SCSI C875 Fast Wide
Differential
target     8  0/4/0/1.7   tgt      CLAIMED    DEVICE
ctl        5  0/4/0/1.7.0 sctl     CLAIMED    DEVICE      Initiator
ba         5  0/5         lba      CLAIMED    BUS_NEXUS   Local PCI Bus Adapter (782)
ba         6  0/6         lba      CLAIMED    BUS_NEXUS   Local PCI Bus Adapter (782)
ba         7  0/7         lba      CLAIMED    BUS_NEXUS   Local PCI Bus Adapter (782)
ext_bus    6  0/7/0/0     c720     CLAIMED    INTERFACE
                                                          SCSI C875 Fast Wide Differential
target     9  0/7/0/0.7   tgt      CLAIMED    DEVICE
ctl        6  0/7/0/0.7.0 sctl     CLAIMED    DEVICE      Initiator
ext_bus    7  0/7/0/1     c720     CLAIMED    INTERFACE
                                                          SCSI C875 Fast Wide Differential
```

```
target      10  0/7/0/1.7    tgt       CLAIMED   DEVICE
ctl          7  0/7/0/1.7.0  sctl      CLAIMED   DEVICE      Initiator
memory       0  8            memory    CLAIMED   MEMORY      Memory
processor    0  160          processor CLAIMED   PROCESSOR   Processor
processor    1  166          processor CLAIMED   PROCESSOR   Processor
#
```

man page

ioscan - 4

I normally run **ioscan** with the *-f* option because it includes the *Driver, S/W State,* and *H/W Type* columns. I am interested in the driver associated with the hardware in the system that the *-f* option produces.

The **ioscan** output shows all of the hardware that comprises the system, including the two processors in the system.

The file **/stand/vmunix** is the currently running kernel. Here is a long listing of the directory **/stand** on the L-Class system, which shows the file **/stand/vmunix**:

```
# ls -l
total 74274
-rw-r--r--   1 root    sys          19 Aug  4 11:37 bootconf
drwxr-xr-x   4 root    sys        2048 Aug 25 11:24 build
drwxr-xr-x   5 root    sys        1024 Aug 24 13:00 dlkm
drwxr-xr-x   5 root    sys        1024 Aug  4 12:45 dlkm.vmunix.prev
-rw-r--r--   1 root    sys        3024 Aug  4 12:26 ioconfig
-r--r--r--   1 root    sys          82 Aug  4 12:27 kernrel
drwxr-xr-x   2 root    sys        1024 Aug 29 11:39 krs
drwxr-xr-x   2 root    root       1024 Aug 29 11:33 krs_lkg
drwxr-xr-x   2 root    root       1024 Aug 29 11:39 krs_tmp
drwxr-xr-x   2 root    root       8192 Aug  4 11:36 lost+found
-rw-------   1 root    root         12 Aug 29 11:33 rootconf
-rw-rw-rw-   1 root    sys        1180 Aug 24 12:52 system
-r--r--r--   1 root    sys        1026 Aug  4 12:21 system.prev
-rwxr-xr-x   1 root    sys    14774416 Aug 24 12:53 vmunix
-rwxr-xr-x   1 root    sys    23184584 Aug  4 12:22 vmunix.prev
#
```

Notice that among the directories shown are two related to Dynamically Loadable Kernel Modules (DLKM.) These are kernel modules that can be included in the kernel without having to reboot the system.

In order to make a change to the kernel, we would change to the **/stand/build** directory, where all work in creating a new kernel is performed, and issue the **system_prep** command as shown below:

```
# cd /stand/build
# /usr/lbin/sysadm/system_prep  -s  system
```

We can now proceed to make the desired changes to the kernel, including adding a driver or subsystem such as cdfs for a CD-ROM filesystem. With the dynamically loadable kernel module (DLKM) structure in place with 11i, we must use **kmsystem** and **kmtune** to make changes to the kernel system and system description files.

You can use **kmtune** to view the value and parameters related to existing kernel parameters as well as make proposed modifications to the kernel. The following listing shows issuing **kmtune** (without the -*l* option to view details) to view a summary of the currently running kernel:

```
# kmtune

Parameter              Current Dyn Planned                        Module     Version
====================================================================================
NSTRBLKSCHED               -   -  2
NSTREVENT                 50   -  50
NSTRPUSH                  16   -  16
NSTRSCHED                  0   -  0
STRCTLSZ                1024   -  1024
STRMSGSZ               65535   -  65535
acctresume                 4   -  4
acctsuspend                2   -  2
aio_listio_max           256   -  256
aio_max_ops             2048   -  2048
aio_physmem_pct           10   -  10
aio_prio_delta_max        20   -  20
allocate_fs_swapmap        0   -  0
alwaysdump                 1   -  1
bootspinlocks              -   -  256
bufcache_hash_locks      128   -  128
bufpages                   0   -  0
chanq_hash_locks         256   -  256
create_fastlinks           0   -  0
dbc_max_pct               50   -  50
dbc_min_pct                5   -  5
default_disk_ir            0   -  0
desfree                    -   -  0
disksort_seconds           0   -  0
dnlc_hash_locks          512   -  512
dontdump                   0   -  0
dskless_node               -   -  0
dst                        1   -  1
effective_maxpid           -   -  ((NPROC<22500)?30000:(NPROC*5/4))
eisa_io_estimate           -   -  0x300
enable_idds                0   -  0
eqmemsize                 15   -  15
executable_stack           1   -  1
fcp_large_config           0   -  0
file_pad                   -   -  10
fs_async                   0   -  0
ftable_hash_locks         64   -  64
```

```
hdlpreg_hash_locks        128     -   128
hfs_max_ra_blocks           8     -   8
hfs_max_revra_blocks        8     -   8
hfs_ra_per_disk            64     -   64
hfs_revra_per_disk         64     -   64
hp_hfs_mtra_enabled         1     -   1
hpux_aes_override           -     -   0
initmodmax                 50     -   50
io_ports_hash_locks        64     -   64
iomemsize                   -     -   40000
ksi_alloc_max            2208     -   2208
ksi_send_max               32     -   32
lotsfree                    -     -   0
max_async_ports            50     -   50
max_fcp_reqs              512     -   512
max_mem_window              0     -   0
max_thread_proc            64     -   64
maxdsiz            0x10000000     -   0x10000000
maxdsiz_64bit      0x40000000     -   0X40000000
maxfiles                   60     -   60
maxfiles_lim             1024     Y   1024
maxqueuetime                -     -   0
maxssiz             0x800000     -   0X800000
maxssiz_64bit       0x800000     -   0X800000
maxswapchunks             512     -   512
maxtsiz            0x4000000     Y   0X4000000
maxtsiz_64bit      0x40000000     Y   0x40000000
maxuprc                    77     Y   77
maxusers                   32     -   32
maxvgs                     10     -   10
mesg                        1     -   1
minfree                     -     -   0
modstrmax                 500     -   500
msgmap                     42     -   42
msgmax                   8192     Y   8192
msgmnb                  16384     Y   16384
msgmni                     50     -   50
msgseg                   2048     -   2048
msgssz                      8     -   8
msgtql                     40     -   40
nbuf                        0     -   0
ncallout                  515     -   515
ncdnode                   150     -   150
nclist                    612     -   612
ncsize                   5596     -   5596
ndilbuffers                30     -   30
netisr_priority             -     -   -1
netmemmax                   -     -   0
nfile                     910     -   910
nflocks                   200     -   200
nhtbl_scale                 0     -   0
ninode                    476     -   476
nkthread                  499     -   499
nni                         -     -   2
no_lvm_disks                0     -   0
nproc                     400     -   500
npty                       60     -   60
nstrpty                    60     -   60
nstrtel                    60     -   60
nswapdev                   10     -   10
nswapfs                    10     -   10
nsysmap                   800     -   800
nsysmap64                 800     -   800
num_tachyon_adapters        0     -   0
o_sync_is_o_dsync           0     -   0
page_text_to_local          -     -   0
pfdat_hash_locks          128     -   128
public_shlibs               1     -   1
region_hash_locks         128     -   128
remote_nfs_swap             0     -   0
rtsched_numpri             32     -   32
scroll_lines              100     -   100
scsi_maxphys          1048576     -   1048576
sema                        1     -   1
semaem                  16384     -   16384
```

```
semmap                       66   -   66
semmni                       64   -   64
semmns                      128   -   128
semmnu                       30   -   30
semume                       10   -   10
semvmx                    32767   -   32767
sendfile_max                  0   -   0
shmem                         1   -   1
shmmax                 0x4000000  Y   0X4000000
shmmni                      200   -   200
shmseg                      120   Y   120
st_ats_enabled                1   -   1
st_fail_overruns              0   -   0
st_large_recs                 0   -   0
streampipes                   0   -   0
swapmem_on                    1   -   1
swchunk                    2048   -   2048
sysv_hash_locks             128   -   128
tcphashsz                     0   -   0
timeslice                    10   -   10
timezone                    420   -   420
unlockable_mem                0   -   0
vas_hash_locks              128   -   128
vnode_cd_hash_locks         128   -   128
vnode_hash_locks            128   -   128
vps_ceiling                  16   -   16
vps_chatr_ceiling       1048576   -   1048576
vps_pagesize                  4   -   4
vx_fancyra_enable             0   -   0
vx_maxlink                32767   -   32767
vx_ncsize                  1024   -   1024
vxfs_max_ra_kbytes         1024   -   1024
vxfs_ra_per_disk           1024   -   1024
#
```

Issuing **kmtune** with the *-l* option produces a detailed listing of the kernel. The following shows just the output for one of the parameters:

```
# kmtune -l
Parameter:      maxuprc
Current:        77
Planned:        77
Default:        75
Minimum:        -
Module:         -
Version:        -
Dynamic:        Yes
#
```

This parameter is *Dynamic* (*Yes*) meaning that the kernel can be dynamically updated. After having viewed this output we can now modify the value of this dynamic parameter. The following command changes the value of the following parameter from *77*, which is the existing value, to *80*:

```
# kmtune -s maxuprc=80
#
```

We can now issue the **kmtune** to again view the existing and proposed value of the *maxuprc* parameter:

```
# kmtune
Parameter              Current Dyn Planned                         Module    Version
=====================================================================================
NSTRBLKSCHED               -    -  2
NSTREVENT                 50    -  50
NSTRPUSH                  16    -  16
NSTRSCHED                  0    -  0
STRCTLSZ                1024    -  1024
STRMSGSZ               65535    -  65535
acctresume                 4    -  4
acctsuspend                2    -  2
aio_listio_max           256    -  256
aio_max_ops             2048    -  2048
aio_physmem_pct           10    -  10
aio_prio_delta_max        20    -  20
allocate_fs_swapmap        0    -  0
alwaysdump                 1    -  1
bootspinlocks              -    -  256
bufcache_hash_locks      128    -  128
bufpages                   0    -  0
chanq_hash_locks         256    -  256
create_fastlinks           0    -  0
dbc_max_pct               50    -  50
dbc_min_pct                5    -  5
default_disk_ir            0    -  0
desfree                    -    -  0
disksort_seconds           0    -  0
dnlc_hash_locks          512    -  512
dontdump                   0    -  0
dskless_node               -    -  0
dst                        1    -  1
effective_maxpid           -    -  ((NPROC<22500)?30000:(NPROC*5/4))
eisa_io_estimate           -    -  0x300
enable_idds                0    -  0
eqmemsize                 15    -  15
executable_stack           1    -  1
fcp_large_config           0    -  0
file_pad                   -    -  10
fs_async                   0    -  0
ftable_hash_locks         64    -  64
hdlpreg_hash_locks       128    -  128
hfs_max_ra_blocks          8    -  8
```

```
hfs_max_revra_blocks          8    -    8
hfs_ra_per_disk              64    -   64
hfs_revra_per_disk           64    -   64
hp_hfs_mtra_enabled           1    -    1
hpux_aes_override             -    -    0
initmodmax                   50    -   50
io_ports_hash_locks          64    -   64
iomemsize                     -    -   40000
ksi_alloc_max              2208    - 2208
ksi_send_max                 32    -   32
lotsfree                      -    -    0
max_async_ports              50    -   50
max_fcp_reqs                512    -  512
max_mem_window                0    -    0
max_thread_proc              64    -   64
maxdsiz             0x10000000    -   0x10000000
maxdsiz_64bit       0x40000000    -   0X40000000
maxfiles                     60    -   60
maxfiles_lim               1024    Y 1200
maxqueuetime                  -    -    0
maxssiz              0x800000    -   0X800000
maxssiz_64bit        0x800000    -   0X800000
maxswapchunks               512    -  512
maxtsiz             0x4000000    Y   0X4000000
maxtsiz_64bit       0x40000000    Y   0X40000000
maxuprc                      77    Y   80
maxusers                     32    -   32
maxvgs                       10    -   10
mesg                          1    -    1
minfree                       -    -    0
modstrmax                   500    -  500
msgmap                       42    -   42
msgmax                     8192    Y 8192
msgmnb                    16384    Y 16384
msgmni                       50    -   50
msgseg                     2048    - 2048
msgssz                        8    -    8
msgtql                       40    -   40
nbuf                          0    -    0
ncallout                    515    -  515
ncdnode                     150    -  150
nclist                      612    -  612
ncsize                     5596    - 5596
ndilbuffers                  30    -   30
netisr_priority               -    -   -1
netmemmax                     -    -    0
nfile                       910    -  910
nflocks                     200    -  200
nhtbl_scale                   0    -    0
ninode                      476    -  476
nkthread                    499    -  499
nni                           -    -    2
no_lvm_disks                  0    -    0
nproc                       400    -  400
npty                         60    -   60
nstrpty                      60    -   60
nstrtel                      60    -   60
nswapdev                     10    -   10
nswapfs                      10    -   10
nsysmap                     800    -  800
nsysmap64                   800    -  800
num_tachyon_adapters          0    -    0
o_sync_is_o_dsync             0    -    0
page_text_to_local            -    -    0
pfdat_hash_locks            128    -  128
public_shlibs                 1    -    1
region_hash_locks           128    -  128
remote_nfs_swap               0    -    0
rtsched_numpri               32    -   32
scroll_lines                100    -  100
scsi_maxphys            1048576    - 1048576
sema                          1    -    1
semaem                    16384    - 16384
semmap                       66    -   66
semmni                       64    -   64
```

```
semmns                        128   -   128
semmnu                         30   -   30
semume                         10   -   10
semvmx                      32767   -   32767
sendfile_max                    0   -   0
shmem                           1   -   1
shmmax                 0x4000000    Y   0X4000000
shmmni                        200   -   200
shmseg                        120   Y   120
st_ats_enabled                  1   -   1
st_fail_overruns                0   -   0
st_large_recs                   0   -   0
streampipes                     0   -   0
swapmem_on                      1   -   1
swchunk                      2048   -   2048
sysv_hash_locks               128   -   128
tcphashsz                       0   -   0
timeslice                      10   -   10
timezone                      420   -   420
unlockable_mem                  0   -   0
vas_hash_locks                128   -   128
vnode_cd_hash_locks           128   -   128
vnode_hash_locks              128   -   128
vps_ceiling                    16   -   16
vps_chatr_ceiling         1048576   -   1048576
vps_pagesize                    4   -   4
vx_fancyra_enable               0   -   0
vx_maxlink                  32767   -   32767
vx_ncsize                    1024   -   1024
vxfs_max_ra_kbytes           1024   -   1024
vxfs_ra_per_disk             1024   -   1024
#
```

This output shows that the change to our parameter is pending.

We can apply the change to the dynamic parameter *maxuprc* from *77* to *80* by issuing **kmtune** with the *-u* option:

```
# kmtune -u
The kernel's value of maxuprc has been set to 80 (0x50).
#
```

This output shows that the change we wanted made to the kernel has been made. We can confirm this by running **kmtune** again and searching for *maxuprc*:

```
# kmtune | grep maxuprc
maxuprc                        80   Y   80
#
```

Both the *Current* and *Planned* values have been updated to *80*. This dynamic update can be done using **kmsystem** to add dynamic drivers to your kernel.

There are many other procedures for which you would have to perform additional steps to include modifications in the kernel and rebuild it. With these non-dynamic changes you would create a new kernel, which will be generated as **/stand/build/vmunix_test,** using the command shown below:

```
# mk_kernel -s system
Compiling conf.c...
Loading the kernel...
Generating kernel symbol table...
#
```

At this point, the new kernel exists in the **/stand/build** directory. The existing kernel is updated with the newly generated kernel with **kmupdate. kmupdate** moves the new kernel files into the **/stand** directory. I would first recommend moving the existing **/stand/system** kernel file to a backup file, and then updating the new kernel as shown below:

```
# mv /stand/system /stand/system.prev       (may want to move additional
# kmupdate /stand/build/vmunix_test         files shown in Figure 3-1)

  Kernel update request is scheduled.

  Default kernel /stand/vmunix will be updated by
  newly built kernel /stand/build/vmunix_test
  at next system shutdown or startup time.
#
```

kmupdate will automatically create backup copies of **/stand/ vmunix** and **/stand/dlkm** for you. These will be created as **/stand/ vmunix.prev** and **/stand/dlkm.vmunix.prev,** respectively.

You can now shut down the system and automatically boot from the new kernel if your update did not take place dynamically and requires a reboot.

Figure 3-1 summarizes the process of building a new kernel in HP-UX 11i.

Step	Comments
1) run **sysdef** and **ioscan -f**	Analyzes and reports tunable parameters of currently running kernel.
2) perform long listing of **/stand** directory	The file **vmunix** is the existing kernel, and **system** is used to build a new kernel.
3) **cd /stand/build**	This is the directory where the new kernel will be built.
4) **/usr/lbin/sysadm/system_prep -s system**	This extracts the **system** file from the currently running kernel.
5) use **kmsystem** and **kmtune** to make changes	Takes place in the **/stand/build** directory. Dyamic update complete here.
6) **mk_kernel -s system**	Makes a new kernel in the **/stand/build** directory called **vmunix_test**. DLKM files are produced in **dlkm.vmunix_test/***.

7) **mv /stand/system /stand/system.prev**
   mv /stand/vmunix /stand/vmunix.prev
   mv /stand/dlkm /stand/dlkm.vmunix.prev
	Saves the existing files as **.prev**.

8) **mv /stand/build/system /stand/system** **kmupdate /stand/build/vmunix_test**	Updates the kernel with the newly generated kernel. Automatically saves the old versions in **/stand** as follows: **vmunix** as **/stand/vmunix.prev** **dlkm** as **/dlkm.vmunix.prev**
9) **cd /** **shutdown -r 0**	Changes directory to **/** and shuts down the sytem so that it comes up with the new kernel. This may not be required if your change could be implemented dynamically.

Figure 3-1   Creating a Kernel in HP-UX 11i

There are really two different procedures for generating your kernel - one for dynamic elements, such as the parameter *maxuprc* shown in the earlier example, and one for static elements. The static procedure consists of several additional steps and a reboot. With HP-UX 11i, more and more kernel objects will be updated dynamically, resulting in fewer reboots when modifying your kernel.

Description of Kernel Parameters

The following is a description of kernel parameters in HP-UX 11i at the time of this writing. The first section is a list of and description of each kernel parameter. The second section is an overview of kernel parameters. The full and most recent descriptions can be found at the following URL:

http://docs.hp.com/hpux/onlinedocs/os/KCparams.OverviewAll.html

I encourage you to use the online help of SAM and the URL above to access the most recent and complete information on kernel parameters. Due to limitations of the amount of material I can include in the book, I eliminated much of the background information related to kernel parameters in order to save space. This information is available in the SAM online help and the URL at the time of this writing.

I performed minimal formatting on this material. It is close to the form in which I received it from my HP associates in the lab. I think it is most effective in this somewhat "raw" form because, after all, we're dealing with kernel-related information.

Kernel Parameters

aio_listio_max specifies the maximum number of POSIX asynchronous I/O operations that can be specified in a "listio()" call.

Acceptable Values:

Minimum 2
Maximum 0x10000
Default 256

This parameter places a limit on the system resources that can be consumed if a large number of POSIX asynchronous I/O operations are requested in a single "listio()" call. The value should be set large enough to meet system programming needs while protecting the system against excessive asynchronous I/O operations initiated by a malfunctioning process.

The value specified must not exceed the value of aio_max_ops.

aio_max_ops specifies the system-wide maximum number of POSIX asynchronous I/O operations that can be queued simultaneously at any given time.

Acceptable Values:

Minimum 1
Maximum 0x100000
Default 2048

Specify integer value.

Description

This parameter places a limit on the system resources that can be consumed if a large number of POSIX asynchronous I/O operations are queued on the system at the same time. This parameter limits the ability of competing processes to overwhelm the system with large numbers of asynchronous I/O operations and the memory they require.

Each enqueued asynchronous operation requires allocation of system memory for its internal control structure, thus making this limit necessary. In addition to the system-wide limit, there is a per-process limit that is controlled using the argument "RLIMIT_AIO_OPS" to "getrlimit()" and "setrlimit()" calls.

aio_physmem_pct specifies the maximum percentage of the total physical memory in the system that can be locked for use in POSIX asynchronous I/O operations.

Acceptable Values:

Minimum 5
Maximum 50
Default 10

Specify integer value.

Description

This parameter places a limit on how much system memory can be locked by
the combined total number of POSIX asynchronous I/O operations that are
in progess at any given time. It is also important to be aware that an
operation remains on the active queue and memory is not released, even
if the operation is complete, until it is properly terminated by an
"aio_return()" call for that operation.

Asynchronous I/O operations that use a request-and-callback mechanism
for I/O must be able to lock the memory they are using. The
request-and-callback mechanism is used only if the device drivers
involved support it. Memory is locked only while the I/O transfer is in
progress. On a large server it is better to increase
"aio_physmem_pct" to higher values (up to 50).

"aio_physmem_pct" imposes a system-wide limit on lockable physical
memory. A per-process lockable-memory limit can also be self-imposed by
using the "setrlimit()" system call within the application program.

Remember too that the total amount of memory that can be locked at any
given time for any reason, not just for asynchronous I/O, is controlled
by the system-wide limit "lockable_mem". Other system activity,
including explicit memory locking with plock() and/or mlock() interfaces
can also affect the amount of lockable memory at any given time.

There is no kernel parameter named "lockable_mem", but there is a parameter
named "unlockable_mem" which affects it. The value of "lockable_mem"
is determined by subtracting the value of "unlockable_mem" from the
amount of system memory available after system startup. During startup,
the system displays on the system console the amount of its lockable
memory (along with available memory and physical memory). These values
can be retrieved while the system is running by using the "/sbin/dmesg"
command.

aio_prio_delta_max specifies the maximum slow-down factor (priority
offset) for POSIX asynchronous I/O operations. This is the maximum
priority-offset value allowed in the "aio_reqprio" field in the
asynchronous I/O control block ("aiocb" structure).

Acceptable values:

Minimum 0
Maximum 20
Default 20
lablist

Specify integer value

Description

This parameter places a limit on how much the priority of a POSIX asynchronous I/O operation can be reduced to slow down it down. This limits the value allowed for "int aio_reqprio" in the asynchronous-I/O control block structure "aiocb".

acctresume

Resume accounting when sufficient free file-system space becomes available.

Acceptable Values:

Minimum -100
Maximum 101
Default 4

Specify integer value.

Description

This parameter is of interest only if process accounting is being used on the system.

"acctresume" specifies the minimum amount of free space that must be available in the file system before the system can resume process accounting if it is suspended due to insufficient free space. The threshold at which accounting is suspended is defined by "acctsuspend".

Related Parameters

"acctsuspend" and "acctresume" are interrelated. To prevent suspend-resume conflicts, the signed, integer value of "acctresume" must always be greater than the signed, integer value of "acctsuspend".

acctsuspend

Suspend accounting when available free file-system space drops below specified amount.

Acceptable Values:

Minimum -100

Maximum 100
Default 2

Specify integer value.

Description

This parameter is of interest only if process accounting is being used
on the system.

"acctsuspend" prevents accounting files from invading file system free
space by specifying the minimum amount of available file system space
that must be kept available for other uses while process accounting is
running. If the available space drops below that value, accounting is
suspended until sufficient file space becomes available again so
accounting can resume.

 Selecting a Value for "acctsuspend"

Related Parameters

"acctsuspend" and "acctresume" are interrelated. To prevent
suspend-resume conflicts, the signed, integer value of "acctsuspend"
must always be less than the signed, integer value of "acctresume".

allocate_fs_swapmap

Preallocate sufficient kernel data structures for file-system swap use.

Acceptable Values:

Minimum 0 (allocate swap data structures as needed)
Maximum 1 (preallocate necessary kernel data structures)
Default 0

Specify integer value of "0" or "1".

Description

"allocate_fs_swapmap" determines whether kernel data structures for
file-system swap are allocated only when needed or reserved in advance
(does not apply to device swap). Only two values are recognized as
valid:

"allocate_fs_swapmap" = 0   (default value) System allocates data

structures as they are needed in order
to conserve system memory. Under
certain conditions, the system could
deny swap requests because it lacks
available data structures, even though
the file system has space available for
swapping.

"allocate_fs_swapmap" = 1   System allocates sufficient data
structures to accommodate the maximum
file system swap limit specified by the
the "swapon()" system call or
"swapon" command. This ensures that
space in memory will support swap
requests as long as the file systems
have swap space available. This mode is
most commonly used on high availability
systems where prevention of process
failures due to unavailable resources is
more important than reduced system
efficiency caused by reserving resources
before they are needed.

alwaysdump

"alwaysdump" is a bit-map value that defines which classes of kernel
memory pages are to be dumped if a kernel panic occurs.

Acceptable Values:

Minimum 0
Maximum none
Default 0

Specify integer value.

Description

On large systems, the time required to dump system memory when a kernel
panic occurs can be excessive or even prohibitive, depending on how much
physical memory is installed in the system. Fast-dump capabilities
controlled by the "dontdump" and "alwaysdump" parameters provides
a means for restricting kernel dumps to specific types of information:

* Unused Physical Memory

* Kernel Static Data
* Kernel Dynamic Data
* File-System Metadata
* Kernel Code
* Buffer Cache
* Process Stack
* User Process

The bit-map value stored in "alwaysdump" specifies which of these
memory classes are to be included in the memory dumps associated with
a kernel panic.

Related Parameters

"alwaysdump" and "dontdump" have opposite effects. If the bit
corresponding to a particular memory-page class is set in one parameter,
it should not be set in the other parameter; otherwise a conflict occurs
and the actual kernel behavior based on parameter values is undefined.
These conflicts do not occur when SAM is used to set the values
([[Modify Page-Class Configuration]] in the [[Actions]] menu, SAM
"Dump Devices" subarea in the kernel-configration area).

bufpages

Define number of 4096-byte memory pages in the file system buffer cache.

Acceptable Values:

Minimum: "0 or 6" ("Nbuf*2" or 64 pages)
Maximum: Memory limited
Default: "0"

Specify integer value or use integer formula expression. Use non-zero
value !!only!! if dynamic buffer cache is !!not!! being used.

Description

"bufpages" specifies how many 4096-byte memory pages are allocated for
the file system buffer cache. These buffers are used for all file
system I/O operations, as well as all other block I/O operations in the
system ("exec", "mount", inode reading, and some device drivers.)

Specifying a Value for "bufpages"

To enable dynamic buffer cache allocation, set "bufpages" to zero.
Otherwise, set "bufpages" to the desired number of 4-Kbyte pages to be
allocated for buffer cache. If the value specified for "bufpages" is

non-zero but less than 64, the number is increased at boot time and a message is printed, announcing the change. If "bufpages" is larger than the maximum supported by the system, the number is decreased at boot time and a message is printed.

Related Parameters and System Values

"bufpages" controls how much actual memory is allocated to the buffer pool.

If "bufpages" is zero at system boot time, the system allocates two pages for every buffer header defined by "nbuf". If "bufpages" and "nbuf" are both zero, the system enables dynamic buffer cache allocation and allocates a percentage of available memory.

The maximum amount of memory that can be allocated to the buffer pool is also affected by the amount of memory allocated to the system for other purposes. Thus, modifying parameters that affect system memory may also affect the maximum amount of memory can be made available to the buffer pool.

clicreservedmem

"clicreservedmem" specifies how many bytes of system memory are to be reserved for I/O-mapping use by user processes in high-speed, distributed-server environments such as those used for running large database-processing programs.

Acceptable Values:

Minimum: "0"
Maximum: none
Default: "0"

Specify integer value.

Description

Normal HP-UX systems reserve a relatively small amount of system memory for I/O mapping. However, some specialized applications (such as large database-processing programs) often run on clusters of high-speed servers that are interconnected by specialized high-speed, wideband communication networks. Because of the intense demands on system resources, these applications often communicate by means of memory-mapped I/O where large blocks of memory are shared by the application and the corresponding I/O or networking sofware.

The configurable parameter "clicreservedmem" provides a means for setting aside as much as 15/16 (approximately 93%) of total system memory for use by applications that perform large-volume, memory-mapped, network I/O. While this value could be as much as 512 Gbytes or even 1 Tbyte, it more commonly ranges from about 1 Gbyte to perhaps 64 Gbytes. Regardless of the value chosen within SAM, the actual memory reserved by the system cannot exceed 15/16 or total system memory.

create_fastlinks

Use fast symbolic links.
Acceptable Values:

Minimum: "0"
Maximum: "1"
Default: "0"

Specify integer value.

Description

When "create_fastlinks" is non-zero, it causes the system to create HFS symbolic links in a manner that reduces the number of disk-block accesses by one for each symbolic link in a pathname lookup. This involves a slight change in the HFS disk format, which makes any disk formatted for fast symbolic links unusable on Series 700 systems prior to HP-UX Release 9.0 and Series 800 systems prior to HP-UX Release 10.0 (this configurable parameter was present on Series 700 Release 9.0 systems, but not on Series 800 HP-UX 9.0 systems).

To provide backward compatibility, the default setting for "create_fastlinks" is zero, which does not create the newer, faster format. However, all HP-UX 10.0 kernels (and all Series 700 HP-UX 9.0 kernels) understand both disk formats, whether "create_fastlinks" is set to zero or non-zero.

dbc_max_pct

Define maximum percentage of memory to be used by dynamic buffer cache.
Acceptable Values:

Minimum: " 2"
Maximum: "90"
Default: "50"

Specify integer value.

Description

When the parameters "bufpages" "nbuf" are both set to their default value of 0, the size of the buffer cache grows or shrinks dynamically, depending on competing requests for system memory.

The value of "dbc_max_pct" sets the maximum percentage of physical memory that can be allocated to the dynamic buffer cache.

dbc_min_pct

Define minimum percentage of memory to be used by dynamic buffer cache.

Acceptable Values:

Minimum: " 2"
Maximum: "90"
Default: " 5"

Specify integer value.
Description

During file-system I/O operations, data is stored in a buffer cache, the size of which can be fixed or dynamically allocated. When the parameters "bufpages" "nbuf" are both set to their default value of 0, the size of the buffer cache grows or shrinks dynamically, depending on competing requests for system memory.

The value of "dbc_min_pct" specifies the minimum percentage of physical memory that is reserved for use by the dynamic buffer cache.

Selecting an Appropriate Value

If "dbc_min_pct" is set to too low a value, very high demand on the buffer cache can effectively hang the system. The is also true when using fixed buffer cache. To determine a reasonable (and conservative) value for the minimum cache size in Mbytes, use the following formula:

(number of system processes) $\times$ (largest file-system block size) / 1024

To determine the value for "dbc_min_pct", divide the result by the number of Mbytes of physical memory installed in the computer and multiply that value by 100 to obtain the correct value in percent.

Only those processes that actively use disk I/O should be included in the calculation. All others can be excluded. Here are some examples what processes should be included in or excluded from the calculation:

Include: NFS daemons, text formatters such as "nroff",
            database management applications, text editors,
            compilers, etc. that access or use source and/or
            output files stored in one or more file systems
            mounted on the system.

Exclude: X-display applications, "hpterm", "rlogin",
            login shells, system daemons, "telnet" or
            "uucp" connections, etc. These process use
            very little, if any, disk I/O.

dst

Enable or disable daylight-savings-time conversion and specify
conversion schedule.

Acceptable Values:

Specify one of the following integer values:

"0"   Disable daylight-saving time
"1"   Set daylight-saving time to USA style (this is the default)
"2"   Set daylight-saving time to Australian style
"3"   Set daylight-saving time to Western-Europe style
"4"   Set daylight-saving time to Middle-Europe style
"5"   Set daylight-saving time to Eastern-Europe style

Description

"dst" specifies whether to convert to daylight savings time, and which
schedule to use when converting between daylight-savings and standard
time.

A zero value disables conversion to daylight-savings time. Non-zero
values enable conversion and select a conversion schedule according to
the following definitions in the file "usr/include/sys/time.h":

```
#define DST_NONE    0   /* not on dst */
#define DST_USA     1   /* USA style dst */
#define DST_AUST    2   /* Australian style dst */
#define DST_WET     3   /* Western European dst */
#define DST_MET     4   /* Middle European dst */
#define DST_EET     5   /* Eastern European dst */
```

default_disk_ir

Enable Immediate Reporting on disk I/O.

Acceptable Values:

Minimum: "0" (off)
Maximum: "1" (on)
Default: "0" (off)

Set to "0" (disable immediate reporting) or "1" (enable immediate reporting).

Description

"default_disk_ir" enables or disables immediate reporting.

With Immediate Reporting ON, disk drives that have data caches return from a "write()" system call when the data is cached, rather than returning after the data is written on the media. This sometimes enhances write performance, especially for sequential transfers, but cached data can be lost if a device power failure or reset occurs before the device writes the cached data to media. The recommended value for this parameter on Series 800 systems is zero (OFF).

Although not an option to the "mount" command, the configurable parameter, "default_disk_ir", has a profound effect upon filesystem (and raw) disk performance and, conversely, data integrity through resets. It may either be turned ON (set to 1) or OFF (set to 0).

If this configurable parameter is omitted from the kernel configuration file used to create the kernel ("/stand/system"), it is assumed to be OFF (0). Thus, the default behavior for Immediate Reporting (also known as Write Cache Enable, WCE) is OFF (disabled).

"default_disk_ir" also affects delayed-write versus write-through-filesystem behavior.

dontdump

"dontdump" is a bit-map value that defines which classes of kernel memory pages are to be dumped if a kernel panic occurs.

Acceptable Values:

Minimum: "0"
Maximum: none
Default: "0"

Specify integer value.

Description

On large systems, the time required to dump system memory when a kernel
panic occurs can be excessive or even prohibitive, depending on how much
physical memory is installed in the system. Fast-dump capabilities
controlled by the "dontdump" and "alwaysdump" parameters provide
a means for restricting kernel dumps to specific types of information:

    * Unused Physical Memory
    * Kernel Static Data
    * Kernel Dynamic Data
    * File-System Metadata
    * Kernel Code
    * Buffer Cache
    * Process Stack
    * User Process

The bit-map value stored in "alwaysdump" specifies which of these
memory classes are to be included in the memory dumps associated with
a kernel panic.

Related Parameters

"alwaysdump" and "dontdump" have opposite effects. If the bit
corresponding to a particular memory-page class is set in one parameter,
it should not be set in the other parameter; otherwise a coflict occurs
and the actual kernel behavior based on parameter values is undefined.
These conflicts do not occur when SAM is used to set the values
([[Modify Page-Class Configuration]] in the [[Actions]] menu, SAM
"Dump Devices" subarea in the kernel-configration area).

enable_idds

enable_idds is reserved for future use.

Acceptable Values:

Default: "0 (off)"

Specify boolean value.

Description

enable_idds is reserved for future use in an optional product.

Customers should not attempt to change this parameter. Enabling this parameter without the optional product provides no benefit and will lower system performance by a few percentage points.

IDDS = Intrusion Detection Data Source

eqmemsize

Specify size, in pages, of the equivalently mapped memory reserve pool.

Acceptable Values:

Minimum:	" 0"
Maximum:	Memory limited
Default:	"15" pages

Specify integer value or use integer formula expression.

Description

"eqmemsize" specifies the minimum amount of memory space, in pages, that is to be reserved as a pool of space for use by drivers and subsystems that require allocated memory where addressing is the same in real and virtual mode. At boot time, the system may increase the actual space reserved, based upon how much physical memory is installed.

Drivers use these pages to transfer information between hardware interfaces. The driver places data on the page, using virtual mode. The hardware then transfers the data, using DMA (Direct Memory Access) in real mode, bypassing the addressing translation. Since the virtual and real addresses are the same, no special address processing is needed. The space is also used to support address aliasing requests issued on behalf of "EXEC_MAGIC" processes.

Normally, the system handles requests for equivalently mapped memory dynamically by trying to obtain a free page with a matching virtual address from the system-wide memory pool. If the system cannot dynamically obtain an equivalently mapped page, it resorts to its reserve pool. Normally this reserve pool should never be exhausted because the system can usually dynamically allocate an equivalently mapped page. However, systems with a relatively high load and/or a physical memory configuration that exceeds 1 Gbyte could potentially deplete this reserve pool.

Depending on the exact nature of applications running on the system, system load, memory and I/O configurations, and other factors, the reserve pool could still become exhausted. If this happens, the system prints a message to the console indicating that the reserve pool has been exhausted and that "eqmemsize" should be increased.

Selecting a Value

executable_stack

Allows or denies program execution on the stack (security feature).

Acceptable Values:

Minimum: "   0"
Maximum: "   2"
Default: "   1"

Specify integer value. "0" is disable, "1" is enable, "2" is enable with warning.

Description

executable_stack provides protection against commonly attempted security breaches. It sets the system-wide default for whether to use system memory-mapping hardware to help protect against one of the most common classes of security breaches, commonly known as 'stack buffer overflow attacks.'

Unless you have a proven need to do otherwise, HP strongly recommends that you set this parameter to a value of '0' (zero). This is the most secure of the settings, incurs no performance penalty, and will very rarely interfere with legitimate applications.

Note that, for compatibility reasons, the default setting of this parameter in this release is '1' (one), which is the most compatible but least secure setting. It is equivalent to system behavior on HP-UX 11.00 and earlier, and does not provide protection against this type of attack.

Refer to the description of the '+es' option in the manual page for chatr(1) for a detailed description of the effects of this parameter, the meanings of the possible settings, how to recognize if a different setting may be needed on your system, and how to combine system-wide and per-application settings for the best tradeoffs between security and compatibility for your system.

fs_async

Select synchronous or asynchronous writes of file-system data structures to disk.

Acceptable Values:

Minimum: "0'' (Use synchronous disk writes only)
Maximum: "1'' (Allow asynchronous disk writes)
Default: "0''

Specify integer value of "0'' or "1''.

Description

"fs_async'' specifies whether or not asychronous writing of file-system data structures to disk is allowed. If no value for "fs_async'' is specified, synchronous writes are used.

Synchronous writes to disk make it easier to restore file system integrity if a system crash occurs while file system data structures are being updated on the file system.

If asynchronous writes are selected, HP-UX file system semantics for NFS cluster environments are preserved. In addition, files opened using "open()'' with the "0_SYNC'' flag (synchronous writing) will continue to be written synchronously when the asynchronous-writes feature has been configured into the kernel.

Asynchronous writes to disk can improve file system performance significantly. However, asynchronous writes can leave file system data structures in an inconsistent state in the event of a system crash. For more information about when to select synchronous or asynchronous writing, refer to the explanatory text later in this help page.

What are Synchronous and Asynchronous Writes?

If a file is open for writing and data is being written to a file, the data is accumulated in buffers and periodically written to disk. When an end-of-file condition occurs and the file is to be closed, any remaining buffer contents are written to the disk, the inode is updated with file size and block pointer information, and the file system's list of free disk blocks is updated. To ensure maximum protection of file system integrity, these operations are handled in a specific sequence

that minimizes the risk of file system corruption on the disk if a
system crash or power failure occurs while writing to the disk. This
sequential update process is called is called !!synchronous writing!!.

HP-UX file systems store free space lists, blocks, inodes, and other
file components at random and widely separate locations on disk devices.
This means that writing file information blocks in a particular sequence
requires additional time to move to the desired location on the disk
before performing the write operation. If a power failure or system
crash occurs during this sequence, one or more blocks may not be
properly updated, leaving a potentially inconsistent file system. The
"fsck" command is used to repair such inconsistencies.

Asynchronous writing as it relates to the "fs_async" kernel parameter
allows the system to update file system information on the disk in a
more convenient (hence faster) sequence rather than in a more secure
(safer but slower) sequence, thus reducing search and move delays
between writes. However, if a system crash occurs while these
operations are being performed, the risk of an inconsistent file system
that cannot be automatically repaired by fsck is significantly greater
than with synchronous writes.

Consequences of a Crash

If only synchronous writing is used, all updates to directories, file
inodes, free space lists, etc. are handled in a sequence that is known
to "fsck". If a crash occurs while updating any disk block in the
sequence, "fsck" can readily determine where the crash occurred and
repair the missing update information, probably without assistance from
the system administrator.

If "fs_async" is set to allow asynchronous writes and a crash occurs,
"fsck" does not know what sequence was used, and thus will probably
require interactive assistance from the administrator while fixing
inconsistent file system information, repairing directory and inode
entries, etc.

Why Allow Asynchronous Writes?

Waiting for synchronous writing and updating of disk blocks when closing
files after writing to them degrades the performance of programs and
applications that require frequent file and directory write and close
operations. Allowing asynchronous writing significantly reduces those
delays, producing a corresponding improvement in performance. However,
when applications are CPU intensive with relatively little disk I/O,
performance improvements are much lower.

When Should I Use Asynchronous Writes?

Asynchronous writing is advisable for improving system performance if:

* Risk of power failure is low (very dependable power source and/or uninterruptible power sources).

* Precautions have been taken to enhance data security (sophisticated file system backup or redundancy strategies), or potential loss of data due to a system crash is less important than system performance.

* User applications require frequent opening, writing, and closing of disk files and directories.

* Elimination of synchronous writing would improve system performance sufficiently to offset any associated risks.

To enable asynchronous writing, set the "fs_async" kernel parameter to "1" instead of the default value of "0").

hfs_max_ra_blocks

Set the maximum number of read-ahead blocks that the kernel may have outstanding for a single HFS filesystem.

Acceptable Values:

Minimum: " 0"
Maximum: "128"
Default: " 8"

Specify integer value or use integer formula expression.

Description

When data is read from a disk drive, the system may read additional data beyond that requested by the operation. This "read-ahead" speeds up sequential disk accesses, by anticipating that additional data will be read, and having it available in system buffers before it is requested.
This parameter limits the number of read-ahead blocks that the kernel is allowed to have outstanding for any given HFS filesystem. The limit applies to each individual HFS filesystem, !!not!! to the system-wide total.

"hfs_max_ra_blocks" and "hfs_ra_per_disk" should be adjusted according to the characteristics of the workload on the system.

Note

To determine the block size of the filesystem containing the
current directory, use the command:

df -g

EXAMPLE ONE

A software development environment typically consists of small or
medium sized I/Os with a fair number of disk seeks. Therefore,
"hfs_max_ra_blocks" should be set to 8-to-16 blocks and "hfs_ra_per_disk"
should be set to 32-to-64 kilobytes.

EXAMPLE TWO

An out-of-core solver for an MCAE application has a significant sequential
I/O component, so "hfs_max_ra_blocks" should be set to 64-to-128 blocks and
"hfs_ra_per_disk" to 128-to-256 kilobytes.

hfs_ra_per_disk

Set the amount of HFS filesystem read-ahead per disk drive, in Kbytes.

Acceptable Values:

Minimum: "   0"
Maximim: "8192"
Default: " 64"

Specify an integer value or use an integer formula expression.

Description

When data is read from a disk drive, the system may read additional data
beyond that requested by the operation. This "read-ahead" speeds up sequential
disk accesses, by anticipating that additional data will be read, and
having it available in system buffers before it is requested.
This parameter specifies the amount of read-ahead permitted per disk drive.

The total amount of read-ahead is determined by multiplying
"hfs_ra_per_disk" by the number of drives in the logical volume.
If the filesystem does not reside in a logical volume, then the
number of drives is effectively one.

hfs_revra_blocks

This parameter sets the maximum blocks read with each HFS reverse read-ahead operation.

Acceptable Values:

Minimum: 0''
Maximum: 128''
Default;   8''

Specify integer value.

Description

This tunable defines the maximum number of Kbytes to be read in a read-ahead operation when sequentially reading backwards.

Only HP Field Engineers should modify the hfs_revra_per_disk kernel parameter. Customers should not change this parameter from its default value.

Purpose

This value should be raised when the workload is known to include frequent reverse-order sequential reading of files. This value should be lowered back to its default value if raising the value does not provide noteworthy performance improvement. Increasing this value has potential additional disk contention and performance penalty due to excess read-ahead.

Interactions

The following additional tunable parameters may also need to be modified when changing the value of ''hfs_revra_per_disk'':

hfs_max_revra_blocks; hfs_ra_per_disk; hfs_max_ra_blocks

hfs_revra_per_disk

This parameter sets the maximum HFS file system blocks read with each reverse read-ahead operation.

Minimum:''0''
Maximum:''8192''
Default:''64''

Specify integer value.

Description

This tunable defines the maximum number of file system blocks to be read in a read-ahead operation when sequentially reading backwards.

Only HP Field Engineers should modify the hfs_revra_per_disk kernel parameter. Customers should not change this parameter from its default value.

Purpose

An increase in the value of this parameter is indicated when there are a large number of reverse sequential file I/Os on file systems with small file system block sizes. Raising the value of this parameter will mean that more memory is used in the buffer cache.

A decrease in the value of this parameter is indicated when there are a small number of reverse sequential file I/Os on files systems with large file system block sizes. Decreasing the value of this parameter can cause a decreased file throughput rate.

Interactions

The following additional tunable parameters may also need to be modified when changing the value of "hfs_revra_per_disk":

hfs_max_revra_blocks; hfs_ra_per_disk; hfs_max_ra_blocks

initmodmax

"initmodmax" specifies the maximum number of kernel modules that the "savecrash" command will handle when a kernel panic causes a system-memory dump.

Acceptable Values:

Minimum: "0"
Maximum: none
Default: "50"

Specify integer value.

Description

When a kernel panic (system crash) occurs, specified areas of system

memory are copied to the dump devices before the system shuts down.
The "savecrash" command can then be used to copy the dump area into
a directory in a file system (requires !!lots!! of space, depending
on system size and what memory classes were dumped).

When the kernel includes dynamically loadable kernel modules (drivers
that are not statically installed in the kernel), "savecrash" must
allocate space in one of its structures to hold information about
those modules. Since there is no means to predict how many modules
might be loaded at any given time, this parameter provides an upper
limit that "savecrash" is prepared to deal with.

If "initmodmax" is set to less than the number of loaded kernel
modules, only the first modules encountered up to the limit are
processed by "savecrash". It is therefore important that
system administrators keep track of how many kernel modules are
being loaded during system operation to ensure that "initmodmax"
has a value sufficient to properly handle them in case of a kernel
panic and dump.

Note that this parameter only affects the operation of the "savecrash"
command. It does not limit the number of modules that can be loaded
into the kernel during normal system operation.

ksi_alloc_max

"ksi_alloc_max" specifies the system-wide maximum number of queued
signals that can be allocated.

Acceptable Values:

Minimum: "32"
Maximum: (memory limited)
Default: "nproc * 8"

Specify integer value.

Description

The kernel allocates storage space for the data structures required to
support queued signals that are sent by processes using the
"sigqueue()" system call. This parameter is used to determine how much space
should be allocated. At any given time during normal system operation,
if the combined total number of queued signals sent by existing
processes and still pending at receivers are enough to fill the
available data-structure space, no new queued signals can be sent.

Note that queued signals are different than traditional HP-UX/UNIX
signals. Traditional signals (such as kill or hangup signals) were sent
to the receiving process. If multiple identical signals were sent to a
single process, there was no way for the process to determine that more
than one signal had been sent. Queued signals eliminate that ambiguity
because a process can handle a queued signal, then examine the queue
again to discover another signal on the queue.

"ksi_alloc_max" specifies the maximum number of queued signals that
can be queued at any given time, system wide, by controlling how much
data-structure space is allocated in the kernel for handling queued
signals. The limit value of "SIGQUEUE_MAX" and
"_POSIX_SIGQUEUE_MAX" defined in "/usr/include/limits.h" are
affected by the value of this parameter.

The default value of this parameter is set to "nproc * 8" which allows
a total large enough to accommodate eight signals pending for every
process running on the system, assuming that the system is running at
full capacity. This should be adequate for nearly all systems unless
system software requirements dictate that a more are needed.

ksi_send_max

"ksi_send_max" specifies the maximum number of queued signals that a
single process can send and have pending at one or more receivers.

Acceptable Values:

Minimum: "32"
Maximum: (memory limited)
Default: "32"

Specify integer value.

Description

The kernel allocates storage space for the data structures required to
support queued signals that are sent by processes using the
"sigqueue()" system call. This parameter is used to determine how much space
should be allocated. At any given time during normal system operation,
if the combined total number of queued signals sent by existing
processes and still pending at receivers are enough to fill the
available data-structure space, no new queued signals can be sent.

Note that queued signals are different than traditional HP-UX/UNIX
signals. Traditional signals (such as kill or hangup signals) were sent
to the receiving process. If multiple identical signals were sent to a

single process, there was no way for the process to determine that more than one signal had been sent. Queued signals eliminate that ambiguity because a process can handle a queued signal, then examine the queue again to discover another signal on the queue.

"ksi_send_max" places a limit on the number of queued signals that a single process can send and/or have pending at one or more receivers. It provides a mechanism for preventing a single process from monopolizing the signals data-structure space by issuing too many signals and thereby preventing other processes from being able to send and receive signals due to insufficient kernel resources.

The default value of "32" is adequate for most common HP-UX applications. If you have specialized applications that require more than that number ("sigqueue()" returns "EAGAIN"), the number should be increased sufficiently to prevent the error unless the "EAGAIN" error returned by "sigqueue()" is due to a run-away process generating signals when it should not.

maxvgs   Maximum number of volume groups configured by the Logical Volume Manager on the system.

no_lvm_disks   Flag that notifies the kernel when no logical volumes exist on the system. If set, all file systems coincide with physical disks on the system and physical disk boundaries. The only exception to this is when disks are configured for partitions or part of the disk is reserved for swap and other non-file-system uses.

max_async_ports

Specify the system-wide maximum number of ports to the asynchronous disk I/O driver that processes can have open at any given time.

Acceptable Values:

Minimum: "1"
Maximum: " "
Default: "50"

Specify integer value.

Description

"max_async_ports" limits the total number of open ports to the ansynchronous disk-I/O driver that processes on the system can have at any given time (this has nothing to do with any RS-232 asynchronous data-communications interfaces). The system allocates an array of port structures for each port when it is opened that is used for all communication between the process and the asynchronous disk driver. The number of asynchronous ports required by a given application is usually specified in the documentation for that application (such as database applications software, video management software, etc.).

To determine a suitable value for "max_async_ports":

* Determine how many ports are required for each application and/or process that uses asynchronous disk I/O.

* Determine which of these applications will be running simultaneously as separate processes. Also determine whether multiple copies of an application will be running at the same time as separate processes.

* Based on these numbers, determine the maximum number of open ports to the asynchronous disk driver that will be needed by all processes at any given time to obtain a reasonable total.

* Set "max_async_ports" to a value that is not less than this number.

maxdsiz and maxdsiz_64bit

Specify the maximum data segment size, in bytes, for an executing process.

Acceptable Values:

"maxdsiz" for 32-bit processes:

Minimum: "0x400000" (4 Mbytes)
Maximum: "0x7B03A000" (approx 2 Gbytes)
Default: "0x4000000" (64 Mbytes)

"maxdsiz_64bit" for 64-bit processes:

Minimum: "0x400000" (4 Mbytes)
Maximum: "4396972769279"
Default: "0x4000000" (64 Mbytes)

Specify integer value.

Description

Enter the value in bytes.

"maxdsiz" and "maxdsiz_64bit" define the maximum size of the
data storage segment of an executing process for 32-bit and 64-bit
processes, respectively.
The data storage segment contains fixed data storage such
as statics and strings, as well as dynamic data space allocated
using "sbrk()" and "malloc()".

Increase the value of "maxdsiz" or "maxdsiz_64bit" only if you have
one or more processes that use large amounts of data storage
space.

Whenever the system loads a process, or an executing process attempts to
expand its data storage segment, the system checks the size of the
process' data storage segment.

If the process' requirements exceed "maxdsiz" or "maxdsiz_64bit",
the system returns an error to the calling process, possibly causing the
process to terminate.

max_fcp_reqs

Define the maximum number of concurrent Fiber-Channel FCP requests that
are to be allowed on any FCP adapter installed in the machine.
Acceptable Values:

Minimum: "   0"
Maximum: "1024"
Default: " 512"

Specify integer value or use integer formula expression.

Description

"max_fcp_reqs" specifies the maximum number of concurrent FCP requests
that are allowed on an FCP adapter. The default value specified when
the system is shipped is 512 requests. To raise or lower the limit,
specify the desired value for this parameter. The optimal limit on
concurrent requests depends on several different factors such as
configuration, device characteristics, I/O load, host memory, and other

values that FCP software cannot easily determine.

Related Parameters and System Values

The system allocates memory for use by Tachyon FCP adapters based on the comination of values specified for "num_tachyon_adapters" and "max_fcp_reqs".

maxssiz and **maxssiz_64bit**

Set the maximum dynamic storage segment (DSS) size in bytes. Acceptable Values:

"maxssiz" for 32-bit processes:

Minimum: "0x4000 (16" Kbytes)
Maximum: "0x17F00000" (approx 200 Mbytes)
Default: "0x800000" (8 Mbytes)

"maxssiz_64bit" for 64-bit processes:

Minimum: "0x4000 (16" Kbytes)
Maximum: "1073741824"
Default: "0x800000" (8 Mbytes)

Specify integer value.

Description

Enter the value in bytes.

"maxssiz" and "maxssiz_64bit" define, for 32-bit and 64-bit processes respectively, the maximum size of the dynamic storage segment (DSS), also called the user-stack segment, or an executing process's run-time stack. This segment contains stack and register storage space, generally used for local variables.

The default DSS size meets the needs of most processes. Increase the value of "maxssiz" or "maxssiz_64bit" only if you have one or more processes that need large amounts of dynamic storage.

The stack grows dynamically. As it grows, the system checks the size of the process' stack segment. If the stack size requirement exceeds "maxssiz" or "maxssiz_64bit", the system terminates the process.

maxswapchunks

Set the maximum amount of swap space configurable on the system.

Acceptable Values:

Minimum: " 1"
Maximum: "16384"
Default: " 256"

Specify integer value.

Description

"maxswapchunks" specifies the maximum amount of configurable swap space on the system. The maximum swap space limit is calculated as follows:

* Disk blocks contain "DEV_BSIZE" (1024) bytes each. "DEV_BSIZE" is the system-wide mass storage block size and is not configurable.

* Swap space is allocated from device to device in chunks, each chunk containing "swchunk" blocks. Selecting an appropriate value for "swchunk" requires extensive knowledge of system internals. Without such knowledge, the value of "swchunk" should not be changed from the standard default value.

* The maximum number of chunks of swap space allowed system-wide is "maxswapchunks" chunks.

* The maximum swap space in bytes is:

"maxswapchunks" × "swchunk" × "DEV_BSIZE"

For example, using default values for "swchunk" (2048) and "maxswapchunks" (256), and assuming "DEV_BSIZE" is 1024 bytes, the total configurable swap space equals 537 Mbytes.

Selecting Values

The amount of swap space available on system disk devices is determined by the contents of file "/etc/fstab", and is not affected by kernel configuration.

On a stand-alone system or on a cluster client with local swap space, "maxswapchunks" should be set to support sufficient swap space to accommodate all swap anticipated. Set the parameter large enough to avoid having to reconfigure the kernel.

For a server node, set the parameter to include not only the server's local swap needs, but also sufficient swap for each client node that will use the swap. At a minimum, allot swap space equal to the amounts of memory used by each client.

max_thread_proc

Specify the maximum number of threads a single process is allowed to have.

Acceptable Values:

Minimum: "64"
Maximum: "30000"
Default: "64"

Specify integer value.

Description

"max_thread_proc" limits the number of threads a single process is allowed to create. This protects the system from excessive use of system resources if a run-away process creates more threads than it should in normal operation. The value assigned to this parameter is the limit value assigned to the limit variables "PTHREAD_THREADS_MAX" and "_SC_THREAD_THREADS_MAX" defined in "/usr/include/limits.h".

When a process is broken into multiple threads, certain portions of the process space are replicated for each thread, requiring additional memory and other system resources. If a run-away process creates too many processes, or if a user is attacking the system by intentionally creating a large number of threads, system performance can be seriously degraded or other malfunctions can be introduced.

Selecting a value for "max_thread_proc" should be based on evaluating the most complex threaded applications the system will be running and determine how many threads will be required or created by such applications under worst-case normal use. The value should be at least that large but not enough larger that it could compromise other system needs if something goes wrong.

maxtsiz

Set maximum shared-text segment size in bytes.

Acceptable Values:

"maxtsiz" for 32-bit processes:

Minimum: "   262144" (256 kbytes)
Maximum: "1073741824" (1 Gbyte)
Default:" 0x4000000" (64 Mbytes)

"maxtsiz_64bit" for 64-bit processess:

Minimum: "   262144" (256 kbytes)
Maximum: "4398046507008" (approx 4 Tbytes)
Default: "   0x4000000" (64 Mbytes)

Specify integer value.

Description

"maxtsiz" and "maxtsiz_64bit" define, for 32-bit and 64-bit
processes respectively, the maximum size of the shared text segment
(program storage space) of an executing process. Program executable
object code is stored as read-only, and thus can be shared by multiple
processes if two or more processes are executing the same program
simultaneously, for example.

The normal default value accommodates the text segments of most
processes. Unless you plan to execute a process with a text segment
larger than 64 Mbytes, do not modify "maxtsiz" or "maxtsiz_64bit".

Each time the system loads a process with shared text, the system checks
the size of its shared text segment. The system issues an error message
and aborts the process if the process' text segment exceeds "maxtsiz"
or "maxtsiz_64bit".

"maxtsiz" and "maxtsiz_64bit" can be set by rebuilding the kernel
or be set in the running kernel with "settune()". "SAM" and
"kmtune" use "settune()". Dynamic changes to "maxtsiz" and
"maxtsiz_64bit" only affect future calls to "exec()".
Dynamically lowering these parameters will not affect any running
processes, until they call "exec()".

maxuprc

Set maximum number of simultaneous user processes.

Acceptable Values:

Minimum: " 3"
Maximum: "Nproc-5"

Default: "50"

Specify integer value.

Description

"maxuprc" establishes the maximum number of simultaneous processes
available to each user on the system. A user is identified by the user
ID number, not by a login instance. Each user requires at
least one process for the login shell, and additional processes for all
other processes spawned in that process group. (the default is usually
adequate).

The super-user is exempt from this limit.

Pipelines need at least one simultaneous process for each side of a
"|". Some commands, such as cc, fc, and pc, use more than one process
per invocation.

If a user attempts to start a new process that would cause the total
number of processes for that user to exceed "maxuprc", the system
issues an error message to the user:

no more processes

If a user process executes a "fork()" system call to create a new
process, causing the total number of processes for the user to exceed
"maxuprc", "fork()" returns −1 and sets "errno" to
"EAGAIN".

"maxuprc" can be set by rebuilding the kernel or be set in the running
kernel with "settune()". "SAM" and "kmtune" use "settune()".
Dynamic changes to "maxuprc" only affect future calls to "fork()".
Lowering "maxuprc" below a user's current number of processes will
not affect any running processes. The user's processes will not be
able to "fork()" until enough of the current processes exit that
the user is below the new limit.

maxusers

Allocate system resources according to the expected number of
simultaneous users on the system.

Acceptable Values:

Minimum: "0"
Maximum: Memory limited

Default: "32"

Specify integer value.
Description

"maxusers" limits system resource allocation, not the actual number of users on the system. "maxusers" does not itself determine the size of any structures in the system; instead, the default value of other global system parameters depend on the value of "maxusers". When other configurable parameter values are defined in terms of "maxusers", the kernel is made smaller and more efficient by minimizing wasted space due to improperly balanced resource allocations.

"maxusers" defines the C-language macro MaxUsers (for example, "#define MaxUsers 8"). It determines the size of system tables. The actual limit of the number of users depends on the version of the HP-UX license that was purchased. To determine the actual limit, use the "uname -a" command.

Rather than varying each configurable parameter individually, it is easier to specify certain parameters using a formula based on the maximum number of expected users (for example, "nproc" "(20+8*MaxUsers)"). Thus, if you increase the maximum number of users on your system, you only need to change the "maxusers" parameter.

"maxvgs"

Specify maximum number of volume groups on the system.

Acceptable Values:

Minimum: " 1"
Maximum: "256"
Default: " 10"

Specify integer value.

Description

"maxvgs" specifies the maximum number of volume groups on the system. A set of data structures is created in the kernel for each logical volume group on the system. Setting this parameter to match the number of volume groups on the system conserves kernel storage space by creating only enough data structures to meet actual system needs.

"maxvgs" is set for to ten volume groups by default. To allow more or fewer, change "maxvgs" to reflect a new maximum number.

Related Parameters

None.

maxfiles

Set soft limit for the number of files a process is allowed to have open simultaneously.

Acceptable Values:

Minimum: " 30"
Maximum: "60000"
Default: " 60"

Specify integer value.

Description

"maxfiles" specifies the system default soft limit for the number of files a process is allowed to have open at any given time. It is possible for a process to increase its soft limit and therefore open more than "maxfiles" files.

Non-superuser processes can increase their soft limit until they reach the hard limit "maxfiles_lim".

maxfiles_lim

Set hard limit for number of files a process is allowed to have open simultaneously.

Acceptable Values:

Minimum: " 30"
Maximum: "nfile"
Default: " 1024"

Specify integer value.

Description

"maxfiles_lim" specifies the system default hard limit for the number of open files a process may have. It is possible for a non-superuser process to increase its soft limit up to this hard limit.

"maxfiles_lim" can be set by rebuilding the kernel or be set in the running kernel with "settune()". "SAM" and "kmtune" use "settune()".

Dynamic changes affect all existing processes in the system with two classes of exceptions: Process that are already over the new limit will be unaffected. Process that have specifically set their limits through a call to "setrlimit()" (or "ulimit") will be unaffected.

mesg

Enable or disable System V IPC message support in kernel at system boot time (Series 700 only).

Acceptable Values:

Minimum: "0" (Exclude System V IPC message parameters from kernel)
Maximum: "1" (Include System V IPC message parameters in kernel)
Default: "1"

Specify integer value of "0" or "1".

Description

"mesg" specifies whether the code for System V IPC message parameters is to be included in the kernel at system boot time (Series 700 systems only).

"mesg" = 1 Code is included in the kernel (enable IPC messages).

"mesg" = 0 Code is not included in the kernel (disable IPC messages).

Series 800 systems: IPC messages are always enabled in the kernel.

Series 700 systems: If "mesg" is set to zero, all other IPC message parameters are ignored.

modstrmax

"modstrmax" specifies the maximum size of the "savecrash" kernel-module table that contains module names and their location in the file system.

Acceptable Values:

Minimum: "500"
Maximum: none
Default: "500"

Specify integer value.

Description

When a kernel panic (system crash) occurs, specified areas of system
memory are copied to the dump devices before the system shuts down.
The "savecrash" command can then be used to copy the dump area into
a directory in a file system (requires !!lots!! of space, depending
on system size and what memory classes were dumped).

When the kernel includes dynamically loadable kernel modules (drivers
that are not statically installed in the kernel), "savecrash"
allocates space to keep track of module names and their locations on the
file system. The space stores full path names to directories containing
modules, and also module names. Space usage has been optimized by
keeping only one copy of a directory path, even if more than one module
is found there.

As more modules are added to the system, and if module names tend to be
long, or if modules are scattered around the file system, "modstrmax"
will need to be increased to accomodate the extra data.

Note that this parameter only affects the operation of the "savecrash"
command. It does not limit the number of modules that can be loaded
into the kernel during normal system operation.

msgmap

Specify size of the free-space resource map used for assigning locations
for new messages in shared memory.

Acceptable Values:

Minimum: "3"
Maximum: Memory limited
Default: "msgtql+2"

Specify integer value or use integer formula expression.

Description

Message queues are implemented as linked lists in shared memory, each
message consisting of one or more contiguous slots in the message queue.
As messages are allocated and deallocated, the shared memory area
reserved for messages may become fragmented.

"msgmap" specifies the size of a resource map used for allocating
space for new messages. This map shows the free holes in the shared

memory message space used by all message queues. Each entry in the map contains a pointer to a corresponding set of contiguous unallocated slots, and includes a pointer to the set plus the size of (number of segments in) the set.

Free-space fragmentation increases as message size variation increases. Since the resource map requires an entry for each fragment of free space, excessive fragmentation can cause the free-space map array to fill up and overflow. If an overflow occurs when the kernel requests space for a new message or releases space used by a received message, the system issues the message:

DANGER: mfree map overflow

If this error message occurs, regenerate the kernel using a larger value for "msgmap".

msgmax

Specify the maximum individual messages size allowed, in bytes.

Acceptable Values:

Minimum: " 0"
Maximum: "min(msgmnb, msgseg * msgssz, 65535) bytes"
Default: " 8192 bytes"

Specify integer value.

Description

"msgmax" defines the maximum allowable size, in bytes, of individual messages in a queue.

Increase the value of "msgmax" only if applications being used on the system require larger messages. This parameter prevents malicious or poorly written programs from consuming excessive message buffer space.

msgmnb

Specify maximum total size, in bytes, of all messages that can be queued simultaneously on a message queue.

Acceptable Values:

Minimum: " 0"

Maximum: "min(msgseg * msgssz, 65535) bytes"
Default: "16384 bytes"

Specify integer value.

Description

"msgmnb" specifies the maximum total combined size, in bytes, of all messages queued in a given message queue at any one time.

Any "msgsnd()" system call that attempts to exceed this limit returns the error:

"EAGAIN"   If "IPC_NOWAIT" is set.
"EINTR"   If "IPC_NOWAIT" is not set.

"msgmnb" can be set by rebuilding the kernel or be set in the running kernel with "settune()". "SAM" and "kmtune" use "settune()". Dynamically changing this parameter will affect only new message queues as they are created. Existing message queues will be unaffected.

msgmni

Specify maximum number of message queues that can exist simultaneously on the system.

Acceptable Values:

Minimum: " 1"
Maximum: Memory limited
Default: "50"

Specify integer value.

Description

"msgmni" defines the maximum number of message queue identifiers allowed on the system at any given time.

One message queue identifier is needed for each message queue created on the system.

msgseg

"msgseg" specifies the system-wide maximum total number of message segments that can exist in all message queues at any given time.

Acceptable Values:

Minimum: " 1"
Maximum: "32767"
Default: " 2048"

Specify integer value.

Description

"msgseg", multiplied by "msgssz", defines the total amount of shared-memory message space that can exist for all message queues, system-wide (not including message header space).

The related parameter, "msgssz" (message segment size in bytes), defines the number of bytes that are reserved for each message segment in any queue. When a message is placed in the queue, the length of the message determines how many "msgssz" segments are used for that message. Space consumed by each message in the queue is always an integer multiple of "msgssz".

"msgseg" (message segments) defines the number of these units that are available for all queues, system-wide.

"msgssz"

Specify message segment size to be used when allocating message space in message queues.

Acceptable Values:

Minimum: "1"
Maximum: Memory limited
Default: "8 bytes"

Specify integer value.

Description

"msgssz", multiplied by "msgseg", defines the total amount of shared-memory message space that can exist for all message queues, system-wide (not including message header space).

"msgssz" specifies the size, in bytes, of the segments of memory space to be allocated for storing IPC messages. Space for new messages is created by allocating one or more message segments containing "msgssz" bytes each as required to hold the entire message.

msgtql

Specify maximum number of messages allowed to exist on the system at any given time.

Acceptable Values:

Minimum: "1"
Maximum: Memory limited
Default: "40"

Specify integer value.

Description

"msgtql" dimensions an area for message header storage. One message header is created for each message queued in the system. Thus, the size of the message header space defines the maximum total number of messages that can be queued system-wide at any given time. Message headers are stored in shared (swappable) memory.

If a "msgsnd()" system call attempts to exceed the limit imposed by "msgtql", it:

  * Blocks waiting for a free header if the "IPC_NOWAIT" flag is
    !!not!! set, or it

  * returns "EAGAIN" if "IPC_NOWAIT" is set.

ndilbuffers

Set maximum number of Device I/O Library device files that can be open simultaneously at any given time.

Acceptable Values:

Minimum: " 1"
Maximum: Memory limited
Default: "30"

Specify integer value.

Description

"ndilbuffers" defines the maximum number of Device I/O Library (DIL)
device files that can be open, system-wide, at any given time.

"ndilbuffers" is used exclusively by the Device I/O Library. If DIL
is not used, no DIL buffers are necessary.

nbuf

Set system-wide number of file-system buffer and cache buffer headers
(determines maximum total number of buffers on system). See note below.

Acceptable Values:

Minimum: "0 or 16"
Maximum: Memory limited
Default: "0"

Specify integer value of zero (see below).

Description

This parameter is for backwards compatibility and should be set to zero
because dynamic buffer cache is preferred.

If set to a non-zero value, "nbuf" specifies the number of buffer
headers to be allocated for the file system buffer-cache. Each buffer
is allocated 4096 bytes of memory unless overridden by a conflicting
value for "bufpages".

If "nbuf" is set to a non-zero value that is less than 16 or greater
than the maximum supported by the system, or to a value that is
inconsistent with the value of "bufpages", the number will be
increased or decreased as appropriate, and a message printed at boot
time.

Related Parameters

"nbuf" interacts with "bufpages" as follows:

  * "bufpages" = 0, "nbuf" = 0: Enables dynamic buffer cache.

  * "bufpages" not zero, "nbuf" = zero: Creates "BufPages/2"
    buffer headers and allocates "bufpages" times 4 Kbytes of buffer
    pool space at system boot time.

  * "bufpages" = 0, "nbuf" not zero: Allocates "Nbuf*2" pages of
    buffer pool space and creates "Nbuf" headers at boot time..

* "bufpages" not zero, "nbuf" not zero: Allocates "BufPages" pages of buffer pool space and creates "Nbuf" buffer headers at boot time. If the two values conflict such that it is impossible to configure a system using both of them, "bufpages" takes precedence.

"ncallout"

Specify the maximum number of timeouts that can be scheduled by the kernel at any given time.

Acceptable Values:

Minimum: "6"
Maximum: Memory limited
Default: "16+nproc"

Specify integer value or use integer formula expression.

Description

"ncallout" specifies the maximum number of timeouts that can be scheduled by the kernel at any given time. Timeouts are used by:

* "alarm()" system call,

* "setitimer()" system call,

* "select()" system call,

* drivers,

* "uucp" processes,

* process scheduling.

When the system exceeds the timeout limit, it prints the following fatal error to the system console:

panic: timeout table overflow

Related Parameters

If the value of "nproc" is increased, "ncallout" should be increased proportionately. A general rule is that one callout per process should be allowed unless you have processes that use multiple callouts.

ncdnode

Maximum number of open CD-ROM file-system nodes that can be in memory.

Acceptable Values:

Minimum: "14"
Maximum: Memory limited
Default: "150"

Specify integer value or use integer formula expression.

Description

"ncdnode" specifies the maximum number of CD-ROM file-system nodes that can be in memory (in the vnode table) at any given time. It is functionally similar to "ninode" but applies only to CD-ROM file systems. Behavior is identical on Series 700 and Series 800 systems.

Each node consumes 288 bytes which means, for example, that if "ncdnodes" is set to 10&sigspace;000, nearly 3 Mbytes of memory is reserved exclusively for CD-ROM file-system node tables.

nclist

Specify number of cblocks for pty and tty data transfers.

Acceptable Values:

Minimum: "132"
Maximum: Limited by available memory
Default: "(100 + 16 * MAXUSERS)"

Specify integer value or use integer formula expression.

Description

"nclist" specifies how many cblocks are allocated in the system. Data traffic is stored in cblocks as it passes through tty and pty devices.

The default value for "nclist", "(100 + 16 * MAXUSERS)", is based on a formula of 100 cblocks for system use in handling traffic to the console, etc., plus an average of 16 cblocks per user session. Note that cblocks are also used for serial connections other than login sessions, such as as SLIP connections, UUCP transfers, terminal

emulators, and such. If your system is using these other kinds of
connections, ``nclist'' should be increased accordingly.

If the cblock pool is exhausted, data being passed through a tty or pty
device might be lost because no cblock was available when it was needed.

nfile

Set maximum number of files that can be open simultaneously on the system
at any given time.

Acceptable Values:

Minimum: ``14''
Maximum: Memory limited
Default:
``((16*(NPROC+16+MAXUSERS)/10)+32+2*(NPTY+NSTRPTY+NSTRTEL)''

Specify integer value or use integer formula expression.

Description

``nfile'' defines the maximum number files that can be open at any one
time, system-wide.

It is the number of slots in the file descriptor table. Be generous
with this number because the required memory is minimal, and not having
enough slots restricts system processing capacity.

nflocks

Specify the maximum combined total number of file locks that are
available system-wide to all processes at any given time.

Acceptable Values:

Minimum: ``2''
Maximum: Memory limited
Default: ``200''

Specify integer value or use integer formula expression.

Description

``nflocks'' gives the maximum number of file/record locks that are available system-wide. When choosing this number, note that one file may have several locks and databases that use ``lockf()'' may need an exceptionally large number of locks.

Open and locked files consume memory and other system resources. These resources must be balanced against other system needs to maintain optimum overall system performance. Achieving an optimum balance can be quite complex, especially on large systems, because of wide variation in the kinds of applications being used on each system and the number and types of applications that might be running simultaneously, the number of local and/or remote users on the system, and many other factors.

ninode

Specify the maximum number of open inodes that can be in memory.

Acceptable Values:

Minimum: ``14''
Maximum: Memory limited
Default: ``nproc+48+maxusers+(2*npty)''

Specify integer value or use integer formula expression.

Description

``ninode'' defines the number of slots in the inode table, and thus the maximum number of open inodes that can be in memory. The inode table is used as a cache memory. For efficiency reasons, the most recent ``Ninode'' (number of) open inodes is kept in main memory. The table is hashed.

Each unique open file has an open inode associated with it. Therefore, the larger the number of unique open files, the larger ``ninode'' should be.

nkthread

Specify the maximum number of threads that all processes combined can run, system-wide, at any given time.

Acceptable Values:

Minimum `` 50''
Maximum ``30000''

Default ``(nproc*2)+16''

Specify integer or formula value.

Description

Processes that use threads for improved performance create multiple
copies of certain portions of their process space, which requires memory
space for thread storage as well as processor and system overhead
related to managing the threads. On systems running large threaded
applications, a large number of threads may be required. The kernel
parameter ``max_thread_proc'' limits the number of threads
that a single process can create, but there may be other threaded
applications on the system that also use a large number of threads or
they may have more modest requirements.

``nkthread'' limits the combined total number of threads that can be
running on the system at any given time from all processes on the
system. This value protects the system against being overwhelmed by
a large number of threads that exceeds normal, reasonable operation.
It protects the system against overload if multiple large applications
are running, and also protects the system from users who might maliciously
attempt to sabotage system operation by launching a large number of
threaded programs, causing resources to become unavailable for normal
system needs.

The default value allows an average of two threads per process plus
an additional system allowance. If you need to use a larger value:

  * Determine the total number of threads required by each threaded
    application on the system; especially any large applications.

  * Determine how many and which of these will be running simultaneously
    at any given time.

  * Add these together and combine with a reasonable allowance for
    other users or processes that might run occasionally using
    threads (``nproc*2'' might be a useful number).

  * Select a value for ``nkthread'' that is large enough to accommodate
    the total, but not so large that it compromises system integrity.

no_lvm_disk

Tell the kernel that no logical volume groups exist on the system
(Series 700 only).

Acceptable Values:

Minimum: ``0'' (check for LVM disks)
Maximum: ``1'' (system has no LVM disks)
Default: ``0''

Specify integer value of ``0'' or ``1''.

Description

By default at boot time, the system checks for LVM data structures on
the configured root, swap, and dump disks. If no LVM disks exist on the
system, setting ``no_lvm_disks'' to 1 speeds up the boot process by
omitting the check for LVM data structures.

Setting this parameter to a non-zero value on systems where LVM is
being used causes kernel panics because the kernel does not obtain
the necessary information about logical volumes on the system during
the normal boot process.

``nproc''

number of processes

Minimum: ``10''
Maximum: Memory limited
Default: ``20+(8 * maxusers)''

Specify integer value or use integer formula expression.

Description

``nproc'' specifies the maximum total number of processes that can exist
simultaneously in the system.

There are at least four system overhead processes at all times, and
one entry is always reserved for the super-user.

When the total number of processes in the system is larger than
``nproc'', the system issues these messages:

At the system console:

proc: table is full

Also, if a user tries to start a new process from a shell, the following
message prints on the user's terminal:

no more processes

If a user is executing ``fork()'' to create a new process, ``fork()''
returns −1 and sets ``errno'' to ``EAGAIN''.

npty

Specifies the maximum number of pseudo-tty data structures available
on the system.

Acceptable Values:

Minimum: `` 1''
Maximum: Memory limited
Default: ``60''

Specify integer value.

Description

``npty'' limits the number of the following structures that can be used
by the pseudo-teletype driver:

```
struct tty      pt_tty[npty];
struct tty      *pt_line[npty];
struct pty_info  pty_info[npty];
```

NSTREVENT'

Set the maximum number of outstanding streams bufcalls that are allowed
to exist on the system at any given time.

Acceptable Values:

Minimum: none
Maximum: none
Default: ``50''

Specify integer value.

Description

This parameter limits the maximum number of outstanding bufcalls that
are allowed to exist in a stream at any given time. The number of

bufcalls that exist in a given stream is determined by the number and nature of the streams modules that have been pushed into that stream.

This parameter is intended to protect the system against resource overload caused if the combination of modules running in all streams issue an excessive number of bufcalls. The value selected should be equal to or greater than the combined maximum number of bufcalls that can be reasonably expected during normal operation from all streams on the system. This value depends on the behavior and structure of each available streams module as well as the number and combinations of modules that can be pushed onto all streams in the system at any given time.

nstrpty

Set the system-wide maximum number of streams-based PTYs that are allowed on the system.

Acceptable Values:

Minimum: ``0"
Maximum: Memory limited
Default: ``0"

Specify integer value.

Description

This parameter limits the number of streams-based PTYs that are allowed system-wide. When sending data to PTY devices (such as windows), a PTY device must exist for every window that is open at any given time.

This parameter should be set to a value that is equal to or greater than the number of PTY devices on the system that will be using streams-based I/O pipes. Using a parameter value significantly larger than the number of PTYs is not recommended. ``nstrpty" is used when creating data structures in the kernel to support those streams-based PTYs, and an excessively large value wastes kernel memory space.

NSTRPUSH

Set the maximum number of streams modules that are allowed to exist in any single stream at any given time on the system.

Acceptable Values:

Minimum: none
Maximum: none
Default: ``16"

Specify integer value.

Description

This parameter defines the maximum number of streams modules that can be
pushed onto any given stream. This provides some protection against
run-away processes that might automatically select modules to push onto
a stream, but it is not intended as a defense against malicious use of
streams modules by system users.

Most systems do not require more than about three or four modules in any
given stream. However, there may be some unusual cases where more
modules are needed. The default value for this parameter allows as many
as 16 modules in a stream, which should be sufficient for even the most
demanding installations.

If your system needs more than 16 modules in a stream, the need should
be carefully evaluated, and the demands on other system resources such
as outstanding bufcalls and other factors should also be carefully
evaluated.

NSTRSCHED

Set the maximum number of streams scheduler daemons (``smpsched") that
are allowed to run at any given time on the system.

Acceptable Values:

Minimum: ``0"
Maximum: ``32"
Default: ``0"

Specify integer value.

Description

This parameter defines the maximum number of multi-processor (MP)
streams-scheduler daemons to run on systems containing more than one
processer. Note that uni-processor (UP) systems do not use an MP
scheduler daemon, but both MP and UP systems always have one UP streams
scheduler (``supsched").

If the parameter value is set to zero, the system determines how many daemons to run, based on the number of processors in the system. The value selected is ``1" for 2-4 processors, ``2" for 5-8 processors, ``3" for 9-16 processors, and ``4" for more than 16 processors.

If the parameter value is set to a positive, non-zero value, that is the number of ``smpsched" daemons that will be created on an MP system.

nstrtel

Specifies the number of telnet device files that the kernel can support for incoming ``telnet" sessions.

Acceptable Values:

Minimum: ``60"
Maximum: `` "
Default: ``60"

Specify integer value.

Description

``nstrtel" specifies the number of kernel data structures that are created at system boot time that are required to support the device files used by incoming telnet sessions on a server. This number should match the number of device files that exist on the system. If the ``insf" command or SAM is used to create more telnet device files, the value of ``nstrtel" must be increased accordingly or the device files cannot be used because there are no kernel data structures available for communicating with the system.

Select a value for ``nstrtel" that is equal to or greater than the number of telnet device files on the system. Selecting a value that exceeds the number of device files actually existing on the system wastes the memory consumed by extra data structures, but it may be justified if you are planning to add more device files.

nswapdev

Specify number of disk devices that can be enabled for device swap.

Acceptable Values:

Minimum: `` 1"
Maximum: ``25"
Default: ``10"

Specify an integer value equal to the number of physical disk devices
that have been configured for device swap up to the maximum limit of 25.
Only an integer value is allowed (formula values do not work for this
parameter).

Description

``nswapdev'' defines the maximum number of devices that can be used for
device swap.

At system boot time, the kernel creates enough internal data structures
to support device swap to the specified number of physical devices that
have reserved system swap areas. If the specified value is greater than
the number of available devices, the extra data structure space is never
used, thus wasting a little bit of memory (<50 bytes per structure). If
the value is less than the number of available devices, some devices
cannot be used for swap due to lack of supporting data structures in the
kernel.

Related Parameters

None.

nswapfs

Specify number of file systems that can be enabled for file-system swap.

Acceptable Values:

Minimum: `` 1''
Maximum: ``25''
Default: ``10''

Specify an integer value equal to the number of file systems that are
available for file-system swap up to the maximum limit of 25.

Description

``nswapfs'' defines the maximum number of file systems that can be used
for file system swap.

At system boot time, the kernel creates enough internal data structures
(about 300 bytes per structure) to support file system swap to the
specified number of file systems. If the specified value is greater
than the number of available file systems, the extra data structure
space is never used, thus wasting that much memory. If the value is

less than the number of available file systems, some file systems cannot
be used for swap due to lack of supporting data structures.

Related Parameters

nsysmap

Set the number of entries in the kernel dynamic memory virtual address
space resource map.

Acceptable Values:

Minimum: `` 800"
Maximum: Memory Limited
Default: `` 2 * nproc"

Specify integer value.

Description

nsysmap and it's 64-bit equivalent, nsysmap64, sets the size of the
kernel dynamic memory resource map, an array of address/length pairs
that describe the free virtual space in the kernel's dynamic address
space. There are different tunables for the 32-bit and 64-bit kernel
because the 64-bit kernel has more virtual address space.

Previously, the kernel dynamic memory resource map was set by the
system solely, and not easily changed. Certain workloads, which
fragmented the kernel address space significantly, resulted in too
many entries in the resource map. When this happened, the last entry
in the resource map was thrown away, resulting in "leaked" kernel
virtual address space. If this overflow happened often enough,
virtual space was exhausted.

The system uses an algorithm to automatically scale the map size, at
boot time, according to the system workload. If the value is still
not set high enough to avoid the problem of overflowing the memory
resource map array, you can tune this parameter to fit a particular
workload.

Note that even when you override the default value, the kernel may
increase the value beyond that value depending on the system size.

Purpose

This tunable was added to address the problem of ``kalloc: out of

virtual space" system panics. Only systems that experience the
resource map overflow will need to modify this tunable parameter.

The following message will appear on the console when the resource map
overflow occurs:

    sysmap32: rmap ovflo, lost [X,Y] *
or
    sysmap64: rmap ovflo, lost [X,Y]

* Where X and Y are hexadecimal numbers.

If this happens rarely, no action is necessary. If this happens
frequently, (for example, several times a day on a system which the
user does not intend to reboot for a long time (a year of more), the
tunable should be increased. If the tunable is not increased, the
following panic may occur:

kalloc: out of kernel virtual space

When increasing nsysmap{32|64}, doubling the tunable value is a
reasonable rule of thumb. If the problem persists after doubling the
tunable several times from the default, there is likely another
kernel problem, and the customer should go through their normal HP
support channels to investigate.

Side-Effects

If the value of this parameter is increased, kernel memory use
increases very slightly. Depending on the workload, if the tunable is
quite large, the performance of kernel memory allocation may be
negatively affected.

Lowering the value of this parameter from the default is risky and
increases the probability of resource map overflows, eventually
leading to a kernel panic. Consult your HP support representative
prior to decreasing the value of nsysmap.

num_tachyon_adapters

Define number of Fiber-Channel Tachyon adapters in the system if system
does not support I/O virtual addressing.

Acceptable Values:

Minimum: ``0"
Maximum: ``5"
Default: ``0"

Specify integer value or use integer formula expression. A non-zero
value is !!required!! if the system does not provide I/O virtual
addressing. Choose a value equal to the number of Tachyon FCP adapters
installed in the system.

Description

``num_tachyon_adapters" specifies how many Tachyon FCP adapters are
installed in the system so that an appropriate amount of memory can be
allocated for them at system start-up if the system does not provide
I/O virtual addressing.

Specifying a Value for ``num_tachyon_adapters"

If your system does not provide I/0 virtual addressing, set
``num_tachyon_adapters" equal to the number of Tachyon FCP adapters
actually installed in the machine. During boot-up, the system then
reserves a corresponding amount of memory for use by those adapters,
varying that amount according to the value of ``max_fcp_reqs".

If the system supports I/O virtual addressing, set this parameter to
zero. The system then automatically allocates memory as needed.

If you do not know whether your system provides I/O virtual addressing,
setting this parameter to a non-zero value is harmless, provided the
value does not exceed the number of Tachyon FCP adapters actually
installed in the system. If the value exceeds the number of installed
adapters, a corresponding amount of memory is wasted because it cannot
be used for other purposes.

Related Parameters and System Values

The system allocates memory for use by Tachyon FCP adapters based on the
comination of values specified for ``num_tachyon_adapters" and
``max_fcp_reqs".

o_sync_is_o_dsync

``o_sync_is_o_dsync" specifies whether the system is allowed to
translate the ``O_SYNC" flag in an ``open()" or ``fcntl()" call
into an ``O_DSYNC" flag.

Acceptable Values:

Minimum: ``0"
Maximum: ``1"
Default: ``0"

Specify integer value.

Description

In an ``open()" or ``fcntl()" call, the ``O_SYNC" and ``O_DSYNC"
flags are used to ensure that data is properly written to disk before
the call returns. If these flags are not set, the function returns as
soon as the disk-access request is initiated, and assumes that the write
operation will be successfully completed by the system software and
hardware.

Setting the ``O_SYNC" or ``O_DSYNC" flag prevents the function from
returning to the calling process until the requested disk I/O operation
is complete, thus ensuring that the data in the write operation has been
successfully written on the disk. Both flags are equivalent in this
regard except for one important difference: if ``O_SYNC" is set, the
function does not return until the disk operation is complete !!and!!
until all all file attributes changed by the write operation (including
access time, modification time, and status change time) are also written
to the disk. Only then does it return to the calling process.

Setting ``o_sync_is_o_dsync" to ``1" allows the system to convert any
``open()" or ``fcntl()" calls containing an ``O_SYNC" flag into the
same call using the ``O_DSYNC" flag instead. This means that the
function returns to the calling process before the file attributes are
updated on the disk, thus introducing the risk that this information
might not be on the disk if a system failure occurs.

Setting this parameter to a non-zero value allows the function to
return before file time-stamp attributes are updated, but still ensures
that actual file data has been committed to disk before the calling
process can continue. This is useful in installations that perform
large volumes of disk I/O and require file data integrity, but which can
gain some performance advantages by not forcing the updating of time
stamps before proceeding. When the benefits of performance improvement
exceeds the risks associated with having incorrect file-access timing
information if a system or disk crash occurs, this parameter can be set
to ``1". If that is not the case, it should remain set to its default
value of zero.

The setting of this parameter does not affect disk I/O operations
where ``O_SYNC" is not used.

page_text_to_local

Enable or disable swapping of program text segments to local swap device on NFS cluster client.

Acceptable Values:

Minimum: ``0'' (stand-alone, or client uses file-system server)
Maximum: ``1'' (use client local swap)
Default: ``1'' (use client local swap)

Specify integer value of ``0'' or ``1''.

Description

Programs usually contain three segments:

Text segment   Unchanging executable-code part of the program.
Data segment   Arrays and other fixed data structures
DSS segment   Dynamic storage, stack space, etc.

To minimize unnecessary network traffic, NFS cluster clients that have no local swap device discard the text segment of programs when it becomes necessary to swap memory in order to make space available for another program or application. Text segments are discarded because swapping to swap space on the server when no local disk is available then later retrieving the same data that exists in the original program file wastes server disk space and increases network data traffic.

However, when adequate swap space is available on a local disk device that is connected to the client machine, it is more efficient to write the text segment to local swap and retrieve it later. This eliminates two separate text-segment data transfers to and from the server, thus improving cluster performance (depending on the particular applications and programs being used). To use local swap this way, the available swap space must be greater than the !!maximum!! total swap space required by !!all!! processes running on the system at any time. If this condition is not met, system memory-allocation errors occur when space conflicts arise.

``page_text_to_local'' is the configurable kernel parameter that determines whether text segments are discarded or swapped to the local device to save network traffic.

``0''   Do not use local client swap device. Client either has no
        local swap device, or sufficient space is not available for

full text swap support. Discard text segment if memory space
is needed, then retrieve original file from server when ready
to execute again.

``1''   Swap text pages to local swap device when memory space is
needed for other purposes, then retrieve from swap device when
the segment is required. This usually improves client
performance and decreases cluster network data traffic. If
you use this value, local swap !!must!! be enabled, and the
available device-swap space on the client's local disk must be
sufficient for the maximum required virtual memory for !!all!!
programs that may be running on the client at any given time.
Otherwise, processes may fail due to insufficient memory.

On stand-alone, non-cluster systems, set ``page_text_to_local'' to ``0''.

pfail_enabled

Disable or enable system power-failure routines (Series 800 only).

Acceptable Values:

Minimum: ``0''
Maximum: ``1''
Default: ``0''

Specify integer value.

Description

``pfail_enabled'' determines whether a Series 800 system can recognize a
local power failure (that halts the computer by affecting its central
bus). The value can be set to zero or ``1'' as follows:

``0''   Disable powerfail detect. This prevents the system from
running the ``/sbin/powerfail'' command (started from
``/etc/inittab'') so that it can provide for recovery when a
power failure occurs. Programs running when power fails
cannot resume execution when power is restored.

``1''   Enable powerfail detection. This causes the system to recognize
a power failure and employ recovery mechanisms related to the
``/sbin/powerfail'' command (started from ``/etc/inittab'') so
that when a power failure occurs, programs running when power
fails can resume execution when power is restored.

Be sure to follow guidelines for correct shutdown and start-up of a system necessitated by powerfail. These guidelines are discussed in the <book|System Administration Tasks| manual.

Note that although powerfail appears in all ``/etc/inittab'' files, the entry is only recognized and used by systems that support powerfail.

public_shlibs

Enable "public" protection IDs on shared libraries.

Acceptable Values:

Minimum: ``0''
Maximum: ``1'' (or non-zero)
Default: ``1''

Specify integer value.

Description

``public_shlibs'' enables the use of "public" protection IDs on shared libraries.

Shared libraries are implemented using ``mmap()'', and each individual ``mmap()'' is given a unique protection ID. Processes have four protection ID registers of which two are hard-coded to text/data. The remaining two are shared back and forth between whatever shared library/shared memory segments the user process is accessing.

A performance problem arose when the shared libraries were introduced, causing increased process ID (pid) thrashing. To minimize this effect, a public protection ID was added to all shared-library mappings, thus effectively removing shared libraries from the pool of objects that were accessing the two protection ID registers.

Setting ``public_shlibs'' to ``1'' allows the system to assign public protection id's to shared libraries. Setting it to ``0'' disables public access and places a unique protection id on every shared library. The default value is ``1'', and any non-zero value is interpreted as ``1''.

Set the parameter to zero value !!only!! if there is some "security hole" or other reason why a public value should not be used.

rtsched_numpri

Specify the number of available, distinct real-time process scheduling priorities.

Acceptable Values:

Minimum: `` 32"
Maximum: ``512"
Default: `` 32"

Specify integer value.

Description

``rtsched_numpri" specifies the number of distinct priorities that can be set for real-time processes running under the real-time scheduler (POSIX Standard, P1003.4).

Appropriate Values

The default value of 32 satisfies the needs of most configurations. In cases where you need more distinct levels of priorities among processes, increase the value accordingly. However, be aware that increasing the value of ``rtsched_numpri" to specify a larger number of priorities can cause the system to spend more time evaluating eligible processes, thus resulting in possible reduced overall system performance.

remote_nfs_swap

``remote_nfs_swap" enables or disables the ability of the system to perform swap to NFS-mounted devices or file systems.

Acceptable Values:

Minimum: ``0"
Maximum: ``1"
Default: ``0"

Specify integer value.

Description

Use ``remote_nfs_swap" to enable or disable the ability of the system to perform swap to NFS-mounted devices or file systems. The default value of zero disables NFS swap. To enable, change the value to ``1".

This parameter was initially created to allow clients in an NFS cluster to use disk space on the server for swap. NFS clusters are no longer supported on HP-UX systems, and this parameter is set to zero by default (remote NFS swap not allowed). Setting this parameter to allow remote NFS swap is not very useful unless the system where it is allowed has extremely fast NFS capabilities.

scsi_maxphys

Set the maximum record size for the SCSI I/O subsystem, in bytes.

Acceptable Values:

Minimum: `` 1048576 (1 MB)"
Maximum: ``16777215 (16MB - 1)"
Default: `` 1048576 (1 MB)"

Specify integer value.

Description

This parameter is used in conjunction with ``st_large_recs" to enable large tape record support without logical record breakup and recombination.

scsi_max_qdepth

Set the maximum number of SCSI commands queued up for SCSI devices.

Acceptable Values:

Minimum: `` 1"
Maximum: ``255"
Default: `` 8"

Specify integer value.

Description

For devices that support a queue depth greater than the system default, this parameter controls how many I/Os the driver will attempt to queue to the device at any one time. Valid values are (1-255). Some disk devices will not support the maximum queue depth settable by this command. Setting the queue depth in software to a value larger than the disk can handle will result in I/Os being held off once a QUEUE FULL condition exists on the disk.

st_fail_overruns

If set, SCSI tape read resulting in data overrun causes failure.

Acceptable Values:

Disabled: ``0''
Enabled: ``1''
Default: ``0''

Specify ``0'' or ``1''.

Description

Certain technical applications depend on the fact that
reading a record smaller than the actual tape record size
should generate an error.

st_large_recs

If set, enables large record support for SCSI tape.

Acceptable Values:

Disabled: ``0''
Enabled: ``1''
Default: ``0''

Specify ``0'' or ``1''.

Description

This parameter is used in conjunction with
``scsi_maxphys''to enable large tape record support without logical
record breakup and recombination.

scroll_lines

Specify the number of display lines in ITE console screen buffer.

Acceptable Values:

Minimum: `` 60''
Maximum: ``999''

Default: ``100"

Specify integer value.

Description

``scroll_lines" defines the scrolling area (the number of lines of
emulated terminal screen memory on each Internal Terminal Emulator (ITE)
port configured into the system).

semmni

Specify maximum number of sets of IPC semaphores that can exist
simultaneously on the system.

Acceptable Values:

Minimum: `` 2"
Maximum: Memory limited
Default: ``64"

Specify integer value or use integer formula expression.

Description

``semmni" defines the number of sets (identifiers) of semaphores
available to system users.

When the system runs out of semaphore sets, the ``semget()" system call
returns a ``ENOSPC" error message.

semmns

Define the system-wide maximum number of individual IPC semaphores that
can be allocated for users.

Acceptable Values:

Minimum: `` 2"
Maximum: Memory limited
Default: ``128"

Specify integer value or use integer formula expression.

Description

``semmns'' defines the system-wide maximum total number of individual semaphores that can be made available to system users.

When the free-space map shows that there are not enough contiguous semaphore slots in the semaphore area of shared memory to satisfy a ``semget()'' request, ``semget()'' returns a ``ENOSPC'' error. This error can occur even though there may be enough free semaphores slots, but they are not contiguous.

semmnu

Define the maximum number of processes that can have undo operations pending on any given IPC semaphore on the system.

Acceptable Values:

Minimum: `` 1''
Maximum: ``nproc-4''
Default: ``30''

Specify integer value.

Description

An !!undo!! is a special, optional, flag in a semaphore operation which causes that operation to be undone if the process which invoked it terminates.

``semmnu'' specifies the maximum number of processes that can have undo operations pending on a given semaphore. It determines the size of the ``sem_undo'' structure.

A ``semop()'' system call using the ``SEM_UNDO'' flag returns an ``ENOSPC'' error if this limit is exceeded.

semmap

Specify size of the free-space resource map used for allocating new System V IPC semaphores in shared memory.

Acceptable Values:

Minimum: ``4''
Maximum: Memory limited
Default: ``SemMNI+2''

Specify integer value or use integer formula expression.

Description

Each set of semaphores allocated per identifier occupies 1 or more contiguous slots in the sem array. As semaphores are allocated and deallocated, the sem array might become fragmented.

``semmap'' dimensions the resource map which shows the free holes in the sem array. An entry in this map is used to point to each set of contiguous unallocated slots; the entry consists of a pointer to the set, plus the size of the set.

If semaphore usage is heavy and a request for a semaphore set cannot be accommodated, the following message appears:

danger: mfree map overflow

You should then configure a new kernel with a larger value for ``semmap''.

Fragmentation of the sem array is reduced if all semaphore identifiers have the same number of semaphores; ``semmap'' can then be somewhat smaller.

Four is the lower limit: 1 slot is overhead for the map and the second slot is always needed at system initialization to show that the sem array is free.

semume

Define the maximum number of IPC semaphores that a given process can have undo operations pending on.

Acceptable Values:

Minimum: `` 1''
Maximum: ``SemMNS''
Default: ``10''

Specify integer value.

Description

An !!undo!! is a special, optional, flag in a semaphore operation which causes that operation to be undone if the process which invoked it terminates.

``semume'' specifies the maximum number of semaphores that any given process can have undos pending on.

``semop'' is the value of the maximum number of semaphores you can change with one system call. This value is specified in the file ``/usr/include/sys/sem.h''.

A ``semop()'' system call using the ``SEM_UNDO'' flag returns an ``EINVAL'' error if the ``semume'' limit is exceeded.

semvmx

Specify maximum possible semaphore value.

Acceptable Values:

Minimum: `` 1''
Maximum: ``65535''
Default: ``32767''

Specify integer value.

Description

``semvmx'' specifies the maximum value a semaphore can have. This limit must not exceed the largest number that can be stored in a 16-bit unsigned integer or undetectable semaphore overflows can occur.

Any ``semop()'' system call that tries to increment a semaphore value to greater than ``semvmx'' returns an ``ERANGE'' error. If ``semvmx'' is greater than 65&sigspace;535, semaphore values can overflow without being detected.

``semop'' is the value of the maximum number of semaphores you can change with one system call. This value is specified in the file ``/usr/include/sys/sem.h''.

sema

Enable or disable System V IPC semaphores support in kernel at system boot time (Series 700 only).

Acceptable Values:

Minimum: ``0'' (exclude System V IPC semaphore code from kernel)

Maximum: ``1" (include System V IPC semaphore code in kernel)
Default: ``1"

Specify integer value of ``0" or ``1".

Description

``sema" determines whether the code for System V IPC semaphore is
to be included in the kernel at system boot time (Series 700 systems
only).

``sema" = 1 Code is included in the kernel (enable IPC shared
memory).

``sema" = 0 Code is not included in the kernel (disable IPC shared
memory).

Series 800 systems: IPC shared memory is always enabled in the kernel.

Series 700 systems: If ``shmem" is set to zero, all other IPC shared
memory parameters are ignored.

Starbase graphics library and some other HP-UX subsystems use
semaphores. Disable only if you are certain that no applications on
your system depend on System V IPC semaphores.

If ``sema" is zero, any program that uses ``semget()" or ``semop()"
system calls, will return a ``SIGSYS" signal.

semaem

Define the maximum amount a semaphore value can be changed by a
semaphore "undo" operation.

Acceptable Values:

Minimum: ``0"
Maximum: ``SEMVMX" or 32767, whichever is smaller"
Default: ``16384"

Specify integer value or use integer formula expression.

Description

An !!undo!! is an optional flag in a semaphore operation which
causes that operation to be undone if the process which invoked it
dies.

``semaem'' specifies the maximum amount the value of a semaphore can be changed by an undo operation.

The undo value is cumulative per process, so if one process has more than one undo operation on a semaphore, the values of each undo operation are added together and the sum is stored in a variable named ``semadj''. ``semadj'' then contains the number by which the semaphore will be incremented or decremented if the process dies.

sendfile_max

``sendfile_max'' defines the maximum number of pages of buffer cache that can be in transit via the ``sendfile()'' system call at any given time.

Acceptable Values:

Minimum: ``   0''
Maximum: ``0x40000''
Default: ``   0''

Specify integer value.

Description

``sendfile_max'' places a limit on the number of pages of buffer cache that can be monopolized by the ``sendfile()'' system call at any given time. ``sendfile()'' is a system call used by web servers so they can avoid the overhead of copying data from user space to kernel space using the ``send()'' system call. The networking software uses the buffer-cache buffer directly while data is in-transit over the wire. Normally this is a very short time period, but when sending data over a slow link or when retransmitting due to errors, the in-transit period can be much longer than usual.

``sendfile_max'' prevents ``sendfile()'' from locking up all of the available buffer cache by limiting the amount of buffer cache memory that sendfile can access at any given time.

``sendfile_max'' is the upper bound on the number of !!pages!! of buffer cache that can be in transit via sendfile at any one time. The minimum value of zero means there is no limit on the number of buffers. Any other value limits buffer-cache access to the number of pages indicated. The default value is 0.

Setting ``sendfile_max'' to ``1'' means, in effect, that no buffers are

available. Every buffer is at least one page, and that value prevents
any access because the first request for buffer space would exceed the
upper bound, forcing ``sendfile()'' to revert back to using ``malloc()''
and data-copy operations, which is what the ``send()'' system call does.

Setting ``sendfile_max'' to any other value up to 0x40000, allows the
adminstrator to protect the system against the possibility of
``sendfile()'' monopolizing too many buffers, if buffer availability
becomes a problem during normal system operation.

shmem

Enable or disable System V IPC shared memory support in kernel at system
boot time (Series 700 only).

Acceptable Values:

Minimum: ``0'' (exclude System V IPC shared memory code from kernel)
Maximum: ``1'' (include System V IPC shared memory code in kernel)
Default: ``1''

Specify integer value of ``0'' or ``1''.

Description

``shmem'' determines whether the code for System V IPC shared memory is
to be included in the kernel at system boot time (Series 700 systems
only).

``shmem'' = ``1''   Code is included in the kernel (enable IPC shared
                    memory).

``shmem'' = ``0''   Code is not included in the kernel (disable IPC
                    shared memory).

Series 800 systems: IPC shared memory is always enabled in the kernel.

Series 700 systems: If ``shmem'' is set to zero, all other IPC shared
memory parameters are ignored.

When to Disable Shared Memory

Some subsystems such as Starbase graphics require shared memory. Others
such as X Windows use shared memory (often in large amounts) for
server-client communication if it is available, or sockets if it is not.
If memory space is at a premium and such applications can operate,
albeit slower, without shared memory, you may prefer to run without

shared memory enabled.

shmmax

Specify system-wide maximum allowable shared memory segment size.

Acceptable Values:

Minimum: ``2048'' (2 Kbytes)
Maximum: ``1 Gbyte'' on 32-bit systems
Maximum: ``4 Tbyte'' on 64-bit systems
Default: ``0x04000000'' (64 Mbytes)

Specify integer value.

Description

``shmmax'' defines the system-wide maximum allowable shared memory
segment size in bytes. Any ``shmget()'' system call that requests a
segment larger than this limit returns an error.

The value used cannot exceed maximum available swap space. For minimum
and maximum allowable values, as well as the default value for any given
system, refer to values in ``/etc/conf/master.d/*'' files.

``shmmax'' can be set by rebuilding the kernel or be set in the running
kernel with ``settune()''. ``SAM'' and ``kmtune'' use ``settune()''.
``shmmax'' is only checked when a new shared memory segment is created.
Dynamically changing this parameter will only limit the size
of shared memory segments created after the call to ``settune()''.

shmmni

Specify system-wide maximum allowable number of shared memory segments
(by limiting the number of segment identifiers).

Acceptable Values:

Minimum: `` 3''
Maximum: (memory limited)
Default: `` 200'' identifiers

Specify integer value.

Description

``shmmni'' specifies the maximum number of shared memory segments allowed
to exist simultaneously, system-wide. Any ``shmget()'' system call
requesting a new segment when ``shmni'' segments already exist returns
an error. This parameter defines the number of entries in the shared memory segment
identifier list which is stored in non-swappable kernel space.

Setting ``shmmni'' to an arbitrarily large number wastes memory and can
degrade system performance. Setting the value too high on systems with
small memory configuration may consume enough memory space that the
system cannot boot. Select a value that is as close to actual system
requirements as possible for optimum memory usage. A value not
exceeding 1024 is recommended unless system requirements dictate
otherwise.

Starbase graphics requires that ``shmmni'' be set to not less than 4.

shmseg

Define maximum number of shared memory segments that can be simultaneously
attached to a single process.

Acceptable Values:

Minimum: ``1''
Maximum: ``shmmni''
Default: ``120''

Specify integer value.

Description

``shmseg'' specifies the maximum number of shared memory segments
that can be attached to a process at any given time. Any calls to
``shmat()'' that would exceed this limit return an error.

``shmseg'' can be set by rebuilding the kernel or be set in the running
kernel with ``settune()''.  ``SAM'' and ``kmtune'' use ``settune()''.
``shmseg'' is only checked in ``shmat()'' whenever a segment is attached
to a process. Dynamically changing this parameter will only affect future
calls to ``shmat()''. Existing shared memory segments will be unaffected.

STRCTLSZ

Set the maximum number of control bytes allowed in the control portion
of any streams message on the system.

Acceptable Values:

Minimum: ``0''
Maximum: Memory limited
Default: ``1024'' bytes

Specify integer value.

Description

This parameter limits the number of bytes of control data that can be
inserted by ``putmsg()'' in the control portion of any streams message
on the system. If the parameter is set to zero, there is no limit on
how many bytes can be placed in the control segment of the message.

``putmsg()'' returns ``ERANGE'' if the buffer being sent is larger
than the current value of ``STRCTLSZ''.

STRMSGSZ

Set the maximum number of data bytes allowed in any streams message on
the system.

Acceptable Values:

Minimum: ``0''
Maximum: Memory limited
Default: ``8192'' bytes

Specify integer value.

Description

This parameter limits the number of bytes of control data that can be
inserted by ``putmsg()'' or ``write()'' in the data portion of any
streams message on the system. If the parameter is set to zero, there
is no limit on how many bytes can be placed in the data segment of the
message.

``putmsg()'' returns ``ERANGE'' if the buffer being sent is larger
than the current value of ``STRMSGSZ''; ``write()'' segments the
data into multiple messages.

``**streampipes**''

Force All Pipes to be Streams-Based.

Acceptable Values:

Minimum: ``0"
Maximum: ``1"
Default: ``0"

Specify integer value.

Description

This parameter determines the type of pipe that is created by the
``pipe()" system call. If set to the default value of zero, all pipes
created by ``pipe()" are normal HP-UX file-system pipes. If the value
is ``1", ``pipe()" creates streams-based pipes and modules can be pushed
onto the resulting stream.

If this parameter is set to a non-zero value, the ``pipemod" and
``pipedev" module and driver must be configured in file
``/stand/system".

swchunk

Specify chunk size to be used for swap.

Acceptable Values:

Minimum: `` 2048"
Maximum: ``65536"
Default: `` 2048"

Specify integer value.

Use the default value of ``2048" unless you need
to configure more than 32Gb of swap. See the help for
``maxswapchunks" before changing this parameter.

Description

``swchunk" defines the chunk size for swap. This value must be an
integer power of two.

Swap space is allocated in "chunks", each containing ``swchunk" blocks
of ``DEV_BSIZE" bytes each. When the system needs swap space, one swap
chunk is obtained from a device or file system. When that chunk has
been used and another is needed, a new chunk is obtained from a
different device or file system, thus distributing swap use over several

devices and/or file systems to improve system efficiency and minimize monopolization of a given device by the swap system.

swapmem_on

Enable pseudo-swap reservation.

Acceptable Values:

Minimum: ``0'' (disable pseudo-swap reservation)
Maximum: ``1'' (enable pseudo-swap reservation)
Default: ``1''

Specify integer value of ``0'' or ``1''.

Description

``swapmem_on'' enables or disables the reservation of pseudo-swap, which is space in system memory considered as available virtual memory space in addition to device swap space on disk. By default, pseudo-swap is enabled.

Virtual memory (swap) space is normally allocated from the device swap area on system disks. However, on systems that have massive amounts of installed RAM and large disks or disk arrays, there may be situations where it would be advantageous to not be restricted to the allocated device swap space.

For example, consider an administrator running a system in single-user mode that has 200 Mbytes of installed RAM, only 20 Mbytes of which is used by the kernel, and 1 Gbyte of swap area on the root disk array. Suppose a process is running that requires 1.1 Gbytes of swap space. Since no other users have processes running on the system, providing access to the unused RAM by the swap system would provide sufficient swap space. ``swapmem_on'' accomplishes this.

Administrators of workstations and smaller systems may prefer to disable this capability, depending on system and user needs.

``**timeslice**''

scheduling timeslice interval

Acceptable Values:

Minimum: ``   -1''

Maximum: ``2147483647" (approximately 8 months)
Default: ``10" (ten 10-msec ticks)

Specify integer value or use integer formula expression.

Description

The ``timeslice" interval is the amount of time one process is allowed
to run before the CPU is given to the next process at the same priority.
The value of ``timeslice" is specified in units of (10 millisecond) clock
ticks. There are two special values:

`` 0"   Use the system default value (currently ten
            10-msec ticks, or 100 milliseconds).

``-1"   Disable round-robin scheduling completely.

Impact on System

``timeslice" imposes a time limit which, when it expires, forces a
process to check for pending signals. This guarantees that any
processes that do not make system calls can be terminated (such as a
runaway process in an infinite loop). Setting ``timeslice" to a very
large value, or to −1, allows such processes to continue operating
without checking for signals, thus causing system performance
bottlenecks or system lock-up.

Use the default value for ``timeslice" unless a different value is
required by system applications having specific real-time needs.

No memory allocation relates to this parameter. Some CPU time is spent
at each timeslice interval, but this time has not been precisely
measured.

timezone

Specify the time delay from Coordinated Universal Time west to the local
time zone.

Acceptable Values:

Minimum: ``-720"
Maximum: `` 720"
Default: `` 420"

Specify integer value.

Description

``timezone'' specifies the time delay in minutes from Coordinated
Universal Time in a westerly direction to the local time zone where the
system is located. A negative value is interpreted as minutes east from
Coordinated Unversal Time. The value is stored in a structure defined
in ``/usr/include/sys/time.h'' as follows:

```
struct  timezone tz = { TimeZone, DST };
struct timezone {
int tz_minuteswest; /* minutes west of Greenwich */
int tz_dsttime;    /* type of dst correction */
};
```

```
#define DST_NONE    0    /* not on dst */
#define DST_USA     1    /* USA style dst */
#define DST_AUST    2    /* Australian style dst */
#define DST_WET     3    /* Western European dst */
#define DST_MET     4    /* Middle European dst */
#define DST_EET     5    /* Eastern European dst */
```

unlockable_mem

Specify minimum amount of memory that is to remain reserved for system
overhead and virtual memory management use.

Acceptable Values:

Minimum: ``0''
Maximum: Available memory indicated at power-up
Default: ``0'' (system sets to appropriate value)

Specify integer value.

Description

``unlockable_mem'' defines the minimum amount of memory that is to
always remain available for virtual memory management and system
overhead. Increasing the amount of unlockable memory decreases the
amount of lockable memory.

Specify ``unlockable_mem'' in 4-Kbyte pages. Note that current amounts
of available and lockable memory are listed along with the physical page
size in startup messages, which you can view later by running
``/etc/dmesg.''

If the value for ``unlockable_mem" exceeds available system memory, it
is set equal to available memory (reducing lockable memory to zero).

Any call that requires lockable memory may fail if the amount of lockable
memory is insufficient. Note that lockable memory is available for
virtual memory except when it is locked.

vas_hash_locks

vas_hash_locks is reserved for future use.

Acceptable Values:

Default: `` 128"

Customers should not attempt to change this parameter.

vmebpn_public_pages

``vmebpn_public_pages" specifies the number of 4-Kbyte pages reserved
for the VME slave I/O memory mapper.

Acceptable Values:

Minimum: `` 0"
Maximum: ``32"
Default: `` 1"

Specify integer value.

Description

``vmebpn_public_pages" specifies the number of 4-Kbyte pages reserved
for the VME slave I/O memory mapper.

Refer to VME documentation for further information about setting
kernel parameters for the optional VME subsystem.

vmebpn_sockets

``vmebpn_sockets" specifies whether the VME socket domain
``AF_VME_LINK" is active or not.

Acceptable Values:

Minimum: ``0'' (``AF_VME_LINK'' inactive)
Maximum: ``1'' (``AF_VME_LINK'' active)
Default: ``1'' (``AF_VME_LINK'' active)

Specify integer value.

Description

``vmebpn_sockets'' enables or disables the VME socket domain
``AF_VME_LINK''.

Refer to VME documentation for further information about setting
kernel parameters for the optional VME subsystem.

vmebpn_tcp_ip

Maximum number of DLPI PPAs allowed.

Acceptable Values:

Minimum: ``0''
Maximum: ``1''
Default: ``1''

Specify integer value.

Description

``vmebpn_tcp_ip'' specifies the maximum number of DLPI PPAs
allowed on the system. If set to zero, TCP-IP is disabled.
Otherwise, the maximum value is ``1''.

Refer to VME documentation for further information about setting
kernel parameters for the optional VME subsystem.

vmebpn_tcp_ip_mtu

``vmebpn_tcp_ip_mtu'' specifies the maximum number of Kbytes allowed
in PPA transmission units.

Acceptable Values:

Minimum: `` 0''
Maximum: ``64''
Default: `` 8''

Specify integer value.

Description

``vmebpn_tcp_ip_mtu" specifies the maximum number of Kbytes allowed in PPA transmission units.

Refer to VME documentation for further information about setting kernel parameters for the optional VME subsystem.

vmebpn_total_jobs

``vmebpn_total_jobs" specifies the system-wide maximum number of VME ports that can be open at any given time.

Acceptable Values:

Minimum: `` 0"
Maximum: ``8096"
Default: `` 16"

Specify integer value.

Description

``vmebpn_total_jobs" specifies the system-wide maximum number of VME ports that can be open at any given time.

Refer to VME documentation for further information about setting kernel parameters for the optional VME subsystem.

vme_io_estimate

``vme_io_estimate" specifies the number of 4-Kbyte pages in the kernel I/O space that are needed by and are to be allocated to the VME subsystem.

Acceptable Values:

Minimum: `` 0"
Maximum: ``0x800"
Default: ``0x800"

Specify integer value.

Description

``vme_io_estimate'' specifies how many 4-Kbyte pages in the kernel I/O space are to be allocated for use by the VME subsystem.

Refer to VME documentation for further information about setting kernel parameters for the optional VME subsystem.

vps_ceiling

Specify the maximum page size (in Kbytes) that the kernel can select when it chooses a page size based on system configuration and object size.

Acceptable Values:

Minimum: `` 4''
Maximum: ``65536''
Default: `` 16''

Specify integer value.

Description

This parameter is provided as a means to minimize lost cycle time caused by TLB (translation look-aside buffer) misses on systems using newer PA-RISC devices such as the PA-8000 that have smaller TLBs and no hardware TLB walker.

If a user application does not use the ``chatr'' command to specify a page size for program text and data segments, the kernel selects a page size that, based on system configuration and object size, appears to be suitable. This is called transparent selection. The selected size is then compared to the default maximum page-size value defined by ``vps_ceiling'' that is configured at system-boot time. If the the value is larger than ``vps_ceiling'', ``vps_ceiling'' is used.

The value is also compared with the default minimum page-size value defined by``vps_pagesize'' that is configured at system-boot time. If the the value is smaller than ``vps_pagesize'', ``vps_pagesize'' is used.

Note also that if the value specified by ``vps_ceiling'' is not a legitimate page size, the kernel uses the next !!lower!! valid value.

For more information about how these parameters are used, and how they affect system operation, refer to the whitepaper entitled !!Performance Optimized Page Sizing: Getting the Most out of your HP-UX Server!!.

This document is available on the World Wide Web at:
http://www.unixsolutions.hp.com/products/hpux/pop.html

vps_chatr_ceiling

Specify the maximum page size (in Kbytes) that can be specified when a
user process uses the ``chatr'' command to specify a page size.

Acceptable Values:

Minimum: `` 4'' Kbytes
Maximum: ``65536'' Kbytes
Default: ``65536'' Kbytes

Specify integer value.

Description

This parameter is provided as a means to minimize lost cycle time
caused by TLB (translation look-aside buffer) misses on systems
using newer PA-RISC devices such as the PA-8000 that have smaller
TLBs and no hardware TLB walker.

vps_pagesize

Specify the default user-page size (in Kbytes) that is used by the
kernel if the user application does not use the ``chatr'' command to
specify a page size.

Acceptable Values:

Minimum: `` 4''
Maximum: ``65536''
Default: `` 4''

Specify integer value.

Description

This parameter is provided as a means to minimize lost cycle time
caused by TLB (translation look-aside buffer) misses on systems
using newer PA-RISC devices such as the PA-8000 that have smaller
TLBs and no hardware TLB walker.

vxfs_max_ra_kbytes

Set the maximum amount of read-ahead data, in kilobytes,
that the kernel may have outstanding for a single VxFS filesystem.

Acceptable Values:

Minimum: `` 0''
Maximum: ``65536''
Default: `` 1024''

Specify integer value or use integer formula expression.

Description

When data is read from a disk drive, the system may read additional data
beyond that requested by the operation. This "read-ahead" speeds up sequential
disk accesses, by anticipating that additional data will be read, and
having it available in system buffers before it is requested.
This parameter limits the number of read-ahead blocks that the kernel
is allowed to have outstanding for any given VxFS filesystem. The
limit applies to each individual VxFS filesystem, !!not!! to the
system-wide total.

vxfs_ra_per_disk

Set the amount of VxFS filesystem

Acceptable Values:

Minimum: `` 0''
Maximum: ``8192''
Default: ``1024''

Specify an integer value or use an integer formula expression.

Description

When data is read from a disk drive, the system may read additional data
beyond that requested by the operation. This "read-ahead" speeds up sequential
disk accesses, by anticipating that additional data will be read, and
having it available in system buffers before it is requested.
This parameter specifies the amount of read-ahead permitted per disk drive.

The total amount of read-ahead is determined by multiplying
``vxfs_ra_per_disk'' by the number of drives in the logical volume.
If the filesystem does not reside in a logical volume, then the number

of drives is effectively one

The total amount of read-ahead that the kernel may have
outstanding for a single VxFS filesystem is constrained by
``vxfs_max_ra_kbytes".

vx_ncsize

Specify the number of bytes to be reserved for the directory path-name
cache used by the VxFS file system.

Acceptable Values:

Minimum: ``0"
Maximum: None
Default: ``1024"

Specify integer value.

Description

The VxFS file system uses a name cache to store directory pathname
information related to recently accessed directories in the file system.
Retrieving this information from a name cache allows the system to
access directories and their contents without having to use direct disk
accesses to find its way down a directory tree every time it needs to
find a directory that is used frequently. Using a name cache in this
way can save considerable overhead, especially in large applications
such as databases where the system is repetitively accessing a
particular directory or directory path.

``vx_ncsize" specifies the how much space, in bytes, is set aside for
the VxFS file system manager to use for this purpose. The default value
is sufficient for most typical HP-UX systems, but for larger systems or
systems with applications that use VxFS disk I/O intensively, some
performance enhancement may result from expanding the cache size. The
efficiency gained, however, depends greatly on the variety of directory
paths used by the application or applications, and what percentage of
total process time is expended while interacting with the VxFS file
system.

Overview of Select Kernel Parameters

Asynchronous I/O Parameters

The following kernel parameters are used for managing asynchronous
I/O operations. The first four are related to POSIX asynchronous
I/O operations; the last pertains to open ports between processes
and the asynchronous disk-I/O driver:

"aio_listio_max"   Specifies how many POSIX asynchronous I/O
                   operations are allowed in a single "listio()"
                   call.

"aio_max_ops"   System-wide maximum number of POSIX asynchronous
                   I/O operations that are allowed at any given time.

"aio_physmem_pct"   Maximum total system memory that can be locked for
                    use in POSIX asynchronous I/O operations.

"aio_prio_delta_max"   Maximum priority offset allowed in a POSIX
                       asynchronous I/O control block ("aiocb").

"max_async_ports"   Maximum number of ports to the asynchronous
                    disk-I/O driver that processes can have open at
                    any given time.

Configurable Parameters for Kernel-Panic Dumps

The following parameters affect dump operations when a kernel panic
occurs and parts of system memory are dumped to disk:

"alwaysdump"   Specifies which classes of system memory are to be
               dumped if a kernel panic occurs.

"dontdump"   Specifies which classes of system memory are !!not!!
               to be dumped if a kernel panic occurs.

"initmodmax"   Maximum number of kernel modules that "savecrash"
               will handle when processing system-crash dump data.

"modstrmax"   Maximum size, in bytes, of the "savecrash"
kernel-module table which contains module names and
their location in the file system.

Overview of Fiber Channel Kernel Parameters

Two kernel configuration parameters pertain to the Fiber Channel SCSI
subsystem and communication between the system processor and any
peripheral devices that interact with it using Fiber-Channel Protocol
(FCP). These parameters are used for adjusting the default amount and
type of memory allocated for supporting concurrent FCP read, write,
and/or control requests.

"num_tachyon_adapters"
Some of the memory that is allocated for FCP requests must meet
certain requirements. The "num_tachyon_adapters" parameter is
used on systems that do not provide I/O virtual addressing so that
memory meeting these requirements can be allocated. The value you
specify controls what type of memory is allocated, and specifies
the number of Tachyon-based Fiber-Channel adapters in the system.

"max_fcp_reqs"
This parameter sets a limit on the number of concurrent FCP requests
that are allowed on an FCP adapter. The default value of 512
requests can be changed by specifying a different value for this
parameter. The optimal limit on concurrent requests depends on a
number of factors such as configuration, device characteristics, I/O
load, host memory, and other values that FCP software cannot easily
determine.

Configurable File-System Parameters

The following parameters control various aspects of file-system
management:

Buffer Cache Group

"bufpages"
Number of 4-Kbyte pages in file-system buffer cache.

"dbc_min_pct"
Mimimum percentage of memory for dynamic buffer cache.

"dbc_max_pct"
Maximum percentage of memory for dynamic buffer cache.

"nbuf"
> System-wide number of file-system buffer and cache buffer headers.

Open/Locked Files Group

"maxfiles"
> Soft limit on how many files a single process can have opened or locked at any given time.

"maxfiles_lim"
> Hard limit on how many files a single process can have opened or locked at any given time.

"nfile"
> Maximum number of files that can be open simultaneously on the system at any given time.

"nflocks"
> Maximum combined total number of file locks that are available system-wide to all processes at any given time.

"ninode"
> Maximum number of open inodes that can be in memory.

Asynchronous Writes Group

"fs_async"
> Specify synchronous or asynchronous writes of file-system data structures to disk.

VxFS (Journaled) File-System Parameter

"vx_ncsize"
> Memory space reserved for VxFS directory path-name cache

Overview of Mass-Storage Kernel Parameters

Configurable parameters related to file system performance fall into the following categories:

File System Buffers   Allocating system physical memory resources for file system buffer cache space.

Open or Locked Files   Number of files that can be open or locked
                simultaneously.

Journal File Systems   Allocate space for the Directory-Name Lookup
                Cache (DNLC) associated with VxFS file-system
                inodes.

Asynchronous Writes   Asynchronous writes to file system allowed or
                not allowed.

Configurable Parameters for Logical Volume Manager (LVM)

Two configurable kernel parameters are provided that relate to kernel interaction
with the Logical Volume Manager:

maxvgs   Maximum number of volume groups configured by the
            Logical Volume Manager on the system.

no_lvm_disks   Flag that notifies the kernel when no logical
            volumes exist on the system. If set, all file
            systems coincide with physical disks on the system
            and physical disk boundaries. The only exception to
            this is when disks are configured for partitions or
            part of the disk is reserved for swap and other
            non-file-system uses.

Overview of LVM Operation

Logical Volume Manager (LVM) is a subsystem for managing file systems
and disk storage space that are structured into logical volumes rather
than being restricted to the beginning and end points of a physical
disk. Logical volumes can be smaller than the disk or disk array on
which they reside, or they can include all or part of several disks or
disk arrays. Logical volume boundaries are not required to coincide
with the boundaries of physical disks when multiple disks or arrays are
used.

Managing logical volumes is done by the Logical Volume Manager, not the
kernel. However, the kernel contains data structures for each volume
group on the system, and the space reserved for LVM data structures must
be sufficient to support the number of volume groups that exist on the
system. This is done by the "maxvgs" kernel configuration parameter.
A second parameter, "no_lvm_disks", is provided for notifying the
kernel at boot time that no logical volumes exist on the system. This
saves the system from having to identify and activate logical volumes at

boot time.
 Volume and Group Boundaries

Logical volume groups consist of one or more logical volumes. Logical
volume boundaries within a volume group can be configured anywhere on a
given disk. However, a single disk device cannot be shared between
volume groups. Disk arrays configured as RAID (redundant array of
independent disks) arrays for data protection are treated as a single
disk device and cannot be shared between volume groups. Individual
disks in any array that is not configured as a RAID array are treated as
individual devices, and individual devices can be assigned to any volume
group as desired by the administrator.

Configurable Parameters for Memory Paging

``allocate_fs_swapmap''   Enable or disable allocation of file-system
                swap space when ``swapon()'' is called as
                opposed to allocating swap space when
                ``malloc()'' is called. Enabling allocation
                reduces risk of insufficient swap space and
                is used primarily where high-availabilility
                is important.

``maxswapchunks''    This parameter, multiplied by ``swchunk''
                times the system block size value
                (``DEV_BSIZE''), determines the combined
                maximum amount device swap and file-system
                swap space that can be configured,
                system-wide.

``nswapdev''   Maximum number of devices, system-wide, that
                can be used for device swap. Set to match
                actual system configuration.

``nswapfs''   Maximum number of mounted file systems,
                system-wide, that can be used for file-system
                swap. Set to match actual system
                configuration.

``page_text_to_local''   Enable or disable program text segment
                swapping to local swap device on cluster
                client. Increases load time for loading
                memory with new contents (text is written to
                local disk instead of discarding and
                reloading later from server), but reduces

network traffic from server to client.

``remote_nfs_swap''   Enable or disable swap to mounted remote NFS
file system. Used on cluster clients for
swapping to NFS-mounted server file systems.

``swapmem_on''   Enable or disable pseudo-swap allocation.
This allows systems with large installed
memory to allocate memory space as well as
disk swap space for virtual memory use
instead of restricting availability to
defined disk swap area.

``swchunk''   Defines amount of space allocated for each
!!chunk!! of swap area. Chunks are
allocated from device to device by the
kernel. Changing this parameter requires extensive
knowledge of system internals. Without such knowledge,
Do not change this parameter from
the normal default value.

Variable-Page-Size Parameters

``vps_ceiling''   Defines the maximum system-selected page size
if the user does not specify a page size.

``vps_chatr_ceiling''   Defines the maximum page size a user can specify
by using the ``chatr'' command in a program.

``page_size''   Defines the default minimum user page-size if
no page size is specified using ``chatr''.

Overview of Memory Paging Parameters

Configurable kernel parameters for memory paging enforce operating
rules and limits related to virtual memory (swap space). They fall
into the following categories:

Total System Swap   Maximum swap space that can be allocated
system-wide.

Device Swap   Swap space allocated on hard disk devices.

File System Swap   Swap space allocated on mounted file
                          systems.

Pseudo-Swap   Use of installed RAM as pseudo-swap,
                          allowing virtual memory space allocation
                          beyond the limit of swap space on disk
                          devices.

Variable Page Sizes   The size of virtual memory pages can be
                          altered to make swap operations more
                          efficient in particular applications.

Undocumented Kernel Parameters

Some of the configurable parameters that appear in the kernel master
file are not documented, and some are not known to or are not supported
by SAM for any of several possible reasons:

* The parameter is obsolete. It is no longer used in current HP-UX
  releases, but might appear in an existing kernel configuration. If
  SAM encounters an obsolete parameter in the current kernel
  configuration, it does not display it in the list of configurable
  parameters that can be changed. It also removes that parameter when
  creating the new configuration file used to build the pending kernel.

* The parameter is not supported by SAM. As with obsolete parameters,
  it is not displayed in the list of configurable parameters, but it
  is retained in the new kernel configuration file to ensure that no
  malfunctions are introduced due to a missing parameter.

* The parameter is assigned a value by kernel configuration software,
  which is frequently based on external factors. The assigned value
  might be used when calculating values for one or more other
  parameters.

* The parameter is for HP factory or support use only. No change from
  the default value should be made unless specifically directed
  otherwise by official HP support personnel.

* The parameter supports obsolete or obsolescent sofware. For
  information about how to select a non-default value, consult the
  documentation furnished with the software that the parameter
  supports.

Manual Pages for Commands Used in Chapter 3

The following section contains copies of the manual pages for commands used in Chapter 3. This makes a quick reference for you to use when issuing the commands commonly used during your system administration day.

sysdef

man page

sysdef - 3

sysdef - Analyze the currently running system and report on its tunable configuration parameters.

```
sysdef(1M)                                                          sysdef(1M)

NAME
      sysdef - display system definition

SYNOPSIS

      /usr/sbin/sysdef [kernel [master]]

DESCRIPTION
      The command sysdef analyzes the currently running system and reports
      on its tunable configuration parameters.  kernel is the file used to
      retrieve the kernel namelist; if not specified, /stand/vmunix is used.
      master is not used, but can be specified for standards compliance.

      For each configuration parameter, the following information is
      printed:

            NAME          The name and description of the parameter.

            VALUE         The current value of the parameter.

            BOOT          The value of the parameter at boot time, if
                          different from the current value.

            MIN           The minimum allowed value of the parameter, if
                          any.

            MAX           The maximum allowed value of the parameter, if
                          any.

            UNITS         Where appropriate, the units by which the
                          parameter is measured.

            FLAGS         Flags that further describe the parameter.   The
                          following flag is defined:

                          M  Parameter can be modified without rebooting.

EXAMPLES
      Analyze the system using the /stand/vmunix kernel file:

            sysdef

      Analyze the system using the kernel file /os_file:

            sysdef /os_file
```

WARNINGS
     Users of sysdef must not rely on the exact field widths and spacing of
     its output, as these will vary depending on the system, the release of
     HP-UX, and the data to be displayed.

FILES
     /stand/vmunix   Default kernel file

     /usr/conf/master.d   Directory containing master files

CHAPTER 4

Device Files and Adding Peripherals

Introduction

HP-UX creates special files for most devices it finds attached at the time the system boots. You may, however, have to create your own device files or, at a minimum, have to understand some device files that exist on your system so the information in this chapter is important for every system administrator to know. A typical installation will have terminals, printers, a tape drive, a DVD drive, etc. Some devices are "standard," meaning that they are HP products or third-party products officially supported by HP. You have to be careful here, though, because what may seem as if it should work may not work after all and may not be supported. Almost always you can find a way to get things working eventually, but beware of devices you may be adding that aren't supported and may cause you trouble.

As you add additional peripherals to your system, you will have to either add device files manually or use SAM to create them for you. Most all devices you add can be added through SAM. I find adding peripherals to be much like setting up networking; that is, I almost always use SAM, but I find it important to know what is going on in the background. As an example, you could add a printer to your system using SAM and never know what has been done to support the new printer. In the event that the printer does not work for some reason, you really can't begin troubleshooting the problem without an understanding of the device files.

The following section is a general overview of device files.

Device Files in HP-UX 11i

What could be more confusing in the UNIX world than device files? Fortunately, in HP-UX, device files for the Series 700 and Series 800 are nearly identical, so if you learn one, your knowledge applies to the other. In this section, I cover:

- The structure of device files.

- Some commands associated with helping you work with device files.

- Some examples of creating device files.

A device file provides the HP-UX kernel with important information about a specific device. The HP-UX kernel needs to know a lot about a device before Input/Output operations can be performed. With HP-UX 11i, the device file naming convention is the same for workstations and server systems. Device files are in the **/dev** directory. There may also be a subdirectory under **/dev** used to further categorize the device files. An example of a subdirectory would be **/dev/dsk,** where disk device files are usually located, and **/dev/rmt**, where tape drive device files are located. Figure 4-1 shows the HP-UX 11i device file-naming convention.

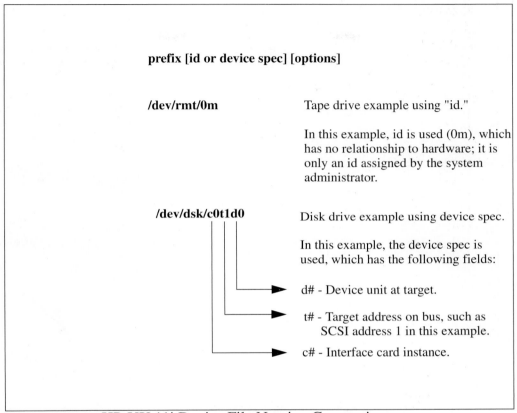

Figure 4-1 HP-UX 11i Device File Naming Convention

There are a number of commands you can use as you go about creating device files. The **ioscan** command is the first of these. Some of the examples in this section were used in Chapter 3, when building a kernel was covered. The following is an **ioscan** output of the same Series 700 for which **sysdef** was run when describing how a kernel is created in Chapter 3. (Using *-f* with **ioscan** would have created a full listing; you should try it with and without *-f*.) I included four **ioscan** outputs so you could see examples from a variety of different systems. The last listing is from a large V-Class system used in some of the examples in Chapter 8, where disks and filesystems are covered.

(on Series 700)

```
$ /usr/sbin/ioscan

H/W Path      Class            Description
================================================================

              bc
1             graphics         Graphics
2             ba
2/0           unknown
2/0/1           ext_bus        Built-in SCSI
2/0/1.1           target
2/0/1.1.0           disk       HP         C2247
2/0/1.2           target
2/0/1.2.0           disk       TOSHIBA CD-ROM XM-3301TA
2/0/1.6           target
2/0/1.6.0           disk       ' HP        C2247
2/0/2           lan            Built-in LAN
2/0/4           tty            Built-in RS-232C
2/0/6           ext_bus        Built-in Parallel Interface
2/0/8           audio          Built-in Audio
2/0/10          pc             Built-in Floppy Drive
2/0/10.1          floppy       HP_PC_FDC_FLOPPY
2/0/11          ps2            Built-in Keyboard
8             processor        Processor
9             memory           Memory
```

man page

ioscan - 4

The following is an **ioscan** output from a Series 800 system. Note the four processors shown in this output.

(on Series 800)

```
$ /usr/sbin/ioscan

H/W Path      Class            Description
================================================================

              bc
8             bc               I/O Adapter
10            bc               I/O Adapter
10/0            ext_bus        GSC built-in Fast/Wide SCSI
10/0.3            target
10/0.3.0            disk       HP         C2490WD
10/0.4            target
10/0.4.0            disk       HP         C2490WD
10/0.5            target
10/0.5.0            disk       HP         C2490WD
```

```
10/0.6                  target
10/0.6.0                    disk       HP        C2490WD
10/4           bc                      Bus Converter
10/4/0                  tty            MUX
10/12          ba                      Core I/O Adapter
10/12/0            ext_bus             Built-in Parallel Interface
10/12/5            ext_bus             Built-in SCSI
10/12/5.0               target
10/12/5.0.0                 tape       HP        HP35480A
10/12/5.2               target
10/12/5.2.0                 disk       TOSHIBA CD-ROM XM-4101TA
10/12/6            lan                 Built-in LAN
10//12/7           ps2                 Built-in Keyboard/Mouse
32             processor               Processor
34             processor               Processor
36             processor               Processor
38             processor               Processor
49             memory                  Memory
```

man page

ioscan - 4

And last is an **ioscan** output from a V-Class server. Note the eight processors shown in this output.

(on V-Class)

$ **/usr/sbin/ioscan**

```
H/W Path    Class                      Description
================================================
            bc
0           ba                         PCI Bus Bridge - epic
0/0/0            lan                    PCI(10110019)
0/1/0            unknown                PCI(107e0008)
2           ba                         PCI Bus Bridge - epic
2/0/0            ext_bus                Ultra Wide SCSI
2/0/0.5             target
2/0/0.5.0              disk            SEAGATE ST34371W
2/0/0.6             target
2/0/0.6.0              disk            SEAGATE ST34371W
2/0/0.7             target
2/0/0.7.0                 ctl          Initiator
2/1/0            lan                    PCI(10110019)
4           ba                         PCI Bus Bridge - epic
4/1/0              fc                   HP Fibre Channel Mass
                                          Storage Adapter
4/1/0.5          lan                    HP Fibre Channel Mass
                                          Storage Cntl
4/1/0.8             fcp                 FCP Protocol Adapter
4/2/0           ext_bus                 Ultra Wide SCSI
```

```
4/2/0.0                  target
4/2/0.0.0                  disk      TOSHIBA CD-ROM XM-5701TA
4/2/0.1                  target
4/2/0.1.0                  tape      HP C1537A
4/2/0.7                  target
4/2/0.7.0                  ctl       Initiator
6            ba                      PCI Bus Bridge - epic
8            memory
15           ba                      Core I/O Adapter
15/1             tty                 Built-in Serial Port DUART
15/2             tty                 Built-in Serial Port DUART
15/3             unknown             Unknown
17           processor               Processor
19           processor               Processor
20           processor               Processor
22           processor               Processor
25           processor               Processor
27           processor               Processor
28           processor               Processor
30           processor               Processor
```

man page

ioscan - 4

        The following is a full **ioscan** output from a V-Class server. This server has a large disk unit attached to it (XP 256), which resulted in a very long output that I had to abbreviate in the places where the three dots are shown.

(on V-Class)

```
# ioscan -f
Class       I  H/W Path    Driver    S/W State  H/W Type    Description
========================================================================================
bc          0              root      CLAIMED    BUS_NEXUS
ba          0  0           saga      CLAIMED    BUS_NEXUS   saga Bridge
lan         0  0/0/0       btlan6    CLAIMED    INTERFACE   PCI Ethernet (10110019)
ba          1  1           saga      CLAIMED    BUS_NEXUS   saga Bridge
ext_bus     0  1/0/0       c720      CLAIMED    INTERFACE   Ultra2 Wide LVD SCSI
target      0  1/0/0.4     tgt       CLAIMED    DEVICE
disk        0  1/0/0.4.0   sdisk     CLAIMED    DEVICE      SEAGATE ST318275LW
target      1  1/0/0.5     tgt       CLAIMED    DEVICE
disk        1  1/0/0.5.0   sdisk     CLAIMED    DEVICE      SEAGATE ST318275LW
target      2  1/0/0.6     tgt       CLAIMED    DEVICE
disk        2  1/0/0.6.0   sdisk     CLAIMED    DEVICE      SEAGATE ST318275LW
target      3  1/0/0.7     tgt       CLAIMED    DEVICE
ctl         0  1/0/0.7.0   sctl      CLAIMED    DEVICE      Initiator
target      4  1/0/0.8     tgt       CLAIMED    DEVICE
disk        3  1/0/0.8.0   sdisk     CLAIMED    DEVICE      SEAGATE ST318275LW
ext_bus     1  1/1/0       c720      CLAIMED    INTERFACE   Ultra2 Wide LVD SCSI
target      5  1/1/0.7     tgt       CLAIMED    DEVICE
ctl         1  1/1/0.7.0   sctl      CLAIMED    DEVICE      Initiator
target      6  1/1/0.9     tgt       CLAIMED    DEVICE
disk        4  1/1/0.9.0   sdisk     CLAIMED    DEVICE      SEAGATE ST318275LW
target      7  1/1/0.10    tgt       CLAIMED    DEVICE
disk        5  1/1/0.10.0  sdisk     CLAIMED    DEVICE      SEAGATE ST318275LW
target      8  1/1/0.11    tgt       CLAIMED    DEVICE
```

```
disk        6    1/1/0.11.0           sdisk     CLAIMED    DEVICE       SEAGATE ST318275LW
target      9    1/1/0.12             tgt       CLAIMED    DEVICE
disk        7    1/1/0.12.0           sdisk     CLAIMED    DEVICE       SEAGATE ST318275LW
ba          2    2                    saga      CLAIMED    BUS_NEXUS    saga Bridge
fc          0    2/0/0                td        CLAIMED    INTERFACE    HP Tachyon TL/TS Fibre
Channel Mass Storage Adapter
fcp         0    2/0/0                fcp       CLAIMED    INTERFACE    FCP Protocol Adapter
ext_bus     7    2/0/0.8.0.0.0        fcparray  CLAIMED    INTERFACE    FCP Array Interface
target      12   2/0/0.8.0.0.0.0      tgt       CLAIMED    DEVICE
disk        9    2/0/0.8.0.0.0.0.0    sdisk     CLAIMED    DEVICE       HP        OPEN-8
disk        77   2/0/0.8.0.0.0.0.1    sdisk     CLAIMED    DEVICE       HP        OPEN-8
disk        78   2/0/0.8.0.0.0.0.2    sdisk     CLAIMED    DEVICE       HP        OPEN-8
disk        105  2/0/0.8.0.0.0.0.3    sdisk     CLAIMED    DEVICE       HP        OPEN-8
disk        106  2/0/0.8.0.0.0.0.4    sdisk     CLAIMED    DEVICE       HP        OPEN-8
disk        10   2/0/0.8.0.0.0.0.5    sdisk     CLAIMED    DEVICE       HP        OPEN-8
disk        107  2/0/0.8.0.0.0.0.6    sdisk     CLAIMED    DEVICE       HP        OPEN-8
disk        108  2/0/0.8.0.0.0.0.7    sdisk     CLAIMED    DEVICE       HP        OPEN-8
target      13   2/0/0.8.0.0.0.1      tgt       CLAIMED    DEVICE
disk        11   2/0/0.8.0.0.0.1.0    sdisk     CLAIMED    DEVICE       HP        OPEN-8
disk        109  2/0/0.8.0.0.0.1.1    sdisk     CLAIMED    DEVICE       HP        OPEN-8
disk        110  2/0/0.8.0.0.0.1.2    sdisk     CLAIMED    DEVICE       HP        OPEN-8
disk        111  2/0/0.8.0.0.0.1.3    sdisk     CLAIMED    DEVICE       HP        OPEN-8
disk        112  2/0/0.8.0.0.0.1.4    sdisk     CLAIMED    DEVICE       HP        OPEN-8
disk        113  2/0/0.8.0.0.0.1.5    sdisk     CLAIMED    DEVICE       HP        OPEN-8
disk        114  2/0/0.8.0.0.0.1.6    sdisk     CLAIMED    DEVICE       HP        OPEN-8
disk        176  2/0/0.8.0.0.0.1.7    sdisk     CLAIMED    DEVICE       HP        OPEN-8
target      14   2/0/0.8.0.0.0.2      tgt       CLAIMED    DEVICE
disk        12   2/0/0.8.0.0.0.2.0    sdisk     CLAIMED    DEVICE       HP        OPEN-8
disk        177  2/0/0.8.0.0.0.2.1    sdisk     CLAIMED    DEVICE       HP        OPEN-8
target      15   2/0/0.8.0.0.0.3      tgt       CLAIMED    DEVICE
disk        13   2/0/0.8.0.0.0.3.0    sdisk     CLAIMED    DEVICE       HP        DISK-SUBSYSTEM
target      16   2/0/0.8.0.0.0.4      tgt       CLAIMED    DEVICE
disk        14   2/0/0.8.0.0.0.4.0    sdisk     CLAIMED    DEVICE       HP        DISK-SUBSYSTEM
target      17   2/0/0.8.0.0.0.5      tgt       CLAIMED    DEVICE
disk        15   2/0/0.8.0.0.0.5.0    sdisk     CLAIMED    DEVICE       HP        DISK-SUBSYSTEM
target      18   2/0/0.8.0.0.0.6      tgt       CLAIMED    DEVICE
disk        16   2/0/0.8.0.0.0.6.0    sdisk     CLAIMED    DEVICE       HP        DISK-SUBSYSTEM
target      19   2/0/0.8.0.0.0.7      tgt       CLAIMED    DEVICE
disk        17   2/0/0.8.0.0.0.7.0    sdisk     CLAIMED    DEVICE       HP        DISK-SUBSYSTEM
target      20   2/0/0.8.0.0.0.8      tgt       CLAIMED    DEVICE
disk        18   2/0/0.8.0.0.0.8.0    sdisk     CLAIMED    DEVICE       HP        OPEN-8
disk        79   2/0/0.8.0.0.0.8.1    sdisk     CLAIMED    DEVICE       HP        OPEN-8
disk        80   2/0/0.8.0.0.0.8.2    sdisk     CLAIMED    DEVICE       HP        OPEN-8
disk        115  2/0/0.8.0.0.0.8.3    sdisk     CLAIMED    DEVICE       HP        OPEN-8
disk        116  2/0/0.8.0.0.0.8.4    sdisk     CLAIMED    DEVICE       HP        OPEN-8
disk        117  2/0/0.8.0.0.0.8.5    sdisk     CLAIMED    DEVICE       HP        OPEN-8
disk        118  2/0/0.8.0.0.0.8.6    sdisk     CLAIMED    DEVICE       HP        OPEN-8
disk        119  2/0/0.8.0.0.0.8.7    sdisk     CLAIMED    DEVICE       HP        OPEN-8
target      21   2/0/0.8.0.0.0.9      tgt       CLAIMED    DEVICE
disk        19   2/0/0.8.0.0.0.9.0    sdisk     CLAIMED    DEVICE       HP        OPEN-8
disk        120  2/0/0.8.0.0.0.9.1    sdisk     CLAIMED    DEVICE       HP        OPEN-8
disk        121  2/0/0.8.0.0.0.9.2    sdisk     CLAIMED    DEVICE       HP        OPEN-8
disk        122  2/0/0.8.0.0.0.9.3    sdisk     CLAIMED    DEVICE       HP        OPEN-8
disk        123  2/0/0.8.0.0.0.9.4    sdisk     CLAIMED    DEVICE       HP        OPEN-8
disk        124  2/0/0.8.0.0.0.9.5    sdisk     CLAIMED    DEVICE       HP        OPEN-8
disk        125  2/0/0.8.0.0.0.9.6    sdisk     CLAIMED    DEVICE       HP        OPEN-8
disk        178  2/0/0.8.0.0.0.9.7    sdisk     CLAIMED    DEVICE       HP        OPEN-8
target      22   2/0/0.8.0.0.0.10     tgt       CLAIMED    DEVICE
disk        20   2/0/0.8.0.0.0.10.0   sdisk     CLAIMED    DEVICE       HP        OPEN-8
disk        179  2/0/0.8.0.0.0.10.1   sdisk     CLAIMED    DEVICE       HP        OPEN-8
target      23   2/0/0.8.0.0.0.11     tgt       CLAIMED    DEVICE
disk        21   2/0/0.8.0.0.0.11.0   sdisk     CLAIMED    DEVICE       HP        DISK-SUBSYSTEM
target      24   2/0/0.8.0.0.0.12     tgt       CLAIMED    DEVICE
disk        22   2/0/0.8.0.0.0.12.0   sdisk     CLAIMED    DEVICE       HP        DISK-SUBSYSTEM
target      25   2/0/0.8.0.0.0.13     tgt       CLAIMED    DEVICE
disk        23   2/0/0.8.0.0.0.13.0   sdisk     CLAIMED    DEVICE       HP        DISK-SUBSYSTEM
target      26   2/0/0.8.0.0.0.14     tgt       CLAIMED    DEVICE
disk        24   2/0/0.8.0.0.0.14.0   sdisk     CLAIMED    DEVICE       HP        DISK-SUBSYSTEM
```

.
.
.

```
memory      0   8          memory     CLAIMED    MEMORY      Memory
ba          8   15         bus_adapter CLAIMED   BUS_NEXUS   Core I/O Adapter
tty         0   15/1       consp1     CLAIMED    INTERFACE   Built-in Serial Port DUART
tty         1   15/2       consp1     CLAIMED    INTERFACE   Built-in Serial Port DUART
unknown    -1   15/3                  UNCLAIMED  UNKNOWN     Built-in Ethernet
processor   0   16         processor  CLAIMED    PROCESSOR   Processor
processor   1   18         processor  CLAIMED    PROCESSOR   Processor
processor   2   21         processor  CLAIMED    PROCESSOR   Processor
processor   3   23         processor  CLAIMED    PROCESSOR   Processor
processor   4   24         processor  CLAIMED    PROCESSOR   Processor
processor   5   26         processor  CLAIMED    PROCESSOR   Processor
processor   6   29         processor  CLAIMED    PROCESSOR   Processor
processor   7   32         processor  CLAIMED    PROCESSOR   Processor
processor   8   34         processor  CLAIMED    PROCESSOR   Processor
processor   9   37         processor  CLAIMED    PROCESSOR   Processor
processor  10   39         processor  CLAIMED    PROCESSOR   Processor
processor  11   40         processor  CLAIMED    PROCESSOR   Processor
processor  12   42         processor  CLAIMED    PROCESSOR   Processor
processor  13   45         processor  CLAIMED    PROCESSOR   Processor
```

man page

lsdev - 4

man page

ioscan - 4

The next command that helps you when creating device files is **lsdev**. **lsdev** lists the drivers configured into your system. When adding a device file, you need to have the driver for the device configured into the system. If it is not configured into the system, you can use SAM to configure it, or you can use the manual kernel configuration process covered earlier. There are columns for the major number for a character device and block device, the driver name, and the class of the driver. The major number, character device, and other parameters are defined later. Here is an example of running **lsdev** on the same Series 700 on which **ioscan** was run:

(on Series 700)

```
$ /usr/sbin/lsdev
```

Character	Block	Driver	Class
0	-1	cn	pseudo
1	-1	ansio0	tty
3	-1	mm	pseudo
16	-1	ptym	ptym
17	-1	ptys	ptys
24	-1	hil	hil
27	-1	dmem	pseudo
46	-1	netdiag1	unknown
52	-1	lan2	lan
64	64	lv	lvm
66	-1	audio	audio
69	-1	dev_config	pseudo
72	-1	clone	pseudo
73	-1	strlog	pseudo

```
 74        -1      sad          pseudo
 75        -1      telm         strtelm
 76        -1      tels         strtels
 77        -1      tlctls       pseudo
 78        -1      tlcots       pseudo
 79        -1      tlcotsod     pseudo
114        -1      ip           pseudo
115        -1      arp          pseudo
116        -1      echo         pseudo
119        -1      dlpi         pseudo
130        -1      rawip        pseudo
136        -1      tcp          pseudo
137        -1      udp          pseudo
138        -1      stcpmap      pseudo
139        -1      nuls         pseudo
140        -1      netqa        pseudo
141        -1      tun          pseudo
142        -1      btlan3       unknown
143        -1      fddi3        unknown
144        -1      fddi0        unknown
145        -1      fcT1_cntl    unknown
156        -1      ptm          strptym
157        -1      ptm          strptys
159        -1      ps2          ps2
164        -1      pipedev      unknown
168        -1      beep         graf_pseudo
169        -1      fcgsc_lan    lan
170        -1      lpr0         unknown
174        -1      framebuf     graf_pseudo
183        -1      diag1        diag
188        31      sdisk        disk
189        -1      klog         pseudo
196        -1      eeprom       da
203        -1      sctl         ctl
205        -1      stape        tape
207        -1      sy           pseudo
216        -1      CentIF       ext_bus
227        -1      kepd         pseudo
229        -1      ite          graf_pseudo
232        -1      diag2        diag
```

man page

lsdev - 4

man page

ioscan - 4

   Here is an example of running **lsdev** on the same Series 800 on which **ioscan** was run:

(on Series 800)

```
$ /usr/sbin/lsdev
```

Character	Block	Driver	Class
0	-1	cn	pseudo
1	-1	asio0	tty
3	-1	mm	pseudo
16	-1	ptym	ptym
17	-1	ptys	ptys
28	-1	diag0	diag
46	-1	netdiag1	unknown
52	-1	lan2	lan
64	64	lv	lvm
69	-1	dev_config	pseudo
72	-1	clone	pseudo
73	-1	strlog	pseudo
74	-1	sad	pseudo
75	-1	telm	strtelm
76	-1	tels	strtels
77	-1	tlctls	pseudo
78	-1	tlcots	pseudo
79	-1	tlcotsod	pseudo
114	-1	ip	pseudo
116	-1	echo	pseudo
119	-1	dlpi	pseudo
130	-1	rawip	pseudo
136	-1	lpr0	unknown
137	-1	udp	pseudo
138	-1	stcpmap	pseudo
139	-1	nuls	pseudo
140	-1	netqa	pseudo
141	-1	tun	pseuod
142	-1	btlan3	unknown
143	-1	fddi3	unknown
144	-1	fddi0	unknown
156	-1	ptm	strptym
157	-1	ptm	strptys
159	-1	ps2	ps2
164	-1	pipedev	unknown
168	-1	beep	graf_pseudo
174	-1	framebuf	graf_pseudo
188	31	sdisk	disk
189	-1	klog	pseudo
193	-1	mux2	tty
203	-1	sctl	ctl
205	-1	stape	tape
207	-1	sy	pseudo
216	-1	CentIF	ext_bus
227	-1	kepd	pseudo
229	-1	ite	graf_pseudo

And last, here is an example of running **lsdev** on the same V class server on which the first **ioscan** was run:

lsdev - 4

(on V-Class)

ioscan - 4

```
$ /usr/sbin/lsdev

    Character      Block      Driver          Class
        0           -1        cn              pseudo
        3           -1        mm              pseudo
       16           -1        ptym            ptym
       17           -1        ptys            ptys
       27           -1        dmem            pseudo
       28           -1        diag0           diag
       46           -1        netdiag1        unknown
       64           64        lv              lvm
       69           -1        dev_config      pseudo
       72           -1        clone           pseudo
       73           -1        strlog          pseudo
       74           -1        sad             pseudo
       75           -1        telm            strtelm
       76           -1        tels            strtels
       77           -1        tlclts          pseudo
       78           -1        tlcots          pseudo
       79           -1        tlcotsod        pseudo
      114           -1        ip              pseudo
      115           -1        arp             pseudo
      116           -1        echo            pseudo
      119           -1        dlpi            pseudo
      130           -1        rawip           pseudo
      136           -1        tcp             pseudo
      137           -1        udp             pseudo
      138           -1        stcpmap         pseudo
      139           -1        nuls            pseudo
      140           -1        netqa           pseudo
      141           -1        tun             pseudo
      142           -1        fddi4           unknown
      143           -1        fcT1_cntl       lan
      144           -1        fcgsc_lan       lan
      145           -1        lpr0            unknown
      156           -1        ptm             strptym
      157           -1        pts             strptys
      164           -1        pipedev         unknown
      169           -1        consp1          tty
      170           -1        btlan6          lan
      171           -1        fcp             fcp
      188           31        sdisk           disk
      189           -1        klog            pseudo
      203           -1        sctl            ctl
```

```
205              -1      stape       tape
207              -1      sy          pseudo
227              -1      kepd        pseudo
232              -1      diag2       diag
```

man page

lsdev - 4

man page

ioscan - 4

From these three **lsdev** outputs, you can observe some minor differences in the devices. The Series 700, for instance, has such classes as audio and floppy, the Series 800 has a multiplexer, and the V-Class has a BaseTen network card.

You can use **ioscan** to show the device files for a particular peripheral. Going back to the Series 800 that had four disks and a CD-ROM attached to it, you could issue the following **ioscan** command to see the device files associated with *disk:*

(on Series 800)

```
$ /usr/sbin/ioscan -fn -C disk

Class   I  H/W Path      Driver  S/W State  H/W Type   Description
====================================================================
disk    0  10/0.3.0      sdisk   CLAIMED    DEVICE     HP C2490WD
                         /dev/dsk/c0t3d0    /dev/rdsk/c0t3d0

disk    1  10/0.4.0      sdisk   CLAIMED    DEVICE     HP C2490WD
                         /dev/dsk/c0t4d0    /dev/rdsk/c0t4d0

disk    2  10/0.5.0      sdisk   CLAIMED    DEVICE     HP C2490WD
                         /dev/dsk/c0t5d0    /dev/rdsk/c0t5d0

disk    3  10/0.6.0      sdisk   CLAIMED    DEVICE     HP C2490WD
                         /dev/dsk/c0t6d0    /dev/rdsk/c0t6d0

disk    3  10/12/5/2/0   sdisk   CLAIMED    DEVICE     CD-ROM
                         /dev/dsk/c1t2d0    /dev/rdsk/c1t2d0
```

You can see from this **ioscan** all of the device files associated with *disk,* including the CD-ROM.

man page

diskinfo - 4

You could find out more information about one of these devices with the **diskinfo** command. Specify the character device you want to know more about, as shown below (using the *-v* option for verbose provides more detailed information).

```
$ diskinfo /dev/rdsk/c0t5d0

SCSI describe of /dev/rdsk/c0t5d0
            vendor: HP
        product id: C2490WD
              type: direct access
              size: 2082636 bytes
   bytes per sector: 512
```

man page

diskinfo - 4

An Example of Adding a Peripheral

In this section, we'll construct a device file for a tape drive. Chapter 8 covers the process of using device files and all Logical Volume Manager commands for adding disk devices that you may want to view as well. Before we construct a device file, let's view two existing device files on the Series 700 and see where some of this information appears. The first long listing is that of the tape drive, and the second is the disk, both of which are on the Series 700 in the earlier listings.

(on Series 700)

$ ll /dev/rmt/0m

crw-rw-rw- 2 bin bin 205 0x003000 Feb 12 03:00 /dev/rmt/0m

(on Series 700)

$ ll /dev/dsk/c0t1d0

brw-r----- 1 bin sys 31 0x001000 Feb 12 03:01 /dev/dsk/c0t1d0

The tape drive device file, **/dev/rmt/0m**, shows a major number of 205 corresponding to that shown for the *character* device driver *stape* from **lsdev**. The disk drive device file, **/dev/dsk/c0t6d0**, shows a major number of *31* corresponding to the *block* device driver *sdisk* from **lsdev**. Since the tape drive requires only a character device file and no major number exists for a block *stape* device, as indicated by the *-1* in the *block* column of **lsdev**, this file is the only device file that exists for the tape drive. The disk, on the other hand, may be used as either a block device or a character device (also referred to as the *raw device*). Therefore, we should see a character device file, **/dev/rdsk/c0t6d0**, with a major number of *188*, as shown in **lsdev** for *sdisk*.

(on Series 700)

```
$ ll /dev/rdsk/c0t0d0

crw-r-----   1   root   sys   188   0x001000   Feb   12   03:01
/dev/rdsk/c0t1d0
```

man page

mksf - 4

We can now create a device file for a second tape drive, this time at SCSI address 2, and a disk device file for a disk drive at SCSI address 5, using the **mksf** command. You can run **mksf** two different ways. The first form of **mksf** requires you to include less specific information such as the minor number. The second form requires you to include more of this specific information. Some of these arguments relate only to the specific form of **mksf** you use.

man page

lsdev - 4

-*d*   Use the device driver specified. A list of device drivers is obtained with the **lsdev** command.

-*C*   The device specified belongs to this class. The class is also obtained with the **lsdev** command.

man page

ioscan - 4

-*H*   Use the hardware path specified. Hardware paths are obtained with the **ioscan** command.

-m   The minor number of the device is supplied.

-r   Create a character, also known as a raw
                          device file. The default is to create a block
                          file.

-v   Use verbose output, which prints the name of
                          each special file as it is created.

We will now create the device files for a disk drive. Both a block
and a character device file are required. The *0x005000* in the example
corresponds to the address of 5 on the disk drive. This number, used in
both the block and character device files, is unique for every disk
drive created.

We can now create a *block* device file for a disk at SCSI address
5 using the following **mksf** command:

man page

mksf - 4

(on Series 700)

```
$ /sbin/mksf -v -C disk -m 0x005000 /dev/dsk/c0t5d0

    making /dev/dsk/c0t5d0 b 31 0x005000
```

Similarly, we can now create a *character* device file for a disk at
SCSI address 5 using form two of **mksf**:

(on Series 700)

```
$ /sbin/mksf -v -r -C disk -m 0x005000 /dev/dsk/c0t5d0

    making /dev/rdsk/c0t5d0 c 188 0x005000
```

man page

mksf - 4

The **-v** option used in these examples prints out each device file as it is created. If you wanted to add a second tape drive at SCSI address 2 to your system in addition to the existing tape drive (**/dev/ rmt/0m**), you might use the following **mksf** command:

(on Series 700)

```
$ /sbin/mksf  -v -C tape -m 0x002000 /dev/rmt/1m

    making /dev/rmt/1m c 205 0x002000
```

man page

lsdev - 4

Character devices are automatically produced for tape drives, since no block device drivers are required. This fact was found in the output from the **lsdev** command, as indicated by a *-1* in the "Block" column.

With this level of device file background, you should have a good understanding of the device files that SAM will build for you when you add peripherals. By the way, printer device files look much different from the device files I covered here, but all the same principles apply.

Memory Management - Kind of Related to Device Files

Memory-related topics are almost never covered in system administration discussion. This is because memory is in too many different forms and there are too many factors affecting how much memory you need, what kind of memory you need, and so on. Let's cover some memory-related topics at a high level and look at some commands related to memory.

To begin with, most memory discussions begin with what is swap and how much do I need? HP-UX system administrators spend a lot of time worrying about swap. It must be very important. Swap is one part of the overall HP-UX memory management scheme, one of three parts to be exact. As any student of computer science will tell you, computers have three types of memory: cache memory, Random Access Memory (RAM), and disk memory. These are listed in order of their speed; that is, cache is much faster than RAM, which is much faster than disk.

Cache Memory

The HP Precision Architecture chip-set is configured with both data and instruction cache, which, I might add, are used very efficiently. You must rely on the operating system to use cache efficiently, since you have very little control over this. If you need information from memory and it is loaded in cache (probably because you recently accessed this information or accessed some information that is located close to what you now want), it will take very little time to get the information out of cache memory. This access, called a cache "hit," is instantaneous for all practical purposes. One of the reasons cache memory is so fast is that it typically is physically on the same chip as the processor. If putting large amounts of cache on-chip with the processor were possible, this would obviate the need for RAM and disk. This, however, is not currently possible, so efficient use of memory is a key to good overall system performance.

Checking Available RAM

man page

dmesg - 4

Your system spells out to you what RAM is available. **/sbin/dmesg** gives you the amount of "physical" memory installed on the system, as shown below for a 64-MByte system:

```
Physical: 65536 Kbytes
```

Don't get too excited when you see this number, because it is not all "available" memory. Available memory is what is leftover after some memory is reserved for kernel code and data structures. You'll also see the available memory, in this case approximately 54 MBytes, with **/sbin/dmesg**:

```
available: 55336 Kbytes
```

Some of the available memory can also be "lockable." Lockable memory is that which can be devoted to frequently accessed programs and data. The programs and data that lock memory for execution will remain memory-resident and run more quickly. You will also see the amount of lockable memory, in this case approximately 44 MBytes, at the time of system startup:

```
lockable: 45228
```

man page

bdf - 8

/sbin/dmesg shows you these values and a summary of system-related messages. You should issue this command on your system to see what it supplies you. The following displays the output of both **bdf** and the **/sbin/dmesg** command issued on a large V-Class system with an XP 256 disk array unit attached to it.

```
# bdf
Filesystem          kbytes     used     avail %used Mounted on
/dev/vg00/lvol3     524288    40899    453231    8% /
/dev/vg00/lvol1      99669    29984     59718   33% /stand
/dev/vg00/lvol7    1048576   272706    728019   27% /var
/dev/vg00/lvol6    1048576   491445    522318   48% /usr
/dev/vgu10/lvol1  35860480    35632  35544976    0% /u10
/dev/vgu09/lvol1  35860480  4358224  31256152   12% /u09
/dev/vgu08/lvol1  35860480    21560  35576720    0% /u08
/dev/vgu07/lvol1  35860480   555544  35029128    2% /u07
/dev/vgu06/lvol1  35860480    13624  35566816    0% /u06
/dev/vgu05/lvol1  35860480   560432  35024280    2% /u05
```

```
/dev/vgu04/lvol1    35860480   575152 35009672    2% /u04
/dev/vgu03/lvol1    35860480    13624 35566816    0% /u03
/dev/vgu02/lvol1    35860480    13632 35566808    0% /u02
/dev/vgu01/lvol1    35860480  5611848 30012328   16% /u01
/dev/vg00/lvol5       204800     2273   189930    1% /tmp
/dev/vg00/lvol4      2097152   466824  1528479   23% /opt
/dev/vg00/lvol8       524288     2887   488858    1% /home
/dev/vgapp/lvol1    35860480  6485880 29146160   18% /app


# /sbin/dmesg

Jun 20 16:26
...
disk
5/0/0.8.0.0.0.9.2 sdisk
5/0/0.8.0.0.0.9.3 sdisk
5/0/0.8.0.0.0.9.4 sdisk
5/0/0.8.0.0.0.9.5 sdisk
5/0/0.8.0.0.0.9.6 sdisk
5/0/0.8.0.0.0.9.7 sdisk
5/0/0.8.0.0.0.10 tgt
5/0/0.8.0.0.0.10.0 sdisk
5/0/0.8.0.0.0.10.1 sdisk
5/0/0.8.0.0.0.10.2 sdisk
5/0/0.8.0.0.0.10.3 sdisk
5/0/0.8.0.0.0.10.4 sdisk
5/0/0.8.0.0.0.10.5 sdisk
5/0/0.8.0.0.0.11 tgt
5/0/0.8.0.0.0.11.0 sdisk
5/0/0.8.0.0.0.12 tgt
5/0/0.8.0.0.0.12.0 sdisk
5/0/0.8.0.0.0.13 tgt
5/0/0.8.0.0.0.13.0 sdisk
5/0/0.8.0.0.0.14 tgt
5/0/0.8.0.0.0.14.0 sdisk
5/0/0.8.0.255.0 fcpdev
5/0/0.8.0.255.0.0 tgt
5/0/0.8.0.255.0.0.0 sctl
Probing epic6
Probe of epic6 complete
6 saga
6/0/0 btlan6
Probing epic7
Probe of epic7 complete
7 saga
7/0/0 td
td: claimed Tachyon TL/TS Fibre Channel Mass Storage card at 7/0/0
7/0/0.8 fcp
7/0/0.8.0.0.0 fcparray
7/0/0.8.0.0.0.0 tgt
7/0/0.8.0.0.0.0.0 sdisk
7/0/0.8.0.0.0.0.1 sdisk
7/0/0.8.0.0.0.0.2 sdisk
7/0/0.8.0.0.0.0.3 sdisk
7/0/0.8.0.0.0.0.4 sdisk
7/0/0.8.0.0.0.0.5 sdisk
7/0/0.8.0.0.0.0.6 sdisk
7/0/0.8.0.0.0.0.7 sdisk
7/0/0.8.0.0.0.1 tgt
7/0/0.8.0.0.0.1.0 sdisk
7/0/0.8.0.0.0.1.1 sdisk
7/0/0.8.0.0.0.1.2 sdisk
7/0/0.8.0.0.0.1.3 sdisk
7/0/0.8.0.0.0.1.4 sdisk
7/0/0.8.0.0.0.1.5 sdisk
7/0/0.8.0.0.0.1.6 sdisk
7/0/0.8.0.0.0.1.7 sdisk
7/0/0.8.0.0.0.2 tgt
7/0/0.8.0.0.0.2.0 sdisk
7/0/0.8.0.0.0.2.1 sdisk
7/0/0.8.0.0.0.3 tgt
7/0/0.8.0.0.0.3.0 sdisk
7/0/0.8.0.0.0.4 tgt
7/0/0.8.0.0.0.4.0 sdisk
7/0/0.8.0.0.0.5 tgt
```

```
7/0/0.8.0.0.0.5.0 sdisk
7/0/0.8.0.0.0.6 tgt
7/0/0.8.0.0.0.6.0 sdisk
7/0/0.8.0.0.0.7 tgt
7/0/0.8.0.0.0.7.0 sdisk
7/0/0.8.0.0.0.8 tgt
7/0/0.8.0.0.0.8.0 sdisk
7/0/0.8.0.0.0.8.1 sdisk
7/0/0.8.0.0.0.8.2 sdisk
7/0/0.8.0.0.0.8.3 sdisk
7/0/0.8.0.0.0.8.4 sdisk
7/0/0.8.0.0.0.8.5 sdisk
7/0/0.8.0.0.0.8.6 sdisk
7/0/0.8.0.0.0.8.7 sdisk
7/0/0.8.0.0.0.9 tgt
7/0/0.8.0.0.0.9.0 sdisk
7/0/0.8.0.0.0.9.1 sdisk
7/0/0.8.0.0.0.9.2 sdisk
7/0/0.8.0.0.0.9.3 sdisk
7/0/0.8.0.0.0.9.4 sdisk
7/0/0.8.0.0.0.9.5 sdisk
7/0/0.8.0.0.0.9.6 sdisk
7/0/0.8.0.0.0.9.7 sdisk
7/0/0.8.0.0.0.10 tgt
7/0/0.8.0.0.0.10.0 sdisk
7/0/0.8.0.0.0.10.1 sdisk
7/0/0.8.0.0.0.11 tgt
7/0/0.8.0.0.0.11.0 sdisk
7/0/0.8.0.0.0.12 tgt
7/0/0.8.0.0.0.12.0 sdisk
7/0/0.8.0.0.0.13 tgt
7/0/0.8.0.0.0.13.0 sdisk
7/0/0.8.0.0.0.14 tgt
7/0/0.8.0.0.0.14.0 sdisk
7/0/0.8.0.255.0 fcpdev
7/0/0.8.0.255.0.0 tgt
7/0/0.8.0.255.0.0.0 sctl
8 memory
15 bus_adapter
15/1 consp1
15/2 consp1
16 processor
18 processor
21 processor
23 processor
24 processor
26 processor
29 processor
32 processor
34 processor
37 processor
39 processor
40 processor
42 processor
45 processor
btlan6: Initializing 10/100BASE-TX card at 0/0/0....
btlan6: Initializing 10/100BASE-TX card at 6/0/0....

System Console is on SPP DUART0 Interface
Entering cifs_init...
Initialization finished successfully... slot is 8
Logical volume 64, 0x3 configured as ROOT
Logical volume 64, 0x2 configured as SWAP
Logical volume 64, 0x2 configured as DUMP
    Swap device table:  (start & size given in 512-byte blocks)
        entry 0 - major is 64, minor is 0x2; start = 0, size = 2097152
    Dump device table:  (start & size given in 1-Kbyte blocks)
        entry 0 - major is 31, minor is 0x6000; start = 105312, size = 1048576
Starting the STREAMS daemons-phase 1
btlan6: NOTE: MII Link Status Not OK - Switch Connection to AUI at 0/0/0....
Create STCP device files
Starting the STREAMS daemons-phase 2
    B2352B/9245XB HP-UX (B.11.00) #1: Wed Nov  5 22:38:19 PST 1997

Memory Information:
```

```
        physical page size = 4096 bytes, logical page size = 4096 bytes
        Physical: 16773120 Kbytes, lockable: 13099368 Kbytes, available: 15031616 Ks

btlan6: timeout: DMA timeout occurred at 0/0/0
btlan6: reset state is 550 at 0/0/0....
btlan6: WARNING: AUI Loopback Failed at 0/0/0....
btlan6: timeout: DMA timeout occurred at 0/0/0
btlan6: reset state is 575 at 0/0/0....
btlan6: WARNING: BNC Loopback Failed at 0/0/0....
Unable to add all swap for device: /dev/vg00/lvol9. Increase the tunable parame.
#
```

man page

dmesg - 4

As you can see, **dmesg** provides a lot of useful information in additional to the memory-related reporting we earlier covered. The memory information in this output is roughly 1.6 GBytes total and 1.3 GBytes lockable.

Managing Cache and RAM

If the information you need is not in cache memory but in RAM, then the access will take longer. The speed of all memory is increasing and RAM speed is increasing at a particularly rapid rate. You have a lot of control over the way in which RAM is used. First, you can decide how much RAM is configured into your system. The entire HP product line, both workstations and server systems, supports more RAM than you will need in the system. RAM, at the time of this writing, is inexpensive and getting less expensive all the time. RAM is not a good area in which to cut corners in the configuration of your system. Moreover, you can use whatever RAM you have configured efficiently. One example is in configuring an HP-UX kernel that is efficient. The HP-UX kernel is always loaded in RAM. This means if it is 2 or 3 MBytes too big for your needs, then this is 2 or 3 MBytes you don't have for other purposes. If you need to access some information in RAM, it will take roughly one order of magnitude longer to access than if it were in cache.

Virtual Memory

If your system had only cache and, say, 64 MBytes of RAM, then you would be able to have user processes that consumed only about 64 MBytes of physical memory. With memory management, you can have user processes that far exceed the size of physical memory by using virtual memory. Virtual memory allows you to load into RAM only parts of a process while keeping the balance on disk. You move blocks of data back and forth between memory and disk in pages.

Swap

Swap is used to extend the size of memory, that is, reserve an area on the disk to act as an extension to RAM. When the load on the system is high, swap space is used for part or all of the processes for which space is not available in physical memory. HP-UX handles all this swapping for you with the **vhand**, **statdaemon**, and **swapper** processes. You want to make sure that you have more than enough swap space reserved on your disk so that memory management can take place without running out of swap space.

Three types of swap space exist: primary swap, secondary swap, and filesystem swap. These are described next:

Primary swap   Swap that is available at boot. Primary swap is located on the same disk as the root file system. If a problem occurs with this primary swap, you may have a hard time getting the system to boot.

Secondary swap   Swap that is located on a disk other than the root disk.

File system swap   This is a filesystem that supports both files and data structures as well as swapping.

Don't labor too much over the amount of swap to configure. At a minimum, swap should be twice the size of physical memory (this is the installation process default size). Also, our primary applications will define the amount of swap required. Most of the applications I've worked with make clear the maximum amount of swap required for the application. If you are running several applications, add together the swap required for each application if they are going to be running simultaneously.

Manual Pages for Commands Used in Chapter 4

The following section contains copies of the manual pages for commands used in Chapter 4. This makes a quick reference for you to use when issuing the commands commonly used during your system administration day.

diskinfo

diskinfo - Describe a disk device.

man page

diskinfo - 4

```
diskinfo(1M)                                                    diskinfo(1M)

NAME
     diskinfo - describe characteristics of a disk device

SYNOPSIS

     /usr/sbin/diskinfo [-b|-v] character_devicefile

DESCRIPTION
     The diskinfo command determines whether the character special file
     named by character_devicefile is associated with a SCSI, CS/80, or
     Subset/80 disk drive. If so, diskinfo summarizes the disk's
     characteristics.

     The diskinfo command displays information about the following
     characteristics of disk drives:

            Vendor name    Manufacturer of the drive (SCSI only)
            Product ID     Product identification number or ASCII name
            Type           CS/80 or SCSI classification for the device
            Disk           Size of disk specified in bytes
            Sector         Specified as bytes per sector

     Both the size of disk and bytes per sector represent formatted media.

     Options
       The diskinfo command recognizes the following options:

            -b             Return the size of the disk in 1024-byte sectors.


            -v             Display a verbose summary of all of the
                           information available from the device. (Since the
                           information returned by CS/80 drives and SCSI
                           drives differs, the associated descriptions also
                           differ.)

                              -  CS/80 devices return the following:
                                      Device name
                                      Number of bytes/sector
                                      Geometry information
                                      Interleave
                                      Type of device
                                      Timing information

                              -  SCSI disk devices return the following:
                                      Vendor and product ID
                                      Device type
                                      Size (in bytes and in logical blocks)
                                      Bytes per sector
                                      Revision level
                                      SCSI conformance level data
```

DEPENDENCIES
   General

      The diskinfo command supports only CS/80, subset/80, and HP SCSI disk
      devices.

   SCSI Devices

      The SCSI specification provides for a wide variety of device-dependent
      formats. For non-HP devices, diskinfo may be unable to interpret all
      of the data returned by the device. Refer to the drive operating
      manual accompanying the unit for more information.

AUTHOR
      diskinfo was developed by HP.

SEE ALSO
      lsdev(1M), disktab(4), disk(7).

dmesg

dmesg - Print system diagnostic information.

```
dmesg(1M)                                                           dmesg(1M)

NAME
     dmesg - collect system diagnostic messages to form error log

SYNOPSIS

     /usr/sbin/dmesg [-] [core] [system]

DESCRIPTION
     dmesg looks in a system buffer for recently printed diagnostic
     messages and prints them on the standard output.  The messages are
     those printed by the system when unusual events occur (such as when
     system tables overflow or the system crashes).  If the - argument is
     specified, dmesg computes (incrementally) the new messages since the
     last time it was run and places these on the standard output.  This is
     typically used with cron (see cron(1)) to produce the error log
     /var/adm/messages by running the command:

          /usr/sbin/dmesg - >> /var/adm/messages

     every 10 minutes.

     The arguments core and system allow substitution for the defaults
     /dev/kmem and /stand/vmunix respectively, where core should be a file
     containing the image of the kernel virtual memory saved by the
     savecore(1M) command and system should be the corresponding kernel.
     If the system is booted with a kernel other than /stand/vmunix say
     /stand/vmunix_new, dmesg must be passed this name, the command must
     be,

          /usr/sbin/dmesg [-] /dev/kmem /stand/vmunix_new

WARNINGS
     The system error message buffer is of small, finite size.  dmesg is
     run only every few minutes, so there is no guarantee that all error
     messages will be logged.

AUTHOR
     dmesg was developed by the University of California, Berkeley.

FILES
     /var/adm/messages          error log (conventional location)
     /var/adm/msgbuf            memory scratch file for - option
     /dev/kmem                  special file containing the image of kernel
                                virtual memory
     /stand/vmunix              the kernel, system name list

SEE ALSO
     savecore(1M).
```

ioscan

ioscan - Scan the system and list the results.

```
ioscan(1M)                                                          ioscan(1M)

NAME
     ioscan - scan I/O system

SYNOPSIS

     /usr/sbin/ioscan [-k|-u] [-d driver|-C class] [-I instance] [-H
     hw_path] [-f[-n]|-F[-n]] [devfile]

     /usr/sbin/ioscan -M driver -H hw_path [-I instance]

DESCRIPTION
     ioscan scans system hardware, usable I/O system devices, or kernel I/O
     system data structures as appropriate, and lists the results.  For
     each hardware module on the system, ioscan displays by default the
     hardware path to the hardware module, the class of the hardware
     module, and a brief description.

     By default, ioscan scans the system and lists all reportable hardware
     found.  The types of hardware reported include processors, memory,
     interface cards and I/O devices.  Scanning the hardware may cause
     drivers to be unbound and others bound in their place in order to
     match actual system hardware.  Entities that cannot be scanned are not
     listed.

     In the second form shown, ioscan forces the specified software driver
     into the kernel I/O system at the given hardware path and forces
     software driver to be bound.  This can be used to make the system
     recognize a device that cannot be recognized automatically; for
     example, because it has not yet been connected to the system, does not
     support autoconfiguration, or because diagnostics need to be run on a
     faulty device.

Options
     ioscan recognizes the following options:

         -C class            Restrict the output listing to those devices
                             belonging to the specified class.  Cannot be
                             used with -d.

         -d driver           Restrict the output listing to those devices
                             controlled by the specified driver.  Cannot be
                             used with -C.

         -f                  Generate a full listing, displaying the
                             module's class, instance number, hardware path,
                             driver, software state, hardware type, and a
                             brief description.

         -F                  Produce a compact listing of fields (described
                             below), separated by colons. This option
                             overrides the -f option.
```

-H hw_path	Restrict the scan and output listing to those devices connected at the specified hardware path. When used with -M, this option specifies the full hardware path at which to bind the software modules.
-I instance	Restrict the scan and output listing to the specified instance, when specified with either -d or -C. When used with -M, specifies the desired instance number for binding.
-k	Scan kernel I/O system data structures instead of the actual hardware and list the results. No binding or unbinding of drivers is performed. The -d, -C, -I, and -H options can be used to restrict listings. Cannot be used with -u.
-M driver	Specifies the software driver to bind at the hardware path given by the -H option. Must be used with the -H option.
-n	List device file names in the output. Only special files in the /dev directory and its subdirectories are listed.
-u	Scan and list usable I/O system devices instead of the actual hardware. Usable I/O devices are those having a driver in the kernel and an assigned instance number. The -d, -C, -I, and -H options can be used to restrict listings. The -u option cannot be used with -k.

The -d and -C options can be used to obtain listings of subsets of the I/O system, although the entire system is still scanned. Specifying -d or -C along with -I, or specifying -H or a devfile causes ioscan to restrict both the scan and the listing to the hardware subset indicated.

Fields

The -F option can be used to generate a compact listing of fields separated by colons (:), useful for producing custom listings with awk. Fields include the module's bus type, cdio, is_block, is_char, is_pseudo, block major number, character major number, minor number, class, driver, hardware path, identify bytes, instance number, module path, module name, software state, hardware type, a brief description, and card instance. If a field does not exist, consecutive colons hold the field's position. Fields are defined as follows:

class	A device category, defined in the files located in the directory /usr/conf/master.d and consistent with the listings output by lsdev (see lsdev(1M)). Examples are disk, printer, and tape.
instance	The instance number associated with the device or card. It is a unique number assigned to a card or device within a class. If no driver is available for the hardware component or an error occurs binding the driver, the kernel will not assign an instance number and a (-1), is listed.
hw path	A numerical string of hardware components, notated sequentially from the bus address to the device address. Typically, the initial number is appended by slash (/), to represent a bus converter (if required by your machine), and

subsequent numbers are separated by periods (.).
Each number represents the location of a hardware
component on the path to the device.

driver   The name of the driver that controls the hardware
                    component. If no driver is available to control
                    the hardware component, a question mark (?) is
                    displayed in the output.

software state The result of software binding.

  CLAIMED   software bound successfully

  UNCLAIMED   no associated software found

  DIFF_HW   software found does not match the
                   associated software

  NO_HW   the hardware at this address is no
                   longer responding

  ERROR   the hardware at this address is
                   responding but is in an error state

  SCAN   node locked, try again later

hardware type Entity identifier for the hardware component. It
               is one of the following strings:

  UNKNOWN   There is no hardware associated or
                   the type of hardware is unknown

  PROCESSOR   Hardware component is a processor

  MEMORY   Hardware component is memory

  BUS_NEXUS   Hardware component is bus converter
                   or bus adapter

  INTERFACE   Hardware component is an interface
                   card

  DEVICE   Hardware component is a device

bus type   Bus type associated with the node.

cdio   The name associated with the Context-Dependent I/O
                   module.

is_block   A boolean value indicating whether a device block
                   major number exists. A T or F is generated in this
                   field.

is_char   A boolean value indicating whether a device
                   character major number exists. A T or F is
                   generated in this field.

is_pseudo   A boolean value indicating a pseudo driver. A T or
                   F is generated in this field.

block major   The device block major number. A -1 indicates that
                   a device block major number does not exist.

character major

The device character major number. A -1 indicates that a device character major number does not exist.

minor	The device minor number.
identify bytes	The identify bytes returned from a module or device.
module path	The software components separated by periods (.).
module name	The module name of the software component controlling the node.
description	A description of the device.
card instance	The instance number of the hardware interface card.

RETURN VALUE
     ioscan returns 0 upon normal completion and 1 if an error occurred.

EXAMPLES
     Scan the system hardware and list all the devices belonging to the disk device class.

         ioscan -C disk

     Forcibly bind driver tape1 at the hardware path 8.4.1.

         ioscan -M tape1 -H 8.4.1

AUTHOR
     ioscan was developed by HP.

FILES
     /dev/config
     /dev/*

SEE ALSO
     config(1M), lsdev(1M), ioconfig(4).

lsdev

lsdev - List devices configured into the system.

```
lsdev(1M)                                                              lsdev(1M)

NAME
     lsdev - list device drivers in the system

SYNOPSIS

     /usr/sbin/lsdev [-h] [-d driver | -C class] [-b block_major]
          [-c char_major] [-e major] [major ...]

DESCRIPTION
     The lsdev command lists, one pair per line, the major device numbers
     and driver names of device drivers configured into the system and
     available for invocation via special files.  A -1 in either the block
     or character column means that a major number does not exist for that
     type.

     If no arguments are specified, lsdev lists all drivers configured into
     the system.

     If the -h option is specified, lsdev will not print a heading.  This
     option may be useful when the output of lsdev will be used by another
     program.

     The -d, -C, -b, -c, and -e options are used to select specific device
     drivers for output.  If more than one option is specified, all drivers
     that match the criteria specified by those options will be listed.
     These search options are divided into two types: name search keys (the
     -d and -C options) and major number search keys (the -b, -c, and -e
     options).  If both types of options are present, only entries that
     match both types are printed.  The same type of option may appear more
     than once on the command line with each occurrence providing an ORing
     effect of that search type.  The -d and -C options may not be
     specified at the same time.

     The ability to process major arguments is provided for compatibility
     and functions like the -e option.

Options
          -C class           List device drivers that match class.

          -d driver          List device drivers with the name driver.

          -b block_major     List device drivers with a block major number
                             of block_major.

          -c char_major      List device drivers with a character major
                             number of char_major.

          -e major           List device drivers with either a character
                             major number or block major equal to major.
```

DIAGNOSTICS

    Invalid combination of options
        The -d and -C options may not be specified at the same time.

    Invalid major number
        A major number is malformed or out of range.

EXAMPLES
    To output entries for all drivers in the pseudo class:

        lsdev -C pseudo

    To output entries that are in the class disk that have either a block
    or character major number of 0:

        lsdev -C disk -e 0

    To get the character major number of my_driver into a shell
    environment variable:

        C_MAJOR=$(lsdev -h -d my_driver | awk '{print $1}')

WARNINGS
    Some device drivers available from the system may be intended for use
    by other drivers. Attempting to use them directly from a special file
    may produce unexpected results.

    A driver may be listed even when the hardware requiring the driver is
    not present. Attempts to access a driver without the corresponding
    hardware will fail.

    lsdev only lists drivers that are configured into the currently
    executing kernel. For a complete list of available drivers, please
    run sam (see sam(1M).

DEPENDENCIES
    Since lsdev relies on the device driver information provided in a
    driver_install routine, lsdev may not list drivers installed by other
    means.

AUTHOR
    lsdev was developed by HP.

SEE ALSO
    sam(1M).

    Section 7 entries related to specific device drivers.

    HP-UX System Administration Tasks

mksf

man page

mksf - 4

mksf - Make a special device file in the devices directory.

```
mksf(1M)                                                          mksf(1M)

NAME
     mksf - make a special (device) file

SYNOPSIS

     /sbin/mksf [-C class | -d driver] [-D directory] [-H hw-path]
         [-I instance] [-q|-v] [driver-options] [special-file]

     /sbin/mksf [-C class | -d driver] [-D directory] [-H hw-path]
         -m minor [-q|-v] [-r] special-file

DESCRIPTION
     The mksf command makes a special file in the devices directory,
     normally /dev, for an existing device, a device that has already been
     assigned an instance number by the system.  The device is specified by
     supplying some combination of the -C, -d, -H, and -I options.  If the
     options specified match a unique device in the system, mksf creates a
     special file for that device; otherwise, mksf prints an error message
     and exits.  If required, mksf creates any subdirectories relative to
     the device installation directory that are defined for the resulting
     special file.

     For most drivers, mksf has a set of built-in driver options,
     driver-options, and special-file naming conventions.  By supplying
     some subset of the driver options, as in the first form above, the
     user can create a special file with a particular set of
     characteristics.  If a special-file name is specified, mksf creates
     the special file with that special file name; otherwise, the default
     naming convention for the driver is used.

     In the second form, the minor number and special-file name are
     explicitly specified.  This form is used to make a special file for a
     driver without using the built-in driver options in mksf.  The -r
     option specifies that mksf should make a character (raw) device file
     instead of the default block device file for drivers that support
     both.

   Options
     mksf recognizes the following options:

          -C class       Match a device that belongs to a given device
                         class, class.  Device classes can be listed with
                         the lsdev command (see lsdev(1M)).  They are
                         defined in the files in the directory
                         /usr/conf/master.d.  This option is not valid for
                         pseudo devices.  This option cannot be used with
                         -d.

          -d driver      Match a device that is controlled by the specified
                         device driver, driver.  Device drivers can be
                         listed with the lsdev command (see lsdev(1M)).
                         They are defined in the files in the directory
```

/usr/conf/master.d. This option cannot be used with -C.

-D directory Override the default device installation directory /dev and install the special files in directory instead. directory must exist; otherwise, mksf displays an error message and exits. See WARNINGS.

-H hw-path Match a device at a given hardware path, hw-path. Hardware paths can be listed with the ioscan command (see ioscan(1M)). A hardware path specifies the addresses of the hardware components leading to a device. It consists of a string of numbers separated by periods (.), such as 52 (a card), 52.3 (a target address), and 52.3.0 (a device). If a hardware component is a bus converter, the following period, if any, is replaced by a slash (/) as in 2, 2/3, and 2/3.0. This option is not valid for pseudo devices.

-I instance Match a device with the specified instance number. Instances can be listed with the -f option of the ioscan command (see ioscan(1M)). This option is not valid for pseudo devices.

-m minor Create the special file with the specified minor number minor. The format of minor is the same as that given in mknod(1M) and mknod(5).

-q Quiet option. Normally, mksf displays a message as each driver is processed. This option suppresses the driver message, but not error messages. See the -v option.

-r Create a character (raw) special file instead of a block special file.

-v Verbose option. In addition to the normal processing message, display the name of each special file as it is created. See the -q option.

Naming Conventions

Many special files are named using the ccardttargetddevice naming convention. These variables have the following meaning wherever they are used.

card The unique interface card identification number from ioscan (see ioscan(1M)). It is represented as a decimal number with a typical range of 0 to 255.

target The device target number, for example the address on a HP-FL or SCSI bus. It is represented as a decimal number with a typical range of 0 to 15.

device A address unit within a device, for example, the unit in a HP-FL device or the LUN in a SCSI device. It is represented as a decimal number with a typical range of 0 to 15.

Special Files

The driver-specific options (driver-options) and default special file names (special-file) are listed below.

asio0

-a access-mode   Port access mode (0-2). The default access mode
is 0 (Direct connect). The access-mode meanings
are:

access-mode	Port Operation
0	Direct connect
1	Dial out modem
2	Dial in modem

-c   CCITT.

-f   Hardware flow control (RTS/CTS).

-i   Modem dialer. Cannot be used with -l.

-l   Line printer. Cannot be used with -i.

-r fifo-trigger

                 fifo-trigger should have a value between 0 and 3.
The following table shows the corresponding FIFO
trigger level for a given fifo-trigger value.

fifo-trigger	Receive FIFO Trigger Level
0	1
1	4
2	8
3	14

-t   Transparent mode (normally used by diagnostics).

-x xmit-limit   xmit-limit should have a value between 0 and 3.
The following table shows the corresponding
transmit limit for a given xmit-limit value.

xmit-limit	Transmit Limit
0	1
1	4
2	8
3	12

special-file   The default special file name depends on the
access-mode and whether the -i and -l options are
used.

access-mode	-i	-l	Special File Name
-	no	yes	ccardp0_lp
2	no	no	ttydcardp0
1	no	no	culcardp0

	0	yes	no	cuacardp0	
	0	no	no	ttycardp0	

audio

    -f format   Audio format (0-3). The format meanings are:

format	Audio Format	File Name Modifier format-mod
0	No change in audio format	
1	8-bit Mu-law	U
2	8-bit A-law	A
3	16-bit linear	L

    -o output-dest Output destination (0-4). The output-dest should
               have a value between 0 and 4. The following table
               shows the corresponding output destinations for a
               given output-dest value.

output-dest	Output Destinations	File Name Modifier output-mod
0	All outputs	B
1	Headphone	E
2	Internal Speaker	I
3	No output	N
4	Line output	L

    -r   Raw, control access. This option cannot be used
               with either the -f or -o options.

    special-file The default special file name depends on the
               options specified.

Options	Special File Name
-r	audioCtl_card
-f 0	audio_card
all others	audiooutput-modformat-mod_card

               The optional output-mod and format-mod values are
               given in the tables above. Note the underscore
               (_) before card in each special file name. Also
               note that for card 0, each file will be linked to
               a simpler name without the trailing _card.

autox0 schgr

    Note that -i cannot be used with either -r or -p.

    -i   Ioctl; create picker control special file.

    -p optical-disk[:last-optical-disk]
               The optical disk number (starts with 1). If the

optional :last-optical-disk is given then special
files for the range of disks specified will be
created.

-r   Raw; create character, not block, special file.

special-file   A special file cannot be given if a range of
                      optical disks is given with the -p option. If one
                      is given for the single disk case, the name will
                      have an a appended to the end for the A-side
                      device and a b appended to the end for the B-side
                      device. The default special file name depends on
                      whether the -r option is used.

-r	Special File Name
yes	rac/ccardttargetddevice_optical-diska rac/ccardttargetddevice_optical-diskb
no	ac/ccardttargetddevice_optical-diska ac/ccardttargetddevice_optical-diskb

Note the underscore (_) between device and
optical-disk.

CentIf

  -h handshake-mode
                Handshake mode. Valid values range from 1 to 6:

handshake-mode	Handshake operation
1	Automatic NACK/BUSY handshaking
2	Automatic BUSY only handshaking
3	Bidirectional read/write
4	Stream mode (NSTROBE only, no handshaking)
5	Automatic NACK/BUSY with pulsed NSTROBE
6	Automatic BUSY with pulsed NSTROBE

special-file   The default special file name is ccardt0d0_lp for
                      handshake-mode 2 and ccardt0d0hhandshake-mode_lp
                      for all others.

disc1

  -c   This option must be present if the unit is a
                        cartridge tape.

  -r   Raw; create character, not block, special file.

  -s section   The section number.

  -t   Transparent mode (normally used by diagnostics).

  -u unit   The CS/80 unit number (for example, unit 0 for
                        disk, unit 1 for tape).

  special-file   The default special file name depends on whether
                        the -c, -r, and -s options are used:

-c	-r	-s	Special File Name
yes	yes	invalid	rct/ccardttargetddevice
no	yes	no	rdsk/ccardttargetddevice
no	yes	yes	rdsk/ccardttargetddevicessection
yes	no	invalid	ct/ccardttargetddevice
no	no	no	dsk/ccardttargetddevice
no	no	yes	dsk/ccardttargetddevicessection

disc2

-r   Raw; create character, not block, special file.

-s section   The section number.

-t   Transparent mode (normally used by diagnostics).

-u unit   The cs80 unit number (typically 0).

special-file   The default special file name depends on whether
                the -r and -s options are used:

-r	-s	Special File Name
yes	no	rdsk/ccardttargetddevice
yes	yes	rdsk/ccardttargetddevicessection
no	no	dsk/ccardttargetddevice
no	yes	dsk/ccardttargetddevicessection

disc3

-f   Floppy.

-r   Raw; create character, not block, special file.

-s section   The section number.

special-file   The default special file name depends on whether
                the -r and -s options are used:

-r	-s	Special File Name
yes	no	rdsk/ccardttargetddevice and rfloppy/ccardttargetddevice
yes	yes	rdsk/ccardttargetddevicessection
no	no	dsk/ccardttargetddevice and floppy/ccardttargetddevice
no	yes	dsk/ccardttargetddevicessection

disc4 sdisc

-r   Raw; create character, not block, special file.

-s section   The section number.

special-file   The default special file name depends on whether the -r and -s options are used:

```
 -r  | -s  |          Special File Name
_____|_____|_____
yes  | no  | rdsk/ccardttargetddevice
yes  | yes | rdsk/ccardttargetddevicessection
no   | no  | dsk/ccardttargetddevice
no   | yes | dsk/ccardttargetddevicessection
_____|_____|_____
```

instr0

    -a address   The HP-IB instrument address (0-30). Cannot be used with the -t option.

    -t   Transparent mode (normally used by diagnostics). Cannot be used with the -a option.

    special-file   The default special file name depends on the arguments -a and -t:

```
 -a  | -t  |          Special File Name
_____|_____|_____
no   | no  | hpib/ccard
no   | yes | diag/hpib/ccard
yes  | no  | hpib/ccardttargetdaddress
_____|_____|_____
```

hil

    Note that only one of -a, -k, or -r is allowed.

    -a address   The link address (1-7).

    -k   Cooked keyboard.

    -n   The hil controller device.

    special-file   The default special file name depends on the -a, -k, and -r options:

```
Option |  Special File Name
_____|_____
  -a   |  hil_card.address
  -k   |  hilkbd_card
  -r   |  rhil_card
_____|_____
```

    Note the underscore (_) before card. Also note that for card 0, each file will be linked to a simpler name without _card, either hiladdress, hilkbd, or rhil.

lan0 lan1 lan2 lan3

    Note that only one of -e or -i is allowed.

    -e   Ethernet protocol.

    -i   IEEE 802.3 protocol.

-t   Transparent mode (normally used by diagnostics).

special-file   The default special file name depends on the -e, -i, and -t options:

Option	-t	Special File Name
-e	no	ethercard
-e	yes	diag/ethercard
-i	no	lancard
-i	yes	diag/lancard

lantty0

-e   Exclusive access.

special-file   The default special file name depends on whether the -e option is used:

-e	Special File Name
no	lanttycard
yes	diag/lanttycard

lpr0 lpr1 lpr2 lpr3

-c   Capital letters. Convert all output to uppercase.

-e   Eject page after paper-out recovery.

-n   No form-feed.

-o   Old paper-out behavior (abort job).

-r   Raw.

-t   Transparent mode (normally used by diagnostics).

-w   No wait. Don't retry errors on open.

special-file   The default special file name depends on whether the -r option is used:

-r	Special File Name
no	ccardttargetddevice_lp
yes	ccardttargetddevice_rlp

mux0 mux2 mux4 eisa_mux0

-a access-mode Port access mode (0-2). The default access mode is 0 (Direct connect). The access-mode meanings are:

```
|access-mode | Port Operation |
|            |                |
|_____|_____|
|     0      | Direct connect |
|     1      | Dial out modem |
|     2      | Dial in modem  |
|            |                |
|_____|_____|
```

-c   CCITT.

-f   Hardware flow control (RTS/CTS).

-i   Modem dialer. Cannot be used with -l.

-l   Line printer. Cannot be used with -i.

-p port   Multiplexer port number (0-15 for mux0 and mux2;
                0-1 for mux4; 0-256 for eisa_mux0). Some MUX
                cards controlled by a particular driver have fewer
                than the maximum supported ports.

-t   Transparent mode (normally used by diagnostics).

special-file   The default special file name depends on the
                access-mode and whether the -i and -l options are
                used.

```
| access-mode | -i  | -l  | Special File Name |
|             |     |     |                   |
|_____|_____|_____|_____|
|      -      | no  | yes | ccardpport_lp     |
|      2      | no  | no  | ttydcardpport     |
|      1      | no  | no  | culcardpport      |
|      0      | yes | no  | cuacardpport      |
|      0      | no  | no  | ttycardpport      |
|             |     |     |                   |
|_____|_____|_____|_____|
```

pflop sflop

  -r   Raw; create character, not block, special file.

  special-file The default special file name depends on whether
                the -r option is used:

```
| -r  |        Special File Name        |
|_____|_____|
| no  | floppy/ccardttargetddevice      |
| yes | rfloppy/ccardttargetddevice     |
|_____|_____|
```

ps2

    Note that only one of -a, or -p is allowed.

    -a auto_device Autosearch device. An auto_device value of 0
                    means first mouse; a value of 1 means first
                    keyboard.

    -p port   PS2 port number.

    special-file   The default special file name depends on the -a,
                    and -p options:

Option	Special File Name
-a 0	ps2mouse
-a 1	ps2kbd
-p	ps2_port

Note the underscore (_) before port.

sccl

    -a access-mode Port access mode (0-2). The default access mode is 0. The access-mode meanings are:

access-mode	Port Operation
0	Direct connect
1	Dial out modem
2	Dial in modem

    -b   Port B.

    -c   CCITT.

    -i   Modem dialer. Cannot be used with -l.

    -l   Line printer. Cannot be used with -i.

    special-file   The default special file name depends on the access-mode and whether the -i and -l options are used.

access-mode	-i	-l	Special File Name
-	no	yes	ccardpport_lp
2	no	no	ttydcardpport
1	no	no	culcardpport
0	yes	no	cuacardpport
0	no	no	ttycardpport

schgr   See autox0.

sdisk   See disc4.

sflop   See pflop.

stape

    -a   AT&T-style rewind/close.

    -b bpi   Bits per inch or tape density. The recognized values for bpi are:
BEST, D1600, D3480, D3480C, D6250, D6250C, D800, D8MM_8200, D8MM_8200C, D8MM_8500, D8MM_8500C, DDS1, DDS1C, DDS2, DDS2C, NOMOD, QIC_1000, QIC_11, QIC_120, QIC_1350, QIC_150, QIC_2100, QIC_24, QIC_2GB, QIC_525, QIC_5GB, or a decimal number density code.

-c [code]   Compression with optional compression code. The
                   optional decimal code is used to select a
                   particular compression algorithm on drives that
                   support more than one compression algorithm. This
                   option must be specified at the end of an option
                   string. See mt(7) for more details.

-e   Exhaustive mode. This option allows the driver to
                   experiment with multiple configuration values in
                   an attempt to access the media. The default
                   behavior is to use only the configuration
                   specified.

-n   No rewind on close.

-p   Partition one.

-s [block-size]
                   Fixed block size mode. If a numeric block-size is
                   given, it is used for a fixed block size. If the
                   -s option is used alone, a device-specific default
                   fixed block size is used. This option must be
                   specified at the end of an option string.

-u   UC Berkeley-style rewind/close.

-w   Wait (disable immediate reporting).

-x index   Use the index value to access the tape device
                   driver property table entry. Recognized values
                   for index are decimal values in the range 0 to 30.

special-file   Put all tape special files in the /dev/rmt
                   directory. This is required for proper
                   maintenance of the Tape Property Table (see
                   mt(7)). Device files located outside the /dev/rmt
                   directory may not provide consistent behavior
                   across system reboots. The default special file
                   names are dependent on the tape drive being
                   accessed and the options specified. All default
                   special files begin with rmt/ccardttargetddevice.
                   See mt(7) for a complete description of the
                   default special file naming scheme for tapes.

tape1 tape2

-a   AT&T-style rewind/close.

-b bpi   Bits per inch or tape density. The recognized
                   values for bpi are:
                   BEST, D1600, D3480, D3480C, D6250, D6250C, D800,
                   D8MM_8200, D8MM_8200C, D8MM_8500, D8MM_8500C,
                   DDS1, DDS1C, DDS2, DDS2C, NOMOD, QIC_1000, QIC_11,
                   QIC_120, QIC_1350, QIC_150, QIC_2100, QIC_24,
                   QIC_2GB, QIC_525, QIC_5GB, DLT_42500_24,
                   DLT_42500_56, DLT_62500_64, DLT_81633_64,
                   DLT_62500_64C, DLT_81633_64C,
                   or a decimal number density code.

-c [code]   Compression with optional compression code. The
                   optional decimal code is used to select a
                   particular compression algorithm on drives that
                   support more than one compression algorithm. This
                   option must be specified at the end of an option

string. See mt(7) for more details.

-n	No rewind on close.
-o	Console messages disabled.
-t	Transparent mode, normally used by diagnostics.
-u	UC Berkeley-style rewind/close.
-w	Wait (disable immediate reporting).
-x index	Use the index value to access the tape device driver property table entry. The recognized values for index are decimal values in the range 0 to 30.
-z	RTE compatible close.
special-file	Put all tape special files in the /dev/rmt directory. This is required for proper maintenance of the Tape Property Table (see mt(7)). Device files located outside the /dev/rmt directory may not provide consistent behavior across system reboots. The default special file names are dependent on the tape drive being accessed and the options specified. All default special files begin with rmt/ccardttargetddevice. See mt(7) for a complete description of the default special file naming scheme for tapes.

RETURN VALUE
    mksf exits with one of the following values:

    0   Successful completion.
    1   Failure. An error occurred.

DIAGNOSTICS
    Most of the diagnostic messages from mksf are self-explanatory.
    Listed below are some messages deserving further clarification.
    Errors cause mksf to abort immediately.

  Errors
  Ambiguous device specification

        Matched more than one device in the system. Use some combination
        of the -d, -C, -H, and -I options to specify a unique device.

  No such device in the system

        No device in the system matched the options specified. Use
        ioscan to list the devices in the system (see ioscan(1M)).

  Device driver name is not in the kernel
  Device class name is not in the kernel

        The indicated device driver or device class is not present in the
        kernel. Add the appropriate device driver and/or device class to
        the config input file and generate a new kernel (see config(1M)).

  Device has no instance number

        The specified device has not been assigned an instance number.
        Use ioscan to assign an instance to the device.

Directory directory doesn't exist

The directory argument of the -D option doesn't exist. Use mkdir
to create the directory (see mkdir(1)).

EXAMPLES
Make a special file named /dev/printer for the line printer device
associated with instance number 2.

mksf -C printer -I 2 /dev/printer

Make a special file, using the default naming convention, for the tape
device at hardware path 8.4.1. The driver-specific options specify
1600 bits per inch and no rewind on close.

mksf -C tape -H 8.4.1 -b D1600 -n

WARNINGS
Many commands and subsystems assume their device files are in /dev;
therefore, the use of the -D option is discouraged.

AUTHOR
mksf was developed by HP.

FILES
/dev/config   I/O system special file

/etc/mtconfig   Tape driver property table database

SEE ALSO
mkdir(1), config(1M), insf(1M), ioscan(1M), lsdev(1M), mknod(1M),
rmsf(1M), mknod(2), ioconfig(4), mknod(5), mt(7).

CHAPTER 5

Users and Groups

Set Up Users and Groups

As you may have guessed by now, performing system administration functions on your HP-UX system is easy; the planning is what takes time and effort. Setting up users and groups is no exception. Thanks to SAM, doing just about anything with users and groups is simple.

One exception exists to this easy setup: HP (Common Desktop Environment) CDE customization. SAM doesn't really help with HP CDE customization and it can be quite tricky to modify one's HP CDE setup manually. I have Chapter 13 to assist you with HP CDE customization.

You need to make a few basic decisions about users. Where should users' data be located? Who needs to access data from whom, thereby defining "groups" of users? What kind of particular startup is required by users and applications? Is there a shell that your users prefer?

You will want to put some thought into these important user-related questions. I spend a lot of time working with my customers, rearranging user data, for several reasons. It doesn't fit on a whole disk (for this reason, I strongly recommend using Logical Volume Manager or Veritas Volume

Manager); users can't freely access one another's data, or even worse, users *can* access one another's data too freely.

We will consider these questions, but first, let's look at the basic steps to adding a user, whether you do this manually or rely on SAM. Here is a list of activities:

- Select a user name to add
- Select a user ID number
- Select a group for the user
- Create an **/etc/passwd** entry
- Assign a user password (including expiration options)
- Select and create a home directory for user
- Select the shell the user will run (I strongly recommend the default POSIX shell)
- Place startup files in the user's home directory
- Test the user account

This list may seem like a lot of work, but there is nothing to it if you run SAM and answer the questions. Most of what you do is entered in the **/etc/passwd** file, where information about all users is stored. You can make these entries to the **/etc/passwd** file with the **/usr/sbin/vipw** command. Figure 5-1 is a sample **/etc/passwd** entry.

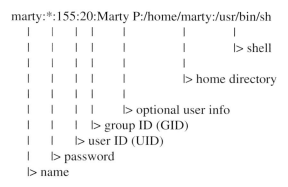

Figure 5-1   Sample **/etc/passwd** Entry

Here is a description of each of these fields:

name.   The user name you assign. This name should be easy for the user and other users on the system to remember. When sending electronic mail or copying files from one user to another, the easier it is to remember the user name the better. If a user has a user name on another system, you may want to assign the same user name on your HP-UX system. Some systems don't permit nice, easy user names, so you may want to break the tie with the old system and start using sensible, easy-to-remember user names on your HP-UX system. Remember, no security is tied to the user name; security is handled through the user's password and the file permissions.

password.   This is the user's password in encrypted form. If an asterisk appears in this field, the account can't be used. If it is empty, the user has no password assigned and can log in by typing only his or her user name. I strongly recommend that each user have a password that he or she changes periodically. Every system has different security needs, but at a minimum, every user on every system should have a password. When setting up a new user, you can force the user to create a password at first login by putting ,.. in the password field. Password aging can easily be set in SAM.

Some features of a good password are:

- A minimum of six characters that should include special characters such as a slash (/), a dot (.), or an asterisk (*).

- No words should be used for a password.

- Don't make the password personal such as name, address, favorite sports team, etc.

- Don't use something easy to type such as 123456, or qwerty.

- Some people say that misspelled words are acceptable, but I don't recommend using them. Spell-check programs that match misspelled words to correctly spelled words can be used to guess at words that might be misspelled for a password.

•A password generator that produces an intelligible passwords works the best.

user ID (UID).   The identification number of the user. Every user on your system should have a unique UID. There are no conventions for UIDs. SAM will assign a UID for you when you add users, but you can always change this. I would recommend that you reserve UIDs less than 100 for system-level users.

group ID (GID).   The identification number of the group. The members of the group and their GID are in the **/etc/group** file. You can change the GID assigned if you don't like it, but you may also have to change the GID of many files. As a user creates a file, his or her UID is assigned to the file as well as the GID. This means if you change the GID well after users of the same group have created many files and directories, you may have to change the GID of all these elements. I usually save GIDs less than 10 for system groups.

optional user info.   In this space, you can make entries, such as the user's phone number or full name. SAM asks you for this information when you create a user. You can leave this blank, but if you manage a system or network with many users, you may want to add the user's full name and extension so that if you need to get in touch with him or her, you'll have the information at your fingertips. (This field is sometimes referred to as the GECOs field.)

home directory.   The home directory defines the default location for all the users' files and directories. This is the present working directory at the time of login.

shell.   This is the startup program the user will run at the time of login. The shell is really a command interpreter for the commands the user issues from the command line. I recommend using the default POSIX shell (**/usr/bin/sh**), but there are also three traditional, popular shells in the HP-

UX environment: the C shell (**/usr/bin/csh**); Bourne shell (**/usr/old/bin/ sh**); and Korn shell (**/usr/bin/ksh**). Shell programming for the system administrator is covered in Chapter 6.

The location of the user's home directory is another important entry in the **/etc/passwd** file. You have to select a location for the user's "home" directory in the file system where the user's files will be stored. With some of the advanced networking technology that exists, such as NFS, the user's home directory does not even have to be on a disk that is physically connected to the computer he or she is using! The traditional place to locate a user's home directory on an HP-UX system is the **/home** directory in HP-UX 11.x.

The **/home** directory is typically the most dynamic area in terms of growth. Users create and delete files in their home directory on a regular basis. This means you have to do more planning related to your user area than in more static areas, such as the root file system and application areas. You would typically load HP-UX and your applications and then perform relatively few accesses to these in terms of adding and deleting files and directories. The user area is continuously updated, making it more difficult to maintain.

Assigning Users to Groups

After defining all user-related information, you need to consider groups. Groups are often overlooked in the HP-UX environment until the system administrator finds that all his or her users are in the very same group, even though from an organizational standpoint, they are in different groups. Before I cover the groups in general, let's look at a file belonging to a user and the way access is defined for a file:

```
$ ll
-rwxr-x--x   1 marty      users     120 Jul 26 10:20 sort
```

For every file on the system, HP-UX supports three classes of access:

- User access (u). Access is granted to the owner of the file

- Group access (g). Access granted to members of the same group as the owner of the file

- Other access (o). Access granted to everyone else

These access rights are defined by the position of r (read), write (w), and execute (x) when the long listing command is issued. For the long listing (**ll**) above, you see the permissions in Table 5-1.

TABLE 5-1 Long Listing Permissions

Access	User Access	Group Access	Other
Read	r	r	-
Write	w	-	-
Execute	x	x	x

You can see that access rights are arranged in groups of three. Three groups of permissions exist with three access levels each. The owner, in this case, marty, is allowed read, write, and execute permissions on the file. Anyone in the group users is permitted read and execute access to the file. Others are permitted only execute access of the file.

These permissions are important to consider as you arrange your users into groups. If several users require access to the same files, then you will want to put those users in the same group. The trade-off here is that you can give all users within a group rwx access to files, but then you run the risk of several users editing a file without other users knowing it, thereby causing confusion. On the other hand, you can make several copies of a file so that each user has his or her personal copy, but then you have multiple versions of a file. If possible, assign users to groups based on their work.

When you run SAM and specify the groups to which each user belongs, the file **/etc/group** is updated. The **/etc/group** file contains the group name, an encrypted password (which is rarely used), a group ID, and a list of users in the group. Here is an example of an **/etc/group** file:

```
root::0:root
other::1:root, hpdb
bin::2:root,bin
sys::3:root,uucp
adm::4:root,adm
daemon::5:root,daemon
mail::6:root
lp::7:root,lp
tty::10:
nuucp::11:nuucp
military::25:jhunt,tdolan,vdallesandro
commercial::30:ccascone,jperwinc,devers
nogroup:*:-2:
```

This **/etc/group** file shows two different groups of users. Although all users run the same application, a desktop publishing tool, some work on documents of "commercial" products while others work on only "military" documents. It made sense for the system administrator to create two groups, one for commercial document preparation and the other for military document preparation. All members of a group know what documents are current and respect one another's work and its importance. You will have few problems among group members who know what the other members are doing and you will find that these members don't delete files that shouldn't be deleted. If you put all users into one group, however, you may find that you spend more time restoring files, because users in this broader group don't find files that are owned by other members of their group to be important. Users can change group with the **newgrp** command.

NIS for Managing Users

One of the most popular ways to manage user-related information in a distributed environment is the Network Information System (NIS). NIS provides a method for multiple systems to share a centralized database of password, group, and other optional databases such as services and/or hosts. By doing so, the administration of user accounts is simplified for both end-users and system administrators. You will also often hear NIS referred to as "Yellow Pages" or "YP"; in fact, most of the NIS commands begin with the letters "yp".

NIS, and other such technology, is required only in a distributed environment where users have to be managed on many systems. This is because changes in information, such as adding and removing users, must be disseminated to many systems. This is normally not required in a centralized environment, where only a small number of copies of such information must be maintained.

NIS on HP-UX is interoperable with Solaris and Sun-licensed NIS implementations, including Linux. Like most of these implementations, HP's NIS is not implemented in C2 or Trusted System mode. Additionally, Microsoft-based operating systems such as Windows do not use or interoperate with NIS.

What Does NIS Manage?

NIS can manage many different databases. We'll focus on the user password and group information. Table 5-2 is a list of some of the databases NIS can manage:

TABLE 5-2   Some NIS Databases NIS Can Manage

File Name	Information Contained in File
/etc/passwd	Usernames, user IDs primary groups and encrypted passwords.
/etc/group	User group memberships.
/etc/hosts	Hostnames and IP addresses.
/etc/services	Network port numbers and service names.
/etc/aliases	Aliases and mailing lists for the mail system.
/etc/netgroup	Netgroup definitions.
/etc/rpc	Remote procedure call program numbers.
/etc/protocols	Network protocol names and numbers.
	The following are optional for HP, but not used by HP-UX NIS clients.
/etc/bootparms	Information about diskless nodes.
/etc/ethers	Ethernet numbers (MAC addresses).
/etc/netmasks	Network masks.

NIS also calls each of these databases a "map". These are called maps because NIS allows you to map a key, such as a username, to a value field, such as the user's **passwd** entry from the **passwd** map on the NIS Master Server.

How Do I Plan For NIS?

NIS requires one NIS Master Server and typically at least one NIS Slave Server per IP subnet. A NIS Master or Slave Server answers requests from NIS clients typically seeking user password information when a user login occurs. NIS is designed in a "top-down" or hierarchical manner, with all changes being made through the NIS Master Server. When a change is made to the NIS Master, the changes can be made visible to the NIS Slaves by "pushing" the updated database to the Slaves. Generally an NIS server should satisfy the demands of 25 to 50 NIS clients. NIS Masters and Slaves are typically also NIS clients.

On the NIS Master server, you need to decide where you want to keep the NIS database "source" files. Most typically, the **/etc** files are used on the NIS Master for all databases except passwords, which are generally put into an "alternate" or "private" password file such as **/etc/passwd.nis**. Put only the user password database there and not the "system" users such as root, sys, bin etc. The "system" users should always be put in **/etc/passwd** on any NIS server or client.

NIS will provide a small additional network and system load on an NIS Slave and Master server. Most typically, this extra load is encountered when updating a map or database and pushing the changes to the Slave servers.

The design of NIS requires that you first configure the NIS Master Server, then the NIS Slave Servers, and finally the NIS clients.

How Do I Configure a NIS Master Or Slave Server?

You can configure an NIS Master and Slave Server either by using SAM or by performing the process manually. If you use SAM to perform this process most of the work will take place for you in the background. You enter the pertinent information and SAM performs the configuration. You perform the steps in the manual procedure. There are many good documents that can help you in this configuration including HP's *Installing and Administering NFS Services* manual. This manual covers configuring Master and Slave Servers and can be obtained from *www.docs.hp.com*. HP support likes when you follow these step-by-step procedures so that, should you encounter a problem, your execution of the steps can be reviewed.

To configure with SAM, select *Networking/Communications*, then *NIS*. You will first be prompted to specify the NIS domain name. After that, you can proceed to the *Enable NIS Master Server* or *Enable NIS Slave Server* menus.

How Do I Configure a NIS Client?

You can also configure an NIS client by either using SAM or by performing the process manually. Once again, the *Installing and Administering NFS Services* manual provides an excellent step-by-step procedure for configuring the client.

To configure with SAM, select *Networking/Communications*, then *NIS*. You will first be prompted to specify the NIS domain name. After that you can proceed to the *Enable NIS Client* menu.

In either case, I have two additional tips. First, HP supplies the following **/etc/nsswitch.compat** file as a template to copy into **/etc/nsswitch.conf**. This allows you to use the "+" and "-" syntax in **/etc/passwd** and **/etc/group**:

```
# /etc/nsswitch.compat:
#
# An example file that could be copied over to
# /etc/nsswitch.conf; it
# uses NIS (YP) in conjunction with files. #

passwd:        compat
group:         compat
hosts:         nis [NOTFOUND=return] files
networks:      nis [NOTFOUND=return] files
protocols:     nis [NOTFOUND=return] files
rpc:           nis [NOTFOUND=return] files
publickey:     nis [NOTFOUND=return] files
netgroup:      nis [NOTFOUND=return] files
automount:     files nis
aliases:       files nis
services:      files nis
```

Second, you may prefer DNS over NIS to manage the hosts database, and will use the following "hosts" entry in **/etc/nsswitch.conf**:

```
hosts:          files [NOTFOUND=continue] dns ...
```

or

```
hosts:          dns     [NOTFOUND=continue,UNAVAILABLE=continue]
files [NOTFOUND=continue,UNAVAILABLE=continue] nis
```

How Do I Maintain My NIS Environment?

The most common user activity is changing a user password. A user can use either the **passwd -r nis** or **yppasswd** command to do this. This will prompt for the old NIS passwd, the new password, make the change on the NIS server, and by default, re-make the NIS map and push it out to all the Slave Servers.

A system administrator can change user passwords either with SAM or with shell scripts or commands such as **passwd -r nis** *<username>* or **yppasswd** *<username>*. You can also use SAM to add new users, or you can do this with shell scripts or commands.

Often, when a user changes a database file by editing with **vi**, the changes need to be compiled into the NIS maps (called "making" a map) and pushing the maps out to the Slave Servers if the "make" does not do this. For example, after modifying some users' home directories in **/etc/passwd.nis**, the system administrator needs to:

```
1. cd /var/yp   # Change to directory of NIS Makefile
2. make passwd  # "make" or compile the passwd map
3. yppush passwd (if step #2 did not push to the NIS slaves)
```

Here is a tip that applies to HP-UX and to any NIS vendor's implementation with group files: There are times when users are members of multiple groups, producing lines in **/etc/group** that are longer than the NIS limitation of 1024 characters per line. To work around this, use different group names for the same GID, for example:

```
102 support:brian,sam,charlie
102 support1:bill,julie,maria
```

Note that you don't need to specify a users' primary group membership in **/etc/group** since that is already specified by their GID in **/etc/passwd**. If users are members of multiple groups, you only need to put their username in **/etc/group** entries for their secondary groups.

NIS provides a centralized database scheme for managing user password and group information. Administration techniques used for NIS setup and administration are well-documented, integrated into SAM, and are generally inter-operable with other NIS implementations.

Manual Pages of Some Commands Used in Chapter 5

Many useful commands are used in this chapter. I provided a brief description of many of the commands along with some examples. The following are the HP-UX manual pages for many of the commands used in the chapter. The manual pages are thorough and provide much more detailed description of each of the commands.

passwd

passwd - Contents of **/etc/passwd** file.

passwd(4)   passwd(4)

NAME
     passwd - password file, pwd.h

DESCRIPTION

     passwd contains the following information for each user:

          - login name
          - encrypted password
          - numerical user ID
          - numerical group ID
          - reserved field, which can be used for identification
          - initial working directory
          - program to use as shell

     This is an ASCII file. Each field within each user's entry is
     separated from the next by a colon. Each user is separated from the
     next by a newline. This file resides in the /etc directory. It can
     and does have general read permission and can be used, for example, to
     map numerical user IDs to names. If the password field is null and
     the system has not been converted to a trusted system, no password is
     demanded.

     If the shell field is null, /usr/bin/sh is used.

     The encrypted password consists of 13 characters chosen from a 64-
     character set of "digits" described below, except when the password is
     null, in which case the encrypted password is also null. Login can be
     prevented by entering in the password field a character that is not
     part of the set of digits (such as *).

     The characters used to represent "digits" are . for 0, / for 1, 0
     through 9 for 2 through 11, A through Z for 12 through 37, and a
     through z for 38 through 63.

     Password aging is put in effect for a particular user if his encrypted
     password in the password file is followed by a comma and a nonnull
     string of characters from the above alphabet. (Such a string must be
     introduced in the first instance by a superuser.) This string defines
     the "age" needed to implement password aging.

     The first character of the age, M, denotes the maximum number of weeks
     for which a password is valid. A user who attempts to login after his
     password has expired is forced to supply a new one. The next
     character, m, denotes the minimum period in weeks that must expire
     before the password can be changed. The remaining characters define
     the week (counted from the beginning of 1970) when the password was
     last changed (a null string is equivalent to zero). M and m have
     numerical values in the range 0 through 63 that correspond to the 64-
     character set of "digits" shown above. If m = M = 0 (derived from the
     string . or ..), the user is forced to change his password next time

he logs in (and the "age" disappears from his entry in the password file). If m > M (signified, for example, by the string ./), then only a superuser (not the user) can change the password. Not allowing the user to ever change the password is discouraged, especially on a trusted system.

Trusted systems support password aging and password generation. For more information on converting to trusted system and on password, see the HP-UX System Administration Tasks Manual and sam(1M).

getpwent(3C) designates values to the fields in the following structure declared in <pwd.h>:

```
struct passwd {
    char    *pw_name;
    char    *pw_passwd;
    uid_t   pw_uid;
    gid_t   pw_gid;
    char    *pw_age;
    char    *pw_comment;
    char    *pw_gecos;
    char    *pw_dir;
    char    *pw_shell;
    aid_t   pw_audid;
    int     pw_audflg;
};
```

It is suggested that the range 0-99 not be used for user and group IDs (pw_uid and pw_gid in the above structure) so that IDs that might be assigned for system software do not conflict.

The user's full name, office location, extension, and home phone stored in the pw_gecos field of the passwd structure can be set by use of the chfn command (see chfn(1)) and is used by the finger(1) command. These two commands assume the information in this field is in the order listed above. A portion of the user's real name can be represented in the pw_gecos field by an & character, which some utilities (including finger) expand by substituting the login name for it and shifting the first letter of the login name to uppercase.

SECURITY FEATURES
    On trusted systems, the encrypted password for each user is stored in the file /tcb/files/auth/c/user_name (where c is the first letter in user_name). Password information files are not accessible to the public. The encrypted password can be longer than 13 characters . For example, the password file for user david is stored in /tcb/files/auth/d/david. In addition to the password, the user profile in /tcb/files/auth/c/user_name also contains:

        - numerical audit ID

        - numerical audit flag

    Like /etc/passwd, this file is an ASCII file. Fields within each user's entry are separated by colons. Refer to authcap(4) and prpwd(4) for details. The passwords contained in /tcb/files/auth/c/* take precedence over those contained in the encrypted password field of /etc/passwd. User authentication is done using the encrypted passwords in this file . The password aging mechanism described in passwd(1), under the section called SECURITY FEATURES, applies to this password .

NETWORKING FEATURES
    NFS
    The passwd file can have entries that begin with a plus (+) or minus (-) sign in the first column. Such lines are used to access the

Network Information System network database. A line beginning with a plus (+) is used to incorporate entries from the Network Information System. There are three styles of + entries:

+   Insert the entire contents of the Network Information
                System password file at that point;

+name   Insert the entry (if any) for name from the Network
                Information System at that point

+@name   Insert the entries for all members of the network
                group name at that point.

If a + entry has a nonnull password, directory, gecos, or shell field, they override what is contained in the Network Information System. The numerical user ID and group ID fields cannot be overridden.

The passwd file can also have lines beginning with a minus (-), which disallow entries from the Network Information System. There are two styles of - entries:

-name   Disallow any subsequent entries (if any) for name.

-@name   Disallow any subsequent entries for all members of
                the network group name.

WARNINGS
Using User ID (uid) 17 is reserved for the Pascal Language operating system. User ID (uid) 18 is reserved for the BASIC Language operating system. These are operating systems for Series 300 and 400 computers that can coexist with HP-UX on the same disk. Using these uids for other purposes may inhibit file transfer and sharing.

The login shell for the root user (uid 0) must be /sbin/sh. Other shells such as sh, ksh, and csh are all located under the /usr directory which may not be mounted during earlier stages of the bootup process. Changing the login shell of the root user to a value other than /sbin/sh may result in a non-functional system.

The information kept in the pw_gecos field may conflict with unsupported or future uses of this field. Use of the pw_gecos field for keeping user identification information has not been formalized within any of the industry standards. The current use of this field is derived from its use within the Berkeley Software Distribution. Future standards may define this field for other purposes.

The following fields have character limitations as noted:

-   Login name field can be no longer than 8 characters;

-   Initial working directory field can be no longer than 63
    characters;

-   Program field can be no longer than 44 characters.

-   Results are unpredictable if these fields are longer than the
    limits specified above.

The following fields have numerical limitations as noted:

-   The user ID is an integer value between -2 and UID_MAX
    inclusive.

-   The group ID is an integer value between 0 and UID_MAX
    inclusive.

-    If either of these values are out of range, the getpwent(3C)
     functions reset the ID value to (UID_MAX).

EXAMPLES
    NFS Example
        Here is a sample /etc/passwd file:

            root:3Km/o4Cyq84Xc:0:10:System Administrator:/:/sbin/sh
            joe:r4hRJr4GJ4CqE:100:50:Joe User,Post 4A,12345:/home/joe:/usr/bin/ksh
            +john:
            -bob:
            +@documentation:no-login:
            -@marketing:
            +:::Guest

        In this example, there are specific entries for users root and joe, in
        case the Network Information System are out of order.

            -    User john's password entry in the Network Information System
                 is incorporated without change.

            -    Any subsequent entries for user bob are ignored.

            -    The password field for anyone in the netgroup documentation
                 is disabled.

            -    Users in netgroup marketing are not returned by getpwent(3C)
                 and thus are not allowed to log in.

            -    Anyone else can log in with their usual password, shell, and
                 home directory, but with a pw_gecos field of Guest.

    NFS Warnings
        The plus (+) and minus (-) features are NFS functionality; therefore,
        if NFS is not installed, they do not work. Also, these features work
        only with /etc/passwd, but not with a system that has been converted
        to a trusted system. When the system has been converted to a trusted
        system, the encrypted passwords can be accessed only from the
        protected password database, /tcb/files/auth/*/*. Any user entry in
        the Network Information System database also must have an entry in the
        protected password database.

        The uid of -2 is reserved for remote root access by means of NFS. The
        pw_name usually given to this uid is nobody. Since uids are stored as
        signed values, the following define is included in <pwd.h> to match
        the user nobody.

            UID_NOBODY   (-2)

FILES
        /tcb/files/auth/*/*   Protected password database used when
                                            system is converted to trusted system.

        /etc/passwd   Standard password file used by HP-UX.

SEE ALSO
        chfn(1), finger(1), login(1), passwd(1), a64l(3C), crypt(3C),
        getprpwent(3), getpwent(3C), authcap(4), limits(5).

STANDARDS CONFORMANCE
        passwd: SVID2, SVID3, XPG2

CHAPTER 6

Backup

Built-In Backup Programs

Most HP-UX system administrators employ a dual backup strategy. The first is to use the **make_recovery** command of Ignite-UX to create a bootable backup tape of their root volume (**make_recovery** is covered in Chapter 10). Secondly, a backup program is used to back up the balance of data on the system. In this chapter I'll give an overview of several backup commands. I won't cover any advanced backup programs such as HP's OmniBack. Advanced backup tools, however, can make tasks such as centralized backup and overall management of backup much easier.

    Here is a brief overview of backup programs I'll cover in upcoming sections:

man page

**make_
recovery
10**

man page

tar - 6

tar   **tar** is widely considered the most *portable* of the backup and restore programs. **tar** is the most popular generic backup utility. You will find that many applications are shipped on **tar** tapes. This is the most widely used format for exchanging data with other UNIX systems. **tar** is the oldest UNIX backup method and therefore runs on all UNIX systems. You can append files to the end of a **tar** tape, which you can't do with **fbackup**. When sending files to another UNIX user, I would strongly recommend **tar**. **tar** is as slow as molasses, so you won't want to use it for your full or incremental backups. One highly desirable aspect of **tar** is that when you load files onto a tape with **tar** and then restore them onto another system, the original users and groups are retained.

fbackup   **fbackup** is the utility used by SAM. It has a lot of functionality associated with it, such as specifying whether the backup is full or incremental, different *levels* of backup, files and directories to be included or excluded, support for a *graph* file which specifies files to be included and excluded, and other advanced features. **fbackup** is an HP-UX-only utility and tapes can be read using **frecover** on HP-UX systems only.

cpio   **cpio** is also portable and easy to use, like **tar**. In addition, **cpio** is much faster than **tar** - not as fast as **fbackup**, but much faster than **tar**. **cpio** is good for replicating directory trees.

dd   This is a bit-for-bit copy. It is not smart in the sense that it does not copy files and ownerships; it just copies bits. You could not, therefore, select an individual file from a **dd** tape as you could with **frecover**, **tar**, **restore** or **cpio**. **dd** is mainly used for converting data such as EBCDIC to ASCII.

man page

vxdump - 6

man page

vxrestore-6

dump **dump** is similar to **fbackup**. If you use **fbackup** on HP-UX, you will see much similarity when you use **dump**. **dump** provides the same level backup scheme as **fbackup** and creates **/var/adm/dump-dates,** which lists the last time a filesystem was backed up. **restore** is used to read information backed up with **dump**. **dump**, however, works only with HFS file systems and not VxFS, and it assumes that you are using a reel tape.

tar

man page

tar - 6

tar is widely considered the most *portable* of the backup and restore programs. You will find that many applications are shipped on **tar** tapes and many UNIX files downloaded from the Internet are in **tar** format. This is the most widely used format for exchanging data with other UNIX systems. **tar** is the oldest UNIX backup method and therefore runs on all UNIX systems. You can append files to the end of a **tar** tape, which you can't do with many other programs. When sending files to another UNIX user, I would strongly recommend **tar**. **tar** is as slow as molasses, so you won't want to use it for your full or incremental backups if you have a lot of data to back up. One highly desirable aspect of **tar** is that when you load files onto a tape with **tar** and then restore them onto another system, the original users and groups are retained.

We'll use several tar commands in the upcoming examples, including the following:

```
# tar cf /dev/rmt/0m /var      ;use tar to create (c) an archive of
                                the directory /var and put it on
                                tape /dev/rmt/0m.


# tar tvf /dev/rmt/0m          ;obtain table of contents (t) from
                                tape /dev/rmt/0m and produce
                                produce verbose (v) output.


# tar xvf /dev/rmt/0m          ;extract (x) the entire contents
                                of the archive on tape /dev/rmt/0m
                                to default destination.


# tar xvf /dev/rmt/0m file1    ;extract (x) only file1
                                from the archive on tape /dev/rmt/0m
                                to default destination.
```

You'll notice when you view the man pages for **tar** that options are preceded by a hyphen. The command works without the hyphen so most **tar** examples, including those in this chapter, omit the hyphen.

Let's take a look at some examples using **tar**. Let's begin by performing a **tar** backup (usually called creating an archive) of the directory **/var** to tape device **/dev/rmt/0m**. We use the *c* option to create a backup and the *f* option to specify the file of the tape drive **/dev/rmt/ 0m**:

```
# tar cf /dev/rmt/0m /var
tar: /var/opt/dce/rpc/local/01060/reaper is not a file. Not dumped
tar: /var/opt/dce/rpc/local/00997/reaper is not a file. Not dumped
tar: /var/opt/dce/rpc/local/00997/c-3/7000 is not a file. Not dumped
tar: /var/opt/dce/rpc/local/00997/c-3/shared is not a file. Not dumped
tar: /var/opt/dce/rpc/local/00997/c-3/7002 is not a file. Not dumped
tar: /var/opt/dce/rpc/local/s-0/135 is not a file. Not dumped
tar: /var/opt/dce/rpc/local/s-0/2121 is not a file. Not dumped
tar: /var/opt/dce/rpc/local/s-3/135 is not a file. Not dumped
tar: /var/opt/dce/rpc/local/s-3/2121 is not a file. Not dumped
tar: /var/spool/sockets/pwgr/client933 is not a file. Not dumped
tar: /var/spool/sockets/pwgr/client1028 is not a file. Not dumped
tar: /var/spool/sockets/pwgr/client1152 is not a file. Not dumped
tar: /var/spool/sockets/pwgr/client1172 is not a file. Not dumped
tar: /var/spool/sockets/pwgr/client1173 is not a file. Not dumped
tar: /var/spool/sockets/pwgr/client1139 is not a file. Not dumped
tar: /var/spool/sockets/pwgr/client2500 is not a file. Not dumped
tar: /var/spool/sockets/pwgr/client2592 is not a file. Not dumped
tar: /var/spool/sockets/pwgr/client2490 is not a file. Not dumped
tar: /var/spool/sockets/pwgr/client2593 is not a file. Not dumped
tar: /var/spool/pwgr/daemon is not a file. Not dumped
#
```

man page

tar - 6

The result of this command printed only problem-related messages to *standard output*. You will often see the *v* option used with **tar** to produce verbose output, which would have listed both the messages above and those related to files that were successfully written to the tape archive.

Next let's take a look at only the files on the tape with the string *eaaa* in them. To produce a table of contents, we will use the *t* option. The following example also uses *v* for verbose output:

```
# tar tvf /dev/rmt/0m | grep eaaa
rw-rw-rw-   0/3      28 Jul 11 15:37 2000 /var/tmp/eaaa01299
rw-rw-rw-   0/3      28 Jul 11 15:37 2000 /var/tmp/eaaa01333
rw-rw-rw-   0/3      28 Jul 11 15:38 2000 /var/tmp/eaaa01354
rw-rw-rw-   0/3      28 Jul 11 15:40 2000 /var/tmp/eaaa01380
rw-rw-rw-   0/3      28 Jul 11 15:40 2000 /var/tmp/eaaa01405
rw-rw-rw-   0/3      28 Jul 11 15:45 2000 /var/tmp/eaaa01487

#
```

man page

tar - 6

This output shows several files that begin with *eaaa* on the tape. We'll delete the last of these files from the computer and restore it from tape using the *x* option to extract the file from the **tar** archive. We'll then list the directory on the system to confirm that the file we deleted has been restored to the directory from tape.

```
# rm /var/tmp/eaaa01487
#
# tar xvf /dev/rmt/0m /var/tmp/eaaa01487

x /var/tmp/eaaa01487, 28 bytes, 1 tape blocks

#
# ls -l /var/tmp/eaaa*
-rw-rw-rw-   1 root        sys              28 Jul 11 15:37 /var/tmp/eaaa01299
-rw-rw-rw-   1 root        sys              28 Jul 11 15:37 /var/tmp/eaaa01333
-rw-rw-rw-   1 root        sys              28 Jul 11 15:38 /var/tmp/eaaa01354
-rw-rw-rw-   1 root        sys              28 Jul 11 15:40 /var/tmp/eaaa01380
-rw-rw-rw-   1 root        sys              28 Jul 11 15:40 /var/tmp/eaaa01405
-rw-rw-rw-   1 root        sys              28 Jul 11 15:45 /var/tmp/eaaa01487

#
```

This backup and restore using **tar** is simple and gets the job done.

A common use for **tar** is to back up files from one directory and restore them to another directory. We'll backup the contents of **/var/ tmp** and restore them to the directory **/tmp/puttarfileshere**. In the following example, we will create a **tar** backup archive to a file rather than to tape. The file is called **tartest**. We will then move this file to the destination directory and extract it there. We don't use a tape at all in this example.

```
# cd /var/tmp
# ls -l
total 72
-rw-------   1 root     sys            0 Jul 11 15:57 OBAMFEAa01630
-rw-------   1 root     sys            0 Jul 11 15:20 OBAMHBAa01020
-rw-------   1 root     sys            0 Jul 11 15:50 OBAMHBAa01540
-rw-rw-rw-   1 root     sys          102 Jul 11 15:20 aaaa01112
-rw-rw-rw-   1 root     sys          102 Jul 11 15:37 aaaa01299
-rw-rw-rw-   1 root     sys          102 Jul 11 15:37 aaaa01333
-rw-rw-rw-   1 root     sys          102 Jul 11 15:38 aaaa01354
-rw-rw-rw-   1 root     sys          102 Jul 11 15:40 aaaa01380
-rw-rw-rw-   1 root     sys           99 Jul 11 15:40 aaaa01405


                .
                .
                .
   1 root       sys           28 Jul 11 15:37 eaaa01333
-rw-rw-rw-   1 root     sys           28 Jul 11 15:38 eaaa01354
-rw-rw-rw-   1 root     sys           28 Jul 11 15:40 eaaa01380
-rw-rw-rw-   1 root     sys           28 Jul 11 15:40 eaaa01405
-rw-rw-rw-   1 root     sys           28 Jul 11 15:45 eaaa01487
-rwxr--r--   1 root     root          28 Jul 11 16:04 envd.action2
-rwxr--r--   1 root     root          28 Jul 11 16:04 envd.action5
dr-xr-xr-x   2 bin      bin           96 Jul 11 13:50 ntp
-rw-r--r--   1 root     sys          600 Jul 11 15:27 swagent.log
#
# tar cvf /tmp/tartest `ls`
a OBAMFEAa01630 0 blocks
a OBAMHBAa01020 0 blocks
a OBAMHBAa01540 0 blocks
a aaaa01112 1 blocks
a aaaa01299 1 blocks
a aaaa01333 1 blocks
a aaaa01354 1 blocks
a aaaa01380 1 blocks
a aaaa01405 1 blocks


                .
                .
                .
a eaaa01354 1 blocks
a eaaa01380 1 blocks
a eaaa01405 1 blocks
a eaaa01487 1 blocks
a envd.action2 1 blocks
a envd.action5 1 blocks
a swagent.log 2 blocks
#
# cd /tmp
# mkdir puttarfileshere
# cp tartest puttarfileshere
# cd puttarfileshere
# ls -l
total 80
-rw-rw-rw-   1 root     sys        40960 Jul 11 17:09 tartest
#
```

```
# tar xvf tartest
x OBAMFEAa01630, 0 bytes, 0 tape blocks
x OBAMHBAa01020, 0 bytes, 0 tape blocks
x OBAMHBAa01540, 0 bytes, 0 tape blocks
x aaaa01112, 102 bytes, 1 tape blocks
x aaaa01299, 102 bytes, 1 tape blocks
x aaaa01333, 102 bytes, 1 tape blocks
x aaaa01354, 102 bytes, 1 tape blocks
x aaaa01380, 102 bytes, 1 tape blocks
x aaaa01405, 99 bytes, 1 tape blocks




                    .
                    .
                    .


x daaa01405, 28 bytes, 1 tape blocks
x daaa01487, 28 bytes, 1 tape blocks
x eaaa01299, 28 bytes, 1 tape blocks
x eaaa01333, 28 bytes, 1 tape blocks
x eaaa01354, 28 bytes, 1 tape blocks
x eaaa01380, 28 bytes, 1 tape blocks
x eaaa01405, 28 bytes, 1 tape blocks
x eaaa01487, 28 bytes, 1 tape blocks
x envd.action2, 28 bytes, 1 tape blocks
x envd.action5, 28 bytes, 1 tape blocks
x swagent.log, 600 bytes, 2 tape blocks
#
```

When creating the **tar** backup, I first changed to the **/var/tmp** directory and then used the **ls** command (a *grav* or *accent*, which is near the upper left of most keyboards on the same key as a *tilde*, appears before and after the **ls**). This produced relative pathnames that I could easily restore to the **/tmp/puttarfileshere** directory. Alternatively, I could also have just changed directory to **/var** and issued the command **tar cf /dev/rmt/0m tmp** to back up the entire contents of the **/var/tmp** directory.

This entire process could have been done on a single command line. The following line is from the **tar** file man page at the end of this chapter and shows the procedure for producing an archive in the *from-dir* and restoring it to the *todir*:

cd *fromdir* ; **tar cf - .** | (**cd** *todir* ; **tar xf -i**)

The "-" in the **tar cf** command tells **tar** to send its data to *standard output*. The "-" in the **tar xf** command tells **tar** to look to *standard input* for data, which is the data produced by **tar cf -** issued earlier on the command line.

man page

tar - 6

cpio

man page

cpio - 6

cpio is a powerful utility that is used in conjunction with **find** (see Chapter 20 dedicated to **find**) in order to perform full and incremental backups. **cpio** is an established UNIX utility that works similarly on most UNIX variants.

We'll use several commands in the upcoming examples, including the following:

```
# find . -print | cpio -oBv > /dev/rmt/0m    ;find the contents of
                                                the current dir and
                                                write them to tape.

# cpio -it < /dev/rmt/0m         ;read table of contents (t) of tape.

# cpio -icvBdum < /dev/rmt/0m ;restore (i) the contents of tape,
                                 this is the most widely used
                                 cpio command.

# find . -print | cpio -oBv | (remsh tapesys dd of=/dev/rmt/0m)
             ;find the contents of the current dir and
              write (o) them to tape on remote machine tapesys.

# remsh tapesys "dd if=/dev/rmt/0m bs=8k" | cpio -icvBdum
                ;restore the contents (i) of a tape on remote system
                 tapesys to the local system.
```

man page

find - 20

The first command we'll issue is to **find** the contents in **/var/tmp** and write them to our tape device **/dev/rmt/0m**. The options to **cpio** used in the following example are *o* for output mode, *B* for block output, and *v* for verbose reporting:

```
# cd /var/tmp
# find . -print | cpio -oBv > /dev/rmt/0m
(Using tape drive with immediate report mode enabled (reel #1).)
            .
envd.action2
envd.action5
swagent.log
ntp
OBAMHBAa01020
aaaa01558
aaaa01426
aaaa01112
OBAMHBAa01540
aaaa01299

                    .
                    .
                    .

eaaa01487
OBAMFEAa01630
cmd_res8215
tmp_cfg_file
cmd_res8708
exclude.temp
arch.include.1
3570 blocks
#
```

In the example, we first changed directory to **/var/tmp**, then issue the **find** command and pipe its output to **cpio**. **cpio** is almost always used in conjunction with **find** in the manner shown in the example. This produced a backup with relative pathnames because we changed to the directory **/var/tmp** before issuing the backup commands.

Next we'll view the contents of the tape to see the files we wrote to it with **cpio**. The *i* option is used for input, and the *t* option is used to get a table of contents in the following listing:

man page

find - 20

man page

cpio - 6

```
# cpio -it < /dev/rmt/0m
    .
envd.action2
envd.action5
swagent.log
```

```
ntp
OBAMHBAa01020
aaaa01558
aaaa01426
aaaa01112
OBAMHBAa01540
aaaa01299

                              .

                              .

                              .

eaaa01487
OBAMFEAa01630
cmd_res8215
tmp_cfg_file
cmd_res8708
exclude.temp
arch.include.1
3570 blocks
#
```

man page

cpio - 6

Now that we have written to the tape and viewed its table of contents, we'll restore the contents of **/var/tmp**. In the following example, we use several options to **cpio**, including *i* for input mode, *c* for ASCII header format, *v* for verbose, *B* for block output, *d* for directories, *u* for unconditional write over existing files, and *m* to restore the original modification times:

```
# cpio -icvBdum < /dev/rmt/0m
 .
envd.action2
envd.action5
swagent.log
ntp
OBAMHBAa01020
aaaa01558
aaaa01426
aaaa01112
OBAMHBAa01540
aaaa01299

                              .

                              .

                              .
```

```
eaaa01487
OBAMFEAa01630
cmd_res8215
tmp_cfg_file
cmd_res8708
exclude.temp
arch.include.1
3570 blocks
#
```

man page

cpio - 6

The **cpio** command produces a list of files that will be read from the tape and restored to the system. Since we included the verbose option, we'll see all the information related to the restore.

Now that we've seen how to write a tape, produce a table of contents, and read the contents of a tape on a local system, let's work with a tape drive on a remote system. We'll perform a backup to a remote tape drive, view the table of contents on the tape, and then restore using the remote tape drive.

First let's perform a backup to a remote tape drive. The local system, which does not have a tape drive attached to it, is *or1*. The remote system, which has a tape drive attached to it, is *tapesys*. We'll run **cpio** (using the same three options earlier described) on *or1* and run a remote shell and **dd** on *tapesys,* which will store the contents of the backup. We'll run these commands from **/var/tmp** on *or1* in the following example:

man page

dd - 6

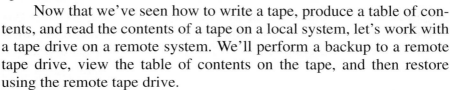

```
# find . -print | cpio -oBv | (remsh tapesys dd of=/dev/rmt/0m)

.
envd.action2
envd.action5
swagent.log
ntp
OBAMHBAa01020
aaaa01558
aaaa01426
aaaa01112
OBAMHBAa01540
aaaa01299
                    .
                    .
                    .
```

```
eaaa01487
OBAMFEAa01630
cmd_res8215
tmp_cfg_file
cmd_res8708
exclude.temp
arch.include.1
3570 blocks
#
```

man page

cpio - 6

man page

tar - 6

man page

remsh-12

man page

dd - 6

Now let's come back to our local system without the tape drive and restore the contents of the **cpio** tape we just produced, but let's restore them to a different directory. The directory to which we'll restore the contents of the tape (originally in **/var/tmp**) is **/tmp/remotecpiofiles**. This is similar to the process we performed in the **tar** section earlier in this chapter in which we restored **tar** files to a different location.

In the following example, we issue a series of commands while on *or1*. The last of these commands is to issue a **remsh** to system *tapesys* which has on it a tape drive with the **cpio** tape we just created. We **dd** the information and pipe it through **cpio** to restore the contents of the tape. In this example, we use the same restore options to **cpio**, including *i* for input mode, *c* for ASCII header format, *v* for verbose, *B* for block output, *d* for directories, *u* for unconditional write over existing files, and *m* to restore original modification times:

```
# hostname
or1
# cd /tmp
# mkdir remotecpiofiles
# cd remotecpiofiles
# pwd
/tmp/remotecpiofiles
# remsh tapesys "dd if=/dev/rmt/0m bs=8k" | cpio -icvBdum
.
envd.action2
envd.action5
swagent.log
ntp
OBAMHBAa01020
aaaa01558
aaaa01426
```

```
aaaa01112
OBAMHBAa01540
aaaa01299

                        .

                        .

                        .

eaaa01487
OBAMFEAa01630
cmd_res8215
tmp_cfg_file
cmd_res8708
exclude.temp
arch.include.1
3570 blocks
#
# pwd
/tmp/remotecpiofiles
# ls
envd.action2
envd.action5
swagent.log
ntp
OBAMHBAa01020
aaaa01558
aaaa01426
aaaa01112
OBAMHBAa01540
aaaa01299

                        .

                        .

                        .

eaaa01487
OBAMFEAa01630
cmd_res8215
tmp_cfg_file
cmd_res8708
exclude.temp
arch.include.1
#
```

The **ls** we issued at the end of this example confirmed that we did indeed write the the contents of the tape on the remote system to the new directory **/tmp/remotecpiofiles**. You may want to add the *-a* command to the **ls** option to ensure the files have contents.

You can build from the simple examples in this **cpio** section to develop backup and restore commands to meet your needs in a modest environment.

man page

ls - 15

man page

cpio - 6

fbackup and frecover

fbackup and **frecover** are the preferred backup and restore programs on HP-UX. Backups produced with **fbackup** are not portable to other UNIX variants. If you're working in a heterogenous environment, you won't be able to take **fbackup** tapes produced on an HP-UX system and recover them to a system running a different UNIX variant.

In this section I'll cover issuing **fbackup** and **frecover** at the command line. You can also manage backups using these commands with SAM (covered in Chapter 3). SAM helps you manage both *Automated Backups* and *Interactive Backup and Recovery.* Although **fbackup** and **frecover** are the most advanced programs bundled with your HP-UX system for backup and restore, your needs may go beyond these programs. There are also advanced backup programs you can procure from both HP and third parties. In general, I find the capabilities of **fbackup** and **frecover** are sufficient for new HP-UX installations. If, however, you have a highly distributed environment or need to back up large amounts of data, perform backups on systems with a variety of operating systems, or need to use several backup devices simultaneously, you may want to consider a more advanced product.

fbackup has the capability of performing backups at different *levels*. The levels define the amount of information to be included in the backup. A full backup, which is covered in this section, is backup level 0. The other levels define various degrees of incremental backups. I am a strong advocate of performing a full backup, and then performing incremental backups of every file that has changed since the *last full backup*. This means that to recover from a completely "hosed" (a technical term meaning *destroyed*) system, you would need your full backup tape and only one incremental tape (you would restore your root volume with a bootable Ignite-UX tape produced with **make_recovery**, which is covered in Chapter 9). If, for instance, you performed a full backup on Sunday and an incremental backups on Monday through Friday, you would need to load only Sunday's full backup tape and Friday's incremental backup tape to completely restore your system. **fbackup** supports this scheme.

Keep in mind that although we'll be issuing **fbackup** and **frecovery** commands at the command line in this chapter, these can be managed more easily through SAM. Here is an explanation of the **fbackup** command and *some* of its options:

man page

fbackup - 6

```
/usr/sbin/fbackup -f device [-0-9] [-u] [-i path] [-e path] [-g graph]
```

-f device	The tape drive for the backup, such as **/dev/rmt/0m** for your local tape drive.

man page

frecover-6

[-0-9]	This is the level of the backup. If you run a full backup on Sunday at level 0, then you would run an incremental backup at level 1 the other days of the week. An incremental backup will back up all information changed since a backup was made at a lower level. You could back up at 0 on Sunday, 1 on Monday, 2 on Tuesday, and so on. However, to recover your system, you would need to load Sunday's tape, then Monday's tape, then Tuesday's tape, and so on, to fully recover.
[-u]	This updates the database of past backups so that it contains such information as the backup level, time of the beginning and end of the backup session, and the graph file (described below) used for the backup session. This is valid only with the *-g* (graph) option.
[-i path]	The specified path is to be included in the backup. This can be issued any number of times.
[-e path]	The specified path is to be excluded from the backup. This can also be specified any number of times.

[-g graph]   The graph file contains the list of files and directories to be included or excluded from the backup.

man page

fbackup - 6

Although **fbackup** is quite thorough and easy to use, it does not have embedded in it the day and time at which full and incremental backups will be run. You have to make a **cron** entry to run **fbackup** automatically. SAM will make a **cron** entry for you, thereby running **fbackup** whenever you like. (**cron** is covered in Chapter 10.)

In its simplest form, we could run **fbackup** and specify only the tape drive with the *f* option and the directory to back up with the *i* option as shown in the following example:

```
# fbackup -f /dev/rmt/0m -i /var/tmp
fbackup(1004): session begins on Wed Jul 12 14:26:30 2000
fbackup(3205): WARNING: unable to read a volume header
fbackup(3024): writing volume 1 to the output file /dev/rmt/0m
fbackup(3055): total file blocks read for backup: 3606
fbackup(3056): total blocks written to output file /dev/rmt/0m: 3857
fbackup(1030): warnings encountered during backup
#
```

man page

frecover-6

fbackup did not produce a list of files included in the backup since we did not include the *v* option for verbose.

To view the contents of the tape, we run **frecover** with the options *r* for read, *N* to prevent the contents of the tape from being restored to the system, and *v* for verbose as shown in the following command:

```
# frecover -rNv -f /dev/rmt/0m
drwxr-xr-x      root     root     /
dr-xr-xr-x      bin      bin      /var
drwxrwxrwx      bin      bin      /var/tmp
-rw-------      root     sys      /var/tmp/OBAMFEAa01630
-rw-------      root     sys      /var/tmp/OBAMHBAa01020
-rw-------      root     sys      /var/tmp/OBAMHBAa01540
```

```
-rw-------           root      sys        /var/tmp/OBAMHBAa07762
-rw-rw-rw-           root      sys        /var/tmp/aaaa01112
                       .
                       .
                       .
-rw-rw-rw-           root      sys        /var/tmp/eaaa01487
-rwxr--r--           root      root       /var/tmp/envd.action2
-rwxr--r--           root      root       /var/tmp/envd.action5
-rw-rw-rw-           root      sys        /var/tmp/exclude.temp
dr-xr-xr-x           bin       bin        /var/tmp/ntp
-rw-r--r--           root      sys        /var/tmp/swagent.log
-rw-rw-rw-           root      sys        /var/tmp/tmp_cfg_file
#
```

Let's now delete a file from the system that was included as part of the **fbackup**. We'll then restore only the file we deleted. We'll use the *x* option for extract and the *i* option to specify the file to include with **frecover** as shown in the following example:

man page

fbackup - 6

man page

frecover-6

```
# cd /var/tmp
# ls -l aa*
-rw-rw-rw-   1 root          sys                  102 Jul 11 15:20 aaaa01112
-rw-rw-rw-   1 root          sys                  102 Jul 11 15:37 aaaa01299
-rw-rw-rw-   1 root          sys                  102 Jul 11 15:37 aaaa01333
-rw-rw-rw-   1 root          sys                  102 Jul 11 15:38 aaaa01354
-rw-rw-rw-   1 root          sys                  102 Jul 11 15:40 aaaa01380
-rw-rw-rw-   1 root          sys                   99 Jul 11 15:40 aaaa01405
-rw-rw-rw-   1 root          sys                  102 Jul 11 14:57 aaaa01426
-rw-rw-rw-   1 root          sys                   99 Jul 11 15:45 aaaa01487
-rw-rw-rw-   1 root          sys                  102 Jul 11 14:24 aaaa01558
# rm aaaa01487
# cd /
# frecover -x -i /var/tmp/aaaa01487 -f /dev/rmt/0m
# cd /var/tmp
# ls -l aaa*
-rw-rw-rw-   1 root          sys                  102 Jul 11 15:20 aaaa01112
-rw-rw-rw-   1 root          sys                  102 Jul 11 15:37 aaaa01299
-rw-rw-rw-   1 root          sys                  102 Jul 11 15:37 aaaa01333
-rw-rw-rw-   1 root          sys                  102 Jul 11 15:38 aaaa01354
-rw-rw-rw-   1 root          sys                  102 Jul 11 15:40 aaaa01380
-rw-rw-rw-   1 root          sys                   99 Jul 11 15:40 aaaa01405
-rw-rw-rw-   1 root          sys                  102 Jul 11 14:57 aaaa01426
-rw-rw-rw-   1 root          sys                   99 Jul 11 15:45 aaaa01487
-rw-rw-rw-   1 root          sys                  102 Jul 11 14:24 aaaa01558
#
```

man page

fbackup - 6

In the previous example, we successfully restored the file **/var/tmp/aaa01487** from the tape using **frestore**.

There are some powerful aspects to **fbackup** that we did not employ in our example. These include *backup levels, graph files,* and *index files*.

fbackup supports backup levels 0-9. 0 is used for full backups and the other digits indicate various incremental backup levels (see the **fbackup** man page at the end of this chapter for additional information).

Graph files are used to specify the files to be included in the backup.

Index files contain a list of files produced as part of the backup.

Let's take a look at an example that employs all of these functions. First, we create a graph file that contains the files we wish to include (*i*) or exclude (*e*) as part of the backup. In our case the file will contain only the following line:

```
i /var/tmp
```

Let's now run **fbackup** with *u* to update the backup database, *0* for a full backup, *f* to specify the file to which we want to write the backup (we'll use a file rather than tape in this example), *g* to specify our graph file, *I* to specify the name of the index file, and finally we'll redirect messages to a file that will contain the backup log. We'll add the date and time to the end of the index and backup log files.

```
# fbackup -0u -f /tmp/testbackup -g /tmp/backupgraph
           -I /tmp/backupindex.`date '+%y%m%d.%H:%M'` 2>
           /tmp/backuplog.`date '+%y%m%d.%H:%M'`
#
```

Let's now see what files were produced as a result of having issued this command. First let's look at the backup index and backup logfiles:

```
# ls /tmp/backup*
backupgraph
backupgraph000712.15.04
backupindex.000712.15:04
backuplog.000712.15:04
#
# cat /tmp/backupindex000712.15:04
1024                       1 /
1024                       1 /var
2048                       1 /var/tmp
0                          1 /var/tmp/OBAMFEAa01630
0                          1 /var/tmp/OBAMHBAa01020
0                          1 /var/tmp/OBAMHBAa01540
336                        1 /var/tmp/OBAMHBAa07762
102                        1 /var/tmp/aaaa01112
                         .
                         .
                         .
28                         1 /var/tmp/eaaa01487
28                         1 /var/tmp/envd.action2
28                         1 /var/tmp/envd.action5
4608                       1 /var/tmp/exclude.temp
96                         1 /var/tmp/ntp
1595                       1 /var/tmp/swagent.log
205                        1 /var/tmp/tmp_cfg_file
#
# cat /tmp/backupgraph000712.15:04
i/var/tmp
#
# cat /tmp/backuplog000712.15:04

fbackup(1004): session begins on Wed Jul 12 14:56:19 2000
fbackup(3024): writing volume 1 to the output file /tmp/testbackup
fbackup(1030): warnings encountered during backup
fbackup(3055): total file blocks read for backup: 3614
fbackup(3056): total blocks written to output file /tmp/testbackup:3876
#
```

The three files with the date appended (*7/12/00 time 15:04*) to the end of the filename were produced by the **fbackup** command issued earlier. The date appended to the end of the file can help in the organization of backup files. We could restore any or all of these files with **frestore** from the file that contains the backup information (**/tmp/testbackup**) as demonstrated earlier.

man page

fbackup - 6

We are not restricted to performing backups to a tape drive attached to the local system. We can backup to a remote tape with **fbackup** by specifying the system name and tape drive, or file, to which we want to store the files. The following example uses **fbackup** options covered earlier and also includes the name of the system with the tape drive:

```
# fbackup -f tapesys:/dev/rmt/0m -i /var/tmp -v
fbackup(1004): session begins on Wed Jul 12 15:56:22 2000
fbackup(3307): volume 1 has been used -1 time(s) (maximum: 100)
fbackup(3024): writing vol 1 to output file tapesys:/dev/rmt/0m
    1: / 2
    2: /var 2
    3: /var/tmp 4
    4: /var/tmp/AAAa11812 0
    5: /var/tmp/AAAa11992 0
    6: /var/tmp/BEQ19522 19
    7: /var/tmp/DCE19522 0
    8: /var/tmp/DEC19522 0
    9: /var/tmp/ISPX19522 0
                  .
                  .
                  .
   73: /var/tmp/eaaa13306 1
   74: /var/tmp/ems_inittab.old 2
   75: /var/tmp/envd.action2 1
   76: /var/tmp/envd.action5 1
   77: /var/tmp/inetd.conf.old 9
   78: /var/tmp/net19522 1799
   79: /var/tmp/swagent.log 16
fbackup(1005): run time: 43 seconds
fbackup(3055): total file blocks read for backup: 1974
fbackup(3056): total blocks written to output file or1:/dev/rmt/0m: 0
#
```

man page

fbackup - 6

This command performs the backup of **/var/tmp** on system *or1* by sending the files to the tape drive on system *tapesys*. We could have used many additional options to **fbackup** as demonstrated in earlier examples, but I wanted to keep the example simple so it would be easy to see the remote tape drive specification.

dd

man page

dd - 6

man page

tar - 6

dd is a utility for writing the contents of a device, such as a disk, to tape. You can also use **dd** to copy an image of a tape to a file on your system, and then you can look at file.

First, let's write the contents of a directory to tape using **tar**, then we'll use **dd** to copy the tape contents as a file. The only option to **dd** required in this example is *if,* which specifies the input file as the tape drive.

```
# cd /var/tmp
# tar cf /dev/rmt/0m `ls`
# cd /tmp
# dd if=/dev/rmt/0m > /tmp/tapecontents
183+0 records in
183+0 records out
# tar tv /tmp/tapecontents
rw-------    0/3        0 Jul 11 15:57 2000 OBAMFEAa01630
rw-------    0/3        0 Jul 11 15:20 2000 OBAMHBAa01020
rw-------    0/3        0 Jul 11 15:50 2000 OBAMHBAa01540
rw-------    0/3      336 Jul 12 13:18 2000 OBAMHBAa07762
rw-------    0/3        0 Jul 12 13:44 2000 OBAMHBAa08333
rw-rw-rw-    0/3      102 Jul 11 15:20 2000 aaaa01112
                  .
                  .
                  .
rw-rw-rw-    0/3       28 Jul 11 15:45 2000 eaaa01487
rwxr--r--    0/0       28 Jul 11 21:53 2000 envd.action2
rwxr--r--    0/0       28 Jul 11 21:53 2000 envd.action5
rw-rw-rw-    0/3     2304 Jul 12 12:42 2000 exclude.temp
r-xr-xr-x    2/2        0 Jul 11 13:50 2000 ntp/
rw-r--r--    0/3     1595 Jul 12 12:23 2000 swagent.log
rw-rw-rw-    0/3      205 Jul 12 12:39 2000 tmp_cfg_file
#
```

Now we can look at the contents of the file with **tar** as shown in an earlier section, with the following command:

```
# tar tv /tmp/tapecontents
```

man page

cpio - 6

Another common use of **dd** is to extract a **cpio** archive from a tape drive on a remote system to a local system. In the following

man page

dd - 6

example the local system without a tape drive is *or1* and the remote system with a tape drive is *tapesys*. We'll read the tape to a directory on *or1* using **dd** and **cpio** (see the earlier **cpio** section for an explanation of the options) in the following example:

man page

cpio - 6

```
# hostname
or1
# pwd
/tmp/remotecpiofiles
# remsh tapesys "dd if=/dev/rmt/0m bs=8k" | cpio -icvBdum
.
envd.action2
envd.action5
swagent.log
ntp
OBAMHBAa01020
aaaa01558

                        .
                        .
                        .

eaaa01487
OBAMFEAa01630
cmd_res8215
tmp_cfg_file
cmd_res8708
OBAMHBAa07762
exclude.temp
arch.include.1
3580 blocks
0+358 records in
0+358 records out
#
```

man page

remsh - 12

This command runs a remote shell (**remsh**) to run the **dd** command on *tapesys*. The output of this command is piped to **cpio** on our local system to extract the archive. In this example, only the *if* option was used to specify the input file. The *of* option, which specifies the output file was not needed. If you were to perform a **dd** of a disk device to a tape drive, the *of* would be the tape drive on your system, such as **/dev/rmt/0m**.

dump and restore

man page

vxdump - 6

man page

vxrestore-6

dump is similar to **fbackup**. If you use **fbackup** on HP-UX, you will see much similarity when you use **dump**. **dump** provides levels as part of the backup scheme and creates **/var/adm/dumpdates,** which lists the last time a filesystem was backed up. **restore** is used to read information backed up with **dump**. **dump**, however, works only with HFS filesystems, and not VxFS, and it assumes that you are using a reel tape. **vxdump** and **vxrestore** are used for VxFS. Generally speaking, you will not find **dump** (and **vxdump**) and **restore** (and **vxrestore**) recommended as backup and restore programs on HP-UX. **fbackup** and **cpio** are the preferred backup programs on HP-UX. There is, however, no reason why you can't use **dump** and **restore** as long as you keep in mind the filesystem type limitation.

Let's take a look at some examples using **dump** and **restore**. Our examples will actually use **vxdump** and **vxrestore**; however. Nearly the same usage applies to both the HFS and VxFS programs. We'll use several commands in the upcoming examples, including the following:

```
# vxdump 0fu /dev/rmt/0m /var        ;dump vxfs file system /var to tape
                                      /dev/rmt/0m using level 0 and
                                      update /var/adm/dumpdates.



# vxrestore tf /dev/rmt/0m | grep eaaa  ;obtain table of contents from
                                         tape /dev/rmt/0m and look for
                                         file name containing "eaaa"

# vxrestore -x -f /dev/rmt/0m ./tmp/eaaa01487   ;restore file to
                                                 current directory
```

Let's take a look at some of these commands in more detail and I'll provide more explanation for what is taking place.

Our first example runs **vxdump** to back up the directory **/var** with a backup level of *0* for full backup, the *f* option to specify the output file **/dev/rmt/0m**, and *u* for a write to **/var/adm/dumpdates**:

```
# vxdump 0fu /dev/rmt/0m /var
   vxdump: Date of this level 0 dump: Tue Jul 11 16:41:27 2000
   vxdump: Date of last level 0 dump: the epoch
   vxdump: Dumping /dev/vg00/rlvol10 to /dev/rmt/0m
   vxdump: mapping (Pass I) [regular files]
   vxdump: mapping (Pass II) [directories]
   vxdump: estimated 428058 blocks (209.01MB).
   vxdump: dumping (Pass III) [directories]
   vxdump: dumping (Pass IV) [regular files]
   vxdump: vxdump: 214146 tape blocks on 1 volumes(s)
   vxdump: level 0 dump on Tue Jul 11 16:41:27 2000
   vxdump: Closing /dev/rmt/0m
   vxdump: vxdump is done
#
```

man page

vxdump - 6

man page

vxrestore-6

vxdump provides information related to the backup to *standard output*.

Next, let's view the table of contents on the tape using **vxrestore**, looking for files that begin with *eaaa*. We'll then delete one of these files from the system and use **vxrestore** to restore it from tape. To produce the table of contents, we use the *t* option, and to extract the file from tape, we use the *x* option to **vxrestore** as shown in the following listing:

```
#
# vxrestore tf /dev/rmt/0m | grep eaaa
      404      ./tmp/eaaa01299
      678      ./tmp/eaaa01333
      700      ./tmp/eaaa01354
      736      ./tmp/eaaa01380
      741      ./tmp/eaaa01405
      717      ./tmp/eaaa01487
#
#
# rm /var/tmp/eaaa01487
#
# vxrestore -x -f /dev/rmt/0m ./tmp/eaaa01487
You have not read any tapes yet.
Unless you know which volume your file(s) are on you should start
with the last volume and work towards the first.
Specify next volume #: 1
set owner/mode for '.'? [yn] y
```

```
# cd /var/tmp
# ls -l eaaa01487
total 2
-rw-rw-rw-   1 root        sys              28 Jul 11 15:45 eaaa01487
#
```

Notice that as part of restoring the file, we had to specify a volume number of *1* and whether or not we wanted to set the mode for the file.

The examples in this section showed creating a backup tape with **vxdump**, producing a table of contents, and restoring with **vxrestore**. Although **fbackup** and **cpio** are the recommended backup solutions on HP-UX, you can use **dump** and **restore** if you are familiar with these programs and would like to use them. Due to the portability of **tar**, it is often used for backup and restore as well.

man page

vxdump - 6

man page

vxrestore- 6

Manual Pages for Commands Used in Chapter 6

The following section contains copies of the manual pages for commands used in Chapter 6. This makes a quick reference for you to use
when issuing the commands commonly used for backup and restore.

cpio

cpio - Save or restore archives.

NAME
     cpio - copy file archives in and out; duplicate directory trees

SYNOPSIS

     cpio -o [-e extarg] [achvxABC]

     cpio -i[bcdfmrstuvxBPRSU6] [pattern...]

     cpio -p [-e extarg] [adlmruvxU] directory

DESCRIPTION
     The cpio command saves and restores archives of files on magnetic
     tape, other devices, or a regular file, and copies files from one
     directory to another while replicating the directory tree structure.

     cpio -o   (copy out, export) Read standard input to obtain a list
                 of path names, and copy those files to standard output
                 together with path name and status information.   The
                 output is padded to a 512-byte boundary.

     cpio -i   (copy in, import) Extract files from standard input,
                 which is assumed to be the result of a previous cpio -o.

                 If pattern..., is specified, only the files with names
                 that match a pattern according to the rules of Pattern
                 Matching Notation (see regexp(5)) are selected. A leading
                 ! on a pattern indicates that only those names that do
                 not match the remainder of the pattern should be selected.
                 Multiple patterns can be specified. The patterns are
                 additive. If no pattern is specified, the default is *
                 (select all files). See the f option, as well.

                 Extracted files are conditionally created and copied into
                 the current directory tree, as determined by the options
                 described below. The permissions of the files match the
                 permissions of the original files when the archive was
                 created by cpio -o unless the U option is used. File
                 owner and group are that of the current user unless the
                 user has appropriate privileges, in which case cpio
                 retains the owner and group of the files of the previous
                 cpio -o.

     cpio -p   (passthrough) Read standard input to obtain a list of
                 path names of files which are then conditionally created
                 and copied into the destination directory tree as
                 determined by the options described below. directory must
                 exist. Destination path names are interpreted relative to
                 directory.

        Options
         cpio recognizes the following options, which can be appended as

appropriate to -i, -o, and -p. Whitespace and hyphens are not
permitted between these options and -i, -o, or -p.

    a   Reset access times of input files after they are copied.

    b   Swap both bytes and half-words. Use only with -i. See
                the P option for details; see also the s and S options.

    c   Write or read header information in ASCII character form
                for portability.

    d   Create directories as needed.

-e extarg
                Specifies the handling of any extent attributes of the
                file(s) to be archived or copied. extarg takes one of
                the following values.

                      warn   Archive or copy the file and issue a
                                   warning message if extent attributes
                                 cannot be preserved.
                    ignore   Do not issue a warning message even if
                                 extent attributes cannot be preserved.
                    force   Any file(s) with extent attributes will
                                 not be archived and a warning message will
                                 be issued.

                When using the -o option, extent attributes are not
                preserved in the archive. Furthermore, the -p option
                will not preserve extent attributes if the files are
                being copied to a file system that does not support
                extent attributes. If -e is not specified, the default
                value for extarg is warn.

    f   Copy in all files except those selected by pattern....

    h   Follow symbolic links as though they were normal files or
                directories. Normally, cpio archives the link.

    l   Whenever possible, link files rather than copying them.
                This option does not destroy existing files. Use only
                with -p.

    m   Retain previous file modification time. This option does
                not affect directories that are being copied.

    r   Rename files interactively. If the user types a null
                line, the file is skipped.

    s   Swap all bytes of the file. Use only with -i. See the P
                option for details; see also the s and S options.

    t   Print only a table of contents of the input. No files
                are created, read, or copied.

    u   Copy unconditionally (normally, an older file does not
                replace a newer file with the same name).

    v   Print a list of file names as they are processed. When
                used with the t option, the table of contents has the
                format:

                numeric-mode owner-name blocks date-time filename

where numeric-mode is the file privileges in numeric
format, owner-name is the name of the file owner, blocks
is the size of the file in 512-byte blocks, date-time is
the date and time the file was last modified, and
filename is the path name of the file as recorded in the
archive.

x   Save or restore device special files. Since mknod() is
used to recreate these files on a restore, -ix and -px
can be used only by users with appropriate privileges
(see mknod(2)). This option is intended for intrasystem
(backup) use only. Restoring device files from previous
versions of the OS, or from different systems can be very
dangerous. cpio may prevent the restoration of certain
device files from the archive.

A   Suppress warning messages regarding optional access
control list entries. cpio does not back up optional
access control list entries in a file's access control
list (see acl(5)). Normally, a warning message is
printed for each file that has optional access control
list entries.

B   Block input/output at 5120 bytes to the record (does not
apply to cpio -p). This option is meaningful only with
data directed to or from devices that support variable-
length records such as magnetic tape.

C   Have cpio checkpoint itself at the start of each volume.
If cpio is writing to a streaming tape drive with
immediate-report mode enabled and a write error occurs,
it normally aborts and exits with return code 2. With
this option specified, cpio instead automatically
restarts itself from the checkpoint and rewrites the
current volume. Alternatively, if cpio is not writing to
such a device and a write error occurs, cpio normally
continues with the next volume. With this option
specified, however, the user can choose to either ignore
the error or rewrite the current volume.

P   Read a file written on a PDP-11 or VAX system (with
byte-swapping) that did not use the c option. Use only
with -i. Files copied in this mode are not changed.
Non-ASCII files are likely to need further processing to
be readable. This processing often requires knowledge of
file contents, and thus cannot always be done by this
program. The b, s, and S options can be used when
swapping all the bytes on the tape (rather than just in
the headers) is appropriate. In general, text is best
processed with P and binary data with one of the other
options.

(PDP-11 and VAX are registered trademarks of Digital
Equipment Corporation.)

R   Resynchronize automatically when cpio goes "out of
phase", (see DIAGNOSTICS).

S   Swap all half-words in the file. Use only with -i. See
the P option for details; see also the b and s options.

U   Use the process's file-mode creation mask (see umask(2))
to modify the mode of files created, in the same manner
as creat(2).

6   Process a UNIX Sixth-Edition-format file. Use only with
           -i.

Note that cpio archives created using a raw device file must be read
using a raw device file.

When the end of the tape is reached, cpio prompts the user for a new
special file and continues.

If you want to pass one or more metacharacters to cpio without the
shell expanding them, be sure to precede each of them with a backslash
(\).

Device files written with the -ox option (such as /dev/tty03) do not
transport to other implementations of HP-UX.

EXTERNAL INFLUENCES
    Environment Variables
        LC_COLLATE determines the collating sequence used in evaluating
        pattern matching notation for file name generation.

        LC_CTYPE determines the interpretation of text as single and/or
        multi-byte characters, and the characters matched by character class
        expressions in pattern matching notation.

        LC_TIME determines the format and content of date and time strings
        output when listing the contents of an archive with the v option.

        LANG determines the language in which messages are displayed.

        If LC_COLLATE, LC_CTYPE, or LC_TIME is not specified in the
        environment or is set to the empty string, the value of LANG is used
        as a default for each unspecified or empty variable. If LANG is not
        specified or is set to the empty string, a default of "C" (see
        lang(5)) is used instead of LANG. If any internationalization
        variable contains an invalid setting, cpio behaves as if all
        internationalization variables are set to "C". See environ(5).

    International Code Set Support
        Single- and multi-byte character code sets are supported.

RETURN VALUE
    cpio returns the following exit codes:

        0   Successful completion. Review standard error for files that
              could not be transferred.

        1   Error during resynchronization. Some files may not have
              been recovered.

        2   Out-of-phase error. A file header is corrupt or in the
              wrong format.

DIAGNOSTICS
    Out of phase--get help
    Perhaps the "c" option should[n't] be used

        cpio -i could not read the header of an archived file. The
        header is corrupt or it was written in a different format.
        Without the R option, cpio returns an exit code of 2.

        If no file name has been displayed yet, the problem may be the
        format. Try specifying a different header format option: null
        for standard format; c for ASCII; b, s, P, or S, for one of the

byte-swapping formats; or 6 for UNIX Sixth Edition.

Otherwise, a header may be corrupt. Use the R option to have cpio attempt to resynchronize the file automatically. Resynchronizing means that cpio tries to find the next good header in the archive file and continues processing from there. If cpio tries to resynchronize from being out of phase, it returns an exit code of 1.

Other diagnostic messages are self-explanatory.

EXAMPLES
Copy the contents of a directory into a tape archive:

    ls | cpio -o > /dev/rmt/c0t0d0BEST

Duplicate a directory hierarchy:

    cd olddir
    find . -depth -print | cpio -pd newdir

The trivial case

    find . -depth -print | cpio -oB >/dev/rmt/c0t0d0BEST

can be handled more efficiently by:

    find . -cpio /dev/rmt/c0t0d0BEST

WARNINGS
Because of industry standards and interoperability goals, cpio does not support the archival of files larger than 2GB or files that have user/group IDs greater than 60K. Files with user/group IDs greater than 60K are archived and restored under the user/group ID of the current process.

Do not redirect the output of cpio to a named cpio archive file residing in the same directory as the original files belonging to that cpio archive. This can cause loss of data.

cpio strips any leading ./ characters in the list of filenames piped to it.

Path names are restricted to PATH_MAX characters (see <limits.h> and limits(5)). If there are too many unique linked files, the program runs out of memory to keep track of them. Thereafter, linking information is lost. Only users with appropriate privileges can copy special files.

cpio tapes written on HP machines with the -ox[c] options can sometimes mislead (non-HP) versions of cpio that do not support the x option. If a non-HP (or non-AT&T) version of cpio happens to be modified so that the (HP) cpio recognizes it as a device special file, a spurious device file might be created.

If /dev/tty is not accessible, cpio issues a complaint and exits.

The -pd option does not create the directory typed on the command line.

The -idr option does not make empty directories.

The -plu option does not link files to existing files.

POSIX defines a file named TRAILER!!! as an end-of-archive marker. Consequently, if a file of that name is contained in a group of files being written by cpio -o, the file is interpreted as end-of-archive, and no remaining files are copied. The recommended practice is to avoid naming files anything that resembles an end-of-archive file name.

To create a POSIX-conforming cpio archive, the c option must be used. To read a POSIX-conforming cpio archive, the c option must be used and the b, s, S, and 6 options should not be used. If the user does not have appropriate privileges, the U option must also be used to get POSIX-conforming behavior when reading an archive. Users with appropriate privileges should not use this option to get POSIX -conforming behavior.

Using Cartridge Tape Drives
For an explanation of the constraints on cartridge tapes, see ct(7).

Using cpio to write directly to a cartridge tape unit can severely damage the tape drive in a short amount of time, and is therefore strongly discouraged. The recommended method of writing to the cartridge tape unit is to use the tcio command (see tcio(1)) in conjunction with cpio (note that the B option must not be used by cpio when tcio is used). tcio buffers data into larger pieces suitable for cartridge tapes. The B option must be used when writing directly (that is, without using tcio) to a CS/80 cartridge tape unit.

DEPENDENCIES
If the path given to cpio contains a symbolic link as the last element, this link is traversed and pathname resolution continues. cpio uses the symbolic link's target, rather than that of the link.

SEE ALSO
ar(1), find(1), tar(1), tcio(1), cpio(4), acl(5), environ(5), lang(5), regexp(5).

STANDARDS CONFORMANCE
cpio: SVID2, SVID3, XPG2, XPG3

dd

dd - Copy the specified input file to the specified output.

```
dd(1)                                                              dd(1)

NAME
     dd - convert, reblock, translate, and copy a (tape) file

SYNOPSIS

     dd [option=value] ...

DESCRIPTION
     dd copies the specified input file to the specified output with
     possible conversions.  The standard input and output are used by
     default.  Input and output block size can be specified to take
     advantage of raw physical I/O.

   Options
     dd recognizes the following option=value pairs:

          if=file       Input file name; default is standard input.

          of=file       Output file name; default is standard output.  The
                        output file will be created using the same owner
                        and group used by creat().

          ibs=n         Input block size is n bytes (default 512).

          obs=n         Output block size is n bytes (default 512).

          bs=n          Set both input and output block size to the same
                        size, superseding ibs and obs.  This option is
                        particularly efficient if no conversion is
                        specified, because no in-core copy is necessary.


          cbs=n         Conversion buffer size is n bytes.

          skip=n        Skip n input blocks before starting copy.

          seek=n        Seek n blocks from beginning of output file before
                        copying.  This option is ignored on a raw magnetic
                        tape device.  See mt(1) for information about
                        operations on raw magnetic tape devices.

          count=n       Copy only n input blocks.

          conv=option   Data conversion option.  Use one of the following:

                        conv=ascii     Convert EBCDIC to ASCII.

                        conv=ebcdic    Convert ASCII to EBCDIC

                        conv=ibm       Convert ASCII to EBCDIC
                                       using an alternate
                                       conversion table
```

conv=lcase	Map US ASCII alphabetics to lowercase
conv=ucase	Map US ASCII alphabetics to uppercase
conv=swab	Swap every pair of bytes
conv=noerror	Do not stop processing on an error
conv=sync	Pad every input block to input block size (ibs)
conv=notrunc	Do not truncate existing file on output
conv=block	Convert input record to a fixed length specified by cbs
conv=unblock	Convert fixed length records to variable length
conv=..., ...	Multiple comma-separated conversions

Where sizes are required, n indicates a numerical value in bytes. Numbers can be specified using the forms:

n	for n bytes
nk	for n Kbytes (n * 1024),
nb	for n blocks (n * 512), or
nw	for n words (n * 2).

To indicate a product, use x to separate number pairs.

The cbs option is used when block , unblock , ascii or ebcdic conversion is specified. In case of ascii , cbs characters are placed into the conversion buffer, converted to ASCII, trailing blanks are trimmed, and a new-line is added before sending the line to the output. In case of ebcdic , ASCII characters are read into the conversion buffer, converted to EBCDIC, and blanks are added to make up an output block of size cbs.

Upon completion, dd reports the number of whole and partial input and output records.

EXTERNAL INFLUENCES
  International Code Set Support
    Single- and multibyte character code sets are supported.

  Environment Variables
    The following environment variables will affect execution of dd :

    LANG determines the locale when LC_ALL and a corresponding variable (beginning with LC_) do not specify a locale.

    LC_ALL determines the locale used to override any values set by LANG or any environment variables beginning with LC_.

    The LC_CTYPE variable determines the locale for the interpretation of sequences of bytes of text data as characters (single/multiple byte characters, upper/lower case characters).

The LC_MESSAGES variable determines the language in which messages should be written.

RETURN VALUE
    Exit values are:

        0   Successful completion.
        >0   Error condition occurred.

DIAGNOSTICS
        f+p records in   Number of full and partial blocks read.
        f+p records out   Number of full and partial blocks written.

EXAMPLES
    Read an EBCDIC tape blocked ten 80-byte EBCDIC card images per block
    into an ASCII file named x:

        dd if=/dev/rmt/c0t0d0BEST of=x ibs=800 cbs=80
        conv=ascii,lcase

    Note the use of the raw magnetic tape device file. dd is especially
    suited to I/O on raw physical devices because it allows reading and
    writing in arbitrary block sizes.

WARNINGS
    You may experience trouble writing directly to or reading directly
    from a cartridge tape. For best results, use tcio(1) as an input or
    output filter. For example, use

        ... |dd ... |tcio -ovVS 256 /dev/rct/c4t1d0

    for output to a cartridge tape, or

        tcio -ivS 256 /dev/rct/c4t1d0 |dd ... | ...

    for input from a cartridge tape.

    Some devices, such as 1/2-inch magnetic tapes, are incapable of
    seeking. Such devices must be positioned prior to running dd by using
    mt(1) or some other appropriate command.

    ASCII and EBCDIC conversion tables are taken from the 256-character
    ACM standard, Nov, 1968. The ibm conversion, while less widely
    accepted as a standard, corresponds better to certain IBM print train
    conventions. There is no universal solution.

    New-line characters are inserted only on conversion to ASCII; padding
    is done only on conversion to EBCDIC. These should be separate
    options.

    If if or of refers to a raw disk, bs should always be a multiple of
    sector size of disk. The default bs size used by dd is 512 bytes. If
    sector size of disk is different from 512 bytes, a bs multiple of
    sector size should be specified. The character special (raw) device
    file should always be used for devices.

    It is entirely up to the user to insure there is enough room in the
    destination file, filesystem and/or device to contain the output since
    dd(1) cannot pre-determine the required space after conversion.

SEE ALSO
    cp(1), mt(1), tr(1), disk(7), mt(7).

STANDARDS CONFORMANCE
    dd: SVID2, SVID3, XPG2, XPG3, XPG4, POSIX.2

fbackup

man page

fbackup - 6

fbackup - Perform a high-speed selective backup.

fbackup(1M)   fbackup(1M)

NAME
     fbackup - selectively back up files

SYNOPSIS
     /usr/sbin/fbackup -f device [-f device] ... [-0-9] [-nsuvyAEl] [-i
     path] [-e path] [-g graph] [-d path] [-I path] [-V path] [-c config]

     /usr/sbin/fbackup -f device [-f device] ... [-R restart] [-nsuvyAEl]
     [-d path] [-I path] [-V path] [-c config]

DESCRIPTION
     fbackup combines features of dump and ftio to provide a flexible,
     high-speed file system backup mechanism (see dump(1M) and ftio(1)).
     fbackup selectively transfers files to an output device. For each
     file transferred, the file's contents and all the relevant information
     necessary to restore it to an equivalent state are copied to the
     output device. The output device can be a raw magnetic tape drive,
     the standard output, a DDS-format tape, a rewritable magneto-optical
     disk or a file.

     The selection of files to backup is done by explicitly specifying
     trees of files to be included or excluded from an fbackup session.
     The user can construct an arbitrary graph of files by using the -i or
     -e options on the command line, or by using the -g option with a graph
     file. For backups being done on a regular basis, the -g option
     provides an easier interface for controlling the backup graph.
     fbackup selects files in this graph, and attempts to transfer them to
     the output device. The selectivity depends on the mode in which
     fbackup is being used; i.e., full or incremental backup.

     When doing full backups, all files in the graph are selected. When
     doing incremental backups, only files in the graph that have been
     modified since a previous backup of that graph are selected. If an
     incremental backup is being done at level 4 and the -g option is used,
     the database file is searched for the most recent previous backup at
     levels 0-3. If a file's modification time is before the time when the
     last appropriate session began and the i-node change time is before
     the time that same session ended, the file is not backed up.
     Beginning at HP-UX Release 8.0, all directories lying on the path to a
     file that qualifies for the incremental backup will also be on the
     backup media, even if the directories do not qualify on their own
     status.

     If fbackup is used for incremental backups, a database of past backups
     must be kept. fbackup maintains this data in the text file
     /var/adm/fbackupfiles/dates, by default. Note that the directory
     /var/adm/fbackupfiles must be created prior to the first time fbackup
     is used for incremental backups. The -d option can be used to specify
     an alternate database file. The user can specify to update this file
     when an fbackup session completes successfully. Entries for each
     session are recorded on separate pairs of lines. The following four

items appear on the first line of each pair: the graph file name,
backup level, starting time, and ending time (both in time(2) format).
The second line of each pair contains the same two times, but in
strftime(3C) format. These lines contain the local equivalent of
STARTED:, the start time, the local equivalent of ENDED:, and the
ending time. These second lines serve only to make the dates file
more readable; fbackup does not use them. All fields are separated by
white space. Graph file names are compared character-by-character
when checking the previous-backup database file to ascertain when a
previous session was run for that graph. Caution must be exercised to
ensure that, for example, graph and ./graph are not used to specify
the same graph file because fbackup treats them as two different graph
files.

The general structure of a fbackup volume is the same, no matter what
type of device is used. There are some small specific differences due
to differing capabilities of devices. The general structure is as
follows:

- Reserved space for ASCII tape label (1024 bytes)
- fbackup specific volume label (2048 bytes)
- session index (size in field of volume label)
- data

Each file entry in the index contains the volume number and the
pathname of the file. At the beginning of every volume, fbackup
assumes that all files not already backed up will fit on that volume;
an erroneous assumption for all but the last volume. Indices are
accurate only for the previous volumes in the same set. Hence, the
index on the last volume may indicate that a file resides on that
volume, but it may not have actually been backed up (for example, if
it was removed after the index was created, but before fbackup
attempted to back it up). The only index guaranteed to be correct in
all cases is the on-line index (-I option), which is produced after
the last volume has been written. Specific minor differences are
listed below:

- When using 9-track tape drives or DDS-format tape drives
  several small differences exist. The main blocks of
  information are separated by EOF. fbackup checkpoints the
  media periodically to enhance error recovery. If a write
  error is detected, the user normally has two options: First, a
  new volume can be mounted and that volume rewritten from the
  beginning. Second, if the volume is not too severely damaged,
  the good data before the error can be saved, and the write
  error is treated as a normal end-of-media condition. The
  blocks of data with their checkpoint records are also
  separated by EOF. In addition if the DDS-format drive
  supports Fast Search Marks these will be used to enhance
  recovery speed by placing them between blocks of files.

- For a magneto-optical device, a disk, a file, or standard
  output, there are no special marks separating the information
  pieces. Using standard output results in only one volume.

fbackup provides the ability to use UCB-mode tape drives. This makes
it possible to overlap the tape rewind times if two or more tape
drives are connected to the system.

Set-up
  There are several things the user will want to consider when setting
  fbackup up for regular use. These include type of device and media,
  full versus incremental frequency, amount of logging information to
  keep on-line, structure of the graph file, and on-line versus off-line
  backup.

The type of device used for backups can affect such things as media
expenses, ability to do unattended backup and speed of the backup.
Using 9-track tapes will probably result in the highest performance,
but require user intervention for changing tapes. A magneto-optical
autochanger can provide an unattended backup for a large system and
long life media, however the media cost is high. The lowest cost will
probably be achieved through DDS-format devices, but at the lowest
performance.

It is also important to consider how often full backups should be
made, and how many incremental backups to make between full backups.
Time periods can be used, such as a full backup every Friday and
incrementals on all other days. Media capacities can be used if
incremental backups need to run unattended. The availability of
personnel to change media can also be an important factor as well as
the length of time needed for the backup. Other factors may affect
the need for full and incremental backup combinations such as
contractual or legal requirements.

If backup information is kept online; i.e., output from the -V or -I
options, the required storage space must also be considered. Index
file sizes are hard to predict in advance because they depend on
system configuration. Each volume header file takes less than 1536
bytes. Of course the more information that is kept on-line, the
faster locating a backup media for a recovery will be.

There are several ways to structure the graph file or files used in a
system backup. The first decision involves whether to use one or more
than one graph files for the backup. Using one file is simpler, but
less flexible. Using two or more graph files simplifies splitting
backups into logical sets. For example, one graph file can be used
for system disks where changes tend to be less frequent, and another
graph file for the users area. Thus two different policies can be
implemented for full and incremental backups.

fbackup was designed to allow backups while the system is in use by
providing the capability to retry an active file. When absolute
consistency on a full backup is important, the system should probably
be in single-user mode. However, incremental backups can be made
while the system is in normal use, thus improving system up-time.

Options
  -c config   config is the name of the configuration file, and can
                       contain values for the following parameters:

                         - Number of 1024-byte blocks per record,
                         - Number of records of shared memory to allocate,
                         - Number of records between checkpoints,
                         - Number of file-reader processes,
                         - Maximum number of times fbackup is to retry an
                            active file,
                         - Maximum number of bytes of media to use while
                            retrying the backup of an active file,
                         - Maximum number of times a magnetic tape volume
                            can be used,
                         - Name of a file to be executed when a volume
                            change occurs. This file must exist and be
                            executable.
                         - Name of a file to be executed when a fatal error
                            occurs. This file must exist and be executable.

                         - The number of files between the Fast Search Marks
                            on DDS-format tapes. The cost of these marks are
                            negligible in terms of space on the DDS-format
                            tape. Not all DDS-format devices support fast
                            search marks.

Each entry in the configuration file consists of one line of text in the following format: identifier, white space, argument. In the following sample configuration file, the number of blocks per record is set to 16, the number of records is set to 32, the checkpoint frequency is set to 32, the number of file reader processes is set to 2, the maximum number of retries is set to 5, the maximum retry space for active files is set to 5,000,000 bytes, the maximum number of times a magnetic tape volume can be used is set to 100, the file to be executed at volume change time is /var/adm/fbackupfiles/chgvol, the file to be executed when a fatal error occurs is /var/adm/fbackupfiles/error, and the number of files between fast search marks is set to 200.

```
blocksperrecord          16
records                  32
checkpointfreq           32
readerprocesses          2 (maximum of 6)
maxretries               5
retrylimit               5000000
maxvoluses               100
chgvol                   /var/adm/fbackupfiles/chgvol

error                    /var/adm/fbackupfiles/error

filesperfsm              200
```

Each value listed is also the default value, except chgvol and error, which default to null values.

-d path   This specifies a path to a database for use with incremental backups. It overrides the default database file /var/adm/fbackupfiles/dates.

-e path   path specifies a tree to be excluded from the backup graph. This tree must be a subtree of part of the backup graph. Otherwise, specifying it will not exclude any files from the graph. There is no limit on how many times the -e option can be specified.

-f device   device specifies the name of an output file. If the name of the file is -, fbackup writes to the standard output. There is no default output file; at least one must be specified. If more than one output file is specified, fbackup uses each one successively and then repeats in a cyclical pattern. Patterns can be used in the device name in a manner resembling file name expansion as done by the shell (see sh-bourne(1) and other shell manual entries. The patterns must be protected from expansion by the shell by quoting them. The expansion of the pattern results in all matching names being in the list of devices used.

There is slightly different behavior if remote devices are used. A device on the remote machine can be specified in the form machine:device. fbackup creates a server process from /usr/sbin/rmt on the remote machine to access the tape device. If /usr/sbin/rmt does not exist on the remote system, fbackup creates a server process from /etc/rmt on the remote machine to access the tape device. Only half-inch 9-track magnetic tapes or DDS-format tapes can be remote devices. The fast search and save set marks

capabilities are not used when remote DDS-format
devices are used.

-g graph   graph defines the graph file. The graph file is a text
                      file containing the list of file names of trees to be
                      included or excluded from the backup graph. These
                      trees are interpreted in the same manner as when they
                      are specified with the -i and -e options. Graph file
                      entries consist of a line beginning with either i or e,
                      followed by white space, and then the path name of a
                      tree. Lines not beginning with i or e are treated as
                      an error. There is no default graph file. For
                      example, to backup all of /usr except for the subtree
                      /usr/lib, a file could be created with the following
                      two records:

                              i /usr
                              e /usr/lib

-i path   path specifies a tree to be included in the backup
                      graph. There is no limit on how many times the -i
                      option can be specified.

-n   Cross NFS mount points. By default fbackup does not
                      cross NFS mount points, regardless of paths specified
                      by the -i or -g options.

-l   Includes LOFS files specified by the backup graph. By
                      default, fbackup does not cross LOFS mount points. If
                      -l is specified, and the backup graph includes files
                      which are also in a LOFS that is in the backup graph,
                      then those files will backed up twice.

-s   Backup the object that a symbolic link refers to. The
                      default behavior is to backup the symbolic link.

-u   Update the database of past backups so that it contains
                      the backup level, the time of the beginning and end of
                      the session, and the graph file used for this fbackup
                      session. For this update to take place, the following
                      conditions must exist: Neither the -i nor the -e option
                      can be used; the -g option must be specified exactly
                      once (see below); the fbackup must complete
                      successfully.

-v   Run in verbose mode. Generates status messages that
                      are otherwise not seen.

-y   Automatically answer yes to any inquiries.

-A   Do not back up optional entries of access control lists
                      (ACLs) for files. Normally, all mode information is
                      backed up including the optional ACL entries. With the
                      -A option, the summary mode information (as returned by
                      stat()) is backed up. Use this option when backing up
                      files from a system that contains ACL to be recovered
                      on a system that does not understand ACL (see acl(5)).

-E   Do not back up extent attributes. Normally, all extent
                      attributes that have been set are included with the
                      file. This option only applies to file systems which
                      support extent attributes.

-I path   path specifies the name of the on-line index file to be

generated. It consists of one line for each file
backed up during the session. Each line contains the
volume number on which that file resides and the file
name. If the -I option is omitted, no index file is
generated.

-V path   The volume header information is written to path at the
                 end of a successful fbackup session. The following
                 fields from the header are written in the format
                 label:value with one pair per line.

Magic Field   On a valid fbackup media it
                           contains the value
                           FBACKUP_LABEL (HP-UX
                           release 10.20 and beyond).
                           Before HP-UX release 10.20,
                           it contained the value
                           FBACKUP LABEL.
Machine Identification This field contains the
                           result of uname -m.
System Identification This field contains the
                           result of uname -s.
Release Identification This field contains the
                           result of uname -r.
Node Identification   This field contains the
                           result of uname -n.
User Identification   This field contains the
                           result of cuserid() (see
                           cuserid(3S)).
Record Size   This field contains the
                           maximum length in bytes of
                           a data record.
Time   This field contains the
                           clock time when fbackup was
                           started.
Media Use   This field contains the
                           number of times the media
                           has been used for backup.
                           Since the information is
                           actually on the media, this
                           field will always contain
                           the value 0.
Volume Number   This field contains a #
                           character followed by 3
                           digits, and identifies the
                           number of volumes in the
                           backup.
Checkpoint Frequency   This field contains the
                           frequency of backup-data-
                           record checkpointing.
Index Size   This field contains the
                           size of the index.
Backup Identification Tag
                           This field is composed of
                           two items: the process ID
                           (pid) and the start time of
                           that process.
Language   This field contains the
                           language used to make the
                           backup.

-R restart   Restart an fbackup session from where it was previously
                 interrupted. The restart file contains all the
                 information necessary to restart the interrupted
                 session. None of the -[ieg0-9] options can be used

          together with the restart option.

`-0-9`   This single-digit number is the backup level. Level 0 indicates a full backup. Higher levels are generally used to perform incremental backups. When doing an incremental backup of a particular graph at a particular level, the database of past backups is searched to find the date of the most recent backup of the same graph that was done at a lower level. If no such entry is found, the beginning of time is assumed. All files in the graph that have been modified since this date are backed up.

   Access Control Lists (ACLs)
     If a file has optional ACL entries, the -A option is required to enable its recovery on a system whose access control lists capability is not present.

EXTERNAL INFLUENCES
   Environment Variables
     LC_COLLATE determines the order in which files are stored in the backup device and the order output by the -I option.

     LC_TIME determines the format and contents of date and time strings.

     LC_MESSAGES determines the language in which messages are displayed.

     If LC_COLLATE and LC_TIME and LC_MESSAGES are not all specified in the environment or if either is set to the empty string, the value of LANG is used as a default for each unspecified or empty variable. If LANG is not specified or is set to the empty string, a default of "C" (see lang(5)) is used instead of LANG. If any internationalization variable contains an invalid setting, fbackup behaves as if all internationalization variables are set to "C". See environ(5).

   International Code Set Support
     Single- and multi-byte character code sets are supported.

RETURN VALUE
     fbackup returns 0 upon normal completion, 1 if it is interrupted but allowed to save its state for possible restart, and 2 if any error conditions prevent the session from completing.

EXAMPLES
     In the following two examples, assume the graph of interest specifies all of /usr except /usr/lib (as described in the g key section above).

     The first example is a simple case where a full backup is done but the database file is not updated. This can be invoked as follows:

          `/usr/sbin/fbackup -0i /usr -e /usr/lib -f /dev/rmt/c0t0d0BEST`

     The second example is more complicated, and assumes the user wants to maintain a database of past fbackup sessions so that incremental backups are possible.

     If sufficient on-line storage is available, it may be desirable to keep several of the most recent index files on disk. This eliminates the need to recover the index from the backup media to determine if the files to be recovered are on that set. One method of maintaining on-line index files is outlined below. The system administrator must do the following once before fbackup is run for the first time (creating intermediate level directories where necessary):

       - Create a suitable configuration file called config in the directory /var/adm/fbackupfiles

- Create a graph file called usr-usrlib in the directory
  /var/adm/fbackupfiles/graphs

- Create a directory called usr-usrlib in the directory
  /var/adm/fbackupfiles/indices

A shell script that performs the following tasks could be run for each
fbackup session:

- Build an index file path name based on both the graph file
  used (passed as a parameter to the script) and the start time
  of the session (obtained from the system). For example:

      /var/adm/fbackupfiles/indices/usr-usrlib/871128.15:17
      (for Nov 28, 1987 at 3:17 PM)

- Invoke fbackup with this path name as its index file name.
  For example:

      cd /var/adm/fbackupfiles
      /usr/sbin/fbackup -0uc config -g graphs/usr-usrlib\
          -I indices/usr-usrlib/871128.15:17\
              -f /dev/rmt/c0t0d0BEST

When the session completes successfully, the index is automatically
placed in the proper location.

Note that fbackup should be piped to tcio when backing up to a CS/80
cartridge tape device see tcio(1)). The following example copies the
entire contents of directory /usr to a cartridge tape:

      /usr/sbin/fbackup i /usr -f - | tcio -oe /dev/rct/c0d1s2

WARNINGS
  With release 10.20, HP-UX supports large files (greater than 2GB) and
  increased UID/GIDs (greater than 60,000). Archives containing files
  with these attributes would cause severe problems on systems that do
  not support the increased sizes. For this reason, fbackup creates
  tapes with a new magic number ("FBACKUP_LABEL"). This prevents
  fbackup tape archives from being restored on pre-10.20 HP-UX systems.
  frecover still reads both tape formats so that fbackup tape archives
  created on pre-10.20 HP-UX systems can be restored.

  Starting with HP-UX Release 8.0, fbackup does not back up network
  special files because RFA networking is obsolete. A warning message
  is issued if a network special file is encountered in the backup graph
  and the file is skipped.

  The use of fbackup for backing up NFS mounted file systems is not
  guaranteed to work as expected if the backup is done as a privileged
  user. This is due to the manner in which NFS handles privileged-user
  access by mapping user root and uid 0 to user nobody, usually uid -2,
  thus disallowing root privileges on the remote system to a root user
  on the local system.

  The utility set comprised of fbackup and frecover was originally
  designed for use on systems equipped with not more than one gigabyte
  of total file system storage. Although the utilities have no
  programming limitations that restrict users to this size, complete
  backups and recoveries of substantially larger systems can cause a
  large amount system activity due to the amount of virtual memory (swap
  space) used to store the indices. Users who want to use these
  utilities, but are noticing poor system-wide performance due to the
  size of the backup, are encouraged to backup their systems in multiple

smaller sessions, rather than attempting to backup the entire system at one time.

Due to present file-system limitations, files whose inode data, but not their contents, are modified while a backup is in progress might be omitted from the next incremental backup of the same graph. Also, fbackup does not reset the inode change times of files to their original value.

fbackup allocates resources that are not returned to the system if it is killed in an ungraceful manner. If it is necessary to kill fbackup, send it a SIGTERM; not a SIGKILL.

For security reasons, configuration files and the chgvol and error executable files should only be writable by their owners.

If sparse files are backed up without using data compression, a very large amount of media can be consumed.

fbackup does not require special privileges. However, if the user does not have access to a given file, the file is not backed up.

fbackup consists of multiple executable objects, all of which are expected to reside in directory /usr/sbin.

fbackup creates volumes with a format that makes duplication of volumes by dd impossible (see dd(1)). Copying an fbackup volume created on one media type to another media type does not produce a valid fbackup volume on the new media because the formats of volumes on 9-track tape, backup to a file, rewritable optical disks and DDS-format tapes are not identical.

When configuring the parameter blocksperrecord (see -c option), the record size is limited by the maximum allowed for the tape drive. Common maximum record sizes include 16 1-Kbyte blocks for tape drive models HP7974 and HP7978A, 32 blocks for the HP7978B, 60 blocks for the HP7980, and 64 blocks for DDS tape drives. Note also that the blocksize used in earlier releases (7.0 and before) was 512 bytes, whereas it is now 1024 bytes. This means that the same value specified in blocksperrecord in an earlier release creates blocks twice their earlier size in the current release (i.e., a blocksperrecord parameter of 32 would create 16-Kbyte blocks at Release 7.0, but now creates 32-Kbyte blocks). If blocksperrecord exceeds the byte count allowed by the tape drive, the tape drive rejects the write, causing an error to be communicated to fbackup which fbackup interprets as a bad tape. The resulting write error message resembles the following:

        fbackup (3013): Write error while writing backup at tape block 0.
        Diagnostic error from tape 11...... SW_PROBLEM   (printed by
        driver on console)
        fbackup (3102): Attempting to make this volume salvageable.
        etc.

DEPENDENCIES
  NFS
        Access control lists of networked files are summarized (as returned in
        st_mode by stat()), but not copied to the new file (see stat(2)).

  Series 800
        On NIO-bus machines there can be problems when a CS/80 cartridge tape
        device is on the same interface card as hard disk devices. If writes
        longer than 16K bytes are made to the tape device, it is possible to
        have disk access time-out errors. This happens because the tape
        device has exclusive access to the bus during write operations.
        Depending on the system activity, this problem may not be seen. The

default write size of fbackup is 16 Kbytes.

Series 700/800
        fbackup does not support QIC-120, and QIC-150 formats on QIC devices.
        If fbackup is attempted for these formats, fbackup fails and the
        following message is displayed :

                mt lu X: Write must be a multiple of 512 bytes in QIC 120 or QIC
                150

AUTHOR
        fbackup was developed by HP.

FILES
        /var/adm/fbackupfiles/dates   database of past backups

SEE ALSO
        cpio(1), ftio(1), tcio(1), dump(1M), frecover(1M), ftio(1M),
        restore(1M), rmt(1M), stat(2), acl(5), mt(7).

frecover

frecover - Recover files saved with **fbackup**.

---

frecover(1M)   frecover(1M)

NAME
     frecover - selectively recover files

SYNOPSIS
     /usr/sbin/frecover -r [-hmosvyAFNOX] [-c config] [-f device] [-S skip]
     [-E extarg]

     /usr/sbin/frecover -R path [-f device]

     /usr/sbin/frecover -x [-hmosvyAFNOX] [-c config] [-e path] [-f device]
     [-g graph] [-i path] [-S skip] [-E extarg]

     /usr/sbin/frecover -I path [-vy] [-f device] [-c config]

     /usr/sbin/frecover -V path [-vy] [-f device] [-c config]

DESCRIPTION
     frecover reads media written by the fbackup(1M) command. Its actions
     are controlled by the selected function -r, -R, -x, -V, or -I.

     The function performed by frecover is specified by one of the
     following letters:

     -r   The backup media is read and the contents are loaded
                       into the directories from which they were backed up.
                       This option should only be used to recover a complete
                       backup onto a clear directory or to recover an
                       incremental backup after a full level-zero recovery
                       (see fbackup(1M)). This is the default behavior.

     -x   The files identified by the -i, -e, and -g options (see
                       below) are extracted or not extracted from the backup
                       media. If a file to be extracted matches a directory
                       whose contents have been written to the backup media,
                       and the -h option is not specified, the directory is
                       recursively extracted. The owner, modification time,
                       and access control list (including optional entries,
                       unless the -A option is specified) are recovered. If
                       no file argument is given (including an empty graph
                       file), all files on the backup media are extracted,
                       unless the -h option is specified.

     -I path   The index on the current volume is extracted from the
                       backup media and is written to path.

     -V path   The volume header on the current volume is extracted
                       from the backup media and is written to path. The
                       following fields from the header are extracted in the
                       format label:value with one pair per line.

                            Magic Field   On a valid fbackup

		media it contains the value FBACKUP_LABEL. On a pre-10.20 fbackup media it contains FBACKUP LABEL.
	Machine Identification	This field contains the result of uname -m.
	System Identification	This field contains the result of uname -s.
	Release Identification	This field contains the result of uname -r.
	Node Identification	This field contains the result of uname -n.
	User Identification	This field contains the result of cuserid(3S).
	Record Size	This field contains the maximum length in bytes of a data record.
	Time	This field contains the time fbackup was started.
	Media Use	This field contains the number of times the media has been used for backup.
	Volume Number	This field contains a # character followed by 3 digits, and identifies the current volume in the backup.
	Checkpoint Frequency	This field contains the frequency of backup-data-record checkpointing.
	Fast Search Mark Frequency	This field contains the number of files between fast search marks for backups made with DDS tape drives.
	Index Size	This field contains the size of the index.
	Backup Identification Tag	This field is composed of 2 items: the process ID (pid), and the start time of that process.
	Language	This field contains the language used to make the backup.

-R path   An interrupted full recovery can be continued using this option. frecover uses the information in file path to continue the recovery from where it was interrupted. The only command line option used by frecover with this option is -f. The values in path override all other options to frecover. Note also that

only full recoveries are restarted with this option,
because no history of include or exclude lists is
stored in the restart file. If a partial recovery
(i.e., using the -x option) is interrupted then
restarted with this option, frecover continues
recovering where the partial recovery left off, but
restores all files on the backup media beyond this
point.

The following characters can be used in addition to the letter that
selects the desired function:

-c config   config specifies the name of a configuration file to be
                 used to alter the behavior of frecover. The
                 configuration file allows the user to specify the
                 action to be taken on all errors, the maximum number of
                 attempts at resynchronizing on media errors (-S
                 option), and changing media volumes. Each entry of a
                 configuration file consists of an action identifier
                 followed by a separator followed by the specified
                 action. Valid action identifiers are error, chgvol,
                 and sync. Separators can be either tabs or spaces. In
                 the following sample configuration file, each time an
                 error is encountered, the script
                 /var/adm/fbackupfiles/frecovererror is executed. Each
                 time the backup media is to be changed, the script
                 /var/adm/fbackupfiles/frecoverchgvol is executed. The
                 maximum number of resynchronization attempts is five.

                     error /var/adm/fbackupfiles/frecovererror
                     chgvol /var/adm/fbackupfiles/frecoverchgvol
                     sync 5

-e path   path is interpreted as a graph to be excluded from the
                 recovery. There is no limit on how many times the -e
                 option can be specified.

-f device   device identifies the backup device to be used instead
                 of the default /dev/rmt/0m. If device is -, frecover
                 reads from standard input. Thus fbackup(1M) and
                 frecover can be used in a pipeline to backup and
                 recover a file system as follows:

                 fbackup -i /usr -f - | (cd /mnt; frecover -Xrf -)

                 If more than one output file is specified, frecover
                 uses each one successively and then repeats in a
                 cyclical pattern. Patterns can be used in the device
                 name in a way similar to file name expansion as done by
                 sh(1). The expansion of the pattern results in all
                 matching names being in the list of devices used. A
                 device on the remote machine can be specified in the
                 form machine:device. frecover creates a server
                 process, /usr/sbin/rmt, on the remote machine to access
                 the tape device. If /usr/sbin/rmt does not exist on
                 the remote system, frecover creates a server process
                 from /etc/rmt on the remote machine to access the tape
                 device. The pattern matching capability does not apply
                 to remote devices. Only half-inch 9-track magnetic
                 tapes or DDS-format tapes can be remote devices. The
                 fast search capability is not used when accessing
                 remote DDS-format devices.

-g graph   graph defines a graph file. Graph files are text files
                 and contain the list of file names (graphs) to be

recovered or skipped. Files are recovered using the -i option; thus if the user wants to recover all of /usr, the graph file contains one record:

    i /usr

It is also possible to skip files by using the -e option. For instance, if a user wants to recover all of /usr except for the subgraph /usr/lib, the graph file contains two records:

    i /usr
    e /usr/lib

If the graph file is missing, frecover exits with an error message. An empty graph file results in recovering all files on the media.

-h
    Extract the actual directory, rather than the files that it references. This prevents hierarchical restoration of complete subtrees from the backup media.

-i path
    path is interpreted as a graph to be included in the recovery. There is no limit on how many times the -i option can be specified.

-m
    Print a message each time a file marker is encountered. Using this option, frecover prints a message each time either a DDS setmark, a file marker, or a checkpoint record is read. Although useful primarily for troubleshooting, these messages can also be used to reassure the user that the backup is progressing during long, and otherwise silent, periods during the recovery.

-o
    Recover the file from the backup media irrespective of age. Normally frecover does not overwrite an existing file with an older version of the file.

-s
    Attempt to optimize disk usage by not writing null blocks of data to sparse files.

-v
    Normally frecover works silently. The -v (verbose) option causes it to display the file type and name of each file it treats.

-y
    Automatically answer yes to any inquiries.

-A
    Do not recover any optional entries in access control lists (ACLs). Normally, all access control information, including optional ACL entries, is recovered. This option drops any optional entries and sets the permissions of the recovered file to the permissions of the backed up file. Use this option when recovering files backed up from a system with ACLs on a system for which ACLs are not desired (see acl(5)).

-F
    Recover files without recovering leading directories. For example, this option would be used if a user wants to recover /usr/bin/vi, /usr/bin/sh, and /etc/passwd to a local directory without creating each of the graph structures.

-E extarg
    Specifies the handling of any extent attributes backed

up by fbackup(1M). The -E option takes the following
keywords as arguments:

warn	Issues a warning message if extent attributes cannot be restored, but restore the file anyway.
ignore	Do not restore extent attributes.
force	Issue an error message and do not restore the file if extent attributes cannot be restored.

Extent attributes cannot be restored if the files are
being restored to a file system which does not support
extent attributes or if the file system's block size is
incompatible with the extent attributes. If -E is not
specified, extarg defaults to warn.

-N   (no recovery) Prevent frecover from actually recovering
any files onto disk, but read the backup as if it was,
in fact, recovering the data from the backup, producing
the same output that it would on a normal recovery.
This option is useful for verifying backup media
contents in terms of validity (block checksum errors
are reported), and contents (a listing of files can be
produced by using the -N and -v options together).
Note that the listing of files produced with the -N and
-v options requires the reading of the entire backup,
but is therefore a more accurate reflection of the
backup's contents than the index stored at the
beginning of the backup (which was created at the start
of the backup session, and is not changed during the
course of the backup).

-O   Use the effective uid and gid for the owner and group
of the recovered file instead of the values on the
backup media.

-S skip   frecover does not ask whether it should abort the
recovery if it gets a media error. It tries to skip
the bad block or blocks and continue. Residual or lost
data is written to the file named by skip. The user
can then edit this file and recover otherwise
irretrievable data.

-X   Recover files relative to the current working
directory. Normally frecover recovers files to their
absolute path name.

EXTERNAL INFLUENCES
  Environment Variables
    LC_COLLATE determines the order in which frecover expects files to be
    stored in the backup device and the order in which file names are
    output by the -I option.

    LC_MESSAGES determines the language in which messages are displayed.

    If LC_COLLATE and LC_MESSAGES are not specified in the environment or
    is set to the empty string, the value of LANG is used as a default for
    each unspecified or empty variable. If LANG is not specified or is
    set to the empty string, a default of "C" (see lang(5)) is used
    instead of LANG. If any internationalization variable contains an
    invalid setting, frecover behaves as if all internationalization
    variables are set to "C". See environ(5).

  International Code Set Support
    Single- and multi-byte character code sets are supported.

WARNINGS
    For incremental backups created prior to installing HP-UX Release 8.0,
    or for recoveries that do not begin with the first volume (such as
    when, reading tape 3 first), it is possible for the preceding
    directories to a recoverable file to not be on the media. This can
    happen, for example, if the directories did not change since the last
    full backup. If frecover encounters a file on the backup that should
    be recovered, but it has not recovered the file's parent directories
    from the backup, it prints a message stating that the recovery will
    continue with that file, and attempts to create the file's parent
    directories as needed.

    Use of frecover does not require special privileges. However, if a
    user does not have access permission to a given file, the file is not
    recovered.

    Network special files are obsolete. Therefore, frecover cannot
    restore these files. A warning message is issued if an attempt is
    made to recover a network special file, and the file is skipped.

    When using a DDS tape written with the current release of fbackup to
    do a partial recovery, frecover attempts to use the DDS fast-search
    capability to find files on the tape more quickly. In order to do
    this, however, frecover needs to create an in-memory copy of the
    index, and mark the files on that index which it needs to recover
    before actually reading through the tape to find the files. This is
    done when the first index is read from the tape, and accounts for a
    period of time just after recovery is begun where the tape is inactive
    while this in-memory index is constructed. The larger the index is,
    the longer this period lasts.

    The utility set comprised of fbackup and frecover was originally
    designed for use on systems equipped with not more than one gigabyte
    of total file system storage. Although the utilities have no
    programming limitations that restrict users to this size, complete
    backups and recoveries of substantially larger systems can cause a
    large amount system activity due to the amount of virtual memory (swap
    space) used to store the indices. Users who want to use these
    utilities, but are noticing poor system-wide performance due to the
    size of the backup, are encouraged to back up their systems in
    multiple smaller sessions, rather than attempting to back up the
    entire system at one time.

    Note that when recovering files with access-control lists, the ACL
    entries are stored on the backup as user login names. If a login name
    cannot be found in the password file, the file is recovered without
    its ACL, and an error is printed. In order to fully recover files
    backed up with ACLs, the password file (/etc/passwd) must be recovered
    before attempting to recover any desired ACLs.

    Care should be taken to match the names specified by the include and
    exclude options with the names in the index on the tape. Since the
    files are stored on the backup in lexographic order as defined by the
    LANG or LC_COLLATE environment variable, frecover uses the exact path
    names to determine when a partial recovery is complete, and when an
    earlier tape needs to be loaded. If a user's specification of a file
    to be recovered is misspelled, this may cause confusing messages, such
    as frecover asking for the previous volume, when volume one is
    mounted.

DEPENDENCIES
    SS Series 700/800 frecover is not supported on QIC devices with QIC-
    120, and QIC-150 formats. If frecover is attempted for these formats,
    frecover fails and the following message is displayed :

> mt lu X:Read must be a multiple of 512 bytes in QIC 120 and QIC 150

AUTHOR
    frecover was developed by HP.

FILES
    /dev/rmt/0m   Default backup device.

SEE ALSO
    cpio(1M), dump(1M), fbackup(1M), restore(1M), rmt(1M), tcio(1M), acl(5).

tar

tar - Save and restore archives of files.

```
tar(1)                                                          tar(1)

NAME
     tar - tape file archiver

SYNOPSIS

     tar [-]key [arg ...] [file | -C directory] ...

DESCRIPTION
     The tar command saves and restores archives of files on a magnetic
     tape, a flexible disk, or a regular file.  The default archive file is
     /dev/rmt/0m.  See the -f option below.  Its actions are controlled by
     the key argument.

   Arguments
     key          is a string of characters containing an optional version
                  letter, exactly one function letter, and possibly one or
                  more function modifiers, specified in any order.
                  Whitespace is not permitted in key.  The key string can
                  be preceded by a hyphen (-), as when specifying options
                  in other HP-UX commands, but it is not necessary.

     arg ...      The b and f function modifiers each require an arg
                  argument (see below).  If both b and f are specified,
                  the order of the arg arguments must match the order of
                  the modifiers.  If specified, the arg arguments must be
                  separated from the key and each other by whitespace.

     file         specifies a file being saved or restored.  If file is a
                  directory name, it refers to the files and (recursively)
                  the subdirectories contained in that directory.

     -C directory causes tar to perform a chdir() to directory (see
                  chdir(2)).  Subsequent file and -C directory arguments
                  must be relative to directory.  This allows multiple
                  directories not related by a close or common parent to
                  be archived using short relative path names.

     The value of file is stored in the archive.  The value of directory is
     not stored.

   Version Keys
     The version portion of the key determines the format in which tar
     writes the archive.  tar can read either format regardless of the
     version.  The version is specified by one of the following letters:

          N    Write a POSIX format archive.  This format allows file names
               of up to 256 characters in length, and correctly archives
               and restores the following file types: regular files,
               character and block special devices, links, symbolic links,
               directories, and FIFO special files.  It also stores the
               user and group name of each file and attempts to use these
```

names to determine the user-ID and group-ID of a file when restoring it with the p function modifier. This is the default format.

O   Write a pre-POSIX format archive.

Function Keys
The function portion of the key is specified by exactly one of the following letters:

c   Create a new archive. Write from the beginning of the archive instead of appending after the last file. Any previous information in the archive is overwritten.

r   Add the named file to the end of the archive. The same blocking factor used to create the archive must be used to append to it.

t   List the names of all the files in the archive. Adding the v function modifier expands this listing to include the file modes and owner numbers. The names of all files are listed each time they occur on the tape.

u   Add any named file to the archive if it is not already present or has been modified since it was last written in the archive. The same blocking factor used to create the archive must be used to update it.

x   Extract the named file from the archive and restore it to the system. If a named file matches a directory whose contents were written to the archive, this directory is (recursively) extracted. If a named file on tape does not exist on the system, the file is created as follows:

- The user, group, and other protections are restored from the tape.

- The modification time is restored from the tape unless the m function modifier is specified.

- The file user ID and group ID are normally those of the restoring process.

- The set-user-ID, set-group-ID, and sticky bits are not set automatically. The o and p function modifiers control the restoration of protection; see below for more details.

If the files exist, their modes are not changed, but the set-user-id, set-group-id and sticky bits are cleared. If no file argument is given, the entire content of the archive is extracted. Note that if several files with the same name are on the archive, the last one overwrites all earlier ones.

Function Modifier Keys
The following function modifiers can be used in addition to the function letters listed above (note that some modifiers are incompatible with some functions):

A   Suppress warning messages that tar did not archive a file's access control list. By default, tar writes a warning message for each file with optional ACL entries.

b   Use the next arg argument as the blocking factor for archive records. The default is 20; the maximum is at least 20. However, if the f - modifier is used to specify standard input, the default blocking factor is 1.

           The blocking factor is determined automatically when reading nine-track tapes (key letters x and t). On nine-track tapes, the physical tape record length is the same as the block size. The block size is defined as the logical record size times the blocking factor (number of logical records per block).

           The blocking factor must be specified when reading flexible disks and cartridge tapes if they were written with a blocking factor other than the default.

           If a tar file is read using a blocking factor not equal to the one used when the file was written, an error may occur at the end of the file but there may or may not be an actual error in the read. To prevent this problem, a blocking factor of 1 can be used, although performance may be reduced somewhat.

           tar writes logical records of 512 bytes, independent of how logical records may be defined elsewhere by other programs (such as variable-length records (lines) within an ASCII text file).

e   Fail if the extent attributes are present in the files to be archived. If tar fails for this reason, the partially created destination file is not be removed.

f   Use the next arg argument as the name of the archive instead of the default, /dev/rmt/0m. If the name of the file is -, tar writes to standard output or reads from standard input, whichever is appropriate, and the default blocking factor becomes 1. Thus, tar can be used as the head or tail of a pipeline (see EXAMPLES).

h   Force tar to follow symbolic links as if they were normal files or directories. Normally, tar does not follow symbolic links.

l   Tell tar to complain if it cannot resolve all of the links to the files being saved. If l is not specified, no error messages are printed.

m   Tell tar not to restore the modification time written on the archive. The modification time of the file will be the time of extraction.

o   Suppress writing certain directory information that older versions of tar cannot handle on input. tar normally writes information specifying owners and modes of directories in the archive. Earlier versions of tar, when encountering this information, give error messages of the form:

                name - cannot create

           When o is used for reading, it causes the extracted file to take on the user and group IDs of the user running the program rather than those on the tape. This is the default for the ordinary user and can be overridden, to the extent that system protections allow, by using the p function modifier.

     p   Cause file to be restored to the original modes and
ownerships written on the archive, if possible. This is the
default for the superuser, and can be overridden by the o
function modifier. If system protections prevent the
ordinary user from executing chown(), the error is ignored,
and the ownership is set to that of the restoring process
(see chown(2)). The set-user-id, set-group-id, and sticky
bit information are restored as allowed by the protections
defined by chmod() if the chown() operation above succeeds.

    nd   Specify a particular nine-track tape drive and density,
where n is a tape drive number: 0-7, and d is the density: l
= low (800 bpi); m = medium (1600 bpi); h = high (6250 bpi).
This modifier selects the drive on which the nine-track tape
is mounted. The default is 0m.

     v   Normally, tar does its work silently. The v (verbose)
function modifier causes tar to type the name of each file
it treats, preceded by the function letter. With the t
function, v gives more information about the archive entries
than just the name.

     V   Same as the v function modifier except that, when using the
t option, tar also prints out a letter indicating the type
of the archived file.

     w   Cause tar to print the action being taken, followed by the
name of the file, then wait for the user's confirmation. If
the user answers y, the action is performed. Any other
input means "no".

When end-of-tape is reached, tar prompts the user for a new special
file and continues.

If a nine-track tape drive is used as the output device, it must be
configured in Berkeley-compatibility mode (see mt(7)).

EXTERNAL INFLUENCES
  Environment Variables
    LC_TIME determines the format and contents of date and time strings
    output when listing the contents of an archive with the -v option.

    LANG determines the language equivalent of y (for yes/no queries).

    If LC_TIME is not specified in the environment or is set to the empty
    string, the value of LANG is used as the default.

    If LANG is not specified or is set to the empty string, it defaults to
    "C" (see lang(5)).

    If any internationalization variable contains an invalid setting, tar
    behaves as if all internationalization variables are set to "C". See
    environ(5).

  International Code Set Support
    Single- and multibyte character code sets are supported.

ERRORS
    tar issues self-explanatory messages about bad key characters, tape
    read/write errors, and if not enough memory is available to hold the
    link tables.

EXAMPLES
    Create a new archive on /dev/rfd.0 and copy file1 and file2 onto it,
    using the default blocking factor of 20. The key is made up of one

function letter (c) and two function modifiers (v and f):

        tar cvf /dev/rfd.0 file1 file2

Archive files from /usr/include and /etc:

        tar cv -C /usr/include -C /etc

Use tar in a pipeline to copy the entire file system hierarchy under fromdir to todir:

        cd fromdir ; tar cf - . | (cd todir ; tar xf -i)

Archive all files and directories in directory my_project in the current directory to a file called my_project.TAR, also in the current directory:

        tar -cvf my_project.TAR my_project

WARNINGS
        Because of industry standards and interoperability goals, tar does not support the archival of files larger than 2GB or files that have user/group IDs greater than 60K. Files with user/group IDs greater than 60K are archived and restored under the user/group ID of the current process.

        The default version has changed from O to N, beginning with HP-UX Release 8.0.

        Due to internal limitations in the header structure, not all file names of fewer than 256 characters fit when using the N version key. If a file name does not fit, tar prints a message and does not archive the file.

        Link names are still limited to 100 characters when using the N version key.

        There is no way to ask for the n-th occurrence of a file.

        Tape errors are handled ungracefully.

        The u function key can be slow.

        If the archive is a file on disk, flexible disk, or cartridge tape, and if the blocking factor specified on output is not the default, the same blocking factor must be specified on input, because the blocking factor is not explicitly stored in the archive. Updating or appending to the archive without following this rule can destroy it.

        Some previous versions of tar have claimed to support the selective listing of file names using the t function key with a list. This appears to be an error in the documentation because the capability does not appear in the original source code.

        There is no way to restore an absolute path name to a relative position.

        tar always pads information written to an archive up to the next multiple of the block size. Therefore, if you are creating a small archive and write out one block of information, tar reports that one block was written, but the actual size of the archive might be larger if the b function modifier is used.

        Note that tar c0m is not the same as tar cm0.

        Do not create archives on block special devices. Attempting to do so

can causes excessive wear, leading to premature drive hardware
failure.

DEPENDENCIES
 Series 700/800
 The r and u function keys are not supported on QIC or 8mm devices. If
 these options are used with QIC or 8mm devices, tar fails and displays
 the message:

 tar: option not supported for this device

AUTHOR
 tar was developed by AT&T, the University of California, Berkeley, HP,
 and POSIX.

FILES
 /dev/rmt/*
 /dev/rfd.*
 /tmp/tar*

SEE ALSO
 ar(1), cpio(1), acl(5), mt(7).

STANDARDS CONFORMANCE
 tar: SVID2, SVID3, XPG2, XPG3

vxdump

vxdump - Backup VxFS files specified.

man page

vxdump - 6

NAME
     vxdump, rvxdump (vxfs) - incremental file system dump, local or across
     network

SYNOPSIS
     /usr/sbin/vxdump [-nuwW] [-0123456789] [-f file_name]
         [-d density] [-s size] [-T time] [-b block_size]
         [-B records] filesystem

     /usr/sbin/rvxdump [-nuwW] [-0123456789] [-f file_name]
         [-d density] [-s size] [-T time] [-b block_size]
         [-B records] filesystem

     /usr/sbin/vxdump [option [argument ...] filesystem]

     /usr/sbin/rvxdump [option [argument ...] filesystem]

DESCRIPTION
     vxdump and rvxdump copy to magnetic tape all files in the vxfs
     filesystem that have been changed after a certain date. This
     information is derived from the files /var/adm/dumpdates and
     /etc/fstab.

     vxdump and rvxdump support both getopt(3C) and traditional dump
     command line invocations as shown above. The original dump command
     line style is supported for compatibility with previous versions of
     vxdump and for synonymy with the existing dump program used for hfs
     file systems. For the traditional command line style, option consists
     of characters from the set 0123456789bBdfnsTuWw without any
     intervening white space.

     On most devices vxdump can detect end-of-media and prompt for the
     media to be changed, so it is not necessary to specify the size of the
     device. However, if the dump will require multiple tapes and the
     tapes are to be read using an older version of vxrestore, or if the
     tape device handles end-of-media in a way that vxdump doesn't
     understand, then the size of the device must be specified using either
     the -B option or a combination of the -d and -s options.

     Options
         -number   Where number is in the range [0-9]. This number is the
                   dump level. All files modified since the last date
                   stored in the file /var/adm/dumpdates for the same file
                   system at a lesser dump level will be dumped. Thus,
                   the option -0 causes the entire file system to be
                   dumped. If no date is determined by the level, the
                   beginning of time is assumed.

         -B records
                   The number of logical records per volume. The vxdump
                   logical record size is 1024 bytes. records can also be

specified with a suffix to indicate a unit of measure
other than 1024 bytes. A k, m, or g can be appended to
the number to indicate that the value is in kilobytes,
megabytes, or gigabytes, respectively. This option
overrides the calculation of tape size based on length
and density.

-b block_size

The blocking factor is taken from the block_size option
argument. (default is 63 if -b is not specified).
Block size is defined as the logical record size times
the blocking factor. vxdump writes logical records of
1024 bytes. Older versions of vxdump used a blocking
factor of 10 for tapes with densities less than 6250
BPI, and 32 for tapes with densities of 6250 BPI or
greater. vxrestore will dynamically determine the
blocking factor.

-d density

The density of the tape (expressed in BPI). This is
used in calculating the amount of tape used per tape
reel. If the -s option is specified, a default density
value of 1600 is assumed a for a reel tape.

-f file_name

Place the dump on the file file_name instead of the
tape. If the name of the file is -, vxdump writes to
the standard output. This option can be of the form
machine:device to specify a tape device on a remote
machine.

-n

Whenever vxdump requires operator attention, notify all
users in group operator by means similar to that
described by wall(1).

-s size

size is the size of the dump tape, specified in feet.
When the specified size is reached, vxdump waits for
reels to be changed. If the -d option is specified, a
default size value of 2300 is assumed a for a reel
tape.

-u

If the dump completes successfully, write on file
/var/adm/dumpdates the date when the dump started.
This file records a separate date for each file system
and each dump level. The format of /var/adm/dumpdates
is user-readable and consists of one free-format record
per line: file system name, increment level and dump
date in ctime(3C) format. The file /var/adm/dumpdates
can be edited to change any of the fields if necessary.

-T date

Use the specified date as the starting time for the
dump instead of the time determined from looking in
/var/adm/dumpdates. The format of date is the same as
that of ctime(3C) This option is useful for automated
dump scripts that wish to dump over a specific period
of time. The -T option is mutually exclusive with the
-u option.

-W

For each file system in /var/adm/dumpdates, print the
most recent dump date and level, indicating which file
systems should be dumped. If the -W option is set, all
other options are ignored and vxdump exits immediately.

-w

Operates like W, but prints only file systems that need

to be dumped.

If no arguments are given, the options are assumed to be -9u and a default file system is dumped to the default tape.

Operator Interaction
  vxdump requires operator intervention for any of the following conditions:

- end of tape,
- end of dump,
- tape-write error,
- tape-open error, or
- disk-read error (if errors exceed threshold of 32).

In addition to alerting all operators implied by the -n option, vxdump interacts with the control terminal operator by posing questions requiring yes or no answers when it can no longer proceed or if something is grossly wrong.

Since making a full dump involves considerable time and effort, vxdump establishes a checkpoint at the start of each tape volume. If, for any reason, writing that volume fails, vxdump will, with operator permission, restart from the checkpoint after the old tape has been rewound and removed and a new tape has been mounted.

vxdump periodically reports information to the operator, including estimates (typically low) of the number of blocks to write, the number of tapes it will require, time needed for completion, and the time remaining until tape change. The output is verbose to inform other users that the terminal controlling vxdump is busy and will be for some time.

Compatibility
  The dump tape format is independent of the VxFS disk layout. A dump of a file system with the Version 3 disk layout can be restored on a file system using the Version 2 disk layout or even a file system of another file system type, with the following exceptions:

- Files larger than 2 Gbyte cannot be restored by earlier versions of vxrestore. If a file larger than 2 Gbyte is encountered, vxrestore will skip the file and produce the diagnostic:
        Resync restore, skipped num blocks

- Files larger than 2 Gbyte cannot be restored on a file system that does not support large files (see mount_vxfs(1m)).

- A file with a large uid (user ID of the file owner) or large gid (group ID of the file owner) cannot be restored correctly on a file system that does not support large IDs. Instead, the owner and/or group of the file will be that of the user invoking vxrestore. (A large ID is a value grater than 65535. The VxFS Version 2 disk layout does not support lage IDs).

- Files with VxFS extent attributes (see setext(1m)) cannot be restored on a file system of a type that does not support extent attributes.

If you use vxdump to produce a dump intended for an earlier version of vxrestore, and if the dump requires multiple tapes, you should use the -s, -d, or -B option.

Dumps produced by older versions of vxdump can be read by the current version of vxrestore.

NOTES

Dumps should be performed with the file system unmounted or the system
in single-user environment (see init(1M)) to insure a consistent dump.
If the VxFS Advanced package is installed, the dump can be performed
in the multi-user environment using a snapshot file system with the
online backup facility (see the snapof=file option of mount_vxfs(1M)).

Up to 32 read errors on the file system are ignored.

Each reel requires a new process; thus parent processes for reels
already written remain until the entire tape is written.

vxdump creates a server, /usr/sbin/rmt, on the remote machine to
access the tape device.

EXAMPLES

In the following example, assume that the file system /mnt is normally
attached to the file tree at the root directory, (/).

This example causes the entire file system (/mnt) to be dumped on
/dev/rmt/0m and specifies that the the size of the tape is 2
gigabytes.

        vxdump -0 -B 2g -f /dev/rmt/0m

Or, using the traditional command line syntax and specifying the tape
size in logical records:

        vxdump 0Bf 2097152 /dev/rmt/0m /mnt

where the option argument ``2097152'' goes with the option letter B as
it is the first option letter that requires an option argument, and
where the option argument ``/dev/rmt/0m'' goes with the option letter
f as it is the second option letter that requires an option argument.

AUTHOR

vxdump and rvxdump are based on the dump and rdump programs from the
4.4 Berkeley Software Distribution, developed by the the University of
California, Berkeley, and its contributors.

FILES

/dev/rdsk/c0t0d0	Default file system to dump from.
/dev/rmt/0m	Default tape unit to dump to.
/var/adm/dumpdates	New format-dump-date record.
/etc/fstab	Dump table: file systems and frequency.
/etc/mnttab	Mounted file system table.
/etc/group	Used to find group operator.

SEE ALSO

rmt(1M), vxrestore(1M), fstab(4).

vxrestore

vxrestore - Restore files written by **vxdump** or **rvxdump**.

```
vxrestore(1M)                                                    vxrestore(1M)

NAME
     vxrestore, rvxrestore (vxfs) - restore file system incrementally,
     local or across network

SYNOPSIS
     /usr/sbin/vxrestore [-rRtxihmvy] [-s number]
          [-b block_size] [-e opt] [-f file] [file_name ...]

     /usr/sbin/rvxrestore [-rRtxihmvy] [-s number]
          [-b block_size] [-e opt] [-f file] [file_name ...]

     /usr/sbin/vxrestore key [file_name ...]

     /usr/sbin/rvxrestore key [file_name ...]

DESCRIPTION
     rvxrestore is another name for vxrestore.  vxrestore reads tapes
     previously dumped by the vxdump or rvxdump command (see vxdump(1M)).

     vxrestore and rvxrestore support both getopt(3C) and traditional
     restore command line invocations as shown above.  The original restore
     command line style is supported for compatibility with previous
     versions of vxrestore and for synonymy with the existing restore
     program used for hfs file systems.

     For the original restore command line style, actions taken are
     controlled by the key argument where key is a string of characters
     containing exactly one function letter from the group rRxtsi, and zero
     or more function modifiers from the group befhmvy.  One or more
     file_name arguments, if present, are file or directory names
     specifying the files that are to be restored.  Unless the h modifier
     is specified (see below), the appearance of a directory name refers to
     the files and (recursively) subdirectories of that directory.

     Options
          -r        Read the tape and load into the current directory.  -r
                    should be used only after careful consideration, and only
                    to restore a complete dump tape onto a clear file system or
                    to restore an incremental dump tape after a full-level zero
                    restore.  Thus,

                         /usr/sbin/newfs -F vxfs /dev/rdsk/c0t0d0
                         /usr/sbin/mount -F vxfs /dev/dsk/c0t0d0 /mnt
                         cd /mnt
                         vxrestore -r

                    is a typical sequence to restore a complete dump.  Another
                    vxrestore can then be performed to restore an incremental
                    dump on top of this.  Note that vxrestore leaves a file
                    restoresymtab in the root directory of the file system to
                    pass information between incremental vxrestore passes.
```

This file should be removed when the last incremental tape
has been restored.

-R   Resume a full restore. vxrestore restarts from a
        checkpoint it created during a full restore (see -r above).
        It requests a particular tape of a multi-volume set on
        which to restart a full restore. This provides a means for
        interrupting and restarting a multi-volume vxrestore.

-x   Extract named files from the tape. If the named file
        matches a directory whose contents had been written onto
        the tape, and the -h option is not specified, the directory
        is recursively extracted. The owner, modification time,
        and mode are restored (if possible). If no file_name
        argument is given, the root directory is extracted, which
        results in the entire contents of the tape being extracted,
        unless -h has been specified.

-t   Names of file_names, as specified on the command line, are
        listed if they occur on the tape. If no file_name is
        given, the root directory is listed, which results in the
        entire content of the tape being listed, unless -h has been
        specified.

-snumber
        number is used as the dump file number to recover. This is
        useful if there is more than one dump file on a tape.

-i   This option allows interactive restoration of files from a
        dump tape. After reading in the directory information from
        the tape, vxrestore provides a shell-like interface that
        allows the user to move around the directory tree selecting
        files to be extracted. The available commands are given
        below; for those commands that require an argument, the
        default is the current directory.

                add [arg]   The current directory or specified
                                argument is added to the list of files
                                to be extracted. If a directory is
                                specified, it and all its descendents
                                are added to the extraction list
                                (unless the h key is specified on the
                                command line). File names on the
                                extraction list are displayed with a
                                leading * when listed by ls.

                cd [arg]   Change the current working directory to
                                the specified argument.

                delete [arg]   The current directory or specified
                                argument is deleted from the list of
                                files to be extracted. If a directory
                                is specified, it and all its
                                descendents are deleted from the
                                extraction list (unless h is specified
                                on the command line). The most
                                expedient way to extract most files
                                from a directory is to add the
                                directory to the extraction list, then
                                delete unnecessary files.

                extract   All files named on the extraction list
                                are extracted from the dump tape.
                                vxrestore asks which volume the user
                                wants to mount. The fastest way to
                                extract a few files is to start with

the last volume, then work toward the
first volume.

help	List a summary of the available commands.
ls [arg]	List the current or specified directory. Entries that are directories are displayed with a trailing /. Entries marked for extraction are displayed with a leading *. If the verbose key is set, the inode number of each entry is also listed.
pwd	Print the full pathname of the current working directory.
quit	vxrestore immediately exits, even if the extraction list is not empty.
set-modes	Set the owner, modes, and times of all directories that are added to the extraction list. Nothing is extracted from the tape. This setting is useful for cleaning up after a restore aborts prematurely.
verbose	The sense of the v modifier is toggled. When set, the verbose key causes the ls command to list the inode numbers of all entries. It also causes vxrestore to print out information about each file as it is extracted.

The following options can be used in addition to the letter that
selects the primary function desired:

-b block_size
    Specify the block size of the tape in Kbytes. If the -b
    option is not specified, vxrestore will determine the tape
    block size dynamically. [This option is exists to preserve
    backwards compatibility with previous versions of
    vxrestore.]

-e opt
    Specify how to handle a vxfs file that has extent attribute
    information. Extent attributes include reserved space, a
    fixed extent size, and extent alignment. It may not be
    possible to preserve the information if the destination
    file system does not support extent attributes, has a
    different block size than the source file system, or lack
    free extents appropriate to satisfy the extent attribute
    requirements. Valid values for opt are:

warn	Issue a warning message if extent attribute information cannot be kept (the default).
force	Fail to restore the file if extent attribute information cannot be kept.
ignore	Ignore extent attribute information entirely.

-f file
    Specify the name of the archive instead of /dev/rmt/0m. If
    the name of the file is -, vxrestore reads from standard

input. Thus, vxdump and vxrestore can be used in a
pipeline to vxdump and vxrestore a file system with the
command

     vxdump 0f - /usr | (cd /mnt; vxrestore xf -)

An archive name of the form machine:device can be used to
specify a tape device on a remote machine.

-h   Extract the actual directory, rather than the files to
which it refers. This prevents hierarchical restoration of
complete subtrees.

-m   Extract by inode numbers rather than by file name. This is
useful if only a few files are being extracted and one
wants to avoid regenerating the complete pathname to the
file.

-v   Type the name of each file restored, preceded by its file
type. Normally vxrestore does its work silently; the -v
option specifies verbose output.

-y   Do not ask whether to abort the operation if vxrestore
encounters a tape error. Normally vxrestore asks whether
to continue after encountering a read error. With this
option, vxrestore continues without asking, attempting to
skip over the bad tape block(s) and continue as best it
can.

vxrestore creates a server, /usr/sbin/rmt, on the remote machine to
access the tape device.

DIAGNOSTICS

vxrestore complains if a read error is encountered. If the -y option
has been specified, or the user responds y, vxrestore attempts to
continue the restore.

If the dump extends over more than one tape, vxrestore asks the user
to change tapes. If the -x or -i option has been specified, vxrestore
also asks which volume the user wants to mount. The fastest way to
extract a few files is to start with the last volume and work towards
the first volume.

There are numerous consistency checks that can be listed by vxrestore.
Most checks are self-explanatory or can ``never happen''. Here are
some common errors:

filename: not found on tape
     The specified file name was listed in the tape directory but
not found on the tape. This is caused by tape read errors
while looking for the file, and from using a dump tape
created on an active file system.

expected next file inumber, got inumber
     A file not listed in the directory showed up. This can
occur when using a dump tape created on an active file
system. Dumps should be performed with the file system
unmounted or the system in single-user environment (see
init(1M)) to insure a consistent dump. If the VxFS Advanced
package is installed, the dump can be performed in the
multi-user environment using a snapshot file system with the
online backup facility (see the snapof=file option of
mount_vxfs(1M)).

Incremental tape too low

When doing an incremental restore, a tape that was written
before the previous incremental tape, or that has too low an
incremental level has been loaded.

Incremental tape too high
When doing an incremental restore, a tape that does not
begin its coverage where the previous incremental tape left
off, or that has too high an incremental level has been
loaded.

Tape read error while restoring filename

Tape read error while skipping over inode inumber

Tape read error while trying to resynchronize
A tape-read error has occurred. If a file name is
specified, the contents of the restored files are probably
partially wrong. If vxrestore is skipping an inode or is
trying to resynchronize the tape, no extracted files are
corrupted, although files may not be found on the tape.

Resync restore, skipped num blocks
After a tape-read error, vxrestore may have to resynchronize
itself. This message indicates the number of blocks skipped
over. This message will also be generated by older versions
of vxrestore while skipping over files larger than 2 Gbyte
dumped by a more recent version of vxdump.

NOTES
If the dump tape contains files larger than 2 Gbyte, and if the file
system being restored to does not support files larger than 2 Gbyte,
the file will not be restored correctly. Instead it will be truncated
to 2 Gbyte.

A file with a large uid (user ID of the file owner) or large gid
(group ID of the file owner) cannot be restored correctly on a file
system that does not support large IDs. Instead, the owner and/or
group of the file will be that of the user invoking vxrestore. (A
large ID is a value grater than 65535. The VxFS Version 2 disk layout
does not support lage IDs).

Dumps produced by older versions of vxdump can be read by the current
version of vxrestore.

vxrestore can restore files to a file system of a type other than
VxFS. If the file system type does not support extent attributes,
than the extent attributes will not be restored (see the -e option).

WARNINGS
vxrestore can get confused when doing incremental restores from dump
tapes that were made on active file systems.

A level-zero dump (see the vxdump(1M) manual page) must be done after
a full restore. Since vxrestore runs in user code, it has no control
over inode allocation; thus a full dump must be done to get a new set
of directories reflecting the new inode numbering, even though the
contents of the files are unchanged.

AUTHOR
vxrestore and rvxrestore are based on the restore program distributed
in the 4.4 Berkeley Software Distribution, developed by the the
University of California, Berkeley, and its contributors.

FILES
/dev/rmt/0m   default tape drive

```
/tmp/rstdr*            file containing directories on the tape

/tmp/rstmd*            owner, mode, and time stamps for directories

./restoresymtab        information passed between incremental restores
```

SEE ALSO
    vxdump(1M), extendfs_vxfs(1M), fsadm_vxfs(1M), mkfs(1M), mount(1M),
    newfs(1M), rmt(1M).

CHAPTER 7

System Startup and Shutdown Scripts

Introduction

A variety of topics related to startup and shutdown scripts are covered in this chapter, including:

- The overall organization of the startup and shutdown mechanism in HP-UX
- Example of a startup file
- **/etc/inittab** file
- **shutdown** command

System Startup and Shutdown Scripts

Startup and shutdown scripts for HP-UX 11.x are based on a mechanism that separates the actual startup and shutdown scripts from configuration information. In order to modify the way your system starts or stops, you don't have to modify scripts, which in general is considered somewhat risky; you can instead modify configuration variables. The startup and shutdown sequence is based on an industry standard that is similar to many other UNIX-based systems, so your knowledge of HP-UX applies to many other systems.

Startup and shutdown are going to become increasingly more important to you as your system administration work becomes more sophisticated. As you load and customize more applications, you will need more startup and shutdown knowledge. What I do in this section is give you an overview of startup and shutdown and the commands you can use to control your system.

The following three components are in the startup and shutdown model:

Execution Scripts

> Execution scripts read variables from configuration variable files and run through the startup or shutdown sequence. These scripts are located in **/sbin/init.d**.

Configuration Variable Scripts

> These are the files you would modify to set variables that are used to enable or disable a subsystem or perform some other function at the time of system startup or shutdown. These are located in **/etc/rc.config.d**.

Link Files

> These files are used to control the order in which scripts execute. These are actually links to execution scripts to be executed when moving from one run level to another. These files are located in the directory for the appropriate run level, such as **/sbin/rc0.d**

for run level 0, **/sbin/rc1.d** for run level 1, and so on.

Sequencer Script

This script invokes execution scripts based on run-level transition. This script is located in **/sbin/rc**.

Figure 7-1 shows the directory structure for startup and shutdown scripts.

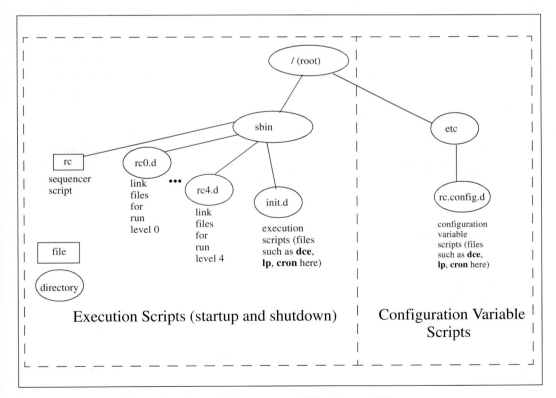

Figure 7-1 Organization of Startup and Shutdown Files

Execution scripts perform startup and shutdown tasks. **/sbin/rc** invokes the execution script with the appropriate start or stop arguments, and you can view the appropriate start or stop messages on the console. The messages you see will have one of the three following values:

OK	This indicates that the execution script started or shut down properly.
FAIL	A problem occurred at startup or shutdown.
N/A	The script was not configured to start.

In order to start up a subsystem, you would simply edit the appropriate configuration file in **/etc/rc.config.d**.

Let's take a look at an example startup and shutdown file for an application loaded onto an HP-UX system that is widely used for Internet applications called Cold Fusion. Like many applications loaded on HP-UX systems, Cold Fusion installs startup and shutdown scripts as a standard part of the installation of the product.

As mentioned earlier, the script used as part of the startup and shutdown process is in **/etc/init.d**. In our case, the name of the program is **/etc/init.d/coldfusion** and is shown in the following listing:

```
# cat /sbin/init.d/coldfusion
#!/bin/sh
#
# Start the Cold Fusion servers
#

# set at install
CFHOME=/apps/coldfusion
CFBIN=$CFHOME/bin

export CFHOME

#
# Start/stop processes for Cold Fusion
#

rval=0

case "$1" in
```

```
    start_msg)
        print "Starting ColdFusion Application Server"
        ;;

    stop_msg)
        print "Stopping ColdFusion Application Server"
        ;;

    'start')
        #First, check "on/off switch", to set CF_AUTOSTART, in config.d file.
        RCFILE=/etc/rc.config.d/coldfusion
        if [ -f $RCFILE ] ; then
                . $RCFILE
        else
                print "Warning: $RCFILE defaults file missing."
                print "         Starting ColdFusion by default."
                CF_AUTOSTART=1
        fi

        # Start CF if switch is on.
        if [ "$CF_AUTOSTART" -eq 1 ]; then
                if [ -x $CFBIN/start ]; then
                    $CFBIN/start
                    rval=$?
                else
                    print "Error: ColdFusion startup script $CFBIN/start missing."
                    print "       ColdFusion not started."
                    rval=1
                fi
        else
                print "Notice: ColdFusion startup disabled in $RCFILE"
                rval=2
        fi
        ;;

    'stop')
        if [ -x $CFBIN/stop ]; then
                $CFBIN/stop -force
        fi
        ;;

    *)
        echo "Usage: $0 { start | stop }"
        rval=1
        ;;
esac

exit $rval

#
```

The startup and shutdown scripts in **/etc/init.d** generally perform both startup and shutdown functions. The startup and shutdown scripts, including the one in our example, recognize the following four arguments:

- *start_msg* - This is an argument passed to scripts so the script can report a message indicating what the "start" action will do.

- *stop_msg* - This is an argument passed to scripts so the script can report a message indicating what the "stop" action will do.

- *start* - The script will start the application.

- *stop* - The script will shut down the application.

All startup and shutdown scripts, including the one in the previous listing, obtain configuration data from variables in **/etc/rc.config.d**. Our example script checks the value of the "on/off" switch in **/etc/rc.confi.d/coldfusion**, which is shown in the following listing to determine if Cold Fusion should be started:

```
# cat /etc/rc.config.d/coldfusion
# ColdFusion Application Server configuration file
#
CF_AUTOSTART=1  #Set to 1 to restart at boot time

#
```

The variable in this file is set to *one,* so the application will start at the time of system boot.

Startup and shutdown scripts are run based on the directory in which a link to the script appears. Our example script should be started at run level *three*. Therefore, a link to the script appears in the directory **/sbin/rc3.d**, shown as the third link in the following listing:

```
# ls -l /sbin/rc3.d
total 0
lrwxr-xr-x  1 root     sys    23 Apr 26 14:32 S100nfs.server -> /sbin/init.d/nfs.server
lrwxr-xr-x  1 root     sys    19 Apr 26 14:52 S200tps.rc -> /sbin/init.d/tps.rc
lrwxrwxrwx  1 root     sys    20 May 16 20:57 S790coldfusion -> ../init.d/coldfusion
lrwxr-xr-x  1 root     sys    23 Apr 26 14:44 S990dtlogin.rc -> /sbin/init.d/dtlogin.rc
#
```

We'll get to the significance of the naming of the link shortly. For the time being, it is sufficient to know that a link called **/sbin/rc3.d/S790coldfusion** points to our script **/init.d/coldfusion**.

Applications are shut down in the opposite order from which they were started. This means that a link to the startup and shutdown script will appear in a lower level directory for shutdown. In our example, the startup link appears in **/sbin/rc3.d** but the shutdown link appears in **/etc/rc1.d** as shown in the following listing:

```
# ls -l /sbin/rc1.d

lrwxr-xr-x   1 root       sys           17 Apr 26 14:52 K220slsd -> /sbin/init.d/slsd
lrwxr-xr-x   1 root       sys           18 Apr 26 14:45 K230audio -> /sbin/init.d/audio
lrwxr-xr-x   1 root       sys        21 Apr 26 14:46 K240auditing -> /sbin/init.d/auditing
lrwxr-xr-x   1 root       sys           17 Apr 26 14:43 K250envd -> /sbin/init.d/envd
lrwxr-xr-x   1 root       sys           17 Apr 26 14:43 K270cron -> /sbin/init.d/cron
lrwxr-xr-x   1 root       sys           15 Apr 26 14:45 K278pd -> /sbin/init.d/pd
lrwxr-xr-x   1 root       sys           15 Apr 26 14:45 K280lp -> /sbin/init.d/lp
lrwxr-xr-x   1 root       sys        21 Apr 26 14:49 K290hparamgr -> /sbin/init.d/hparamgr
lrwxr-xr-x   1 root       sys        20 Apr 26 14:43 K290hparray -> /sbin/init.d/hparray
lrwxrwxrwx   1 root       sys        20 May 16 20:57 K300coldfusion -> ../init.d/coldfusion
                  .
                  .
                  .
```

The link called **/sbin/rc3.d/K300coldfusion** points to our script **/init.d/coldfusion**. Startup for this application takes place at run level 3 and shutdown takes place at run level 1.

There is significance associated with the names of the links shown in the previous two listings. Let's take a look at the startup link in our example:

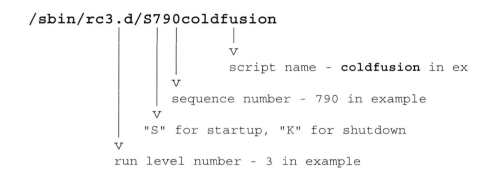

```
/sbin/rc3.d/S790coldfusion
    |      |  |        |
    |      |  |        v
    |      |  |      script name - coldfusion in ex
    |      |  v
    |      | sequence number - 790 in example
    |      v
    |    "S" for startup, "K" for shutdown
    v
  run level number - 3 in example
```

This example is for our Cold Fusion startup script. Startup links begin with an "S" for startup. The shutdown script has a similar entry in **/sbin/rc1.d**, it but has a "K" as the first character of the link name to indicate kill.

Scripts are executed in lexicographical order. Gaps are left between startup scripts at a given run level and between shutdown scripts at a given run level, so when additional scripts are added, you don't have to renumber any existing scripts within a run level.

Because applications are shut down in the opposite order in which they are started, shutdown scripts do not usually have the same numbers as their startup counterparts. Two applications that start in a given order due to dependencies will usually be shut down in the opposite order in which they were started. In our example, the startup number is *S790coldfusion* and the shutdown number is *K300coldfusion*.

man page

inittab - 7

Scripts are run when there is a change in run level. **/sbin/rc** is a program that is run whenever there is a change in run level. The following listing shows **/etc/inittab**, which which invokes **/sbin/rc** on the system used in our example:

```
init:3:initdefault:
ioin::sysinit:/sbin/ioinitrc >/dev/console 2>&1
tape::sysinit:/sbin/mtinit > /dev/console 2>&1
muxi::sysinit:/sbin/dasetup   </dev/console >/dev/console 2>&1 # mux init
stty::sysinit:/sbin/stty 9600 clocal icanon echo opost onlcr ixon icrnl ignpar </dev/
systty
brc1::bootwait:/sbin/bcheckrc </dev/console >/dev/console 2>&1 # fsck, etc.
link::wait:/sbin/sh -c "/sbin/rm -f /dev/syscon; \
                /sbin/ln /dev/systty /dev/syscon" >/dev/console 2>&1
cprt::bootwait:/sbin/cat /etc/copyright >/dev/syscon        # legal req
sqnc::wait:/sbin/rc </dev/console >/dev/console 2>&1        # system init
#powf::powerwait:/sbin/powerfail >/dev/console 2>&1         # powerfail
cons:123456:respawn:/usr/sbin/getty console console         # system console
#ttp1:234:respawn:/usr/sbin/getty -h tty0p1 9600
#ttp2:234:respawn:/usr/sbin/getty -h tty0p2 9600
#ttp3:234:respawn:/usr/sbin/getty -h tty0p3 9600
#ttp4:234:respawn:/usr/sbin/getty -h tty0p4 9600
#ttp5:234:respawn:/usr/sbin/getty -h tty0p5 9600
#ups::respawn:rtprio 0 /usr/lbin/ups_mond -f /etc/ups_conf
```

man page

inittab - 7

The **/sbin/rc** line is always present in the **/etc/inittab** file. There is more information about **/etc/inittab** coming shortly.

If you are booting your system to run level 3, then **/sbin/rc** will run the startup scripts present in **/sbin/rc1.d**, **/sbin/rc2.d**, and **/sbin/rc3.d**.

I have mentioned run levels several times in this discussion. Both the startup and shutdown scripts described here, as well as the **/etc/inittab** file, depend on run levels. In HP-UX 11.x, the following run levels exist:

0	Halted run level.
s	Run level s, also known as single-user mode, is used to ensure that no one else is on the system so you can proceed with system administration tasks.
1	Run level 1 starts various basic processes.
2	Run level 2 allows users to access the system. This is also known as multi-user mode.
3	Run level 3 is for exporting NFS file systems.

4	Run level 4 starts the graphical manager, including HP Common Desktop Environment (HP CDE).
5 and 6	Not currently used.

man page

inittab - 7

/etc/inittab is also used to define a variety of processes that will be run, and is it used by **/sbin/init**. The **/sbin/init** process ID is 1. It is the first process started on your system and it has no parent. The **init** process looks at **/etc/inittab** to determine the run level of the system.

Entries in the **/etc/inittab** file have the following format:

id:run state:action:process

id	The name of the entry. The id is up to four characters long and must be unique in the file. If the line in **/etc/inittab** is preceded by a "#", the entry is treated as a comment.
run state	Specifies the run level at which the command is executed. More than one run level can be specified. The command is executed for every run level specified.
action	Defines which of 11 actions will be taken with this process. The 11 choices for action are: *initdefault, sysinit, boot, bootwait, wait, respawn, once, powerfail, powerwait, ondemand,* and *off.*
process	The shell command to be executed *if* the run level and/or action field so indicates.

Here is an example of an **/etc/inittab** entry:

cons:123456:respawn:/usr/sbin/getty   console console

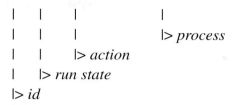

man page

inittab - 7

This is in the **/etc/inittab** file, as opposed to being defined as a startup script, because the console may be killed and have to be restarted whenever it dies, even if no change has occurred in run level. **respawn** starts a process if it does not exist and restarts the process after it dies. This entry shows all run states, since you want the console to be activated at all times.

Another example is the first line from **/etc/inittab**:

```
init:3:initdefault:
```

The default run level of the system is defined as *3*.

The basics of system startup and shutdown described here are important to understand. You will be starting up and shutting down your system and possibly even modifying some of the files described here. Please take a close look at the startup and shutdown files before you begin to modify them.

Now let's take a look at the commands you can issue to shut down your system.

System Shutdown

man page

shutdown-7

What does it mean to shut down the system? Well, in its simplest form, a shutdown of the system simply means issuing the **/sbin/shutdown** command. The **shutdown** command is used to terminate all processing. It has many options, including the following:

-r	Automatically reboots the system; that is, brings it down and brings it up.
-h	Halts the system completely.
-y	Completes the shutdown without asking you any questions it would normally ask.
grace	Specifies the number of seconds you wish to wait before the system is shut down, in order to give your users time to save files, quit applications, and log out.

Here are some of the things your system does when you issue the **shutdown** command:

- Checks to see whether the user who executed **shutdown** does indeed have permission to execute the command.
- Changes the working directory to root (/).
- Sets *PATH* to **/usr/bin/:/usr/sbin:/sbin**.
- Updates all superblocks.
- Informs users that a **shutdown** has been issued and asks them to log out.
- Executes **/sbin/rc,** which does such things as shut down subsystems via shutdown scripts such as the spooler and CDE, unmount file systems and other such tasks.
- Runs **/sbin/reboot** if the *-r* option is used.

To shut down and automatically reboot the system, you would type:

```
$ shutdown -r
```

To halt the system, you would type:

```
$ shutdown -h
```

You will be asked whether you want to type a message to users, informing them of the impending system shutdown. After you type the message, it is immediately sent to all users. After the specified time elapses (60 seconds is the default), the system begins the shutdown process. Once you receive a message that the system is halted, you can power off all your system components.

To shut down the system in two minutes without being asked any questions or sending any message, type:

```
$ shutdown -h -y 120
```

man page

shutdown-7

At times, you will need to go into single-user mode with **shutdown** to perform some task such as a backup or to expand a logical volume, and then reboot the system to return it to its original state.

To shut down the system into single-user mode, you would type:

```
$ shutdown
```

The **shutdown** command with no options puts you into single-user mode. On older versions of the operating system, you could go to single-user mode by using the **init** command with the *s* option (**init s**). However, this is highly discouraged because this command does not terminate other system activity nor does it log users off; therefore, it does not result in a true single-user state.

If the system is already in single-user mode or you like to live dangerously, you can execute **/usr/sbin/reboot**. I strongly suggest that you issue **shutdown,** which will call **reboot**. The **reboot** command abruptly terminates all processes and then halts or reboots the system. Also, with dynamically loadable kernel modules, **reboot** will not load these modules; only **shutdown** will.

Again, I recommend using the **shutdown** command, not **reboot**.

Manual Pages for Commands Used in Chapter 7

The following section contains copies of the manual pages for commands used in Chapter 7. This makes a quick reference for you to use when issuing the commands commonly used during your system administration day.

inittab

man page

inittab - 7

inittab - File that supplies scripts to init.

inittab(4)   inittab(4)

NAME
     inittab - script for the boot init process

DESCRIPTION

     The /etc/inittab file supplies the script to the boot init daemon in
     its role as a general process dispatcher (see init(1M)). The process
     that constitutes the majority of boot init's process dispatching
     activities is the line process /usr/sbin/getty that initiates
     individual terminal lines. Other processes typically dispatched by
     boot init are daemons and shells.

     The inittab file is composed of entries that are position-dependent
     and have the following format:

          id:rstate:action:process

     Each entry is delimited by a newline; however, a backslash (\)
     preceding a newline indicates a continuation of the entry. Up to 1024
     characters per entry are permitted. Comments can be inserted in the
     process field by starting a "word" with a # (see sh(1)). Comments for
     lines that spawn gettys are displayed by the who command (see who(1)).
     It is expected that they will contain some information about the line
     such as the location. There are no limits (other than maximum entry
     size) imposed on the number of entries within the inittab file.

     The entry fields are:

          id   A one- to four-character value used to uniquely
                    identify an entry. Duplicate entries cause an error
                    message to be issued, but are otherwise ignored. The
                    use of a four-character value to identify an entry is
                    strongly recommended (see WARNINGS below).

          rstate   Defines the run level in which this entry is to be
                    processed. Run levels correspond to a configuration of
                    processes in the system where each process spawned by
                    boot init is assigned one or more run levels in which
                    it is allowed to exist. Run levels are represented by
                    a number in the range 0 through 6. For example, if the
                    system is in run level 1, only those entries having a 1
                    in their rstate field are processed.

                    When boot init is requested to change run levels, all
                    processes that do not have an entry in the rstate field
                    for the target run level are sent the warning signal
                    (SIGTERM) and allowed a 20-second grace period before
                    being forcibly terminated by a kill signal (SIGKILL).
                    You can specify multiple run levels for a process by
                    entering more than one run level value in any
                    combination. If no run level is specified, the process
                    is assumed to be valid for all run levels, 0 through 6.

Three other values, a, b and c, can also appear in the
rstate field, even though they are not true run levels.
Entries having these characters in the rstate field are
processed only when a user init process requests them
to be run (regardless of the current system run level).
They differ from run levels in that boot init can never
enter "run level" a, b, or c. Also, a request for the
execution of any of these processes does not change the
current numeric run level.

Furthermore, a process started by an a, b, or c option
is not killed when boot init changes levels. A process
is killed only if its line in inittab is marked off in
the action field, its line is deleted entirely from
inittab, or boot init goes into the single-user state.

action   A keyword in this field tells boot init how to treat
the process specified in the process field. The
following actions can be specified:

boot   Process the entry only at boot init's
                  boot-time read of the inittab file.
                  Boot init starts the process, does
                  not wait for its termination, and
                  when it dies, does not restart the
                  process. In order for this
                  instruction to be meaningful, the
                  rstate should be the default or it
                  must match boot init's run level at
                  boot time. This action is useful for
                  an initialization function following
                  a hardware boot of the system.

bootwait   Process the entry only at boot init's
                  boot-time read of the inittab file.
                  Boot init starts the process, waits
                  for its termination, and, when it
                  dies, does not restart the process.

initdefault   An entry with this action is only
                  scanned when boot init is initially
                  invoked. Boot init uses this entry,
                  if it exists, to determine which run
                  level to enter initially. It does
                  this by taking the highest run level
                  specified in the rstate field and
                  using that as its initial state. If
                  the rstate field is empty, boot init
                  enters run level 6.

                  The initdefault entry cannot specify
                  that boot init start in the single-
                  user state. Additionally, if boot
                  init does not find an initdefault
                  entry in inittab, it requests an
                  initial run level from the user at
                  boot time.

off   If the process associated with this
                  entry is currently running, send the
                  warning signal (SIGTERM) and wait 20
                  seconds before forcibly terminating
                  the process via the kill signal

		(SIGKILL). If the process is nonexistent, ignore the entry.
	once	When boot init enters a run level that matches the entry's rstate, start the process and do not wait for its termination. When it dies, do not restart the process. If boot init enters a new run level but the process is still running from a previous run level change, the process is not restarted.
	ondemand	This instruction is really a synonym for the respawn action. It is functionally identical to respawn but is given a different keyword in order to divorce its association with run levels. This is used only with the a, b, or c values described in the rstate field.
	powerfail	Execute the process associated with this entry only when boot init receives a power-fail signal (SIGPWR see signal(5)).
	powerwait	Execute the process associated with this entry only when boot init receives a power-fail signal (SIGPWR) and wait until it terminates before continuing any processing of inittab.
	respawn	If the process does not exist, start the process; do not wait for its termination (continue scanning the inittab file). When it dies, restart the process. If the process currently exists, do nothing and continue scanning the inittab file.
	sysinit	Entries of this type are executed before boot init tries to access the console. It is expected that this entry will be only used to initialize devices on which boot init might attempt to obtain run level information. These entries are executed and waited for before continuing.
	wait	When boot init enters the run level that matches the entry's rstate, start the process and wait for its termination. Any subsequent reads of the inittab file while boot init is in the same run level cause boot init to ignore this entry.
process		This is a sh command to be executed. The entire process field is prefixed with exec and passed to a forked sh as "sh -c 'exec command'". For this reason, any sh syntax that can legally follow exec can appear

in the process field. Comments can be inserted by using the ; #comment syntax.

WARNINGS
    The use of a four-character id is strongly recommended. Many pty servers use the last two characters of the pty name as an id. If an id chosen by a pty server collides with one used in the inittab file, the /etc/utmp file can become corrupted. A corrupt /etc/utmp file can cause commands such as who to report inaccurate information.

FILES
    /etc/inittab   File of processes dispatched by boot init.

SEE ALSO
    sh(1), getty(1M), exec(2), open(2), signal(5).

shutdown

man page

shutdown-7

shutdown - Terminate all running processes in an orderly fashion.

---

shutdown(1M)   shutdown(1M)

NAME
     shutdown - terminate all processing

SYNOPSIS

     /sbin/shutdown [-h|-r] [-y] [-o] [grace]

DESCRIPTION
     The shutdown command is part of the HP-UX system operation procedures.
     Its primary function is to terminate all currently running processes
     in an orderly and cautious manner. shutdown can be used to put the
     system in single-user mode for administrative purposes such as backup
     or file system consistency checks (see fsck(1M)), and to halt or
     reboot the system. By default, shutdown is an interactive program.

     Options and Arguments
     shutdown recognizes the following options and arguments.

          -h   Shut down the system and halt.

          -r   Shut down the system and reboot automatically.

          -y   Do not require any interactive responses from the user.
                    (Respond yes or no as appropriate to all questions,
                    such that the user does not interact with the shutdown
                    process.)

          -o   When executed on the cluster server in a diskless
                    cluster environment, shutdown the server only and do
                    not reboot clients. If this argument is not entered the
                    default behavior is to reboot all clients when the
                    server is shutdown.

          grace   Either a decimal integer that specifies the duration in
                    seconds of a grace period for users to log off before
                    the system shuts down, or the word now. The default is
                    60. If grace is either 0 or now, shutdown runs more
                    quickly, giving users very little time to log out.

     If neither -r (reboot) nor -h (halt) is specified, standalone and
     server systems are placed in single-user state. Either -r
     (reboot) or -h (halt) must be specified for a client; shutdown to
     single-user state is not allowed for a client. See dcnodes(1M),
     init(1M).

     Shutdown Procedure
     shutdown goes through the following steps:

          -    The PATH environment variable is reset to
               /usr/bin:/usr/sbin:/sbin.

          -    The IFS environment variable is reset to space, tab, newline.

- The user is checked for authorization to execute the shutdown
  command. Only authorized users can execute the shutdown
  command. See FILES for more information on the
  /etc/shutdown.allow authorization file.

- The current working directory is changed to the root directory
  (/).

- All file systems' super blocks are updated; see sync(1M).
  This must be done before rebooting the system to ensure file
  system integrity.

- The real user ID is set to that of the superuser.

- A broadcast message is sent to all users currently logged in
  on the system telling them to log out. The administrator can
  specify a message at this time; otherwise, a standard warning
  message is displayed.

- The next step depends on whether a system is standalone, a
  server, or a client.

  - If the system is standalone, /sbin/rc is executed to shut
    down subsystems, unmount file systems, and perform other
    tasks to bring the system to run level 0.

  - If the system is a server, the optional -o argument is used
    to determine if all clients in the cluster should also be
    rebooted. The default behavior (command line parameter -o
    is not entered) is to reboot all clients using
    /sbin/reboot; entering -o results in the server only being
    rebooted and the clients being left alone. Then /sbin/rc
    is executed to shut down subsystems, unmount file systems,
    and perform other tasks to bring the system to run level 0.

  - If the system is a client, /sbin/rc is executed to bring
    the system down to run-level 2, and then /sbin/reboot is
    executed. Shutdown to the single-user state is not an
    allowed option for clients.

- The system is rebooted or halted by executing /sbin/reboot if
  the -h or -r option was chosen. If the system was not a
  cluster client and the system was being brought down to
  single-user state, a signal is sent to the init process to
  change states (see init(1M)).

DIAGNOSTICS

device busy

This is the most commonly encountered error diagnostic, and
happens when a particular file system could not be unmounted; see
mount(1M).

user not allowed to shut down this system

User is not authorized to shut down the system. User and system
must both be included in the authorization file
/etc/shutdown.allow.

EXAMPLES
Immediately reboot the system and run HP-UX again:

```
shutdown -r 0
```

Halt the system in 5 minutes (300 seconds) with no interactive
questions and answers:

```
shutdown -h -y 300
```

Go to run-level s in 10 minutes:

```
shutdown 600
```

FILES

/etc/shutdown.allow

Authorization file.

The file contains lines that consist of a system host name
and the login name of a user who is authorized to reboot or
halt the system. A superuser's login name must be included
in this file in order to execute shutdown. However, if the
file is missing or of zero length, the root user can run the
shutdown program to bring the system down.

This file does not affect authorization to bring the system
down to single-user state for maintenance purposes; that
operation is permitted only when invoked by a superuser.

A comment character, #, at the beginning of a line causes
the rest of the line to be ignored (comments cannot span
multiple lines without additional comment characters).
Blank lines are also ignored.

The wildcard character + can be used in place of a host name
or a user name to specify all hosts or all users,
respectively (see hosts.equiv(4)).

For example:

```
# user1 can shut down systemA and systemB
systemA user1
systemB user1
# root can shut down any system
+ root
# Any user can shut down systemC
systemC  +
```

WARNINGS

The user name compared with the entry in the shutdown.allow file is
obtained using getlogin() or, if that fails, using getpwuid() (see
getlogin(3) and getpwuid(3)).

The hostname in /etc/shutdown.allow is compared with the hostname
obtained using gethostbyname() (see gethostbyname(3)).

shutdown must be executed from a directory on the root volume, such as
the / directory.

The maximum broadcast message that can be sent is approximately 970
characters.

When executing shutdown on an NFS diskless cluster server and the -o
option is not entered, clients of the server will be rebooted. No
clients should be individually rebooted or shutdown while the cluster
is being shutdown.

SEE ALSO
        dcnodes(1M), fsck(1M), init(1M), killall(1M), mount(1M), reboot(1M),
        sync(1M), dcnodes(3), gethostbyname(3), getpwuid(3), hosts.equiv(4).

CHAPTER 8

Logical Volume Manager and Veritas Volume Manager

Introduction

If you haven't worked with the HP-UX filesystem, then you'll immediately want to jump ahead to Chapter 15, which covers the three following topics in detail:

- UNIX File Types - This section describes the different types of files in HP-UX and using the **file** command to determine the file type.

man page

file - 15

- Filesystem Layout - This section discusses the layout of the filesystem, including important directories and their contents.

man page

ls - 15

- The **ls** command.

In this chapter we'll focus on the following:

- Veritas Volume Manager overview

- Logical Volume Manager (LVM) - You will probably be using LVM to manange the data on your system. I provide LVM background in this section.

- Example of adding XP 256 disks to your system using LVM.

- Example of Using LVM to Reconfigure Disks - I include an example of a complex disk reconfiguration performed on a real system to show how many LVM commands are used. Although this disk reconfiguration may not be required on your system(s), it is a good example of using LVM commands.

- Some Additional File System Commands.

Veritas Volume Manager

New to HP-UX 11i is the Veritas Volume Manager, which is bundled with the operating system.

Unlike Logical Volume Manager, most of the work you perform with Vertias Volume Manager is performed through the Java-based graphical interface. The examples in this section all use the graphical interface to introduce you to Veritas Volume Manager.

Logical Volume Manager Background

Logical Volume Manager is a disk management subsystem that allows you to manage physical disks as logical volumes. This means that a file system can span multiple physical disks. You can view Logical Volume Manager as a flexible way of defining boundaries of disk space that are independent of one another. Not only can you specify the size of a logical volume, but you can also change its size if the need arises. This possibility is a great advancement over dedicating a disk to a filesystem or having fixed-size partitions on a disk. Logical volumes can hold filesystems, raw data, or swap space. You can now specify a logical volume to be any size you wish, have logical volumes that span multiple physical disks, and then change the size of the logical volume if you need to do so!

So what do you need to know in order to set up Logical Volume Manager and realize all these great benefits? First, you need to know the terminology, and second, you need to know Logical Volume Manager commands. As with many other system administration tasks, you can use SAM to set up Logical Volume Manager for you. In fact, I recommend that you use SAM to set up Logical Volume Manager on your system(s). But, as usual, I recommend that you read this overview and at least understand the basics of Logical Volume Manager before you use SAM to set up Logical Volume Manager on your system. The SAM chapter (Chapter 3) has an example of using SAM to create logical volumes. After reading this section, you may want to take a quick look at that example.

For use with the Journaled Filesystem (JFS), Hewlett-Packard has an add-on product called HP OnLineJFS. This handy product allows you to perform many of the LVM functions without going into single-user mode. For example, when a filesystem needs to be expanded, the logical volume on which it resides needs to be unmounted before the expansion takes place. Normally, that unmounting would mean shutting the system down into single-user mode so that no user or process could access the volume and it could then be unmounted. With OnLineJFS, the logical volumes and file systems are simply expanded with the system up and running and no interruption to users or processes.

Logical Volume Manager Terms

The following terms are used when working with Logical Volume Manager. They are only some of the terminology associated with Logical Volume Manager, but they are enough for you to get started with Logical Volume Manager. You can work with Logical Volume Manager without knowing all these terms if you use SAM. It is a good idea, however, to read the following brief overview of these terms if you plan to use Logical Volume Manager, so you have some idea of what SAM is doing for you.

Volume

A volume is a device used for a filesystem, swap, or raw data. Without Logical Volume Manager, a volume would be either a disk partition or an entire disk drive.

Physical Volume

A disk that has been not been initialized for use by Logical Volume Manager. An entire disk must be initialized if it is to be used by Logical Volume Manager; that is, you can't initialize only part of a disk for Logical Volume Manager use and the rest for fixed partitioning.

Volume Group

A volume group is a collection of logical volumes that are managed by Logical Volume Manager. You would typically define which disks on your system are going to be used by Logical Volume Manager and then define how you wish to group these into volume groups. Each individual disk may be a volume group, or more than one disk may form a volume group. At this point, you have created a pool of disk space called a *volume group*. A disk can belong to only one volume group. A volume group may span multiple physical disks.

Logical Volume

This is space that is defined within a volume group. A volume group is divided up into logical volumes. This is like a disk partition, which is of a fixed size, but you have the flexibility to change its size. A logical volume is contained within a volume group, but the volume group may span multiple physical disks. You can have a logical volume that is bigger than a single disk.

Physical Extent   A set of contiguous disk blocks on a physical volume. If you define a disk to be a physical volume, then the contiguous blocks within that disk form a physical extent. Logical Volume Manager uses the physical extent as the unit for allocating disk space to logical volumes. If you use a small physical extent size, such as 1 MByte, then you have a fine granularity for defining logical volumes. If you use a large physical extent size such as 256 MBytes, then you have a coarse granularity for defining logical volumes. The default size is 4 MBytes.

Logical Extents   A logical volume is a set of logical extents. Logical extents and physical extents are the same size within a volume group. Although logical and physical extents are the same size, this doesn't mean that two logical extents will map to two contiguous physical extents. It may be that you have two logical extents that end up being mapped to physical extents on different disks!

Figure 8-1 graphically depicts some of the logical volume terms we just covered. In this diagram, you can see clearly that logical extents are not mapped to contiguous physical extents, because some of the physical extents are not used.

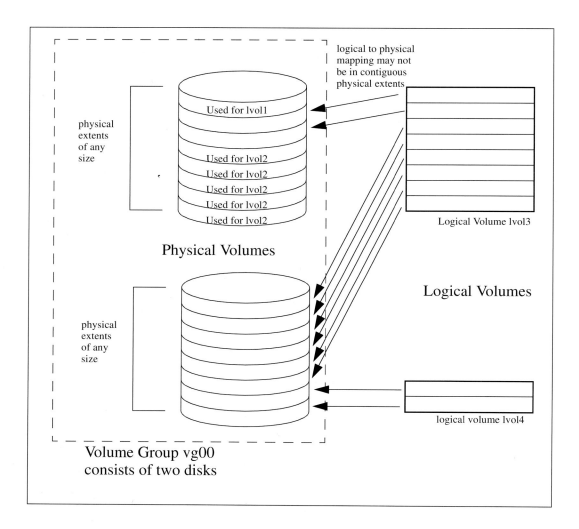

Figure 8-1 Logical Volume Manager Partial Logical to Physical Mapping

Disk Mirroring

Logical volumes can be mirrored one or more times, creating an identical image of the logical volume. This means a logical extent can map to more than one physical extent if mirrored.

You may have an environment where you wish to mirror some or all of the logical volumes. SAM can be used to set up disk mirroring for you. You must first, however, decide the characteristics of your mirroring. There is a mirroring policy called "strict." You define one of the following three strict policies when you create the logical volume using the following options:

<table>
<tr><td>n</td><td>No, this is not a strict allocation policy, meaning that mirrored copies of a logical extent can share the same physical volume. This means that your original data and mirrored data may indeed be on the same physical disk. If you encounter a disk mechanism problem of some type, you may lose both your original and mirrored data.</td></tr>
<tr><td>y</td><td>Yes, this is a strict allocation policy, meaning that mirrored copies of a logical extent may not share the same physical volume. This is safer than allowing mirrored copies of data to share the same physical volume. If you have a problem with a disk in this scenario, you are guaranteed that your original data is on a different physical disk from your mirrored data. Original data and mirrored data are always part of the same volume group even if you want them on different physical volumes.</td></tr>
</table>

>   *g*   Mirrored data will not be on the same Physical Volume Group (PVG) as the original data. This policy is called a PVG-strict allocation policy.

The strict allocation policy depends on your environment. Most installations that employ mirroring buy sufficient disk drives to mirror all data. In an environment such as this, I would create two volume groups, one for the original data and one for the mirrored data, and use the "strict -g" option when creating logical volumes so that the original data is on one volume group and the mirrored data on the other.

Logical Volume Manager Commands

The following are definitions of some of the more common Logical Volume Commands. Many of these commands are found in the log file that SAM creates when setting up logical volumes for you. I am giving a description of these commands here so that when you see them, you'll have an idea of each command's use. Although these are not all of the Logical Volume Manager commands, these are the ones I use most often and are the commands you should have knowledge of when using Logical Volume Manager. The commands are grouped by physical volume (pv) commands, volume group (vg) commands, and logical volume (lv) commands. These commands are found in the manual pages. Some of the commands such as **vgdisplay**, **pvdisplay**, and **lvdisplay** were issued so that you could see examples of these. The following output of **bdf** will be helpful to you when you view the output of Logical Volume Manager commands that are issued. The output of **bdf** shows several logical volumes mounted (**lvol1**, **lvol3**, **lvol4**, **lvol5**, **lvol6**, **lvol7**, **lvol8**), all of which are in volume group **vg00** (see the **bdf** command overview later in this chapter).

man page

lv, pv, vg- 8

man page

bdf- 8

$ **bdf**

Filesystem	kbytes	used	avail	%used	Mounted on
/dev/vg00/lvol3	47829	18428	24618	43%	/
/dev/vg00/lvol1	67733	24736	36223	41	/stand
/dev/vg00/lvol8	34541	8673	22413	28%	/var
/dev/vg00/lvol7	299157	149449	119792	56%	/usr
/dev/vg00/lvol4	23013	48	20663	0%	/tmp
/dev/vg00/lvol6	99669	32514	57188	36%	/opt
/dev/vg00/lvol5	19861	9	17865	0%	/home
/dev/dsk/c0t6d0	802212	552120	169870	76%	/mnt/9.x

Physical Volume Commands

pvchange   This command is used to change a physical volume in some way. For example, you may wish to allow additional physical extents to be added to a physical volume if they are not permitted, or prohibit additional physical extents from being added to a physical volume if, indeed, they are allowed.

pvcreate   This command is used to create a physical volume that will be part of a volume group. Remember that a volume group may consist of several physical volumes. The physical volumes are the disks on your system.

man page

"pv" - 8

pvdisplay   This command shows information about the physical volumes you specify. You can get a lot of information about the logical to physical mapping with this command if you use the verbose (-v) option. With -v **pvdisplay** will show you the mapping of logical to physical extents for the physical volumes specified.

You get a lot of other useful data from this command, such as the name of the physical volume; the name of the volume group to which the physical volume belongs; the status of the physical volume; the size of physical extents on the physical volume; the total number of physical extents; and the number of free physical extents.

The following is a partial example of running **pvdisplay**:

```
$ pvdisplay -v /dev/dsk/c0t6d0

--- Physical volumes ---
PV Name                 /dev/dsk/c0t1d0
VG Name                 /dev/vg00
PV Status               available
Allocatable             yes
VGDA                    2
Cur LV                  7
PE Size (Mbytes)        4
Total PE                157
Free PE                 8
Allocated PE            149
Stale PE                0

   --- Distribution of physical volume ---
   LV Name              LE of LV    PE for LV
   /dev/vg00/lvol1      12          12
   /dev/vg00/lvol2      17          17
   /dev/vg00/lvol6      75          75
   /dev/vg00/lvol7      9           9
   /dev/vg00/lvol4      25          25
```

```
/dev/vg00/lvol5      6            6
/dev/vg00/lvol3      5            5

--- Physical extents ---
PE     Status   LV                    LE
0000   current  /dev/vg00/lvol1       0000
0001   current  /dev/vg00/lvol1       0001
0002   current  /dev/vg00/lvol1       0002
0003   current  /dev/vg00/lvol1       0003
0004   current  /dev/vg00/lvol1       0004
0005   current  /dev/vg00/lvol1       0005
0006   current  /dev/vg00/lvol1       0006
0007   current  /dev/vg00/lvol1       0007
0008   current  /dev/vg00/lvol1       0008
0009   current  /dev/vg00/lvol1       0009
0010   current  /dev/vg00/lvol1       0010
0011   current  /dev/vg00/lvol1       0011
0012   current  /dev/vg00/lvol2       0000
0013   current  /dev/vg00/lvol2       0001
0014   current  /dev/vg00/lvol2       0002
0015   current  /dev/vg00/lvol2       0003
0016   current  /dev/vg00/lvol2       0004
0017   current  /dev/vg00/lvol2       0005
0018   current  /dev/vg00/lvol2       0006
0019   current  /dev/vg00/lvol2       0007
0020   current  /dev/vg00/lvol2       0008
0021   current  /dev/vg00/lvol2       0009
0022   current  /dev/vg00/lvol2       0010
0023   current  /dev/vg00/lvol2       0011
0024   current  /dev/vg00/lvol3       0000
0025   current  /dev/vg00/lvol3       0001
0026   current  /dev/vg00/lvol3       0002
0027   current  /dev/vg00/lvol3       0003
0028   current  /dev/vg00/lvol3       0004
0029   current  /dev/vg00/lvol4       0000
0030   current  /dev/vg00/lvol4       0001
0031   current  /dev/vg00/lvol4       0002
0032   current  /dev/vg00/lvol4       0003
0033   current  /dev/vg00/lvol4       0004
0034   current  /dev/vg00/lvol4       0005
0035   current  /dev/vg00/lvol4       0006



               .
               .
               .

0156   free                           0000
```

From this listing, you can see that *lvol1*, which is roughly 48 MBytes, has many more physical extents assigned to it than *lvol3*, which is roughly 20 MBytes.

pvmove   You can move physical extents from one physical volume to other physical volumes with this command. By specifying the source physical volume and one or more destination physical volumes, you can spread data around to the various physical volumes you wish with this command.

Volume Group Commands

vgcfgbackup   This command is used to save the configuration information for a volume group. Remember that a volume group is made up of one or more physical volumes. SAM automatically runs this command after you make an LVM change.

vgcfgrestore   This command is used to restore the configuration information for a volume group.

vgchange   This command makes a volume group active or inactive. With the *-a* option, you can deactivate (*-a n*) a volume group or activate (*-a y*) a volume group.

vgcreate   You can create a volume group and specify all of its parameters with this command. You specify a volume group name and all of the associated parameters for the volume group when creating it.

vgdisplay   This displays all information related to the volume group if you use the verbose (*-v*) option, including the volume group name; the status of the volume group; the maximum, current, and open logical volumes in the volume group; the maximum, current, and active physical volumes in the volume group; and physical extent-related information.

The following is an example of using **vgdisplay** for the volume group *vg00*:

```
$ vgdisplay /dev/vg00

--- Volume groups ---
VG Name                /dev/vg00
VG Write Access        read/write
VG Status              available
Max LV                 255
Cur LV                 7
Open LV                7
Max PV                 16
Cur PV                 1
Act PV                 1
Max PE per PV          2000
VGDA                   2
PE Size (Mbytes)       4
Total PE               157
Alloc PE               149
Free PE                8
Total PVG              0
```

vgexport   This command removes a logical volume group from the system, but does not modify the logical volume information on the physical volumes. These physical volumes can then be imported to another system using **vgimport.**

man page

"vg" - 8

vgextend   Physical volumes can be added to a volume group with this command by specifying the physical volume to be added to the volume group.

vgimport   This command can be used to import a physical volume to another system.

vgreduce   The size of a volume group can be reduced with this command, by specifying which physical volume(s) to remove from a volume group. Make sure that the physical volume to be removed has no data on it before doing this.

vgremove   A volume group definition can be completely removed from the system with this command.

vgscan   In the event of a catastrophe of some type, you can use this command to scan your system in an effort to rebuild the **/etc/lvmtab** file.

vgsync   There are times when mirrored data in a volume group becomes "stale" or out-of-date. **vgsync** is used to synchronize the physical extents in each mirrored logical volume in a volume group.

Logical Volume Commands

man page

"lv" - 8

lvcreate   This command is used to create a new logi-
                     cal volume. A logical volume is created
                     within a volume group. A logical volume
                     may span multiple disks, but must exist
                     within a volume group. SAM will execute
                     this command for you when you create a log-
                     ical volume using SAM. Many options exist
                     for this command, and two that you would
                     often use are -L to define the size of the logi-
                     cal volume and -n to define the name of the
                     logical volume.

lvchange   This command is used to change the logical vol-
                     ume in some way. For example, you may
                     wish to change the permission on a logical
                     volume to read-write (w) or read (r) with the
                     -p option. Or, you may want to change the
                     strict policy (described under Disk Mirror-
                     ing) to strict (y), not strict (n), or PVG strict
                     (g).

lvdisplay   This command shows the status and charac-
                     teristics of every logical volume that you
                     specify. If you use the verbose (-v) option of
                     this command, you get a lot of useful data in
                     many categories, including:

                     1) Information about the way in which the
                     logical volumes are set up, such as the physi-
                     cal volume on which the logical extents
                     appear; the number of local extents on a
                     physical volume; and the number of physical
                     extents on the physical volume.

man page

"lv" - 8

man page

bdf- 8

2) Detailed information for logical extents, including the logical extent number and some information about the physical volume and physical extent for the logical extent.

The following is an example of **lvdisplay** for the first of the logical volumes (*lvol1*) shown in the earlier **bdf** example:

```
$  lvdisplay -v /dev/vg00/lvol1

--- Logical volumes ---
LV Name                    /dev/vg00/lvol1
VG Name                    /dev/vg00
LV Permission              read/write
LV Status                  available/syncd
Mirror copies              0
Consistency Recovery       MWC
Schedule                   parallel
LV Size (Mbytes)           48
Current LE                 12
Allocated PE               12
Stripes                    0
Stripe Size (Kbytes)       0
Bad block                  off
Allocation                 strict/contiguous

    --- Distribution of logical volume ---
    PV Name              LE on PV  PE on PV
    /dev/dsk/c0t1d0      12        12

    --- Logical extents ---
    LE    PV1                      PE1    Status 1
    0000 /dev/dsk/c0t1d0           0000   current
    0001 /dev/dsk/c0t1d0           0001   current
    0002 /dev/dsk/c0t1d0           0002   current
    0003 /dev/dsk/c0t1d0           0003   current
    0004 /dev/dsk/c0t1d0           0004   current
    0005 /dev/dsk/c0t1d0           0005   current
    0006 /dev/dsk/c0t1d0           0006   current
    0007 /dev/dsk/c0t1d0           0007   current
    0008 /dev/dsk/c0t1d0           0008   current
    0009 /dev/dsk/c0t1d0           0009   current
    0010 /dev/dsk/c0t1d0           0010   current
    0011 /dev/dsk/c0t1d0           0011   current
```

Although most of what is shown in this example is self-explanatory, some entries require explanation. The size of the logical volume is 48 MBytes, which consists of 12 Logical Extents (LE,) and 12 Physical Extents (PE). This means that each physical extent is 4 MBytes in size (4 MBytes x 12 extents = 48 MBytes). We can verify this by running the command to display the characteristics of the physical volume. At the bottom of this listing, you can see the mapping of logical extents onto physical extents. In this case there is a direct mapping takes place between logical extents *0000 - 0011* and physical extents *0000 - 0011*.

lvextend This command is used to increase the number of physical extents allocated to a logical volume. We sometimes underestimate the size required for a logical volume, and with this command, you can easily correct this problem. You may want to extend a logical volume to increase the number of mirrored copies (using the *-m* option), to increase the size of the logical volume (using the *-L* option), or to increase the number of logical extents (using the *-l* option).

man page

"lv" - 8

extendfs Use this command after **lvextend**. Whereas the **lvextend** command expands the logical volume, **extendfs** expands the filesystem within the logical volume. If you forget to issue the **extendfs** command, the logical volume inside SAM will look expanded, but issuing the **bdf** command will not show the expansion.

man page
"lv" - 8

lvlnboot   Use this to set up a logical volume to be a root, boot, primary swap, or dump volume (this can be undone with **lvrmboot**). Issuing the **lvlnboot** command with the *-v* option gives the current settings.

lvsplit and **lvmerge**

These commands are used to split and merge mirrored logical volumes, respectively. If you have a mirrored logical volume, **lvsplit** will split this into two logical volumes. **lvmerge** merges two logical volumes of the same size, increasing the number of mirrored copies.

lvmmigrate   This command prepares a root file system in a disk partition for migration to a logical volume. You would use this if you had a partition to convert into a logical volume.

lvreduce   Use this to decrease the number of physical extents allocated to a logical volume. When creating logical volumes, we sometimes overestimate the size of the logical volume. This command can be used to set the number of mirrored copies (with the *-m* option), decrease the number of logical extents (with the *-l* option), or decrease the size of the logical volume (with the *-L* option). Be careful when decreasing the size of a logical volume. You may make it smaller than the data in it. If you choose to do this, make sure that you have a good backup of your data.

lvremove   After emptying a logical volume, you can use this command to remove logical volumes from a volume group.

lvrmboot   Use this if you don't want a logical volume to be root, boot, primary swap, or a dump device (this is the converse of the **lvlnboot** command). However, unless you have a disk partition to boot from, don't leave the system without a root or boot device designated with the **lvlnboot** command or the system won't know where to boot from.

lvsync   There are times when mirrored data in a logical volume becomes "stale" or out-of-date. **lvsync** is used to synchronize the physical extents in a logical volume.

Adding Disks

In this section, we're going to do some work with XP 256 disks. We want to create ten volume groups with five primary disks and five alternate disks per volume group.

Let's take a look at the file that contains the physical disks to be used for the primary and alternate paths on the XP 256. The XP 256 is an advanced storage device that has in it the capability to fail over to an alternate controller should the primary controller fail. The same set of disks are connected to the primary and alternate controllers but the disks are given two different sets of device files. One set is for the disks when connected to the primary controller and the second set is for the same disks when connected to the alternate controller. This is the same concept that you may have come across if you are a Service-Guard user. There are a set of disks connected through two different paths, so you must define the disks with different names depending on whether they are connected through the primary or alternate path. The following is a listing of the file **pri**, containing the primary disks in groups of five:

```
c9t0d0   c9t0d1   c9t0d2   c8t0d0    c8t0d1
c7t0d0   c7t0d1   c7t0d2   c10t0d0   c10t0d1
c9t0d3   c9t0d4   c9t0d5   c8t0d3    c8t0d4
c7t0d3   c7t0d4   c7t0d5   c10t0d3   c10t0d4
c9t0d6   c9t0d7   c9t1d0   c8t0d6    c8t0d7
c7t0d6   c7t0d7   c7t1d0   c10t0d6   c10t0d7
c9t1d1   c9t1d2   c9t1d3   c8t1d1    c8t1d2
c7t1d1   c7t1d2   c7t1d3   c10t1d1   c10t1d2
c9t1d4   c9t1d5   c9t1d6   c8t1d4    c8t1d5
c7t1d4   c7t1d5   c7t1d6   c10t1d4   c10t1d5
```

Notice that in this listing, the disks have been grouped in fives. Each group of five disks will constitute a volume group. There are a total of *10* groups of five disks that will be placed in volume groups *vgu01* through *vgu10*.

There will also be an alternate group of five disks. The alternate disks will be used in the event of a disk controller failover as described earlier. The following is a listing of the file **alt**, which contains a list of alternate disks in groups of five:

```
c8t8d0    c8t8d1    c8t8d2    c9t8d0   c9t8d1
c10t8d0   c10t8d1   c10t8d2   c7t8d0   c7t8d1
c8t8d3    c8t8d4    c8t8d5    c9t8d3   c9t8d4
c10t8d3   c10t8d4   c10t8d5   c7t8d3   c7t8d4
c8t8d6    c8t8d7    c8t9d0    c9t8d6   c9t8d7
c10t8d6   c10t8d7   c10t9d0   c7t8d6   c7t8d7
c8t9d1    c8t9d2    c8t9d3    c9t9d1   c9t9d2
```

```
c10t9d1  c10t9d2  c10t9d3  c7t9d1  c7t9d2
c8t9d4   c8t9d5   c8t9d6   c9t9d4  c9t9d5
c10t9d4  c10t9d5  c10t9d6  c7t9d4  c7t9d5
```

There are a total of *10* groups of alternate disks shown in this listing that will also be part of volume groups *vgu01* through *vgu10*. Using these primary and alternate disks that have been set up on the XP 256, we'll set up the appropriate volumes on the host system. In this example, the host system is a V-Class system.

Let's now cover the steps to create one of these volume groups. First, we'll create a physical volume for each of the disks in the volume group with the **pvcreate** command. Next, we'll create a directory for the volume group with **mkdir**, then we'll create a device special file for the volume group within the directory with **mknod**. This will set up the directory and special file required for the first of the *10* volume groups. Then we'll create the volume group in which the five primary disks will be contained using **vgcreate**. We'll specify the first disk when we create the volume group and then include the other disks in the volume group with **vgextend**. Then we extend the volume group with **vgextend** to include the five alternate disks. The final step is to create a single logical volume for the entire volume group. You might want to create several logical volumes within a volume group, but in our example, we need only one logical volume that consumes the entire capacity of the volume group, which is 8755 physical extents. The following procedure is the list of manual steps to create the first volume group:

man page

"pv" - 8

man page

mkdir - 16

man page

"vg" - 8

```
# pvcreate /dev/rdsk/c9t0d0     # run for each of the 5 pri disks


# mkdir /dev/vgu01              # make dir for first vol group


# mknod /dev/vgu01/group -c 64 0x01000
                                # create special file with major
                                    and minor numbers shown

# vgcreate /dev/vgu01 /dev/dsk/c9t0d0
                                # Place first disk in volume group
```

```
# vgextend /dev/vgu01 /dev/dsk/c9t0d1
                              # extend volume with remaining four
                                primary disks disks


# vgextend /dev/vgu01 /dev/dsk/c8t8d0
                              # extend volume group to include five
                                alternte disks

# lvcreate -l 8755 /dev/vgu01  # creates lvol1 (lvol1 by default)
                                 that consumes all 8755 extents
```

We completed the procedure for only one disk, and there are nine additional disks in this volume group. In addition, there are another nine volume groups for which this procedure must be completed. That is a total of an additional 99 disks for which various commands must be run. There is a lot of room for error with that much typing involved so this is an ideal process to automate.

-- Read this only if you wish to see how to automate the procedure --

Since there are a primary set of disks and an alternate set of disks we'll write a short program to automate each procedure. The following program performs all of the steps required to create a physical volume for each disk, create a volume group, and include the primary disks in it:

```
#!/bin/ksh
set -x              ;set tracing on

  vgnum=$1          ;first item on each line is the volume group no.
  shift             ;shift to get to first disk


  for i in $*       ;run pvcreate for every disk name in first line
  do
     pvcreate /dev/rdsk/$i
  done
```

```
reada                  ;pause program to view what has been run

mkdir /dev/vgu$vgnum                         ;mkdir for volume group
mknod /dev/vgu$vgnum/group c 0x$(vgnum)0000  ;mknod for volume group
vgcreate /dev/vgu$vgnum /dev/dsk/$1          ;vgcreate 1st disk in vg

shift              ;shift over to second disk

for i in $*        ;extend volume group to include remaining four disks
do
   vgextend /dev/vgu$vgnum /dev/dsk/$i
done

lvcreate -l 8755 /dev/vgu$vgnum   ;create single log vol for entire vg
```

I use **set -x** in this file to turn on execution tracing. I always do this when first debugging a shell program so I can see the lines in the shell program as they are executed. The line being executed will appear with a "+" in front of it, followed by the what you would normally see when the program is run. The **read a** is a way of pausing the program to wait for input so I can review what has been run to that point of the program.

In order for this program to run, we must slightly modify the file containing the primary disk devices and add the volume group number to the beginning of each line. In addition, I decided to call the program from the file that has the primary disks in it and operate on one line of disks at a time. The following listing shows the updated file containing the name of the shell program in the previous listing (**vg.sh**), followed by the volume group number and then the list of five primary disks names for each volume group:

```
#vg.sh 01 c9t0d0 c9t0d1 c9t0d2 c8t0d0 c8t0d1
#read a
#vg.sh 02 c7t0d0 c7t0d1 c7t0d2 c10t0d0 c10t0d1
#read a
#vg.sh 03 c9t0d3 c9t0d4 c9t0d5 c8t0d3 c8t0d4
#read a
#vg.sh 04 c7t0d3 c7t0d4 c7t0d5 c10t0d3 c10t0d4
#read a
#vg.sh 05 c9t0d6 c9t0d7 c9t1d0 c8t0d6 c8t0d7
```

```
#read a
#vg.sh 06 c7t0d6 c7t0d7 c7t1d0 c10t0d6 c10t0d7
#read a
#vg.sh 07 c9t1d1 c9t1d2 c9t1d3 c8t1d1 c8t1d2
#read a
#vg.sh 08 c7t1d1 c7t1d2 c7t1d3 c10t1d1 c10t1d2
#read a
#vg.sh 09 c9t1d4 c9t1d5 c9t1d6 c8t1d4 c8t1d5
#read a
#vg.sh 10 c7t1d4 c7t1d5 c7t1d6 c10t1d4 c10t1d5
```

The **read a** between lines of this file will pause and wait for you to enter a *Return* before the next line will be executed. I did this in case I decided to run several lines and I wanted to check the results between the execution of lines.

We can now uncomment the first line of the file and type the file name **pri**, which will call **vg.sh** and run the program (you must give appropriate permissions to the files and make sure both **vg.sh** and **pri** are executable). I like to run such files one line at a time and check the volume groups as they are created. The script is written to run one line at a time but is easily modifyable to run all ten lines.

We need to do much less work with the alternate disk names. The physical volumes have already been created, and the volume group and single logical volume have already been setup in **vg.sh**. We'll create another script called **vga.sh**, "a" for alternate), in which we'll extend the volume group to include the alternate name for each disk. This script is shown in the listing below:

```
#!/bin/ksh
set -x              ;set tracing on

  vgnum=$1          ;first item on each line is the volume group number
  shift             ;shift to get to first disk


  for i in $*       ;extend vol group to include all five disks on line

    vgextend /dev/vgu$vgnum /dev/dsk/$i

  done
```

This script performs only the task of extending the volume group *vgnum* to include all five disks that appear on the line. Much like the file **pri**, the file **alt** will call the script **vga.alt** as shown in the following listing:

```
#vga.sh 01 c8t8d0   c8t8d1   c8t8d2   c9t8d0  c9t8d1
#vga.sh 02 c10t8d0  c10t8d1  c10t8d2  c7t8d0  c7t8d1
#vga.sh 03 c8t8d3   c8t8d4   c8t8d5   c9t8d3  c9t8d4
#vga.sh 04 c10t8d3  c10t8d4  c10t8d5  c7t8d3  c7t8d4
#vga.sh 05 c8t8d6   c8t8d7   c8t9d0   c9t8d6  c9t8d7
#vga.sh 06 c10t8d6  c10t8d7  c10t9d0  c7t8d6  c7t8d7
#vga.sh 07 c8t9d1   c8t9d2   c8t9d3   c9t9d1  c9t9d2
#vga.sh 08 c10t9d1  c10t9d2  c10t9d3  c7t9d1  c7t9d2
#vga.sh 09 c8t9d4   c8t9d5   c8t9d6   c9t9d4  c9t9d5
#vga.sh 10 c10t9d4  c10t9d5  c10t9d6  c7t9d4  c7t9d5
```

You would uncomment the line for which you wanted to run the script. Again, you could run all ten lines, but I like to check what has taken place after each line has been run. You could add **read a** between the lines of this file if you wanted to run several lines and have a pause between them to check the results.

These two scripts automate a lot of typing. There are 100 disks for which commands must be run as well as other Logical Volume Manager commands. This is the type of HP-UX system administration task that is ideally suited to shell programming.

----------- End of Automated Procedure -----------

I completed the steps that had to be run for the additional disks to complete the work, such as the **vgcreate** for the additional four disks and the **vgextend** for the additional nine disk devices. I included only the first disk in the examples so you could see the initial step that had to be run.

We don't have to set up any RAID levels within the primary or alternate volume because this is being done internally to the XP 256.

man page

"vg" - 8

The following **vgdisplay** listing shows the disks we set up for volume group *vgu01* with both the group of five primary and alternate disks:

```
# vgdisplay /dev/vgu01 -v


VG Name                     /dev/vgu01
VG Write Access             read/write
VG Status                   available
Max LV                      255
Cur LV                      1
Open LV                     1
Max PV                      16
Cur PV                      5
Act PV                      5
Max PE per PV               1751
VGDA                        10
PE Size (Mbytes)            4
Total PE                    8755
Alloc PE                    8755
Free PE                     0
Total PVG                   0
Total Spare PVs             0
Total Spare PVs in use      0

    --- Logical volumes ---
    LV Name                 /dev/vgu01/lvol1
    LV Status               available/syncd
    LV Size (Mbytes)        35020
    Current LE              8755
    Allocated PE            8755
    Used PV                 5


    --- Physical volumes ---
    PV Name                 /dev/dsk/c9t0d0
    PV Name                 /dev/dsk/c8t8d0Alternate Link
    PV Status               available
    Total PE                1751
    Free PE                 0

    PV Name                 /dev/dsk/c9t0d1
    PV Name                 /dev/dsk/c8t8d1Alternate Link
    PV Status               available
    Total PE                1751
    Free PE                 0

    PV Name                 /dev/dsk/c9t0d2
    PV Name                 /dev/dsk/c8t8d2Alternate Link
    PV Status               available
    Total PE                1751
    Free PE                 0
```

```
PV Name                        /dev/dsk/c8t0d0
PV Name                        /dev/dsk/c9t8d0Alternate Link
PV Status                      available
Total PE                       1751
Free PE                        0

PV Name                        /dev/dsk/c8t0d1
PV Name                        /dev/dsk/c9t8d1Alternate Link
PV Status                      available
Total PE                       1751
Free PE                        0
```

There are some points of interest to cover in this **vgdisplay**. The first is that there is a primary and alternate path to the same disk because we defined them earlier. For instance, the first disk in the volume group has a primary pathname of *c9t0d0* and an alterate path name of *c8t8d0*. Next, both the volume group *vgu01* and the only logical volume in it, *lvol1*, consist of a total of 8755 PE or phsical extents (the size of volume group is PE x PE size, or 8755 x 4MB in our case).

We should also check one logical volume on *vgu01*, called *lvol1*. We can check the parameters of this logical volume with the **lvdisplay** command as shown in the following example:

```
# lvdisplay -v /dev/vgu01/l*

--- Logical volumes ---
LV Name                        /dev/vgu01/lvol1
VG Name                        /dev/vgu01
LV Permission                  read/write
LV Status                      available/syncd
Mirror copies                  0
Consistency Recovery           MWC
Schedule                       parallel
LV Size (Mbytes)               35020
Current LE                     8755
Allocated PE                   8755
Stripes                        0
Stripe Size (Kbytes)           0
Bad block                      on
Allocation                     strict
IO Timeout (Seconds)           default

    --- Distribution of logical volume ---
    PV Name           LE on PV   PE on PV
    /dev/dsk/c9t0d0     1751      1751
    /dev/dsk/c9t0d1     1751      1751
    /dev/dsk/c9t0d2     1751      1751
```

```
/dev/dsk/c8t0d0      1751        1751
/dev/dsk/c8t0d1      1751        1751

--- Logical extents ---
LE     PV1                  PE1     Status 1
00000  /dev/dsk/c9t0d0      00000   current
00001  /dev/dsk/c9t0d0      00001   current
00002  /dev/dsk/c9t0d0      00002   current
00003  /dev/dsk/c9t0d0      00003   current
00004  /dev/dsk/c9t0d0      00004   current
00005  /dev/dsk/c9t0d0      00005   current
00006  /dev/dsk/c9t0d0      00006   current
00007  /dev/dsk/c9t0d0      00007   current
00008  /dev/dsk/c9t0d0      00008   current
00009  /dev/dsk/c9t0d0      00009   current
00010  /dev/dsk/c9t0d0      00010   current
00011  /dev/dsk/c9t0d0      00011   current
00012  /dev/dsk/c9t0d0      00012   current
00013  /dev/dsk/c9t0d0      00013   current
00014  /dev/dsk/c9t0d0      00014   current
00015  /dev/dsk/c9t0d0      00015   current
00016  /dev/dsk/c9t0d0      00016   current
00017  /dev/dsk/c9t0d0      00017   current
00018  /dev/dsk/c9t0d0      00018   current
00019  /dev/dsk/c9t0d0      00019   current
00020  /dev/dsk/c9t0d0      00020   current
00021  /dev/dsk/c9t0d0      00021   current
00022  /dev/dsk/c9t0d0      00022   current
00023  /dev/dsk/c9t0d0      00023   current
00024  /dev/dsk/c9t0d0      00024   current
00025  /dev/dsk/c9t0d0      00025   current
00026  /dev/dsk/c9t0d0      00026   current
00027  /dev/dsk/c9t0d0      00027   current
00028  /dev/dsk/c9t0d0      00028   current
00029  /dev/dsk/c9t0d0      00029   current
00030  /dev/dsk/c9t0d0      00030   current
00031  /dev/dsk/c9t0d0      00031   current
00032  /dev/dsk/c9t0d0      00032   current
                    .
                    .
                    .
08733  /dev/dsk/c8t0d1      01729   current
08734  /dev/dsk/c8t0d1      01730   current
08735  /dev/dsk/c8t0d1      01731   current
08736  /dev/dsk/c8t0d1      01732   current
08737  /dev/dsk/c8t0d1      01733   current
08738  /dev/dsk/c8t0d1      01734   current
08739  /dev/dsk/c8t0d1      01735   current
08740  /dev/dsk/c8t0d1      01736   current
08741  /dev/dsk/c8t0d1      01737   current
08742  /dev/dsk/c8t0d1      01738   current
08743  /dev/dsk/c8t0d1      01739   current
08744  /dev/dsk/c8t0d1      01740   current
08745  /dev/dsk/c8t0d1      01741   current
08746  /dev/dsk/c8t0d1      01742   current
08747  /dev/dsk/c8t0d1      01743   current
08748  /dev/dsk/c8t0d1      01744   current
08749  /dev/dsk/c8t0d1      01745   current
```

```
08750 /dev/dsk/c8t0d1      01746 current
08751 /dev/dsk/c8t0d1      01747 current
08752 /dev/dsk/c8t0d1      01748 current
08753 /dev/dsk/c8t0d1      01749 current
08754 /dev/dsk/c8t0d1      01750 current
```

man page

"lv" - 8

This listing has been abbreviated where the three dots are shown. Only the beginning of the first disk and end of the last disk are shown. The **lvdisplay** does indeed show the five primary disks of which the logical volume is comprised.

The final step is to place a file system on the logical volume we set up in *vgu00*. This is a task for which SAM is ideally suited. Figure 8-2 shows the SAM screen shot of the logical volumes we created. There is one logical volume created for each of the ten volume groups.

```
  ═══════════════ Disks and File Systems (o2) (1) ══════════════
 File List View Options Actions                              Help
                  Press CTRL-K for keyboard help.


 Logical Volumes                                  0 of 19 selected

                                      Total    Mirror    Mount
    Logical Volume   Volume Group  Use  Mbytes   Copies   Directory

    lvol1            vgu01       Unused   35020     0                  ▲
    lvol1            vgu02       Unused   35020     0                  █
    lvol1            vgu03       Unused   35020     0                  █
    lvol1            vgu04       Unused   35020     0                  █
    lvol1            vgu05       Unused   35020     0                  █
    lvol1            vgu06       Unused   35020     0                  █
    lvol1            vgu07       Unused   35020     0                  █
    lvol1            vgu08       Unused   35020     0                  █
    lvol1            vgu09       Unused   35020     0                  █
    lvol1            vgu10       Unused   35020     0                  ▼
    ◄                                                                 ►►
```

Figure 8-2   *lvol1* on *vgu01* through *vgu10*

lvol1 appears for volume groups *vgu01* through *vgu10*. We want a file system on each of the logical volumes for the application we are running. Although we could issue the appropriate commands at the command line, we'll use SAM for this task.

Figure 8-3 shows the SAM screen used to add a file system to one of the logical volumes:

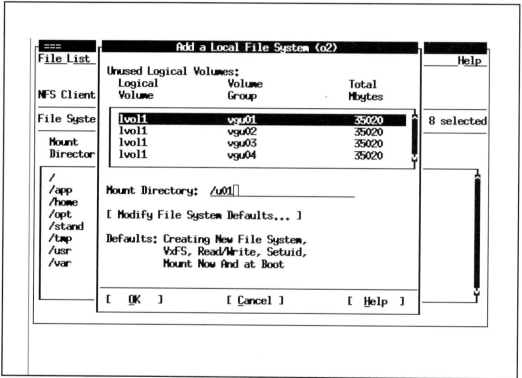

Figure 8-3   Adding a Filesystem to *lvol1* on *vgu01*

We have selected *lvol1* on *vgu01* to add a file system as shown in this figure. Next, we want to modify the defaults for the logical volume as shown in Figure 8-4:

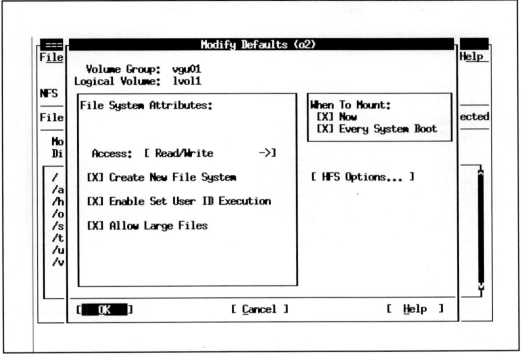

Figure 8-4 Modify File System Defaults

We want to be sure to *Allow Large Files* in this screen because we'll be running a database application that creates many large files. If we were to create a filesystem without large files, we could use the **fsadm** command to convert to large files if we're running Online JFS. We want to mount this file system now and at the time of system boot so an entry gets made in **/etc/fstab** for us.

Figure 8-5 shows the result of having created the ten filesystems on the ten logical volumes:

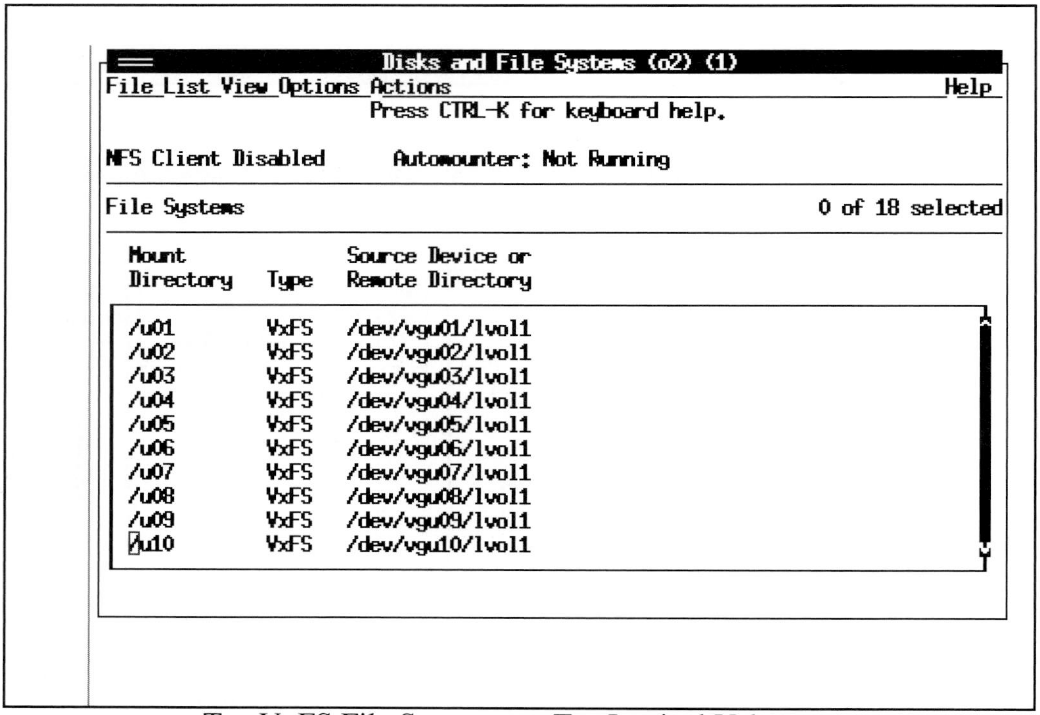

Figure 8-5 Ten VxFS File Systems on Ten Logical Volumes

Using SAM, we created ten VxFS filesystems on all ten *lvol1*s. We had to create all ten individually in SAM, so this may have been a good candidate for automating with a shell program.

SAM automatically adds these entries to **/etc/fstab** because we specified them to be mounted both now and at the time of system boot as shown in the following listing:

```
# System /etc/fstab file.  Static information about the file systems
# See fstab(4) and sam(1M) for further details on configuring devices.
/dev/vg00/lvol3 / vxfs delaylog 0 1
/dev/vg00/lvol1 /stand hfs defaults 0 1
/dev/vg00/lvol4 /opt vxfs delaylog 0 2
/dev/vg00/lvol5 /tmp vxfs delaylog 0 2
/dev/vg00/lvol6 /usr vxfs delaylog 0 2
/dev/vg00/lvol7 /var vxfs delaylog 0 2
/dev/vg00/lvol8 /home vxfs delaylog 0 2
/dev/vg00/lvol9 ... swap pri=0 0 0
/dev/vgapp/lvol1 /app vxfs rw,suid,largefiles,delaylog,datainlog 0 2
```

```
/dev/vgu01/lvol1  /u01 vxfs rw,suid,largefiles,delaylog,datainlog 0 2
/dev/vgu02/lvol1  /u02 vxfs rw,suid,largefiles,delaylog,datainlog 0 2
/dev/vgu03/lvol1  /u03 vxfs rw,suid,largefiles,delaylog,datainlog 0 2
/dev/vgu04/lvol1  /u04 vxfs rw,suid,largefiles,delaylog,datainlog 0 2
/dev/vgu05/lvol1  /u05 vxfs rw,suid,largefiles,delaylog,datainlog 0 2
/dev/vgu06/lvol1  /u06 vxfs rw,suid,largefiles,delaylog,datainlog 0 2
/dev/vgu07/lvol1  /u07 vxfs rw,suid,largefiles,delaylog,datainlog 0 2
/dev/vgu08/lvol1  /u08 vxfs rw,suid,largefiles,delaylog,datainlog 0 2
/dev/vgu09/lvol1  /u09 vxfs rw,suid,largefiles,delaylog,datainlog 0 2
/dev/vgu10/lvol1  /u10 vxfs rw,suid,largefiles,delaylog,datainlog 0 2
```

This listing shows our ten logical volumes with the parameters we set up such as VxFS and support for large files as the last ten entries.

There is no reason why we could not have run the filesystem-related commands such as **newfs** and **fsadm** at the command line as we did with the volume-related commands earlier. Since most people use SAM for these procedures, I thought it would be best illustrated using SAM.

The next section provides tips on various procedures you may want to perform using logical volume manager. These are procedures I have used many times and they may help you when you need to perform similar tasks.

Commonly Used LVM Procedures

System administrators tend to be careful before running any intrusive (there is a chance something LVM-related will be changed) LVM commands. Always back up your system and create a bootable recovery tape with Ignite-UX before you run any intrusive LVM commands. The following are some procedures for tasks I have encountered on a regular basis. Please modify them to suit your needs. Don't run the commands as shown. You will need to prepare your system, substitute the names of your volumes, and perform additional steps. These commands, however, serve as good examples for ways in which the tasks shown can be performed.

The first task we'll perform is to replace a bad disk in a system that is not mirrored (Figure 8-6).

```
# vgcfgrestore - /dev/vgXX  /dev/rdsk/cxtxdx    ; volume group configuration restore
# vgchange -a y /dev/vgXX                       ; change volume group to available (-a y)
# newfs -F fstype /dev/vgXX/rlvolx              ; create filesystem for every lvol on physical volume
# mount /mountpointname                         ; mount every new filesystem
```

Notes:

Confirm you have **/etc/lvmconf/vgXX.conf**

vgcfgbackup is run automatically

Defective disk was not mirrored before it failed

Additional steps may be required on your system

Figure 8-6 Replace a Non-Mirrored Disk

man page

newfs- 8

In this example, we had a non-mirrored and non-root disk that was defective and had to be replaced. After replacing the disk, the volume group information was restored for the specific disk with **vgcfgrestore**. We then changed the volume group to available, ran a **newfs** on the disk, and mounted the filesystems that used the disk.

In Figure 8-7 we will again replace a defective non-root disk, but this time, the disk will be mirrored.

---

vgcfgrestore - /dev/vgXX /dev/rdsk/cxtxdx   ; volume group configuration restore

vgchange -a y /dev/vgXX   ; change volume group to available (-*a y*)

vgsync /dev/vgXX   ; resync logical volumes in volume group

Notes:

Defective disk was mirrored before it failed

Additional steps may be required on your system

Figure 8-7   Replace a Mirrored Disk

In this example, we performed the same first two steps of restoring the volume group configuration and changing the volume group to available. Because the disk was mirrored, we only have to synchronize the data on the new disk with that on its mirror with **vgsync**.

In Figure 8-8 we will again replace a mirrored disk, but this time, the disk will have a boot area on it.

```
# vgcfgrestore - /dev/vgXX /dev/rdsk/cxtxdx        ; volume group configuration restore
# vgchange -a y /dev/vgXX                          ; change volume group to available (-a y)
# vgsync /dev/vgXX                                 ; resync logical volumes in volume group
# mkboot /dev/rdsk/cxtxdx                          ; create boot area on disk
# mkboot -a "hpux lq" /dev/rdsk/cxtxdx             ; specify low quorum in boot area
# shutdown <desired options>                       ; reboot system to take effect
vgcfgbackup is run automatically

Notes:
Confirm you have /etc/lvmconf/vgXX.conf
Defective disk was mirrored before it failed
Addtional steps may be required on your system
```

Figure 8-8   Replace Mirrored Disk Boot Disk

In this example, we performed the same first three steps as the previous example, but we also have to create a boot area on the disk. The system has to be rebooted in order for this to take effect.

In Figure 8-9, we want to move a volume group onto a different system.

On system 1:

vgchange -a n /dev/vgXX   ; change volume group to unavailable (*-a n*) on 1st sys

vgexport -v -m mapfile -s /dev/vgXX   ; make volume group unavailable on 1st system,
                                               mapfile will have to be copied to 2nd system, but
                                               you don't have to specify here if standard
                                               volume names are used

On system 2:

mkdir /dev/vgXX   ; make directory on 2nd system for volume group

mknod /dev/vgXX/group c 64 0xyy0000   ; create special file for vol group (*yy*=group number
                                               such as *00* for *vg00*, *01* for *vg01*, and so on)

vgimport -v -m mapfile -s /dev/vgXX   ; import volume group using mapfile copied from
                                               1st system or specify device filenames

vgchange -a y /dev/vgXX   ; make volume group available

edit **/etc/fstab** or use SAM to include new filesystems

Notes:

vgcfgbackup is run automatically

Addtional steps may be required on your system

Figure 8-9 Exporting (Removing) and Importing a Volume Group Onto Another System

In this example, we performed the first two steps on the system from which we're moving the volume group. We make the volume group unavailable and then export the volume group. The mapfile from the first system needs to be copied to the second system. You don't have to specify the mapfile name if standard names such as **/dev/vg01** are used. In any event, the mapfile has to be copied to the system to which the volume group is being migrated.

On the second system we create a directory and device special file for the new volume group. We then import the mapfile for the volume group and make the volume group active. The last step involved making additions to **fstab** for the filesystems to be mounted.

Fgiure 8-10 shows extending a VxFS filesystem by 800 MBytes.

lvextend -L 800 /dev/vgXX/rlvolY   ; extend logical volume *rlvolY* by 800 MBytes

fsadm -F vxfs -b 800M */mountpointname*   ; use **fsadm** to extend or **extendfs** on non-JFS

Notes:

This is a VxFS filesystem and Online JFS is installed on system

Additional steps may be required on your system

Figure 8-10 Extend VxFS File System Using Online JFS

man page

'lv'- 8

First we use **lvextend** to specify the size and raw logical volume to be extended. Next we use **fsadm** to make the change.

The Figure 8-11 shows changing a VxFS filesystem to support large files.

---

fsadm -F vxfs -o largefiles /dev/vgXX/rlvolY   ; use *fsadm* and specify *largefile* option

Notes:

This is VxFS filesystem, you can substitute *hfs* for *vxfs* in above example for an *hfs* filesystem and use *lvolY* in place of *rlvolY*
Unmount filesystem before running

Additional steps may be required on your system

Figure 8-11   Change a Logical Volume to Support Large Files

Using **fsadm**, we specify the raw logical volume on which we want lardge files supported.

This change would be unnecessary had the logical volume been created to support large files.

Reconfiguring Some Disks - An Example of Using Some Logical Volume Commands

I have always advised in my books and articles to take great care when you first set up disks on your HP-UX systems to make sure the disk layout you select is one you can live with for a long time. No matter how careful you are, however, you often need to perform some logical volume reconfiguration. It is much more difficult to make changes to an existing logical volume layout than it is to set up your system correctly when it is first installed. This section describes the steps performed to make some changes to the dump and mirror on an existing system.

This is not a procedure you should follow. It is an example of some advanced Logical Volume Manager (LVM) commands used to reconfigure some disks on a specific system. It is a good procedure for illustrating how several LVM commands can be used.

Why Change?

Figure 8-12 shows the original configuration of disks on a system and the updated configuration we wish to implement.

The overall objective here is to move the 4 GByte disk used as the mirror of the root disk to a different SCSI channel and to install a 2 GByte dump device on the same SCSI channel as the root disk.

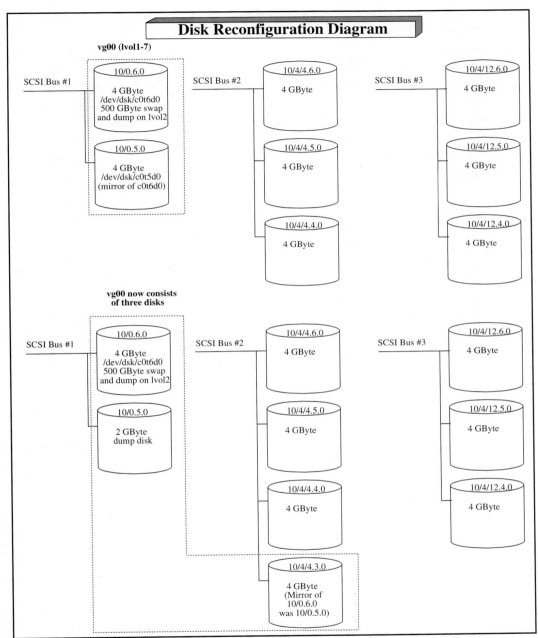

Figure 8-12 Disk Reconfiguration Diagram

The procedure consists of several parts. The first is to obtain a snapshot of the system before any reconfigurations. This serves two purposes. The first is to have documentation of the original system configuration that can be included in the system administration notebook. Should any questions arise in the future as to the original configuration and changes made to it, the original configuration will be in the system administration notebook. The second purpose of having this information is to have all of the relevant information about the configuration available as you proceed with the reconfiguration process.

The second part of the procedure is to shut down the system, install the new 2 GByte disk, and move the 4 GByte disk.

The last part of the procedure is to perform the system administration reconfiguration of the dump and mirror.

Figures 8-13, 8-14, and 8-15 show a flowchart depicting the procedure we'll follow throughout this section. The step numbers in the upcoming procedure correspond to the step numbers shown in these figures. Let's now proceed beginning with the snapshot of the system.

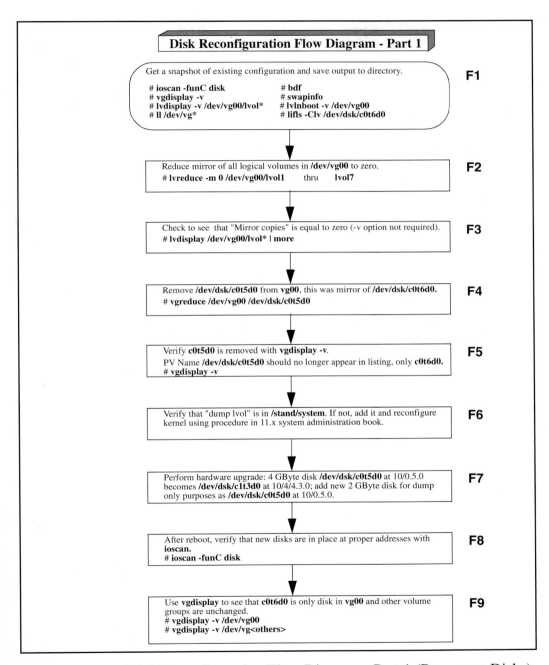

Disk Reconfiguration Flow Diagram - Part 1

Get a snapshot of existing configuration and save output to directory.   **F1**
```
# ioscan -funC disk          # bdf
# vgdisplay -v               # swapinfo
# lvdisplay -v /dev/vg00/lvol*   # lvlnboot -v /dev/vg00
# ll /dev/vg*                # lifls -Clv /dev/dsk/c0t6d0
```

Reduce mirror of all logical volumes in **/dev/vg00** to zero.   **F2**
```
# lvreduce -m 0 /dev/vg00/lvol1      thru      lvol7
```

Check to see that "Mirror copies" is equal to zero (-v option not required).   **F3**
```
# lvdisplay /dev/vg00/lvol* | more
```

Remove **/dev/dsk/c0t5d0** from **vg00**, this was mirror of **/dev/dsk/c0t6d0**.   **F4**
```
# vgreduce /dev/vg00 /dev/dsk/c0t5d0
```

Verify **c0t5d0** is removed with **vgdisplay -v**.   **F5**
PV Name **/dev/dsk/c0t5d0** should no longer appear in listing, only **c0t6d0**.
```
# vgdisplay -v
```

Verify that "dump lvol" is in **/stand/system**. If not, add it and reconfigure   **F6**
kernel using procedure in 11.x system administration book.

Perform hardware upgrade: 4 GByte disk **/dev/dsk/c0t5d0** at 10/0.5.0   **F7**
becomes **/dev/dsk/c1t3d0** at 10/4/4.3.0; add new 2 GByte disk for dump
only purposes as **/dev/dsk/c0t5d0** at 10/0.5.0.

After reboot, verify that new disks are in place at proper addresses with   **F8**
ioscan.
```
# ioscan -funC disk
```

Use **vgdisplay** to see that **c0t6d0** is only disk in **vg00** and other volume   **F9**
groups are unchanged.
```
# vgdisplay -v /dev/vg00
# vgdisplay -v /dev/vg<others>
```

Figure 8-13   Disk Reconfiguration Flow Diagram - Part 1 (Rearrange Disks)

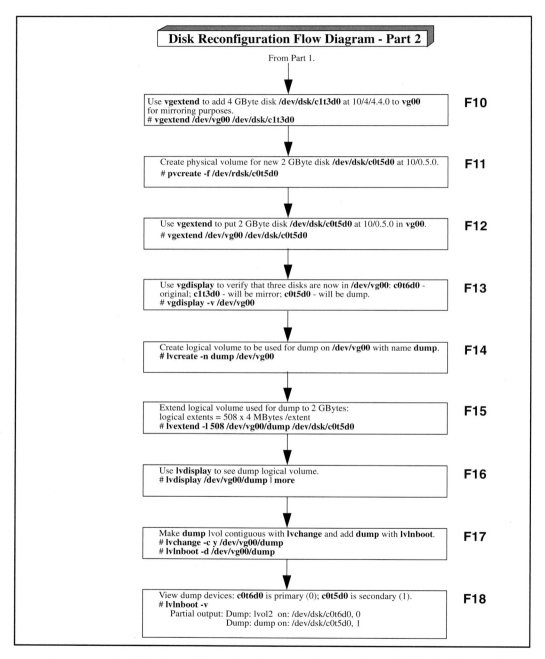

Disk Reconfiguration Flow Diagram - Part 2

From Part 1.

Use **vgextend** to add 4 GByte disk **/dev/dsk/c1t3d0** at 10/4/4.4.0 to **vg00** for mirroring purposes.
vgextend /dev/vg00 /dev/dsk/c1t3d0
F10

Create physical volume for new 2 GByte disk **/dev/dsk/c0t5d0** at 10/0.5.0.
pvcreate -f /dev/rdsk/c0t5d0
F11

Use **vgextend** to put 2 GByte disk **/dev/dsk/c0t5d0** at 10/0.5.0 in **vg00**.
vgextend /dev/vg00 /dev/dsk/c0t5d0
F12

Use **vgdisplay** to verify that three disks are now in **/dev/vg00**: **c0t6d0** - original; **c1t3d0** - will be mirror; **c0t5d0** - will be dump.
vgdisplay -v /dev/vg00
F13

Create logical volume to be used for dump on **/dev/vg00** with name **dump**.
lvcreate -n dump /dev/vg00
F14

Extend logical volume used for dump to 2 GBytes:
logical extents = 508 x 4 MBytes /extent
lvextend -l 508 /dev/vg00/dump /dev/dsk/c0t5d0
F15

Use **lvdisplay** to see dump logical volume.
lvdisplay /dev/vg00/dump | more
F16

Make **dump** lvol contiguous with **lvchange** and add **dump** with **lvlnboot**.
lvchange -c y /dev/vg00/dump
lvlnboot -d /dev/vg00/dump
F17

View dump devices: **c0t6d0** is primary (0); **c0t5d0** is secondary (1).
lvlnboot -v
    Partial output: Dump: lvol2 on: /dev/dsk/c0t6d0, 0
                    Dump: dump on: /dev/dsk/c0t5d0, 1
F18

Figure 8-14 Disk Reconfiguration Flow Diagram - Part 2 (Set Up Dump)

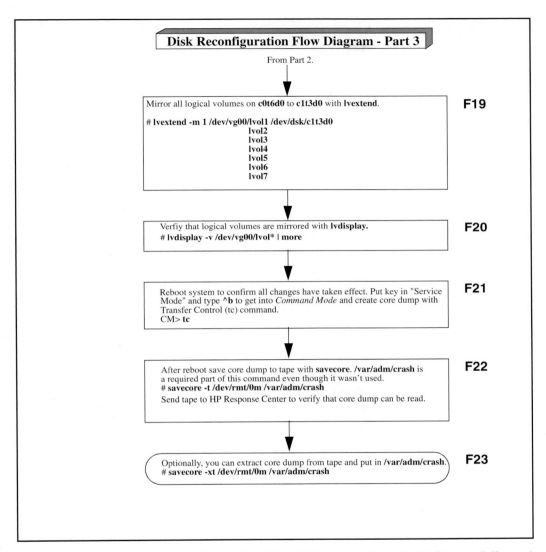

Disk Reconfiguration Flow Diagram - Part 3

From Part 2.

Mirror all logical volumes on **c0t6d0** to **c1t3d0** with **lvextend**.

```
# lvextend -m 1 /dev/vg00/lvol1 /dev/dsk/c1t3d0
                lvol2
                lvol3
                lvol4
                lvol5
                lvol6
                lvol7
```

F19

Verfiy that logical volumes are mirrored with **lvdisplay**.
```
# lvdisplay -v /dev/vg00/lvol* | more
```

F20

Reboot system to confirm all changes have taken effect. Put key in "Service Mode" and type **^b** to get into *Command Mode* and create core dump with Transfer Control (tc) command.
```
CM> tc
```

F21

After reboot save core dump to tape with **savecore**. **/var/adm/crash** is a required part of this command even though it wasn't used.
```
# savecore -t /dev/rmt/0m /var/adm/crash
```
Send tape to HP Response Center to verify that core dump can be read.

F22

Optionally, you can extract core dump from tape and put in **/var/adm/crash**.
```
# savecore -xt /dev/rmt/0m /var/adm/crash
```

F23

Figure 8-15   Disk Reconfiguration Flow Diagram - Part 3 (Reinstate Mirrors)

F1 - to scan

First let's run **ioscan** to see the disks on the system.

```
$ /usr/sbin/ioscan -funC disk
```

```
Class     I  H/W Path    Driver      S/W State H/W Type  Description
===================================================================
disk      2  10/0.5.0    sdisk       CLAIMED   DEVICE    SEAGATE ST15150W
                         /dev/dsk/c0t5d0    /dev/rdsk/c0t5d0
disk      3  10/0.6.0    sdisk       CLAIMED   DEVICE    SEAGATE ST15150W
                         /dev/dsk/c0t6d0    /dev/rdsk/c0t6d0
disk      6  10/4/4.4.0  sdisk       CLAIMED   DEVICE    SEAGATE ST15150W
                         /dev/dsk/c1t4d0    /dev/rdsk/c1t4d0
disk      7  10/4/4.5.0  sdisk       CLAIMED   DEVICE    SEAGATE ST15150W
                         /dev/dsk/c1t5d0    /dev/rdsk/c1t5d0
disk      8  10/4/4.6.0  sdisk       CLAIMED   DEVICE    SEAGATE ST15150W
                         /dev/dsk/c1t6d0    /dev/rdsk/c1t6d0
disk      9  10/4/12.4.0 sdisk       CLAIMED   DEVICE    SEAGATE ST15150W
                         /dev/dsk/c2t4d0    /dev/rdsk/c2t4d0
disk     10  10/4/12.5.0 sdisk       CLAIMED   DEVICE    SEAGATE ST15150W
                         /dev/dsk/c2t5d0    /dev/rdsk/c2t5d0
disk     11  10/4/12.6.0 sdisk       CLAIMED   DEVICE    SEAGATE ST15150W
                         /dev/dsk/c2t6d0    /dev/rdsk/c2t6d0
disk      5  10/12/5.2.0 sdisk       CLAIMED   DEVICE    TOSHIBA CD-ROM XM-5401TA
                         /dev/dsk/c3t2d0    /dev/rdsk/c3t2d0
```

Note that the disks in this configuration correspond to those on the top of Figure 8-4. We haven't yet looked at the logical volume information related to these disks, only their physical addresses.

F1 - vgdisplay

Next run **vgdisplay** to see the volume groups. **lvol2** on **vg00** is the dump logical volume we are going to move to a separate 2 GByte disk. We don't yet know if **lvol1-7** on **vg00** are all mirrored.

```
# vgdisplay -v
   --- Volume groups ---
VG Name                 /dev/vg00
VG Write Access         read/write
VG Status               available
Max LV                  255
Cur LV                  7
Open LV                 7
Max PV                  16
Cur PV                  2
```

```
Act PV                  2
Max PE per PV           1023
VGDA                    4
PE Size (Mbytes)        4
Total PE                2046
Alloc PE                688
Free PE                 1358
Total PVG               0

    --- Logical volumes ---
LV Name                 /dev/vg00/lvol1
LV Status               available/syncd
LV Size (Mbytes)        92
Current LE              23
Allocated PE            46
Used PV                 2

LV Name                 /dev/vg00/lvol2
LV Status               available/syncd
LV Size (Mbytes)        500
Current LE              125
Allocated PE            250
Used PV                 2

LV Name                 /dev/vg00/lvol3
LV Status               available/syncd
LV Size (Mbytes)        20
Current LE              5
Allocated PE            10
Used PV                 2

LV Name                 /dev/vg00/lvol4
LV Status               available/syncd
LV Size (Mbytes)        252
Current LE              63
Allocated PE            126
Used PV                 2

LV Name                 /dev/vg00/lvol5
LV Status               available/syncd
LV Size (Mbytes)        32
Current LE              8
Allocated PE            16
Used PV                 2

LV Name                 /dev/vg00/lvol6
LV Status               available/syncd
LV Size (Mbytes)        320
Current LE              80
Allocated PE            160
Used PV                 2
LV Name                 /dev/vg00/lvol7
LV Status               available/syncd
LV Size (Mbytes)        160
Current LE              40
Allocated PE            80
Used PV                 2

    --- Physical volumes ---
PV Name                 /dev/dsk/c0t6d0
PV Status               available
Total PE                1023
Free PE                 679

PV Name                 /dev/dsk/c0t5d0
PV Status               available
Total PE                1023
Free PE                 679
```

F1 - lvdisplay

View detailed logical volume information with **lvdisplay**. Note that all of these logical volumes are mirrored and that each has "current" status. Only **lvol1** and **lvol2** are shown in the listing. **lvol3** through **lvol7** are not shown.

```
# lvdisplay -v /dev/vg00/lvol*
 --- Logical volumes ---
LV Name                    /dev/vg00/lvol1
VG Name                    /dev/vg00
LV Permission              read/write
LV Status                  available/syncd
Mirror copies              1
Consistency Recovery       MWC
Schedule                   parallel
LV Size (Mbytes)           92
Current LE                 23
Allocated PE               46
Stripes                    0
Stripe Size (Kbytes)       0
Bad block                  off
Allocation                 strict/contiguous

--- Distribution of logical volume ---
PV Name            LE on PV  PE on PV
/dev/dsk/c0t6d0      23         23
/dev/dsk/c0t5d0      23         23


--- Logical extents ---
LE    PV1                  PE1   Status 1 PV2               PE2   Status 2
0000 /dev/dsk/c0t6d0       0000  current  /dev/dsk/c0t5d0  0000  current
0001 /dev/dsk/c0t6d0       0001  current  /dev/dsk/c0t5d0  0001  current
0002 /dev/dsk/c0t6d0       0002  current  /dev/dsk/c0t5d0  0002  current
0003 /dev/dsk/c0t6d0       0003  current  /dev/dsk/c0t5d0  0003  current
0004 /dev/dsk/c0t6d0       0004  current  /dev/dsk/c0t5d0  0004  current
0005 /dev/dsk/c0t6d0       0005  current  /dev/dsk/c0t5d0  0005  current
0006 /dev/dsk/c0t6d0       0006  current  /dev/dsk/c0t5d0  0006  current
0007 /dev/dsk/c0t6d0       0007  current  /dev/dsk/c0t5d0  0007  current
0008 /dev/dsk/c0t6d0       0008  current  /dev/dsk/c0t5d0  0008  current
0009 /dev/dsk/c0t6d0       0009  current  /dev/dsk/c0t5d0  0009  current
0010 /dev/dsk/c0t6d0       0010  current  /dev/dsk/c0t5d0  0010  current
0011 /dev/dsk/c0t6d0       0011  current  /dev/dsk/c0t5d0  0011  current
0012 /dev/dsk/c0t6d0       0012  current  /dev/dsk/c0t5d0  0012  current
0013 /dev/dsk/c0t6d0       0013  current  /dev/dsk/c0t5d0  0013  current
0014 /dev/dsk/c0t6d0       0014  current  /dev/dsk/c0t5d0  0014  current
0015 /dev/dsk/c0t6d0       0015  current  /dev/dsk/c0t5d0  0015  current
0016 /dev/dsk/c0t6d0       0016  current  /dev/dsk/c0t5d0  0016  current
0017 /dev/dsk/c0t6d0       0017  current  /dev/dsk/c0t5d0  0017  current
0018 /dev/dsk/c0t6d0       0018  current  /dev/dsk/c0t5d0  0018  current
0019 /dev/dsk/c0t6d0       0019  current  /dev/dsk/c0t5d0  0019  current
0020 /dev/dsk/c0t6d0       0020  current  /dev/dsk/c0t5d0  0020  current
0021 /dev/dsk/c0t6d0       0021  current  /dev/dsk/c0t5d0  0021  current
0022 /dev/dsk/c0t6d0       0022  current  /dev/dsk/c0t5d0  0022  current

LV Name                    /dev/vg00/lvol2
VG Name                    /dev/vg00
LV Permission              read/write
LV Status                  available/syncd
Mirror copies              1
Consistency Recovery       MWC
Schedule                   parallel
LV Size (Mbytes)           500
```

```
Current LE              125
Allocated PE            250
Stripes                 0
Stripe Size (Kbytes)    0
Bad block               off
Allocation              strict/contiguous

--- Distribution of logical volume ---

PV Name            LE on PV  PE on PV
/dev/dsk/c0t6d0    125       125
/dev/dsk/c0t5d0    125       125

--- Logical extents ---

LE    PV1                 PE1   Status 1  PV2               PE2   Status 2

0000  /dev/dsk/c0t6d0     0023  current   /dev/dsk/c0t5d0   0023  current
0001  /dev/dsk/c0t6d0     0024  current   /dev/dsk/c0t5d0   0024  current
0002  /dev/dsk/c0t6d0     0025  current   /dev/dsk/c0t5d0   0025  current
0003  /dev/dsk/c0t6d0     0026  current   /dev/dsk/c0t5d0   0026  current
0004  /dev/dsk/c0t6d0     0027  current   /dev/dsk/c0t5d0   0027  current
0005  /dev/dsk/c0t6d0     0028  current   /dev/dsk/c0t5d0   0028  current
0006  /dev/dsk/c0t6d0     0029  current   /dev/dsk/c0t5d0   0029  current
0007  /dev/dsk/c0t6d0     0030  current   /dev/dsk/c0t5d0   0030  current
0008  /dev/dsk/c0t6d0     0031  current   /dev/dsk/c0t5d0   0031  current
0009  /dev/dsk/c0t6d0     0032  current   /dev/dsk/c0t5d0   0032  current
0010  /dev/dsk/c0t6d0     0033  current   /dev/dsk/c0t5d0   0033  current
0011  /dev/dsk/c0t6d0     0034  current   /dev/dsk/c0t5d0   0034  current
0012  /dev/dsk/c0t6d0     0035  current   /dev/dsk/c0t5d0   0035  current
0013  /dev/dsk/c0t6d0     0036  current   /dev/dsk/c0t5d0   0036  current
                             .
                             .
                             .
0111  /dev/dsk/c0t6d0     0134  current   /dev/dsk/c0t5d0   0134  current
0112  /dev/dsk/c0t6d0     0135  current   /dev/dsk/c0t5d0   0135  current
0113  /dev/dsk/c0t6d0     0136  current   /dev/dsk/c0t5d0   0136  current
0114  /dev/dsk/c0t6d0     0137  current   /dev/dsk/c0t5d0   0137  current
0115  /dev/dsk/c0t6d0     0138  current   /dev/dsk/c0t5d0   0138  current
0116  /dev/dsk/c0t6d0     0139  current   /dev/dsk/c0t5d0   0139  current
0117  /dev/dsk/c0t6d0     0140  current   /dev/dsk/c0t5d0   0140  current
0118  /dev/dsk/c0t6d0     0141  current   /dev/dsk/c0t5d0   0141  current
0119  /dev/dsk/c0t6d0     0142  current   /dev/dsk/c0t5d0   0142  current
0120  /dev/dsk/c0t6d0     0143  current   /dev/dsk/c0t5d0   0143  current
0121  /dev/dsk/c0t6d0     0144  current   /dev/dsk/c0t5d0   0144  current
0122  /dev/dsk/c0t6d0     0145  current   /dev/dsk/c0t5d0   0145  current
0123  /dev/dsk/c0t6d0     0146  current   /dev/dsk/c0t5d0   0146  current
0124  /dev/dsk/c0t6d0     0147  current   /dev/dsk/c0t5d0   0147  current
```

F1 - ll /dev/vg00

Next, view **/dev/vg00** to have a record of the logical volumes.

```
# ll /dev/vg00

/dev/vg00:
total 0
crw-r--r--   1 root    sys        64 0x000000 May 29 04:44 group
brw-r-----   1 root    sys        64 0x000001 May 29 04:44 lvol1
brw-r-----   1 root    sys        64 0x000002 Jul  9 17:10 lvol2
brw-r-----   1 root    sys        64 0x000003 May 29 04:44 lvol3
brw-r-----   1 root    sys        64 0x000004 May 29 04:44 lvol4
brw-r-----   1 root    sys        64 0x000005 May 29 04:44 lvol5
brw-r-----   1 root    sys        64 0x000006 May 29 04:44 lvol6
brw-r-----   1 root    sys        64 0x000007 May 29 04:44 lvol7
crw-r-----   1 root    sys        64 0x000001 May 29 04:44 rlvol1
```

```
crw-r-----    1 root      sys         64 0x000002 Jul  9 17:10 rlvol2
crw-r-----    1 root      sys         64 0x000003 May 29 04:44 rlvol3
crw-r-----    1 root      sys         64 0x000004 May 29 04:44 rlvol4
crw-r-----    1 root      sys         64 0x000005 May 29 04:44 rlvol5
crw-r-----    1 root      sys         64 0x000006 May 29 04:44 rlvol6
crw-r-----    1 root      sys         64 0x000007 May 29 04:44 rlvol7
```

F1 - ll /dev/vg_nw

Next, view **/dev/vg_nw** and any other volume groups.

```
# ll /dev/vg_nw

/dev/vg_nw:
total 0
crw-rw-rw-    1 root      sys         64 0x010000 Jul  9 12:03 group
brw-r-----    1 root      sys         64 0x010003 Jul  9 13:01 lv_nwbackup
brw-r-----    1 root      sys         64 0x010004 Jul  9 13:01 lv_nwlog
brw-r-----    1 root      sys         64 0x010002 Jul  9 12:54 lv_nwsys
brw-r-----    1 root      sys         64 0x010001 Jul  9 12:53 lv_nwtext
crw-r-----    1 root      sys         64 0x010003 Jul  9 13:01 rlv_nwbackup
crw-r-----    1 root      sys         64 0x010004 Jul  9 13:01 rlv_nwlog
crw-r-----    1 root      sys         64 0x010002 Jul  9 12:55 rlv_nwsys
crw-r-----    1 root      sys         64 0x010001 Jul  9 12:54 rlv_nwtext
```

F1 - bdf

Next, view the file systems with **bdf**. Notice that **lvol2** is not shown because this is a swap and dump device.

```
# bdf
Filesystem                kbytes      used    avail %used Mounted on
/dev/vg00/lvol1            91669     31889    50613  39% /
/dev/vg00/lvol7           159509     83630    59928  58% /var
/dev/vg00/lvol6           319125    197912    89300  69%
/usr /dev/vg00/lvol5       31829     11323    17323  40% /tmp
/dev/vg00/lvol4           251285     67854   158302  30% /opt
/dev/vg_nw/lv_nwtext     4099465   2070905  1618613  56% /nwtext
/dev/vg_nw/lv_nwsys      4099465   1063909  2625609  29% /nwsys
/dev/vg_nw/lv_nwlog        99669     17313    72389  19% /nwlog
/dev/vg_nw/lv_nwbackup   2552537    377388  1919895  16% /nwbackup
/dev/vg00/lvol3            19861      2191    15683  12% /home
```

F1 - swapinfo

Next, run **swapinfo** to see that **lvol2** is the only swap device.

```
# swapinfo
               Kb        Kb        Kb   PCT  START/        Kb
TYPE        AVAIL      USED      FREE  USED  LIMIT  RESERVE  PRI  NAME
dev        512000         0    512000   0%      0        -    1  /dev/vg00/lvol2
reserve         -    512000   -512000
memory    1670828   1474704    196124  88%
```

F1 - lvlnboot

Next, look at the boot information with **lvlnboot**. **lvol2** on **vg00** is the dump device.

```
# lvlnboot -v /dev/vg00
Boot Definitions for Volume Group /dev/vg00:
Physical Volumes belonging in Root Volume Group:
        /dev/dsk/c0t6d0 (10/0.6.0) -- Boot Disk
        /dev/dsk/c0t5d0 (10/0.5.0) -- Boot Disk
Root: lvol1      on: /dev/dsk/c0t6d0
                     /dev/dsk/c0t5d0
Swap: lvol2      on: /dev/dsk/c0t6d0
                     /dev/dsk/c0t5d0
Dump: lvol2      on: /dev/dsk/c0t6d0, 0
```

F1 - lifls

Look at the boot area with **lifls**.

```
#lifls -Clv /dev/dsk/c0t6d0

volume ISL10 data size 7984 directory size 8 94/11/04 15:46:53
filename   type    start   size    implement  created
=====================================================================
ODE        -12960  584     496     0          95/05/19 13:36:50
MAPFILE    -12277  1080    32      0          95/05/19 13:36:50
SYSLIB     -12280  1112    224     0          95/05/19 13:36:50
CONFIGDATA -12278  1336    62      0          95/05/19 13:36:50
SLMOD      -12276  1400    70      0          95/05/19 13:36:50
SLDEV      -12276  1472    68      0          95/05/19 13:36:50
SLDRIVERS  -12276  1544    244     0          95/05/19 13:36:50
MAPPER     -12279  1792    93      0          95/05/19 13:36:51
IOTEST     -12279  1888    150     0          95/05/19 13:36:51
PERFVER    -12279  2040    80      0          95/05/19 13:36:51
PVCU       -12801  2120    64      0          95/05/19 13:36:51
SSINFO     -12286  2184    1       0          96/09/16 09:04:01
ISL        -12800  2192    240     0          94/11/04 15:46:53
AUTO       -12289  2432    1       0          94/11/04 15:46:53
HPUX       -12928  2440    800     0          94/11/04 15:46:54
LABEL      BIN     3240    8       0          96/05/29 01:49:55
```

F2

After all the appropriate information has been saved for the existing configuration, we can begin the reconfiguration. First, we break the mirror with **lvreduce** and the **-m** option.

```
# lvreduce -m 0 /dev/vg00/lvol1
Logical volume "/dev/vg00/lvol1" has been successfully reduced.
Volume Group configuration for /dev/vg00 has been saved in /etc/lvmconf/vg00.conf
# lvreduce -m 0 /dev/vg00/lvol2
Logical volume "/dev/vg00/lvol2" has been successfully reduced.
Volume Group configuration for /dev/vg00 has been saved in /etc/lvmconf/vg00.conf
# lvreduce -m 0 /dev/vg00/lvol3
Logical volume "/dev/vg00/lvol3" has been successfully reduced.
Volume Group configuration for /dev/vg00 has been saved in /etc/lvmconf/vg00.conf
# lvreduce -m 0 /dev/vg00/lvol4
Logical volume "/dev/vg00/lvol4" has been successfully reduced.
Volume Group configuration for /dev/vg00 has been saved in /etc/lvmconf/vg00.conf
# lvreduce -m 0 /dev/vg00/lvol5
Logical volume "/dev/vg00/lvol5" has been successfully reduced.
Volume Group configuration for /dev/vg00 has been saved in /etc/lvmconf/vg00.conf
# lvreduce -m 0 /dev/vg00/lvol6
Logical volume "/dev/vg00/lvol6" has been successfully reduced.
Volume Group configuration for /dev/vg00 has been saved in /etc/lvmconf/vg00.conf
# lvreduce -m 0 /dev/vg00/lvol7
Logical volume "/dev/vg00/lvol7" has been successfully reduced.
Volume Group configuration for /dev/vg00 has been saved in /etc/lvmconf/vg00.conf
```

You can type each command or make a file with the **lvreduce** commands in it and run the file. You can call the file **/tmp/reduce** with the following entries:

```
lvreduce -m 0 /dev/vg00/lvol1
lvreduce -m 0 /dev/vg00/lvol2
lvreduce -m 0 /dev/vg00/lvol3
lvreduce -m 0 /dev/vg00/lvol4
lvreduce -m 0 /dev/vg00/lvol5
lvreduce -m 0 /dev/vg00/lvol6
lvreduce -m 0 /dev/vg00/lvol7
```

After you create this file, change it to executable and then run with the following two commands.

```
# chmod 555 /tmp/reduce
# /tmp/reduce
```

You will then see all the output of having run the **lvreduce** commands.

F3

Check to see that mirroring of **lvol1-7** has been reduced with **lvdisplay**. Look to see that mirrored copies are equal to 0. Only **lvol1** through **lvol3** are shown in this listing.

```
# lvdisplay -v /dev/vg00/lvol* | more

--- Logical volumes ---
LV Name                   /dev/vg00/lvol1
VG Name                   /dev/vg00
LV Permission             read/write
LV Status                 available/syncd
Mirror copies             0
Consistency Recovery      MWC
Schedule                  parallel
LV Size (Mbytes)          92
Current LE                23
Allocated PE              23
Stripes                   0
Stripe Size (Kbytes)      0
Bad block                 off
Allocation                strict/contiguous

LV Name                   /dev/vg00/lvol2
VG Name                   /dev/vg00
LV Permission             read/write
LV Status                 available/syncd
Mirror copies             0
Consistency Recovery      MWC
Schedule                  parallel
LV Size (Mbytes)          500
Current LE                125
Allocated PE              125
Stripes                   0
Stripe Size (Kbytes)      0
Bad block                 off
Allocation                strict/contiguous

LV Name                   /dev/vg00/lvol3
VG Name                   /dev/vg00
LV Permission             read/write
LV Status                 available/syncd
Mirror copies             0
Consistency Recovery      MWC
Schedule                  parallel
LV Size (Mbytes)          20
Current LE                5
Allocated PE              5
Stripes                   0
Stripe Size (Kbytes)      0
Bad block                 on
Allocation                strict
```

F4

Now remove **c0t5d0** from **vg00** with **vgreduce**. Since there is no mirroring in place, this approach will work. This disk will be put on a different SCSI controller and again used for mirroring later in the procedure.

```
# vgreduce /dev/vg00 /dev/dsk/c0t5d0
Volume group "/dev/vg00" has been successfully reduced.
Volume Group configuration for /dev/vg00 has been saved in /etc/lvmconf/vg00.conf
```

F5

At this point **c0t5d0** is no longer in **vg00**. Verify that "PV Name" **c0t5d0** is no longer in **vg00** with **vgdisplay**.

```
# vgdisplay -v
```

There should be no **c0t5d0** in **vg00**.

F6

Verify that "dump lvol" is in **/stand/system**. If not, add "dump vol" and reconfigure the kernel. See kernel the rebuild procedure in Chapter 1.

F7

Now the hardware upgrade takes place. The system is shut down, disk drives are added and moved, and the system is rebooted. The 4 GByte disk **/dev/dsk/c0t5d0** becomes **/dev/dsk/c1t3d0** at address 10/4/4.3.0, and a new 2 GByte disk is introduced as 10/0.5.0 with the device name **/dev/dsk/c0t5d0**. The second half of Figure 8-4 depicts this change.

F8

The first activity to perform after the hardware upgrade is to view the new disks with **ioscan**. There is now a 2 GByte disk at 10/0.5.0 and a 4 GByte disk at 10/4/4.3.0.

```
# ioscan -funC disk
Class    I  H/W Path   Driver     S/W State H/W Type  Description
=====================================================================
disk     2  10/0.5.0   sdisk      CLAIMED   DEVICE SEAGATE   ST32550W
                       /dev/dsk/c0t5d0    /dev/rdsk/c0t5d0
disk     3  10/0.6.0   sdisk      CLAIMED   DEVICE    SEAGATE ST15150W
                       /dev/dsk/c0t6d0    /dev/rdsk/c0t6d0
disk    12  10/4/4.3.0 disc3      CLAIMED   DEVICE    SEAGATE ST15150W
                       /dev/dsk/c1t3d0    /dev/rdsk/c1t3d0
                       /dev/floppy/c1t3d0 /dev/rfloppy/c1t3d0
disk     6  10/4/4.4.0 disc3      CLAIMED   DEVICE    SEAGATE ST15150W
                       /dev/dsk/c1t4d0    /dev/rdsk/c1t4d0
                       /dev/floppy/c1t4d0 /dev/rfloppy/c1t4d0
disk     7  10/4/4.5.0 disc3      CLAIMED   DEVICE    SEAGATE ST15150W
                       /dev/dsk/c1t5d0    /dev/rdsk/c1t5d0
                       /dev/floppy/c1t5d0 /dev/rfloppy/c1t5d0
disk     8  10/4/4.6.0 disc3      CLAIMED   DEVICE    SEAGATE ST15150W
                       /dev/dsk/c1t6d0    /dev/rdsk/c1t6d0
                       /dev/floppy/c1t6d0 /dev/rfloppy/c1t6d0
disk     9  10/4/12.4.0 disc3     CLAIMED   DEVICE    SEAGATE ST15150W
                       /dev/dsk/c2t4d0    /dev/rdsk/c2t4d0
                       /dev/floppy/c2t4d0 /dev/rfloppy/c2t4d0
disk    10  10/4/12.5.0 disc3     CLAIMED   DEVICE    SEAGATE ST15150W
                       /dev/dsk/c2t5d0    /dev/rdsk/c2t5d0
                       /dev/floppy/c2t5d0 /dev/rfloppy/c2t5d0
disk    11  10/4/12.6.0 disc3     CLAIMED   DEVICE    SEAGATE ST15150W
                       /dev/dsk/c2t6d0    /dev/rdsk/c2t6d0
                       /dev/floppy/c2t6d0 /dev/rfloppy/c2t6d0
disk     5  10/12/5.2.0 sdisk     CLAIMED   DEVICE    TOSHIBA CD-ROM XM-5401TA
                       /dev/dsk/c3t2d0    /dev/rdsk/c3t2d0
```

F9

Now we run **vgdisplay** to see new volume group information. Only **c0t6d0** is in **vg00** and no mirroring is yet configured. The other volume groups have remained the same. Only **lvol1** through **lvol3** are shown in our example.

```
# vgdisplay -v /dev/vg00

--- Volume groups ---
VG Name                 /dev/vg00
VG Write Access         read/write
VG Status               available
Max LV                  255
Cur LV                  7
Open LV                 7
Max PV                  16
Cur PV                  1
Act PV                  1
Max PE per PV           1023
VGDA                    2
PE Size (Mbytes)        4
Total PE                1023
Alloc PE                344
Free PE                 679
Total PVG               0

--- Logical volumes ---
LV Name                 /dev/vg00/lvol1
LV Status               available/syncd
LV Size (Mbytes)        92
Current LE              23
Allocated PE            23
Used PV                 1

LV Name                 /dev/vg00/lvol2
LV Status               available/syncd
LV Size (Mbytes)        500
Current LE              125
Allocated PE            125
Used PV                 1

LV Name                 /dev/vg00/lvol3
LV Status               available/syncd
LV Size (Mbytes)        20
Current LE              5
Allocated PE            5
Used PV                 1
```

(F9 continued)

Only the first three logical volumes in **/dev/vg_nw** are shown.

```
# vgdisplay -v /dev/vg_nw
VG Name                 /dev/vg_nw
VG Write Access         read/write
VG Status               available
Max LV                  255
Cur LV                  4
Open LV                 4
Max PV                  16
Cur PV                  6
Act PV                  6
Max PE per PV           1023
VGDA                    12
PE Size (Mbytes)        4
```

```
Total PE                6138
Alloc PE                5416
Free PE                 722
Total PVG               2
   --- Logical volumes ---
LV Name                 /dev/vg_nw/lv_nwtext
LV Status               available/syncd
LV Size (Mbytes)        4092
Current LE              1023
Allocated PE            2046
Used PV                 2

LV Name                 /dev/vg_nw/lv_nwsys
LV Status               available/syncd
LV Size (Mbytes)        4092
Current LE              1023
Allocated PE            2046
Used PV                 2

LV Name                 /dev/vg_nw/lv_nwbackup
LV Status               available/syncd
LV Size (Mbytes)        2548
Current LE              637
Allocated PE            1274
Used PV                 2
```

F10

Use **vgextend** to add the 4 GByte disk to **vg00** for mirroring (you may also have to run **pvcreate** here, too).

```
# vgextend /dev/vg00 /dev/dsk/c1t3d0
Volume group "/dev/vg00" has been successfully extended. Volume Group configuration for
/dev/vg00 has been saved in /etc/lvmconf/vg00.conf
```

F11

Now we can create the new 2 GByte disk and add it to **vg00** using the two following commands: **pvcreate** (F11) to create the physical volume and **vgextend** (F12) to extend the volume group.

```
# pvcreate -f /dev/rdsk/c0t5d0
Physical volume "/dev/rdsk/c0t5d0" has been successfully created.
```

F12

```
# vgextend /dev/vg00 /dev/dsk/c0t5d0
Volume group "/dev/vg00" has been successfully extended.
Volume Group configuration for /dev/vg00 has been saved in /etc/lvmconf/vg00.conf
```

F13

We can check to see that these two disks have indeed been added to **vg00** with **vgdisplay**. Only **lvol1** through **lvol3** are shown in our example. The end of the display is the significant part of the listing showing three physical volumes.

```
# vgdisplay -v /dev/vg00

   --- Volume groups ---
VG Name                  /dev/vg00
VG Write Access          read/write
VG Status                available
Max LV                   255
Cur LV                   7
Open LV                  7
Max PV                   16
Cur PV                   3
Act PV                   3
Max PE per PV            1023
VGDA                     6
PE Size (Mbytes)         4
Total PE                 2554
Alloc PE                 344
Free PE                  2210
Total PVG                0

--- Logical volumes ---

LV Name                  /dev/vg00/lvol1
LV Status                available/syncd
LV Size (Mbytes)         92
Current LE               23
Allocated PE             23
Used PV                  1

LV Name                  /dev/vg00/lvol2
LV Status                available/syncd
LV Size (Mbytes)         500
Current LE               125
Allocated PE             125
Used PV                  1

LV Name                  /dev/vg00/lvol3
LV Status                available/syncd
LV Size (Mbytes)         20
Current LE               5
```

```
Allocated PE            5
Used PV                 1

                .
                .
                .

--- Physical volumes ---

PV Name                 /dev/dsk/c0t6d0
PV Status               available
Total PE                1023
Free PE                 679

PV Name                 /dev/dsk/c1t3d0
PV Status               available
Total PE                1023
Free PE                 1023

PV Name                 /dev/dsk/c0t5d0
PV Status               available
Total PE                508
Free PE                 508
```

F14

We can now create the dump logical volume in **vg00** with **lvcreate** (F14), extend it to 2 GBytes with **lvextend** (F15), and view it with **lvdisplay** (F16).

```
# lvcreate -n dump  /dev/vg00
Logical volume "/dev/vg00/dump" has been successfully created with character de-
vice
"/dev/vg00/rdump".
Volume Group configuration for /dev/vg00 has been saved in /etc/lvmconf/vg00.conf
```

F15

```
# lvextend -l 508 /dev/vg00/dump /dev/dsk/c0t5d0
Logical volume "/dev/vg00/dump" has been successfully extended.
Volume Group configuration for /dev/vg00 has been saved in /etc/lvmconf/vg00.conf
```

F16

```
# lvdisplay /dev/vg00/dump | more

--- Logical volumes ---
LV Name                 /dev/vg00/dump
VG Name                 /dev/vg00
```

```
LV Permission           read/write
LV Status               available/syncd
Mirror copies           0
Consistency Recovery    MWC
Schedule                parallel
LV Size (Mbytes)        2032
Current LE              508
Allocated PE            508
Stripes                 0
Stripe Size (Kbytes)    0
Bad block               on
Allocation              strict


--- Distribution of logical volume ---
PV Name             LE on PV  PE on PV
/dev/dsk/c0t5d0      508       508
                      .
                      .
                      .
```

F17

In order to make **/dev/vg00/dump** the dump device, we must first make it contiguous with **lvchange** and then make it a dump device with **lvlnboot**.

```
# lvchange -C y /dev/vg00/dump
```

```
# lvlnboot -d /dev/vg00/dump
```

F18

View dump devices.

```
# lvlnboot -v | more
Boot Definitions for Volume Group /dev/vg00:
Physical Volumes belonging in Root Volume Group:
        /dev/dsk/c0t6d0 (10/0.6.0) -- Boot Disk
        /dev/dsk/c1t3d0 (10/4/4.3.0) -- Boot Disk
        /dev/dsk/c0t5d0 (10/0.5.0)
Root: lvol1     on:     /dev/dsk/c0t6d0
Swap: lvol2     on:     /dev/dsk/c0t6d0
Dump: lvol2     on:     /dev/dsk/c0t6d0, 0
Dump: dump      on:     /dev/dsk/c0t5d0, 1
```

This may not be what we want. The primary dump device, as indicated by the "0" is **/dev/dsk/c0t6d0** and the secondary dump device, indicated by the "1," is **/dev/dsk/c0t5d0**. We can optionally redo this. Let's proceed with mirroring the lvols on **/dev/vg00** and come back to dump devices.

F19

Let's now extend all the volumes in **vg00** for one mirror using **lvextend**.

```
# lvextend -m 1 /dev/vg00/lvol1 /dev/dsk/c1t3d0
The newly allocated mirrors are now being synchronized.
This operation will take some time. Please wait ....
Logical volume "/dev/vg00/lvol1" has been successfully extended.
Volume Group configuration for /dev/vg00 has been saved in /etc/lvmconf/vg00.conf
```

Put the following in **/tmp/mirror** and run. **lvol1** was extended earlier; **lvol2** is swap and doesn't need to be extended:

```
lvextend -m 1 /dev/vg00/lvol3 /dev/dsk/c1t3d0
lvextend -m 1 /dev/vg00/lvol4 /dev/dsk/c1t3d0
lvextend -m 1 /dev/vg00/lvol5 /dev/dsk/c1t3d0
lvextend -m 1 /dev/vg00/lvol6 /dev/dsk/c1t3d0
lvextend -m 1 /dev/vg00/lvol7 /dev/dsk/c1t3d0

The newly allocated mirrors are now being synchronized.
This operation will take some time.
Please wait .... Logical volume "/dev/vg00/lvol2" has been successfully extended.
Volume Group configuration for /dev/vg00 has been saved in /etc/lvmconf/vg00.conf
          .
          .
          .
```

F20

Let's now verify that the mirroring is in place with **lvdisplay** (only **lvol1** and **lvol2** are shown).

```
# lvdsisplay -v /dev/vg00/lvol* | more

--- Logical volumes ---
LV Name                 /dev/vg00/lvol1
VG Name                 /dev/vg00
LV Permission           read/write
```

```
LV Status                  available/syncd
Mirror copies              1
Consistency Recovery       MWC
Schedule                   parallel
LV Size (Mbytes)           92
Current LE                 23
Allocated PE               46
Stripes                    0
Stripe Size (Kbytes)       0
Bad block                  off
Allocation                 strict/contiguous

--- Distribution of logical volume ---
PV Name            LE on PV  PE on PV
/dev/dsk/c0t6d0    23          23
/dev/dsk/c1t3d0    23          23

--- Logical extents ---
LE    PV1              PE1   Status 1  PV2              PE2   Status 2
0000  /dev/dsk/c0t6d0  0000  current   /dev/dsk/c1t3d0  0000  current
0001  /dev/dsk/c0t6d0  0001  current   /dev/dsk/c1t3d0  0001  current
0002  /dev/dsk/c0t6d0  0002  current   /dev/dsk/c1t3d0  0002  current
0003  /dev/dsk/c0t6d0  0003  current   /dev/dsk/c1t3d0  0003  current
                        .
                        .
                        .
```

You can see from this listing that **c0t6d0** is mirrored on **c1t3d0**.

F21

Reboot the system to confirm that all changes have taken effect.

After reboot, do the following to create a dump. The key must be in the "Service" position for **^b** to work (you must be on a server and at the system console for this to work).

Use **^b** to get the **CM>** prompt.

Use the **tc** command at the **CM>** prompt to create core dump

F22

The system will automatically reboot after a core dump. Use the following command to save the core dump to tape. The **/var/adm/crash** file name is required even though the core dump is in the dump logical volume and not in the **/var/adm/crash** directory.

```
# savecore -t /dev/rmt/0m /var/adm/crash
```

F23

Then use **savecore -xt** and the directory name to the extract core dump. If you do not have room for the core dump, or you want a more thorough check, you can place a call and ask the HP Response Center to verify the **savecore** to tape has worked.

```
# savecore -xt /dev/rmt/0m /var/adm/crash
```

The core dump space requirement is calculated from the end of dump back toward the front. For this reason about roughly 1.5 GBytes is written to the **dump** logical volume and then roughly 600 MBytes are written to **lvol2**.

Optional Procedure to Exchange Dump Priorities

This procedure removes all boot definitions, including swap and dump, from **/dev/vg00** with **lvrmboot** and recreates them with **lvlnboot**. This needs to be done because **lvol2** is the primary dump logical volume (0) and dump is the secondary dump logical volume (1).

You must reboot in order for these changes to take effect. Figure 8-16 shows the steps required to complete this optional procedure.

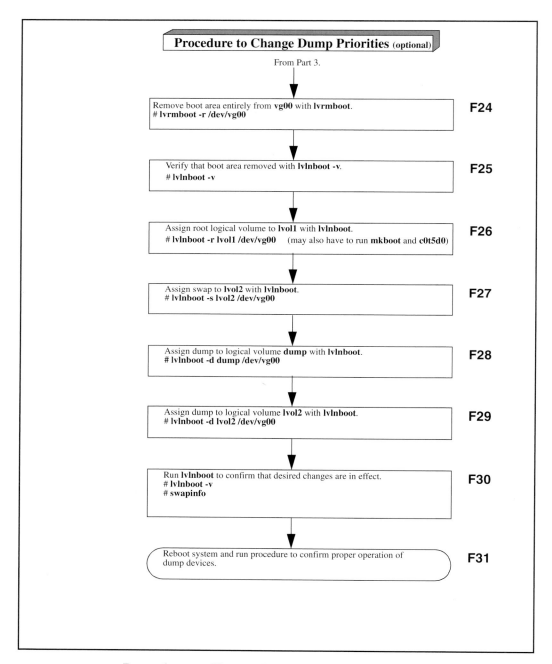

Figure 8-16   Procedure to Change Dump Priorities (Optional)

F24

    Remove the boot area entirely from **vg00** with **lvrmboot**.

```
# lvrmboot -r /dev/vg00
```

F25

    Verify that the boot area was removed with **lvlnboot.**

```
# lvlnboot -v
Boot Definitions for Volume Group /dev/vg00: The Boot Data Area is empty.
```

F26

    Assign the root logical volume to **lvol1** on **/dev/vg00** with **lvln-boot**.

```
# lvlnboot -r lvol1 /dev/vg00
```

F27

    Assign the swap to **lvol2** on **/dev/vg00**.

```
# lvlnboot -s lvol2 /dev/vg00

# swapinfo
           Kb        Kb       Kb   PCT   START/     Kb
TYPE    AVAIL      USED     FREE  USED   LIMIT RESERVE  PRI  NAME
dev    512000         0   512000   0%       0       -    1  /dev/vg00/lvol2
reserve     -     23144   -23144
memory 1671008    27324  1643684   2%
```

F28

    Assign the dump to the logical volume **dump** on **/dev/vg00**.

```
# lvlnboot -d dump /dev/vg00
```

F29

Assign the secondary dump device as **lvol2** (primary swap) on **lvol2**.

```
# lvlnboot -d lvol2 /dev/vg00
```

F30

Run **lvlnboot** to confirm that the dump and swap are properly configured with priority "0" on 2 GByte disk **c0t5d0** and "1" on **c0t6d0**.

```
# lvlnboot -v       # after adding lvol2 as secondary dump

Boot Definitions for Volume Group /dev/vg00:
Physical Volumes belonging in Root Volume Group:
                /dev/dsk/c0t6d0 (10/0.6.0) -- Boot Disk
                /dev/dsk/c1t3d0 (10/4/4.3.0) -- Boot Disk
                /dev/dsk/c0t5d0 (10/0.5.0)
Root: lvol1     on:      /dev/dsk/c0t6d0
                         /dev/dsk/c1t3d0
Swap: lvol2     on:      /dev/dsk/c0t6d0
                         /dev/dsk/c1t3d0
Dump: dump      on:      /dev/dsk/c0t5d0, 0
Dump: dump      on:      /dev/dsk/c0t6d0, 1
```

F31

Reboot the system and run steps F21-F23 to confirm proper operation of dump devices.

Although this procedure to reconfigure disks is for a specific system, it is useful for illustrating the many LVM commands required to perform such tasks. LVM, and disk management in general, are the areas I find consumes the most system administration time in mature HP-UX installations. There are many commands used in this procedure for which there is no way to "back out," so use caution whenever using LVM commands.

HP VERITAS Volume Manager

At the time of this writing HP Veritas Volume Manager (what I'll call VxVM throughout much of this chapter) is a software product loaded from the HP-UX 11i Application CD-ROM. There is a version of VxVM bundled with 11i called Base HP VERITAS Volume Manager and a full version called HP VERITAS Volume Manager. The Base product is a subset of the full version. With both versions of VxVM there is a Java-based administration interface, striping (RAID 0), concatenation, path failover support, online resizing of volumes, and a task monitor. The full version performs all of the functions in the Base product and also supports load balancing, hot relocation and unrelocation, mirroring of up to 32 copies (RAID 1), mirrored stripes, striped mirrors, RAID 5, online migration, and online relayout. The features of each are described in the *HP VERITAS Volume Manager Release Notes*.

On the system used for the examples compiled for the VxVM part of this chapter the root disk setup at the time 11i was originally loaded on the system was under control of Logical Volume Manager (LVM.) After loading HP Veritas Volume Manager as an application we can then perform storage administration on other disks on the system. The root disk will remain under LVM control and not be placed under VxVM control.

In the upcoming sections, we'll load HP Veritas Volume Manager and perform some basic storage management tasks so you can get a feel for this product. This is a product that has a lot of functionality and manuals devoted to using it, so in this part of the chapter we'll cover some of the basics. Please see *docs.hp.com* for a complete list of manuals on VxVm. Two that contain much more detailed information on configuring and using VxVM are *HP VERITAS Volume Manager Release Notes* and *HP VERITAS Volume Manager Administrator's Guide*.

HP VERITAS Volume Manager Setup

After loading HP Veritas from the Applications CD-ROM we have to decide what disk(s) we want to control with VxVM. Let's run **ioscan** to view the disks in our L-Class system:

```
# ioscan -funC disk
Class     I  H/W Path      Driver S/W State  H/W Type     Description


=====================================================================

disk      0  0/0/1/1.2.0   sdisk CLAIMED     DEVICE       SEAGATE ST318203LC

                           /dev/dsk/c1t2d0   /dev/rdsk/c1t2d0

disk      1  0/0/2/0.2.0   sdisk CLAIMED     DEVICE       SEAGATE ST318203LC

                           /dev/dsk/c2t2d0   /dev/rdsk/c2t2d0

disk      2  0/0/2/1.4.0   sdisk CLAIMED     DEVICE       TOSHIBA CD-ROM XM-6201TA

                           /dev/dsk/c3t4d0   /dev/rdsk/c3t4d0
```

This output shows two internal disks and a CD-ROM drive (we'll later add two more disks to demonstrate a setup of mirroring and striping). The root disk under LVM control is *c1t2d0*. We want to use VxVM to perform various storage management functions on disk *c2t2d0*. If there is any LVM header information on this disk, it must be removed prior to proceeding with any VxVM functions on the disk. The following two LVM-related commands were issued to create and remove this disk from LVM:

```
# pvcreate -f /dev/rdsk/c2t2d0
```

Physical volume "/dev/rdsk/c2t2d0" has been successfully created.

```
# pvremove /dev/rdsk/c2t2d0
```

The physical volume associated with "/dev/rdsk/c2t2d0" has been removed.

```
#
```

You may not have to issue the **pvcreate** command; however, I have found that issuing both commands works every time. This procedure is outlined in the *Release Notes* I mentioned earlier.

Next, we run **vxinstall** to perform the initial setup of VxVM. In the following procedure, we run **vxinstall** and select a *Quick Installation,* which walks us through evaluating the disks on the system and allows us to select those that we want to put under VxVM control:

```
# vxinstall

Populating VxVM DMP device directories ....
Generating list of attached controllers....
Volume Manager Installation


Menu: VolumeManager/Install

The Volume Manager names disks on your system using the controller
and disk number of the disk, substituting them into the following


    pattern:
            c<controller>t<disk>d<disk>


NOTE:  With the Dynamic Multipathing (DMP) facility of VxVM, the
controller number represents a multipath pseudo controller number
for those disk devices with multiple access paths.  For example,
if a disk has 2 paths from controllers c0 and c1, then the Volume
Manager displays only one of them, such as c0, to represent both
of the controllers.



    Some examples would be:

            c0t0d0- first controller, first target, first disk
            c1t0d0- second controller, first target, first disk
            c1t1d0- second controller, second target, first disk

    The Volume Manager has detected the following controllers on your
system:

            c1:
            c2:

Hit RETURN to continue.
```

```
Volume Manager Installation
Menu: VolumeManager/Install
   You will now be asked if you wish to use Quick Installation or
   Custom Installation.  Custom Installation allows you to select how
   the Volume Manager will handle the installation of each disk
   attached to your system.

   Quick Installation examines each disk attached to your system and
   attempts to create volumes to cover all disk partitions that might
   be used for file systems or for other similar purposes.


   If you do not wish to use some disks with the Volume Manager, or if
   you wish to reinitialize some disks, use the Custom Installation
   option Otherwise, we suggest that you use the Quick Installation
   option.


Hit RETURN to continue.
```

```
Volume Manager Installation Options
Menu: VolumeManager/Install


    1               Quick Installation
    2               Custom Installation
    ?               Display help about menu
    ??              Display help about the menuing system
    q               Exit from menus


Select an operation to perform: 1
```

```
Volume Manager Quick Installation
Menu: VolumeManager/Install/QuickInstall/c1

Generating list of attached disks on c1....
<excluding c1t2d0>
No disks were found attached to controller c1 !


Hit RETURN to continue.
```

```
Volume Manager Quick Installation
Menu: VolumeManager/Install/QuickInstall/c2

Generating list of attached disks on c2....
  The Volume Manager has detected the following disks on controller
c2:
  c2t2d0

Hit RETURN to continue.
```
_____

```
Volume Manager Quick Installation For Controller c2


Menu: VolumeManager/Install/QuickInstall/c2

Initialize all disks on this controller ? (destroys data on these
disks)
[y,n,q,?] (default: n) y


Are you sure ? (destroys data on these disks)
[y,n,q,?] (default: n) y


 Volume Manager will now initialize all the disks on this controller

Hit RETURN to continue.
```
_____

```
Volume Manager Quick Installation
Menu: VolumeManager/Install/QuickInstall/c2/Init

Use default disk names for these disks? [y,n,q,?] (default: y) y

  The c2t2d0 disk will be given disk name disk01

Hit RETURN to continue.
```
_____

```
Volume Manager Quick Installation
Menu: VolumeManager/Install/QuickInstall


  The following is a summary of your choices.
           c2t2d0New Disk
Is this correct [y,n,q,?] (default: y)
  The Volume Manager is now reconfiguring (partition phase)...
```

```
Volume Manager: Initializing c2t2d0 as a new disk.
The Volume Manager is now reconfiguring (initialization phase)...
Volume Manager: Adding disk01 (c2t2d0) as a new disk.

The Volume Daemon has been enabled for transactions
Starting the relocation daemon, vxrelocd.
#
```

Notice that **vxinstall** found the one disk on our system not under LVM control and asked us if we wanted to initialize this disk. Since we have only one potential disk to place under VxVM control, it is the only disk found by **vxinstall**. The *Quick Installation* we chose, as opposed to *Custom Installation*, makes some of the decisions for us, and in this case, helped us configure the disk quickly.

After running **vxinstall**, we can view the processes that have been started to support VxVM:

```
# ps -ef | grep vx
root      34       0   0 12:52:28 ?              0:01 vxfsd
root    2978       0   0 12:58:59 ?              0:00 vxiod
root    4170    4156   0 13:07:35 ttyp4          0:00 vxnotify
root    4079       1   0 13:05:51 ?              0:00 vxconfigd -k -m enable
root    4165       1   0 13:07:35 ttyp4          0:00 /sbin/sh -
                                        /usr/lib/vxvm/bin/vxrelocd root
root    4173    4165   0 13:07:35 ttyp4          0:00 vxnotify -f -w 15
root    4628    2900   1 13:16:12 ttyp4          0:00 grep vx
#
```

The initial load and setup of VxVM is quick and easy. I suggest that you obtain documents from *docs.hp.com* if you don't have them in hardcopy in case you need to refer to them as part of the setup. Without the *Release Notes* I would have not known the procedure to free the second disk from LVM control so I could place it under VxVM control.

Volume Manager Storage Administrator

After the setup of HP Veritas Volume Manager is complete, its graphical interface is invoked with **/opt/HPvmsa/bin/vmsa** for Volume

Manager Storage Administrator (I'll call this vmsa occasionally in this section). Figure 8-17 shows the interface for our L-Class system:

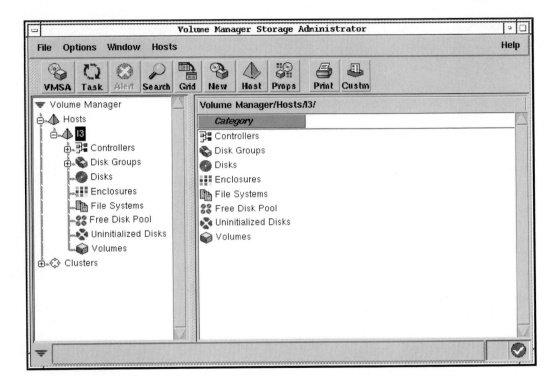

Figure 8-17   *Volume Manager Storage Administrator*

Figure 8-17 shows the many areas of administration that can be performed in this interface under our system name *l3*. We could also perform storage administration on additional systems, *Hosts*, and *Clusters*, which would be shown in the left-hand window along with system *l3* which is now shown.

Let's now select some of the administration icons and see what is reported for our L-Class system. Figure 8-18 shows the *Controllers* on our system:

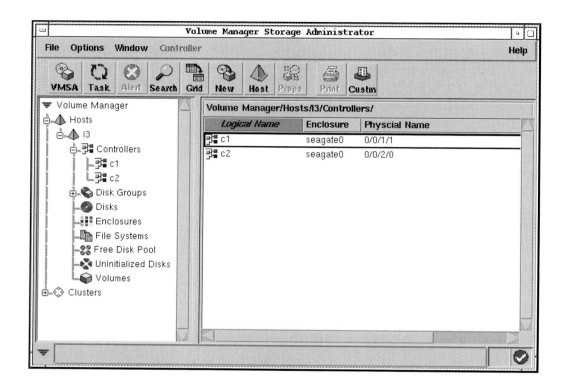

Figure 8-18 *Controllers*

Figure 8-18 shows two internal controllers on our system, *c1* and *c2*. All L-Class systems have two internal controllers, and in our case, there are no additional controllers. We could also select these controllers individually to see what disks are connected to them if we so desired.

Let's now view the *Disk Groups* on our system as shown in Figure 8-19:

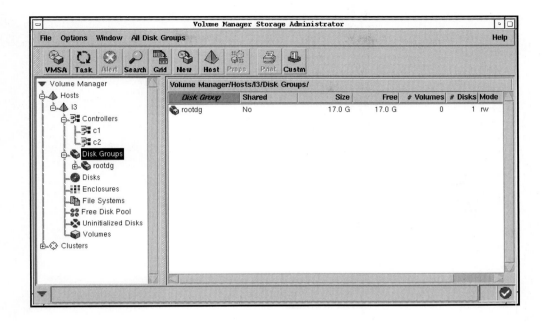

Figure 8-19 *Disk Groups*

Figure 8-19 shows one disk group, called *rootdg* which consists of one 17 GByte disk drive. This is the VxVM disk group we set up earlier. Notice that the LVM disk is not shown because it is not under VxVM control.

Next we'll view *Disks* in Figure 8-20:

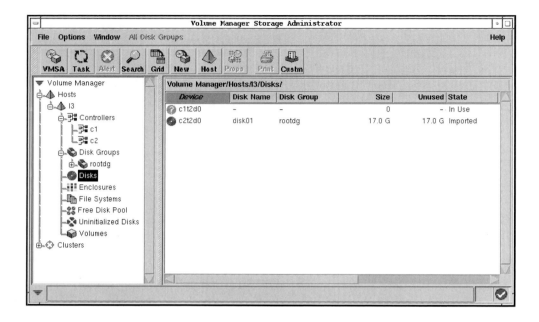

Figure 8-20 *Disks*

Figure 8-20 shows the two internal disks of our L-Class system. The first is in use by the Logical Volume Manager (root disk) and is not under the control of Veritas Volume Manager. It therefore has very little information associated with it because the VxVM interface does not recognize any of the LVM information. The second is our unused disk in *rootdg* that is called *disk01*.

Figure 8-21 shows the *File Systems* in use on our system:

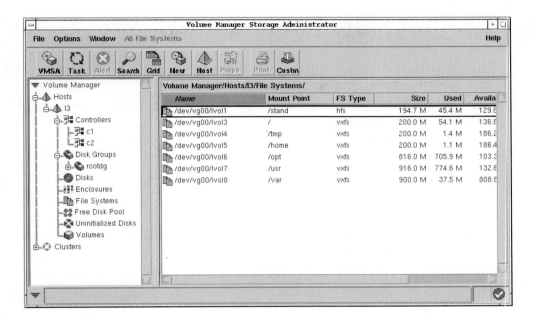

Figure 8-21   *File Systems*

Figure 8-21 shows many filesystems in use. Notice that all but one of these filesystems is a Veritas filesystem as indicated by the *vxfs*. This is sometimes a point of confusion. There is a Veritas file system (*vxfs*) that defines the type of filesystem and there is the Veritas Volume Manager, which we're covering in this section and is used to manage filesystems. You can also manage Veritas filesystems on HP-UX using LVM.

We know that we have one disk in *rootdg* that is unused at this time. Let's issue a couple of **vx** commands and compare these to what we see in the graphical interface. Table 8-1 at the end of this section that describes the use of some **vx** commands.

First, let's get a list of disks on the system with **vxdisk**:

```
# vxdisk list
DEVICE        TYPE         DISK          GROUP         STATUS
c1t2d0        simple       -             -             LVM
c2t2d0        simple       disk01        rootdg        online
#
```

The output of **vxdisk** shows two disks in our system. The first is the root disk, which is under LVM control, and the second is *disk01*, which is under VxVM control.

Next let's get some detailed information with **vxprint -ht**:

```
# vxprint -ht
Disk group: rootdg
DG NAME           NCONFIG       NLOG      MINORS    GROUP-ID
DM NAME           DEVICE        TYPE      PRIVLEN   PUBLEN    STATE
RV NAME           RLINK_CNT     KSTATE    STATE     PRIMARY   DATAVOLS   SRL
RL NAME           RVG           KSTATE    STATE     REM_HOST  REM_DG     REM_RLNK
V  NAME           RVG           KSTATE    STATE     LENGTH    USETYPE    PREFPLEX  RDPOL
PL NAME           VOLUME        KSTATE    STATE     LENGTH    LAYOUT     NCOL/WID  MODE
SD NAME           PLEX          DISK      DISKOFFS  LENGTH    [COL/]OFF  DEVICE    MODE
SV NAME           PLEX          VOLNAME   NVOLLAYR  LENGTH    [COL/]OFF  AM/NM     MODE
dg rootdg         default       default   0         969390349.1025.13
dm disk01         c2t2d0        simple    1024      17782088  -
#
```

Notice that only the information related to *rootdg*, which is under the control of the Veritas Volume Manager, has been produced. The *dg* is information related to the *disk group* and *dm* is information about the *disk mechanism*. In an upcoming **vxprint** , we'll add the *-q* option to eliminate the extensive header information produced with this output.

Next let's see what we have free on *rootdg* with the **vxdg** command:

```
# vxdg free
GROUP         DISK         DEVICE        TAG          OFFSET      LENGTH     FLAGS
rootdg        disk01       c2t2d0        c2t2d0       0           17782088   -
```

This output shows that we have nearly the full 18 GBytes of the disk free at this time.

We can now go back to the graphical interface and create a usable volume by selecting *rootdg* and entering information related to the new volume as shown in Figure 8-22:

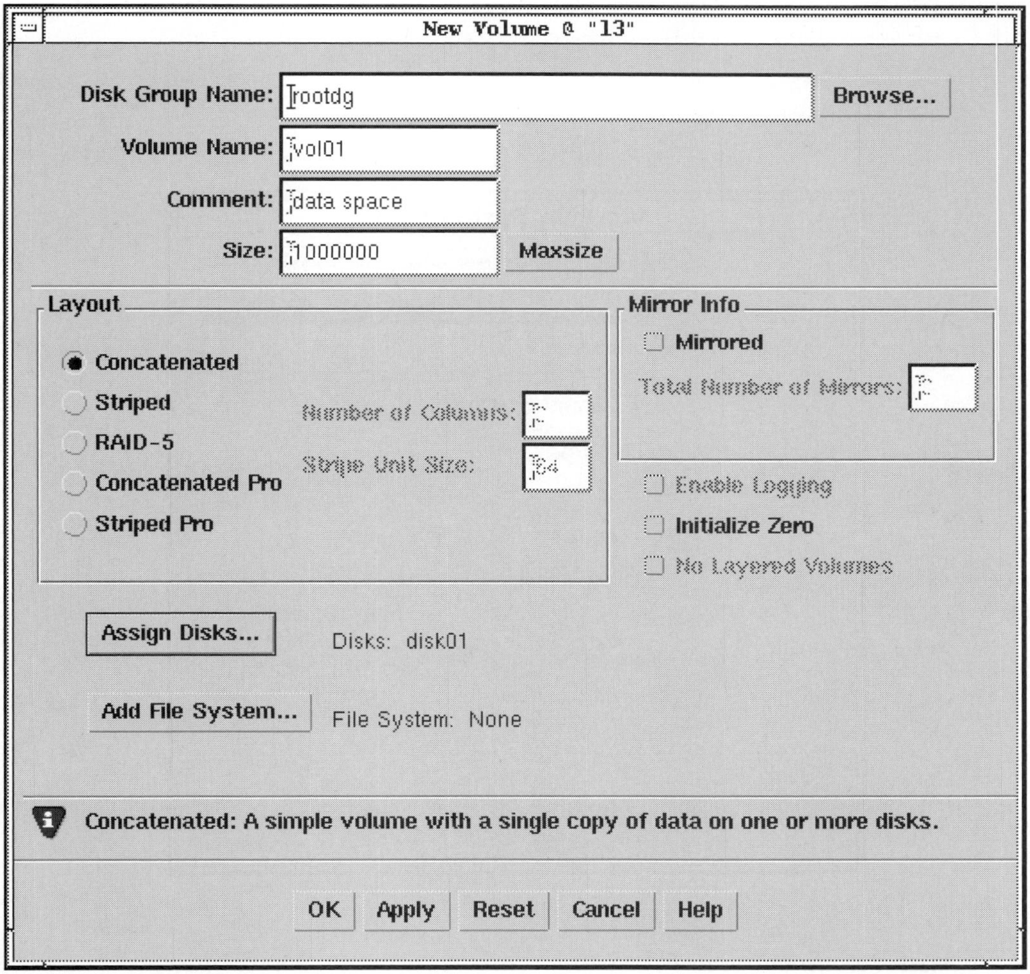

Figure 8-22   *Creating a New Volume*

The maximum size we could have made this volume is the total size of the unused disk of which *rootdg* is comprised, which is 17781760 bytes. We have selected about 1 GByte without RAID 5 because another disk would have been required. The default name of *vol011* is used. In addition, selecting *Add File System...* from the bottom of Figure 8-22 brought up the window in Figure 8-23:

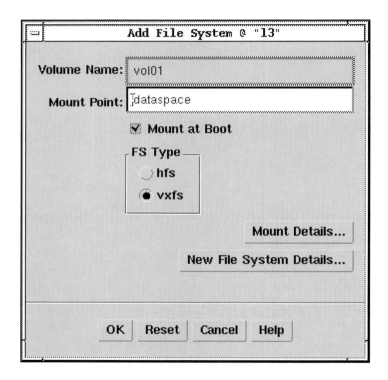

Figure 8-23 *Specifying File System Information of a New Volume*

In Figure 8-23 we selected a name of *Idataspace* as the mount point and have selected *vxfs* as the file systemtype. After clicking *OK*, a new volume is created as shown in Figure 8-24:

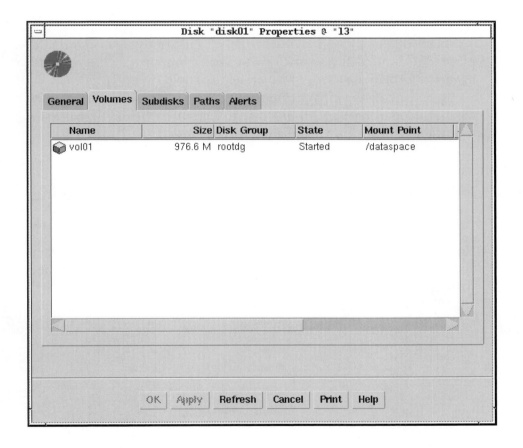

Figure 8-24 *vol01*

Figure 8-24 shows *vol01* with a mount point of */dataspace*. We can use the **vxprint** command with some useful options to see volume information. This includes information on the volume we just created. The following **vxprint** shows some useful options in the following listing:

```
# vxprint -AGtsq
Disk group: rootdg

dg rootdg        default      default  0        969390349.1025.13
sd disk01-01     vol01-01     disk01   0        1000000  0          c2t2d0   ENA
#
```

This output shows that our roughly 1 GByte area on *c2t2d0* is in place. We issued this **vxprint** with the *-q* option to eliminate the header information shown in the earlier example.

This simple example demonstrates the ease with which volumes can be added using VxVM. In the next section, we'll add two disks to the system and perform some additional setup.

HP VERITAS Volume Manager Mirroring and Striping

Now that we've covered the basics of VxVM, let's take the next step and add two additional disks to our system and use mirroring and striping.

To begin with let's again use the **vxdisk** command to see the two new disks we've added to the system:

```
# vxdisk list
DEVICE      TYPE      DISK        GROUP       STATUS
c1t0d0      simple    -           -           online invalid
c1t2d0      simple    -           -           LVM
c2t0d0      simple    -           -           online invalid
c2t2d0      simple    disk01      rootdg      online
#
```

At this point, the disks are listed, but they have not been configured in any way. These disks were physically added to the system, and no additional commands were issued prior to the **vxdisk**.

Let's now go to the graphical interface and configure these disks. Figure 8-25 shows a total of four disks, including our two new unconfigured disks:

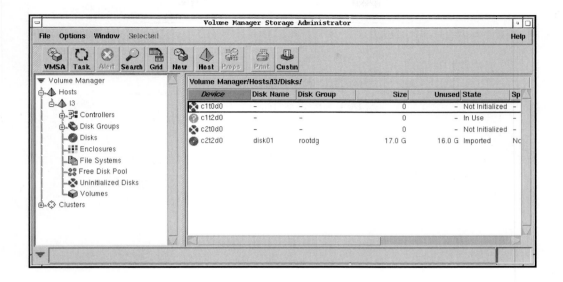

Figure 8-25 *Two New Disks in **vmsa***

Figure 8-25 shows that disks *c1t0d0* and *c2t0d0* are installed and *Not Initialized*. Let's now add these disks to a new disk group, called *test*, using the graphical interface as shown in Figure 8-26 for the first of the two disks:

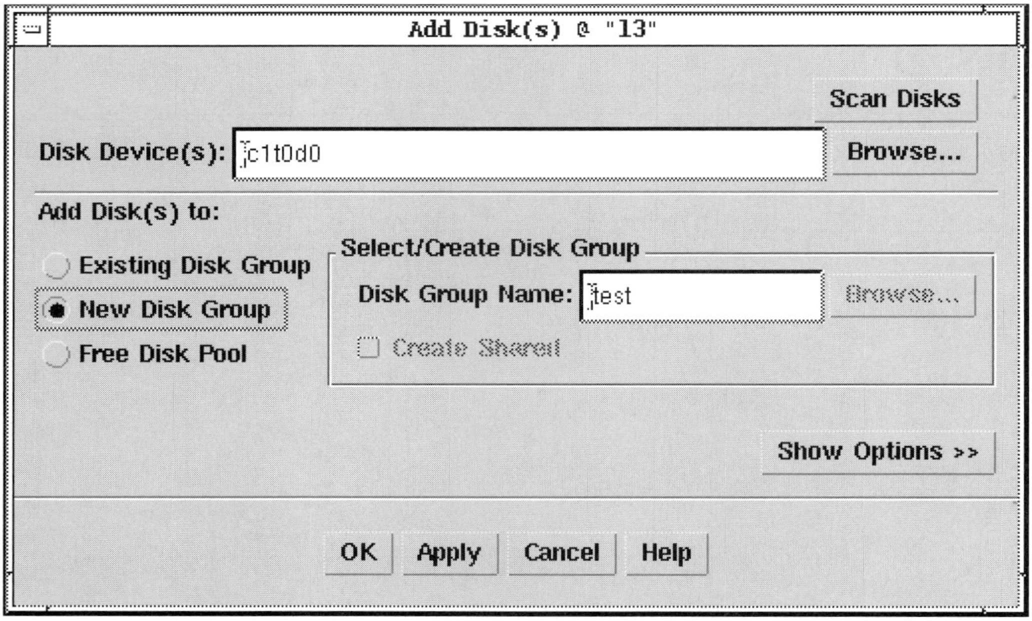

Figure 8-26   Adding New Disk to Group *test*

We add both disks to *test* graphically using the *Add Disk(s)* window. This results in the screen shown in Figure 8-27, in which both new disks, *test01* and *test02,* are part of *test*:

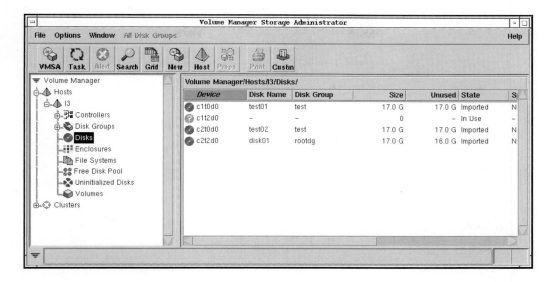

Figure 8-27   Two new disks Added to Group *test*

We can confirm the disks in *test* with the **vxdisk** command as shown in the following listing:

```
# vxdisk list
DEVICE      TYPE      DISK       GROUP        STATUS
c1t0d0      simple    test01     test         online
c1t2d0      simple    -          -            LVM
c2t0d0      simple    test02     test         online
c2t2d0      simple    disk01     rootdg       online
#
```

The disks are now shown as configured with names of *test01* and *test02* and both are *online*. Both of these disks are part of *Group test*.

Next, let's create a striped and mirrored volume in our new *disk group test*. Selecting *New* from the items on the *vmsa* window brings up the dialog box shown in Figure 8-28.

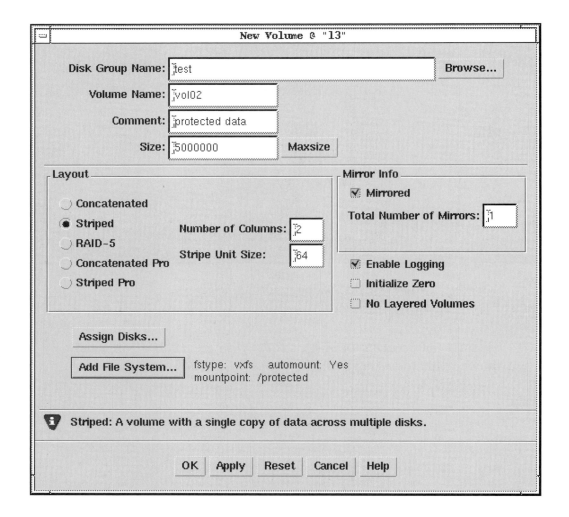

Figure 8-28 *Creating a New Volume That is Striped and Mirrored*

From Figure 8-28, you can see all of the characteristics specified for *vol02*. It is roughly 5 GBytes in size, it is striped, and it has one mirror copy. It is a filesystem type of *vxfs* and has a mount point of **/protected**.

After adding this volume, it appears in the *vmsa* window as shown in Figure 8-29:

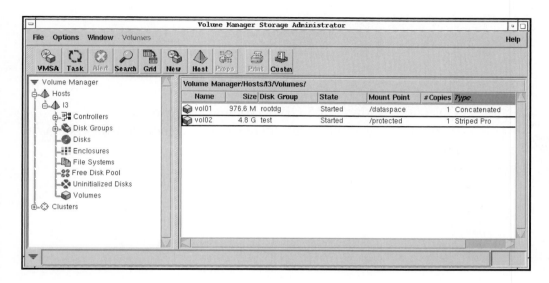

Figure 8-29   Volume *vol02*

We could go to the command line to confirm the presence of *vol02* with **vxprint** and no options as shown in the following listing:

```
# vxprint
Disk group: rootdg

TY NAME        ASSOC       KSTATE    LENGTH    PLOFFS    STATE     TUTIL0    PUTIL0
dg rootdg      rootdg      -         -         -         -         -         -

dm disk01      c2t2d0      -         17782088  -         -         -         -

v  vol01       fsgen       ENABLED   1000000   -         ACTIVE    -         -
pl vol01-01    vol01       ENABLED   1000000   -         ACTIVE    -         -
sd disk01-01   vol01-01    ENABLED   1000000   0         -         -         -

Disk group: test

TY NAME        ASSOC       KSTATE    LENGTH    PLOFFS    STATE     TUTIL0    PUTIL0
dg test        test        -         -         -         -         -         -

dm test01      c1t0d0      -         17782088  -         -         -         -
dm test02      c2t0d0      -         17782088  -         -         -         -

v  vol02       fsgen       ENABLED   5000000   -         ACTIVE    -         -
pl vol02-03    vol02       ENABLED   5000064   -         ACTIVE    -         -
```

```
sv vol02-S01      vol02-03       ENABLED   2500032   0      -         -      -
sv vol02-S02      vol02-03       ENABLED   2500032   0      -         -      -

v  vol02-L01      fsgen          ENABLED   2500032   -      ACTIVE    -      -
pl vol02-P01      vol02-L01      ENABLED   LOGONLY   -      ACTIVE    -      -
sd test01-03      vol02-P01      ENABLED   33        LOG    -         -      -
pl vol02-P02      vol02-L01      ENABLED   2500032   -      ACTIVE    -      -
sd test01-04      vol02-P02      ENABLED   2500032   0      -         -      -

v  vol02-L02      fsgen          ENABLED   2500032   -      ACTIVE    -      -
pl vol02-P03      vol02-L02      ENABLED   LOGONLY   -      ACTIVE    -      -
sd test01-05      vol02-P03      ENABLED   33        LOG    -         -      -
pl vol02-P04      vol02-L02      ENABLED   2500032   -      ACTIVE    -      -
sd test02-02      vol02-P04      ENABLED   2500032   0      -         -      -
#
```

man page

bdf - 8

This output shows our 5 GByte volume as mirrored.

In addition we want to see **/protected** as a mounted filesystem with **bdf**:

```
# bdf

Filesystem            kbytes     used     avail %used Mounted on
/dev/vg00/lvol3       204800    55509    140002   28% /
/dev/vg00/lvol1       199381    46526    132916   26% /stand
/dev/vg00/lvol8       921600    38739    827833    4% /var
/dev/vg00/lvol7       937984   793162    135806   85% /usr
/dev/vg00/lvol4       204800     1529    190628    1% /tmp
/dev/vg00/lvol6       835584   722803    105775   87% /opt
/dev/vg00/lvol5       204800     1162    190917    1% /home
/dev/vx/dsk/rootdg/vol01
                     1000000     1349    936243    0% /dataspace
/dev/vx/dsk/test/vol02
                     5000000     2693   4685038    0% /protected
#
```

Our new volume, *vol02*, has been created with a size of 5 GBytes and a mount point of **/protected**.

Several of the basics of using VxVM were covered in the previous examples. This by no means is an exhaustive coverage of VxVM, but hopefully it serves as a good introduction. Please refer to the detailed information in the manuals related to VxVM.

Although we focused mostly on *vmsa* in this section there are a number of **vx** commands that you can issue that perform the same functions as the graphical interface. I sometimes like to issue commands to view volume-related work I have performed in the graphical interface just to confirm the results. Table 8-1 lists some of the most commonly used **vx** commands and their functions.

TABLE 8-1 **VxVM** Commands

Command	Description
vxassist	Create and change volumes.
vxdctl	Manage the vxconfigd daemon.
vxdg	Perform tasks related to disk groups.
vxdisk	Perform tasks related to disks.
vxdiskadd	Used to add disks.
vxedit	Change VxVM objects.
vxmake	Create VxVM objects.
vxmend	Correct configuration problems.
vxplex	Perform plex-related tasks.
vxprint	Print configuration information.
vxsd	Perform tasks on subdisks.
vxstat	Print volume statistics.
vxtrace	Trace volume tasks.
vxunrelocate	Move relocated subdisks.
vxvol	Perform volume tasks.

These commands are covered in the HP documentation set, and there are also man pages available which provide detailed usage information on the commands.

Some Additional File System-Related Commands

Viewing File Systems with bdf

man page

bdf - 8

You can manually view the file systems you have mounted with the **bdf** command. **bdf** provides the following output:

File system	Block device file system name. In the following example, several logical volumes are shown.
KBytes	Number of KBytes of total disk space on the file system.
used	The number of used KBytes on the file system.
avail	The number of available KBytes on the file system.
%used	The percentage of total available disk space that is used on the file system.
Mounted on	The directory name on which the file system is mounted.
iused	Number of inodes in use (only if you use the -i option with **bdf**).
ifree	Number of free inodes (only if you use the -i option with **bdf**).
%iuse	Percentage of inodes in use (only if you use the **-i** option with **bdf**).

Here is an example of **bdf** that is also in "Logical Volume Manager Background," covered earlier in this chapter:

$ **/usr/bin/bdf**

File system	kbytes	used	avail	%used	Mounted on
/dev/vg00/lvol3	47829	18428	24618	43%	/
/dev/vg00/lvol1	67733	24736	36223	41%	/stand
/dev/vg00/lvol8	34541	8673	22413	28%	/var
/dev/vg00/lvol7	299157	149449	119792	56%	/usr
/dev/vg00/lvol4	23013	48	20663	0%	/tmp
/dev/vg00/lvol6	99669	32514	57188	36%	/opt
/dev/vg00/lvol5	19861	9	17865	0%	/home
/dev/dsk/c0t6d0	802212	552120	169870	76%	/mnt/9.x

File System Maintenance with fsck

man page

fsck - 8

fsck is a program used for file system maintenance on HP-UX systems. **fsck** checks file system consistency and can make many "life-saving" repairs to a corrupt file system. **fsck** can be run with several options, including the following:

-F   This option allows you to specify the file system type (see the explanation of file system types in Chapter 15. Be sure to specify a file system type. On some UNIX variants **/etc/fstab** will be used to determine the file system type on others it will not be used. See the **fstab** description later in this section.

-m   This is a sanity check of the file system. If you run this, you'll be told whether your file system is okay or not. I did the following to check lvol5, which is mounted as **/home**:

$ `umount /home`

```
$ fsck -m /dev/vg00/lvol5
```

```
vxfs fsck: sanity check: /dev/vg00/lvol5 OK
```

man page

fsck - 8

        -y   **fsck** will ask questions if run in interactive mode, which is the default. Using the *-y* option causes a "yes" response to all questions asked by **fsck**. Don't use this! If you have a serious problem with your file system, data will probably have to be removed, and the *-y* indicates that the response to every question, including removing data, will be "yes".

        -n   The response to all questions asked by **fsck** will be "no." Don't use this, either. If your file system is in bad shape, you may have to respond "yes" to some questions in order to repair the file system. All "no" responses will not do the job.

    Since your system runs **fsck** on any file systems that were not marked as clean at the time you shut down the system, you can rest assured that when your system boots, any disks that were not properly shut down will be checked. It is a good idea to run **fsck** interactively on a periodic basis just so you can see firsthand that all of your file systems are in good working order.

    Should **fsck** find a problem with a directory or file, it would place these in the **lost+found** directory, which is at the top level of each file system. If a file or directory appears in **lost+found,** you may be able to identify the file or directory by examining it and move it back to its original location. You can use the **file, what,** and **strings** commands on a file to obtain more information about it to help identify its origin.

    How are file system problems created? The most common cause of a file system problem is improper shutdown of the system. The information written to file systems is first written to a buffer cache in memory. It is later written to the disk with the **sync** command by unmounting the disk, or through the normal use of filling the buffer and writing it to the disk. If you walk up to a system and shut off the power, you will surely end up with a file system problem. Data in the buffer that was not synchronized to the disk will be lost, the file system will not be marked as properly shut down, and **fsck** will be run when the system boots. A sudden loss of power can also cause an improper system shutdown.

man page

fsck - 8

Proper shutdown of the system is described with the **shutdown** command. Although **fsck** is a useful utility that has been known to work miracles on occasion, you don't want to take any unnecessary risks with your file systems. So be sure to properly shut down your system.

The **/etc/fstab** file mentioned earlier is used by **fsck** to determine the sequence of the file system check if it is required at the time of boot. The sequence of entries in **/etc/fstab** is important if a "pass number" for any of the entries does not exist. Here is an example of the **/etc/fstab** file:

```
# System /etc/fstab file. Static information about the file
# systems. See fstab(4) and sam(1m) for further details.

/dev/vg00/lvol3     /           vxfs   delaylog    0   1
/dev/vg00/lvol1     /stand      hfs    defaults    0   1
/dev/vg00/lvol4     /tmp        vxfs   delaylog    0   2
/dev/vg00/lvol6     /opt        vxfs   delaylog    0   2
/dev/vg00/lvol5     /home       vxfs   delaylog    0   2
/dev/vg00/lvol7     /usr        vxfs   delaylog    0   2
/dev/vg00/lvol8     /var        vxfs   delaylog    0   2
/dev/dsk/c0tt6d0    /tmp/mnt9.x hfs    rw, suid    0   2

        |               |           |          |        |     |

        v               v           v          v        v     v
```

device special file	directory	type	options	backup frequency	pass #

device special file

This is the device block file, such as **/dev/vg00/lvol1** in the example.

directory   The name of the directory under which the device special file is mounted.

type   Can be one of several types including:
                       cdfs (local CD-ROM file system)
                       hfs (high performance local file system)
                       nfs (network file system)
                       vxfs (journaled file system)
                       swap or
                       swapfs

options   Several options are available, including those shown in the example. *rw* is read and write; *ro* is read only.

backup frequency

                       To be used by backup utilities in the future.

pass #   Used by **fsck** to determine the order in which file system checks (**fsck**) will take place.

comment   Anything you want, as long as it's preceded by a #.

Initialize with mediainit

A command you probably won't use, but should be aware of, is **mediainit**. When you use SAM to set up disks for you, the **mediainit** command may be run to initialize new media.

Here are some of the options of **mediainit**:

-v

This is the verbose option. **mediainit** normally just prints error messages to the screen. You can get continuous feedback on what **mediainit** is doing with the **-v** option.

man page

mediainit-8

-i interleave

This allows you to specify the interleave factor, which is the relationship between sequential logical and physical records. **mediainit** will provide this if one is not specified.

-f format

The format option allows you to specify format options for devices, such as floppy disks, that support different format options. This is not required for hard disks.

pathname

This is the character device file to be used for **mediainit**.

man page

newfs - 8

newfs, which was used in some of the earlier examples, is used to create a new file system. **newfs** calls the **mksf** command earlier covered. **newfs** builds a file system of the type you specify (this is one of the commands that uses the *-F* option, so you can specify the file system type).

Manual Pages for Commands Used in Chapter 8

The following section contains copies of the manual pages for commands used in Chapter 8. This makes a quick reference of commands commonly used during your system administration day. The manual pages, more commonly referred to as man pages, are listed in detail with the exception of the LVM commands. Since I strongly encourage you to use SAM to make any LVM alterations, I am giving a synopsis of these commands only. They are listed under "vg command summaries," "lv command summaries," and "pv command summaries."

bdf

bdf - Produce a report of free disk blocks.

man page

bdf - 8

bdf(1M)   bdf(1M)

NAME
     bdf - report number of free disk blocks (Berkeley version)

SYNOPSIS

     /usr/bin/bdf [-b] [-i] [-l] [-t type | [filesystem|file] ...]

DESCRIPTION
     The bdf command displays the amount of free disk space available
     either on the specified filesystem (/dev/dsk/c0d0s0, for example) or
     on the file system in which the specified file (such as $HOME), is
     contained. If no file system is specified, the free space on all of
     the normally mounted file systems is printed. The reported numbers
     are in kilobytes.

   Options
     The bdf command recognizes the following options:

          -b   Display information regarding file system
                         swapping.

          -i   Report the number of used and free inodes.

          -l   Display information for local file systems only
                         (for example, HFS and CDFS file systems).

          -t type   Report on the file systems of a given type (for
                         example, nfs or hfs).

RETURN VALUE
     The bdf command returns 0 on success (able to get status on all file
     systems), or returns 1 on failure (unable to get status on one or more
     file systems).

WARNINGS
     If file system names are too long, the output for a given entry is
     displayed on two lines.

     The bdf command does not account for any disk space reserved for swap
     space, or used for the HFS boot block (8 KB, 1 per file system), HFS
     superblocks (8 KB each, 1 per disk cylinder), HFS cylinder group
     blocks (1 KB - 8 KB each, 1 per cylinder group), and inodes (currently
     128 bytes reserved for each inode). Non-HFS file systems may have
     other items not accounted for by this command.

AUTHOR
     bdf was developed by the University of California, Berkeley.

FILES
     /etc/fstab   Static information about the file systems.
     /etc/mnttab   Mounted file system table.
     /dev/dsk/*   File system devices.

SEE ALSO
     df(1M), fstab(4), mnttab(4).

fsck

fsck - File system check and repair (this is a generic man page; there are also man pages for hfs and vxfs).

man page

fsck - 8

---

fsck(1M)   fsck(1M)

NAME
     fsck (generic) - file system consistency check and interactive repair

SYNOPSIS

     /usr/sbin/fsck [-F FSType] [-m] [-V] [special]

     /usr/sbin/fsck [-F FSType] [-o FSspecific-options] [-V] [special ...]

DESCRIPTION
     The fsck command audits and interactively repairs inconsistent
     conditions for HP-UX file systems on mass storage device files
     identified by special. If the file system is consistent, the number
     of files on that file system and the number of used and free blocks
     are reported. If the file system is inconsistent, fsck provides a
     mechanism to fix these inconsistencies, depending on which form of the
     fsck command is used.

     special represents a special device (e.g., /dev/rdsk/c1d0s8).

   Options
     fsck recognizes the following options:

          -F FStype   Specify the file system type on which to operate
                           (see fstyp(1M) and fs_wrapper(5)). If this option
                           is not included on the command line, then the file
                           system type is determined from the file /etc/fstab
                           by matching special with an entry in that file.
                           If there is no entry in /etc/fstab, then the file
                           system type is determined from the file
                           /etc/default/fs.

          -m   Perform a sanity check only. fsck will return 0 if
                           the file system is suitable for mounting. If the
                           file system needs additional checking, the return
                           code is 32. If the file system is mounted, the
                           return code is 33. Error codes larger than 33
                           indicate that the file system is badly damaged.

          -o FSspecific-options
                           Specify options specific to each file system type.
                           FSspecific-options is a list of suboptions and/or
                           keyword/attribute pairs intended for a file-
                           system-specific version of the command. See the
                           file-system-specific manual entries for a
                           description of the specific_options supported, if
                           any.

          -V   Echo the completed command line, but perform no
                           other action. The command line is generated by
                           incorporating the user-specified options and other
                           information derived from /etc/fstab. This option

allows the user to verify the command line.

RETURN VALUES
The following values are returned by the -m option to fsck:

0   Either no errors were detected or all errors were corrected.

32   The file system needs additional checking.

33   The file system is mounted.

Return values greater that 33 indicate that file system is badly corrupted. File system specific versions of fsck will have their own additional return values (see fsck_FSType(1M)).

WARNINGS
This command may not be supported for all file system types.

FILES
| /etc/default/fs | Specifies the default file system type |
| /etc/fstab | Default list of file systems to check |

STANDARDS CONFORMANCE
fsck: SVID3

SEE ALSO
fsck_FSType(1M), mkfs(1M), newfs(1M), fstab(4), fs_wrapper(5).

"lv" command summaries

"lv" commands - Command summaries related to logical volumes.

```
lvchange(1M)                                                      lvchange(1M)

NAME
     lvchange - change LVM logical volume characteristics

SYNOPSIS

     /sbin/lvchange [-a availability] [-A autobackup]
          [-c mirror_consistency] [-C contiguous] [-d schedule]
          [-M mirror_write_cache] [-p permission] [-r relocate] [-s strict]
          lv_path
```

```
lvcreate(1M)                                                      lvcreate(1M)

NAME
     lvcreate - create logical volume in LVM volume group

SYNOPSIS

     /sbin/lvcreate [-A autobackup] [-c mirror_consistency] [-C contiguous]
          [-d schedule] [-i stripes -I stripe_size]
          [-l le_number | -L lv_size] [-m mirror_copies]
          [-M mirror_write_cache] [-n lv_name] [-p permission]
          [-r relocate] [-s strict] vg_name
```

```
lvdisplay(1M)                                                     lvdisplay(1M)

NAME
     lvdisplay - display information about LVM logical volumes

SYNOPSIS

     /sbin/lvdisplay [-k] [-v] lv_path  ...
```

lvextend(1M)   lvextend(1M)

NAME
     lvextend - increase space, increase mirrors for LVM logical volume

SYNOPSIS

     /sbin/lvextend [-A autobackup]
         {-l le_number | -L lv_size | -m mirror_copies}
         lv_path [pv_path ... | pvg_name ...]

lvlnboot(1M)   lvlnboot(1M)

NAME
     lvlnboot - prepare LVM logical volume to be root, boot, primary swap,
     or dump volume

SYNOPSIS

     /sbin/lvlnboot [[-A autobackup]
         { -b boot_lv | -d dump_lv | -r root_lv | -R | -s swap_lv }] [-v]
         [vg_name]

lvmerge(1M)   lvmerge(1M)
               Requires Optional HP MirrorDisk/UX Software

NAME
     lvmerge - merge two LVM logical volumes into one logical volume

SYNOPSIS

     /sbin/lvmerge [-A autobackup] dest_lv_path src_lv_path

lvmmigrate(1M)   lvmmigrate(1M)

NAME
     lvmmigrate - prepare root file system for migration from partitions to
     LVM logical volumes

SYNOPSIS

     /usr/sbin/lvmmigrate [-d disk_special_file] [-e file_system ...] [-f]
         [-i file_system ...] [-n] [-v]

lvreduce(1M)   lvreduce(1M)

NAME
     lvreduce - decrease number of physical extents allocated to LVM
     logical volume

SYNOPSIS

     /sbin/lvreduce [-A autobackup] [-f] -l le_number lv_path

     /sbin/lvreduce [-A autobackup] [-f] -L lv_size lv_path

     /sbin/lvreduce [-A autobackup] -m mirror_copies lv_path [pv_path ...]

     /sbin/lvreduce [-A autobackup] -k pvkey -m mirror_copies lv_path
     [pv_path ...]

lvremove(1M)   lvremove(1M)

NAME
     lvremove - remove one or more logical volumes from LVM volume group

SYNOPSIS

     /sbin/lvremove [-A autobackup] [-f] lv_path ...

lvrmboot(1M)   lvrmboot(1M)

NAME
     lvrmboot - remove LVM logical volume link to root, primary swap, or
     dump volume

SYNOPSIS

     /sbin/lvrmboot [-A autobackup] [-d dump_lv] [-r] [-s] [-v] vg_name

lvsplit(1M)   lvsplit(1M)
                    Requires Optional HP MirrorDisk/UX Software

NAME
     lvsplit - split mirrored LVM logical volume into two logical volumes

SYNOPSIS

     /sbin/lvsplit [-A autobackup] [-s suffix] lv_path ...

lvsync(1M)
lvsync(1M)

                    Requires Optional HP MirrorDisk/UX Software

NAME
     lvsync - synchronize stale mirrors in LVM logical volumes

SYNOPSIS

     /sbin/lvsync lv_path ...

mediainit

mediainit - Initialize mass storage media.

mediainit(1)   mediainit(1)

NAME
     mediainit - initialize disk or cartridge tape media, partition DDS
     tape

SYNOPSIS

     mediainit [-vr] [-f fmt_optn] [-i interleave] [-p size] pathname

DESCRIPTION
     mediainit initializes mass storage media by formatting the media,
     writing and reading test patterns to verify media integrity, then
     sparing any defective blocks found. This process prepares the disk or
     tape for error-free operation. Initialization destroys all existing
     user data in the area being initialized.

     mediainit can also used for partitioning DDS tape media. See the -p
     option below for further details.

   Options
     The following command options are recognized. They can be specified
     in any order, but all must precede the pathname. Options without
     parameters can be listed individually or grouped together. Options
     with parameters must be listed individually, but white space between
     the option and its parameter is discretionary.

            -v   Normally, mediainit provides only fatal error
                              messages which are directed to standard error.
                              The -v (verbose) option sends device-specific
                              information related to low-level operation of
                              mediainit to standard output (stdout). This
                              option is most useful to trained service personnel
                              because it usually requires detailed knowledge of
                              device operation before the information can be
                              interpreted correctly.

            -r   (re-certify) This option forces a complete tape
                              certification whether or not the tape has been
                              certified previously. All record of any
                              previously spared blocks is discarded, so any bad
                              blocks will have to be rediscovered. This option
                              should be used only if:

                                 - It is suspected that numerous blocks on
                                    the tape have been spared which should not
                                    have been, or

                                 - It is necessary to destroy (overwrite) all
                                    previous data on the tape.

            -f fmt_optn   The format option is a device-specific number in
                              the range 0 through 239. It is intended solely

for use with certain SS/80 devices that support
multiple media formats (independent from
interleave factor). For example, certain
microfloppy drives support 256-, 512-, and 1024-
byte sectors. mediainit passes any supplied
format option directly through to the device. The
device then either accepts the format option if it
is supported, or rejects it if it is not
supported. Refer to device operating manuals for
additional information. The default format option
is 0.

-i interleave   The interleave factor, interleave, refers to the
relationship between sequential logical records
and sequential physical records. It defines the
number of physical records on the media that lie
between the beginning points of two consecutively
numbered logical records. The choice of
interleave factor can have a substantial impact on
disk performance. For CS/80 and SS/80 drives,
consult the appropriate device operating manual
for details. For Amigo drives, see WARNINGS.

-p size   Partition DDS cartridge media into two logical
separate volumes: partition 0 and partition 1:

- size specifies the minimum size of
  partition 1 (in Mbytes).

- Partition 0 is the remainder of the tape
  (partition 0 physically follows partition
  1 on the tape).

The actual size of partition 1 is somewhat larger
than the requested size to allow for tape media
errors during writing. Thus, a size of 400
formats the DDS tape into two partitions where
partition 1 holds at least 400 Megabytes of data,
and the remainder of the tape is used for
partition 0 (for a 1300 Mbyte DDS cartridge, this
means that partition 0 has a size somewhat less
than 900 Mbytes).

Note that it is unnecessary to format a DDS tape
before use unless the tape is being partitioned.
Unformatted DDS media does not require
initialization when used as a single partition
tape. Accessing partition 1 on a single-partition
tape produces an error. To change a two-partition
tape to single-partition, use mediainit with 0
specified as the size.

pathname   pathname is the path name to the character (raw)
device special file associated with the device
unit or volume that is to be initialized.
mediainit aborts if you lack either read or write
permission to the device special file, or if the
device is currently open for any other process.
This prevents accidental initialization of the
root device or any mounted volume. mediainit
locks the unit or volume being initialized so that
no other processes can access it.

Except for SCSI devices, pathname must be a device
special file whose minor number of the device
being initialized has the diagnostic bit set. For

device special files with the diagnostic bit set, the section number is meaningless. The entire device is accessed.

When a given CS/80 or SS/80 device contains multiple units, or a given unit contains multiple volumes as defined by the drive controller, any available unit or volume associated with that controller can be initialized, independent of other units and volumes that share the same controller. Thus, you can initialize one unit or volume to any format or interleave factor without affecting formats or data on companion units or volumes. However, be aware that the entire unit or volume (as defined by the drive controller) is initialized without considering the possibility that it may be subdivided into smaller structures by the the operating software. When such structures exist, unexpected loss of data is possible.

mediainit dominates controller resources and limits access by competing processes to other units or volumes sharing the same controller. If other simultaneous processes need access to the same controller, some access degradation can be expected until initialization is complete; especially if you are initializing a tape cartridge in a drive that shares the root disk controller.

In general, mediainit attempts to carefully check any -f (format option) or -i (interleave options) supplied, and aborts if an option is out of range or inappropriate for the media being initialized. Specifying an interleave factor or format option value of 0 has the same effect as not specifying the option at all.

For disks that support interleave factors, the acceptable range is usually 1 (no interleave) through n-1, where n is the number of sectors per track. With SS/80 hard disks, the optimum interleave factor is usually determined by the speed (normal or high) of the HP-IB interface card used and whether DMA is present in the system. The optimum interleave factor for SS/80 flexible disk drives is usually a constant (often 2), and is independent of the type of HP-IB interface used. The optimum interleave factor for CS/80 disks is usually 1 and is also usually not related to the type of HP-IB interface being used. In any case, refer to the appropriate device operating manual for recommended values.

If a disk being initialized requires an interleave factor but none is specified, mediainit provides an appropriate, though not necessarily optimum default. For CS/80 and SS/80 disks, mediainit uses whatever the device reports as its current interleave factor. SS/80 floppy drives report their minimum (usually best) interleave factor, if the currently installed media is unformatted.

When a given device supports format options, the allowable range of interleave factors may be related to the specified format option. In such instances, mediainit cannot check the interleave factor if one is specified.

Notes

Most types of mass storage media must be initialized before they can be used. HP hard disks, flexible disks, and cartridge tapes require some form of initialization, but 9-track tapes do not. Initialization usually involves formatting the media, writing and reading test patterns, then sparing any defective blocks. Depending upon the media and device type, none, some, or all of the initialization process may have been performed at the factory. mediainit completes whatever steps are appropriate to prepare the media for error-free operation.

Most HP hard disks are formatted and exhaustively tested at the factory by use of a process more thorough but also more time-consuming than appropriate for mediainit. However, mediainit is still valuable

for ensuring the integrity of the media after factory shipment,
formatting with the correct interleave factor, and sparing any blocks
which may have become defective since original factory testing was
performed.

HP flexible disks are not usually formatted prior to shipment, so they
must undergo the entire initialization process before they can be
used.

All HP CS/80 cartridge tapes are certified and formatted prior to
shipment from the factory. When a tape is certified, it is thoroughly
tested and defective blocks are spared. mediainit usually certifies a
tape only if it has not been certified previously. If the tape has
been previously certified and spared, mediainit usually reorganizes
the tape's spare block table, retaining any previous spares, and
optimizing their assignment for maximum performance under sequential
access. Reorganizing the spare block table takes only a few seconds,
whereas complete certification takes about a half-hour for 150-foot
tapes, and over an hour for 600-foot tapes.

HP CS/80 cartridge tape drives have a feature called "auto-sparing".
If under normal usage the drive has trouble reading a block, the drive
logs the fact and automatically spares out that block the next time
data is written to it. Thus, as a tape is used, any marginal blocks
that were not spared during certification are spared automatically if
they cause problems. This sparing is automatic within the device, and
is totally independent of mediainit.

Reorganization of a tape's spare block table technically renders any
existing data undefined, but the data is not usually destroyed by
overwriting. To ensure that old tape data is destroyed, which is
useful for security, complete tape re-certification can be forced with
the -r option.

Some applications may require that a file system be placed on the
media before use. mediainit does not create a file system; it only
prepares media for writing and reading. If such a file system is
required, other utilities such as newfs, lifinit, or mkfs must be
invoked after running mediainit (see newfs(1M), lifinit(1), and
mkfs(1M)).

RETURN VALUE
     mediainit returns one of the following values:

          0   Successful completion.
          1   A device-related error occurred.
          2   A syntax-related error was encountered.

ERRORS
     Appropriate error messages are printed on standard error during
     execution of mediainit.

EXAMPLES
     Format an HP 9122 SS/80 3-1/2-inch flexible disk with an interleave
     factor of 2, 1024-byte sectors, and double-sided HP format:

          mediainit -i 2 -f 3 /dev/rdsk/9122

WARNINGS
     For a device that contains multiple units on a single controller, each
     unit can be initialized independently from any other unit. It should
     be noted, however, that mediainit requires that there be no other
     processes accessing the device before initialization begins,
     regardless of which unit is being initialized. If there are accesses
     currently in progress, mediainit aborts.

Aborting mediainit is likely to leave the medium in a corrupt state, even if it was previously initialized. To recover, the initialization must be restarted.

During the initialization process, open() rejects all other accesses to the device being initialized, producing the error EACCES (see open(2)).

DEPENDENCIES
   Series 800
     Partitioning of DDS tape media (-p option) is not supported.

AUTHOR
    mediainit was developed by HP.

SEE ALSO
    lifinit(1), mkfs(1M), newfs(1M).

mount

mount - Mount and umount file systems (this is a generic man page; there are also man pages for hfs and vxfs).

.

```
mount(1M)                                                          mount(1M)

NAME
     mount (generic), umount (generic) - mount and unmount file systems

SYNOPSIS
     /usr/sbin/mount [-l] [-p|-v]

     /usr/sbin/mount -a [-F FStype] [-eQ]

     /usr/sbin/mount [-F FStype] [-eQrV] [-o specific_options]
         {special|directory}

     /usr/sbin/mount [-F FStype] [-eQrV] [-o specific_options]
         special directory

     /usr/sbin/umount [-v] [-V] {special|directory}

     /usr/sbin/umount -a [-F FStype] [-v]

DESCRIPTION
     The mount command mounts file systems.  Only a superuser can mount
     file systems.  Other users can use mount to list mounted file systems.

     The mount command attaches special, a removable file system, to
     directory, a directory on the file tree.  directory, which must
     already exist, will become the name of the root of the newly mounted
     file system.  special and directory must be given as absolute path
     names.  If either special or directory is omitted, mount attempts to
     determine the missing value from an entry in the /etc/fstab file.
     mount can be invoked on any removable file system, except /.

     If mount is invoked without any arguments, it lists all of the mounted
     file systems from the file system mount table, /etc/mnttab.

     The umount command unmounts mounted file systems.  Only a superuser
     can unmount file systems.

   Options (mount)
     The mount command recognizes the following options:

         -a              Attempt to mount all file systems described in
                         /etc/fstab.  All optional fields in /etc/fstab
                         must be included and supported.  If the -F option
                         is specified, all file systems in /etc/fstab with
                         that FStype are mounted.  File systems are not
                         necessarily mounted in the order listed in
                         /etc/fstab.
```

-e   Verbose mode. Write a message to the standard output indicating which file system is being mounted.

-F FStype   Specify FStype, the file system type on which to operate. See fstyp(1M). If this option is not included on the command line, then it is determined from either /etc/fstab, by matching special file with, or from file system statistics of special, obtained by statfsdev() (see statfsdev(3C)).

-l   Limit actions to local file systems only.

-o specific_options

               Specify options specific to each file system type. specific_options is a list of comma separated suboptions and/or keyword/attribute pairs intended for a FStype-specific version of the command. See the FStype-specific manual entries for a description of the specific_options supported, if any.

-p   Report the list of mounted file systems in the /etc/fstab format.

-Q   Prevent the display of error messages that result from an attempt to mount already mounted file systems.

-r   Mount the specified file system as read-only. Physically write-protected file systems must be mounted in this way or errors occur when access times are updated, whether or not any explicit write is attempted.

-v   Report the regular output with file system type and flags; however, the directory and special fields are reversed.

-V   Echo the completed command line, but perform no other action. The command line is generated by incorporating the user-specified options and other information derived from /etc/fstab. This option allows the user to verify the command line.

Options (umount)

The umount command recognizes the following options:

-a   Attempt to unmount all file systems described in /etc/mnttab. All optional fields in /etc/mnttab must be included and supported. If FStype is specified, all file systems in /etc/mnttab with that FStype are unmounted. File systems are not necessarily unmounted in the order listed in /etc/mnttab.

-F FStype   Specify FStype, the file system type on which to operate. If this option is not included on the command line, then it is determined from /etc/mnttab by matching special with an entry in that file. If no match is found, the command fails.

-v   Verbose mode. Write a message to standard output indicating which file system is being unmounted.

-V   Echo the completed command line, but perform no other action. The command line is generated by incorporating the user-specified options and other information derived from /etc/fstab. This option allows the user to verify the command line.

EXAMPLES

List the file systems currently mounted:

```
mount
```

Mount the HFS file system /dev/dsk/c1d2s0 at directory /home:

```
mount -F hfs /dev/dsk/c1d2s0 /home
```

Unmount the same file system:

```
umount /dev/dsk/c1d2s0
```

AUTHOR

mount was developed by HP, AT&T, the University of California, Berkeley, and Sun Microsystems.

FILES

/etc/fstab   Static information about the systems

/etc/mnttab   Mounted file system table

SEE ALSO

mount_FStype(1M), mount(2), fstab(4), mnttab(4), fs_wrapper(5), quota(5).

STANDARDS COMPLIANCE

mount: SVID3

umount: SVID3

newfs

newfs - Build a new file system by invoking **mkfs** command (this is generic man page; there are also man pages for hfs and vxfs).

man page

newfs - 8

```
newfs(1M)                                                          newfs(1M)

NAME
     newfs (generic) - construct a new file system

SYNOPSIS

     /usr/sbin/newfs [-F FStype] [-o specific_options] [-V] special

DESCRIPTION
     The newfs command is a "friendly" front-end to the mkfs command (see
     mkfs(1M)).  The newfs command calculates the appropriate parameters
     and then builds the file system by invoking the mkfs command.

     special represents a character (raw) special device.

   Options
     newfs recognizes the following options:

         -F FStype     Specify the file system type on which to operate
                       (see fstyp(1M) and fs_wrapper(5)).  If this option
                       is not included on the command line, then the file
                       system type is determined from the file /etc/fstab
                       by matching special with an entry in that file.
                       If there is no entry in /etc/fstab, then the file
                       system type is determined from the file
                       /etc/default/fs.

         -o specific_options
                       Specify options specific to the file system type.
                       specific_options is a list of suboptions and/or
                       keyword/attribute pairs intended for an FStype-
                       specific module of the command.  See the file
                       system specific manual entries for a description
                       of the specific_options that are supported, if
                       any.

         -V            Echo the completed command line, but perform no
                       other actions.  The command line is generated by
                       incorporating the specified options and arguments
                       and other information derived from /etc/fstab.
                       This option allows the user to verify the command
                       line.

EXAMPLES
     Execute the newfs command to create an HFS file system on
     /dev/rdsk/c1d0s2

         newfs -F hfs /dev/rdsk/c1d0s2
```

AUTHOR
     newfs was developed by HP and the University of California, Berkeley.

FILES
     /etc/default/fs   File that specifies the default file system
                                  type.
     /etc/fstab   Static information about the file systems.

SEE ALSO
     fsck(1M), fstyp(1M), mkfs(1M), newfs_FStype(1M), fstab(4),
     fs_wrapper(5).

"pv" command summaries

"pv" commands - Command summaries related to physical volumes.

man page

"pv" - 8

```
pvchange(1M)                                                    pvchange(1M)

NAME
      pvchange - change characteristics and access path of physical volume
      in LVM volume group

SYNOPSIS

      /sbin/pvchange [-A autobackup] -s pv_path

      /sbin/pvchange [-A autobackup] -S autoswitch pv_path

      /sbin/pvchange [-A autobackup] -x extensibility pv_path

      /sbin/pvchange [-A autobackup] -t IO_timeout pv_path
```

```
pvcreate(1M)                                                    pvcreate(1M)

NAME
      pvcreate - create physical volume for use in LVM volume group

SYNOPSIS

      /sbin/pvcreate [-b] [-B] [-d soft_defects] [-s disk_size] [-f]
            [-t disk_type] pv_path
```

```
pvdisplay(1M)                                                  pvdisplay(1M)

NAME
      pvdisplay - display information about physical volumes within LVM
      volume group

SYNOPSIS

      /sbin/pvdisplay [-v] [-b BlockList] pv_path ...
```

pvmove(1M)   pvmove(1M)

NAME
     pvmove - move allocated physical extents from one LVM physical volume
     to other physical volumes

SYNOPSIS

     /sbin/pvmove [-A autobackup] [-n lv_path] source_pv_path
          [dest_pv_path ... | dest_pvg_name ...]

"vg" command summaries

"vg" commands - Command summaries related to volume groups.

man page

"vg" - 8

```
vgcfgbackup(1M)                                                    vgcfgbackup(1M)

NAME
     vgcfgbackup - create or update LVM volume group configuration backup
     file

SYNOPSIS

     /sbin/vgcfgbackup [-f vg_conf_path] [-u] vg_name



vgcfgrestore(1M)                                                  vgcfgrestore(1M)

NAME
     vgcfgrestore - display or restore LVM volume group configuration from
     backup file

SYNOPSIS

     /sbin/vgcfgrestore -n vg_name -l

     /sbin/vgcfgrestore -n vg_name [-o old_pv_path] pv_path

     /sbin/vgcfgrestore -f vg_conf_path -l

     /sbin/vgcfgrestore -f vg_conf_path [-o old_pv_path] pv_path



vgchange(1M)                                                        vgchange(1M)

NAME
     vgchange - set LVM volume group availability

SYNOPSIS

   Activate volume group
     /sbin/vgchange -a availability [-l] [-p] [-q quorum] [-s] [-P
     resync_daemon_count] [vg_name ...]

   Assign to high availability cluster and mark volume group sharable
     /sbin/vgchange -c cluster -S cluster vg_name



vgcreate(1M)                                                        vgcreate(1M)

NAME
     vgcreate - create LVM volume group
```

```
SYNOPSIS

     /sbin/vgcreate [-A autobackup] [-x extensibility] [-e max_pe]
         [-l max_lv] [-p max_pv] [-s pe_size] [-g pvg_name]
         vg_name pv_path ...
```

vgdisplay(1M)   vgdisplay(1M)

NAME
     vgdisplay - display information about LVM volume groups

SYNOPSIS

     /sbin/vgdisplay [-v] [vg_name ...]

vgexport(1M)   vgexport(1M)

NAME
     vgexport - export an LVM volume group and its associated logical
     volumes

SYNOPSIS

     /sbin/vgexport [-m mapfile] [-p] [-v] vg_name

     /sbin/vgexport -m mapfile -s -p -v vg_name

vgextend(1M)   vgextend(1M)

NAME
     vgextend - extend an LVM volume group by adding physical volumes

SYNOPSIS

     /sbin/vgextend [-A autobackup] [-g pvg_name] [-x extensibility]
         vg_name pv_path ...

vgimport(1M)   vgimport(1M)

NAME
     vgimport - import an LVM volume group onto the system

SYNOPSIS

     /sbin/vgimport [-m mapfile] [-p] [-v] vg_name pv_path ...

     /sbin/vgimport -m mapfile -s -v vg_name

```
vgreduce(1M)                                                      vgreduce(1M)

NAME
     vgreduce - remove physical volumes from an LVM volume group

SYNOPSIS

     /sbin/vgreduce vg_name pv_path ...

     /sbin/vgreduce -f vg_name




vgremove(1M)                                                      vgremove(1M)

NAME
     vgremove - remove LVM volume group definition from the system

SYNOPSIS

     /sbin/vgremove vg_name ...




vgscan(1M)                                                          vgscan(1M)

NAME
     vgscan - scan physical volumes for LVM volume groups

SYNOPSIS

     /sbin/vgscan [-a] [-p] [-v]




vgsync(1M)                                                          vgsync(1M)
                  Requires Optional HP MirrorDisk/UX Software

NAME
     vgsync - synchronize stale logical volume mirrors in LVM volume groups

SYNOPSIS

     /sbin/vgsync vg_name ...
```

CHAPTER 9

Ignite-UX

Ignite-UX Overview

Ignite-UX is quite a versatile product. It has a great deal of functionality associated with it that would take an entire book to cover. I'll cover what I believe to be the two major functional areas of Ignite-UX that I see used. These are:

- Network installation of client, or target, systems from a server that has on it software depots. These depots are usually created by copying software from media into depots on the Ignite-UX server. This is somewhat the same as the software installation covered in Chapter 2, except that the software is on a server rather than media. There is also a graphical user interface that allows you to control this process from the server. This technique would allow you to select the specific software that you want to load on each individual client. You can either "push" software from the server to the client or "pull" software to the client from the server. In addition to creating software depots from media, you can create an operating system archive from a "golden image." The "golden image" is a perfectly running system that you wish to replicate to many systems. The **make_sys_image** command produces a compressed image of the "golden system." In this chapter we'll focus on the software depots created from copying media into depots on the server.

• Creating a bootable system recovery tape. This feature allows you to create an image of your root volume on tape. You could later boot off of this tape and restore the root volume group directly from tape.

Let's take a look at these two aspects of Ignite-UX in the upcoming sections. Be sure to check *www.docs.hp.com* to obtain some good documents available on Ignite-UX and *www.software.hp.com* to obtain the latest Ignite-UX software. Some of these documents have much more detail than I do in my upcoming "how to" sections.

I'll assume that you already have the Ignite-UX product loaded on your server system. This software comes bundled with HP-UX 11i and 11.0, so it is just a matter of loading it on your server system from media. You can be sure you're getting the latest version of Ignite-UX if you download it from the *software.hp.com* Web site. The process of working with Ignite-UX in this chapter is nearly identical for HP-UX 10.20, 11.0, and 11i. You'll find this chapter applicable regardless of which version of HP-UX you're running.

After installing Ignite-UX, you may want to update your path so you don't have to type the full path for every Ignite-UX command. For the default POSIX shell, you would issue the following:

```
# export PATH=${PATH}:/opt/ignite/bin
```

This command updates your path to include the directory for most Ignite-UX executables, **/opt/ignite/bin**.

Set up Server with Depots and Install Clients

You can use most any system as your Ignite-UX server. You can have depots on your server for HP-UX 11i, 11.0, and 10.20. I would recommend using an 11.00 or 11i system as an Ignite-UX server because I have seen problems with a 10.20 system acting as a server for loading clients with 11.00 and 11i. I have never seen a problem with an 11.0 or 11i system acting as a server for loading clients with any version of HP-UX. In general though, the server acts as a host for depots and its operating system is not an integral part of loading software onto clients. We'll use a workstation (model J2240) running 11.00 in our examples. From the 11.00 depot we create on this system, we can load a variety of clients. The fact that we're using a workstation rather than a server doesn't matter as far as loading clients is concerned. I find that many system administrators use a workstation as an Ignite-UX server even though they're loading primarily servers, such as N-Class systems.

The software depots you create on your Ignite-UX server consume a lot of disk space. A core operating system with many applications could take up several GBytes of disk space. I like to devote several GBytes of disk space to Ignite servers so I don't have to increase the size of **/var** (the default location for software depots) when additional depots are loaded on a system. My rule of thumb is **/var** at 6 GBytes to support several depots.

Just to give you an idea of the disk space consumed by depots, I have issued the following **bdf** commands upon initial system installation without any software depots and then again after creating a core operating system and application depot. The location of the software depots is **/var** by default; however, you can load the depots in any directory. I would recommend creating a filesystem such as **/var/ depots** as a depot area. In the following example, we'll focus on the capacity of **/var** since it is used as the destination for depots in upcoming examples.

man page

bdf - 8

```
# bdf
Filesystem            kbytes    used    avail %used Mounted on
/dev/vg00/lvol3       204800   19830   173464   10% /
/dev/vg00/lvol1        83733   13654    61705   18% /stand
/dev/vg00/lvol8      6553600  156292  5998347    3% /var
/dev/vg00/lvol7       512000  341251   160127   68% /usr
/dev/vg00/lvol4       102400    1522    94578    2% /tmp
/dev/vg00/lvol6       602112  186976   389238   32% /opt
/dev/vg00/lvol5       204800    1157   190923    1% /home
/dev/dsk/c1t2d0      2457600 2457600        0  100% /var/tmp/
cddirAAAa02574
```

man page

bdf - 8

The following **bdf**, which was taken immediately after the core operating system depot for 11.0 was created shows **/var** availability has been reduced to about 5.667 GBytes from 5.998 GBytes. This represents roughly 330 MBytes of data that were loaded as part of the core operating system.

```
# bdf
Filesystem            kbytes    used    avail %used Mounted on
/dev/vg00/lvol3       204800   19943   173357   10% /
/dev/vg00/lvol1        83733   13654    61705   18% /stand
/dev/vg00/lvol8      6553600  507003  5668779    8% /var
/dev/vg00/lvol7       512000  341255   160123   68% /usr
/dev/vg00/lvol4       102400    3350    92862    3% /tmp
/dev/vg00/lvol6       602112  186976   389238   32% /opt
/dev/vg00/lvol5       204800    1157   190923    1% /home
/dev/dsk/c1t2d0      2457600 2457600        0  100% /iuxcdrom0
#
```

The disk space consumed by the core operating system depot can be confirmed by viewing the location of the depot as shown in the following listing:

man page

cd - 16

```
# cd /var/opt/ignite/depots
# du -s *
688842  Rel_B.11.00
#
```

This listing of the **du** command shows that roughly 330 MBytes (688K blocks divided by 2048 bytes/block) are in the core operating system directory. This 330 MBytes of disk space consumed by the core operating system depot is nothing compared with all of the application software we're going to load into the **depots** directory. We're going to put both the core operating system and applications in this directory so substantially more space will be consumed.

To further drive home the point of the amount of disk space consumed, the following **du** command shows the amount of disk space consumed by both the core operating system depot (still about 330 MBytes) and the total applications contained on the three CD-ROMs that came with the release of the operating system for which we're creating our depots. The **/var/opt/ignite/depots/app** directory, which is the depot for the contents of the three application CD-ROMs, is roughly 3.7 GBytes!

man page

cd -16

```
# cd /var/opt/ignite/depots
# du -s *
688874   Rel_B.11.00
3722622 app
#
```

The space consumed by the applications is over 10 times the space consumed by the core operating system. This 3.7 GBytes consists of every application available for the 11.0 release of the operating system; however, this gives you an idea of the space required when using Ignite-UX to create depots.

Run Ignite-UX GUI

man page

ignite - 9

After loading the Ignite-UX tool, you can type **ignite** if you have set up your path for **/opt/ignite/bin**, or you can type the full path **/opt/ignite/bin/ignite** to bring-up the graphical interface for Ingite-UX as shown in Figure 9-1:

Figure 9-1   Ignite-UX Welcome Screen

From this window we can make various selections to configure Ignite-UX for our environment. The first configuration we'll perform is *Server Setup*. When we select *Server Setup*, we're shown the screen in Figure 9-2, Which allows use to set up IP addresses for the clients we wish to manage from Ignite-UX under option 1.

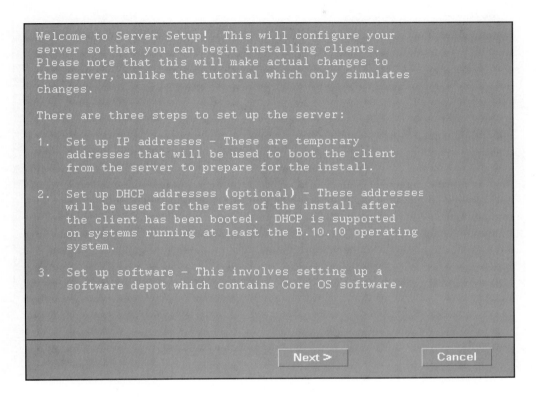

```
Welcome to Server Setup!  This will configure your
server so that you can begin installing clients.
Please note that this will make actual changes to
the server, unlike the tutorial which only simulates
changes.

There are three steps to set up the server:

1.  Set up IP addresses - These are temporary
    addresses that will be used to boot the client
    from the server to prepare for the install.

2.  Set up DHCP addresses (optional) - These addresses
    will be used for the rest of the install after
    the client has been booted.  DHCP is supported
    on systems running at least the B.10.10 operating
    system.

3.  Set up software - This involves setting up a
    software depot which contains Core OS software.
```

                                    Next >   Cancel

Figure 9-2 Setup Client IP Address

We'll set up a bank of addresses for several clients we anticipate loading through the Ignite-UX interface as shown in Figure 9-3. Be sure to put entries for these clients in your host database, such as the file **/etc/hosts** as well.

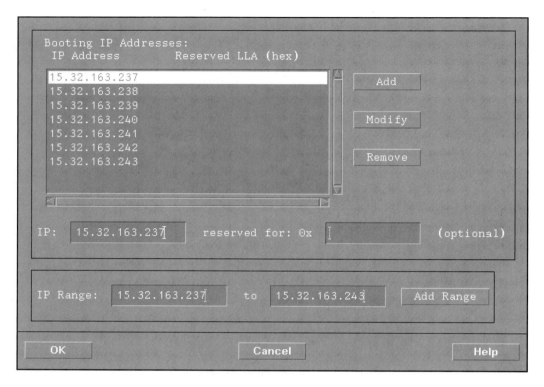

Figure 9-3 A Bank of Client Ip Addresses

We have set up a bank of seven clients that we wish to manage from Ignite-UX.

Next, let's create a core operating system depot for HP-UX 11.0 through the graphical interface. We'll copy the core operating system from the orginal CD-ROM, which is the selection we make in Figure 9-4:

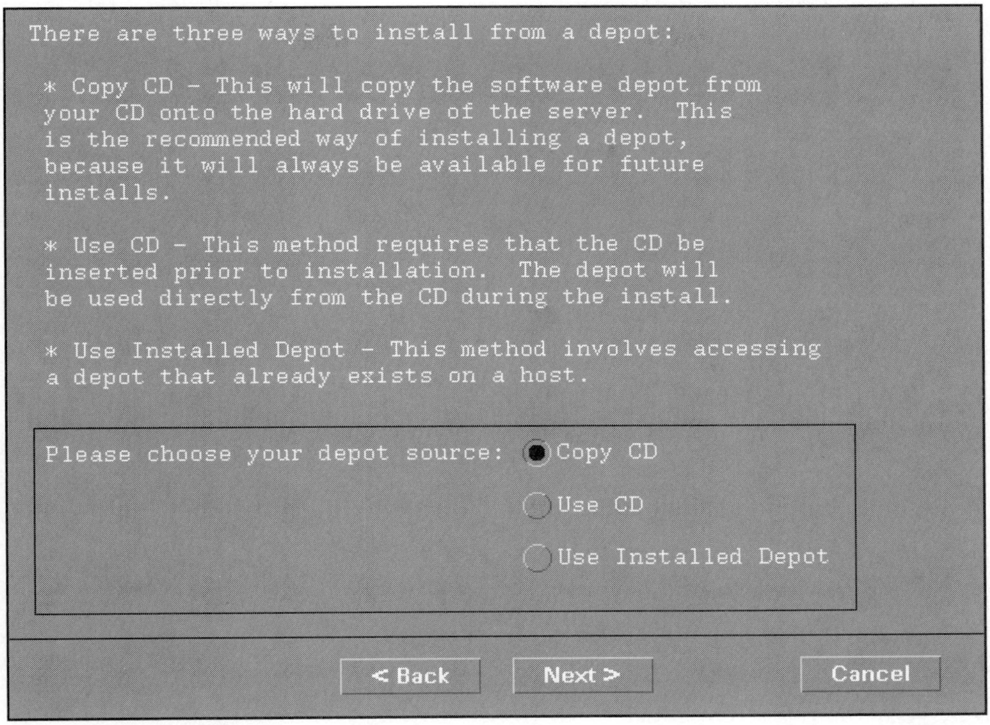

```
There are three ways to install from a depot:

* Copy CD - This will copy the software depot from
your CD onto the hard drive of the server.  This
is the recommended way of installing a depot,
because it will always be available for future
installs.

* Use CD - This method requires that the CD be
inserted prior to installation.  The depot will
be used directly from the CD during the install.

* Use Installed Depot - This method involves accessing
a depot that already exists on a host.

Please choose your depot source:  ● Copy CD

                                   ○ Use CD

                                   ○ Use Installed Depot

            < Back        Next >              Cancel
```

Figure 9-4 Install a Software Depot

After making the selection to load from the CD-ROM, another window appears, which is not shown in our example. Here, we specify the location in which the depot will be loaded. By default the directory is **/var/opt/ignite/depots** (full path **/var/opt/ignite/depots/ Rel_B.11.11/core** as an example for the 11.11 release of HP-UX); however, we can specify any directory location for the depots. If you have a lot of unused disk space in **/localapps** for instance, you could make the full path **/localapps/depots/Rel_B.11.11/core**. Next, we receive a status window showing the progression of the software copy and depot creation shown in Figure 9-5:

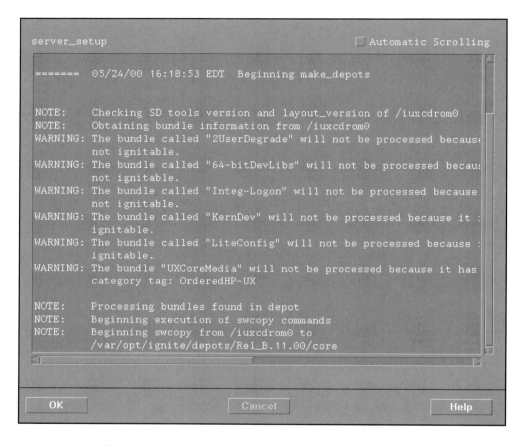

server_setup   ☐ Automatic Scrolling

    ======= 05/24/00 16:18:53 EDT Beginning make_depots

    NOTE: Checking SD tools version and layout_version of /iuxcdrom0
    NOTE: Obtaining bundle information from /iuxcdrom0
    WARNING: The bundle called "2UserDegrade" will not be processed because
              not ignitable.
    WARNING: The bundle called "64-bitDevLibs" will not be processed because
              not ignitable.
    WARNING: The bundle called "Integ-Logon" will not be processed because
              not ignitable.
    WARNING: The bundle called "KernDev" will not be processed because it :
              ignitable.
    WARNING: The bundle called "LiteConfig" will not be processed because :
              ignitable.
    WARNING: The bundle "UXCoreMedia" will not be processed because it has
              category tag: OrderedHP-UX

    NOTE: Processing bundles found in depot
    NOTE: Beginning execution of swcopy commands
    NOTE: Beginning swcopy from /iuxcdrom0 to
              /var/opt/ignite/depots/Rel_B.11.00/core

          OK   Cancel   Help

Figure 9-5   Status of Software Depot Creation

Upon completion of software copy and depot setup, we are given the window shown in Figure 9-6:

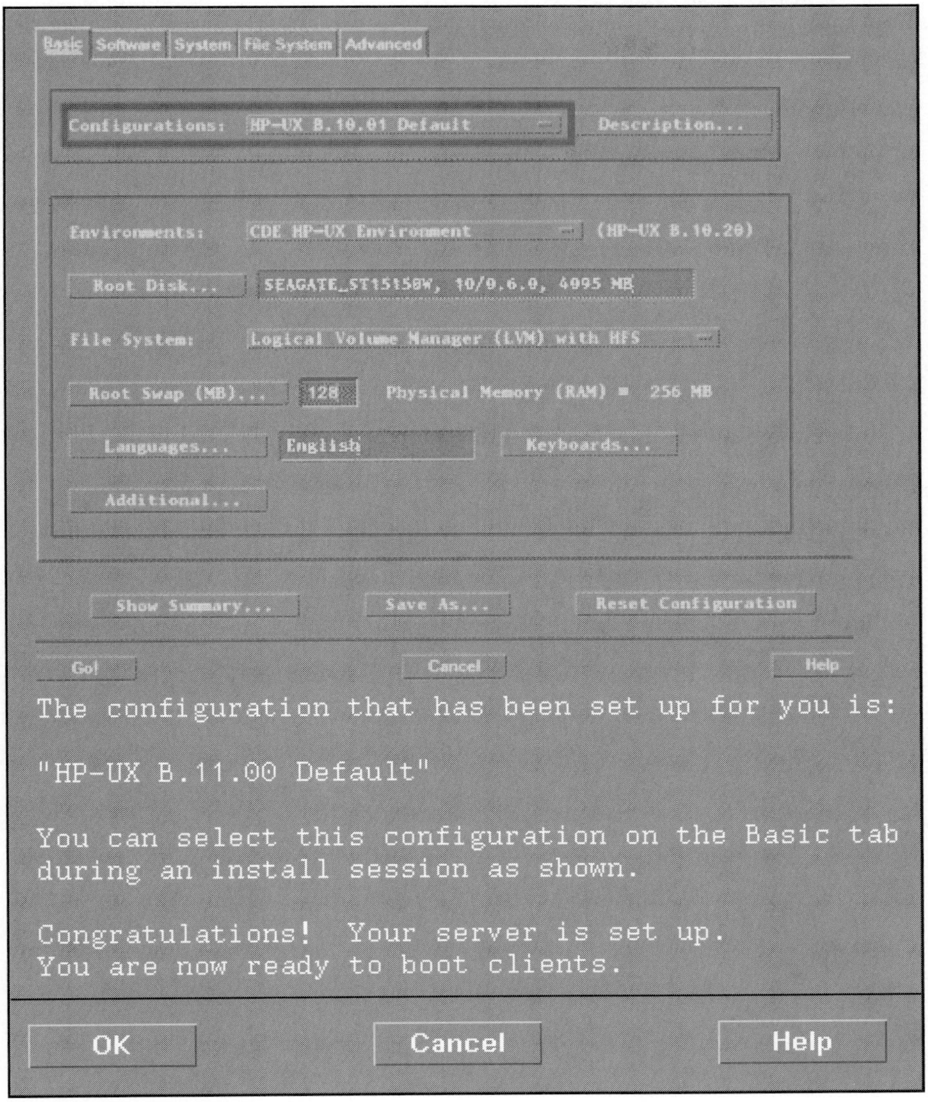

Figure 9-6 The Software Depot is Complete

The depot for the core operating system was automatically created under **/var/opt/ignite/depots/Rel_B.11.00**. As described earlier in the chapter, this depot consumes about 330 MBytes of disk space.

At this point, we have created only the core operating system depot and configured the clients all through the graphical interface on the Ignite-UX server. At the time of this writing, there is no way to use the graphical interface to create the applications software depot. We'll use three Ignite-UX commands to create the applications depot. First we'll run the **make_depots** command for all three applications CD-ROMs we wish to load into the depot. Then we'll run the **make_config** command one time for the applications depot we have created. Finally, we'll run the **manage_index** one time for the applications depot we created. Let's take a look at each of these commands in the upcoming listings.

```
# /opt/ignite/bin/make_depots -d /var/opt/ignite/depots/app -s /dev/dsk/c1t2d0
# /opt/ignite/bin/make_depots -d /var/opt/ignite/depots/app -s /dev/dsk/c1t2d0
# /opt/ignite/bin/make_depots -d /var/opt/ignite/depots/app -s /dev/dsk/c1t2d0
```

We add the -d option to specify a destination directory called **app** for the contents of the application media. We could also specify an alternate destination directory. Using the earlier example, we could specify the destination with **-d /localapps/depots/app**, for instance. We'll load the entire application media, in this case, three CD-ROMs. Next we run **make_config**:

```
# /opt/ignite/bin/make_config -s /var/opt/ignite/depots/app
             -c /var/opt/ignite/data/Rel_B.11.00/app_cfg

NOTE:    make_config can sometimes take a long time to complete. Please be
         patient!
```

We placed the **app_cfg** file in the directory for our specific release of the operating system. This is a method of organizing the configuration files in such a way that those pertaining to a specific release of the operating system are grouped together. If we had used a different location for the application directory, we would have specified it with **-s /localapps/depots/app**, but left the **app_cfg** file in the same location. You will want to take a look at the configuration files in **/var/opt/ignite/data/<***yourHP-UXrelease***>** to see their contents. These files contain the information about all of the software you have loaded as part of your Ignite-UX depot.

The **manage_index** command is required to manage the index file used by Ignite-UX as shown in the following example:

```
# /opt/ignite/bin/manage_index -a -f /var/opt/ignite/data/Rel_B.11.00/app_cfg
```

We have now set up the core operating system depot using the Ignite-UX graphical interface and the application depot using the three Ignite-UX commands at the command line. You now also have an entry for your release of the operating system in **/var/opt/ignite/ INDEX**. This is a file you will want to view so you can see the entry made for your release of the operating system.

Let's now get back to using the Ignite-UX graphical interface on the server. We can get information about a specific client through the Ignite-UX interface on the server. The window that appears on the server is shown in Figure 9-7 for the client we'll be booting through Ignite-UX:

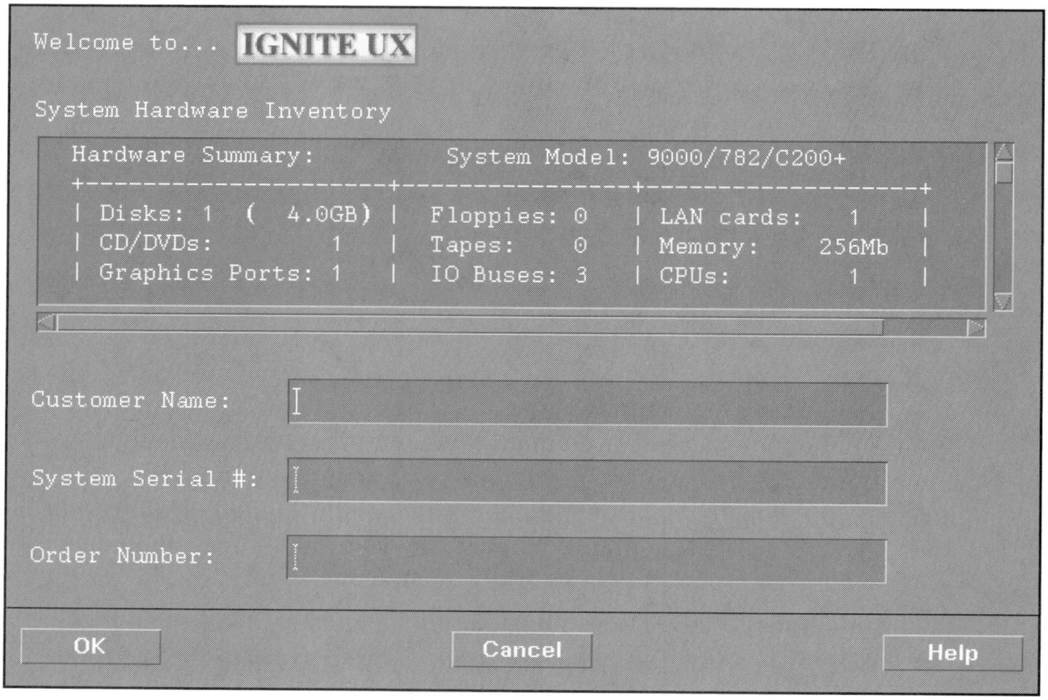

```
Welcome to...  IGNITE UX

System Hardware Inventory

    Hardware Summary:          System Model: 9000/782/C200+
    +-------------------+----------------+-------------------+
    | Disks: 1 (  4.0GB) |  Floppies: 0  | LAN cards:   1    |
    | CD/DVDs:        1  |  Tapes:    0  | Memory:    256Mb  |
    | Graphics Ports: 1  |  IO Buses: 3  | CPUs:        1    |


  Customer Name:    [                                        ]


  System Serial #:  [                                        ]


  Order Number:     [                                        ]


  [    OK    ]              [   Cancel   ]              [  Help  ]
```

Figure 9-7 Information About Client

Now that we've created both a core operating system and applications depot we can boot and load one of our clients through Ignite-UX on the server.

In addition to controlling the client as we have done using the Ignite-UX graphical interface in "push" fashion from the server, you can also work from the client in "pull" fashion. In order to boot the client from the server while sitting at the server, you would issue the following command from PDC (Processor Dependent Code; see Chapter 1)after interrupting the boot process:

man page

boot - 1

BOOT ADMIN> **boot lan 15.32.163.26 install**

The IP address specified is that of the server where we set up the software depot. While sitting at the client, you would see the Ignite-UX interface in character mode and proceed with the installation while sitting at the client using the software depot we set up on the server.

Getting back to the GUI, we select the software we wish to load through the familiar Ignite-UX interface that is part of any initial operating system load as shown in Figure 9-8:

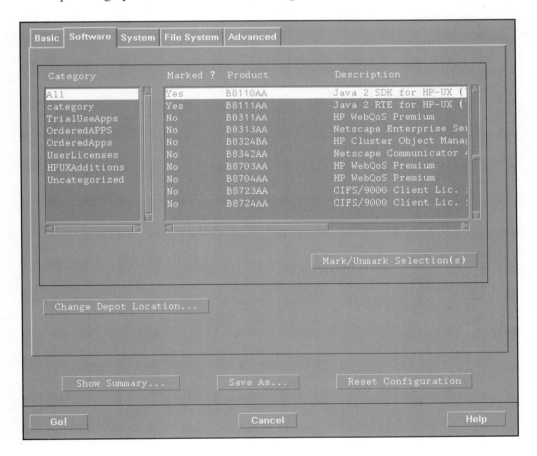

Figure 9-8 Selecting Software to Load on Client

Notice in Figure 9-8 that we are in the *Software* tab at the top of the screen. We'll progress through the *System* and *File System* tabs in two upcoming figures. Remember, all of this work is being done on the Ignite-UX server we set up.

We have selected a Java product that was part of the applications depot we created in Figure 9-8. The core operating system and other software selections were also made in the *Software* window.

In addition to the software load, we can also perform additional configuration on the server for the client we are loading such as providing the system name under the *System* tab as shown in Figure 9-9:

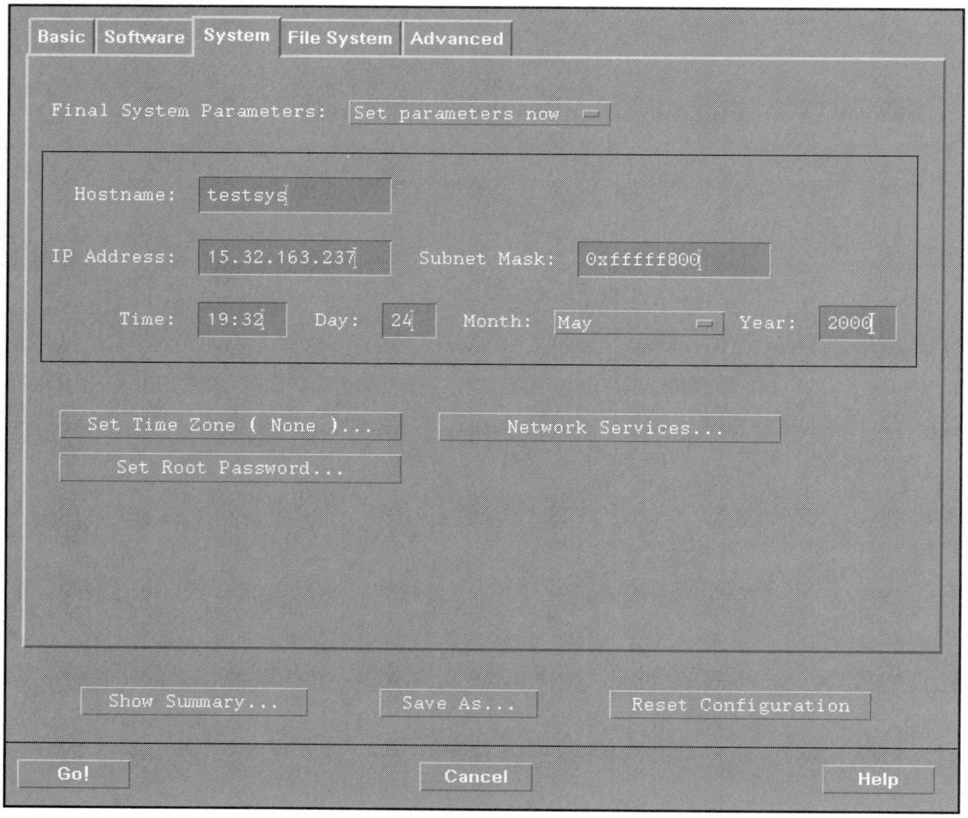

Figure 9-9 Setup the Client System

Next we can perform file system-related configuration under the *File System* tab as shown in Figure 9-10:

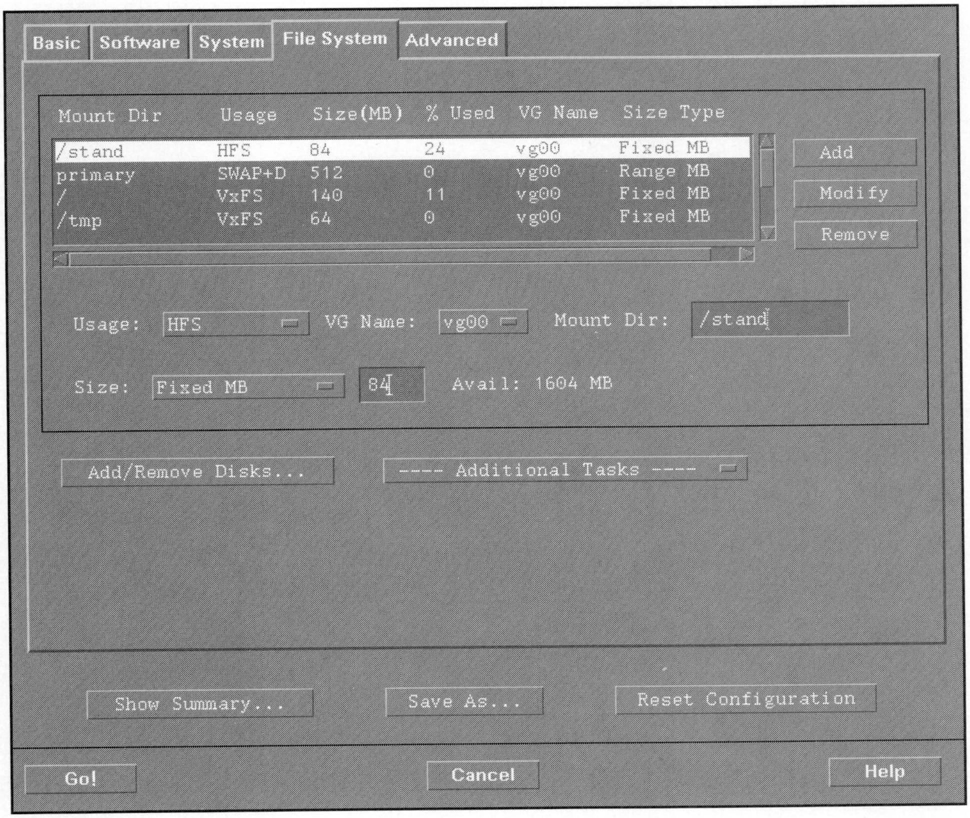

Figure 9-10   Setup the Client File Systems

After we have completed all of our initial work in the Ignite-UX for the client while working on the server, we can proceed with the

client load. Figure 9-11 shows two Ignite-UX windows that appear on
the server when we begin configuring and loading the client:

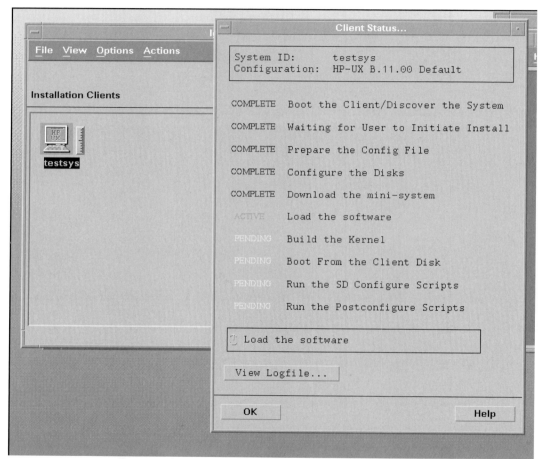

Figure 9-11   Status of Client Load

The left-most window in Figure 9-11 shows the icon for the system we are working on and the right-most window provides the status
of the client load. Since we are working on only one system, only one

icon appears in the left-most window. The status of the software load in the right-most window indicates that *Load the software* is an *ACTIVE* process. Serveral process have been *COMPLETE,* and several others are *PENDING.*

Although you can't see the colors in the original screen shot, the status messages are color-coded.

There is substantially more that you can accomplish with Ignite-UX such as grouping the configuration files into sets that you can select when loading clients, installing patch depots, and many other useful tasks. The *Ignite-UX Administrator Guide* at *www.docs.hp.com* covers many additional topics.

From the procedure we performed in this section, however, you can see how easy it is to create software depots and manage clients.

System Recovery with Ignite-UX

Ignite-UX is a product bundled with HP-UX 11i that provides a process to create a bootable system recovery tape. The tape contains a boot area and an operating system archive. Should your root disk fail or corruption of the root disk take place, you can recover using the bootable system recovery tape.

make_recovery is the Ignite-UX tool that is used to create the bootable system recovery tape. You could boot and restore from the system recovery tape and then use your system backup to fully restore the system. If your root disk were to fail, in a non-mirrored environment, you would perform the following steps to recover from the failure:

- Replace the defective root disk.

- Boot from the recovery tape by selecting the tape device.

- Monitor the restoration of the operating system archive from the recovery tape.

- Restore the balance of data on the system with backup information.

The bootable system recovery tape consists of both a Logical Interchange Format (LIF) volume as well as the operating system archive. The LIF volume contains all the components necessary to boot from the tape. The operating system archive contains only the core operating system by default.

You can include additional files in the operating system archive, if you wish, using two different techniques. The first is to edit the file **/var/opt/ignite/recovery/makrec.append** and add to it the file name, directory name, or software distributor product name you wish to include in the operating system archive. The second technique is to run **make_recovery** in preview mode with the *-p* option, manually add files to include and/or exclude from the archive, and resume **make_recovery** with the *-r* option. The manual pages for **/opt/ignite/**

bin/make_recovery and **/opt/ignite/bin/ignite** appear at the end of this chapter.

You can also determine whether your recovery tape is up-to-date by using the **check_recovery** command. Running **make_recovery** with the *-C* option produces a system recovery status file. **check_recovery** compares the system recovery status file to the current state of the system and produces a list of discrepancies. From this list, you can determine whether or not you should produce another system recovery tape. The manual page for **/opt/ignite/bin/ check_recovery** is also included at the end of this chapter.

man page

ignite - 9

man page

make_ recovery 9

man page

check_ recovery 9

The recovery feature is only one component of the Ignite-UX product. Ignite-UX provides a means to install systems over the network by either pushing the installation to a client from an Ignite server or pulling the installation from the Ignite server to the client. With Ignite-UX, "golden images" of your standard installation setup can be created and systems can be set up in a matter of minutes by "igniting" them from this image over the network. More information about Ignite-UX can be viewed on the Internet at *http://www.soft-ware.hp.com/products/IUX* and read about in the "Configuring an Ignite-UX Server" and "Installing from the Ignite-UX Server" chapters as well as Appendix C: "Ignite-UX System Administration" of the *Installing HP-UX 11.0 and Upgrading 10.x to 11.0* manual from Hewlett-Packard. The "HP-UX System Recovery" chapter of the same manual gives additional information about the **make_recovery** feature of Ignite-UX.

An Example of Creating a Bootable System Recovery Tape

Now that we have covered the basic components and capabilities of the Ignite-UX recovery process, let's look at an example of creating a bootable system recovery tape.

Let's first run **make_recovery** with the *-p* option so that we can-see the way Ignite-UX reports the information it is including on the tape. I'll also use the *-A* option, which specifies that the entire root

man page

make_
recovery
9

volume group is to be included. I sometimes use **make_recovery** to clone identical systems by producing a recovery tape with the *-A* option and then loading the tape on systems that I want to be identical to the original system. You would not use the *-A* option if you have a large root volume group or if you perform normal backups and don't need to include all root volume group information on the recovery tape. In addition to *-p* for preview and *-A* for all, I'll also use the *-v* for the verbose option and *-C* to create the system status file in the following preview command example:

```
# make_recovery -p -v -A -C


        *** Previewing only ***
        Option -A specified. Entire Core Volume Group/disk will be backed up.


        ****************************************
        HP-UX System Recovery
        Validating append file
                Done

        File Systems on Core OS Disks/Volume Groups:

                vg name = vg00
                pv_name = /dev/dsk/c0t5d0

                vg00        /dev/vg00/lvol3        /
                vg00        /dev/vg00/lvol4        /home
                vg00        /dev/vg00/lvol5        /opt
                vg00        /dev/vg00/lvol1        /stand
                vg00        /dev/vg00/lvol6        /tmp
                vg00        /dev/vg00/lvol7        /usr
                vg00        /dev/vg00/lvol8        /var

        Create mount points
        /apps
        /work
        /spill
        /spill2
        /rbdisk01
        /rbdisk02
        /rbdisk03
        /rbdisk04
        /rbdisk05
        /rbdisk06
        /rbdisk07
        /rbdisk09
        /rbdisk10
        /rbdisk11
        /rbdisk12
        /rbdisk13
        /rbdisk14
        /rbdisk15
        /rbdisk16
        /rbdisk17
```

```
      /rbdisk18
      /nfs

            /opt is a mounted directory
               It is in the Core Volume Group
               Mounted at /dev/vg00/lvol5

            /var is a mounted directory
               It is in the Core Volume Group
               Mounted at /dev/vg00/lvol8

   Destination = /dev/rmt/0m
   Boot LIF location = /var/tmp/uxinstlf.recovery


   ******************************************
      Preview only. Tape not created

   The /var/opt/ignite/recovery/arch.include file has been created.
   This can be modified to exclude known files.
   Only delete files or directories that are strictly user created.
   The creation of the System Recovery tape can then be
   resumed using the -r option.

   No further checks will be performed by the commands.
            Cleanup
```

The **arch.include** file has been produced at this point. This file lists the files that will be part of the archive that you can modify. The following is an abbreviated listing of **arch.include**, showing just the very beginning and very end of the file:

```
/
/lost+found
/etc
/etc/vue
/etc/vue/config
/etc/vue/config/types
/etc/vue/config/types/tools
/etc/vue/config/types/tools/System_Admin
/etc/vue/config/types/tools/System_Admin/FontClientSrvr
/etc/vue/config/types/tools/System_Admin/SetNetworking
/etc/vue/config/types/tools/System_Admin/ShutdownSystem
/etc/vue/config/types/tools/System_Admin/VerifyPEX
/etc/vue/config/types/tools/System_Admin/VerifyPEX
/etc/vue/config/types/tools/Media

   .
   .
   .


/spp/scripts/tc_standalone
```

```
/spp/scripts/sppconsole.old
/spp/unsupported
/spp/unsupported/cbus
/spp/unsupported/clear_pid
/spp/unsupported/ex_shm
/spp/unsupported/rdr_dumper.fw
/spp/unsupported/rdr_formatter
/spp/unsupported/reset_jtag
/spp/unsupported/scan_sram
/users
/users/sppuser
/users/sppuser/.Xdefaults
/users/sppuser/.cshrc
/users/sppuser/.kshrc
/users/sppuser/.login
/users/sppuser/.mwmrc
/users/sppuser/.profile
/users/sppuser/.x11start
/users/sppuser/.x11startlog
/users/sppuser/.sh_history
/users/sppuser/.sw
/users/sppuser/.sw/sessions
/users/sppuser/.sw/sessions/swlist.last
/users/sppuser/.history
/.sh_history
/.profile
/lib
/lib
/bin
/bin
/core
/ignite_10.20.tar
/var/tmp/makrec.lasttmp
/var/opt/ignite/recovery/chkrec.include
/var/opt/ignite/recovery/config.recover
```

man page

make_
recovery
9

On the system on which this **make_recovery** was performed, the **arch.include** file had over 44,000 lines in it, as shown below:

```
# cat /var/opt/igntite/recovery/arch.include | wc
44142 44146 1730818
```

Now let's resume **make_recovery**, which was running in pre-view mode with the -*r* option for resume, the -*v* option for verbose, and the -*C* option to create the system status file. The -*d* option will not be specified because the default tape device will be used. The *-A* option, which was specified earlier in preview mode, specifies that the entire root volume group is to be included.

```
# make_recovery -r -C -v
make_recovery(306): In Resume mode. Do you wish to continue?y


        ****************************************
        HP-UX System Recovery

        File Systems on Core OS Disks/Volume Groups:

                vg name = vg00
                pv_name =  /dev/dsk/c0t5d0

                vg00        /dev/vg00/lvol3         /
                vg00        /dev/vg00/lvol4         /home
                vg00        /dev/vg00/lvol5         /opt
                vg00        /dev/vg00/lvol1         /stand
                vg00        /dev/vg00/lvol6         /tmp
                vg00        /dev/vg00/lvol7         /usr
                vg00        /dev/vg00/lvol8         /var

        Create mount points
         /apps
         /work
         /spill
         /spill2
         /rbdisk01
         /rbdisk02
         /rbdisk03
         /rbdisk04
         /rbdisk05
         /rbdisk06
         /rbdisk07
         /rbdisk09
         /rbdisk10
         /rbdisk11
         /rbdisk12
         /rbdisk13
         /rbdisk14
         /rbdisk15
         /rbdisk16
         /rbdisk17
         /rbdisk18
         /nfs

                /opt is a mounted directory
                   It is in the Core Volume Group
                   Mounted at /dev/vg00/lvol5


                /var is a mounted directory
                   It is in the Core Volume Group
                   Mounted at /dev/vg00/lvol8

        Destination = /dev/rmt/0m
        Boot LIF location = /var/tmp/uxinstlf.recovery
```

```
*****************************************
Creating the configuration file.
        Done
Modifying the configuration file.
        Done
Backing up vg configurations
        Volume Group vg00
        Volume Group vg01
        Volume Group vg03
        Volume Group vg02
        Done
Creating the /var/opt/ignite/recovery/makrec.last file
        Done
Going to create the tape.
Processing tape
        Invoking instl_adm -T
        Creating boot LIF
        Done
        Writing boot LIF to tape /dev/rmt/0mn
        Done
        Creating archive - this may take about 30 minutes.
        Done
System Recovery Tape successfully created.
#
```

A system recovery tape has now been produced. You could now boot from the system recovery tape and restore the entire volume group **vg00** on this system.

Running the check_recovery Command

You can run the **check_recovery** command any time to view the changes that have been made to the system since the last time the system recovery status file was created with the -C option. The following example shows running the **check_recovery** command:

```
# check_recovery

Since the last System Recovery Image was created, the following software
product changes have been detected.

(Added)     Auxiliary-OptB.11.01.01     Auxiliary Optimizer for HP Languages.
(Added)     OBJCOBOLB.12.50                 Object COBOL Developer

Since the last System Recovery Image was created, the following system
files (or links) have been added to the current system.

  /apps/informix7.3/lib/iosm07a.sl
  /apps/informix7.3/lib/ipldd07a.sl
  /apps/informix7.3/lib/liborb_r.sl
```

```
/dev/vg13/lvol01
/dev/vg13/rlvol01
/etc/sam/custom/scjjs.cf
/etc/sam/custom/scrar.cf
/sbin/init.d/flex
/sbin/rc2.d/S989flex
/usr/lib/iosm07a.sl
/usr/lib/iosm07a.sl.980709
/usr/lib/ipldd07a.sl.980709
/usr/lib/liborb_r.sl
/usr/local/adm/bin/user_watch.pl
/usr/local/adm/etc/rept
/usr/local/flexlm/bin/lmcksum
/usr/local/flexlm/bin/lmdiag
/usr/local/flexlm/bin/lmdown
/usr/local/flexlm/bin/lmgrd
/usr/local/flexlm/bin/lmhostid
/usr/local/flexlm/bin/lmremove
/usr/local/flexlm/bin/lmreread
/usr/local/flexlm/bin/lmstat
/usr/local/flexlm/bin/lmswitchr
/usr/local/flexlm/bin/lmutil
/usr/local/flexlm/bin/lmver
/usr/local/flexlm/daemons/HPCUPLANGS
/usr/local/flexlm/licenses/license.dat
/usr/local/flexlm/licenses/license.log
/usr/share/man/cat1.Z/X.1
/usr/share/man/cat1.Z/Xserver.1
/usr/share/man/cat1.Z/grep.1
/usr/share/man/cat1.Z/mwm.1
/usr/share/man/cat1.Z/xhost.1
/usr/share/man/cat1.Z/xset.1
/usr/share/man/cat2.Z/exec.2
```

Since the last System Recovery Image was created, the following system files (or links) have been deleted from the current system.

```
/dev/vg13/lvol1
/dev/vg13/rlvol1
/stand/build/conf.o
```

Since the last System Recovery Image was created, the following system files (or links) have been modified on the current system.

```
                        Current         makrec.last
                        -------         -----------
/dev/pty/ttyp2
        permissions     crw-rw-rw-      crw--w----
        uid             0               102
        gid             0               10
/dev/pty/ttyp3
        permissions     crw--w----      crw-rw-rw-
        uid             102             0
        gid             10              0
/dev/pty/ttyp4
        permissions     crw--w----      crw-rw-rw-
        gid             10              0
/dev/pty/ttyp5
        permissions     crw-rw-rw-      crw--w----
        uid             0               102
        gid             0               10
/dev/pty/ttyp6
        permissions     crw-rw-rw-      crw--w----
        uid             0               102
        gid             0               10
```

```
/dev/pty/ttyp8
        uid                 0                       2
        gid                 0                       10
/dev/ttyp2
        permissions         crw-rw-rw-              crw--w----
        uid                 0                       102
        gid                 0                       10
/dev/ttyp3
        permissions         crw--w----              crw-rw-rw-
        uid                 102                      0
        gid                 10                       0
/dev/ttyp4
        permissions         crw--w----              crw-rw-rw-
        gid                 10                       0
/dev/ttyp5
        permissions         crw-rw-rw-              crw--w----
        uid                 0                       102
        gid                 0                       10
/dev/ttyp6
        permissions         crw-rw-rw-              crw--w----
        uid                 0                       102
        gid                 0                       10
/dev/ttyp8
        uid                 0                       2
        gid                 0                       10
/etc/MANPATH
        checksum            1982379524              497249200
/etc/PATH
        checksum            562953260               2784298760
/etc/SHLIB_PATH
        checksum            2664385509              241316845
/etc/fstab
        checksum            3014086519              200239819
/etc/fstab.old
        checksum            682979636               2528618126
/etc/group
        checksum            368341889               127908837
/etc/lvmconf/vg13.conf
        checksum            1522028984              929609311
/etc/lvmconf/vg13.conf.old
        checksum            1830986219              3891043243
/etc/lvmtab
        checksum            4141778997              3277790772
/etc/passwd
        checksum            1661378396              2350540120
/etc/profile
        checksum            510591831               2645970599
/stand/build/conf.SAM.c
        checksum            3973853979              4022316306
/stand/build/conf.SAM.o
        checksum            4142700410              118504989
/stand/build/conf.o.old
        checksum            2526740160              1129366190
/stand/build/config.SAM.mk
        checksum            2849240259              1706527948
/stand/build/function_names.c
        checksum            2434797998              1240646943
        permissions         rw-rw-rw-               rw-r--r--
/stand/build/function_names.o
        checksum            3857693076              1165263911
        permissions         rw-rw-rw-               rw-r--r--
/stand/build/space.h
        permissions         rw-rw-rw-               rw-r--r--
/stand/build/tune.h
        checksum            2763942582              2084822502
/stand/dlkm.vmunix.prev/symtab
```

```
        checksum            2086890351              1785861028
        permissions         rw-r--r--               rw-rw-rw-
/stand/dlkm.vmunix.prev/system
        checksum            3376707916              2873910478
/stand/dlkm/symtab
        checksum            2368412414              2086890351
        permissions         rw-rw-rw-               rw-r--r--
/stand/dlkm/system
        checksum            2855591959              3376707916
/stand/system
        checksum            4141126356              1910321628
        permissions         rw-rw-rw-               r--r--r--
/stand/system.prev
        checksum            1910321628              253499711
        permissions         r--r--r--               rw-rw-rw-
/stand/vmunix
        checksum            2977157561              2742478025
/stand/vmunix.prev
        checksum            2742478025              3594881120
/usr/lib/ipldd07a.sl
        linkname        /apps/informix7.3/lib/ipldd07a.sl
        /apps/informix/lib/ipldd07a.sl
/usr/local/samba.1.9.18p3/var/locks/browse.dat
        checksum            2594069517              2221092461
/usr/local/samba.1.9.18p3/var/log.nmb
        checksum            4219117043              2190854115
/usr/local/samba.1.9.18p3/var/log.smb
        checksum            2251415300              1791314631
/var/spool/cron/crontabs/root
        checksum            2015828837              1660287231
#
```

man page

check_
recovery
9

This output indicates that many changes have been made to the system, including software additions and system file additions, deletions, and modifications. If **check_recovery** produces any significant changes to the system, you should rerun the **make_recovery** command so that the system recovery tape reflects the current state of your system. As a result of completing the procedure covered in this section, many files were produced. Some that you may want to take a look at are in the **/var/opt/ignite/recovery** directory shown in the following listing:

man page

make_
recovery
9

```
# cd /var/opt/ignite/recovery
# ll
total 5412
-rw-rw-rw-   1 root     sys          1737051 Jul 13 16:17 arch.include
-rw-rw-rw-   1 root     sys              250 Jul 13 16:12 chkrec.include
-rw-rw-rw-   1 root     sys             4872 Jul 13 16:17 config.recover
-rw-rw-rw-   1 root     sys             4872 Jul 13 16:17 config.recover.prev
-rw-rw-rw-   1 root     sys             1682 Jul 13 16:12 fstab
-rw-rw-rw-   1 root     sys              390 Jul 13 16:29 group.makrec
-r--r--r--   1 root     sys             1971 Jun 25 12:27 makrec.append
-r--r--r--   1 bin      bin             1971 Apr 24 00:32 makrec.append.org
-rw-rw-rw-   1 root     sys          1010844 Jul 13 16:28 makrec.last
-rw-rw-rw-   1 root     sys             2573 Jul 13 16:29 passwd.makrec
```

Manual Pages for Commands Used in Chapter 9

The following section contains copies of the manual pages for Ignite-UX commands used in Chapter 9.

check_recovery

check_recovery - Compare the current system to the system recovery status file created by **make_recovery**.

check_recovery(1M)   check_recovery(1M)

NAME
     check_recovery - compare the current system to the System Recovery
     status file created by the last invocation of make_recovery.

SYNOPSIS
     /opt/ignite/bin/check_recovery

DESCRIPTION
     check_recovery compares the current state of the system to the System
     Recovery status file (created by the last invocation of make_recovery)
     to determine if a new System Recovery Tape needs to be created. Only
     Core OS and User Core OS files are validated. Refer to make_recovery
     for an explanation of these terms.

     check_recovery displays all discrepancies found between the current
     system and the status file to stderr. Based on these, the System
     Administrator can then make a determination as to whether a new System
     Recovery Tape needs to be created.

     check_recovery detects the following discrepancies:

   + Additions: A file existing on the current system and not
      listed in the System Recovery status file is a file added to
      the system since the last System Recovery Tape was created.

   + Deletions: A file not existing on the current system and
      listed in the System Recovery status file is a file deleted
      from the system since the last System Recovery Tape was
      created.

   + Modifications: A file existing on the current system but with
      a different "last modification date" is further validated via
      its checksum. If the file's checksum is different from the
      value in the System Recovery status file, then the file has
      been modified.

     check_recovery can be invoked only by a user who has superuser
     privileges.

   Options
     check_recovery has no options.

EXAMPLES

Check the current system to determine whether a new System Recovery
Tape needs to be created.

    check_recovery

NOTES
        make_recovery must have been previously executed with the -C option to
        create the System Recovery status file.

AUTHOR
        check_recovery was developed by HP.

FILES
        /var/opt/ignite/recovery/makrec.last
    System Recovery status file created by
    make_recovery during the last System Recovery
    archive creation

        /var/opt/ignite/recovery/chkrec.include
    List of files to be included for validation by
    check_recovery

        /opt/ignite/recovery/chkrec.exclude
    List of files to be excluded for validation by
    check_recovery

SEE ALSO
        make_recovery(1M).

ignite

ignite - Invoke the Graphical User Interface (GUI) of Ignite-UX.

man page

ignite - 9

ignite(5)   ignite(5)

NAME
     ignite - HP-UX configuration and installation manager

SYNOPSIS
     /opt/ignite/bin/ignite

DESCRIPTION
  Introduction
     ignite is part of the Ignite-UX product, a client-server application
     that provides the ability to configure and install HP-UX systems.
     Ignite-UX is available on all HP-UX 10.XX platforms (with the
     exception of HP-UX 10.00) and supports the installation of all 10.XX
     releases and 10.XX applications.

     The ignite command is the graphical user interface of this client-
     server application. It provides the ability to build software
     configurations and to use these configurations to install HP-UX
     systems.

     Key features:

   + True client-server framework enabling an install session for
     multiple targets to be controlled from a single server.

   + Support of client standalone installation by enabling an
     installation to be controlled from a terminal user interface
     running on the target machine.

   + Support for non-interactive installations initiated from the
     client or server.

   + Support for multiple sources within a single install session.
     This allows end customers to install multiple applications at
     the same time they install the base OS.

   + Support for Software Distributor (SD) and non-SD sources, by
     providing the ability to load SD software, as well as software
     from a non-SD sources (tar, cpio, or pax). One use of this
     feature is the ability to load a system with an OS and
     applications, capture that system into an archive and then use
     that archive to install to multiple targets.

   + Support for user-defined configurations by allowing a system
     administrator to construct a description (configuration) for a
     target system including disk and networking layout, software to
     install, kernel modifications and post-installation
     customizations. Once this configuration has been defined it
     may then be applied to one or more target machines.

+ Support for user-defined customization both by defining what a
target system should look like and by allowing execution of
user-supplied scripts at pre-defined points in the installation
process.

+ Support for saved configurations by enabling a user to modify
an existing configuration, save these changes, and then quickly
apply the new configuration to a target system.

+ Support for system manifest creation by providing a simple
method to capture a snapshot of the currently loaded software
along with a complete hardware inventory.

Hardware/Software Requirements
    For doing 10.XX loads, the following hardware is required to set up
    either a Series 700 or Series 800 Ignite-UX server. If a Series 800
    Ignite-UX server is set up, it needs a graphics display or the display
    can be redirected to another X(1) windows system. The redirection is
    accomplished by setting the DISPLAY environment variable. For
    example, in the Korn Shell or Posix Shell you would type: export
    DISPLAY=hpfcdn:0.0

    Ignite-UX server requirements:

+ A Series 700/800 system running HP-UX 10.XX.

+ An X11 display server (workstation, X-terminal, PC running an
    X server, etc). Can be the same system as above.

+ Sufficient disk space to load Ignite-UX, and any software
depots and/or archives to be used during the install.

+ Access to the Ignite-UX tool set.The tool set can be loaded
onto any 10.XX system.

+ Tape/CD-ROM in order to load Ignite-UX and any software depots
you plan to distribute onto the server.

+ Network access to any clients to be installed. Client and
    Server must be on the same subnet if you plan to do the initial
    boot of the client over the network.

Server Setup: Overview
1.   Install HP-UX 10.XX.

2.   Install Ignite-UX tools and data.

3.   Set up core software.

4.   Add additional applications (optional).

5.   Run ignite to complete the configuration and to start the
    process.

    Note: All operations are executed as "root" on the Ignite-UX
    server.Except where noted, all commands referenced here are
    located in /opt/ignite/bin.

Server Setup: Details
    1. Install HP-UX 10.XX
Refer to the manual for instructions on how to update a system to
HP-UX 10.XX.

2. Install Ignite-UX Software
The Ignite-UX tool-set is contained on the HP-UX application set
of CD-ROMs.The software bundles are named as such: Ignite-UX-
10-01, Ignite-UX-10-10, Ignite-UX-10-20, etc. Each software
bundle contains the Ignite-UX tools plus the data files required
for support of the particular HP-UX release indicated by the
bundle name. You may load one or more of the Ignite-UX-10-XX
bundles onto your server depending on which releases of HP-UX you
plan on installing onto clients.

The Ignite-UX product replaces the capability previously supplied
by the NetInstall bundle that came with HP-UX releases 10.01,
10.10 and 10.20. Loading one of the Ignite-UX software bundles
will cause the NetInstall bundle to be automatically removed.

Once the application CD-ROM containing Ignite-UX has been
mounted, you may use the swinstall command to load the desired
Ignite-UX bundles. For example, the command below would load the
support needed for installing HP-UX 10.20 onto clients:

swinstall -s /cdromIgnite-UX-10-20

3. Set up "core" HP-UX software
Before Ignite-UX can be used, you must configure the software for
it to load onto the clients. Since both SD sources and archive
(non-SD) sources (tar, cpio, or pax) may be used, both cases will
be considered separately below.

For SD OS software:
For Ignite-UX to use an SD source, you must have a
registered SD depot available, and an Ignite-UX
configuration file generated from that depot.

If you already have an SD depot containing the core HP-UX
software, then you can enable Ignite-UX to access it by
using the make_config and manage_index commands. If you do
not already have a depot available, you may want to use the
add_release command to lead you though copying the software
from the distribution media into a depot and then
configuring Ignite-UX to use it. Both methods are outlined
below.

Enabling (or updating) an existing depot
If you already have an SD depot available, or if you
have made changes to a depot that Ignite-UX knows
about, then you can use the make_config and
manage_index commands to generate a configuration file
that Ignite-UX will use in accessing the depot. For
example:
make_config -s server:/depot_700 \
-c /var/opt/ignite/data/Rel_B.10.20/core_700
manage_index -a -f /var/opt/ignite/data/Rel_B.10.20/core_700

If at a later time, you modify the contents of a depot
(you use swcopy to add software, for example), then the
same make_config step will need to be rerun in order
for Ignite-UX to be aware of the modifications.

Note: The make_config command only operates on software
that is contained in a bundle. If you have a depot
that has products not in a bundle, then you can run the
make_bundles command on the depot prior to running
make_config.

Using add_release to do it all
    If you need to copy the core HP-UX software off the
    distribution media into a depot, and configure Ignite-
    UX to use it, then the add_release command can be used
    to lead you though all the steps.

    To run add_release to see what it would do and not
    actually modify anything, you can specify the -p option
    (preview mode).

    For example:
    /opt/ignite/bin/add_release -s /dev/dsk/c0t2s0 -p

    To use a depot other than /dev/rmt/0m to read the
    software, you can specify it with the -s option.

    For example:
    /opt/ignite/bin/add_release -s jupiter:/depot/s700_10.XX_final

   For non-SD (archive) OS software:
Ignite-UX has the capability of loading a system from an
archive image taken from a system that represents your
standard configuration. This method gives significantly
faster install times, but may not be as flexible as using an
SD source.

You will first need to generate the archive image of a
system in the desired state. It is recommended that the
/opt/ignite/data/scripts/make_sys_image script be used to
accomplish this task.

Once an archive image is created, then a configuration file
that represents the location and attributes of that image
must be created before Ignite-UX can use it.

A sample of a config file that can be used with a core
archive can be found at:
/opt/ignite/data/examples/core.cfg

The comments in this example file describe where to copy the
file and what to change in the file to make it reference
your archive and to work in your environment.

    4. Add additional applications (optional)
    If you have other software that you would like to have loaded
    during the system installation then you can create configuration
    files similar to what was done for the core-OS software by using
    make_config and manage_index or by using an example configuration
    file and modifying it.

   For SD application software
Run the following commands for each depot you plan to load
SD software from during the installation. The make_config
command only handles SD software which is packaged in bundle
form. If the SD depot you want to use has software not
contained in a bundle (for example: a collection of
patches), then the make_bundles command may be used to
create bundles in the depot.

If the contents are not 700/800 specific then the
make_config -a[78]00 option should not be used.

For example, to make a depot containing patches available:
make_bundles /depots/s700_10.20_patches

make_config -s hpfcxxx.hp.com:/depots/s700_10.20_patches

```
   -a 700 -c /opt/ignite/data/Rel_B.10.20/patches_700_cfg
```

manage_index -a -f /opt/ignite/data/Rel_B.10.20/patches_700_cfg

For example, to make a depot containing compilers available
which are already in bundles (no need to use make_bundles):
make_config -s hpfcxxx.hp.com:/depots/compiler
  -c /opt/ignite/data/Rel_B.10.XX/compilers_cfg

manage_index -a -f /opt/ignite/data/Rel_B.10.XX/compilers_cfg

The depot server (in this example hpfcxxx) should be
replaced with the server you have the SD software on. The
make_bundles script must be run on the same system where the
depot exists. If the depot is not on the Ignite-UX server,
you may need to copy the make_bundles script to the depot
server and run it there.

Note: The make_config command will need to be re-run each
time new software is added or modified in the depots.

make_config constructs Ignite-UX config files which
correspond to SD depots. When an SD depot is used as part
of the Ignite-UX process, it must have a config file which
describes the contents of the depot to Ignite-UX. This
command can automatically construct such a config file given
the name of an SD depot to operate on.This command should
be run when adding or changing a depot which will be used by
Ignite-UX.

manage_index is used to manipulate the /var/opt/ignite/INDEX
file. This utility is primarily called by other Ignite-UX
tools but can also be called directly.

    For non-SD application software:
If the source is not an "SD" depot, the make_config command
is not applicable. You will need to create a unique config
file that includes the non-SD software. A sample of a
config file that does a non-core archive can be found at:

/opt/ignite/data/examples/noncore.cfg

The comments in this example file describe where to copy the
file and what to change in the file to make it reference
your archive and to work in your environment.

    5. Run ignite to complete the configuration and to start the process
    On the Series 700 server run: /opt/ignite/bin/ignite. This will start
    the Ignite-UX server program.

    Complete the Configuration:
When the GUI display titled "Ignite-UX" appears, do the following
in that window:

a)Choose Options: Server Configuration

b)Look over both the Server Options and the Session Options to
see if they are suitable.

    About the Screen: 'Add Booting IP Addresses':

    Booting Clients: xx.xx.xx.xx to xx.xx.xx.xx
These IP addresses are used to initially boot the target
systems. They are used until the system is assigned one of
the DHCP-assigned addresses. One address is required for

each simultaneous boot. Typically one to three are needed, depending on the usage.

    DHCP Addresses: xx.xx.xx.xx to xx.xx.xx.xx
These IP addresses are used during the OS download and application loading. These addresses are in use for most of the Ignite-UX download to a target machine.

One address is required for each simultaneous download. You should set more, if the addresses are assigned permanently.

    DHCP Class ID:
The unique name for the DHCP server that serves these DHCP Addresses. Not necessarily the install server.

If you will not be using the install server as the DHCP server, then either do not set class ID at all, or you need to know what the client ID is set to on your real DHCP server.

Do not apply the class ID unless you are configuring the install server to be a DHCP server.

    DHCP Addresses are temporary:
If these DHCP Addresses are only used for doing installs, and the clients will get reassigned new addresses when deployed. Keep this field set.

If you want to set up the Ignite-UX server as a departmental DHCP server, in which case the IP address leases are permanent, and isolated to the department's DHCP server, set this field to false.

    Boot the S700 or S800 client system that supports network boot: If the system you plan to install is running HP-UX version 9.X or 10.X, then you can use the bootsys command to remotely reboot the client to run Ignite-UX.

If the client system is new, or disabled such that bootsys cannot be used, then you can boot it over the network (note, that currently the only S800 systems that are capable of network boot are the K and D class systems).

To do a network boot, Go to the console for that client and enter the appropriate command. (You will find the exact boot ROM commands for your system in

In general:

1)   Stop the auto-boot by pressing <escape>.

2)   For older Series 700s (non-bootp), type the following:

      search lan

      It will typically require three searches for the server to be found and listed, on older Series 700s.

      Boot the client either by using the index displayed in the search or by using the following:

      boot lan.080009-XXXYYY

3)   For newer Series 700s, type the following to search for servers on your network. If you already know the server's IP address, or you are on a S800 (K and D class) that do not

support the search command, then just issue the boot command
below:

search lan install

Note: Some C-class systems had a firmware defect such that
the search lan install install does not display any servers.
However, doing an explicit boot using the server's IP address
works correctly. A firmware upgrade is available for systems
with this defect.

Choose the preferred boot server (if you have more than one)
and enter the following:

boot lan.IP-Address install

If only one server appears in the listing, just type the
following:

boot lan install

If the client cannot find the server, check the following
items:

+ Client is on the same subnet as the server.

+ Any instl_bootd errors in /var/adm/syslog/syslog.log.

+ Your /var/adm/inetd.sec file to make sure that IP address
0.0.0.0 is not being disallowed for the instl_boots
service.

+ If /etc/services comes from NIS, make sure that the NIS
server has instl_boot* entries.

+ rbootd is running.

  Booting a system remotely using bootsys:
    If a system you need to reinstall is up and running HP-UX 9.X or 10.X
    and available on the network, then you can use the bootsys command
    from the server to cause the client system to boot Ignite-UX. Using
    the bootsys command has the advantages of:

+ Can be done remotely from the Ignite-UX server. Does not
  require access to the client console.

+ It is able to boot S800's that are not capable of a network
  boot.

+ It allows booting clients that are on different subnets (since
  it is not really doing a true network boot).

+ The bootsys command may also be used to schedule installations
  to happen at a later time by calling it from at or cron.

The bootsys command has options to initiate an automated
installation (-a), or an installation controlled from the ignite
user interface (-w).

  Booting a system from customer-created install
    An install image used to boot a system can be created using
    make_medialif. When transferred to physical media, it can be used to:

+ Automatically load an archive image also stored on the media
  without intervention.

+ Initiate an install from an Ignite-UX server. The install can
  be either automated or interactive.

    This is a way for shipping user-customized install media to remote
    sites. See make_medialif(1M) for more information.

Start the Installation:
    After the client is booted, its icon should appear on the ignite
    interface. If the server has not been set up completely, or if the
    client could not obtain enough networking parameters via DHCP, then
    the client may require interaction on the client console.

    After the client icon appears on the server screen, select it by
    clicking on the icon for that client. Use the Actions menu to select a
    task for the selected client. The first task would be to choose
    "Install Client". Then choose "New Install".

    During the installation, choose a configuration file for this
    installation. Clients will be installed per the description given in
    the configuration file. If you want to reuse this configuration, save
    the file.

    Once installation is proceeding, check the client's status on the
    server.

    When the installation completes, you can print a manifest, and either
    save the client's data in a history directory or remove the client and
    its data from the server.

    Refer to the online help: "Ignite-UX Concepts", or "Getting Started"
    for more information.

Standalone Installation
    The standalone type of installation is invoked by booting the system
    from the network, as described in the previous section, or by booting
    from the Ignite-UX media. After choosing "Install HP-UX", select
    "Local interaction at console, installing from network server" on the
    next screen.

    Or if you are installing from media, select "Media installation, with
    user interaction at local console".

    A basic interface, "wizard mode" can be chosen at this point. This
    will direct you though the required system setup steps. This mode is
    for the novice user, and proceeds though a more limited set of
    configuration steps, while giving you recommended choices based on
    your system's hardware.

    Additionally, a more sophisticated interface can be selected if the
    user needs to modify the filesystem configuration, or would like to
    set the system hostname and networking parameters prior to completing
    the installation.

    If you find that you have selected the wrong interface to accomplish
    your task, you may use the "Cancel" button which will allow you to
    switch to the other interface mode.

    The standalone installation uses an ASCII (TUI) interface, and
    requires a keyboard for navigation.

    The following keys can be used to navigate in the various screens:

+ <return> and <space> keys select an item

+ <tab> key moves to the next item on the screen.

+ <right> arrow and <down> arrow keys cycle to the next item in
  the "Tab Group"

  A Tab Group is defined as all of the selectable options within
  an area of the screen defined by dotted lines. To move to the
  next Tab Group, the <tab> key must be used.

+ <left> arrow and <up> arrow keys cycle to the previous item in
  the Tab Group. To move to the next Tab Group, the <tab> key
  must be used.

+ Additionally, any key with an underlined character, can be
  chosen by typing that underlined character.

Manifest Generation
    Included in the Ignite-UX tool set is a command: print_manifest(1M).
    This utility prints a formatted ascii system manifest to stdout.The
    manifest includes information on hardware and software installed and
    configured on the system. It gathers information about the system
    every time it is run.

    ignite can display and/or print the manifest of a just-installed
    system with the action "View/Print Manifest". If the client's data is
    moved to history, that data includes both the client's manifest and
    config file. Both these files can be recalled at a later time.

EXTERNAL INPUTS AND INFLUENCES
  Default Options:
    The server maintains a defaults file, ignite.defs, located at
    /var/opt/ignite/server/ignite.defs. This file contains a subset of
    the values that are entered on the Server Configuration screen.

    The following values and their defaults are shipped in the Ignite-UX
    product:

    client_timeout:30
    Time (in mins) until the client is declared hung.

    halt_when_done:false
    Halt the client after installation rather than reboot to invoke
    set_parms.

    ignite_welcome:true
    Show the server's welcome screen.

    itool_welcome:true
    Ask for customer information during client installation.

    new_client_notification:true
    Asks whether the user be notified when new clients boot.

  Locking
    In order to allow multiple ignite sessions to run concurrently with
    the currently installing process, ignite will lock a client during a
    New Install or a Repeat Install.This lock is tested in the actions:
    New Install, Repeat Installation, Stop Client and Remove Client.
    The lock is removed when the client is stopped or COMPLETE. For
    stopped clients, it is possible for someone, other than the installer,
    to remove them. For COMPLETE clients, it is possible for someone,
    other than the installer, to remove them or move them to history.

RETURN VALUES
    ignite returns the following values:

  0ignite completed successfully.

```
    lignite failed.

DIAGNOSTICS
   Logging:
       All major events are logged to the server logfile located at
       /var/opt/ignite/logs/server.

FILES
       /opt/ignite/bin
     Contains Ignite-UX commands.

       /opt/ignite/lbin
     Contains Ignite-UX commands used by other commands.

       /var/opt/ignite/depots
     Contains the software depots used by Ignite-UX.

       /var/opt/ignite/logs
     Contains logfiles for each command.

       /var/opt/ignite/clients
     Contains the per-client directories.

       /var/opt/ignite/server
     Contains the file ignite.defs (server defaults).

AUTHOR
       Ignite-UX was developed by the Hewlett-Packard Company.

SEE ALSO
       add_release(1M), archive_impact(1M), bootsys(1M), instl_adm(1M),
       instl_adm(4), instl_bootd(1M), make_bundles(1M), make_config(1M),
       make_depots(1M), make_medialif(1M), manage_index(1M),
       print_manifest(1M), remove_release(1M), save_config(1M), sd(5),
       setup_server(1M).
```

make_recovery

make_recovery - Create an Ignite-UX system recovery tape.

make_recovery(1M)   make_recovery(1M)

NAME
     make_recovery - create the System Recovery Tape

SYNOPSIS
     /opt/ignite/bin/make_recovery [-AprvC] [-d destination] [-b
boot_destination]

DESCRIPTION
     make_recovery creates the System Recovery Tape. This tape can be used
     to:

   restore a non-bootable system with little or no human
   intervention.

   restore a system in the event of a hardware failure of the root
   disk or volume group when a disk has to be replaced.

   Clone the software from one system to another.

   Convert from hfs to vxfs file systems.

   Modify root file system size.

   Modify primary swap space allocation.

        It makes use of the installation technology provided by the Ignite-UX
        product, and can be considered a "customized" installation media. A
        system can be recovered by booting and installing from the tape
        without user intervention. All information regarding disk
        configuration, software, and system identity is stored on the tape at
        the time that make_recovery is executed.

        The System Recovery tape consists of a Boot Image, followed by an
        archive of system files that comprise a "Minimum Core OS". Minimum
        Core OS is defined as: /stand, /sbin, /dev, /etc, and subsets of /usr,
        /opt and /var that are required during the install process. The
        devices or volume groups that correspond to the file
        systems/directories /, /dev, /etc, /sbin, /stand and /usr are
        considered "Core" devices/volume groups. These devices or volume
        groups are recreated during the recovery process. All non-OS data on
        these devices or volume groups would be removed unless specifically
        appended to the recovery tape (as described below).

        Since non-core Applications reside in /opt /<application> and system
        dynamic files such as administration files, data bases etc. reside in

/var, these file systems have not been considered part of the Minimum
Core OS.

If these reside in the "Core" disk/volume group, they will be
recreated during the recovery installation process and the data must
be recovered. The data can be included in the archive by using the -A
option (described below). In that case, if the system has to be
recovered, then these directories will be recreated by the install
process, and the data will be recovered from the archive.
Alternatively, the data can be recovered from normal backups if the -A
option is not used while creating the recovery tape.

Any file system that resides in a "non-Core" disk/volume group will
not be recreated by the install process. The original file system will
be remounted after final re-boot and the data will be preserved.

make_recovery provides a mechanism for the user to include user
specified non-system files in the archive via the
/var/opt/ignite/recovery/makrec.append file. These are limited to
files or directories that belong to file systems in the "Core"
devices/volume groups, /opt and /var.

make_recovery also provides a mechanism for the user to exclude
selected files from the archive via the -p and -r options.

Non-Core File Systems, which are not on the Core device/volume groups
are expected to be backed up and recovered using normal backup
utilities.

The System Recovery tape is only as good as the last time it was
created.The tape should be recreated if the software, hardware,
patches, etc. on the system are changed. The check_recovery command
can be used to determine if the system has changed enough that the
tape needs to be recreated.

To recover a failed system disk or volume group, the user would
- mount the System Recovery tape on the tape drive
- boot the system
- interrupt the boot sequence to redirect it to the tape drive
- elect no intervention with ISL
- allow the install process to complete.

To clone a system disk or volume group, the user would
- mount the System Recovery tape on the tape drive
- boot the system
- interrupt the boot sequence to redirect it to the tape drive
- Cancel the non-interactive installation by hitting the return
key when the following messages are displayed:

WARNING: The configuration information calls for a non-
interactive installation.

Press <Return> within 10 seconds to cancel batch-mode
installation:

- The "Ignite-UX Welcome" screen will be presented.

As a "customized" installation is being performed, select the
option
[Install HP-UX]
  and then the option
[   ] Advanced Installation (recommended for disk and
filesystem management)
  Then configure/change disks, file systems, hostname, IP address,
  timezone, root password, DNS server, gateway information. These

can also be configured by using /etc/set_parms after the system
has been finally re-booted.
- allow the install process to complete.

The System Recovery tape can be used to clone the software on a system
on to another system, with manual configuration to be performed by the
user during the interactive installation.

Progress and errors are logged to /var/opt/ignite/logs/makrec.log1.

make_recovery requires superuser privilege.

Options
  make_recovery recognizes the following options:

 -A Specifies that the entire root disk/volume group
is to be included in the System Recovery tape.
This creates a complete bootable backup of the
disk or volume group.

In the case of large root disks or volume groups,
or when other utilities are used for normal
backups, this option should not be used. Instead,
the default minimum core OS should be backed up,
to recover a minimum system, and then the full
recovery should be done from the backups.

 -p Previews what processing would take place, without
actually creating the tape. This is a way of
verifying /var/opt/ignite/recovery/makrec.append,
and getting /var/opt/ignite/recovery/arch.include
created. The latter file determines what goes into
the archive. This file can be edited to exclude
some files/directories from the archive if desired
by deleting them from the file. Only files or
directories that are known to be user created
should be deleted. No further checks are done by
make_recovery. The creation of the System
Recovery tape can then be resumed using the -r
option.

 -r Resumes creation of the System Recovery tape after
the -p option has been used to create
/var/opt/ignite/recovery/arch.include, and it has
been possibly edited. If the -A and -r options
are both used, the -A option will override the -r
option, and the entire root disk/volume group will
be backed up.

 -v Specifies verbose mode that displays progress
messages.

 -d destination Specifies the device file of a DDS tape drive
where the System Recovery Tape is to be created.
A no-rewind device file is required. The default
is /dev/rmt/0mn.

 -b destination Specifies the location where the boot LIF volume
is to be assembled, before it is written out to
tape. 32Mb is required. The default location is
/var/tmp/uxinstlf.recovery.

 -C Create the System status file
/var/opt/ignite/recovery/makrec.last. This file
reflects the current state of the system. It
contains the names, dates of last modification,

and checksums of all the files on the tape that
are considered "Core OS" files. It may also
contain the file information for the user files
specified in the
/var/opt/ignite/recovery/makrec.append file if the
file exists. This option would be used if the user
plans to use check_recovery to determine if the
system has been changed such that the System
Recovery tape needs to be recreated.

The /var/opt/ignite/recovery/makrec.append file is provided for the
user to append selected data files to the archive. This has the
format:

```
** User Core OS **
file: filename
file: filename
file: filename
dir: dirname
product: productname
** User Data **
file: filename
file: filename
product: productname
dir: dirname
```

The headers ** User Core OS ** and ** User Data ** are fixed form. The
files/directories listed in the ** User Core OS ** section are
considered Users system files, and are appended to the System Recovery
archive, as well as to the /var/opt/ignite/recovery/makrec.last file,
which is used by the check_recovery command for system validation.

The files/directories listed in the ** User Data ** section are not
considered system files, and while they are appended to the archive,
they are not validated by check_recovery.

Adding unnecessary files/directories to the ** User Core OS ** section
indiscriminately will significantly increase the amount of time
required for both tape generation and check_recovery execution, and is
not advised.

The product tag is provided to allow a user to append a backup utility
to the System Recovery tape. This is limited to utilities that have
been installed using SD (Software Distributor), and follow the SD
guidelines.

Lines starting with "#" are treated as comments and ignored. Blank
lines are also ignored.

EXAMPLES

To create a Minimum OS System Recovery tape at /dev/rmt/0mn. This
tape includes only the minimum OS required to boot the system. A
system recovery from this tape would mean booting from the tape to
recover the minimum Core OS, and then following up with a user data
recovery from normal backup media.

make_recovery

To create a Minimum OS System Recovery tape at /dev/rmt/c0t1d1BESTn
(assuming a writable DDS tape is in the drive pointed to by
/dev/rmt/c0t1d1BESTn.) User data recovery is done as described above.

make_recovery -d /dev/rmt/c0t1d1BESTn

To preview the creation of a System Recovery tape at
/dev/rmt/c0t1d1BESTn (assuming a writable DDS tape is in the drive

pointed to by /dev/rmt/c0t1d1BESTn), review the list of files that
will be included in the archive, possibly modify the list, and then
subsequently continue the creation.

```
make_recovery -p -d /dev/rmt/c0t1d1BESTn
vi /var/opt/ignite/arch.include
make_recovery -r -d /dev/rmt/c0t1d1BESTn
```

To create a System Recovery tape, at the default device /dev/rmt/0m,
and include the entire root disk in the archive.
```
make_recovery -A
```

To create a System Recovery tape that
- includes the entire root file system in the disk,
- adds the file /mnt/fileA as a users system file,
- adds the data directory /mnt/dirB to the archive as non-system
data. (assuming that /mnt is mounted on the same volume group as
the core File Systems),
- creates the system status file.

Edit the /var/opt/ignite/recovery/makrec.append file to include:

```
** User Core OS **
file: /mnt/fileA
** User Data **
dir: /mnt/dirB
```

Then issue the command:
```
make_recovery -v -C
```

To clone a system, create the System Recovery tape.
```
make_recovery -v -A
```
Install it on the new system. Invoke the user interface by hitting any
key during the 10 second interval given for this purpose during the
installation. Configure the hostname, IP address, root password etc.
using the "system" screen of the user interface.

The installation can be non-interactive if the configuration of the
system being installed is the same as that of the original system.

If the system is installed non-interactively, immediately run
/etc/set_parms to configure the new hostname, IP address etc for the
system. This method is not recommended. (See WARNINGS).

If the configuration of the system being installed is not the same as
that of the original system, the normal user interface for
installation will be presented, and the user has the opportunity to
provide the configuration information via the "system" installation
configuration screen.

WARNINGS
make_recovery relies on the Installed Products Database (IPD) to
extract files relevant to a product added to the System Recovery tape
via the "product" tag in the append file. It is only as reliable as
the IPD.Only products installed via SD (Software Distributor) are
logged into the IPD. It is also necessary that the SD commands be
used to add, modify, remove these products, so that the IPD is
correctly updated to reflect these changes. If there is any
possibility that the product has been manipulated without using SD, or
that the products' installation/configuration scripts are not
modifying the IPD reliably, then it is better to set up
/var/opt/ignite/recovery/makrec.append with all the filenames for the
product as a one time effort.

If the System Recovery tape is used to clone the software on another
system, the newly installed system will have the same hostname and IP
address as the original system. These should be immediately changed
using /etc/set_parms. Introducing a second system into the network
with the same hostname or IP address will very possibly disable
networking on both systems.

The -p and -r options can be used to exclude some non OS
files/directories from the System Recovery archive. These should only
be used by knowledgeable System Administrators as excluding required
files/directories from the boot tape could render it useless.

On systems that support Large UID/GIDs or Large Files (>2GB), the
System Recovery tape should be created for only the Minimum OS, and
remaining user data recovered from Normal Backup Media that support
these features. make_recovery does not directly support these
features since pax (used to generate the archive) does not as yet
support them.

make_recovery does not support mirrored disks. V-class systems are
not supported at first release.

NOTES

If a non-root disk is corrupted, it should be recovered from normal
backups.

The System Recovery tape should be used when the root disk or volume
group is corrupted and the system cannot be booted. The install
process recreates the disk or volume group from scratch, and no data
on the disks is salvaged. The file systems /, /stand, /sbin, /etc and
/dev are always mounted on the root volume group, and are always
recreated.

/usr is always recreated. If it is mounted on a non-root volume group,
that volume group will also be considered Core, and will be recreated.

The entire / file system is not archived by default. This can be done
via the append file, or by using the -A option.

If /opt and /var are mounted on the root volume group, these can
either be included in the System Recovery archive, or recovered from
normal backups after the system is brought up.

/opt and /var tend to grow large, and are occasionally mounted on a
separate disk or in a non root volume group. In such cases, it is
essential that the user data on these disks should not be "wiped out"
during the process of reinstalling the root disk/volume group. Some
files from these file systems are required for Ignite-UX processing
and make_recovery would automatically include them in the archive.
Other files from these file systems can be included in the archive for
cloning purposes, but if the same system is being recovered, the files
will not be restored onto these file systems. These file systems will
be left unaltered.

If the disks on the system have been changed, the install process can
detect that the hardware is different, and starts up the install user
interface to allow changes to the configuration.If the hardware
configuration is the same, the installation can complete non-
interactively.

The user can also elect to invoke the user interface by hitting any
key during the 10 second interval given for this purpose during the
installation. The user can then make configuration choices, but the
archives will be recovered in a manner similar to a cold install. The
software, data files and so forth will be recovered, but the user will

manually complete the configuration of hostname, IP address, DNS
server, date and time, root password. The /etc/fstab and /etc/hosts
files will have to be re-created. A copy of the original /etc/fstab
file is saved in /var/opt/ignite/recovery/fstab for reference.

Minimum Core OS consists of:
/.profile, /.rhosts,
/dev, /etc, /sbin,

/usr/bin, /usr/sbin,
/usr/lib, /usr/obam,
/usr/sam, /usr/share,
/usr/ccs, /usr/conf,
/usr/lbin, /usr/contrib,
/usr/local, /usr/newconfig

/var/adm/sw, /var/opt/ignite/local/manifest,
/var/adm/cron, /var/spool/cron

The following files/directories are considered part of minimum Core OS
if they exist on the system.

/opt/ignite/bin/print_manifest,
/opt/ignite/share/man/man1m.Z/print_manifest.1m,
/opt/upgrade

All of the above files/directories are included in the archive as
default.

DEPENDENCIES
make_recovery requires that the following filesets of the Ignite-UX
product be installed on the system.

Ignite-UX.BOOT-KERNEL
Ignite-UX.BOOT-SERVICES
Ignite-UX.FILE-SRV-release
Ignite-UX.MGMT-TOOLS
Ignite-UX.IGNT-ENG-A-MAN

For 10.x systems, the current patch for pax that fixes problems with
hardlinks is required.

FILES
/var/opt/ignite/recovery/makrec.append
User created file for appending
files/directories/products to the System Recovery
archive.

/var/opt/ignite/logs/makrec.log1
Progress and error log.

/var/opt/ignite/logs/makrec.log2
Archive content log.

/var/opt/ignite/recovery/makrec.last
System status file created with the -C option.
This file will be used by check_recovery for
system validation.

/var/opt/ignite/recovery/arch.include
List of files to be included in the System
Recovery archive.

/var/opt/ignite/recovery/chkrec.include
List of files that will be validated by
check_recovery.

```
     /var/opt/ignite/recovery/config.recover
File that describes the System configuration.

     /var/opt/ignite/recovery/fstab
A copy of the current /etc/fstab file for
reference in case the Interactive mode was used,
causing the /etc/fstab file to be re-created.

     /var/tmp/uxinstlf.recovery
Default location for Boot LIF volume creation.

SEE ALSO
     check_recovery(1M), save_config(1M), make_medialif(1M), instl_adm(1M),
     instl_adm(5), ignite(5), pax(1).
```

CHAPTER 10

System Administration
Manager (SAM) and
ServiceControl Manager (SCM)

SAM Overview

SAM is a program you can use to automate and perform various system administration tasks. SAM has been refined over many releases of HP-UX and is now a highly functional and reliable tool for performing routine system administration tasks. As you'll see in the upcoming sections, SAM has many *functional areas* in which you can perform system administration tasks. Since there is a lot of "coverage" with SAM, meaning most system administration tasks can be performed with SAM, combined with its reliability in performing these tasks, I have found more and more system administrators using SAM for performing system administration tasks.

Four features of SAM that make it particularly useful are:

1. It provides a central point from which system administration tasks can be performed. This includes both the built-in tasks that come with SAM as well as those you can add into the SAM menu hierarchy. You can run SAM on a remote system and display it locally so that you truly have a central point of control.

2. It provides an easy way to perform tasks that are difficult, in that you would have to perform many steps. SAM performs these steps for you.

3. It provides a summary of what your system currently looks like for any of the categories of administration tasks you wish to perform. If you want to do something with the disks on your system, SAM first lists the disks you currently have connected. If you want to play with a printer, SAM first lists all your printers and plotters for you. This capability cuts down on mistakes by putting your current configuration right in front of you.

4. You can assign non-root users to perform some of the system administration functions in SAM. If, for instance, you feel comfortable assigning one of your associates to manage users, you can give them permission to perform user-related tasks and give another user permission to perform backups, and so on.

There are some tasks SAM can't perform for you. SAM does most routine tasks for you, but troubleshooting a problem is not considered routine. Troubleshooting a problem gives you a chance to show off and hone your system administration skills.

When SAM is performing routine tasks for you, it isn't doing anything you couldn't do yourself by issuing a series of HP-UX commands. SAM provides a simple user interface that allows you to perform tasks by selecting menu items and entering pertinent information essential to performing the task.

Running and Using SAM as Superuser

To run SAM, log in as root and type:

sam   (or **sam &**)

This will invoke SAM. If you have a graphics display, SAM will run with the Motif interface. If you have a character-based display, SAM will run in character mode. You have nearly all the same functionality in both modes, but the Motif environment is much more pleasant to use.

If you have a graphics display and SAM does not come up in a Motif window, you probably don't have your *DISPLAY* variable set for root.

Type the following to set the *DISPLAY* variable for default POSIX, Korn, and Bourne shells:

```
# DISPLAY=system_name:0.0
# export DISPLAY
```

Just substitute the name of your computer for *system_name*. This can be set in your local **.profile** file. If you're running HP CDE, you may want to put these lines in your **.dtprofile** file.

Type the following to set the *DISPLAY* variable for C shell:

```
# setenv DISPLAY system_name:0.0
```

Again, you would substitute the name of your computer for *system_name*. This would typically be done in your **.login** file, but if you're running HP CDE, you may want to put this in your **.dtprofile** file. Most CDE users, however, have **.dtprofile** as the source for **.profile** or **.login**.

Figure 10-1 shows the System Administration Manager running in graphics mode. This is the top-level window of the hierarchical SAM environment called the *Functional Area Launcher* (*FAL*). The are many categories, or areas, of management shown are the default functional areas managed by SAM. You can select one of these functional areas to be placed in a subarea. Because SAM is hierarchical, you may find yourself working your way down through several levels of the hierarchy before you reach the desired level. I'll cover each of these categories, or areas, in this chapter.

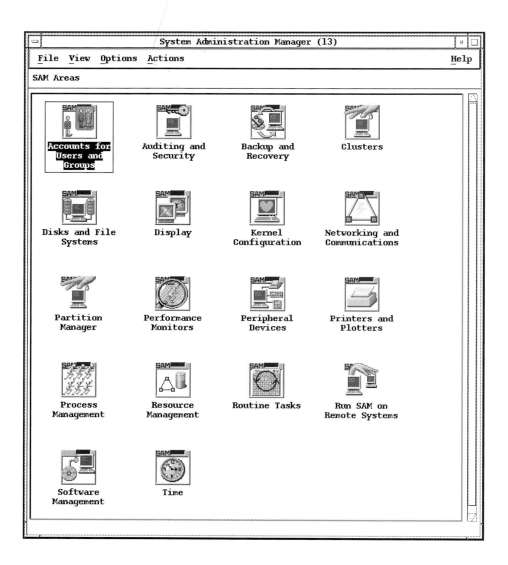

Figure 10-1 HP-UX 11i SAM Startup Window in Graphics Mode

In addition to selecting a functional area, you can select from the pull-down menu bar across the top of the SAM window. I will indicate selections made in SAM and keyboard keys in this chapter with italics. The five selections are *File, View, Options, Actions,* and *Help.* The title line shown in Figure 10-1 reads *SAM Areas.* If you're running Restricted SAM Builder, you will also see a status line with the message *"Privileges for user: <username>."* As you progress down the hierarchy, the title line will change to reflect your level in the SAM hierarchy. You can move into one of the areas shown, such as *Backup and Recovery,* by double-clicking the left mouse button on this functional area. You move back up the hierarchy by double-clicking the *..(go up)* icon, if available, or by selecting the *Actions-Close Level* menu commands.

You don't need a graphics display to run SAM. You have access to nearly all the same functionality on a text terminal as you do on a graphics terminal. Figure 10-2 is SAM running in character mode with the same functional areas you have in graphics mode, although the bottom selections are not shown in the figure:

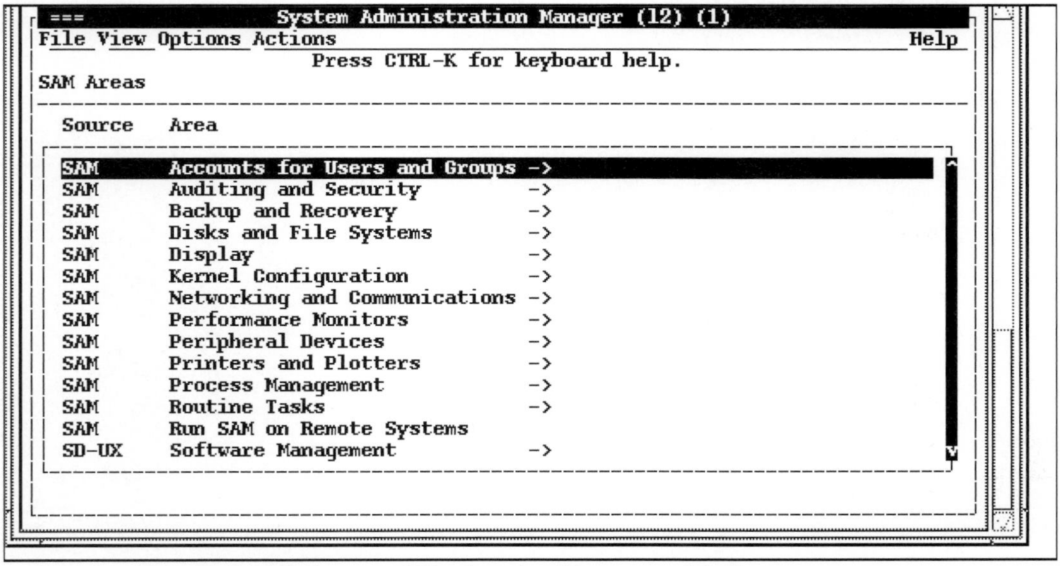

```
  ===           System Administration Manager (12) (1)
 File View Options Actions                                   Help
                  Press CTRL-K for keyboard help.
 SAM Areas
 ----------------------------------------------------------------
   Source    Area
 ----------------------------------------------------------------
   SAM       Accounts for Users and Groups ->
   SAM       Auditing and Security          ->
   SAM       Backup and Recovery            ->
   SAM       Disks and File Systems         ->
   SAM       Display                        ->
   SAM       Kernel Configuration           ->
   SAM       Networking and Communications  ->
   SAM       Performance Monitors           ->
   SAM       Peripheral Devices             ->
   SAM       Printers and Plotters          ->
   SAM       Process Management             ->
   SAM       Routine Tasks                  ->
   SAM       Run SAM on Remote Systems
   SD-UX     Software Management            ->
```

Figure 10-2 SAM Startup Window in Character Mode

The *View* menu can be used in character mode to tailor the information desired, filter out some entries, or search for particular entries.

Because you don't have a mouse on a text terminal, you use the keyboard to make selections. The point-and-click method of using SAM when in graphics mode is highly preferable to using the keyboard; however, the same structure to the functional areas exists in both environments. When you see an item in reverse video on the text terminal (such as *Accounts for Users and Groups* in Figure 10-2), you know that you have that item selected.   After having selected *Accounts for Users and Groups* as shown in Figure 10-2, you would then use the *tab* key (or *F4*) to get to the menu bar, use the <- -> *(arrow)* keys to select the desired menu, and use the *space bar* to display the menu. This situation is where having a mouse to make your selections is highly desirable. Figure 10-3 shows a menu bar selection for both text and graphic displays. In both cases, the *Actions* menu has been selected.

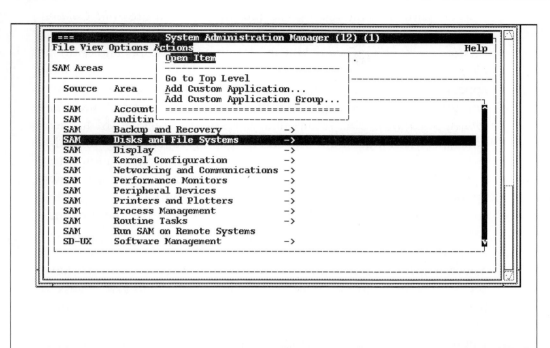

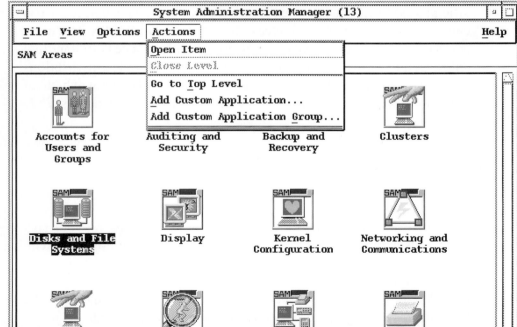

Figure 10-3 SAM Menu Selection for Text and Graphics Displays

Of particular interest on the pull-down menu are *Add Custom Application* and *Add Custom Application Group*. When you use *Add Custom Application Group,* you are prompted for a *Label* and optional *Help File* for the group. After you enter this information, a new icon appears, if you have a graphics display, with the name of your application group. You can then go into this application group and *Add Custom Applications*. This means that you can customize SAM to meet your specific administration needs by adding functionality to SAM. After you familiarize yourself with the aspects of system administration SAM can help you with, you'll want to test adding your own application to SAM. Adding a simple application like opening a log file or issuing the **/usr/bin/find** command will take you only seconds to create.

You can also create users who have restricted access to SAM. You can specify areas within SAM to which specific users can have access. You may have users to whom you would like to give access to backup and restore, or managing users, or handling the print spooler. Invoking SAM with the *-r* option will allow you to select a user to whom you want to give access to a SAM area and then select the specific area(s) to which you want to enable that user to have access. You can also give a user partial access to some areas, such as providing access to backup and recovery, but not providing access to handling automated backups. As you progress through the detailed descriptions of SAM areas in this chapter, you'll want to think about which of these areas may be appropriate for some of your users to access.

Author's Disclaimer - SAM is a Moving Target

SAM is improving all the time. The SAM you are using on your HP-UX 11i system may have been enhanced and may therefore differ in some ways from what I cover in this chapter. The HP 9000 product line also improves requiring SAM to be enhanced. In the functional area *Partitions* for instance, I could not provide any information at the time of this writing because there were no systems available for me to test. I instead refer you to Appendix A, which has in it background information on Virtual Partitions (vPars). By the time you're reading this book, there will be many systems for which partitions are supported. Since the very nature of the computer business is to change rapidly I know you appreciate the fact that no document can be 100% current.

Running Restricted SAM Builder

SAM can be configured to provide a subset of its overall functionality to specified users such as operators. You may, for instance, wish to give a user the ability to start a backup, but not the ability to manage disks and file systems. With the Restricted SAM Builder, you have control of the functional areas to which specified users have access.

When specifying the functionality you wish to give a user, you invoke SAM with the -r option, initiating a Restricted SAM Builder session. After you have set up a user with specific functionality, you can then invoke SAM with both the -r and -f options with the login name of a user you wish to test. The functionality of the user can be tested using these two options along with the login name.

man page

sam - 10

Initially Setting User Privileges

When you invoke SAM with the -r option, you are first asked to select the user to whom you want to assign privileges. You will then be shown a list of default privileges for a new restricted SAM user. Figure 10-4 shows the default privileges SAM recommends for a new restricted user; note that custom SAM functional areas are disabled by default.

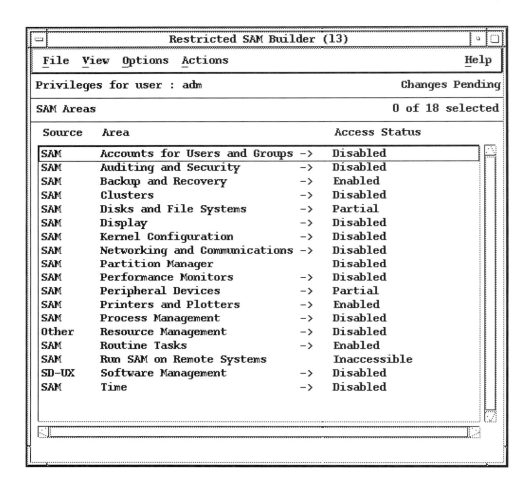

Figure 10-4 Restricted SAM Builder Screen

You can select from the *Actions* shown in Figure 10-4 to control access to functional areas. Of particular interest is the ability to save the privileges, which you may later use as a template for other users with *Load User Privileges* from the *Actions* menu.

The user will now have only access to the functional areas specified and therefore be able to execute tasks in only the areas to which
they have access.

Accounts for Users and Groups

In Chapter 5, I explained the information that is associated with each
user and group. There is an entry in the **/etc/passwd** file for each
user and an entry in **/etc/group** for each group. To save you the trouble of flipping back to Chapter 5, Figure 10-5 is an example of a
user entry from **/etc/passwd** and an example of a group entry from
/etc/group:

User Example:

```
vinny:*:204:20:Vinny Emmaddebra,,,:/home/vinny:/usr/bin/sh
    |   |   |   |               |               |       |
    |   |   |   |               |               |       |> shell
    |   |   |   |               |               |
    |   |   |   |               |               |> home directory
    |   |   |   |               |
    |   |   |   |               |> optional user info
    |   |   |   |> group ID (GID)
    |   |   |> user ID (UID)
    |   |> password
    |> name
```

Group Example:

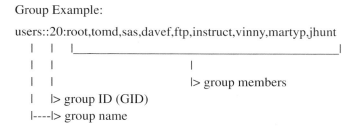

Figure 10-5   Sample **/etc/passwd** and **/etc/group** Entry

The *Accounts for Users and Groups* top-level SAM category, or area, has beneath it only two picks: *Groups* and *Users*. The menu hierarchy for "Users and Groups" is shown in Figure 10-6.

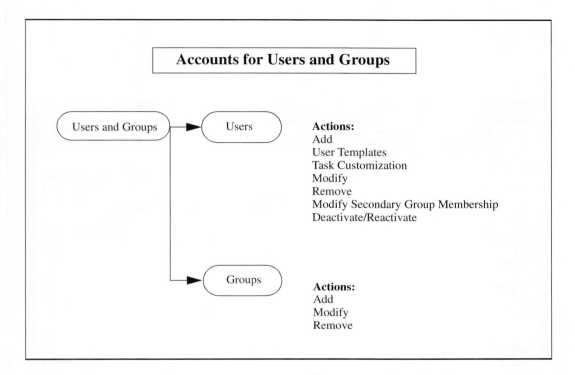

Figure 10-6 Accounts for Users and Groups

When you select *Accounts for Users and Groups* and then *Users* from the SAM menu, you are provided a list of all the users on your system. Figure 10-7 is a list of users provided by SAM for a system including Oracle users:

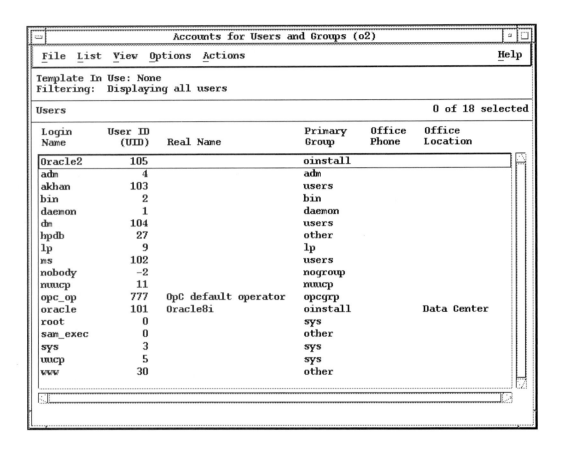

Figure 10-7   List of Users

Adding a User

SAM is ideal for performing administration tasks related to users and groups. These are routine tasks that are not complex but require you to edit the **/etc/passwd** and **/etc/group** files, make directories, and copy default files, all of which SAM performs for you. Finally, take a minute to check what SAM has done for you, especially if you modify an existing user or group.

To add an additional user, you would select *Add* from the *Actions* menu under *Users* and then fill in the information as shown in Figure 10-8:

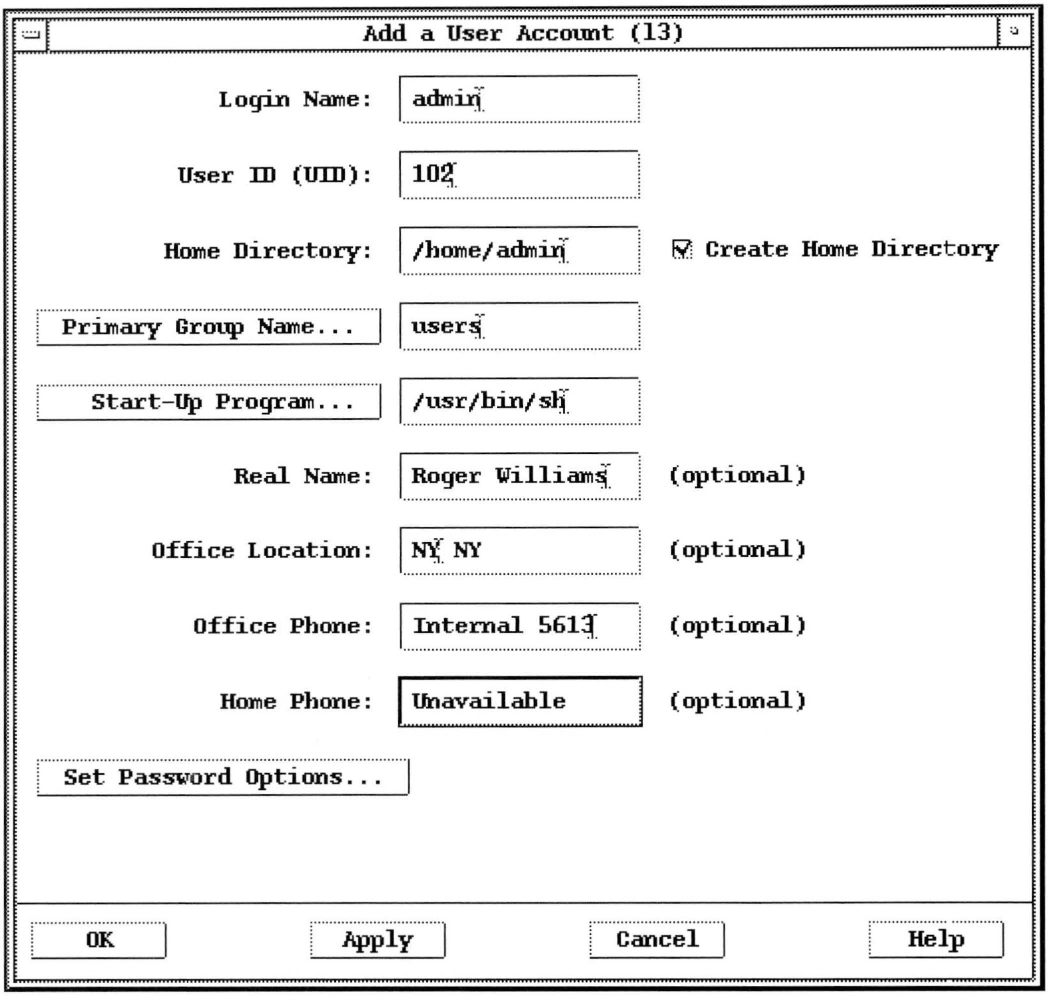

```
┌─────────────────────────────────────────────────────────────────────┐
│ ▭│            Add a User Account (13)                              │ ◷ │
│                                                                       │
│            Login Name:    │ admin                │                    │
│                                                                       │
│          User ID (UID):   │ 102                  │                    │
│                                                                       │
│         Home Directory:   │ /home/admin          │  ☑ Create Home Directory │
│                                                                       │
│  │ Primary Group Name... │ │ users               │                    │
│                                                                       │
│  │ Start-Up Program...   │ │ /usr/bin/sh         │                    │
│                                                                       │
│             Real Name:    │ Roger Williams       │  (optional)         │
│                                                                       │
│        Office Location:   │ NY NY                │  (optional)         │
│                                                                       │
│          Office Phone:    │ Internal 5613        │  (optional)         │
│                                                                       │
│            Home Phone:    │ Unavailable          │  (optional)         │
│                                                                       │
│  │ Set Password Options... │                                          │
│                                                                       │
│                                                                       │
│  ┌──────┐      ┌────────┐        ┌────────┐         ┌────────┐         │
│  │  OK  │      │ Apply  │        │ Cancel │         │  Help  │         │
│  └──────┘      └────────┘        └────────┘         └────────┘         │
└─────────────────────────────────────────────────────────────────────┘
```

Figure 10-8 Example of Adding a New User

There are some restrictions when entering this information. For instance, a comma and colon are not permitted in the *Office Location* field. When I tried to enter a comma, SAM informed me this was not permitted.

To see the **/etc/passwd** entry that was made I issued the following **cat** and **grep** commands that showed two users who had *admin* in their names:

```
# cat /etc/passwd | grep admin
webadmin:*:40:1::/usr/obam/server/nologindir:/usr/bin/false
admin::102:20:Roger Williams,NY NY,Internal 5613,Unavailable:/home/admin:/usr/
bin/sh
#
```

This user admin has no password entry, as indicated by the **::**, which is a poor practice. You want to make sure there are passwords for all users.

You can view the log file that SAM produces with the menu selection *Options - View SAM Log.* Figure 10-9 show the end of the log file indicating that our user was successfully added:

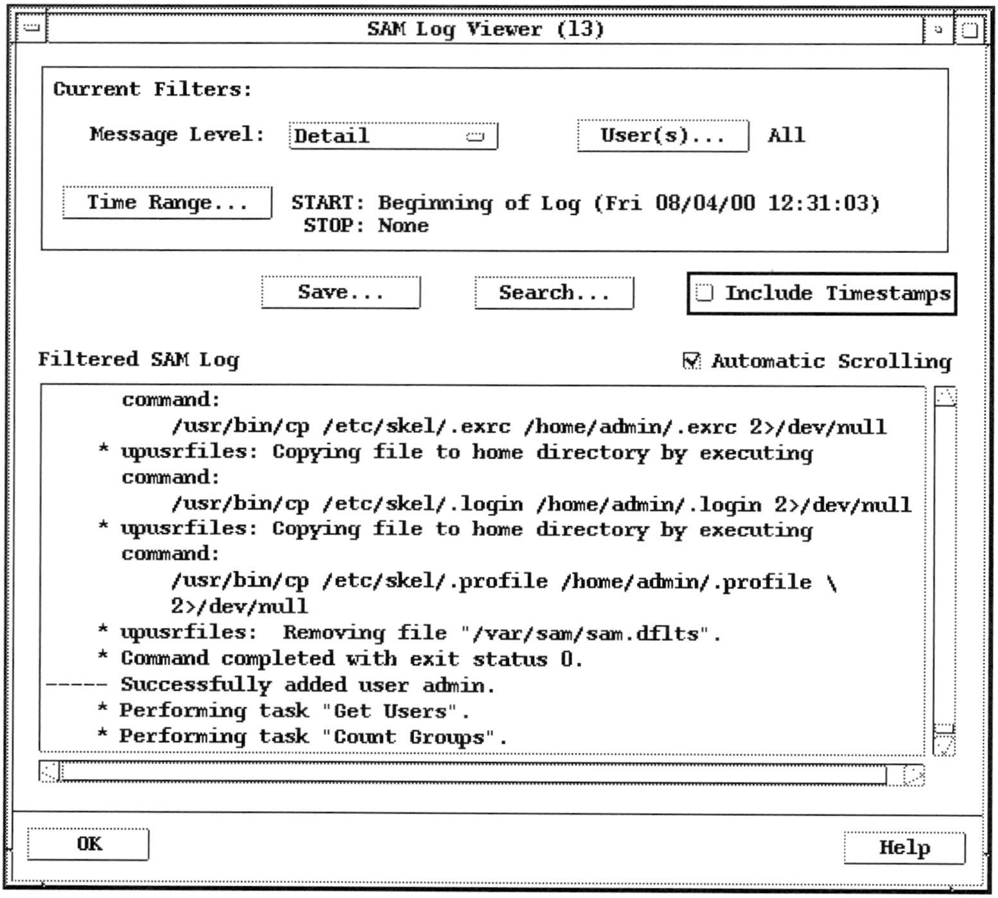

```
┌─────────────────────────────────────────────────────────────────────────┐
│ ▢                        SAM Log Viewer (13)                      ▫  ▢   │
│  ┌──────────────────────────────────────────────────────────────────┐   │
│  │ Current Filters:                                                 │   │
│  │                                                                  │   │
│  │     Message Level: │Detail         ▭│    │ User(s)... │  All     │   │
│  │                                                                  │   │
│  │     │ Time Range... │  START: Beginning of Log (Fri 08/04/00 12:31:03)│
│  │                       STOP: None                                 │   │
│  └──────────────────────────────────────────────────────────────────┘   │
│                                                                          │
│           │   Save...   │      │  Search...  │   │ ▢ Include Timestamps│  │
│                                                                          │
│  Filtered SAM Log                               ☑ Automatic Scrolling    │
│  ┌────────────────────────────────────────────────────────────────┐┌─┐ │
│  │    command:                                                    ││▲│ │
│  │          /usr/bin/cp /etc/skel/.exrc /home/admin/.exrc 2>/dev/null││ │ │
│  │   * upusrfiles: Copying file to home directory by executing    ││ │ │
│  │    command:                                                    ││ │ │
│  │          /usr/bin/cp /etc/skel/.login /home/admin/.login 2>/dev/null││ │
│  │   * upusrfiles: Copying file to home directory by executing    ││ │ │
│  │    command:                                                    ││ │ │
│  │          /usr/bin/cp /etc/skel/.profile /home/admin/.profile \ ││ │ │
│  │          2>/dev/null                                           ││ │ │
│  │   * upusrfiles:  Removing file "/var/sam/sam.dflts".           ││ │ │
│  │   * Command completed with exit status 0.                     ││ │ │
│  │ ----- Successfully added user admin.                          ││ │ │
│  │   * Performing task "Get Users".                              ││ │ │
│  │   * Performing task "Count Groups".                           ││▼│ │
│  └────────────────────────────────────────────────────────────────┘└─┘ │
│  ◁▯                                                              ▯▷    │
│                                                                          │
│  │  OK  │                                              │  Help  │        │
└─────────────────────────────────────────────────────────────────────────┘
```

Figure 10-9   SAM Log Viewer for Adding a User

The scroll bar on the right-hand side of the SAM Log Viewer allows you to scroll to any point in the log file. We are viewing only the part of the log file that pertains to adding the user *Roger Williams*. You can select the level of detail you wish to view with the log file. The four levels are *Summary, Detail, Verbose,* and *Commands Only*.

The level shown in Figure 10-9 is *Detail*. I like this level because you can see what has taken place without getting mired down in too much detail. When you view the log file you typically see the calls to SAM scripts that SAM has made as well as other commands SAM is issuing.

Adding a Group

Adding an additional group is similar to adding a new user. To add an additional group, you would select *Add* from the *Actions* menu under *Groups*. Figure 10-10 shows the Add a New Group window:

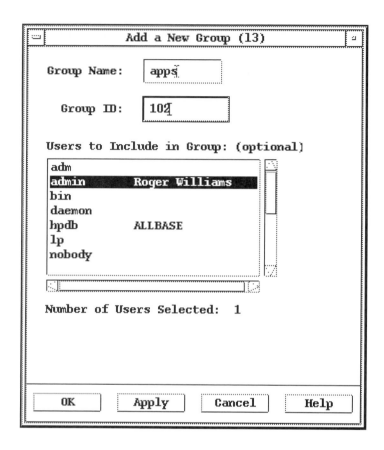

Figure 10-10 Example of Adding a New Group

In Figure 10-10, I added a new group called *apps* with a group ID of *102*, and into that group I added the user *admin* that we had earlier created.

Auditing and Security

Under *Auditing and Security,* you manage the security of your system. This is becoming an increasingly important aspect of system management. Some installations care very little about security because of well-known, limited groups of users who will access a system. Other installations, such as those connected to the Internet, may go to great pains to make their systems into fortresses, with firewalls checking each and every user who attempts to access a system. I suggest that you take a close look at all the ramifications of security, and specifically a trusted system, before you enable security. You'll want to review the "Managing System Security" section of the "Administering A System" chapter of the *Managing Systems and Workgroups* manual, which replaces the 10.x manual *HP-UX System Administration Tasks Manual.* Although SAM makes creating and maintaining a trusted system easy, a lot of files are created for security management, which takes place under the umbrella of Auditing and Security. Among the modifications that will be made to your system, should you choose to convert to a trusted system, is the **/etc/rc.config.d/ auditing** file, which will be updated by SAM. In addition, passwords in the **/etc/passwd** file will be replaced with "*," and the encrypted passwords are moved to a password database. All users are also given audit ID numbers. Figure 10-11 shows the menu hierarchy of Auditing and Security.

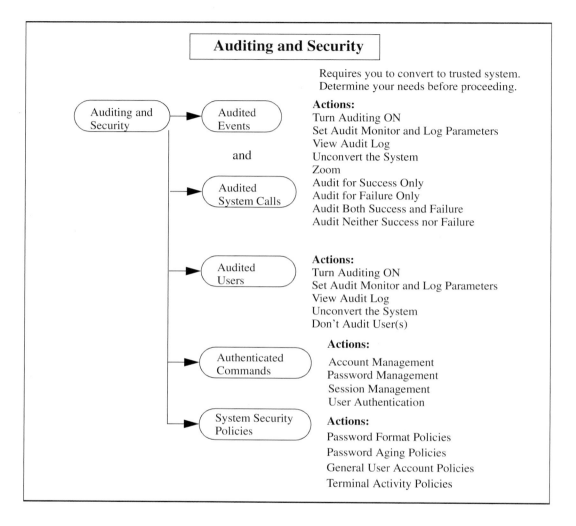

Figure 10-11 Auditing and Security Menu Structure

One choice to observe in Figure 10-11 is an *Actions* menu choice to *Unconvert the System*. This means to reverse the trusted system environment. I have tried this on various systems and it seems to work fine, but you should have a good idea of what a trusted system can do for and to you before you make the conversion.

I hope that I have given you a reasonably good overview of Auditing and Security, because in order to investigate it yourself, you must first convert to a trusted system. Before you do, please read this section to get an idea of the functionality this will provide and then convert to a trusted system if you think there is adequate benefit.

Audited Events and Audited System Calls

Under *Audited Events,* you can select the particular events you wish to analyze and detect which may cause security breaches. Under *Audited System Calls,* you can monitor system calls. This option is a function of the trusted system to which you must convert in order to perform auditing. You may have in mind particular events and system calls that are most vital to your system's security that you wish to audit, and not bother with the balance. There are a number of events and system calls that you may wish to keep track of for security reasons.

Auditing these events gives you a detailed report of each event. The same is true of system calls. SAM uses the auditing commands of HP-UX such as **audsys**, **audusr**, **audevent**, **audomon**, and **audisp** to perform auditing.

Audited Users

Under *Audited Users,* you can use the *Actions* menu to turn auditing on and off for specific users. Since the audit log files, which you can also control and view through the *Actions* menu, grow large very quickly, you may want to select specific users to monitor to better understand the type of user audit information that is created.

Authenticated Commands

This security feature is the ability to perform authentication based on user, password, session, or account. This industry-standard authentication framework is known as the Pluggable Authentication Module, or PAM. The PAM framework allows for authentication modules to be implemented without modifying any applications. Authentication is currently provided for CDE components, HP-UX standard commands, trusted systems, and DCE (the Distributed Computing Environment), as well as third-party modules.

System Security Policies

The most important part of HP-UX security is the policies you put in place. If, for instance, you choose to audit each and every system call, but don't impose any restrictions on user passwords, then you are potentially opening up your system to any user. You would be much better off restricting users and not worrying so much about what they're doing. Being proactive is more important in security than being reactive.

Password Aging Policies, when enabled, allows you to set:

• Time between Password Changes

• Password Expiration Time

• Password Expiration Warning Time

• Password Life Time

• Expire All User Passwords Immediately

General User Account Policies, when enabled, allows you to specify the time at which an account will become inactive and lock it. In addition, you can specify the number of unsuccessful login tries that are permitted.

Terminal Security Policies allows you to set:

• Number of unsuccessful Login Tries Allowed

• Delay between Login Tries

• Login Timeout Value in Seconds

• Required Login upon Boot to Single-User State

Backup and Recovery

The most important activities you'll perform as a system administrator are system backup and recovery. The SAM team put a lot of thought into giving you all the options you need to ensure the integrity of your system through backup and recovery. You may also want to see Chapter 6, which covers various backup commands available on HP-UX. Figure 10-12 shows the hierarchy of the *Backup and Recovery* SAM menu:

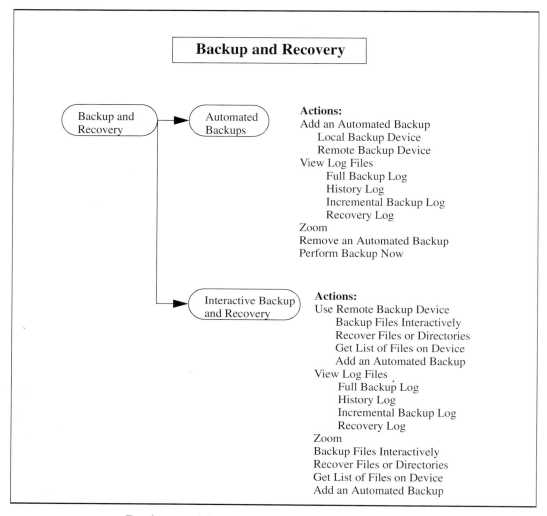

Figure 10-12 Backup and Recovery Menu Structure

Scheduling a Backup

The first step is to enter the *Automated Backups* subarea. You won't see any automated backups appear in the list until you have specified one. Using the *Actions* menu and selecting *Add an Automated Backup,* you can specify all the information about your automated backup. When you select *Add an Automated Backup,* you have to specify whether your backup will be to a local or a remote backup device. You will have to enter information pertaining to the backup scope, backup device, backup time, and additional parameters.

Select Backup Scope

You can view the backup scope as the files that will be included and excluded from the backup. This can include Network File System (NFS)-mounted file systems as well. Figure 10-13 shows the window used to specify files to be included and excluded from a backup:

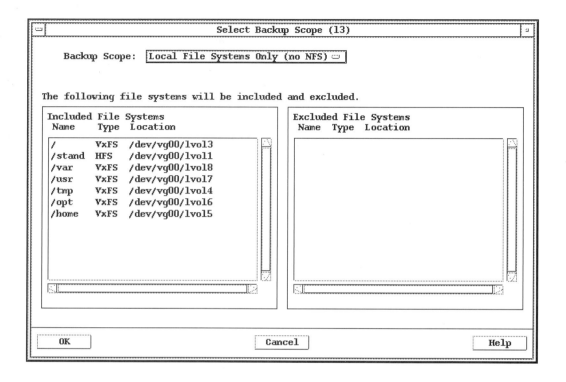

Figure 10-13 Selecting the Backup Scope

In the selections shown in Figure 10-13 are several directories specified under *Included Files*. These were selected with the *Local File Systems Only (no NFS)* option. We could easily have excluded files and directories from the backup scope as well.

Select Backup Device

If you plan to back up to a local backup device, then those attached to your system will be listed and you select the desired device from the list.

If you plan to use a remote backup device, then you will be asked to specify the remote system name and device file.

Select Backup Time

As with the backup scope, you are provided with a window in which you can enter all the information about backup time for both full and incremental backups, as shown in Figure 10-14. If *Incremental Backup* is *Enabled,* then you must provide all pertinent information about both the full and incremental backup, as shown in the figure.

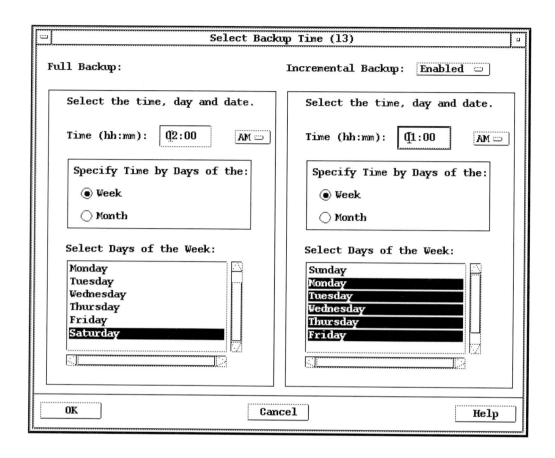

Figure 10-14　Selecting the Backup Time

A key point to keep in mind here is that the incremental backup that SAM creates for you includes files that have been changed *since the last full backup*. This means that you need only the full backup and last incremental backup to recover your system; that is, you do not need to restore the full backup and each incremental backup.

Set Additional Parameters

You can also specify additional parameters such as whether or not to create an index log, which I strongly suggest you do, and to whom to mail the results of a backup. After specifying backup information, you can view the **crontab** entry SAM has made for root for your backups. The **crontab** file is used to schedule jobs that are automatically executed by **cron**. **crontab** files are in the **/var/spool/cron/crontabs** directory. **cron** is a program that runs other programs at the specified time. **cron** reads files that specify the operation to be performed and the date and time it is to be performed. Since we want to perform backups on a regular basis, SAM will activate **cron**.

man page

crontab-10

The format of entries in the **crontab** file are as follows:

minute   hour   monthday   month   weekday   user name   command

minute - the minute of the hour, from 0-59

hour - the hour of the day, from 0-23

monthday - the day of the month, from 1-31

month - the month of the year, from 1-12

weekday - the day of the week, from 0 (Sunday) - 6 (Saturday)

user name - the user who will run the command if necessary
(not used in the example)

command - specifies the command line or script file to run

You have many options in the **crontab** for specifying the *minute, hour, monthday, month,* and *weekday* to perform a task. You could list one entry in a field and then a space, several entries in any field separated by a comma, two entries separated by a dash indicating a range, or an asterisk, which corresponds to all possible entries for the field.

To list the contents of the **crontab** file, you would issue the command **crontab -l**. following command. SAM will create a **crontab** entry for any backups you specify.

man page

crontab-10

You will see various *crontab* **commands** when you use the *SAM Log Viewer* to see what SAM has done for you to create the **crontab** files. For instance, if you change your backup plan, SAM will remove the old **crontab** file with the command:

```
$ crontab -r
```

This will remove the **crontab** file for the user from the **/var/ spool/cron/crontabs** directory.

To place a file in the **crontab** directory, you would simply issue the **crontab** command and the name of the **crontab** file:

```
$ crontab crontabfile
```

You can schedule cron jobs using SAM. The section in this chapter covering *Process Management* has a section called *Scheduling Cron Jobs*.

Interactive Backup and Recovery

The *Interactive Backup and Recovery* subarea is used to perform a backup interactively or restore information that was part of an earlier backup. When you enter this area, you are asked to select a backup device from a list that is produced, in the same way that you are asked to select a backup device when you first enter the *Automated Backups* subarea.

After selecting a device from the list, you may select an item from the *Actions* menu shown earlier. If you decide to use *Backup Files Interactively,* you are again provided a window from which you can specify files to be included and excluded from the backup. You are asked to *Select Backup Scope, Specify Tape Device Options*, and *Set Additional Parameters*. You are not, however, asked to *Select Backup Time,* since the backup is taking place interactively.

The steps in this area will vary, depending on the tape devices you have selected.

The index files can be reviewed from the *Actions* menu. These are stored in the **/var/sam/log** directory. The following shows the very top and bottom of an index file for an interactive backup:

```
#  1 /
#  1 /.profile
#  1 /.rhosts
#  1 /.sh_history
#  1 /.sw
#  1 /.sw/sessions
#  1 /.sw/sessions/swinstall.last
#  1 /.sw/sessions/swlist.last
#  1 /.sw/sessions/swmodify.last
#  1 /.sw/sessions/swreg.last
#  1 /.dt
#  1 /.dt/Desktop
#  1 /.dt/Desktop/Two                        TOP
#  1 /.dt/Desktop/Four
#  1 /.dt/Desktop/One
#  1 /.dt/Desktop/Three


                  .
                  .
                  .


#  1 /var/uucp/.Log/uucico
#  1 /var/uucp/.Log/uucp
#  1 /var/uucp/.Log/uux
#  1 /var/uucp/.Log/uuxqt
#  1 /var/uucp/.Old
#  1 /var/uucp/.Status
#  1 /var/varspool/sw
#  1 /var/varspool/sw/catalog/dfiles
#  1 /var/varspool/sw/catalog/swlock
#  1 /var/varspool/sw/swagent.log
#  1 /var/yp
#  1 /var/yp/Makefile                        BOTTOM
#  1 /var/yp/binding
#  1 /var/yp/securenets
#  1 /var/yp/secureservers
#  1 /var/yp/updaters
#  1 /var/yp/ypmake
#  1 /var/yp/ypxfr_1perday
#  1 /var/yp/ypxfr_1perhour
#  1 /var/yp/ypxfr_2perday
```

Performing a Restore

A full or incremental backup, however, is only as good as the files it restores. To retrieve a file from the backup tape, you specify a backup device and then many options related to the backup. Figure 10-15 shows one device selected from among four DLT units connected to a system:

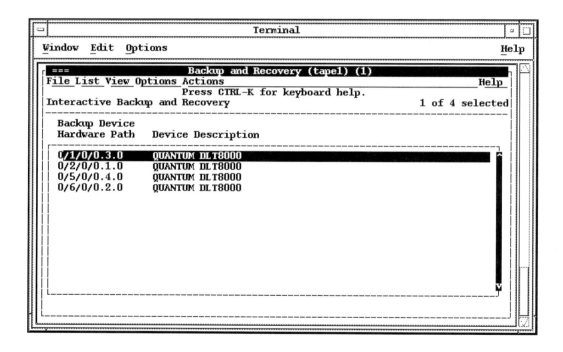

Figure 10-15   Selecting From Among Four DLT Units

After selecting a device, there are a number of options from which you can select, including those shown in Figure 10-16:

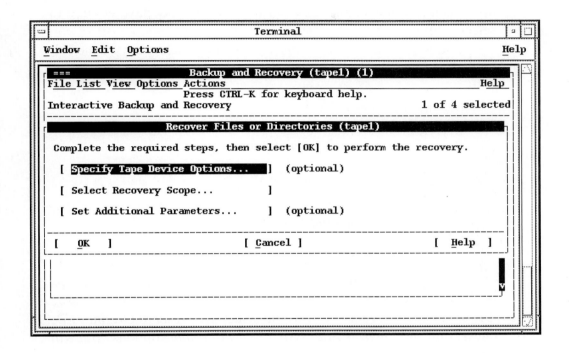

Figure 10-16 *Recover Files Interactively*

In this window you supply information in three areas: *Select Recovery Scope; Specify Tape Device Options*; and *Set Additional Parameters*. The device options you specify will depend on the tape device you are using.

Select Recovery Scope allows you to either enter a file name that contains the files to be recovered or manually list the files to be included in the recovery. You can optionally list files to be excluded from the recovery as well.

A list of tape device files is provided in *Specify Tape Device Options,* from which you can select the tape device. In this step, you may select the tape device file; in other cases, you might make selections such as a magneto-optical surface, or you may have nothing to select at all.

Under *Set Additional Parameters,* you can select any of the following options:

Overwrite Newer Files

Preserve Original File Ownership

Recover Files Using Full Path Name

Place Files in Non-Root Directory

After you make all the desired selections, the recovery operation begins. If a file has been inadvertently deleted and you wish to restore it from the recovery tape, you would select the *Preserve Original File Ownership* and *Recover Files Using Full Path Name* options. You will receive status of the recovery as it takes place and may also *View Recovery Log* from the *Actions* menu after the recovery has completed. If you *View Recovery Log,* you will receive a window that provides the name of the index log and the names of the files recovered.

Clusters

High availability clusters can be managed through SAM. Such tasks as adding applications and adding application groups can be performed using SAM. Since high availability is a highly customized aspect of a computing environment, I won't cover this area of SAM. If, however, you have to manage clusters of systems, you will want to review this SAM area to see if it would help in your cluster-related work.

Disks and File Systems

Disks and File Systems helps you manage disk devices, file systems, logical volumes, swap, and volume groups (you may also manage other HP disk devices such as XP and disk arrays through SAM if you have these installed on your system). There is no reason to manually work with these, since SAM does such a good job of managing these for you. Figures 10-17 and 10-18 show the hierarchy of *Disks and File Systems*:

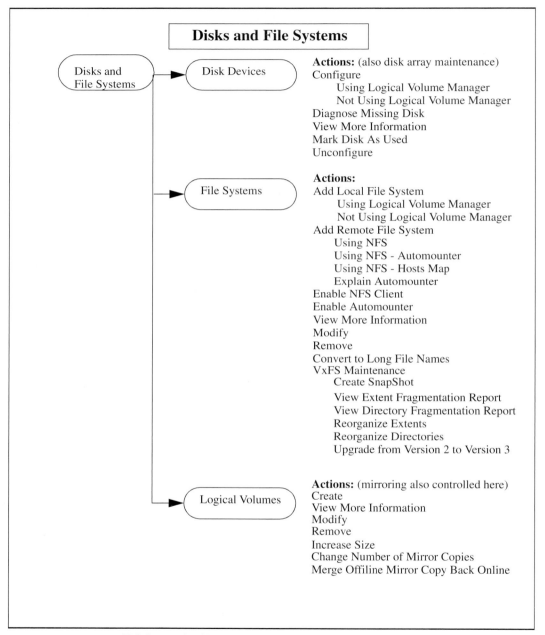

Figure 10-17 Disks and File Systems Menu Structure

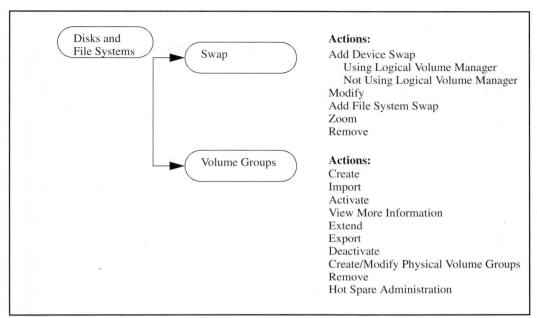

Figure 10-18 Disks and File Systems Menu Structure (continued)

Disk Devices

When you enter this subarea, SAM shows you the disk devices connected to your system. Figure 10-19 shows a listing of the disks for a Series 800 unit:

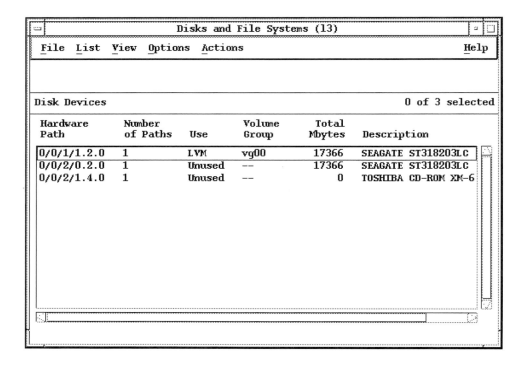

Figure 10-19 *Disk Devices* Window

man page

ioscan - 4

The first two entries refer to internal disks in an L-Class system. The third entry is a CD-ROM drive. Let's compare this output to what we would see when we run **ioscan**:

```
$ /usr/sbin/ioscan -funC disk

Class     I  H/W Path     Driver S/W State   H/W Type       Description
=======================================================================
disk      1  0/0/1/1.2.0  sdisk CLAIMED      DEVICE         SEAGATE ST318203LC
                          /dev/dsk/c1t2d0    /dev/rdsk/c1t2d0
disk      2  0/0/2/0.2.0  sdisk CLAIMED      DEVICE         SEAGATE ST318203LC
                          /dev/dsk/c2t2d0    /dev/rdsk/c2t2d0
disk      3  0/0/2/1.4.0  sdisk CLAIMED      DEVICE         TOSHIBA CD-ROM XM-6201TA
                          /dev/dsk/c3t4d0    /dev/rdsk/c3t4d0
```

man page

ioscan - 4

The **ioscan** output jives with the disk information produced by SAM. The SAM output also indicates that the first disk is used and the second unused, which **ioscan** does not show.

We can now add one of the unused disks in SAM by selecting *Add* from the *Actions* menu. Using Logical Volume Manager, we can create a new volume group or select the volume group to which we wish to add the new disk. We would then select the new logical volumes we wanted on the volume group or extend the size of existing logical volumes. Other information such as the mount directory and size of the logical volume would be entered as well.

Most disks connected to your system can be managed through SAM. Figure 10-20 shows a SAM screen shot of a V-Class system with an XP-256 attached to it:

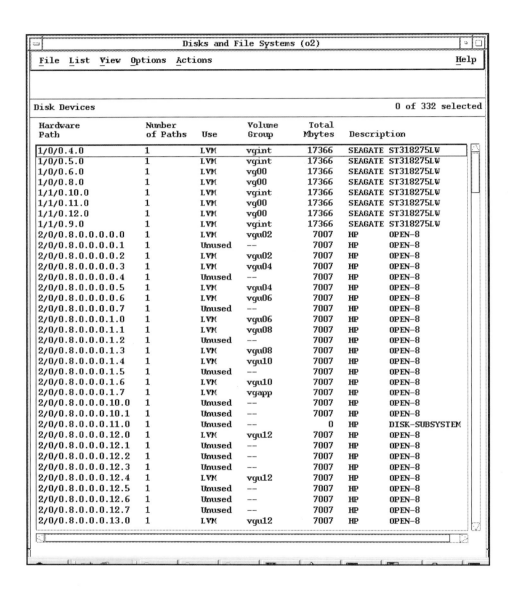

Hardware Path	Number of Paths	Use	Volume Group	Total Mbytes	Description
1/0/0.4.0	1	LVM	vgint	17366	SEAGATE ST318275LW
1/0/0.5.0	1	LVM	vgint	17366	SEAGATE ST318275LW
1/0/0.6.0	1	LVM	vg00	17366	SEAGATE ST318275LW
1/0/0.8.0	1	LVM	vg00	17366	SEAGATE ST318275LW
1/1/0.10.0	1	LVM	vgint	17366	SEAGATE ST318275LW
1/1/0.11.0	1	LVM	vg00	17366	SEAGATE ST318275LW
1/1/0.12.0	1	LVM	vg00	17366	SEAGATE ST318275LW
1/1/0.9.0	1	LVM	vgint	17366	SEAGATE ST318275LW
2/0/0.8.0.0.0.0.0	1	LVM	vgu02	7007	HP OPEN-8
2/0/0.8.0.0.0.0.1	1	Unused	--	7007	HP OPEN-8
2/0/0.8.0.0.0.0.2	1	LVM	vgu02	7007	HP OPEN-8
2/0/0.8.0.0.0.0.3	1	LVM	vgu04	7007	HP OPEN-8
2/0/0.8.0.0.0.0.4	1	Unused	--	7007	HP OPEN-8
2/0/0.8.0.0.0.0.5	1	LVM	vgu04	7007	HP OPEN-8
2/0/0.8.0.0.0.0.6	1	LVM	vgu06	7007	HP OPEN-8
2/0/0.8.0.0.0.0.7	1	Unused	--	7007	HP OPEN-8
2/0/0.8.0.0.0.1.0	1	LVM	vgu06	7007	HP OPEN-8
2/0/0.8.0.0.0.1.1	1	LVM	vgu08	7007	HP OPEN-8
2/0/0.8.0.0.0.1.2	1	Unused	--	7007	HP OPEN-8
2/0/0.8.0.0.0.1.3	1	LVM	vgu08	7007	HP OPEN-8
2/0/0.8.0.0.0.1.4	1	LVM	vgu10	7007	HP OPEN-8
2/0/0.8.0.0.0.1.5	1	Unused	--	7007	HP OPEN-8
2/0/0.8.0.0.0.1.6	1	LVM	vgu10	7007	HP OPEN-8
2/0/0.8.0.0.0.1.7	1	LVM	vgapp	7007	HP OPEN-8
2/0/0.8.0.0.0.10.0	1	Unused	--	7007	HP OPEN-8
2/0/0.8.0.0.0.10.1	1	Unused	--	7007	HP OPEN-8
2/0/0.8.0.0.0.11.0	1	Unused	--	0	HP DISK-SUBSYSTEM
2/0/0.8.0.0.0.12.0	1	LVM	vgu12	7007	HP OPEN-8
2/0/0.8.0.0.0.12.1	1	Unused	--	7007	HP OPEN-8
2/0/0.8.0.0.0.12.2	1	Unused	--	7007	HP OPEN-8
2/0/0.8.0.0.0.12.3	1	Unused	--	7007	HP OPEN-8
2/0/0.8.0.0.0.12.4	1	LVM	vgu12	7007	HP OPEN-8
2/0/0.8.0.0.0.12.5	1	Unused	--	7007	HP OPEN-8
2/0/0.8.0.0.0.12.6	1	Unused	--	7007	HP OPEN-8
2/0/0.8.0.0.0.12.7	1	Unused	--	7007	HP OPEN-8
2/0/0.8.0.0.0.13.0	1	LVM	vgu12	7007	HP OPEN-8

Figure 10-20   *Disk Devices* Window with XP-256 Disks Shown

A small subset of the total disks attached is shown in the screen shot. The first eight disks are internal to the V-Class and the remainder are XP disks. All of the devices shown in this figure can be managed through SAM.

File Systems

File Systems shows the *Mount Directory*, *Type* of file system, and *Source Device or Remote Directory*. Figure 10-21 shows the information you see when you enter *File Systems* for the L-Class system used in earlier examples:

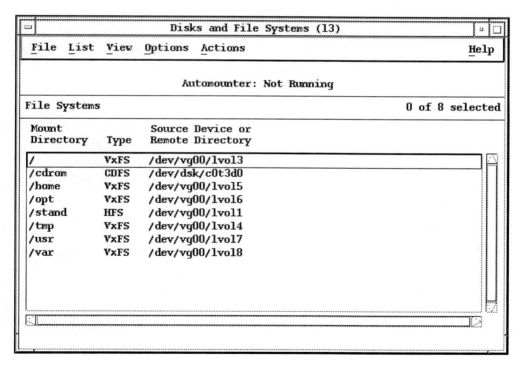

Figure 10-21 *File Systems* Window

At this level, you can perform such tasks as *Add Local File System* and *Add Remote File System,* and you can perform *VxFS Maintenance* from the *Actions* menu.

Several types of file systems may be listed under the Type column. The most common are:

Auto-Indirect	Directory containing auto-mountable remote NFS file systems. You may see the **/net** directory here if you have auto-mounter running.
Auto-Mount	Auto-mountable remote NFS file system.
CDFS	CD-ROM file system if it is currently mounted. If, for instance, you have a CD-ROM mounted as /SD_CDROM, you will see this as type CDFS in the list.
HFS	Local HFS file system. These are local HFS file systems that are part of your system. HP's version of the UNIX File System. This was the most common file system under earlier versions of HP-UX.
NFS	Remote NFS file system that is currently mounted.
LOFS	Loopback file system that allows you to have the same file system in multiple places.

VxFS   Local Journaled File System (JFS). This is
                    the HP-UX implementation of the Veritas
                    journaled file system (VxFS), which sup-
                    ports fast file system recovery. JFS is the
                    default HP-UX file system.

Add Local File System allows you to mount an unmounted, local file
system. *Add Remote File System* gives you the ability to mount a file
system from another host. The *VxFS Maintenance* subarea is where
you can perform some file system maintenance tasks on your JFS file
system. Here, you can create reports on extent and directory fragmentation. Once these are reviewed and you find that you do indeed need
to perform maintenance, you can choose the option to reorganize
either the extents or the directory.

Logical Volumes

You can perform several functions related to logical volume manipulation in SAM. Such tasks as *Create, Modify, Remove,* and *Increase
Size* can be performed in SAM. Figure 10-22 shows increasing the
size of lvol5 (**/home**) from 52 MBytes to 6 MBytes:

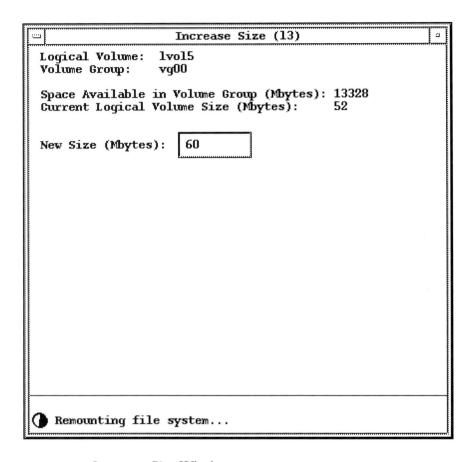

Figure 10-22 *Increase Size* Window

SAM will increase the size of the logical volume only if it can be unmounted. Viewing the log file after this task has been completed shows that SAM ran such commands as **/sbin/lvextend** and **/sbin/extendfs** to extend the size of the logical volume and file system, and **/usr/sbin/umount** and **/usr/sbin/mount** to unmount and mount the file system.

See the Logical Volume Manager detail in Chapter 8 for definitions of Logical Volume Manager terms. There is also a description of some Logical Volume Manager commands.

Increasing the Size of a Logical Volume in SAM

SAM may create a unique set of problems when you attempt to increase the size of a logical volume. Problems may be encountered when increasing the size of a logical volume if it can't be unmounted. If, for instance, you wanted to increase the size of the **/opt** logical volume, it would first have to be unmounted by SAM. If SAM can't **umount /opt**, you will receive a message from SAM indicating that the device is busy. You can go into single-user state, but you will have to have some logical volumes mounted, such as **/usr** and **/var,** in order to get SAM to run. You would then need to reboot your system with `shutdown -r` after you have completed your work. This works for directories such as **/opt**, which SAM does not need in order to run.

man page

shutdown-7

Alternatively, you could exit SAM and kill any processes accessing the logical volume you wish to extend the size of, and then manually unmount that logical volume. You could then use SAM to increase the size of the logical volume.

The HP OnLineJFS add-on product allows you to perform many of these LVM functions without going into single-user mode. For example, with OnLineJFS, logical volumes and file systems are simply expanded with the system up and running and no interruption to users or processes.

Swap

Both device swap and file system swap are listed when you enter *Swap*. Listed for you are the *Device File/Mount Directory, Type, Mbytes Available*, and *Enabled.* You can get more information about an item by highlighting it and selecting *Zoom* from the *Actions* menu.

Volume Groups

Listed for you when you enter volume groups are *Name, Mbytes Available, Physical Volumes*, and *Logical Volumes*. If you have an unused disk on your system, you can extend an existing volume group or create a new volume group. This window is useful to see how much disk space within a volume group has not been allocated yet. Another function here is the ability to import volume groups from other systems or ready a volume group for export to a remote system. You would use this when moving a volume group contained on an entire disk drive or set of disk drives from one system to another.

Display

In this SAM area, you can perform work related to the graphics display(s) on your system. This work is self-explanatory in SAM, so I won't cover this functional area of SAM.

Kernel Configuration

Your HP-UX kernel is a vitally important part of your HP-UX system that is often overlooked by HP-UX administrators. Perhaps this is because administrators are reluctant to tinker with such a critical and sensitive part of their system. Your HP-UX kernel, however, can have a big impact on system performance, so you want to be sure that you know how it is configured. This doesn't mean that you have to make a lot of experimental changes, but you should know how your kernel is currently configured so that you can assess the possible impact that changes to the kernel may have on your system.

SAM allows you to view and modify the four basic elements of your HP-UX kernel. There is a great deal of confusion among new HP-UX system administrators regarding these four elements. Before I get into the details of each of these four areas, I'll first give you a brief description of each.

- *Configurable Parameters* - These are parameters that have a <u>value</u> associated with them. When you change the value, there is a strong possibility you will affect the performance of your system. An example of a *Configurable Parameter* is **nfile**, which is the maximum number of open files on the system. Many configurable parameters in HP-UX 11i can be modified and included in the kernel without a reboot required. We'll cover this in one of the upcoming examples.

- *Drivers* - Drivers are used to control the hardware on your system. You have a driver called **CentIF** for the parallel interface on your system, one called **sdisk** for your SCSI disks, and so on.

- *Dump Devices* - A dump device is used to store the contents of main memory in the event that a serious kernel problem is encountered. If no dump device is configured, then the contents of main memory are saved on the primary swap device, and this information is copied into one of the directories (usually **/var/adm/crash**) when the system is booted. It is not essential that you have a dump device, but the system will boot faster after a crash if you have a dump device because the contents of main memory don't need to be copied to a file after a crash. A dump device is different from a swap device.

- *Subsystems* - A subsystem is different from a driver. A subsystem is an area of functionality or support on your system such as **CD-ROM/9000**, which is CD-ROM file system support; **LVM,** which is Logical Volume Manager support; and so on.

When you go into one of the four subareas described above, the configuration of your system for the respective subarea is listed for you. The first thing you should do when entering *Kernel Configuration* is to go into each of the subareas and review the list of information about your system in each.

In *Kernel Configuration* is a *current* kernel and *pending* kernel. The *current* kernel is the one you are now running, and the *pending* kernel is the one for which you are making changes.

Figure 10-23 shows the SAM menu hierarchy for *Kernel Configuration*.

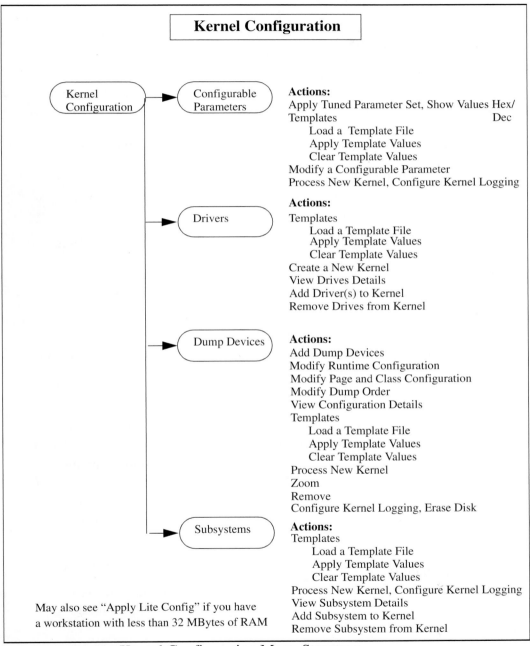

Kernel Configuration

Kernel Configuration

Configurable Parameters

Actions:
Apply Tuned Parameter Set, Show Values Hex/
Templates   Dec
    Load a Template File
    Apply Template Values
    Clear Template Values
Modify a Configurable Parameter
Process New Kernel, Configure Kernel Logging

Drivers

Actions:
Templates
    Load a Template File
    Apply Template Values
    Clear Template Values
Create a New Kernel
View Drives Details
Add Driver(s) to Kernel
Remove Drives from Kernel

Dump Devices

Actions:
Add Dump Devices
Modify Runtime Configuration
Modify Page and Class Configuration
Modify Dump Order
View Configuration Details
Templates
    Load a Template File
    Apply Template Values
    Clear Template Values
Process New Kernel
Zoom
Remove
Configure Kernel Logging, Erase Disk

Subsystems

Actions:
Templates
    Load a Template File
    Apply Template Values
    Clear Template Values
Process New Kernel, Configure Kernel Logging
View Subsystem Details
Add Subsystem to Kernel
Remove Subsystem from Kernel

May also see "Apply Lite Config" if you have
a workstation with less than 32 MBytes of RAM

Figure 10-23 Kernel Configuration Menu Structure

Configurable Parameters

Selecting *Configurable Parameters* lists all your configurable kernel parameters. For each configurable parameter, the following information is listed:

- Name - Name of the parameter.

- Current Value - Value of the parameter in **/stand/vmunix**.

- Pending Value - Value of the parameter in the kernel to be built.

- Type - Shows whether parameters are part of the static kernel or a loadable module.

- Associated Module - Lists module parameter is part of if type is loadable.

- Description - A few words describing the parameter.

You can then take a number of *Actions,* including the following:

Apply Tuned Parameter Set

Several sets of configurable parameters have been tuned for various environments. When you select this from the *Actions* menu, the tuned parameter sets on your system, such as a database server system, are listed for you and you can select from among them.

Templates   You can select a kernel template to load that is basically a different kernel configuration from the one you are currently running.

Process New Kernel

> After making whatever changes you like to the *Pending Value* of a configurable parameter, you can have SAM create a new kernel for you.

Modify Configurable Parameter

> You can change the value of a parameter in the *pending* kernel. You simply highlight a parameter and select this from the *Actions* menu.

Modifying a configurable parameter is made much easier by SAM. But although the logistics of changing the parameter are easier, determining the value of the parameter is still the most important part of this process.

Many applications recommend modifying one or more of these parameters for optimal performance of the application. Keep in mind, though, that many of these parameters are related; modifying one may adversely affect another parameter. Many applications will request that you change the *maxuprc* to support more processes. Keep in mind that if you have more processes running, you may end up with more open files and also you may have to change the *maxfiles* per process. If you have a system primarily used for a single application, you can feel more comfortable in modifying these. But if you run many applications, make sure that you don't improve the performance of one application at the expense of another.

When you do decide to modify the value of a configurable parameter, be careful. The range on some of these values is broad. The *maxuprc* (maximum number of user processes) can be reduced as low as three processes. I can't imagine what a system could be used for with this low a value, but SAM ensures that the parameter is set within supported HP-UX ranges for the parameter. "Let the administrator beware" when changing these values. You may find that you'll want to undo some of your changes. Here are some tips: Keep careful notes of the values you change, in case you have to undo a change. In addition, change as few values at a time as possible. That way, if you're not happy with the results, you know which configurable parameter caused the problem.

In Chapter 3, when covering the kernel, we manually modified the *maxuprc* kernel parameter. Since this parameter is dynamic, there was not a reboot required in order for it to take effect. Let's now use SAM to modify this parameter and again demonstrate that since it is dynamic, no reboot is required if it is modified with SAM.

Figure 10-24 shows *maxuprc* selected in a SAM screen shot:

```
┌─┬──────────────────────────────────────────────────────────────────────┬───┬──┐
│ ▭ │              Kernel Configuration (13)                            │ ▫ │▢ │
├───┴──────────────────────────────────────────────────────────────────────┴───┴──┤
│  File  List  View  Options  Actions                              Help           │
├──────────────────────────────────────────────────────────────────────────────────┤
│  Pending Kernel Based Upon:     Current Kernel                                    │
│                                                                                   │
│  Configurable Parameters                               1 of 128 selected          │
│                                                                                   │
│                      Current       Pending            Associated                  │
│  Name                Value         Value     Type     Module      D               │
│  max_thread_proc          64            64   Static   N/A         M               │
│  maxdsiz            268435456     268435456  Static   N/A         M               │
│  maxdsiz_64bit     1073741824    1073741824  Static   N/A         M               │
│  maxfiles                 60            60   Static   N/A         S               │
│  maxfiles_lim           1024          1024   Dynamic  N/A         H               │
│  maxssiz             8388608       8388608   Static   N/A         M               │
│  maxssiz_64bit       8388608       8388608   Static   N/A         M               │
│  maxswapchunks           512           512   Static   N/A         M               │
│  maxtsiz            67108864      67108864   Dynamic  N/A         M               │
│  maxtsiz_64bit     1073741824    1073741824  Dynamic  N/A         M               │
│  maxuprc                  80            80   Dynamic  N/A         M               │
│  maxusers                 32            32   Static   N/A         V               │
│  maxvgs                   10            10   Static   N/A         M               │
│  mesg                      1             1   Static   N/A         E               │
│  modstrmax               500           500   Static   N/A         M               │
│  msgmap                   42            42   Static   N/A         M               │
│  msgmax                 8192          8192   Dynamic  N/A         M               │
│  msgmnb                16384         16384   Dynamic  N/A         M               │
│  msgmni                   50            50   Static   N/A         N               │
│  msgseg                 2048          2048   Static   N/A         N               │
│  msgssz                    8             8   Static   N/A         M               │
│  msgtql                   40            40   Static   N/A         N               │
│  nbuf                      0             0   Static   N/A         N               │
└──────────────────────────────────────────────────────────────────────────────────┘
```

Figure 10-24 *maxuprc* Selected in SAM Window

Let's now increase the value of *maxuprc* from *80* to *100* as shown in Figure 10-25:

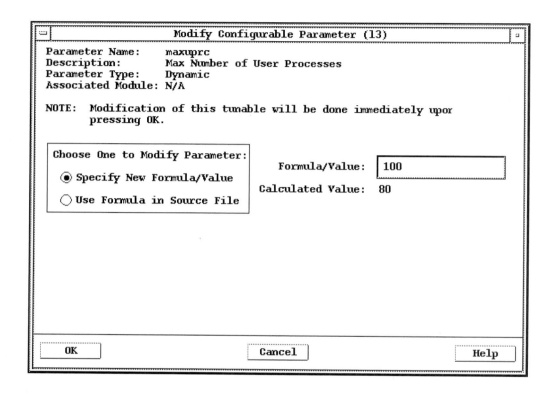

Figure 10-25 *maxuprc* from *80* to *100*

Clicking *OK* results in changing *maxuprc* from *80* to *100* on the system immediately, without a reboot required, as shown in Figure 10-26:

```
┌─────────────────────────────────────────────────────────────────────────┐
│ ⊟                  Kernel Configuration (13)                    ▫ ▯       │
│  File  List  View  Options  Actions                         Help         │
├─────────────────────────────────────────────────────────────────────────┤
│ Pending Kernel Based Upon:    Current Kernel                             │
│                                                                          │
│ Configurable Parameters                         1 of 128 selected        │
│                                                                          │
│                    Current      Pending            Associated            │
│   Name              Value        Value     Type     Module      D        │
│ max_thread_proc        64           64    Static    N/A         M        │
│ maxdsiz         268435456    268435456    Static    N/A         M        │
│ maxdsiz_64bit  1073741824   1073741824    Static    N/A         M        │
│ maxfiles               60           60    Static    N/A         S        │
│ maxfiles_lim         1024         1024    Dynamic   N/A         H        │
│ maxssiz           8388608      8388608    Static    N/A         M        │
│ maxssiz_64bit     8388608      8388608    Static    N/A         M        │
│ maxswapchunks         512          512    Static    N/A         M        │
│ maxtsiz          67108864     67108864    Dynamic   N/A         M        │
│ maxtsiz_64bit  1073741824   1073741824    Dynamic   N/A         M        │
│ maxuprc               100          100    Dynamic   N/A         M        │
│ maxusers               32           32    Static    N/A         V        │
│ maxvgs                 10           10    Static    N/A         M        │
│ mesg                    1            1    Static    N/A         E        │
│ modstrmax             500          500    Static    N/A         M        │
│ msgmap                 42           42    Static    N/A         M        │
│ msgmax               8192         8192    Dynamic   N/A         M        │
│ msgmnb              16384        16384    Dynamic   N/A         M        │
│ msgmni                 50           50    Static    N/A         N        │
│ msgseg               2048         2048    Static    N/A         N        │
│ msgssz                  8            8    Static    N/A         M        │
│ msgtql                 40           40    Static    N/A         N        │
│ nbuf                    0            0    Static    N/A         N        │
└─────────────────────────────────────────────────────────────────────────┘
```

Figure 10-26 *maxuprc* Increase Takes Effect Immediately

Figure 10-26 shows that both the *Current Value* and *Pending Value* of *maxuprc* are *100,* without a reboot required. Dynamic configurable parameters and dynamically loadable kernel modules can be updated in this fashion without a reboot required.

Drivers

When you select *Drivers*, the drivers for your current kernel, the template file on which your current kernel is based, and the pending kernel are listed. You'll know that the drivers displayed are for more than your current kernel because you'll see that some of the drivers listed are *Out* of both your current and pending kernels. The following information is listed for you when you enter the *Drivers* subarea:

- Name - Name of the driver.
- Current State - Lists whether the driver is *In* or *Out* of **/stand/vmunix**.
- Pending State - Lists whether the driver is *In* or *Out* of the pending kernel to be built.
- Class - Identifies element as a driver or module.
- Type - Identifies driver as part of the static kernel or a loadable module.
- Load Module at Boot? - Lists whether driver is automatically loaded at boot time if it is a loadable module.
- Description - A few words describing the driver.

The *Current State* indicates whether or not the driver selected is in **/stand/vmunix.**

The *Pending State* indicates whether or not you have selected this driver to be added to or removed from the kernel. *In* means that the driver is part of the kernel or is pending to be part of the kernel. *Out* means that the driver is not part of the kernel or is pending to be removed from the kernel.

Typically, drivers are added statically. In other words, they are added to the kernel and left there. However, if the driver is a specially created module for a particular purpose, then it may be configured as loadable. This means that it can be loaded and unloaded from the kernel without rebooting the system. This advanced feature is discussed in detail in the "Managing Dynamically Loadable Kernel Modules" chapter of the *Managing Systems and Workgroups* book from Hewlett-Packard.

Using the *Actions* menu, you can select one of the drivers and add or remove it. You can also pick *View Driver Details* from the *Actions* menu after you select one of the drivers. You can select *Process New Kernel* from the *Actions* menu. If you have indeed modified this screen by adding or removing drivers, you want to recreate the kernel. SAM asks whether you're sure that you want to rebuild the kernel before it does this for you. The only recommendation I can make here is to be sure that you have made your selections carefully before you rebuild the kernel.

Dump Devices

When you enter this subarea, both the *Current Dump Devices* and *Pending Dump Devices* are listed for you. A dump device is used when a serious kernel problem occurs with your system, and main memory is written to disk. This information is a core dump that can later be read from disk and used to help diagnose the kernel problem.

Prior to HP-UX 11.x, memory dumps contained the entire image of physical memory. As a result, in order to get a full memory dump, you needed to create a dump area at least as large as main memory. With systems with memory size into the gigabits, a large amount of disk space was wasted just waiting around for a system panic to occur. With HP-UX 11.x comes a new, fast dump feature. This allows you to pick and choose what to dump. The fast dump feature not only prevents such things as unused memory pages and user text pages from being dumped, but it also allows you to configure what memory page classes to dump.

The sizes of the dump areas can be configured somewhat smaller than main memory in your system. You can specify a disk or logical volume as a dump device (you can also specify a disk section, but I don't recommend that you use disk sections at all). The entire disk or logical volume is then reserved as a dump device.

If no dump device is specified or if the size of the dump area is less than what is configured to be dumped, then the core dump is written to primary swap. At the time of system boot, the core dump is written out to a core file, usually in **/var/adm/crash**. This is the way most systems I have worked on operate; that is, there is no specific dump device specified and core dumps are written to primary swap and then to **/var/adm/crash**. This approach has sometimes been a point of confusion; that is, primary swap may indeed be used as a dump device, but a dump device is used specifically for core dump purposes whereas primary swap fills this role in the event there is no dump device specified. As long as you don't mind the additional time it takes at boot to write the core dump in primary swap to a file, you may want to forego adding a specific dump device to your system.

Since you probably won't be allocating an entire disk as a dump device, you may be using a logical volume. You must select a logical volume in the root volume group that is unused or is used for non-file-system swap. This is done by selecting *Add* from the *Actions* menu to add a disk or logical volume to the list of dump devices.

You will want to get acquainted with the *View Dump Configuration Details* subarea of *Dump Devices*. It is here where you can see what the current dump configuration is, what the current and pending kernel dump configurations are, and what the current runtime dump configuration is.

Subsystems

Selecting *Subsystems* lists all of your subsystems. For each subsystem, the following information is listed:

- *Name* - Name of the subsystem.

- *Current Value* - Lists whether the subsystem is *In* or *Out* of **/stand/vmunix**.

• *Pending Value* - Lists whether the subsystem is *In* or *Out* of the pending kernel.

• *Description* - A few words describing the parameter.

You can then take a number of *Actions,* including the following:

Templates
: You can select a kernel template to load that is basically a different kernel configuration from the one you are currently running.

Process New Kernel
: After making whatever changes you like to the *Pending State* of a subsystem, you can have SAM create a new kernel for you.

View Subsystem Details
: You get a little more information about the subsystem when you select this.

Add Subsystem to Kernel
: When you highlight one of the subsystems and select this from the menu, the *Pending State* is changed to *In* and the subsystem will be added to the kernel when you rebuild the kernel.

Remove Subsystem from Kernel
: When you highlight one of the subsystems and select this from the menu, the *Pending State* is changed to *Out* and the subsystem will be removed from the kernel when you rebuild the kernel.

After making selections, you can rebuild the kernel to include your pending changes or back out of them without making the changes.

Networking and Communications

The menu hierarchy for *Networking and Communications* is shown in Figures 10-27 through 10-29. This area contains many advanced networking features. Because there are so many networking areas to cover in SAM, I'll go over just a few so you can get a feel for working in this area. The bubble diagram shows the many areas related to networking configuration for which you can use SAM so you can refer back to it if you have a question about whether or not some specific networking can be configured using SAM.

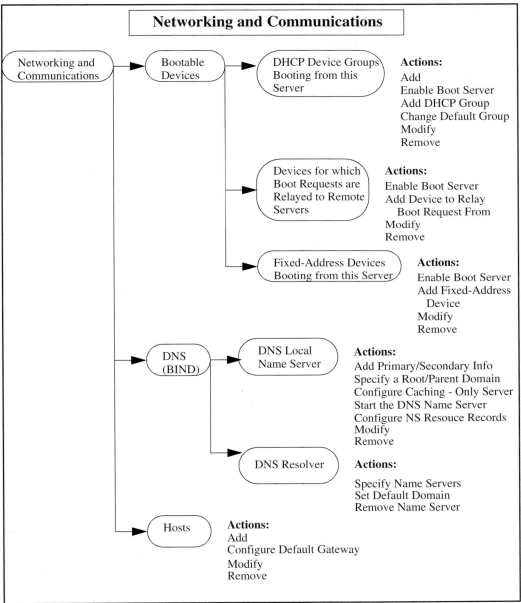

Figure 10-27 Networking and Communications Menu Structure

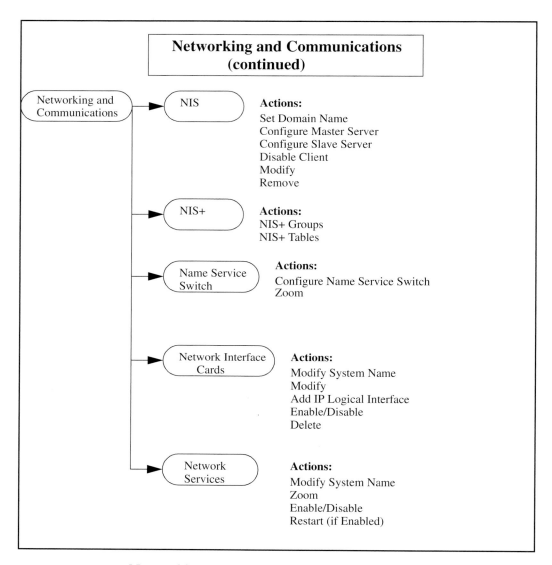

Figure 10-28 Networking and Communications Menu Structure (cont)

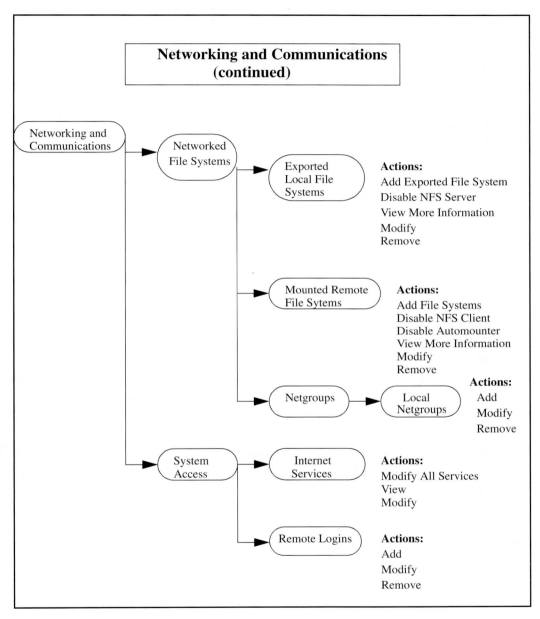

Figure 10-29 Networking and Communications Menu Structure (cont)

Bootable Devices

The *Bootable Devices* area is further subdivided into three subareas: *DHCP Device Groups Booting from this Server, Devices for which Boot Requests are Relayed to Remote Servers*, and *Fixed-Address Devices Booting from this Server*. I will briefly describe each subarea and its use. DHCP (Dynamic Host Configuration Protocol) is now available on HP-UX and is used by many services.

The *DHCP Device Groups Booting from this Server* subarea is where the device groups can be configured. Each group would contain a set of IP addresses for use by that device group. Devices could be such things as specific types of printers or specific types of terminals.

In the *Devices for which Boot Requests are Relayed to Remote Servers* subarea, you can view information about Bootstrap Protocol (Bootp) client devices that get their booting information from remote Bootp or DHCP servers. Information is displayed on the client or client groups, including the IP addresses of the remove servers and the maximum number of hops a boot request from a client or client group can be relayed.

In the *Fixed-Address Devices Booting from this Server* subarea, you can specify systems that will boot from your system using Bootstrap Protocol (Bootp) or DHCP. Bootp is a means by which a system can discover network information and boot automatically. The Bootp software must be loaded on your system in order for other devices to use it as a boot source (see the **swlist** command in Chapter 2 regarding how to list software installed on your system). In this subarea, you can add, modify, or remove a Bootp device. In addition, you can enable or disable the Bootp Server. Similarly, DHCP allows the client to use one of a pool of IP addresses in order to boot automatically. Applications such as Ignite-UX can be configured to use this protocol.

When you enter the *Fixed-Address Devices Booting from this Server* subarea, you immediately receive a list of devices that can boot off your system. You can choose *Add* from the *Actions* menu and you'll be asked to enter the following information about the device you are adding:

- Host Name

- Internet Address

- Subnet Mask (this is optional)

- Station Address in hex or client ID (this is optional)

- Boot File Name

- Whether you'll be using Ethernet or IEEE 802.3 for booting

- Whether to send the hostname to the client or device

You can select *Enable Protocol Server* or *Disable Protocol Server* from the *Actions* menu, depending on whether your system is currently disabled or enabled to support this functionality. When you *Enable Protocol Server,* you also enable Trivial File Transfer Protocol (TFTP), which boot devices use to get boot files. When you enable or disable this, the **/etc/inetd.conf** is edited. This file contains configuration information about the networking services running on your system. If a line in **/etc/inetd.conf** is preceded by a "#", then it is viewed as a comment. The daemon that reads the entries in this file is **/usr/sbin/inetd**. Before enabling or disabling Bootp, you may want to view the **/etc/inetd.conf** file and see what services are enabled. After you make your change through SAM, you can again view **/etc/inetd.conf** to see what has been modified. See *System Access* for security related to **/etc/inetd.conf.** The following is the *beginning* of the **/etc/inetd.conf** file from a system showing Bootp and TFTP enabled. Also, a brief explanation of the fields in this file appears at the beginning of the file:

```
## Configured using SAM by root
##
#
# Inetd  reads its configuration information from this file upon ex-
# ecution and at some later time if it is reconfigured.
#
# A line in the configuration file has the following fields separated
# by tabs and/or spaces:
```

```
#
#     service name          as in /etc/services
#     socket type           either "stream" or "dgram"
#     protocol              as in /etc/protocols
#     wait/nowait            only applies to datagram sockets, stream
#                           sockets should specify nowait
#     user                   name of user as whom the server should run
#     server program        absolute pathname for the server inetd
#                           will execute
#   server program args.    arguments server program uses as they
#                            normally are starting with argv[0] which
#                           is the name of the server.
#
# See the inetd.conf(4) manual page for more information.
##


##
#
#               ARPA/Berkeley services
#
##
ftp          stream tcp nowait root /usr/lbin/ftpd      ftpd -l
telnet       stream tcp nowait root /usr/lbin/telnetd   telnetd

# Before uncommenting the "tftp" entry below, please make sure
# that you have a "tftp" user in /etc/passwd. If you don't
# have one, please consult the tftpd(1M) manual entry for
# information about setting up this service.

tftp         dgram  udp wait    root   /usr/lbin/tftpd    tftpd
bootps       dgram  udp wait    root   /usr/lbin/bootpd   bootpd
#finger      stream tcp nowait  bin    /usr/lbing/fingerd fingerd
login        stream tcp nowait  bin    /usr/lbin/rlogind  rlogind
shell        stream tcp nowait  bin    /usr/lbin/remshd   remshd
exec         stream tcp nowait  root   /usr/lbin/rexecd   rexecd
#uucp        stream tcp nowait  bin    /usr/sbin/uucpd    uucpd
```

.
.
.

If you select *Fixed-Address Device Client Names*, you can then select *Modify* or *Remove* from the *Actions* menu and either change one of the parameters related to the client, such as its address or subnet mask, or completely remove the client.

DNS (BIND)

Domain Name Service (DNS) is a name server used to resolve hostname-to-IP addressing. HP-UX uses BIND, Berkeley InterNetworking Domain, one of the name services that can be used to implement DNS. A DNS server is responsible for the resolution of all hostnames on a network or subnet. Each DNS client would rely on the server to resolve all IP address-to-hostname issues on the client's behalf. A boot file is used by the server to locate database files. The database files map hostnames to IP addresses and IP addresses to hostnames. Through SAM, a DNS server can be easily set up.

Information about DNS and its setup and administration is described in the HP-UX manual *Installing and Administering Internet Services*.

Hosts

This subarea is for maintaining the default gateway and remote hosts on your system. When you enter this subarea, you receive a list of hosts specified on your system. This information is retrieved from the **/etc/hosts** file on your system.

You can then *Add* a new host, *Specify Default Gateway, Modify* one of the hosts, or *Remove* one of the hosts, all from the *Actions* menu. When adding a host, you'll be asked for information pertaining to the host, including its Internet Address, system name, aliases for the system, and comments.

NIS

Network Information Service (NIS) is a database system used to propagate common configuration files across a network of systems. Managed on a master server are such files as **/etc/passwd**, **/etc/hosts**, and **/etc/auto***, files used by automounter. Formerly called "yellow pages," NIS converts these files to its own database files, called maps, for use by clients in the NIS domain. When a client requests information, such as when a user logs in and enters their password, the information is retrieved from the server rather than from the client's system. Thus, this information only needs to be maintained only on the server.

Through SAM, the NIS master server, slave servers, and clients can be configured, enabled, disabled, and removed. Once the master, slaves, and clients are established, you can easily build, modify, and push the various maps to the slaves.

NIS is not available on trusted systems.

NIS+

HP-UX 11i supports NIS+. This is not an enhancement of NIS, but rather a new service that includes standard and trusted systems and non-HP-UX systems. If you already use NIS, a compatibility mode version of NIS+ allows servers to answer requests from both NIS and NIS+ clients. When NIS+ is configured on a trusted system, in the *Auditing and Security* area of SAM, a new subarea, *Audited NIS+ Users*, is displayed.

Name Service Switch

The Name Service Switch file, **/etc/nsswitch.conf**, can now be configured through SAM. This service allows you to prioritize which name service (FILES, NIS, NIS+, DNS, or COMPAT) to use to look up information. Unless you specifically use one of these services, the default of FILES should be used. The FILES designation supports the use of the local **/etc** directory for such administrative files as **/etc/passwd**, **/etc/hosts**, and **/etc/services**. (COMPAT is used with the compatibility mode of NIS+.)

More information about Name Service Switch file and its setup is described in the HP-UX manual *Installing and Administering NFS Services*.

Network Interface Cards

This subarea is used for configuring any networking cards in your system. You can *Enable, Disable*, and *Modify* networking cards as well as *Modify System Name,* all from the *Actions* menu. Under *Add IP Logical Interface,* you can add additional logical IP addresses to an existing network card.

The *Network Interface Cards* screen lists the network cards installed on your system, including the information listed below. You may have to expand the window or scroll over to see all this information.

- Card Type such as Ethernet, IEEE 802.3, Token Ring, FDDI, etc.

- Card Name

- Hardware Path

- Status, such as whether or not the card is enabled

- Internet Address

- Subnet Mask

- Station Address in hex

Included under *Configure* for Ethernet cards is *Advanced Options,* which will modify the Maximum Transfer Unit (MTU) for this card. Other cards included in your system can also be configured here, such as ISDN, X.25, ATM, and so on.

Network Services

This subarea is used to enable or disable *some* of the network services on your system. You will recognize some of the network services in Figure 10-30 from the **/etc/inetd.conf** file shown earlier. This screen has three columns, which are the Name, Status, and Description of the network services. Figure 10-30 from the *Network Services* subarea shows some of the network services that can be managed:

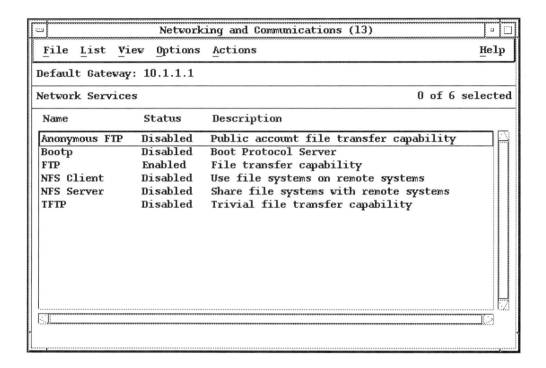

Figure 10-30   Network Services Window

After selecting one of the network services shown, you can *Enable* or *Disable* the service, depending on its current status, *Restart* the service if it is currently enabled, get more information about the service with *Zoom*, or *Modify System Name*, all from the *Actions* menu.

Network File Systems

This subarea is broken down into *Exported Local File Systems, Mounted Remote File Systems,* and *Netgroups.* NFS is broken down into these first two areas because you can export a local file system without mounting a remote file system, and vice versa. This means you can manage these independently of one another. You may have an NFS server in your environment that won't mount remote file systems, and you may have an NFS client that will mount only remote file systems and never export its local file system. *Entropies,* a part of NIS, allows you to group a set of systems or users to be used together. Among other things, netgroup designations can be used to export file systems to.

Under *Exported Local File Systems,* you can select the file systems you want to export. The first time you enter this screen you have no exported file systems listed. When you select *Add Exported File System* from the *Actions* menu, you enter such information as:

- Local directory name

- User ID

- Whether or not to allow asynchronous writes

- Permissions

After this exported file system has been added, you can select it and choose from a number of *Actions,* including *Modify* and *Remove.*

Under *Mounted Remote File Systems,* you have listed for you all of the directories and files that are mounted using NFS. These can be either mounted or unmounted on demand with automounter. After selecting one of the mounted file systems, you can perform various *Actions.* For every remote file system mounted, you have the following columns:

- *Mount Directory,* which displays the name of the local directory name used to mount the remote directory.

- *Type*, which is either *NFS* for standard NFS or *Auto* for auto-mounter (see the paragraph below).

- *Remote Server*, which displays the name of the remote system where the file or directory is mounted.

- *Remote Directory*, which is the name of the directory under which the directory is remotely mounted.

You should think about whether or not you want to use the NFS automounter. With automounter, you mount a remote file or directory on demand, that is, when you need it. Using a master map, you can specify which files and directories will be mounted when needed. The files and directories are not continuously mounted with automounter, resulting in more efficiency as far as how system resources are being used. There is, however, some overhead time associated with mounting a file or directory on-demand, as opposed to having it continuously mounted. From a user standpoint, this may be slightly more undesirable, but from an administration standpoint, using the automounter offers advantages. Since the automounter is managed through SAM, there is very little additional work you need to perform to enable it.

System Access

This subarea is broken down into *Internet Services* and *Remote Logins*.

When you select *Internet Services,* the screen lists the networking services that are started by the Internet daemon **/usr/sbin/inetd**. I earlier covered **/etc/inetd.conf**, which is a configuration file that lists all of the network services supported by a system that is read by **inetd**. There is also a security file, **/var/adm/inetd.sec**, that serves as a security check for **inetd**. Although many other components are involved, you can view **inetd**, **/etc/inetd.conf**, and **/var/adm/inetd.sec** as working together to determine what network services are supported and the security level of each.

Listed for you in the *System Access* subarea are *Service Name, Description, Type*, and *System Permission*. Figure 10-31 shows the defaults for my system:

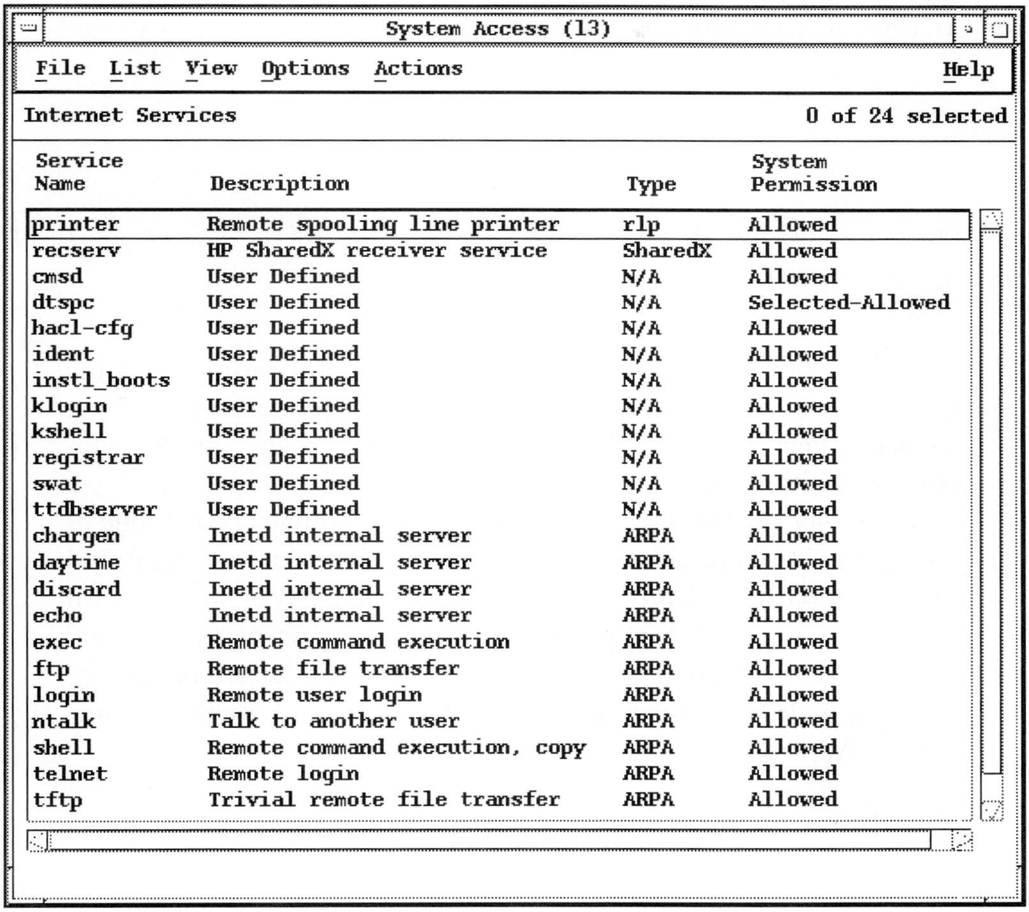

```
┌─────────────────────────────────────────────────────────────────┐
│ ⊟            System Access (13)                          ▫ □     │
├─────────────────────────────────────────────────────────────────┤
│  File  List  View  Options  Actions                        Help  │
├─────────────────────────────────────────────────────────────────┤
│ Internet Services                              0 of 24 selected   │
│                                                                   │
│  Service                                   System                 │
│  Name          Description          Type   Permission            │
│ ┌──────────────────────────────────────────────────────────┐   │
│ │printer       Remote spooling line printer  rlp      Allowed│▲  │
│ │recserv       HP SharedX receiver service    SharedX  Allowed│   │
│ │cmsd          User Defined                   N/A      Allowed│   │
│ │dtspc         User Defined                   N/A  Selected-Allowed│
│ │hacl-cfg      User Defined                   N/A      Allowed│   │
│ │ident         User Defined                   N/A      Allowed│   │
│ │instl_boots   User Defined                   N/A      Allowed│   │
│ │klogin        User Defined                   N/A      Allowed│   │
│ │kshell        User Defined                   N/A      Allowed│   │
│ │registrar     User Defined                   N/A      Allowed│   │
│ │swat          User Defined                   N/A      Allowed│   │
│ │ttdbserver    User Defined                   N/A      Allowed│   │
│ │chargen       Inetd internal server          ARPA     Allowed│   │
│ │daytime       Inetd internal server          ARPA     Allowed│   │
│ │discard       Inetd internal server          ARPA     Allowed│   │
│ │echo          Inetd internal server          ARPA     Allowed│   │
│ │exec          Remote command execution       ARPA     Allowed│   │
│ │ftp           Remote file transfer           ARPA     Allowed│   │
│ │login         Remote user login              ARPA     Allowed│   │
│ │ntalk         Talk to another user           ARPA     Allowed│   │
│ │shell         Remote command execution, copy ARPA     Allowed│   │
│ │telnet        Remote login                   ARPA     Allowed│   │
│ │tftp          Trivial remote file transfer   ARPA     Allowed│▼  │
│ └──────────────────────────────────────────────────────────┘   │
│ ◁                                                            ▷   │
└─────────────────────────────────────────────────────────────────┘
```

Figure 10-31 System Access - Internet Services Window

You could change the permission for any of these entries by selecting them, using the *Modify* command from the *Actions* menu, and selecting the desired permissions.

Remote Logins is used to manage security restrictions for remote users who will access the local system. Two HP-UX files are used to manage users. The file **/etc/hosts.equiv** handles users, and **/.rhosts** handles superusers (root). When you enter this subarea, you get a list of users and the restrictions on each. You can then *Add, Remove*, or *Modify* login security.

Partition Manager

Many HP 9000 systems running HP-UX 11i support partitions. At the time of this writing, however, partitions were just emerging as an advanced technology and I did not have access to any systems supporting partitions. The two partition types supported on HP 9000 systems running HP-UX 11i are hard and virtual partitions. At the time of this writing, hard partitions are available on Superdome systems and consist primarily of hardware components that are combined to form the hard partition. Virtual partitions are available on many HP 9000 systems and are meant to be created, modified, and deleted on-the-fly. I have provided as much background information as possible on partitions in Appendix A.

Performance Monitors

Under *Performance Monitors,* you can view the performance of your system in several different areas such as disk and virtual memory. Figure 10-32 shows the menu hierarchy of *Performance Monitors*:

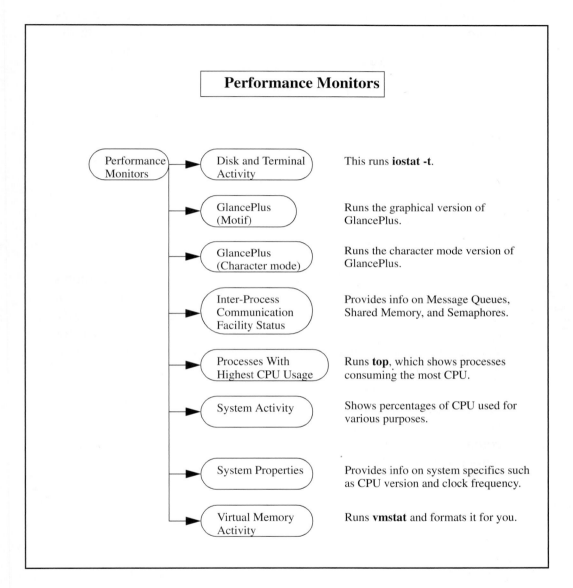

Figure 10-32 Performance Monitors Menu Structure

Performance Monitors provides you with a window into several areas of your system. If you are serious about becoming familiar with the tools available on your system to help you understand how your system resources are being used, you should take a close look at Chapter 11. Chapter 11 is devoted to getting a handle on how your system resources are being used, including many built-in HP-UX commands. Some of the performance monitors you can select in this subarea are HP-UX commands, which you'll need some background in before you can use them. I'll cover these areas only briefly because this material will be covered in more detail in Chapter 11.

Disk and Terminal Activity

Selecting *Disk and Terminal Activity* opens a window that shows the output of **iostat -t**. I have included the description of **iostat** from Chapter 11 to save you the trouble of flipping ahead. When the *Disks and Terminal Activity* window with the output of **iostat** is opened for you, it shows a single **iostat** output. When you press *Return,* the window is automatically closed for you.

The **iostat** command gives you an indication of the level of effort the CPU is putting into I/O and the amount of I/O taking place among your disks and terminals. The following example shows the **iostat -t** command, which will be executed every three seconds, and associated output from an HP-UX 11.x system:

 # iostat -t 3

	tty			cpu		
	tin	tout	us	ni	sy	id
	78	42	2	0	28	70

/dev/dsk/c0t1d0			/dev/dsk/c0t4d0			/dev/dsk/c0t6d0		
bps	sps	msps	bps	sps	msps	bps	sps	msps
0	0	0	33	8.3	25.2	7	1	19.5

	tty			cpu		
	tin	tout	us	ni	sy	id
	66	24	0	0	30	70

/dev/dsk/c0t1d0			/dev/dsk/c0t4d0			/dev/dsk/c0t6d0

bps	sps	msps		bps	sps	msps		bps	sps	msps
5	12	15.9		36	9.7	21		7	1.2	13.8

tty					cpu			
tin	tout		us		ni	sy	id	
90	29		1		0	25	73	

/dev/dsk/c0t1d0				/dev/dsk/c0t4d0				/dev/dsk/c0t6d0		
bps	sps	msps		bps	sps	msps		bps	sps	msps
12	1.7	15.5		24	3	19.1		14	2.1	14.6

tty					cpu			
tin	tout		us		ni	sy	id	
48	16		1		0	16	83	

/dev/dsk/c0t1d0				/dev/dsk/c0t4d0				/dev/dsk/c0t6d0		
bps	sps	msps		bps	sps	msps		bps	sps	msps
0	0	0		62	9.3	18		12	2	17.2

tty					cpu			
tin	tout		us		ni	sy	id	
32	48		7		0	14	79	

/dev/dsk/c0t1d0				/dev/dsk/c0t4d0				/dev/dsk/c0t6d0		
bps	sps	msps		bps	sps	msps		bps	sps	msps
1	0.3	14.4		5	.9	16.2		171	29.4	18.2

tty					cpu			
tin	tout		us		ni	sy	id	
2	40		20		1	42	27	

/dev/dsk/c0t1d0				/dev/dsk/c0t4d0				/dev/dsk/c0t6d0		
bps	sps	msps		bps	sps	msps		bps	sps	msps
248	30.9	20.8		203	29.2	18.8		165	30.6	22.1

man page

iostat - 11

Descriptions of the reports you receive with **iostat** for terminals, the CPU, and mounted file systems follow.

For every terminal you have connected (tty), you see a "tin" and "tout," which represent the number of characters read from your terminal and the number of characters written to your terminal, respectively. The -t option produces this terminal report.

For your CPU, you see the percentage of time spent in user mode ("us"), the percentage of time spent running user processes at a low priority called nice ("ni"), the percentage of time spent in system mode ("sy"), and the percentage of time the CPU is idle ("id").

man page

iostat - 11

For every locally mounted file system, you receive information on the kilobytes transferred per second ("bps"), number of seeks per second ("sps"), and number of milliseconds per average seek ("msps"). For disks that are NFS-mounted or disks on client nodes of your server, you will not receive a report; **iostat** reports only on locally mounted file systems.

GlancePlus

GlancePlus is available here if it is installed on your system. You are given the choice of using either the Motif (graphical) version or the character mode version of GlancePlus. GlancePlus and other HP VantagePoint products are covered in Chapter 11.

Inter-Process Communication Facility Status

Inter-Process Communication Facility Status shows categories of information related to communication between processes. You receive status on Message Queues, Shared Memory, and Semaphores. This is a status window only, so again, when you press *Return,* and the window closes.

Processes with Highest CPU Usage

Processes with Highest CPU Usage is a useful window that lists the processes consuming the most CPU on your system. Such useful information as the *Process ID*, its *Resident Set Size*, and the *Percentage of CPU* it is consuming are listed.

System Activity

System Activity provides a report of CPU utilization. You receive the following list:

%usr	Percent of CPU spent in user mode.
%sys	Percent of CPU spent in system mode.
%wio	Percent of CPU idle with some processes waiting for I/O, such as virtual memory pages moving in or moving out.
%idle	Percent of CPU completely idle.

System Properties

System Properties gives you a great overview of system specifics. Included here are those hard-to-find items such as processor information, CPU version, clock frequency, kernel support (32-bit or 64-bit), memory information, operating system version, and network IP and MAC addresses.

Virtual Memory Activity

Virtual Memory Activity runs the **vmstat** command. This too is covered in Chapter 11, but I have included the **vmstat** description here so that you don't have to flip ahead. Some of the columns of **vmstat** are moved around a little when the *Virtual Memory Activity* window is opened for you.

man page

vmstat - 11

man page

.iostat - 11

vmstat provides virtual memory statistics. It provides information on the status of processes, virtual memory, paging activity, faults, and a breakdown of the percentage of CPU time. In the following example, the output was produced ten times at five-second intervals. The first argument to the **vmstat** command is the interval; the second is the number of times you would like output produced.

vmstat 5 10:

procs			memory				page					faults			cpu		
r	b	w	avm	free	re	at	pi	po	fr	de	sr	in	sy	cs	us	sy	id
4	0	0	1161	2282	6	22	48	0	0	0	0	429	289	65	44	18	38
9	0	0	1161	1422	4	30	59	0	0	0	0	654	264	181	18	20	62
6	0	0	1409	1247	2	19	37	0	0	0	0	505	316	130	47	10	43
1	0	0	1409	1119	1	10	19	0	0	0	0	508	254	180	69	15	16
2	0	0	1878	786	0	1	6	0	0	0	0	729	294	217	75	17	8
2	0	0	1878	725	0	0	3	0	0	0	0	561	688	435	67	32	1
2	0	0	2166	98	0	0	20	0	0	0	66	728	952	145	8	14	78
1	0	0	2310	90	0	0	20	0	0	0	171	809	571	159	16	21	63
1	0	0	2310	190	0	0	8	1	3	0	335	704	499	176	66	14	20
1	0	0	2316	311	0	0	3	1	5	0	376	607	945	222	4	11	85

You will get more out of the **vmstat** command than you want. Here is a brief description of the categories of information produced by **vmstat**:

Processes are classified into one of three categories: runnable ("r"), blocked on I/O or short-term resources ("b"), or swapped ("w").

Next you will see information about memory. "avm" is the number of virtual memory pages owned by processes that have run within the last 20 seconds. If this number is roughly the size of physical memory minus your kernel, then you are near paging. The "free" column indicates the number of pages on the system's free list. It doesn't mean that the process has finished running and these pages won't be accessed again; it just means that they have not been accessed recently.

Next is paging activity. The first field (*re*) shows the pages that were reclaimed. These pages made it to the free list but were later referenced and had to be salvaged. Check to see that "re" is a low number. If you are reclaiming pages that were thought to be free by the system, then you are wasting valuable time salvaging these. Reclaiming pages is also a symptom that you are short on memory.

Next you see the number of faults in three categories: interrupts per second, which usually come from hardware ("in"); system calls per second ("sy"); and context switches per second ("cs").

The final output is CPU usage percentage for user ("us"), system ("sy"), and idle ("id"). This is not as complete as the **iostat** output, which also shows **nice** entries.

Peripheral Devices

With *Peripheral Devices,* you can view any I/O cards installed in your system and peripherals connected to your system. These include both used and unused devices. You can also quickly configure any peripheral, including printers, plotters, tape drives, terminals, modems, and disks. This is a particularly useful area in SAM, because configuring peripherals in HP-UX is tricky. You perform one procedure to connect a printer, a different procedure to connect a disk, and so on, when you use the command line. In SAM, these procedures are menu-driven and therefore much easier.

Two of the six subareas, *Disks and File Systems* and *Printers and Plotters,* have their own dedicated hierarchy within SAM and are covered in this chapter. I don't cover these again in this section. The other four subareas, *Cards, Device List, Tape Drives*, and *Terminals and Modems,* are covered in this section.

It's impossible for me to cover every possible device that can be viewed and configured in SAM. What I'll do is give you examples of what you would see reported as devices on a server so that you can get a feel for what you can do under *Peripheral Devices* with SAM. From what I show here, you should be comfortable that SAM can help you configure peripherals.

Figure 10-33 shows the hierarchy of *Peripheral Devices*:

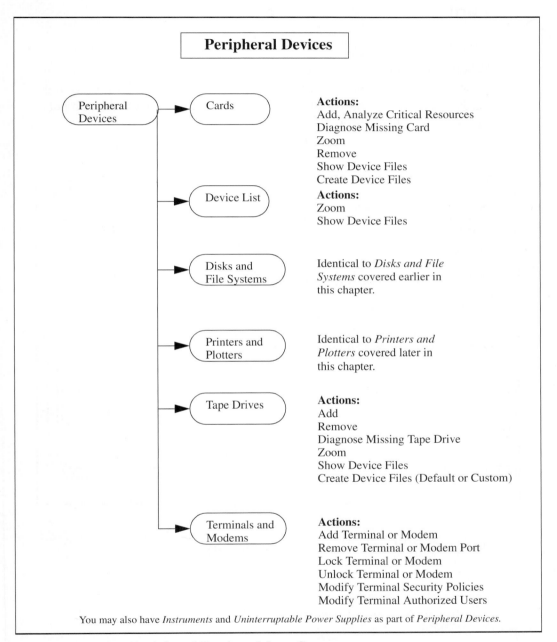

Figure 10-33 Peripheral Devices Menu Structure

Cards

When you select *Cards,* you are provided with a list of I/O cards in your system. You can also perform such tasks as adding and removing cards. Having this list of I/O cards is useful. Figure 10-34 shows a listing of I/O cards for an L-Class system:

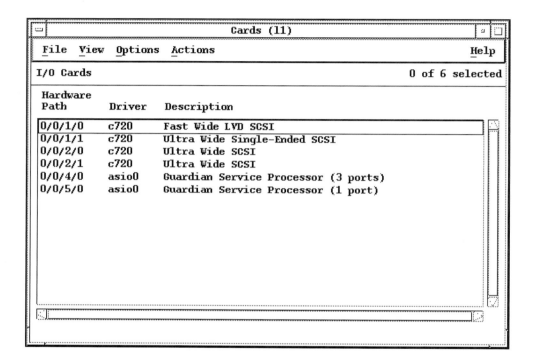

Figure 10-34 *I/O Cards* Window for L-Class System

In *Cards,* you can perform the following *Actions*:

Add	You can add a new I/O card in the window that is opened for you.

Diagnose Missing Card

> If a card you have installed is not included in the list, you can select this to determine the reason.

Zoom

> If you highlight a card and select *Zoom,* you will be provided such information as the hardware path, driver, and description of the card.

Remove

> If you highlight a card and select *Remove,* a window will appear that walks you through removing the card from the system.

Show Device Files

> If you select this, a window will be opened in which the device files associated with the card will be listed.

Create Device Files

> Creates device files for the selected card. This takes place without any user interaction.

Device List

Device List shows all the peripherals configured into the system. Figure 10-35 shows a device list for an L-Class system:

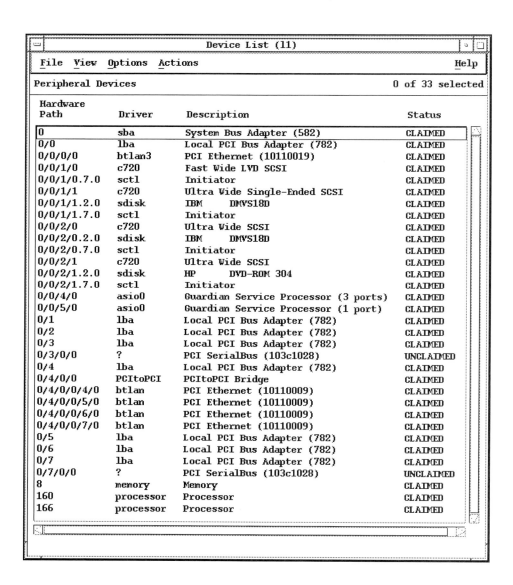

Figure 10-35 *Peripheral Devices* Window

The two *Action* menu picks here are *Zoom* and *Show Device Files*. Selecting *Zoom* produces a window with such information as hardware path, driver, description, and status. The devices files associated with the item you have highlighted will be shown if you select *Show Device Files*.

Disks and File Systems was covered earlier in this chapter.

Instruments may appear if your system supports HP-IB cards.

Printers and Plotters is covered later in this chapter.

Tape Drives

Tape Drives lists the tape drives connected to your system. You are shown the *Hardware Path*, *Driver*, and *Description* for each tape drive. You can add, remove, diagnose tape drives, list tape drive device files, and add new tape drive device files. Figure 10-36 shows a four-drive DLT unit attached to the system:

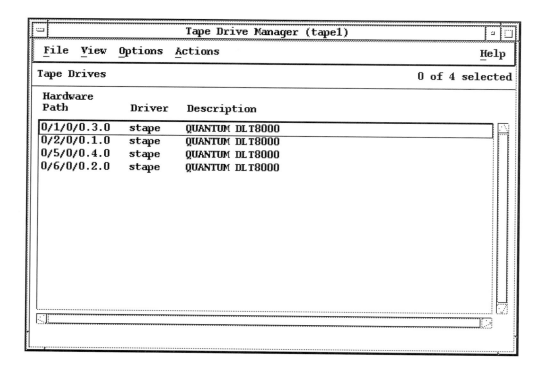

Figure 10-36 *Tape Drives* Window

Terminals and Modems

Your system's terminals and modems are listed for you when you enter this subarea. You can perform a variety of tasks from the *Actions* menu, including the following:

- *Add Terminal or Modem*

- *Remove Terminal or Modem Port*

- *Lock Terminal or Modem Port*

- *Unlock Terminal or Modem Port*

- *Modify Terminal Security Policies*

- *Modify Terminal Security Policies*

- *Modify Terminal Authorized Users*

- *Additional Information*

Uninterruptable Power Supplies

Your system's uninterruptable power supplies are listed for you when you enter this area, including the UPS type, device file of the UPS, hardware path, port number, and whether or not shutdown is enabled. The *Actions* you can select are: *Modify Global Configuration, Add, Zoom, Remove,* and *Modify.*

Printers and Plotters

Printers and Plotters is divided into two subareas: *HP Distributed Print Service* and *LP Spooler. HP Distributed Print Service* (HPDPS) is part of the Distributed Computing Environment (DCE). It is not covered in this book. *LP Spooler* is covered in this section; Figure 10-37 shows the hierarchy of *Printers and Plotters*:

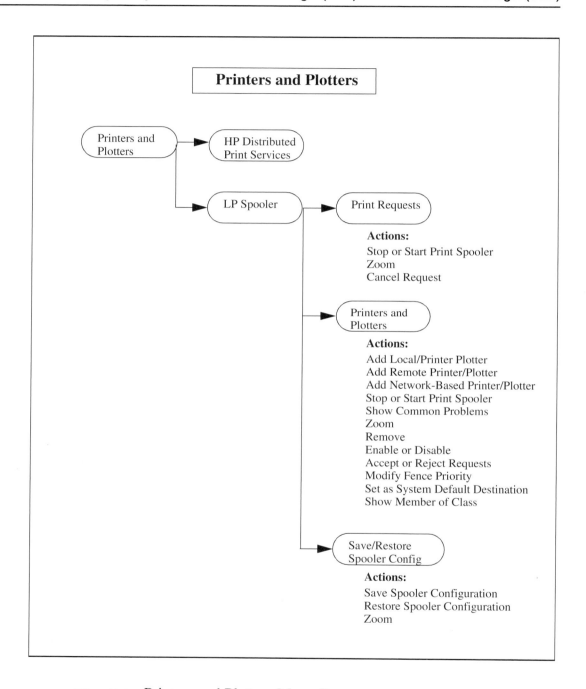

Figure 10-37   Printers and Plotters Menu Structure

Print Requests

Under *Print Requests,* you can manage the print spooler and specific print jobs. You can start or stop the print spooler and cancel print jobs. The following information on print requests is listed for you:

Request ID	An ID is associated with each print job. This is the Printer Name followed by a number.
Owner	The name of the user who requested the print job.
Priority	The priority of a print job is assigned when the job is submitted. The **-p** option of **lp** can be used to assign a priority to a job. Each print destination has a default priority that is assigned to jobs when **-p** is not used on the **lp** command.
File	The name of the file sent to the print queue.
Size	The size of the print job in bytes.

The *Actions* menu allows you to act on print jobs by cancelling them. In addition, the print spooler can be stopped and started.

Printers and Plotters

You can configure both local and remote printers in *Printers and Plotters*. When you select *Add Local Printer/Plotter* from the *Actions* menu and then the appropriate type of printer, a window is opened for you in which you can supply the specifics about the printer. Before this window is opened, however, you must specify whether the *type* of printer to be added is: parallel serial; HP-IB; non-standard device file; or a printer connected to a TSM terminal, as well as to which I/O card to add the printer. One huge advantage to adding the printer using SAM is that this process is entirely menu-driven, so you only have to select from among the information that is supplied.

The window appears to ask you for the following information:

Printer Name   You can pick any name for the printer. I usually like to use a name that is somewhat descriptive, such as *ljet5* for a LaserJet 5. The name is limited to 14 alphanumeric characters and underscores.

Printer Model/Interface

SAM supplies a list of all interface models for you when this window is opened. These models are located in the **/usr/lib/lp/model** directory. Each printer has an interface program that is used by the spooler to send a print job to the printer. When an interface model is selected, the model is copied to **/etc/lp/interface/**<*printername*>, where it becomes the printer's interface program. Models can be used without modification, or you can create customized interface programs.

Printer Class   You can define a group of printers to be in a class, which means that print requests won't go to a specific printer but instead they will go to the first available printer within the class. This is optional.

Default Request Priority

This defines the default priority level of all requests sent to this printer.

Default Destination

Users who do not specify a printer when requesting a print job will have the print request sent to the default printer.

man page

lpstat - 10

You could use SAM to view printers or you could use the **lpstat** command showing printers configured on a system as shown in the following example:

```
$ /usr/bin/lpstat -t
scheduler is running
system default destination: ljet5
members of class laser:
        ljet5
device for ljet5: /dev/c1t0d0_lp
ljet5 accepting requests since Nov 21 22:45
printer ljet5 is idle. enabled since Nov 21 22:45
        fence priority : 0
no entries
```

As with all the other tasks SAM helps you with, you can manage printers and plotters manually or you can use SAM. Not only does SAM make this easier for you, but I have also had nothing but good results having SAM do this for me. As you go through the SAM Log

man page

lpstat - 10

file, you will see a variety of **lp** commands that were issued. Some of the more common commands, including the **lpstat** command issued earlier, are listed in Table 10-1:

TABLE 10-1 **lp** Commands

COMMAND	DESCRIPTION
/usr/sbin/accept	Start accepting jobs to be queued
/usr/bin/cancel	Cancel a print job that is queued
/usr/bin/disable	Disable a device for printing
/usr/bin/enable	Enable a device for printing
/usr/sbin/lpfence	Set minimum priority for spooled file to be printed
/usr/bin/lp	Queue a job or jobs for printing
/usr/sbin/lpadmin	Configure the printing system with the options provided
/usr/sbin/lpmove	Move printing jobs from one device to another
/usr/sbin/lpsched	Start the **lp** scheduling daemon
/usr/sbin/lpshut	Stop the **lp** scheduling daemon
/usr/bin/lpstat	Show the status of printing based on the options provided
/usr/sbin/reject	Stop accepting jobs to be queued

Save/Restore Spooler Configuration

Occasionally, the spooler can get into an inconsistent state (usually something else has to go wrong with your system that ends up somehow changing or renaming some of the spooler configuration files). SAM keeps a saved version of the spooler's configuration each time it is used to make a change (only the most recent one is saved). This saved configuration can be restored by SAM to recover from the spooler having gotten into an inconsistent state. Your latest configuration is automatically saved by SAM, provided you used SAM to create the configuration, as opposed to issuing **lp** commands at the command line, and it can be restored with *Restore Spooler Configuration* from *Save/Restore Spooler Config.* This screen allows you to save your current spooler configuration or restore a previously saved spooler configuration information.

Process Management

Process Management is broken down into two areas that allow you to control and schedule processes. *Process Control* allows you to control an individual process by performing such tasks as viewing it, changing its *nice* priority, killing it, stopping it, or continuing it. You can also view and schedule **cron** jobs under *Scheduled Cron Jobs.* Figure 10-38 shows the menu hierarchy of *Process Management*:

man page

crontab-10

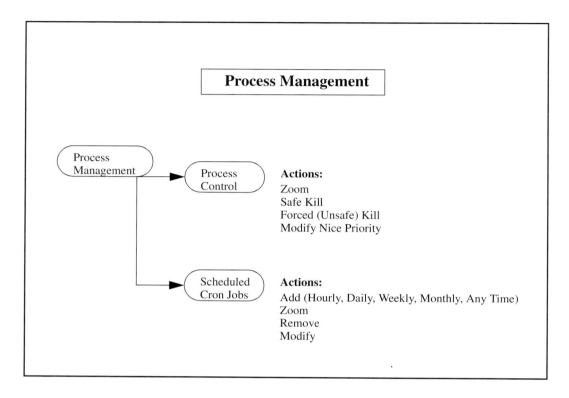

Figure 10-38 Process Management Menu Structure

Process Control

man page

ps - 11

When you pick *Process Control,* SAM lists the processes on your system and allows you to perform various actions. Using *Process Control* is a much easier way of controlling the processes on your system than executing commands such as **ps, nice,** etc. Figure 10-39 shows a partial listing of processes:

```
┌─────────────────────────────────────────────────────────────────────────┐
│ ⊐                           Process Management (13)                ▫ │□│ │
├─────────────────────────────────────────────────────────────────────────┤
│  File  List  View  Options  Actions                                Help  │
├─────────────────────────────────────────────────────────────────────────┤
│ Process Control                                        0 of 91 selected   │
│                                                                           │
│                      Nice                                                 │
│  User    Priority  Priority   Command                                     │
│ ┌───────────────────────────────────────────────────────────────────┐▲── │
│ │root       128       20     swapper                                  │▒  │
│ │root       168       20     init                                     │   │
│ │root       152       20       /usr/sbin/syncer                       │   │
│ │root       154       20       /usr/sbin/syslogd -D                   │   │
│ │root       155       20       /usr/sbin/ptydaemon                    │   │
│ │root       127       20       /usr/lbin/nktl_daemon 0 0 0 0 0 1 -2   │   │
│ │root       127       20       /usr/lbin/ntl_reader 0 1 1 1 1000 2 /var/adm/ne│
│ │root       127       20         /usr/sbin/netfmt -C -F -f /var/adm/nettl.LOGO│
│ │root       154       20       /usr/sbin/rpcbind                      │   │
│ │root       154       20       /usr/sbin/inetd                        │   │
│ │root       154       20       /usr/sbin/snmpdm                       │   │
│ │root       154       20       /usr/sbin/hp_unixagt                   │   │
│ │root       154       20       /usr/sbin/mib2agt                      │   │
│ │root       154       20       /usr/sbin/trapdestagt                  │   │
│ │root       154       20       /usr/lbin/cmsnmpd                      │   │
│ │root       154       20       /opt/dce/sbin/rpcd                     │   │
│ │root       152       20       /usr/dmi/bin/dmisp                     │   │
│ │root       152       20       /var/dmi/bin/hpuxci                    │   │
│ │root       152       20       /var/dmi/bin/sdci                      │   │
│ │root       152       20       /var/dmi/bin/swci                      │   │
│ │root       168       20       /opt/scr/lbin/scrdaemon                │   │
│ │root        64       20       /usr/sbin/rbootd                       │   │
│ │root       154       20       /usr/sbin/pwgrd                        │   │
│ │root       154       20       /usr/sbin/cron                         │   │
│ │root       154       20       /usr/sbin/envd                         │   │
│ │root       154       20       /opt/perf/bin/ttd                      │   │
│ │root       154       20       /opt/perf/bin/perflbd                  │   │
│ │root       154       20         /opt/perf/bin/rep_server -t SCOPE /var/opt/pe│
│ │root       154       20         /opt/perf/bin/agdbserver -t alarmgen /var/opt│
│ │root       154       20           /opt/perf/bin/alarmgen -svr 1811 -t alarmge│
│ │root       -16       20       /opt/perf/bin/midaemon                 │   │
│ │root       152       20       /opt/prm/bin/prm3d                     │   │
│ │root       127       20       /opt/perf/bin/scopeux                  │   │
│ │root       154       20       /usr/sbin/swagentd -r                  │   │
│ │root       154       20       /etc/opt/resmon/lbin/emsagent          │   │
│ │root       152       20       opcctla -start                        │   │
│ │root       152       20         opcmsga                              │   │
│ │root       152       20         opcacta                              │▒  │
│ └───────────────────────────────────────────────────────────────────┘▼── │
│ ┌──┬──────────────────────────────────────────────────────────────┬───┐ │
│ └──┴──────────────────────────────────────────────────────────────┴───┘ │
└─────────────────────────────────────────────────────────────────────────┘
```

Figure 10-39 Partial *Process Control* Listing.

There are the four columns of information listed for.

- *User* - The name of the user who owns the process.

- *Priority* - The priority of the process determines its scheduling by the CPU. The lower the number, the higher the priority. Unless you have modified these priorities, they will be default priorities. Changing the priority is done with the **nice** command, which will be covered shortly.

- *Nice Priority* - If you have a process that you wish to run at a lower or higher priority, you could change this value. The lower the value, the higher the CPU scheduling priority.

- *Command* - Lists the names of all the commands currently being run or executed on the system.

In addition to these four columns, there are several others you can specify to be included in the list by selecting *Columns* from the *View* menu. You can include such information as the *Process ID, Parent Process ID, Processor Utilization, Core Image Size*, and so on. Adding *Processor Utilization* as a column, for instance, shows me how much of the processor all processes are consuming, including SAM.

You can now select one of the processes and an *Actions* to perform.

When you select a process to kill and pick *Safe Kill* from the *Actions* menu, you will see a message that indicates the process number killed and that it may take a few minutes to kill it in order to terminate cleanly. If you select a process to kill and pick *Forced Kill* from the *Actions* menu, you don't get any feedback; SAM just kills the process and you move on.

man page

kill - 22

Chapter 5 covered the **kill** command. To save you the trouble of flipping ahead, I have included some of the information related to **kill** here. The **kill** command can be either **/usr/bin/kill** or **kill** which is part of the POSIX shell. The POSIX shell is the default shell for HP-UX 11i. The other shells provide their own **kill** commands as well. We use the phrase "kill a process" in the UNIX world all the time, I think, because it has a powerful connotation associated with it. What we are really saying is we want to terminate a process. This termination is done with a signal. The most common signal to send is "SIGKILL," which terminates the process. There are other signals you can send to the process, but SIGKILL is the most common. As an alternative to sending the signal, you could send the corresponding signal number. A list of signal numbers and corresponding signals is shown below:

Signal Number	Signal
0	SIGNULL
1	SIGHUP
2	SIGINT
3	SIGQUIT
9	SIGKILL
15	SIGTERM
24	SIGSTOP
25	SIGTSTP
26	SIGCONT

man page

kill - 22

I obtained this list of processes from the **kill** manual page.

To **kill** a process with a process ID of *234*, you would issue the following command:

```
$ kill -9 234
    |    |   |
    |    |   |> process id (PID)
    |    |> signal number
    |> kill command to terminate the process
```

The final selection from the *Actions* menu is to *Modify Nice Priority* of the process you have selected. If you were to read the manual page on **nice,** you would be very happy to see that you can modify this with SAM. Modifying the **nice** value in SAM simply requires you to select a process and specify its new **nice** value within the acceptable range.

Scheduling Cron Jobs

The *Scheduled Cron Jobs* menu selection lists all the **cron** jobs you have scheduled and allows you to *Add, Zoom, Remove,* and *Modify* **cron** jobs through the *Actions* menu. **cron** was described earlier in this chapter in "Backup and Recovery." I have included some of the **cron** background covered earlier to save you the trouble of flipping back.

The **crontab** file is used to schedule jobs that are automatically executed by **cron**. **crontab** files are in the **/var/spool/cron/crontabs** directory. **cron** is a program that runs other programs at the specified time. **cron** reads files that specify the operation to be performed and the date and time it is to be performed.

The format of entries in the **crontab** file are as follows:

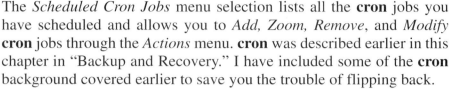

minute - the minute of the hour, from 0-59

hour - the hour of the day, from 0-23

monthday - the day of the month, from 1-31

month - the month of the year, from 1-12

weekday - the day of the week, from 0 (Sunday) - 6 (Saturday)

user name - the user who will run the command if necessary

command - specifies the command line or script file to run

You have many options in the **crontab** file for specifying the *minute, hour, monthday, month,* and *weekday* to perform a task. You could list one entry in a field and then a space, several entries in any field separated by a comma, two entries separated by a dash indicating a range, or an asterisk, which corresponds to all possible entries for the field.

To list the contents of a **crontab** file, you would issue the **crontab -l** command.

Routine Tasks

The following subareas exist under *Routine Tasks* in SAM:

- Backup and Recovery
- Find and Remove Unused Filesets
- Selective File Removal
- System Log Files
- System Shutdown

The hierarchy of *Routine Tasks* is shown in Figure 10-40. Please note that *Backup and Recovery* is identical to the SAM top-level *Backup and Recovery* area discussed earlier in this chapter.

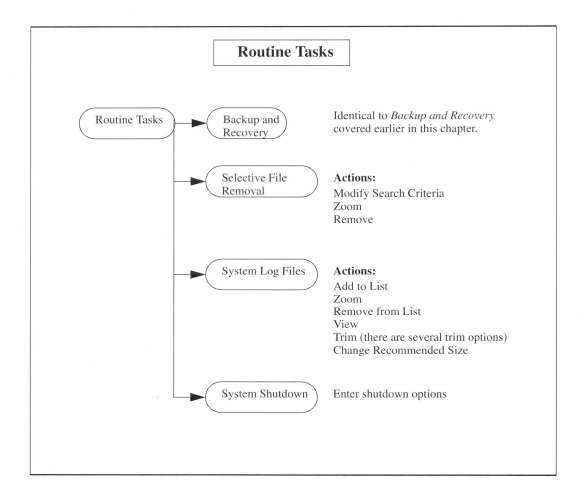

Figure 10-40   Routine Tasks Menu Structure

Backup and Recovery

This is identical to the *Backup and Recovery* area covered earlier in this chapter.

Selective File Removal

Selective File Removal allows you to search for files to remove. You can specify a variety of criteria for selecting files to remove including the following:

Type of file	There are three different file types you can search for: *Large Files, Unowned Files*, and *Core Files*. A pop-up menu allows you to select which of these to search for. With *Large Files,* you are searching for files of a minimum size that haven't been modified in the specified time. *Unowned Files* are files owned by someone other than a valid system user. *Core Files* contain a core image of a terminated process when the process was terminated under certain conditions. Core files are usually related to a problem with a process and contain such information as data, stack, etc.
Mount Points	Specify whether or not you want to search across non-NFS mount points. If you select *Yes,* this means that the search will include mount points on your system, but not extend to NFS mount points. I chose not to include other mount points in the example.
Beginning Path	Your search can begin at any point in the system hierarchy. You can specify the start point of the search in this field. If you want to search only the **/home** directory for files, then change this entry to **/home** and you will

search only that directory, as I did in the example.

Minimum Size   Specify the smallest size file in bytes that you want to search for. Files smaller than this size will not be reported as part of the search. The minimum size in the example is 500,000 bytes.

Last Modification

If you select *Large Files*, you can make an entry in this field. You enter the minimum number of days since the file was last modified, and files that have been modified within that time period will be excluded from the search. This is *30* days in the example.

Figure 10-41 shows an example of specifying which files to search for:

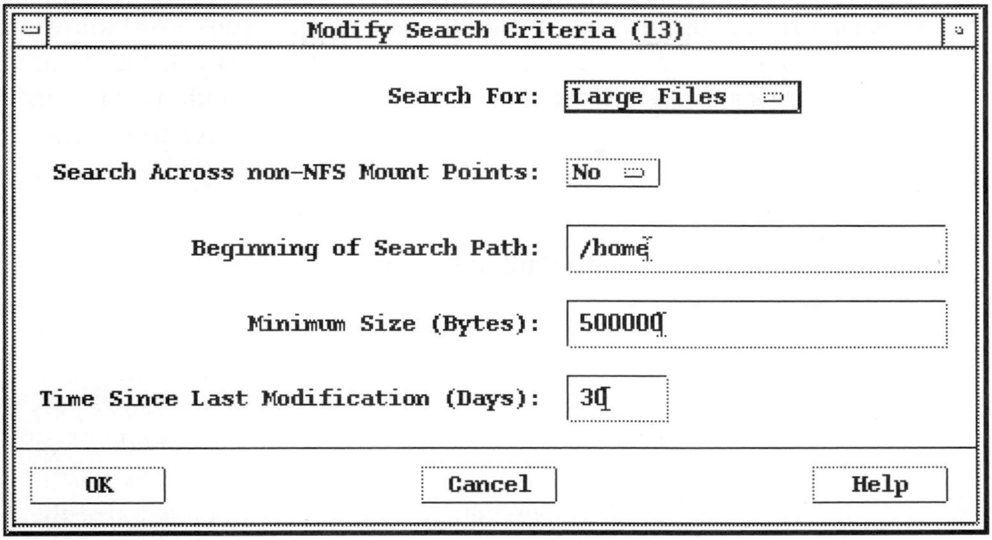

Figure 10-41 Searching for Files to Remove

The way to approach removing files is to start with an exceptionally large file size and work your way down in size. It may be that you have a few "unexpected" large files on your system that you can remove and ignore the smaller files.

System Log Files

System Log Files is used to manage the size of your system log files. Log files are generated by HP-UX for a variety of reasons, including backup, shutdown, **cron**, etc. Your applications may very well be generating log files as well. Some of these log files can grow in size indefinitely, creating a potential catastrophe on your system by growing and crashing your system. You can be proactive and manage these log files in this subarea.

SAM is aware of many of the log files generated by HP-UX. When you enter the *System Log Files* subarea, information related to these log files is listed. You can add to the list of log files SAM knows about and have a complete list of log files presented to you each time you enter this subarea. SAM lists the following information related to log files each time you enter this subarea. (You may have to increase the size of the window to see all this information:)

File Name   The full path name of the log file.

Percent Full   SAM has what it thinks should be the maximum size of a log file. You can change this size by selecting *Change Recommended Size* from the *Actions* menu. The *Percent Full* is the percentage of the recommended size the log file consumes.

Current Size   The size of the file in bytes is listed for you. You may want to take a look at this. The current size of a log file may be much bigger than you would like. You could then change the recommended size and quickly see which files are greater than 100 percent. The converse may also be true. You may think the recommended size for a log file is far too small and change the recommended size to a larger value. In either case, you would like to quickly see which files are much bigger than recommended.

Recommended Size

                   This is what you define as the recommended size of the file. Check to make sure that you agree with this value.

Present on System

> *Yes* if this file is indeed present on your system; *No* if it is not present on your system. If a file is not present on your system and it simply does not apply to you, then you can select *Remove from List* from the *Actions* menu. For example, you may not be running UUCP and therefore want to remove all the UUCP related log files.

File Type

> The only file types listed are *ASCII* and *Non-ASCII*. I found it interesting that **/var/sam/log/samlog** was not one of the log files listed. This is not an ASCII file and must be viewed through *View SAM Log* from the *Actions* menu, but it is indeed a log file that I thought would appear in the list.

You can trim a log file using the *Trim* command from the *Actions* menu. You then have several options for trimming the file having to do with the size of the file when the trim is complete, and so on.

System Shutdown

SAM offers you the following three ways to shut down your system:

- *Halt the System*
- *Reboot (Restart) the System*
- *Go to Single-User State*

In addition, you can specify the number of minutes before shutdown occurs.

Run SAM on Remote Systems

I think SAM is great. If it works well on one system, then you, as the system administrator, may as well use it on other systems from a central point of control. *Run SAM on Remote Systems* allows you to set up the system on which you will run SAM remotely from a central point of control.

You can specify any number of remote systems to be controlled by a central system. With the *Actions* menu, you can:

Add System	A window opens up in which you can specify the name of the remote system you wish to administer locally.
Run SAM	You can select the remote system on which you want to run SAM.
Remove System(s)	Remote systems can be removed from the list of systems on which you will run SAM remotely.

Software Management

man page
sw - 2

Software Management under SAM uses Software Distributor-HP-UX (I'll call this Software Distributor), which was covered in detail in Chapter 2. SAM is giving you an interface to Software Distributor that allows you to perform software management by selecting the task you want to perform. In the end, all of the same Software Distributor commands are run, so I won't cover those again in this section. The following subareas exist under *Software Management* in SAM:

- Copy Software to Depot
- Install Software to Local Host
- List Software
- Remove Software

The hierarchy of *Software Management* is shown in Figure 10-42:

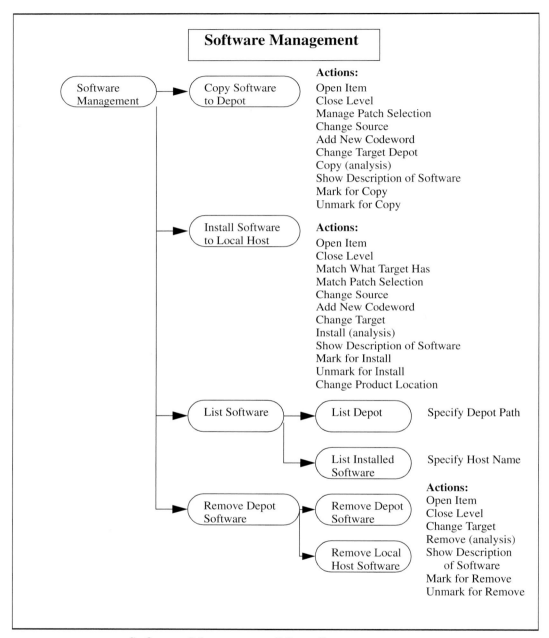

Figure 10-42 Software Management Menu Structure

As you can see from this diagram, when you select a task you want to perform SAM is selecting the Software Distributor command to run. Chapter 2 covers many of these commands.

Time

The *Time* area of SAM allows you to configure Network Time Protocol, or NTP, and set the system clock. NTP is a service that allows you to synchronize the time on all your systems utilizing a Universal Coordinated Time server. I won't cover this area of SAM other than to say that NTP can be a little tricky to configure, so using SAM for this greatly simplifies NTP.

NFS Diskless Concepts

Rather than cover NFS Diskless as an area to manage, I'm going to deviate from the format found throughout this chapter and instead provide a brief description of NFS Diskless.

This topic was introduced with HP-UX 10.x. Diskless nodes were implemented with Distributed HP-UX (DUX) in HP-UX 9.x and earlier releases. Distributed HP-UX was first introduced in HP-UX 6.0 in 1986 and was successfully used in many HP installations. The new implementation of diskless nodes as of HP-UX 10.x is NFS Diskless. It has many desirable features, including the following:

- NFS Diskless is the current de facto standard.

- It is not a proprietary solution.

- High-end diskless servers and clients can be symmetric multi-processing systems.

- Many file system types and features are available, such as UNIX File System, Journaled File System, Logical Volume Manager, disk mirroring, etc.

- The System V Release 4 file system layout described through-out this book is implemented. This file system layout is condu-cive to extensive file sharing, which is used in NFS Diskless.

- Read-only NFS mounts, such as **/usr** and **/opt/**<*application*> are supported.

- Distributed HP-UX functionality, such as context-dependent files, has been removed.

- Servers can be both Series 700 and Series 800 units.

- The physical link doesn't matter, so servers can use many interfaces such as IEEE 802.3 and FDDI. A server can also assign some diskless systems to one network card, and other systems to other network cards.

- Diskless systems can boot across a gateway, thereby allowing subnets to be used.

- Booting is implemented with standard Boot Protocol (BOOTP) and Trivial File Transfer Protocol (TFTP) proto-cols.

- Clients can swap to a local disk or swap using NFS to a remote disk.

Many additional features of NFS Diskless exist; however, since our focus is on management, let's take a closer look at this. Using SAM, all tasks related to NFS Diskless administration can be per-formed. This means you have a single point of administration for the cluster. You have cluster-wide resources, such as printers and file sys-tems, that can be managed from any node in the cluster. You can defer some operations until a later point in time if a node is unreachable. And, of course, you can add and delete clients in SAM.

Using SAM, you get a single point of administration for several NFS Diskless systems. This means that performing an operation in SAM affects all systems in the cluster. The single point of administra-tion areas in SAM include:

- Printers/Plotters

- File Systems

- Users/Groups

- Home Directories

- Electronic Mail

- Backups

Although a great deal could be covered on NFS Diskless and the many improvements in this area over Distributed HP-UX, the key point from an administrative perspective is that SAM provides a central point of administration for NFS Diskless administration. All tasks related to NFS Diskless administration can be performed through SAM.

ServiceControl Manager (SCM) Overview

man page

find - 20

SCM allows you to replicate tasks over multiple systems. Tasks that have traditionally been performed individually on many systems can now be performed across multiple systems in a cluster managed by SCM.

You can take a command or tool that runs on an individual system, such as the **find** or **df** command, dispatch it to run on multiple systems, and collect the results for review in SCM.

More advanced tools that were designed to run on multiple system, such as Ignite-UX, can also be run in the same manner using SCM.

Specific tasks can be assigned to specific individuals with SCM, thus creating a role-based environment. This obviates the need for root access to systems because specific management activities are assigned to specific users on specific nodes. These user roles provide great flexibility in defining the tasks individual users can perform.

You can define the systems of which an SCM cluster is composed. The Central Management Server (CMS) in an SCM environment is the focal point in which management takes place. Agents on the managed nodes communicate with CMS to perform management functions.

SCM is available on the applications media of 11i and loaded with Software Distributor like any other application.

After having loaded SCM from the Applications CD-ROM for HP-UX 11i, we'll run the program to set up SCM called **mxsetup**. Most of the programs related to SCM begin with "*mx*" and the application itself is loaded in **/opt/mx**, and the repository of SCM data is kept in **/var/opt/mx**.

```
# mxsetup

Please enter the ServiceControl repository password

Please re-enter the ServiceControl repository password

Please enter a name for your Managed Cluster
```

```
(default name: 'HP Managed Cluster'): servicecluster

Please enter the login name of the initial ServiceControl trusted user
martyp

Would you like mxsetup to backup the ServiceControl repository after
it has initially configured it?(Y/N) [Y]:

Please enter the file path where mxsetup will store the backup data
(default path: /var/opt/mx/data/scm.backup) :

  ----------------------------------------------------------------
  You have entered,

  ServiceControl Managed Cluster Name  : servicecluster
  Initial ServiceControl trusted user  : martyp
  Backup the ServiceControl repository : y
  Backup file path                     : /var/opt/mx/data/scm.backup
  ----------------------------------------------------------------
  Would you like to continue? (Y/N) [Y] :

Please enter the file path where mxsetup will store the backup data
(default path: /var/opt/mx/data/scm.backup) :

  ----------------------------------------------------------------
  You have entered,

  ServiceControl Managed Cluster Name  : servicecluster
  Initial ServiceControl trusted user  : martyp
  Backup the ServiceControl repository : y
  Backup file path                     : /var/opt/mx/data/scm.backup
  ----------------------------------------------------------------
  Would you like to continue? (Y/N) [Y] :

  ================================================================
  ServiceControl Manager configuration has '8' Tasks and
  it may take a while to do the configuration.

  Please wait while mxsetup configures the ServiceControl Manager...
  ================================================================

1: Creating Agent Depots..

2: Naming the ServiceControl Managed Cluster
   as  'servicecluster'........................ OK

3: Configuring the ServiceControl daemons.......... OK

4: Starting the ServiceControl daemons............. OK

5: Installing the AgentConfig..................... OK

6: Initializing ServiceControl................... OK

7: Adding Tools ................................. OK

8: Backing up the Repository..................... OK
```

```
The ServiceControl Manager was successfully configured
Please see /var/opt/mx/logs/scmgr-setup.log for details.

To start the ServiceControl Manager:
    - set DISPLAY environment variable
    - and enter '/opt/mx/bin/scmgr'

#
```

After the setup is complete you can issue a **ps** to view processes that begin with an *mx* to see the daemons started in order to run SCM.

With SCM having been set up we can now run the graphical interface to it with **/opt/mx/bin/scmgr** as shown in Figure 10-43:

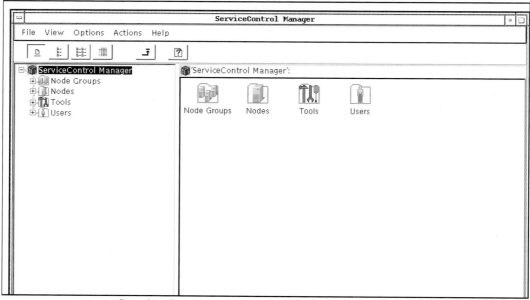

Figure 10-43   ServiceControl Manager scmgr Screen

The four icons shown are launch points for the tasks you'll perform in SCM as described below:

1. *Node Groups* provides a view of the managed nodes as groups. Once the node groups are displayed a user can perform a task on a selected group of nodes.

2. *Nodes View* provides a view of all nodes that are managed. This is the point from which you can perform a variety of node-related tasks such as adding and removing nodes.

3. *Tools View* provides a view of SCM tools.

4. *Users View* provides a view of HP-UX users who are part of SCM. A trusted user can perform a variety of user-related tasks from this view, such as adding or removing users.

If all of your systems are 11i, you won't have to load any software on clients in order to manage them from the central SCM system. If you have 11.0 or 10.20 systems, additional software is required on client systems. You can obtain the *Planning, Installing, Configuring and Updating ServiceControl Manager* document from *docs.hp.com* provides procedures for installing all SCM-related software.

In order to add managed nodes, you would go to the *Actions - New - Node...* menu pick and then select the nodes you wish to add.

Also under this menu pick is a tab area for *Users and Roles*. In Figure 10-44, we've added a user *martyp* with an *operator* role:

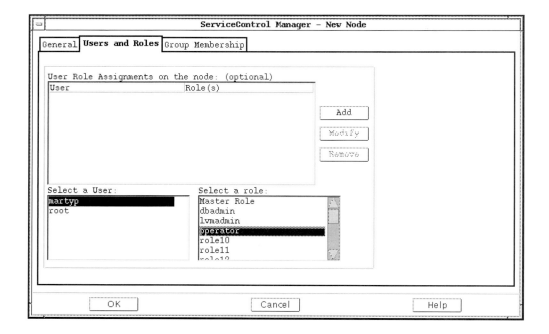

Figure 10-44   Selecting an *operator* Role for a User on a New Node

After adding nodes and grouping them, and adding users and defining their roles, you have set up the SCM management environment. You can use the pre-defined tools for users and add your own custom tools as well.

Figure 10-45 shows some of the software management tools that are predefined in SCM:

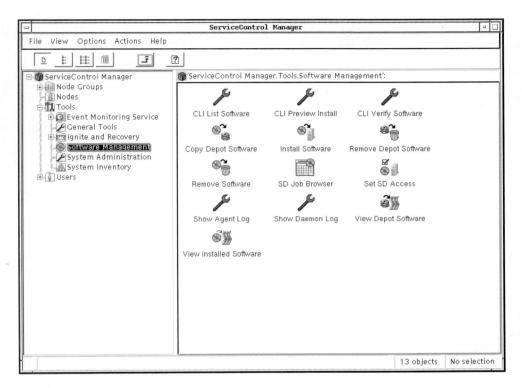

Figure 10-45 SCM *Software Management* Tools

The tools shown in Figure 10-45 are the default tools for software management. You can define and add your own tools as well. Note the categories of tools shown at the left-hand side of the figure.

From the graphical environment shown in the previous figure you can launch into SCM-related work. You can also work with SCM from the command line. Table 10-2 lists some of the more commonly used SCM commands you can issue at the command line:

TABLE 10-2   Commonly Used SCM Commands

COMMAND	DESCRIPTION
mxauth	Add, remove, or list authorizations in SCM.
mxexec	Run an SCM tool.
mxngroup	Add, modify, remove, or list node groups in SCM.
mxnode	Add, remove, or list nodes in SCM.
mxrepositoryrestore	Restore the SCM repository.
mxrepositorysave	Backup the SCM repository.
mxrole	List or modify SCM roles.
mxsetup	Set up or uninstall the Central Management Server of an SCM managed cluster.
mxtool	Add, modify, remove, or list tools in SCM.
mxuser	Add, modify, remove, or list users in SCM.

To view SCM roles, you would issue the following command:

```
# mxrole -lt

NAME           ENABLED?   DESCRIPTION
role16         true       For use by ServiceControl administrators
role15         true       For use by ServiceControl administrators
role14         true       For use by ServiceControl administrators
role13         true       For use by ServiceControl administrators
role12         true       For use by ServiceControl administrators
role11         true       For use by ServiceControl administrators
role10         true       For use by ServiceControl administrators
role9          true       For use by ServiceControl administrators
role8          true       For use by ServiceControl administrators
role7          true       For use by ServiceControl administrators
role6          true       For use by ServiceControl administrators
lvmadmin       true       A role for LVM Administrators
operator       true       A read-only role for operators
webadmin       true       A role for WEB Server Administrators
dbadmin        true       A role for Database Administrators
Master Role    true       The ServiceControl Master Role
#
```

This output shows the default roles that have been set up for SCM and a brief description of each. Since you can perform most any function you want in the graphical version of SCM, I don't expect you'll be running many functions at the command line; however, it's good to know these commands exist.

Manual Pages for Commands Used in Chapter 10

The following section contains copies of the manual pages for commands used in Chapter 10. This makes a quick reference for you to use when issuing commands commonly used during your system administration day.

crontab

crontab - Schedule jobs that are executed automatically on a regular basis.

man page

crontab-10

NAME
     crontab - user job file scheduler

SYNOPSIS

     crontab [file]

     crontab -e

     crontab -l

     crontab -r

DESCRIPTION
     The crontab command manages a crontab file for the user. You can use
     a crontab file to schedule jobs that are executed automatically by
     cron (see cron(1M)) on a regular basis. The command has four forms:

          crontab [file]   Create or replace your crontab file by copying
                            the specified file, or standard input if file
                            is omitted or - is specified as file , into the
                            crontab directory, /var/spool/cron/crontabs.
                            The name of your crontab file in the crontab
                            directory is the same as your effective user
                            name.

          crontab -e   Edit a copy of your crontab file, or create an
                            empty file to edit if the crontab file does not
                            exist. When editing is complete, the file will
                            be copied into the crontab directory as your
                            crontab file.

          crontab -l   List your crontab file.

          crontab -r   Remove your crontab file from the crontab
                            directory.

     The entries in a crontab file are lines of six fields each. The
     fields are separated by spaces or tabs. The lines have the following
     format:

          minute hour monthday month weekday command

     The first five are integer patterns that specify when the sixth field,
     command, should be executed. They can have the following ranges of
     values:

          minute   The minute of the hour, 0-59

          hour   The hour of the day, 0-23

```
monthday          The day of the month, 1-31

month             The month of the year, 1-12

weekday           The day of the week, 0-6, 0=Sunday
```

Each pattern can be either an asterisk (*), meaning all legal values, or a list of elements separated by commas. An element is either a number in the ranges shown above, or two numbers in the range separated by a hyphen (meaning an inclusive range). Note that the specification of days can be made in two fields: monthday and weekday. If both are specified in an entry, they are cumulative. For example,

```
0    0    1,15    *    1    command
```

runs command at midnight on the first and fifteenth of each month, as well as every Monday. To specify days in only one field, set the other field to asterisk (*). For example,

```
0    0    *    *    1    command
```

runs command only on Mondays.

The sixth field, command (the balance of a line including blanks in a crontab file), is a string that is executed by the shell at the specified times. A percent character (%) in this field (unless escaped by a backslash (\)) is translated to a newline character, dividing the field into "lines". Only the first "line" (up to a % or end-of-line) of the command field is executed by the shell. Any other "lines" are made available to the command as standard input.

Blank lines and those whose first non-blank character is # will be ignored.

cron invokes the command from the user's HOME directory with the POSIX shell, (/usr/bin/sh). It runs in the c queue (see queuedefs(4)).

cron supplies a default environment for every shell, defining:

```
HOME=user's-home-directory
LOGNAME=user's-login-id
PATH=/usr/bin:/usr/sbin:.
SHELL=/usr/bin/sh
```

Users who desire to have their .profile executed must explicitly do so in the crontab entry or in a script called by the entry.

You can execute crontab if your name appears in the file /var/adm/cron/cron.allow. If that file does not exist, you can use crontab if your name does not appear in the file /var/adm/cron/cron.deny. If only cron.deny exists and is empty, all users can use crontab. If neither file exists, only the root user can use crontab. The allow/deny files consist of one user name per line.

EXTERNAL INFLUENCES
  Environment Variables
    LC_CTYPE determines the interpretation of text within file as single- and/or multi-byte characters.

    LC_MESSAGES determines the language in which messages are displayed.

    If LC_CTYPE or LC_MESSAGES is not specified in the environment or is set to the empty string, the value of LANG is used as a default for each unspecified or empty variable. If LANG is not specified or is set to the empty string, a default of "C" (see lang(5)) is used instead of LANG.

If any internationalization variable contains an invalid setting, crontab behaves as if all internationalization variables are set to "C". See environ(5). EDITOR determines the editor to be invoked when -e option is specified. The default editor is vi.

International Code Set Support
Single-byte and multi-byte character code sets are supported.

WARNINGS
Be sure to redirect the standard output and standard error from commands. If this is not done, any generated standard output or standard error is mailed to the user.

FILES
/var/adm/cron	Main cron directory
/var/adm/cron/cron.allow	List of allowed users
/var/adm/cron/cron.deny	List of denied users
/var/adm/cron/log	Accounting information
/var/spool/cron/crontabs	Directory containing the crontab files

SEE ALSO
sh(1), cron(1M), queuedefs(4).

STANDARDS CONFORMANCE
crontab: SVID2, SVID3, XPG2, XPG3, XPG4

lpstat

man page

lpstat - 10

lpstat - List the current status of the line printer system.

```
lpstat(1)                                                          lpstat(1)

NAME
     lpstat - report line printer status information

SYNOPSIS

     lpstat [-drst] [-a[list]] [-c[list]] [-o[list]] [-p[list]] [-u[list]]
     [-v[list]] [ID...]

DESCRIPTION
     The lpstat utility writes to standard output information about the
     current status of the line printer system.

     If no arguments are given, lpstat writes the status of all requests
     made to lp by the user that are still in the output queue.

OPTIONS
     The lpstat utility supports the XBD specification, Section 10.2,
     Utility Syntax Guidelines, except the option-arguments are optional
     and cannot be presented as separate arguments.

     Some of the options below can be followed by an optional list that can
     be in one of two forms: a list of items separated from one another by
     a comma, or a quoted list of items separated from one another by a
     comma or one or more blank  characters, or combinations of both. See
     EXAMPLES.

     The omission of a list following such options causes all information
     relevant to the option to be written to standard output; for example:

         lpstat -o

     writes the status of all output requests that are still in the output
     queue.

         -a[list]     Write the acceptance status of destinations for
                      output requests.  The list argument is a list of
                      intermixed printer names and class names.

         -c[list]     Write the class names and their members. The list
                      argument is a list of class names.

         -d           Write the system default destination for output
                      requests.

         -o[list]     Write the status of output requests. The list
                      argument is a list of intermixed printer names, class
                      names and request IDs.

         -p[list]     Write the status of printers. The list argument is a
                      list of printer names.
```

-r	Write the status of the line printer request scheduler.
-s	Write a status summary, including the status of the line printer scheduler, the system default destination, a list of class names and their members and a list of printers and their associated devices.
-t	Write all status information.
-u[list]	Write the status of output requests for users. The list argument is a list of login names.
-v[list]	Write the names of printers and the pathnames of the devices associated with them. The list argument is a list of printer names.

OPERANDS

The following operand is supported:

ID	A request ID, as returned by lp.

STDIN

Not used.

INPUT FILES

None.

ENVIRONMENT VARIABLES

The following environment variables affect the execution of lpstat:

LANG	Provide a default value for the internationalisation variables that are unset or null. If LANG is unset or null, the corresponding value from the implementation-specific default locale will be used. If any of the internationalisation variables contains an invalid setting, the utility will behave as if none of the variables had been defined.
LC_ALL	If set to a non-empty string value, override the values of all the other internationalisation variables.
LC_CTYPE	Determine the locale for the interpretation of sequences of bytes of text data as characters (for example, single- as opposed to multi-byte characters in arguments).
LC_MESSAGES	Determine the locale that should be used to affect the format and contents of diagnostic messages written to standard error, and informative messages written to standard output.
LC_TIME	Determine the format of date and time strings output when displaying line printer status information with the -a, -o, -p, -t, or -u options.
NLSPATH	Determine the location of message catalogues for the processing of

LC_MESSAGES.

TZ   Determine the timezone used with date
                                  and time strings.

ASYNCHRONOUS EVENTS
     Default.

STDOUT
     The standard output is a text file containing the information
     described in OPTIONS, in an unspecified format.

STDERR
     Used only for diagnostic messages.

OUTPUT FILES
     None.

EXTENDED DESCRIPTION
     None.

EXIT STATUS
     The following exit values are returned:

     0   Successful completion.

     >0   An error occurred.

CONSEQUENCES OF ERRORS
     Default.

APPLICATION USAGE
     The lpstat utility cannot reliably determine the status of print
     requests in all conceivable circumstances. When the printer is under
     the control of another operating system or resides on a remote system
     across a network, it need not be possible to determine the status of
     the print job after it has left the control of the local operating
     system. Even on local printers, spooling hardware in the printer may
     make it appear that the print job has been completed long before the
     final page is printed.

EXAMPLES

     1.   Obtain the status of two printers, the pathnames of two
          printers, a list of all class names and the status of the
          request named HiPri-33:

          lpstat -plaser1,laser4 -v"laser2 laser3" -c HiPri-33

     2.   Obtain user print job status using the obsolescent mixed
          blank and comma form:

          lpstat -u"ddg,gmv, maw"

FUTURE DIRECTIONS
     A version of lpstat that fully supports the XBD specification, Section
     10.2, Utility Syntax Guidelines may be introduced in a future issue.

SEE ALSO
     cancel, lp.

CHANGE HISTORY
     First released in Issue 2.

Issue 3
   The operation of this utility in an 8-bit transparent manner has been
   noted.

   The operation of this utility in an internationalised environment has
   been described.

Issue 4
   Format reorganised.

   Exceptions to Utility Syntax Guidelines conformance noted.

   Internationalised environment variable support mandated.

STANDARDS CONFORMANCE
   lpstat: SVID2, SVID3, XPG2, XPG3, XPG4

lpstat(1)   lpstat(1)

HP-UX EXTENSIONS

DESCRIPTION
   Any arguments that are not options are assumed to be request ids (as
   returned by lp). lpstat prints the status of such requests. options
   can appear in any order and can be repeated and intermixed with other
   arguments.

       -i   Inhibit the reporting of remote status.

       -o[list]   Also see the -i option.

       -t   Print all status information. Same as specifying -r,
                   -s, -a, -p, -o. See the -i option.

   Security Restriction
   Only users who have the lp subsystem authorization or the printqueue
   secondary subsystem authorization can view the entire queue.
   Unauthorized users can view only their own jobs whose sensitivity
   levels are dominated by the user's current sensitivity level.

   The allowmacaccess privilege allows viewing jobs at higher sensitivity
   levels.

EXAMPLES
   Check whether your job is queued:

       lpstat

   Check the relative position of a queued job:

       lpstat -t

   Verify that the job scheduler is running:

       lpstat -r

```
FILES
      /var/spool/lp/*
      /var/adm/lp/*
      /etc/lp/*
      /usr/lib/lp/*




SEE ALSO
      enable(1), lp(1), rlpstat(1M).

STANDARDS CONFORMANCE
      lpstat: SVID2, SVID3, XPG2, XPG3, XPG4
```

sam

sam - Start the menu-driven System Administration Manager (SAM).

man page

sam - 10

NAME
     sam - system administration manager

SYNOPSIS

     /usr/sbin/sam [-display display] [-f login] [-r]

DESCRIPTION
     The sam command starts a menu-driven System Administration Manager
     program (SAM) that makes it easy to perform system administration
     tasks with only limited, specialized knowledge of the HP-UX operating
     system. SAM discovers most aspects of a system's configuration
     through automated inquiries and tests. Help menus describe how to use
     SAM and perform the various management tasks. Context-sensitive help
     on the currently highlighted field is always available by pressing the
     F1 function key. Status messages and a log file monitor keep the user
     informed of what SAM is doing.

  Running SAM
     SAM has been tuned to run in the Motif environment, but it can be run
     on text terminals as well. To run SAM in the Motif environment, be
     sure that Motif has been installed on your system, and that the
     DISPLAY environment variable is set to the system name on which the
     SAM screens should be displayed (or use the -display command line
     option).

     Generally, SAM requires superuser (user root) privileges to execute
     successfully. However, SAM can be configured (through the use of
     "Restricted SAM"; see below) to allow subsets of its capabilities to
     be used by non-root users. When Restricted SAM is used, non-root
     users are promoted to root when necessary to enable them to execute
     successfully.

  Options
     sam recognizes the following options.

          -display display   Set the DISPLAY value for the duration of the
                                SAM session.

          -f login   Execute SAM with the privileges associated
                                with the specified login. When used in
                                conjunction with -r, the Restricted SAM
                                Builder is invoked and initialized with the
                                privileges associated with the specified
                                login. You must be a superuser to use this
                                option. See "Restricted SAM" below for more
                                information.

          -r   Invoke the Restricted SAM Builder. This
                                enables the system administrator to provide
                                limited nonsuperuser access to SAM
                                functionality. You must be a superuser to

use this option. See "Restricted SAM" below
for more information.

SAM Functional Areas
SAM performs system administration tasks in the following areas:

Auditing and Security (Trusted Systems)

- Set global system security policies

    - Maximum account inactivity period
    - Password generation policies
    - Null password usage and use of password restriction rules

    - Password aging
    - Maximum unsuccessful login attempts
    - Single-user boot authorization
    - Terminal security policies

- Turn the Auditing system on or off

- Set the parameters for the Audit Logs and Size Monitor

- View all or selected parts of the audit logs

- Modify (or view) which users, events, and/or system calls get
  audited

- Convert your system to a Trusted System

- Convert your system to a non-Trusted System

Backup and Recovery

- Interactively back up files to a valid backup device
  (cartridge tape, cartridge tape autochanger, magnetic tape,
  DAT, magneto-optical disk, or magneto-optical disk
  autochanger). The SAM interface is suspended so that you can
  read and/or respond to the interactive messages produced by
  fbackup (see fbackup(1M)).

- Recover files online from a valid backup device. The SAM
  interface is suspended so that you can read/respond to the
  interactive messages produced by frecover (see frecover(1M)).

- Add to, delete from, or view the automated backup schedule.

- Obtain a list of files from a backup tape.

- View various backup and recovery log files.

Disk and File Systems Management

- Add, configure, or unconfigure disk devices. This includes
  hard drives, floppy drives, CD-ROMs, magneto-optical devices,
  and disk arrays.

- Add, modify, or remove local file systems, or convert them to
  long file names.

- Configure HFS or VxFS file systems.

- Remote (NFS) file systems configuration, including:

- Add, modify, or remove remote (NFS) file systems.

- Allow or disallow access by remote systems to local file systems.

- Modify RPC (Remote Procedure Call) services' security.

- Add, remove, or modify device or file system swap.

- Change the primary swap device.

- Add, modify, or remove dump devices.

- Examine, create, extend, or reduce a volume-group pool of disks.

- Create, extend or change number of mirrored copies of a logical volume and associated file system.

- Remove a logical volume or increase its size.

- Split or merge mirrored copies of a logical volume.

- Share or unshare volume groups (only on ServiceGuard clusters running MC/LockManager distributed lock-manager software).

Diskless Cluster Configuration

- Add or remove cluster clients. You can customize the tasks of adding and removing cluster clients by specifying steps to be performed before and/or after SAM does its processing for the task. The Task Customization action leads you through this capability. See "Customizing SAM Tasks" below for more information.

Kernel and Device Configuration

- Change the configuration for I/O device and pseudo drivers.

- Modify operating system parameters.

- Modify dump device configuration in the kernel.

- Minimize kernel and system configuration to reduce memory usage (Series 700 only).

- Add or remove optional subsystems such as NFS, LAN, NS, CD-ROM, etc.

- Generate a new kernel.

Networks/Communications

- Configure one or more LAN cards.

- Configure ARPA services.

- Configure the Network File System (NFS).

- Configure X.25 card or cards and PAD (Packet Assembler/Disassembler) services (if X.25 has been purchased).

Peripheral Devices Management

- Administer the LP spooler or Distributed Print Services and associated printers and plotters (see "Printer and Plotter Management" below).

- Add, modify, or remove the configuration of disk devices.

- Add or remove terminals and modems.

- Configure terminal security policies (Trusted Systems only).

- Lock and unlock terminals (Trusted Systems only).

- Add or remove tape drives.

- Add or remove hardware interface cards and HP-IB instruments.

- View current configuration of peripherals and disk space information.

Printer and Plotter Management
SAM supports two methods for managing printers and plotters:

LP Spooler

- Add and remove local, remote, and networked printers and plotters to/from the LP spooler.

- Enable and disable printers and plotters from printing requests accepted by the LP spooler.

- Accept and reject requests for printers, plotters, and print classes.

- Modify the fence priority of printers and plotters.

- Set the system default print destination.

- Start and stop the LP scheduler.

HP Distributed Print Service (HPDPS)

- Add and remove physical printers (parallel, serial, or network interface and remote printers), logical printers, print queues, spoolers, and supervisors.

- Enable and disable logical printers, print queues, and physical printers to accept print jobs.

- Pause and resume print queues, physical printers, and print jobs.

- Start and stop spoolers and supervisors

- Modify attributes of physical printers, logical printers, print queues, spoolers, and supervisors.

- Remove a single print job or all print jobs assigned to a physical printer, logical printer, print queue, spooler or supervisor.

Process Management

- Kill, stop or continue processes.

- Change the nice priority of processes.

- View the current status of processes.

- Schedule periodic tasks via cron.

- View current periodic (cron) tasks.

- Run performance monitors.

- Display system properties such as: machine model and ID;
  number of installed processors, their version and speed;
  operating-system release version; swap statistics, real,
  physical, and virtual memory statistics; network connection
  information.

Remote Administration

- Configure remote systems for remote administration.

- Execute SAM on systems configured for remote administration.

Routine Tasks

- Shut down the system.

- View and remove large files. Specify size and time-since-
  accessed of large files to display or remove.

- View and remove unowned files. Specify size and time-since-
  accessed of unowned files to display or remove.

- View and remove core files.

- View and trim ASCII or non-ASCII log files. Add or remove
  files from the list of files to monitor. Set recommended size
  for trimming.

User and Group Account Management

- Add, remove, view, and modify user accounts.

- Remove or reassign ownership of files belonging to removed or
  modified user accounts.

- Modify a user account's group membership.

- Set up password aging for a user account.

- Add, remove, view, and modify groups.

- Customize adding and removing users by specifying steps to be
  performed before and/or after SAM does its processing for the
  task. The Task Customization action items in SAM Users and
  Groups leads you through this capability. See "Customizing
  SAM Tasks" below for more information.

- Deactivate and reactivate user accounts.

- Manage trusted system security policies on a per-user basis.
  The policies that can be managed include:

    - Account lifetime
    - Maximum account inactivity period
    - Password generation policies
    - Null password usage and use of password restriction rules

- Maximum password length
- Password aging
- Maximum unsuccessful login attempts
- Generation of admin numbers for new or reactivated accounts
- Single-user boot authorization
- Authorized login times

Adding New Functionality to SAM

You can easily add stand-alone commands, programs, and scripts to SAM. SAM is suspended while the executable program is running. When it finishes, the SAM interface is restored. You can also write your own help screen for each menu item you create. To add functionality to SAM, select the "Add Custom Menu Item" or "Add Custom Menu Group" action items from the SAM Areas menu. (Note that the new item is added to the hierarchy that is currently displayed, so you need to navigate to the desired hierarchy before adding the item.)

Single-Point Administration of NFS Diskless Clusters

SAM provides some special capabilities for managing an NFS diskless cluster as a single entity.

For printers and file systems, you can use a feature of the "add" tasks to add a resource to all members of a cluster, making the printer or file system a "cluster-wide" resource. Not only can the resource be added to all systems in the cluster in a single task, but when a cluster-wide resource is selected and a task requested, that task can be performed automatically on all members of the cluster.

For users/groups and electronic mail, SAM provides the choice between shared data and private data when the first client is configured. Choosing shared data results in clients being configured in such a way that they and the cluster server share such things as /etc/passwd, /etc/group, and user mailboxes, and such that sendmail is configured on clients so that all email passes through the server.

Finally, for backups, all publicly-available file systems that belong to systems in the cluster can be backed up from the cluster server.

Online help in the various SAM areas contains more details about single-point administration of NFS diskless clusters (for example, the online help in the Printers/Plotters area provides more information about managing printers as cluster-wide resources and what it means to perform a task on a cluster-wide resource).

File System Protection When Removing Users

When removing users or files from a system, there is always the unfortunate possibility that the wrong user may be removed or that files belonging to a user who is removed are deleted inadvertently during the removal process. For example, user bin is the owner of (from the operating system's perspective) the majority of the executable commands on the system. Removing this user would obviously be disastrous. On the other hand, suppose user joe owns all of the files comprising the test suite for a project. It may be appropriate to remove joe, but the test suite should be left intact and assigned to a new owner. SAM provides two features to help protect against inadvertent removal of users or files when removing users:

- When prompting for the name of a user to remove from the system, SAM checks the name given against a list of names specified in the file /etc/sam/rmuser.excl. If the name matches one within the file, SAM does not remove the user.

- When SAM removes a user, all files (or a subset thereof) for that user are also removed, unless the ownership is given to another user. Before removing a file belonging to the user,

SAM checks to see if the file resides in a path that has been excluded from removal. SAM uses the file /etc/sam/rmfiles.excl to determine which paths have been excluded from removal. So, for example, if the path /users/joe/test is named in the file, SAM will not remove any files residing beneath that directory. SAM logs a list of all files it removes in the file /var/tmp/sam_remove.log.

- SAM does not remove or reassign any files if the user being removed has the same user ID as another user on the system.

Files /etc/sam/rmuser.excl and /etc/sam/rmfiles.excl can be edited to contain users and directories that you want to exclude from removal by SAM.

Customizing SAM Tasks
  You can customize the following SAM tasks:

- Add a New User Account to the System

- Remove a User Account from the System

- Add a Cluster Client

- Remove a Cluster Client

For each of these tasks, you can specify steps you want performed before and/or after SAM does its processing for the task. Before SAM performs one of the tasks, it checks to see if a pretask step (executable file) was defined. If so, SAM invokes the executable, passes it a set of parameters (see below), and waits for its completion. You can halt SAM's processing of a task by exiting from your executable with a nonzero value (for example if an error occurs during execution of your executable).

After SAM has finished processing, it checks for a posttask step, performing the same type of actions as for the pretask step.

The executable file must have these characteristics:

- Must be owned by root.

- Must be executable only by root, and if writable, only by root.

- Must reside in a directory path where all the directories are writable only by owner.

- The full path name of the executable file must be given in the SAM data entry form.

The same parameters are passed from SAM to your program for both the pretask and posttask steps. Here are the parameters passed for each task:

- Add a New User Account to the System

    -l login_name
    -v user_id
    -h home_directory
    -g group
    -s shell
    -p password
    -R real_name
    -L office_location
    -H home_phone

```
        -O office_phone
```

The file /usr/sam/lib/ct_adduser.ex contains an example of how to process these parameters.

- Remove a User Account From the System

    There can be one of three possible parameters, depending on the option selected in the SAM data entry form. The parameter can be one of these three:

-f user_name	Option supplied when all of user_name's files are being removed.
-h user_name	Option supplied when user_name's home directory and files below it are being removed.
-n new_owner user_name	Option supplied when all of user_name's files are being assigned to new_owner.

    The file /usr/sam/lib/ct_rmuser.ex contains an example of how to process these parameters.

- Add a Cluster Client

    When adding multiple clients, the customized task is invoked once for each client. If any pretask command fails (returns nonzero), the corresponding client is not added.

    The parameters are:

-n client_nodename	Name of the cluster client being added.
-i internet_address	Unique network address for the cluster client, in the form ddd.ddd.ddd.ddd.
-s server	Name of the server.
-h link_level_address	12-character hardware address associated with the LAN card in the cluster client.

    The file /usr/sam/lib/ct_addnode.ex contains an example of how to process these parameters. The task customize command is run with standard output and standard error sent to the SAM log file.

- Remove a Cluster Client

    When removing multiple clients, the customized task is invoked once for each client. If any pretask command fails (returns nonzero), the corresponding client is not removed. The format of the parameter string for this task is:

-n client_nodename	Name of the cluster client being removed.

    File /usr/sam/lib/ct_rmnode.ex contains an example of how to process these parameters. The task customize command is run with standard output and standard error sent to the SAM log file.

Restricted SAM
   SAM can be configured to provide a subset of its functionality to
   certain users or groups of users. It can also be used to build a
   template file for assigning SAM access restrictions on multiple
   systems. This is done through the Restricted SAM Builder. System
   administrators access the Restricted SAM Builder by invoking SAM with
   the -r option (see "Options" above). In the Builder, system
   administrators may assign subsets of SAM functionality on a per-user
   or per-group basis. Once set up, the -f option (see "Options" above)
   can then be used by system administrators to verify that the
   appropriate SAM functional areas, and only those areas, are available
   to the specified user.

   A nonroot user that has been given Restricted SAM privileges simply
   executes /usr/sbin/sam and sees only those areas the user is
   privileged to access. For security reasons, the "List" and "Shell
   Escape" choices are not provided. (Note that some SAM functional
   areas require the user to be promoted to root in order to execute
   successfully. SAM does this automatically as needed.)

   SAM provides a default set of SAM functional areas that the system
   administrator can assign to other users. Of course, system
   administrators are able to assign custom lists of SAM functional areas
   to users as necessary.

SAM Logging
   All actions taken by SAM are logged into the SAM log file
   /var/sam/log/samlog. The log entries in this file can be viewed via
   the SAM utility samlog_viewer (see samlog_viewer(1M)). samlog_viewer
   can filter the log file by user name, by time of log entry creation,
   and by level of detail.

   The "Options" menu in the SAM Areas Menu enables you to start a log
   file viewer and to control certain logging options. These options
   include whether or not SAM should automatically start a log file
   viewer whenever SAM is executed, whether or not SAM should trim the
   log file automatically, and what maximum log file size should be
   enforced if automatic log file trimming is selected.

VT320 Terminal Support
   Because the VT320 terminal has predefined local functions for keys
   labeled as F1, F2, F3 and F4, users should use following mapping when
   they desire to use function keys:

HP or Wyse60	VT320 or HP 700/60 in VT320 mode
F1	PF2 (1)
F2	PF1 (1)
F3	spacebar
F4	PF3 (1)
F5	F10, [EXIT], F5 (2)
F6	none
F7	F18, first unlabeled key to right of Pause/Break (2)
F8	F19, second unlabeled key to right of Pause/Break (2)

         (1)   See the "Configuration: HP 700/60 in DEC mode, or DEC
               terminals with PC-AT-type keyboard" subsection below.

         (2)   When using PC-AT keyboard with HP 700/60 in VT320 mode.

Since DEC terminals do not support the softkey menu, that menu is not displayed on those terminals.

Many applications use TAB for forward navigation (moving from one field to another) and shift-TAB for backward navigation. Users having DEC terminals or using terminals in DEC emulation modes such as VT100 or VT320 may note that these terminals/emulators may produce the same character for TAB and shift-TAB. As such, it is impossible for an application to distinguish between the two and both of them are treated as if the TAB key was pressed. This presents an inconvenience to users if they want to go backward. In most cases, they should complete rest of the input fields and get back to the desired field later.

VT100 Terminal Support
  VT100 does not allow the F1-F8 function keys to be configured. Therefore, the following keyboard mappings apply to VT100 terminals:

HP or Wyse60	VT100 or HP 700/60 in VT100 mode
F1	PF2 (1)
F2	PF1 (1)
F3	spacebar
F4	PF3, spacebar or PF3, = (1)
F5	Return
F6	none
F7	none
F8	none

(1) See the "Configuration: HP 700/60 in DEC mode, or DEC terminals with PC-AT-type keyboard" subsection below.

See the comments on softkeys and TAB keys in the "VT320 Terminal Support" subsection above.

Configuration: HP 700/60 Terminal in DEC Mode, or DEC Terminal with PC-AT-Type Keyboard
Customers using the following configuration may want to be aware of the following keyboard difference.

It may be possible for a user with the "HP 700/60 terminal in DEC mode, or DEC terminal with PC-AT-type keyboard" configuration to be told to press function key F1 through F4 to achieve some desired result. For an HP 700/60 terminal in DEC mode or DEC terminals, these functions keys may be mapped onto PF1-PF4 keys. However, the PC-AT-type keyboard does not provide PF1-PF4 keys, as does the DEC/ANSI keyboard.

Key	Maps to
Num Lock	PF1
/	PF2
*	PF3
-	PF4

The Num Lock, /, *, and - keys are located on the keyboard, in a row above the number pad on the right side of the keyboard. Please note that although this keyboard is called a PC-AT-type keyboard, it is supplied by HP. A PC-AT-type keyboard can be recognized by location of ESC key at the left-top of the keyboard.

Wyse60 Terminal Support
  On Wyse60, use the DEL key (located next to Backspace) to backspace.

On an HP 700/60 with a PC-AT-type keyboard in Wyse60 mode, the DEL key is located in the bottom row on the number pad.

Wyse60 terminals provide a single line to display softkey labels unlike HP terminals which provide two lines. Sometimes this may result in truncated softkey labels. For example, the Help on Context label for F1 may appear as Help on C. Some standard labels for screen-oriented applications, such as SAM and swinstall are as follows:

The SAM label:	May appear on the Wyse60 as:
Help On Context	Help On C
Select/Deselect	Select/D
Menubar on/off	Menubar

DEPENDENCIES
  SAM runs in an X Window environment as well as on the following kinds of terminals or terminal emulators:

  - HP-compatible terminal with programmable function keys and on-screen display of function key labels.

  - VT-100 and VT-320

  - WY30 and WY60

  Depending on what other applications are running concurrently with SAM, more swap space may be required. SAM requires the following amounts of internal memory:

  8 MB   If using terminal based version of SAM.
  16 MB   If using Motif X Window version of SAM.

  For more detailed information about how to use SAM on a terminal, see the System Administration Tasks manual.

AUTHOR
  sam was developed by HP.

FILES

/etc/sam/custom	Directory where SAM stores user privileges.
/etc/sam/rmfiles.excl	File containing a list of files and directories that are excluded from removal by SAM.
/etc/sam/rmuser.excl	File containing a list of users that are excluded from removal by SAM.
/usr/sam/bin	Directory containing executable files, which can be used outside of any SAM session.
/usr/sam/help/$LANG	Directory containing SAM language specific online help files.
/usr/sam/lbin	Directory containing SAM executables, which are intended only for use by SAM and are not supported in any other context.
/usr/sam/lib	Directory for internal configuration files.

/var/sam	Directory for working space, including lock files (if a SAM session dies, it may leave behind a spurious lock file), preferences, logging, and temporary files.
/var/sam/log/samlog	File containing unformatted SAM logging messages. This file should not be modified by users. Use samlog_viewer to view the contents of this file (see samlog_viewer(1M)).
/var/sam/log/samlog.old	Previous SAM log file. This file is created by SAM when /var/sam/log/samlog is larger than the user specified limit. Use samlog_viewer with its -f option to view the contents of this file (see samlog_viewer(1M)).

```
SEE ALSO
     samlog_viewer(1M).

     System Administration Tasks
     Installing and Administering ARPA Services
     Installing and Administering LAN/9000
     Installing and Administering NFS Services
     Installing and Administering Network Services
     Installing and Administering X.25/9000
     How HP-UX Works: Concepts for the System Administrator
```

CHAPTER 11

Introduction to UNIX Performance Tools

Introduction

You can take a variety of approaches to performance analysis on your system. These choices range from quick snapshots that take but a few seconds to create, to long-range capacity planning programs that you may want to run for weeks or months before you even begin to analyze the data they produce. This chapter contains examples from a variety of systems, including HP-UX 11i systems. I left in the examples from non-HP-UX systems because some readers of my books are coming from UNIX variants other than HP-UX. Most of the HP-UX examples in this chapter have been updated to reflect 11i systems, however, I'm not aware of any differences between these performance examples on 11i vs. 11.0.

In this chapter, we'll focus on some commonly used UNIX commands and a couple of advanced tools that run on several UNIX variants. These are by no means an exhaustive list of UNIX commands and tools related to performance management; however, I provide enough good information to give you an overview. Your UNIX system may support additional commands and have advanced performance analysis tools. This chapter will give a good overview of performance analysis, including examples of the most commonly used UNIX performance-related commands.

Standard UNIX Commands

To begin, let's look at some commands you can issue from the UNIX prompt to give you some information about your system. The commands I'll cover are:

- **iostat**
- **vmstat**
- **netstat**
- **ps**
- **kill**
- **showmount**
- **swapinfo and swap**
- **sar**

We'll first look at each of these commands so that you get an understanding of the output produced by them and how this output may be used. There are manual pages for many of the commands covered at the end of this chapter.

Please keep in mind that, like all topics we have covered, the output of these commands may differ somewhat among UNIX variants. The basic information produced on most UNIX variants is the same; however, the format of the outputs may differ somewhat. This usually is not significant if you're viewing the outputs; however, if you're writing programs that accept these outputs and manipulate them in some way, then the format of the outputs is important.

I/O and CPU Statistics with iostat

man page

iostat - 11

The **iostat** command gives you an indication of the level of effort the
CPU is putting into I/O and the amount of I/O taking place among
your disks and terminals. **iostat** provides a lot of useful information;
however, it acts somewhat differently among UNIX variants. The following examples show issuing **iostat** on a Solaris system, an HP-UX
system, and an AIX system. **iostat** was not supported on the Linux
system I was using for this chapter. Note that on some systems, using
the -*t* option for terminal information produces just terminal information, and on some systems it produces a full output. You will, of
course, have to determine the best options for your needs on your
UNIX variant. The following examples show the **iostat** command:

Here is a Solaris example executed ten times at five-second intervals:

```
# iostat 5 10
        tty          fd0           sd1           sd3           sd6           cpu
  tin tout kps tps serv  kps tps serv  kps tps serv  kps tps serv  us sy wt id
    0    0   0   0    0    0   0    0    3   0   57    0  79    0    0  7 49 43
    0   47   0   0    0    0   0    0   14   2   75    0   0    0    0  2  0 98
    0   16   0   0    0    0   0    0    0   0    0    0   0    0    0  1  0 98
    0   16   0   0    0    0   0    0    0   0    0    0   0    0    0  2  0 98
    0   16   0   0    0    0   0    0    0   0    0    0   0    0    0  0  0 100
    0   16   0   0    0    0   0    0    0   0    0    0   0    0    0  0  0 100
    0   16   0   0    0    0   0    0    0   0    0    0   0    0    0  1  0 99
    0   16   0   0    0    0   0    0    0   0    0    0   0    0    0  0  0 100
    0   16   0   0    0    0   0    0    6   1   35    0   0    0    0  4  0 96
    0   16   0   0    0    0   0    0    0   0    0    0   0    0    0  0  0 100
```

An HP-UX example includes the -*t* option executed five times at five-
second intervals:

```
# iostat -t 5 5
                tty              cpu
            tin tout        us  ni  sy  id
              1   58         5   1  10  84

    device    bps     sps    msps

    c1t2d0      0     0.0     1.0


                tty              cpu
            tin tout        us  ni  sy  id
              0   30         0   2  26  72
```

```
device      bps      sps      msps

c1t2d0      484      249.6     1.0


                tty              cpu
              tin tout        us  ni  sy  id
               0   31          1   3  23  73

device      bps      sps      msps

c1t2d0      517      256.1     1.0


                tty              cpu
              tin tout        us  ni  sy  id
               0   35          0   2  23  75

device      bps      sps      msps

c1t2d0      456      254.4     1.0


                tty              cpu
              tin tout        us  ni  sy  id
               0  744          1   6  38  55

device      bps      sps      msps

c1t2d0      155      83.1      1.0


#
```

Here is an AIX example executed ten times at five-second intervals:

man page

iostat - 11

```
# iostat 5 10
tty:       tin          tout     avg-cpu: % user      % sys      % idle      % iowait
           0.0          0.0               0.3        1.0        98.4        0.3

Disks:        % tm_act      Kbps       tps     Kb_read    Kb_wrtn
hdisk0          0.4         2.7        0.4     2366635     959304
hdisk1          0.0         0.0        0.0       18843      37928
hdisk2          0.1         0.6        0.1      269803     423284
hdisk3          0.0         0.0        0.0       20875        172
cd0             0.0         0.0        0.0          14          0

tty:       tin          tout     avg-cpu: % user      % sys      % idle      % iowait
           0.0        108.2               0.0        0.2        99.8        0.0

Disks:        % tm_act      Kbps       tps     Kb_read    Kb_wrtn
hdisk0          0.0         0.0        0.0           0          0
hdisk1          0.0         0.0        0.0           0          0
hdisk2          0.0         0.0        0.0           0          0
hdisk3          0.0         0.0        0.0           0          0
cd0             0.0         0.0        0.0           0          0

tty:       tin          tout     avg-cpu: % user      % sys      % idle      % iowait
           0.0        108.4               0.2        0.8        99.0        0.0

Disks:        % tm_act      Kbps       tps     Kb_read    Kb_wrtn
```

```
hdisk0          0.0         0.0         0.0         0           0
hdisk1          0.0         0.0         0.0         0           0
hdisk2          0.0         0.0         0.0         0           0
hdisk3          0.0         0.0         0.0         0           0
cd0             0.0         0.0         0.0         0           0

tty:     tin          tout   avg-cpu:  % user    % sys     % idle    % iowait
         0.0         108.4              0.4       0.2       99.4      0.0

Disks:        % tm_act    Kbps        tps    Kb_read    Kb_wrtn
hdisk0          0.0         0.0         0.0         0           0
hdisk1          0.0         0.0         0.0         0           0
hdisk2          0.0         0.0         0.0         0           0
hdisk3          0.0         0.0         0.0         0           0
cd0             0.0         0.0         0.0         0           0

tty:     tin          tout   avg-cpu:  % user    % sys     % idle    % iowait
         0.0         108.2              0.4       0.6       99.0      0.0

Disks:        % tm_act    Kbps        tps    Kb_read    Kb_wrtn
hdisk0          0.0         0.0         0.0         0           0
hdisk1          0.0         0.0         0.0         0           0
hdisk2          0.0         0.0         0.0         0           0
hdisk3          0.0         0.0         0.0         0           0
cd0             0.0         0.0         0.0         0           0

tty:     tin          tout   avg-cpu:  % user    % sys     % idle    % iowait
         0.0         108.4              0.0       0.4       99.6      0.0

Disks:        % tm_act    Kbps        tps    Kb_read    Kb_wrtn
hdisk0          0.0         0.0         0.0         0           0
hdisk1          0.0         0.0         0.0         0           0
hdisk2          0.0         0.0         0.0         0           0
hdisk3          0.0         0.0         0.0         0           0
cd0             0.0         0.0         0.0         0           0

tty:     tin          tout   avg-cpu:  % user    % sys     % idle    % iowait
         0.0         108.4              0.6       0.0       99.4      0.0

Disks:        % tm_act    Kbps        tps    Kb_read    Kb_wrtn
hdisk0          0.0         0.0         0.0         0           0
hdisk1          0.0         0.0         0.0         0           0
hdisk2          0.0         0.0         0.0         0           0
hdisk3          0.0         0.0         0.0         0           0
cd0             0.0         0.0         0.0         0           0

tty:     tin          tout   avg-cpu:  % user    % sys     % idle    % iowait
         0.0         108.2              0.2       0.8       99.0      0.0

Disks:        % tm_act    Kbps        tps    Kb_read    Kb_wrtn
hdisk0          0.0         0.0         0.0         0           0
hdisk1          0.0         0.0         0.0         0           0
hdisk2          0.0         0.0         0.0         0           0
hdisk3          0.0         0.0         0.0         0           0
cd0             0.0         0.0         0.0         0           0

tty:     tin          tout   avg-cpu:  % user    % sys     % idle    % iowait
         0.0         108.4              0.4       0.0       99.6      0.0

Disks:        % tm_act    Kbps        tps    Kb_read    Kb_wrtn
hdisk0          0.0         0.0         0.0         0           0
hdisk1          0.0         0.0         0.0         0           0
hdisk2          0.0         0.0         0.0         0           0
hdisk3          0.0         0.0         0.0         0           0
cd0             0.0         0.0         0.0         0           0

tty:     tin          tout   avg-cpu:  % user    % sys     % idle    % iowait
         0.0         108.4              0.4       0.4       99.2      0.0

Disks:        % tm_act    Kbps        tps    Kb_read    Kb_wrtn
hdisk0          0.0         0.0         0.0         0           0
hdisk1          0.0         0.0         0.0         0           0
hdisk2          0.0         0.0         0.0         0           0
hdisk3          0.0         0.0         0.0         0           0
cd0             0.0         0.0         0.0         0           0
```

man page

iostat - 11

Here are descriptions of the reports you receive with **iostat** for terminals, the CPU, and mounted file systems. Because the reports are somewhat different, I have included detailed information from the HP-UX output. A more detailed description of these fields is included in the **iostat** manual page at the end of this chapter. Most of the fields appear in the outputs; however, the outputs of the commands differ somewhat among UNIX variants.

For every terminal you have connected (*tty*), you see a "tin" and "tout," which represent the number of characters read from your terminal and the number of characters written to your terminal, respectively.

For your CPU, you see the percentage of time spent in user mode ("us"), the percentage of time spent running user processes at a low priority called nice ("ni"), the percentage of time spent in system mode ("sy"), and the percentage of time the CPU is idle ("id").

For every locally mounted file system, you receive information on the kilobytes transferred per second ("bps"), number of seeks per second ("sps"), and number of milliseconds per average seek ("msps"). For disks that are NFS-mounted or disks on client nodes of your server, you will not receive a report; **iostat** reports only on locally mounted file systems.

When viewing the output of **iostat**, there are some parameters to take note of.

First, note that the time that your CPU is spending in the four categories shown. The CPU report is produced with the *-t* option. I have worked on systems with poor performance that the administrator assumed to be a result of a slow CPU because the "id" number was very high, indicating that the CPU was actually idle most of the time. If the CPU is mostly idle, the chances are that the bottleneck is not the CPU, but may be I/O, memory, or networking. If the CPU is indeed busy most of the time ("id" is very low), see whether any processes are running "nice" (check the "ni" number). It may be that there are some background processes consuming a lot of CPU time that can be changed to run "nice."

Second, compare the number of transfers taking place. These are usually indicated by something like blocks per second (bps), transfers per second (*tps*), or seeks per second (*sps*). These numbers give an indication of the amount of activity taking place on a disk. If one volume is consistently much higher than other volumes, then it may be performing an inordinate amout of the workload. Notice on HP-UX that the milliseconds per average seek (*msps*) for all disks is always equal to one.

Virtual Memory Statistics with vmstat

man page

vmstat - 11

vmstat provides virtual memory statistics. It provides information on the status of processes, virtual memory, paging activity, faults, and a breakdown of the percentage of CPU time. **vmstat** acts somewhat differently among UNIX variants. The following examples show issuing **vmstat** on a Solaris system, an HP-UX system, an AIX system, and a Linux system. You will, of course, have to determine the best options for your needs on your UNIX variant. In the following examples, the output was produced nine times at five-second intervals. The first argument to the **vmstat** command is the interval; the second is the number of times you would like the output produced.

Solaris example:

```
# vmstat 5 9
 procs     memory            page            disk          faults      cpu
 r b w   swap  free  re  mf pi po fr de sr f0 s1 s3 s6   in   sy   cs us sy id
 0 0 0   4480  4696   0   0  1  0  0  0  0  0  0  0 79  864  130  297  0  7 92
 0 0 0 133020  5916   0   3  0  0  0  0  0  0  0  3  0  102   42   24  0  2 98
 0 0 0 133020  5916   0   0  0  0  0  0  0  0  0  0  0   70   48   24  0  0 100
 0 0 0 133020  5916   0   0  0  0  0  0  0  0  0  0  0   74   42   24  0  0 100
 0 0 0 133020  5916   0   0  0  0  0  0  0  0  0  0  0   35   45   23  0  0 99
 0 0 0 133020  5916   0   0  0  0  0  0  0  0  0  0  0   65   66   26  0  0 100
 0 0 0 133020  5916   0   0  0  0  0  0  0  0  0  0  0   52   44   23  0  1 99
 0 0 0 133020  5916   0   0  0  0  0  0  0  0  0  0  0   53   54   24  0  1 99
 0 0 0 133020  5916   0   0  0  0  0  0  0  0  0  1  0   60   53   25  0  2 98
```

HP-UX example:

```
# vmstat 5 9

 procs      memory             page                 faults       cpu
 r  b  w   avm    free   re  at  pi  po  fr  de  sr   in   sy   cs  us sy id
 5 240 0 17646   3979    2   0   0   0   0   0   0    0  778  193  17  3 80
```

```
4 242 0 16722    4106    0   0   0   0   0   0   0   814  20649  258  89 10  2
4 240 0 16649    4106    0   0   0   0   0   0   0    83  18384  218  91  9  0
4 240 0 16468    4106    0   0   0   0   0   0   0   792  19552  273  89 11  1
5 239 0 15630    4012    9   0   0   0   0   0   0   804  18295  270  93  8 -1
5 241 0 16087    3934    6   0   0   0   0   0   0   920  21044  392  89 10  0
5 241 0 15313    3952   11   0   0   0   0   0   0   968  20239  431  90 10  0
4 242 0 16577    4043    3   0   0   0   0   0   0   926  19230  409  89 10  0
6 238 0 17453    4122    0   0   0   0   0   0   0   837  19269  299  89  9  2
```

AIX example:

```
martyp $ vmstat 5 9
kthr    memory                page                   faults        cpu
----- ----------- ------------------------------ ------------ -----------
 r  b   avm   fre  re pi po  fr  sr cy  in   sy  cs us sy id wa
 0  0 16604   246   0  0  0   0   2   0 149   79  36  0  1 98  0
 0  0 16604   246   0  0  0   0   0   0 153  125  41  0  0 99  0
 0  0 16604   246   0  0  0   0   0   0 143   83  33  0  0 99  0
 0  0 16604   246   0  0  0   0   0   0 140   94  35  0  1 99  0
 0  0 16604   246   0  0  0   0   0   0 166   62  32  0  0 99  0
 0  0 16604   246   0  0  0   0   0   0 150  102  38  1  0 99  0
 0  0 16604   246   0  0  0   0   0   0 183   78  34  0  0 99  0
 0  0 16604   246   0  0  0   0   0   0 132   87  33  0  1 99  0
 0  0 16604   246   0  0  0   0   0   0 147   84  38  0  0 99  0
```

Linux example:

```
# vmstat 5 5
   procs                   memory      swap        io    system       cpu
 r  b  w   swpd   free  buff  cache  si  so   bi   bo   in    cs  us sy id
 1  0  0   9432   1160   656  12024   1   2   14    1  138   274   3  1 96
 1  0  0   9684    828   652  12148   0  50    0   14  205  8499  82 18  0
 1  0  0   9684    784   652  11508   0   0    0    1  103  8682  81 19  0
 1  0  0   9684    800   652  10996   0   0    0    0  101  8683  80 20  0
 0  0  0   9772    796   652   9824  12  18    3    4  160  6577  66 17 18
```

man page

vmstat - 11

You certainly get a lot for your money out of the **vmstat** command. Here is a brief description of the categories of information produced by **vmstat**. I have included a description of the fields in the HP-UX example because of the manual page that appears at the end of this chapter for HP-UX. You can see, however, that the outputs are very similar.

Processes are classified into one of three categories: runnable ("r"), blocked on I/O or short-term resources ("b"), or swapped ("w").

Next you will see information about memory. "avm" is the number of virtual memory pages owned by processes that have run within the last 20 seconds. If this number is roughly the size of physical memory minus your kernel, then you are near forced paging. The "free" column indicates the number of pages on the system's free list.

It doesn't mean that the process is finished running and these pages won't be accessed again; it just means that they have not been accessed recently. I suggest that you ignore this column.

Next is paging activity. The first field ("re") shows the pages that were reclaimed. These pages made it to the free list but were later referenced and had to be salvaged.

Next you see the number of faults in three categories: interrupts per second, which usually come from hardware ("in"), system calls per second ("sy"), and context switches per second ("cs").

The final output is CPU usage percentage for user ("us"), system ("sy"), and idle ("id"). This is not as complete as the **iostat** output, which also shows **nice** entries.

man page

iostat - 11

If you are running an I/O intensive workload you may indeed see a lot of activity in runnable processes ("r"), blocked processes("b"), and the runnable but swapped ("w") processes. If you have many runnable but swapped processes, then you probably have an I/O bottleneck.

Network Statistics with netstat

netstat provides information related to network statistics. Because network bandwidth has as much to do with performance as the CPU and memory in some networks, you want to get an idea of the level of network traffic you have.

man page

netstat - 12

I use two forms of **netstat** to obtain network statistics. The first is **netstat -i**, which shows the state of interfaces that are autoconfigured. Although **netstat -i** gives a good rundown of the primary LAN interface, such as the network it is on, its name, and so on, it does not show useful statistical information.

The following shows the output of **netstat -i**:

 # netstat -i

Name	Mtu	Network	Address	Ipkts	Ierrs	Opkts	Oerrs	Col
lan0	1497	151.150	a4410.e.h.c	242194	120	107665	23	19884

man page

netstat - 12

netstat provides a concise output. Put another way, most of what you get from **netstat** is useful. Here is a description of the nine fields in the **netstat** example:

Name	The name of your network interface (Name), in this case, "lan0."
Mtu	The "maximum transmission unit," which is the maximum packet size sent by the interface card.
Network	The network address of the LAN to which the interface card is connected (151.150).
Address	The host name of your system. This is the symbolic name of your system as it appears in the **/etc/hosts** file if your networking is configured to use **/etc/hosts**.

Below is the statistical information. Depending on the system you are using, or revision of OS, you may not see some of these commands:

Ipkts	The number of packets received by the interface card, in this case, "lan0."
Ierrs	The number of errors detected on incoming packets by the interface card.
Opkts	The number of packets transmitted by the interface card.
Oerrs	The number of errors detected during the transmission of packets by the interface card.
Col	The number of collisions that resulted from packet traffic.

netstat provides cumulative data since the node was last powered up; therefore you might have a long elapsed time over which data was accumulated. If you are interested in seeing useful statistical information, you can use **netstat** with different options. You can also specify an interval to report statistics. I usually ignore the first entry, because it shows all data since the system was last powered up. This means that the data includes non-prime hours when the system was idle. I prefer to view data at the time the system is working its hardest. The following examples show running **netstat -I** and specifying the *lan* interface for Solaris, HP-UX, and AIX. These outputs are nearly identical, although the name of the network interface does vary among UNIX variants. The **netstat** command is run at an interval of five seconds. The Linux version of this command, which is not shown, does not allow me to specify an interval.

man page

netstat - 12

Solaris example:

```
# netstat -I le0 5
    input   le0        output              input  (Total)     output
packets errs  packets errs  colls  packets errs  packets errs  colls
116817990 0   3299582 11899 1653100 116993185 0   3474777 11899 1653100
185      0    3       0     0      185      0    3       0     0
273      0    8       0     0      273      0    8       0     0
153      0    3       0     0      153      0    3       0     0
154      0    3       0     0      154      0    3       0     0
126      0    3       0     0      126      0    3       0     0
378      0    2       0     0      378      0    2       0     0
399      0    4       0     0      399      0    4       0     0
286      0    2       0     0      286      0    2       0     0
```

HP-UX example (10.x):

```
# netstat -I lan0 5

(lan0)-> input          output       (Total)-> input          output
    packets errs  packets errs  colls      packets errs  packets errs  colls
    269841735 27  256627585 1   5092223    281472199 27  268258048 1   5092223
    1602    0     1238    0     49         1673    0     1309    0     49
    1223    0     1048    0     25         1235    0     1060    0     25
    1516    0     1151    0     42         1560    0     1195    0     42
    1553    0     1188    0     17         1565    0     1200    0     17
    2539    0     2180    0     44         2628    0     2269    0     44
    3000    0     2193    0     228        3000    0     2193    0     228
    2959    0     2213    0     118        3003    0     2257    0     118
    2423    0     1981    0     75         2435    0     1993    0     75
```

AIX example:

```
# netstat -I en0 5
    input   (en0)      output              input  (Total)     output
packets errs  packets errs colls  packets errs  packets errs colls
46333531 0    1785025 0    0  47426087 0    2913405 0    0
    203  0    1       0    0      204  0    2       0    0
    298  0    1       0    0      298  0    1       0    0
    293  0    1       0    0      304  0    12      0    0
    191  0    1       0    0      191  0    1       0    0
```

150	0	2	0	0	151	0	3	0	0
207	0	3	0	0	218	0	15	0	0
162	0	3	0	0	162	0	4	0	0
120	0	2	0	0	120	0	2	0	0

With this example, you get multiple outputs of what is taking place on the LAN interface, including the totals on the right side of the output. As I mentioned earlier, you may want to ignore the first output, because it includes information over a long time period. This may include a time when your network was idle, and therefore the data may not be important to you.

You can specify the network interface on which you want statistics reported by using **-I interface**; in the case of the example, it was **-I** and either *le0, lan0,* or *en0.* An interval of five seconds was also used in this example.

Analyzing **netstat** statistical information is intuitive. You want to verify that the collisions (Colls) are much lower than the packets transmitted (Opkts). Collisions occur on output from your LAN interface. Every collision your LAN interface encounters slows down the network. You will get varying opinions about what is too many collisions. If your collisions are less than 5 percent of "Opkts," you're probably in good shape and better off spending your time analyzing some other system resource. If this number is high, you may want to consider segmenting your network in some way such as installing networking equipment between portions of the network that don't share a lot of data.

As a rule of thumb, if you reduce the number of packets you are receiving and transmitting ("Ipkts" and "Opkts"), then you will have less overall network traffic and fewer collisions. Keep this in mind as you plan your network or upgrades to your systems. You may want to have two LAN cards in systems that are in constant communication. That way, these systems have a "private" LAN over which to communicate and do not adversely affect the performance of other systems on the network. One LAN interface on each system is devoted to intra-system communication. This provides a "tight" communication path among systems that usually act as servers. The second LAN interface is used to communicate with any systems that are usually clients on a larger network.

man page

netstat - 12

You can also obtain information related to routing with **netstat** (see Chapter 12). The *-r* option to **netstat** shows the routing tables, which you usually want to know about, and the *-n* option can be used to print network addresses as numbers rather than as names. In the following examples, **netstat** is issued with the *-r* option (this will be used when describing the **netstat** output) and the *-rn* options, so that you can compare the two outputs:

$ netstat -r

Routing tables

Destination	Gateway	Flags	Refs	Use	Interface	Pmtu
hp700	localhost	UH	0	28	lo0	4608
default	router1	UG	0	0	lan0	4608
128.185.61	system1	U	347	28668	lan0	1500

$ netstat -rn

Routing tables

Destination	Gateway	Flags	Refs	Use	Interface	Pmtu
127.0.0.1	127.0.0.1	UH	0	28	lo0	4608
default	128.185.61.1	UG	0	0	lan0	4608
128.185.61	128.185.61.2	U	347	28668	lan0	1500

With **netstat**, some information is provided about the router, which is the middle entry. The *-r* option shows information about routing, but there are many other useful options to this command are available. Of particular interest in this output is "Flags," which defines the type of routing that takes place. Here are descriptions of the most common flags, which may be different among UNIX variants, from the manual page at the end of this chapter.

1=*U*   Route to a *network* via a gateway that is the local
             host itself.

3=*UG*   Route to a *network* via a gateway that is the remote
             host.

5=*UH*   Route to a *host* via a gateway that is the local host
             itself.

7=*UGH*   Route to a *host* via a remote gateway that is a host.

man page

netstat - 12

        The first line is for the local host, or loopback interface called,
lo0 at address 127.0.0.1 (you can see this address in the **netstat -rn**
example). The *UH* flags indicate that the destination address is the
local host itself. This Class A address allows a client and server on the
same host to communicate with one another via TCP/IP. A datagram
sent to the loopback interface won't go out onto the network; it will
simply go through the loopback.

        The second line is for the default route. This entry says to send
packets to Router 1 if a more specific route can't be found. In this
case, the router has a *UG* under *Flags*. Some routers are configured
with a *U*; others, such as the one in this example, with a *UG*. I've
found that I usually end up determining through trial and error
whether a *U* or *UG* is required. If there is a *U* in *Flags* and I am unable
to ping a system on the other side of a router, a *UG* entry usually fixes
the problem.

        The third line is for the system's network interface, *lan0*. This
means to use this network interface for packets to be sent to
128.185.61.

Check Processes with ps

Knowing about the processes running on your system, and knowing
how to stop them, are important to both system administration and
performance.

To find the answer to "What is my system doing?," use **ps -ef**. This command provides information about every running process on your system. If, for instance, you want to know whether NFS is running, you simply type **ps -ef** and look for NFS daemons. Although **ps** tells you every process that is running on your system, it doesn't provide a good summary of the level of system resources being consumed. I would guess that **ps** is the most often issued system administration command. There are a number of options you can use with **ps**. I normally use *e* and *f*, which provide information about every ("*e*") running process and lists this information in full ("*f*"). **ps** outputs are almost identical from system to system. The following three examples are from a Solaris, AIX, and HP-UX system, respectively:

man page

ps - 11

Solaris example:

```
martyp $ ps -ef
     UID    PID  PPID  C    STIME TTY       TIME CMD
    root      0     0  0   Feb 18 ?        0:01 sched
    root      1     0  0   Feb 18 ?        1:30 /etc/init -
    root      2     0  0   Feb 18 ?        0:02 pageout
    root      3     0  1   Feb 18 ?      613:44 fsflush
    root   3065  3059  0   Feb 22 ?        5:10 /usr/dt/bin/sdtperfmeter -f -H -r
    root     88     1  0   Feb 18 ?        0:01 /usr/sbin/in.routed -q
    root    478     1  0   Feb 18 ?        0:00 /usr/lib/saf/sac -t 300
    root     94     1  0   Feb 18 ?        2:50 /usr/sbin/rpcbind
    root    150     1  0   Feb 18 ?        6:03 /usr/sbin/syslogd
    root     96     1  0   Feb 18 ?        0:00 /usr/sbin/keyserv
    root    144     1  0   Feb 18 ?       50:37 /usr/lib/autofs/automountd
    root   1010     1  0   Apr 12 ?        0:00 /opt/perf/bin/midaemon
    root    106     1  0   Feb 18 ?        0:02 /usr/lib/netsvc/yp/ypbind -broadt
    root    156     1  0   Feb 18 ?        0:03 /usr/sbin/cron
    root    176     1  0   Feb 18 ?        0:00 /usr/lib/lpsched
    root    129     1  0   Feb 18 ?        0:00 /usr/lib/nfs/lockd
  daemon    130     1  0   Feb 18 ?        0:01 /usr/lib/nfs/statd
    root  14798     1  0   Mar 09 ?       31:10 /usr/sbin/nscd
    root    133     1  0   Feb 18 ?        0:10 /usr/sbin/inetd -s
    root    197     1  0   Feb 18 ?        0:00 /usr/lib/power/powerd
    root    196     1  0   Feb 18 ?        0:35 /etc/opt/licenses/lmgrd.ste -c /d
    root    213     1  0   Feb 18 ?     4903:09 /usr/sbin/vold
    root    199   196  0   Feb 18 ?        0:03 suntechd -T  4 -c /etc/optd
    root    219     1  0   Feb 18 ?        0:08 /usr/lib/sendmail -bd -q15m
    root    209     1  0   Feb 18 ?        0:05 /usr/lib/utmpd
    root   2935   266  0   Feb 22 ?       48:08 /usr/openwin/bin/Xsun :0 -nobanna
    root  16795 16763  1  07:51:34 pts/4   0:00 ps -ef
    root   2963  2954  0   Feb 22 ?        0:17 /usr/openwin/bin/fbconsole
    root    479     1  0   Feb 18 console  0:00 /usr/lib/saf/ttymon -g -h -p sunc
    root  10976     1  0   Jun 01 ?        0:00 /opt/perf/bin/ttd
    root   7468     1  0   Feb 24 ?        0:13 /opt/perf/bin/pvalarmd
    root    266     1  0   Feb 18 ?        0:01 /usr/dt/bin/dtlogin -daemon
  martyp  16763 16761  0  07:46:46 pts/4   0:01 -ksh
    root  10995     1  0   Jun 01 ?        0:01 /opt/perf/bin/perflbd
    root    484   478  0   Feb 18 ?        0:00 /usr/lib/saf/ttymon
    root    458     1  0   Feb 18 ?       20:06 /usr/lib/snmp/snmpdx -y -c /etc/f
    root  16792  3059  0  07:50:37 ?        0:00 /usr/dt/bin/dtscreen -mode blank
    root    471     1  0   Feb 18 ?        0:07 /usr/lib/dmi/dmispd
    root    474     1  0   Feb 18 ?        0:00 /usr/lib/dmi/snmpXdmid -s
    root    485   458  0   Feb 18 ?      739:44 mibiisa -r -p 32874
```

```
root  2954  2936  0  Feb 22 ?         0:01 /bin/ksh /usr/dt/bin/Xsession
root  2936   266  0  Feb 22 ?         0:00 /usr/dt/bin/dtlogin -daemon
root  3061  3059  0  Feb 22 ?         1:32 dtwm
root  3058     1  0  Feb 22 pts/2     0:01 /usr/dt/bin/ttsession
root   712   133  0  Feb 18 ?         0:01 rpc.ttdbserverd
root 11001 11000  0                   0:01 <defunct>
root  2938     1  0  Feb 22 ?         0:00 /usr/openwin/bin/fbconsole -d :0
root  2999  2954  0  Feb 22 pts/2     0:16 /usr/dt/bin/sdt_shell -c       unt
root  3059  3002  0  Feb 22 pts/2   283:35 /usr/dt/bin/dtsession
root  3063  3059  0  Feb 22 ?         0:03 /usr/dt/bin/dthelpview -helpVolur
root  3099  3062  0  Feb 22 ?         0:13 /usr/dt/bin/dtfile -geometry +700
root 11000 10995  0  Jun 01 ?         0:02 /opt/perf/bin/agdbserver -t alar/
root  3002  2999  0  Feb 22 pts/2     0:01 -ksh -c         unset DT;      DISPLg
root   730   133  0  Feb 18 ?         1:37 rpc.rstatd
root  3062  3059  0  Feb 22 ?         2:17 /usr/dt/bin/dtfile -geometry +700
root  3067     1  0  Feb 22 ?         0:00 /bin/ksh /usr/dt/bin/sdtvolcheckm
root  3000     1  0  Feb 22 ?         0:00 /usr/dt/bin/dsdm
root  3078  3067  0  Feb 22 ?         0:00 /bin/cat /tmp/.removable/notify0
root 10984     1  0  Jun 01 ?        12:42 /opt/perf/dce/bin/dced -b
root 16761   133  0 07:46:45 ?        0:00 in.telnetd
martyp $
```

AIX example:

```
martyp $ ps -ef
   UID   PID  PPID  C    STIME    TTY  TIME CMD
  root     1     0  0  Feb 24      -   5:07 /etc/init
  root  2208 15520  0  Feb 24      -   8:21 dtwm
  root  2664     1  0  Feb 24      -   0:00 /usr/dt/bin/dtlogin -daemon
  root  2882     1  0  Feb 24      - 158:41 /usr/sbin/syncd 60
  root  3376  2664  5  Feb 24      - 3598:41 /usr/lpp/X11/bin/X -D /usr/lib/
  root  3624  2664  0  Feb 24      -   0:00 dtlogin <:0>         -daemon
  root  3950     1  6  Feb 24      - 5550:30 /usr/lpp/perf/bin/llbd
  root  4144     1  0  Feb 24      -   0:00 /usr/lpp/perf/bin/midaemon
  root  4490     1  0  Feb 24      -   0:48 /usr/lpp/perf/bin/perflbd
  root  4906     1  0  Feb 24      -   0:00 /usr/lib/errdemon
  root  5172     1  0  Feb 24      -   0:00 /usr/sbin/srcmstr
  root  5724  5172  0  Feb 24      -   9:54 /usr/sbin/syslogd
  root  6242  5172  0  Feb 24      -   0:00 /usr/sbin/biod 6
  root  6450  5172  0  Feb 24      -   0:02 sendmail: accepting connections
  root  6710  5172  0  Feb 24      -   7:34 /usr/sbin/portmap
  root  6966  5172  0  Feb 24      -   0:23 /usr/sbin/inetd
  root  7224  5172  0  Feb 24      -   1:09 /usr/sbin/timed -S
  root  7482  5172  0  Feb 24      -  11:55 /usr/sbin/snmpd
  root  8000     1  0  Feb 24      -   9:17 ovspmd
  root  8516  8782  0  Feb 24      -   0:00 netfmt -CF
  root  8782     1  0  Feb 24      -   0:00 /usr/OV/bin/ntl_reader 0 1 1 1
  root  9036  8000  0  Feb 24      -  10:09 ovwdb -O -n5000
  root  9288  8000  0  Feb 24      -   0:44 pmd -Au -At -Mu -Mt -m
  root  9546  8000  0  Feb 24      -  20:05 trapgend -f
  root  9804  8000  0  Feb 24      -   0:28 trapd
  root 10062  8000  0  Feb 24      -   0:47 orsd
  root 10320  8000  0  Feb 24      -   0:33 ovesmd
  root 10578  8000  0  Feb 24      -   0:30 ovelmd
  root 10836  8000  0  Feb 24      -  13:12 ovtopmd -O
  root 11094  8000  0  Feb 24      -  17:50 netmon -P
  root 11352  8000  0  Feb 24      -   0:02 snmpCollect
  root 11954     1  0  Feb 24      -   1:22 /usr/sbin/cron
  root 12140  5172  0  Feb 24      -   0:01 /usr/lib/netsvc/yp/ypbind
  root 12394  5172  0  Feb 24      -   1:39 /usr/sbin/rpc.mountd
  root 12652  5172  0  Feb 24      -   0:29 /usr/sbin/nfsd 8
  root 12908  5172  0  Feb 24      -   0:00 /usr/sbin/rpc.statd
  root 13166  5172  0  Feb 24      -   0:29 /usr/sbin/rpc.lockd
  root 13428     1  0  Feb 24      -   0:00 /usr/sbin/uprintfd
  root 14190  5172  0  Feb 24      -  72:59 /usr/sbin/automountd
  root 14452  5172  0  Feb 24      -   0:17 /usr/sbin/qdaemon
  root 14714  5172  0  Feb 24      -   0:00 /usr/sbin/writesrv
  root 14992     1  0  Feb 24      - 252:26 /usr/lpp/perf/bin/scopeux
  root 15520  3624  1  Feb 24      -  15:29 /usr/dt/bin/dtsession
  root 15742     1  0  Feb 24      -   0:00 /usr/lpp/diagnostics/bin/diagd
  root 15998     1  0  Feb 24    lft0  0:00 /usr/sbin/getty /dev/console
```

```
      root 16304 18892    0    Feb 24  pts/0  0:00 /bin/ksh
      root 16774     1    0    Feb 24    -    0:00 /usr/lpp/perf/bin/ttd
      root 17092  4490    0    Feb 24    - 68:54 /usr/lpp/perf/bin/rep_server -t
      root 17370 19186    3                    0:00 <defunct>
      root 17630 15520    0    Mar 25    -    0:00 /usr/dt/bin/dtexec -open 0 -ttp
      root 17898 15520    0    Mar 20    -    0:00 /usr/dt/bin/dtexec -open 0 -ttp
      root 18118 19888    0    Feb 24  pts/1  0:00 /bin/ksh
      root 18366  6966    0    Feb 24    -    0:00 rpc.ttdbserver 100083 1
      root 18446 15520    0    Mar 15    -    0:00 /usr/dt/bin/dtexec -open 0 -ttp
      root 18892 15520    0    Feb 24    -    3:46 /usr/dt/bin/dtterm
      root 19186 16304    0    Feb 24  pts/0  0:01 /usr/lpp/X11/bin/msmit
      root 19450     1    0    Feb 24    - 26:53 /usr/dt/bin/ttsession -s
      root 19684  2208    0    Feb 24    -    0:00 /usr/dt/bin/dtexec -open 0 -ttp
      root 19888 19684    0    Feb 24    -    0:00 /usr/dt/bin/dtterm
      root 20104 15520    0    Feb 27    -    0:00 /usr/dt/bin/dtexec -open 0 -ttp
      root 20248 20104    0    Feb 27    -    0:03 /usr/dt/bin/dtscreen
      root 20542 29708    0    May 14    -    0:03 /usr/dt/bin/dtscreen
      root 20912 26306    0    Apr 05    -    0:03 /usr/dt/bin/dtscreen
      root 33558     1    0    May 18    -    3:28 /usr/atria/etc/lockmgr -a /var/
      root 33834  6966    3 07:55:49    -    0:00 telnetd
      root 34072     1    0    May 18    -    0:00 /usr/atria/etc/albd_server
    martyp 36296 36608   13 07:56:07  pts/2  0:00 ps -ef
    martyp 36608 33834    1 07:55:50  pts/2  0:00 -ksh
      root 37220 15520    0    May 28    -    0:00 /usr/dt/bin/dtexec -open 0 -ttp
  martyp $
```

HP-UX example (partial listing):

```
  martyp $ ps -ef
      UID    PID  PPID C   STIME  TTY    TIME   COMMAND
      root     0    0  0   Mar  9  ?   107:28 swapper
      root     1    0  0   Mar  9  ?     2:27 init
      root     2    0  0   Mar  9  ?    14:13 vhand
      root     3    0  0   Mar  9  ?   114:55 statdaemon
      root     4    0  0   Mar  9  ?     5:57 unhashdaemon
      root     7    0  0   Mar  9  ?   154:33 ttisr
      root    70    0  0   Mar  9  ?     0:01 lvmkd
      root    71    0  0   Mar  9  ?     0:01 lvmkd
      root    72    0  0   Mar  9  ?     0:01 lvmkd
      root    13    0  0   Mar  9  ?     9:54 vx_sched_thread
      root    14    0  0   Mar  9  ?     1:54 vx_iflush_thread
      root    15    0  0   Mar  9  ?     2:06 vx_ifree_thread
      root    16    0  0   Mar  9  ?     2:27 vx_inactive_cache_thread
      root    17    0  0   Mar  9  ?     0:40 vx_delxwri_thread
      root    18    0  0   Mar  9  ?     0:33 vx_logflush_thread
      root    19    0  0   Mar  9  ?     0:07 vx_attrsync_thread
                            .
                            .
                            .
      root    69    0  0   Mar  9  ?     0:09 vx_inactive_thread
      root    73    0  0   Mar  9  ?     0:01 lvmkd
      root    74    0 19   Mar  9  ?  3605:29 netisr
      root    75    0  0   Mar  9  ?     0:18 netisr
      root    76    0  0   Mar  9  ?     0:17 netisr
      root    77    0  0   Mar  9  ?     0:14 netisr
      root    78    0  0   Mar  9  ?     0:48 nvsisr
      root    79    0  0   Mar  9  ?     0:00 supsched
      root    80    0  0   Mar  9  ?     0:00 smpsched
      root    81    0  0   Mar  9  ?     0:00 smpsched
      root    82    0  0   Mar  9  ?     0:00 sblksched
      root    83    0  0   Mar  9  ?     0:00 sblksched
      root    84    0  0   Mar  9  ?     0:00 strmem
```

man page

ps - 11

```
  root     85     0   0  Mar  9  ?       0:00 strweld
  root   3730     1   0  16:39:22 console  0:00 /usr/sbin/getty console console
  root    404     1   0  Mar  9  ?       3:57 /usr/sbin/swagentd
oracle    919     1   0  15:23:23 ?      0:00 oraclegprd (LOCAL=NO)
  root    289     1   2  Mar  9  ?      78:34 /usr/sbin/syncer
  root    426     1   0  Mar  9  ?       0:10 /usr/sbin/syslogd -D
  root    576     1   0  Mar  9  ?       0:00 /usr/sbin/portmap
  root    429     1   0  Mar  9  ?       0:00 /usr/sbin/ptydaemon
  root    590     1   0  Mar  9  ?       0:00 /usr/sbin/biod 4
  root    442     1   0  Mar  9  ?       0:00 /usr/lbin/nktl_daemon 0 0 0 0 0 1 -2
oracle   8145     1   0  12:02:48 ?      0:00 oraclegprd (LOCAL=NO)
  root    591     1   0  Mar  9  ?       0:00 /usr/sbin/biod 4
  root    589     1   0  Mar  9  ?       0:00 /usr/sbin/biod 4
  root    592     1   0  Mar  9  ?       0:00 /usr/sbin/biod 4
  root    604     1   0  Mar  9  ?       0:00 /usr/sbin/rpc.lockd
  root    598     1   0  Mar  9  ?       0:00 /usr/sbin/rpc.statd
  root    610     1   0  Mar  9  ?       0:16 /usr/sbin/automount -f /etc/auto_master
  root    638     1   0  Mar  9  ?       0:06 sendmail: accepting connections
  root    618     1   0  Mar  9  ?       0:02 /usr/sbin/inetd
  root    645     1   0  Mar  9  ?       5:01 /usr/sbin/snmpdm
  root    661     1   0  Mar  9  ?      11:28 /usr/sbin/fddisubagtd
  root    711     1   0  Mar  9  ?      30:59 /opt/dce/sbin/rpcd
  root    720     1   0  Mar  9  ?       0:00 /usr/sbin/vtdaemon
  root    867   777   1  Mar  9  ?       0:00 <defunct>
    lp    733     1   0  Mar  9  ?       0:00 /usr/sbin/lpsched
  root    777     1   0  Mar  9  ?       8:55 DIAGMON
  root    742     1   0  Mar  9  ?       0:15 /usr/sbin/cron
oracle   7880     1   0  11:43:47 ?      0:00 oraclegprd (LOCAL=NO)
  root    842     1   0  Mar  9  ?       0:00 /usr/vue/bin/vuelogin
oracle   5625     1   0  07:00:14 ?      0:01 ora_smon_gprd
  root    781     1   0  Mar  9  ?       0:00 /usr/sbin/envd
  root    833   777   0  Mar  9  ?       0:00 DEMLOG  DEMLOG;DEMLOG;0;0;
  root    813     1   0  Mar  9  ?       0:00 /usr/sbin/nfsd 4
  root    807     1   0  Mar  9  ?       0:00 /usr/sbin/rpc.mountd
  root    815   813   0  Mar  9  ?       0:00 /usr/sbin/nfsd 4
  root    817   813   0  Mar  9  ?       0:00 /usr/sbin/nfsd 4
  root    835   777   0  Mar  9  ?       0:13 PSMON  PSMON;PSMON;0;0;
```

Here is a brief description of the headings:

UID	The user ID of the process owner.
PID	The process ID (you can use this number to kill the process).
PPID	The process ID of the parent process.
C	Processor utilization. On a multi-processor system, you may see this number go beyond 100%. It could potentially go to 100% per processor, so a two-processor system may show 200% utilization. This varies among UNIX variants.
STIME	Start time of the process.
TTY	The controlling terminal for the process.

TIME   The cumulative execution time for the process.

COMMAND   The command name and arguments.

man page

ps - 11

ps gives a quick profile of the processes running on your system. To get more detailed information, you can include the "*l*" option, which includes a lot of useful additional information as shown in the following example:

```
martyp $ ps -efl
 F S     UID   PID   PPID  C PRI NI   ADDR     SZ   WCHAN    STIME TTY        D
19 T    root     0     0   0   0 SY f026f7f0    0           Feb 18 ?          d
 8 S    root     1     0   0  41 20 f5b90808  175 f5b90a30  Feb 18 ?          -
19 S    root     2     0   0   0 SY f5b90108    0 f0283fd0  Feb 18 ?          t
19 S    root     3     0   0   0 SY f5b8fa08    0 f0287a44  Feb 18 ?          6h
 8 S    root  3065  3059   0  40 20 f626d040 1639 f62aab96  Feb 22 ?          c
 8 S    root    88     1   0  40 20 f5b8d708  377 f5b59df6  Feb 18 ?          q
 8 S    root   478     1   0  41 20 f5b8ec08  388 f5b51bb8  Feb 18 ?          0
 8 S    root    94     1   0  41 20 f5b8d008  527 f5b59e46  Feb 18 ?          d
 8 S    root   150     1   0  41 20 f5da1a10  808 f5b59806  Feb 18 ?          d
 8 S    root    96     1   0  67 20 f5da2810  535 f5b59ad6  Feb 18 ?          v
 8 S    root   144     1   0  41 20 f5da0c10 2694 ef69f61c  Feb 18 ?          5d
 8 S    root  1010     1   0   0 RT f61da330  496 f5dbec1c  Apr 12 ?          n
 8 S    root   106     1   0  41 20 f5da1310  485 f5b59e96  Feb 18 ?          s
 8 S    root   156     1   0  51 20 f5b8de08  446 f5b51eb8  Feb 18 ?          n
 8 S    root   176     1   0  53 20 f5da2110  740 f5b59036  Feb 18 ?          d
 8 S    root   129     1   0  56 20 f5d9fe10  447 f5b59cb6  Feb 18 ?          d
 8 S  daemon   130     1   0  41 20 f5d9f710  564 f5b59b76  Feb 18 ?          d
 8 S    root 14798     1   0  45 20 f5b8e508  616 f5b8e730  Mar 09 ?          3d
 8 S    root   133     1   0  51 20 f5e18818  507 f5b59c66  Feb 18 ?          s
 8 S    root   197     1   0  63 20 f5e15e18  284 f5e16040  Feb 18 ?          d
 8 S    root   196     1   0  41 20 f5da0510  429 f5c68f8e  Feb 18 ?          c
 8 S    root   213     1   0  41 20 f5e16518  586 f5c68b2e  Feb 18 ?          4d
 8 S    root   199   196   0  41 20 f5e16c18  451 f5b59f86  Feb 18 ?          i
 8 S    root   219     1   0  41 20 f5e17318  658 f5b59d06  Feb 18 ?          m
 8 S    root   209     1   0  41 20 f5e18118  234 f5c68e4e  Feb 18 ?          d
 8 S    root  2935   266   0  40 20 f61db130 2473 f62aaa56  Feb 22 ?          4
 8 S    root 16800  3059   1  81 30 f626f340 1466 f61b345e 07:59:40 ?         k
 8 S    root  2963  2954   0  40 20 f5f52028  513 f61b313e  Feb 22 ?          e
 8 S    root   479     1   0  55 20 f5ee7120  407 f5fde2c6  Feb 18 console    g
 8 S    root 10976     1   0  65 20 f5f55828  478 f5c6853e  Jun 01 ?          d
 8 S    root  7468     1   0  46 20 f621da38 2851    8306c  Feb 24 ?          d
 8 S    root   266     1   0  41 20 f5ee5520 1601 f5c6858e  Feb 18 ?          n
 8 S  martyp 16763 16761   0  51 20 f6270140  429 f62701ac 07:46:46 pts/4     h
 8 S    root 10995     1   0  41 20 f5b8f308 2350 f5fde5e6  Jun 01 ?          d
 8 S    root   484   478   0  41 20 f5ee4e20  408 f5ee5048  Feb 18 ?          n
 8 S    root   458     1   0  41 20 f5f54a28  504 f5fde906  Feb 18 ?          2m
 8 O    root 16802 16763   1  61 20 f5ee7820  220          08:00:05 pts/4     l
 8 S    root   471     1   0  41 20 f5f53c28  658 f5fde726  Feb 18 ?          d
 8 S    root   474     1   0  51 20 f5f53528  804 f61a58b6  Feb 18 ?          g
 8 S    root   485   458   0  40 20 f5f52e28  734 f607ecde  Feb 18 ?          74
 8 S    root  2954  2936   0  40 20 f626e540  433 f626e5ac  Feb 22 ?          n
 8 S    root  2936   266   0  66 20 f5ee4720 1637 f5ee478c  Feb 22 ?          n
 8 S    root  3061  3059   0  40 20 f5e17a18 2041 f61b359e  Feb 22 ?          m
 8 S    root  3058     1   0  40 20 f61daa30 1067 f62aadc6  Feb 22 pts/2      n
 8 S    root   712   133   0  41 20 f61d8e30  798 f61b390e  Feb 18 ?          d
 8 Z    root 11001 11000   0   0                                              >
 8 S    root  2938     1   0  60 20 f5ee6320  513 f601bfb6  Feb 22 ?          0
 8 S    root  2999  2954   0  40 20 f621e138 1450 f61b33be  Feb 22 pts/2      t
 8 S    root  3059  3002   1  51 20 f626de40 4010 f62aafa6  Feb 22 pts/2      2n
 8 S    root  3063  3059   0  50 20 f621e838 1952 f62aa556  Feb 22 ?
 8 S    root  3099  3062   0  40 20 f5f52728 2275 f60a1d18  Feb 22 ?          0
 8 S    root 11000 10995   0  48 20 f626d740 2312    55694  Jun 01 ?          e
 8 S    root  3002  2999   0  43 20 f61d8730  427 f61d879c  Feb 22 pts/2      =
```

```
8 S     root    730   133   0  40 20 f61d9530    422 f62aa9b6   Feb 18 ?         d
8 S     root   3062  3059   0  61 20 f621b738   2275 f62aa506   Feb 22 ?         0
8 S     root   3067     1   0  40 20 f5ee5c20    424 f5ee5c8c   Feb 22 ?         d
8 S     root   3000     1   0  40 20 f61d8030    518 f62aa8c6   Feb 22 ?         m
8 S     root   3078  3067   0  40 20 f61d9c30    211 f5b512b8   Feb 22 ?         0
8 S     root  10984     1   0  41 20 f5f54328   2484 eee46e84   Jun 01 ?        1b
8 S     root  16761   133   0  44 20 f5ee4020    411 f5c6894e 07:46:45 ?         d
martyp $
```

In this example, the first column is *F* for flags. *F* provides octal information about whether the process is swapped, in core, a system process, and so on. The octal value sometimes varies from system to system, so check the manual pages for your system to see the octal value of the flags.

S is for state. The state can be sleeping, as indicated by *S* for most of the processes shown in the example, waiting, running, intermediate, terminated, and so on. Again, some of these values may vary from system to system, so check your manual pages.

Some additional useful information in this output are: *NI* for the nice value, *ADDR* for the memory address of the process, *SZ* for the size of the process in physical pages, and *WCHAN*, which is the event for which the process is waiting.

Killing a Process

ps - 11

kill - 22

If you issue the **ps** command and find that one of your processes is hung, or if you started a large job that you wish to stop, you can do so with the **kill** command. **kill** is a utility that sends a signal to the process you identify. You can **kill** any process that you own. In addition, the superuser can kill almost any process on the system.

To kill a process that you own, simply issue the **kill** command and the Process ID (PID). The following example shows issuing the

ps command to find all processes owned by *martyp*, killing a process, and checking to see that it has disappeared:

man page

grep - 19

```
martyp $ ps -ef | grep martyp
   martyp 19336 19334 0 05:24:32 pts/4  0:01 -ksh
   martyp 19426 19336 0 06:01:01 pts/4  0:00 grep martyp
   martyp 19424 19336 5 06:00:48 pts/4  0:01 find / -name .login
martyp $ kill 19424
martyp $ ps -ef | grep martyp
   martyp 19336 19334 0 05:24:32 pts/4  0:01 -ksh
   martyp 19428 19336 1 06:01:17 pts/4  0:00 grep martyp
[1] + Terminated              find / -name .login &
martyp $
```

man page

ps - 11

The example shows killing process *19424,* which is owned by *martyp*. We confirm that the process has indeed been killed by reissuing the **ps** command. You can also use the *-u* option to **ps** to list processes with the login name you specify.

You can kill several processes on the command line by issuing **kill** followed by a space-separated list of all the process numbers you wish to kill.

Take special care when killing processes if you are logged in as superuser. You may adversely affect the way the system runs and have to manually restart processes or reboot the system.

Signals

man page

kill - 22

man page

find - 20

When you issue the **kill** command and process number, you are also sending a *signal* associated with the **kill**. We did not specify a *signal* in our **kill** example; however, the default *signal* of 15, or *SIGTERM,* was used. These *signals* are used by the system to communicate with processes. The *signal* of 15 we used to terminate our process is a software termination *signal* that is usually enough to terminate a user process such as the **find** we had started. A process that is difficult to kill may require the *SIGKILL,* or 9 *signal*. This *signal* causes an immediate termination of the process. I use this only as a last resort because processes killed with *SIGKILL* do not always terminate smoothly. To kill such processes as the shell, you sometimes have to use *SIGKILL*.

You can use either the *signal* name or number. These signal numbers sometimes vary from system to system, so view the manual page for *signal*, usually in section 5, to see the list of *signals* on your system. A list of some of the most frequently used *signal* numbers and corresponding *signals* follows:

Signal Number	Signal
1	SIGHUP
2	SIGINT
3	SIGQUIT
9	SIGKILL
15	SIGTERM
24	SIGSTOP

To kill a process with id *234* with *SIGKILL*, you would issue the following command:

```
$ kill -9 234
    |    |   |
    |    |   |> process id (PID)
    |    |> signal number
    |> kill command to terminate the process
```

Show Remote Mounts with showmount

showmount is used to show all remote systems (clients) that have mounted a local file system. **showmount** is useful for determining the file systems that are most often mounted by clients with NFS. The output of **showmount** is particularly easy to read because it lists the host name and directory that was mounted by the client.

NFS servers often end up serving many NFS clients that were not originally intended to be served. This situation ends up consuming additional UNIX system resources on the NFS server, as well as additional network bandwidth. Keep in mind that any data transferred from an NFS server to an NFS client consumes network bandwidth, and in some cases, may be a substantial amount of bandwith if large files or applications are being transferred from the NFS server to the client. The following example is a partial output of **showmount** taken from a system. **showmount** runs on the HP-UX, AIX, and Linux systems I have been using throughout this chapter, but not on the Solaris system:

```
# showmount -a
sys100.ct.mp.com:/applic
sys101.ct.mp.com:/applic
sys102.cal.mp.com:/applic
sys103.cal.mp.com:/applic
sys104.cal.mp.com:/applic
sys105.cal.mp.com:/applic
sys106.cal.mp.com:/applic
sys107.cal.mp.com:/applic
sys108.cal.mp.com:/applic
sys109.cal.mp.com:/applic
sys200.cal.mp.com:/usr/users
sys201.cal.mp.com:/usr/users
sys202.cal.mp.com:/usr/users
sys203.cal.mp.com:/usr/users
sys204.cal.mp.com:/usr/users
sys205.cal.mp.com:/usr/users
sys206.cal.mp.com:/usr/users
```

showmount -a

sys207.cal.mp.com:/usr/users

sys208.cal.mp.com:/usr/users

sys209.cal.mp.com:/usr/users

man page

showmount
- 11

The three following options are available for the **showmount** command:

-**a** prints output in the format "name:directory," as shown above.

-**d** lists all the local directories that have been remotely mounted by clients.

-**e** prints a list of exported file systems.

The following are examples of **showmount -d** and **showmount -e**:

showmount -d

/applic

/usr/users

/usr/oracle

/usr/users/emp.data

/network/database

/network/users

/tmp/working

showmount -e

export list for server101.cal.mp.com

/applic

/usr/users

/cdrom

Show System Swap

If your system has insufficient main memory for all the information it needs to work with, it will move pages of information to your swap area or swap entire processes to your swap area. Pages that were most recently used are kept in main memory, and those not recently used will be the first moved out of main memory.

System administrators spend a lot of time determining the right amount of swap space for their systems. Insufficient swap may prevent a system from starting additional processes, hang applications, or not permit additional users to get access to the system. Having sufficient swap prevents these problems from occurring. System administrators usually go about determining the right amount of swap by considering many important factors, including the following:

1. How much swap is recommended by the application(s) you run? Use the swap size recommended by your applications. Application vendors tend to be realistic when recommending swap space. There is sometimes competition among application vendors to claim the lowest memory and CPU requirements in order to keep the overall cost of solutions as low as possible, but swap space recommendations are usually realistic.

2. How many applications will you run simultaneously? If you are running several applications, sum the swap space recommended for each application you plan to run simultaneously. If you have a database application that recommends 200 MBytes of swap and a development tool that recommends 100 MBytes of swap, then configure your system with 300 MBytes of swap, minimum.

3. Will you be using substantial system resources on peripheral functionality such as NFS? The nature of NFS is to provide access to file systems, some of which may be very large, so this use may have an impact on your swap space requirements.

Swap is listed and manipulated on different UNIX variants with different commands. The following example shows listing the swap area on a Solaris system with **swap -l**:

```
# swap -l
swapfile              dev  swaplo blocks    free
/dev/dsk/c0t3d0s1    32,25      8 263080 209504
```

These values are all in 512 KByte blocks. In this case, the free blocks are *209504*, which is a significant amount of the overall swap allocated on the system.

man page

swapinfo
- 11

You can view the amount of swap being consumed on your HP-UX system with **swapinfo**. The following is an example output of **swapinfo**:

```
# swapinfo

            Kb      Kb      Kb  PCT  START/     Kb
TYPE     AVAIL    USED    FREE USED  LIMIT RESERVE  PRI  NAME
dev      49152   10532   38620  21%      0       -    1  /dev/vg00/lvol2
dev     868352   10888  759160   1%      0       -    1  /dev/vg00/lvol8
reserve      -  532360 -532360
memory  816360  469784  346576  58%
```

Following is a brief overview of what **swapinfo** gives you.

In the previous example, the "TYPE" field indicated whether the swap was "dev" for device, "reserve" for paging space on reserve, or "memory." Memory is a way to allow programs to reserve more virtual memory than you have hard disk paging space setup for on your system.

"Kb AVAIL" is the total swap space available in 1024-byte blocks. This includes both used and unused swap.

"Kb USED" is the current number of 1024-byte blocks in use.

"Kb FREE" is the difference between "Kb AVAIL" and "Kb USED."

"PCT USED" is "Kb USED" divided by "Kb AVAIL."

"START/LIMIT" is the block address of the start of the swap area.

"Kb RESERVE" is "-" for device swap or the number of 1024-byte blocks for file system swap.

"PRI" is the priority given to this swap area.

"NAME" is the device name of the swap device.

man page

swapinfo - 11

You can also issue the **swapinfo** command with a series of options. Here are some of the options you can include:

-*m* to display output of **swapinfo** in MBytes rather than in 1024-byte blocks.

-*d* prints information related to device swap areas only.

-*f* prints information about file system swap areas only.

man page

sar - 11

sar: The System Activity Reporter

sar is another UNIX command for gathering information about activities on your system. You can gather data over an extended time period with **sar** and later produce reports based on the data. **sar** is similar among UNIX variants in that the options and outputs are similar. The Linux system I was using for the examples did not support **sar**, but the Solaris, HP-UX, and AIX systems had the same options and nearly identical outputs. The following are some useful options to **sar,** along with examples of reports produced with these options where applicable:

sar -o	Saves data in a file specified by "o." After the file name, you would usually also enter the time interval for samples and the number of samples. The following example shows saving the binary data in file **/tmp/sar.data** at an interval of 60 seconds 300 times:

```
# sar -o /tmp/sar.data 60 300
```

The data in **/tmp/sar.data** can later be extracted from the file.

sar -f

Specify a file from which you will extract data.

sar -u

Report CPU utilization with the headings %usr, %sys, %wio, %idle with some processes waiting for block I/O, %idle. This report is similar to the **iostat** and **vmstat** CPU reports. You extract the binary data saved in a file to get CPU information, as shown in the following example. The following is a **sar -u** example:

```
# sar -u -f /tmp/sar.data

Header Information for your system

12:52:04     %usr     %sys     %wio     %idle
12:53:04       62        4        5        29
12:54:04       88        5        3         4
12:55:04       94        5        1         0
12:56:04       67        4        4        25
12:57:04       59        4        4        32
12:58:04       61        4        3        32
12:59:04       65        4        3        28
13:00:04       62        5       16        17
13:01:04       59        5        9        27
13:02:04       71        4        3        22
13:03:04       60        4        4        32
13:04:04       71        5        4        20
13:05:04       80        6        8         7
13:06:04       56        3        3        37
13:07:04       57        4        4        36
13:08:04       66        4        4        26
13:09:04       80       10        2         8
13:10:04       73       10        2        15
13:11:04       64        6        3        28
13:12:04       56        4        3        38
```

```
13:13:04          55          3          3          38
13:14:04          57          4          3          36
13:15:04          70          4          5          21
13:16:04          65          5          9          21
13:17:04          62          6          2          30
13:18:04          60          5          3          33
13:19:04          77          3          4          16
13:20:04          76          5          3          15

                  .
                  .
                  .

14:30:04          50          6          6          38
14:31:04          57         12         19          12
14:32:04          51          8         20          21
14:33:04          41          4          9          46
14:34:04          43          4          9          45
14:35:04          38          4          6          53
14:36:04          38          9          7          46
14:37:04          46          3         11          40
14:38:04          43          4          7          46
14:39:04          37          4          5          54
14:40:04          33          4          5          58
14:41:04          40          3          3          53
14:42:04          44          3          3          50
14:43:04          27          3          7          64

Average           57          5          8          30
```

sar -b   Report buffer cache activity. A database application such as Oracle would recommend that you use this option to see the effectiveness of buffer cache use. You extract the binary data saved in a file to get CPU information, as shown in the following example:

man page

sar - 11

```
# sar -b -f /tmp/sar.data

Header information for your system

12:52:04 bread/s lread/s %rcache bwrit/s lwrit/s %wcache pread/s pwrit/s
12:53:04       5     608      99       1      11      95       0       0
12:54:04       7     759      99       0      14      99       0       0
12:55:04       2    1733     100       4      24      83       0       0
```

```
12:56:04        1        836      100        1        18       96        0        0
12:57:04        0        623      100        2        21       92        0        0
12:58:04        0        779      100        1        16       96        0        0
12:59:04        0       1125      100        0        14       98        0        0
13:00:04        2       1144      100        9        89       89        0        0
13:01:04       10        898       99       11        76       86        0        0
13:02:04        0       1156      100        0        14       99        0        0
13:03:04        1        578      100        2        22       88        0        0
13:04:04        5       1251      100        0        12       99        0        0
13:05:04        3       1250      100        0        12       97        0        0
13:06:04        1        588      100        0        12       98        0        0
13:07:04        1        649      100        2        15       86        0        0
13:08:04        1        704      100        2        15       86        0        0
13:09:04        1       1068      100        0        18      100        0        0
13:10:04        0        737      100        1        44       99        0        0
13:11:04        0        735      100        1        13       95        0        0
13:12:04        0        589      100        1        15       93        0        0
13:13:04        0        573      100        0        16       99        0        0
13:14:04        1        756      100        1        16       91        0        0
13:15:04        1       1092      100        9        49       81        0        0
13:16:04        2        808      100        6        82       93        0        0
13:17:04        0        712      100        1         9       93        0        0
13:18:04        1        609      100        0        13       97        0        0
13:19:04        1        603      100        0        10       99        0        0
13:20:04        0       1127      100        0        14       98        0        0
                                      .
                                      .
                                      .
14:30:04        2        542      100        1        22       94        0        0
14:31:04       10        852       99       12       137       92        0        0
14:32:04        2        730      100       10       190       95        0        0
14:33:04        4        568       99        2        26       91        0        0
14:34:04        4        603       99        1        13       91        0        0
14:35:04        1        458      100        1        13       89        0        0
14:36:04       13        640       98        1        24       98        0        0
14:37:04       21        882       98        1        18       95        0        0
14:38:04        7        954       99        0        19       98        0        0
14:39:04        3        620      100        1        11       94        0        0
14:40:04        3        480       99        2        15       85        0        0
14:41:04        1        507      100        0         9       98        0        0
14:42:04        1       1010      100        1        10       91        0        0
14:43:04        5        547       99        1         9       93        0        0

Average         3        782      100        3        37       91        0        0
```

man page

sar - 11

sar -d

Report disk activity. You get the device name, percent that the device was busy, average number of requests outstanding for the device, number of data transfers per second for the device, and other information. You extract the binary data saved in a file to get CPU information, as shown in the following example:

```
# sar -d -f /tmp/sar.data
```

Header information for your system

12:52:04	device	%busy	avque	r+w/s	blks/s	avwait	avserv
12:53:04	c0t6d0	0.95	1.41	1	10	16.76	17.28
	c5t4d0	100.00	1.03	20	320	8.36	18.90
	c4t5d1	10.77	0.50	13	214	5.02	18.44
	c5t4d2	0.38	0.50	0	3	4.61	18.81
12:54:04	c0t6d0	0.97	1.08	1	11	10.75	14.82
	c5t4d0	100.00	1.28	54	862	9.31	20.06
	c4t5d1	12.43	0.50	15	241	5.21	16.97
	c5t4d2	0.37	0.50	0	3	3.91	18.20
12:55:04	c0t6d0	1.77	1.42	1	22	13.32	14.16
	c5t4d0	100.00	0.79	26	421	8.33	16.00
	c4t5d1	14.47	0.51	17	270	5.30	13.48
	c5t4d2	0.72	0.50	0	7	4.82	15.69
12:56:04	c0t6d0	1.07	21.57	1	22	72.94	19.58
	c5t4d0	100.00	0.60	16	251	6.80	13.45
	c4t5d1	8.75	0.50	11	177	5.05	10.61
	c5t4d2	0.62	0.50	0	6	4.79	15.43
12:57:04	c0t6d0	0.78	1.16	1	9	13.53	14.91
	c5t4d0	100.00	0.66	15	237	7.60	13.69
	c4t5d1	9.48	0.54	13	210	5.39	13.33
	c5t4d2	0.87	0.50	1	10	4.86	14.09
12:58:04	c0t6d0	1.12	8.29	1	17	54.96	14.35
	c5t4d0	100.00	0.60	11	176	7.91	14.65
	c4t5d1	5.35	0.50	7	111	5.23	10.35
	c5t4d2	0.92	0.50	1	10	4.63	16.08
12:59:04	c0t6d0	0.67	1.53	1	8	18.03	16.05
	c5t4d0	99.98	0.54	11	174	7.69	14.09
	c4t5d1	3.97	0.50	5	83	4.82	9.54
	c5t4d2	1.05	0.50	1	11	4.69	16.29
13:00:04	c0t6d0	3.22	0.67	3	39	8.49	16.53
	c5t4d0	100.00	0.60	65	1032	8.46	14.83
	c4t5d1	21.62	0.50	31	504	5.30	8.94
	c5t4d2	6.77	0.50	5	78	4.86	14.09
13:01:04	c0t6d0	4.45	3.08	5	59	25.83	11.49
	c5t4d0	100.00	0.65	42	676	7.85	14.52
	c4t5d1	21.34	0.55	30	476	5.87	18.49
	c5t4d2	4.37	0.50	3	51	5.32	13.50

                       .
                       .
                       .

| 14:42:04 | c0t6d0 | 0.53 | 0.83 | 0 | 7 | 12.21 | 16.33 |
```
```

```
              c5t4d0    100.00     0.56       7     107     6.99    14.65
              c4t5d1      6.38     0.50       7     113     4.97    15.18
              c5t4d2      0.15     0.50       0       2     4.53    16.50
   14:43:04   c0t6d0      0.52     0.92       0       7    11.50    15.86
              c5t4d0     99.98     0.92      17     270     8.28    18.64
              c4t5d1     10.26     0.50       9     150     5.35    16.41
              c5t4d2      0.12     0.50       0       1     5.25    14.45

   Average    c0t6d0      1.43   108.80       2      26     0.00    14.71
   Average    c5t4d0    100.00     0.74      25     398     7.83   -10.31
   Average    c4t5d1     19.11     0.51      25     399     5.26   -13.75
   Average    c5t4d2      1.71     0.53       1      21     5.29    13.46
```

man page

sar - 11

sar -q   Report average queue length. You may have
a problem any time the run queue length is
greater than the number of processors on the
system:

```
# sar -q -f /tmp/sar.data

Header information for your system

12:52:04 runq-sz %runocc swpq-sz %swpocc
12:53:04    1.1      20    0.0       0
12:54:04    1.4      51    0.0       0
12:55:04    1.3      71    0.0       0
12:56:04    1.1      22    0.0       0
12:57:04    1.3      16    0.0       0
12:58:04    1.1      14    0.0       0
12:59:04    1.2      12    0.0       0
13:00:04    1.2      21    0.0       0
13:01:04    1.1      18    0.0       0
13:02:04    1.3      20    0.0       0
13:03:04    1.2      15    0.0       0
13:04:04    1.2      20    0.0       0
13:05:04    1.2      43    0.0       0
13:06:04    1.1      14    0.0       0
13:07:04    1.2      15    0.0       0
13:08:04    1.2      26    0.0       0
13:09:04    1.5      38    0.0       0
13:10:04    1.5      30    0.0       0
13:11:04    1.2      23    0.0       0
13:12:04    1.3      11    0.0       0
```

```
13:13:04      1.3        12       0.0          0
13:14:04      1.4        16       0.0          0
13:15:04      1.4        27       0.0          0
13:16:04      1.5        20       0.0          0
13:17:04      1.3        21       0.0          0
13:18:04      1.1        15       0.0          0
13:19:04      1.2        19       0.0          0
13:20:04      1.4        22       0.0          0

                         .
                         .
                         .

14:30:04      1.5         5       0.0          0
14:31:04      1.6        12       0.0          0
14:32:04      1.4         9       0.0          0
14:33:04      1.1         6       0.0          0
14:34:04      1.3         3       0.0          0
14:35:04      1.1         4       0.0          0
14:36:04      1.2         6       0.0          0
14:37:04      1.4         5       0.0          0
14:38:04      1.2        10       0.0          0
14:39:04      1.3         4       0.0          0
14:40:04      1.1         3       0.0          0
14:41:04      1.6         3       0.0          0
14:42:04      1.1         4       0.0          0
14:43:04      1.3         1       0.0          0

Average       1.3        17       1.2          0
```

sar -w   Report system swapping activity.

man page

sar - 11

```
# sar -w -f /tmp/sar.data

Header information for your system

12:52:04 swpin/s bswin/s swpot/s bswot/s pswch/s
12:53:04    1.00     0.0    1.00     0.0     231
12:54:04    1.00     0.0    1.00     0.0     354
12:55:04    1.00     0.0    1.00     0.0     348
12:56:04    1.00     0.0    1.00     0.0     200
12:57:04    1.00     0.0    1.00     0.0     277
12:58:04    1.00     0.0    1.00     0.0     235
```

12:59:04	1.02	0.0	1.02	0.0	199
13:00:04	0.78	0.0	0.78	0.0	456
13:01:04	1.00	0.0	1.00	0.0	435
13:02:04	1.02	0.0	1.02	0.0	216
13:03:04	0.98	0.0	0.98	0.0	204
13:04:04	1.02	0.0	1.02	0.0	239
13:05:04	1.00	0.0	1.00	0.0	248
13:06:04	0.97	0.0	0.97	0.0	170
13:07:04	1.00	0.0	1.00	0.0	166
13:08:04	1.02	0.0	1.02	0.0	209
13:09:04	0.98	0.0	0.98	0.0	377
13:10:04	1.00	0.0	1.00	0.0	200
13:11:04	1.00	0.0	1.00	0.0	192
13:12:04	0.87	0.0	0.87	0.0	187
13:13:04	0.93	0.0	0.93	0.0	172
13:14:04	1.00	0.0	1.00	0.0	170
13:15:04	1.00	0.0	1.00	0.0	382
13:16:04	1.00	0.0	1.00	0.0	513
13:17:04	1.00	0.0	1.00	0.0	332
13:18:04	1.00	0.0	1.00	0.0	265
13:19:04	1.02	0.0	1.02	0.0	184
13:20:04	0.98	0.0	0.98	0.0	212

.
.
.

14:30:04	0.00	0.0	0.00	0.0	301
14:31:04	0.00	0.0	0.00	0.0	566
14:32:04	0.00	0.0	0.00	0.0	539
14:33:04	0.00	0.0	0.00	0.0	400
14:34:04	0.00	0.0	0.00	0.0	242
14:35:04	0.00	0.0	0.00	0.0	286
14:36:04	0.00	0.0	0.00	0.0	295
14:37:04	0.00	0.0	0.00	0.0	249
14:38:04	0.00	0.0	0.00	0.0	300
14:39:04	0.00	0.0	0.00	0.0	296
14:40:04	0.00	0.0	0.00	0.0	419
14:41:04	0.00	0.0	0.00	0.0	234
14:42:04	0.00	0.0	0.00	0.0	237
14:43:04	0.00	0.0	0.00	0.0	208
Average	0.70	0.0	0.70	0.0	346

timex to Analyze a Command

man page

timex - 11

If you have a specific command you want to find out more about, you can use **timex**, which reports the elapsed time, user time, and system time spent in the execution of any command you specify.

timex is a good command for users because it gives you an idea of the system resources you are consuming when issuing a command. The following two examples show issuing **timex** with no options to get a short output of the amount of *cpu* consumed; the second example shows issuing **timex -s** to report "total" system activity on a Solaris system:

```
martyp $ timex listing

real       0.02
user       0.00
sys        0.02


martyp $ timex -s listing

real       0.02
user       0.00
sys        0.01


SunOS 5.7 Generic sun4m      08/21
```

07:48:30	%usr	%sys	%wio	%idle
07:48:31	32	68	0	0

07:48:30	bread/s	lread/s	%rcache	bwrit/s	lwrit/s	%wcache	pread/s	pwrit/s
07:48:31	0	0	100	0	0	100	0	0
Average	0	0	100	0	0	100	0	0

07:48:30	device	%busy	avque	r+w/s	blks/s	avwait	avserv
07:48:31	fd0	0	0.0	0	0	0.0	0.0
	nfs1	0	0.0	0	0	0.0	0.0
	nfs219	0	0.0	0	0	0.0	0.0
	sd1	0	0.0	0	0	0.0	0.0
	sd1,a	0	0.0	0	0	0.0	0.0
	sd1,b	0	0.0	0	0	0.0	0.0
	sd1,c	0	0.0	0	0	0.0	0.0
	sd1,g	0	0.0	0	0	0.0	0.0
	sd3	0	0.0	0	0	0.0	0.0
	sd3,a	0	0.0	0	0	0.0	0.0
	sd3,b	0	0.0	0	0	0.0	0.0
	sd3,c	0	0.0	0	0	0.0	0.0
	sd6	0	0.0	0	0	0.0	0.0
Average	fd0	0	0.0	0	0	0.0	0.0
	nfs1	0	0.0	0	0	0.0	0.0
	nfs219	0	0.0	0	0	0.0	0.0
	sd1	0	0.0	0	0	0.0	0.0
	sd1,a	0	0.0	0	0	0.0	0.0
	sd1,b	0	0.0	0	0	0.0	0.0
	sd1,c	0	0.0	0	0	0.0	0.0
	sd1,g	0	0.0	0	0	0.0	0.0
	sd3	0	0.0	0	0	0.0	0.0

```
              sd3,a          0      0.0      0        0      0.0     0.0
              sd3,b          0      0.0      0        0      0.0     0.0
              sd3,c          0      0.0      0        0      0.0     0.0
              sd6            0      0.0      0        0      0.0     0.0

07:48:30 rawch/s canch/s outch/s rcvin/s xmtin/s mdmin/s
07:48:31       0       0     147       0       0       0

Average        0       0     147       0       0       0

07:48:30 scall/s sread/s swrit/s  fork/s  exec/s rchar/s wchar/s
07:48:31    2637       0      95   15.79   15.79       0   19216

Average     2637       0      95   15.79   15.79       0   19216

07:48:30 swpin/s bswin/s swpot/s bswot/s pswch/s
07:48:31    0.00     0.0    0.00     0.0     116

Average     0.00     0.0    0.00     0.0     116

07:48:30  iget/s namei/s dirbk/s
07:48:31       0     195     121

Average        0     195     121

07:48:30 runq-sz %runocc swpq-sz %swpocc
07:48:31     2.0     526

Average      2.0     526

07:48:30  proc-sz     ov inod-sz     ov file-sz     ov  lock-sz
07:48:31   45/986      0 973/4508     0 357/357      0    0/0


07:48:30   msg/s  sema/s
07:48:31    0.00    0.00

Average     0.00    0.00

07:48:30  atch/s  pgin/s ppgin/s  pflt/s  vflt/s slock/s
07:48:31    0.00    0.00    0.00  505.26 1036.84    0.00

Average     0.00    0.00    0.00  505.26 1036.84    0.00

07:48:30 pgout/s ppgout/s pgfree/s pgscan/s %ufs_ipf
07:48:31    0.00    0.00    0.00    0.00    0.00

Average     0.00    0.00    0.00    0.00    0.00

07:48:30 freemem freeswap
07:48:31   15084 1224421

Average    15084 1224421

07:48:30 sml_mem   alloc  fail  lg_mem   alloc  fail ovsz_alloc fail
07:48:31 2617344 1874368     0 17190912 10945416    0   3067904    0

Average   186953  133883     0 1227922  781815     0    219136    0
```

More Advanced and Graphical Performance Tools

The command line is a way of life when working with UNIX. UNIX grew out of the command line and is still primarily command line-based. Although you need to know a lot when issuing commands, especially when it comes to system performance, you can dig deeply very quickly with many of the commands I just covered.

You have the option with most UNIX variants to buy graphical performance tools. Some systems come with basic graphical performance tools, but will usually end up buying an advaced performance analysis tool if you want to perform advanced performance analysis. We'll take a quick look at a few performance tools in upcoming sections.

Figure 11-1 shows three performance tools that came with the Red Hat Linux system I used for many of the examples in this chapter:

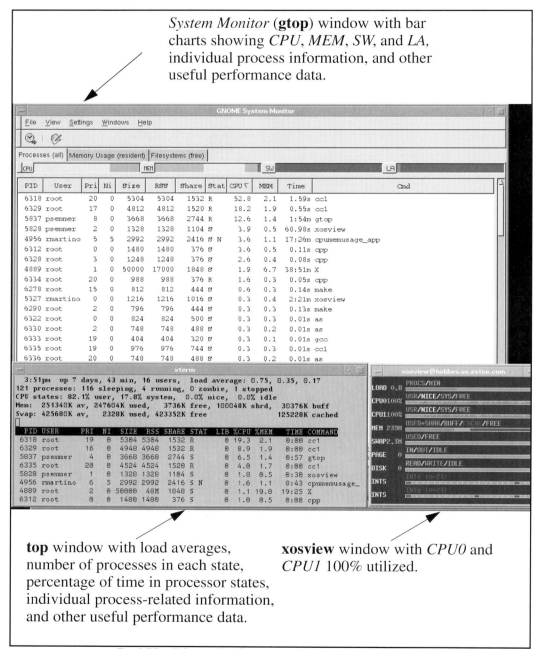

System Monitor (**gtop**) window with bar charts showing *CPU*, *MEM*, *SW*, and *LA*, individual process information, and other useful performance data.

top window with load averages, number of processes in each state, percentage of time in processor states, individual process-related information, and other useful performance data.

xosview window with *CPU0* and *CPU1* 100% utilized.

Figure 11-1   Red Hat Linux Performance Tools Screen Shot

The three performance tools shown in this diagram are **xosview** in the lower right, the *System Monitor* across the top of the screen, and **top** shown in the lower left. The *System Monitor* provides bar charts across the top of the screen that indicate the amount of CPU, Memory, Swap, and LAN utilization taking place. There is then tabular data supplied for every process on the system. The *System Monitor* is a graphical version of **top** that I invoked with the command **gtop** for graphical **top**. **xosview** is a small load meter that you can keep running that provides bar charts of system activity shown in the bottom right window. This is the **X** Windows **o**perating **s**ystem **view** program, hence the name **xosview**. You can't see the bar charts clearly in this diagram, because this is a color-based application and the book is printed in only black and white. The bar charts are, however, clear on the computer screen. The final, and most often used, tool on UNIX systems is the character version of **top** that is running in the bottom left **xterm**. **top** is found on many UNIX variants and supplies a lot of useful system information.

man page

top - 11

Among the useful **top** system data displayed is the following:

- Load averages in the last one, five, and fifteen minutes.

- Number of existing processes and the number of processes in each state.

- Percentage of time spent in each of the processor states per processor on the system.

This same information is included in the bottom of the *System Monitor* window, which is covered by the **top** and **xosview** windows.

Next in the **top** window is memory data, including used, free, and shared.

Data is also provided for individual processes in a format similar to **ps**, including the following:

man page

ps - 11

PID - Process ID number.

USER - Name of the owner of the process.

PRI - Current priority of the process.

NI - Nice value, ranging from -20 to +20.

SIZE - Total size of the process in kilobytes.

RSS - Resident size of the process in kilobytes.

STATE - Current state of the process.

TIME - Number of system and CPU seconds the process has consumed.

%CPU - CPU percentage.

%MEM - Memory percentage.

COMMAND - Name of the command the process is currently running.

man page

top - 11

   As with most of the commands we have been covering, **top** is different among UNIX variants. You may see some different fields on the different UNIX variants. I am usually confident when I sit down at any UNIX system that I can run **top** and quickly see how the system is running. Most versions of **top** I have run are character-based applications, so you don't even need a graphics terminal to run them. I have run **top** in this example in character mode within an X terminal.

   The system used in this example has two CPUs. If you look carefully in the **xosview** window, you'll see that both *CPU0* and *CPU1* are 100 percent used. At the time this screen shot was obtained, I was compiling the Linux kernel on this system, which consumed all the

CPU resources on the system for a short period of time. You can see from both the **top** and *System Monitor* windows that the program **cc1**, used to compile the kernel, was consuming a substantial amount of the CPU resources on the system.

Figure 11-1 helps illustrate how different tools can help with viewing how system resources are consumed. **xosview** provides a quick reference, graphical overview of how many system resources are being consumed. **top** and *System Monitor* can then be used to determine the specific process consuming the most system resources.

HP GlancePlus/UX

Using UNIX commands to get a better understanding of what your system is doing requires you to do a lot of work. In the first case, issuing UNIX commands gives you the advantage of obtaining data about what is taking place on your system that very second. Unfortunately, you can't always issue additional commands to probe more deeply into an area, such as a process, about which you want to know more.

Now I'll describe another technique - a tool that can help get useful data in real time, allow you to investigate a specific process, and not bury you in reports. This tool is HP GlancePlus/UX (GlancePlus). This tool runs on several UNIX variants, including Solaris, HP-UX, and AIX.

GlancePlus can be run in character mode or in graphic mode. I chose to use the character-based version of GlancePlus, because this will run on any display, either graphics- or character-based, and the many colors used by the Motif version of GlancePlus do not show up well in a book. My examples are displayed much more clearly in the book when using the character mode. I recommend that you try both versions of GlancePlus to see which you prefer.

The system used in the examples has eight processors, 4 GBytes of RAM, and a substantial amount of EMC Symmetrix disk connected to it.

Figure 11-2 shows one of several interactive screens of Glance-Plus. This one is the *Process List* screen, also referred to as the *Global* screen. This is the default screen when bringing up GlancePlus.

Two features of the screen shown in Figure 11-2 are worth noticing immediately:

man page

ps - 11

1. Four histograms at the top of the screen give you a graphical representation of your CPU, Disk, Memory, and Swap Utilization in a format much easier to assimilate than a column of numbers.

2. The "Process Summary" has columns similar to **ps -ef**, with which many system administrators are familiar and comfortable. GlancePlus, however, gives you the additional capability of filtering out processes that are using very few resources by specifying thresholds.

Using GlancePlus, you can take a close look at your system in many areas, including the following:

- *Process List*
- *CPU Report*
- *Memory Report*
- *Swap Space*
- *Disk Report*
- *LAN Detail*
- *NFS by System*
- *PRM Summary (Process Resource Manager)*
- *I/O by File System*
- *I/O by Disk*
- *I/O by Logical Volume*

• *System Tables*

Figure 11-2 is a GlancePlus screen shot.

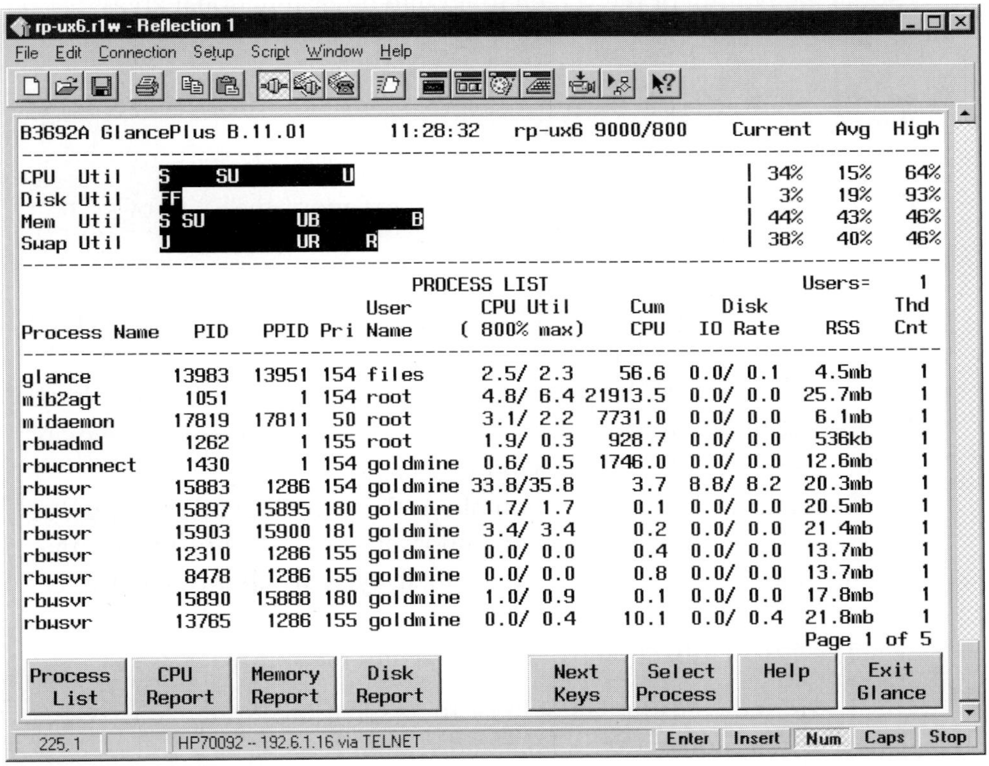

Figure 11-2 HP GlancePlus/UX *Process List* Screen Shot

Because the *Process List* shown in the example tells you where
your system resources are going at the highest level, I'll start my
description here. I am using a terminal emulator on my portable computer to display GlancePlus. I find that many system administrators
use a PC and a terminal emulator to perform UNIX management functions. Keep in mind that the information shown on this screen can be

updated at any interval you choose. If your system is running in a steady-state mode, you may want to have a long interval because you don't expect things to much change. On the other hand, you may have a dynamic environment and want to see the histograms and other information updated every few seconds. In either case, you can change the update interval to suit your needs. You can use the function keys at the bottom of the screen to go into other functional areas.

Process List **Description**

The *Process List* screen provides an overview of the state of system resources and active processes.

The top section of the screen (the histogram section) is common to the many screens of GlancePlus. The bottom section of the screen displays a summary of active processes.

Line 1 provides the product and version number of GlancePlus, the time, name of your system, and system type. In this case, we are running version 11.01 of GlancePlus.

Line 3 provides information about the overall state of the CPU. This tends to be the single most important piece of information that administrators want to know about their system - Is my CPU over-worked?

The CPU Utilization bar is divided into the following parts:

1. "S" indicates the amount of time spent on "system" activities such as context switching and system calls.

2. "N" indicates the amount of time spent running "nice" user processes (those run at a low priority).

3. "U" indicates the amount of time spent running user processes.

4. "R" indicates real-time processes.

5. "A" indicates the amount of time spent running processes at a negative "nice" priority.

The far right of line 3 shows the percentage of CPU utilization. If your system is "CPU-Bound," you will consistently see this number near 100 percent. You get statistics for Current, Average (since analysis was begun), and High.

Line 4 shows Disk Utilization for the busiest mounted disk. This bar indicates the percentage of File System and Virtual Memory disk I/O over the update interval. This bar is divided into two parts:

1. "F" indicates the amount of file system activity of user reads and writes and other non-paging activities.

2. "V" indicates the percentage of disk I/O devoted to paging virtual memory.

The Current, Avg, and High statistics have the same meaning as in the CPU Utilization description.

Line 5 shows the system memory utilization. This bar is divided into three parts:

1. "S" indicates the amount of memory devoted to system use.

2. "U" indicates the amount of memory devoted to user programs and data.

3. "B" indicates the amount of memory devoted to buffer cache.

The Current, Avg, and High statistics have the same meaning as in the CPU Utilization description.

Line 6 shows Swap Util information, which is divided into two parts:

1. "R" indicates reserved, but not in use.

2. "U" indicates swap space in use.

All three of these areas (CPU, Memory, and Disk) may be further analyzed by using the F2, F3, and F4 function keys, respectively. Again, you may see different function keys, depending on the version of GlancePlus you are running. When you select one of these keys, you move from the *Process List* screen to a screen that provides more in-depth functions in the selected area. In addition, more detailed screens are available for many other system areas. Because most investigation beyond the *Process List* screen takes place on the CPU, Memory, and Disk screens, I'll describe these in more detail shortly.

The bottom of the *Process List* screen shows the active processes running on your system. Because there are typically many processes running on a UNIX system, you may want to consider using the **o** command to set a threshold for CPU utilization. If you set a threshold of five percent, for instance, then only processes that exceed the average CPU utilization of five percent over the interval will be displayed. There are other types of thresholds that can be specified such as the amount of RAM used (Resident Size). If you specify thresholds, you see only the processes you're most interested in, that is, those consuming the greatest system resources.

There is a line for each active process that meets the threshold requirements you defined. There may be more than one page of processes to display. The message in the bottom-right corner of the screen indicates which page you are on. You can scroll forward to view the next page with **f** and backwards with **b**. Usually only a few processes consume most of your system resources, so I recommend setting the thresholds so that only one page of processes is displayed. There are a whole series of commands you can issue in GlancePlus. The final figure in this section shows the commands recognized by GlancePlus.

Here is a brief summary of the process headings:

Process Name The name or abbreviation used to load the executable program.

PID   The process identification number.

PPID   The PID of the parent process.

Pri   The priority of the process. The lower the number, the higher the priority. System-level processes usually run between 0 and 127. Other processes usually run between 128 and 255. "Nice" processes are those with the lowest priority and they have the largest number.

User Name   Name of the user who started the process.

CPU Util   The first number is the percentage of CPU utilization that this process consumed over the update interval. Note that this is 800% maximum for our eight-processor system. The second number is the percentage of CPU utilization that this process consumed since GlancePlus was invoked. Most system administrators leave GlancePlus running continuously on their systems with a low update interval. Since GlancePlus uses very little system overhead, there is virtually no penalty for this.

Cum CPU   The total CPU time used by the process. Glance-Plus uses the "midaemon" to gather information. If the **midaemon** started before the process, you will get an accurate measure of cumulative CPU time used by the process.

Disk IO Rate   The first number is the average disk I/O rate per second over the last update interval. The second number is the average disk I/O rate since Glance-Plus was started or since the process was started. Disk I/O can mean a lot of different things. Disk I/O could mean taking blocks of data off the disk for the first time and putting them in RAM, or it could be entirely paging and swapping. Some processes will simply require a lot more Disk I/O than others. When this number is very high, however, take a close look at whether or not you have enough RAM. Keep in mind that pageout activity, such as deactivation and swapping, are attributed to the *vhand* process.

RSS Size   The amount of RAM in KBytes that is consumed by the process. This is called the Resident Size. Everything related to the process that is in RAM is included in this column, such as the process's data, stack, text, and shared memory segments. This is a good column to inspect. Because slow systems are often erroneously assumed to be CPU-bound, I always make a point of looking at this column to identify the amount of RAM that the primary applications are using. This is often revealing. Some applications use a small amount of RAM but use large data sets, a point often overlooked when RAM calculations are made. This column shows all the RAM your process is currently using.

Block On   The reason the process was blocked (unable to run). If the process is currently blocked, you will see why. If the process is running, you will see why it was last blocked. There are many reasons a process could be blocked. After *Thd Cnt* is a list of the most common reasons for the process being blocked.

Thd Cnt   The total number of threads for this current process.

Abbreviation	Reason for the Blocked Process
CACHE	Waiting for a cache buffer to become available
DISK	Waiting for a disk operation to complete
INODE	Waiting for an inode operation to complete
IO	Waiting for a non-disk I/O to complete
IPC	Waiting for a shared memory operation to complete
LAN	Waiting for a LAN operation to complete
MESG	Waiting for a message queue operation to complete
NFS	Waiting for an NFS request to complete
PIPE	Waiting for data to or from a pipe
PRI	Waiting because a higher-priority process is running
RFA	Waiting for a Remote File Access to complete
SEM	Waiting for a semaphore to become available

SLEEP	Waiting because the process called **sleep** or **wait**
SOCKT	Waiting for a socket operation to complete
SYS	Waiting for system resources
TERM	Waiting for a terminal transfer
VM	Waiting for a virtual memory operation to complete
OTHER	Waiting for a reason GlancePlus can't determine

CPU Report Screen Description

If the *Process List* screen indicates that the CPU is overworked, you'll want to refer to the *CPU Report* screen shown in Figure 11-3. It can provide useful information about the seven types of states on which GlancePlus reports.

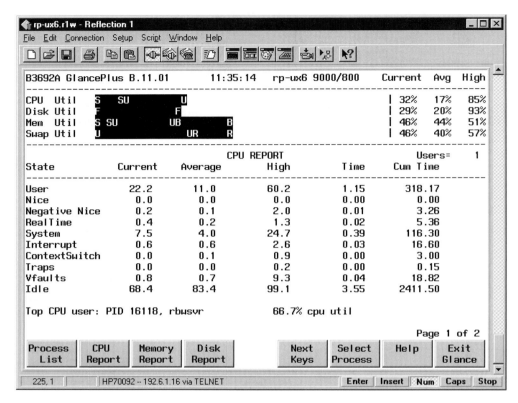

Figure 11-3 HP GlancePlus/UX *CPU Report* Screen Shot

For each of the seven types of states, there are columns that provide additional information. Following is a description of the columns:

Current   Displays the percentage of CPU time devoted to this state over the last time interval.

Average   Displays the average percentage of CPU time spent in this state since GlancePlus was started.

High	Displays the highest percentage of CPU time devoted to this state since GlancePlus was started.
Time	Displays the CPU time spent in this state over the last interval.
Cum Time	Displays the total amount of CPU time spent in this state since GlancePlus was started.

A description of the seven states follows:

User	CPU time spent executing user activities under normal priority.
Nice	CPU time spent running user code in nice mode.
Negative Nice	CPU time spent running code at a high priority.
Realtime	CPU time spent executing real-time processes that run at a high priority.
System	CPU time spent executing system calls and programs.
Interrupt	CPU time spent executing system interrupts. A high value here may indicate of a lot of I/O, such as paging and swapping.
ContSwitch	CPU time spent context switching between processes.
Traps	CPU time spent handling traps.
Vfaults	CPU time spent handling page faults.
Idle	CPU time spent idle.

The *CPU Report* screen also shows your system's run queue length or load average. This is displayed on the second page of the *CPU Report* screen. The Current, Average, and High values for the number of runnable processes waiting for the CPU are shown. You may want to get a gauge of your system's run queue length when the system is mostly idle and compare these numbers with those you see when your system is in normal use.

The final area reported on the *CPU Report* screen is load average, system calls, interrupts, and context switches. I don't inspect these too closely, because if one of these is high, it is normally the symptom of a problem and not the cause of a problem. If you correct a problem, you will see these numbers reduced.

You can use GlancePlus to view all the CPUs in your system, as shown in Figure 11-4. This is an eight-processor system.

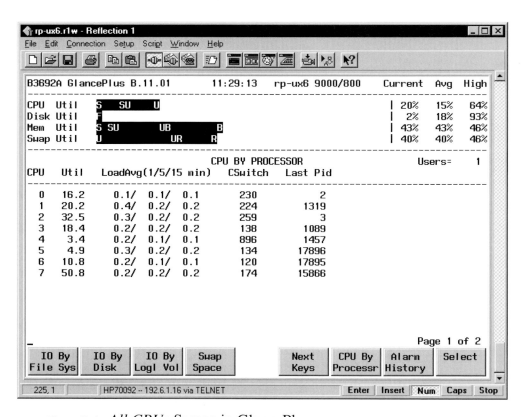

Figure 11-4 *All CPUs* Screen in GlancePlus

Memory Report Screen Description

The *Memory Report* Screen, shown in Figure 11-5 provides information on several types of memory management events. The statistics shown are in the form of counts, not percentages. You may want to look at these counts for a mostly idle system and then observe what takes place as the load on the system is incrementally increased. My experience has been that many more memory bottlenecks occur than CPU bottlenecks, so you may find this screen revealing.

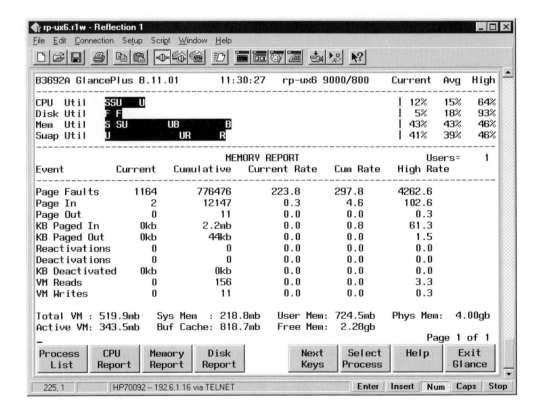

Figure 11-5 HP GlancePlus/UX *Memory Report* Screen Shot

The following five statistics are shown for each memory management event:

Current	The number of times an event occurred in the last interval. The count changes if you update the interval, so you may want to select an interval you are comfortable with and stick with it.
Cumulative	The sum of all counts for this event since GlancePlus was started.
Current Rate	The number of events per second.
Cum Rate	Average of the rate over the cummulative collection interval.
High Rate	The highest rate recorded.

Following are brief descriptions of the memory management events for which statistics are provided:

Page Faults	Any address translation fault such as reclaims, pid faults, and so on.
Page In/Page Out	Pages of data moved from virtual memory (disk) to physical memory (page in), or vice versa.
KB Paged In	The amount of data paged in because of page faults.
KB Paged Out	The amount of data paged out to disk.
Reactivations/Deactivations	The number of processes swapped in and out of memory. A system low on RAM will spend a lot of time swapping processes in and out of RAM. If a lot of this type of swapping is taking place, you may high CPU utilization and see some other statistics may increase as well. These may only be symptoms that a lot of swapping is taking place.

KB Reactivated	The amount of information swapped into RAM as a result of processes having been swapped out earlier due to insufficient RAM.
KB Deactivated	The amount of information swapped out when processes are moved to disk.
VM Reads	The total count of the number of vitual memory reads to disk. The higher this number, the more often your system is going to disk.
VM Writes	The total count of memory management I/O.

The following values are also on the Memory screen:

Total VM	The amount of total virtual memory used by all processes.
Active VM	The amount of virtual memory used by all active processes.
Sys Mem	The amount of memory devoted to system use.
Buf Cache Size	The current size of buffer cache.
User Mem	The amount of memory devoted to user use.
Free Memory	The amount of RAM not currently allocated for use.
Phys Memory	The total RAM in your system.

This screen gives you a lot of information about how your memory subsystem is being used. You may want to view some statistics when your system is mostly idle and when it is heavily used and compare the two. Some good numbers to record are "Free Memory" (to see whether you have any free RAM under either condition) and "Total VM" (to see how much virtual memory has been allocated for all your processes). A system that is RAM-rich will have available memory; a system that is RAM-poor will allocate a lot of virtual memory.

Disk Report **Screen Description**

The *Disk Report* screen appears in Figure 11-6. You may see group-ings of "local" and "remote" information.

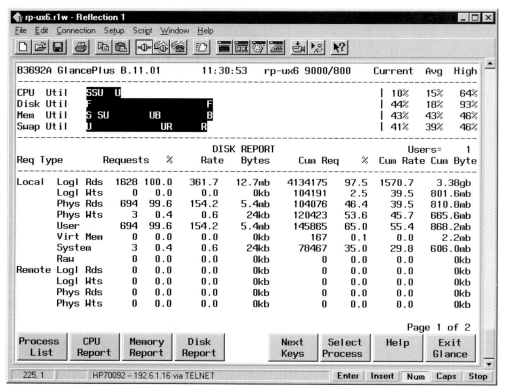

Figure 11-6   HP GlancePlus/UX *Disk Report* Screen Shot

There are eight disk statistics provided for eight events related to logical and physical accesses to all the disks mounted on the local sys-tem. These events represent all the disk activity taking place on the system.

Here are descriptions of the eight disk statistics provided:

Requests   The total number of requests of that type over the last interval.

%	The percentage of this type of disk event relative to other types.
Rate	The average number of requests of this type per second.
Bytes	The total number of bytes transferred for this event over the last interval.
Cum Req	The cumulative number of requests since GlancePlus started.
%	The relative percentage of this type of disk event since GlancePlus started.
Cum Rate	Average of the rate over the cummulative collection interval.
Cum Bytes	The total number of bytes transferred for this type of event since GlancePlus started.

Next are descriptions of the disk events for which these statistics are provided, which may be listed under "Local" on your system:

Logl Rds and Logl Wts

	The number of logical reads and writes to a disk. Because disks normally use memory buffer cache, a logical read may not require physical access to the disk.
Phys Rds	The number of physical reads to the disk. These physical reads may be due to either file system logical reads or to virtual memory management.
Phys Wts	The number of physical writes to the disk. This may be due to file system activity or virtual memory management.
User	The amount of physical disk I/O as a result of user file I/O operations.
Virtual Mem	The amount of physical disk I/O as a result of virtual memory management activity.

System   Housekeeping I/O such as inode updates.

Raw   The amount of raw mode disk I/O.

A lot of disk activity may also take place as a result of NFS mounted disks. Statistics are provided for "Remote" disks as well.

Disk access is required on all systems. The question to ask is: What disk activity is unnecessary and slowing down my system? A good place to start is to compare the amount of "User" disk I/O with "Virtual Mem" disk I/O. If your system is performing much more virtual memory I/O than user I/O, you may want to investigate your memory needs.

GlancePlus Summary

In addition to the Process List, or Global, screen and the CPU, Memory, and Disk screens described earlier, there are many other useful screens including the following:

Swap Space   Shows details of all swap areas. May be called by another name in other releases.

Netwk By Intrface   Gives details about each LAN card configured on your system. This screen may have another name in other releases.

NFS Global   Provides details on inbound and outbound NFS-mounted file systems. May be called by another name in other releases.

Select Process   Allows you to select a single process to investigate. May be called by another name in other releases.

I/O By File Sys   Shows details of I/O for each mounted disk partition.

I/O By Disk   Shows details of I/O for each mounted disk.

I/O By Logl Vol   Shows details of I/O for each mounted logical volume.

System Tables   Shows details of internal system tables.

Process Threshold   Defines which processes will be displayed on the Process List screen. May be called by another name, such as the Global screen, in other releases.

As you can see, although I described the four most commonly used screens in detail, you can use many others to investigate your system further.

There are also many commands you can issue within GlancePlus. Figures 11-7 and 11-8 show the *Command List* screens in GlancePlus.

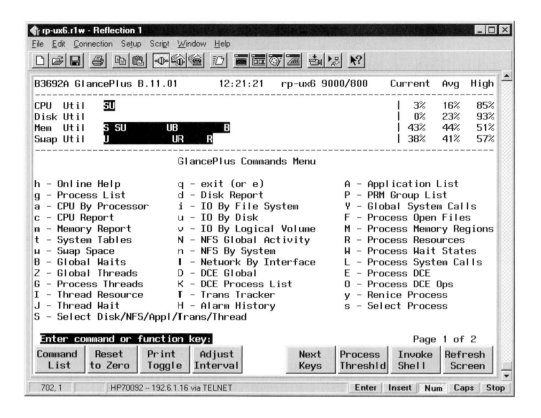

Figure 11-7 HP GlancePlus/UX *Command List* Screen 1

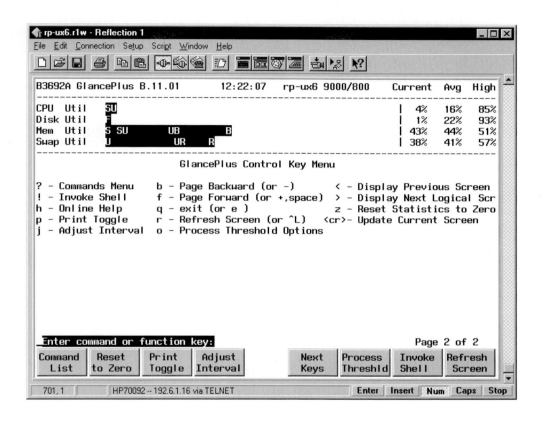

Figure 11-8 HP GlancePlus/UX *Command List* Screen 2

Using VantagePoint Performance Agent to Identify Bottlenecks

VantagePoint Performance Agent allows you to view many metrics related to system performance that can help you identify the source of bottlenecks in your system. You can use the graphical version of GlancePlus, called gpm, to specify the metrics you want to keep track of. You can then view them in the gpm interface and sort them a variety of different ways.

The following are the most important types of bottlenecks you can encounter on a system and the metrics associated with each type of bottleneck. This information was provided by Doug Grumann and Stephen Ciullo of Hewlett Packard, who are two performance experts.

1. CPU bottleneck Using VantagePoint Performance Agent:

   - Consistent High global CPU utilization with *GBL_CPU_TOTAL_UTIL*>90% and next bullet.

   - Significant *Run Queue* or *Load Average* indicated by *GBL_PRI_QUEUE* or *GBL_RUN_QUEUE*>3.

   - Look for processes blocked on priority with *PROC_STOP_REASON=PRI*.

2. System CPU bottleneck using VantagePoint Performance Agent (same as 1 with addition of first bullet):

   - Most of the CPU time spent in kernel mode with *GBL_CPU_SYS_MODE_UTIL*>50%.

   - Consistent High global CPU utilization with *GBL_CPU_TOTAL_UTIL*>90% and next bullet.

   - Significant *Run Queue* or *Load Average* indicated by *GBL_PRI_QUEUE* or *GBL_RUN_QUEUE*>3.

   - Look for processes blocked on priority with *PROC_STOP_REASON=PRI*.

3. Context switching bottleneck using VantagePoint Performance Agent (same as 2 with addition of first bullet):

   - Significant CPU time spent switching with *GBL_CPU_CSWITCH*>30%.

   - Most of the CPU time spend in kernel mode with *GBL_CPU_SYS_MODE_UTIL*>50%.

- Consistent High global CPU utilization with *GBL_CPU_TOTAL_UTIL*>90% and next bullet.

- Significant *Run Queue* or *Load Average* indicated by *GBL_PRI_QUEUE* or *GBL_RUN_QUEUE*>3.

- Look for processes blocked on priority with *PROC_STOP_REASON=PRI*.

4. User CPU bottleneck Using VantagePoint Performance Agent (same as 1 with addition of first bullet):

- Most of the CPU time spent in user mode with *GBL_CPU_USER_MODE_UTIL*>50%.

- Consistent High global CPU utilization with *GBL_CPU_TOTAL_UTIL*>90% and next bullet.

- Significant *Run Queue* or *Load Average* indicated by *GBL_PRI_QUEUE* or *GBL_RUN_QUEUE*>3.

- Look for processes blocked on priority with *PROC_STOP_REASON=PRI*.

5. Disk bottleneck Using VantagePoint Performance Agent:

- At least one disk device with consistently high utilization with *BYDSK_UTIL*>50%.

- Queue lengths greater than zero with *BYDSK_QUEUE*>0.

- Processes or threads blocked on I/O for a variety of reasons with *PROC_STOP_REASON=CACHE, DISK* or *IO*.

- Look for processes blocked on priority with *PROC_STOP_REASON=PRI*.

6. Buffer Cache bottleneck Using VantagePoint Performance Agent:

- Moderate utilization of at least one disk with *BYDSK_UTIL>25%*.

- Queue lengths greater than zero with *BYDSK_QUEUE>0*.

- Low Buffer cache read hit percentage with *GBL_MEM_CACHE_HIT_PCT<90%*.

- Processes or threads blocked on cache with *PROC_STOP_REASON=CACHE*.

7. Memory bottleneck Using VantagePoint Performance Agent:

- High physical memory utiliztion with *GBL_MEM_UTIL>95%*.

- Significant pageouts or any deactivations with *GBL_MEM_PAGEOUT_RATE>1* or *GBL_MEM_SWAPOUT_RATE>0*.

- vhand processes consistently active with vhand's *PROC_CPU_TOTAL_UTIL>5%*.

- Processes or threads blocked on virtual memory with *PROC_STOP_REASON=VM*.

8. Networking bottleneck Using VantagePoint Performance Agent:

- High network packet rates with *GBL_NET_PACKET_RATE>2* average. Keep in mind this varies greatly depending on configuration.

- Any output queuing taking place with *GBL_NET_OUTQUEUE>0*.

- Higher than normal number of processes or threads blocked on networking with *PROC_STOP_REASON=NFS, LAN, RPC* or *SOCKET GBL_NETWORK_SUBSYSTEM_QUEUE>*average.

- One CPU with a high system mode CPU utilization while other CPUs are mostly idle with *BYCPU_CPU_INTERRUPT_TIME>30.*

- Using *lanadmin,* check for frequent incrementing of *Outbound Discards* or excessive *Collisions.*

In order to identify a problem on your system, you must first characterize your system when it is running smoothly and has no problems. Should your system start to perform poorly in some respect or another, you can compare the performance data of a smoothly running system to one with potential problems.

HP VantagePoint Performance Agent and HP VantagePoint Performance Analyzer/UX

There are performance tools that track and chart data over a long period of time. System Administrators often call this exercise "capacity planning." The goal of capacity planning is to view what system resources have been consumed over a long period of time and determine what adjustments or additions can be made to the system to improve performance and plan for the future. We'll use HP VantagePoint Performance Agent (what used to be MeasureWare Agent) and HP VantagePoint Performance Analyzer/UX (what used to be PerfView Analyzer) together to take a look at the performance of a system. These tools run on HP-UX and are similar to many advanced tools that run on other UNIX variants.

The VantagePoint Performance Agent is installed on individual systems throughout a distributed environment. It collects resource and performance measurement data on the individual systems. The VantagePoint Performance Analyzer/UX management console, which you would typically install on a management system, is then used to display the historical VantagePoint Performance Agent data. You could also set alarms to be triggered off by exception conditions using the VantagePoint Performance agent. For instance, if the VantagePoint Performance agent detects an exception condition, such as CPU utilization greater than 90%, it produces an alarm message. The alarm messages are then displayed with VantagePoint Performance Analyzer/UX. We're going to use the VantagePoint Performance Analyzer/UX in our upcoming examples; however, there are really three VantagePoint Performance components:

Monitor	Provides alarm monitoring capability by accepting alarms from VantagePoint Performance and displays alarms.
Planner	Provides forecasting capability by extrapolating VantagePoint Performance data for forecasts.
Analyzer	Analyzes VantagePoint Performance data from multiple systems and displays data. You can view the data from multiple systems simultaneously.

In our example, we will be working with a single system. We'll take the VantagePoint Performance data, collected over roughly a one-week period, and display some of it. In this example, we won't take data from several distributed systems and we'll use only one server in the example.

HP VantagePoint Performance Agent produces log files that contain information about the system resource consumption. The longer HP VantagePoint Performance Agent runs, the longer it records data in the log files. I am often called to review systems that are running poorly to propose system upgrades. I usually run HP VantagePoint Performance Agent for a minimum of a week so that I obtain log information over a long enough period of time to obtain useful data.

For some systems, this time period is months. For other systems with a regular load, a week may be enough time.

After having run VantagePoint Performance for a week, I invoked VantagePoint Performance Analyzer/UX to see the level of system resource utilization that took place over the week. The graphs we'll review are CPU, Memory, and Disk. Figure 11-9 shows *Global CPU Summary* for the week:

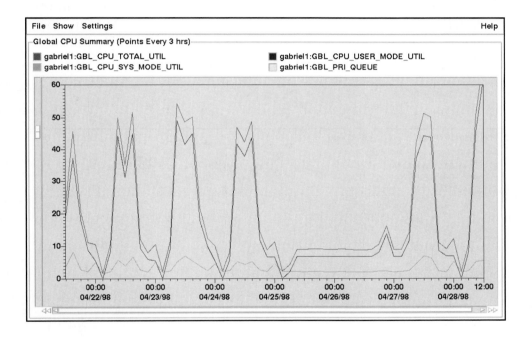

Figure 11-9 Global CPU Summary Screen

You can adjust every imaginable feature of this graph with VantagePoint Performance Analyzer/UX. Unfortunately, the color in this graph is lost in the book. The colors used allow you to discern the parameters when viewing the graph on the computer screen. Total CPU utilization is always the top point in the graph and it is the sum of system and user mode utilization.

Figure 11-9 shows classic CPU utilization with prime hours reflecting high CPU utilization and non-prime hours reflecting low CPU utilization. In some respects, however, this graph can be deceiving. Because there is a data point occurs every three hours, hence the eight ticks per 24-hour period, you don't get a view of the actual CPU utilization during a much smaller window of time. We can't, for instance, see precisely what time in the morning the CPU becomes heavily used. We can see that it is between the second and third tick, but this is a long time period - between 6:00 and 9:00 am. The same lack of granularity is true at the end of the day. We see a clear fall-off in CPU utilization between the fifth and seventh ticks, but this does not give us a well defined view. Figure 11-10 shows CPU utilization during a much shorter time window.

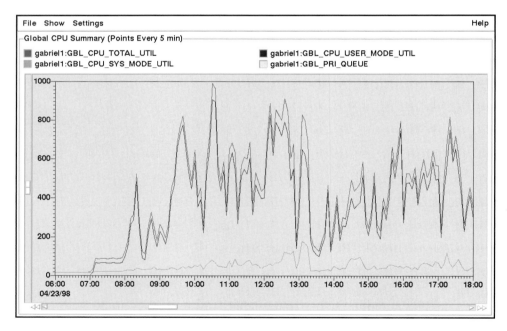

Figure 11-10 *Global CPU Summary* - Short Time Period

Figure 11-10 shows a finer granularity of CPU utilization during the shorter time window. The much finer granularity of this window makes clear the activity spikes that occur throughout the day. For instance, a clear login spike occurs at 8:30 am.

Memory utilization can also be graphed over the course of the week, as shown in Figure 11-11.

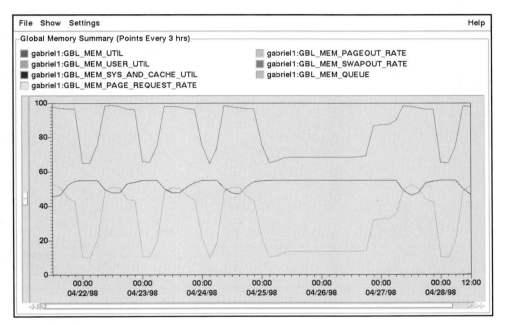

Figure 11-11 Global Memory Summary

The user memory utilization is the bottom line of the graph, which roughly corresponds to the CPU utilization shown earlier. User memory utilization is low during non-prime hours and high during prime hours.

System memory utilization is the middle line of the graph, which remains fairly steady throughout the week.

Total memory utilization is always the top line of the graph, and it is the sum of system and user utilization. It rises and drops with user utilization, because system memory utilization remains roughly the same.

The three-hour interval between data points on this graph may not give us the granularity we require. Figure 11-12 shows memory utilization during a much shorter time window.

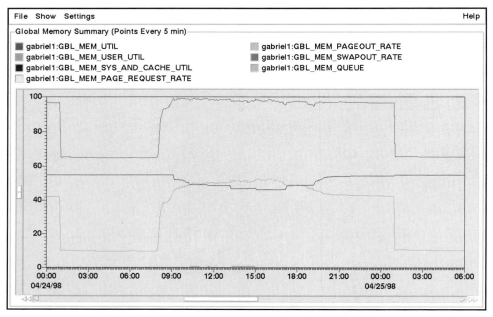

Figure 11-12 *Global Memory Summary* - Short Time Period

Figure 11-12 shows a finer granularity of memory utilization during the shorter time window. You can now see precisely how memory utilization is changing over roughly one day.

Disk utilization can also be graphed over the course of the week, as shown in Figure 11-13.

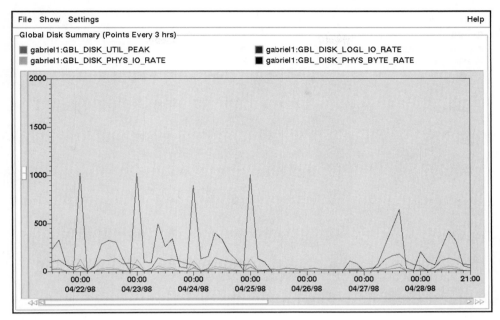

Figure 11-13 Global Disk Summary

Like the CPU and memory graph, this is an entire week of disk usage. Because many spikes occur on this graph, we would surely want to view and analyze much shorter time windows.

Figure 11-14 shows disk utilization during a much shorter time window.

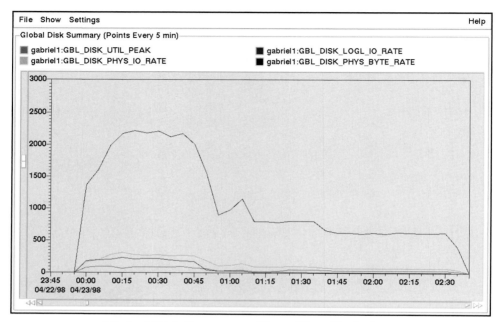

Figure 11-14 *Global Disk Summary* - Short Time Period

This much shorter time window, of roughly three hours, shows a lot more detail. There are tremendous spikes in disk activity occurring in the middle of the night. These could take place for a variety of reasons, including batch job processing or system backup.

You are not limited to viewing parameters related to only one system resource at a time. You can also view the way many system resources are used simultaneously, as shown in Figure 11-15.

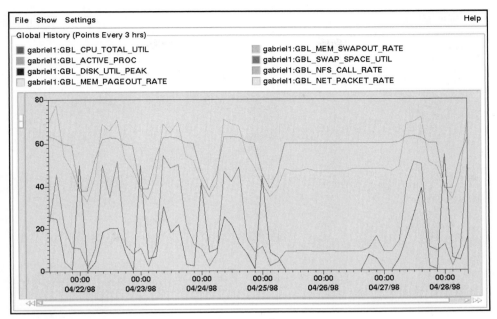

Figure 11-15 *Global Summary History* Screen

Many system resources are present on this graph, including CPU, disk, and memory. You would surely want to view a much shorter time period when displaying so many system resources simultaneously.

Figure 11-16 shows the same parameters during a much shorter time window.

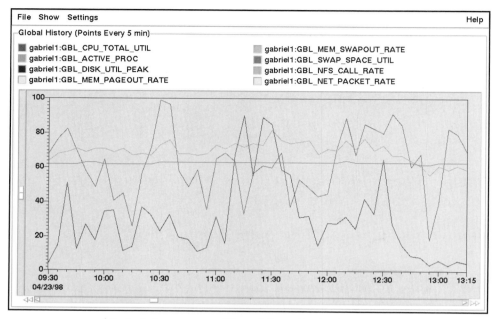

Figure 11-16 *Global Summary* - Short Time Period

Figure 11-16 shows a finer granularity of the utilization of many system resources during the shorter time window. You can now view the ways in which various system resources are related to other system resources.

You can find the status of VantagePoint Performance Analyzer/ UX running on your system with a useful command called **perfstat**. The following example shows issuing the **perfstat** command with the -? option to see all **perfstat** options:

```
# perfstat -?

usage: perfstat [options]

   Unix option  Function
   -----------  --------
      -?        List all perfstat options.
      -c        Show system configuration information.
      -e        Search for warnings and errors from
                  performance tool status files.
```

```
        -f              List size of performance tool status files.
        -p              List active performance tool processes.
        -t              Display last few lines of performance tool
                          status files.
        -v              List version strings for performance tool files.
        -z              Dump perfstat info to a file and tar tape.
```

Using the *-c* option, you get information about your system configuration, as shown in the following listing:

```
# perfstat -c

****************************************************************
** perfstat for rp-ux6 on Fri May 15 12:20:06 EDT
****************************************************************

system configuration information:

uname -a: HP-UX ux6 B.11.00 E 9000/800 71763 8-user license

mounted file systems with disk space shown:
Filesystem              kbytes       used    avail %used Mounted on
/dev/vg00/lvol3          86016      27675    54736  34% /
/dev/vg00/lvol1          67733      44928    16031  74% /stand
/dev/vg00/lvol8         163840      66995    90927  42% /var
/dev/vg00/lvol7         499712     358775   132155  73% /usr
/dev/rp06vgtmp/tmp     4319777    1099297  3134084  26% /tmp
/dev/vg00/lvol6         270336     188902    76405  71% /opt
/dev/vgroot1/var        640691      15636   605834   3% /newvar
/dev/vgroot1/usr        486677     356866   115210  76% /newusr
/dev/vgroot1/stand       67733      45109    15850  74% /newstand
/dev/vgroot1/root        83733      21181    54178  28% /newroot
/dev/vgroot1/opt        263253     188109    67246  74% /newopt
/dev/vg00/lvol5          20480       1109    18168   6% /home


LAN interfaces:
Name    Mtu     Network     Address       Ipkts      Opkts
lo0     4136    127.0.0.0   localhost     7442       7442
lan0    1500    192.60.11.0 rp-ux6        7847831    12939169


************* (end of perfstat -c output) ***************
```

Using the *-f* option shows the size of the performance tools status files, as shown in the following listing:

```
# perfstat -f

* * * * * * * * * * * * * * * * * * * * * * * * * * * * * * * * * * * * * * * * * * * * * * * * *
** perfstat for ux6 on Fri May 15 12:20:08 EDT
* * * * * * * * * * * * * * * * * * * * * * * * * * * * * * * * * * * * * * * * * * * * * * * * *

ls -l list of performance tool status files in /var/opt/perf:

-rw-rw-rw-   1 root    root     7812 May 10 19:35 status.alarmgen
-rw-r--r--   1 root    root        0 May 10 02:40 status.mi
-rw-rw-rw-   1 root    root     3100 May 10 02:40 status.perflbd
-rw-rw-rw-   1 root    root     3978 May 10 02:40 status.rep_server
-rw-r--r--   1 root    root     6079 May 11 23:30 status.scope
-rw-r--r--   1 root    root        0 Mar 31 07:26 status.ttd

* * * * * * * * * * * * *  (end of perfstat -f output)  * * * * * * * * * * * * * * *
```

Using the *-v* option displays the version strings for the performance tools running, as shown in the following listing:

```
# perfstat -v

* * * * * * * * * * * * * * * * * * * * * * * * * * * * * * * * * * * * * * * * * * * * * * * * *
** perfstat for ux6 on Fri May 15 12:20:08 EDT
* * * * * * * * * * * * * * * * * * * * * * * * * * * * * * * * * * * * * * * * * * * * * * * * *

listing version strings for performance tool files:

NOTE:   The following software version information can be com-
pared
with the version information shown in the /opt/perf/ReleaseNotes
file(s).

MeasureWare executables in the directory /opt/perf/bin
        scopeux  C.01.00      12/17/97 HP-UX 11.0+
           ttd  A.11.00.15   12/15/97 HP-UX 11.00
       perflbd  C.01.00      12/17/97 HP-UX 11.0+
      alarmgen  C.01.00      12/17/97 HP-UX 11.0+
    agdbserver  C.01.00      12/17/97 HP-UX 11.0+
       agsysdb  C.01.00      12/17/97 HP-UX 11.0+
    rep_server  C.01.00      12/17/97 HP-UX 11.0+
       extract  C.01.00      12/17/97 HP-UX 11.0+
       utility  C.01.00      12/17/97 HP-UX 11.0+
           mwa  A.10.52      12/05/97
      perfstat  A.11.01      11/19/97
        dsilog  C.01.00      12/17/97 HP-UX 11.0+
       sdlcomp  C.01.00      12/17/97 HP-UX 11.0+
```

```
           sdlexpt   C.01.00      12/17/97 HP-UX 11.0+
        sdlgendata   C.01.00      12/17/97 HP-UX 11.0+
            sdlutil  C.01.00      12/17/97 HP-UX 11.0+

Measureware libraries in the directory /opt/perf/lib
          libmwa.sl  C.01.00      12/17/97 HP-UX 11.0+
          libarm.a   A.11.00.15   12/15/97 HP-UX 11.00
          libarm.sl  A.11.00.15   12/15/97 HP-UX 11.00

Measureware metric description file in the directory /var/opt/
perf
          metdesc  C.01.00      12/17/97

All critical MeasureWare files are accessible

      libnums.sl  B.11.00.15   12/15/97 HP-UX 11.00
      midaemon    B.11.00.15   12/15/97 HP-UX 11.00
        glance  B.11.01      12/16/97 HP-UX 11.00
           gpm  B.11.01      12/16/97 HP-UX 11.00

************* (end of perfstat -v output) ***************
```

Manual Pages of Some Commands Used in Chapter 11

Many useful commands are in this chapter. I provided a brief description of many of the commands along with some of the examples. The following are the HP-UX manual pages for many of the commands used in this chapter. The manual pages are thorough and provide much more detailed description of each of the commands.

iostat

iostat - Interactively report I/O and CPU statistics.

man page

iostat - 11

```
iostat(1)                                                          iostat(1)

NAME
     iostat - report I/O statistics

SYNOPSIS

     iostat [-t] [interval [count]]

DESCRIPTION
     iostat iteratively reports I/O statistics for each active disk on the
     system.  Disk data is arranged in a four-column format:

          Column Heading            Interpretation
             device                 Device name
             bps                    Kilobytes transferred per second
             sps                    Number of seeks per second
             msps                   Milliseconds per average seek

     If two or more disks are present, data is presented on successive
     lines for each disk.

     To compute this information, seeks, data transfer completions, and the
     number of words transferred are counted for each disk.  Also, the
     state of each disk is examined HZ times per second (as defined in
     <sys/param.h>) and a tally is made if the disk is active.  These
     numbers can be combined with the transfer rates of each device to
     determine average seek times for each device.

     With the advent of new disk technologies, such as data striping, where
     a single data transfer is spread across several disks, the number of
     milliseconds per average seek becomes impossible to compute
     accurately. At best it is only an approximation, varying greatly,
     based on several dynamic system conditions.  For this reason and to
     maintain backward compatibility, the milliseconds per average seek (
     msps ) field is set to the value 1.0.

     Options
       iostat recognizes the following options and command-line arguments:

          -t                Report terminal statistics as well as disk
                            statistics.  Terminal statistics include:

                            tin    Number of characters read from terminals.

                            tout   Number of characters written to
                                   terminals.
                            us     Percentage of time system has spent in
                                   user mode.
                            ni     Percentage of time system has spent in
                                   user mode running low-priority (nice)
                                   processes.
                            sy     Percentage of time system has spent in
```

                              system mode.
                      id   Percentage of time system has spent
                              idling.

              interval   Display successive lines which are summaries of the
                          last interval seconds. The first line reported is
                          for the time since a reboot and each subsequent line
                          is for the last interval only.

              count   Repeat the statistics count times.

EXAMPLES
     Show current I/O statistics for all disks:

          iostat

     Display I/O statistics for all disks every 10 seconds until INTERRUPT
     or QUIT is pressed:

          iostat 10

     Display I/O statistics for all disks every 10 seconds and terminate
     after 5 successive readings:

          iostat 10 5

     Display I/O statistics for all disks every 10 seconds, also show
     terminal and processor statistics, and terminate after 5 successive
     readings:

          iostat -t 10 5

WARNINGS
     Users of iostat must not rely on the exact field widths and spacing of
     its output, as these will vary depending on the system, the release of
     HP-UX, and the data to be displayed.

AUTHOR
     iostat was developed by the University of California, Berkeley, and
     HP.

FILES
     /usr/include/sys/param.h

SEE ALSO
     vmstat(1).

ps

ps - Report the status of processes.

ps(1)   ps(1)

NAME
     ps - report process status

SYNOPSIS

     ps [-adeflP] [-g grplist] [-p proclist] [-R prmgrplist] [-t termlist]
     [-u uidlist]

XPG4 SYNOPSIS
     ps [-aAcdefHjlP] [-C cmdlist] [-g grplist] [-G gidlist] [-n namelist]
     [-o format] [-p proclist] [-R prmgrplist] [-s sidlist] [-t termlist]
     [-u uidlist] [-U uidlist]

DESCRIPTION
     ps prints information about selected processes. Use options to
     specify which processes to select and what information to print about
     them.

   Process Selection Options
     Use the following options to choose which processes should be
     selected.

     NOTE: If an option is used in both the default (standard HP-UX) and
     XPG4 environments, the description provided here documents the default
     behavior. Refer to the UNIX95 variable under EXTERNAL INFLUENCES for
     additional information on XPG4 behavior.

          (none)   Select those processes associated with the current
                         terminal.

          -A   (XPG4 Only.) Select all processes. (Synonym for
                         -e.)

          -a   Select all processes except process group leaders
                         and processes not associated with a terminal.

          -C cmdlist   (XPG4 Only.) Select processes executing a command
                         with a basename given in cmdlist.

          -d   Select all processes except process group leaders.

          -e   Select all processes.

          -g grplist   Select processes whose process group leaders are
                         given in grplist.

          -G gidlist   (XPG4 Only.) Select processes whose real group ID
                         numbers or group names are given in gidlist.

          -n namelist   (XPG4 Only.) This option is ignored; its presence
                         is allowed for standards compliance.

-p proclist   Select processes whose process ID numbers are
                   given in proclist.

-R prmgrplist   Select processes belonging to PRM process resource
                   groups whose names or ID numbers are given in
                   prmgrplist. See DEPENDENCIES.

-s sidlist   (XPG4 Only.) Select processes whose session
                   leaders are given in sidlist. (Synonym for -g).

-t termlist   Select processes associated with the terminals
                   given in termlist. Terminal identifiers can be
                   specified in one of two forms: the device's file
                   name (such as tty04) or if the device's file name
                   starts with tty, just the rest of it (such as 04).
                   If the device's file is in a directory other than
                   /dev or /dev/pty, the terminal identifier must
                   include the name of the directory under /dev that
                   contains the device file (such as pts/5).

-u uidlist   Select processes whose effective user ID numbers
                   or login names are given in uidlist.

-U uidlist   (XPG4 Only.) Select processes whose real user ID
                   numbers or login names are given in uidlist.

If any of the -a, -A, -d, or -e options is specified, the -C, -g, -G,
-p, -R, -t, -u, and -U options are ignored.

If more than one of -a, -A, -d, and -e are specified, the least
restrictive option takes effect.

If more than one of the -C, -g, -G, -p, -R, -t, -u, and -U options are
specified, processes will be selected if they match any of the options
specified.

The lists used as arguments to the -C, -g, -G, -p, -R, -t, -u, and -U
options can be specified in one of two forms:

   - A list of identifiers separated from one another by a comma.

   - A list of identifiers enclosed in quotation marks (") and
     separated from one another by a comma and/or one or more
     spaces.

Output Format Options
  Use the following options to control which columns of data are
  included in the output listing. The options are cumulative.

(none)   The default columns are: pid, tty, time, and comm,
                   in that order.

-f   Show columns user, pid, ppid, cpu, stime, tty,
                   time, and args, in that order.

-l   Show columns flags, state, uid, pid, ppid, cpu,
                   intpri, nice, addr, sz, wchan, tty, time, and
                   comm, in that order.

-fl   Show columns flags, state, user, pid, ppid, cpu,
                   intpri, nice, addr, sz, wchan, stime, tty, time,
                   and args, in that order.

-c	(XPG4 Only.) Remove columns cpu and nice; replace column intpri with columns cls and pri.
-j	(XPG4 Only.) Add columns pgid and sid after column ppid (or pid, if ppid is not being displayed).
-P	Add column prmid (for -l) or prmgrp (for -f or -fl) immediately before column pid. See DEPENDENCIES.
-o format	(XPG4 Only.) format is a comma- or space-separated list of the columns to display, in the order they should be displayed. (Valid column names are listed below.) A column name can optionally be followed by an equals sign (=) and a string to use as the heading for that column. (Any commas or spaces after the equals sign will be taken as a part of the column heading; if more columns are desired, they must be specified with additional -o options.) The width of the column will be the greater of the width of the data to be displayed and the width of the column heading. If an empty column heading is specified for every heading, no heading line will be printed. This option overrides options -c, -f, -j, -l, and -P; if they are specified, they are ignored.
-H	(XPG4 Only.) Shows the process hierarchy. Each process is displayed under its parent, and the contents of the args or comm column for that process is indented from that of its parent. Note that this option is expensive in both memory and speed.

The column names and their meanings are given below. Except where noted, the default heading for each column is the uppercase form of the column name.

addr	The memory address of the process, if resident; otherwise, the disk address.
args	The command line given when the process was created. This column should be the last one specified, if it is desired. Only a subset of the command line is saved by the kernel; as much of the command line will be displayed as is available. The output in this column may contain spaces. The default heading for this column is COMMAND if -o is specified and CMD otherwise.
cls	Process scheduling class, see rtsched(1).
comm	The command name. The output in this column may contain spaces. The default heading for this column is COMMAND if -o is specified and CMD otherwise.
cpu	Processor utilization for scheduling. The default heading for this column is C.
etime	Elapsed time of the process. The default heading for this column is ELAPSED.
flags	Flags (octal and additive) associated with the process:

```
                              0    Swapped
                              1    In core
                              2    System process
                              4    Locked in core (e.g., for physical I/O)

                              10   Being traced by another process
                              20   Another tracing flag
```

The default heading for this column is F.

intpri   The priority of the process as it is stored
                internally by the kernel. This column is provided
                for backward compatibility and its use is not
                encouraged.

gid   The group ID number of the effective process
                owner.

group   The group name of the effective process owner.

nice   Nice value; used in priority computation (see
                nice(1)). The default heading for this column is
                NI.

pcpu   The percentage of CPU time used by this process
                during the last scheduling interval. The default
                heading for this column is %CPU.

pgid   The process group ID number of the process group
                to which this process belongs.

pid   The process ID number of the process.

ppid   The process ID number of the parent process.

pri   The priority of the process. The meaning of the
                value depends on the process scheduling class; see
                cls, above, and rtsched(1).

prmid   The PRM process resource group ID number.

prmgrp   The PRM process resource group name.

rgid   The group ID number of the real process owner.

rgroup   The group name of the real process owner.

ruid   The user ID number of the real process owner.

ruser   The login name of the real process owner.

sid   The session ID number of the session to which this
                process belongs.

state   The state of the process:

```
                              0    Nonexistent
                              S    Sleeping
                              W    Waiting
                              R    Running
                              I    Intermediate
                              Z    Terminated
                              T    Stopped
```

          X   Growing

          The default heading for this column is S.

stime	Starting time of the process. If the elapsed time is greater than 24 hours, the starting date is displayed instead.
sz	The size in physical pages of the core image of the process, including text, data, and stack space. Physical page size is defined by _SC_PAGE_SIZE in the header file <unistd.h> (see sysconf(2) and unistd(5)).
time	The cumulative execution time for the process.
tty	The controlling terminal for the process. The default heading for this column is TT if -o is specified and TTY otherwise.
uid	The user ID number of the effective process owner.
user	The login name of the effective process owner.
vsz	The size in kilobytes (1024 byte units) of the core image of the process. See column sz, above.
wchan	The event for which the process is waiting or sleeping; if there is none, a hyphen (-) is displayed.

Notes

  ps prints the command name and arguments given at the time of the process was created. If the process changes its arguments while running (by writing to its argv array), these changes are not displayed by ps.

  A process that has exited and has a parent, but has not yet been waited for by the parent, is marked <defunct> (see zombie process in exit(2)).

  The time printed in the stime column, and used in computing the value for the etime column, is the time when the process was forked, not the time when it was modified by exec*().

  To make the ps output safer to display and easier to read, all control characters in the comm and args columns are displayed as "visible" equivalents in the customary control character format, ^x.

EXTERNAL INFLUENCES

  Environment Variables

    UNIX95 specifies to use the XPG4 behavior for this command. The changes for XPG4 include support for the entire option set specified above and include the following behavioral changes:

      - The TIME column format changes from mmmm:ss to [dd-]hh:mm:ss.

      - When the comm, args, user, and prmgrp fields are included by default or the -f or -l flags are used, the column headings of those fields change to CMD, CMD, USER, and PRMGRP, respectively.

      - -a, -d, and -g will select processes based on session rather than on process group.

- The uid or user column displayed by -f or -l will display
  effective user rather than real user.

- The -u option will select users based on effective UID rather
  than real UID.

- The -C and -H options, while they are not part of the XPG4
  standard, are enabled.

LC_TIME determines the format and contents of date and time strings.
If it is not specified or is null, it defaults to the value of LANG.

If LANG is not specified or is null, it defaults to C (see lang(5)).

If any internationalization variable contains an invalid setting, all
internationalization variables default to C (see environ(5)).

International Code Set Support
    Single-byte character code sets are supported.

EXAMPLES
    Generate a full listing of all processes currently running on your
    machine:

        ps -ef

    To see if a certain process exists on the machine, such as the cron
    clock daemon, check the far right column for the command name, cron,
    or try

        ps -f -C cron

WARNINGS
    Things can change while ps is running; the picture it gives is only a
    snapshot in time. Some data printed for defunct processes is
    irrelevant.

    If two special files for terminals are located at the same select
    code, that terminal may be reported with either name. The user can
    select processes with that terminal using either name.

    Users of ps must not rely on the exact field widths and spacing of its
    output, as these will vary depending on the system, the release of
    HP-UX, and the data to be displayed.

DEPENDENCIES
    HP Process Resource Manager
    The -P and -R options require the optional HP Process Resource Manager
    (PRM) software to be installed and configured. See prmconfig(1) for a
    description of how to configure HP PRM, and prmconf(4) for the
    definition of "process resource group."

    If HP PRM is not installed and configured and -P or -R is specified, a
    warning message is displayed and (for -P) hyphens (-) are displayed in
    the prmid and prmgrp columns.

sar

sar - System activity reporter.

sar(1M)   sar(1M)

NAME
     sar - system activity reporter

SYNOPSIS

     sar [-ubdycwaqvmAMS] [-o file] t [n]

     sar [-ubdycwaqvmAMS] [-s time] [-e time] [-i sec] [-f file]

DESCRIPTION
     In the first form above, sar samples cumulative activity counters in
     the operating system at n intervals of t seconds. If the -o option is
     specified, it saves the samples in file in binary format. The default
     value of n is 1. In the second form, with no sampling interval
     specified, sar extracts data from a previously recorded file, either
     the one specified by -f option or, by default, the standard system
     activity daily data file /var/adm/sa/sadd for the current day dd. The
     starting and ending times of the report can be bounded via the -s and
     -e time arguments of the form hh[:mm[:ss]]. The -i option selects
     records at sec-second intervals. Otherwise, all intervals found in
     the data file are reported.

     In either case, subsets of data to be printed are specified by option:

          -u   Report CPU utilization (the default); portion of time
                 running in one of several modes. On a multi-processor
                 system, if the -M option is used together with the -u
                 option, per-CPU utilization as well as the average CPU
                 utilization of all the processors are reported. If the -M
                 option is not used, only the average CPU utilization of all
                 the processors is reported:

                      cpu   cpu number (only on a multi-processor
                                 system with the -M option);

                      %usr   user mode;

                      %sys   system mode;

                      %wio   idle with some process waiting for I/O
                                 (only block I/O, raw I/O, or VM
                                 pageins/swapins indicated);

                      %idle   otherwise idle.

          -b   Report buffer activity:

                      bread/s   Number of physical reads per second
                                 from the disk (or other block devices)
                                 to the buffer cache;

bwrit/s	Number of physical writes per second from the buffer cache to the disk (or other block device);
lread/s	Number of reads per second from buffer cache;
lwrit/s	Number of writes per second to buffer cache;
%rcache	Buffer cache hit ratio for read requests e.g., 1 - bread/lread;
%wcache	Buffer cache hit ratio for write requests e.g., 1 - bwrit/lwrit;
pread/s	Number of reads per second from character device using the physio() (raw I/O) mechanism;
pwrit/s	Number of writes per second to character device using the physio() (i.e., raw I/O) mechanism; mechanism.

-d   Report activity for each block device, e.g., disk or tape drive. One line is printed for each device that had activity during the last interval. If no devices were active, a blank line is printed. Each line contains the following data:

device	Logical name of the device and its corresponding instance. Devices are categorized into the following four device types:

                              disk1 - HP-IB disks (CS/80)
                              disk2 - CIO HP-FL disks (CS/80)
                              disk3 - SCSI and NIO FL disks
                              sdisk - SCSI disks;

%busy	Portion of time device was busy servicing a request;
avque	Average number of requests outstanding for the device;
r+w/s	Number of data transfers per second (read and writes) from and to the device;
blks/s	Number of bytes transferred (in 512-byte units) from and to the device;
avwait	Average time (in milliseconds) that transfer requests waited idly on queue for the device;
avserv	Average time (in milliseconds) to service each transfer request (includes seek, rotational latency, and data transfer times) for the device.

-y   Report tty device activity:

	rawch/s	Raw input characters per second;
	canch/s	Input characters per second processed by canon();
	outch/s	Output characters per second;
	rcvin/s	Receive incoming character interrupts per second;
	xmtin/s	Transmit outgoing character interrupts per second;
	mdmin/s	Modem interrupt rate (not supported; always 0).

-c   Report system calls:

	scall/s	Number of system calls of all types per second;
	sread/s	Number of read() and/or readv() system calls per second;
	swrit/s	Number of write() and/or writev() system calls per second;
	fork/s	Number of fork() and/or vfork() system calls per second;
	exec/s	Number of exec() system calls per second;
	rchar/s	Number of characters transferred by read system calls block devices only) per second;
	wchar/s	Number of characters transferred by write system calls (block devices only) per second.

-w   Report system swapping and switching activity:

	swpin/s	Number of process swapins per second;
	swpot/s	Number of process swapouts per second;
	bswin/s	Number of 512-byte units transferred for swapins per second;
	bswot/s	Number of 512-byte units transferred for swapouts per second;
	pswch/s	Number of process context switches per second.

-a   Report use of file access system routines:

	iget/s	Number of file system iget() calls per second;

| namei/s | Number of file system lookuppn() (pathname translation) calls per second; |
| dirblk/s | Number of file system blocks read per second doing directory lookup. |

-q   Report average queue length while occupied, and percent of time occupied. On a multi-processor machine, if the -M option is used together with the -q option, the per-CPU run queue as well as the average run queue of all the processors are reported. If the -M option is not used, only the average run queue information of all the processors is reported:

cpu	cpu number (only on a multi-processor system and used with the -M option)
runq-sz	Average length of the run queue(s) of processes (in memory and runnable);
%runocc	The percentage of time the run queue(s) were occupied by processes (in memory and runnable);
swpq-sz	Average length of the swap queue of runnable processes (processes swapped out but ready to run);
%swpocc	The percentage of time the swap queue of runnable processes (processes swapped out but ready to run) was occupied.

-v   Report status of text, process, inode and file tables:

text-sz	(Not Applicable);
proc-sz	The current-size and maximum-size of the process table;
inod-sz	The current-size and maximum-size of the inode table (inode cache);
file-sz	The current-size and maximum-size of the system file table;
text-ov	(Not Applicable);
proc-ov	The number of times the process table overflowed (number of times the kernel could not find any available process table entries) between sample points;
inod-ov	The number of times the inode table (inode cache) overflowed (number of times the kernel could not find any available inode table entries) between sample points;
file-ov	The number of times the system file table overflowed (number of times the kernel could not find any available file table entries) between sample

points.

-m   Report message and semaphore activities:

        msg/s   Number of System V msgrcv() calls per
                        second;

        sema/s   Number of System V semop() calls per
                        second;

        select/s   Number of System V select() calls per
                        second. This value will only be
                        reported if the "-S" option is also
                        explicitly specified.

-A   Report all data. Equivalent to -udqbwcayvm.

-M   Report the per-processor data on a multi-processor system
        when used with -q and/or -u options. If the -M option is
        not used on a multi-processor system, the output format of
        the -u and -q options is the same as the uni-processor
        output format and the data reported is the average value of
        all the processors.

EXAMPLES

Watch CPU activity evolve for 5 seconds:

    sar 1 5

Watch CPU activity evolve for 10 minutes and save data:

    sar -o temp 60 10

Review disk and tape activity from that period later:

    sar -d -f temp

Review cpu utilization on a multi-processor system later:

    sar -u -M -f temp

WARNINGS

Users of sar must not rely on the exact field widths and spacing of
its output, as these will vary depending on the system, the release of
HP-UX, and the data to be displayed.

FILES

/var/adm/sa/sadd   daily data file, where dd is two digits
                                    representing the day of the month.

SEE ALSO

sa1(1M).

STANDARDS CONFORMANCE

sar: SVID2, SVID3

showmount

man page

showmount - 11

showmount- Show all remote mounts.

---

showmount(1M)   showmount(1M)

NAME
     showmount - show all remote mounts

SYNOPSIS

     /usr/sbin/showmount [-a] [-d] [-e] [host]

DESCRIPTION
     showmount lists all clients that have remotely mounted a filesystem
     from host. This information is maintained by the mountd server on
     host (see mountd(1M)). The default value for host is the value
     returned by hostname (see hostname(1)).

   Options
     -a   Print all remote mounts in the format

               name:directory

          where hostname is the name of the client, and directory is the
          directory or root of the file system that was mounted.

     -d   List directories that have been remotely mounted by clients.

     -e   Print the list of exported file systems.

WARNINGS
     If a client crashes, executing showmount on the server will show that
     the client still has a file system mounted. In other words, the
     client's entry is not removed from /etc/rmtab until the client reboots
     and executes:

          umount -a

     Also, if a client mounts the same remote directory twice, only one
     entry appears in /etc/rmtab. Doing a umount of one of these
     directories removes the single entry and showmount no longer indicates
     that the remote directory is mounted.

AUTHOR
     showmount was developed by Sun Microsystems, Inc.

SEE ALSO
     hostname(1), exportfs(1M), mountd(1M), exports(4), rmtab(4).

swapinfo

swapinfo - Report system paging information.

```
swapinfo(1M)                                                      swapinfo(1M)

NAME
     swapinfo - system paging space information

SYNOPSIS
     /usr/sbin/swapinfo [-mtadfnrMqw]

DESCRIPTION
     swapinfo prints information about device and file system paging space.
     (Note:  the term `swap' refers to an obsolete implementation of
     virtual memory; HP-UX actually implements virtual memory by way of
     paging rather than swapping.  This command and others retain names
     derived from `swap' for historical reasons.)

     By default, swapinfo prints to standard output a two line header as
     shown here, followed by one line per paging area:

                   Kb      Kb      Kb      PCT    START/  Kb
           TYPE    AVAIL   USED    FREE    USED   LIMIT   RESERVE PRI      NAME

     The fields are:

     TYPE      One of:

               dev       Paging space residing on a mass storage device,
                         either taking up the entire device or, if the
                         device contains a file system, taking up the
                         space between the end of the file system and
                         the end of the device.  This space is
                         exclusively reserved for paging, and even if it
                         is not being used for paging, it cannot be used
                         for any other purpose.  Device paging areas
                         typically provide the fastest paging.

               fs        Dynamic paging space available from a file
                         system.  When this space is needed, the system
                         creates files in the file system and uses them
                         as paging space.  File system paging is
                         typically slower than device paging, but allows
                         the space to be used for other things (user
                         files) when not needed for paging.

               localfs   File system paging space (see fs above) on a
                         file system residing on a local disk.

               network   File system paging space (see fs above) on a
                         file system residing on another machine.  This
                         file system would have been mounted on the
                         local machine via NFS.

               reserve   Paging space on reserve.  This is the amount of
                         paging space that could be needed by processes
```

that are currently running, but that has not
yet been allocated from one of the above paging
areas. See "Paging Allocation" below.

memory   Memory paging area (also known as pseudo-swap).
            This is the amount of system memory that can be
            used to hold pages in the event that all of the
            above paging areas are used up. See "Paging
            Allocation" below. This line appears only if
            memory paging is enabled.

Kb AVAIL   The total available space from the paging area, in blocks
              of 1024 bytes (rounded to nearest whole block if
              necessary), including any paging space already in use.

              For file system paging areas the value is not necessarily
              constant. It is the current space allocated for paging
              (even if not currently used), plus the free blocks
              available on the file system to ordinary users, minus
              RESERVE (but never less than zero). AVAIL is never more
              than LIMIT if LIMIT is non-zero. Since paging space is
              allocated in large chunks, AVAIL is rounded down to the
              nearest full allocation chunk.

              For the memory paging area this value is also not
              necessarily constant, because it reflects allocation of
              memory by the kernel as well as by processes that might
              need to be paged.

Kb USED   The current number of 1-Kbyte blocks used for paging in
              the paging area. For the memory paging area, this count
              also includes memory used for other purposes and thus
              unavailable for paging.

Kb FREE   The amount of space that can be used for future paging.
              Usually this is the difference between Kb AVAIL and Kb
              USED. There could be a difference if some portion of a
              device paging area is unusable, perhaps because the size
              of the paging area is not a multiple of the allocation
              chunk size, or because the tunable parameter maxswapchunks
              is not set high enough.

PCT USED   The percentage of capacity in use, based on Kb USED
              divided by Kb AVAIL; 100% if Kb AVAIL is zero.

START/LIMIT   For device paging areas, START is the block address on the
              mass storage device of the start of the paging area. The
              value is normally 0 for devices dedicated to paging, or
              the end of the file system for devices containing both a
              file system and paging space.

              For file system paging areas, LIMIT is the maximum number
              of 1-Kbyte blocks that will be used for paging, the same
              as the limit value given to swapon. A file system LIMIT
              value of none means there is no fixed limit; all space is
              available except that used for files, less the blocks
              represented by minfree (see fs(4)) plus RESERVE.

RESERVE   For device paging areas, this value is always ``-''. For
              file system paging areas, this value is the number of 1-
              Kbyte blocks reserved for file system use by ordinary
              users, the same as the reserve value given to swapon.

PRI   The same as the priority value given to swapon. This
              value indicates the order in which space is taken from the

devices and file systems used for paging. Space is taken
from areas with lower priority values first. priority can
have a value between 0 and 10. See "Paging Allocation"
below.

NAME   For device paging areas, the block special file name whose
                major and minor numbers match the device's ID. The
                swapinfo command searches the /dev tree to find device
                names. If no matching block special file is found,
                swapinfo prints the device ID (major and minor values),
                for example, 28,0x15000.

                For file system swap areas, NAME is the name of a
                directory on the file system in which the paging files are
                stored.

Paging Allocation
   Paging areas are enabled at boot time (for device paging areas
   configured into the kernel) or by the swapon command (see swapon(1M)),
   often invoked by /sbin/init.d/swap_start during system initialization
   based on the contents of /etc/fstab. When a paging area is enabled,
   some portion of that area is allocated for paging space. For device
   paging areas, the entire device is allocated, less any leftover
   fraction of an allocation chunk. (The size of an allocation chunk is
   controlled by the tunable parameter swchunk, and is typically 2 MB.)
   For file system paging areas, the minimum value given to swapon
   (rounded up to the nearest allocation chunk) is allocated.

   When a process is created, or requests additional space, space is
   reserved for it by increasing the space shown on the reserve line
   above. When paging activity actually occurs, space is used in one of
   the paging areas (the one with the lowest priority number that has
   free space available, already allocated), and that space will be shown
   as used in that area.

   The sum of the space used in all of the paging areas, plus the amount
   of space reserved, can never exceed the total amount allocated in all
   of the paging areas. If a request for more memory occurs which would
   cause this to happen, the system tries several options:

   1.   The system tries to increase the total space available by
        allocating more space in file system paging areas.

   2.   If all file system paging areas are completely allocated and the
        request is still not satisfied, the system will try to use memory
        paging as described on the memory line above. (Memory paging is
        controlled by the tunable parameter swapmem_on, which defaults to
        1 (on). If this parameter is turned off, the memory line will
        not appear.)

   3.   If memory paging also cannot satisfy the request, because it is
        full or turned off, the request is denied.

   Several implications of this procedure are noteworthy for
   understanding the output of swapinfo:

   -    Paging space will not be allocated in a file system paging area
        (except for the minimum specified when the area is first enabled)
        until all device paging space has been reserved, even if the file
        system paging area has a lower priority value.

   -    When paging space is allocated to a file system paging area, that
        space becomes unavailable for user files, even if there is no
        paging activity to it.

   -    Requests for more paging space will fail when they cannot be satisfied by reserving device, file system, or memory paging, even if some of the reserved paging space is not yet in use. Thus it is possible for requests for more paging space to be denied when some, or even all, of the paging areas show zero usage - space in those areas is completely reserved.

- System available memory is shared between the paging subsystem and kernel memory allocators. Thus, the system may show memory paging usage before all available disk paging space is completely reserved or fully allocated.

Options

swapinfo recognizes the following options:

-m   Display the AVAIL, USED, FREE, LIMIT, and RESERVE values in Mbytes instead of Kbytes, rounding off to the nearest whole Mbyte (multiples of 1024^2). The output header format changes from Kb to Mb accordingly.

-t   Add a totals line with a TYPE of total. This line totals only the paging information displayed above it, not all paging areas; this line might be misleading if a subset of -dfrM is specified.

-a   Show all device paging areas, including those configured into the kernel but currently disabled. (These are normally omitted.) The word disabled appears after the NAME, and the Kb AVAIL, Kb USED, and Kb FREE values are 0. The -a option is ignored unless the -d option is present or is true by default.

-d   Print information about device paging areas only. This modifies the output header appropriately.

-f   Print information about file system paging areas only. This modifies the output header appropriately.

-n   Categorize file system paging area information into localfs areas and network areas, instead of calling them both fs areas.

-r   Print information about reserved paging space only.

-M   Print information about memory paging space only.

       The -d, -f, -n, -r and -M options can be combined. The default is -dfnrM.

-q   Quiet mode. Print only a total "Kb AVAIL" value (with the -m option, Mb AVAIL); that is, the total paging space available on the system (device, file system, reserve, or memory paging space only if -d, -f, -r, or -M is specified), for possible use by programs that want a quick total. If -q is specified, the -t and -a options are ignored.

-w   Print a warning about each device paging area that contains wasted space; that is, any device paging area whose allocated size is less than its total size. This option is effective only if -d is also specified or true by default.

RETURN VALUE

swapinfo returns 0 if it completes successfully (including if any warnings are issued), or 1 if it reports any errors.

DIAGNOSTICS

swapinfo prints messages to standard error if it has any problems.

EXAMPLES
List all file system paging areas with a totals line:

swapinfo -ft

WARNINGS
swapinfo needs kernel access for some information. If the user does
not have appropriate privileges for kernel access, swapinfo will print
a warning and assume that the defaults for that information have not
been changed.

Users of swapinfo must not rely on the exact field widths and spacing
of its output, as these will vary depending on the system, the release
of HP-UX, and the data to be displayed.

The information in this manual page about paging allocation and other
implementation details may change without warning; users should not
rely on the accuracy of this information.

AUTHOR
swapinfo was developed by HP.

SEE ALSO
swapon(1M), swapon(2), fstab(4), fs(4).

timex

timex - Time a command and produce a system activity report.

```
timex(1)                                                              timex(1)

NAME
     timex - time a command; report process data and system activity

SYNOPSIS

     timex [-o] [-p[fhkmrt]] [-s] command

DESCRIPTION
     timex reports in seconds the elapsed time, user time, and system time
     spent in execution of the given command.  Optionally, process
     accounting data for command and all its children can be listed or
     summarized, and total system activity during the execution interval
     can be reported.

     The output of timex is written on the standard error.

   Options
          -o             Report the total number of blocks read or written
                         and total characters transferred by command and
                         all its children.

          -p[fhkmrt]     List process accounting records for command and
                         all its children.  The suboptions f, h, k, m, r,
                         and t modify the data items reported.  They behave
                         as defined in acctcom(1M).  The number of blocks
                         read or written and the number of characters
                         transferred are always reported.

          -s             Report total system activity (not just that due to
                         command) that occurred during the execution
                         interval of command.  All the data items listed in
                         sar(1) are reported.

EXAMPLES
     A simple example:

          timex -ops sleep 60

     A terminal session of arbitrary complexity can be measured by timing a
     sub-shell:

          timex -opskmt sh

               session commands

          EOT
```

WARNINGS
      Process records associated with command are selected from the
      accounting file /var/adm/pacct by inference, since process genealogy
      is not available. Background processes having the same user-ID,
      terminal-ID, and execution time window are spuriously included.

SEE ALSO
      sar(1), acctcom(1M).

STANDARDS CONFORMANCE
      timex: SVID2, SVID3

top

man page

top - 11

top - Provide information about top processes on the system.

```
top(1)                                                              top(1)

NAME
     top - display and update information about the top processes on the
     system

SYNOPSIS

     top [-s time] [-d count] [-q] [-u] [-n number]

DESCRIPTION
     top displays the top processes on the system and periodically updates
     the information.  Raw CPU percentage is used to rank the processes.

   Options
     top recognizes the following command-line options:

          -s time     Set the delay between screen updates to time seconds.
                      The default delay between updates is 5 seconds.

          -d count    Show only count displays, then exit.  A display is
                      considered to be one update of the screen.  This
                      option is used to select the number of displays to be
                      shown before the program exits.

          -q          This option runs the top program at the same priority
                      as if it is executed via a nice -20 command so that
                      it will execute faster (see nice(1)).  This can be
                      very useful in discovering any system problem when
                      the system is very sluggish.  This option is
                      accessibly only to users who have appropriate
                      privileges.

          -u          User ID (uid) numbers are displayed instead of
                      usernames.  This improves execution speed by
                      eliminating the additional time required to map uid
                      numbers to user names.

          -n number   Show only number processes per screen.  Note that
                      this option is ignored if number is greater than the
                      maximum number of processes that can be displayed per
                      screen.

   Screen-Control Commands
     When displaying multiple-screen data, top recognizes the following
     keyboard screen-control commands:

          j           Display next screen if the current screen is not the
                      last screen.

          k           Display previous screen if the current screen is not
                      the first screen.

          t           Display the first (top) screen.
```

Program Termination
  To exit the program and resume normal user activities, type q at any
  time.

Display Description
  Three general classes of information are displayed by top:

    System Data:
        The first few lines at the top of the display show general
        information about the state of the system, including:

            - System name and current time.

            - Load averages in the last one, five, and fifteen
               minutes.

            - Number of existing processes and the number of
               processes in each state (sleeping, waiting, running,
               starting, zombie, and stopped).

            - Percentage of time spent in each of the processor
               states (user, nice, system, idle, interrupt and
               swapper) per processor on the system.

            - Average value for each of the processor states (only
               on multi-processor systems).

    Memory Data
        Includes virtual and real memory in use (with the amount of
        memory considered "active" in parentheses) and the amount of
        free memory.

    Process Data
        Information about individual processes on the system. When
        process data cannot fit on a single screen, top divides the
        data into two or more screens. To view multiple-screen
        data, use the j, k, and t commands described previously.
        Note that the system- and memory-data displays are present
        in each screen of multiple-screen process data.

        Process data is displayed in a format similar to that used
        by ps(1):

            CPU   Processor number on which the process is
                        executing (only on multi-processor
                        systems).

            TTY   Terminal interface used by the process.

            PID   Process ID number.

            USERNAME   Name of the owner of the process. When the
                        -u option is specified, the user ID (uid)
                        is displayed instead of USERNAME.

            PRI   Current priority of the process.

            NI   Nice value ranging from -20 to +20.

            SIZE   Total size of the process in kilobytes.
                        This includes text, data, and stack.

            RES   Resident size of the process in kilobytes..
                        The resident size information is, at best,

	an approximate value.
STATE	Current state of the process. The various states are sleep, wait, run, idl, zomb, or stop.
TIME	Number of system and CPU seconds the process has consumed.
%WCPU	Weighted CPU (central processing unit) percentage.
%CPU	Raw CPU percentage. This field is used to sort the top processes.
COMMAND	Name of the command the process is currently running.

EXAMPLES
    top can be executed with or without command-line options. To display
    five screens of data at two-second intervals then automatically exit,
    use:

        top -s2 -d5

AUTHOR
    top was developed by HP and William LeFebvre of Rice University.

vmstat

vmstat - Report process, virtual memory, trap, and CPU activity.

man page

vmstat - 11

---

vmstat(1)   vmstat(1)

NAME
     vmstat - report virtual memory statistics

SYNOPSIS

     vmstat [-dnS] [interval [count]]

     vmstat -f | -s | -z

DESCRIPTION
     The vmstat command reports certain statistics kept about process,
     virtual memory, trap, and CPU activity. It also can clear the
     accumulators in the kernel sum structure.

  Options
     vmstat recognizes the following options:

          -d   Report disk transfer information as a separate section,
                    in the form of transfers per second.

          -n   Provide an output format that is more easily viewed on
                    an 80-column display device. This format separates the
                    default output into two groups: virtual memory
                    information and CPU data. Each group is displayed as a
                    separate line of output. On multiprocessor systems,
                    this display format also provides CPU utilization on a
                    per CPU basis.

          -S   Report the number of processes swapped in and out (si
                    and so) instead of page reclaims and address
                    translation faults (re and at).

          interval Display successive lines which are summaries over the
                    last interval seconds. If interval is zero, the output
                    is displayed once only. If the -d option is specified,
                    the column headers are repeated. If -d is omitted, the
                    column headers are not repeated.

                    The command vmstat 5 prints what the system is doing
                    every five seconds. This is a good choice of printing
                    interval since this is how often some of the statistics
                    are sampled in the system; others vary every second.

          count   Repeat the summary statistics count times. If count is
                    omitted or zero, the output is repeated until an
                    interrupt or quit signal is received. From the
                    terminal, these are commonly ^C and ^\, respectively
                    (see stty(1)).

          -f   Report on the number of forks and the number of pages
                    of virtual memory involved since boot-up.

-s   Print the total number of several kinds of paging-
            related events from the kernel sum structure that have
            occurred since boot-up or since vmstat was last
            executed with the -z option.

-z   Clear all accumulators in the kernel sum structure.
            This requires write file access permission on
            /dev/kmem. This is normally restricted to users with
            appropriate privileges.

If none of these options is given, vmstat displays a one-line summary
of the virtual memory activity since boot-up or since the -z option
was last executed.

Column Descriptions
   The column headings and the meaning of each column are:

procs   Information about numbers of processes in various
            states.

                r   In run queue

                b   Blocked for resources (I/O, paging, etc.)

                w   Runnable or short sleeper (< 20 secs) but
                        swapped

memory   Information about the usage of virtual and real
            memory. Virtual pages are considered active if they
            belong to processes that are running or have run in
            the last 20 seconds.

                avm   Active virtual pages

                free   Size of the free list

page   Information about page faults and paging activity.
            These are averaged each five seconds, and given in
            units per second.

                re   Page reclaims (without -S)

                at   Address translation faults (without -S)

                si   Processes swapped in (with -S)

                so   Processes swapped out (with -S)

                pi   Pages paged in

                po   Pages paged out

                fr   Pages freed per second

                de   Anticipated short term memory shortfall

                sr   Pages scanned by clock algorithm, per
                        second

faults	Trap/interrupt rate averages per second over last 5 seconds.	
	in	Device interrupts per second (nonclock)
	sy	System calls per second
	cs	CPU context switch rate (switches/sec)
cpu	Breakdown of percentage usage of CPU time	
	us	User time for normal and lów priority processes
	sy	System time
	id	CPU idle

EXAMPLES

The following examples show the output for various command options. For formatting purposes, some leading blanks have been deleted.

1. Display the default output.

vmstat

```
    procs              memory                      page
           faults          cpu
 r    b    w      avm     free    re   .at    pi    po    fr    de    sr
      in   sy    cs   us sy id
 0    0    0     1158      511     0     0     0     0     0     0     0
     111   18     7    0   0 100
```

2. Add the disk tranfer information to the default output.

vmstat -d

```
    procs              memory                      page
           faults          cpu
 r    b    w      avm     free    re    at    pi    po    fr    de    sr
      in   sy    cs   us sy id
 0    0    0     1158      511     0     0     0     0     0     0     0
     111   18     7    0   0 100
```

Disk Transfers
```
  device    xfer/sec
  c0t6d0        0
  c0t1d0        0
  c0t3d0        0
  c0t5d0        0
```

3. Display the default output in 80-column format.

vmstat -n

```
VM
    memory                      page                          faults
   avm    free    re    at    pi    po    fr    de    sr    in     sy    cs
  1158     430     0     0     0     0     0     0     0   111     18     7
CPU
     cpu          procs
 us sy id     r     b      w
```

```
 0  0 100    0     0     0
```

4. Replace the page reclaims and address translation faults with
   process swapping in the default output.

```
vmstat -S
```

procs			memory				page					
		faults		cpu								
r	b	w	avm	free	si	so	pi	po	fr	de	sr	
	in	sy	cs	us sy id								
0	0	0	1158	430	0	0	0	0	0	0	0	
	111	18	7	0 0 100								

5. Display the default output twice at five-second intervals. Note
   that the headers are not repeated.

```
vmstat 5 2
```

procs			memory				page					
		faults		cpu								
r	b	w	avm	free	re	at	pi	po	fr	de	sr	
	in	sy	cs	us sy id								
0	0	0	1158	456	0	0	0	0	0	0	0	
	111	18	7	0 0 100								
0	0	0	1221	436	5	0	5	0	0	0	0	
	108	65	18	0 1 99								

6. Display the default output twice in 80-column format at five-
   second intervals. Note that the headers are not repeated.

```
vmstat -n 5 2
```

```
VM
   memory              page                    faults
  avm    free   re   at   pi   po   fr   de   sr    in    sy   cs
  1221    436    0    0    0    0    0    0    0    111    18    7
CPU
     cpu         procs
 us sy id    r    b    w
  0  0 100    0    0    0
  1221    435    2    0    2    0    0    0    0    109    35   17
    0  1 99    0    0    0
```

7. Display the default output and disk transfers twice in 80-column
   format at five-second intervals. Note that the headers are
   repeated.

```
vmstat -dn 5 2
```

```
VM
   memory              page                    faults
  avm    free   re   at   pi   po   fr   de   sr    in    sy   cs
  1221    435    0    0    0    0    0    0    0    111    18    7
CPU
     cpu         procs
 us sy id    r    b    w
  0  0 100    0    0    0

Disk Transfers
   device    xfer/sec
   c0t6d0        0
```

```
   c0t1d0          0
   c0t3d0          0
   c0t5d0          0
```

```
VM
   memory                      page                        faults
  avm    free    re   at    pi   po   fr   de   sr     in    sy    cs
 1219     425     0    0     0    0    0    0    0    111    54    15
CPU
     cpu          procs
  us sy id    r     b     w
   1  8 92    0     0     0
```

```
Disk Transfers
   device     xfer/sec
   c0t6d0         0
   c0t1d0         0
   c0t3d0         0
   c0t5d0         0
```

8.   Display the number of forks and pages of virtual memory since
     boot-up.

vmstat -f

24558 forks, 1471595 pages, average= 59.92

9.   Display the counts of paging-related events.

vmstat -s

```
0 swap ins
0 swap outs
0 pages swapped in
0 pages swapped out
1344563 total address trans. faults taken
542093 page ins
2185 page outs
602573 pages paged in
4346 pages paged out
482343 reclaims from free list
504621 total page reclaims
124 intransit blocking page faults
1460755 zero fill pages created
404137 zero fill page faults
366022 executable fill pages created
71578 executable fill page faults
0 swap text pages found in free list
162043 inode text pages found in free list
196 revolutions of the clock hand
45732 pages scanned for page out
4859 pages freed by the clock daemon
36680636 cpu context switches
1497746186 device interrupts
1835626 traps
87434493 system calls
```

WARNINGS
     Users of vmstat must not rely on the exact field widths and spacing of
     its output, as these will vary depending on the system, the release of
     HP-UX, and the data to be displayed.

AUTHOR
     vmstat was developed by the University of California, Berkeley and HP.

FILES
     /dev/kmem

SEE ALSO
     iostat(1).

CHAPTER 12

Networking

Networking varies greatly from installation to installation. Some installations, such as highly centralized and isolated systems that have only ASCII terminals connected to the system, require the system administrator to pay very little attention to networking. Other installations, such as highly distributed environments in which thousands of systems are connected to a network that may span many geographic sites, may require the system administrator to pay a great deal of attention to networking. In this second scenario, the amount of time a system administrator devotes to networking may exceed the amount of time spent on all other system administration functions combined! Rather than ignoring networking altogether, as the first system administrator might, or covering all aspects of network administration, as the second system administrator may require, I cover in this chapter the aspects of networking that apply to most UNIX systems. This content is based on my experience of working in a variety of new UNIX installations. In the event that you require more networking background than I cover in this chapter, I recommend the following book as an excellent source of networking information - *UNIX Networks* by Bruce H. Hunter and Karen Bradford Hunter (Prentice Hall, ISBN 0-13-08987-1).

In this chapter, I provide primarily background rather than setup information on many networking topics, because setup is predominantly performed by system administrators. Most of what I cover is sometimes called "Internet Services." In general, I am going to cover the basics of networking in this chapter. This includes ARPA and Berkeley Services. Here is a list of topics I cover:

- General UNIX networking background

- Internet Protocol (IP) addressing (classes A, B, and C)

- Subnet mask

- ARPA Services

- Berkeley commands

- Host name mapping

- Network File System (NFS) background

- UNIX networking commands

I provide summaries and examples of many UNIX commands in this chapter. A great deal more detail can be found in the manual pages for these commands. I provide the full manual pages at the end of this chapter for many of the commands covered.

I use a variety of systems in the examples in this chapter, including Solaris, AIX, and HP-UX.

UNIX Networking

Connecting to other machines is an important part of every UNIX network. This means connecting both to other UNIX machines as well as to non-UNIX machines. The machines must be physically connected to one another as well as functionally connected to one another, so that you can perform such tasks as transferring files and logging into other systems. Many commands exist on your UNIX system that provide you with the functionality to log in and transfer files between systems. These are known as the ARPA commands, **telnet** and **ftp**.

The **telnet** command allows remote logins in a heterogeneous environment. From your UNIX system, for instance, you can **telnet** to non-UNIX systems and log in. After login on the remote system, you need to have an understanding of the operating system running on that system. If you need to connect to a different computer only for the purpose of transferring files to and from the system, then you can use **ftp**. This command allows you to transfer files between any two systems without having an understanding of the operating system running on the remote system.

These commands are somewhat primitive compared to the commands that can be issued between UNIX systems. To UNIX systems, networking is not an afterthought that needs to be added on to the system. The **ftp** and **telnet** commands come with your UNIX system, as well as more advanced commands and functionality you can use to communicate between your UNIX system and other UNIX systems. These more advanced commands, known as Berkeley commands, allow you to perform many commands remotely, such as copying files and directories and logging in. This functionality continues to increase to a point where you are working with files that can be stored on any system on the network, and your access to these files is transparent to you with the Network File System (NFS).

Let's take a look at some of the basics of UNIX networking.

An Overview of IEEE802.3, TCP/IP

In order to understand how the networking on your UNIX system works, you first need to understand the components of your network that exist on your UNIX system. Seven layers of network functionality exist on your UNIX system, as shown in Figure 12-1. I cover the bottom four layers at a cursory level so that you can see how each plays a part in the operation of your network and, therefore, be more informed when you configure and troubleshoot networking on your UNIX system. The top layers are the ones that most UNIX system administrators spend time working with because those layers are closest to the functionality to which you can relate. The bottom layers are, however, also important to understand at some level, so that you can perform any configuration necessary to improve the network performance of your system, which has a major impact on the overall performance of your system.

Layer Number	Layer Name	Data Form	Comments
7	Application		User applications here.
6	Presentation		Applications prepared.
5	Session		Applications prepared.
4	Transport	Packet	Port-to-port transportation handled by TCP.
3	Network	Datagram	Internet Protocol (IP) handles routing by going directly to either the destination or default router.
2	Link	Frame	Data encapsulated in Ethernet or IEEE 802.3 with source and destination addresses.
1	Physical		Physical connection between systems. Usually thinnet or twisted pair.

Figure 12-1 ISO/OSI Network Layer Functions

I start reviewing Figure 9-1 at the bottom with layer 1 and then describe each of the four bottom layers. This is the International Standards Organization Open Systems Interconnection (ISO/OSI) model. It is helpful to visualize the way in which networking layers interact.

Physical Layer

The beginning is the physical interconnection between the systems on your network. Without the **physical layer,** you can't communicate between systems, and all the great functionality you would like to implement is not possible. The physical layer converts the data you would like to transmit to the analog signals that travel along the wire (I'll assume for now that whatever physical layer you have in place uses wires). The information traveling into a network interface is taken off the wire and prepared for use by the next layer.

Link Layer

In order to connect to other systems local to your system, you use the link layer that is able to establish a connection to all the other systems on your local segment. This is the layer where you have either IEEE 802.3 or Ethernet. Your UNIX system supports both of these "encapsulation" methods. This is called encapsulation because your data is put in one of these two forms (either IEEE 802.3 or Ethernet). Data is transferred at the link layer in frames (just another name for data), with the source and destination addresses and some other information attached. You might think that because two different encapsulation methods exist, they must be very different. This assumption, however, is not the case. IEEE 802.3 and Ethernet are nearly identical. For this reason, many UNIX systems can handle both types of encapsulation. So with the bottom two layers, you have a physical connection between your systems and data that is encapsulated into one of two formats with a source and destination address attached. Figure 9-2 lists the components of an **Ethernet** encapsulation and makes comments about IEEE802.3 encapsulation where appropriate:

destination address	6 bytes	address data is sent to
source address	6 bytes	address data is sent from
type	2 bytes	this is the "length count" in 802.3

data	46-1500 bytes	38-1492 bytes for 802.3; the difference in these two data sizes (MTU) can be seen with the **ifconfig** command
crc	4 bytes	checksum to detect errors

Figure 12-2   Ethernet Encapsulation

One interesting item to note is the difference in the maximum data size between IEEE 802.3 and Ethernet of 1492 and 1500 bytes, respectively. This is the Maximum Transfer Unit (MTU). The **ifconfig** command covered shortly displays the MTU for your interface. The data in Ethernet is called a *frame* (the re-encapsulation of data at the next layer up is called a *datagram* in IP, and encapsulation at two levels up is called a *packet* for TCP).

Keep in mind that Ethernet and IEEE 802.3 will run on the same physical connection, but there are indeed differences between the two encapsulation methods. With your UNIX systems, you don't have to spend much, if any, time setting up your network interface for encapsulation.

Network Layer

Next we work up to the third layer, which is the network layer. This layer on UNIX systems is synonymous with the Internet Protocol (IP). Data at this layer is transported as *datagrams*. This is the layer that handles the routing of data around the network. Data that gets routed with IP sometimes encounters an error of some type, which is reported back to the source system with an Internet Control Message Protocol (ICMP) message. We will see some ICMP messages shortly. **ifconfig** and **netstat** are two UNIX commands that are commonly used to configure this routing.

Unfortunately, the information that IP uses does not conveniently fit inside an Ethernet frame, so you end up with fragmented data. This is really re-encapsulation of the data, so you end up with a lot of inefficiency as you work your way up the layers.

IP handles routing in a simple fashion. If data is sent to a destination connected directly to your system, then the data is sent directly to that system. If, on the other hand, the destination is not connected directly to your system, the data is sent to the default router. The default router then has the responsibility of getting the data to its destination. This routing can be a little tricky to understand, so I'll cover it in detail shortly.

Transport Layer

The *trasport level* is the next level up from the network layer. It communicates with *ports*. TCP is the most common protocol found at this level, and it forms packets that are sent from port to port. The port used by a program is usually defined in **/etc/services**, along with the protocol (such as TCP). These ports are used by network programs such as **telnet**, **rlogin**, **ftp**, and so on. You can see that these programs, associated with ports, are the highest level we have covered while analyzing the layer diagram.

man page
telnet - 12

man page
rlogin - 12

man page
ftp - 12

Internet Protocol (IP) Addressing

The Internet Protocol address (IP address) is either a class "A," "B," or "C" address (there are also class "D" and "E" addresses I will not cover). A class "A" network supports many more nodes per network than either a class "B" or "C" network. IP addresses consist of four fields. The purpose of breaking down the IP address into four fields is to define a node (or host) address and a network address. Figure 12-3 summarizes the relationships between the classes and addresses.

Address Class	Networks	Nodes per Network	Bits Defining Network	Bits Defining Nodes per Network
A	a few	the most	8 bits	24 bits

Address Class	Networks	Nodes per Network	Bits Defining Network	Bits Defining Nodes per Network
B	many	many	16 bits	16 bits
C	the most	a few	24 bits	8 bits
Reserved	-	-	-	-

Figure 12-3   Comparison of Internet Protocol (IP) Addresses

These bit patterns are significant in that the number of bits defines the ranges of networks and nodes in each class. For instance, a class A address uses 8 bits to define networks, and a class C address uses 24 bits to define networks. A class A address therefore supports fewer networks than a class C address. A class A address, however, supports many more nodes per network than a class C address. Taking these relationships one step further, we can now view the specific parameters associated with these address classes in Figure 12-4.

Figure 12-4   Address Classes

Address Class	Networks Supported	Nodes per Network	Address Range		
A	127	16777215	0.0.0.1	-	127.255.255.254
B	16383	65535	128.0.0.1	-	191.255.255.254
C	2097157	255	192.0.0.1	-	223.255.254.254
Reserved	-	-	224.0.0.0	-	255.255.255.255
Looking at the 32-bit address in binary form, you can see how to determine the class of an address:					

Figure 12-4 Address Classes (Continued)

Class "A"

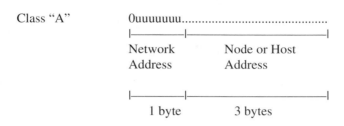

net.host.host.host

A class "A" address has the first bit set to 0. You can see how so many nodes per network can be supported with all the bits devoted to the node or host address. The first bit of a class A address is 0, and the remaining 7 bits of the network portion are used to define the network. Then a total of 3 bytes are devoted to defining the nodes with a network.

Class "B"

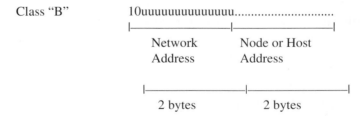

net.net.host.host

A class "B" address has the first bit set to a 1 and the second bit to a 0. More networks are supported here than with a class A address, but fewer nodes per network. With a class B address, 2 bytes are devoted to the network portion of the address and 2 bytes devoted to the node portion of the address.

Figure 12-4   Address Classes (Continued)

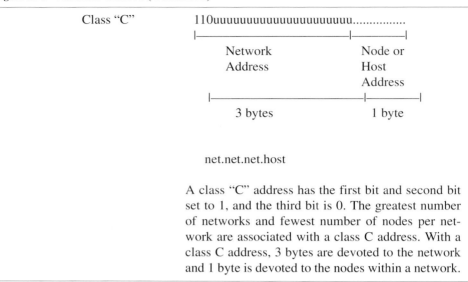

net.net.net.host

A class "C" address has the first bit and second bit set to 1, and the third bit is 0. The greatest number of networks and fewest number of nodes per network are associated with a class C address. With a class C address, 3 bytes are devoted to the network and 1 byte is devoted to the nodes within a network.

These addresses are used in various setup files that are covered later when the **/etc/hosts** file is described. Every interface on your network must have a unique IP address. Systems that have two network interfaces must have two unique IP addresses.

Subnet Mask

Your UNIX system uses the subnet mask to determine whether an IP datagram is for a host on its own subnet, a host on a different subnet but the same network, or a host on a different network. Using subnets, you can have some hosts on one subnet and other hosts on a different subnet. The subnets can be separated by routers or other networking electronics that connect the subnets.

To perform routing, the only aspects of an address that your router uses are the net and subnet. The subnet mask is used to mask the host part of the address. Because you can set up network addresses in such a way that you are the only one who knows which part of the address is the host, subnet, and network, you use the subnet mask to make your system aware of the bits of your IP address that are for the host and which are for the subnet.

In its simplest form, what you are really doing with subnet masking is specifying which portion of your IP address defines the host, and which part defines the network. One of the most confusing aspects of working with subnet masks is that most books show the subnet masks in Figure 12-5 as the most common.

Address Class	Decimal	Hex
A	255.0.0.0	0xff000000
B	255.255.0.0	0xffff0000
C	255.255.255.0	0xffffff00

Figure 12-5 Subnet Masks

This way of thinking, however, assumes that you are devoting as many bits as possible to the network and as many bits as possible to the host, and that no subnets are used. Figure 12-6 shows an example of using subnetting with a class B address.

Address Class	Class B		
host IP address	152.128.	12.	1
breakdown	network	subnet	hostid
number of bits	16 bits	8 bits	8 bits
subnet mask in decimal	255.255.	255.	0
subnet mask in hexadecimal	0xffffff00		
Example of different host on same subnet	152.128.	12.	2

Address Class	Class B		
Example of host on different subnet	152.128.	13.	1

Figure 12-6 Class B IP Address and Subnet Mask Example

In Figure 12-6, the first two bytes of the subnet mask (255.255) define the network, the third byte (255) defines the subnet, and the fourth byte (0) is devoted to the host ID. Although this subnet mask for a class B address did not appear in the earlier default subnet mask figure, the subnet mask of 255.255.255.0 is widely used in class B networks to support subnetting.

How does your UNIX system perform the comparison using the subnet mask of 255.255.255.0 to determine that 152.128.12.1 and 152.128.13.1 are on different subnets? Figure 12-7 shows this comparison.

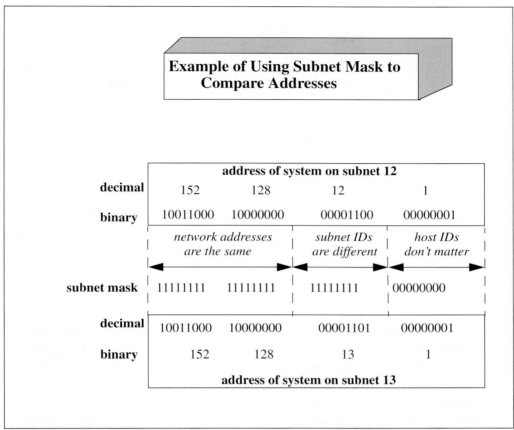

Figure 12-7 Example of Using Subnet Mask to Compare Addresses

Figure 12-8 shows these two systems on the different subnets:

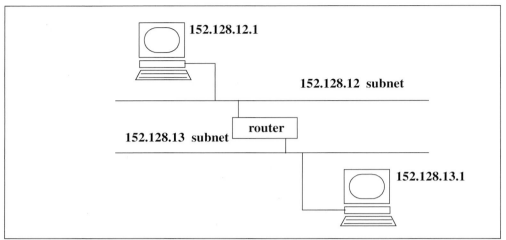

Figure 12-8 Class B Systems on Different Subnets

You don't have to use the 8-bit boundaries to delineate the network, subnet, and host ID fields. If, for instance, you want to use part
of the subnet field for the host ID, you can do so. A good reason for
this approach would be to accommodate future expandability. You
might want subnets 12, 13, 14, and 15 to be part of the same subnet
today and make these into separate subnets in the future. Figure 12-9
shows this setup:

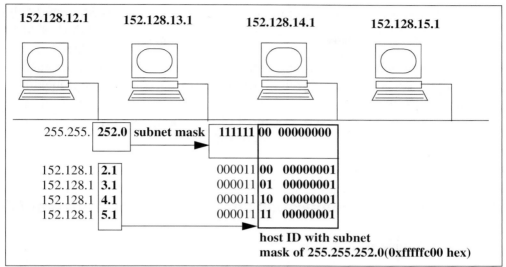

Figure 12-9 Future Expandability Using Subnet Mask

These systems are connected to the same subnet, even though part of the third byte, normally associated with the subnet, is used for the host ID. In the future, the subnet mask could be changed to 255.255.252.0 and have four separate subnets of 12, 13, 14, and 15. This arrangement would require putting routers in place to route to these separate subnets.

Let's now switch to a higher levels of the ISO/OSI model and look at some networking functionality.

Using Networking

The ISO/OSI model is helpful for visualizing the way in which the networking layers interact. The model does not, however, tell you how to use the networking. Two widely used networking services that may be running on your system(s) and are worth taking a look at are ARPA and NFS.

The first networking product to try on your system is what is sometimes called ARPA Services - what I have been calling ARPA.

ARPA is a combination of "ARPA Services" and "Berkeley Services." ARPA Services supports communications among systems running different operating systems, and Berkeley Services supports UNIX systems. The following sections are a list of the most common ARPA and Berkeley commands. Although many programs can be run under each of these services, the following are the most commonly used ones in the UNIX world. In some cases, there are examples that show how these commands are used. For most of the examples, the local host is **system1** and the remote host is **system2**.

ARPA Services (Communication among Systems w/ Different OS)

man page

ftp - 12

File Transfer Protocol (ftp)   Transfer a file, or multiple files, from one system to another. This is often used when transferring files between a UNIX workstation and a Windows PC, VAX, etc. The following example shows copying the file **/tmp/krsort.c** from system2 (remote host) to the local directory on system1 (local host):

	Comments
$ ftp system2	Issue ftp command
Connected to system2.	
system2 FTP server (Version 4.1) ready.	
Name (system2:root): root	Log in to system2
Password required for root.	
Password:	Enter password
User root logged in.	
Remote system type is UNIX.	
Using binary mode to transfer files.	
ftp> **cd /tmp**	**cd** to **/tmp** on system2
CWD command successful	
ftp> **get krsort.c**	Get krsort.c file
PORT command successful	
Opening BINARY mode data connection for **krsort.c**	
Transfer complete.	
2896 bytes received in 0.08 seconds	

	Comments
ftp> **bye**	Exit ftp
Goodbye.	
$	

man page

ftp - 12

In this example, both systems are running UNIX; however, the commands you issue through **ftp** are operating system-independent. The **cd** for change directory and **get** commands used above work for any operating system on which **ftp** is running. If you become familiar with just a few **ftp** commands, you may find that transferring information in a heterogeneous networking environment is not difficult.

Chances are that you are using your UNIX system(s) in a heterogeneous environment and may therefore use **ftp** to copy files and directories from one system to another. Because **ftp** is so widely used, I describe some of the more commonly used **ftp** commands:

ascii   Set the type of file transferred to ASCII. This means that you are transferring an ASCII file from one system to another. This is usually the default, so you don't have to set it.

Example: **ascii**

binary   Set the type of file transferred to binary. This means that you are transferring a binary file from one system to another. If, for instance, you want to have a directory on your UNIX system that holds applications that you copy to non-UNIX systems, then you want to use binary transfer.

Example: **binary**

cd	Change to the specified directory on the remote host.
	Example: **cd /tmp**
dir	List the contents of a directory on the remote system to the screen or to a file on the local system, if you specify a local file name.
get	Copy the specified remote file to the specified local file. If you don't specify a local file name, then the remote file name will be used.
lcd	Change to the specified directory on the local host.
	Example: **lcd /tmp**
ls	List the contents of a directory on the remote system to the screen or to a file on the local system, if you specify a local file name.
mget	Copy multiple files from the remote host to the local host.
	Example: **mget *.c**
put	Copy the specified local file to the specified remote file. If you don't specify a remote file name, then the local file name will be used.
	Example: **put test.c**

mput Copy multiple files from the local host to the remote host.

Example: **mput *.c**

bye/quit Close the connection to the remote host.

Example: **bye**

Other **ftp** commands are available in addition to those I have covered here. If you need more information on these commands or wish to review additional **ftp** commands, the UNIX manual pages for **ftp** are helpful.

man page

ftp - 12

man page

telnet - 12

telnet Used for communication with another host using the telnet protocol. Telnet is an alternative to using **rlogin**, described later. The following example shows how to establish a telnet connection with the remote host, system2:

man page

rlogin - 12

	Comments
$ telnet system2	
Connected to system2.	Telnet to system2
AIX version 4 system2	
login: **root**	Log in as root on system2
password:	Enter password
Welcome to system2. - rs6000 aix 4.3.1.0	
$	AIX prompt on system2

Berkeley Commands (Communication between UNIX Systems)

Remote Copy (rcp)

This program is used to copy files and directories from one UNIX system to another. To copy **/tmp/krsort.c** from system1 to system2, you could do the following:

$ rcp   system2:/tmp/krsort.c /tmp/krsort.c

man page

rcp - 12

Some networking configuration needs to be made to files to get this level of functionality. In this example, the user who issues the command is considered "equivalent" on both systems and has permission to copy files from one system to the other with **rcp** (These terms are described shortly).

Remote login (rlogin)

Supports login to a remote UNIX system. To remotely log in to system2 from system1, you would do the following:

man page

rogin - 12

$ rlogin system2

password:

Welcome to system2

$

If a password is requested when the user issues the **rlogin** command, the users are not equivalent on the two systems. If no password is requested, then the users are indeed equivalent. You can also issue **rlogin** *system* **-l** *user* to specify the *system* and *user* as part of the command.

Remote shell (remsh)

With the **remsh** command, you can sit on one UNIX system and issue a command to be run remotely on a different UNIX system and have the results displayed locally. In this case, a **remsh** is issued to show a long listing of **/tmp/krsort.c**. The command is run on system2, but the result is displayed on system1, where the command was typed:

man page

remsh - 12

$ remsh system2 ll /tmp/krsort.c

-rwxrwxrwx 1 root sys 2896 Sept 1 10:54 /tmp/krsort.c

$

In this case, the users on system1 and system2 must be equivalent, or else permission is denied to issue this command.

Remote who (rwho)

Find out who is logged in on a remote UNIX system. Here is the output of issuing **rwho**:

man page

rwho - 12

$ rwho

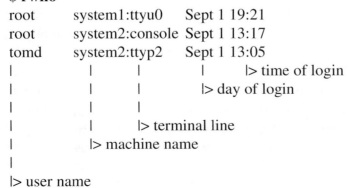

```
root        system1:ttyu0     Sept 1 19:21
root        system2:console   Sept 1 13:17
tomd        system2:ttyp2     Sept 1 13:05
 |           |     |            |      |> time of login
 |           |     |            |> day of login
 |           |     |
 |           |     |> terminal line
 |           |> machine name
 |
 |> user name
```

man page

rwho - 12

For **rwho** to work, the **rwho** daemon (**rwhod**) must be running.

Other "r" commands, in addition to those covered are available. Also, variations of these commands occur going from one UNIX variant to another, so you may not run exactly the same "r" command on your UNIX system.

Host Name Mapping

The most important decision related to networking is how host name mapping is implemented on your system in ARPA. Three techniques are available for host name mapping:

- Berkeley Internet Named Domain (BIND)

- Network Information Service (NIS)

- UNIX file **/etc/hosts**

The most common and simplest way to implement host name mapping is with **/etc/hosts**, so I cover this technique in the next section. Keep in mind that there are probably networking manuals for your UNIX variant devoted to many networking topics including NFS, ARPA, and others. These manuals serve as good reference material if you need to know more about networking than is covered here.

Using the **/etc/hosts** file, as you are about to see, becomes very difficult for environments where there are many systems deployed. With this solution there is one **/etc/hosts** file that must be kept up-to-date and propagated to all other systems.

The Domain Name System (DNS) is widely used in large environments. DNS uses Berkeley Internet Name Domain Service (BIND) to resolve names to addresses. There are name servers that fill a request for name data. This is the server side to BIND. There is a client side to BIND, called the resolver, that accesses the name server(s) to resolve names. Using this client/server model, it is much easier to maintain naming information, because it only needs to be kept in a few places as opposed to on each system.

Clients use a file called **/etc/resolv.conf** to configure the resolver. The name server and its corresponding address are the keys to resolving information.

This solution makes it much easier to maintain system names and addresses in large environments. DNS and BIND are primarily a system administration exercise to setup. From a user standpoint, you don't need to know much about them. What I will instead focus on in the upcoming sections are some of the programs in which users are more interested. I will supply some background so that the way in which the programs are used has more meaning. In general, though, I'll concentrate on the user aspect of these networking topics, as opposed to the system administration aspect of them.

/etc/hosts

This file contains information about the other systems to which you are connected. It contains the Internet address of each system, the system name, and any aliases for the system name. If the **/etc/hosts** file is modified to contain the names of the systems on your network, they have provided the basis for **rlogin** to another system. Although you can now **rlogin** to other UNIX systems, you cannot yet **rcp** or **remsh** to another system. Although adding **remsh** and **rcp** functionality is easy, it does indeed compromise security, so it is not always set up on all systems. Here is an example **/etc/hosts** file:

```
127.0.0.1            localhost        loopback
15.32.199.42         a4410827
15.32.199.28         a4410tu8
15.32.199.7          a4410922
15.32.199.21         a4410tu1
15.32.199.22         a4410tu2
15.32.199.62         a4410730
```

15.32.199.63	hpxterm1	
15.32.199.64	a4410rd1	
15.32.199.62	a4410750	hp1

This file is in the following format:

<internet_address>   <official_hostname>   <alias>

The Internet Protocol address (IP address) is a class "A," "B," or "C" address. A class "A" network supports many more nodes per network than either a class "B" or "C" network. The purpose of breaking down the IP address into four fields is to define a node (or host) address and a network address. Figures 9-3 through 9-6 described these classes in detail.

Assuming that the above **/etc/hosts** file contains class "C" addresses, the rightmost field is the host or node address, and the other three fields comprise the network address.

You could use either the official_hostname or alias from the **/etc/hosts** file when issuing one of the ARPA or Berkeley commands described earlier. For instance, either of the following ARPA commands work:

man page

telnet - 12

$ **telnet a4410750**

or

$ **telnet hp1**

Similarly, either of the following Berkeley commands works:

man page

rogin - 12

$ **rlogin a4410750**

or

$ **rlogin hp1**

/etc/hosts.equiv

Your system may be setup so user's don't have to issue a password when they **rlogin** to a remote system, they can set up equivalent hosts by editing this file. As I mentioned earlier, this is technique sometimes considered a security risk, so it is not always employed. The login names must be the same on both the local and remote systems for **/etc/hosts.equiv** to allow the user to bypass entering a password. You can either list all the equivalent hosts in **/etc/ hosts.equiv** or list the host and user name you wish to be equivalent. Users can now use **rcp** and **remsh**, because they are equivalent users on these systems. I usually just enter all the host names on the network. Here is an example of **/etc/hosts.equiv**:

        a4410730
        a4410tu1
        a4410tu2
        hpxterm1
        a4410827
        a4410750

Keep in mind the potential security risks of using **/etc/ hosts.equiv**. If a user can log into a remote system without a password, you have reduced the overall level of security on your network. Even though users may find it convenient to not have to enter a password when logging into a remote system, you have given every user in **/etc/hosts.equiv** access to the entire network. If you could ensure that all the permissions on all the files and directories on all systems were properly set up, then you wouldn't care who had access to what system. In the real UNIX world, however, permissions are sometimes not what they are supposed to be. Users have a strong tendency to "browse around," invariably stumbling upon a file they want to copy to which they really shouldn't have access.

/.rhosts

This file is the **/etc/hosts.equiv** for superuser. If you log in as root, you want to have this file configured with exactly the same information as **/etc/hosts.equiv**. If you do, however, you have compounded your network security risk by allowing superuser on any system to log in to a remote system without a root password. If you are the undisputed ruler of your network and you're 100 percent certain that no security holes exist, then you may want to set up **/.rhosts** so that you don't have to issue a password when you log in remotely to a system as superuser. From a security standpoint, however, you should know that this setup is frowned upon.

If the appropriate changes have been made to the appropriate entries in **/etc/hosts**, **/etc/hosts.equiv**, and **/.rhosts**, you can use the ARPA Services commands **ftp** and **telnet**, as well as the Berkeley commands **rcp**, **rlogin**, **remsh**, and **rwho**.

I have described the process of setting up the appropriate files to get the most commonly used ARPA Services up and running. There is sometimes even more advanced functionality, such as DNS/BIND, required. You system may have DNS/BIND or similar functionality set up that gives you access to some or all of the commands covered throughout this section.

Network File System (NFS)

NFS allows you to mount disks on remote systems so that they appear as though they are local to your system. Similarly, NFS allows remote systems to mount your local disk so that it looks as though it is local to the remote system. Configuring NFS to achieve this functionality is simple. Here are the steps to go through in order to configure NFS:

1. Start NFS.

2. Specify whether your system will be an NFS Client, NFS Server, or both.

3. Specify which of your local file systems can be mounted by remote systems.

4. Specify the remote disks you want to mount and view as if they were local to your system.

As with ARPA, you could enable other aspects to NFS, but again, I cover what I know to be the NFS functionality that nearly every UNIX installation uses.

Because NFS may be setup on your system to meet the needs of many users, you may want to understand the terminology associated with NFS. The following are commonly used NFS terms:

Node	A computer system that is attached to or is part of a computer network.
Client	A node that requests data or services from other nodes (servers).
Server	A node that provides data or services to other nodes (clients) on the network.
File System	A disk partition or logical volume.
Export	Makes a file system available for mounting on remote nodes using NFS.
Mount	Accesses a remote file system using NFS.
Mount Point	The name of a directory on which the NFS file system is mounted.

Import   Mounts a remote file system.

Some of the specific configuration tasks and related files are different among UNIX variants. The following are some general tasks and examples related to configuring NFS. Your system administrator, of course, has to deal with the specifics of configuration on the UNIX variants.

Your system must be an NFS client, NFS server, or both. There are also daemons which must be running to support NFS. Both of these tasks are performed somewhat differently among the UNIX variants.

Your system then imports remote file systems to which you have local access and exports local file systems that are accessed by other systems.

A remote file system that you are mounting locally has an entry similar to the one that follows in **/etc/fstab**, **/etc/vfstab**, **/etc/filesystems**, or whatever file is used to mount file systems:

```
system2:/opt/app3   /opt/app3    nfs  rw,suid   0 0
```

man page

showmount
- 13

In this case, we are mounting **/opt/app3** on *system2* locally as **/opt/app3**. This is an NFS mount with the permissions shown.

You can use the **showmount** command to show all remote systems (clients) that have mounted a local file system. This command is supported on most UNIX variants. **showmount** is useful for determining the file systems that are most often mounted by clients with NFS. The output of **showmount** is particularly easy to read, because it lists the host name and the directory that was mounted by the client. You have the three following options to the **showmount** command:

-a prints output in the format "name:directory"

-d lists all the local directories that have been remotely mounted by clients

-e prints a list of exported file systems

Set Up DNS Servers Using BIND 8.1.2 on HP-UX 11.0 and 11i

This procedure documents how to setup a Master (primary), a Slave (secondary), and a Caching-only DNS server on HP-UX 11.0/11i platforms with the latest supported BIND version 8.1.2 release for HP-UX. BIND 8.1.2 is loaded on 11.0 via a patch from *http://software.hp.com* and is provided on the 11i release media. For a more detailed discussion on BIND 8.1.2, please refer to the O'Reilly and Associates 3rd Edition book DNS and BIND, by Albitz and Liu. BIND 8.1.2 is available on the 11.0/11i platforms only and not on 10.20. 10.20 uses the older 4.9.7 version. It is important to be aware that the older 4.9.X versions of BIND have a different configuration file (boot file) format. There are also some terminology differences. The "boot" file is now called a "config" or "conf" file. HP Primary nameservers are now called Master nameservers; Secondary name servers are now called Slaves.

In most cases, DNS implementation is fairly straightforward, i.e., resource records and database files, etc. The real test comes in planning. Considerations such as whether the DNS system will be protected behind a firewall, whether or not you wish your resolvers to "peer" out on the Internet, and nslookup remote domains and addresses must be considered. Some administrators choose to turn off looking out on the internet to reduce the network traffic it creates. If you are directly attached to the Internet, you will need to register at least two nameservers with an authorized Internet Domain Name provider. A list of these providers can be found at http://www.icann.org/registrars/accredited-list.html. If you are not directly attached, i.e., sitting behind a firewall, an ISP is a good choice for DNS services and will do most of the work for you.

When you have completed your planning you need to configure your DNS server. What names should you use? Some people use planets, locational references, and sometimes people use names for their network computers and printers. The decision is up to you, but do not use underscores in your hostnames (see "check-names" boot file options), and make the names easy to remember.. Here are the steps to creating a Master (Primary) DNS server for your network:

1. Populate **/etc/hosts** with all of the hosts that you want to administer, separated by network segment and domains, and keep everything in an orderly fashion so that a tool such as hosts_to_named can safely and efficiently administer database files for you as in the following example:

/etc/hosts
```
15.17.186.159 wtec712-rtr

127.0.0.1 localhost loopback
# 812 Bogus Domain BASEBALL.HP.COM

# NL - EAST DIVISION
10.1.1.1 atlantabraves atlantabraves.baseball.hp.com

10.1.1.2 newyork newyorkmets.baseball.hp.com
# NL - CENTRAL DIVISION

10.1.2.1 houstonastros houstonastros.baseball.hp.com

10.1.2.2 chicagocubs chicagocubs.baseball.hp.com

10.1.2.3 stlouiscardinals stlouscardinals.baseball.hp.com
```

2. Create a *param* file with the parameters for your domain as shown in the following example for **/tmp/parm**:

/tmp/param

```
-d baseball.hp.com    <--------- Your domain.
-n 10.1.1             <--------- Your subnet(s).
-n 10.1.2
-n 10.1.3
-n 15.17.186
-H /etc/hosts.dnstest <--------- hosts file you will use.
-r                    <--------- If this nameserver is a
                                 root NS. Our examples
                                 below are NOT for root NS.
```

3. Run **hosts_to_named** with your newly created **param** file from the directory in which you want to place the database. Note that the **param** file is not necessary, but, it is a good idea; the options can be run from the command line instead of including a file. Another common error with **hosts_to_named** is not running it in a "clean" directory. If you need to preserve results before you run it, **mkdir /etc/ named.data.old**; **mv /etc/named.data/* /etc/named.data.old** to preserve the prior configuration.

```
# cd /etc/named.data

# hosts_to_named -f /tmp/param

Translating /tmp/hosts.dns to lower case ...

Collecting network data ...

10.1.1
10.1.2
10.1.3
15.17.186

Creating list of multi-homed hosts ...
Creating "A" data (name to address mapping) for net 10.1.1 ...
Creating "PTR" data (address to name mapping) for net 10.1.1 ...
Creating "A" data (name to address mapping) for net 10.1.2 ...
Creating "PTR" data (address to name mapping) for net 10.1.2 ...
Creating "A" data (name to address mapping) for net 10.1.3 ...
Creating "PTR" data (address to name mapping) for net 10.1.3 ...
Creating "A" data (name to address mapping) for net 15.17.186 ...
Creating "PTR" data (address to name mapping) for net 15.17.168 ...
Creating "MX" (mail exchanger) data ...
Building default named.boot file …

Building default db.cache file ...
WARNING: db.cache must be filled in withthe name(s) and address(es)
of the rootserver(s)
Building default boot.cacheonly for caching only servers ...
done
```

4. **hosts_to_named** will produce both a BIND 4.X **named.boot** file and a BIND 8.X **named.conf** file. Match the db files created in **/etc/ named.data** with those found in **/etc/named.data/named.conf.** Here is an example for a non-root name server:

```
// generated by named-bootconf.pl

options {
check-names response fail;    // do not change this
check-names slave warn;
```

```
directory "/etc/named.data"; // running directory for named
/*
 * If there is a firewall between you and nameservers you want
 * to talk to, you might need to uncomment the query-source
 * directive below. Previous versions of BIND always asked
 * questions using port 53, but BIND 8.1 uses an unprivileged
 * port by default.
 */
// query-source address * port 53;
};


//
// type domain source file
//

zone "0.0.127.IN-ADDR.ARPA" {
type master;
file "db.127.0.0";
};

zone "baseball.hp.com" {
type master;
file "db.baseball";
};

zone "1.1.10.IN-ADDR.ARPA" {
type master;
file "db.10.1.1";
};

zone "2.1.10.IN-ADDR.ARPA" {
type master;
file "db.10.1.2";
};

zone "3.1.10.IN-ADDR.ARPA" {
type master;
file "db.10.1.3";
};

zone "186.17.15.IN-ADDR.ARPA" {
type master;
file "db.15.17.186";
};

zone "." {
type hint;
file "db.cache";
};

(wtec712-rtr)named.data- ls
```

```
boot.cacheonly db.10.1.2 db.15.17.186 named.boot
conf.cacheonly db.10.1.3 db.baseball named.conf
db.10.1.1 db.127.0.0 db.cache params-file
```

As you can see, **hosts_to_named** created reverse lookup (IP addresses to names) db files with one parent domain, **baseball.hp.com**. Each of the nodes in our network will have the fully-qualified name **shortname.baseball.hp.com**.

5. Since many installations still use underscores in hostnames, we highly recommend you allow for this by modifying the *check-names* options lists in the **named.conf** file that **hosts_to_named** generates. For example, you may want to change these lines:

```
options {
check-names response fail          // do not change this
check-names slave warn
  .
  .
  .

to:

options {
check-names response ignore   //change "fail" to "ignore"
check-names slave ignore      //change "warn" to "ignore"
check-names master ignore     //add this whole new line
  .
  .
  .
```

6. Fill in **db.cache** with the addresses of the root name servers. If you are directly connected to the Internet and will be querying the root nameservers at the NIC, obtain an updated list from the site ftp://internic.net/domain/named.cache.

Next, copy the file to **db.cache** after you have downloaded. If you are not directly connected to the Internet and have to go through a firewall to query the root name servers, make the firewall your root name server and point your **db.cache** entry at the firewall in the same fashion that you would specify the root name servers. It is very important to configure **db.cache** correctly or services such as mail and name resolution will be affected. Here is an example of this:

```
; FILL IN THE NAMES AND ADDRESSES OF THE ROOT SERVERS

;

; . 99999999 IN NS root.server.

; root.server. 99999999 IN A ??.??.??.??

;

. 99999999 IN NS firewall.baseball.hp.com.

firewall.baseball.hp.com. 99999999 IN A 15.17.186.99
```

In this case, **firewall.baseball.hp.com.** is my firewall and since my name server cannot directly query the root nameservers, **db.cache** is directed to my firewall.

7. If you are going to have a Master (primary) name server which will not talk to the internet in any way, shape, or form, then you need to setup your name server as a root name server by doing a couple of things. Either use the -*r* option in your **params** file to **hosts_to_named** or make the following changes:

In your **named.conf** file, change:

```
zone "." {

type hint;

file "db.cache";
```

to:

```
zone "." {

type master;

file "db.root";
```

The root name server database file **db.root** would contain:

```
.   IN   SOA   m3107ced.baseball.hp.com.   root.m3107ced.base-
ball.hp.com.

(

            1          ; Serial
            10800      ; Refresh every 3 hours
            3600       ; Retry every hour
            604800     ; Expire after a week
            86400 )    ; Minimum ttl of 1 day

    IN NS m3107ced.baseball.hp.com.
m3107ced.baseball.hp.com. IN A 15.50.73.92
```

What we have done is set up an internal root name server, **db.root**, with one record, **m3107ced.baseball.hp.com.**

8. The next consideration is where to send queries for domains that you are not authoritative for. If your domain is **baseball.hp.com** and someone asks for **jughead.ibm.com**, what happens to the request? Well, if you've configured a root nameserver with no forwarder statements, the answer is nothing. The query will fail with host not found. This might be a good thing if you do not want your internal systems querying internet domains. Security and network congestion are usually the reason. What if you want to resolve Internet names and addresses, however? Easy, configure a forwarders statement in your /**etc/named.conf** to point to the firewall or whichever system is talking directly to the root name servers as shown in the following example:

```
options {
check-names response ignore ;     // change fail to ignore

check-names slave ignore          // change warn to ignore

check-names master ignore         // add this line

forwards 15.253.24.10 15.253.32.10 15.253.24.10 15.253.32.10

directory "/etc/named.data"; // running directory for named

/*
```

```
 * If there is a firewall between you and nameservers you want
 * to talk to, you might need to uncomment the query-source
 * directive below. Previous versions of BIND always asked
 * questions using port 53, but BIND 8.1 uses an unprivileged
 * port by default.
 */
// query-source address * port 53;
};
```

What's happening here is that queries for domains that we are not authoritative for, basically anything outside **baseball.hp.com**, we are sending to the forwarders to let them handle it. As you can see, there are two forwarders, each listed twice. The reason for this is that forwarders tend to be quite busy and by specifying two of them, you prevent the query from timing out. Be sure to copy **/etc/named.data/named.conf** to **/etc/named.conf**. All versions of BIND will look for the boot file in **/etc/** by default, so don't forget to copy it to **/etc** when you are ready.

9. Configure **/etc/resolv.conf** and **/etc/nsswitch.conf** on your name server and all clients that will be pointed at the name server:

/etc/resolv.conf

```
domain baseball.hp.com
search baseball.hp.com atl.hp.com hp.com rose.hp.com cup.hp.com
external.hp.com

nameserver 15.50.73.92 # authoritative name server 4 atl.hp.com
nameserver 15.51.240.8 # non-authoritate cache only servers
```

/etc/resolv.conf is pretty simple: the domain statement identifies which domain the system is part of; the search statements are used to simplify typing when ther is more than one domain. When you issue a query for say, *jughead*, it will search for *jughead* first in **baseball.hp.com**, then **atl.hp.com**, **rose.hp.com**, and finally, **cup.hp.com**. **/etc/nsswitch.conf** modifies the switch order you will use to look up hosts and IP addresses. There are four possible sources for this information: 1) **/etc/hosts**, 2) **nis**, 3) **nisplus**, 4) and **dns** By default, the hard coded order is **dns nis files**. To modify the switch order, you need to copy in a fresh **/etc/nsswitch.conf** file from **/usr/newconfig/ etc/nsswitch.hp_defaults** and modify the *hosts* entry:

```
# /etc/nsswitch.hp_defaults:

#

# An example file that could be copied over to /etc/nss-
witch.conf; it

# uses NIS (YP) in conjunction with files.

#

passwd: compat

group: compat

hosts: files [NOTFOUND=return] dns

networks: nis [NOTFOUND=return] files

protocols: nis [NOTFOUND=return] files

rpc: nis [NOTFOUND=return] files

publickey: nis [NOTFOUND=return] files

netgroup: nis [NOTFOUND=return] files

automount: files nis

aliases: files nis

services: nis [NOTFOUND=return] files
```

As you can see, the *hosts* line has been modified so that we consult the **/etc/hosts** file first then continue on to *dns* if the query is unsuccessful. There are many ways to modify the switch order and many ways to mess things up. Use discretion when changing the switch order and consult the man pages on *switch* for more information.

10. Start up the DNS name server process as follows:

```
# /usr/sbin/named.
# ps -eaf|grep named
root 8074 1 0 08:42:08 ? 0:00 /usr/sbin/named <--- check to make
                                           sure it is running..
```

```
root 8077 8072 2 08:42:13 ttyp7 0:00 grep named
```

After the name server is started, you use can **sig_named** to perform various functions. After you modify any of the *db* files or **/etc/named.boot**, you need to tell named to refresh its databases. You can accomplish this using either of the two following commands:

```
# sig_named restart

# kill -HUP `/var/run/named.pid`
```

This will reload the databases, which you can verify by viewing the end of file **/var/adm/syslog/syslog.log** as shown below:

```
Oct 12 08:49:13 m3107ced named[8074]: primary zone "0.0.127.IN-AD-
DR.ARPA" loaded (serial 1)

Oct 12 08:49:13 m3107ced named[8074]: primary zone "baseball.hp.com"
loaded (serial 1)

Oct 12 08:49:13 m3107ced named[8074]: primary zone "1.1.10.IN-AD-
DR.ARPA" loaded(serial 1)

Oct 12 08:49:13 m3107ced named[8074]: primary zone "2.1.10.IN-AD-
DR.ARPA" loaded(serial 1)

Oct 12 08:49:13 m3107ced named[8074]: primary zone "3.1.10.IN-AD-
DR.ARPA" loaded(serial 1)

Oct 12 08:49:13 m3107ced named[8074]: primary zone "1.168.192.IN-AD-
DR.ARPA" loaded (serial 1)

Oct 12 08:49:13 m3107ced named[8074]: primary zone "2.168.192.IN-AD-
DR.ARPA" loaded (serial 1)

Oct 12 08:49:13 m3107ced named[8074]: primary zone "3.168.192.IN-AD-
DR.ARPA" loaded (serial 1)

Oct 12 08:49:13 m3107ced named[8074]: Ready to answer queries.
```

As you can see, **named** loaded each of our databases, or zones, and is ready to answer queries.

11. Test queries both by name and IP address.

```
# nslookup atlantabraves
Using /etc/hosts on: wtec712-rtr
looking up FILES
Trying DNS

Name: atlantabraves.baseball.hp.com

Address: 10.1.1.1

# nslookup 10.1.1.1

Using /etc/hosts on: wtec712-rtr
looking up FILES
Trying DNS
Trying DNS
Name: atlantabraves.baseball.hp.com
Address: 10.1.1.1
```

Looking up *atlantabraves* by name and IP address worked and generally we are done.

We always check **/var/adm/syslog/syslog.log** for messages from **named**. **named** logs a lot of seemingly unimportant chatter, but it always deserves at least a short look.

A Word on Slave (Secondary) Name Servers

Once you have created a Master (primary) DNS server, you have completed all the hard work. Creating Slaves and cache-only servers is simple. Let's walk through this process step-by-step:

1. Use **ftp** to copy the **named.conf** file and **db.cache** from the Master (primary).

2. Edit the **named.conf** file as follows:

- Change each instance of "master" to "slave", except for the loopback domain db.127.0.0 and the cache entry.
- Add a "masters" entry for each zone with the IP address of the Master DNS server.
Using our example from above:

```
# cat /etc/named.conf

// generated by named-bootconf.pl

options {

check-names response fail; // do not change this
check-names slave warn;
directory "/etc/named.data"; // running directory for named

/*
 * If there is a firewall between you and nameservers you want
 * to talk to, you might need to uncomment the query-source
 * directive below. Previous versions of BIND always asked
 * questions using port 53, but BIND 8.1 uses an unprivileged
 * port by default.
 */
// query-source address * port 53;
};

//
// type domain source file
//
zone "0.0.127.IN-ADDR.ARPA" {
type master;
file "db.127.0.0";
};

zone "baseball.hp.com" {
type slave;
file "db.baseball";
masters ( 15.17.186.159);
};

zone "1.1.10.IN-ADDR.ARPA" {
type slave;
file "db.10.1.1";
masters ( 15.17.186.159);
};

zone "2.1.10.IN-ADDR.ARPA" {
type slave;
file "db.10.1.2";
masters ( 15.17.186.159);
};

zone "3.1.10.IN-ADDR.ARPA" {
type slave;
file "db.10.1.3";
masters ( 15.17.186.159);
};

zone "186.17.15.IN-ADDR.ARPA" {
type slave;
file "db.15.17.186";
masters ( 15.17.186.159);
```

```
};

zone "." {
type hint;
file "db.cache";
};
```

2. Now, all you need to do, once your **named.boot** has been copied to **/etc/named.boot** and your **/etc/named.data** directory has been created, is kick off a zone transfer.

To kick off a zone transfer, all you need to do is **kill named** with

```
# sig_named restart
```

or

```
# kill -HUP `/var/run/named.pid`
```

to start the transfer.

Take a look at **/etc/named.data** and you should see all the database files there now. Also, check **/var/adm/syslog/sylog.log** to make sure the zones were loaded properly as shown in the following example:

```
Oct 12 09:21:34 stimpy named[1893]: secondary zone "1.1.10.IN-AD-
DR.ARPA" loaded (serial 1)

Oct 12 09:21:35 stimpy named[1893]: secondary zone "baseball.hp.com"
loaded (ser ial 1)

Oct 12 09:21:35 stimpy named[1893]: secondary zone "2.1.10.IN-AD-
DR.ARPA" loaded (serial 1)

Oct 12 09:21:35 stimpy named[1893]: secondary zone "1.168.192.IN-AD-
DR.ARPA" loaded (serial 1)

Oct 12 09:21:35 stimpy named[1893]: secondary zone "3.1.10.IN-AD-
DR.ARPA" loaded (serial 1)

Oct 12 09:21:36 stimpy named[1893]: secondary zone "2.168.192.IN-AD-
DR.ARPA" loaded (serial 1)

Oct 12 09:21:36 stimpy named[1893]: secondary zone "3.168.192.IN-AD-
DR.ARPA" loaded (serial 1)
```

Notice the serial number entries. They should match on the Master (primary) and Slaves (secondaries).

A Word On Cache-Only Nameservers

Why in the world would you want a cache-only name server? In a word, performance. If you want to maintain a local cache but do not want to manage database files, this is the way to go. It will act as any other name server, responding to queries in the same fashion, except queries that are built in the cache will be non-authoritative. Any query that comes back with a non-authoritative reply is a query received from cache. Is that a bad thing? No, but be aware that the data may have changed on the Master (primary) and the cache replies may be outdated. The Time To Live (TTL) flag for each query is a way to manipulate the time, in seconds, that a name server may cache the answer to a query, versus having to contact an authoritative name server. The default TTL for records is usually 86400 seconds, or 24 hours. You may want to play with this value, depending on how frequently or infrequently the records are updated. A good rule of thumb is to have at least one name server per subnet, and cache-only name servers are an excellent choice.

To configure a cache-only nameserver, copy down the **conf.cacheonly** file and db.cache from the Master (primary) nameserver .

```
// generated by named-bootconf.pl

options {
check-names response fail; // do not change this
check-names slave warn;
directory "/tmp/testhack"; // running directory for named
/*
* If there is a firewall between you and nameservers you want
* to talk to, you might need to uncomment the query-source
* directive below. Previous versions of BIND always asked
* questions using port 53, but BIND 8.1 uses an unprivileged
* port by default.
```

```
*/
// query-source address * port 53;
};

//
// type domain source file
//
zone "0.0.127.IN-ADDR.ARPA" {
type master;
file "db.127.0.0";
};

zone "." {
type hint;
file "db.cache";
};
```

Please don't forget to fill in **db.cache** with the name server(s) that you will be caching data for.

A Final Word on Name Server Setup

This section in no way offers a comprehensive discussion on setting up DNS. It is only intended to act as a cookbook after all your planning has been completed. Please refer to the book <u>HP Installing and Administering Internet Services</u> at *http://docs.hp.com*. DNS is pretty straightforward, but any syntax errors or problems with **/etc/named.boot** can have dramatic consequences. The **syslog** can be your best friend when zones are not transferring or there are problems with the data.

Other Networking Commands and Setup

Setting up a network is an intensive planning exercise for both network and system administrators. No two networking environments
are alike. There is typically a lot of networking electronics to which
your system is connected. There are many useful commands related to
testing connectivity to other systems and networking configuration.
Should you encounter a problem, you want to have an understanding
of some networking commands that can be lifesavers. In addition, you
can encounter some tricky aspects to networking setup if you have
some networking hardware that your UNIX systems must interface to,
such as routers, gateways, bridges, etc. I give an example of one such
case: connecting a UNIX system to a router. At the same time, I cover
some of the most handy networking commands as part of this description.

Consider Figure 12-10, in which a UNIX system is connected
directly to a router.

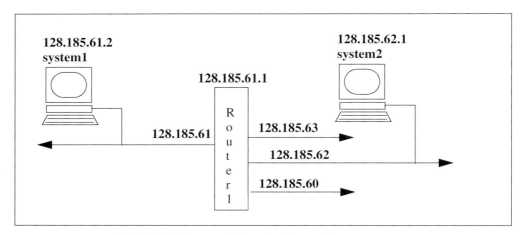

Figure 12-10 UNIX System and Router Example

Here we have a UNIX system connected to segment 128.185.61. This
is a class "B" Internet address with subnetting enabled.

The **/etc/hosts** file needs to have in it the UNIX system with node ID 2, the router, and any other systems on this segment or segments on the other side of the router.

If the router is properly configured, we should be able to seamlessly connect from 61 to systems on segments 60, 62, and 63. The router should be configured to allow our system to connect to systems on other segments (60, 62, and 63) by going through the router. Some unforeseen configuration was required to make this simple network operate seamlessly. In this case, a problem occurred getting system1 to connect to systems on the other side of the router on 60, 62, and 63. Before discussing the additional configuration that needed to be done, I first show the **/etc/hosts** file and then use some very useful UNIX commands that show the state of the network. Here is the **/etc/hosts** file showing just the UNIX system and router:

$ cat /etc/hosts

```
127.0.0.1    localhosts loopback
128.185.61.1  router1      # router
128.185.61.2  system1      # UNIX system on 61
128.185.62.1  system2      # UNIX system on 62
```

This host file is simple and allows system1 to connect to router1 and system2. The connection from system1 to system2 is accomplished by going through the router.

ping

Let's look at one of the most commonly used networking commands - **ping**. This command is used to determine whether or not a connection exists between two networking components. **ping** is a simple command that sends an ICMP echo packet to the host you specify once per second. You may recall that ICMP was covered earlier under the network, or third layer. **ping** stands for Packet InterNet Groper. **ping** differs somewhat among UNIX variants, mostly in the reporting that **ping** produces when no options are provided.

Some systems provide performance information when **ping** is issued with no options; others report that the system "is alive". The following is an example of checking the connection between the local system and another system on the network called *austin*:

```
martyp $ ping austin
austin is alive
martyp $
```

You can adjust the packet size and number of iterations on most UNIX variants as in the HP-UX example shown below specifying a packet size of *4096* and interval of *5*:

```
# ping 12 4096 5
PING 12: 4096 byte packets
4096 bytes from 10.1.1.12: icmp_seq=0. time=2. ms
4096 bytes from 10.1.1.12: icmp_seq=1. time=2. ms
4096 bytes from 10.1.1.12: icmp_seq=2. time=2. ms
4096 bytes from 10.1.1.12: icmp_seq=3. time=2. ms
4096 bytes from 10.1.1.12: icmp_seq=4. time=2. ms

----12 PING Statistics----
5 packets transmitted, 5 packets received, 0% packet loss
round-trip (ms)  min/avg/max = 2/2/2
#
```

AIX allows you to specify the interval with *-I* as well as other options, including packet size, and number of iterations. These options are shown for an AIX system in the following example:

```
martyp $ ping -I 5 austin 4096 10
PING austin: 4096 data bytes
4104  bytes  from  austin  (128.185.61.5):  icmp_seq=0.
time=8. ms
4104  bytes  from  austin  (128.185.61.5):  icmp_seq=1.
time=9. ms
4104 bytes from austin (128.15.61.5): icmp_seq=2. time=9.
ms
4104 bytes from austin (128.15.61.5): icmp_seq=3. time=9.
ms
4104 bytes from austin (128.15.61.5): icmp_seq=4. time=8.
```

```
ms
4104 bytes from austin (128.15.61.5): icmp_seq=5. time=9.
ms
4104 bytes from austin (128.15.61.5): icmp_seq=6. time=9.
ms
4104 bytes from austin (128.15.61.5): icmp_seq=7. time=9.
ms
4104 bytes from austin (128.15.61.5): icmp_seq=8. time=9.
ms
4104 bytes from austin (128.15.61.5): icmp_seq=9. time=9.
ms

----austin PING Statistics----

10 packets transmitted, 10 packets received, 0% packet
loss
round-trip (ms)  min/avg/max = 9/9/15
martyp $
```

man page

ping - 9

In this example, we **ping** *austin* every five seconds, with a packet size of *4096* bytes for a total of ten times.

Let's now get back to our example.

How do I know that I have a connection between system1 and the router and the other systems on the other side of the router? I use the **ping** command. Here is how I know that system1 is connected to router1:

$ ping router1

PING router1: 64 byte packets
64 bytes from 128.185.61.2: icmp_seq=0. time=0. ms
64 bytes from 128.185.61.2: icmp_seq=1. time=0. ms
64 bytes from 128.185.61.2: icmp_seq=2. time=0. ms

Each line of output here represents a response that was returned from the device that was pinged. This means that the device responded. You continue to get this response indefinitely and have to type **^c** (control c) to terminate the **ping**. If no output is produced, as shown below, then no response occurred and you may have a problem between your system and the device to which you are checking the connection:

$ ping system2

PING router1: 64 byte packets

In this scenario, you would see this message and that is as far as you would get. A **^c** will kill the **ping**, and you see that some number of packets were sent and none were received. I did indeed get this response when issuing the **ping** command, so I know that a problem exists with the connection between system1 and router1.

man page

ping - 12

ping should be used only for testing purposes such as manual fault isolation, because it generates a substantial amount of network traffic. You do not want to use **ping** on an ongoing basis, such as in a script that is running continuously.

A nice variation of **ping** that I use is to specify a packet size of 4096 bytes, rather than the default of 64 bytes shown in the previous examples, and count the number of times **ping** transmits before terminating, rather than having to type **^c** to terminate **ping**. The following example shows this:

$ ping router1 4096 5

PING router1: 64 byte packets
4096 bytes from 128.185.51.2: icmp_seq=0. time=8. ms
4096 bytes from 128.185.51.2: icmp_seq=1. time=8. ms
4096 bytes from 128.185.51.2: icmp_seq=2. time=9. ms
4096 bytes from 128.185.51.2: icmp_seq=3. time=8. ms
4096 bytes from 128.185.51.2: icmp_seq=4. time=8. ms

Notice that the time required to transmit and receive a response, the round-trip time, is substantially longer than with only 64 bytes transmitted. I usually find that the round-trip time for 64 bytes is 0 ms, although this depends on a number of factors, including network topology and network traffic.

netstat

From the earlier description of the subnet mask, you can see that routing from one host to another can be configured in a variety of ways. The path that information takes in getting from one host to another depends on routing.

man page

netstat - 9

You can obtain information related to routing with the **netstat** command. The *-r* option to **netstat** shows the routing tables, which you usually want to know, and the *-n* option can be used to print network addresses as numbers rather than as names. With the *-v* option, you get additional information related to routing, such as the subnet mask. In the following examples, **netstat** is issued with the *-r* option (this is used when describing the **netstat** output), the *-rn* options, and the   *-rnv* options, so you can compare the outputs:

```
# netstat -r
Routing tables
Dest/Netmask        Gateway         Flags  Refs       Use  Interface  Pmtu
o2                  o2              UH     0      1890905  lo0        4136
o2                  o2              UH     0          343  lan1       4136
o2                  o2              UH     0            0  lan0       4136
10.1.1.0            o2              U      2            0  lan0       1500
10.1.1.0            o2              U      2            0  lan1       1500
127.0.0.0           o2              U      0            0  lo0        4136
default             10.1.1.1        UG     0            0  lan1       1500
#
```

```
# netstat -rn
Routing tables
Dest/Netmask        Gateway         Flags  Refs       Use  Interface  Pmtu
127.0.0.1           127.0.0.1       UH     0      1891016  lo0        4136
10.1.1.10           10.1.1.10       UH     0          343  lan1       4136
10.1.1.110          10.1.1.110      UH     0            0  lan0       4136
10.1.1.0            10.1.1.110      U      2            0  lan0       1500
10.1.1.0            10.1.1.10       U      2            0  lan1       1500
127.0.0.0           127.0.0.1       U      0            0  lo0        4136
default             10.1.1.1        UG     0            0  lan1       1500
#
```

```
# netstat -rnv
Routing tables
Dest/Netmask              Gateway         Flags  Refs       Use  Interface  Pmtu
127.0.0.1/255.255.255.255   127.0.0.1     UH     0      1891036  lo0        4136
10.1.1.10/255.255.255.255   10.1.1.10     UH     0          343  lan1       4136
10.1.1.110/255.255.255.255  10.1.1.110    UH     0            0  lan0       4136
10.1.1.0/255.255.255.0      10.1.1.110    U      2            0  lan0       1500
```

```
10.1.1.0/255.255.255.0        10.1.1.10        U      2        0  lan1    1500
127.0.0.0/255.0.0.0           127.0.0.1        U      0        0  lo0     4136
default/0.0.0.0               10.1.1.1         UG     0        0  lan1    1500
#
```

The first and second outputs show that our system, *o2*, has three interfaces: The first is the loopback interface called *lo0*. The second. is at *.10*, and the third is at *.110* (which we can see from the *-rn* output). The next two lines show that our destination of *10.1.1.0*, which is a network, can be accessed through either the card at *.10* or *.110*. The third output provides verbose information. The last line is for the default route. This entry says to send packets to *10.1.1.1* if a more direct route can't be found.

man page

netstat - 12

With **netstat**, some information is provided about the router. The *-r* option shows information about routing, but many other useful options to this command are also available. Of particular interest in this output is "Flags," which defines the type of routing that takes place. Here are descriptions of the most common flags from the UNIX manual pages:

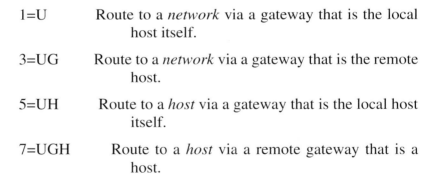

1=U	Route to a *network* via a gateway that is the local host itself.
3=UG	Route to a *network* via a gateway that is the remote host.
5=UH	Route to a *host* via a gateway that is the local host itself.
7=UGH	Route to a *host* via a remote gateway that is a host.

Also, I use two forms of **netstat** to obtain network statistics, as opposed to routing information. The first is **netstat -i**, which shows the state of interfaces that are autoconfigured. Because I am most often interested in getting a summary of **lan0**, I issue this command.

netstat -i gives a good rundown of *lan0*, such as the network it is on, its name, and so on.

The following example shows the output of **netstat -i** on a Solaris and HP-UX system, respectively:

```
# netstat -i

Name  Mtu    Network      Address            Ipkts  Ierrs    Opkts  Oerrs  Coll
ni0*  0      none         none                   0      0        0      0     0
ni1*  0      none         none                   0      0        0      0     0
lo0   4608   loopback     127.0.0.1            232      0      232      0     0
lan0  1500   169.200.112  169.200.112.2    3589746      2    45630      0   104


# netstat -i
Name        Mtu  Network        Address             Ipkts       Opkts
lan1        1500 10.1.1.0       o2               59935480   163641547
lan0        1500 10.1.1.0       o2                 139173    12839358
lo0         4136 127.0.0.0      o2                1892333     1892345
#
```

Here is a description of the fields in the **netstat** example:

man page

netstat - 9

Name	The name of your network interface (Name), in this case, *lan0*.
MTU	The "maximum transmission unit," which is the maximum packet size sent by the interface card.
Network	The network address of the LAN to which the interface card is connected (169.200).
Address	The host name of your system. This is the symbolic name of your system as it appears in the file **/etc/hosts**.

The statistical information includes:

Ipkts	The number of packets received by the interface card, in this case **lan0**.
Ierrs	The number of errors detected on incoming packets by the interface card (on some UNIX variants).

Opkts	The number of packets transmitted by the interface card.
Oerrs	The number of errors detected during the transmission of packets by the interface card (on some UNIX variants.)
Collis	The number of collisions that resulted from packet traffic (on some UNIX variants.)

netstat provides cumulative data since the node was last powered up; you might have a long elapsed time over which data was accumulated. If you are interested in seeing useful statistical information, you can use **netstat** with different options. You can also specify an interval over which to report statistics. I usually ignore the first entry, because it shows all data since the system was last powered up. Therefore, the data includes non-prime hours when the system was idle. I prefer to view data at the time the system is working its hardest. The following **netstat** example provides network interface information every five seconds on a Solaris system:

man page

netstat - 12

```
# netstat -I lan0 5
```

(lan0)-> input		output			(Total)-> input		output		
packets	errs	packets	errs	colls	packets	errs	packets	errs	colls
3590505	2	45714	0	104	3590737	2	45946	0	104
134	0	5	0	0	134	0	5	0	0
174	0	0	0	0	174	0	0	0	0
210	0	13	0	0	210	0	13	0	0
165	0	0	0	0	165	0	0	0	0
169	0	0	0	0	169	0	0	0	0
193	0	0	0	0	193	0	0	0	0
261	0	7	0	0	261	0	7	0	0
142	0	8	0	0	142	0	8	0	0
118	0	0	0	0	118	0	0	0	0
143	0	0	0	0	143	0	0	0	0
149	0	0	0	0	149	0	0	0	0

With this example, you get multiple outputs of what is taking place on the LAN interface. As I mentioned earlier, you may want to ignore the first output, because it includes information over a long time period. This may include a time when your network was idle, and therefore the data is not important to you.

The following **netstat** example provides network interface information every five seconds on an HP-UX 11i system:

man page

netstat - 12

```
# netstat -I lan0 5
(lan0)-> input      output      (Total)-> input      output
        packets     packets               packets     packets
        139185      12841621              61968131    178375605
        139185      12841714              61968172    178375698
        139185      12841810              61968213    178375794
        139185      12841877              61968247    178375861
        139185      12841912              61968265    178375896
        139185      12842095              61968358    178376079
        139187      12842244              61968413    178376240
        139189      12842352              61968470    178376360
        139189      12842453              61968525    178376461
        139190      12842482              61968565    178376498
        139190      12842539              61968594    178376555
        139190      12842671              61968667    178376699
```

You can specify the network interface on which you want statistics reported by using **-I interface**; in the case of the example, it was *-I lan0*. An interval of five seconds was also used in this example.

Yet another use of **netstat** is to show the state of network sockets. **netstat -a** produces a list of protocols, queues, local and remote addresses, and protocol states. All this information is useful for showing active communications, as shown in the following example:

```
# netstat -a
Active Internet connections (including servers)
Proto Recv-Q Send-Q  Local Address            Foreign Address          (state)
tcp        0      2   system1.telnet           atlm0081.atl.hp..1319    ESTABLISHED
tcp        0      0   *.1095                   *.*                      LISTEN
tcp        0      0   *.psmond                 *.*                      LISTEN
tcp        0      0   *.mcsemon                *.*                      LISTEN
tcp        0      0   localhost.8886           localhost.1062           ESTABLISHED
tcp        0      0   localhost.1062           localhost.8886           ESTABLISHED
tcp        0      0   *.8886                   *.*                      LISTEN
tcp        0      0   *.8887                   *.*                      LISTEN
tcp        0      0   *.1006                   *.*                      LISTEN
tcp        0      0   *.978                    *.*                      LISTEN
tcp        0      0   *.22370                  *.*                      LISTEN
tcp        0      0   *.389                    *.*                      LISTEN
tcp        0      0   *.8181                   *.*                      LISTEN
tcp        0      0   *.1054                   *.*                      LISTEN
tcp        0      0   *.1053                   *.*                      LISTEN
tcp        0      0   *.diagmond               *.*                      LISTEN
tcp        0      0   *.1045                   *.*                      LISTEN
tcp        0      0   *.1038                   *.*                      LISTEN
tcp        0      0   *.135                    *.*                      LISTEN
tcp        0      0   *.smtp                   *.*                      LISTEN
tcp        0      0   *.1036                   *.*                      LISTEN
tcp        0      0   *.appconn                *.*                      LISTEN
tcp        0      0   *.spc                    *.*                      LISTEN
tcp        0      0   *.dtspc                  *.*                      LISTEN
tcp        0      0   *.recserv                *.*                      LISTEN
tcp        0      0   *.klogin                 *.*                      LISTEN
tcp        0      0   *.kshell                 *.*                      LISTEN
```

```
tcp       0       0   *.chargen                 *.*                        LISTEN
tcp       0       0   *.discard                 *.*                        LISTEN
tcp       0       0   *.echo                    *.*                        LISTEN
tcp       0       0   *.time                    *.*                        LISTEN
tcp       0       0   *.daytime                 *.*                        LISTEN
tcp       0       0   *.printer                 *.*                        LISTEN
tcp       0       0   *.auth                    *.*                        LISTEN
tcp       0       0   *.exec                    *.*                        LISTEN
tcp       0       0   *.shell                   *.*                        LISTEN
tcp       0       0   *.login                   *.*                        LISTEN
tcp       0       0   *.telnet                  *.*                        LISTEN
tcp       0       0   *.ftp                     *.*                        LISTEN
tcp       0       0   *.795                     *.*                        LISTEN
tcp       0       0   *.792                     *.*                        LISTEN
tcp       0       0   *.*                       *.*                        CLOSED
tcp       0       0   *.787                     *.*                        LISTEN
tcp       0       0   *.783                     *.*                        LISTEN
tcp       0       0   *.779                     *.*                        LISTEN
tcp       0       0   *.portmap                 *.*                        LISTEN
tcp       0       0   *.2121                    *.*                        LISTEN
udp       0       0   *.1127                    *.*
udp       0       0   *.177                     *.*
udp       0       0   *.1003                    *.*
udp       0       0   *.*                       *.*
udp       0       0   *.*                       *.*
udp       0       0   *.*                       *.*
udp       0       0   *.nfsd                    *.*
udp       0       0   *.976                     *.*
udp       0       0   *.22370                   *.*
udp       0       0   *.1097                    *.*
udp       0       0   *.1095                    *.*
udp       0       0   *.1079                    *.*
udp       0       0   *.135                     *.*
udp       0       0   *.*                       *.*
udp       0       0   *.1045                    *.*
udp       0       0   *.snmp                    *.*
udp       0       0   *.1040                    *.*
udp       0       0   *.tftp                    *.*
udp       0       0   *.chargen                 *.*
udp       0       0   *.discard                 *.*
udp       0       0   *.echo                    *.*
udp       0       0   *.time                    *.*
udp       0       0   *.daytime                 *.*
udp       0       0   *.ntalk                   *.*
udp       0       0   *.bootps                  *.*
udp       0       0   *.1023                    *.*
udp       0       0   *.787                     *.*
udp       0       0   *.798                     *.*
udp       0       0   *.797                     *.*
udp       0       0   *.1037                    *.*
udp       0       0   *.*                       *.*
udp       0       0   *.1036                    *.*
udp       0       0   *.1035                    *.*
udp       0       0   *.777                     *.*
udp       0       0   *.portmap                 *.*
udp       0       0   *.1034                    *.*
udp       0       0   *.syslog                  *.*
udp       0       0   *.2121                    *.*
```

Active UNIX domain sockets

Address	Type	Recv-Q	Send-Q	Inode	Conn	Refs	Nextref	Addr
bb9c00	stream	0	0	af9000	0	0	0	/tmp/.AgentSoA
ced700	dgram	0	0	c99400	0	0	0	/opt/dcelocalr
ce9e00	dgram	0	0	d23000	0	0	0	/opt/dcelocalr
b0d200	dgram	0	0	b87000	0	0	0	/opt/dcelocalr
997a00	stream	0	0	b84800	0	0	0	/opt/dcelocal1
b24e00	dgram	0	0	b84000	0	0	0	/opt/dcelocal1
d59400	dgram	0	0	b66400	0	0	0	/var/tmp/psb_t
d85c00	dgram	0	0	b67000	0	0	0	/var/tmp/psb_t
c8b200	dgram	0	0	b12000	0	0	0	/opt/dcelocalr
c8b400	stream	0	0	b78400	0	0	0	/opt/dcelocal5
c8b300	dgram	0	0	b78000	0	0	0	/opt/dcelocal5
c90900	dgram	0	0	d22400	0	0	0	/opt/dcelocalr
c78c00	dgram	0	0	ba1000	c4a180	0	0	/opt/dcelocal0
b1e900	dgram	0	0	9a4400	0	c32e80	0	/opt/dcelocald

```
        d64100 stream      0      0  d24c00        0        0        0 /opt/dcelocal5
        9e1600 dgram       0      0  9a4000   d4d940        0        0 /opt/dcelocal2
        d64200 dgram       0      0  cfc800        0   c32c80        0 /opt/dcelocal9
        d12d00 dgram       0      0  cfc000   c32c00        0        0 /opt/dcelocal1
        c5ee00 stream      0      0  b1c000        0        0        0 /opt/dcelocal4
        d19d00 dgram       0      0  ce4800        0        0        0 /opt/dcelocald
        cf0c00 dgram       0      0  a92800        0   af15c0        0 /opt/dcelocal7
        d2d600 dgram       0      0  a93800   c32c00        0   d4db80 /opt/dcelocal0
        c9b900 dgram       0      0  a93c00        0        0        0 /opt/dcelocald
        d6c800 stream      0      0  ba3000        0        0        0 /var/opt/OV/sT
#
```

A lot of information is in this output. You can refer to the manual page at the end of this chapter if you want a detailed explanation of the fields.

The first line shows the *Proto tcp* to the *Local Address system1.telnet* as having a *(state)* of *ESTABLISHED*. This is the connection we have initiated to this system. We are sitting on *system1* with a telnet session open to the system on which we ran **netstat**.

man page

netstat - 12

Most of the remaining *tcp* protocol entries are listening. This means that they are listening for incoming connections, as indicated by the *LISTEN*. They have a wildcard in the *Foreign Address* field, which will contain the address when a connection has been established. We are one of the few connections that has been made, as indicated by the *ESTABLISHED*.

All the send and receive queues, shown as *Recv-Q* and *Send-Q*, are empty as indicated by *0*.

The UNIX domain sockets at the end of the output are stream and datagram connections for a variety of services such as NFS.

This output gives you an appreciation of the immense amount of activity taking place from a networking perspective on your UNIX system. Networking and connectivity have been among the most advanced aspects of UNIX since its inception.

netstat - 12

ifconfig -12

man page

route - 12

route

The information displayed with **netstat** is the routing tables for your system. Some are automatically created with the **ifconfig** command when your system is booted or when the network interface is initialized. Routes to networks and hosts that are not directly connected to your system are entered with the **route** command.

Routing changes can be made on the fly, as I did to change the *Flags* from *U* to *UG*:

```
$ /usr/sbin/route add default 128.185.61.1 3
```

First is the **route** command. Second, we specify that we wish to add a route; the other option is to delete a route. Third, we specify the destination, in this case, the default. This could be a specific host name, a network name, an IP address, or default that signifies the wildcard gateway route that is shown in our example. Fourth is the gateway through which the destination is reached. In the above example, the IP address was used, but this could also be a host name. The 3 corresponds to the count that is used to specify whether the gateway is the local host or a remote gateway. If the gateway is the local host, then a count of 0 is used. If the gateway is a remote host, which is the case in the example, a count of >0 is used. This corresponds to *UG* for *Flags*. This manually changed the network routing table by adding a default route with the appropriate *Flags*. Issuing this command fixed the problem I encountered trying to get system1 to talk to the systems on the other side of the router (remember Figure 12-10?).

Before issuing **/usr/sbin/route** with the **add** option, you can first use the **delete** option to remove the existing default route, which is not working.

route commands usually appear in one of the system's startup files so that every time the system boots, **route** commands are issued. This ensures that the right connectivity information is in place every time the system starts.

ifconfig

The **ifconfig** command provides additional information on a LAN interface. The following example provides the configuration of a network interface:

man page

ifconfig - 9

```
$ /etc/ifconfig lan0
lan0:    flags=863<UP,BROADCAST,NOTRAILERS,RUNNING>
         inet 128.185.61.2 netmask ffff0000 broadcast 128.185.61.255
```

From this example, we can quickly see that the interface is up, it has an address of 128.185.61.2, and it has a netmask of *ffff0000*. Again, keep in mind that your network interface may have a different name, such as *le0*.

You can use **ifconfig** to get the status of a network interface as I have done here to assign an address to a network interface, or to configure network interface parameters. The network address you have falls into classes such as "A," "B," or "C," as mentioned earlier. You want to be sure that you know the class of your network before you start configuring your LAN interface. This example is a class "B" network, so the netmask is defined as ffff0000 (typical for a class "B" address), as opposed to ffffff00, which is typical for a class "C" network. The netmask is used to determine how much of the address to reserve for subdividing the network into smaller networks. The netmask can be represented in hex, as shown above, or in decimal format, as in the **/etc/hosts** file. Here is the **ifconfig** command I issued to configure the interface:

```
$ /etc/ifconfig lan0 inet 128.185.61.2 netmask 255.255.0.0
```

- The *255.255.0.0* corresponds to the hex *ffff000* shown earlier for the class "B" subnet mask.

- *lan0* is the interface being configured.

- *inet* is the address family, which is currently the only one supported for this system.

- *128.185.61.2* is the address of the LAN interface for system1.

- **netmask** shows how to subdivide the network.

- *255.255.0.0* is the same as *ffff0000*, which is the netmask for a class "B" address.

netstat - 12

ping - 12

ifconfig -12

route -12

I have made good use of **netstat**, **ping**, and **ifconfig** to help get the status of the network. **ifconfig**, **route**, and **/etc/hosts** are used to configure the network, should you identify any changes you need to make. The subnet examples show how flexible you can be when configuring your network for both your current and future needs. In simple networks, you may not need to use many of these commands or complex subnetting. In complex networks, or at times when you encounter configuration difficulties, you may have to make extensive use of these commands. In either case, network planning is an important part of setting up UNIX systems.

Most of the commands used throughout this chapter are a part of every system administrator's tool box. Networking is so vital to the use of UNIX systems, however, that having background in this area can help with your overall understanding of the system and how to use it more effectively.

rpcinfo -12

rcp - 12

rpcinfo

As a user, you may have a need to NFS mount a directory on another system or perform some other function that you haven't before used on your system. You can determine whether various pieces of functionality have been enabled by evaluating the daemons running on your system. **rpcinfo** allows you to generate a Remote Procedure Call (RPC) on a system, including your local system, by issuing the command **rpc -p** *system_name*.

The following example shows issuing **rpcinfo -p** on our local system:

```
# rpcinfo -p
   program vers proto    port   service
    100000   2   tcp      111   portmapper
    100000   2   udp      111   portmapper
    100024   1   udp      777   status
    100024   1   tcp      779   status
    100021   1   tcp      783   nlockmgr
    100021   1   udp     1035   nlockmgr
    100021   3   tcp      787   nlockmgr
    100021   3   udp     1036   nlockmgr
    100020   1   udp     1037   llockmgr
    100020   1   tcp      792   llockmgr
    100021   2   tcp      795   nlockmgr
    100068   2   udp     1040   cmsd
    100068   3   udp     1040   cmsd
    100068   4   udp     1040   cmsd
    100068   5   udp     1040   cmsd
    100083   1   tcp     1036   ttdbserver
    100005   1   udp      976   mountd
    100005   1   tcp      978   mountd
    100003   2   udp     2049   nfs
    150001   1   udp     1003   pcnfsd
    150001   2   udp     1003   pcnfsd
    150001   1   tcp     1006   pcnfsd
    150001   2   tcp     1006   pcnfsd
#
```

Many daemons are running on the system that are important to the functionality I like to use. **mountd** is running, which indicates that a server could NFS mount file systems on this computer. There is other setup required for the mount to take place, but at least the daemon is running to support this functionality. In addition, **pcnfsd** is running, meaning that we have support for Windows-based NFS access.

arp

The mechanism used to maintain a list of IP addresses and their corresponding MAC addresses is the *ARP cache*. The mapped addresses are only held in the cache for minutes, so if you want to see what

addresses have been mapped recently, you can use the **arp** command
as shown in the following example:

```
# arp -a
o2 (10.1.1.10) at 0:10:83:f7:a2:f8 ether
l1 (10.1.1.11) at 0:10:83:f7:2e:d0 ether
63.88.85.1 (63.88.85.1) at 0:30:94:b0:b8:a0 ether
l3 (10.1.1.200) at 0:10:83:fc:92:88 ether
tape1 (10.1.1.14) at 0:10:83:f7:e:32 ether
tape1 (10.1.1.14) at 0:10:83:f7:e:32 ether
tape1 (10.1.1.14) at 0:10:83:f7:e:32 ether
tape1 (10.1.1.14) at 0:10:83:f7:e:32 ether
63.88.85.18 (63.88.85.18) -- no entry
```

Current *arp* entries are displayed with the *-a* command. You can
create an entry with the *-s* option.

lanadmin

lanadmin is used to view and perform administration on network
cards. Issuing **lanadmin** with no options brings you into the interactive interface as shown the following example:

```
# lanadmin

        LOCAL AREA NETWORK ONLINE ADMINISTRATION, Version 1.0


             Copyright 1994 Hewlett Packard Company.
                  All rights are reserved.

Test Selection mode.

        lan      = LAN Interface Administration
        menu     = Display this menu
        quit     = Terminate the Administration
        terse    = Do not display command menu
        verbose  = Display command menu

Enter command: lan

LAN Interface test mode. LAN Interface PPA Number = 0
```

```
     clear    = Clear statistics registers
     display  = Display LAN Interface status and statistics registers
     end      = End LAN Interface Administration, return to Test Selection
     menu     = Display this menu
     ppa      = PPA Number of the LAN Interface
     quit     = Terminate the Administration, return to shell
     reset    = Reset LAN Interface to execute its selftest
     specific = Go to Driver specific menu

Enter command: d

                LAN INTERFACE STATUS DISPLAY


PPA Number                        = 0
Description                       = lan0 Hewlett-Packard 10/100 TX Half-Duplex  TT = 1500
Type (value)                      = ethernet-csmacd(6)
MTU Size                          = 1500
Speed                             = 100000000
Station Address                   = 0x1083ffcaae
Administration Status (value)     = up(1)
Operation Status (value)          = down(2)
Last Change                       = 237321866
Inbound Octets                    = 0
Inbound Unicast Packets           = 0
Inbound Non-Unicast Packets       = 0
Inbound Discards                  = 0
Inbound Errors                    = 0
Inbound Unknown Protocols         = 0
Outbound Octets                   = 820
Outbound Unicast Packets          = 20
Outbound Non-Unicast Packets      = 0
Outbound Discards                 = 1
Outbound Errors                   = 0
Outbound Queue Length             = 0
Specific                          = 655367

Press <Return> to continue
```

In this example, we issued **lanadmin** and specified that we wanted to go into the *lan* interface administration and that we wanted to *d*isplay information about the interface.

lanadmin can also be used to perform such tasks as to change the MTU or speed of a lan interface with the *-M* and *-s* options, respectively.

ndd

ndd is used to perform network tuning and view information about network parameters. To view information about all supported tunable parameters with **ndd**, you would issue **ndd -h supported**. You can get

the value of a parameter using the *-get* option you can set the value of
a parameter with the *-set* option.

nslookup

nslookup is used to resolve a host name into an IP address. You issue
nslookup *hostname* and **nslookup** will access either the **/etc/
resolv.conf** file or **/etc/hosts** to resolve the host name. The following
example shows a system using **/etc/hosts** to produce the IP address of
system *l2*:

```
# nslookup l2
Using /etc/hosts on:  l3

looking up FILES
Name:     l2
Address:  10.1.1.12

#
```

You can also run **nslookup** in interactive mode by issuing the
command with no command-line arguments. The following example
shows issuing the command with no command line arguments to get
into interactive mode and then typing **help** to get information on commands you can issue:

```
# nslookup l2
> help
NAME              - print address information about NAME
IP-ADDRESS        - print hostname information about IP-ADDRESS
policy            - print switch policy information
server NAME       - set default server to NAME, using current de-
fault server
lserver NAME      - set default server to NAME, using initial serv-
er
set OPTION        - sets the OPTION
    all           -  print options, current server and host
    [no]swtrace   -  print lookup result and lookup switch messages
>
```

Manual Pages of Some Commands Used in Chapter 12

The following are the HP-UX manual pages for many of the commands used in this chapter. Commands often differ among UNIX variants, so you may find differences in the options or other areas for some commands; however, the following manual pages serve as an excellent reference.

ftp

man page

ftp - 12

ftp - Interface for file transfer program.

```
ftp(1)                                                                    ftp(1)

NAME
      ftp - file transfer program

SYNOPSIS

      ftp [-g] [-i] [-n] [-v] [-B size] [server-host]

DESCRIPTION
      ftp is a user interface to the File Transfer Protocol.  ftp copies
      files over a network connection between the local ``client'' host and
      a remote ``server'' host.  ftp runs on the client host.

   Options
      The ftp command supports the following options:

               -g    Disable file name ``globbing''; see the glob command, below.
                     By default, when this option is not specified, globbing is
                     enabled.

               -i    Disable interactive prompting by multiple-file commands; see
                     the prompt command, below.  By default, when this option is
                     not specified, prompting is enabled.

               -n    Disable ``auto-login''; see the open command, below.  By
                     default, when this option is not specified, auto-login is
                     enabled.

               -v    Enable verbose output; see the verbose command, below.  If
                     this option is not specified, ftp displays verbose output
                     only if the standard input is associated with a terminal.

               -B    Set the buffer size of the data socket to size blocks of
                     1024 bytes. The valid range for size is an integer from 1 to
                     64 (default is 56).
                     Note: A large buffer size will improve the performance of
                     ftp on fast links (e.g., FDDI), but may cause long
                     connection times on slow links (e.g., X.25).

      The name of the server host that ftp communicates with can be
      specified on the command line.  If the server host is specified, ftp
      immediately opens a connection to the server host; see the open
      command, below.  Otherwise, ftp waits for commands from the user.

      File Transfer Protocol specifies file transfer parameters for type,
      mode, form, and struct.  ftp supports the ASCII, binary, and tenex
      File Transfer Protocol types.  ASCII is the default FTP type.  (It
      should be noted though that, whenever ftp establishes a connection
      between two similar systems, it switches automatically to the more
      efficient binary type.) ftp supports only the default values for the
      file transfer parameters mode which defaults to stream, form which
      defaults to non-print, and struct which defaults to file.
```

COMMANDS

ftp supports the following commands. Command arguments with embedded spaces must be enclosed in quotes (for example, "argument with embedded spaces").

! [command [args]]
>   Invoke a shell on the local host. The SHELL environment variable specifies which shell program to invoke. ftp invokes /usr/bin/sh if SHELL is undefined. If command is specified, the shell executes it and returns to ftp. Otherwise, an interactive shell is invoked. When the shell terminates, it returns to ftp.

$ macro-name [args]
>   Execute the macro macro-name that was defined with the macdef command. Arguments are passed to the macro unglobbed.

account [passwd]
>   Supply a supplemental password required by a remote system for access to resources once a login has been successfully completed. If no argument is included, the user is prompted for an account password in a non-echoing input mode.

append local-file [remote-file]
>   Copy local-file to the end of remote-file. If remote-file is left unspecified, the local file name is used in naming the remote file after being altered by any ntrans or nmap setting.

ascii
>   Set the file transfer type to network ASCII. This is the default type.

bell Sound a bell after each file transfer completes.

binary
>   Set the file transfer type to binary.

bye Close the connection to the server host if a connection was open, and exit. Typing an end-of-file (EOF) character also terminates and exits the session.

case Toggle remote computer file name case mapping during mget commands. When case is on (the default is off), remote computer file names with all letters in uppercase are written in the local directory with the letters mapped to lowercase.

cd remote-directory
>   Set the working directory on the server host to remote-directory.

cdup Set the working directory on the server host to the parent of the current remote working directory.

chmod mode file-name
>   Change the permission modes of the file file-name on the remote system to mode.

close
>   Terminate the connection to the server host. The close command does not exit ftp. Any defined macros are erased.

cr   Toggle carriage return stripping during ascii type file retrieval. Records are denoted by a carriage-return/line-feed sequence during ascii type file transfer. When cr is on (the default), carriage returns are stripped from this sequence to conform with the UNIX single line-feed record delimiter. Records on non-UNIX remote systems may contain single line-feeds; when an

ascii type transfer is made, these line-feeds can be
distinguished from a record delimiter only when cr is off.

delete remote-file
    Delete remote-file. The remote-file can be an empty directory.
    No globbing is done.

dir [remote-directory] [local-file]
    Write a remote-directory listing to standard output or optionally
    to local-file. If neither remote-directory nor local-file is
    specified, list the remote working directory to standard output.
    If interactive prompting is on, ftp prompts the user to verify
    that the last argument is indeed the target file for dir output.
    Globbing characters are always expanded.

disconnect
    A synonym for close.

form format
    Set the file transfer form to format. The only supported format
    is non-print

get remote-file [local-file]
    Copy remote-file to local-file. If local-file is unspecified,
    ftp uses the specified remote-file name as the local-file name,
    subject to alteration by the current case, ntrans, and nmap
    settings.

glob Toggle file name globbing. When file name globbing is enabled,
    ftp expands csh(1) metacharacters in file and directory names.
    These characters are *, ?, [,], ~, {, and }. The server host
    expands remote file and directory names. Globbing metacharacters
    are always expanded for the ls and dir commands. If globbing is
    enabled, metacharacters are also expanded for the multiple-file
    commands mdelete, mdir, mget, mls, and mput.

hash Toggle printing of a hash-sign (#) for each 1024 bytes
    transferred.

help [command]
    Print an informative message about the ftp command called ftp-
    command. If ftp-command is unspecified, print a list of all ftp
    commands.

idle [seconds]
    Set the inactivity timer on the remote server to seconds seconds.
    If seconds is omitted, ftp prints the current inactivity timer.

lcd [local-directory]
    Set the local working directory to local-directory. If local-
    directory is unspecified, set the local working directory to the
    user's local home directory.

ls [remote-directory] [local-file]
    Write a listing of remote-directory to local-file. The listing
    includes any system-dependent information that the server chooses
    to include; for example, most UNIX systems produce output from
    the command ls -l (see also nlist). If neither remote-directory
    nor local-file is specified, list the remote working directory.
    If globbing is enabled, globbing metacharacters are expanded.

macdef macro-name
    Define a macro. Subsequent lines are stored as the macro macro-
    name; an empty input line terminates macro input mode. There is
    a limit of 16 macros and 4096 total characters in all defined

macros. Macros remain defined until a close command is executed.
The macro processor interprets $ and \ as special characters. A
$ followed by a number (or numbers) is replaced by the
corresponding argument on the macro invocation command line. A $
followed by an i signals to the macro processor that the
executing macro is to be looped. On the first pass $i is
replaced by the first argument on the macro invocation command
line, on the second pass it is replaced by the second argument,
and so on. A \ followed by any character is replaced by that
character. Use the \ to prevent special treatment of the $.

mdelete [remote-files]
     Delete remote-files. If globbing is enabled, globbing
     metacharacters are expanded.

mdir remote-files local-file
     Write a listing of remote-files to local-file. If globbing is
     enabled, globbing metacharacters are expanded. If interactive
     prompting is on, ftp prompts the user to verify that the last
     argument is indeed the target local file for mdir output.

mget remote-files
     Copy remote-files to the local system. If globbing is enabled,
     globbing metacharacters are expanded. The resulting local file
     names are processed according to case, ntrans, and nmap settings.

mkdir directory-name
     Create remote directory-name.

mls remote-files local-file
     Write an abbreviated listing of remote-files to local-file. If
     globbing is enabled, globbing metacharacters are expanded. If
     interactive prompting is on, ftp prompts the user to verify that
     the last argument is indeed the target local file for mls output.

mode [mode-name]
     Set the FTP file transfer mode to mode-name. The only supported
     mode is stream.

modtime remote-file
     Show the last modification time of remote-file.

mput local-files
     Copy local-files from the local system to the remote system. The
     remote files have the same name as the local files processed
     according to ntrans and nmap settings. If globbing is enabled,
     globbing characters are expanded.

newer file-name
     Get the file only if the modification time of the remote file is
     more recent that the file on the current system. If the file
     does not exist on the current system, the remote file is
     considered newer. Otherwise, this command is identical to get.

nlist [remote-directory] [local-file]
     Write an abbreviated listing of remote-directory to local-file.
     If remote-directory is left unspecified, the current working
     directory is used. If interactive prompting is on, ftp prompts
     the user to verify that the last argument is indeed the target
     local file for nlist output.

nmap [inpattern outpattern]
     Set or unset the filename mapping mechanism. If no arguments are

specified, the filename mapping mechanism is unset. If arguments
are specified, remote filenames are mapped during mput commands
and put commands issued without a specified remote target
filename. If arguments are specified, local filenames are mapped
during mget commands and get commands issued without a specified
local target filename. This command is useful when connecting to
a non-UNIX remote computer with different file naming conventions
or practices. The mapping follows the pattern set by inpattern
and outpattern. inpattern is a template for incoming filenames
(which may have already been processed according to the ntrans
and case settings). Variable templating is accomplished by
including the sequences $1, $2, ..., $9 in inpattern. Use \ to
prevent this special treatment of the $ character. All other
characters are treated literally, and are used to determine the
nmap inpattern variable values. For example, given inpattern
$1.$2 and the remote file name mydata.data, $1 would have the
value mydata, and $2 would have the value data. The outpattern
determines the resulting mapped filename. The sequences $1,
$2, ..., $9 are replaced by any value resulting from the
inpattern template. The sequence $0 is replaced by the original
filename. Additionally, the sequence [seq1,seq2] is replaced by
seq1 if seq1 is not a null string; otherwise it is replaced by
seq2. For example, the command nmap $1.$2.$3 [$1,$2].[$2,file]
would yield the output filename myfile.data for input filenames
myfile.data and myfile.data.old, myfile.file for the input
filename myfile, and myfile.myfile for the input filename
.myfile. Spaces can be included in outpattern, as in the
example: nmap $1 | sed "s/ *$//" > $1 . Use the \ character to
prevent special treatment of the $, [,], and , characters.

ntrans [inchars [outchars]]
     Set or unset the filename character translation mechanism. If no
     arguments are specified, the filename character translation
     mechanism is unset. If arguments are specified, characters in
     remote filenames are translated during mput commands and put
     commands issued without a specified remote target filename. If
     arguments are specified, characters in local filenames are
     translated during mget commands and get commands issued without a
     specified local target filename. This command is useful when
     connecting to a non-UNIX remote computer with different file
     naming conventions or practices. Characters in a filename
     matching a character in inchars are replaced with the
     corresponding character in outchars. If the character's position
     in inchars is longer than the length of outchars, the character
     is deleted from the file name.

open server-host [port-number]
     Establish a connection to server-host, using port-number (if
     specified). If auto-login is enabled, ftp attempts to log into
     the server host.

prompt
     Toggle interactive prompting. By default, ftp prompts the user
     for a yes or no response for each output file during multiple-
     file commands. If interactive prompting is disabled, ftp
     performs the command for all specified files.

proxy ftp-command
     Execute an ftp command on a secondary control connection. This
     command allows simultaneous connection to two remote FTP servers
     for transferring files between the two servers. The first proxy
     command should be an open, to establish the secondary control
     connection. Enter the command proxy ? to see other FTP commands
     executable on the secondary connection. The following commands
     behave differently when prefaced by proxy: open does not define
     new macros during the auto-login process, close does not erase

existing macro definitions, get and mget transfer files from the
host on the primary control connection to the host on the
secondary control connection, and put, mput, and append transfer
files from the host on the secondary control connection to the
host on the primary control connection. Third party file
transfers depend upon support of the FTP protocol PASV command by
the server on the secondary control connection.

put local-file [remote-file]
    Copy local-file to remote-file. If remote-file is unspecified,
    ftp assigns the local-file name, processed according to any
    ntrans or nmap settings, to the remote-file name.

pwd Write the name of the remote working directory to stdout.

quit A synonym for bye.

quote arguments
    Send arguments, verbatim, to the server host. See ftpd(1M).

recv remote-file [local-file]
    A synonym for get.

reget remote-file [local-file]
    reget acts like get, except that if local-file exists and is
    smaller than remote-file, local-file is presumed to be a
    partially transferred copy of remote-file and the transfer is
    continued from the apparent point of failure. This command is
    useful when transferring very large files over networks that tend
    to drop connections.

rhelp [command-name]
    Request help from the server host. If command-name is specified,
    supply it to the server. See ftpd(1M).

rstatus [file-name]
    With no arguments, show status of remote machine. If file-name
    is specified, show status of file-name on remote machine.

rename remote-from remote-to
    Rename remote-from, which can be either a file or a directory, to
    remote-to.

reset
    Clear reply queue. This command re-synchronizes command/reply
    sequencing with the remote FTP server. Resynchronization may be
    necessary following a violation of the FTP protocol by the remote
    server.

restart marker
    Restart the immediately following get or put at the indicated
    marker. On UNIX systems, marker is usually a byte offset into
    the file.

rmdir remote-directory
    Delete remote-directory. remote-directory must be an empty
    directory.

runique
    Toggle storing of files on the local system with unique
    filenames. If a file already exists with a name equal to the
    target local filename for a get or mget command, a .1 is appended
    to the name. If the resulting name matches another existing
    file, a .2 is appended to the original name. If this process
    continues up to .99, an error message is printed, and the
    transfer does not take place. ftp reports the unique filename.

Note that runique does not affect local files generated from a
shell command (see below). The default value is off.

send local-file [remote-file]
     A synonym for put.

sendport
     Toggle the use of PORT commands. By default, ftp attempts to use
     a PORT command when establishing a connection for each data
     transfer. If the PORT command fails, ftp uses the default data
     port. When the use of PORT commands is disabled, ftp makes no
     attempt to use PORT commands for each data transfer. This is
     useful for certain FTP implementations that ignore PORT commands
     but (incorrectly) indicate that they've been accepted. See
     ftpd(1M). Turning sendport off may cause delays in the execution
     of commands.

site arguments
     Send arguments, verbatim, to the server host as a SITE command.
     See ftpd(1M).

size remote-file
     Show the size of remote-file.

status
     Show the current status of ftp.

struct [struct-name]
     Set the FTP file transfer struct to struct-name. The only
     supported struct is file.

sunique
     Toggle storing of files on remote machine under unique file
     names. The remote server reports the unique name. By default,
     sunique is off.

system
     Show the type of operating system running on the remote machine.

tenex
     Set the FTP file transfer type to tenex.

type [type-name]
     Set the FTP file transfer type to type-name. If type-name is
     unspecified, write the current type to stdout. Ascii, binary,
     and tenex are the types currently supported.

umask [newmask]
     Set the default umask on the remote server to newmask. If
     newmask is omitted, the current umask is printed.

user user-name [password] [account]
     Log into the server host on the current connection, which must
     already be open. A .netrc file in the user's local home
     directory can provide the user-name, password, and optionally the
     account; see netrc(4). Otherwise ftp prompts the user for this
     information. The HP-UX FTP server does not require an account.
     For security reasons, ftp always requires a password. It does
     not log into remote accounts that do not have a password.

verbose
     Toggle verbose output. If verbose output is enabled, ftp
     displays responses from the server host, and when a file transfer
     completes it reports statistics regarding the efficiency of the
     transfer.

? [command]
>   A synonym for the help command. Prints the help information for
>   the specified command.

Aborting A File Transfer
  To abort a file transfer, use the terminal interrupt key (usually
  Ctrl-C). Sending transfers are halted immediately. ftp halts
  incoming (receive) transfers by first sending a FTP protocol ABOR
  command to the remote server, then discarding any further received
  data. The speed at which this is accomplished depends upon the remote
  server's support for ABOR processing. If the remote server does not
  support the ABOR command, an ftp> prompt does not appear until the
  remote server completes sending the requested file.

  The terminal interrupt key sequence is ignored while ftp awaits a
  reply from the remote server. A long delay in this mode may result
  from the ABOR processing described above, or from unexpected behavior
  by the remote server, including violations of the FTP protocol. If
  the delay results from unexpected remote server behavior, the local
  ftp program must be killed manually.

File Naming Conventions
  Files specified as arguments to ftp commands are processed according
  to the following rules.

  - If the file name - is specified, ftp uses the standard input (for
     reading) or standard output (for writing).

  - If the first character of the file name is |, ftp interprets the
     remainder of the argument as a shell command. ftp forks a shell,
     using popen() (see popen(3S)) with the supplied argument, and reads
     (writes) from standard output (standard input). If the shell
     command includes spaces, the argument must be quoted, as in:

         "| ls -lt".

     A particularly useful example of this mechanism is:

         "| dir . | more".

  - Otherwise, if globbing is enabled, ftp expands local file names
     according to the rules used by the C shell (see csh(1)); see the
     glob command, below. If the ftp command expects a single local
     file (e.g. put), only the first filename generated by the globbing
     operation is used.

  - For mget commands and get commands with unspecified local file
     names, the local filename is named the same as the remote filename,
     which may be altered by a case, ntrans, or nmap setting. The
     resulting filename may then be altered if runique is on.

  - For mput commands and put commands with unspecified remote file
     names, the remote filename is named the same as the local filename,
     which may be altered by a ntrans or nmap setting. The resulting
     filename may then be altered by the remote server if sunique is on.

WARNINGS
     Correct execution of many commands depends upon proper behavior by the
     remote server.

AUTHOR
     ftp was developed by the University of California, Berkeley.

SEE ALSO
     csh(1), rcp(1), ftpd(1M), netrc(4), ftpusers(4), hosts(4).

ifconfig

ifconfig - Display or configure network interface parameters.

man page

ifconfig - 12

```
ifconfig(1M)                                                    ifconfig(1M)

NAME
     ifconfig - configure network interface parameters

SYNOPSIS

     ifconfig interface address_family [address [dest_address]] [parameters]

     ifconfig interface [address_family]

DESCRIPTION
     The first form of the ifconfig command assigns an address to a network
     interface and/or configures network interface parameters.  ifconfig
     must be used at boot time to define the network address of each
     interface present on a machine.  It can also be used at other times to
     redefine an interface's address or other operating parameters.

     The second form of the command, without address_family, displays the
     current configuration for interface.  If address_family is also
     specified, ifconfig reports only the details specific to that address
     family.

     Only a user with appropriate privileges can modify the configuration
     of a network interface.  All users can run the second form of the
     command.

   Arguments
     ifconfig recognizes the following arguments:

          address        Either a host name present in the host name
                         database (see hosts(4)), or a DARPA Internet
                         address expressed in Internet standard dot
                         notation (see inet(3N)).  The host number can be
                         omitted on 10MB/second Ethernet interfaces (which
                         use the hardware physical address), and on
                         interfaces other than the first.

          address_family Name of protocol on which naming scheme is based.
                         An interface can receive transmissions in
                         differing protocols, each of which may require
                         separate naming schemes.  Therefore, it is
                         necessary to specify the address_family, which
                         may affect interpretation of the remaining
                         parameters on the command line.  The only address
                         family currently supported is inet (DARPA-
                         Internet family).

          dest_address   Address of destination system.  Consists of
                         either a host name present in the host name
                         database (see hosts(4)), or a DARPA Internet
                         address expressed in Internet standard dot
                         notation (see inet(3N)).

          interface      A string of the form nameunit, such as lan0.
```

(See the LAN Card Numbering subsection.)

parameters   One or more of the following operating
                    parameters:

          up   Mark an interface "up". Enables
                              interface after an ifconfig down.
                              Occurs automatically when setting
                              the address on an interface.
                              Setting this flag has no effect if
                              the hardware is "down".

          down   Mark an interface "down". When an
                              interface is marked "down", the
                              system will not attempt to
                              transmit messages through that
                              interface. If possible, the
                              interface will be reset to disable
                              reception as well. This action
                              does not automatically disable
                              routes using the interface.

          broadcast   (Inet only) Specify the address
                              that represents broadcasts to the
                              network. The default broadcast
                              address is the address with a host
                              part of all 1's.

          debug   Enable driver-dependent debugging
                              code. This usually turns on extra
                              console error logging.

          -debug   Disable driver-dependent debugging
                              code.

          ipdst   (NS only) This is used to specify
                              an Internet host that is willing
                              to receive IP packets
                              encapsulating NS packets bound for
                              a remote network. In this case,
                              an apparent point-to-point link is
                              constructed, and the address
                              specified is taken as the NS
                              address and network of the
                              destination.

          metric n   Set the routing metric of the
                              interface to n. The default is 0.
                              The routing metric is used by the
                              routing protocol (see gated(1m)).
                              Higher metrics have the effect of
                              making a route less favorable;
                              metrics are counted as additional
                              hops to the destination network or
                              host.

          netmask mask   (Inet only) Specify how much of
                              the address to reserve for
                              subdividing networks into sub-
                              networks or aggregating networks
                              into supernets. mask can be
                              specified as a single hexadecimal
                              number with a leading 0x, with a
                              dot-notation Internet address, or
                              with a pseudo-network name listed
                              in the network table (see

networks(4)). For subdividing
networks into sub-networks, mask
must include the network part of
the local address, and the subnet
part which is taken from the host
field of the address. mask must
contain 1's in the bit positions
in the 32-bit address that are to
be used for the network and subnet
parts, and 0's in the host part.
The 1's in the mask must be
contiguous starting from the
leftmost bit position in the 32-
bit field. mask must contain at
least the standard network
portion, and the subnet field must
be contiguous with the network
portion. The subnet field must
contain at least 2 bits. The
subnet part after performing a
bit-wise AND operation between the
address and the mask must not
contain all 0's or all 1's. For
aggregating networks into
supernets, mask must only include
a portion of the network part.
mask must contain contiguous 1's
in the bit positions starting from
the leftmost bit of the 32-bit
field.

trailers   Request the use of a "trailer"
                        link-level encapsulation when
                        sending. If a network interface
                        supports trailers, the system
                        will, when possible, encapsulate
                        outgoing messages in a manner that
                        minimizes the number of memory-
                        to-memory copy operations
                        performed by the receiver. On
                        networks that support the Address
                        Resolution Protocol, this flag
                        indicates that the system should
                        request that other systems use
                        trailers when sending to this
                        host. Similarly, trailer
                        encapsulations will be sent to
                        other hosts that have made such
                        requests. Currently used by
                        Internet protocols only. See
                        WARNINGS section.

-trailers   Disable the use of a "trailer"
                        link-level encapsulation
                        (default).

LAN Card Numbering
   The name of an interface associated with a LAN card is lan, and its
   unitnumber is determined as follows. The LAN card installed first in
   the system is given interface unit number 0; the next LAN card
   installed is given interface unit number 1; and so on. When there are
   two or more LAN cards installed at the same time, interface unit
   numbers are assigned according to card positions in the backplane:
   the LAN card that appears "first" in the backplane is given the
   interface unit number N; the next LAN card in the backplane is given
   the number N+1.

The lanscan command can be used to display the name and unit number of
each interface that is associated with a LAN card (see lanscan(1M)).

Supernets
A supernet is a collection of smaller networks. Supernetting is a
technique of using the netmask to aggregate a collection of smaller
networks into a supernet. This technique is particularly useful for
class C networks. A Class C network can only have 254 hosts. This
can be too restrictive for some companies. For these companies, a
netmask that only contains a portion of the network part can be
applied to the hosts in these class C networks to form a supernet.
This supernet netmask should be applied to those interfaces that
connect to the supernet using the ifconfig command. For example, a
host can configure its interface to connect to a class C supernet,
192.6, by configuring an IP address of 192.6.1.1 and a netmask of
255.255.0.0 to its interface.

DIAGNOSTICS
Messages indicate if the specified interface does not exist, the
requested address is unknown, or the user is not privileged and tried
to alter an interface's configuration.

WARNINGS
Currently, all HP 9000 systems can receive trailer packets but do not
send them. Setting the trailers flag has no effect.

SEE ALSO
netstat(1), lanconfig(1m), lanscan(1m) hosts(4), routing(7).

netstat

netstat - Display statistics related to networking.

```
netstat(1)                                                              netstat(1)

NAME
     netstat - show network status

SYNOPSIS
     netstat [-aAn] [-f address-family] [system [core]]
     netstat [-mMnrsv] [-f address-family] [-p protocol] [system [core]]
     netstat [-gin] [-I interface] [interval] [system [core]]

DESCRIPTION
     netstat displays statistics for network interfaces and protocols, as
     well as the contents of various network-related data structures.  The
     output format varies according to the options selected.  Some options
     are ignored when used in combination with other options.

     Generally, the netstat command takes one of the three forms shown
     above:

         -   The first form of the command displays a list of active
             sockets for each protocol.

         -   The second form displays the contents of one of the other
             network data structures according to the option selected.

         -   The third form displays configuration information for each
             network interface.  It also displays network traffic data on
             configured network interfaces, optionally updated at each
             interval, measured in seconds.

     Options are interpreted as follows:

         -a                  Show the state of all sockets, including
                             passive sockets used by server processes.  When
                             netstat is used without any options (except -A
                             and -n), only active sockets are shown.  This
                             option does not show the state of X.25
                             programmatic access sockets.  The option is
                             ignored if the -g, -i, -I, -m, -M, -p, -r, -s
                             or interval option is specified.

         -A                  Show the address of the protocol control block
                             associated with sockets.  This option is used
                             for debugging.  It does not show the X.25
                             programmatic access control blocks.  This
                             option is ignored if the -g, -i, -I, -m, -M,
                             -p, -r, -s or interval option is specified.

         -f address-family   Show statistics or address control block for
                             only the specified address-family.  The
                             following address families are recognized: inet
                             for AF_INET, and unix for AF_UNIX.  This option
```

applies to the -a, -A and -s options.

-g	Show multicast information for network interfaces. Only the address family AF_INET is recognized by this option. This option may be combined with the -i option to display both kinds of information. The option is ignored if the -m, -M or -p option is specified.
-i	Show the state of network interfaces. Interfaces that are statically configured into a system, but not located at boot time, are not shown. This option is ignored if the -m, -M or -p option is specified.
-I interface	Show information about the specified interface only. This option applies to the -g and -i options.
-m	Show statistics recorded by network memory management routines. If this option is specified, all other options are ignored.
-M	Show the multicast routing tables. When -s is used with the -M option, netstat displays multicast routing statistics instead. This option is ignored if the -m or -p option is specified.
-n	Show network addresses as numbers. Normally, netstat interprets addresses and attempts to display them symbolically. This option applies to the -a, -A, -i, -r and -v options.
-p protocol	Show statistics for the specified protocol. The following protocols are recognized: tcp, udp, ip, icmp, igmp, arp, and probe. This option is ignored if the -m option is specified.
-r	Show the routing tables. When -v is used with the -r option, netstat also displays the network masks in the route entries. When -s is used with the -r option, netstat displays routing statistics instead. This option is ignored if the -g, -m, -M, -i, -I, -p or interval option is specified.
-s	Show statistics for all protocols. When this option is used with the -r option, netstat displays routing statistics instead. When this option is used with the -M option, netstat displays multicast routing statistics instead. This option is ignored if the -g, -i, -I, -m, -p or interval option is specified.
-v	Show additional routing information. When -v is used with the -r option, netstat also displays the network masks in the route entries. This option only applies to the -r option.

The arguments system and core allow substitutes for the defaults, /stand/vmunix and /dev/kmem.

If no options or only the -A or -n option is specified, netstat displays the status of only active sockets. The display of active and passive sockets status shows the local and remote addresses, send and receive queue sizes (in bytes), protocol, and the internal state of the protocol. Address formats are of the form host.port, or network.port if the host portion of a socket address is zero. When known, the host and network addresses are displayed symbolically by using gethostbyname() and getnetbyname(), respectively (see gethostbyname(3N) and getnetbyname(3N)). If a symbolic name for an address is unknown, or if the -n option is specified, the address is displayed numerically according to the address family. For more information regarding the Internet ``dot format'', refer to inet(3N). Unspecified or ``wildcard'' addresses and ports appear as an asterisk (*).

The interface display provides a table of cumulative statistics regarding packets transferred, errors, and collisions. The network addresses of the interface and the maximum transmission unit (MTU) are also displayed. When the interval argument is specified, netstat displays a running count of statistics related to network interfaces. This display consists of a column for the primary interface (the first interface found during auto-configuration) and a column summarizing information for all interfaces. To replace the primary interface with another interface, use the -I option. The first line of each screen of information contains a summary since the system was last rebooted. Subsequent lines of output show values accumulated over the preceding interval.

The routing table display indicates the available routes and their status. Each route consists of a destination host or network, a netmask and a gateway to use in forwarding packets. The Flags field shows whether the route is up (U), whether the route is to a gateway (G), whether the route is a host or network route (with or without H), whether the route was created dynamically (D) by a redirect or by Path MTU Discovery, and whether a gateway route has been modified (M), or it has been marked doubtful (?) due to the lack of a timely ARP response.

The Netmask field shows the mask to be applied to the destination IP address of an IP packet to be forwarded. The result will be compared with the destination address in the route entry. If they are the same, then the route is one of the candidates for routing this IP packet. If there are several candidate routes, then the route with the longest Netmask field (contiguous 1's starting from the leftmost bit position) will be chosen. (see routing (7).)

The Gateway field shows the address of the immediate gateway for reaching the destination. It can be the address of the outgoing interface if the destination is on a directly connected network.

The Refs field shows the current number of active uses of the route. Connection-oriented protocols normally hold on to a single route for the duration of a connection, while connectionless protocols normally obtain a route just while sending a particular message. The Use field shows a count of the number of packets sent using the route. The Interface field identifies which network interface is used for the route.

The Pmtu and PmtuTime fields apply only to host routes. The Pmtu field for network and default routes is the same as the MTU of the network interface used for the route. If the route is created with a static PMTU value (see route(1M)), the corresponding PmtuTime field contains the word perm, and the PMTU value permanently overrides the interface MTU. If the route is created dynamically (D in the Flags field), the value in the corresponding PmtuTime field is the number of minutes remaining before the PMTU expires. When the PMTU expires, the system rediscovers the current PMTU for the route, in case it has

changed. The PmtuTime field is left blank when the PMTU is identical
to the MTU of the interface. An asterisk (*) in the Pmtu field
indicates that user has disabled the PMTU Discovery for the route.

DEPENDENCIES
    X.25:
        -A and -a options do not list X.25 programmatic access information.

AUTHOR
    netstat was developed by the University of California, Berkeley.

SEE ALSO
    hosts(4), networks(4), gethostbyname(3N), getnetbyname(3N),
    protocols(4), route(1M), services(4).

ping

ping - Send information over a network and get a response.

man page

ping - 12

ping(1M)   ping(1M)

NAME
     ping - send ICMP Echo Request packets to network host

SYNOPSIS

     ping [-oprv] [-i address] [-t ttl] host [-n count]
     ping [-oprv] [-i address] [-t ttl] host packet-size [[-n] count]

DESCRIPTION
     The ping command sends ICMP Echo Request (ECHO_REQUEST) packets to
     host once per second. Each packet that is echoed back via an ICMP
     Echo Response packet is written to the standard output, including
     round-trip time.

     ICMP Echo Request datagrams ("pings") have an IP and ICMP header,
     followed by a struct timeval (see gettimeofday(2)) and an arbitrary
     number of "pad" bytes used to fill out the packet. The default
     datagram length is 64 bytes, but this can be changed by using the
     packet-size option.

     Options
        The following options and parameters are recognizaed by ping:

            -i address If host is a multicast address, send multicast
                        datagrams from the interface with the local IP
                        address specified by address in ``dot'' notation (see
                        inet_addr(3N)). If the -i option is not specified,
                        multicast datagrams are sent from the default
                        interface, which is determined by the route
                        configuration.

            -o   Insert an IP Record Route option in outgoing packets,
                        summarizing routes taken when the command terminates.

                        It may not be possible to get the round-trip path if
                        some hosts on the route taken do not implement the IP
                        Record Route option. A maximum of 9 Internet
                        addresses can be recorded due to the maximum length
                        of the IP option area.

            -p   The new Path MTU information is displayed when a ICMP
                        "Datagram Too Big" message is received from a
                        gateway. The -p option must be used in conjunction
                        with a large packetsize and with the -v option.

            -r   Bypass the normal routing tables and send directly to
                        a host on an attached network. If the host is not on
                        a directly-connected network, an error is returned.
                        This option can be used to ping the local system
                        through an interface that has no route through it,
                        such as after the interface was dropped by gated (see

gated(1M)).

-t ttl   If host is a multicast address, set the time-to-live
              field in the multicast datagram to ttl. This
              controls the scope of the multicast datagrams by
              specifying the maximum number of external systems
              through which the datagram can be forwarded.

              If ttl is zero, the datagram is restricted to the
              local system. If ttl is one, the datagram is
              restricted to systems that have an interface on the
              network directly connected to the interface specified
              by the -i option. If ttl is two, the datagram can
              forwarded through at most one multicast router; and
              so forth. Range: zero to 255. The default value is
              1.

-v   Verbose output. Show ICMP packets other than Echo
              Responses that are received.

host   Destination to which the ICMP Echo Requests are sent.
              host can be a hostname or an Internet address. All
              symbolic names specified for host are looked up by
              using gethostbyname() (see gethostbyname(3N)). If
              host is an Internet address, it must be in "dot"
              notation (see inet_addr(3N)).

              If a system does not respond as expected, the route
              might be configured incorrectly on the local or
              remote system or on an intermediate gateway, or there
              might be some other network failure. Normally, host
              is the address assigned to a local or remote network
              interface.

              If host is a broadcast address, all systems that
              receive the broadcast should respond. Normally,
              these are only systems that have a network interface
              on the same network as the local interface sending
              the ICMP Echo Request.

              If host is a multicast address, only systems that
              have joined the multicast group should respond.
              These may be distant systems if the -t option is
              specified, and there is a multicast router on the
              network directly connected to the interface specified
              by the -i option.

packet-size   The size of the transmitted packet, in bytes. By
              default (when packet-size is not specified), the size
              of transmitted packets is 64 bytes. The minimum
              value allowed for packet-size is 8 bytes, and the
              maximum is 4095 bytes. If packet-size is smaller
              than 16 bytes, there is not enough room for timing
              information. In that case, the round-trip times are
              not displayed.

count   The number of packets ping will transmit before
              terminating. Range: zero to 2147483647. The default
              is zero, in which case ping sends packets until
              interrupted.

When using ping for fault isolation, first specify a local address for
host to verify that the local network interface is working correctly.
Then specify host and gateway addresses further and further away to
determine the point of failure. ping sends one datagram per second,
and it normally writes one line of output for every ICMP Echo Response

that is received. No output is produced if there are no responses.
If an optional count is given, only the specified number of requests
is sent. Round-trip times and packet loss statistics are computed.
When all responses have been received or the command times out (if the
count option is specified), or if the command is terminated with a
SIGINT, a brief summary is displayed.

This command is intended for use in testing, managing and measuring
network performance. It should be used primarily to isolate network
failures. Because of the load it could impose on the network, it is
considered discourteous to use ping unnecessarily during normal
operations or from automated scripts.

AUTHOR
     ping was developed in the Public Domain.

FILES
     /etc/hosts

SEE ALSO
     gethostbyname(3N), inet(3N).

rcp

rcp - Copy files and directories from one system to another.

rcp(1)   rcp(1)

NAME
     rcp - remote file copy

SYNOPSIS

  Copy Single File
     rcp [-p] source_file1 dest_file

  Copy Multiple Files
     rcp [-p] source_file1 [source_file2]... dest_dir

  Copy One or More Directory Subtrees
     rcp [-p] -r source_dir1 [source_dir2]... dest_dir

  Copy Files and Directory Subtrees
     rcp [-p] -r file_or_dir1 [file_or_dir2]... dest_dir

DESCRIPTION
     The rcp command copies files, directory subtrees, or a combination of
     files and directory subtrees from one or more systems to another. In
     many respects, it is similar to the cp command (see cp(1)).

     To use rcp, you must have read access to files being copied, and read
     and search (execute) permission on all directories in the directory
     path.

  Options and Arguments
     rcp recognizes the following options and arguments:

          source_file   The name of an existing file or directory on a
          source_dir   local or remote machine that you want copied to
                         the specified destination. Source file and
                         directory names are constructed as follows:

                              user_name@hostname:pathname/filename

                         or

                              user_name@hostname:pathname/dirname

                         Component parts of file and directory names are
                         described below. If multiple existing files
                         and/or directory subtrees are specified
                         (source_file1, source_file2, ..., etc.), the
                         destination must be a directory. Shell file name
                         expansion is allowed on both local and remote
                         systems. Multiple files and directory subtrees
                         can be copied from one or more systems to a single
                         destination directory with a single command.

          dest_file   The name of the destination file. If host name
                         and path name are not specified, the existing file

is copied into a file named dest_file in the
current directory on the local system. If
dest_file already exists and is writable, the
existing file is overwritten. Destination file
names are constructed the same way as source files
except that file name expansion characters cannot
be used.

dest_dir   The name of the destination directory. If host
name and path name are not specified, the existing
file is copied into a directory named dest_dir in
the current directory on the local system. If
dest_dir already exists in the specified directory
path (or current directory if not specified), a
new directory named dest_dir is created underneath
the existing directory named dest_dir.
Destination directory names are constructed the
same way as source directory tree names except
that file name expansion characters cannot be
used.

file_or_dir   If a combination of files and directories are
specified for copying (either explicitly or by
file name expansion), only files are copied unless
the -r option is specified. If the -r option is
present, all files and directory subtrees whose
names match the specified file_or_dir name are
copied.

-p   Preserve (duplicate) modification times and modes
(permissions) of source files, ignoring the
current setting of the umask file creation mode
mask. If this option is specified, rcp preserves
the sticky bit only if the target user is
superuser.

If the -p option is not specified, rcp preserves
the mode and owner of dest_file if it already
exists; otherwise rcp uses the mode of the source
file modified by the umask on the destination
host. Modification and access times of the
destination file are set to the time when the copy
was made.

-r   Recursively copy directory subtrees rooted at the
source directory name. If any directory subtrees
are to be copied, rcp recursively copies each
subtree rooted at the specified source directory
name to directory dest_dir. If source_dir is
being copied to an existing directory of the same
name, rcp creates a new directory source_dir
within dest_dir and copies the subtree rooted at
source_dir to dest_dir/source_dir. If dest_dir
does not exist, rcp creates it and copies the
subtree rooted at source_dir to dest_dir.

Constructing File and Directory Names
  As indicated above, file and directory names contain one, two, or four
  component parts:

user_name   Login name to be used for accessing directories and
files on remote system.

hostname   Hostname of remote system where directories and
files are located.

pathname   Absolute directory path name or directory path name
                relative to the login directory of user user_name.

filename   Actual name of source or destination file. File
                name expansion is allowed on source file names.

dirname   Actual name of source or destination directory
                subtree. File name expansion is allowed on source
                directory names.

Each file or directory argument is either a remote file name of the
form hostname:path, or a local file name (with a slash (/) before any
colon (:)). hostname can be either an official host name or an alias
(see hosts(4)). If hostname is of the form ruser@rhost, ruser is used
on the remote host instead of the current user name. An unspecified
path (that is, hostname:) refers to the remote user's login directory.
If path does not begin with /, it is interpreted relative to the
remote user's login directory on hostname. Shell metacharacters in
remote paths can be quoted with backslash (\), single quotes (''), or
double quotes (""), so that they will be interpreted remotely.

The rcp routine does not prompt for passwords. The current local user
name or any user name specified via ruser must exist on rhost and
allow remote command execution via remsh(1) and rcmd(3). remshd(1M)
must be executable on the remote host.

Third-party transfers in the form:

       rcp ruser1@rhost1:path1 ruser2@rhost2:path2

are performed as:

       remsh rhost1 -l ruser1 rcp path1 ruser2@rhost2:path2

Therefore, for a such a transfer to succeed, ruser2 on rhost2 must
allow access by ruser1 from rhost1 (see hosts.equiv(4)).

WARNINGS
       The rcp routine is confused by any output generated by commands in a
       .cshrc file on the remote host (see csh(1)).

       Copying a file onto itself, for example:

              rcp path `hostname`:path

       may produce inconsistent results. The current HP-UX version of rcp
       simply copies the file over itself. However, some implementations of
       rcp, including some earlier HP-UX implementations, corrupt the file.
       In addition, the same file may be referred to in multiple ways, for
       example, via hard links, symbolic links, or NFS. It is not guaranteed
       that rcp will correctly copy a file over itself in all cases.

       Implementations of rcp based on the 4.2BSD version (including the
       implementations of rcp prior to HP-UX 7.0) require that remote users
       be specified as rhost.ruser. If the first remote host specified in a
       third party transfer (rhost1 in the example below) uses this older
       syntax, the command must have the form:

              rcp ruser1@rhost1:path1 rhost2.ruser2:path2

       since the target is interpreted by rhost1. A common problem that is
       encountered is when two remote files are to be copied to a remote
       target that specifies a remote user. If the two remote source
       systems, rhost1 and rhost2, each expect a different form for the
       remote target, the command:

```
rcp rhost1:path1 rhost2:path2 rhost3.ruser3:path3
```

will certainly fail on one of the source systems. Perform such a transfer using two separate commands.

AUTHOR
    rcp was developed by the University of California, Berkeley.

SEE ALSO
    cp(1), ftp(1), remsh(1), remshd(1M), rcmd(3), hosts(4), hosts.equiv(4).

    ftp chapter in Using Internet Services.

rcp(1)   Secure Internet Services with Kerberos Authentication   rcp(1)

NAME
    rcp - remote file copy

SYNOPSIS

  Copy Single File
    rcp [-k realm] [-P] [-p] source_file1 dest_file

  Copy Multiple Files
    rcp [-k realm] [-P] [-p] source_file1 [source_file2]... dest_dir

  Copy One or More Directory Subtrees
    rcp [-k realm] [-P] [-p] -r source_dir1 [source_dir2]... dest_dir

  Copy Files and Directory Subtrees
    rcp [-k realm] [-P] [-p] -r file_or_dir1 [file_or_dir2]... dest_dir

DESCRIPTION
    The rcp command copies files, directory subtrees, or a combination of files and directory subtrees from one or more systems to another. In many respects, it is similar to the cp command (see cp(1)).

    To use rcp, you must have read access to files being copied, and read and search (execute) permission on all directories in the directory path.

    In a Kerberos V5 Network Authentication environment, rcp uses the Kerberos V5 protocol while initiating the connection to a remote host. The authorization mechanism is dependent on the command line options used to invoke remshd on the remote host (i.e., -K, -R, -r, or -k). Kerberos authentication and authorization rules are described in the Secure Internet Services man page, sis(5).

    Although Kerberos authentication and authorization may apply, the Kerberos mechanism is not applied when copying files. The files are still transferred in cleartext over the network.

  Options and Arguments
    rcp recognizes the following options and arguments:

        source_file   The name of an existing file or directory on a
        source_dir   local or remote machine that you want copied to
                    the specified destination. Source file and
                    directory names are constructed as follows:

                            user_name@hostname:pathname/filename

                or

> user_name@hostname:pathname/dirname

> Component parts of file and directory names are
> described below. If multiple existing files
> and/or directory subtrees are specified
> (source_file1, source_file2, ..., etc.), the
> destination must be a directory. Shell file name
> expansion is allowed on both local and remote
> systems. Multiple files and directory subtrees
> can be copied from one or more systems to a single
> destination directory with a single command.

dest_file
> The name of the destination file. If host name
> and path name are not specified, the existing file
> is copied into a file named dest_file in the
> current directory on the local system. If
> dest_file already exists and is writable, the
> existing file is overwritten. Destination file
> names are constructed the same way as source files
> except that file name expansion characters cannot
> be used.

dest_dir
> The name of the destination directory. If host
> name and path name are not specified, the existing
> file is copied into a directory named dest_dir in
> the current directory on the local system. If
> dest_dir already exists in the specified directory
> path (or current directory if not specified), a
> new directory named dest_dir is created underneath
> the existing directory named dest_dir.
> Destination directory names are constructed the
> same way as source directory tree names except
> that file name expansion characters cannot be
> used.

file_or_dir
> If a combination of files and directories are
> specified for copying (either explicitly or by
> file name expansion), only files are copied unless
> the -r option is specified. If the -r option is
> present, all files and directory subtrees whose
> names match the specified file_or_dir name are
> copied.

-k realm
> Obtain tickets from the remote host in the
> specified realm instead of the remote host's
> default realm as specified in the configuration
> file krb.realms.

-P
> Disable Kerberos authentication. Only applicable
> in a secure environment based on Kerberos V5. If
> the remote host has been configured to prevent
> non-secure access, using this option would result
> in the generic error,

> rcmd: connect: <hostname>: Connection refused

> See DIAGNOSTICS in remshd(1M) for more details.

-p
> Preserve (duplicate) modification times and modes
> (permissions) of source files, ignoring the
> current setting of the umask file creation mode
> mask. If this option is specified, rcp preserves
> the sticky bit only if the target user is
> superuser.

> If the -p option is not specified, rcp preserves

the mode and owner of dest_file if it already
exists; otherwise rcp uses the mode of the source
file modified by the umask on the destination
host. Modification and access times of the
destination file are set to the time when the copy
was made.

-r   Recursively copy directory subtrees rooted at the
                        source directory name. If any directory subtrees
                        are to be copied, rcp recursively copies each
                        subtree rooted at the specified source directory
                        name to directory dest_dir. If source_dir is
                        being copied to an existing directory of the same
                        name, rcp creates a new directory source_dir
                        within dest_dir and copies the subtree rooted at
                        source_dir to dest_dir/source_dir. If dest_dir
                        does not exist, rcp creates it and copies the
                        subtree rooted at source_dir to dest_dir.

Constructing File and Directory Names
  As indicated above, file and directory names contain one, two, or four
  component parts:

        user_name   Login name to be used for accessing directories and
                        files on remote system.

        hostname   Hostname of remote system where directories and
                        files are located.

        pathname   Absolute directory path name or directory path name
                        relative to the login directory of user user_name.

        filename   Actual name of source or destination file. File
                        name expansion is allowed on source file names.

        dirname   Actual name of source or destination directory
                        subtree. File name expansion is allowed on source
                        directory names.

Each file or directory argument is either a remote file name of the
form hostname:path, or a local file name (with a slash (/) before any
colon (:)). hostname can be either an official host name or an alias
(see hosts(4)). If hostname is of the form ruser@rhost, ruser is used
on the remote host instead of the current user name. An unspecified
path (that is, hostname:) refers to the remote user's login directory.
If path does not begin with /, it is interpreted relative to the
remote user's login directory on hostname. Shell metacharacters in
remote paths can be quoted with backslash (\), single quotes (''), or
double quotes (""), so that they will be interpreted remotely.

rcp does not prompt for passwords. In a non-secure or traditional
environment, user authorization is checked by determining if the
current local user name or any user name specified via ruser exists on
rhost. In a Kerberos V5 Network Authentication or secure environment,
the authorization method is dependent upon the command line options
for remshd (see remshd(1M) for details). In either case, remote
command execution via remsh(1) and rcmd(3) must be allowed and
remshd(1M) must be executable on the remote host.

Third-party transfers in the form:

        rcp ruser1@rhost1:path1 ruser2@rhost2:path2

are performed as:

```
remsh rhost1 -l ruser1 rcp path1 ruser2@rhost2:path2
```

Therefore, for a such a transfer to succeed, ruser2 on rhost2 must allow access by ruser1 from rhost1 (see hosts.equiv(4)).

WARNINGS

The rcp routine is confused by any output generated by commands in a .cshrc file on the remote host (see csh(1)).

Copying a file onto itself, for example:

```
rcp path `hostname`:path
```

may produce inconsistent results. The current HP-UX version of rcp simply copies the file over itself. However, some implementations of rcp, including some earlier HP-UX implementations, corrupt the file. In addition, the same file may be referred to in multiple ways, for example, via hard links, symbolic links, or NFS. It is not guaranteed that rcp will correctly copy a file over itself in all cases.

Implementations of rcp based on the 4.2BSD version (including the implementations of rcp prior to HP-UX 7.0) require that remote users be specified as rhost.ruser. If the first remote host specified in a third party transfer (rhost1 in the example below) uses this older syntax, the command must have the form:

```
rcp ruser1@rhost1:path1 rhost2.ruser2:path2
```

since the target is interpreted by rhost1. A common problem that is encountered is when two remote files are to be copied to a remote target that specifies a remote user. If the two remote source systems, rhost1 and rhost2, each expect a different form for the remote target, the command:

```
rcp rhost1:path1 rhost2:path2 rhost3.ruser3:path3
```

will certainly fail on one of the source systems. Perform such a transfer using two separate commands.

AUTHOR

rcp was developed by the University of California, Berkeley.

SEE ALSO

cp(1), ftp(1), remsh(1), remshd(1M), rcmd(3), hosts(4), hosts.equiv(4), sis(5).

ftp chapter in Using Internet Services.

remsh

remsh - Connect to a remote host and execute a command.

remsh(1)   remsh(1)

NAME
     remsh - execute from a remote shell

SYNOPSIS

     remsh host [-l username] [-n] command
     host [-l username] [-n] command

     rexec host [-l username] [-n] command

DESCRIPTION
     remsh connects to the specified host and executes the specified
     command. The host name can be either the official name or an alias as
     understood by gethostbyname() (see gethostent(3N) and hosts(4)).
     remsh copies its standard input (stdin) to the remote command, and the
     standard output of the remote command to its standard output (stdout),
     and the standard error of the remote command to its standard error
     (stderr). Hangup, interrupt, quit, terminate, and broken pipe signals
     are propagated to the remote command. remsh exits when the sockets
     associated with stdout and stderr of the remote command are closed.
     This means that remsh normally terminates when the remote command does
     (see remshd(1M)).

     By default, remsh uses the following path when executing the specified
     command:

          /usr/bin:/usr/ccs/bin:/usr/bin/X11:

     remsh uses the default remote login shell with the -c option to
     execute the remote command. If the default remote shell is csh, csh
     sources the remote .cshrc file before the command. remsh cannot be
     used to run commands that require a terminal interface (such as vi) or
     commands that read their standard error (such as more). In such
     cases, use rlogin or telnet instead (see rlogin(1) and telnet(1)).

     The remote account name used is the same as your local account name,
     unless you specify a different remote name with the -l option. This
     remote account name must be equivalent to the originating account; no
     provision is made for specifying a password with a command. For more
     details about equivalent hosts and how to specify them, see
     hosts.equiv(4). The files inspected by remshd on the remote host are
     /etc/hosts.equiv and $HOME/.rhosts (see remshd(1M)).

     If command, is not specified, instead of executing a single command,
     you will be logged in on the remote host using rlogin (see rlogin(1)).
     Any rlogin options typed in on the command line are transmitted to
     rlogin. If command is specified, options specific to rlogin are
     ignored by remsh.

     By default, remsh reads its standard input and sends it to the remote
     command because remsh has no way to determine whether the remote
     command requires input. The -n option redirects standard input to

remsh from /dev/null. This is useful when running a shell script
containing a remsh command, since otherwise remsh may use input not
intended for it. The -n option is also useful when running remsh in
the background from a job control shell, /usr/bin/csh or /usr/bin/ksh.
Otherwise, remsh stops and waits for input from the terminal keyboard
for the remote command. /usr/bin/sh automatically redirects its input
from /dev/null when jobs are run in the background.

Host names for remote hosts can also be commands (linked to remsh) in
the directory /usr/hosts. If this directory is specified in the $PATH
environment variable, you can omit remsh. For example, if remotehost
is the name of a remote host, /usr/hosts/remotehost is linked to
remsh, and if /usr/hosts is in your search path, the command

    remotehost command

executes command on remotehost, and the command

    remotehost

is equivalent to

    rlogin remotehost

The rexec command, a link to remsh, works the same as remsh except
that it uses the rexec() library routine and rexecd for command
execution (see rexec(3N) and rexecd(1M)). rexec prompts for a
password before executing the command instead of using hosts.equiv for
authentication. It should be used in instances where a password to a
remote account is known but there are insufficient permissions for
remsh.

EXAMPLES
Shell metacharacters that are not quoted are interpreted on the local
host; quoted metacharacters are interpreted on the remote host. Thus
the command line:

    remsh otherhost cat remotefile >> localfile

appends the remote file remotefile to the local file localfile, while
the command line

    remsh otherhost cat remotefile ">>" otherremotefile

appends remotefile to the remote file otherremotefile.

If the remote shell is /usr/bin/sh, the following command line sets up
the environment for the remote command before executing the remote
command:

    remsh otherhost . .profile 2>&- \; command

The 2>&- throws away error messages generated by executing .profile
when stdin and stdout are not a terminal.

The following command line runs remsh in the background on the local
system, and the output of the remote command comes to your terminal
asynchronously:

    remsh otherhost -n command &

The background remsh completes when the remote command does.

The following command line causes remsh to return immediately without
waiting for the remote command to complete:

```
              remsh otherhost -n "command 1>&- 2>&- &"
```

(See remshd(1M) and sh(1)). If your login shell on the remote system
is csh, use the following form instead:

```
              remsh otherhost -n "sh -c \"command 1>&- 2>&- &\""
```

RETURN VALUE

If remsh fails to set up the secondary socket connection, it returns
2. If it fails in some other way, it returns 1. If it fully succeeds
in setting up a connection with remshd, it returns 0 once the remote
command has completed. Note that the return value of remsh bears no
relation to the return value of the remote command.

DIAGNOSTICS

Besides the errors listed below, errors can also be generated by the
library functions rcmd() and rresvport() which are used by remsh (see
rcmd(3N)). Those errors are preceded by the name of the library
function that generated them. remsh can produce the following
diagnostic messages:

rlogin: ...
    Error in executing rlogin (rlogin is executed when the user
    does not specify any commands to be executed). This is
    followed by the error message specifying why the execution
    failed.

shell/tcp: Unknown service
    The ``shell'' service specification is not present in the
    /etc/services file.

Can't establish stderr
    remsh cannot establish secondary socket connection for
    stderr.

<system call>: ...
    Error in executing system call. Appended to this error is a
    message specifying the cause of the failure.

There is no entry for you (user ID uid) in /etc/passwd
    Check with the system administrator to see if your entry in
    the password file has been deleted by mistake.

WARNINGS

For security reasons, the /etc/hosts.equiv and .rhosts files should
exist, even if empty, and should be readable and writable only by the
owner. Note also that all information, including any passwords asked
for, is passed unencrypted between the two hosts.

If remsh is run with an interactive command it hangs.

DEPENDENCIES

remsh is the same service as rsh on BSD systems. The name was changed
due to a conflict with the existing System V command rsh (restricted
shell).

AUTHOR

remsh was developed by the University of California, Berkeley.

FILES

/usr/hosts/*   for version of the command invoked only with
                    hostname

SEE ALSO

rlogin(1), remshd(1M), rexecd(1M), gethostent(3N), rcmd(3N),

```
        rexec(3N), hosts.equiv(4), hosts(4).
```

remsh(1)   Secure Internet Services with Kerberos Authentication   remsh(1)

NAME
     remsh - execute from a remote shell

SYNOPSIS

     remsh host [-l username] [-f/F] [-k realm] [-P] [-n] command
     host [-l username] [-f/F] [-k realm] [-P] [-n] command

     rexec host [-l username] [-n] command

DESCRIPTION
     remsh connects to the specified host and executes the specified
     command. The host name can be either the official name or an alias as
     understood by gethostbyname() (see gethostent(3N) and hosts(4)).
     remsh copies its standard input (stdin) to the remote command, and the
     standard output of the remote command to its standard output (stdout),
     and the standard error of the remote command to its standard error
     (stderr). Hangup, interrupt, quit, terminate, and broken pipe signals
     are propagated to the remote command. remsh exits when the sockets
     associated with stdout and stderr of the remote command are closed.
     This means that remsh normally terminates when the remote command does
     (see remshd(1M)).

     By default, remsh uses the following path when executing the specified
     command:

          /usr/bin:/usr/ccs/bin:/usr/bin/X11:

     remsh uses the default remote login shell with the -c option to
     execute the remote command. If the default remote shell is csh, csh
     sources the remote .cshrc file before the command. remsh cannot be
     used to run commands that require a terminal interface (such as vi) or
     commands that read their standard error (such as more). In such
     cases, use rlogin or telnet instead (see rlogin(1) and telnet(1)).

     The remote account name used is the same as your local account name,
     unless you specify a different remote name with the -l option. In
     addition, the remote host account name must also conform to other
     rules which differ depending upon whether the remote host is operating
     in a Kerberos V5 Network Authentication, i.e., secure environment or
     not. In a non-secure, or traditional environment, the remote account
     name must be equivalent to the originating account; no provision is
     made for specifying a password with a command. For more details about
     equivalent hosts and how to specify them, see hosts.equiv(4). The
     files inspected by remshd on the remote host are /etc/hosts.equiv and
     $HOME/.rhosts (see remshd(1M)).

     In a Kerberos V5 Network Authentication environment, the local host
     must be successfully authenticated before the remote account name is
     checked for proper authorization. The authorization mechanism is
     dependent on the command line options used to invoke remshd on the
     remote host (i.e., -K, -R, -r, or -k). For further information on
     Kerberos authentication and authorization see the Secure Internet
     Services man page, sis(5) and remshd(1M).

     Although Kerberos authentication and authorization may apply, the
     Kerberos mechanism is not applied to the command or to its response.
     All information transferred between the local and remote host is still
     sent in cleartext over the network.

     In a secure or Kerberos V5-based environment, the following command
     line options are available:

-f   Forward the ticket granting ticket (TGT) to the remote system. The TGT is not forwardable from there.

-F   Forward the TGT to the remote system and have it forwardable from there to another remote system. -f and -F are mutually exclusive.

-k realm   Obtain tickets from the remote host in the specified realm instead of the remote host's default realm as specified in the configuration file krb.realms.

-P   Disable Kerberos authentication.

If a command is not specified, instead of executing a single command, you will be logged in on the remote host using rlogin (see rlogin(1)). Any rlogin options typed in on the command line are transmitted to rlogin. If no command and the option -P is specified, rlogin will be invoked with -P to indicate that Kerberos authentication (or secure access) is not required. This will mean that if a password is requested, the password will be sent in cleartext. If a command is specified, options specific to rlogin are ignored by remsh.

If a command and the option -n are specified, then standard input is redirected to remsh by /dev/null. If -n is not specified (the default case), remsh reads its standard input and sends the input to the remote command. This is because remsh has no way to determine whether the remote command requires input. This option is useful when running a shell script containing a remsh command, since otherwise remsh may use input not intended for it. The -n option is also useful when running remsh in the background from a job control shell, /usr/bin/csh or /usr/bin/ksh. Otherwise, remsh stops and waits for input from the terminal keyboard for the remote command. /usr/bin/sh automatically redirects its input from /dev/null when jobs are run in the background.

Host names for remote hosts can also be commands (linked to remsh) in the directory /usr/hosts. If this directory is specified in the $PATH environment variable, you can omit remsh. For example, if remotehost is the name of a remote host, /usr/hosts/remotehost is linked to remsh, and if /usr/hosts is in your search path, the command

    remotehost command

executes command on remotehost, and the command

    remotehost

is equivalent to

    rlogin remotehost

The rexec command, a link to remsh, works the same as remsh except that it uses the rexec() library routine and rexecd for command execution (see rexec(3N) and rexecd(1M)) and does not support Kerberos authentication. rexec prompts for a password before executing the command instead of using hosts.equiv for authentication. It should be used in instances where a password to a remote account is known but there are insufficient permissions for remsh.

EXAMPLES

Shell metacharacters that are not quoted are interpreted on the local host; quoted metacharacters are interpreted on the remote host. Thus the command line:

    remsh otherhost cat remotefile >> localfile

appends the remote file remotefile to the local file localfile, while
the command line

        remsh otherhost cat remotefile ">>" otherremotefile

appends remotefile to the remote file otherremotefile.

If the remote shell is /usr/bin/sh, the following command line sets up
the environment for the remote command before executing the remote
command:

        remsh otherhost . .profile 2>&- \; command

The 2>&- throws away error messages generated by executing .profile
when stdin and stdout are not a terminal.

The following command line runs remsh in the background on the local
system, and the output of the remote command comes to your terminal
asynchronously:

        remsh otherhost -n command &

The background remsh completes when the remote command does.

The following command line causes remsh to return immediately without
waiting for the remote command to complete:

        remsh otherhost -n "command 1>&- 2>&- &"

(See remshd(1M) and sh(1)). If your login shell on the remote system
is csh, use the following form instead:

        remsh otherhost -n "sh -c \"command 1>&- 2>&- &\""

RETURN VALUE
        If remsh fails to set up the secondary socket connection, it returns
        2. If it fails in some other way, it returns 1. If it fully succeeds
        in setting up a connection with remshd, it returns 0 once the remote
        command has completed. Note that the return value of remsh bears no
        relation to the return value of the remote command.

DIAGNOSTICS
        Besides the errors listed below, errors can also be generated by the
        library functions rcmd() and rresvport() which are used by remsh (see
        rcmd(3N)). Those errors are preceded by the name of the library
        function that generated them. remsh can produce the following
        diagnostic messages:

            rlogin: ...
                    Error in executing rlogin (rlogin is executed when the user
                    does not specify any commands to be executed). This is
                    followed by the error message specifying why the execution
                    failed.

            shell/tcp: Unknown service
                    The ``shell'' service specification is not present in the
                    /etc/services file.

            Can't establish stderr
                    remsh cannot establish secondary socket connection for
                    stderr.

            <system call>: ...
                    Error in executing system call. Appended to this error is a

message specifying the cause of the failure.

There is no entry for you (user ID uid) in /etc/passwd
    Check with the system administrator to see if your entry in
    the password file has been deleted by mistake.

rcmd: connect: <hostname>: Connection refused
    One cause for display of this generic error message could be
    due to the absence of an entry for shell in /etc/inetd.conf
    on the remote system. This entry may have been removed or
    commented out to prevent non-secure access.

Kerberos-specific errors are listed in sis(5).

WARNINGS
For security reasons, the /etc/hosts.equiv and .rhosts files should
exist, even if empty, and should be readable and writable only by the
owner.

If remsh is run with an interactive command it hangs.

DEPENDENCIES
remsh is the same service as rsh on BSD systems. The name was changed
due to a conflict with the existing System V command rsh (restricted
shell).

AUTHOR
remsh was developed by the University of California, Berkeley.

FILES
/usr/hosts/*   for version of the command invoked only with
                     hostname

SEE ALSO
rlogin(1), remshd(1M), rexecd(1M), gethostent(3N), rcmd(3N),
rexec(3N), hosts.equiv(4), hosts(4), sis(5).

rlogin

man page

rlogin - 12

rlogin - Log in to a remote host.

NAME
      rlogin - remote login

SYNOPSIS

      rlogin rhost [-7] [-8] [-ee] [-l username]

      rhost [-7] [-8] [-ee] [-l username]

DESCRIPTION
      The rlogin command connects your terminal on the local host to the
      remote host (rhost). rlogin acts as a virtual terminal to the remote
      system. The host name rhost can be either the official name or an
      alias as listed in the file /etc/hosts (see hosts(4)).

      In a manner similar to the remsh command (see remsh(1)), rlogin allows
      a user to log in on an equivalent remote host, rhost, bypassing the
      normal login/password sequence. For more information about equivalent
      hosts and how to specify them in the files /etc/hosts.equiv and
      .rhosts, see hosts.equiv(4). The searching of the files
      /etc/hosts.equiv and .rhosts occurs on the remote host, and the
      .rhosts file must be owned by the remote user account or by a remote
      superuser.

      If the originating user account is not equivalent to the remote user
      account, the originating user is prompted for the password of the
      remote account. If this fails, a login name and password are prompted
      for, as when login is used (see login(1)).

      The terminal type specified by the current TERM environment variable
      is propagated across the network and used to set the initial value of
      your TERM environment variable on the remote host. Your terminal baud
      rate is also propagated to the remote host, and is required by some
      systems to set up the pseudo-terminal used by rlogind (see
      rlogind(1M)).

      All echoing takes place at the remote site, so that (except for
      delays) the remote login is transparent.

      If at any time rlogin is unable to read from or write to the socket
      connection on the remote host, the message Connection closed is
      printed on standard error and rlogin exits.

   Options
     rlogin recognizes the following options. Note that the options follow
     the rhost argument.

            -7   Set the character size to seven bits. The eighth
                                    bit of each byte sent is set to zero (space
                                    parity).

            -8   Use an eight-bit data path. This is the default
                                    HP-UX behavior.

To use eight-bit characters, the terminal must be configured to generate either eight-bit characters with no parity, or seven bit characters with space parity. The HP-UX implementation of rlogind (see rlogind(1M)) interprets seven bit characters with even, odd, or mark parity as eight-bit non-USASCII characters. You may also need to reconfigure the remote host appropriately (see stty(1) and tty(7)). Some remote hosts may not provide the necessary support for eight-bit characters. In this case, or if it is not possible to disable parity generation by the local terminal, use the -7 option.

-ee   Set the escape character to e. There is no space separating the option letter and the argument character. To start a line with the escape character, two of the escape characters must be entered. The default escape character is tilde (~). Some characters may conflict with your terminal configuration, such as ^S, ^Q, or backspace. Using one of these as the escape character may not be possible or may cause problems communicating with the remote host (see stty(1) and tty(7)).

-l username   Set the user login name on the remote host to username. The default name is the current account name of the user invoking rlogin.

Escape Sequences
   rlogin can be controlled with two-character escape sequences, in the form ex, where e is the escape character and x is a code character described below. Escape sequences are recognized only at the beginning of a line of input. The default escape character is tilde (~). It can be changed with the -e option.

   The following escape sequences are recognized:

        ey   If y is NOT a code character described below, pass the escape character and y as characters to the remote host.

        ee   Pass the escape character as a character to the remote host.

        e.   Disconnect from the remote host.

        e!   Escape to a subshell on the local host. Use exit to return to the remote host.

        If rlogin is run from a shell that supports job control (see csh(1), ksh(1), and sh-posix(1)), escape sequences can be used to suspend rlogin. The following escape sequences assume that ^Z and ^Y are set as the user's susp and dsusp characters, respectively (see stty(1) and termio(7)).

        e^Z   Suspend the rlogin session and return the user to the shell that invoked rlogin. The rlogin job can be resumed with the fg command (see csh(1), ksh(1), and sh-posix(1)). e^Z suspends both rlogin processes: the one transmitting user input to the remote login, and the one displaying output from the remote login.

        e^Y   Suspend the rlogin session and return the user to the shell that invoked rlogin. The rlogin job can be resumed with the fg command (see csh(1), ksh(1), and sh-posix(1)). e^Y suspends only the input process; output from the remote login continues to be displayed.

If you "daisy-chain" remote logins (for example, you rlogin from host A to host B and then rlogin from host B to host C) without setting unique escape characters, you can repeat the escape character until it reaches your chosen destination. For example, the first escape character, e, is seen as an escape character on host A; the second e is passed as a normal character by host A and seen as an escape character on host B; a third e is passed as a normal character by hosts A and B and accepted as a normal character by host C.

Remote Host Name As Command
The system administrator can arrange for more convenient access to a remote host (rhost) by linking remsh to /usr/hosts/rhost, allowing use of the remote host name (rhost) as a command (see remsh(1)). For example, if remotehost is the name of a remote host and /usr/hosts/remotehost is linked to remsh, and if /usr/hosts is in your search path, the command:

    remotehost

is equivalent to:

    rlogin remotehost

RETURN VALUES
rlogin sends an error message to standard error and returns a nonzero value if an error occurs before the connection to the remote host is completed. Otherwise, it returns a zero.

DIAGNOSTICS
Diagnostics can occur from both the local and remote hosts. Those that occur on the local host before the connection is completely established are written to standard error. Once the connection is established, any error messages from the remote host are written to standard output, like any other data.

login/tcp: Unknown service

    rlogin was unable to find the login service listed in the /etc/services database file.

There is no entry for you (user ID username) in /etc/passwd

    rlogin was unable to find your user ID in the password file.

    Next Step: Contact your system administrator.

system call:...
An error occurred when rlogin attempted the indicated system call. See the appropriate manual entry for information about the error.

EXAMPLES
Log in as the same user on the remote host remote:

    rlogin remote

Set the escape character to a !, use a seven-bit data connection, and attempt a login as user guest on host remhost:

    rlogin remhost -e! -7 -l guest

Assuming that your system administrator has set up the links in
/usr/hosts, the following is equivalent to the previous command:

    remhost -e! -7 -l guest

WARNINGS
    For security purposes, the /etc/hosts.equiv and .rhosts files should
    exist, even if they are empty. These files should be readable and
    writable only by the owner. See host.equiv(4) for more information.

    Note also that all information, including any passwords asked for, is
    passed unencrypted between the two hosts.

    rlogin is unable to transmit the Break key as an interrupt signal to
    the remote system, regardless of whether the user has set stty brkint
    on the local system. The key assigned to SIGINT with the command stty
    intr c should be used instead (see stty(1)).

AUTHOR
    rlogin was developed by the University of California, Berkeley.

FILES
    $HOME/.rhosts   User's private equivalence list
    /etc/hosts.equiv   List of equivalent hosts
    /usr/hosts/*   For rhost version of the command

SEE ALSO
    csh(1), ksh(1), login(1), remsh(1), sh(1), sh-bourne(1), sh-posix(1),
    stty(1), telnet(1), rlogind(1M), hosts(4), hosts.equiv(4),
    inetd.conf(4), services(4), termio(7), tty(7).

rlogin(1)   Secure Internet Services with Kerberos Authentication   rlogin(1)

NAME
    rlogin - remote login

SYNOPSIS

    rlogin rhost [-7] [-8] [-ee] [-f/F] [-k realm] [-l username] [-P]

    rhost [-7] [-8] [-ee] [-f/F] [-k realm] [-l username] [-P]

DESCRIPTION
    The rlogin command connects your terminal on the local host to the
    remote host (rhost). rlogin acts as a virtual terminal to the remote
    system. The host name rhost can be either the official name or an
    alias as listed in the file /etc/hosts (see hosts(4)).

    The terminal type specified by the current TERM environment variable
    is propagated across the network and used to set the initial value of
    your TERM environment variable on the remote host. Your terminal baud
    rate is also propagated to the remote host, and is required by some
    systems to set up the pseudo-terminal used by rlogind (see
    rlogind(1M)).

    All echoing takes place at the remote site, so that (except for
    delays) the remote login is transparent.

    If at any time rlogin is unable to read from or write to the socket
    connection on the remote host, the message Connection closed is
    printed on standard error and rlogin exits.

    In a Kerberos V5 Network Authentication environment, rlogin uses the
    Kerberos V5 protocol to authenticate the connection to a remote host.
    If the authentication is successful, user authorization will be
    performed according to the command line options selected for rlogind

(i.e., -K, -R, -r, or -k). A password will not be required, so a password prompt will not be seen and a password will not be sent over the network where it can be observed. For further information on Kerberos authentication and authorization see the Secure Internet Services man page, sis(5) and rlogind(1M).

Although Kerberos authentication and authorization may apply, the Kerberos mechanism is not applied to the login session. All information transferred between your host and the remote host is sent in cleartext over the network.

Options
   rlogin recognizes the following options. Note that the options follow the rhost argument.

-7	Set the character size to seven bits. The eighth bit of each byte sent is set to zero (space parity).
-8	Use an eight-bit data path. This is the default HP-UX behavior.
	To use eight-bit characters, the terminal must be configured to generate either eight-bit characters with no parity, or seven bit characters with space parity. The HP-UX implementation of rlogind (see rlogind(1M)) interprets seven bit characters with even, odd, or mark parity as eight-bit non-USASCII characters. You may also need to reconfigure the remote host appropriately (see stty(1) and tty(7)). Some remote hosts may not provide the necessary support for eight-bit characters. In this case, or if it is not possible to disable parity generation by the local terminal, use the -7 option.
-ee	Set the escape character to e. There is no space separating the option letter and the argument character. To start a line with the escape character, two of the escape characters must be entered. The default escape character is tilde (~). Some characters may conflict with your terminal configuration, such as ^S, ^Q, or backspace. Using one of these as the escape character may not be possible or may cause problems communicating with the remote host (see stty(1) and tty(7)).
-f	Forward the ticket granting ticket (TGT) to the remote system. The TGT is not forwardable from there.
-F	Forward the TGT to the remote system and have it forwardable from there to another remote system. -f and -F are mutually exclusive.
-k realm	Obtain tickets from the remote host in the specified realm instead of the remote host's default realm as specified in the configuration file krb.realms.
-l username	Set the user login name on the remote host to username. The default name is the current account name of the user invoking rlogin.
-P	Disable Kerberos authentication. Only applicable

in a secure environment based on Kerberos V5.
When this option is specified, a password is
required and the password is sent across the
network in cleartext. To bypass the normal
login/password sequence, you can login to a remote
host using an equivalent account in a manner
similar to remsh. See hosts.equiv(4) for details.

rlogin can be controlled with two-character escape sequences, in the
form ex, where e is the escape character and x is a code character
described below. Escape sequences are recognized only at the
beginning of a line of input. The default escape character is tilde
(~). It can be changed with the -e option.

The following escape sequences are recognized:

ey If y is NOT a code character described below, pass the
escape character and y as characters to the remote host.

ee Pass the escape character as a character to the remote host.

e. Disconnect from the remote host.

e! Escape to a subshell on the local host. Use exit to return
to the remote host.

If rlogin is run from a shell that supports job control (see
csh(1), ksh(1), and sh-posix(1)), escape sequences can be used to
suspend rlogin. The following escape sequences assume that ^Z
and ^Y are set as the user's susp and dsusp characters,
respectively (see stty(1) and termio(7)).

e^Z Suspend the rlogin session and return the user to the shell
that invoked rlogin. The rlogin job can be resumed with the
fg command (see csh(1), ksh(1), and sh-posix(1)). e^Z
suspends both rlogin processes: the one transmitting user
input to the remote login, and the one displaying output
from the remote login.

e^Y Suspend the rlogin session and return the user to the shell
that invoked rlogin. The rlogin job can be resumed with the
fg command (see csh(1), ksh(1), and sh-posix(1)). e^Y
suspends only the input process; output from the remote
login continues to be displayed.

If you "daisy-chain" remote logins (for example, you rlogin from host
A to host B and then rlogin from host B to host C) without setting
unique escape characters, you can repeat the escape character until it
reaches your chosen destination. For example, the first escape
character, e, is seen as an escape character on host A; the second e
is passed as a normal character by host A and seen as an escape
character on host B; a third e is passed as a normal character by
hosts A and B and accepted as a normal character by host C.

Remote Host Name As Command
The system administrator can arrange for more convenient access to a
remote host (rhost) by linking remsh to /usr/hosts/rhost, allowing use
of the remote host name (rhost) as a command (see remsh(1)). For
example, if remotehost is the name of a remote host and
/usr/hosts/remotehost is linked to remsh, and if /usr/hosts is in your
search path, the command:

remotehost

is equivalent to:

        rlogin remotehost

RETURN VALUES
    rlogin sends an error message to standard error and returns a nonzero
    value if an error occurs before the connection to the remote host is
    completed. Otherwise, it returns a zero.

DIAGNOSTICS
    Diagnostics can occur from both the local and remote hosts. Those
    that occur on the local host before the connection is completely
    established are written to standard error. Once the connection is
    established, any error messages from the remote host are written to
    standard output, like any other data.

    login/tcp: Unknown service

        rlogin was unable to find the login service listed in the
        /etc/services database file.

    There is no entry for you (user ID username) in /etc/passwd

        rlogin was unable to find your user ID in the password file.

        Next Step: Contact your system administrator.

    system call:...
        An error occurred when rlogin attempted the indicated system
        call. See the appropriate manual entry for information about the
        error.

    rcmd: connect <hostname>: Connection refused.
        One cause for display of this generic error message could be due
        to the absence of an entry for login in /etc/inetd.conf on the
        remote system. This entry may have been removed or commented out
        to prevent non-secure access.

    Kerberos-specific errors are listed in sis(5).

EXAMPLES
    Log in as the same user on the remote host remote:

        rlogin remote

    Set the escape character to a !, use a seven-bit data connection, and
    attempt a login as user guest on host remhost:

        rlogin remhost -e! -7 -l guest

    Assuming that your system administrator has set up the links in
    /usr/hosts, the following is equivalent to the previous command:

        remhost -e! -7 -l guest

WARNINGS
    For security purposes, the /etc/hosts.equiv and .rhosts files should
    exist, even if they are empty. These files should be readable and
    writable only by the owner. See host.equiv(4) for more information.

    Note also that all information, including passwords, is passed
    unencrypted between the two hosts. In a Kerberos V5 Network
    Authentication environment, a password is not transmitted across the
    network, so it will be protected.

rlogin is unable to transmit the Break key as an interrupt signal to
the remote system, regardless of whether the user has set stty brkint
on the local system. The key assigned to SIGINT with the command stty
intr c should be used instead (see stty(1)).

AUTHOR
    rlogin was developed by the University of California, Berkeley.

FILES
    $HOME/.rhosts   User's private equivalence list
    /etc/hosts.equiv   List of equivalent hosts
    /usr/hosts/*   For rhost version of the command

SEE ALSO
    csh(1), ksh(1), login(1), remsh(1), sh(1), sh-bourne(1), sh-posix(1),
    stty(1), telnet(1), rlogind(1M), hosts(4), hosts.equiv(4),
    inetd.conf(4), services(4), termio(7), tty(7), sis(5).

route

man page

route - 12

route - Manipulate network routing tables.

```
route(1M)                                                            route(1M)

NAME
     route - manually manipulate the routing tables

SYNOPSIS

     /usr/sbin/route [-f] [-n] [-p pmtu] add [net|host] destination
          [netmask mask] gateway [count]

     /usr/sbin/route [-f] [-n] delete [net|host] destination
          [netmask mask] gateway [count]

     /usr/sbin/route -f [-n]

DESCRIPTION
     The route command manipulates the network routing tables manually.
     You must have appropriate privileges.

   Subcommands
     The following subcommands are supported.

         add                Add the specified host or network route to the
                            network routing table.  If the route already
                            exists, a message is printed and nothing changes.


         delete             Delete the specified host or network route from
                            the network routing table.

   Options and Arguments
     route recognizes the following options and arguments.

         -f                 Delete all route table entries that specify a
                            remote host for a gateway.  If this is used with
                            one of the subcommands, the entries are deleted
                            before the subcommand is processed.

         -n                 Print any host and network addresses in Internet
                            dot notation, except for the default network
                            address, which is printed as default.

         -p pmtu            Specifies a path maximum transmission unit (MTU)
                            value for a static host route.  The minimum value
                            allowed is 68 bytes; the maximum is the MTU of the
                            outgoing interface for this route.  This option
                            only applies to adding a host route.  In all other
                            cases, this option is ignored and has no effect on
                            a system.

                            You can also disable the Path MTU Discovery for a
                            host route by specifying pmtu as zero.
```

net or host	The type of destination address. If this argument is omitted, routes to a particular host are distinguished from those to a network by interpreting the Internet address associated with destination. If the destination has a local address part of INADDR_ANY(0), the route is assumed to be to a network; otherwise, it is treated as a route to a host.
destination	The destination host system where the packets will be routed. destination can be one of the following:

- A host name (the official name or an alias, see gethostbyname(3N)).
- A network name (the official name or an alias, see getnetbyname(3N)).
- An Internet address in dot notation (see inet(3N)).
- The keyword default, which signifies the wildcard gateway route (see routing(7)).

netmask mask	The mask that will be bit-wise ANDed with destination to yield a net address where the packets will be routed. mask can be specified as a single hexadecimal number with a leading 0x, with a dot-notation Internet address, or with a pseudo-network name listed in the network table (see networks(4)). The length of the mask, which is the number of contiguous 1's starting from the leftmost bit position of the 32-bit field, can be shorter than the default network mask for the destination address. (see routing (7)). If the netmask option is not given, mask for the route will be derived from the netmasks associated with the local interfaces. (see ifconfig (1)). mask will be defaulted to the longest netmask of those local interfaces that have the same network address. If there is not any local interface that has the same network address, then mask will be defaulted to the default network mask of destination.
gateway	The gateway through which the destination is reached. gateway can be one of the following:

- A host name (the official name or an alias, see gethostbyname(3N)).
- An Internet address in dot notation (see inet(3N)).

count	An integer that indicates whether the gateway is a remote host or the local host. If the route leads to a destination through a remote gateway, count should be a number greater than 0. If the route leads to destination and the gateway is the local host, count should be 0. The default for count is zero. The result is not defined if count is negative.

Operation

All symbolic names specified for a destination or gateway are looked up first as a host name using gethostbyname(); if the host name is not

found, the destination is searched for as a network name using
getnetbyname(). destination and gateway can be in dot notation (see
inet(3N)).

If the -n option is not specified, any host and network addresses are
displayed symbolically according to the name returned by
gethostbyaddr() and getnetbyaddr(), respectively, except for the
default network address (printed as default) and addresses that have
unknown names. Addresses with unknown names are printed in Internet
dot notation (see inet(3N)).

If the -n option is specified, any host and network addresses are
printed in Internet dot notation except for the default network
address which is printed as default.

If the -f option is specified, route deletes all route table entries
that specify a remote host for a gateway. If it is used with one of
the subcommands described above, the entries are deleted before the
subcommand is processed.

Path MTU Discovery is a technique for discovering the maximum size of
an IP datagram that can be sent on an internet path without causing
datagram fragmentation in the intermediate routers. In essence, a
source host that utilizes this technique initially sends out datagrams
up to the the size of the outgoing interface. The Don't Fragment (DF)
bit in the IP datagram header is set. As an intermediate router that
supports Path MTU Discovery receives a datagram that is too large to
be forwarded in one piece to the next-hop router and the DF bit is
set, the router will discard the datagram and send an ICMP Destination
Unreachable message with a code meaning "fragmentation needed and DF
set". The ICMP message will also contain the MTU of the next-hop
router. When the source host receives the ICMP message, it reduces
the path MTU of the route to the MTU in the ICMP message. With this
technique, the host route in the source host for this path will
contain the proper MTU.

By default, Path MTU Discovery is enabled for TCP sockets and disabled
for UDP sockets.

If the -p pmtu option is specified for a host route, the pmtu value is
considered permanent for the host route. Even if the Path MTU
Discovery process discovers a smaller pmtu for this route at a later
time, the pmtu field in the host route will not be updated. A warning
message will be logged with the new pmtu value.

The -p pmtu option is useful only if you knows the network environment
well enough to enter an appropriate pmtu for a host route. IP will
fragment a datagram to the pmtu specified for the route on the local
host before sending the datagram out to the remote. It will avoid
fragmentation by routers along the path, if the pmtu specified in the
route command is correct.

ping can be used to find the pmtu information for the route to a
remote host. The pmtu information in the routing table can be
displayed with the netstat -r command (see netstat(1)).

Output
  add destination: gateway gateway

        The specified route is being added to the tables.

  delete destination: gateway gateway

        The specified route is being deleted from the tables.

Flags

The values of the count and destination type fields in the route command determine the presence of the G and H flags in the netstat -r display and thus the route type, as shown in the following table.

Count	Destination Type	Flags	Route Type
=0	network	U	Route to a network directly from the local host
>0	network	UG	Route to a network through a remote host gateway
=0	host	UH	Route to a remote host directly from the local host
>0	host	UGH	Route to a remote host through a remote host gateway
=0	default	U	Wildcard route directly from the local host
>0	default	UG	Wildcard route through a remote host gateway

DIAGNOSTICS

The following error diagnostics can be displayed.

add a route that already exists

The specified entry is already in the routing table.

add too many routes

The routing table is full.

delete a route that does not exist

The specified route was not in the routing table.

WARNINGS

Reciprocal route commands must be executed on the local host, the destination host, and all intermediate hosts if routing is to succeed in the cases of virtual circuit connections or bidirectional datagram transfers.

The HP-UX implementation of route does not presently support a change subcommand.

AUTHOR

route was developed by the University of California, Berkeley.

FILES

/etc/networks
/etc/hosts

SEE ALSO

netstat(1), ifconfig(1M), ping(1M), getsockopt(2), recv(2), send(2), gethostbyaddr(3N), gethostbyname(3N), getnetbyaddr(3N), getnetbyname(3N), inet(3N), routing(7).

rpcinfo

man page

rpcinfo - 9

rpcinfo - Report Remote Procedure Call (RPC) information.

```
rpcinfo(1M)                                                           rpcinfo(1M)

NAME
     rpcinfo - report RPC information

SYNOPSIS

     /usr/sbin/rpcinfo -p [host]
     /usr/sbin/rpcinfo [-n portnum] -u host program [version]
     /usr/sbin/rpcinfo [-n portnum] -t host program [version]
     /usr/sbin/rpcinfo -b program version
     /usr/sbin/rpcinfo -d program version

DESCRIPTION
     rpcinfo makes an RPC call to an RPC server and reports what it finds.

   Options
     rpcinfo recognizes the following command-line options and arguments:

            -p host      Probe the portmapper on host and print a list of
                         all registered RPC programs.  If host is not
                         specified, it defaults to the value returned by
                         hostname (see hostname(1)).

            -n portnum   Use portnum as the port number for the -t and -u
                         options instead of the port number given by the
                         portmapper.

            -u           Make an RPC call to procedure 0 of program on the
                         specified host using UDP and report whether a
                         response was received.

            -t           Make an RPC call to procedure 0 of program on the
                         specified host using TCP and report whether a
                         response was received.

            -b           Make an RPC broadcast to procedure 0 of the
                         specified program and version using UDP and report
                         all hosts that respond.

            -d           Delete registration for the RPC service of the
                         specified program and version.  Only users with
                         appropriate privileges can use this option.

            program      Can be either a name or a number.

            version      If specified, rpcinfo attempts to call that
                         version of the specified program.  Otherwise,
                         rpcinfo attempts to find all the registered
                         version numbers for the specified program by
                         calling version 0, then attempts to call each
                         registered version.  (Version 0 is presumed to not
                         exist, but if version 0 does exist, rpcinfo
```

attempts to obtain the version number information
by calling an extremely high version number
instead.) Note that version must be specified when
the -b and -d options are used.

EXAMPLES

Show all of the RPC services registered on the local machine:

        rpcinfo -p

Show all of the RPC services registered on the machine named klaxon:

        rpcinfo -p klaxon

Show all machines on the local net that are running the Network
Information Service (NIS):

        rpcinfo -b ypserv 1 | sort | uniq

where 1 is the current NIS version obtained from the results of the -p
option in the previous example.

Delete the registration for version 1 of the walld service:

        rpcinfo -d walld 1

[Note that walld is the RPC program name for rwalld (see rwalld(1m))].

WARNINGS

In releases prior to Sun UNIX 3.0, the Network File System (NFS) did
not register itself with the portmapper; rpcinfo cannot be used to
make RPC calls to the NFS server on hosts running such releases. Note
that this does not apply to any HP releases of NFS.

AUTHOR

rpcinfo was developed by Sun Microsystems, Inc.

FILES

/etc/rpc   names for RPC program numbers

SEE ALSO

rpc(4), portmap(1M),
Programming and Protocols for NFS Services.

rwho

rwho - Produce a list of users on a remote system.

```
rwho(1)                                                            rwho(1)

NAME
     rwho - show who is logged in on local machines

SYNOPSIS

     rwho [-a]

DESCRIPTION
     rwho produces output similar to the output of the HP-UX who command
     for all machines on the local network that are running the rwho daemon
     (see who(1) and rwhod(1M)).  If rwhod has not received a report from a
     machine for 11 minutes, rwho assumes the machine is down and rwho does
     not report users last known to be logged into that machine.

     rwho's output line has fields for the name of the user, the name of
     the machine, the user's terminal line, the time the user logged in,
     and the amount of time the user has been idle.  Idle time is shown as:

          hours:minutes

     If a user has not typed to the system for a minute or more, rwho
     reports this as idle time.  If a user has not typed to the system for
     an hour or more, the user is omitted from rwho's output unless the -a
     flag is given.

     An example output line from rwho would look similar to:

          joe_user    machine1:tty0p1  Sep 12  13:28   :11

     This output line could be interpreted as joe_user is logged into
     machine1 and his terminal line is tty0p1.  joe_user has been logged on
     since September 12  at 13:28 (1:28 p.m.).  joe_user has not typed
     anything into machine1 for 11 minutes.

WARNINGS
     rwho's output becomes unwieldy when the number of users for each
     machine on the local network running rwhod becomes large.  One line of
     output occurs for each user on each machine on the local network that
     is running rwhod.

AUTHOR
     rwho was developed by the University of California, Berkeley.

FILES
     /var/spool/rwho/whod.*            Information about other machines.

SEE ALSO
     ruptime(1), rusers(1), rwhod(1M).
```

telnet

telnet - User interface for TELNET.

NAME
     telnet - user interface to the TELNET protocol

SYNOPSIS

     telnet [[options]host [port]]

DESCRIPTION
     telnet is used to communicate with another host using the TELNET
     protocol. If telnet is invoked without arguments, it enters command
     mode, indicated by its prompt (telnet>). In this mode, it accepts and
     executes the commands listed below. If telnet is invoked with
     arguments, it performs an open command (see below) with those
     arguments.

     Once a connection has been opened, telnet enters an input mode. The
     input mode will be either ``character at a time'' or ``line by line'',
     depending on what the remote system supports.

     In ``character at a time'' mode, most text typed is immediately sent
     to the remote host for processing.

     In ``line by line'' mode, all text is echoed locally, and (normally)
     only completed lines are sent to the remote host. The ``local echo
     character'' (initially ^E) can be used to turn off and on the local
     echo (this would mostly be used to enter passwords without the
     password being echoed).

     In either mode, if the localchars toggle is TRUE (the default in line
     mode; see below), the user's quit and intr characters are trapped
     locally, and sent as TELNET protocol sequences to the remote side.
     There are options (see toggle autoflush and toggle autosynch below)
     which cause this action to flush subsequent output to the terminal
     (until the remote host acknowledges the TELNET sequence) and flush
     previous terminal input (in the case of quit and intr).

     While connected to a remote host, telnet command mode can be entered
     by typing the telnet ``escape character'' (initially ^]). When in
     command mode, the normal terminal editing conventions are available.

     telnet supports eight-bit characters when communicating with the
     server on the remote host. To use eight-bit characters you may need
     to reconfigure your terminal or the remote host appropriately (see
     stty(1)). Furthermore, you may have to use the binary toggle to
     enable an 8-bit data stream between telnet and the remote host. Note
     that some remote hosts may not provide the necessary support for
     eight-bit characters.

     If, at any time, telnet is unable to read from or write to the server
     over the connection, the message Connection closed by foreign host. is
     printed on standard error. telnet then exits with a value of 1.

telnet supports the TAC User ID (also known as the TAC Access Control
System, or TACACS User ID) option. Enabling the option on a host
server allows the user to telnet into that host without being prompted
for a second login sequence. The TAC User ID option uses the same
security mechanism as rlogin for authorizing acces by remote hosts and
users. The system administrator must enable the (telnetd) option only
on systems which are designated as participating hosts. The system
administrator must also assign to each user of TAC User ID the very
same UID on every system for which he is allowed to use the feature.
(See telnetd(1M) and the System Administration Tasks manual, PN 2355-
90051.)

The following telnet options are available:

-8   Enable cs8 (8 bit transfer) on local tty.

-ec   Set the telnet command mode escape character to be ^c
            instead of its default value of ^].

-l   Disable the TAC User ID option if enabled on the client, to
            cause the user to be prompted for login username and
            password. Omitting the -l option executes the default
            setting.

Commands
  The following commands are available in command mode. You need only
  type enough of each command to uniquely identify it (this is also true
  for arguments to the mode, set, toggle, and display commands).

open host [port]
                    Open a connection to the named host at the indicated
                    port. If no port is specified, telnet attempts to
                    contact a TELNET server at the standard TELNET port.
                    The hostname can be either the official name or an
                    alias as understood by gethostbyname() (see
                    gethostent(3N)), or an Internet address specified in
                    the dot notation as described in hosts(4). If no
                    hostname is given, telnet prompts for one.

close   Close a TELNET session. If the session was started
                    from command mode, telnet returns to command mode;
                    otherwise telnet exits.

quit   Close any open TELNET session and exit telnet. An end
                    of file (in command mode) will also close a session and
                    exit.

z   Suspend telnet. If telnet is run from a shell that
                    supports job control, (such as csh(1) or ksh(1)), the z
                    command suspends the TELNET session and returns the
                    user to the shell that invoked telnet. The job can
                    then be resumed with the fg command (see csh(1) or
                    ksh(1)).

mode mode   Change telnet's user input mode to mode, which can be
                    character (for ``character at a time'' mode) or line
                    (for ``line by line'' mode). The remote host is asked
                    for permission to go into the requested mode. If the
                    remote host is capable of entering that mode, the
                    requested mode is entered. In character mode, telnet
                    sends each character to the remote host as it is typed.
                    In line mode, telnet gathers user input into lines and
                    transmits each line to the remote host when the user
                    types carriage return, linefeed, or EOF (normally ^D;
                    see stty(1)). Note that setting line-mode also sets

local echo. Applications that expect to interpret user input character by character (such as more, csh, ksh, and vi) do not work correctly in line mode.

status Show current status of telnet. telnet reports the current escape character. If telnet is connected, it reports the host to which it is connected and the current mode. If telnet is not connected to a remote host, it reports No connection. Once telnet has been connected, it reports the local flow control toggle value.

display [argument ...]
Displays all or some of the set and toggle values (see below).

? [command] Get help. With no arguments, telnet prints a help summary. If a command is specified, telnet prints the help information available about that command only. Help information is limited to a one-line description of the command.

! [shell_command]
Shell escape. The SHELL environment variable is checked for the name of a shell to use to execute the command. If no shell_command is specified, a shell is started and connected to the user's terminal. If SHELL is undefined, /usr/bin/sh is used.

send arguments Sends one or more special character sequences to the remote host. Each argument can have any of the following values (multiple arguments can be specified with each send command):

escape Sends the current telnet escape character (initially ^]).

synch Sends the TELNET SYNCH sequence. This sequence causes the remote system to discard all previously typed (but not yet read) input. This sequence is sent as TCP urgent data (and may not work to some systems -- if it doesn't work, a lower case ``r'' may be echoed on the terminal).

brk Sends the TELNET BRK (Break) sequence, which may have significance to the remote system.

ip Sends the TELNET IP (Interrupt Process) sequence, which should cause the remote system to abort the currently running process.

ao Sends the TELNET AO (Abort Output) sequence, which should cause the remote system to flush all output from the remote system to the user's terminal.

ayt Sends the TELNET AYT (Are You There) sequence, to which the remote system may or may not choose to respond.

ec Sends the TELNET EC (Erase Character) sequence, which should cause the remote

                       system to erase the last character
                       entered.

    el   Sends the TELNET EL (Erase Line)
               sequence, which should cause the remote
               system to erase the line currently being
               entered.

    ga   Sends the TELNET GA (Go Ahead) sequence,
               which likely has no significance to the
               remote system.

    nop   Sends the TELNET NOP (No OPeration)
               sequence.

    ?   Prints out help information for the send
               command.

set variable_name value
    Set any one of a number of telnet variables to a
    specific value. The special value off turns off the
    function associated with the variable. The values of
    variables can be shown by using the display command.
    The following variable_names can be specified:

    echo This is the value (initially ^E) which, when in
        line-by-line mode, toggles between doing local
        echoing of entered characters (for normal
        processing), and suppressing echoing of entered
        characters (for entering, for example, a
        password).

    escape
        This is the telnet escape character (initially ^])
        which causes entry into telnet command mode (when
        connected to a remote system).

    interrupt
        If telnet is in localchars mode (see toggle
        localchars below) and the interrupt character is
        typed, a TELNET IP sequence (see send ip above) is
        sent to the remote host. The initial value for
        the interrupt character is taken to be the
        terminal's intr character.

    quit If telnet is in localchars mode (see toggle
        localchars below) and the quit character is typed,
        a TELNET BRK sequence (see send brk above) is sent
        to the remote host. The initial value for the
        quit character is taken to be the terminal's quit
        character.

    flushoutput
        If telnet is in localchars mode (see toggle
        localchars below) and the flushoutput character is
        typed, a TELNET AO sequence (see send ao above) is
        sent to the remote host. The initial value for
        the flush character is ^O.

    erase
        If telnet is in localchars mode (see toggle
        localchars below), and if telnet is operating in
        character-at-a-time mode, then when this character
        is typed, a TELNET EC sequence (see send ec above)

Name	Description	Default
NSTREVENT	Max Number of Outstanding Streams	50
NSTRPUSH	Max Number of Streams Modules in Single Stream	16
NSTRSCHED	Number of Streams Scheduler Daemons to Run	0
STRCTLSZ	Max Size of Streams Message Control (in Bytes)	1024
STRMSGSZ	Max Size of Streams Message Data (in Bytes)	0
acctresume	Threshold to Resume Accounting	4
acctsuspend	Threshold to Suspend Accounting	2
aio_listio_max	Max Number of AIO Ops That Can be Specified in lio_list Call	256
aio_max_ops	Max Number of AIO Ops That Can be Queued at Any Time	2048
aio_physmem_pct	Percentage of Physical Memory Lockable for Request Call-Back Operations	10
aio_prio_delta_max	Max Slowdown Factor; Greatest Delta Allowed in aiocb's aio_reqprio Field	20
allocate_fs_swapmap	Allocates Swapmap Space at Swapon	0
alwaysdump	Bit-Mask of Kernel Memory Pages Included in Dumps	1
bufcache_hash_locks	Buffer Cache Spinlock Pool Size	128
bufpages	Number of Buffer Pages	(NBUF*2)
chanq_hash_locks	Channel Queue Spinlock Pool Size	256
core_addshmem_read	Boolean; If Set, Includes Read-Protected Shared Memory Segments in Application Core File	0
core_addshmem_write	Boolean; If Set, Includes Write-Protected Shared Memory Segments in Application Core File	0
create_fastlinks	Creates Fast Symbolic Links	0
dbc_max_pct	Max Dynamic Buffer Cache Size as Percent of System RAM Size	50
dbc_min_pct	Min Dynamic Buffer Cache Size as Percent of System RAM Size	5
default_disk_ir	Immediately Report (Write Cache-Enable) Behavior for SCSI Disks	0
disksort_seconds	Max Wait Time for Disk Requests	0
dnlc_hash_locks	Number of Locks for Directory Cache Synchronization	4*128
dontdump	Bit-Mask of Kernel Memory Pages Excluded from Dumps	0
dst	Daylight Savings Time Policy	1
effective_maxpid	Max Allowed Process ID Value	((NPROC<=30000)? 30000:(NPROC*5/4))
enable_idds	Boolean; Turns Off/On Intrusion Detection Data Source (IDDS) Kernel Subsystem	0
eqmemsize	Min Number of Equivalently Mapped Memory Pages on Reserve List	15
executable_stack	Allows or Denys Program Execution on Stack (Security Feature)	1
fcp_large_config	Boolean; 0 if Small (<=64 Nodes) Loop, 1 if Large (<=126 Nodes) Loop	0
fs_async	Selects Asynchronous Writes	0

Name	Description	Default
ftable_hash_locks	File Table Spinlock Pool Size	64
hdlpreg_hash_locks	Number (Given as Power of Two) of Spinlocks Allocated to Pregion Hash Table Objects	128
hfs_max_ra_blocks	Max Number of Read-Ahead Blocks Outstanding for HFS Filesystems (in Blocks)	8
hfs_max_revra_blocks	Max Number of Kbytes Read with Each Read-Ahead Operation for HFS Filesystems	8
hfs_ra_per_disk	Amount of HFS Filesystem Read-Ahead (in Kbytes)	64
hfs_revra_per_disk	Max Number of HFS Filesystem Blocks Read with Each Reverse Read-Ahead Operation	64
hp_hfs_mtra_enabled	Boolean; Enables/Disables HFS Multi-Threaded Read-Ahead	1
initmodmax	Max Number of Kernel Modules Saved by System Crash Dump	50
io_ports_hash_locks	I/O Ports Spinlock Pool Size	64
ksi_alloc_max	System-Wide Limit of Queued Signal That Can be Allocated	(NPROC*8)
ksi_send_max	Max Number of Queued Signals a Process May Send and Have Pending at Receiver(s)	32
max_async_ports	Max Number of asyncdsk Ports That Can be Open at One Time	50
max_fcp_reqs	Max Number of Concurrent Fiber Channel Requests Per Adapter	512
max_mem_window	Max Number of Memory Windows Configurable by User	0
max_thread_proc	Max Number of Threads Allowed in Each Process	64
maxdsiz	Max Data Segment Size for 32-bit Processes (in Bytes)	0x10000000
maxdsiz_64bit	Max Data Segment Size for 64-bit Processes (in Bytes)	0x40000000
maxfiles	Soft File Limit Per Process	60
maxfiles_lim	Hard File Limit Per Process	1024
maxssiz	Max Stack Segment Size for 32-bit Processes (in Bytes)	0x00800000
maxssiz_64bit	Max Stack Segment Size for 64-bit Processes (in Bytes)	0x00800000
maxswapchunks	Max Number of Swap Chunks	256
maxtsiz	Max Text Segment Size for 32-bit Processes (in Bytes)	0x04000000
maxtsiz_64bit	Max Text Segment Size for 64-bit Processes (in Bytes)	0x40000000
maxuprc	Max Number of User Processes	75
maxusers	Value of MAXUSERS Macro (Does Not Affect Max User Logins)	32
maxvgs	Max Number of Volume Groups	10
mesg	Enable Sys V Messages	1
modstrmax	Max Size of Kernel-Module Savecrash Table (in Bytes)	500
msgmap	Max Number of Message Map Entries	(2+MSGTQL)
msgmax	Message Max Size (in Bytes)	8192
msgmnb	Max Number of Bytes on Message Queue	16384
msgmni	Number of Message Queue Identifiers	50

Name	Description	Default
msgseg	Number of Segments Available for Messages	2048
msgssz	Message Segment Size	8
msgtql	Number of Message Headers	40
nbuf	Number of Buffer Cache Headers	0
ncallout	Max Number of Pending Timeouts	(16+NKTHREAD)
ncdnode	Max Number of Open CDFS Files	150
nclist	Number of cblocks for pty and tty Data Transfers	(100+16*MAXUSERS)
ncsize	Directory Name Lookup Cache (DNLC) Space Needed for Inodes	(NINODE+VX_NCSIZE)+(8*DNLC_HASH_LOCKS)
ndilbuffers	Number of DIL Buffers	30
nfile	Max Number of Open Files	(16*(NPROC+16+MAXUSERS)/10+32+2*(NPTY+NSTRPTY+NSTRTEL))
nflocks	Max Number of File Locks	200
ninode	Max Number of Open Inodes	((NPROC+16+MAXUSERS)+32+(2*NPTY))
nkthread	Max Number of Kernel Threads Supported by the System	(((NPROC*7)/4)+16)
no_lvm_disks	Boolean; Set Only If System Has No LVM Disks	0
nproc	Max Number of Processes	(20+8*MAXUSERS)
npty	Number of ptys (Pseudo ttys)	60
nstrpty	Max Number of Streams-Based ptys	0
nstrtel	Number of Telnet Session Device Files	60
nswapdev	Max Devices That Can be Enabled for Swap	10
nswapfs	Max Filesystems That Can be Enabled for Swap	10
nsysmap	Number of Entries in Kernel Dynamic Memory Allocation Map	((NPROC)>800?2*(NPROC):800)
nsysmap64	Number of Entries in Kernel Dynamic Memory Allocation Map	((NPROC)>800?2*(NPROC):800)
o_sync_is_o_dsync	Enables/Disables Translation of O_SYNC to O_DSYNC in open(2)/fcntl(2) Calls	0
pfdat_hash_locks	Pfdat Spinlock Pool Size	128
public_shlibs	Public Shared Libraries	1
region_hash_locks	Region Spinlock Pool Size	128
remote_nfs_swap	Enables Swapping across NFS	0
rtsched_numpri	Number of POSIX.1b Realtime Priorities to Support	32
scroll_lines	Number of ITE Off-Screen Lines	100
scsi_max_qdepth	Max Number of SCSI Commands Queued Up for SCSI Devices	8
scsi_maxphys	Max Record Size for SCSI I/O Subsystem (in Bytes)	1048576

Name	Description	Default
sema	Enables Sys V Semaphores	1
semaem	Max Value for Adjust on Exit Semaphores	16384
semmap	Max Number of Semaphore Map Entries	(SEMMNI+2)
semmni	Number of Semaphore Identifiers	64
semmns	Max Number of Semaphores	128
semmnu	Number of Semaphore Undo Structures	30
semmsl	Max Number of Semaphores Per ID	2048
semume	Semaphore Undo Entries Per Process	10
semvmx	Semaphore Max Value	32767
sendfile_max	Max Number of Buffer Cache Pages Usable by sendfile System Call	0
shmem	Enables Sys V Shared Memory	1
shmmax	Max Shared Memory Segment (in Bytes)	0X4000000
shmmni	Number of Shared Memory Identifiers	200
shmseg	Shared Memory Segments Per Process	120
st_ats_enabled	Boolean; If Set, SCSI Tape Open Will Try to Reserve the Tape Device	1
st_fail_overruns	Boolean; If Set, SCSI Tape Read Resulting in Data Overrun Causes Failure	0
st_large_recs	Boolean; If Set, Enables Large Record Support for SCSI Tape	0
streampipes	Forces All Pipes to be Streams-Based	0
swapmem_on	Allows Memory to Exceed Swap Space	1
swchunk	Swaps Chunk Size (1K Blocks)	2048
sysv_hash_locks	System V IPC Spinlock Pool Size	128
tcphashsz	TCP Hash Table Size (in Bytes)	0
timeslice	Scheduling Interval (10-mS Ticks)	(100/10)
timezone	Minutes West of Greenwich	420
unlockable_mem	Non-Lockable Memory (4096-Byte Pages)	0
vas_hash_locks	VAS Spinlock Pool Size	128
vnode_cd_hash_locks	Vnode Clean/Dirty Spinlock Pool Size	128
vnode_hash_locks	Vnode Spinlock Pool Size	128
vps_ceiling	Max System-Selected Page Size (in Kbytes)	16
vps_chatr_ceiling	Max chatr-Selected Page Size (in Kbytes)	1048576
vps_pagesize	Default User Page Size (in Kbytes)	4
vx_fancyra_enable	Boolean; If Set, Enables VXFS Filesystem Read-Ahead	0
vx_ncsize	Directory Name Lookup Cache (DNLC) Space Needed for VxFS Inodes	1024
vxfs_max_ra_kbytes	Max Amount of VxFS Filesystem Read-Ahead Outstanding (in Kbytes)	1024
vxfs_ra_per_disk	Amount of VxFS Filesystem Read-Ahead (in Kbytes)	1024

is sent to the remote system. The initial value
for the erase character is taken to be the
terminal's erase character.

kill If telnet is in localchars mode (see toggle
localchars below), and if telnet is operating in
character-at-a-time mode, then when this character
is typed, a TELNET EL sequence (see send el above)
is sent to the remote system. The initial value
for the kill character is taken to be the
terminal's kill character.

eof If telnet is operating in line-by-line mode,
entering this character as the first character on
a line causes this character to be sent to the
remote system. The initial value of the eof
character is taken to be the terminal's eof
character.

toggle arguments ...
Toggle (between TRUE and FALSE) various flags that
control how telnet responds to events. More than one
argument can be specified. The state of these flags
can be shown by using the display command. Valid
arguments are:

localchars
If TRUE, the flush, interrupt, quit, erase,
and kill characters (see set above) are
recognized locally, and transformed into
appropriate TELNET control sequences
(respectively ao, ip, brk, ec, and el; see
send above). The initial value for this
toggle is TRUE in line-by-line mode, and
FALSE in character-at-a-time mode.

autoflush
If autoflush and localchars are both TRUE,
whenever the ao, intr, or quit characters are
recognized (and transformed into TELNET
sequences - see set above for details),
telnet refuses to display any data on the
user's terminal until the remote system
acknowledges (via a TELNET Timing Mark
option) that it has processed those TELNET
sequences. The initial value for this toggle
is TRUE.

autosynch
If autosynch and localchars are both TRUE,
when either the intr or quit character is
typed (see set above for descriptions of the
intr and quit characters), the resulting
TELNET sequence sent is followed by the
TELNET SYNCH sequence. This procedure should
cause the remote system to begin discarding
all previously typed input until both of the
TELNET sequences have been read and acted
upon. The initial value of this toggle is
FALSE.

binary
Enable or disable the TELNET BINARY option on
both input and output. This option should be

enabled in order to send and receive 8-bit
characters to and from the TELNET server.

crlf If TRUE, end-of-line sequences are sent as an
ASCII carriage-return and line-feed pair. If
FALSE, end-of-line sequences are sent as an
ASCII carriage-return and NUL character pair.
The initial value for this toggle is FALSE.

crmod
Toggle carriage return mode. When this mode
is enabled, any carriage return characters
received from the remote host are mapped into
a carriage return and a line feed. This mode
does not affect those characters typed by the
user; only those received. This mode is only
required for some hosts that require the
client to do local echoing, but output
``naked'' carriage returns. The initial
value for this toggle is FALSE.

echo Toggle local echo mode or remote echo mode.
In local echo mode, user input is echoed to
the terminal by the local telnet before being
transmitted to the remote host. In remote
echo, any echoing of user input is done by
the remote host. Applications that handle
echoing of user input themselves, such as C
shell, Korn shell, and vi (see csh(1),
ksh(1), and vi(1)), do not work correctly
with local echo.

options
Toggle viewing of TELNET options processing.
When options viewing is enabled, all TELNET
option negotiations are displayed. Options
sent by telnet are displayed as ``SENT'',
while options received from the TELNET server
are displayed as ``RCVD''. The initial value
for this toggle is FALSE.

netdata
Toggles the display of all network data (in
hexadecimal format). The initial value for
this toggle is FALSE.

?   Displays the legal toggle commands.

RETURN VALUE
In the event of an error, or if the TELNET connection is closed by the
remote host, telnet returns a value of 1. Otherwise it returns zero
(0).

DIAGNOSTICS
The following diagnostic messages are displayed by telnet:

telnet/tcp: Unknown service
telnet was unable to find the TELNET service entry in the
services(4) database.

hostname: Unknown host
telnet was unable to map the host name to an Internet
address. Your next step should be to contact the system
administrator to check whether there is an entry for the

remote host in the hosts database (see hosts(4)).

?Invalid command
          An invalid command was typed in telnet command mode.

system call>: ...
          An error occurred in the specified system call. See the
          appropriate manual entry for a description of the error.

AUTHOR
     telnet was developed by the University of California, Berkeley.

SEE ALSO
     csh(1), ksh(1), login(1), rlogin(1), stty(1), telnetd(1M), hosts(4),
     services(4), termio(7).

telnet(1) Secure Internet Services with Kerberos Authentication telnet(1)

NAME
     telnet - user interface to the TELNET protocol

SYNOPSIS

     telnet [[options]host [port]]

DESCRIPTION
     telnet is used to communicate with another host using the TELNET
     protocol. If telnet is invoked without arguments, it enters command
     mode, indicated by its prompt (telnet>). In this mode, it accepts and
     executes the commands listed below. If telnet is invoked with
     arguments, it performs an open command (see below) with those
     arguments.

     Once a connection has been opened, telnet enters an input mode. The
     input mode will be either ``character at a time'' or ``line by line'',
     depending on what the remote system supports.

     In ``character at a time'' mode, most text typed is immediately sent
     to the remote host for processing.

     In ``line by line'' mode, all text is echoed locally, and (normally)
     only completed lines are sent to the remote host. The ``local echo
     character'' (initially ^E) can be used to turn off and on the local
     echo (this would mostly be used to enter passwords without the
     password being echoed).

     In either mode, if the localchars toggle is TRUE (the default in line
     mode; see below), the user's quit and intr characters are trapped
     locally, and sent as TELNET protocol sequences to the remote side.
     There are options (see toggle autoflush and toggle autosynch below)
     which cause this action to flush subsequent output to the terminal
     (until the remote host acknowledges the TELNET sequence) and flush
     previous terminal input (in the case of quit and intr).

     While connected to a remote host, telnet command mode can be entered
     by typing the telnet ``escape character'' (initially ^]). When in
     command mode, the normal terminal editing conventions are available.

     telnet supports eight-bit characters when communicating with the
     server on the remote host. To use eight-bit characters you may need
     to reconfigure your terminal or the remote host appropriately (see
     stty(1)). Furthermore, you may have to use the binary toggle to
     enable an 8-bit data stream between telnet and the remote host. Note
     that some remote hosts may not provide the necessary support for
     eight-bit characters.

If, at any time, telnet is unable to read from or write to the server over the connection, the message Connection closed by foreign host. is printed on standard error. telnet then exits with a value of 1.

By default (or by use of the -a option or the -l option), this Kerberos version of telnet behaves as a client which supports authentication based on Kerberos V5. As a Kerberos client, telnet will authenticate and authorize the user to access the remote system. (See sis(5) for details on Kerberos authentication and authorization.) However, it will not support integrity-checked or encrypted sessions. telnet supports the TAC User ID (also known as the TAC Access Control System, or TACACS User ID) option. Enabling the option on a host server allows the user to telnet into that host without being prompted for a second login sequence. The TAC User ID option uses the same security mechanism as rlogin for authorizing access by remote hosts and users. The system administrator must enable the (telnetd) option only on systems which are designated as participating hosts. The system administrator must also assign to each user of TAC User ID the very same UID on every system for which he is allowed to use the feature. (See telnetd(1M) and the System Administration Tasks manual)

The following telnet options are available:

-8   Enable cs8 (8 bit transfer) on local tty.

-a   Attempt automatic login into the Kerberos realm and disable
          the TAC User ID option. (Note: this is the default login
          mode.)

          Sends the user name via the NAME subnegotiation of the
          Authentication option. The name used is that of the current
          user as returned by the USER environment variable. If this
          variable is not defined, the name used is that returned by
          getpwnam(3) if it agrees with the current user ID.
          Otherwise, it is the name associated with the user ID.

-e c   Set the telnet command mode escape character to be ^c
          instead of its default value of ^].

-l user   Attempt automatic login into the Kerberos realm as the
          specified user and disable the TAC User ID option. The user
          name specified is sent via the NAME subnegotiation of the
          Authentication option. Omitting the -l option executes the
          default setting. Only one -l option is allowed.

-P   Disable use of Kerberos authentication and authorization.
          When this option is specified, a password is required which
          is sent across the network in a readable form. (See sis(5).)

-f   Allows local credentials to be forwarded to the remote
          system. Only one of -f or -F is allowed.

-F   Allows local credentials to be forwarded to the remote
          system including any credentials that have already been
          forwarded into the local environment. Only one of -f or -F
          is allowed.

Commands
    The following commands are available in command mode. You need only
    type enough of each command to uniquely identify it (this is also true
    for arguments to the mode, set, toggle, and display commands).

    open [-l user] host [port]
                    Open a connection to the named host at the indicated
                    port. If no port is specified, telnet attempts to

contact a TELNET server at the standard TELNET port.
The hostname can be either the official name or an
alias as understood by gethostbyname() (see
gethostent(3N)), or an Internet address specified in
the dot notation as described in hosts(4). If no
hostname is given, telnet prompts for one. The -l
option can be used to specify the user name to use when
automatically logging in to the remote system. Using
this option disables the TAC User ID option.

close
: Close a TELNET session. If the session was started
from command mode, telnet returns to command mode;
otherwise telnet exits.

quit
: Close any open TELNET session and exit telnet. An end
of file (in command mode) will also close a session and
exit.

z
: Suspend telnet. If telnet is run from a shell that
supports job control, (such as csh(1) or ksh(1)), the z
command suspends the TELNET session and returns the
user to the shell that invoked telnet. The job can
then be resumed with the fg command (see csh(1) or
ksh(1)).

mode mode
: Change telnet's user input mode to mode, which can be
character (for ``character at a time'' mode) or line
(for ``line by line'' mode). The remote host is asked
for permission to go into the requested mode. If the
remote host is capable of entering that mode, the
requested mode is entered. In character mode, telnet
sends each character to the remote host as it is typed.
In line mode, telnet gathers user input into lines and
transmits each line to the remote host when the user
types carriage return, linefeed, or EOF (normally ^D;
see stty(1)). Note that setting line-mode also sets
local echo. Applications that expect to interpret user
input character by character (such as more, csh, ksh,
and vi) do not work correctly in line mode.

status
: Show current status of telnet. telnet reports the
current escape character. If telnet is connected, it
reports the host to which it is connected and the
current mode. If telnet is not connected to a remote
host, it reports No connection. Once telnet has been
connected, it reports the local flow control toggle
value.

display [argument ...]
: Displays all or some of the set and toggle values (see
below).

? [command]
: Get help. With no arguments, telnet prints a help
summary. If a command is specified, telnet prints the
help information available about that command only.
Help information is limited to a one-line description
of the command.

! [shell_command]
: Shell escape. The SHELL environment variable is
checked for the name of a shell to use to execute the
command. If no shell_command is specified, a shell is
started and connected to the user's terminal. If SHELL
is undefined, /usr/bin/sh is used.

send arguments Sends one or more special character sequences to the

remote host. Each argument can have any of the
following values (multiple arguments can be specified
with each send command):

escape   Sends the current telnet escape
            character (initially ^]).

synch   Sends the TELNET SYNCH sequence. This
            sequence causes the remote system to
            discard all previously typed (but not
            yet read) input. This sequence is sent
            as TCP urgent data (and may not work to
            some systems -- if it doesn't work, a
            lower case ``r'' may be echoed on the
            terminal).

brk   Sends the TELNET BRK (Break) sequence,
            which may have significance to the
            remote system.

ip   Sends the TELNET IP (Interrupt Process)
            sequence, which should cause the remote
            system to abort the currently running
            process.

ao   Sends the TELNET AO (Abort Output)
            sequence, which should cause the remote
            system to flush all output from the
            remote system to the user's terminal.

ayt   Sends the TELNET AYT (Are You There)
            sequence, to which the remote system may
            or may not choose to respond.

ec   Sends the TELNET EC (Erase Character)
            sequence, which should cause the remote
            system to erase the last character
            entered.

el   Sends the TELNET EL (Erase Line)
            sequence, which should cause the remote
            system to erase the line currently being
            entered.

ga   Sends the TELNET GA (Go Ahead) sequence,
            which likely has no significance to the
            remote system.

nop   Sends the TELNET NOP (No OPeration)
            sequence.

?   Prints out help information for the send
            command.

set variable_name value
            Set any one of a number of telnet variables to a
            specific value. The special value off turns off the
            function associated with the variable. The values of
            variables can be shown by using the display command.
            The following variable_names can be specified:

            echo This is the value (initially ^E) which, when in
                 line-by-line mode, toggles between doing local
                 echoing of entered characters (for normal

processing), and suppressing echoing of entered
characters (for entering, for example, a
password).

escape
    This is the telnet escape character (initially ^])
    which causes entry into telnet command mode (when
    connected to a remote system).

interrupt
    If telnet is in localchars mode (see toggle
    localchars below) and the interrupt character is
    typed, a TELNET IP sequence (see send ip above) is
    sent to the remote host. The initial value for
    the interrupt character is taken to be the
    terminal's intr character.

quit If telnet is in localchars mode (see toggle
    localchars below) and the quit character is typed,
    a TELNET BRK sequence (see send brk above) is sent
    to the remote host. The initial value for the
    quit character is taken to be the terminal's quit
    character.

flushoutput
    If telnet is in localchars mode (see toggle
    localchars below) and the flushoutput character is
    typed, a TELNET AO sequence (see send ao above) is
    sent to the remote host. The initial value for
    the flush character is ^O.

erase
    If telnet is in localchars mode (see toggle
    localchars below), and if telnet is operating in
    character-at-a-time mode, then when this character
    is typed, a TELNET EC sequence (see send ec above)
    is sent to the remote system. The initial value
    for the erase character is taken to be the
    terminal's erase character.

kill If telnet is in localchars mode (see toggle
    localchars below), and if telnet is operating in
    character-at-a-time mode, then when this character
    is typed, a TELNET EL sequence (see send el above)
    is sent to the remote system. The initial value
    for the kill character is taken to be the
    terminal's kill character.

eof If telnet is operating in line-by-line mode,
    entering this character as the first character on
    a line causes this character to be sent to the
    remote system. The initial value of the eof
    character is taken to be the terminal's eof
    character.

toggle arguments ...
    Toggle (between TRUE and FALSE) various flags that
    control how telnet responds to events. More than one
    argument can be specified. The state of these flags
    can be shown by using the display command. Valid
    arguments are:

        localchars
            If TRUE, the flush, interrupt, quit, erase,

and kill characters (see set above) are
recognized locally, and transformed into
appropriate TELNET control sequences
(respectively ao, ip, brk, ec, and el; see
send above). The initial value for this
toggle is TRUE in line-by-line mode, and
FALSE in character-at-a-time mode.

autoflush

If autoflush and localchars are both TRUE,
whenever the ao, intr, or quit characters are
recognized (and transformed into TELNET
sequences - see set above for details),
telnet refuses to display any data on the
user's terminal until the remote system
acknowledges (via a TELNET Timing Mark
option) that it has processed those TELNET
sequences. The initial value for this toggle
is TRUE.

autologin

Enable or disable automatic login into the
Kerberos realm. Using this option yields the
same results as using the -a option. The
initial value for this toggle is TRUE.

autosynch

If autosynch and localchars are both TRUE,
when either the intr or quit character is
typed (see set above for descriptions of the
intr and quit characters), the resulting
TELNET sequence sent is followed by the
TELNET SYNCH sequence. This procedure should
cause the remote system to begin discarding
all previously typed input until both of the
TELNET sequences have been read and acted
upon. The initial value of this toggle is
FALSE.

binary

Enable or disable the TELNET BINARY option on
both input and output. This option should be
enabled in order to send and receive 8-bit
characters to and from the TELNET server.

crlf If TRUE, end-of-line sequences are sent as an
ASCII carriage-return and line-feed pair. If
FALSE, end-of-line sequences are sent as an
ASCII carriage-return and NUL character pair.
The initial value for this toggle is FALSE.

crmod

Toggle carriage return mode. When this mode
is enabled, any carriage return characters
received from the remote host are mapped into
a carriage return and a line feed. This mode
does not affect those characters typed by the
user; only those received. This mode is only
required for some hosts that require the
client to do local echoing, but output
``naked'' carriage returns. The initial
value for this toggle is FALSE.

echo Toggle local echo mode or remote echo mode.
In local echo mode, user input is echoed to

the terminal by the local telnet before being
transmitted to the remote host. In remote
echo, any echoing of user input is done by
the remote host. Applications that handle
echoing of user input themselves, such as C
shell, Korn shell, and vi (see csh(1),
ksh(1), and vi(1)), do not work correctly
with local echo.

options
      Toggle viewing of TELNET options processing.
      When options viewing is enabled, all TELNET
      option negotiations are displayed. Options
      sent by telnet are displayed as ``SENT'',
      while options received from the TELNET server
      are displayed as ``RCVD''. The initial value
      for this toggle is FALSE.

netdata
      Toggles the display of all network data (in
      hexadecimal format). The initial value for
      this toggle is FALSE.

?   Displays the legal toggle commands.

RETURN VALUE

In the event of an error, or if the TELNET connection is closed by the
remote host, telnet returns a value of 1. Otherwise it returns zero
(0).

DIAGNOSTICS

Diagnostic messages displayed by telnet are displayed below. Kerberos
specific errors are listed in sis(5).

telnet/tcp: Unknown service
      telnet was unable to find the TELNET service entry in the
      services(4) database.

hostname: Unknown host
      telnet was unable to map the host name to an Internet
      address. Your next step should be to contact the system
      administrator to check whether there is an entry for the
      remote host in the hosts database (see hosts(4)).

?Invalid command
      An invalid command was typed in telnet command mode.

system call>: ...
      An error occurred in the specified system call. See the
      appropriate manual entry for a description of the error.

AUTHOR

telnet was developed by the University of California, Berkeley.

SEE ALSO

csh(1), ksh(1), login(1), rlogin(1), stty(1), telnetd(1M), hosts(4),
services(4), termio(7), sis(5).

Keep in mind that you may need to start the telnet daemon, telnetd,
in order to run telnet.

See the manual page for telnetd for startup instructions if you do
not have telnetd running.

telnetd sends options to the client of a telnet session in order to
set up a proper communication exchange during a telnet session.

CHAPTER 13

Common Desktop Environment

The Common Desktop Environment (CDE) represents the effort of major UNIX vendors to unify UNIX at the desktop level. CDE is widely used by X terminal and workstation users on many UNIX systems. Because you may be managing many UNIX variants that run CDE, I'll cover CDE on IBM's AIX systems, Hewlett Packard's HP-UX systems, and Sun Microsystems' Solaris systems. This chapter provides an introduction to CDE: it touches on teh basics of CDE's look and feel, describes making changes to the CDE environment, and a bit of background about the X, Motif, and CDE relationships. CDE versions used to write this chapter are: AIX CDE 1.0, HP-UX CDE 2.1.0, and Solaris CDE 1.3. Newer releases will have enhanced features, but in general, they should still work the same.

Several features make it easy to customize CDE. The Style Manager, which every user has access to, makes it easy to customize CDE on an individual user basis. Sooner or later, however, you may want to provide some common denominator of CDE functionality for your users. If, for instance, you have an application that most users will run, you can set up environment variables, prepare pull-down menus, provide suitable fonts, etc., that will make your users more productive. Users can then perform additional customizations such as defining File Manager characteristics and selecting backgrounds.

To help you thoroughly understand CDE, I'll cover the following topics:

1. Why a Graphical User Interface (GUI)?

2. CDE Basics

3. Customizing CDE

4. CDE - Advanced Topics

> •The Relationship among X, Motif, and CDE
>
> •X, Motif, and CDE Configuration Files
>
> •The Sequence of Events When CDE Starts
>
> •CDE and Performance

First I'll provide you with the reasoning behind providing a graphical interface rather than the more common, but also more cumbersome, line by line terminal interface. An overview of the CDE desktop workspaces follows. This is divided into two sections: AIX and HP-UX (because they are so similar) and Solaris. Each will give an overview of the front panel features. Next I'll guide you through making some CDE customizations. These customizations will give you a working basis for making more advanced changes on your own. I'll show you how to make some basic, simple changes, and then more complex changes, ending with modifying the login screen with a new logo and new welcome messages. Last, I'll delve into the more advanced topics of X, Motif, and CDE relationships, configuration file usage and location, what happens internally when CDE starts up, and some CDE performance tips.

Why a Graphical User Interface (GUI)?

For computers to be used on every desktop, they had to be made easier to use. A new method of accessing computer power was required, one that avoided the command-line prompt, didn't require users to memorize complex commands, and didn't require a working knowledge of technological infrastructures such as networking. Not that this information was unimportant; far from it. The information was both too important and too specialized to be of use to the average worker-bee computer user. A knowledge of their applications was all that was important for these users. After all, so the reasoning goes, to drive a car, one doesn't have to be a mechanic, so why should a computer user have to understand computer technology? The graphical user interface (GUI) makes computers accessible to the application end-user.

Figure 13-1 illustrates the relationship among the computer hardware, the operating system, and the graphical user interface. The computer is the hardware platform on the bottom. The operating system, the next layer up, represents a character-based user interface. To control the computer at this level, users must type commands at the keyboard. The next several layers, beginning with the X Window System, represent the graphical user interface. To control the computer at these levels, users manipulate graphical controls with a mouse.

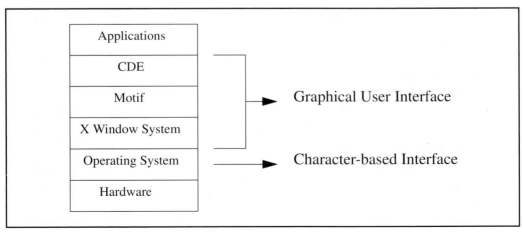

Figure 13-1 User Interface Components

GUIs replaced memorization with exploration. A user could now use pull-down menus, push buttons, sliding scroll bars, and other direct manipulation to use a computer. Typing operating system commands to perform a function is greatly reduced. With a GUI, to use a computer is both easier to learn and easier to use.

While fairly inexpensive in terms of dollars (CDE is bundled "free" with the operating system), GUIs are not without cost in terms of RAM usage and performance. Despite this performance expense, GUIs have become a permanent part of the computing environment. The benefits of their utility are worth the cost.

Beyond the graphical controls that reduce training, make mundane tasks simpler to do, and generally ease the stress of using a computer, two other benefits of GUIs are worth mentioning: multiple windows per display and client-server topology.

The benefit of multiple windows that GUIs provide is that each window (literally a rectangular area surrounded by a window frame) contains a separate application. The user can work with multiple windows open. CDE goes one step further: its multiple workspaces allow users to separate application windows by task into specific workspaces. For instance, in a workspace named "Mail," users may have application windows showing the list of incoming electronic mail, a mail message they are currently reading, and a message they are composing for later transmission. In another workspace called "Financials," they could be working on several spreadsheets, each in its own window.

Client-server topology enables the computing resources spread around a network to be accessed efficiently to meet computing needs. In a client-server topology, powerful computers on the network are dedicated to a specific purpose (file management on a file server and running applications on an application server). Users working on less powerful client computers elsewhere on the network access the files or applications remotely. A file server reduces system administration by centralizing file backup, enabling the system administrator to back up only the file server, not each individual client computer. This setup also ensures that files will be backed up at regular intervals. An application server reduces operating costs by reducing the number and size of storage disks required and the size of RAM required on each client computer. A single version of an application resides and runs on the application server and is accessed by multiple users throughout the network.

Although this topology sounds complicated, the CDE GUI makes it easy. To access a file, users "drag and drop" a file icon from the file manager window. To start an application, users double-click the application icon. To print a file, users drag the file to the icon of the appropriate printer in the front panel and drop it there. Users don't have to know where these files and applications are, what directories they are in, what computers they are on, or how they are accessed. The underlying infrastructure and control you have put in place, along with the power of the GUI, allow users to concentrate on their work and not on the mechanics of their computer.

CDE Basics

Because most systems come with a set of CDE user guides, I'm only going to give an overview of what CDE looks like and the main areas we will be working with when we do some customizations. Along the way, I'll point out similarities and differences among the different flavors of CDE.

The CDE login screen presents you with several choices before you even log in. Under the area where you enter your user name are four buttons: **OK**, **Start Over**, **Options**, and **Help**. **OK** is just the same as pressing *Enter* when you enter your login and then password. The **Start Over** button clears your user login and allows you to start over. **Options** provides you with some initial session configuration that would need to be made before you log in. **Language** allows you to change your default language. Suppose that you need to test your company's software in another language. Assuming that the proper language is preloaded on your system, you can swap between the languages for testing by simply choosing CDE to come up in a different language. **Session** allows you to choose to come up in the CDE desktop session or into a **Failsafe** session, which is an X session but without the CDE desktop. Solaris also has options to log in to their

OpenWindow Desktop or into the **User's Last Desktop**. **Command Line Login** allows you to log in without CDE being invoked. This would be just a regular terminal mode session. **Reset Login Screen** does just what its name suggests. And finally, **Help** lists all these features with a brief description of each.

The login screen itself displays a CDE logo, an operating system logo such as AIX, or possibly your company's logo. A welcome message appears along with a place to enter your user login. After entering your user name, you are prompted for your password. Once entered and verified as correct, CDE is started and the desktop is displayed. On Solaris systems, the first time you log in, you are presented with a choice as to whether you want to log into CDE or OpenWindows Desktop.

The CDE desktop is comprised of four desktop workspaces and a front panel shared by each. The front panel is an easy-to-use interface to various applications, commands, and tools. The various components are easily accessed by the simple point-and-click method. Front panel components are a collection of objects, subpanels, and access to desktop workspaces. Some objects are used only to display items such as the clock, whereas others, when clicked, either bring up an application, such as the calendar or dtmail, or perform an action, such as the lock or the exit action icons. Subpanels pop up a menu of objects that can be accessed. These objects can also simply display items or bring up applications. By default, on AIX and HP-UX, you see Personal Printer subpanels, Personal Applications subpanels, and Help subpanels. On Solaris, all panels contain subpanels. Subpanels can be added to the other panels on AIX and HP-UX as you will see in the next section "Customizing CDE." You can tell that these have subpanels, because they each have a little arrow above the panel where you click to pop it up. In the center of the front panel are four workspaces. These provide areas in which to perform related tasks, enabling the user to separate work and not clutter up the desktop.

CDE on AIX and HP-UX is very similar and, in general, what is displayed on the front panel on one is the same as on the other. Solaris, however, while retaining the basic CDE look and feel, has greatly expanded what is included on the default front panel and the subpanels behind it. I'm going to give an overview of CDE as found on HP-UX and AIX first. Then I'll point out the Solaris enhancements to CDE.

CDE on AIX and HP-UX

The front panel is divided into 11 main areas: 5 panels, 1 workspaces area, and 5 more panels. I'll give an overview of each area from left to right, beginning with the Clock and ending with the Trash Can, as shown in Figure 13-2.

Figure 13-2 Front Panel

Clock - As you would expect, this displays the current time.

Calendar - The Calendar icon displays the current date, and when clicked, brings up an appointment calendar. The calendar allows you to set appointments and reminders and to create a task list. Appointments can be set as a one-time-only events or as recurring. You can be notified of an appointment by a beep, a pop-up message, or an e-mail. The calendar and associated appointments can be displayed by the day, the week, or the month. A yearly calendar can also be displayed, but without appointments.

File Manager - The File Manager opens a window that displays your home directory and associated files. From here, you can do any number of basic file manipulations, such as copy a file, move a file, delete a file, or execute a program or script. More infrequently used operations, such as creating a symbolic link or changing file permissions or ownership, can also be done here. Removing a file from within File Manager moves it to the Trash Can rather than permanently deleting the file. This way, if you decide that you need it back, you can simply retrieve it from the Trash Can rather than having it restored from a backup - a more time-consuming operating. However, note that the Trash Can is automatically "emptied" at the end of every session. So when you log off, the files are permanently removed.

Personal Application - The Personal Application subpanel contains the CDE's text editor, **dtpad,** and terminal emulator, **dtterm**. It also contains the Icon Editor. The **dtpad** is an easy-to-use, full-screen text editor. As in a PC-based word processor, **dtpad** allows you to move the cursor anywhere to add, change, and delete text, unlike the popular **vi**, which is a line-by-line text editor. CDE's dtterm is a good basic terminal emulator. The Icon Editor opens bitmap (.bm) or pixmap (.pm) files and allows you to edit them.

man page

vi - 21

The Personal Applications subpanel is the first place we find the Install Icon application. This is where new icons are added to the subpanel. This allows the application associated with the icon to be executed when the icon is double clicked. We'll be using this when we modify the desktop in "Customizing CDE."

Mail - The CDE mailer, **dtmail**, is invoked when this icon is clicked. From here, mail messages can be composed, messages replied to, and messages forwarded. Most advanced mail features that you've come to think of as basic features are included: items such as adding attachments to messages, replying to just the sender or all recipients, and setting automatic messages saying that you're on vacation. Another feature is when a new message arrives, the **dtmail** icon changes to show a letter popping into the mailbox.

Workspace Area - The next four items comprise the workspace area.

Lock Button - The Lock button allows you to lock your session while you're away from your desk. This security feature keeps others from viewing or accessing your work when you're not there. It saves you from logging off and on every time you need to step away. Your login password, or root's password, must be entered to unlock it again.

Workspace Switch - Four in number, these are the separate workspaces created by default. These allow you to organize your work so that your workspace doesn't get cluttered up. By using the workspaces, you can keep work on different tasks, applications, or systems separated from each other. You change from one workspace to another simply by clicking on the workspace number: One, Two, Three, or Four. You'll notice that no matter what workspace you are in, the Front Panel follows you. In "Customizing CDE," you'll see how easy you can increase the number of workspaces and to change the names.

Activity Light - The Activity light, quite simply, blinks when the system is busy doing work.

Exit button - The Exit button is where you log out of CDE, terminating your CDE session. Upon exiting, depending on how you have CDE configured, you are prompted to resume your current session or return to your home session. If you choose to resume your current session, the next time you login, the desktop looks exactly the same as it does when you log out - as closely as possible. Some things, such as remote logins, are not possible, but others are, such as having an application automatically executed. If you choose to return to your home session, the next time you log in, you are returned to a known, preset configuration. This configuration is set in the Style Manager panel, discussed shortly.

Personal Printers - This subpanel contains printers that you have configured on your system, including the default printer designated as such and the Print Manager. The front panel icon is that of the default printer. To print one of your documents, simply drag it from the File Manager and drop it on the printer icon. The Print Manager allows you to view queued print files and remove them before they print. However, this works only with printers directly managed by your system. In today's networked offices, printers are usually shared and the print manager function is on a server, probably in the next building.

Style Manager - The Style Manager is one of those places where you can either get really creative getting your desktop to look just like you want or waste a lot of time - depending on your point of view. Here is where you personalize your login to the system to your own preferences. You can change your font size, your background, your mouse speed, and whether or not your session automatically locks after a certain amount of non-activity, or idle time. This is where you can set your home session, as referred to earlier, to come back to every time you log in or set your system to return to the current session or choose the option of being asked every time you log out. One other configuration you can make here is whether your window focus follows your mouse or whether you have to click on a window before it is the active window. On AIX systems, you can toggle on or off whether the workspaces are displayed on the front panel.

Application Manager - When opened, the Application Manager displays folders with useful applications and actions. Although they differ among manufacturers and even operating systems for that matter, AIX, HP-UX, and Solaris all have some basic features: Desktop Applications, Desktop Tools, Information, and System Administration. Desktop Applications contains such applications and tools as Calculator, Man Page Viewer, Icon Editor, and Create Action. Desktop Tools includes tools like **xterm**, **xwd** capture, compress files, and reload resources. System Administration contains operating system-specific applications such as SAM in HP-UX, SMIT in AIX, and Admintool in Solaris, besides more generic actions such as change password. Take the time to look around here. You'll find many items you may want to incorporate on your customized CDE front panel. I, for one, have found the Man Page Viewer to be an invaluable resource and moved it to my front panel, where it can be readily accessed.

Help - The Help subpanel is a compilation of the Help Manager, a Desktop Introduction, Front Panel help, and an On-Item Front Panel help mechanism. The Help Manager is the main online help facility for CDE. This is a comprehensive help system with topic trees and the ability to search the index using keywords or pattern matching, backtrack where you've been in the help manager, and view the history of items for which you requested help. The Desktop Introduction is an overview of CDE and how it works. The Front Panel help facility gives information about how to use the front panel icons, subpanels, and workspaces. The On-Item Front Panel help mechanism allows you to click on the front panel item about which you wish assistance. Along with the Help Subpanel, Help can also be requested by pressing the F1 function key. If installed on your system, AIX may also include Basic Desktop Customization help and Base Library.

Trash Can - The Trash Can, used with the File Manager, holds files and folders that you have deleted during the current session. Using the facility allows you to quickly retrieve files that you should not have removed. The Trash Can can be "emptied" at any time to permanently remove items. Also, the Trash Can is "emptied" when you log out of your session.

CDE on Solaris

As mentioned earlier, Solaris has embellished CDE, adding many more subpanels and items to the subpanels, as shown in Figure 13-3. Where Solaris has greatly changed the panel and subpanels, I'll give an overview of what you'll find, as I did in the previous section on AIX and HP-UX. Where they are the same, I'll simply note that they are the same.

Figure 13-3 Front Panel

Like AIX and HP-UX, Solaris' front panel is divided into 11 main areas: 5 panels, 1 workspaces area, and 5 more panels. I'll give an overview of each area from left to right, beginning with the World and ending with the Trash Can.

Links - As you might guess by the World icon, this is where you access the world. Solaris' Web browser, HotJava, lives here. There are also actions included to access Personal Bookmarks for the web browser, and a Find Web Page search engine. As indicated on the front panel icon, the world has a clock on it, too.

Cards - The calendar is the same as on AIX and HP-UX. However, included in the subpanel is Find Card, which is a rolodex-type address manager.

Files - Although the title is slightly different, this is where the File Manager resides. In the subpanel are special icons to perform file actions associated with: Properties, Encryption, Compress File, Archive, and Find File. Solaris has also included actions to manage your floppy disk drive and CD-ROM.

Applications - Renamed simply Applications, here is where you'll not only find the Text Editor, but also Text Note and Voice Note. For the audio enabled, Voice Note allows you to play, record, or save audio files with WAV, AU, and AIFF formats. On this subpanel, you'll also find the Applications subpanel found under Application Manager on the AIX and HP-UX systems. As on the others, this includes Desktop Applications, Desktop Tools, Information, and System Administration. These are basically the same on all systems.

Mail - This subpanel, in addition to **dtmail**, has been enhanced to include a Suggestion Box. A very clever idea, this automatically opens up a message, pre-addressed to Sun Microsystems, Inc., so that you can send them your suggestions.

Workspace Area - The next five items comprise the workspace area:

Lock button - Same as on AIX and HP-UX.

Workspace switch - Same as on AIX and HP-UX.

Progress Indicator - This is the same as the Busy Indicator on AIX and HP-UX.

Exit button - Same as on AIX and HP-UX.

Personal Printers - Same as on AIX and HP-UX.

Tools - The Style Manager is located here and is displayed on the front panel. You'll also find easy access to the CDE error log, and Find Process allows you to view all processes running on your system and kill selected ones. The Customized Workspace Menu and Add Item to Menu actions allow you to easily modify the Workspace Menu. The Workspace Menu is accessed by placing the mouse over a blank area of the desktop and pressing the right mouse key. Whereas AIX and HP-UX come with a generic menu, Solaris has incorporated the front panel and subpanel actions into the Workspace Menu as another way to access these actions.

Hosts - Here, Solaris differs greatly from AIX and HP-UX. The Hosts subpanel contains system-related actions. On the front panel, you'll find the Performance Monitor icons indicating how busy your CPU and disk drives are. From the subpanel, this Host opens up the *dtterm* terminal emulator, and Console opens up a *dtterm* specifically for displaying console messages. System Information provides system information including system name, hardware model, network IP address and domain, physical and virtual memory, operating system version, and date and time last rebooted. Find Host is the same as Find Card in the Cards subpanel.

Help - Same as on AIX and HP-UX.

Trash - The Trash Can is the same, with the addition of a sub-panel icon to "empty" the Trash Can.

This concludes the overview of the look and feel of CDE. Armed with this knowledge, you can easily navigate around your desktop environment with confidence and ease. Next, you'll learn how to change that look and feel to conform to your work environment.

Customizing CDE

Before you modify any CDE configuration files, first develop a strategy. I know that I've mentioned this before, but it's important enough to mention again.

The following questions should get you started:

1. What are your users' needs?

2. Which of those needs can be met by reconfiguring CDE?

3. At what level should these changes be made (system-wide, groups of users, individual users only)?

4. Which CDE files do you need to modify (names and locations)?

5. What are the changes and what is their order within the file?

It's also a good idea to have handy a binder containing man pages for each of the CDE components (for looking up resources and their values) and a copy of each of the CDE configuration files.

Now that you have a good understanding as to how CDE works, I'll lead you through making changes and customizing the system for either the entire user community or each individual user.

I'll precede each change with a discussion of what is involved in making the change. I'll be making some basic, simple changes as well as some more advanced changes to show you how versatile CDE can be.

One thing I need to mention is that all these changes can be made on any system. And knowing how to do these tasks "the hard way" increases your understanding of what these tools are doing for you in the background. So be sure to give each one a try.

Making Changes Using Style Manager

Font Size

When we first log in to CDE and the workspace comes up, as shown in Figure 13-4, one of the first things many users change is the size of the font. Initially set to 4, most users want a bigger font. This change is easy.

Figure 13-4   Style Manager

    1. **Click on the Style Manager icon** on the front panel. This action brings up the Style Manager.

    2. **Click on Font.**

    3. **Highlight 5**.

    4. **Click on OK**.

Backdrop and Colors

The Style Manager is also where we can change the backdrop and colors:

1. **Click on Backdrop** and we are presented with a variety of backdrop choices.

2. After we see one we like, such as Pebbles, we can **click on apply** and then **click on close** to change our backdrop. Notice, however, that this action changes the backdrop only for the workspace that we are in.

To change the other workspaces, we can either go to them and bring up the Style Manager in that workspace or, because we already have Style Manager up, we can click in the top right corner on the little "-" on the window itself, above "File," and access the pull-down menu. From here, we can choose Occupy All Workspaces. Then we can simply go to the other workspaces, and Style Manager is already up and ready for us there. The Backdrop area is the only place we have to worry about moving to other workspaces.

3. To change colors, **click on the Color icon**. We are given a list of different color schemes from which to choose. And if one isn't quite to our liking, we can easily modify the color, hue, brightness, and contrast. We can even grab a color from somewhere else, such as an image off the Internet, to include in the color scheme. Once we have the colors we like, we can save the scheme with its own name.

Adding Objects to or Removing Objects from the Front Panel

The front panel can make life just a little easier for us by including frequently used items on it. One of the most frequent actions is opening up a terminal window. And although CDE comes with dtterm as the default terminal window, we sometimes might want to use an xterm window. We'll add it to the Personal Applications subpanel, where dtterm lives on AIX and HP-UX systems. Solaris users can do the same by putting the **xterm** on the Hosts subpanel, where the This Host terminal emulator lives.

You have two ways to add objects to the CDE front panel:

- Drag and drop them into a slideup subpanel and then make them the default for that subpanel.

- Modify the **/etc/dt/appconfig/types/C/dtwm.fp** configuration file. This approach will be used later when we create actions and file types.

The basic actions to add a control button through drag and drop are as follows:

•Drag the application icon you want as a front panel button from an application manager view and drop the icon onto the installation section (the top section) of the appropriate subpanel.

•Place the mouse pointer over the icon and press mouse button 3 to display the subpanel menu.

• Select *Copy to Main Panel.*

1. **Click on the up arrow** of the Personal Applications subpanel on AIX or HP-UX or on the Hosts subpanel on Solaris so that it pops up.

2. **Click on the Application Manager** icon, where Desktop Applications and Desktop Tools live.

3. **Double click on Desktop_Tools**. Here you'll find **Xterm**.

4. **Drag and drop the Xterm** icon from Desktop_Tools to the Install Icon box at the top of the Personal Applications subpanel on HP-UX and AIX, or Hosts on Solaris.

Now if we want to include **xterm** on the front panel:

1. **Right click on the Xterm** icon in the Personal Applications or Hosts subpanel.

2. **Select Copy to Main Panel** or **Promote to Front Panel** depending on which CDE you are using.

Adding Another Workspace

Another easy change to the front panel is to add another workspace. CDE comes with a default of four workspaces, but this is easy to change. We'll add one more and call it "Web View." This can be the window where we'll access the Internet.

1. **Place the mouse in the Workspace area of the front panel** and **press the right mouse button**.

2. **Select Add Workspace** from the pull-down menu. The workspace "New" has been added.

3. **Right click on the new workspace labeled "New"** and select **Rename. Type Web View** and **press Return**.

If we want to delete a Workspace, simply right-click on the Workspace to be removed and then select delete.

Making these kinds of changes is easy, and they help personalize the workspace for the individual user.

Changing the Front Panel in Other Ways

In addition to adding and removing buttons, you can shape the front panel in other ways. These other ways use Workspace Manager resources to modify default values. The following resources relate to the front panel:

- **clientTimeoutInterval** - Length of time the Busy light blinks and the pointer remains an hourglass when a client is started from the front panel.

- **geometry** - x and y coordinate location of the front panel.

- **highResFontList** - Font to use on a high-resolution display.

- **lowResFontList** - Font to use on a low-resolution display.

- **mediumResFontList** - Font to use on a medium-resolution display.

- **name** - Name of the front panel to use when multiple front panels are in **dtwm.fp**.

- **pushButtonClickTime** - Time interval distinguishing two single mouse clicks from a double click (to avoid double launching an application accidently).

- **waitingBlinkRate** - Blink rate of the front panel Busy light.

- **workspaceList** - List of workspace names.

- **title** - Title to appear on a workspace button.

Like all other workspace manager resources, these front-panel resources have the following syntax:

```
Dtwm*screen*resource: value
```

For example, suppose instead of the default four workspaces, all that your users need a front panel with six workspaces named Mail, Reports, Travel, Financials, Projects, and Studio. Further, they prefer a large font and have decided upon New Century Schoolbook 10-point bold. As system administrator, you'd make everyone happy with the following resource specifications:

```
Dtwm*0*workspaceList: One Two Three Four Five Six
Dtwm*0*One*title: Mail
Dtwm*0*Two*title: Reports
Dtwm*0*Three*title: Travel
Dtwm*0*Four*title: Financials
Dtwm*0*Five*title: Projects
Dtwm*0*Six*title: Studio
Dtwm*0*highResFontList:
          -adobe-new century schoolbook-bold-r-normal\
          --10-100-75-75-p-66-iso8859-1
```

The screen designation is usually *0*, except for displays capable of both image and overlay planes. The order of screens in the **X*screens** file is what determines the screen number; the first screen, typically the image plane, is designated as 0. Note also the inclusion of workspace names (One, Two, Three, Four, Five, and Six) in the six title resource specifications.

These changes can be added to the **sys.resources** file, which is discussed in detail in "Advanced Topics" later in this chapter. These changes can also be made by use of the **EditResources** action to insert the new resource lines into each user's **RESOURCE_MANAGER** property and then restart the workspace manager.

The obvious disadvantage is that you have to physically go to each user's work area and take over the machine for a few minutes. However, on the plus side, the changes are immediate and are automatically saved in the correct **dt.resources** for users who restore their current session. You also avoid having your changes overwritten, which could happen if you modify the right **dt.resources** file at the wrong time, while the user is still logged in.

Modifying Things in Slide-up Subpanels

Subpanels are defined in **dtwm.fp** after the front panel and front-panel control definitions. To associate a subpanel with a front panel control button, the front-panel control name is listed as the container name in the subpanel definition.

Note: **/etc/dt** is where global changes are made. **$HOME/.dt** is where local or individual user changes are made.

To add a slideup subpanel to the front panel, follow these steps:

1. Copy the file **/usr/dt/appconfig/types/C/dtwm.fp** to either **/etc/dt/appconfig/types/C/dtwm.fp**   or   **$HOME/.dt/types/dtwm.fp**.

2. Decide which control button with which the slide-up is to be associated.

3. Create the subpanel definition file in **dtwm.fp**. This will take the following form:

```
SUBPANEL     SubPanelName
{
```

```
CONTAINER_NAME  AssociatedFrontPanelControlButton
TITLE  SubPanelTitle
}
```

4. Create subpanel control definitions for the subpanel. These will take the following form:

```
CONTROL  ControlName
{
TYPE  icon
CONTAINER_NAME    SubPanelName
CONTAINER_TYPE    SUBPANEL
ICON  BitmapName
PUSH_ACTION   ActionName
}
```

As with front panel control buttons, it's easier to copy and modify an existing subpanel file than to start from scratch.

Changing the Default Printer Name Display

We'll now make an easy change to one of the slide-up subpanels. If we pop up the Personal Printers subpanel, it shows that we have a default printer configured, but not the name of it. Let's go back into the front panel file, **dtwm.fp**, and change that:

1. Bring up your favorite editor, such as **dtpad** or **vi**, and edit **/$HOME/.dt/types/dtwm.fp**.

2. Scroll down to CONTROL Printer. You'll see that the LABEL is Default. Change or add to that the name of your default printer. My printer is called *a464*.

LABEL   Default - a464

3. **Save the file** and **restart Workspace Manager**. Position the mouse over a blank area on your workspace and press the right mouse button. Select Restart Workspace Manager. On Solaris, press the right mouse button to bring up the Custom-

ized Workspace Menu. From here, select Windows, where you'll find the Restart Workspace Manager key.

Pop up the Personal Printers subpanel to see what the default printer really is. Of course, if we change the default, we'll have to change the front panel again. But we know how to do that now, don't we! Figure 13-5 shows the Front Panel.

Figure 13-5 Front Panel with Changes

Front Panel Animation

Animation for front panel or slide-up subpanel drop zones is created by displaying a progressive series of bitmaps. By convention, the bit-maps are in **/usr/dt/appconfig/icons**. The list of bitmaps to display is contained in animation definitions at the end of **dtwm.fp**.

To create an animation sequence for a drop zone:

1. Create a progressive series of bitmaps.

2. Add a list of these bitmap files to the appropriate configuration file using the following syntax:

```
ANIMATION AnimationName
{
 bitmap0
 bitmap1
 bitmap2
 bitmap3
 bitmap4
 bitmap5
}
```

3. Add a line to the appropriate control definition using the syntax:

```
DROP_ANIMATION AnimationName
```

Adding Items to the Workspace Menu

The workspace menu is defined in the **sys.dtwmrc** file. As mentioned in the overview of the front panel for Solaris, the Workspace Menu is accessed by placing the mouse over a blank area of the desktop and pressing the right mouse key. Where AIX and HP-UX come with a generic menu, Solaris has incorporated the front panel and subpanel actions into the Workspace Menu as another way to access these actions. However, we can create customized Workspace Menu for all three systems using the left mouse key to access it. We'll be doing this task next.

A cusotmized Workspace menu can contain frequently used commands and applications. The customized menu is usually accessed by pressing the left mouse button, which pops up the menu for viewing and selection. A Workspace menu comes in handy for those who have a set number of things they do regularly. For instance,

man page

vi - 21

man page

ps - 13

man page

netstat -12

a programmer who uses **C++**, **vi**, and **isql** may have a menu with those items, or a system administrator may have a menu with **df**, **ps -ef**, and **netstat** on it. Or those on an expansive network may want a menu of system logins.

For one or two changes, you can modify the existing Workspace menu. For major changes, it's probably easier to insert an entirely new menu definition in **sys.dtwmrc**.

A menu definition has the following syntax:

```
Menu MenuName
{
  "Menu Name"          f.title
  "Frame"              f.exec /nfs/system1/usr/frame/bin/maker
  "Second Item"        action
  "Third Item"         action
}
```

The first line specifies the menu name, following the keyword **Menu**. The lines between the curly braces list the items that appear in the menu in their order of appearance; thus the first line is the title as designated by the function **f.title**. The second line is an example of a definition that would start **FrameMaker** from a remote application server in a distributed environment. Numerous other functions exist, approximately 45 in all. For a complete list, see the **dtwmrc** (4) man page.

For users to display the menu, you need to bind the menu definition to a mouse button and a screen location using the action **f.menu MenuName**. For example, if your users want to post the menu by pressing mouse button 3 when the pointer is on the workspace background, you would insert the following line in the Mouse Button Bindings Description section at the end of **sys.dtwmrc**:

```
<Btn3Down> root f.menu MenuName
```

(Actually, it would be easier to modify the line that's already there by exchanging **MenuName** for **DtRootMenu** on the second line.)

Now we'll create a simple menu. Our menu is going to include running FrameMaker, running the **vi** editor, and logging into a remote system.

1. First we need a copy of the **/usr/dt/config/C/sys.dtwmrc** file to **/etc/dt/config/C**:

man page

cp - 16

> cp /usr/dt/config/C/sys.dtwmrc /etc/dt/config/C/sys.dtwmrc

If we were going to make this a local change for one user only, it would be copied to **/$HOME/.dt** and renamed **dtwmrc**. For the admin1 user, that would be **/home/admin1/.dt/dtwmrc** or on Solaris in **/home/admin1/.dt/C/dtwmrc**.

2. Go into our favorite editor and **modify the file**. We're going to add our new menu just after the DtRootMenu entry, which we see on our system as the left mouse button's "Workspace Menu." Add the following:

```
Menu AdminMenu
{
  "Admin1's Menu"        f.title
  "Frame Maker"          f.exec  "/nfs/system1/usr/frame/bin/maker"
  "VI Editor"            f.exec  "xterm -e /usr/bin/vi"
  "Login systemA"        f.exec  "xterm -geometry 80x50+830+0 -sl 200 -bg
DarkOrchid4 -fg white -n SYSTEMA -T SYSTEMA -e remsh systemA &"
}
```

The **f.title** function shows that this is the menu title. **f.exec** means to execute the following string. Notice that FrameMaker does not need a terminal window because it uses its own, whereas **vi** and the login both need a terminal window in which to run. Also, I embellished on the **xterm** for the login, making the terminal window very large, with lots of terminal memory and using specific colors.

man page

vi - 21

Now, let's restart the Workspace Manager and try out our new menu:

3. Position the mouse over a blank area on the workspace and press the left mouse button. Select **Restart Workspace Manager**.

Creating pull-down menus is easy and can easily be expanded by adding submenus to the menu. Just use the function **f.menu** followed by the menu name. Add the following just after "Admin1's Menu":

"Work Menu"   f.menu   WorkMenu"

And then after the } from the Menu AdminMenu section, add:
Menu WorkMenu
{
.
}

Performing these advanced functions really isn't so hard. The hardest part is remembering which directories to put the files in: **/etc/dt** for global changes or **$HOME/.dt** for individual changes.

Creating Control Buttons, Actions, and File Types

An action starts a process such as a shell script or an application. An action can be connected to a front-panel button to start when the button is clicked. An action can be connected to a front panel drop zone to be performed when a data file is dropped on the drop zone. An action can be associated with an icon in a file manager window so tht the action can be started by double clicking the icon. An action can be associated with a particular data type so that double-clicking the data file icon starts the action and opens the data file.

In addition to setting up a front panel and default session to meet your users needs, the single most important thing you can do to make computing life easier for the people who depend on you is to create actions and data types.

CDE actions and data types are defined in files that end in **.dt**. Similar to most other CDE configuration files, ***.dt** files have a system-wide version that can be copied into a user's personal directory and customized for personal use. Most system-wide ***.dt** files are found in **/usr/dt/appconfig/types/C**; personal ***.dt** files are created by copying **user-prefs.dt** from **/usr/dt/appconfig/types/C** to **$HOME/ .dt/types**.

The default search path that CDE uses to look for actions and file types includes the following main directories in the order listed:

- $HOME/.dt/types

- /etc/dt/appconfig/types

- /usr/dt/appconfig/types

You can add more directories to the search path using the **DTDATABASESEARCHPATH** environment variable. Insert this environment variable and the new search path into **/etc/dt/config/ Xsession** for a system-wide influence. Insert the environment variable and search path into **$HOME/.dtprofile** for individual users.

Control Buttons - The basic control definition has six parts:

- **CONTROL name** - The definition name. This is the only part of the definition outside the curly braces.

- **TYPE** - The type of control. Several types exist. The most useful for customizing the front panel are probably blank and icon. A blank is useful as a space holder. An icon can start an action or application or be a drop zone.

- **ICON** - The bitmap to display on the front panel. Front-panel bitmaps are located in the **/usr/dt/appconfig/icons** directory.

- **CONTAINER_NAME** - The name of the container that holds the control. This must correspond to the name of an actual container listed in **dtwm.fp**.

- **CONTAINER_TYPE** - The type of container that holds the control. This can be **BOX**, **SWITCH**, or **SUBPANEL**, but it must agree with the type of the container name.

- **PUSH_ACTION** - This is what happens when the control button is pushed. **PUSH_ACTION** is just one of several possible actions. For more information, see the **dtwm** man page.

To remove a control button from the front panel, type a pound sign (#) in the left-most column of the **CONTROL** definition line. The (#) turns the control specification into a comment line.

Add a control button by editing the **dtwm.fp** file:

1. Copy **dtwm.fp** from **/usr/dt/appconfig/types/C** to **/etc/dt/appconfig/types/C**.

2. Add the new control definition using the following format:

```
CONTROL NewControl
{
TYPE            icon
CONTAINER_NAME Top
CONTAINER_TYPE BOX
ICON            NewControlBitmap
PUSH_ACTION     NewControlExecutable
}
```

Action and File Types have their own peculiarities in that each has a couple of parts, and each must live in its own directory location. These peculiarities will be come clear as we create an action on the subpanel. The following are the recommended locations in which to create an action or file type definition:

- Create a completely new file in the **/etc/dt/appconfig/types** directory. This file has a system-wide influence. Remember, the file must end with the **.dt** extension.

- Copy **user-prefs.dt** from **/usr/dt/appconfig/types** to the **/etc/dt/appconfig/types** directory and insert the definition there for system-wide use.

- Copy **user-prefs.vf** to **$HOME/.dt/types** and insert the definition there for individual users.

A typical action has the following syntax:

```
ACTION     ActionName
{
 TYPE     type
```

```
  keyword     value
  keyword     value
}
```

For example, here's a FrameMaker action:

```
ACTION      FRAME
{
  TYPE        COMMAND
  WINDOW-TYPE NO-STDIO
  EXEC-STRING /nfs/hpcvxmk6/usr/frame/bin/maker
}
```

A typical data type has the following syntax:

```
DATA_ATTRIBUTES            AttributesName
{
  keyword        value
  keyword        value
  ACTIONS        action, action
}
DATA_CRITERIA
{
 DATA_ATTRIBUTES AttributesName
 keyword        value

 keyword        value
}
```

Note that all definitions have the following general syntax:

```
  KEYWORD value
```

Notice that a data type definition is actually in two parts: an attribute part and a criteria part. The attribute portion of the data type definition specifies the look of the datatype; the criteria portion specifies the behavior of the data type.

For example, here's a file type for FrameMaker files that uses the FRAME action:

```
DATA_ATTRIBUTES       FRAME_Docs
{
  DESCRIPTION         This file type is for FrameMaker documents.
  ICON                makerIcon
  ACTIONS             FRAME
}
DATA_CRITERIA
{
DATA_ATTRIBUTES_NAME  FRAME_Docs
NAME_PATTERN  *.fm
MODE    f
}
```

You can create actions and file types from scratch using these formats. However, the easiest way to create an action is to use the **CreateAction** tool. **CreateAction** is located in the Desktop Applications folder of the Applications Manager and presents you with a fill-in-the-blank dialog box that guides you through creating an **action.dt** file containing the action definition. You can then move this file to the appropriate directory for the range of influence you want the action to have: **/etc/dt/appconfig/types** for a system-wide influence; **$HOME/.dt/types** for individual users.

Creating a New Icon and Action

Creating an icon is a challenging task. We could use the Icon Editor found in Desktop_Apps to create a new icon, or we could find a picture we like and use it. One thing to be careful of when pulling in a picture, in order for it to be seen correctly on the front panel, is that it has to be no larger than 32x32 pixels or only a portion of the icon will be displayed. Viewing the picture in the Icon Editor shows you the size of the picture. You may want to search through the application directories for useful icons or pull one down from the Internet.

For this entire example, I'm going to use the Instant Information software that comes with HP-UX. This is the manual set on the CD. Other application software will work just as well; just make sure that your paths correspond with the software you are using. Also, I'm going to use a fictitious user's home directory: **/home/admin1**.

1. **Bring up the Icon Editor** from the Desktop_Apps (HP-UX), Desktoptools (AIX), or from the Desktop_Tools, on Solaris all in the Application Manager.

2. Choose **File -> Open**.

3. Enter a path or folder name: **/opt/dynatext/data/bitmaps**.

4. Enter the file name: **logoicon.bm**

5. Choose **Open**.

We'll see the icon and that it is indeed 32x32. Now we need to save the icon to our own **.dt** directory.

6. Choose **File -> Save As**.

7. Enter path or folder name: **/$HOME/.dt/icons**. For the admin1 user, that would be in **/home/admin1/.dt/icons**.

If we were going to do this task globally, we'd put this in **/etc/dt/appconfig/types/C**.

8. Leave the file name as is.

9. **Save**.

Now that we have the icon, we need to create an action file and a description file to go with it.

1. **Using your favorite Text Edito**r, enter the following:

```
ACTION instinfo
{
LABEL          instinfo
TYPE           COMMAND
```

```
WINDOW_TYPE    NO_STDIO
EXEC_STRING    /opt/dynatext/bin/dynatext
DESCRIPTION    This action starts Instant Information
}
```

The LABEL is the name of the action, the TYPE is a command, the WINDOW_TYPE is none (no standard I/O or NO_STDIO) because the application has its own window, EXEC_STRING is the command to be executed, and the DESCRIPTION is just a description of what this action does. Make sure that the NO_STDIO has an underscore and not a dash, and don't forget the last }. I've done both of these and then had fun trying to figure out why the action either didn't appear to exist or, if it did appear, why it wouldn't work.

2. **Save this file as /$HOME/.dt/types/instinfo.dt**. For the admin1 user, that would be **/home/admin1/.dt/types/ instinfo.dt**. If this were a global configuration, we'd save the file as **/etc/dt/appconfig/types/C/instinfo.dt**.

Now that we have an action, we need to create a description file. Note that this is a new file with just these 2 lines in it. The contents of this file are irrelevant, but the permissions *must* include executable.

3. Again, **using your favorite editor**, enter:

```
ACTION instinfo
DESCRIPTION  This action starts Instant Information
```

4. **Save this file as /$HOME/.dt/appmanager/instinfo**. For the admin1 user, that would be **/home/admin1/.dt/appmanager/ instinfo**. If this were a global configuration, we'd save the file as   **/etc/dt/appconfig/appmanager/instinfo**.

5. Change the permissions to include execute as follows:

chmod 555 /$HOME/.dt/appmanager/instinfo

Now it's time to modify the front panel to include the icon and action we just created. The front panel file, **dtwm.fp**, is located in the **/usr/dt/appconfig/types/C** directory. Because don't want to overwrite the system file, we need to copy it locally and then modify it for our use.

1. Copy this to **/$HOME/.dt/types/dtwm.fp** for AIX and HP-UX and to **/$HOME/.dt/types/fp-dynamic/dtwm.fp** for Solaris. For the admin1 user, that would be:

   cp /usr/dt/appconfig/types/C/dtwm.fp   /home/admin1/.dt/types/dtwm.fp

man page

cp - 16

   or on Solaris:

   cp /usr/dt/appconfig/types/C/dtwm.fp   /home/admin1/.dt/types/fp-dynamic/dtwm.fp

2. **Using your favorite edito**r, modify the local **dtwm.fp** file.

As we look at the file, we notice that it is in the same order as the front panel is displayed. The clock is the first CONTROL in the file and the first item on the front panel. Also notice that the POSITION_HINTS is 1. Date is next and so is POSITION_HINTS 2. What we want to do is put our new icon and action after POSITION_HINTS 4, the TextEditor CONTROL.

3. Go down just past the } ending CONTROL TextEditor and before CONTROL Mail. At this point, **insert the following exactly as shown below**. Make sure that the uppercase letters are capitalized and the lowercase letters aren't.

```
CONTROL  Info
{
  TYPE              icon
  CONTAINER_NAME    Top
  CONTAINER_TYPE     BOX
  POSITION_HINTS    5
  ICON              logoicon.bm
  LABEL             Instant Info
  PUSH_ACTION       instinfo
}
```

4. Now be careful; this part is tricky. The next items have to have their POSITION_HINTS renumbered. But we are going to **renumber only the next eight items, beginning with Mail and ending with Trash**. Instead of 5 through 12, these are going to become 6 through 13.

5. **Save** the file.

Now, let's restart the Workspace Manager. If we did everything right, we'll have a new icon, which, when clicked, will bring up Instant Information shown in Figure 13-6.

6. Position the mouse over a blank area on the workspace and press the right mouse button. Select **Restart Workspace Manager**.

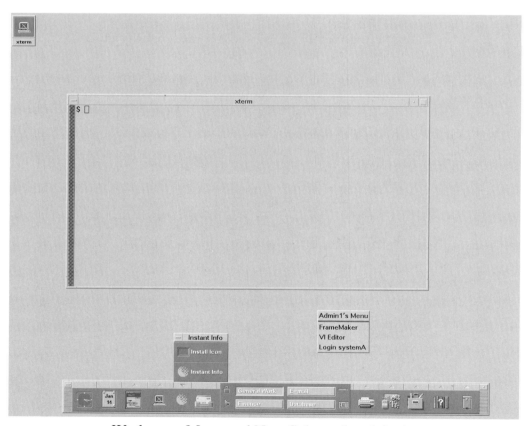

Figure 13-6 Workspace Menu and New Subpanel and Action

A couple of things to remember when creating actions: first and foremost, make sure the PUSH_ACTION and the file names are the same. That similarity is how they find each other. Make sure the that action file ends with **.dt** and make sure that the description file is executable. If any of these are wrong, the action either won't work or won't appear.

To avoid a lot of typing, sometimes the easiest approach is just to copy an existing definition and insert it where you want your new control to be and then modify it. As you move down the list of control definitions, you're moving from left to right across the front panel (notice that the POSITION_HINTS value increases in each definition). So if you want your new control to be to the right of the date on the front panel, you insert the control on the line below "date" and add a POSITION_HINTS 3 line to your definition; if you wanted your new control to be to the left of "date," insert the control on the line above "date" with a POSITION_HINTS of 1.

The new control definition can be located anywhere in the list of control definitions. The POSITION_HINTS line keeps it from getting inadvertently bumped to a new position. It's still a good idea to copy an existing definition and avoid extra typing; it reduces the chance of typing mistakes. And don't forget to include the curly braces.

Using Different Fonts

Although CDE fonts have been carefully selected for readability, you may have valid reasons to prefer other fonts. To make your fonts available system-wide throughout the CDE environment, put them in **/etc/dt/app-defaults/Dtstyle** so that they will appear in the style manager's font dialog box. To make fonts available only for a particular X client application, specify the font in the **app-defaults** file for the application. Just remember, this overrides the fonts in the style manager.

The font dialog box can contain a maximum of seven font sizes. You can adjust this number downward by resetting the value of **Dtstyle*NumFonts** in **/etc/dt/app-defaults/Dtstyle**; however, you can't increase the number higher than seven.

The Font Dialog section of the **Dtstyle** configuration file has seven **SystemFont** resources and seven **UserFont** resources. Again, you can have fewer than seven system and seven user fonts, but you can't have more.

To specify fonts for a particular application, use the ***FontList** resource in the **app-defaults** file for the application.

To modify font resources on an individual user basis, you can use the **EditResources** action as described in the earlier section "Changing the Front Panel in Other Ways."

Changing the Login Messages

One of the nice things about CDE is the ability to modify so many parts. You can customize individual login accounts or the entire system. By customizing the login screen, you can show those about to log in the name of the system they are accessing, the company logo, and a personalized greeting. These modifications take place in the **Xresources** file:

1. As we've done already with the **dtwm.fp** and **dtwmrc** files, we will need to copy the system file from **/usr/dt/config/C** to **/etc/dt/config/C** as follows:

man page

cp - 16

cp /usr/dt/config/C/Xresources   /etc/dt/config/C/Xresources

2. **Go into your favorite editor** and bring up the **Xresources** file so that it can be edited.

3. **Go to the GREETING area**. Here we'll find the following lines:

```
!!Dtlogin*greeting.labelString:        Welcome to %LocalHost%
!!Dtlogin*greetingpersLabelString:     Welcome %s
```

The first line is the message on the initial login screen. Let's change that so that it welcomes us to our company, ABC, Inc.:

1. **Remove the comment notations**. Unlike shell scripts that most of us are used to, the Xresources file uses two exclamation points as comment notation. Remove the !!.

2. Next, **modify "Welcome to %LocalHost%"**. The %Local-Host% variable is replaced with our system name in the login screen. The line should look like this:

Dtlogin*greeting.labelString: **ABC, Inc, Welcomes You to %LocalHost%**

3. Next let's **change the second line** to include the department that this system is dedicated to: finance. This second line shows what is displayed when we are prompted for our password. The %s variable is our user name. The line should now look like this:

Dtlogin*greetingpersLabelString: **The Finance Department Welcomes %s**

4. **Save the file**.

5. **Now log out and back in**. We should see the changes in the login screen. We didn't need to "reload" the file, because the act of logging out and back in does that action.

Changing the Login Picture

Adding a new picture to the login screen is easy if you know one thing. The file has to be a bitmap (.bm) or pixmap (.pm) file. A bitmap file is black and white, and the pixmap file is color. I've tried using other kinds of pictures (.gif and .jpg formats), but they just don't display. The good news is that these can be imported from other systems or the Internet for our use. To make things simple, we're going to use one already on the system. A bitmap showing a birthday cake was found in **/usr/lib/X11/bitmaps** on an HP-UX workstation. However, I have also successfully pulled down pictures of flowers, the Grand

Canyon, and country music singers (note Donna wrote this chapter not Marty) from the Internet and put them on my system login screen.

1. Once more, let's go into our favorite editor and modify **/etc/dt/ config/C/Xresources**.

2. **Go to the MISC area.** Here we'll find the following lines:

!!Dtlogin*logo*bitmapFile: < bitmap or pixmap file >

3. **Delete the leading !!**, which are the comment designators.

4. **Replace < bitmap or pixmap file >** with the name of the bit-map file using the entire path location. The line should look as follows:

Dtlogin*logo*bitmapFile: /usr/lib/X11/bitmap/cake.bm

5. **Save the file.**

6. **Now log out and back in.** We should see the birthday cake in the login screen. Again, we didn't need to "reload" the file, because the act of logging out and back in does that task.

Now that we've seen how easily we can make some simple cus-tomizations in CDE for our end users, we should be able to take this knowledge and really make their CDE environments a productive and friendly place to work.

CDE - Advanced Topics

The Relationship among X, Motif, and CDE

X, OSF/Motif, and CDE are enabling framework technologies. Taken together, X, Motif, and CDE make up the three graphical layers on top of the operating system and hardware platform.

The GUI layers provide increasingly richer ease-of-use functions in a progressive series of layers that buffer the end user from the "user-hostile," character-based interface of the operating system layer.

The X Window System

The X Window System consists of the following:

- Xlib - Low-level library for programming window manipulation; graphics capabilities such as line drawing and text placement; controlling display output, mouse, and keyboard input; and application network transparency.

- Xt Intrinsics - Higher-level library for programming widgets and gadgets (graphical controls components like menus, scrollbars, and push buttons).

- Display servers - Hardware-specific programs, one per display, that manage the graphical input and output.

- Interclient communication conventions (ICCC) - A manual specifying standards for how X client programs should communicate with each other.

- Configuration files - One configuration file that specifies the default session to start (**sys.x11start**) and another specifying values for resources used to shape the X environment (**sys.Xdefaults**).

Through these mechanisms, X provides the standard upon which the graphical part of the network-oriented, client/server, distributed computing paradigm is based. A knowledge of **Xlib** and the **Xt** Intrinsics is important for programming in X and for programming at the Motif level. For system administrators, however, as long as the display servers work and X client applications are ICCC-compliant, you shouldn't need to delve into the X layer. CDE enables you to view X pretty much as part of "all that underlying technological infrastructure stuff" and focus on developing appropriate configurations of CDE to meet your users' work contexts.

Motif

Motif consists of the following:

- mwm window manager - Executable program that provides Motif-based window frames, window management, and a workspace menu in the X environment.

- Motif widget toolkit - Higher-level library of widgets and gadgets, the graphical components used to control the user environment.

- Motif style guide - A manual defining the Motif appearance and behavior for programmers.

- Configuration files - The **system.mwmrc** file containing configuration information for the workspace menu and key and button bindings. Resources for the window manager are in **mwm** in the **/usr/lib/X11/app-defaults** directory.

Motif provides the window manager for the end user, the widget toolkit for application developers, and the style guide to help developers design and build proper Motif-conformant applications. As with X, system administrators can view Motif mostly as "programmer's stuff," part of the underlying infrastructure, and focus on developing appropriate CDE configuration files.

CDE

As we have already seen, CDE consists of the following:

- Workspace Manager - Executable program that provides Motif-based window frames, window management, a workspace menu, and the front panel.

- File Manager - Program that iconically manages files and directories through direct manipulation.

- Style Manager - Container of dialog boxes that control elements of the CDE environment, like workspace color and fonts.

- Help Manager - This program provides context-sensitive help text on CDE components.

- Login Manager - Daemon-like application that handles login and password verification.

- Session Manager - Manager that handles saving and restoring user sessions.

- Application Manager - Manager that registers and keeps track of applications in the CDE environment.

- Configuration Files - A big bunch, most of which you can avoid dealing with (see the next section).

CDE also provides a number of basic, end-user productivity-enhancing applications. In general, CDE provides a graphical environment into which users, or you, their system administrator, can incorporate the software tools needed to do their work.

X, Motif, and CDE Configuration Files

X, Motif, and CDE all use configuration files to shape their appearance and behavior. Elements of appearance and behavior such as foreground color, keyboard focus policy, and client decoration are resources that can be controlled by values in the appropriate configuration file. In X, Motif, and CDE, the word "resource" has a special meaning. It doesn't refer to vague natural resources or generic system resources, but to rather specific elements of appearance and behavior. Some examples are the **foreground** resource, the **keyboardFocusPolicy** resource, and the **clientDecoration** resource. For example, the foreground color could be black, keyboard focus policy could be explicit, and client decoration could be plus-title (title bar only). These would appear in some appropriate configuration file as the following:

```
*foreground:          black

*keyboardFocusPolicy:explicit

*clientDecoration:    +title
```

Which configuration file these resources appear in depends on the scope of the effect desired (system-wide or individual user) and the graphical interface level being used (X, Motif, or CDE).

X Configuration Files

The X Window System has the following configuration files:

sys.x11start
sys.Xdefaults
system.mwmrc
X*screens
X*devices
X*pointerkey

By convention, these files are located in the **/usr/lib/X11** directory; however, I have noticed that many systems have eliminated this directory and moved many of the X-related files elsewhere in the system. In addition, each X client application has its own app-defaults configuration file located, also by convention, in the **/usr/lib/X11/app-defaults** directory. Although six files are listed above, unless you're configuring a workstation for multiple-display screens (X*screens), multiple-input devices (X*devices), or keyboard-only pointer navigation (X*pointerkey), you'll typically need to work with only **sys.x11start**, **sys.Xdefaults**, and **system.mwmrc**.

The **sys.x11start** file was a script used to start X and X clients before the advent of CDE. System administrators or knowledgeable users modified **sys.x11start** so that the appropriate mix of X clients started "automatically." The **sys.Xdefaults** file was read as X started to obtain values for various appearance and behavior resources. Modifications to **sys.Xdefaults** ensured that the X environment and clients had the proper appearance and behavior. **system.mwmrc** contained the configuration of the Workspace menu and button and key bindings. **system.mwmrc** has been replaced by the Motif version also, **system.mwmrc**.

Motif Configuration Files

Motif added only one new configuration file to the X list: **system.mwmrc**.

By convention, this file is kept with the X configuration files in **/usr/lib/X11**. Actually, this file isn't new; it is the Motif version of **system.mwmrc,** which simply replaced **system.mwmrc** in Motif environments.

Whereas X brought network and interclient communication standards to the graphical user interface, Motif brought a standard for appearance and behavior, the standard originally defined in IBM's System Application Architecture Common User Access (SAACUA), which forms the basis of most PC-based GUIs. Thus, push buttons and scroll bars have a defined look and a defined behavior, and double-clicking always causes the default action to happen.

From a programmer's point of view, the Motif Widget Toolkit represents quite an advance over programming in "raw" X. From a user's or system administrator's point of view, the Motif user environment is about the same as the X environment, except that the **mwm** Window Manager is replaced with the Motif window manager.

CDE Configuration Files

It is possible to point to over 80 files that, in one way or another, contribute to configuring some aspect of CDE. By convention, these files reside in the **/usr/dt** directory. However, if you remove from this list such files as those that:

• Configure CDE applications as opposed to the environment itself

- Establish default actions and datatype definitions that, although you create your own definitions in separate files, you never modify

- Are CDE working files and should not be customized

- Are more appropriately associated with configuring the UNIX, X, and Motif environments underlying CDE, including the various shell environments, then CDE has approximately 19 configuration files, as shown in Table 13-1

Table 13-1   CDE Configuration Files

* .Xauthority	* sys.font	* Xresources
* .Xdefaults	* sys.resources	* Xservers
* .dtprofile	* sys.sessions	* Xsession
* dtwm.fp	* Xaccess	* Xsetup
* dt.wmrc	* Xconfig	* Xstartup
* sys.dtprofile	* Xfailsafe	
* sys.dtwmrc	* Xreset	

Although 19 configuration files are still a lot, don't be alarmed by the number. You won't need to modify many of them, and can ignore a couple that you modify once and then forget. You need to understand in depth for periodic modification only one or two, perhaps a system-wide *.**dt** file for custom actions and datatypes or maybe **dtwm.fp**, if you are required to modify the front panel on a regular basis for some reason.

Still, configuring CDE is not something you want to start hacking at without a little preparation and a good idea of what you want to accomplish. All CDE configuration files are pretty well commented, so a good first step is to print the ones you want to modify.

Table 13-2 organizes CDE configuration files according to their content and the breadth of their influence:

Table 13-2   CDE Configuration File Influence

Nature of Configuration File	System-Wide Influence	User's Personal Influence
Environment Variables	sys.dtprofile Xconfig Xsession	.dtprofile
Appearance & Behavior Resources	sys.resources Xconfig Xresources sys.fonts	.Xdefaults
File Types & Action Definitions	misc *.dt files	user-prefs.dt
Client Startup at Login	sys.sessions Xstartup Xsession Xreset Xfailsafe	.xsession sessionetc
Workspace Manager & Front Panel	sys.dtwmrc dtwm.fp	dtwmrc user-prefs.fp
Clients/Servers & Access	Xaccess Xservers	.Xauthority

The file **sys.dtwmrc** controls the configuration of the Workspace Manager at the system level. This includes all of the following:

Workspace Menu   A menu that displays when mouse button 3 is pressed while the mouse pointer is over the workspace backdrop.

Button Bindings   Definitions of what action happens when a particular mouse button is pressed or released while the mouse pointer is over a particular area (frame, icon, window, or root).

Key Bindings   Definitions of what action happens when a particular key or key sequence is pressed while the mouse pointer is over a particular area (frame, icon, window, or root).

Unlike configuration files for X or Motif, **sys.dtwmrc** does not control the following configuration elements:

Front Panel   The box, usually at the bottom of the work-space, that contains commonly referenced indicators and frequently used graphical con-trols, including a six-button workspace switch.

Slideup Subpanels Menus that slide up from the front panel at various locations to provide more functional-ity without consuming more screen space.

Instead, to avoid a massively large and overly complex configu-ration file, these elements were separated into their own configuration file in CDE, **dtwm.fp**.

Some front panel configuration elements, like the number of workspaces and their arrangement in the workspace switch, are con-trolled through resources in a **sys.resources**, **dt.resources**, or **.Xde-faults** file. Like other Workspace Manager configuration files, **sys.dtwmrc** can be copied to a user's home directory, actually to **$HOME/.dt/** as **dtwmrc**, and modified to personalize the user's envi-ronment beyond the system-wide configuration of **sys.dtwmrc**.

The **sys.resources** file is one of those files you might modify once, and then never again. The **dt.resources** file is one of those files you won't ever need to modify and can ignore. The **.Xdefaults** file is one you or your users may modify on occasion.

The **sys.resources** file is where you put any non-default resources that you want in effect when a brand new user logs into CDE for the very first time. For example, as system administrator, you may want your users to have a CDE front panel with prenamed work-spaces, special colors, particular fonts, or application windows in cer-tain locations. After the first-time login, **sys.resources** is ignored in favor of **dt.resources**. This file, **dt.resources**, resides in **$HOME/.dt/ sessions/current** (or **$HOME/.dt/sessions/home** when the home ses-sion is restored) and is created automatically by CDE. You can consider it a CDE working file and forget about it. The **.Xdefaults** file is where you or an end-user would list X resources specific to the user's personal CDE environment. **sys.resources**, **dt.resources**, and **.Xdefaults** contain a list of resources and their values.

The **sys.sessions** file controls which clients start the very first time a new user logs into CDE. The **dt.sessions** file is to **sys.sessions** as **dt.resources** is to **sys.resources**.

It may be efficient to configure CDE to start particular applications for your users. You would specify these applications in **sys.sessions**. When a new user logs in for the first time, the CDE environment includes the specified clients. At the end of this first session by logging out, the remaining clients would be recorded in **$HOME/.dt/sessions/current** for CDE (**$HOME/.dt/sessions/home** when the home session is restored).

The **sys.dtprofile** file is a template that is automatically copied at first login into each new user's home directory as **.dtprofile**. **sys.dtprofile** replaces **.profile** or **.login** in the CDE environment (although either **.profile** or **.login** can be sourced in **.dtprofile** by removing the # comment symbol in front of **DTSOURCEPROFILE=true**). The **.dtprofile** file holds the personal environment variables that would, in a character-based environment, be found in **.profile** or **.login**. Use **.dtprofile** to avoid the interference that terminal I/O commands cause to CDE's graphical environment.

The CDE login manager, **dtlogin**, presets the following environment variables to default values:

DISPLAY	The name of the local display
EDITOR	The default text editor
HOME	The user's home directory as specified in **/etc/passwd**
KBD_LANG	The current language of the keyboard
LANG	The current NLS language
LC_ALL	The value of LANG
LC_MESSAGES	The value of LANG
LOGNAME	The user's login name as specified in **/etc/passwd**
MAIL	The default file for mail (usually **/var/mail/$USER**)

PATH	The default directories to search for files and applications
USER	The user name
SHELL	The default shell as specified in **/etc/passwd**
TERM	The default terminal emulation
TZ	The time zone in effect

Variations to these default values belong in each user's **.dtprofile**. Additional environment variables can be added as needed to shape the user's environment to the needs of the work context. Just beware of using commands that cause any terminal I/O.

Like **.dtprofile**, **Xsession** is a shell script that sets user environment variables. The environment variables in **Xsession** apply system-wide. The environment variables in **.dtprofile** apply only to a user's personal environment. Furthermore, Because the login manager runs **Xsession** after the X server has started, the variables in **Xsession** are not available to the X server. Variables typically set in **Xsession** include the following:

EDITOR	The default text editor.
KBD_LANG	The language of the keyboard (usually set to the value of $LANG).
TERM	The default terminal emulation.
MAIL	The default file for mail, which is usually **/var/mail/$USER**.
DTHELPSEARCHPATH	The locations to search for CDE help files.
DTAPPSEARCHPATH	The locations to search for applications registered with the CDE application manager.
DTDATABASESEARCHPATH	The locations to search for additional action and datatype definitions.
XMICONSEARCHPATH	The locations to search for additional icons.
XMICONBMSEARCHPATH	Same as above.

As an example, suppose that you are the system administrator for several mixed workstation and X terminal clusters located at a single site. As usually happens, most users have grown accustomed to certain text editors. Some like **vi**, others prefer **emacs**, and a couple wouldn't be caught dead without **dmx**. An easy way to provide each user with his or her favored text editor would be to reset their EDITOR variable to the appropriate value in the individual **.dtprofile** files.

man page

vi - 21

Xconfig contains resources that control the behavior of **dtlogin** and it also provides a place to specify the locations for any other **dtlogin** configuration files you create. The **Xconfig** file works on a system-wide basis, so it's one of those files that you modify only once and then forget about. When, during login, **Xconfig** is run, several CDE configuration files get referenced: **Xaccess**, **Xservers**, **Xresources**, **Xstartup**, **Xsession**, **Xreset**, and **Xfailsafe**. Like **Xconfig** itself, most of these files are the type that you modify once when installing CDE and then, unless the network topology changes, you never deal with again.

Xaccess, as the name implies, is a remote display access control file. **Xaccess** contains a list of the host names allowed or denied XDMCP connection access to the local computer. For example, when an X terminal requests login service, **dtlogin** consults the **Xaccess** file to determine whether service should be granted.

The primary use of the **Xservers** file is to list the display screens on the local system that **dtlogin** is responsible for managing. **dtlogin** reads the **Xservers** file and starts an X server for each display listed there. It then starts a child **dtlogin** process to manage the server and display the login screen. Note that **dtlogin** works only locally; **dtlogin** can't start an X server on a remote system or X terminal. For remote display servers, some other mechanism must be used to start the server, which then uses the X Display Management Control Protocol (XDMCP) to request a login screen from **dtlogin**.

The **Xservers** file is another of those files that you may spend some time with initially and then, unless the topology of your network changes, never deal with again. When do you use **Xservers**? When a display doesn't match the default configuration. The default configuration assumes that each system has a single bitmap display and is the system console. X terminals, multiple displays (heads), multiple screens, and Starbase applications all require configuration lines in the **Xservers** file.

The **Xresources** file contains the list of resources that control the appearance and behavior of the login screen. After you substitute your company's logo for the CDE logo and change the fonts and colors, you'll probably never have to deal with **Xresources** again (unless your company changes its logo).

Xstartup is a system-wide configuration file executed by the login manager, from which it receives several environment variables:

DISPLAY	The name of the local display.
USER	The login name of the user.
HOME	The user's home directory.
PATH	The value of the **systemPath** resource in **Xconfig**.
SHELL	The value of the **systemShell** resource in **Xconfig**.
XAUTHORITY	The file to access for authority permissions.
TZ	The local time zone.

Because it can execute scripts and start clients on a system-wide basis, **Xstartup** is similar to **sys.sessions**. The difference is that **Xstartup** runs as root. Thus, modifications to **Xstartup** should be reserved for actions like mounting file systems.

Xreset is a system-wide companion script to **Xstartup**. It runs as root and essentially undoes what **Xstartup** put in motion.

The **Xfailsafe** file contains customizations to the standard fail-safe session. The failsafe session provides a way to correct improper CDE sessions caused by errors in the login and session configuration files. As such, **Xfailsafe** is something that your users are not ever going to use, but you can make your life a little easier with a few judicious customizations.

The **sessionetc** file resides in a user's **.dt/sessions** directory and personalizes that user's CDE session. **sessionetc** handles the starting of additional X clients like **sys.session**, but on a per-user basis, as opposed to system-wide. Although **dt.session** also starts clients on a per-user basis, the clients are those of the default or current session. **dt.session** resides in **.dt/session/current**. **sessionetc**, which resides in **.dt/session**, and should contain only those clients that are not automatically restored. Typically, these are clients that do not set the **WM_COMMAND** properly, so the session manager can't save or restore them; thus, they need to be restarted in **sessionetc**.

The **sys.font** file contains the system-wide, default session font configuration. These default fonts were based on usability studies, so **sys.font** is a file you may never change. However, should you encounter a situation that requires a different mix of fonts on a system-wide basis, this is where you'd change them. Note that the font resources and values mentioned in **sys.font** must match exactly the default font resources specified in the **/usr/dt/app-defaults/C/Dtstyle** file.

CDE has a bunch of files that specify CDE action and data type definitions. All these files end with the file extension ***.dt**. A ***.dt** ("dt" for "desk top") contains both data type and action definitions. The default ***.dt** files are in **/usr/dt/appconfig/types/C** and act on a system-wide basis. Similarly, **user-prefs.dt**, the master copy of which is also located in **/usr/dt/appconfig/types/C**, is used at the personal user level.

The **.Xauthority** file is a user-specific configuration file containing authorization information needed by clients that require an authorization mechanism to connect to the server.

CDE Configuration File Locations

Where CDE looks for particular configuration files depends on the nature of the configuration files, principally what the files configure and how wide their influence is. Table 13-3 shows the location of system and user configuration files based on the nature of the file content.

For each of the default system-wide file locations listed in Table 13-3, a corresponding location exists for custom system-wide configuration files. These custom files should be located in the appropriate subdirectory under **/etc/dt**. The basic procedure is to copy the file you need to customize from **/usr/dt/something** to **/etc/dt/something** and then do your modifications there. For example, to change the default logo in **Xresources**, copy **/usr/dt/config/C/Xresources** to **/etc/dt/**

config/C/Xresources, open **/etc/dt/config/C/Xresources**, and make your changes.

Table 13-3   CDE System and User Configuration Files

Nature of Configuration File	System-Wide Influence	User's Personal Influence
Environment Variables	/usr/dt/config/	$HOME/
Appearance & Behavior Resources	/usr/dt/config/C /usr/dt/app-defaults/C	$HOME/.dt/ $HOME/.dt/sessions/current/ $HOME/.dt/sessions/home/
File Types & Action Definitions	/usr/dt/appconfig/ types/C	$HOME/.dt/types
Client Startup at Login	/usr/dt/config/ /usr/dt/config/C	$HOME/.dt/session/ $HOME/.dt/session/current/ $HOME/.dt/session/home/
Workspace Manager	/usr/dt/config	$HOME/.dt/

This is an important point. Files located under **/usr/dt** are considered CDE system files and will be overwritten during updates. Thus, any customizations you do there will be lost. Make all modifications to system-wide configuration files in **/etc/dt** and its subdirectories.

How Configuration Files Play Together

From the material covered so far, you've probably concluded correctly that CDE configuration files aren't something to go hacking at without a plan - a well thought-out plan. You've probably figured out that the element you want to configure and the breadth of influence you want it to have determine which configuration file you modify.

For instance, if you wanted to set an environment variable, you have a choice of four configuration files: **sys.dtprofile**, **Xconfig**, **Xsession**, and **.dtprofile**. But if you want to set environment variables that affect only a particular user, your choice immediately narrows to a single file, **.dtprofile**.

Now the only remaining piece of the puzzle is to understand the order in which CDE reads its configuration files. When a configuration element (an environment variable, resource, action, or data type) is specified twice but with different values, you obviously want the correct value used and the incorrect value ignored.

The following rules apply:

- For environment variables, the last specified value is used.

- For resources, the last specified value is used. However, this is influenced by specificity. Thus, **emacs*foreground** takes precedence over just ***foreground** for *emacs* clients, regardless of the order in which the resources were encountered.

- For actions, the first specified is used.

- For data types, the first specified is used.

Table 13-4 illustrates which specification is used when CDE reads multiple specifications of configuration elements in its configuration files:

Table 13-4 What CDE Uses for Configuration

Configuration Element	Element Used
resource	last encountered or most specific
environment	last encountered
action	first encountered
file type	first encountered

Put in terms of scope, a user configuration file overrides a system-wide configuration file. Looking at the order of precedence of just system-wide configuration files, the files in **/etc/dt** have precedence over those in **/usr/dt**, so global custom configurations have precedence over the CDE default configuration. And, **$HOME/.dt** files take precedence over those in **/etc/dt.**

For resources, the elements used to specify a GUI's appearance and behavior, CDE sets values according to the following priorities:

1. **Command line** -   When you start a client from the command line, options listed on the command line have top priority.

2. **Xresources, .Xdefaults, dt.resources, sys.resources,**   - When CDE starts, it reads these resource configuration files to determine the value of X resources to use for the session.

3. **RESOURCE MANAGER** - Resources already in the property **RESOURCE_MANAGER** may affect an application that is just starting.

4. **app-defaults** - Specifies "default" resource values that differ from built-in resource values.

5. **built-in defaults** - Default resources that are "hard-coded" have the lowest priority.

Specific resource specifications take precedence over general resource specifications. For example, suppose that you want a certain font in your text entry areas. You could correctly specify a ***FontList** resource in your personal **.Xdefaults** file, only to have it overwritten by an ***XmText*FontList** in an **app-defaults** file. Although **app-defaults** is of lower priority than **.Xdefaults**, the resource specification set there is more specific, so it takes precedence.

For environment variables, CDE sets values according to the following priorities:

1. **$HOME/.dtprofile** - User-specific variables have top priority.

2. **/etc/dt/config/C/Xsession -** Custom system-wide variables not read by X server.

3. **/etc/dt/config/C/Xconfig** - Custom system-wide variables read by X server.

4. **/usr/dt/config/C/Xsession -** Default system-wide variables not read by X server.

5. **/usr/dt/config/C/Xconfig** - Default system-wide variables read by X server.

6. **/usr/dt/bin/dtlogin** - Built-in default variables have the lowest priority.

For data type and action definitions, CDE looks for **.dt** files according to the following priority:

1. $HOME/.dt/types

2. /etc/dt/appconfig/types/C

3. /usr/dt/appconfig/types/C

Remember, for data types or actions, the first value that it finds is the one it uses. So if you just can't get a file type or action to work, check for a duplicate entry earlier in the file or for an entry in a file with higher priority. Note also that the environment variable DTDATABASESEARCHPATH can be set either in **/etc/dt/config/Xsession** or **$HOME/.dtprofile**, to add directories where CDE can search for file type and action definition information.

Specifying Appearance and Behavior

You need to know only two tricks to specifying appearance and behavior resources in configuration files. The first is to specify the resource and its value correctly. The second is to specify the resource and value in the correct configuration file.

Two caveats involve colors and fonts. The CDE style manager provides a graphical interface for modifying colors and fonts. However, if you specify an application's color or font directly, this specification will override the ability of the style manager to manage that resource for the application.

Typical ways to specify a color or font directly include the following:

- Type the specification on the command line as a startup option.

- Include the specification in the application's **app-defaults** file.

- Use the **xrdb** utility to add resources for the application to the resource database.

The Sequence of Events When CDE Starts

The following section is a blow-by-blow account of what happens when a user logs into CDE. In this particular account, assume a distributed topology like a diskless cluster. The account begins with the boot of the hub system and nodes in step 1. By step 4, X servers are running on each node and login screens are being displayed. By step 6, the user is logged in. By step 11, the session manager is busy re-creating the user's session.

1. The **dtlogin** executable is started as part of the **init** process that occurs during the system boot sequence on the hub machine and each cluster node.

2. **dtlogin** reads **/usr/dt/config/Xconfig** to get a list of resources with which to configure the login process. This is where **dtlogin** first learns about files like **Xaccess**, **Xservers**, **Xresources**, **Xstartup**, **Xsession**, and **Xreset** and gets the values of a number of appearance and behavior resources.

3. **dtlogin** reads two files in **/usr/dt/config**:

   - **Xservers** or the file identified by the **Dtlogin*servers** resource setting in **Xconfig**.

   - **Xresources** or the file identified by the **Dtlogin*resources** resource setting in **Xconfig**.

4. **dtlogin** starts an X server and a child **dtlogin** for each local display.

5. Each child **dtlogin** invokes **dtgreet**, the login screen.

6. When a login and password are validated, a child **dtlogin** sets certain environment variables to default values.

7. The child **dtlogin** runs **/usr/dt/config/Xstartup**.

8. The child **dtlogin** runs **/usr/dt/config/Xsession**.

9. **Xsession** runs **dthello**, the copyright screen.

10. **Xsession** reads **$HOME/.dtprofile**, setting any additional environment variables or overwriting those set previously by **dtlogin**.

11. The child **dtlogin** invokes the session manager, **dtsession**.

12. **dtsession** restores the appropriate session. For example, to restore the current session, **dtsession** reads **dt.resources** and **dt.session** in **$HOME/.dt/sessions/current**.

At logout, the reverse happens. The session is saved and **dtlogin** runs **/usr/dt/config/Xreset**. After **Xreset** completes, **dtlogin** again displays the login screen as in step 4.

CDE and Performance

CDE isn't a monolithic application; it's a set of components layered on top of the operating system, the X Window System, and Motif. Each underlying layer takes its share of RAM before CDE or any other client even starts. Because of the low-level nature of these layers, the RAM they use is hardly ever regained through swapping to disk.

In some cases, operating system overhead and user application requirements restrict the amount of RAM available for a graphical user interface to little more than enough to run a window manager such as Motif. Because the CDE workspace manager and the Motif window manager take roughly the same amount of RAM, users can enjoy an enriched graphical environment with the added value of CDE's multiple workspaces at essentially no extra RAM cost over running the Motif window manager.

Tactics for Better Performance

Unless all your users have RAM-loaded powerhouses for systems, you will need to spend some time developing a performance strategy. If you conceive of performance as a bell-shaped curve, satisfaction lies on the leading edge. Your performance strategy should do everything it can to keep your users on the leading edge.

Probably the most logical approach is to start small and grow. In other words, start out with minimal user environments on all the systems on your network. Gradually add software components until you or your users begin to notice performance degradation. Then back off a little. Such an approach might take several weeks or more to evaluate, as you add components and as your users spend several days actually working in the environment to determine the effect of your changes on system performance and their frustration levels.

The most RAM-expensive pieces of CDE are the workspace manager, the session manager, and the file manager. The workspace manager is expensive because portions of it are always in RAM (assuming that you are moving windows around and switching workspaces). The CDE workspace manager is no more expensive than the Motif window manager; if you want a GUI, it's just a price you have to pay. The session manager is expensive only during logout and login, as it saves and restores sessions. The rest of the time, the session manager is dormant and gets swapped out of RAM. Saving your current work session is nice at the end of the day, but it's something to consider giving up if you want to improve your login and logout performance. The file manager is expensive because it wakes up periodically and jumps into RAM to check the status of the file system and update its file manager windows. When it jumps into RAM, it pushes something else out, for example, maybe the desktop publishing program you're using.

Here are some other ideas that you may find useful:

Terminal Emulators	**xterms** are a little less RAM-expensive than **dtterms**. Unless you need the block mode functionality of a **dtterm**,

	xterm might be a better choice for terminal emulation.
Automatic Saves	Some applications automatically save data at periodic intervals. Although this feature can be beneficial, you need to evaluate its effect in light of performance. If the application is central to your users' work, fine, but if not, you might want to disable the automatic save feature.
Scroll Buffers	Large scroll buffers in terminal emulators can be a real convenience, but they can also take up a lot of RAM. Even modestly sized scroll buffers, when multiplied by three or four terminal emulators, consume a lot of RAM.
Background Bitmaps	Avoid large bitmaps; they increase the X server size. Especially avoid switching large bitmaps frequently within a session. If you are hunting for a new background, be sure to restart the X server after you've found the one you want and have included it in the proper **sessionetc** file. The most efficient bitmaps are small ones that can be repeated to tile the background.
Front Panel	Reconfigure the front panel to minimize the number of buttons. Keep just enough to meet user needs. This tactic decreases the workspace manager size in RAM and speeds login and logout.
Pathnames	Whenever possible, use absolute pathnames for bitmap specifications. Although this approach decreases the

flexibility of the system, it speeds access time.

Conclusion

The default CDE is ready to use, but given its power and flexibility, you will inevitably want to customize the CDE environment for your users' work context and optimum performance. Take the time to develop a good idea of what changes you need to make, the order in which to make them, and exactly where to make them. In so doing, all the power and flexibility of CDE will be open to you.

CHAPTER 14

HP-UX System Auditing and System Configuration Repository

Introduction

In this chapter, I first cover a great tool that automatically gathers system information called *System Configuration Repository*. *System Configuration Repository* is a free HP product that you can load on your system from the Application media or from the HP web site. *System Configuration Repository* is both a data collection system and a database query system. In the second half of this chapter I define the aspects of systems that I audit and then give some example scripts you can use as the basis for your own audit program.

System Configuration Repository (SCR)

System Configuration Repository, which I'll call SCR in this chapter, gathers a lot of system information that can be used for viewing and can be compared to previously gathered data to produce a list of differences. SCR is easy to use so the best way to learn about it is to run some SCR commands.

You can obtain documents related to SCR from *www.docs.hp.com.* When writing this chapter I obtained two documents that were helpful for installing and using SCR. The first is *Troubleshooting Guide for SCR+DMI* and the second is *System Configuration Repository User's Reference.* I insalled SCR and DMI directly from the Application media as well as a DCE library that was required. I obtained two required patches from the HP web site. I found out that these additional software products were required when the configuration of SCR and DMI failed at the time of installation. The **swagentd.log** file provided a list of patches and the library required for SCR and DMI to configure properly. You can obtain SCR and DMI from *www.software.hp.com* if you don't have access to Application media.

Using SCR

SCR is easy to use. The first command to issue is **scrconfig** with the option *-n* to register nodes to be managed by SCR. Since you can have a central system act as the SCR server on which information for all managed nodes will be kept you can issue the **scrconfig** command on the central system for all systems to be managed. We'll issue it only for the L-Class system for which we want to gather informaton:

```
# scrconfig -n +l1
scrconfig: Node "l1" is registered.
#
```

To register additional nodes, you would list the node names preceded by the plus sign on the same line in the format:

```
# scrconfig -n +node1 +node2 +node3 ...
```

You can schedule data collection for a node to take place at any time. The **scrconfig** command is also used to schedule data collection. We'll specify the node name with the *-n* option and use *-s* to specify the date and time at which we want collection to take place. The following example collects data on *08/02/2000* at *14:45* on node *11*:

```
# scrconfig -n 11 -s 200008021445
Parameter for "11" is set to:
    Schedule time:        08/02/2000 14:45 EDT
#
```

This command has scheduled collection on *11* on the specified date and time. Note that the time is in 24-hour format. We could initiate data collection on-demand on node 11 by omitting the *-s* option and date and time with **scrconfig -n 11**. Each time data is collected from a node, it is callled a *snapshot*. A *snapshot* will not be saved if there are no changes since the last snapshot that was obtained from the system. If you try to obtain snapshots in very close succession with one another, the second snapshot will probably not be obtained because no changes have occurred to the system.

Let's now issue **scrconfig** for node 11 with the *-l* option to list the details for 11:

```
# scrconfig -n 11 -l
NODE    SCHEDULE    TIME          INTERVAL    EXPIRATION  TIMEOUT
11      08/02/2000 14:45 EDT      1 week      3 months    15 minutes
#
```

The output shows our scheduled collection for node *11*. If we had other scheduled collections, they would show up in this output as well.

Next we'll check the data collection status of all nodes that have been registered, in our case only *11*, to see what collections have taken place and what collections are scheduled:

```
# scrstatus
TIME       (START - STOP)      NODE    STATUS       DETAIL
07/02/2000  14:30 - 14:31 EDT  ll      Completed

08/02/2000  14:45 -       EDT  ll      Scheduled
#
```

This output shows our scheduled collection as the second entry and a collection that had been run earlier that is complete on the first line. If a collection were taking place at the time **scrstatus** was run, the *STATUS* column would be *Executing*.

Next we'll use the command **scrviewer** to see data that has been collected for system *ll*. We specify the system for which we want the collection produced as well as collection we want to view. Because the output is long (very long) I have also redirected the output to a file:

```
# scrviewer ll:latest > /tmp/scrviewer.txt &
[1]    2728
#
```

You'll be amazed at the amount of data that has been collected for your system. The following is a very small subset of the data collected by SCR for system *ll*:

```
ll : 07/02/2000 14:24 EDT (latest oldest)
No filter applied.
COMPONENT NAME                           VALUE
    GROUP NAME
        ATTRIBUTE NAME
"HP-UX Installed Software Definition"
    "Bundle Contents"
        "scr dmi class"                  HPUX_BundleContents_
        "scr dmi version"                001
        "scr dmi key"                    "Bundle Software Specification,Index"

[Bundle Software Specification]          A5506A,r=B.11.00.01,a=HP-UX_B.11.00_32/64,v=HP
[Index]                                  1
[Content]                                100BASE-T,r=B.11.00.01,a=HP-UX_B.11.00_32/64,v=HP

                    .
                    .
                    .
```

```
"Host Processor"
     "scr dmi class"                          "HPUX_Host Processor_"
     "scr dmi version"                        001
     "scr dmi key"                            "Host Processor Index"

     [Host Processor Index]                   1
     [Processor Firmware ID]                  "HP PA_RISC2.0"

     [Host Processor Index]                   2
     [Processor Firmware ID]                  "HP PA_RISC2.0"
"Host Storage"
     "scr dmi class"                          "HPUX_Host Storage_"
     "scr dmi version"                        001
     "scr dmi key"                            "Host Storage Index"

     [Host Storage Index]                     1
     [Storage Type]                           4:FixedDisk
     [Description]                            "  IBM        DMVS18D        "
     [Allocation Unit Size]                   1024
     [Total Allocation Units]                 17366
     [Allocation Units Used]                  17268
     [Storage Allocation Failures]            0

     [Host Storage Index]                     2
     [Storage Type]                           4:FixedDisk
     [Description]                            "  IBM        DMVS18D        "
     [Allocation Unit Size]                   1024
     [Total Allocation Units]                 17366
     [Allocation Units Used]                  13172
     [Storage Allocation Failures]            0

     [Host Storage Index]                     3
     [Storage Type]                           7:CompactDisc
     [Description]                            "  HP        DVD-ROM 304    "
     [Allocation Unit Size]                   0
     [Total Allocation Units]                 0
     [Allocation Units Used]                  0
     [Storage Allocation Failures]            0
"Host System"
     "scr dmi class"                          "HPUX_Host System_"
     "scr dmi version"                        002
     "scr dmi key"                            "Security Token"

     [Initial Load Device]                    0
     [Initial Load Parameters]                "/stand/system"
     [Max Processes]                          532
     [Mounted File Systems]                   10
"Host Volume Group"
     "scr dmi class"                          "HPUX_Host Volume Group_"
     "scr dmi version"                        001
     "scr dmi key"                            "Host Volume Group Index"

     [Host Volume Group Index]                1
     [Volume Group Name]                      /dev/vg00
     [Volume Group Access Permission]         1:Read-Write
     [Volume Group Status]                    0:Available
     [Physical Extent Size]                   4
     [Volume Group Capacity]                  8680
     [Volume Group Allocated]                 7610
     [Volume Group Free Space]                1070
     [Max Number of Physical Volume]          16
     [Max Number of Physical Extent per Physical Volume]
                                              4350
     [Number of Defined Physical Volume]      2
     [Number of Active Physical Volume]       2
     [Max Number of Logical Volume]           255
     [Number of Defined Logical Volume]       11
     [Number of Active Logical Volume]        11
     [Number of Physical Volume Group]        0
"Network Interface"
     "scr dmi class"                          "HPUX_Network Interface_"
     "scr dmi version"                        001
     "scr dmi key"                            "Network Interface Index"
```

```
[Network Interface Index]                1
[Interface Name]                         lan0
[IP Address]                             10.1.1.11
[Subnet Mask]                            255.255.255.0
[Broadcast Address]                      10.255.255.255
[Interface State]                        2:Down
[DHCP Enabled]                           1:Disabled
[Station Address]                        0x001083FEDCB7
[Interface Card Hardware Path]           0/0/0/0

[Network Interface Index]                2
[Interface Name]                         lan1
[IP Address]                             10.1.1.11
[Subnet Mask]                            255.255.255.0
[Broadcast Address]                      10.1.1.255
[Interface State]                        1:Up
[DHCP Enabled]                           0:Unknown
[Station Address]                        0x001083F72ED0
[Interface Card Hardware Path]           0/4/0/0/4/0

[Network Interface Index]                3
[Interface Name]                         lan2
[IP Address]                             63.88.85.16
[Subnet Mask]                            255.255.255.0
[Broadcast Address]                      63.88.85.255
[Interface State]                        1:Up
[DHCP Enabled]                           0:Unknown
[Station Address]                        0x001083F72E9B
[Interface Card Hardware Path]           0/4/0/0/5/0
```

Among the data produced for *ll* is extensive software-related information early in the listing, logical volume-related information, and hardware-related information at the end of the listing.

To get a collection history for managed nodes, we use the **scrhist** command. The following output is for *ll*:

```
# scrhist
NODE            TIME                    ERR   TAG
ll              07/02/2000 14:24 EDT          latest oldest
#
```

The collection performed on *ll* on *07/02/2000* is both the *latest* and the *oldest* listed in the **scrhist** output. When our new data collection takes place, it will be listed as the *latest* and the collection shown in the example will be listed as the *oldest* only.

There are several other SCR-related commands and options to commands we've covered that you can issue. Among the most useful commands is **scrdiff**, which produces a report of differences between collections. The following command would produce a report of differences between the collection taken on 08/02/00 and the latest for *ll*:

```
# scrdiff l1:200008021445 l1:latest
[1]     2728
#
```

Table 14-1 summarizes SCR-related commands. There are manual pages loaded for these commands along with SCR.

TABLE 14-1 System Configuration Repository Commands

Command	Use
scrconfig	Configure and query configuration information.
scrdelete	Delete configuration information.
scrdiff	Report differences between two configuration reports.
scrfilter	Generate, modify, or delete view filter.
scrhist	Produce configuration history.
scrstatus	Produce data collection status report.
scrtag	Manage tag names for snapshots.
scrviewer	Display configuration information.
scrlog_viewer	SCR log file viewer.
scr (not command)	System Configuration Repository.

SCR uses the Desktop Management Interface (DMI) to obtain collection data from nodes. DMI provides the Application Programming Interfaces (APIs) that are called by SCR to obtain data. The central management system, which is *l1* in our examples, requires both DMI and SCR.

Introduction to System Audits

Let's now cover some aspects of systems that I audit and then give some example scripts you can use as the basis for your own audit program. The aspects of auditing that I cover in this chapter are the same for HP-UX 11.0 and 11i. The aspects of the system you audit and the programs are the same for the two releases. I have prefaced pretty much every system administration topic I've covered by saying, "Every installation is unique." Having given my standard disclaimer, let me list some areas to audit that apply to virtually every installation. You surely have others that are peculiar to your installation that should be included in an audit of your system(s).

Important Files The first thing any audit program should do is save the most important files on your system. You need to determine what files are important. When I cover this topic, I give a listing of some important files you should consider saving on a regular basis.

Security Who can shut down your HP-UX system? Who has switched to superuser in the last 24 hours. Have there been any failed attempts to login as root in the last 24 hours? Are there old users in the **/etc/password** file? Most system administrators can't answer these questions (I know I can't answer them about the system in my office). There are simple security checks you can perform to answer these questions.

Logical Volume Review One Logical Volume Manager change can have a big impact on your system. I have worked at installations that had several unused disks on their system and the

system administrator didn't know it! An
audit program should document your existing Logical Volume Manager configuration
and perform some checks.

Performance   How is swap set up? If you put two swap
sections on one disk, this setup will provide
lower performance. Have you run **sar**,
vmstat, or **iostat** recently? An audit should
include a performance snapshot.

Disk Usage   Who are the disk hogs on your system?
There is a command to help you quickly
determine this. You don't want old files,
especially core files, floating around your
system. An audit program should look for
these.

Kernel   Was your HP-UX kernel built with your
existing **/stand/system** file? A different **system** file may have been used. Can you use all
of your hardware? You may have hardware
attached to your system for which you do not
have a driver built into your kernel.

System Boot   Does your system boot smoothly? Run
dmesg to see information produced at the
last system boot.

System Crash   See if the directory exists where core files
would be placed, and if so, see if there are
core files in it.

Printers   Get printer status. Should you encounter a system disaster, it will be easier to rebuild your system printer configurations if you have documented your printers.

Patches   Report all patches currently installed on the system.

Networking   Run all networking commands to get a snapshot of what is configured.

These are all worthwhile areas to document and audit. Even if you do not find a single problem with your system, the audit will produce a document providing a snapshot of your system.

Let's take a closer look at some of these areas.

Important Files

In the event of a system catastrophe, it would be helpful to have saved all of your important system files. Here is a listing of some files that I have copied from their original locations to **/tmp/IMPORTANT**:

```
-rw-------   1   root   syts       502   Apr   24   19:19   /tmp/IMPORTANT/PATCHES_ONLY
-rw-------   1   root   syts     52561   Apr   24   19:19   /tmp/IMPORTANT/archive.imp
-rw-------   1   root   syts     14317   Apr   24   19:19   /tmp/IMPORTANT/bootptab
-rw-------   1   root   syts      1617   Apr   24   19:19   /tmp/IMPORTANT/hosts
-rw-------   1   root   syts      3653   Apr   24   19:19   /tmp/IMPORTANT/inetd.conf
-rw-------   1   root   syts      1347   Apr   24   19:19   /tmp/IMPORTANT/inittab
-rw-------   1   root   syts      1462   Apr   24   19:19   /tmp/IMPORTANT/lvmrc
```

```
-rw-------   1   root   syts      59667   Apr   24   19:19  /tmp/IMPORTANT/lvdisplay.out

-rw-------   1   root   syts       2947   Apr   24   19:19  /tmp/IMPORTANT/netconf

-rw-------   1   root   syts       5707   Apr   24   19:19  /tmp/IMPORTANT/passwd

-rw-------   1   root   syts       2642   Apr   24   19:19  /tmp/IMPORTANT/profile

-rw-------   1   root   syts      75759   Apr   24   19:19  /tmp/IMPORTANT/rc.log

-rw-------   1   root   syts       7779   Apr   24   19:19  /tmp/IMPORTANT/services

-rw-------   1   root   syts        257   Apr   24   19:19  /tmp/IMPORTANT/syslog.conf

-rw-------   1   root   syts        615   Apr   24   19:19  /tmp/IMPORTANT/system

-rw-------   1   root   syts       4996   Apr   24   19:19  /tmp/IMPORTANT/vgdisplay.out

-rw-------   1   root   syts       2061   Apr   24   19:19  /tmp/IMPORTANT/vue

-rw-------   1   root   syts       2061   Apr   24   19:19  /tmp/IMPORTANT/cde
```

man page

"lv" - 8

Some of these files, like **lvdisplay.out** and **vgdisplay.out**, contain a full listing of the logical volume information for this system. You never know when you will have to rebuild a volume group, and having this information in a file can be handy. Notice also there are several files which contain patch-related information.

Security

Who can shut down the system? The **/etc/shutdown.allow** file has in it a list of those who have permission to shut down the system. Verify that only the users you want to shut down a system have entries in this file.

When has the system been shut down and by whom is in **shutdownlog**. Part of **shutdownlog** with a panic is shown below:

```
16:58 Mon Feb  12,  2000.  Reboot:  (by system1!root)

21:49 Mon Feb  12,  2000.  Reboot:  (by system1!root)
```

```
16:46 Tue Feb  13,  2000.  Reboot after panic:  steven:
invalid relocation status

16:28 Sun Mar  24,  2000.  Reboot:  (by system1!root)

17:08 Thu Mar  28,  2000.  Reboot:  (by system1!root)
```

Very few users should be switching to superuser. You may have users that need to make system adjustments in a development environment. In a production environment, however, you should very seldom see a switch to superuser. The **/var/adm/sulog** file has in it all **su** commands issued. All of the following entries have switched from a user name to root.

```
SU 04/22 19:57 - ttyp2 mike-root

SU 04/22 19:57 - ttyp2 mike-root

SU 04/22 19:57 + ttyp2 mike-root

SU 04/23 11:00 + ttyu1 chang-root

SU 04/23 11:12 + ttyu2 denise-root
```

A log of bad login attempts in quick succession, or as root, can be viewed with the **lastb** command. The following example shows several bad login attempts as root:

```
root ttyp6    Tue Apr 16 13:00-13:00 (00:00)

root ttyp6    Tue Apr 16 13:01-13:01 (00:00)

root ttyp6    Tue Apr 16 13:01-13:01 (00:00)

root ttyp6    Tue Apr 16 13:02-13:02 (00:00)

root ttyp6    Tue Apr 16 13:02-13:02 (00:00)

root ttyp6    Tue Apr 16 13:03-13:03 (00:00)
```

```
root ttyp6    Tue Apr 16 13:03-13:03 (00:00)
                    .

                    .

                    .
```

Use **pwck** to check the **/etc/passwd** file, looking for all types of problems. This command performs a sanity check on the **passwd** file that, although it is not a log file, is an important file that should be monitored closely. The following are two errors in the **passwd** file that were found by running the **pwck** command. The first is a user with a **passwd** entry, but with no files on the system. The second is a user with an incorrect home directory name.

```
denise - Login name not found on system

jlance:Hhadsf4353hadsfae:110:20:Joe  Lance,,,:/net/sys1/net/
sys1/home/jlance:/usr/bin/sh
Login directory not found
```

Use **grpck** to check the **/etc/group** file, looking for all types of problems.

This command performs a check of the **group** file, which must also be carefully monitored. The following example shows a **group** entry in which there are no users present and a group that contains a user for which there is no entry in the **passwd** file:

```
database:10:
        No users in this group

development1:*:200:nadmin,charles,william
        william - Login name not found in password file
```

Logical Volume Review

Check the integrity of the **/etc/lvmtab** file. One way of doing so is to compare **strings lvmtab** with **vgscan -v -p**. In the following example, the output of **strings lvmtab** is used as input to **vgscan**, and this yields an unused volume group:

```
# vgscan -v -p

/dev/vgsys
/dev/dsk/c2d0s2
/dev/dsk/c3d0s2

/dev/vgtext
/dev/dsk/c4d0s2
/dev/dsk/c5d0s2

/dev/vgroot
/dev/dsk/c4d0s2
/dev/dsk/c7d0s2


The volume group /dev/vg00 was not matched with any
Physical Volumes.

Scan of the Physical Volumes complete.


# ls -l -d /dev/vg*

drwxrwxrwx  2 root       root   1024 Nov 7   /dev/vg00
drwxrwxrwx  2 root       sys    1024 Jan 20  /dev/vgroot
drwxrwxrwx  2 root       root   1024 Nov 7   /dev/vgsys
drwxrwxrwx  2 root       root   1024 Nov 7   /dev/vgtext
```

man page

ls - 15

The command **ls -l /dev/vg*** shows four volume groups, only three of which are used. **/dev/vg00** exists, but is not in use.

A common problem with a mirrored root volume is that the data is mirrored, but there is no boot area on the mirror. This means that if the primary root volume becomes unbootable then you won't be able to boot off the mirror. You can identify *boot lif* areas on disks with **lifls -Clv /dev/rdsk/***. You can also run the **lvlnboot** command to see all disks that are bootable. The following example shows a root disk (*c0t6d0*) as bootable as well as its mirror (*c1t3d0*).

```
# lvlnboot -v

Boot Definitions for Volume Group /dev/vg00:
Physical Volumes belonging in Root Volume Group:

            /dev/dsk/c0t6d0 (10/0.6.0)    -- Boot Disk
            /dev/dsk/c1t3d0 (10/4/4.3.0) -- Boot Disk
                         .
                         .
                         .
```

I am surprised at the number of times that unused disks are found on a system. The following subroutine of an audit program identifies unused disks with the output of **ioscan** providing input to **pvdisplay**:

man page

ioscan - 4

man page

"pv" - 8

```
pvtest ()
{
for me in `ioscan -fkC disk | awk '{print $3}' `
do
    if [ "$me" != "H/W" ]
    then
    echo "\n$PROG>>>>> from ioscan -fkC , check PV info" | tee -a $DESTF
    diskn=`lssf /dev/dsk/* | grep $me | grep 'section 0' | awk '{print $16}'`
     echo "$PROG>>>>> the disk is $diskn" | tee -a $DESTF
     echo "$PROG>>>>> listing first 25 lines by: pvdisplay -v $diskn |\ head -25" |
tee -a $DESTF

    pvdisplay -v $diskn 2>&1 | head -25 | tee -a $DESTF
```

```
        fi
done
}
```

Here is the result for a disk that was not identified as part of a volume group:

```
pvdisplay: Couldn't query physical volume "/dev/dsk/c0d0s2":
```

The specified path does not correspond to a physical volume attached to any volume group. This fact means that the disk is physically attached to the system, but is not in a volume group.

Performance

man page

vmstat - 11

man page

iostat - 11

man page

sar - 11

Performance is a discipline unto itself. You are not going to perform a detailed performance analysis as part of a system audit. You can get a snapshot of your system that you can later sit down and review, however, which may provide some interesting results.

As part of an audit, you should run the following performance-related commands: **vmstat**, **iostat**, **uptime**, **sar -u** and **sar -b**. The following are examples of running **sar -u** and **sar -b**:

```
# sar -u 5 5

HP-UX system1  9000/819

19:08:02    %usr    %sys    %wio    %idle
19:08:07       1       2       1      96
```

```
        19:08:12        1       1       0       99
        19:08:17        0       1       0       99
        19:08:22        1       1       0       98
        19:08:27        0       1       0       99

        Average         1       1       0       98
# sar -b 5 10


HP-UX system1   9000/819

19:08:27 bread/s lread/s %rcache bwrit/s lwrit/s %wcache pread/s pwrit/s

        19:08:32        0      46     100      0       5      100      0      0
        19:08:37        0      28     100      1       4       80      0      0
        19:08:42        0      13     100      0       0        0      0      0
        19:08:47        0       0       0      0       0        0      0      0
        19:08:52        0      37     100      0       0        0      0      0
        19:08:57        0       6     100      1       2       50      0      0
        19:09:02        0      29     100      0       0        0      0      0
        19:09:07        0      27     100      2       4       59      0      0
        19:09:12        0      13     100      0       0        0      0      0
        19:09:17        0       0       0      0       0        0      0      0

        Average         0      20     100      0       2       77      0      0
```

An area that is often overlooked regarding performance is swap space. If swap is properly configured, you can realize better performance than if it is inefficiently configured.

Run **swapinfo -at** and **swapinfo -m**. Swap is sometimes added to systems in a random fashion. The following example shows two swap sections on **/dev/dsk/c0t6d0**, which is a bad practice:

man page
swapinfo-11

```
# swapinfo -at

          Kb        Kb        Kb  PCT   START/       Kb
TYPE      AVAIL     USED      FREE USED  LIMIT RESERVE PRI    NAME                 ( disk )

dev       512000    0         512000  0%        0       -     1     /dev/vg00/lvol2   c0t6d0

dev       274432    0         274432  0%        0       -     0     /dev/vg00/lvol8   c0t6d0

dev       262144    0         262144  0%        0       -     0     /dev/vg03/lvol20  c1t4d0

dev       524288    0         524288  0%        0       -     0     /dev/vg02/lvol21  c1t2d0
```

It is not a good practice to put two swap sections on the same disk as has been done with *c0t6d0* in this example. It is better is distribute the load among multiple disks and to have the sections the same size to enhance interleaving swap. This size should also be big enough to hold a core dump.

Disk and File System Information

The first thing you need to know about how your disks are being used is which users are consuming the most space. The following subroutine from an audit program uses the **diskusg** command to determine the disk hogs:

```
#!/usr/bin/ksh
# 1st print stats concerning the disk's file systems
echo "This program produces logical volume statistics and the amount of disk"
echo "space consumed by users on each logical volume. \n"
for fs in `bdf| grep '^/' | awk '{print $1}'`
do
fsys=`fstyp $fs`
echo "\n $printing logical volume stats for $fs using fstyp -v \n"
fstyp -v $fs 2>&1
if [ $fsys = vxfs ]
then
echo "\n finding space consumed per user for logical volume "
echo " $fs with vxdiskusg $fs \n"
/usr/sbin/acct/vxdiskusg $fs 2>&1 | tee -a $DESTF
else
# assume hfs type
echo "\n finding space consumed per user for logical volume "
echo " $fs with diskusg $fs \n"
echo "\nUserID login number of blocks "
echo "------ -------------------- \n"
       /usr/sbin/acct/diskusg $fs 2>&1
fi
done
```

Here is an example of finding hogs for filesystem **/dev/vg00/ lvol6**, mounted as **/usr**. In this example, *mike* is consuming substantially more space than *jclairmo*.

```
# diskusg /dev/vg00/lvol6

0            root       105254

1            daemon     304

2            bin        375704

5            uucp       882

9            lp         386

101          jclairmo   36

102          mike       43580
```

Use **find** to search for old and large files, core files, and so on. **find** can be used to uncover such information as large old files, such as those greater than 1MB and older than 120 days, as in the following example:

man page

find - 20

```
# find / \( -fsonly hfs -o -fsonly vxfs \) -a \( -atime +120 -a -size +1000000c \) -
print |    xargs -nl ll

-rw-------    1 jhowell  users     2150400 Nov  1 00:44 /home/jjersey/acrobat/READ.TAR
-rw-------    1 jhowell  users     3921920 Nov  1 00:44 /home/jjersey/acrobat/HPUXR.TAR
```

The following command can be used to find all core files on your system:

```
find / \( -fsonly hfs -o -fsonly vxfs \) -name core -exec what {} \ ;
```

Please see chapter 20, which is dedicated to **find**, to get more information on this command.

Kernel, Boot, and Printer Information

This section could almost be called "Miscellaneous" because it checks several different areas.

man page

ioscan - 4

Run **ioscan -fk** to check the kernel. You may find errors such as hardware for which there is no driver installed, as in the following example.

```
Class      I  H/W Path    Driver    S/W State H/W Type Description
============================================================================
           .
           .
           .

disk       4  10/4/4.1.0  disc3     CLAIMED   DEVICE   HP C2490WD
unknown    -  9           ?         No_Driver
           .
           .
           .
```

The two lines left in this **ioscan** output show that there is an "unknown" device at hardware path 9 for which there is no driver installed. Although you don't know what this is, and it is probably not serious, this is the purpose of the audit program - to identify any potential problems on your system.

man page

ioscan - 4

I very seldom watch a system boot, yet there can be some revealing information produced at boot time. Running **dmesg** can show problems uncovered at boot such as the following message showing that the **/var** logical volume is full:

man page

dmesg - 4

```
/var
file: table is full
file: table is full
file: table is full
file: table is full
file: table is full
file: table is full
file: table is full
file: table is full
file: table is full
file: table is full
file: table is full
file: table is full
file: table is full
```

You can determine whether the existing kernel was built with **/stand/system**. Run **system_prep -s** and compare it to **/stand/system**. The following routine performs this check:

```
#!/bin/ksh
DESTF="$home/audit.ker.out"
export DESTF
{
  /usr/lbin/sysadm/system_prep -s system.tmp
```

```
diffs=`diff system.tmp /stand/system`
if [ ! -z "$diffs" ]
then
echo "the system file is different: $diffs"
echo "/stand/vmunix WAS NOT built with /stand/system"
else
echo "/stand/vmunix was built with /stand/system"
fi
}
```

One area of your system that you might have a difficult time
rebuilding is printer-related setup. Run the following commands and
save the output for future reference:

man page

lpstat - 10

lpstat -s
lpstat -d
lpstat -t

If you should encounter a system crash, **/var/adm/crash** can be
used to save the core dump to your file system. The following routine
checks whether this directory exists:

```
#!/usr/bin/ksh
echo "\n\n"
echo "The /var/adm/crash directory is needed by savecore in order to save the status"
echo "if a system crash occurs. The coredump can then be copied to a file and"
echo "sent to HP for analysis."
echo "See the savecore manual page to get more information about saving a core dump."

REMEMBERCORE=0
if [ -d /var/adm/crash ]
    then
                echo "\n\t/var/adm/crash exists \c"
                if [ -r /var/adm/crash/core.? ]
                then
                echo "and contains a dump."
                echo "\n\tPlease copy the dump in /var/adm/crash to tape."
                echo "\n\nHere is a listing of the core dump(s) on `hostname`. \n"
                ll /var/adm/crash/core.?
                REMEMBERCORE=1
    else
                echo "and contains NO dump."
    fi

else
                echo "\n\n WARNING: /var/adm/crash did not exist."
                echo " use mkdir -p /var/adm/crash "
    fi
```

Patches

Whether or not the appropriate patches are on your system, you need to include an inventory of patches as part of the audit. Patches are difficult to keep up with but are essential to the proper operation of your system. The first few lines of each patch you have installed give a description of the patch, including its number. A good audit program will read this information and save it in a file so that you can have this in the directory with your other important files.

Networking

System administrators spend a lot of time setting up networking. If you encountered a system disaster of some type, it would be helpful to have a section that thoroughly documented your networking setup. The following bullet items describe some of the more common areas of networking to check:

- See whether your system is an NFS server and check **/etc/ exports** for exported file systems.

- Check **syslog** for errors with the following command:

man page

grep - 19

```
# grep err /var/adm/syslog/syslog.log
```

man page

rpcinfo - 12

- Check rpc registration with:

```
# rpcinfo -p
```

- Check your system information with DNS:

```
# nslookup $HOSTNAME
```

- Check for the existence of **/etc/resolv.conf**, which would indicate that your system uses DNS:

```
# ll /etc/resolv.conf
```

man page

ls - 15

- View LAN devices with:

```
# ls -l /dev/lan*
```

- Check LAN cards by running **lanscan** for all interfaces.

man page

ioscan - 4

- Check the kernel for LAN card configuration with:

```
# ioscan -funC lan
```

man page

netstat - 12

- Show routes with:

```
# netstat -r
```

- Check for SNA with:

```
# snapshownet
```

- Check for uucp with:

```
# /usr/lbin/uucp/uucheck -v
```

Auditing your system becomes increasingly more important as you make changes to it. The auditing I have covered in this section does not even address the applications you are running. Having a well-documented system and putting effort into reviewing the audit results will pay dividends in the long run. Fixing the small problems you find as a result of the audit may prevent much bigger problems down the road.

Some Example Scripts

You would ultimately like to have a full audit program that you could run on all your HP-UX systems on a regular basis. The topics I have suggested in this chapter are a good place to start. You may also have additional aspects of your systems that should be audited periodically.

The following sections contain several short scripts that could be run to get a feel for the type of output you could produce with your audit scripts. Many such short scripts could then be combined to produce a larger, more comprehensive audit program. The short scripts you craft could be used as subroutines called by a main program.

The following sections show example scripts and the result of having run the scripts. The earlier discussions in this chapter cover the topics of auditing your system, so I do not include much additional explanation in the upcoming sections.

Every system is different, so *you may have to modify these scripts* in order to get them to meet your needs. Any program that checks system-related information will vary somewhat going from system to system.

Kernel

The following script, called **audker.sh**, determines whether the existing kernel was built with **/stand/system**. The program runs **system_prep -s** and compares it to the file **/stand/system**.

```ksh
#!/bin/ksh
DESTF="$home/audit.ker.out"
export DESTF
{
 /usr/lbin/sysadm/system_prep -s system.tmp
diffs=`diff system.tmp /stand/system`
if [ ! -z "$diffs" ]
then
echo "the system file is different: $diffs"
echo "/stand/vmunix WAS NOT built with /stand/system"
else
echo "/stand/vmunix was built with /stand/system"
fi
}
```

The following output was received from having run **audker.sh**.

```
# audker.sh

the system file is different: 51a52
> spt0
/stand/vmunix WAS NOT built with /stand/system
```

This output indicates that the original **system** file is different from the **system** file just generated from the currently running kernel. The following listings show both **system** files. The first listing is the original **system** file which includes the *spt0* driver.

The second listing does not include the *spt0* driver, meaning that it is not part of the current HP-UX kernel.

First listing: Original system file

```
* Drivers and Subsystems

CentIf
CharDrv
asp
c720
ccio
cdfs
cio_ca0
clone
core
diag0
diag2
disc3
dlpi
dmem
echo
ffs
hpstreams
inet
inet_clts
inet_cots
klog
lan2
lasi
ldterm
lv
lvm
mux2
netdiag1
```

```
netman
nfs
ni
pa
pckt
pfail
pipedev
pipemod
ps2
ptem
ptm
pts
sad
sc
scsi1
scsi2
scsi3
sctl
sdisk
sio
spt
spt0                              <---- spt0 driver in old system file
stape
strlog
strpty_included
tape2
tape2_included
target
timod
tirdwr
tpiso
uipc
vxbase
wsio


* Kernel Device info

dump lvol


* Tunable parameters

dbc_max_pct      10
dbc_min_pct      10
maxswapchunks    1024
maxuprc          100
maxusers         250
msgmax           32768
msgmnb           32768
msgmni           100
msgseg           7168
msgtql           256
nfile            (24*(NPROC+16+MAXUSERS)/10+32+2*(NPTY+NSTRPTY))
npty             250
nstrpty          60
semmni           96
semmns           192
swapmem_on       0
```

Second listing: New system file

```
* Drivers and Subsystems

CentIf
CharDrv
asp
c720
ccio
cdfs
cio_ca0
clone
core
diag0
diag2
disc3
dlpi
dmem
echo
ffs
hpstreams
inet
inet_clts
inet_cots
klog
lan2
lasi
ldterm
lv
lvm
mux2
netdiag1
netman
nfs
ni
pa
pckt
pfail
pipedev
pipemod
ps2
ptem
ptm
pts
sad
sc
scsi1
scsi2
scsi3
sctl
sdisk
sio
spt                              <--- spt0 driver not in current kernel
stape
strlog
strpty_included
tape2
tape2_included
target
timod
tirdwr
tpiso
uipc
```

```
vxbase
wsio


* Kernel Device info

dump lvol


* Tunable parameters

dbc_max_pct      10
dbc_min_pct      10
maxswapchunks    1024
maxuprc          100
maxusers         250
msgmax           32768
msgmnb           32768
msgmni           100
msgseg           7168
msgtql           256
nfile            (24*(NPROC+16+MAXUSERS)/10+32+2*(NPTY+NSTRPTY))
npty             250
nstrpty          60
semmni           96
semmns           192
swapmem_on       0
```

Disk Information

The following script, called **auddisk.sh**, lists all disks on the system and then provides a detailed description of each disk.

```
#!/bin/ksh

{
echo "The following is a description of disks by ioscan -fkC disk\n"
ioscan -fkC disk
echo "\n\n"
echo "The following is a detailed description of the disks earlier"
        echo "identified by ioscan."

echo "\n\nHardware disk information:\n"
for DEV in `ioscan -funC disk | awk '{print $2}' | \
                grep '\/dev\/rdsk'`
do
IS_THERE=$(/etc/diskinfo $DEV 2>&1)
                        if [ ${IS_THERE%% *} != "diskinfo:" ]
                                then
                                        /etc/diskinfo -v $DEV 2>&1
                        fi
echo "  - - - - - - - - - - - - - -"
echo ""
done
        }
```

The following output was received from running **auddisk.sh**.

```
# auddisk.sh

The following is a description of disks by ioscan -fkC disk

Class      I   H/W Path      Driver      S/W State H/W Type  Description
========================================================================
disk       3   10/0.1.0      sdisk       CLAIMED   DEVICE    SEAGATE ST32550W
disk       4   10/0.2.0      sdisk       CLAIMED   DEVICE    HP      C2490WD
disk       0   10/0.5.0      sdisk       CLAIMED   DEVICE    SEAGATE ST32550W
disk       1   10/0.6.0      sdisk       CLAIMED   DEVICE    SEAGATE ST32550W
disk       9   10/4/12.5.0   disc3       CLAIMED   DEVICE    DGC     C2300WDR5
disk      10   10/4/12.5.1   disc3       CLAIMED   DEVICE    DGC     C2300WDR5
disk      11   10/4/12.6.0   disc3       CLAIMED   DEVICE    DGC     C2300WDR5
disk      12   10/4/12.6.1   disc3       CLAIMED   DEVICE    DGC     C2300WDR5
disk      13   10/8.0.0      sdisk       CLAIMED   DEVICE    HP      C3586A
disk      14   10/8.0.1      sdisk       CLAIMED   DEVICE    HP      C3586A
disk      15   10/8.1.0      sdisk       CLAIMED   DEVICE    HP      C3586A
disk      16   10/8.1.1      sdisk       CLAIMED   DEVICE    HP      C3586A
disk       2   10/12/5.2.0   sdisk       CLAIMED   DEVICE    TOSHIBA CD-ROM


The following is a detailed description of the disks earlier
identified by ioscan.


Hardware disk information:

SCSI describe of /dev/rdsk/c0t1d0:
            vendor: SEAGATE
        product id: ST32550W
              type: direct access
              size: 2082636 Kbytes
  bytes per sector: 512
         rev level: HP07
   blocks per disk: 4165272
       ISO version: 0
      ECMA version: 0
      ANSI version: 2
   removable media: no
   response format: 2
  (Additional inquiry bytes: (32)31 (33)34 (34)34 (35)37 (36)31 (37)30 (38)32
(39)0 (40)0 (41)0 (42)0 (43)0 (44)0 (45)0 (46)0 (47)0 (48)0 (49)0 (50)0 (51)0 (52)0
(53)0 (54)0 (55)0 (56)0 (57)0 (58)0 (59)0 (60)0 (61)0 (62)0 (63)0 (64)0 (65)0 (66)0
(67)0 (68)0 (69)0 (70)0 (71)0 (72)0 (73)0 (74)0 (75)0 (76)0 (77)0 (78)0 (79)0 (80)0
(81)0 (82)0 (83)0 (84)0 (85)0 (86)0 (87)0 (88)0 (89)0 (90)0 (91)0 (92)43 (93)6f (94)70
(95)79 (96)72 (97)69 (98)67 (99)68 (100)74 (101)20 (102)28 (103)63 (104)29 (105)20
(106)31 (107)39 (108)39 (109)35 (110)20 (111)53 (112)65 (113)61 (114)67 (115)61
(116)74 (117)65 (118)20 (119)41 (120)6c (121)6c (122)20 (123)0 (124)3f (125)8e (126)98
(127)0 (128)0 (129)2 (130)0 (131)0 (132)0 (133)0 (134)0 (135)0 (136)0 (137)0 (138)0
(139)0 (140)0 (141)0 (142)0 )
    - - - - - - - - - - - - - -

SCSI describe of /dev/rdsk/c0t2d0:
```

```
                        vendor: HP
                    product id: C2490WD
                          type: direct access
                          size: 2082636 Kbytes
              bytes per sector: 512
                     rev level: 4250
               blocks per disk: 4165272
                   ISO version: 0
                  ECMA version: 0
                  ANSI version: 2
              removable media: no
              response format: 2
         - - - - - - - - - - - - - -

        SCSI describe of /dev/rdsk/c0t5d0:
                        vendor: SEAGATE
                    product id: ST32550W
                          type: direct access
                          size: 2082636 Kbytes
              bytes per sector: 512
                     rev level: HP06
               blocks per disk: 4165272
                   ISO version: 0
                  ECMA version: 0
                  ANSI version: 2
              removable media: no
              response format: 2
              (Additional inquiry bytes: (32)30 (33)37 (34)32 (35)35 (36)30 (37)36 (38)30
(39)0  (40)0  (41)0  (42)0  (43)0  (44)0  (45)0  (46)0  (47)0  (48)0  (49)0  (50)0  (51)0  (52)0
(53)0  (54)0  (55)0  (56)0  (57)0  (58)0  (59)0  (60)0  (61)0  (62)0  (63)0  (64)0  (65)0  (66)0
(67)0  (68)0  (69)0  (70)0  (71)0  (72)0  (73)0  (74)0  (75)0  (76)0  (77)0  (78)0  (79)0  (80)0
(81)0  (82)0  (83)0  (84)0  (85)0  (86)0  (87)0  (88)0  (89)0  (90)0  (91)0  (92)43 (93)6f (94)70
(95)79 (96)72 (97)69 (98)67 (99)68 (100)74 (101)20 (102)28 (103)63 (104)29 (105)20
(106)31 (107)39 (108)39 (109)35 (110)20 (111)53 (112)65 (113)61 (114)67 (115)61
(116)74 (117)65 (118)20 (119)41 (120)6c (121)6c (122)20 (123)0 (124)3f (125)8e (126)98
(127)0  (128)0  (129)2 (130)0  (131)0  (132)0  (133)0  (134)0  (135)0  (136)0  (137)0  (138)0
(139)0  (140)0  (141)0  (142)0 )
         - - - - - - - - - - - - - -

        SCSI describe of /dev/rdsk/c0t6d0:
                        vendor: SEAGATE
                    product id: ST32550W
                          type: direct access
                          size: 2082636 Kbytes
              bytes per sector: 512
                     rev level: HP06
               blocks per disk: 4165272
                   ISO version: 0
                  ECMA version: 0
                  ANSI version: 2
              removable media: no
              response format: 2
              (Additional inquiry bytes: (32)31 (33)34 (34)33 (35)33 (36)38 (37)37 (38)32
(39)0  (40)0  (41)0  (42)0  (43)0  (44)0  (45)0  (46)0  (47)0  (48)0  (49)0  (50)0  (51)0  (52)0
(53)0  (54)0  (55)0  (56)0  (57)0  (58)0  (59)0  (60)0  (61)0  (62)0  (63)0  (64)0  (65)0  (66)0
(67)0  (68)0  (69)0  (70)0  (71)0  (72)0  (73)0  (74)0  (75)0  (76)0  (77)0  (78)0  (79)0  (80)0
(81)0  (82)0  (83)0  (84)0  (85)0  (86)0  (87)0  (88)0  (89)0  (90)0  (91)0  (92)43 (93)6f (94)70
(95)79 (96)72 (97)69 (98)67 (99)68 (100)74 (101)20 (102)28 (103)63 (104)29 (105)20
(106)31 (107)39 (108)39 (109)35 (110)20 (111)53 (112)65 (113)61 (114)67 (115)61
(116)74 (117)65 (118)20 (119)41 (120)6c (121)6c (122)20 (123)0 (124)3f (125)8e (126)98
(127)0  (128)0  (129)2 (130)0  (131)0  (132)0  (133)0  (134)0  (135)0  (136)0  (137)0  (138)0
(139)0  (140)0  (141)0  (142)0 )
         - - - - - - - - - - - - - -

        SCSI describe of /dev/rdsk/c4t5d0:
                        vendor: DGC
```

```
              product id: C2300WDR5
                    type: direct access
                    size: 8146176 Kbytes
        bytes per sector: 512
               rev level: HP02
         blocks per disk: 16292352
             ISO version: 0
            ECMA version: 0
            ANSI version: 2
          removable media: no
          response format: 2
    (Additional inquiry bytes: (32)41 (33)55 (34)4e (35)41 (36)20 (37)43 (38)4f
(39)4e (40)54 (41)52 (42)4f (43)4c (44)4c (45)45 (46)52 (47)20 (48)20 (49)20 (50)20
(51)0 (52)0 (53)0 (54)0 (55)0 (56)0 (57)0 (58)0 (59)0 (60)0 (61)0 (62)0 (63)0 (64)0
(65)0 (66)0 (67)0 (68)0 (69)0 (70)0 (71)0 (72)0 (73)0 (74)0 (75)0 (76)0 (77)0 (78)0
(79)0 (80)0 (81)0 (82)0 (83)0 (84)0 (85)0 (86)0 (87)0 (88)0 (89)0 (90)0 (91)2 (92)1
(93)6 (94)0 (95)39 (96)34 (97)2d (98)33 (99)31 (100)36 (101)35 (102)2d (103)31 (104)31
(105)30 (106)0 (107)a (108)f5 (109)17 (110)0 (111)35 (112)7 (113)10 (114)0 (115)0
(116)0 (117)0 (118)0 (119)0 (120)0 (121)0 (122)0 )
             - - - - - - - - - - - - -

    SCSI describe of /dev/rdsk/c4t5d1:
                  vendor: DGC
              product id: C2300WDR5
                    type: direct access
                    size: 8146176 Kbytes
        bytes per sector: 512
               rev level: HP02
         blocks per disk: 16292352
             ISO version: 0
            ECMA version: 0
            ANSI version: 2
          removable media: no
          response format: 2
    (Additional inquiry bytes: (32)41 (33)55 (34)4e (35)41 (36)20 (37)43 (38)4f
(39)4e (40)54 (41)52 (42)4f (43)4c (44)4c (45)45 (46)52 (47)20 (48)20 (49)20 (50)20
(51)0 (52)0 (53)0 (54)0 (55)0 (56)0 (57)0 (58)0 (59)0 (60)0 (61)0 (62)0 (63)0 (64)0
(65)0 (66)0 (67)0 (68)0 (69)0 (70)0 (71)0 (72)0 (73)0 (74)0 (75)0 (76)0 (77)0 (78)0
(79)0 (80)0 (81)0 (82)0 (83)0 (84)0 (85)0 (86)0 (87)0 (88)0 (89)0 (90)0 (91)2 (92)1
(93)6 (94)0 (95)39 (96)34 (97)2d (98)33 (99)31 (100)36 (101)35 (102)2d (103)31 (104)31
(105)30 (106)0 (107)a (108)f5 (109)17 (110)0 (111)35 (112)7 (113)10 (114)0 (115)0
(116)0 (117)0 (118)0 (119)0 (120)0 (121)0 (122)0 )
             - - - - - - - - - - - - -

    SCSI describe of /dev/rdsk/c4t6d0:
                  vendor: DGC
              product id: C2300WDR5
                    type: direct access
                    size: 8146176 Kbytes
        bytes per sector: 512
               rev level: HP02
         blocks per disk: 16292352
             ISO version: 0
            ECMA version: 0
            ANSI version: 2
          removable media: no
          response format: 2
    (Additional inquiry bytes: (32)41 (33)55 (34)4e (35)41 (36)20 (37)43 (38)4f
(39)4e (40)54 (41)52 (42)4f (43)4c (44)4c (45)45 (46)52 (47)20 (48)20 (49)20 (50)20
(51)0 (52)0 (53)0 (54)0 (55)0 (56)0 (57)0 (58)0 (59)0 (60)0 (61)0 (62)0 (63)0 (64)0
(65)0 (66)0 (67)0 (68)0 (69)0 (70)0 (71)0 (72)0 (73)0 (74)0 (75)0 (76)0 (77)0 (78)0
(79)0 (80)0 (81)0 (82)0 (83)0 (84)0 (85)0 (86)0 (87)0 (88)0 (89)0 (90)0 (91)1 (92)0
(93)5 (94)0 (95)39 (96)34 (97)2d (98)33 (99)31 (100)36 (101)35 (102)2d (103)31 (104)31
(105)30 (106)0 (107)35 (108)7 (109)10 (110)0 (111)a (112)f5 (113)17 (114)0 (115)0
(116)0 (117)0 (118)0 (119)0 (120)0 (121)0 (122)0 )
             - - - - - - - - - - - - -
```

```
SCSI describe of /dev/rdsk/c4t6d1:
              vendor: DGC
          product id: C2300WDR5
                type: direct access
                size: 8146176 Kbytes
    bytes per sector: 512
           rev level: HP02
     blocks per disk: 16292352
         ISO version: 0
        ECMA version: 0
        ANSI version: 2
      removable media: no
     response format: 2
         (Additional inquiry bytes: (32)41 (33)55 (34)4e (35)41 (36)20 (37)43 (38)4f
(39)4e (40)54 (41)52 (42)4f (43)4c (44)4c (45)45 (46)52 (47)20 (48)20 (49)20 (50)20
(51)0 (52)0 (53)0 (54)0 (55)0 (56)0 (57)0 (58)0 (59)0 (60)0 (61)0 (62)0 (63)0 (64)0
(65)0 (66)0 (67)0 (68)0 (69)0 (70)0 (71)0 (72)0 (73)0 (74)0 (75)0 (76)0 (77)0 (78)0
(79)0 (80)0 (81)0 (82)0 (83)0 (84)0 (85)0 (86)0 (87)0 (88)0 (89)0 (90)0 (91)1 (92)0
(93)5 (94)0 (95)39 (96)34 (97)2d (98)33 (99)31 (100)36 (101)35 (102)2d (103)31 (104)31
(105)30 (106)0 (107)35 (108)7 (109)10 (110)0 (111)a (112)f5 (113)17 (114)0 (115)0
(116)0 (117)0 (118)0 (119)0 (120)0 (121)0 (122)0 )
         - - - - - - - - - - - - - -

SCSI describe of /dev/rdsk/c5t0d0:
              vendor: HP
          product id: C3586A
                type: direct access
                size: 2097152 Kbytes
    bytes per sector: 512
           rev level: HP02
     blocks per disk: 4194304
         ISO version: 0
        ECMA version: 0
        ANSI version: 2
      removable media: no
     response format: 2
         - - - - - - - - - - - - - -

SCSI describe of /dev/rdsk/c5t0d1:
              vendor: HP
          product id: C3586A
                type: direct access
                size: 10485760 Kbytes
    bytes per sector: 512
           rev level: HP02
     blocks per disk: 20971520
         ISO version: 0
        ECMA version: 0
        ANSI version: 2
      removable media: no
     response format: 2
         - - - - - - - - - - - - - -

SCSI describe of /dev/rdsk/c5t1d0:
              vendor: HP
          product id: C3586A
                type: direct access
                size: 2097152 Kbytes
    bytes per sector: 512
           rev level: HP02
     blocks per disk: 4194304
         ISO version: 0
        ECMA version: 0
        ANSI version: 2
      removable media: no
```

```
            response format: 2
    - - - - - - - - - - - - -

SCSI describe of /dev/rdsk/c5t1d1:
              vendor: HP
          product id: C3586A
                type: direct access
                size: 10485760 Kbytes
    bytes per sector: 512
           rev level: HP02
     blocks per disk: 20971520
         ISO version: 0
        ECMA version: 0
        ANSI version: 2
      removable media: no
     response format: 2
    - - - - - - - - - - - - -

SCSI describe of /dev/rdsk/c1t2d0:
              vendor: TOSHIBA
          product id: CD-ROM XM-4101TA
                type: CD-ROM
                size: 347936 Kbytes
    bytes per sector: 2048
           rev level: 1084
     blocks per disk: 173968
         ISO version: 0
        ECMA version: 0
        ANSI version: 2
     removable media: yes
     response format: 2
     (Additional inquiry bytes: (32)34 (33)2f (34)31 (35)38 (36)2f (37)39 (38)34
(39)0 (40)0 (41)0 (42)0 (43)0 (44)0 (45)0 (46)0 (47)0 (48)0 (49)0 (50)0 (51)0 (52)0
(53)0 (54)0 (55)0 (56)0 (57)0 (58)0 (59)0 (60)0 (61)0 (62)0 (63)0 (64)0 (65)0 (66)0
(67)0 (68)0 (69)0 (70)0 (71)0 (72)0 (73)0 (74)0 (75)0 (76)0 (77)0 (78)0 (79)0 (80)0
(81)0 (82)0 (83)0 (84)0 (85)0 (86)0 (87)0 (88)0 (89)0 (90)0 )
    - - - - - - - - - - - - -
```

Logical Volume Summary

After viewing the physical disks connected to the system, it would be helpful to see some summary information on logical volumes, including the physical disks to which the logical volumes have been assigned. The following script, called **audlvsum.sh**, provides a concise summary of the logical volumes on a system:

```
#!/usr/bin/ksh

USAGE="Usage: $0 [-d]"

VOLORDER='y'    #default - sort by logical volume
           #           n = sort by disk

while (( $# > 0 ))
do
  case "$1" in
```

```
      -d ) VOLORDER='n'
      ;;
    * ) echo unrecognized option: "$1"
        echo $USAGE
      exit 1
    ;;
  esac
  shift
done

if [ "$VOLORDER" = "y" ]     #determine sorting order based on cmdline option
then
  FINISH=sort
else
  FINISH=cat
fi

# width specifiers to make the output align better
#
# LVMINFO = LV + USE + 6
# DISKINFO = HW + ID + 8
#
typeset -L28 LVMINFO
typeset -L18 LV
typeset -L30 DISKINFO
typeset -L10 ID
typeset -L12 HW
typeset -R9  SZ
typeset -R4  USE FRE

ioscan -f|grep -e disk -e ext_bus|awk '{print $1" "$2" "$3}'|while read LINE
do set $LINE
  TY="$1"
  if [ "$TY" = "ext_bus" ]
  then
    C="$2"
  else
    HW="$3"
    T="`echo $HW | cut -f 2 -d .`"
    D="`echo $HW | cut -f 3 -d .`"
    INFO="`diskinfo /dev/rdsk/c${C}t${T}d${D}`"
    ID=`echo $INFO | sed -e 's/^.*product id: //' -e 's/ .*$//'`
    PVD="`pvdisplay -v /dev/dsk/c${C}t${T}d${D} 2>&1|sed '/Physical ext/,$d'`"


    DISKINFO="HW $HW  ID $ID"
    if echo $PVD |grep "find the volume group" > /dev/null
    then
      SZ=`echo $INFO | sed -e 's/^.*size: //' -e 's/ .*$//'`
      LVMINFO="Non-LVM disk $SZ KB"
      DEVFILE=" /dev/rdsk/c${C}t${T}d${D}"
      echo "$LVMINFO$DISKINFO$DEVFILE"
      if [ "$VOLORDER" = "n" ]
      then
        echo
      fi
    else
      PE=`echo $PVD | sed -e 's/^.*PE Size[^0-9]*//' -e 's/ .*$//'`
      TOT=`echo $PVD | sed -e 's/^.*Total PE[^0-9]*//' -e 's/ .*$//'`
      FRE=`echo $PVD | sed -e 's/^.*Free PE[^0-9]*//' -e 's/ .*$//'`
      VG=`echo $PVD | sed -e 's/^.*VG Name *//' -e 's/ .*$//'`
      VG=`basename $VG`

      echo "$PVD" | sed '1,/^   LV Name/d' | while read LVINFO
      do
        set $LVINFO
```

```
                LV="$VG/`basename $1`"
                FULLLV="/dev/$VG/`basename $1`"  #Version without spaces
                USE="$3"
                LVMINFO="$LV${USE}x${PE}MB"
                SYSUSE=`sed 's/#.*//' < /etc/fstab |
                            grep "$FULLLV[        ]" | awk '{ print $2 }'`
                echo "$LVMINFO$DISKINFO$SYSUSE"
            done
            LV="$VG/UNUSED"
            LVMINFO="$LV${FRE}x${PE}MB"
            echo "$LVMINFO$DISKINFO"
            if [ "$VOLORDER" = "n" ]
            then
                echo
            fi
        fi
    fi
done | $FINISH
```

I redirected the output of this script to **audlvsum.out**, shown in the following listing. This output produces a lot of useful information, including unused areas of physical volume groups.

```
Non-LVM disk     347936 KB    HW 10/12/5.2.0   ID CD-ROM      /dev/rdsk/c1t2d0
Non-LVM disk    2097152 KB    HW 10/8.1.0      ID C3586A      /dev/rdsk/c5t1d0
Non-LVM disk   10485760 KB    HW 10/8.1.1      ID C3586A      /dev/rdsk/c5t1d1
vg00/UNUSED          0x4MB    HW 10/0.5.0      ID ST32550W
vg00/UNUSED          0x4MB    HW 10/0.6.0      ID ST32550W
vg00/lvol1          12x4MB    HW 10/0.6.0      ID ST32550W    /stand
vg00/lvol2         128x4MB    HW 10/0.6.0      ID ST32550W
vg00/lvol3          25x4MB    HW 10/0.6.0      ID ST32550W    /
vg00/lvol4         256x4MB    HW 10/0.6.0      ID ST32550W    /opt
vg00/lvol5          50x4MB    HW 10/0.6.0      ID ST32550W    /tmp
vg00/lvol6          36x4MB    HW 10/0.6.0      ID ST32550W    /usr
vg00/lvol6         220x4MB    HW 10/0.5.0      ID ST32550W    /usr
vg00/lvol7         188x4MB    HW 10/0.5.0      ID ST32550W    /var
vg00/lvol8         100x4MB    HW 10/0.5.0      ID ST32550W    ...
vg01/UNUSED        256x4MB    HW 10/4/12.5.0   ID C2300WDR5
vg01/UNUSED        256x4MB    HW 10/4/12.6.0   ID C2300WDR5
vg01/UNUSED        327x4MB    HW 10/8.0.0      ID C3586A
vg01/add           125x4MB    HW 10/8.0.0      ID C3586A      /add
vg01/lvol10       1023x4MB    HW 10/4/12.5.0   ID C2300WDR5   /dev01
vg01/lvol10       1023x4MB    HW 10/4/12.6.0   ID C2300WDR5   /dev01
vg01/lvol12        256x4MB    HW 10/4/12.5.0   ID C2300WDR5   /mdd
vg01/lvol12        256x4MB    HW 10/4/12.6.0   ID C2300WDR5   /mdd
vg01/lvol14         59x4MB    HW 10/8.0.0      ID C3586A      /npscm
vg01/lvol14        453x4MB    HW 10/4/12.5.0   ID C2300WDR5   /npscm
vg01/lvol14        453x4MB    HW 10/4/12.6.0   ID C2300WDR5   /npscm
vg03/UNUSED         90x4MB    HW 10/4/12.5.1   ID C2300WDR5
vg03/UNUSED         90x4MB    HW 10/4/12.6.1   ID C2300WDR5
vg03/lvol11       1023x4MB    HW 10/4/12.5.1   ID C2300WDR5   /dev02
vg03/lvol11       1023x4MB    HW 10/4/12.6.1   ID C2300WDR5   /dev02
vg03/lvol31        375x4MB    HW 10/4/12.5.1   ID C2300WDR5   /ccur
vg03/lvol31        375x4MB    HW 10/4/12.6.1   ID C2300WDR5   /ccur
vg03/lvol41        500x4MB    HW 10/4/12.5.1   ID C2300WDR5   /usr/wind
vg03/lvol41        500x4MB    HW 10/4/12.6.1   ID C2300WDR5   /usr/wind
```

```
vg04/UNUSED         0x4MB     HW 10/0.1.0    ID ST32550W
vg04/UNUSED         0x4MB     HW 10/0.2.0    ID C2490WD
vg04/lvol1         25x4MB     HW 10/0.2.0    ID C2490WD     /OLDROOT
vg04/lvol2        125x4MB     HW 10/0.2.0    ID C2490WD
vg04/lvol4         88x4MB     HW 10/0.1.0    ID ST32550W    /OLDOPT
vg04/lvol4        125x4MB     HW 10/0.2.0    ID C2490WD     /OLDOPT
vg04/lvol5          6x4MB     HW 10/0.2.0    ID C2490WD     /OLDTMP
vg04/lvol5         19x4MB     HW 10/0.1.0    ID ST32550W    /OLDTMP
vg04/lvol6        215x4MB     HW 10/0.1.0    ID ST32550W    /OLDUSR
vg04/lvol7          2x4MB     HW 10/0.2.0    ID C2490WD     /OLDVAR
vg04/lvol7        186x4MB     HW 10/0.1.0    ID ST32550W    /OLDVAR
vg04/lvol8         67x4MB     HW 10/0.2.0    ID C2490WD
vg04/lvol9        157x4MB     HW 10/0.2.0    ID C2490WD
vg05/UNUSED         0x4MB     HW 10/8.0.1    ID C3586A
vg05/lvol10      2431x4MB     HW 10/8.0.1    ID C3586A      /home
vg05/lvol21       128x4MB     HW 10/8.0.1    ID C3586A      ...
```

Logical Volume Detail

The previous script provided a useful summary of logical volumes. The next useful information to have would be detailed information on the logical volumes of the system. The following script, called **audlv-dis.sh**, provides detailed information on the logical volumes connected to a system:

```
#!/usr/bin/ksh
echo "a listing by: lvdisplay -v " >$ARCHDIR/lvdisplay_v.txt
for lv in `vgdisplay -v | grep 'LV Name' | awk '{print $3}'`
do
entry=`bdf | grep $lv`
if [ ! -z "$entry" ]
then
echo "\n$PROG>>>>> $lv IS mounted, line from bdf is:\n$entry"
else
echo "\n$PROG>>>>> $lv IS NOT mounted"
fi
echo "$PROG>>>>> documenting first 30 lines of lvm information \
by: lvdisplay -v $lv | head -30"
echo "the logical volume is:$lv"
lvdisplay -v $lv | head -30
lvdisplay -v $lv >>$ARCHDIR/lvdisplay_v.txt
done
echo "PROG>>>>> archived by lvdisplay -v >$ARCHDIR/lvdisplay_v.txt"
```

I redirected the output of this script to **audlvdis.out**, shown in the following listing. Only the first few logical volumes are listed.

```
      >>>>> /dev/vg00/lvol3 IS mounted, line from bdf is:
      /dev/vg00/lvol3      99669    33110    56592   37% /
      >>>>> documenting first 30 lines of lvm information by: lvdisplay -v /dev/vg00/
lvol3 | head -30
      the logical volume is:/dev/vg00/lvol3
      --- Logical volumes ---
      LV Name                   /dev/vg00/lvol3
      VG Name                   /dev/vg00
      LV Permission             read/write
      LV Status                 available/syncd
      Mirror copies             0
      Consistency Recovery      MWC
      Schedule                  parallel
      LV Size (Mbytes)          100
      Current LE                25
      Allocated PE              25
      Stripes                   0
      Stripe Size (Kbytes)      0
      Bad block                 off
      Allocation                strict/contiguous

         --- Distribution of logical volume ---
         PV Name          LE on PV  PE on PV
         /dev/dsk/c0t6d0   25        25

         --- Logical extents ---
         LE    PV1                  PE1  Status 1
         0000 /dev/dsk/c0t6d0       0140 current
         0001 /dev/dsk/c0t6d0       0141 current
         0002 /dev/dsk/c0t6d0       0142 current
         0003 /dev/dsk/c0t6d0       0143 current
         0004 /dev/dsk/c0t6d0       0144 current
         0005 /dev/dsk/c0t6d0       0145 current
         0006 /dev/dsk/c0t6d0       0146 current
         0007 /dev/dsk/c0t6d0       0147 current

      >>>>> /dev/vg00/lvol2 IS NOT mounted
      >>>>> documenting first 30 lines of lvm information by:
            lvdisplay -v /dev/vg00/lvol2 | head -30
      the logical volume is:/dev/vg00/lvol2
      --- Logical volumes ---
      LV Name                   /dev/vg00/lvol2
      VG Name                   /dev/vg00
      LV Permission             read/write
      LV Status                 available/syncd
      Mirror copies             0
      Consistency Recovery      MWC
      Schedule                  parallel
      LV Size (Mbytes)          512
      Current LE                128
      Allocated PE              128
      Stripes                   0
      Stripe Size (Kbytes)      0
      Bad block                 off
      Allocation                strict/contiguous

         --- Distribution of logical volume ---
         PV Name          LE on PV  PE on PV
         /dev/dsk/c0t6d0   128       128

         --- Logical extents ---
         LE    PV1                  PE1  Status 1
```

```
0000 /dev/dsk/c0t6d0    0012 current
0001 /dev/dsk/c0t6d0    0013 current
0002 /dev/dsk/c0t6d0    0014 current
0003 /dev/dsk/c0t6d0    0015 current
0004 /dev/dsk/c0t6d0    0016 current
0005 /dev/dsk/c0t6d0    0017 current
0006 /dev/dsk/c0t6d0    0018 current
0007 /dev/dsk/c0t6d0    0019 current

>>>>> /dev/vg00/lvol1 IS mounted, line from bdf is:
/dev/vg00/lvol1    47829    29893    13153    69% /stand
>>>>> documenting first 30 lines of lvm information by:
      lvdisplay -v /dev/vg00/lvol1 | head -30
the logical volume is:/dev/vg00/lvol1
--- Logical volumes ---
LV Name                      /dev/vg00/lvol1
VG Name                      /dev/vg00
LV Permission                read/write
LV Status                    available/syncd
Mirror copies                0
Consistency Recovery         MWC
Schedule                     parallel
LV Size (Mbytes)             48
Current LE                   12
Allocated PE                 12
Stripes                      0
Stripe Size (Kbytes)         0
Bad block                    off
Allocation                   strict/contiguous

   --- Distribution of logical volume ---
   PV Name              LE on PV  PE on PV
   /dev/dsk/c0t6d0      12        12

   --- Logical extents ---
   LE   PV1                  PE1   Status 1
   0000 /dev/dsk/c0t6d0      0000  current
   0001 /dev/dsk/c0t6d0      0001  current
   0002 /dev/dsk/c0t6d0      0002  current
   0003 /dev/dsk/c0t6d0      0003  current
   0004 /dev/dsk/c0t6d0      0004  current
   0005 /dev/dsk/c0t6d0      0005  current
   0006 /dev/dsk/c0t6d0      0006  current
   0007 /dev/dsk/c0t6d0      0007  current

>>>>> /dev/vg00/lvol6 IS mounted, line from bdf is:
/dev/vg00/lvol6    1025617   605780   317275   66% /usr
>>>>> documenting first 30 lines of lvm information by:
      lvdisplay -v /dev/vg00/lvol6 | head -30
the logical volume is:/dev/vg00/lvol6
--- Logical volumes ---
LV Name                      /dev/vg00/lvol6
VG Name                      /dev/vg00
LV Permission                read/write
LV Status                    available/syncd
Mirror copies                0
Consistency Recovery         MWC
Schedule                     parallel
LV Size (Mbytes)             1024
Current LE                   256
Allocated PE                 256
Stripes                      0
Stripe Size (Kbytes)         0
Bad block                    on
Allocation                   strict
```

```
    --- Distribution of logical volume ---
    PV Name            LE on PV  PE on PV
    /dev/dsk/c0t6d0       36        36
    /dev/dsk/c0t5d0      220       220

    --- Logical extents ---
    LE    PV1              PE1  Status 1
    0000 /dev/dsk/c0t6d0   0471 current
    0001 /dev/dsk/c0t6d0   0472 current
    0002 /dev/dsk/c0t6d0   0473 current
    0003 /dev/dsk/c0t6d0   0474 current
    0004 /dev/dsk/c0t6d0   0475 current
    0005 /dev/dsk/c0t6d0   0476 current
    0006 /dev/dsk/c0t6d0   0477 current

>>>>> /dev/vg00/lvol4 IS mounted, line from bdf is:
/dev/vg00/lvol4   1025617 667722 255333   72% /opt
>>>>> documenting first 30 lines of lvm information by:
     lvdisplay -v /dev/vg00/lvol4 | head -30
the logical volume is:/dev/vg00/lvol4
--- Logical volumes ---
LV Name                    /dev/vg00/lvol4
VG Name                    /dev/vg00
LV Permission              read/write
LV Status                  available/syncd
Mirror copies              0
Consistency Recovery       MWC
Schedule                   parallel
LV Size (Mbytes)           1024
Current LE                 256
Allocated PE               256
Stripes                    0
Stripe Size (Kbytes)       0
Bad block                  on
Allocation                 strict

    --- Distribution of logical volume ---
    PV Name            LE on PV  PE on PV
    /dev/dsk/c0t6d0      256       256

    --- Logical extents ---
    LE    PV1              PE1  Status 1
    0000 /dev/dsk/c0t6d0   0165 current
    0001 /dev/dsk/c0t6d0   0166 current
    0002 /dev/dsk/c0t6d0   0167 current
    0003 /dev/dsk/c0t6d0   0168 current
    0004 /dev/dsk/c0t6d0   0169 current
    0005 /dev/dsk/c0t6d0   0170 current
    0006 /dev/dsk/c0t6d0   0171 current
    0007 /dev/dsk/c0t6d0   0172 current
```

Patches

The following script, called **audpatch.sh**, is used to produce a list of patches installed on your system. The program categorizes the patches as well as listing them.

```
#!/bin/ksh

echo "\nThis is a list of patches installed on system `hostname`\n"

swlist > swlist.out

        WORD_COUNT=$(cat swlist.out | grep PHKL | wc -l)
        echo "\n\nNumber of kernel patches on `hostname` is $WORD_COUNT."
echo "\nKernel patches : \n"
        echo " Patch Number \t\t\t\t Revision \t Description"
        cat swlist.out | grep PHKL

        WORD_COUNT=$(cat swlist.out | grep PHCO | wc -l)
        echo "\n\nNumber of command patches on `hostname` is $WORD_COUNT."
echo "\nCommand patches : \n"
        echo " Patch Number \t\t\t\t Revision \t Description"
        cat swlist.out | grep PHCO

        WORD_COUNT=$(cat swlist.out | grep PHNE | wc -l)
        echo "\n\nNumber of network patches on `hostname` is $WORD_COUNT."
echo "\nNetwork patches : \n"
        echo " Patch Number \t\t\t\t Revision \t Description"
        cat swlist.out | grep PHNE

        WORD_COUNT=$(cat swlist.out | grep PHSS | wc -l)
        echo "\n\nNumber of subsystem patches on `hostname` is $WORD_COUNT."
echo "\nSubsystem patches : \n"
        echo " Patch Number \t\t\t\t Revision \t Description"
        cat swlist.out | grep PHSS
```

The following output was received from running **audpatch.sh**:

```
# audpatch.sh

This is a list of patches installed on system hpux1


Number of kernel patches on hpux1 is 25.

Kernel patches :

  Patch Number   Revision          Description
  PHKL_10258     B.10.00.00.AA     exec, ptrace, MMF, large shmem, large buf cache
  PHKL_10443     B.10.00.00.AA     SCSI Passthru driver cumulative patch
  PHKL_10453     B.10.00.00.AA     LVM kernel and pstat cumulative patch
  PHKL_10459     B.10.00.00.AA     cumulative patch for SystemV semaphores, semop()
  PHKL_10464     B.10.00.00.AA     HP-PB SCSI cumulative patch (scsi1/scsi3)
  PHKL_10670     B.10.00.00.AA     disc3/disc30 cumulative patch
  PHKL_7764      B.10.00.00.AA     Data loss when truncating VxFS (JFS) files
  PHKL_7765      B.10.00.00.AA     hpux(1M) for kernels larger than 13 MBytes
  PHKL_7900      B.10.00.00.AA     JFS KI, page fault, deadlock, & setuid fixes
  PHKL_8188      B.10.00.00.AA     B_NDELAY and Zalon chip hang workaround.
  PHKL_8204      B.10.00.00.AA     Fix for system hang during panic
  PHKL_8377      B.10.00.00.AA     Fix vmtrace bug. Release malloc memory.
  PHKL_8656      B.10.00.00.AA     panic with autochanger connected to FW interface
  PHKL_8684      B.10.00.00.AA     Two panics page fault on ICS - sysmemunreserve.
```

```
     PHKL_8780   B.10.00.00.AA   panic on GSC/HSC MP machines on kernel semaphore
     PHKL_9076   B.10.00.00.AA   MMF performance, large SHMEM, large buffer cache
     PHKL_9152   B.10.00.00.AA   Performance enhancements for PA-8000 systems.
     PHKL_9156   B.10.00.00.AA   NFS Kernel Cumulative Megapatch
     PHKL_9362   B.10.00.00.AA   Fix panic caused by MP race
     PHKL_9366   B.10.00.00.AA   Data corruption on PA-8000 based systems.
     PHKL_9371   B.10.00.00.AA   Various fixes for unmountable VxFS file systems
     PHKL_9570   B.10.00.00.AA   NFS and VxFS (JFS) cumulative patch
     PHKL_9712   B.10.00.00.AA   VxFS (JFS) patch for "edquota -t"
     PHKL_9724   B.10.00.00.AA   select() system call performance improvement
     PHKL_SP20   B.10.00.00.AA   Unofficial_test_patch


Number of command patches on hpux1 is 11.

Command patches :

     Patch Number   Revision            Description
     PHCO_10016   A.01.20        HP Disk Array Utilities w/AutoRAID Manager
     PHCO_10027   B.10.00.00.AA  libc cumulative patch
     PHCO_10048   B.10.00.00.AA  LVM commands cumulative patch
     PHCO_10175   B.10.00.00.AA  libc year2000 white paper
     PHCO_10295   B.10.00.00.AA  Allows umounting a disabled vxfs snapshot FS
     PHCO_7817    B.10.00.00.AA  fixes LVM maintenance mode HFS fsck error
     PHCO_8549    B.10.00.00.AA  extendfs_hfs fix for large file systems
     PHCO_9228    B.10.00.00.AA  Fbackup(1M) Long User or Group Name Patch
     PHCO_9396    B.10.00.00.AA  Fix for umountable VxFS file systems
     PHCO_9543    B.10.00.00.AA  Allows umount to unmount a Stale NFS FS
     PHCO_9895    B.10.00.00.AA  Cumulative SAM Patch 4.


Number of network patches on hpux1 is 6.

Network patches :

     Patch Number   Revision            Description
     PHNE_10512   B.10.00.00.AA   LAN products cumulative Patch
     PHNE_6190    B.10.00.00.AA   cumulative ocd(1M) patch
     PHNE_8328    B.10.00.00.AA   cumulative telnetd(1M) patch
     PHNE_9060    B.10.00.00.AA   Fix a panic in STREAMS
     PHNE_9107    B.10.00.00.AA   cumulative ARPA Transport patch
     PHNE_9438    B.10.00.00.AA   Cumulative Mux and Pty Patch


Number of subsystem patches on hpux1 is 12.

Subsystem patches :

     Patch Number   Revision            Description
     PHSS_7789    C.10.20.02     Predictive Support: SCSISCAN-Switch Log
     PHSS_8490    B.10.00.00.AA  cumulative pxdb patch.
     PHSS_8590    B.10.00.00.AA  third diagnostic patch
     PHSS_8709    B.10.00.00.AA  X11R5/Motif1.2 Development Nov96 Patch
     PHSS_8711    B.10.00.00.AA  X11R6/Motif1.2 Development Nov96 Patch
     PHSS_9096    B.10.00.00.AA  HP C++ core library components (A.10.24)
     PHSS_9356    B.10.00.00.AA  X11R5/Xt/Motif Nov-D Point patch
     PHSS_9400    B.10.00.00.AA  ld(1) cumulative patch
     PHSS_9778    B.10.00.00.AA  X11R6/Xt/Motif Nov96-D Point patch
     PHSS_9803    B.10.00.00.AA  CDE Runtime Mar97 Patch
     PHSS_9855    B.10.00.00.AA  HP C++ (A.10.24) with a correct eh/lib++.a
     PHSS_9977    B.10.00.00.AA  HP aC++ (A.01.02) to fix numerous defects
```

man page

"sw' - 2

The following is the file **swlist.out**, which was produced in the script by running the **swlist** command. You can see that the summary list of patches produced by **audpatch.sh** is much easier to read than this **swlist** output.

```
# Initializing...
# Contacting target "hpux1"...
#
# Target:  hpux1:/
#

#
# Bundle(s):
#

  2UserDegradeB.10.20       HP-UX 2-User License (For degrading user license level)
  A3516A_APZA.01.16         HP Disk Array Utilities for Unix (S800)
  B2491A_APZB.10.20         MirrorDisk/UX
  B3191A_APZB.10.20         DCE/9000 Core Services Media and Manuals, International version
  B3193A_APZB.10.20         DCE/9000 Application Development Tools Media and Manuals
  B3395AA_APZB.10.20.02     HP-UX Developer's Toolkit for 10.0 Series 800
  B3519AA_APZB.10.20        DCE/9000 Quickstart Bundle, International version,
                            Media and Manuals
  B3701AA_APZ_TRYB.10.20.89    Trial HP GlancePlus/UX Pak for s800 10.20
  B3900AA_APZB.10.20.02     HP C/ANSI C Developer's Bundle for HP-UX 10.20 (S800)
  B3912AA_APZB.10.20.02     HP C++ Compiler S800
  B3912BA_APZA.01.00        HP aC++ Compiler S800
  B3919CA_AGLB.10.20        HP-UX 8-User License
  B3920CAB.10.20            HP-UX Media Kit (Reference Only. See Description)
  B4085CBEngC.05.25         English C SoftBench S800 10.x
  B4087CBEngC.05.25         English C++ SoftBench S800 10.x
  B4474EA_APZ7.09           ENWARE X Station Software
  B5050BBEngC.05.25         English SoftBench CM S800 10.x
  DCEProgB.10.20            DCE Programming and Archive Libraries
  DCESystemAdminB.10.20     DCE System Administration Utilities
  GSLDevEnvB.10.20          GSL Starbase/PEX Development Environment
  HPUXEngGS800B.10.20       English HP-UX VUE Runtime Environment
  Integ-LogonB.10.20        Integrated Logon Bundle
  J2559CD.01.08             Hewlett-Packard JetAdmin for Unix Utility
  MiscDiagB.10.20.02        HPUX 10.0 Support Tools Bundle
  OnlineDiagB.10.20.02      HPUX 10.0 Support Tools Bundle
  SoftBenchRefC.05.25       SoftBench 5.0 (Reference Only.  See Description)
  VUE-to-CDE-ToolsB.10.20   VUE to CDE Migration Tools (for all languages)
#
# Product(s) not contained in a Bundle:
#

  LROMB.02.01               HP LaserROM/UX
  OVOPC-UX10-NODA.03.01     OpC Mgd Node SW running on HP-UX 10.0
  PHCO_10016A.01.20         HP Disk Array Utilities w/AutoRAID Manager
  PHCO_10027B.10.00.00.AA   libc cumulative patch
  PHCO_10048B.10.00.00.AA   LVM commands cumulative patch
  PHCO_10175B.10.00.00.AA   libc year2000 white paper
  PHCO_10295B.10.00.00.AA   Allows umounting a disabled vxfs snapshot FS
  PHCO_7817B.10.00.00.AA    fixes LVM maintenance mode HFS fsck error
  PHCO_8549B.10.00.00.AA    extendfs_hfs fix for large file systems
  PHCO_9228B.10.00.00.AA    Fbackup(1M) Long User or Group Name Patch
  PHCO_9396B.10.00.00.AA    Fix for umountable VxFS file systems
  PHCO_9543B.10.00.00.AA    Allows umount to unmount a Stale NFS FS
  PHCO_9895B.10.00.00.AA    Cumulative SAM Patch 4.
  PHKL_10258B.10.00.00.AA   exec, ptrace, MMF, large shmem, large buf cache
```

```
PHKL_10443B.10.00.00.AA    SCSI Passthru driver cumulative patch
PHKL_10453B.10.00.00.AA    LVM kernel and pstat cumulative patch
PHKL_10459B.10.00.00.AA    cumulative patch for SystemV semaphores, semop()
PHKL_10464B.10.00.00.AA    HP-PB SCSI cumulative patch (scsi1/scsi3)
PHKL_10670B.10.00.00.AA    disc3/disc30 cumulative patch
PHKL_7764B.10.00.00.AA     Data loss when truncating VxFS (JFS) files
PHKL_7765B.10.00.00.AA     hpux(1M) for kernels larger than 13 MBytes
PHKL_7900B.10.00.00.AA     JFS KI, page fault, deadlock, & setuid fixes
PHKL_8188B.10.00.00.AA     B_NDELAY and Zalon chip hang workaround.
PHKL_8204B.10.00.00.AA     Fix for system hang during panic
PHKL_8377B.10.00.00.AA     Fix vmtrace bug. Release malloc memory.
PHKL_8656B.10.00.00.AA     panic with autochanger connected to FW interface
PHKL_8684B.10.00.00.AA     Two panics page fault on ICS - sysmemunreserve.
PHKL_8780B.10.00.00.AA     panic on GSC/HSC MP machines on kernel semaphore
PHKL_9076B.10.00.00.AA     MMF performance, large SHMEM, large buffer cache
PHKL_9152B.10.00.00.AA     Performance enhancements for PA-8000 systems.
PHKL_9156B.10.00.00.AA     NFS Kernel Cumulative Megapatch
PHKL_9362B.10.00.00.AA     Fix panic caused by MP race
PHKL_9366B.10.00.00.AA     Data corruption on PA-8000 based systems.
PHKL_9371B.10.00.00.AA     Various fixes for unmountable VxFS file systems
PHKL_9570B.10.00.00.AA     NFS and VxFS (JFS) cumulative patch
PHKL_9712B.10.00.00.AA     VxFS (JFS) patch for "edquota -t"
PHKL_9724B.10.00.00.AA     select() system call performance improvement
PHKL_SP20B.10.00.00.AA     Unofficial_test_patch
PHNE_10512B.10.00.00.AA    LAN products cumulative Patch
PHNE_6190B.10.00.00.AA     cumulative ocd(1M) patch
PHNE_8328B.10.00.00.AA     cumulative telnetd(1M) patch
PHNE_9060B.10.00.00.AA     Fix a panic in STREAMS
PHNE_9107B.10.00.00.AA     cumulative ARPA Transport patch
PHNE_9438B.10.00.00.AA     Cumulative Mux and Pty Patch
PHSS_7789C.10.20.02        Predictive Support: SCSISCAN-Switch Log
PHSS_8490B.10.00.00.AA     cumulative pxdb patch.
PHSS_8590B.10.00.00.AA     third diagnostic patch
PHSS_8709B.10.00.00.AA     X11R5/Motif1.2 Development Nov96 Patch
PHSS_8711B.10.00.00.AA     X11R6/Motif1.2 Development Nov96 Patch
PHSS_9096B.10.00.00.AA     HP C++ core library components (A.10.24)
PHSS_9356B.10.00.00.AA     X11R5/Xt/Motif Nov-D Point patch
PHSS_9400B.10.00.00.AA     ld(1) cumulative patch
PHSS_9778B.10.00.00.AA     X11R6/Xt/Motif Nov96-D Point patch
PHSS_9803B.10.00.00.AA     CDE Runtime Mar97 Patch
PHSS_9855B.10.00.00.AA     HP C++ (A.10.24) with a correct eh/lib++.a
PHSS_9977B.10.00.00.AA     HP aC++ (A.01.02) to fix numerous defects
```

Software Check

The following script, called **audswchk.sh**, runs the **swverify** command to verify the software installed on a system:

man page

"sw' - 2

```
#!/usr/bin/ksh
# testing of swverify command
echo " About to verify installed software using swverify"
echo " Please be patient, this can take 10-20 minutes"
swverify -x allow_incompatible=true -x autoselect_dependencies=false \* 1>/dev/null 2>&1
begnum=`grep -n 'BEGIN verify AGENT SESSION' /var/adm/sw/swagent.log | \
tail -1 | cut -d: -f1`
endnum=`cat /var/adm/sw/swagent.log | wc -l`
let tailnum='endnum-begnum'
```

```
if [ "$tailnum" -gt 0 ]; then
echo "Writing swverify data to file audswchk.out"
tail -n $tailnum /var/adm/sw/swagent.log >audswchk.out 2>&1
fi
```

The following output was created by running **audswchk.sh**. In addition to this output file, there is also a message written to the screen indicating that it may take some time for this script to complete. The system on which this **audswchk.sh** was run is a smooth-running system with no known errors, yet this output is very long and shows some warnings and errors that could result in serious problems.

```
WARNING: Fileset "VUEHelpDevKit.VUE-HELP-PRG,l=/,r=B.10.20.01" had file
         warnings.
WARNING: Directory "/" should have mode "1363" but the actual mode is
         "755".
WARNING: Directory "/" should have owner,uid "xbuild,3395" but the
         actual owner,uid is "root,0".
WARNING: Directory "/" should have group,gid "users,20" but the actual
         group,gid is "root,0".
WARNING: Fileset "VUEHelpDevKit.VUE-PRG-MAN,l=/,r=B.10.20.01" had file
         warnings.
WARNING: Directory "/" should have mode "555" but the actual mode is
         "755".
WARNING: Directory "/" should have owner,uid "xbuild,3395" but the
         actual owner,uid is "root,0".
WARNING: Directory "/" should have group,gid "users,20" but the actual
         group,gid is "root,0".
WARNING: Directory "/usr" should have owner,uid "root,0" but the actual
         owner,uid is "bin,2".
WARNING: Directory "/usr" should have group,gid "other,1" but the
         actual group,gid is "bin,2".
WARNING: Directory "/usr/lib" should have owner,uid "root,0" but the
         actual owner,uid is "bin,2".
WARNING: Directory "/usr/lib" should have group,gid "other,1" but the
         actual group,gid is "bin,2".
WARNING: Directory "/usr/lib/X11" should have owner,uid "xbuild,3395"
         but the actual owner,uid is "bin,2".
WARNING: Directory "/usr/lib/X11" should have group,gid "users,20" but
         the actual group,gid is "bin,2".
WARNING: Fileset "X11MotifDevKit.IMAKE,l=/,r=B.10.20.02" had file
         warnings.
WARNING: Directory "/" should have mode "555" but the actual mode is
         "755".
WARNING: Directory "/" should have group,gid "other,1" but the actual
         group,gid is "root,0".
ERROR:   File "/usr/lib/libXm.a" missing.
ERROR:   Fileset "X11MotifDevKit.MOTIF12-PRG,l=/,r=B.10.20.02" had file
         errors.
WARNING: Directory "/" should have mode "555" but the actual mode is
         "755".
WARNING: Directory "/" should have owner,uid "xbuild,3395" but the
         actual owner,uid is "root,0".
WARNING: Directory "/" should have group,gid "users,20" but the actual
         group,gid is "root,0".
```

```
WARNING: Directory "/usr/dt" should have owner,uid "root,0" but the
         actual owner,uid is "bin,2".
WARNING: Directory "/usr/dt" should have group,gid "other,1" but the
         actual group,gid is "bin,2".
WARNING: Directory "/usr/dt/share" should have owner,uid "root,0" but
         the actual owner,uid is "bin,2".
WARNING: Directory "/usr/dt/share" should have group,gid "other,1" but
         the actual group,gid is "bin,2".
WARNING: Directory "/usr/dt/share/man" should have owner,uid "root,0"
         but the actual owner,uid is "bin,2".
WARNING: Directory "/usr/dt/share/man" should have group,gid "other,1"
         but the actual group,gid is "bin,2".
WARNING: Directory "/usr/share" should have owner,uid "xbuild,3395" but
         the actual owner,uid is "bin,2".
WARNING: Directory "/usr/share" should have group,gid "users,20" but
         the actual group,gid is "bin,2".
WARNING: Directory "/usr/share/man/man3.Z" should have owner,uid
         "xbuild,3395" but the actual owner,uid is "bin,2".
WARNING: Directory "/usr/share/man/man3.Z" should have group,gid
         "users,20" but the actual group,gid is "bin,2".
WARNING: Fileset "X11MotifDevKit.MOTIF12-PRGMAN,l=/,r=B.10.20.02" had
         file warnings.
WARNING: Directory "/" should have mode "555" but the actual mode is
         "755".
WARNING: Directory "/" should have group,gid "other,1" but the actual
         group,gid is "root,0".
WARNING: Fileset "X11MotifDevKit.X11R5-PRG,l=/,r=B.10.20.02" had file
         warnings.
WARNING: Directory "/" should have mode "555" but the actual mode is
         "755".
WARNING: Directory "/" should have group,gid "other,1" but the actual
         group,gid is "root,0".
WARNING: Directory "/usr/newconfig" should have owner,uid "root,0" but
         the actual owner,uid is "bin,2".
WARNING: Directory "/usr/newconfig" should have group,gid "other,1" but
         the actual group,gid is "bin,2".
WARNING: Fileset "X11MotifDevKit.X11R6-PRG,l=/,r=B.10.20.02" had file
         warnings.
WARNING: Directory "/" should have mode "555" but the actual mode is
         "755".
WARNING: Directory "/" should have group,gid "other,1" but the actual
         group,gid is "root,0".
WARNING: Directory "/usr/contrib/lib" should have owner,uid
         "xbuild,3395" but the actual owner,uid is "bin,2".
WARNING: Directory "/usr/contrib/lib" should have group,gid "users,20"
         but the actual group,gid is "bin,2".
WARNING: Fileset "X11MotifDevKit.X11R6-PRG-CTRB,l=/,r=B.10.20.02" had
         file warnings.
WARNING: Directory "/" should have mode "555" but the actual mode is
         "755".
WARNING: Directory "/" should have group,gid "other,1" but the actual
         group,gid is "root,0".
ERROR:   File "/usr/share/man/man3.Z/XHPSSChange.3x" had a different
         mtime than expected.
ERROR:   Fileset "X11MotifDevKit.X11R6-PRG-MAN,l=/,r=B.10.20.02" had
         file errors.

       * Summary of Analysis Phase:
ERROR:         Verify failed Diag-Sys-800.SUP-CORE-800,l=/,r=B.10.20.02
ERROR:         Verify failed OS-Core.CORE-KRN,l=/,r=B.10.20
ERROR:         Verify failed OS-Core.C2400-UTIL,l=/,r=B.10.20
ERROR:         Verify failed OS-Core.Q4,l=/,r=B.10.20
ERROR:         Verify failed LVM.LVM-RUN,l=/,r=B.10.20
ERROR:         Verify failed LVM.LVM-MIRROR-RUN,l=/,r=B.10.20
ERROR:         Verify failed PHKL_10258.PHKL_10258,l=/,r=B.10.00.00.AA
ERROR:         Verify failed PHKL_10464.PHKL_10464,l=/,r=B.10.00.00.AA
```

```
ERROR:        Verify failed PHKL_10670.PHKL_10670,l=/,r=B.10.00.00.AA
ERROR:        Verify failed PHKL_SP20.PHKL_SP20,l=/,r=B.10.00.00.AA
ERROR:        Verify failed
              Sup-Tool-Mgr-800.STM-UUT-800-RUN,l=/,r=B.10.20.02
ERROR:        Verify failed UserLicense.08-USER,l=/,r=B.10.20
WARNING:      Verified with warnings ACXX.ACXX,l=/opt/aCC,r=A.01.00
WARNING:      Verified with warnings ACXX.ACXX-HELP,l=/opt/aCC,r=A.01.00
WARNING:      Verified with warnings
              ACXX.ACXX-JPN-E-MAN,l=/opt/aCC,r=A.01.00
WARNING:      Verified with warnings
              ACXX.ACXX-JPN-S-MAN,l=/opt/aCC,r=A.01.00
WARNING:      Verified with warnings ACXX.ACXX-MAN,l=/opt/aCC,r=A.01.00
WARNING:      Verified with warnings ACXX.ACXX-SC,l=/opt/aCC,r=A.01.00
WARNING:      Verified with warnings
              ACXX.ACXX-STDLIB,l=/opt/aCC,r=A.01.00
WARNING:      Verified with warnings
              AudioDevKit.AUDIO-PGMAN,l=/opt/audio,r=B.10.10.00
WARNING:      Verified with warnings
              AudioDevKit.AUDIO-PRG,l=/opt/audio,r=B.10.10.00
WARNING:      Verified with warnings
              C-ANSI-C.C,l=/opt/ansic,r=B.10.20.00
ERROR:        Verify failed C-Plus-Plus.HPCXX,l=/opt/CC,r=B.10.20.00
ERROR:        Verify failed C-Plus-Plus.HPCXX-MAN,l=/opt/CC,r=B.10.20.00
ERROR:        Verify failed CDE.CDE-RUN,l=/,r=B.10.20
WARNING:      Verified with warnings
              CDEDevKit.CDE-DEMOS,l=/,r=B.10.20.02
WARNING:      Verified with warnings
              CDEDevKit.CDE-HELP-PRG,l=/,r=B.10.20.02
WARNING:      Verified with warnings CDEDevKit.CDE-INC,l=/,r=B.10.20.02
WARNING:      Verified with warnings
              CDEDevKit.CDE-MAN-DEV,l=/,r=B.10.20.02
WARNING:      Verified with warnings CDEDevKit.CDE-PRG,l=/,r=B.10.20.02
WARNING:      Verified with warnings
              COBOLRT.COBRT,l=/opt/cobol,r=B.11.25
WARNING:      Verified with warnings
              COBOLCRT.COBCRT,l=/opt/cobol,r=B.11.25
WARNING:      Verified with warnings
              COBOLDEV.COBDEV,l=/opt/cobol,r=B.11.25
WARNING:      Verified with warnings
              COBOLTBOX.COBTBOX,l=/opt/cobol,r=B.11.25
WARNING:      Verified with warnings
              CustomerServ.CUST-SERV,l=/opt/secustserv,r=C.05.25
WARNING:      Verified with warnings
              CustomerServ.CUST-SERV-J,l=/opt/secustserv,r=C.05.25
ERROR:        Verify failed
              DCE-CoreAdmin.DCE-CORE-DIAG,l=/opt/dce,r=B.10.20
WARNING:      Verified with warnings
              DigitalVideoDK.DVC-PRG,l=/,r=B.10.20.01
WARNING:      Verified with warnings
              DigitalVideoDK.DVC-PRGMAN,l=/,r=B.10.20.01
WARNING:      Verified with warnings
              DigitalVideoDK.DVC-SHLIBS,l=/,r=B.10.20.01
WARNING:      Verified with warnings
              DigitalVideoDK.DVC-SRV,l=/,r=B.10.20.01
WARNING:      Verified with warnings
              DigitalVideoDK.DVIDEO-FILES,l=/,r=B.10.20.01
WARNING:      Verified with warnings
              DigitalVideoDK.DVIDEO-PGMAN,l=/,r=B.10.20.01
WARNING:      Verified with warnings
              DigitalVideoDK.DVIDEO-PRG,l=/,r=B.10.20.01
WARNING:      Verified with warnings
              DigitalVideoDK.VIDEOOUT-PGMAN,l=/,r=B.10.20.01
WARNING:      Verified with warnings
              DigitalVideoDK.VIDEOOUT-PRG,l=/,r=B.10.20.01
WARNING:      Verified with warnings
              DigitalVideoDK.VIDEOOUT-SHLIBS,l=/,r=B.10.20.01
```

```
ERROR:        Verify failed ENWARE.HPXT-SUPPL,l=/opt/hpxt/enware,r=7.09
ERROR:        Verify failed ENWARE.HPXT-700RX,l=/opt/hpxt/enware,r=7.09
ERROR:        Verify failed ENWARE.HPXT-AUDIO,l=/opt/hpxt/enware,r=7.09
ERROR:        Verify failed ENWARE.HPXT-CDE,l=/opt/hpxt/enware,r=7.09
ERROR:        Verify failed
              ENWARE.HPXT-CLIENTS,l=/opt/hpxt/enware,r=7.09
ERROR:        Verify failed ENWARE.HPXT-ENVIZE,l=/opt/hpxt/enware,r=7.09
ERROR:        Verify failed ENWARE.HPXT-NFS,l=/opt/hpxt/enware,r=7.09
ERROR:        Verify failed ENWARE.HPXT-FLOPPY,l=/opt/hpxt/enware,r=7.09
ERROR:        Verify failed
              ENWARE.HPXT-HP8FONTS,l=/opt/hpxt/enware,r=7.09
ERROR:        Verify failed
              ENWARE.HPXT-ISOFONTS,l=/opt/hpxt/enware,r=7.09
ERROR:        Verify failed
              ENWARE.HPXT-MISCFONT,l=/opt/hpxt/enware,r=7.09
ERROR:        Verify failed ENWARE.HPXT-MPEG,l=/opt/hpxt/enware,r=7.09
ERROR:        Verify failed
              ENWARE.HPXT-PRINTER,l=/opt/hpxt/enware,r=7.09
ERROR:        Verify failed
              ENWARE.HPXT-SCANNER,l=/opt/hpxt/enware,r=7.09
ERROR:        Verify failed ENWARE.HPXT-TOKN,l=/opt/hpxt/enware,r=7.09
ERROR:        Verify failed ENWARE.HPXT-VT320,l=/opt/hpxt/enware,r=7.09
ERROR:        Verify failed ENWARE.HPXT-XLOCK,l=/opt/hpxt/enware,r=7.09
ERROR:        Verify failed ENWARE.HPXT-XTOUCH,l=/opt/hpxt/enware,r=7.09
WARNING:      Verified with warnings
              MeasureWare.MWA,l=/opt/perf,r=B.10.20.89
WARNING:      Verified with warnings
              GraphicsPEX5DK.PEX5-EXAMPLES,l=/opt/graphics/PEX5,r=B.10.20
WARNING:      Verified with warnings
              GraphicsPEX5DK.PEX5-HELP,l=/opt/graphics/PEX5,r=B.10.20
WARNING:      Verified with warnings
              GraphicsPEX5DK.PEX5-PRG,l=/opt/graphics/PEX5,r=B.10.20
WARNING:      Verified with warnings
              GraphicsSBaseDK.FAFM-MAN,l=/opt/graphics/starbase,r=B.10.20
WARNING:      Verified with warnings
              GraphicsSBaseDK.FAFM-PRG,l=/opt/graphics/starbase,r=B.10.20
WARNING:      Verified with warnings
              GraphicsSBaseDK.SBDL-DEMO,l=/opt/graphics/starbase,r=B.10.20
WARNING:      Verified with warnings
              GraphicsSBaseDK.SBDL-MAN,l=/opt/graphics/starbase,r=B.10.20
WARNING:      Verified with warnings
              GraphicsSBaseDK.SBDL-PRG,l=/opt/graphics/starbase,r=B.10.20
WARNING:      Verified with warnings
              GraphicsSBaseDK.STAR-DEMO,l=/opt/graphics/starbase,r=B.10.20
WARNING:      Verified with warnings
              GraphicsSBaseDK.STAR-HARDCOPY,l=/opt/graphics/starbase,r=B.10.20

WARNING:      Verified with warnings
              GraphicsSBaseDK.STAR-MAN,l=/opt/graphics/starbase,r=B.10.20
WARNING:      Verified with warnings
              GraphicsSBaseDK.STAR-PRG,l=/opt/graphics/starbase,r=B.10.20
WARNING:      Verified with warnings
              GraphicsSBaseDK.STAR-WEBDOC,l=/opt/graphics/starbase,r=B.10.20
ERROR:        Verify failed
              HPAutoRAID.HPAutoRAID-MAN,l=/opt/hparray,r=A.01.16
ERROR:        Verify failed
              HPAutoRAID.HPAutoRAID-RUN,l=/opt/hparray,r=A.01.16
ERROR:        Verify failed HPNP.HPNP-RUN,l=/opt/hpnp,r=D.01.08
WARNING:      Verified with warnings
              ImagingDevKit.IMAGE-FILES,l=/,r=B.10.20.02
WARNING:      Verified with warnings
              ImagingDevKit.IMAGE-PGMAN,l=/,r=B.10.20.02
WARNING:      Verified with warnings
              ImagingDevKit.IMAGE-PRG,l=/,r=B.10.20.02
ERROR:        Verify failed LSSERV.LSSERV-ADMIN,l=/opt/ifor,r=B.10.20
WARNING:      Verified with warnings
```

```
                  LSSERV.LSSERV-SERVER,l=/opt/ifor,r=B.10.20
ERROR:            Verify failed OVOPC-UX10-NOD.OVOPC-UX10,l=/,r=A.03.01
ERROR:            Verify failed PHCO_10048.PHCO_10048,l=/,r=B.10.00.00.AA
WARNING:          Verified with warnings SystemAdmin.SAM-HELP,l=/,r=B.10.20
WARNING:          Verified with warnings SystemAdmin.SAM,l=/,r=B.10.20
ERROR:            Verify failed PHSS_8709.PHSS_8709,l=/,r=B.10.00.00.AA
ERROR:            Verify failed PHSS_9855.PHSS_9855,l=/,r=B.10.00.00.AA
WARNING:          Verified with warnings
                  SB-BMSFramework.BMS-ENG-A-MAN,l=/opt/softbench,r=C.05.25
WARNING:          Verified with warnings
                  SB-BMSFramework.BMS-JPN-E-MAN,l=/opt/softbench,r=C.05.25
WARNING:          Verified with warnings
                  SB-BMSFramework.BMS-JPN-E-MSG,l=/opt/softbench,r=C.05.25
WARNING:          Verified with warnings
                  SB-BMSFramework.BMS-JPN-S-MAN,l=/opt/softbench,r=C.05.25
WARNING:          Verified with warnings
                  SB-BMSFramework.BMS-JPN-S-MSG,l=/opt/softbench,r=C.05.25
WARNING:          Verified with warnings
                  SB-BMSFramework.SB-BMS,l=/opt/softbench,r=C.05.25
WARNING:          Verified with warnings
                  SB-BMSFramework.SB-BMSFW,l=/opt/softbench,r=C.05.25
ERROR:            Verify failed
                  SB-BMSFramework.SB-FONTS,l=/opt/softbench,r=C.05.25
WARNING:          Verified with warnings
                  SB-BMSFramework.SB-MSGCONN,l=/opt/softbench,r=C.05.25
WARNING:          Verified with warnings
                  SB-BMSFramework.SBM-ENG-A-MAN,l=/opt/softbench,r=C.05.25
WARNING:          Verified with warnings
                  SB-CM.SBCM-CLT,l=/opt/softbench,r=B.01.55
WARNING:          Verified with warnings
                  SB-CM.SBCM-ENG-A-HLP,l=/opt/softbench,r=B.01.55
WARNING:          Verified with warnings
                  SB-CM.SBCM-ENG-A-MAN,l=/opt/softbench,r=B.01.55
WARNING:          Verified with warnings
                  SB-CM.SBCM-GUI,l=/opt/softbench,r=B.01.55
WARNING:          Verified with warnings
                  SB-CM.SBCM-J,l=/opt/softbench,r=B.01.55
WARNING:          Verified with warnings
                  SB-CM.SBCM-JPN-E-HLP,l=/opt/softbench,r=B.01.55
WARNING:          Verified with warnings
                  SB-CM.SBCM-JPN-E-MAN,l=/opt/softbench,r=B.01.55
WARNING:          Verified with warnings
                  SB-CM.SBCM-JPN-E-MSG,l=/opt/softbench,r=B.01.55
WARNING:          Verified with warnings
                  SB-CM.SBCM-JPN-S-HLP,l=/opt/softbench,r=B.01.55
WARNING:          Verified with warnings
                  SB-CM.SBCM-JPN-S-MAN,l=/opt/softbench,r=B.01.55
WARNING:          Verified with warnings
                  SB-CM.SBCM-JPN-S-MSG,l=/opt/softbench,r=B.01.55
WARNING:          Verified with warnings
                  SB-CM.SBCM-SRV,l=/opt/softbench,r=B.01.55
WARNING:          Verified with warnings
                  SB-SoftBenchCore.SB40-LIBS,l=/opt/softbench,r=C.05.25
WARNING:          Verified with warnings
                  SB-SoftBenchCore.SB-LSMGR,l=/opt/softbench,r=C.05.25
WARNING:          Verified with warnings
                  SB-SoftBenchCore.SB-GNUBIN,l=/opt/softbench,r=C.05.25
ERROR:            Verify failed
                  SB-SoftBenchCore.SB-CORE,l=/opt/softbench,r=C.05.25
WARNING:          Verified with warnings
                  SB-SoftBenchCore.SB-COMMON,l=/opt/softbench,r=C.05.25
WARNING:          Verified with warnings
                  SB-SoftBenchCore.SB-DT,l=/opt/softbench,r=C.05.25
WARNING:          Verified with warnings
                  SB-SoftBenchCore.SB-DEMO,l=/opt/softbench,r=C.05.25
WARNING:          Verified with warnings
```

```
          SB-SoftBenchCore.SB-ENG-A-MAN,l=/opt/softbench,r=C.05.25
WARNING:       Verified with warnings
          SB-SoftBenchCore.SB-GNUBIN-MAN,l=/opt/softbench,r=C.05.25
WARNING:       Verified with warnings
          SB-SoftBenchCore.SB-GNUSRC,l=/opt/softbench,r=C.05.25
WARNING:       Verified with warnings
          SB-SoftBenchCore.SB-JPN-E-MAN,l=/opt/softbench,r=C.05.25
WARNING:       Verified with warnings
          SB-SoftBenchCore.SB-JPN-E-MSG,l=/opt/softbench,r=C.05.25
WARNING:       Verified with warnings
          SB-SoftBenchCore.SB-JPN-S-MAN,l=/opt/softbench,r=C.05.25
WARNING:       Verified with warnings
          SB-SoftBenchCore.SB-JPN-S-MSG,l=/opt/softbench,r=C.05.25
WARNING:       Verified with warnings
          SB-SoftBenchCore.SB40-EDL,l=/opt/softbench,r=C.05.25
WARNING:       Verified with warnings
          SB-SoftBenchCore.SBL-ENG-A-MAN,l=/opt/softbench,r=C.05.25
WARNING:       Verified with warnings
          SB-CPersonality.SB-ADA,l=/opt/softbench,r=C.05.25
WARNING:       Verified with warnings
          SB-CPersonality.SB-C,l=/opt/softbench,r=C.05.25
WARNING:       Verified with warnings
          SB-CPersonality.SB-CBTC,l=/opt/softbench,r=C.05.25
WARNING:       Verified with warnings
          SB-CPersonality.SB-DDE,l=/opt/softbench,r=C.05.25
WARNING:       Verified with warnings
          SB-CPersonality.SBC-ENG-A-HLP,l=/opt/softbench,r=C.05.25
WARNING:       Verified with warnings
          SB-CPersonality.SBC-ENG-A-MAN,l=/opt/softbench,r=C.05.25
WARNING:       Verified with warnings
          SB-CPersonality.SBC-JPN-E-HLP,l=/opt/softbench,r=C.05.25
WARNING:       Verified with warnings
          SB-CPersonality.SBC-JPN-E-MAN,l=/opt/softbench,r=C.05.25
WARNING:       Verified with warnings
          SB-CPersonality.SBC-JPN-E-MSG,l=/opt/softbench,r=C.05.25
WARNING:       Verified with warnings
          SB-CPersonality.SBC-JPN-S-HLP,l=/opt/softbench,r=C.05.25
WARNING:       Verified with warnings
          SB-CPersonality.SBC-JPN-S-MAN,l=/opt/softbench,r=C.05.25
WARNING:       Verified with warnings
          SB-CPersonality.SBC-JPN-S-MSG,l=/opt/softbench,r=C.05.25
WARNING:       Verified with warnings
          SB-CXXAdvisor.SB-RLCK,l=/opt/softbench,r=C.05.25
WARNING:       Verified with warnings
          SB-CXXAdvisor.SBA-ENG-A-HLP,l=/opt/softbench,r=C.05.25
WARNING:       Verified with warnings
          SB-CXXAdvisor.SBA-ENG-A-MAN,l=/opt/softbench,r=C.05.25
WARNING:       Verified with warnings
          SB-CXXPersnlty.SB-CBTCXX,l=/opt/softbench,r=C.05.25
WARNING:       Verified with warnings
          SB-CXXPersnlty.SB-CXX,l=/opt/softbench,r=C.05.25
WARNING:       Verified with warnings
          SB-CXXPersnlty.SBX-JPN-E-MSG,l=/opt/softbench,r=C.05.25
WARNING:       Verified with warnings
          SB-CXXPersnlty.SBX-JPN-S-MSG,l=/opt/softbench,r=C.05.25
WARNING:       Verified with warnings
          SB-CobolPersnlty.SB-CBTCOBOL,l=/opt/softbench,r=C.05.25
WARNING:       Verified with warnings
          SB-CobolPersnlty.SB-COBOL,l=/opt/softbench,r=C.05.25
WARNING:       Verified with warnings
          SB-CobolPersnlty.SB-COBOL-J,l=/opt/softbench,r=C.05.25
WARNING:       Verified with warnings
          SB-CobolPersnlty.SBO-ENG-A-HELP,l=/opt/softbench,r=C.05.25
WARNING:       Verified with warnings
          SB-CobolPersnlty.SBO-JPN-E-HELP,l=/opt/softbench,r=C.05.25
WARNING:       Verified with warnings
```

```
                       SB-CobolPersnlty.SBO-JPN-E-MAN,l=/opt/softbench,r=C.05.25
        WARNING:       Verified with warnings
                       SB-CobolPersnlty.SBO-JPN-E-MSG,l=/opt/softbench,r=C.05.25
        WARNING:       Verified with warnings
                       SB-CobolPersnlty.SBO-JPN-S-HELP,l=/opt/softbench,r=C.05.25
        WARNING:       Verified with warnings
                       SB-CobolPersnlty.SBO-JPN-S-MAN,l=/opt/softbench,r=C.05.25
        WARNING:       Verified with warnings
                       SB-CobolPersnlty.SBO-JPN-S-MSG,l=/opt/softbench,r=C.05.25
        WARNING:       Verified with warnings SW-DIST.SD-FAL,l=/,r=B.10.20
        ERROR:         Verify failed VUE.VUE-RUN,l=/,r=B.10.20
        WARNING:       Verified with warnings
                       VUEHelpDevKit.VUE-HELP-PRG,l=/,r=B.10.20.01
        WARNING:       Verified with warnings
                       VUEHelpDevKit.VUE-PRG-MAN,l=/,r=B.10.20.01
        WARNING:       Verified with warnings
                       X11MotifDevKit.IMAKE,l=/,r=B.10.20.02
        ERROR:         Verify failed X11MotifDevKit.MOTIF12-PRG,l=/,r=B.10.20.02
        WARNING:       Verified with warnings
                       X11MotifDevKit.MOTIF12-PRGMAN,l=/,r=B.10.20.02
        WARNING:       Verified with warnings
                       X11MotifDevKit.X11R5-PRG,l=/,r=B.10.20.02
        WARNING:       Verified with warnings
                       X11MotifDevKit.X11R6-PRG,l=/,r=B.10.20.02
        WARNING:       Verified with warnings
                       X11MotifDevKit.X11R6-PRG-CTRB,l=/,r=B.10.20.02
        ERROR:         Verify failed
                       X11MotifDevKit.X11R6-PRG-MAN,l=/,r=B.10.20.02
        ERROR:   47 of 952 filesets had Errors.
        WARNING: 124 of 952 filesets had Warnings.
               * 781 of 952 filesets had no Errors or Warnings.
        ERROR:   The Analysis Phase had errors and warnings.  See the above
                 output for details.


        =======  19:18:13 EDT  END verify AGENT SESSION (pid=21385)
                 (jobid=hpux1-0144)
```

Password and Group Check

The following script, called **audpassw.sh**, checks the **/etc/passwd** and **/etc/group** files, looking for potential problems:

```
#!/usr/bin/ksh

echo   "*******************************************************************" >
    audpasswd.out
echo  "  This program performs password and group checks on system `hostname`." >>
    audpasswd.out
echo  "*******************************************************************\n\n\n" >>
    audpasswd.out
echo  "Check for multiple root users by using awk on /etc/passwd." >> audpasswd.out
echo  "The following users have a user ID of 0.\n" >> audpasswd.out
awk -F: '{ if ( $3 == 0 ) print $1 }' /etc/passwd >> audpasswd.out

echo "\n\nThe following users do not have a password assigned. " >> audpasswd.out
echo "This could be a serious security problem on the system.\n" >> audpasswd.out
awk -F: '{ if ( $2 == "" ) print $1 }' /etc/passwd >> audpasswd.out
```

```
echo "\n\n\nRunning password consistency check using pwck program." >> audpasswd.out
echo "This program prints the password entry and corresponding" >> audpasswd.out
echo "problem such as login directory not found or bad character" >> audpasswd.out
echo "in login name.\n" >> audpasswd.out
pwck 2>> audpasswd.out

echo "\n\n\nRunning group consistency check using grpck program." >> audpasswd.out
echo "This program prints the group entry and corresponding" >> audpasswd.out
echo "problem such as invalid GID, login name not in password" >> audpasswd.out
echo "file, and groups in which there are no users.\n" >> audpasswd.out
grpck 2>>audpasswd.out
```

This script produces the file **audpasswd.out**. This file has in it several potential user and group-related problems, such as a user without a password:

```
********************************************************************
   This program performs password and group checks on system hpux1.
********************************************************************


   Check for multiple root users by using awk on /etc/passwd.
   The following users have a user ID of 0.

   root
   sam_exec


   The following users do not have a password assigned.
   This could be a serious security problem on the system.

   tburns



   Running password consistency check using pwck program.
   This program prints the password entry and corresponding
   problem such as login directory not found or bad character
   in login name.

   mcohn:2c4hWtfYlRwks:148:101:Mike,Cohn,,:/home/mcohn:/usr/local/bin/tcsh
   Login directory not found

   sam_exec:*:0:1::/home/sam_exec:/usr/bin/sh
   1 Bad character(s) in logname

   opc_op:*:777:77:OpC default operator:/home/opc_op:/usr/bin/ksh
   1 Bad character(s) in logname



   Running group consistency check using grpck program.
   This program prints the group entry and corresponding
   problem such as invalid GID, login name not in password
   file, and groups in which there are no users.
```

```
tty::10:
Null login name

users::20:root,testhp,addadm,mflahert,tdolan,clloyd,eschwartz,jperwinc,denise
denise - Logname not found in password file

nogroup:*:-2:
Invalid GID
Null login name
```

Check for Disk Hogs

With the shell program in this section, you can regularly check the characteristics of each logical volume as well as the amount of disk space consumed by each user. The following script, called **aud-hogs.sh**, uses the **fstyp**, **diskusg**, and **vxdiskusg** programs to produce reports:

```
#!/usr/bin/ksh
# 1st print stats concerning the disk's file systems
echo "This program produces logical volume statistics and the amount of disk"
echo "space consumed by users on each logical volume. \n"
for fs in `bdf| grep '^/' | awk '{print $1}'`
do
fsys=`fstyp $fs`
echo "\n $printing logical volume stats for $fs using fstyp -v \n"
fstyp -v $fs 2>&1
if [ $fsys = vxfs ]
then
echo "\n finding space consumed per user for logical volume "
echo " $fs with vxdiskusg $fs \n"
/usr/sbin/acct/vxdiskusg $fs 2>&1 | tee -a $DESTF
else
# assume hfs type
echo "\n finding space consumed per user for logical volume "
echo " $fs with diskusg $fs \n"
echo "\nUserID login number of blocks "
echo "------ ------------------- \n"
        /usr/sbin/acct/diskusg $fs 2>&1
fi
done
```

I redirected the output of this script to **audhogs.out**. This file contains a summary of each logical volume and the amount of disk space on each logical volume consumed by each user. Only the first few logical volumes are shown.

```
This program produces logical volume statistics and the amount of disk
space consumed by users on each logical volume.

   logical volume stats for /dev/vg00/lvol3 using fstyp -v

hfs
f_bsize: 8192
f_frsize: 1024
f_blocks: 99669
f_bfree: 66562
f_bavail: 56595
f_files: 16128
f_ffree: 12525
f_favail: 12525
f_fsid: 1073741827
f_basetype: hfs
f_namemax: 255
f_magic: 95014
f_featurebits: 1
f_flag: 0
f_fsindex: 0
f_size: 102400

  finding space consumed per user for logical volume
  /dev/vg00/lvol3 with diskusg /dev/vg00/lvol3


UserID login number of blocks
------ ----- --------------

0       root      35014
1001    softcm    2
2       bin       30782
5       uucp      2
9       lp        410
100     adduser   4


   logical volume stats for /dev/vg00/lvol1 using fstyp -v

hfs
f_bsize: 8192
f_frsize: 1024
f_blocks: 47829
f_bfree: 17936
f_bavail: 13153
f_files: 7680
f_ffree: 7654
f_favail: 7654
f_fsid: 1073741825
f_basetype: hfs
f_namemax: 255
f_magic: 95014
f_featurebits: 1
f_flag: 0
f_fsindex: 0
f_size: 49152

  finding space consumed per user for logical volume
  /dev/vg00/lvol1 with diskusg /dev/vg00/lvol1
```

```
UserID login number of blocks
------ ----- --------------

0      root    59784
2      bin     2


   logical volume stats for /dev/vg00/lvol7 using fstyp -v

hfs
f_bsize: 8192
f_frsize: 1024
f_blocks: 723288
f_bfree: 431130
f_bavail: 358801
f_files: 351168
f_ffree: 340324
f_favail: 340324
f_fsid: 1073741831
f_basetype: hfs
f_namemax: 255
f_magic: 95014
f_featurebits: 1
f_flag: 0
f_fsindex: 0
f_size: 770048


 finding space consumed per user for logical volume
 /dev/vg00/lvol7 with diskusg /dev/vg00/lvol7


UserID login number of blocks
------ ----- --------------

0      root     318706
1      daemon   344
1001   softcm   4696
2      bin      197450
4      adm      1754
5      uucp     38
9      lp       328
100    adduser  2
102    user1    164
103    user2    6
104    user3    2
105    user4    68
107    user5    84
109    user6    288
113    user7    192
115    user8    416
116    user9    112
119    user10   110
```

.
.
.

Ignite-UX Check

Ignite-UX is a product bundled with HP-UX that provides a process to create a bootable system recovery tape. Chapter 9 is devoted to Ignite-UX, and the shell programming chapter includes some example shell programs using Ignite-UX commands. In this section, I will first see if Ignite-UX is loaded on the system. If indeed Ignite-UX is loaded on the system, I'll check to see whether the **make_recovery** command has been run, which produces a bootable system recovery tape. The final check determines whether **make_recovery** was run with the *-C* option. This option produces a snapshot of the system and allows us to run **check_recovery** to see whether any important system files have been modified.

man page

make_
recovery
9

man page

check_
recovery
9

```
#!/bin/sh
{

echo "PROG>>>>> determining if Ignite-UX loaded on system."


igtest=`swlist  | grep Ignite`
echo $igtest
if [ -n "$igtest" ]; then
echo "Ignite-UX installed"
else
echo "Ignite-UX is not installed"
fi

echo "PROG>>>>> determining if make_recovery has been run by
                checking for /var/opt/ignite/arch.include."

if [ -f /var/opt/ignite/recovery/arch.include ]; then
echo "make_recovery has been run."
else
echo "make_recovery has not been run."
fi

echo "PROG>>>>> determining if make_recovery was run with the
                -C (for check_recovery) option."

if [ -f /var/opt/ignite/recovery/makrec.last ]; then
echo "make_recovery with -C has been run. We'll now
                run check_recovery."
/opt/ignite/bin/check_recovery 2>&1
else
echo "make_recovery with -C has not been run. We can't
                run check_recovery."
fi

} | tee -a /tmp/IMPORTANT/igtest.out
```

man page

**check_
recovery
9**

The following output of the script shows that **make_recovery** is loaded and was run with the *-C* option. **check_recovery** was then run, showing that three important system files have changed.

```
PROG>>>>> determining if Ignite-UX loaded on system.
B5725AA B.1.48 HP-UX Installation Utilities (Ignite-UX) Ignite-UX-11-00 B.1.48
        HP-UX Installation Utilities for Installing 11.00 Systems
Ignite-UX installed
PROG>>>>> determining if make_recovery has been run by
               checking for /var/opt/ignite/arch.include.
make_recovery has been run.
PROG>>>>> determining if make_recovery was run with the
               -C (for check_recovery) option.
make_recovery with -C has been run. We'll now
               run check_recovery.

Since the last System Recovery Image was created, the following system
files (or links) have been added to the current system.

   /.rhosts
   /etc/hosts.equiv
   /usr/share/man/cat1.Z/lifcp.1
```

Running the commands to produce a recovery tape ensure that you can recover your root volume to a similar system. I encourage you to review the portion of Chapter 9 that describes producing a recovery tape.

CHAPTER 15

UNIX File System Introduction - File System Layout, file and ls Commands

The Basis of UNIX

Most everything in UNIX comes down to files and directories. If you understand the hierarchical UNIX file system layout and how to manipulate files and directories, then you're a long way toward UNIX understanding.

A lot goes into working with UNIX files and directories. This chapter covers the basics and background of files and directories in UNIX, including:

- The **file** command
- The **ls** command
- The file system layout

There are references to a number of UNIX operating systems in this chapter including Linux because the commands covered apply to most all UNIX variants.

man page

file - 15

The next chapter covers commands related to files and directories. The only commands covered in this chapter are the **file** and **ls** commands. **file** is used to determine the type of file and **ls** is used to list files and directories.

File Types

A file is a means by which information is stored on a UNIX system. The commands you issue, the applications you use, the data you store, and the devices you access such as printers and keyboard are all contained in files. One aspect of UNIX that makes it both simple and complex; simple because you know everything out there is a file, complex because the contents of a file could be anything ranging from ASCII text files to executable programs.

Every file on the system has a filename. The operating system takes care of all file-system-related tasks; you just need to know the name of the file and how to use it. Many types of files are on UNIX systems. Some file types are peculiar to the UNIX variant you are using. Device files, for instance, contain information about the specific hardware platform on which you are running your UNIX variant. In general, however, most file types are similar going from system to system. The file types we will look at are:

- Text Files

- Data Files

- Source Code Files

- Executable Files

- Shell Programs

- Links

- Device Files

Many times when dealing with various types of files there are extensions associated with those files. Many applications, for instance, associate a specific extension with that application. Text files, for instance, sometimes have a **.txt** extension. Most C source code programs have a **.c** extension, and most C++ programs have a **.cc** extension. Although the extension can be useful for determining the type of a file, no written requirements state that a particular type of file must contain an assigned extension or that you must have any extension at all.

The following table shows some commonly used extensions for various types of files:

Extension	File Type
.1 to .n	Online manual source.
.a	An archive or library.
.c	C program source.
.cc	C++ program source.
.csh	C shell script.
.f	FORTRAN program source.
.ksh	Korn shell script.
.o	Object file of compiled source.
.ps	Postscript source.

Extension	File Type
.1 to .*n*	Online manual source.
.shar	Shell archive.
.sh	Bourne shell script.
.tar	**tar** archive.
.txt	ASCII text file.
.Z	Compressed file.

man page

file - 15

A useful technique for determining the file type is to use the **file** command. Most UNIX variants support the **file** command, although the outputs differ somewhat, so I suggest that you use the **file** command to determine file type. The best way to learn about file types and the **file** command is through example, which we'll do later in this chapter after discussing some common file types in more detail.

Text Files

What could be simpler than a file that contains characters, just like the ones you're now reading in this chapter? These ASCII characters are letters and numerals that represent the work you perform. If, for instance, you use a UNIX editor to create an electronic mail message or a letter, you are creating a text file in most cases. Here is an example of part of an ASCII text file from a Linux system:

```
Thu Nov  5 07:29:53 1999 debug: FTS: appending '/dev/hda1'
Thu Nov  5 07:29:53 1999 debug: FTS: appending '/tmp/LST/swap.sel'
Thu Nov  5 07:29:53 1999 debug: Building partition-list with argument <Linux>
Thu Nov  5 07:29:53 1999 debug: Respecting exclude file /tmp/LST/targets.sel:
/dev/hdd
/dev/hda1
/dev/hda2
Thu Nov  5 07:29:53 1999 debug: No ADDITIONAL partitions available
Thu Nov  5 07:29:59 1999 debug: added '8390' to '/root/tmp/modules.handled'
Thu Nov  5 07:29:59 1999 debug: added '8390' to '/root/etc/modules/2.0.29/#1 Tue
Feb 11 20:36:48 MET 1997.default'
Thu Nov  5 07:29:59 1999 debug: added 'scsi_mod' to '/root/tmp/modules.handled'
Thu Nov  5 07:29:59 1999 debug: added 'scsi_mod' to '/root/etc/modules/2.0.29/#1
Tue Feb 11 20:36:48 MET 1997.default'
Thu Nov  5 07:29:59 1999 debug: added 'sd_mod' to '/root/tmp/modules.handled'
Thu Nov  5 07:29:59 1999 debug: added 'sd_mod' to '/root/etc/modules/2.0.29/#1 Tue
Feb 11 20:36:48 MET 1997.default'
Thu Nov  5 07:29:59 1999 debug: added 'sr_mod' to '/root/tmp/modules.handled'
Thu Nov  5 07:29:59 1999 debug: added 'sr_mod' to '/root/etc/modules/2.0.29/#1 Tue
Feb 11 20:36:48 MET 1997.default'
Thu Nov  5 07:29:59 1999 debug: added 'st' to '/root/tmp/modules.handled'
Thu Nov  5 07:29:59 1999 debug: added 'st' to '/root/etc/modules/2.0.29/#1 Tue Feb
11 20:36:48 MET 1997.default'
Thu Nov  5 07:29:59 1999 debug: added 'sg' to '/root/tmp/modules.handled'
Thu Nov  5 07:29:59 1999 debug: added 'sg' to '/root/etc/modules/2.0.29/#1 Tue Feb
11 20:36:48 MET 1997.default'
Thu Nov  5 07:29:59 1999 debug: added 'nfs' to '/root/tmp/modules.handled'
Thu Nov  5 07:29:59 1999 debug: added 'nfs' to '/root/etc/modules/2.0.29/#1 Tue
Feb 11 20:36:48 MET 1997.default'
Thu Nov  5 07:29:59 1999 debug: added 'isofs' to '/root/tmp/modules.handled'
Thu Nov  5 07:29:59 1999 debug: added 'isofs' to '/root/etc/modules/2.0.29/#1 Tue
Feb 11 20:36:48 MET 1997.default'
Thu Nov  5 07:29:59 1999 debug: 'isofs' is already handled
Thu Nov  5 07:29:59 1999 debug: 'nfs' is already handled
Thu Nov  5 07:29:59 1999 debug: 'sg' is already handled
Thu Nov  5 07:29:59 1999 debug: 'st' is already handled
```

Data Files

A file that contains data used by one of your applications is a data file. If you use a sophisticated desktop publishing tool such as FrameMaker® to write a book, you create data files that FrameMaker uses. These data files contain data, which you can usually read, and formatting information, which you can sometimes read but is usually hidden from you. If your UNIX installation uses a database program, then you may have data files that you can partially read.

Source Code File

A source code file is a text file that contains information related to a programming language such as C, C++, Pascal, FORTRAN, and so on. These files are readable - at least to the programmer who wrote it. When a programmer develops a source code file, they create a file that conforms to the naming convention of the program language being used, such as adding a ".c" to the end of the file if creating a C program.

The following is an example of a C source code file:

```
/* this is K & R sort program */

# include <stdio.h>
# include <stdlib.h>

        int N;
        int v[1000000];         /* v is array to be sorted */
        int left = 0;           /* left pointer */
        int right;
        int swapcount, comparecount = 0;
                                /* count swaps and compares*/
         int i, j, t;
        char print;
        char pr_incr_sorts;
main()


{
   printf("Enter number of numbers to sort : ");
   scanf("%10d", &N);                   /* 10d used for a BIG input */
   printf ("\n");                         /* select type of input to sort */

   printf("Enter rand(1), in-order(2), or reverse order (3)    sort : ");
   scanf("%2d", &type);
   printf ("\n");                       /* select type of input to sort */

   if (type == 3)
             for (i=0; i<N; ++i)        /* random         */
               v[i] = (N - i);

   else if (type == 2)
             for (i=0; i<N; ++i)
               v[i]= (i + 1);           /* in order       */

   else if (type == 1)
             for (i=0; i<N; ++i)
               v[i]=rand();             /* reverse order */
   fflush(stdin);
   printf("Do you want to see the numbers before sorting (y or n)? : ");
   scanf("%c", &print);
   printf ("\n");                       /* View unsorted numbers?   */
   if (print == 'y')
      {
           printf ("\n");
        for (i=0; i<N; ++i)
           printf("a[%2d]= %2d\n", i, v[i]);
           printf ("\n");
      }
```

```
        fflush(stdin);
      printf("Do you want to see the array at each step as it sorts? (y or n)? : ");
       scanf("%c", &pr_incr_sorts);
       printf ("\n");                        /* View incremental sorts?  */


        right = N-1;                       /* right pointer           */

                    qsort(v, left, right);




        {

          fflush(stdin);
          printf ("Here is the sorted list of %2d items\n", N);
             printf ("\n");
          for (i=0; i<N; ++i)
             printf ("%2d\n ", v[i]);
             printf ("\n");
             printf ("\n");                      /* print sorted list       */
             }
                   printf ("number of swaps = %2d\n ", swapcount);
                   printf ("number of compares = %2d\n ", comparecount);
        }

/* qsort function */

            void qsort( v, left, right)
                     int v[], left, right;
      {
                int i, last;
                if (left > right)
                 return;

                swap(v, left, (left + right)/2);
                last = left;
                for (i=left+1; i <= right; i++)
                {
                    comparecount = ++comparecount;
                      if (v[i] < v[left])
                   swap(v, ++last, i);
                }
                swap(v, left, last);
                qsort(v, left, last-1);
                qsort(v, last+1, right);
                }

                /* swap function  */


                swap(v, i, j)
                   int v[], i, j;

                  {int temp;
                      swapcount = swapcount++;
                      temp = v[i];
                      v[i] = v[j];
                      v[j] = temp;


    if (pr_incr_sorts == 'y')
      {
                   printf("Incremental sort of array = ");
          printf ("\n");
          for (i=0; i<N; ++i)
             printf("a[%2d]= %2d\n", i, v[i]);
             printf ("\n");
      }
}
```

Executable Files

Executable files are compiled or interpreted programs that can be run. You can't read executable files and you'll typically get a bunch of errors, unreadable characters, and beeps from your UNIX system when you try to look at one of these. You may also lose your screen settings and cause other problems.

You don't have to go far in UNIX to find executable files, they are everywhere. Many of the UNIX commands you issue are executable files that you can't read. In addition, if you are developing programs on your system, you are creating your own executables.

Here is an example of what you see if you attempt to send an executable to the screen:

```
unknown/etc/ttytyperunknown<@=>|<@=>|:unknown<@=>
callocLINESCOLUMNSunknownPackaged for
argbad aftger%3
parmnumber missing <@=>|<@=>|:
@ @ 3### @@@A:2TTO|>@#<|2X00R
EraseKillOOPS<@=>|<@=>|:
<@=>|<@=>|:
<@=>|<@=>|:<@=>|ATOO<@=>|:<@=>|<@=>|:<@=>|<@=>|:<@=>|<@=
>|:
```

Shell Programs

A shell program is both a file you can run to perform a task and a file that you can read. So yes, even though you can run this file because it is executable, you can also read it. I'm going to describe shell programming in more detail in an upcoming chapter.

I consider shell programming to be an important skill for every user to have. I'll spend some time going over the basics of shell programming. Some of the background I'm about to cover relating to file

types and permissions is important when it comes to shell programming, so this is important information for you to understand.

Here is an example of part of a shell program that performs an
audit of a system:

```
#!/bin/sh
{

echo "PROG>>>>> determining if Ignite-UX loaded on sys-
tem."


igtest=`swlist  | grep Ignite`
echo $igtest
if [ -n "$igtest" ]; then
echo "Ignite-UX installed"
else
echo "Ignite-UX is not installed"
fi

echo "PROG>>>>> determining if make_recovery has been run
by
           checking for /var/opt/ignite/arch.include."

if [ -f /var/opt/ignite/recovery/arch.include ]; then
echo "make_recovery has been run."
else
echo "make_recovery has not been run."
fi

echo "PROG>>>>> determining if make_recovery was run with
the
           -C (for check_recovery) option."

if [ -f /var/opt/ignite/recovery/makrec.last ]; then
echo "make_recovery with -C has been run. We'll now
           run check_recovery."
/opt/ignite/bin/check_recovery 2>&1
else
echo "make_recovery with -C has not been run. We can't
           run check_recovery."
fi

}  | tee -a /tmp/IMPORTANT/igtest.out
```

The shell program is text you can read and modify if indeed you have permission to do so. In addition to programming information, shell programs contain comments indicated by lines beginning with a #.

Links

A link is a pointer to a file stored elsewhere on the system. Instead of having two or more copies of a file on your system, you can link to a file that already exists on your system.

One particularly useful way links have been used in UNIX is related to new releases of the operating system. The locations of files sometimes change going from one release to another, and rather than learn all the new locations, links are produced from the old location to the new one. When you run a command using the old location, the link points to the new location.

Links are also useful for centralizing files. If a set of identical files has to be updated often, it is easier to link to a central file and update it, rather than having to update several copies of the file in several different locations.

Device Files

Device files, sometimes called device special files, contain information about the hardware connected to your system. Because device special files are associated with system administration functions they are usually not covered much in user, as opposed to system administration, material. I think the situation should be otherwise. It is very frustrating for a user to want to write a file to a floppy disk or a tape and not have any idea how to access a device file. I'll cover some use of device files so you are not completely in the dark in this area.

Devices on your system can often be accessed with different device files. A disk, for instance, can be accessed with either a block device file or a character device file. Most of this access is the responsibility of your system administrator; however, when you attempt to determine the file type, you may encounter special files of different types such as character and block.

Other types of files are on your system as well, but for the purposes of getting started with UNIX, the file types I will describe supply sufficient background to get you started.

The file Command

The **file** command is used to determine the file type. This command is useful because the name of a file does not always indicate its file type. The following examples perform a long listing of a file to provide some background information on the file, and then the **file** command is run to show the file type. I don't cover the command used to list files until the next chapter, but I include it in these examples. The **ls** command provides a listing of files. **ls** is covered in detail in the next chapter. We need to use it in this chapter in only its basic form. I have included the man page for **ls** at the end of this chapter if you need to view it. Combined with the "-l" option, you can produce a long listing that provides a lot of information about files. Using **ls -l** in the following examples, you will see the name of each file, file type, permissions, number of hard links, owner name, group name, size in bytes, and time stamp. You may not know what much of this information is for now; however, some of this information may be useful when viewing the output of the **file** command. Examples in this chapter for the **file** command show that different UNIX variants may produce somewhat different outputs of the **file** command. The following examples show an HP-UX output for the "UNIX example" and then a Linux output where available.

man page

file - 15

Text File (UNIX example)

(Described by the **file** command as *ascii text*.)

```
# ls -l .mosaic-global-history
-rw-r--r--   1 201      users        587 Dec 22  1999 .mosaic-
global-history
# file  .mosaic-global-history
.mosaic-global-history: ascii text
#
```

Text File (Linux example)

(Described by the **file** command as *ASCII text*.)

```
# ls -l *
-rw-r--r--   1 root     root      251367 Nov  5 07:11 debug
-rw-r--r--   1 root     root        2020 Nov  5 07:11 history
# file *
debug:      ASCII text
history:    ASCII text
```

Data File (UNIX example)

(Described by the **file** command as *data*.)

```
# ls -l Static.dat
-rw-r--r--   1 201      users     235874 Aug 26  1999 Static.dat
# file Static.dat
Static.dat:     data
#
```

Source Code File (UNIX example)

(Described by the **file** command as *c program text*.)

```
# ls -l krsort.c
-rwxrwxrwx   1 201      users       3234 Nov 16  1999 krsort.c
# file krsort.c
krsort.c:       c program text
#
```

Source Code File (Linux example)

(Described by the **file** command as *C program text*.)

man page

file - 15

man page

ls - 15

```
# ls -l *.c
-rw-r--r--   1 root      root        4521 Jul 12  1999 intl-bindtextdom.c
-rw-r--r--   1 root      root        6234 Jul 12  1999 intl-cat-compat.c
-rw-r--r--   1 root      root       14128 Jul 12  1999 intl-dcgettext.c
-rw-r--r--   1 root      root        1750 Jul 12  1999 intl-dgettext.c
-rw-r--r--   1 root      root       12759 Jul 12  1999 intl-finddomain.c
-rw-r--r--   1 root      root        1907 Jul 12  1999 intl-gettext.c
-rw-r--r--   1 root      root        1646 Jul 12  1999 intl-intl-compat.c
-rw-r--r--   1 root      root        5361 Jul 12  1999 intl-loadmsgcat.c
-rw-r--r--   1 root      root        7271 Jul 12  1999 intl-localealias.c
-rw-r--r--   1 root      root        2914 Jul 12  1999 intl-textdomain.c
# file *.c
intl-bindtextdom.c: C program text
intl-cat-compat.c:  C program text
intl-dcgettext.c:   C program text
intl-dgettext.c:    C program text
intl-finddomain.c:  C program text
intl-gettext.c:     C program text
intl-intl-compat.c: C program text
intl-loadmsgcat.c:  C program text
intl-localealias.c: C program text
intl-textdomain.c:  C program text
#
```

Executable File (UNIX example)

(Described by the **file** command as *shared executable*.)

```
# ls -l krsort
-rwxr-xr-x   1 201        users        34592 Nov 16  1999 krsort
# file krsort
krsort:         PA-RISC1.1 shared executable dynamically linked
-not stripped
#
```

Executable File (LInux example)

(Described by the **file** command as *executable*.)

```
# ls -l a*
-rwxr-xr-x   1 root      root        3888 Jul 24  1999 activate
-rwxr-xr-x   1 root      root        4452 Feb 25  1999 adjtimex
# file a*
activate: ELF 32-bit LSB executable, Intel 80386, version 1,
stripped
```

```
adjtimex:  ELF 32-bit LSB executable,  Intel 80386,  version 1,
stripped
#
```

Shell Program (UNIX example)

(Described by the **file** command as *commands text*.)

```
# ls -l llsum
-rwxrwxrwx   1 root        sys          1267 Feb 23  1999 llsum
# file llsum
llsum:            commands text
#
```

Shell Program (Linux example)

(Described by the **file** command as *Bourne shell script text*.)

```
# ls -l request-route
-rwx------   1 root       root         1046 Sep 19  1999 request-route
# file request-route
request-route: Bourne shell script text
#
```

Link (UNIX example)

(The link is not referenced by the **file** command; this is shown as a *shared executable dynamically linked*. The reference to *dynamically linked* does not mean that this is a link.)

```
# ls -l /usr/bin/ar
lr-xr-xr-t   1 root       sys          15 Mar 23  1999 ar -> /
usr/ccs/bin/ar
# file /usr/bin/ar
/usr/bin/ar:            s800 shared executable dynamically linked
#
```

Link (Linux example)

(The link shown is a *symbolic link*.)

```
# ls -l reboot
lrwxrwxrwx   1 root      root              4 Nov  5 01:31 reboot -> halt
# file * | grep link
depmod:               symbolic link to modprobe
ksyms:                symbolic link to insmod
pidof:                symbolic link to killall5
reboot:               symbolic link to halt
rmmod:                symbolic link to insmod
swapoff:              symbolic link to swapon
telinit:              symbolic link to init
udosctl:              symbolic link to /sbin/umssync
umssetup:             symbolic link to /sbin/umssync
#
```

man page

ls - 15

man page

file - 15

Block Device File (UNIX example)

(Described by the **file** command as *block special*.)

```
# ls -l /dev/dsk/c0t1d0
brw-r--r--   1 bin      sys       31 0x001000 Apr 17  1999 /dev/
dsk/c0t1d0
# file /dev/dsk/c0t1d0
/dev/dsk/c0t1d0:        block special (31/4096)
#
```

Block Device File (Linux example)

(Described by the **file** command as *block special*.)

```
# ls -l loop*
brw-rw----   1 root      disk      7,    0 Sep 23  1999 loop0
brw-rw----   1 root      disk      7,    1 Sep 23  1999 loop1
brw-rw----   1 root      disk      7,    2 Sep 23  1999 loop2
brw-rw----   1 root      disk      7,    3 Sep 23  1999 loop3
brw-rw----   1 root      disk      7,    4 Sep 23  1999 loop4
```

```
brw-rw----    1 root        disk         7,    5 Sep 23   1999 loop5
brw-rw----    1 root        disk         7,    6 Sep 23   1999 loop6
brw-rw----    1 root        disk         7,    7 Sep 23   1999 loop7
# file loop*
loop0: block special (7/0)
loop1: block special (7/1)
loop2: block special (7/2)
loop3: block special (7/3)
loop4: block special (7/4)
loop5: block special (7/5)
loop6: block special (7/6)
loop7: block special (7/7)
#
```

Character Device File (UNIX example)

(Described by the **file** command as *character special*.)

```
# ls -l /dev/rdsk/c0t1d0
crw-r-----    1 root        sys          188 0x001000 Mar 23   1999 /dev/
rdsk/c0t1d0
# file /dev/rdsk/c0t1d0
/dev/rdsk/c0t1d0:        character special (188/4096)
#
```

Character Device File (Linux example)

(Described by the **file** command as *character special*.)

```
# ls -l mi*
crw-rw-rw-    1 root        sys         14,    2 Sep 23   1999 midi00
crw-rw-rw-    1 root        sys         14,   18 Sep 23   1999 midi01
crw-rw-rw-    1 root        sys         14,   34 Sep 23   1999 midi02
crw-rw-rw-    1 root        sys         14,   50 Sep 23   1999 midi03
crw-rw-rw-    1 root        sys         14,    0 Sep 23   1999 mixer
crw-rw-rw-    1 root        sys         14,   16 Sep 23   1999 mixer1
# file mi*
midi00: character special (14/2)
midi01: character special (14/18)
midi02: character special (14/34)
midi03: character special (14/50)
mixer:  character special (14/0)
mixer1: character special (14/16)
#
```

The ls Command

The **ls** command brings with it a lot to discuss. I haven't yet described the options to **ls,** yet we have already used this command and the *-l* option as part of the **file** command discussion. You can't do much on a UNIX system without **ls** so I'll cover it now. The best way to cover the most important options to **ls** is to show examples. I do just that in the upcoming description of the **ls** command.

man page

ls - 15

ls

The following is an example of **ls** without any options other than the directory to list:

```
# ls /home/denise

27247b.exe
410pt1.exe
410pt2.exe
41ndir.exe
41nds1.exe
41nds4.exe
41nwad.exe
41rtr2.exe
HPDA1.EXE
Mail
N3212B6.EXE
SCSI4S.EXE
clean
clean2
clean3
content.exe
dsenh.exe
eg1
eg2
en0316bz.exe
en0316tb.exe
explore.exe
flexi_cd.exe
fred.h
hal.c
hpdl0117.exe
hpdlinst.txt
hpux.patches
j2577a.exe
ja95up.exe
```

```
msie10.exe
n32e12n.exe
nfs197.exe
pass.sb
plusdemo.exe
ps4x03.exe
psg
quik_res.exe
rclock.exe
rkhelp.exe
roni.mak
sb.txt
smsup2.exe
softinit.remotesoftcm
srvpr.exe
steve.h
target.exe
tcp41a.exe
tnds2.exe
upgrade.exe
whoon
win95app.exe
total 46718
```

man page

ls - 2

Which of these are files? Which are directories? Have all of the entries been listed? There are many options to **ls** that will answer these questions.

There is not a lot of information reported as a result of having issued this command. **ls** lists the contents of the directory specified, or the current working directory if no directory is specified.

ls -a

man page

ls - 15

To list all the entries of a directory, you would use the *-a* option. Files that begin with a "." are called hidden files and are not usually listed with **ls**. The following example shows the output of **ls -a**:

```
$ ls -a /home/denise

.Xauthority
.cshrc
```

```
.dt
.dtprofile
.elm
.exrc
.fmrc.orig
.glancerc
.gpmhp
.history
.login
.lrom
.mailrc
.netscape-bookmarks.html
.netscape-cache
.netscape-cookies
.netscape-history
.netscape-newsgroups-news.spry.com
.netscape-newsgroups-newsserv.hp.com
.netscape-preferences
.newsrc-news.spry.com
.newsrc-newsserv.hp.com
.profile
.rhosts
.sh_history
.softbuildrc
.softinit.orig
.sw
.xinitrc
.xsession
27247b.exe
410pt1.exe
410pt2.exe
41ndir.exe
41nds1.exe
41nds4.exe
41nwad.exe
41rtr2.exe
HPDA1.EXE
Mail
N3212B6.EXE
SCSI4S.EXE
clean
clean2
clean3
content.exe
dsenh.exe
eg1
eg2
en0316bz.exe
en0316tb.exe
explore.exe
flexi_cd.exe
fred.h
hal.c
hpdl0117.exe
hpdlinst.txt
hpux.patches
j2577a.exe
ja95up.exe
```

```
msie10.exe
n32e12n.exe
nfs197.exe
pass.sb
plusdemo.exe
ps4x03.exe
psg
quik_res.exe
rclock.exe
rkhelp.exe
roni.mak
sb.txt
smsup2.exe
softinit.remotesoftcm
srvpr.exe
steve.h
target.exe
tcp41a.exe
tnds2.exe
upgrade.exe
whoon
win95app.exe
total 46718
```

man page

ls - 15

Notice that this output includes hidden files, those that begin with a ".", as well as all other files listed with just **ls**. These did not appear when **ls** was issued without the *-a* option. All subsequent examples include the *-a* option.

ls -l

To list all information about the contents of directory, you use the *-l* option to **ls**, as shown in the following example (some of these file names were shortened to fit on the page):

```
$ ls -al /home/denise

-rw-------    1 denise    users          98 Oct  6 09:19 .Xauthority
-r--r--r--    1 denise    users         814 May 19 10:10 .cshrc
drwxr-xr-x    7 denise    users        1024 Sep 26 11:14 .dt
-rwxr-xr-x    1 denise    users        8705 Jul  7 12:04 .dtprofile
drwx------    2 denise    users        1024 Jul 31 18:48 .elm
-r--r--r--    1 denise    users         347 May 19 10:10 .exrc
-rwxrwxrwx    1 denise    users         170 Jun  6 14:20 .fmrc.orig
-rw-------    1 denise    users          97 Jun 12 18:59 .glancerc
-rw-------    1 denise    users       17620 Sep 21 16:11 .gpmhp
-rwxr-xr-x    1 denise    users         391 Sep 19 09:55 .history
-r--r--r--    1 denise    users         341 May 19 10:10 .login
drwx--x--x    2 denise    users        1024 Jul 31 18:48 .lrom
-rw-r--r--    1 denise    users         768 Jul 28 12:54 .mailrc
-rw-------    1 denise    users        1450 Oct  6 13:58 .netscape-bookmarks.html
drwx------    2 denise    users       10240 Oct 10 15:24 .netscape-cache
-rw-------    1 denise    users          91 Sep 18 14:16 .netscape-cookies
-rw-------    1 denise    users       43906 Oct 10 15:32 .netscape-history
```

```
-rw-r--r--    1 denise   users         566 Aug 25 14:36 .netscape--news.spry.com
-rw-------    1 denise   users       46514 Jun 28 12:35 .netscape-.hp.com
-rw-------    1 denise   users        1556 Sep 28 15:02 .netscape-preferences
-rw-------    1 denise   users         104 Jul 11 11:01 .newsrc-news.spry.com
-rw-r--r--    1 denise   users         223 Sep 26 13:26 .newsrc-newv.hp.com
-r--r--r--    1 denise   users         446 May 19 10:10 .profile
-rw-------    1 denise   users          21 Jul  6 13:21 .rhosts
-rw-------    1 denise   users        2328 Oct 10 15:22 .sh_history
-rw-r--r--    1 denise   users        1052 Sep 22 15:00 .softbuildrc
-rwxrwxrwx    1 denise   users         161 Jul 11 12:19 .softinit.orig
drwxr-xr-x    3 denise   users        1024 Aug 31 15:44 .sw
-rw-------    1 denise   users          23 Jun  2 15:01 .xinitrc
-rwxr-xr-x    1 denise   users       11251 May 19 10:41 .xsession
-rw-r--r--    1 denise   users      611488 Oct  3 12:00 27247b.exe
-rw-r--r--    1 denise   users      114119 Sep 29 12:49 410pt1.exe
-rw-r--r--    1 denise   users      136979 Sep 29 12:53 410pt2.exe
-rw-r--r--    1 denise   users      173978 Sep 29 12:40 41ndir.exe
-rw-r--r--    1 denise   users      363315 Sep 29 12:52 41nds1.exe
-rw-r--r--    1 denise   users      527524 Sep 29 12:57 41nds4.exe
-rw-r--r--    1 denise   users     1552513 Sep 29 12:50 41nwad.exe
-rw-r--r--    1 denise   users      853424 Sep 29 12:24 41rtr2.exe
-rw-r--r--    1 denise   users     1363011 Sep 20 12:20 HPDA1.EXE
drwx------    2 denise   users          24 Jul 31 18:48 Mail
-rw-r--r--    1 denise   users     1787840 Aug 31 09:35 N3212B6.EXE
-rw-r--r--    1 denise   users       13543 Sep 23 09:46 SCSI4S.EXE
-rw-r--r--    1 denise   users       28395 Aug 30 15:07 cabview.exe
-rwx--x--x    1 denise   users          66 Jun  8 17:40 clean
-rwx--x--x    1 denise   users          99 Jun 20 17:44 clean2
-rwx--x--x    1 denise   users          66 Jun 20 17:51 clean3
-rw-r--r--    1 denise   users       15365 Aug 30 15:07 content.exe
-rw-r--r--    1 denise   users      713313 Sep 29 12:56 dsenh.exe
-rwx------    1 denise   users         144 Aug 14 17:10 eg1
-rwx------    1 denise   users         192 Aug 15 12:13 eg2
-rw-r--r--    1 denise   users      667890 Sep 20 12:41 en0316bz.exe
-rw-r--r--    1 denise   users      641923 Sep 20 12:42 en0316tb.exe
-rw-r--r--    1 denise   users        6251 Aug 30 15:07 explore.exe
-rw-r--r--    1 denise   users       23542 Aug 30 15:08 flexi_cd.exe
-rw-r--r--    1 denise   users          30 Aug 14 17:02 fred.h
-rw-r--r--    1 denise   users           0 Aug 14 17:24 hal.c
-rw-r--r--    1 denise   users      895399 Sep 20 12:32 hpdl0117.exe
-rw-r--r--    1 denise   users       14135 Sep 20 12:39 hpdlinst.txt
-rw-------    1 denise   users        2943 Jun 19 14:42 hpux.patches
-rw-r--r--    1 denise   users      680279 Sep 20 12:26 j2577a.exe
-rw-r--r--    1 denise   users      930728 Sep 20 15:16 ja95up.exe
-rw-r--r--    1 denise   users       53575 Oct 10 10:37 mbox
-rw-r--r--    1 denise   users     1097728 Aug 30 15:03 msie10.exe
-rw-r--r--    1 denise   users     1790376 Sep 18 14:32 n32e12n.exe
-rw-r--r--    1 denise   users     1393835 Sep 29 12:59 nfs197.exe
-rw-------    1 denise   users         977 Jul  3 14:25 pass.sb
-rw-r--r--    1 denise   users     1004544 Aug 30 15:00 plusdemo.exe
-rw-r--r--    1 denise   users      229547 Sep 29 12:27 ps4x03.exe
-rwxr--r--    1 denise   users         171 Aug  9 13:43 psg
-rw-r--r--    1 denise   users       16645 Aug 30 15:08 quik_res.exe
-rw-r--r--    1 denise   users       14544 Aug 30 15:08 rclock.exe
-rw-r--r--    1 denise   users     2287498 Aug 30 15:12 rkhelp.exe
-rw-r--r--    1 denise   users           0 Aug 15 12:10 roni.mak
-rw-r--r--    1 denise   users        1139 Sep 28 10:35 sb.txt
-rw-r--r--    1 denise   users      569855 Sep 29 12:55 smsup2.exe
-rw-------    1 root     sys          161 Jul 11 12:18 softinit.remotesoftcm
-rw-r--r--    1 denise   users          39 Sep 29 12:48 srvpr.exe
-rw-r--r--    1 denise   users          38 Aug 15 12:14 steve.h
-rw-r--r--    1 denise   users       14675 Aug 30 15:08 target.exe
-rw-r--r--    1 denise   users      229630 Sep 29 12:54 tcp41a.exe
-rw-r--r--    1 denise   users     1954453 Sep 29 12:26 tnds2.exe
-rw-r--r--    1 denise   users      364270 Sep 23 09:50 upgrade.exe
-rwx-----x    1 denise   users          88 Aug  9 13:43 whoon
-rw-r--r--    1 denise   users      191495 Aug 30 15:00 win95app.exe
total 46718
```

man page

ls - 15

Because I find this to be the most commonly used option with the **ls** command, I describe each of the fields produced by **ls -l**. I'll use the earlier example of the **ls -l** command, which showed only one file when describing the fields:

```
$ ls -l sort
-rwxr-x--x   1 marty      users      120 Jul 26 10:20 sort
```

The first field defines the access rights of the file, which I covered in "Permissions" in an earlier chapter. The *owner* has read, write, and execute permissions on the file. The *group* has read and execute permissions on the file. *other* has execute permissions.

The second field is the link count. This lists how many files are symbolically linked to the file. We will get into the details of the **ln** command used to link files later. In this case, the link count is *1*, which means that this file is linked only to itself. For directories such as **.dt** shown below, the number of subdirectories is shown rather than the link count. This number includes one for the directory itself as well as one for the parent directory. This means that a total of five directories are below **.dt** .

```
drwxr-x--x   7 denise     users      1024 Jul 26 10:20 .dt
```

The subdirectories below **/home/denise/.dt** are:

> **/home/denise/.dt/Desktop**
> **/home/denise/.dt/appmanager**
> **/home/denise/.dt/palettes**
> **/home/denise/.dt/sessions**
> **/home/denise/.dt/types**

These five subdirectories plus the directory itself and the parent directory make a total of seven.

The third field lists the owner of the file. Your login name, such as *denise*, is listed here. When you create a file, your login name is listed by default as the owner of the file.

The fourth field lists the group to which the file belongs. Groups were covered earlier in "Permissions."

The fifth field shows the size of the file. The file **sort** is *120* bytes in size.

The sixth field (which includes a date and time such as *Jul 26 10:20*) lists the date and time the file was created or last changed.

The seventh field lists the files and directories in alphabetical order. You first see the files that begin with a ".", then the files that begin with numbers, then the files that begin with uppercase letters, and finally the files that begin with lower case letters. There are a lot of characters a file can begin with in UNIX, so if you perform an **ls -l** and don't see the file you are looking for, it may appear at a different spot in the listing from what you expected.

man page

ls - 15

ls -i

To get information about the inode of a file, you use the **-i** option to **ls**. The following example includes both the *-i* and *-l* options to **ls**:

```
$ls -ail /home/denise

137717 -rw-------   1 denise   users      98 Oct  6 09:19 .Xauthority
137623 -r--r--r--   1 denise   users     814 May 19 10:10 .cshrc
140820 drwxr-xr-x   7 denise   users    1024 Sep 26 11:14 .dt
137629 -rwxr-xr-x   1 denise   users    8705 Jul  7 12:04 .dtprofile
180815 drwx------   2 denise   users    1024 Jul 31 18:48 .elm
137624 -r--r--r--   1 denise   users     347 May 19 10:10 .exrc
137652 -rwxrwxrwx   1 denise   users     170 Jun  6 14:20 .fmrc.orig
137650 -rw-------   1 denise   users      97 Jun 12 18:59 .glancerc
137699 -rw-------   1 denise   users   17620 Sep 21 16:11 .gpmhp
137640 -rwxr-xr-x   1 denise   users     391 Sep 19 09:55 .history
137625 -r--r--r--   1 denise   users     341 May 19 10:10 .login
```

```
185607 drwx--x--x   2 denise   users      1024 Jul 31 18:48 .lrom
137642 -rw-r--r--    1 denise   users       768 Jul 28 12:54 .mailrc
137641 -rw-------    1 denise   users      1450 Oct  6 13:58 .netscaperks.html
179207 drwx------    2 denise   users     10240 Oct 10 15:24 .netscape-cache
137656 -rw-------    1 denise   users        91 Sep 18 14:16 .netscape-cookies
137635 -rw-------    1 denise   users     43906 Oct 10 15:32 .netscape-history
137645 -rw-r--r--    1 denise   users       566 Aug 25 14:36 .netscapes.spry.com
137646 -rw-------    1 denise   users     46514 Jun 28 12:35 .netsca
137634 -rw-------    1 denise   users      1556 Sep 28 15:02 .netscaperences
137637 -rw-------    1 denise   users       104 Jul 11 11:01 .newsrcws.spry.com
137633 -rw-r--r--    1 denise   users       223 Sep 26 13:26 .newsrc-hp.com
137626 -r--r--r--    1 denise   users       446 May 19 10:10 .profile
137649 -rw-------    1 denise   users        21 Jul  6 13:21 .rhosts
137694 -rw-------    1 denise   users      2328 Oct 10 15:22 .sh_history
137698 -rw-r--r--    1 denise   users      1052 Sep 22 15:00 .softbuildrc
137636 -rwxrwxrwx    1 denise   users       161 Jul 11 12:19 .softinit.orig
 33600 drwxr-xr-x   3 denise   users      1024 Aug 31 15:44 .sw
137648 -rw-------    1 denise   users        23 Jun  2 15:01 .xinitrc
137628 -rwxr-xr-x    1 denise   users     11251 May 19 10:41 .xsession
137715 -rw-r--r--    1 denise   users    611488 Oct  3 12:00 27247b.exe
137707 -rw-r--r--    1 denise   users    114119 Sep 29 12:49 410pt1.exe
137710 -rw-r--r--    1 denise   users    136979 Sep 29 12:53 410pt2.exe
137705 -rw-r--r--    1 denise   users    173978 Sep 29 12:40 41ndir.exe
137709 -rw-r--r--    1 denise   users    363315 Sep 29 12:52 41nds1.exe
137714 -rw-r--r--    1 denise   users    527524 Sep 29 12:57 41nds4.exe
137708 -rw-r--r--    1 denise   users   1552513 Sep 29 12:50 41nwad.exe
137696 -rw-r--r--    1 denise   users    853424 Sep 29 12:24 41rtr2.exe
137654 -rw-r--r--    1 denise   users   1363011 Sep 20 12:20 HPDA1.EXE
182429 drwx------    2 denise   users        24 Jul 31 18:48 Mail
137683 -rw-r--r--    1 denise   users   1787840 Aug 31 09:35 N3212B6.EXE
137702 -rw-r--r--    1 denise   users     13543 Sep 23 09:46 SCSI4S.EXE
137638 -rwx--x--x    1 denise   users        66 Jun  8 17:40 clean
137651 -rwx--x--x    1 denise   users        99 Jun 20 17:44 clean2
137632 -rwx--x--x    1 denise   users        66 Jun 20 17:51 clean3
137688 -rw-r--r--    1 denise   users     15365 Aug 30 15:07 content.exe
137713 -rw-r--r--    1 denise   users    713313 Sep 29 12:56 dsenh.exe
137667 -rwx------    1 denise   users       144 Aug 14 17:10 eg1
137671 -rwx------    1 denise   users       192 Aug 15 12:13 eg2
137662 -rw-r--r--    1 denise   users    667890 Sep 20 12:41 en0316bz.exe
137665 -rw-r--r--    1 denise   users    641923 Sep 20 12:42 en0316tb.exe
137689 -rw-r--r--    1 denise   users      6251 Aug 30 15:07 explore.exe
137690 -rw-r--r--    1 denise   users     23542 Aug 30 15:08 flexi_cd.exe
137670 -rw-r--r--    1 denise   users        30 Aug 14 17:02 fred.h
137673 -rw-r--r--    1 denise   users         0 Aug 14 17:24 hal.c
137660 -rw-r--r--    1 denise   users    895399 Sep 20 12:32 hpdl0117.exe
137661 -rw-r--r--    1 denise   users     14135 Sep 20 12:39 hpdlinst.txt
137647 -rw-------    1 denise   users      2943 Jun 19 14:42 hpux.patches
137659 -rw-r--r--    1 denise   users    680279 Sep 20 12:26 j2577a.exe
137697 -rw-r--r--    1 denise   users    930728 Sep 20 15:16 ja95up.exe
137684 -rw-r--r--    1 denise   users   1097728 Aug 30 15:03 msie10.exe
137658 -rw-r--r--    1 denise   users   1790376 Sep 18 14:32 n32e12n.exe
137643 -rw-r--r--    1 denise   users   1393835 Sep 29 12:59 nfs197.exe
137639 -rw-------    1 denise   users       977 Jul  3 14:25 pass.sb
137664 -rw-r--r--    1 denise   users   1004544 Aug 30 15:00 plusdemo.exe
137704 -rw-r--r--    1 denise   users    229547 Sep 29 12:27 ps4x03.exe
137666 -rwxr-xr-x    1 denise   users       171 Aug  9 13:43 psg
137691 -rw-r--r--    1 denise   users     16645 Aug 30 15:08 quik_res.exe
137692 -rw-r--r--    1 denise   users     14544 Aug 30 15:08 rclock.exe
137693 -rw-r--r--    1 denise   users   2287498 Aug 30 15:12 rkhelp.exe
137669 -rw-r--r--    1 denise   users         0 Aug 15 12:10 roni.mak
137657 -rw-r--r--    1 denise   users      1139 Sep 28 10:35 sb.txt
137712 -rw-r--r--    1 denise   users    569855 Sep 29 12:55 smsup2.exe
137644 -rw-------    1 root     sys        161 Jul 11 12:18 softinittesoftcm
137706 -rw-r--r--    1 denise   users        39 Sep 29 12:48 srvpr.exe
137682 -rw-r--r--    1 denise   users        38 Aug 15 12:14 steve.h
137685 -rw-r--r--    1 denise   users     14675 Aug 30 15:08 target.exe
137711 -rw-r--r--    1 denise   users    229630 Sep 29 12:54 tcp41a.exe
137700 -rw-r--r--    1 denise   users   1954453 Sep 29 12:26 tnds2.exe
137703 -rw-r--r--    1 denise   users    364270 Sep 23 09:50 upgrade.exe
137663 -rwx-----x    1 denise   users        88 Aug  9 13:43 whoon
137678 -rw-r--r--    1 denise   users    191495 Aug 30 15:00 win95app.exe
```

The inode number contains the following: the location of files and directories on the disk; access permissions; owner and group IDs; file link count; time of last modification; time of last access; device identification number for special files; and a variety of other information. inode numbers are used extensively by the system as you change directories and perform various tasks.

ls -p

Because you may have subdirectories within the directory you are listing, you may want to use the *-p* option to **ls,** which puts a "/" (slash) in after directory names, as shown in the following example:

man page

ls - 15

```
$ ls -ap /home/denise

.Xauthority
.cshrc
.dt/
.dtprofile
.elm/
.exrc
.fmrc.orig
.glancerc
.gpmhp
.history
.login
.lrom/
.mailrc
.netscape-bookmarks.html
.netscape-cache/
.netscape-cookies
.netscape-history
.netscape-newsgroups-news.spry.com
.netscape-newsgroups-newsserv.hp.com
.netscape-preferences
.newsrc-news.spry.com
.newsrc-newsserv.hp.com
.profile
.rhosts
.sh_history
.softbuildrc
.softinit.orig
.sw/
.xinitrc
.xsession
27247b.exe
410pt1.exe
410pt2.exe
41ndir.exe
41nds1.exe
41nds4.exe
41nwad.exe
41rtr2.exe
HPDA1.EXE
Mail/
N3212B6.EXE
SCSI4S.EXE
clean
clean2
```

```
clean3
content.exe
dsenh.exe
eg1
eg2
en0316bz.exe
en0316tb.exe
explore.exe
flexi_cd.exe
fred.h
hal.c
hpdl0117.exe
hpdlinst.txt
hpux.patches
j2577a.exe
ja95up.exe
msie10.exe
n32e12n.exe
nfs197.exe
pass.sb
plusdemo.exe
ps4x03.exe
psg
quik_res.exe
rclock.exe
rkhelp.exe
roni.mak
sb.txt
smsup2.exe
softinit.remotesoftcm
srvpr.exe
steve.h
target.exe
tcp41a.exe
tnds2.exe
upgrade.exe
whoon
win95app.exe
```

ls -R

man page

ls - 15

Because the subdirectories you are listing probably have files and sub-directories beneath them, you may want to recursively list these. The *-R* option to **ls** shown in the following example performs this recursive listing. This listing is truncated because it would be too long if it included all the subdirectories under **/home/denise**:

```
$ ls -aR /home/denise

.Xauthority
.cshrc
.dt
.dtprofile
.elm
.exrc
```

```
.fmrc.orig
.glancerc
.gpmhp
.history
.login
.lrom
.mailrc
.netscape-bookmarks.html
.netscape-cache
.netscape-cookies
.netscape-history
.netscape-newsgroups-news.spry.com
.netscape-newsgroups-newsserv.hp.com
.netscape-preferences
.newsrc-news.spry.com
.newsrc-newsserv.hp.com
.profile
.rhosts
.sh_history
.softbuildrc
.softinit.orig
.sw
.xinitrc
.xsession
27247b.exe
410pt1.exe
410pt2.exe
41ndir.exe
41nds1.exe
41nds4.exe
41nwad.exe
41rtr2.exe
HPDA1.EXE
Mail
N3212B6.EXE
SCSI4S.EXE
clean
clean2
clean3
content.exe
dsenh.exe
eg1
eg2
en0316bz.exe
en0316tb.exe
explore.exe
flexi_cd.exe
fred.h
```

.
.
.   **(skip some of the listing)**

```
/home/denise/.lrom:
LRAAAa27637.CC
LRBAAa27637.CC
LROM.AB
LROM.AB.OLD
LROM.AB.1k1
LROM.SET

/home/denise/.netscape-cache:
cache306C05510015292.gif
cache306C05560025292.gif
cache306C05560035292.gif

/home/denise/.sw:
sessions
```

.
.
.   **(skip remainder of the listing)**

ls Summary

man page

ls - 15

I have shown you what I believe to be the most important, and most often used, **ls** options. Because you may have future needs to list files and directories based on other criteria, I provide you with a list of most **ls** options. There is no substitute, however, for issuing the **man ls** command. Whatever I provide is only a summary. Viewing the man pages for **ls** gives you much more information. The following is a summary of the more commonly used **ls** options:

ls - List the contents of a directory

Options

-a	List all entries.
-b	Print non-graphic characters.
-c	Use the time the file was last modified for producing order in which files are listed.
-d	List only the directory name, not its contents.
-f	Assume that each argument is a directory.
-g	Only the group is printed and not the owner.
-i	Print the inode number in the first column of the report.
-m	List the contents across the screen, separated by commas.
-n	Numbers for UID and GID are printed instead of names.
-o	List the information in long form (-l), except that group is omitted.
-p	Put a slash (/) at the end of directory names.
-q	Non-printing characters are represented by a "?".
-r	Reverse the order in which files are printed.
-s	Show the size in blocks instead of bytes.
-t	List in order of time saved, with most recent first.
-u	Use the time of last access instead of last modification for determining order in which files are printed.

-x	List files in multi-column format as shown in examples.
-A	Same as -a, except that current and parent directories aren't listed (only used on some UNIX variants).
-C	Multicolumn output produced.
-F	Directory followed by a "/", executable by an "*", symbolic link by an "@", and FIFO by a "|".
-L	List file or directory to which link points.
-R	Recursively list subdirectories.
-1	Output will be listed in single-column format.

Also, some shorthand command names are available for issuing **ls** with options. For instance, **ll** is equivalent to **ls -l**, and **lsr** is equivalent to **ls -R** in some UNIX variants. We will also cover creating an "alias," whereby you can define your own shorthand for any command in an upcoming chapter.

You can selectively list and perform other file-related commands with wildcards. The following section covers filename expansion and wildcards.

File System Layout

Before I begin describing the file system layout, you need to know that you do not necessarily have a single file system. Your system administrator may have set up a variety of file system types on your system. As a beginning user, you don't care too much about the different types of file systems; however, before proceeding to the file system layout, let me briefly cover some of the different file system types. Your system administrator cares a lot about the different file system types because the commands he or she issues allow them to specify an option such as "-F" followed by the file system type. One good place to start when looking for the different file system types supported by your UNIX variant is the manual page for the **mount** command. The "-F" option, or another option such as "-t" for type in Linux, is usually following by a list of file system types supported. The different file system types and command options to file system types depend on the UNIX variant that you are using. Some commands that commonly support a file system type option are **dcopy**, **fsck**, **mksf**, **mount**, **newfs**, and others, some of which you may need to know as an advanced user if you are going to perform system administration in the future. The following is a description of some of the commonly supported file systems on UNIX variants:

man page

mount - 8

• Personal Computer File System (PCFS) is a file system type that allows direct access to PC formatted disks.

• UNIX File System (UFS) is the standard or basic default UNIX file system on some UNIX variants.

• CD-ROM File System (CDFS) is used when you mount a CD-ROM. Most CD-ROMs are read-only, so you can't write to them. This is called High Sierra File System (HSFS) on some UNIX variants.

• Network File System (NFS) is a way of accessing files on other systems on the network from your local system. An NFS mounted file system looks as though it is local to your system even though it is located on another system.

• Loopback File System (LOFS) allows you to have the same file system in multiple places using alternate path names.

• VxFS is an extent-based Journal File System that supports fast file system recovery and on-line features such as backup on HP-UX.

• High Performance File System (HFS) is HP's version of the UNIX File System. This is used in most of the examples.

• TMPFS is a memory-based file system.

• CacheFS is a file system present in cache.

File system types is an area of high customization on UNIX variants. You will find some of the file systems listed on some UNIX variants and others on other UNIX variants. Although UNIX and its associated commands are very similar, going from one UNIX variant to another, file system types are generally peculiar to a specific UNIX variant. A good place to start when determining what file system types are included with your UNIX variant is to view the file system types listed in the manual page for **mount**.

The manual page for **mount** on the Caldera Linux system we are using lists many file system types. With the Linux **mount** command, you would use the *-t vfstype* option to specify one of the file system types to mount:

man page

mount - 8

- minix

- ext

- ext2

- xiafs

- hpfs

- fat

- msdos

- umsdos

- vfat

- proc

- nfs

- iso9660

- smb

- ncp

- affs

- ufs

- sysv

- xenix

- coherent

One common file system I often mount on Linux systems is a DOS floppy disk. For example, we would go through the following sequence of events to mount a DOS floppy, copy a file to it, and unmount it:

```
# mount -t msdos /dev/fd0 /mnt/floppy
# cp * /mnt/floppy
# ls /mnt/floppy
file1      file2      file3      file4
# umount /dev/fd0
```

This sequence of commands first mounts **/dev/fd0**, which is the floppy disk device file, under the mount point **/mnt/floppy**. **/dev/fd0** is mounted as type *msdos,* as specified by the *-t msdos*. I next copy all files in the current directory to the floppy. All the files on the floppy are then listed with **ls,** producing the list of four files shown. I then unmount the floppy disk with the **umount** command so that I can take the floppy to a DOS system and read the files. Because the floppy was mounted as type *msdos,* the files were written to the floppy in DOS format.

Similarly, to mount a CD-ROM on a Linux system you would issue the following **mount** command, unless it's mounted at boot:

```
# mount /dev/hdd /cdrom
mount: block device /dev/hdd is write-protected, mounting read-
only
#
```

You would substitute your CD-ROM device file for **/dev/hdd**. This CD-ROM is, of course, a read-only device, as the message from **mount** indicates.

The file system layout of most UNIX variants is based on the AT&T SVR4 layout. This means that going from one UNIX variant to the next, you see pretty much the same names used in the file system layouts.

Figure 15-1 is a high-level depiction of the file system.

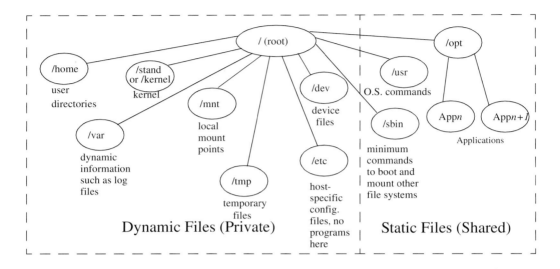

Figure 15-1   General UNIX File System Layout (differs somewhat among UNIX variants)

Here are some of the more important features of the UNIX file system layout:

• Files and directories are organized by category. The two most obvious categories that appear in Figure 15-1 are static vs. dynamic files. Also, other categories are executable, configuration, data files, and so on. The static files are also labeled "shared," because other hosts on the network may share these. The directories **/usr**, **/sbin**, and **/opt** are shared directories.

• The operating system (OS) and applications are kept separate from one another. Application vendors don't care where their applications are loaded; that is up to you. But to a system administrator, it is highly desirable to keep applications separate from the operating system so you don't inadvertently have application files overwriting operating system files. In addition, if applications are loaded in a separate area, they are "modular," meaning that a system administrator can add, remove, and modify them without affecting the operating system or other applications. Applications are kept in the **/opt** directory.

• Intra-system files are kept in a separate area from inter-system, or network-accessible files. **/usr** and **/sbin** are shared operating system directories. No host-specific information is in these two directories. **/etc** is used to hold the host-specific configuration files.

• Executable files are kept separate from system configuration files so that the executables may be shared among hosts. Having the configuration files separate from the programs that use them also means that updates to the operating system won't affect the configuration files.

I provide descriptions of some of the most important directories of the file system layout and their contents:

/   This is the root directory, which is the base of the file system's hierarchical tree structure. A directory is logically viewed as being part of /. Regardless of the disk on which a directory or logical volume is stored, it is

logically viewed as a part of the root hierarchy.

/dev   Contains host-specific device files.

/etc   Contains host-specific system and application configuration files. The information in
this directory is important to the operation of
the system and is of a permanent nature.
There are also additional configuration directories below **/etc**. There are two **/etc** subdirectories of particular interest:

/export Servers export root directories for networked
clients. For instance, a server might export
user directories such as **/export/home/***username*.

/home Users' home directories are located here.
Because the data stored in users' home directories will be modified often, you can expect
this directory to grow in size.

/kernel Contains kernel configuration and binary
files that are required to bring up a system
such as genunix.

/lost+found This is the lost files directory. Here you
find files that are in use but are not associated with a directory. These files typically

become "lost" as a result of a system crash that caused the link between the physical information on the disk and the logical directory to be severed. The program **fsck**, which is run at the time of boot, finds these files and places them in the **lost+found** directory.

man page

fsck - 8

/mnt This directory is reserved as a mount point for local file systems. You can either mount directly to **/mnt** or have **/mnt** subdirectories as mount points such as **/mnt1**, **/mnt2**, **/mnt3**, etc.

/net Name reserved as mount points for remote file systems.

/opt The directory under which applications are installed. As a rule, application vendors never specify a particular location for their applications to be installed. Now, with **/opt**, there is a standard directory under which applications should be installed. This is an organizational improvement for system administrators because they can now expect applications to be loaded under **/opt** and the application name.

/sbin Contains commands and scripts used to boot, shut down, and fix file system mounting problems. **/sbin** is available when a system boots, because it contains commands required to bring up a system.

/stand Contains kernel configuration and binary files that are required to bring up a system. Two significant files contained in this directory are the **system** and **vmunix** (kernel) files.

/tmp This is a free-for-all directory, where any user can *temporarily store* files. Because of the loose nature of this directory, it should not be used to store anything important, and users should know that whatever they have stored in **/tmp** can be deleted without notice. Application working files should go in **/var/tmp** or **/var/opt/appname**, not in **/tmp**.

/usr Most of the UNIX operating system is contained in **/usr**. Included in this directory are commands, libraries, and documentation. A limited number of subdirectories can appear in **/usr**.

/var Holds files that are primarily temporary. Files such as log files, which are frequently deleted and modified, are stored here. Think of this as a directory of "variable" size. Files that an application or command create at runtime should be placed in this directory, including logfile and spool files. However, some applications may store state information in **/var**.

Linux File System Layout

The Linux file system layout is very similar to the other UNIX variants described earlier, both in concept and in implementation. Files are contained in directories, and directories can have any number of subdirectories. Most operating systems are arranged this way, including UNIX.

The following is a long listing at the root level of a Caldera Linux system:

man page

ls - 15

```
# ls -l /
total 439
-rw-rw-rw-    1 root     root           23 Nov   5 07:10 .lgdb
dr-xr-xr-x    3 root     root         1024 Nov   5 07:10 amd
dr-xr-xr-x    2 root     root          512 Nov   5 07:10 auto
drwxr-xr-x    2 root     root         2048 Nov   5 07:12 bin
drwxr-xr-x    2 root     root         1024 Nov   5 01:44 boot
drwxr-xr-x    2 root     root        10240 Nov   6 22:27 dev
drwxr-xr-x   15 root     root         2048 Nov   7 00:15 etc
drwxr-xr-x    5 root     root         1024 Nov   5 01:43 home
drwxr-xr-x    2 root     root         1024 Nov   5 01:29 initrd
lrwxrwxrwx    1 root     root           11 Nov   5 01:29 install ->
                                                          /var/lib/LST
drwxr-xr-x    4 root     root         1024 Nov   5 01:44 lib
drwxr-xr-x    2 root     root        12288 Nov   5 01:29 lost+found
drwxr-xr-x    4 root     root         1024 Nov   5 01:44 mnt
drwxr-xr-x    4 root     root         1024 Sep  10  1996 opt
dr-xr-xr-x    5 root     root            0 Nov   5 01:59 proc
drwxr-xr-x    5 root     root         1024 Nov   6 20:56 root
drwxr-xr-x    2 root     root         2048 Nov   7 00:03 sbin
drwxrwxrwt    6 root     root         1024 Nov   7 00:10 tmp
drwxr-xr-x   21 root     root         1024 Nov   5 01:40 usr
drwxr-xr-x   14 root     root         1024 Nov   5 01:32 var
-rw-r--r--    1 root     root       404158 Nov   5 01:29 vmlinuz
```

Most of the directories are the same as those described earlier. A couple of directory names did not appear earlier that are significant, however. The Linux kernel, **vmlinuz**, appears at the root level. The directory **/root** is the home directory of the user *root*.

The **/proc** directory contains information about the Linux system. The **/proc** directory is really a set of data structure information that looks like a directory. The following is a long listing of the **/proc** directory:

man page

ls - 15

```
# ls -l /proc
total 0
dr-xr-xr-x    3 root      root             0 Nov   7 00:13 1
dr-xr-xr-x    3 root      root             0 Nov   7 00:16 1011
dr-xr-xr-x    3 root      root             0 Nov   7 00:13 104
dr-xr-xr-x    3 bin       root             0 Nov   7 00:13 106
dr-xr-xr-x    3 root      root             0 Nov   7 00:13 116
dr-xr-xr-x    3 root      root             0 Nov   7 00:13 118
dr-xr-xr-x    3 root      root             0 Nov   7 00:13 146
dr-xr-xr-x    3 root      root             0 Nov   7 00:13 155
dr-xr-xr-x    3 root      root             0 Nov   7 00:13 156
dr-xr-xr-x    3 daemon    root             0 Nov   7 00:13 162
dr-xr-xr-x    3 root      root             0 Nov   7 00:13 167
dr-xr-xr-x    3 root      root             0 Nov   7 00:13 170
dr-xr-xr-x    3 root      65535            0 Nov   7 00:13 178
dr-xr-xr-x    3 root      root             0 Nov   7 00:13 18
dr-xr-xr-x    3 root      root             0 Nov   7 00:13 19
dr-xr-xr-x    3 nobody    65535            0 Nov   7 00:13 193
dr-xr-xr-x    3 root      root             0 Nov   7 00:13 199
dr-xr-xr-x    3 root      root             0 Nov   7 00:13 2
dr-xr-xr-x    3 root      root             0 Nov   7 00:13 20
dr-xr-xr-x    3 root      root             0 Nov   7 00:13 200
dr-xr-xr-x    3 root      root             0 Nov   7 00:13 201
dr-xr-xr-x    3 root      root             0 Nov   7 00:13 202
dr-xr-xr-x    3 root      root             0 Nov   7 00:13 203
dr-xr-xr-x    3 root      root             0 Nov   7 00:13 204
dr-xr-xr-x    3 root      root             0 Nov   7 00:13 205
dr-xr-xr-x    3 root      root             0 Nov   7 00:13 21
dr-xr-xr-x    3 root      root             0 Nov   7 00:13 273
dr-xr-xr-x    3 root      root             0 Nov   7 00:13 274
dr-xr-xr-x    3 root      root             0 Nov   7 00:13 276
dr-xr-xr-x    3 root      root             0 Nov   7 00:13 3
dr-xr-xr-x    3 root      root             0 Nov   7 00:13 307
dr-xr-xr-x    3 root      root             0 Nov   7 00:13 327
dr-xr-xr-x    3 root      root             0 Nov   7 00:13 358
dr-xr-xr-x    3 root      root             0 Nov   7 00:13 375
dr-xr-xr-x    3 root      root             0 Nov   7 00:13 443
dr-xr-xr-x    3 root      root             0 Nov   7 00:13 444
dr-xr-xr-x    3 root      root             0 Nov   7 00:13 445
dr-xr-xr-x    3 root      root             0 Nov   7 00:13 45
dr-xr-xr-x    3 root      root             0 Nov   7 00:13 482
dr-xr-xr-x    3 root      root             0 Nov   7 00:13 483
dr-xr-xr-x    3 root      root             0 Nov   7 00:16 996
dr-xr-xr-x    3 root      root             0 Nov   7 00:16 997
dr-xr-xr-x    3 root      root             0 Nov   7 00:16 998
-r--r--r--    1 root      root             0 Nov   7 00:13 cmdline
-r--r--r--    1 root      root             0 Nov   7 00:13 cpuinfo
-r--r--r--    1 root      root             0 Nov   7 00:13 devices
-r--r--r--    1 root      root             0 Nov   7 00:13 dma
-r--r--r--    1 root      root             0 Nov   7 00:13 filesys
-r--r--r--    1 root      root             0 Nov   7 00:13 interrupt
-r--r--r--    1 root      root             0 Nov   7 00:13 ioports
-r--------    1 root      root      33558528 Nov   7 00:13 kcore
```

```
-r--------  1 root    root          0 Nov  5 07:00 kmsg
-r--r--r--  1 root    root          0 Nov  7 00:13 ksyms
-r--r--r--  1 root    root          0 Nov  7 00:05 loadavg
-r--r--r--  1 root    root          0 Nov  7 00:13 locks
-r--r--r--  1 root    root          0 Nov  7 00:13 mdstat
-r--r--r--  1 root    root          0 Nov  7 00:13 meminfo
-r--r--r--  1 root    root          0 Nov  7 00:13 modules
-r--r--r--  1 root    root          0 Nov  7 00:13 mounts
dr-xr-xr-x  2 root    root          0 Nov  7 00:13 net
-r--r--r--  1 root    root          0 Nov  7 00:13 pci
dr-xr-xr-x  2 root    root          0 Nov  7 00:13 scsi
lrwxrwxrwx  1 root    root         64 Nov  7 00:13 self->110
-r--r--r--  1 root    root          0 Nov  7 00:13 stat
dr-xr-xr-x  5 root    root          0 Nov  7 00:13 sys
-r--r--r--  1 root    root          0 Nov  7 00:13 uptime
-r--r--r--  1 root    root          0 Nov  7 00:13 version
```

The directories in the long listing, which have a *"d"* at the beginning of the line, are processes. The file **/proc/kcore** represents the physical memory of your Linux system. Files in **/proc** contain some interesting information about your system. One file you'll want to take a look at is the **/proc/cpuinfo** file. An example of this file is shown in the following listing:

man page

more - 17

```
# more /proc/cpuinfo
processor      : 0
cpu            : 686
model          : 3
vendor_id      : GenuineIntel
stepping       : 4
fdiv_bug       : no
hlt_bug        : no
fpu            : yes
fpu_exception  : yes
cpuid          : yes
wp             : yes
flags          : fpu vme de pse tsc msr pae mce cx8 11 mtrr pge
mca cmov mmx
bogomips       : 266.24
```

more is covered in the next chapter. For now, you just need to know that **more** is used for viewing files.

The **/boot** directory contains the Linux kernel and other files used by the LILO boot manager. The following is a listing of **/boot**:

man page

ls - 15

```
# ls -l /boot
total 452
-rw-r--r--    1 root      root        15954 Feb 11  1997 WHATSIN
-rw-r--r--    1 root      root        15954 Feb 11  1997
                                            WHATSIN-2.0.29-modular
-rw-r--r--    1 root      root          204 Jul 24  1996 any_b.b
-rw-r--r--    1 root      root          204 Jul 24  1996 any_d.b
-rw-r--r--    1 root      root          512 Nov  5 01:44 boot.0300
-rw-r--r--    1 root      root         4416 Jul 24  1996 boot.b
-rw-r--r--    1 root      root           88 Jul 24  1996 chain.b
-rw-------    1 root      root         7680 Nov  5 01:44 map
-r--r--r--    1 root      root         1565 Mar  7  1997 message
-rw-r--r--    1 root      root          192 Jul 24  1996 os2_d.b
-rw-r--r--    1 root      root       404158 Feb 11  1997 vmlinuz-
                                            2.0.29-modular
```

As a user, you are probably most concerned with your home directory, assigned to you by your system administrator, which is most likely in the **/home** directory. I think, however, that as a UNIX user you need to understand the overall UNIX file system layout. Keep in mind that you may find minor differences in the file system layout going from one UNIX variant to another, but in general the layout is similar.

If you're running a graphical user interface on your Linux system, you can view the file system graphically. Figure 15-2 shows the Red Hat Linux *File Manager* that is part of the *Gnome* user interface.

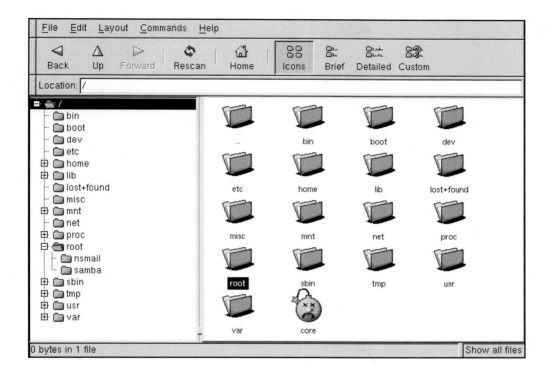

Figure 15-2 *File Manager* in *Gnome* Showing the Red Hat Linux File System

You can see that many of the directories shown on the left-hand side of Figure 15-2 are the same as those described earlier for UNIX systems in general. Although you may be working with any number of different UNIX variants, you'll find most of the system structures to be similar.

Manual Pages for Some Commands Used in Chapter 15

The following are the HP-UX manual pages for many of the commands used in this chapter. Commands often differ among UNIX variants, so you may find differences in the options or other areas for some commands; however, the following manual pages serve as an excellent reference.

file

file - Run test to classify file.

file(1)   file(1)

NAME
     file - determine file type

SYNOPSIS

     file [-m mfile] [-c] [-f ffile] file ...

DESCRIPTION
     file performs a series of tests on each file in an attempt to classify
     it. If file appears to be an ASCII file, file examines the first 512
     bytes and tries to guess its language. If file is an executable a.out
     file, file prints the version stamp, provided it is greater than 0
     (see the description of the -V option in ld(1)).

     file uses the file /etc/magic to identify files that have some sort of
     magic number, that is, any file containing a numeric or string
     constant that indicates its type. Commentary at the beginning of
     /etc/magic explains the format.

   Options
     file recognizes the following command-line options:

          -m mfile   use alternate magic file mfile.

          -c   Check the magic file for format errors. This
                         validation is not normally carried out for reasons
                         of efficiency. No file classification is done
                         when this option is specified.

          -f ffile   Obtain the list of files to be examined from file
                         ffile. file classifies each file whose name
                         appears in ffile.

EXTERNAL INFLUENCES
   Environment Variables
     LC_MESSAGES determines the language in which messages are displayed.

     If LC_MESSAGES is not specified in the environment or is set to the
     empty string, the value of LANG is used as a default for each
     unspecified or empty variable. If LANG is not specified or is set to
     the empty string, a default of "C" (see lang(5)) is used instead of
     LANG.

     If any internationalization variable contains an invalid setting, file
     behaves as if all internationalization variables are set to "C". See
     environ(5).

International Code Set Support
> Single- and multi-byte character code sets are supported. However,
> all non-ASCII text files are identified as "data".

SEE ALSO
> ld(1).

STANDARDS CONFORMANCE
> file: SVID2, SVID3, XPG2, XPG4

ls - List the contents of a directory.

ls(1)   ls(1)

NAME
     ls, l, ll, lsf, lsr, lsx - list contents of directories

SYNOPSIS

     ls [-abcdefgilmnopqrstuxACFLR1] [names]

     l [ls_options] [names]
     ll [ls_options] [names]
     lsf [ls_options] [names]
     lsr [ls_options] [names]
     lsx [ls_options] [names]

DESCRIPTION
     For each directory argument, the ls command lists the contents of the
     directory. For each file argument, ls repeats its name and any other
     information requested. The output is sorted in ascending collation
     order by default (see Environment Variables below). When no argument
     is given, the current directory is listed. When several arguments are
     given, the arguments are first sorted appropriately, but file
     arguments appear before directories and their contents.

     If you are a user with appropriate privileges, all files except . and
     .. are listed by default.

     There are three major listing formats. The format chosen depends on
     whether the output is going to a login device (determined by whether
     output device file is a tty device), and can also be controlled by
     option flags. The default format for a login device is to list the
     contents of directories in multicolumn format, with entries sorted
     vertically by column. (When individual file names (as opposed to
     directory names) appear in the argument list, those file names are
     always sorted across the page rather than down the page in columns
     because individual file names can be arbitrarily long.) If the
     standard output is not a login device, the default format is to list
     one entry per line. The -C and -x options enable multicolumn formats,
     and the -m option enables stream output format in which files are
     listed across the page, separated by commas. In order to determine
     output formats for the -C, -x, and -m options, ls uses an environment
     variable, COLUMNS, to determine the number of character positions
     available on each output line. If this variable is not set, the
     terminfo database is used to determine the number of columns, based on
     the environment variable TERM. If this information cannot be
     obtained, 80 columns is assumed.

     Options
     ls recognizes the following options:

          -a   List all entries; usually entries whose names begin with a
                period (.) are not listed.

-b   Force printing of nongraphic characters to be in the octal
\ddd notation.

-c   Use time of last modification of the inode (file created,
mode changed, etc.) for sorting (-t) or printing (-l
(ell)).

-d   If an argument is a directory, list only its name (not its
contents); often used with -l (ell) to get the status of a
directory.

-e   Print the extent attributes of the file. If any of the
files has a extent attribute, this option prints the extent
size, space reserved and allocation flags. This option
must be used with the -l (ell) option.

-f   Force each argument to be interpreted as a directory and
list the name found in each slot. This option disables -l
(ell), -t, -s, and -r, and enables -a; the order is the
order in which entries appear in the directory.

-g   Same as -l, (ell) except that only the group is printed
(owner is omitted). If both -l (ell) and -g are specified,
the owner is not printed.

-i   For each file, print the inode number in the first column
of the report. When used in multicolumn output, the number
precedes the file name in each column.

-l   (ell) List in long format, giving mode, number of links,
owner, group, size in bytes, and time of last modification
for each file (see further DESCRIPTION and Access Control
Lists below). If the time of last modification is greater
than six months ago, or any time in the future, the year is
substituted for the hour and minute of the modification
time. If the file is a special file, the size field
contains the major and minor device numbers rather than a
size.

-m   Stream output format.

-n   The same as -l, (ell) except that the owner's UID and
group's GID numbers are printed, rather than the associated
character strings.

-o   The same as -l, (ell) except that only the owner is printed
(group is omitted). (If both -l (ell) and -o are
specified, the group is not printed).

-p   Put a slash (/) after each file name if that file is a
directory.

-q   Force printing of nongraphic characters in file names as
the character (?).

-r   Reverse the order of sort to get reverse (descending)
collation or oldest first, as appropriate.

-s   Give size in blocks, including indirect blocks, for each
entry. The first entry printed is the total number of
blocks in the directory. When used in multicolumn output,
the number of blocks precedes the file name in each column.

-t   Sort by time modified (latest first) before sorting
alphabetically.

-u   Use time of last access instead of last modification for
       sorting (-t option) or printing (-l (ell) option).

-x   Multicolumn output with entries sorted across rather than
       down the page.

-A   The same as -a, except that the current directory "." and
       parent directory ".." are not listed. For a user with
       appropriate privileges, this flag defaults to ON, and is
       turned off by -A.

-C   Multicolumn output with entries sorted down the columns.

-F   Put a slash (/) after each file name if that file is a
       directory or a symbolic link to a directory; put an
       asterisk (*) after each file name if that file is
       executable; put an at sign (@) after each file name if that
       file is a symbolic link to a file; put a vertical bar (|)
       after each file name if that file is a FIFO.

-L   If the argument is a symbolic link, list the file or
       directory to which the link refers rather than the link
       itself.

-R   Recursively list subdirectories encountered.

-1   (one) The file names will be listed in single column format
       regardless of the output device. This forces single column
       format to the user's terminal.

Specifying more than one of the options in the following mutually
exclusive pairs is not considered an error: -C and -1 (ell), -m and -1
(ell), -x and -1 (ell), -C and -1 (one), -c and -u.

ls is normally known by several shorthand-version names for the
various formats:

    l   equivalent to ls -m.
    ll   equivalent to ls -1 (ell).
    lsf   equivalent to ls -F.
    lsr   equivalent to ls -R.
    lsx   equivalent to ls -x.

The shorthand notations are implemented as links to ls. Option
arguments to the shorthand versions behave exactly as if the long form
above had been used with the additional arguments.

Mode Bits Interpretation (-l option)
The mode printed in listings produced by the -l (ell) option consists
of 10 characters. The first character indicates the entry type:

    d   Directory
    b   Block special file
    c   Character special file
    l   Symbolic link
    p   Fifo (also called a "named pipe") special file
    n   Network special file
    s   socket
    -      Ordinary file.

The next 9 characters are interpreted as three sets of three bits each
which identify access permissions for owner, group, and others as
follows:

    +----------------- 0400   read by owner (r or -)

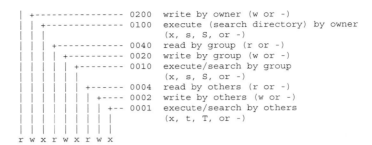

```
| +--------------- 0200  write by owner (w or -)
| | +-------------- 0100  execute (search directory) by owner
| | |                      (x, s, S, or -)
| | | +------------ 0040  read by group (r or -)
| | | | +---------- 0020  write by group (w or -)
| | | | | +-------- 0010  execute/search by group
| | | | | |                (x, s, S, or -)
| | | | | | +------ 0004  read by others (r or -)
| | | | | | | +---- 0002  write by others (w or -)
| | | | | | | | +-- 0001  execute/search by others
| | | | | | | | |          (x, t, T, or -)
| | | | | | | | |
r w x r w x r w x
```

Mode letters are interpreted as follows:

-      Permission not granted in corresponding position.

r   Read permission granted to corresponding user class.

w   Write permission granted to corresponding user class.

x   Execute (or search in directory) permission granted to corresponding user class.

s   Execute (search) permission granted to corresponding user class. In addition, SUID (Set User ID) permission granted for owner, or SGID (Set Group ID) permission granted for group, as indicated by position.

S   Same as s except that execute (search) permission is denied to corresponding user class.

t   (last position only) Execute (search) permission granted to others and "sticky bit" is set (see chmod(2) S_ISVTX description).

T   Same as t except execute (search directory) permission denied to others.

When an option is specified that results in a listing of directory and/or file sizes in bytes or blocks (such as the -s or -l (ell) option), a total count of blocks, including indirect blocks, is also printed at the beginning of the listing.

Access Control Lists (ACLs)
If a file has optional ACL entries, the -l (ell) option displays a plus sign (+) after the file's permissions. The permissions shown are a summary representation of the file's access control list, as returned by stat() in the st_mode field (see stat(2)). To list the contents of an access control list, use the lsacl command (see lsacl(1) and acl(5)).

EXTERNAL INFLUENCES
Environment Variables
If the COLUMNS variable is set, ls uses the width provided in determining positioning of columnar output.

LANG determines the locale to use for the locale categories when both LC_ALL and the corresponding environment variable (beginning with LC_) do not specify a locale. If LANG is not set or is set to the empty string, a default of "C" (see lang(5)) is used.

LC_COLLATE determines the order in which the output is sorted.

LC_CTYPE determines which characters are classified as nongraphic for

the -b and -q options, and the interpretation of single- and/or
multibyte characters within file names.

LC_TIME determines the date and time strings output by the -g, -l
(ell), -n, and -o options.

LC_MESSAGES determines the language in which messages (other than the
date and time strings) are displayed.

If any internationalization variable contains an invalid setting, ls
behaves as if all internationalization variables are set to "C" (see
environ(5)).

International Code Set Support
    Single- and multibyte character code sets are supported.

RETURN VALUE
    ls exits with one of the following values:

    0   All input files were listed successfully.

    >0   ls was aborted because errors occurred when accessing files.
         The following conditions cause an error:

         - Specified file not found.

         - User has no permission to read the directory.

         - Process could not get enough memory.

         - Invalid option specified.

EXAMPLES
    Print a long listing of all the files in the current working directory
    (including the file sizes). List the most recently modified
    (youngest) file first, followed by the next older file, and so forth,
    to the oldest. Files whose names begin with a . are also printed.

        ls -alst

WARNINGS
    Setting options based on whether the output is a login (tty) device is
    undesirable because ls -s is very different from ls -s | lp. On the
    other hand, not using this setting makes old shell scripts that used
    ls almost inevitably fail.

    Unprintable characters in file names may confuse the columnar output
    options.

DEPENDENCIES
    NFS The -l (ell) option does not display a plus sign (+) after the
         access permission bits of networked files to represent existence
         of optional access control list entries.

AUTHOR
    ls was developed by AT&T, the University of California, Berkeley and
    HP.

FILES
    /etc/passwd   to get user IDs for ls -l (ell) and ls -o.
    /etc/group   to get group IDs for ls -l (ell) and ls -g.

    /usr/share/lib/terminfo/?/*
                                to get terminal information.

SEE ALSO
    chmod(1), find(1), lsacl(1), stat(2), acl(5).

STANDARDS CONFORMANCE
    ls: SVID2, SVID3, XPG2, XPG3, XPG4, POSIX.2

CHAPTER 16

Working with Files and Directories - Permissions, Commands, File Name Expansion, and Wild Cards

Introduction

A variety of topics related to UNIX file system strucutre, navigation, and daily use are covered in this chapter, including:

- Permissions

- Absolute and relative path names

- File name expansion and wildcards

- Several commands including: **pwd**, **cd**, **chmod**, **cp**, **mv**, **mkdir**, **rm**, **rmdir**

- Examples of using many commands

Permissions

man page

ls - 15

The best place to begin discussing permissions is by issuing the **ls** command, which lists the contents of directories. Permissions are the means by which files and directories are made secure on your UNIX system. Because UNIX is multi-user, potentially thousands of users could be accessing the files on a system. Permissions controls who has access to what files.

Here is an example **ls -l** command and output:

```
$ ls -l sort
-rwxr-x--x   1 marty      users      120 Jul 26 10:20 sort
```

Issuing this command has produced a lot of information relating to a file called **sort**. Let's begin to understand what this listing has produced by analyzing the first set of characters (-rwxr-x--x). This set of characters is made up of four distinct fields, as shown in Figure 16-1.

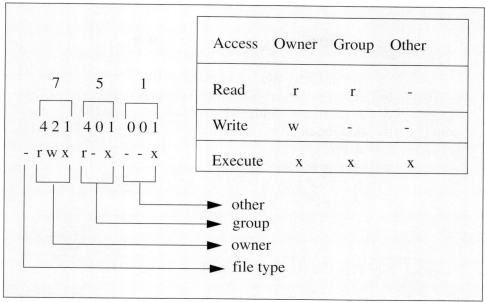

Figure 16-1 Permissions for File **sort**

The first character in this group is related to the file type. I covered some file types earlier, but the **ls -l** command does not analyze files to the same level of detail. Among the types of files **ls -l** will list are shown in Figure 16-2:

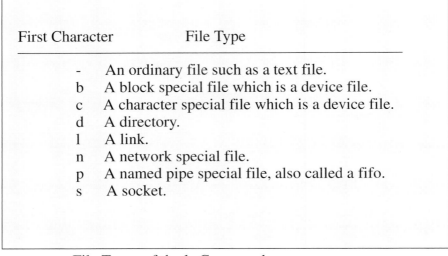

First Character	File Type
-	An ordinary file such as a text file.
b	A block special file which is a device file.
c	A character special file which is a device file.
d	A directory.
l	A link.
n	A network special file.
p	A named pipe special file, also called a fifo.
s	A socket.

Figure 16-2 File Types of the ls Command

Keep in mind the file types can vary slightly from one UNIX variant to another. The file types listed in Figure 16-2 are common to most UNIX variants. For every file on the system, UNIX supports three classes of access:

- User access (u). Access granted to the owner of the file.

- Group access (g). Access granted to members of the same group as the owner of the file.

- Other access (o). Access granted to everyone else.

man page

ls - 15

These access rights are defined by the position of read (r), write (w), and execute (x) when the long listing command is issued. For the long listing (**ls -l**) issued earlier, you see the permissions in Table 16-1.

TABLE 16-1   Long Listing Permissions for the File **sort**

Access	User Access	Group Access	Other
Read	r	r	-
Write	w	-	-
Execute	x	x	x

Permissions are not granted where a "-" (hyphen) appears. In addition, there are other permissions such as s, S, t, and T, which I don't cover at this time.

You can see that access rights are arranged in groups of three: three groups of permissions with three access levels each. The owner, in this case *marty*, has read, write, and execute permissions on the file. Anyone in the group *users* is permitted read and execute access to the file. *other* is permitted only execute access of the file.

The definitions of read, write, and execute differ somewhat for files and directories. Here is what you can do if you have read, write, and execute permissions for files:

read   You have permission to read the file.

write   You have permission to change and to write to the file.

execute   You can run, or execute, the program.

Here is what you can do if you have read, write, and execute permissions for directories:

read   You can list the contents of the directory.

write   You can create files in the directory, delete files in the directory, and create subdirectories in the directory.

execute   You can change to this directory using the **cd** command, which we'll cover shortly.

We will cover permissions again when the **chmod** command is described.

Absolute and Relative Path Names

We have already covered two topics that can serve as the basis for a discussion of absolute and relative path names: some important directories on the system and user login. If you take a look at the user *denise* and the way some of her files can be organized, we can get to the bottom of relative and absolute path names quickly.

The UNIX file system covered in Chapter 2 showed a hierarchy. In this hierarchy, there was the root (/) directory at the top, and files and directories were below root. The two means by which you can traverse this hierarchy to get to a "lower" point are with absolute path names and relative path names. Let's take a closer look at the files and directories that *denise* may have in her user area.

First of all we'll assume that *denise* has many files. This activity is one of the things users do - create files. In addition, your system administrator has provided several default files for purposes such as defining your user environment after login (we'll get into this in a lot more detail in upcoming chapters). *denise* probably has many files under her user area, and subdirectories as well. Her user area may look something like that shown in Figure 16-3:

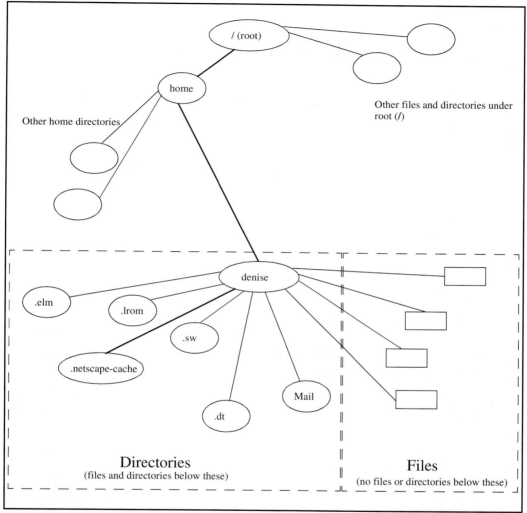

Figure 16-3 Home Directory for *denise*

Most users will have their home directory under **/home** (and who said UNIX doesn't make any sense?). If you want to get to a subdirectory of *denise* using an absolute path name, you traverse the hierarchy using the complete path. To get to the directory **.netscape-cache** under *denise*, you could view the absolute path as shown in Figure 16-4:

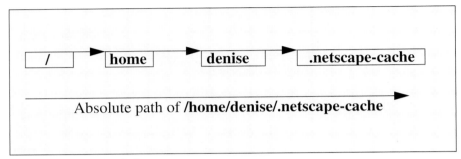

Figure 16-4   Absolute Path

You are progressing from root (**/**), to **home**, to **denise**, and finally to the directory **.netscape-cache**. The change directory (**cd**) command you issue looks like the following:

man page

cd - 16

```
$ cd /home/denise/.netscape-cache
```

This is an absolute path because it starts at root and progresses through the hierarchy. No matter what directory you are currently working in, even if it is **.netscape-cache**, you could use the absolute path name. In many cases, however, you may not need to issue an absolute path name. You may be so close to the file or directory you wish to access that the absolute path would be a waste of time for you. If, for instance, you are already in **/home/denise**, then you could change to **.netscape-cache** using a relative path name easily:

```
$ cd .netscape-cache
```

The relative path name is shorter because you don't begin with a slash (/) that brings you back up to the top of the hierarchy to work your way down. Instead, you are starting at some point in the file system hierarchy, such as **/home/denise**, and entering a path relative to that directory, such as **.netscape-cache**.

File Name Expansion and Wild Cards

Before we cover additional file system related commands, it is worth taking a look at file name expansion. An overview of file name expansion is useful to ensure that you're comfortable with this topic before we cover additional commands.

Table 16-2 lists some common file name expansion and pattern matching.

Table 16-2   File Name Expansion and Pattern Matching

Character(s)	Example	Description
*	1) ls *.c	Match zero or more characters
?	2) ls conf.?	Match any single character
[list]	3) ls conf.[co]	Match any character in list
[lower-upper]	4) ls libdd.9873[5-6].sl	Match any character in range
str{str1,str2,str3,...}	5) ls ux*.{700,300}	Expand str with contents of { }
~	6) ls -a ~	Home directory
~username	7) ls -a ~gene	Home directory of username

The following descriptions of the examples shown in Table 16-2 are more detailed:

1) To list all files in a directory that end in ".c", you could do the following:

man page

ls - 15

```
$  ls *.c
            conf. SAM.c  conf.c
```

2) To find all the files in a directory named "conf" with an extension of one character, you could do the following:

```
$  ls conf.?
            conf.c  conf.o  conf.1
```

3) To list all the files in a directory named "conf" with only the extension "c" or "o," you could do the following:

```
$  ls conf.{co}
            conf.c  conf.o
```

4) To list files with similar names but a field that covers a range, you could do the following:

```
$  ls libdd9873[5-6].sl
            libdd98735.sl  libdd98736.sl
```

5) To list files that start with "ux" and have the extension "300" or "700," you could do the following:

```
$  ls ux*.{700,300}
            uxbootlf.700  uxinstfs.300
```

6) To list the files in your home directory, you could use ~ (tilde:

```
$  ls -a ~
            .            .cshrc.org  .login       .shrc.org
            ..           .exrc       .login.org   .cshrc
                         .history    .profile
```

7) To list the files in the home directory of a user, you could do the following:

```
$  ls  -a  ~gene
                          .history      splinedat    under.des
               ..         .login        trail.txt    xtra.part
        .chsrc            .login.org    ESP-File
        .cshrc.org  .profile            Mail
        .exrc             .shrc.org     opt
```

pwd and cd

When we covered absolute and relative path names, we used the **cd** command to **c**hange **d**irectory. You can be at any point in the file system hierarchy and use **cd** to change to the desired directory, provided that you have the necessary permissions to change to that directory.

We can change directory using an absolute path name as shown in the following example:

```
$ cd /home/denise/.netscape-cache
```

Regardless of your current location in the file system hierarchy, this changes you to the directory **/home/denise/.netscape-cache**. If, however, your current location in the file system hierarchy is **/home/denise**, then you could use a relative pathname to change to **.netscape-cache**, as shown in the following example:

```
$ cd .netscape-cache
```

In order to change directory to a place in the file system relative to your current location, you need a way to determine your current location. The **pwd** command, for **p**resent **w**orking **d**irectory, can do this for you. Going back to the previous example in which we changed directories using the relative path, we could have first issued the **pwd**

command to see that our location was **/home/denise**, as shown in the following example:

man page

pwd - 16

man page

cd - 16

```
$ pwd
/home/denise
$ cd .netscape-cache
$ pwd
$ /home/denise/.netscape-cache
$
```

pwd takes some of the mystery out of determining your current directory.

Let's now take a look at moving up a level in the directory tree using two dots:

```
$ pwd
/home/denise/.netscape-cache
$ cd ..
$ pwd
/home/denise
$
```

The two-dot notation moves you to the parent directory of your current directory.

To return to your home directory, you could issue the **cd** command with no arguments as shown in the following example:

```
$ pwd
/tmp
$ cd
$ pwd
/home/denise
$
```

This shows that no matter what your current location in the file system hierarchy, you can always get back quickly to your home directory. I don't get into shell parameters for some time, but there is a shell parameter which defines your *home* location, as shown in the following example:

```
$ pwd
/tmp
$ cd $HOME
$ pwd
/home/denise
$
```

Using the **pwd** and **cd** commands, you can always obtain your current directory and change to any directory.

cd - Change to a new current directory.

Arguments

none	Change to home directory. This is defined by the HOME environment variable
..	The two dot notation moves you to the parent directory of your current directory.
path	You can specify either an absolute or relative path to change to.

pwd - Present Working Directory, so you know your current location.

Examples

```
$ pwd
/home/denise/.netscape-cache
$ cd ..
```

```
$ pwd
/home/denise
$
```

chmod

The **chmod** command is used to change the permissions on a file. Let's start our discussion of **chmod** with the listing of the file **sort** shown earlier:

```
$ ls -l sort
-rwxr-x--x   1 marty     users      120 Jul 26 10:20 sort
```

Figure 16-5 shows a breakdown of the permissions on **sort**.

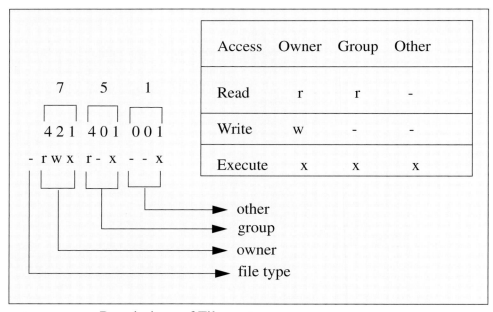

Figure 16-5   Permissions of File **sort**

You have very little control over the type of file defined. You do, however, have a great deal of control over the permissions of this file if it belongs to you. The **chmod** command is used to change the permissions on a file or directory. If you are the owner of the file, you can have a field day changing the permissions on the file.

man page

chmod -16

There are two means by which you can change the permissions: symbolic or numeric. I focus first on the numeric mode, because the numbers involved are easy to manage and I sometimes find that new UNIX users get hung up on the meaning of some of the symbols. I'll then cover the symbols and include the symbol meanings in the **chmod** summary. I decided to use the symbols in the summary because the numeric mode, which I much prefer, is becoming obsolete. In some UNIX variants, the **chmod** manual page is strewn with references to "obsolescent form" whenever the numeric mode is covered.

First of all, what do I mean by numbers? Looking at the numbers for **sort**, we see permissions of 751: 7 for *owner* (hundreds position), 5 for *group* (tens position), and 1 for *other* (ones position). Figure 16-6 helps with the meanings of the positions:

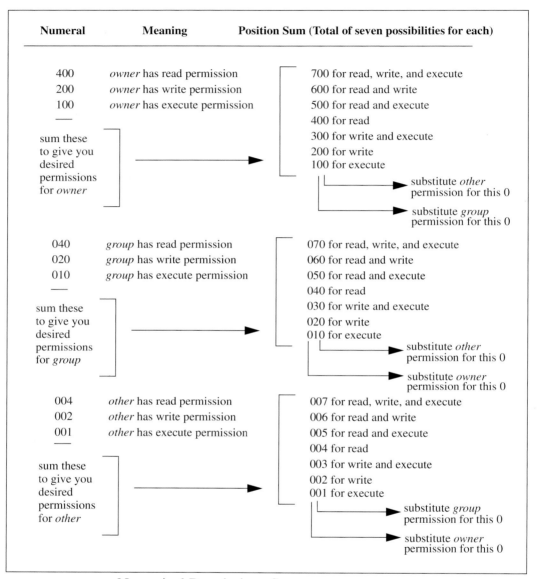

Figure 16-6   Numerical Permissions Summary

Selecting the desired permissions for *owner*, *group*, and *other*, you use the **chmod** command to assign those permissions to a file or directory. Some of these permission possibilities are infrequently used, such as execute only, because you usually need to have read access to a file in order to execute it; however, I included all possibilities in Figure 16-6 for completeness. In addition to the permission mode bits shown in figure 16-6, some miscellaneous mode bits also exist that you don't need to be concerned with at this time.

If you decided that you would like to add write permission of the file **sort** for *group* and remove all permissions for *other*, you would simply execute the **chmod** command with the appropriate numeric value. The following set of commands first lists the existing permissions for **sort**, then it changes the permissions on **sort**, and finally it lists the new permissions on **sort**:

```
$ ls -l sort
-rwxr-x--x   1 marty      users      120 Jul 26 10:20 sort

$ chmod 770 sort

$ ls -l sort
-rwxrwx---  1 marty      users      120 Jul 26 10:20 sort
```

The same set of commands to change the permissions using the symbolic mode would be:

```
$ ls -l sort
-rwxr-x--x   1 marty      users      120 Jul 26 10:20 sort

$ chmod g+w,o-x sort

$ ls -l sort
-rwxrwx---  1 marty      users      120 Jul 26 10:20 sort
```

In symbolic mode, you issue the **chmod** command and specify who will be affected by the change [user (u), group (g), other (o), or all (a)], the operation you wish to perform [add (+), delete (-), or replace (=)] on permissions, and the permission you wish to specify [read (r), write (w), or execute (x)]. In the previous example using symbolic mode, write (w) permission is being added (+) for *group* (g), and execute (x) permission is being removed (-) for *other* (o).

The following is a summary of some of the more commonly used symbols of **chmod**:

chmod - Change permissions of specified files using the following symbolic mode list.

Symbol of who is affected:

u	User is affected.
g	Group is affected.
o	Other is affected.
a	All users are affected.

Operation to perform:

+	Add permission.
-	Remove permission.
=	Replace permission.

Permission specified:

r	Read permission.
w	Write permission.
x	Execute permission.
u	Copy user permissions.
g	Copy group permissions.
o	Copy other permissions.

cp

The **cp** command is used to copy a file from one location to another location. You do not alter the original file when you perform a copy. Provided that you have access to the destination directory to which you wish to copy a file, you can place as many copies of a file in that destination as you wish.

man page

cp - 16

The following bullet list describes some of the types of copies you can perform with **cp**. Because there are many file types in UNIX (as covered in Chapter 2) and you have many ways to specify path names for the source and destination files being copied, this list might help you understand the many ways **cp** can be used:

- Copy a source file to a new file name.

- Copy several source files to a different directory.

- Copy several source files to the same directory.

- Copy an entire directory to a different directory.

- Copy several directories to different directories.

The following is an example of copying a file to a new file name within the same directory:

```
$ cp krsort krsort.sav
```

What if the file **krsort.sav** already exists? The answer is that it is replaced by the new **krsort.sav** being copied. To prevent such mishaps (officially called an overwrite) from occurring, you use the *-i* option to **cp**. *-i* asks you whether you wish to overwrite the file before the copy takes place. If your response is affirmative, then the old file is overwritten with the new file.

The following example first shows a listing of the contents of a directory. Using **cp** with the *-i* option, we copy the file **krsort.c** to **krsortorig.c**, a file that already exists. By responding *n* when asked whether we want to over write **krsortorig.c,** the file is not overwritten and no copy takes place:

```
$ ls -l
total 168
-rwxr-xr-x    1 denise    users       34592 Oct 31 11:27 krsort
-rwxr-xr-x    1 denise    users        3234 Oct 31 11:27 krsort.c
-rwxr-xr-x    1 denise    users       32756 Oct 31 11:27 krsort.dos
-rw-r--r--    1 denise    users        9922 Oct 31 11:27 krsort.q
-rwxr-xr-x    1 denise    users        3085 Oct 31 11:27 krsortorig.c
$ cp -i krsort.c krsortorig.c
overwrite krsortorig.c? (y/n) n
$
```

cp - Copy files and directories.

Options

-i	Interactive copy whereby you are prompted to confirm that you wish to overwrite an existing file.
-f	Force existing files to be overwritten by files being copied if there is a conflict in file names occurs.
-p	Preserve permissions when copying.
-r	Copy recursively.
-R	Copy recursively, except when permissions are different.

mv

The **mv** command is used to move a file or directory from one location to another location. You can also move multiple files.

The following example shows a listing of a directory, the move of file **krsort.c** to **krsort.test.c** within this directory, and a listing of the directory showing the file has been moved:

man page

ls - 15

```
$ ls -l
total 168
-rwxr-xr-x    1 denise    users      34592 Oct 31 15:17 krsort
-rwxr-xr-x    1 denise    users       3234 Oct 31 15:17 krsort.c
-rwxr-xr-x    1 denise    users       2756 Oct 31 15:17 krsort.dos
-rw-r--r--    1 denise    users       9922 Oct 31 15:17 krsort.q
-rwxr-xr-x    1 denise    users       3085 Oct 31 15:17 krsortorig.c
$ mv krsort.c krsort.test.c
$ ls -l
total 168
-rwxr-xr-x    1 denise    users      34592 Oct 31 15:17 krsort
-rwxr-xr-x    1 denise    users      32756 Oct 31 15:17 krsort.dos
-rw-r--r--    1 denise    users       9922 Oct 31 15:17 krsort.q
-rwxr-xr-x    1 denise    users       3234 Oct 31 15:17 krsort.test.c
-rwxr-xr-x    1 denise    users       3085 Oct 31 15:17 krsortorig.c
$
```

man page

mv - 16

What if the destination file already exists? You guessed it, UNIX is more than happy to write over the destination file. Using the *-i* option, **mv** asks you to confirm overwriting a file before it does so. The following example shows an attempt to move **krsort.test.c** to **krsortorig.c**. The user is alerted to the fact that **krsortorig.c** already exists and chooses not to let the move take place:

```
$ ls -l
total 168
-rwxr-xr-x    1 denise    users      34592 Oct 31 15:17 krsort
-rwxr-xr-x    1 denise    users      32756 Oct 31 15:17 krsort.dos
-rw-r--r--    1 denise    users       9922 Oct 31 15:17 krsort.q
-rwxr-xr-x    1 denise    users       3234 Oct 31 15:17 krsort.test.c
-rwxr-xr-x    1 denise    users       3085 Oct 31 15:17 krsortorig.c
$ mv -i krsort.test.c krsortorig.c
remove krsortorig.c? (y/n) n
$ ls -l
total 168
-rwxr-xr-x    1 denise    users      34592 Oct 31 15:17 krsort
-rwxr-xr-x    1 denise    users      32756 Oct 31 15:17 krsort.dos
-rw-r--r--    1 denise    users       9922 Oct 31 15:17 krsort.q
-rwxr-xr-x    1 denise    users       3234 Oct 31 15:17 krsort.test.c
-rwxr-xr-x    1 denise    users       3085 Oct 31 15:17 krsortorig.c
$
```

Because the response was not in the affirmative, the move does not take place, and the original **krsortorig.c** remains intact.

mv - Move files and directories.

Options

-i		Interactive move whereby you are prompted to confirm that you wish to overwrite an existing file.
-f		Force existing files to be overwritten by files being moved if a conflict in file names occurs.
-p		Preserve permissions when moving.

mkdir

How nice it would be to have a command to make a directory any time you wish. You could then use this command to create directories and thereby organize your files in multiple directories in a way similar to organizing files in a filing cabinet. The **mkdir** command allows you to do just that - make a directory.

This is an incredibly simple command. You specify the name of the directory to create. In the following example, we'll look at the contents of a directory with the **ls** command, use **mkdir** to make the directory named **default.permissions**, and then perform another **ls** to see the new directory:

```
$ ls -l
total 2
drwxr-xr-x   2 denise   users      1024 Oct 31 11:27 krsort.dir.old
$ mkdir default.permissions
$ ls -l
total 4
drwxr-xr-x   2 denise   users      1024 Oct 31 11:27 krsort.dir.old
drwxr-xr-x   2 denise   users        24 Oct 31 11:32 default.permissions
$
```

The new directory has been produced with default permissions for the user *denise*. *group* and *other* have both read and execute permissions for this directory.

What if you wanted to create a directory with specific permissions on it instead of default permissions? You could use the *-m* option to **mkdir** and specify the mode or permissions you wanted. To give all users read permission on the **krsort.dir.new** directory, you issue the following:

```
$ mkdir -m "a=r" read.permissions
$ ls -l
total 6
drwxr-xr-x   2 denise    users         1024 Oct 31 11:27 krsort.dir.old
drwxr-xr-x   2 denise    users           24 Oct 31 11:32 default.permissions
dr--r--r--   2 denise    users           24 Oct 31 11:33 read.permissions
$
```

Remember the symbolic versus numeric mode of permissions? This **mkdir** command shows the symbolic mode, which although I do not like as much as the numeric mode, should be used because the numeric mode is becoming obsolete.

You don't have to stop at creating a directory with only one level of depth. With the *-p* option, you can create a new directory with any number of subdirectories in it. Intermediate directories are created with the *-p* option. Let's now create a directory named **level1**, with the directory **level2** beneath it, and the directory **level3** below **level2** in the following example. The **ls** command with the *-R* option recursively lists the directories below **level1**:

```
$ mkdir -p level1/level2/level3
$ ls -R level1
level2

level1/level2:
level3

level1/level2/level3:
$
```

After creating the directory **level1** and issuing the **ls** command, we can see that **level2** is indeed beneath **level1**, and **level3** is beneath **level2**.

mkdir - Create specified directories.

Options

-m	Specify the mode (permissions) of the directory.
-p	Create intermediate directories to achieve the full path. If you want to create several layers of directories down, you use -*p*.

rm

The **rm** command removes one or more files from a directory and can also be used to remove the directory itself. Going back to our earlier discussion on permissions, you must have both *write* and *execute* permissions on a directory in order to remove a file from it. If you own the directory from which you are going to remove files, then you can probably remove files from it. If, however, you don't have the appropriate permissions on a directory, then the **rm** fails.

As with some of the other commands we have covered, you can use the -*i* option, which asks you to confirm each file as it is removed. This means that if you are asked whether you really wish to remove a file and you respond *n*, then the file is not removed. If you respond *y*, the file is removed.

You can also use the -*r* (or -*R*) option to recursively delete the contents of directories and then delete the directories. This means you can recursively delete the files and directories specified. If there is any question in your mind about whether or not you wish to recursively delete files and directories, then use the -*i* option along with -*r*.

You can use the *-f* option to remove files and directories, which performs removes *without* asking you to confirm them.

The following example performs a long listing of the directory **krsort.dir.new**, interactively prompts the user to see whether he or she wants to delete the files in this directory, and then lists the contents of this directory again, showing that all files have *not* been deleted because the user responded *n*:

```
$ ls -l krsort.dir.new
total 168
-rwxr-xr-x    1 denise    users     34592 Oct 27 18:44 krsort
-rwxr-xr-x    1 denise    users      3234 Oct 27 18:46 krsort.c
-rwxr-xr-x    1 denise    users     32756 Oct 27 18:46 krsort.dos
-rw-r--r--    1 denise    users      9922 Oct 27 18:46 krsort.q
-rwxr-xr-x    1 denise    users      3085 Oct 27 18:46 krsortorig.c
$ rm -i krsort.dir.new/*
../krsort.dir.new/krsort: ? (y/n) n
../krsort.dir.new/krsort.c: ? (y/n) n
../krsort.dir.new/krsort.dos: ? (y/n) n
../krsort.dir.new/krsort.q: ? (y/n) n
../krsort.dir.new/krsortorig.c: ? (y/n) n
$ ls -l krsort.dir.new
total 168
-rwxr-xr-x    1 denise    users     34592 Oct 27 18:44 krsort
-rwxr-xr-x    1 denise    users      3234 Oct 27 18:46 krsort.c
-rwxr-xr-x    1 denise    users     32756 Oct 27 18:46 krsort.dos
-rw-r--r--    1 denise    users      9922 Oct 27 18:46 krsort.q
-rwxr-xr-x    1 denise    users      3085 Oct 27 18:46 krsortorig.c
$
```

man page

ls - 15

man page

rm - 16

Note that the response to being asked whether the file should be deleted was *n* in all cases. This means that none of the files have been removed. A *y* response to any question results in that file being removed from the directory. To interactively delete a directory, you combine the options *-i* and *-r* of the **rm** command. If, however, you do not delete every file in a directory, then the directory is not removed if the *-i* option is used. The first part of the following example shows all but the file **krsort** being removed from the directory **krsort.dir.new**. The directory is not deleted because this file still exists. When the file is removed in the second part of this example, the directory itself is then deleted:

```
$ rm -ir krsort.dir.new
directory krsort.dir.new: ? (y/n) y
krsort.dir.new/krsort: ? (y/n) n
krsort.dir.new/krsort.c: ? (y/n) y
krsort.dir.new/krsort.dos: ? (y/n) y
krsort.dir.new/krsort.q: ? (y/n) y
krsort.dir.new/krsortorig.c: ? (y/n) y
krsort.dir.new: ? (y/n) y
rm: directory krsort.dir.new not removed.  Directory not
empty

$ rm -ir krsort.dir.new
directory krsort.dir.new: ? (y/n) y
krsort.dir.new/krsort: ? (y/n) y
krsort.dir.new: ? (y/n) y
$
```

rm - Remove files and directories.

Options

    -i   Interactive remove whereby you are prompted to con-
               firm that you wish to remove an existing file.

    -f   Force files to be removed.

    -r (-R) Recursively remove the contents of the directory and
               then the directory itself.

rmdir

The **rmdir** command removes one or more directories. The directory
must be empty in order to be removed or you must use the *-f* option.
You can also specify more than one directory to be removed. Going
back to our earlier discussion on permissions, you must have both
write and *execute* permissions on the parent of a directory to be
removed in order to remove it.

As with some of the other commands we have covered, you can use the *-i* option, which asks you to confirm each directory as it is removed. This means that if you are asked whether you really wish to remove a directory and you respond *n,* then it is not removed. If you respond *y,* it is removed.

The order in which you specify directories are to be removed is significant. If you want to remove both a directory and its subdirectory, you must specify the subdirectory to be removed first. If you specify the parent directory rather than its subdirectory to be removed first, the removal of the parent directory fails because it is not empty.

You can use the *-f* option to force the removal of directories, an action that performs removal *without* asking you to confirm them.

The following example performs a long listing of the directory **krsort.dir.new**, showing that this directory has in it a file called **.dotfile**. When we attempt to remove this directory with **rmdir,** a message is displayed informing us that this directory is not empty. The file **.dotfile** in this directory prevents the **rmdir** command from removing **krsort.dir.new**. After removing **.dotfile,** we are able to remove the directory with **rmdir**:

man page

rmdir - 16

```
$ ls -al ../krsort.dir.new
total 4
drwxr-xr-x    2 denise    users       1024 Oct 27 18:57 .
drwxrwxr-x    4 denise    users       1024 Oct 27 18:40 ..
-rw-r--r--    1 denise    users          0 Oct 27 18:56 .dotfile
$ rmdir -i ../krsort.dir.new
../krsort.dir.new: ? (y/n) y
rmdir: ../krsort.dir.new: Directory not empty
$ rm ../krsort.dir.new/.dotfile
$ rmdir -i ../krsort.dir.new
../krsort.dir.new: ? (y/n) y
$
```

man page

ls - 15

rmdir has now successfully removed **krsort.dir.new** because **.dotfile** is gone:

rmdir - Remove directories.

Options

-i   Interactive remove whereby you are prompted to confirm that you wish to remove a directory

-f   Force directories to be removed.

-p   If, after removing a directory, the parent directory is empty, then remove it also. This goes on until a parent directory is encountered that is not empty.

Using Commands

Using the cd, pwd, ls, mkdir, and cp Commands

Now that we have covered some of these commands in an "isolated" fashion, let's put some of the commands together.

Let's start by viewing the hierarchy of a directory under *denise's* home directory, called **krsort.dir.old,** as shown in Figure 16-7:

```
$ cd /home/denise/krsort.dir.old
$ pwd
/home/denise/krsort.dir.old
$ ls -l
total 168
-rwxr-xr-x    1 denise    users      34592 Oct 27 18:20 krsort
-rwxr-xr-x    1 denise    users       3234 Oct 27 17:30 krsort.c
-rwxr-xr-x    1 denise    users      32756 Oct 27 17:30 krsort.dos
-rw-r--r--    1 denise    users       9922 Oct 27 17:30 krsort.q
-rwxr-xr-x    1 denise    users       3085 Oct 27 17:30 krsortorig.c
$
```

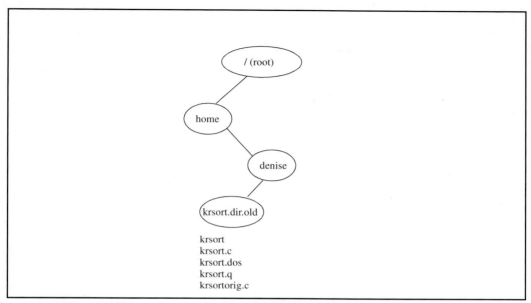

Figure 16-7 **/home/denise/krsort.dir.old**

We can then make a new directory called **krsort.dir.new** and copy a file to it as shown in Figure 16-8:

```
$ mkdir ../krsort.dir.new
$ cp krsort ../krsort.dir.new
$ ls -l ../krsort.dir.new
total 68
-rwxr-xr-x   1 denise    users         34592 Oct 27 18:27 krsort
$
```

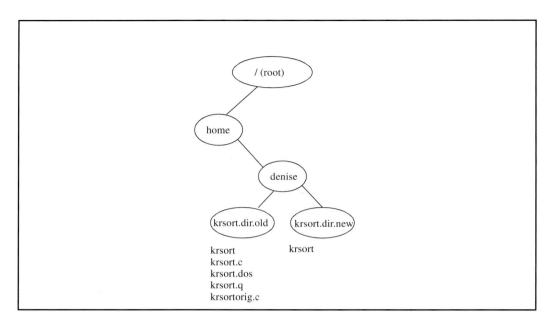

Figure 16-8   **/home/denise/krsort.dir.new**

Now let's try the *-i* option to **cp**. If we attempt to copy a file to an existing file name, we'll be asked if we wish to overwrite the destination file. We are alerted to the fact that the destination file already exists and we can then select a new name for the file we wish to copy, as shown in Figure 16-9:

```
$ pwd
/users/denise/krsort.dir.old
$ cp -i krsort ../krsort.dir.new
overwrite ../krsort.dir.new/krsort? (y/n) n
$ cp krsort ../krsort.dir.new/krsort.new.name
$ ls -l ../krsort.dir.new
total 136
-rwxr-xr-x   1 denise   users     34592 Oct 27 18:27 krsort
-rwxr-xr-x     1 denise      users      34592 Oct 27 18:29
krsort.new.name
$
```

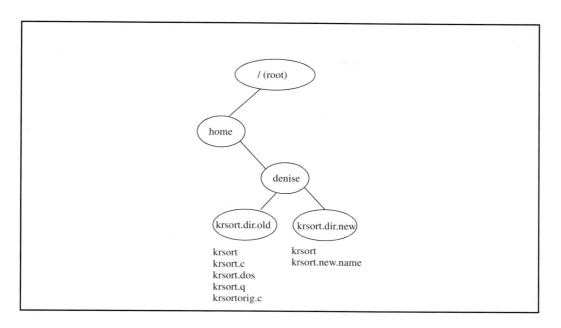

Figure 16-9 **/home/denise/krsort.dir.new/krsort.new.name** Added

We can also use a wild card with **cp** to copy all files in **krsort.dir.old** to **krsort.dir.new** as shown in Figure 16-10:

```
$ cp * ../krsort.dir.new
$ ls -l ../krsort.dir.new
total 236
-rwxr-xr-x   1 denise    users      34592 Oct 27 18:30 krsort
-rwxr-xr-x   1 denise    users       3234 Oct 27 18:30 krsort.c
-rwxr-xr-x   1 denise    users      32756 Oct 27 18:30 krsort.dos
-rwxr-xr-x   1 denise    users      34592 Oct 27 18:29
krsort.new.name
-rw-r--r--   1 denise    users       9922 Oct 27 18:30 krsort.q
-rwxr-xr-x   1 denise    users       3085 Oct 27 18:30 krsortorig.c
$
```

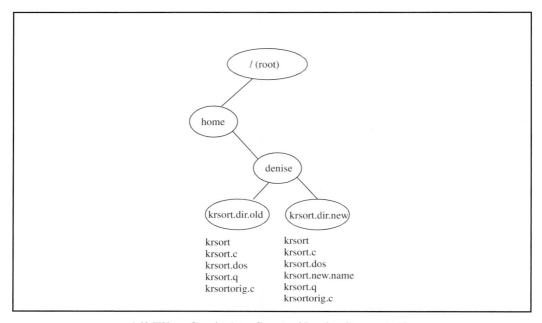

Figure 16-10   All Files Copied to **/home/denise/krsort.dir.new**

Using the mv Command

Let's start over at the point where the **krsort.dir.new** directory is empty, as shown in Figure 16-11:

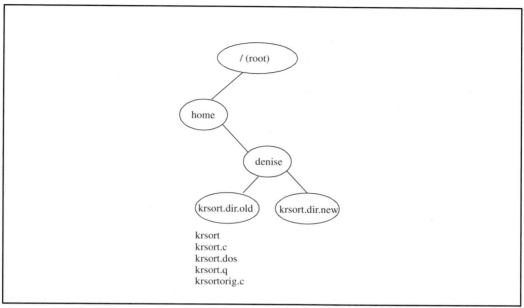

Figure 16-11   Empty **/home/denise/krsort.dir.new** Directory

We can now move the file **krsort** to the **krsort.dir.new** directory
as shown in Figure 16-12:

```
$ mv krsort ../krsort.dir.new
$ ls -l ../krsort.dir.new
total 68
-rwxr-xr-x   1 denise    users        34592 Oct 27 18:20 krsort
$
```

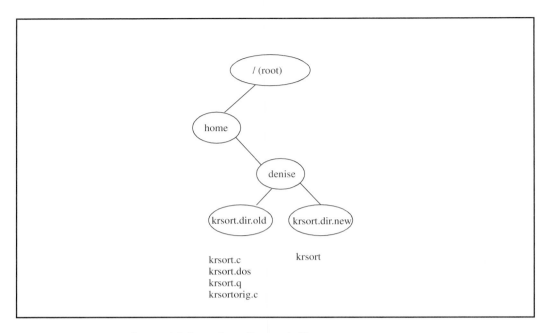

Figure 16-12   **krsort** Moved to **/krsort.dir.new**

If we now attempt to move **krsort** to the **krsort.dir.new** directory with the *-i* option and write over the file **krsort**, we get the following:

man page

mv -16

```
$ mv -i krsort ../krsort.dir.new/krsort
remove ../krsort.dir.new/krsort? (y/n) n
$
```

Because we used the *-i* option to **mv**, we are asked whether we wish to allow a file to be overwritten with the move. Because we responded *n* to the question, the file is not overwritten.

We can also use a wild card with the **mv** command to copy all files from the **krsort.dir.old** directory to the **krsort.dir.new** directory. Without the *-i* option, any files in the **krsort.dir.new** directory are overwritten by files that have the same name, as shown in Figure 16-13:

```
$ mv * ../krsort.dir.new
$ ls -l ../krsort.dir.new
total 168
-rwxr-xr-x    1 denise    users    34592 Oct 27 18:44 krsort
-rwxr-xr-x    1 denise    users     3234 Oct 27 18:46 krsort.c
-rwxr-xr-x    1 denise    users    32756 Oct 27 18:46 krsort.dos
-rw-r--r--    1 denise    users     9922 Oct 27 18:46 krsort.q
-rwxr-xr-x    1 denise    users     3085 Oct 27 18:46 krsortorig.c
$
```

man page

mv - 16

man page

ls - 15

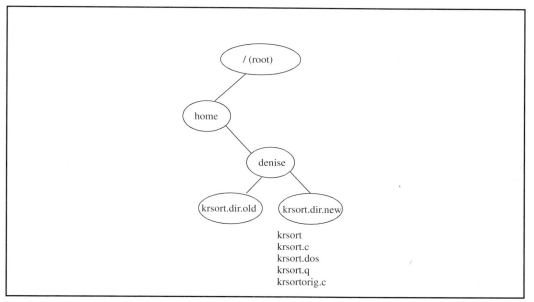

Figure 16-13   All Files Moved to **/home/denise/krsort.dir.new**

Down and Dirty with the rm and rmdir Commands

The most feared command in the UNIX world, with good reason I
might add, is the **rm** command. **rm** removes whatever you want
whenever you want, with no questions asked unless you use the *-i*
option.

man page

rm - 16

    Want to blow away your system instantly? **rm** would be more
than happy to help you. As an average user, and not the system admin-

istrator, you probably do not have the permissions to do so. It is, how-ever, unnerving to know that this is a possibility. In addition, it is likely that you have permissions remove all of your own files and directories. All of this can be easily avoided by simply using the **-i** option to **rm**.

Let's assume that **krsort.dir.new** and **krsort.dir.old** are identical directories as shown in Figure 16-14:

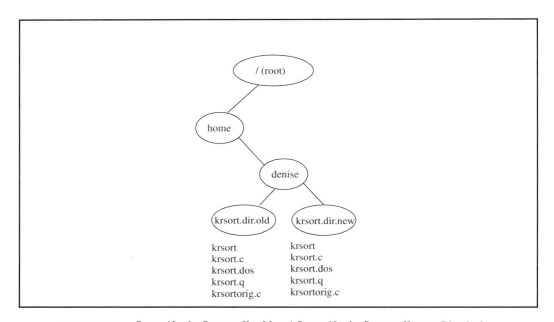

Figure 16-14   **/home/denise/krsort.dir.old** and **/home/denise/krsort.dir.new** Identical

To interactively remove files from **krsort.dir.new**, you do the following:

```
$ rm -i ../krsort.dir.new/*
../krsort.dir.new/krsort: ? (y/n) n
../krsort.dir.new/krsort.c: ? (y/n) n
../krsort.dir.new/krsort.dos: ? (y/n) n
../krsort.dir.new/krsort.q: ? (y/n) n
../krsort.dir.new/krsortorig.c: ? (y/n) n
$ ls -l ../krsort.dir.new
total 168
-rwxr-xr-x   1 denise     users      34592 Oct 27 18:44 krsort
-rwxr-xr-x   1 denise     users       3234 Oct 27 18:46 krsort.c
-rwxr-xr-x   1 denise     users      32756 Oct 27 18:46 krsort.dos
-rw-r--r--   1 denise     users       9922 Oct 27 18:46 krsort.q
```

```
-rwxr-xr-x   1 denise    users      3085 Oct 27 18:46 krsortorig.c
$
```

This obviously resulted in nothing being removed from **krsort.dir.new** because we responded *n* when asked whether we wanted to delete files.

Let's now go ahead and add a file beginning with a "." (period) to **krsort.dir.new**. The **touch** command does just that, it touches a file to create it with no contents, as shown in Figure 16-15 (**touch** can also be used to update the time stamp of an existing file):

```
$ touch ../krsort.dir.new/.dotfile
$ ls -al ../krsort.dir.new
total 172
drwxr-xr-x   2 denise    users      1024 Oct 27 18:54 .
drwxrwxr-x   4 denise    users      1024 Oct 27 18:40 ..
-rw-r--r--   1 denise    users         0 Oct 27 18:56 .dotfile
-rwxr-xr-x   1 denise    users     34592 Oct 27 18:44 krsort
-rwxr-xr-x   1 denise    users      3234 Oct 27 18:46 krsort.c
-rwxr-xr-x   1 denise    users     32756 Oct 27 18:46 krsort.dos
-rw-r--r--   1 denise    users      9922 Oct 27 18:46 krsort.q
-rwxr-xr-x   1 denise    users      3085 Oct 27 18:46 krsortorig.c
$
```

man page

ls - 15

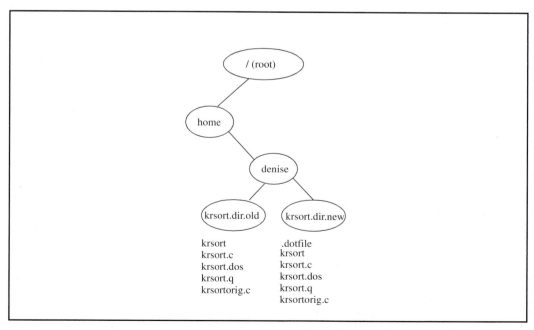

Figure 16-15 **/home/denise/krsort.dir.new** with **.dotfile**

If we now attempt to remove files using the same **rm** command earlier issued, we'll see the following, as shown in Figure 16-16:

man page

rm - 16

man page

ls - 15

```
$ rm -i ../krsort.dir.new/*
../krsort.dir.new/krsort: ? (y/n) y
../krsort.dir.new/krsort.c: ? (y/n) y
../krsort.dir.new/krsort.dos: ? (y/n) y
../krsort.dir.new/krsort.q: ? (y/n) y
../krsort.dir.new/krsortorig.c: ? (y/n) y
$ ls -al ../krsort.dir.new
total 4
drwxr-xr-x    2 denise    users         1024 Oct 27 18:57 .
drwxrwxr-x    4 denise    users         1024 Oct 27 18:40 ..
-rw-r--r--    1 denise    users            0 Oct 27 18:56 .dotfile
```

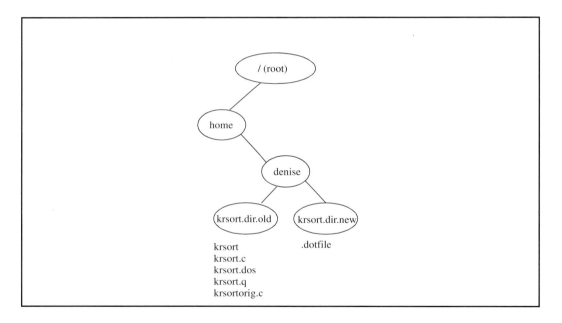

Figure 16-16   Only **.dotfile** Left in **/home/denise/krsort.dir.new**

man page

mkdir - 16

The "*" used as a wild card with the **rm** command does not remove the file **.dotfile**. The file **.dotfile** in this directory prevents the **rmdir** command from removing **krsort.dir.new**. This file must first

be removed before the **rmdir** command can successfully delete
krsort.dir.new.

```
$ rmdir -i ../krsort.dir.new
../krsort.dir.new: ? (y/n) y
rmdir: ../krsort.dir.new: Directory not empty
$ rm ../krsort.dir.new/.dotfile
$ rmdir -i ../krsort.dir.new
../krsort.dir.new: ? (y/n) y
$
```

rmdir has now successfully removed **krsort.dir.new** because **.dotfile**
is gone, as shown in Figure 16-17:

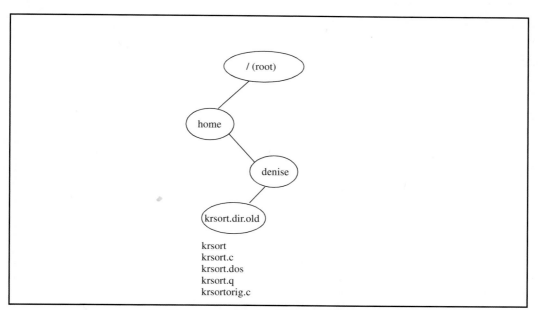

Figure 16-17 **rmdir** Removes **/home/denise/krsort.dir.new**

Manual Pages for Some Commands Used in Chapter 16

The following are the HP-UX manual pages for many of the commands used in the chapter. Commands often differ among UNIX variants, so you may find differences in the options or other areas for some commands; however, the following manual pages serve as an excellent reference.

cd

cd - Change working directory.

cd(1)   cd(1)

NAME
     cd - change working directory

SYNOPSIS

     cd [directory]

DESCRIPTION
     If directory is not specified, the value of shell parameter HOME is
     used as the new working directory. If directory specifies a complete
     path starting with /, ., .., directory becomes the new working
     directory. If neither case applies, cd tries to find the designated
     directory relative to one of the paths specified by the CDPATH shell
     variable. CDPATH has the same syntax as, and similar semantics to,
     the PATH shell variable. cd must have execute (search) permission in
     directory.

     cd exists only as a shell built-in command because a new process is
     created whenever a command is executed, making cd useless if written
     and processed as a normal system command. Moreover, different shells
     provide different implementations of cd as a built-in utility.
     Features of cd as described here may not be supported by all the
     shells. Refer to individual shell manual entries for differences.

     If cd is called in a subshell or a separate utility execution
     environment such as:

         find . -type d -exec cd {}; -exec foo {};

         (which invokes foo on accessible directories)

     cd does not affect the current directory of the caller's environment.
     Another usage of cd as a stand-alone command is to obtain the exit
     status of the command.

EXTERNAL INFLUENCES
   International Code Set Support
     Single- and multi-byte character code sets are supported.

EXAMPLES
     Change the current working directory to the HOME directory from any
     location in the file system:

         cd

     Change to new current working directory foo residing in the current
     directory:

         cd foo

or

```
cd ./foo
```

Change to directory foobar residing in the current directory's parent directory:

```
cd ../foobar
```

Change to the directory whose absolute pathname is /usr/local/lib/work.files:

```
cd /usr/local/lib/work.files
```

Change to the directory proj1/schedule/staffing/proposals relative to home directory:

```
cd $HOME/proj1/schedule/staffing/proposals
```

VARIABLES

The following environment variables affect the execution of cd:

HOME   The name of the home directory, used when no
                        directory operand is specified.

CDPATH   A colon-separated list of pathnames that refer to
                        directories. If the directory operand does not
                        begin with a slash (/) character, and the first
                        component is not dot or dot-dot, cd searches for
                        directory relative to each directory named in the
                        CDPATH variable, in the order listed. The new
                        working directory is set to the first matching
                        directory found. An empty string in place of a
                        directory pathname represents the current
                        directory. If CDPATH is not set, it is treated as
                        if it was an empty string.

RETURN VALUE

Upon completion, cd exits with one of the following values:

0   The directory was successfully changed.
>0   An error occurred. The working directory remains
                        unchanged.

SEE ALSO

csh(1), pwd(1), ksh(1), sh-posix(1), sh(1), chdir(2).

STANDARDS CONFORMANCE

cd: SVID2, SVID3, XPG2, XPG3, XPG4, POSIX.2

chmod

chmod - Change permissions.

NAME
     chmod - change file mode access permissions

SYNOPSIS

     /usr/bin/chmod [-A] [-R] symbolic_mode_list file ...

     Obsolescent form:
     /usr/bin/chmod [-A] [-R] numeric_mode file ...

DESCRIPTION
     The chmod command changes the permissions of one or more files
     according to the value of symbolic_mode_list or numeric_mode. You can
     display the current permissions for a file with the ls -l command (see
     ls(1)).

     Symbolic Mode List
     A symbolic_mode_list is a comma-separated list of operations in the
     following form. Whitespace is not permitted.

          [who] op [permission] [,...]

     The variable fields can have the following values:

          who   One or more of the following letters:

                             u   Modify permissions for user (owner).
                             g   Modify permissions for group.
                             o   Modify permissions for others.
                             a   Modify permissions for all users (a is
                                  equivalent to ugo).

          op   Required; one of the following symbols:

                             +   Add permission to the existing file mode
                                  bits of who.
                             -    Delete permission from the existing file
                                  mode bits of who.
                             =   Replace the existing mode bits of who with
                                  permission.

          permission   One or more of the following letters:

                             r   Add or delete the read permission for who.

                             w   Add or delete the write permission for who.

x   Add or delete the execute file (search
        directory) permission for who.
s   Add or delete the set-owner-id or set-
        group-id on file execution permission for
        who. Useful only if u or g is expressed or
        implied in who.
t   Add or delete the save-text-image on file
        execution (sticky bit) permission. Useful
        only if u is expressed or implied in who.
        See chmod(2).
X   Conditionally add or delete the
        execute/search permission as follows:
        - If file is a directory, add or delete
           the search permission to the existing
           file mode for who. (Same as x.)
        - If file is not a directory, and the
           current file permissions include the
           execute permission (ls -l displays an x
           or an s) for at least one of user,
           group, or other, then add or delete the
           execute file permission for who.
        - If file is not a directory, and no
           execute permissions are set in the
           current file mode, then do not change
           any execute permission.

Or one only of the following letters:

u   Copy the current user permissions to who.

g   Copy the current group permissions to who.

o   Copy the current other permissions to who.

The operations are performed in the order specified, and can override
preceding operations specified in the same command line.

If who is omitted, the r, w, x, and X permissions are changed for all
users if the changes are permitted by the current file mode creation
mask (see umask(1)). The s and t permissions are changed as if a was
specified in who.

Omitting permission is useful only when used with = to delete all
permissions.

Numeric Mode (Obsolescent)
   Absolute permissions can be set by specifying a numeric_mode, an octal
   number constructed from the logical OR (sum) of the following mode
   bits:

Miscellaneous mode bits:

     4000 (= u=s) Set-user-id on file execution (file only)
     2000 (= g=s) Set-group-id on file execution
     1000 (= u=t) Set sticky bit; see chmod(2)

Permission mode bits:

     0400 (= u=r) Read by owner
     0200 (= u=w) Write by owner
     0100 (= u=x) Execute (search in directory) by owner
     0040 (= g=r) Read by group
     0020 (= g=w) Write by group
     0010 (= g=x) Execute/search by group
     0004 (= o=r) Read by others

```
        0002  (= o=w)  Write by others
        0001  (= o=x)  Execute/search by others
```

Options

- -A   Preserve any optional access control list (ACL) entries
        associated with the file. By default, in conformance with
        the IEEE Standard POSIX 1003.1-1988, optional ACL entries
        are deleted. For information about access control lists,
        see acl(5).

- -R   Recursively change the file mode bits. For each file
        operand that names a directory, chmod alters the file mode
        bits of the named directory and all files and subdirectories
        in the file hierarchy below it.

Only the owner of a file, or a user with appropriate privileges, can
change its mode.

Only a user having appropriate privileges can set (or retain, if
previously set) the sticky bit of a regular file.

In order to set the set-group-id on execution bit, the group of the
file must correspond to your current group ID.

If chmod is used on a symbolic link, the mode of the file referred to
by the link is changed.

EXTERNAL INFLUENCES
    Environment Variables
        LC_MESSAGES determines the language in which messages are displayed.

        If LC_MESSAGES is not specified in the environment or is set to the
        empty string, the value of LANG is used as a default for each
        unspecified or empty variable. If LANG is not specified or is set to
        the empty string, a default of "C" (see lang(5)) is used instead of
        LANG.

        If any internationalization variable contains an invalid setting,
        chmod behaves as if all internationalization variables are set to "C".
        See environ(5).

    International Code Set Support
        Single- and multi-byte character code sets are supported.

RETURN VALUE
    Upon completion, chmod returns one of the following values:

        0   Successful completion.
        >0   An error condition occurred.

EXAMPLES
    Deny write permission to others:

        chmod o-w file

    Make a file executable by everybody:

        chmod a+x file

    Assign read and execute permission to everybody, and set the set-
    user-id bit:

        chmod a=rx,u+s file
```
```

Assign read and write permission to the file owner, and read permission to everybody else:

```
chmod u=rw,go=r file
```
or
```
chmod 644 file     (obsolescent form)
```

Traverse a directory subtree making all regular files readable by user and group only, and all executables and directories executable (searchable) by everyone:

```
chmod -R ug+r,o-r,a+X pathname
```

If the current value of umask is 020 (umask -S displays u=rwx,g=rx,o=rwx; do not change write permission for group) and the current permissions for file mytest are 444 (a=r), displayed by ls -l as -r--r--r--, then the command

```
chmod +w mytest
```

sets the permissions to 646 (uo=rw,g=r), displayed by ls -l as -rw-r--rw-.

If the current value of umask is 020 (umask -S displays u=rwx,g=rx,o=rwx; do not change write permission for group) and the current permissions for file mytest are 666 (a=rw), displayed by ls -l as -rw-rw-rw-, then the command

```
chmod -w mytest
```

sets the permissions to 464 (uo=r,g=rw), displayed by ls -l as -r--rw-r--.

DEPENDENCIES

The -A option causes chmod to fail on file systems that do not support ACLs.

AUTHOR

chmod was developed by AT&T and HP.

SEE ALSO

chacl(1), ls(1), umask(1), chmod(2), acl(5).

STANDARDS CONFORMANCE

chmod: SVID2, SVID3, XPG2, XPG3, XPG4, POSIX.2

cp

cp - Copy files and directories.

```
cp(1)                                                              cp(1)

NAME
      cp - copy files and directory subtrees

SYNOPSIS
      cp [-f|-i] [-p] [-e extarg ] file1 new_file
      cp [-f|-i] [-p] [-e extarg ] file1 [file2 ...] dest_directory
      cp [-f|-i] [-p] [-R|-r] [-e extarg ] directory1 [directory2 ...]
      dest_directory

DESCRIPTION
      cp copies:

              -  file1 to new or existing new_file,
              -  file1 to existing dest_directory,
              -  file1, file2, ...  to existing dest_directory,
              -  directory subtree directory1, to new or existing
                 dest_directory.  or
              -  multiple directory subtrees directory1, directory2, ...  to
                 new or existing dest_directory.

      cp fails if file1 and new_file are the same (be cautious when using
      shell metacharacters).  When destination is a directory, one or more
      files are copied into that directory.  If two or more files are
      copied, the destination must be a directory.  When copying a single
      file to a new file, if new_file exists, its contents are destroyed.

      If the access permissions of the destination dest_directory or
      existing destination file new_file forbid writing, cp aborts and
      produces an error message ``cannot create file''.

      To copy one or more directory subtrees to another directory, the -r
      option is required.  The -r option is ignored if used when copying a
      file to another file or files to a directory.

      If new_file is a link to an existing file with other links, cp
      overwrites the existing file and retains all links.  If copying a file
      to an existing file, cp does not change existing file access
      permission bits, owner, or group.

      When copying files to a directory or to a new file that does not
      already exist, cp creates a new file with the same file permission
      bits as file1, modified by the file creation mask of the user if the
      -p option was not specified, and then bitwise inclusively ORed with
      S_IRWXU.  The owner and group of the new file or files are those of
      the user.  The last modification time of new_file (and last access
      time, if new_file did not exist) and the last access time of the
      source file1 are set to the time the copy was made.

      Options
```

-i   (interactive copy) Cause cp to write a prompt to standard
            error and wait for a response before copying a file that would
            overwrite an existing file. If the response from the standard
            input is affirmative, the file is copied if permissions allow
            the copy. If the -i (interactive) and -f (forced-copy)
            options are both specified, the -i option is ignored.

-f   Force existing destination pathnames to be removed before
            copying, without prompting for confirmation. This option has
            the effect of destroying and replacing any existing file whose
            name and directory location conflicts with the name and
            location of the new file created by the copy operation.

-p   (preserve permissions) Causes cp to preserve in the copy as
            many of the modification time, access time, file mode, user
            ID, and group ID as allowed by permissions.

-r   (recursive subtree copy) Cause cp to copy the subtree rooted
            at each source directory to dest_directory. If dest_directory
            exists, it must be a directory, in which case cp creates a
            directory within dest_directory with the same name as file1
            and copies the subtree rooted at file1 to
            dest_directory/file1. An error occurs if dest_directory/file1
            already exists. If dest_directory does not exist, cp creates
            it and copies the subtree rooted at file1 to dest_directory.
            Note that cp -r cannot merge subtrees.

            Usually normal files and directories are copied. Character
            special devices, block special devices, network special files,
            named pipes, symbolic links, and sockets are copied, if the
            user has access to the file; otherwise, a warning is printed
            stating that the file cannot be created, and the file is
            skipped.

            dest_directory should not reside within directory1, nor should
            directory1 have a cyclic directory structure, since in both
            cases cp attempts to copy an infinite amount of data.

-R   (recursive subtree copy) The -R option is identical to the -r
            option with the exception that directories copied by the -R
            option are created with read, write, and search permission for
            the owner. User and group permissions remain unchanged.

            With the -R and -r options, in addition to regular files and
            directories, cp also copies FIFOs, character and block device
            files and symbolic links. Only superusers can copy device
            files. All other users get an error. Symbolic links are
            copied so the target points to the same location that the
            source did.

            Warning: While copying a directory tree that has device
            special files, use the -r option; otherwise, an infinite
            amount of data is read from the device special file and is
            duplicated as a special file in the destination directory
            occupying large file system space.

-e extarg
            Specifies the handling of any extent attributes of the file[s]
            to be copied. extarg takes one of the following values.

                warn   Issues a warning message if extent attributes
                            cannot be copied, but copies the file anyway.

                ignore   Does not copy the extent attributes.
                force   Fails to copy the file if the extent attribute
                            can not be copied.

Extent attributes can not be copied if the files are being copied to a file system which does not support extent attributes or if that file system has a different block size than the original. If -e is not specified, the default value for extarg is warn.

Access Control Lists (ACLs)
If new_file is a new file, or if a new file is created in dest_directory, it inherits the access control list of the original file1, file2, etc., altered to reflect any difference in ownership between the two files (see acl(5)).

EXTERNAL INFLUENCES
Environment Variables
LC_CTYPE determines the interpretation of text as single and/or multi-byte characters.

LANG and LC_CTYPE determine the local language equivalent of y (for yes/no queries).

LANG determines the language in which messages are displayed.

If LC_CTYPE is not specified in the environment or is set to the empty string, the value of LANG is used as a default for each unspecified or empty variable. If LANG is not specified or is set to the empty string, a default of "C" (see lang(5)) is used instead of LANG. If any internationalization variable contains an invalid setting, cp behaves as if all internationalization variables are set to "C". See environ(5).

International Code Set Support
Single- and multi-byte character code sets are supported.

EXAMPLES
The following command moves the directory sourcedir and its contents to a new location (targetdir) in the file system. Since cp creates the new directory, the destination directory targetdir should not already exist.

        cp -r sourcedir targetdir && rm -rf sourcedir

The -r option copies the subtree (files and subdirectories) in directory sourcedir to directory targetdir. The double ampersand (&&) causes a conditional action. If the operation on the left side of the && is successful, the right side is executed (and removes the old directory). If the operation on the left of the && is not successful, the old directory is not removed.

This example is equivalent to:

        mv sourcedir targetdir

To copy all files and directory subtrees in the current directory to an existing targetdir, use:

        cp -r * targetdir

To copy all files and directory subtrees in sourcedir to targetdir, use:

        cp -r sourcedir/* targetdir

Note that directory pathnames can precede both sourcedir and targetdir.

To create a zero-length file, use any of the following:

```
cat /dev/null >file
cp /dev/null file
touch file
```

DEPENDENCIES
   NFS
      Access control lists of networked files are summarized (as returned in
      st_mode by stat()), but not copied to the new file. When using mv or
      ln on such files, a + is not printed after the mode value when asking
      for permission to overwrite a file.

AUTHOR
      cp was developed by AT&T, the University of California, Berkeley, and
      HP.

SEE ALSO
      cpio(1), ln(1), mv(1), rm(1), link(1M), lstat(2), readlink(2),
      stat(2), symlink(2), symlink(4), acl(5).

STANDARDS CONFORMANCE
      cp: SVID2, SVID3, XPG2, XPG3, XPG4, POSIX.2

mkdir

mkdir - Make a directory.

mkdir(1)   mkdir(1)

NAME
     mkdir - make a directory

SYNOPSIS

     mkdir [-p] [-m mode] dirname ...

DESCRIPTION
     mkdir creates specified directories in mode 0777 (possibly altered by
     umask unless specified otherwise by a -m mode option (see umask(1)).
     Standard entries, . (for the directory itself) and .. (for its parent)
     are created automatically. If dirname already exists, mkdir exits
     with a diagnostic message, and the directory is not changed.

   Options
     mkdir recognizes the following command-line options:

          -m mode   After creating the directory as specified, the
                         file permissions are set to mode, which is a
                         symbolic mode string as defined for chmod (see
                         chmod(1)). The umask(1) has precedence over -m.

          -p   Intermediate directories are created as necessary.
                         Otherwise, the full path prefix of dirname must
                         already exist. mkdir requires write permission in
                         the parent directory.

                         For each directory name in the pathname prefix of
                         the dirname argument that is not the name of an
                         existing directory, the specified directory is
                         created using the current umask setting, except
                         that the equivalent of chmod u+wx is done on each
                         component to ensure that mkdir can create lower
                         directories regardless of the setting of umask.
                         Each directory name in the pathname prefix of the
                         dirname argument that matches an existing
                         directory is ignored without error. If an
                         intermediate path component exists, but has
                         permissions set to prevent writing or searching,
                         mkdir fails with an error message. If the dirname
                         argument (including pathname prefix) names an
                         existing directory, mkdir fails with an error
                         message.

                         If the -m option is used, the directory specified
                         by dirname (excluding directories in the pathname
                         prefix) is created with the permissions specified
                         by mode.

Only LINK_MAX subdirectories can be created (see limits(5)).

EXTERNAL INFLUENCES

    Environment Variables

        LANG provides a default value for the internationalization variables that are unset or null. If LANG is unset or null, the default value of "C" (see lang(5)) is used. If any of the internationalization variables contains an invalid setting, mkdir will behave as if all internationalization variables are set to "C". See environ(5).

        LC_ALL If set to a non-empty string value, overrides the values of all the other internationalization variables.

        LC_CTYPE determines the interpretation of text as single and/or multi-byte characters, the classification of characters as printable, and the characters matched by character class expressions in regular expressions.

        LC_MESSAGES determines the locale that should be used to affect the format and contents of diagnostic messages written to standard error and informative messages written to standard output.

        NLSPATH determines the location of message catalogues for the processing of LC_MESSAGES.

    International Code Set Support

        Single- and multi-byte character code sets are supported.

DIAGNOSTICS

    mkdir returns exit code 0 if all directories were successfully made. Otherwise, it prints a diagnostic and returns non-zero.

EXAMPLES

    Create directory gem beneath existing directory raw in the current directory:

        mkdir raw/gem

    Create directory path raw/gem/diamond underneath the current directory and set permissions on directory diamond to read-only for all users (a=r):

        mkdir -p -m "a=r" raw/gem/diamond

    which is equivalent to (see chmod(1)):

        mkdir -p -m 444 raw/gem/diamond

    If directories raw or raw and gem already exist, only the missing directories in the specified path are created.

SEE ALSO

    rm(1), sh(1), umask(1).

STANDARDS CONFORMANCE

    mkdir: SVID2, SVID3, XPG2, XPG3, XPG4, POSIX.2

mv

mv - Move or rename files and directories.

mv(1)   mv(1)

NAME
     mv - move or rename files and directories

SYNOPSIS
     mv [-f|-i] [-e extarg] file1 new-file

     mv [-f|-i] [-e extarg] file1 [file2 ...] dest-directory

     mv [-f|-i] [-e extarg] directory1 [directory2 ...] dest-directory

DESCRIPTION
     The mv command moves:

          - One file (file1) to a new or existing file (new-file).

          - One or more files (file1, [file2, ...]) to an existing
             directory (dest-directory).

          - One or more directory subtrees (directory1, [directory2, ...])
             to a new or existing directory (dest-directory).

     Moving file1 to new-file is used to rename a file within a directory
     or to relocate a file within a file system or across different file
     systems. When the destination is a directory, one or more files are
     moved into that directory. If two or more files are moved, the
     destination must be a directory. When moving a single file to a new
     file, if new-file exists, its contents are destroyed.

     If the access permissions of the destination dest-directory or
     existing destination file new-file forbid writing, mv asks permission
     to overwrite the file. This is done by printing the mode (see
     chmod(2) and Access Control Lists below), followed by the first
     letters of the words yes and no in the language of the current locale,
     prompting for a response, and reading one line from the standard
     input. If the response is affirmative and the action is permissible,
     the operation occurs; if not, the command proceeds to the next source
     file, if any.

     If file1 is a file and new-file is a link to another file with other
     links, the other links remain and new-file becomes a new file. If
     file1 is a file with links or a link to a file, the existing file or
     link remains intact, but the name is changed to new-file which may or
     may not be in the directory where file1 resided, depending on
     directory path names used in the mv command. The last access and
     modification times of the file or files being moved remain unchanged.

     Options
     mv recognizes the following options:

          -f   Perform mv commands without prompting for

permission. This option is assumed when the
standard input is not a terminal.

-i   Causes mv to write a prompt to standard output
before moving a file that would overwrite an
existing file. If the response from the standard
input is affirmative, the file is moved if
permissions allow the move.

-e extarg   Specifies the handling of any extent attributes of
the files(s) to be moved. extarg can be one of
the following values:

warn   Issue a warning message if extent
attributes cannot be preserved,
but move the file anyway.

ignore   Do not preserve extent
attributes.

force   Do not move the file if the
extent attributes cannot be
preserved.

If multiple source files are
specified with a single target
directory, mv will move the files
that either do not have extent
attributes or that have extent
attributes that can be preserved.
mv will not move the files if it
cannot preserve their extent
attributes.

Extent attributes cannot be preserved if the
files are being moved to a file system that
does not support extent attributes or if that
file system has a different block size than
the original. If -e is not specified, the
default value for extarg is warn.

Access Control Lists (ACLs)
If optional ACL entries are associated with new-file, mv displays a
plus sign (+) after the access mode when asking permission to
overwrite the file.

If new-file is a new file, it inherits the access control list of
file1, altered to reflect any difference in ownership between the two
files (see acl(5)).

EXTERNAL INFLUENCES
Environment Variables
LC_CTYPE determines the interpretation of text as single byte and/or
multibyte characters.

LANG and LC_CTYPE determine the local language equivalent of y (for
yes/no queries).

LANG determines the language in which messages are displayed.

If LC_CTYPE is not specified in the environment or is set to the empty
string, the value of LANG is used as a default for each unspecified or
empty variable. If LANG is not specified or is set to the empty
string, a default of C (see lang(5)) is used instead of LANG. If any
internationalization variable contains an invalid setting, mv behaves
as if all internationalization variables are set to C. See

environ(5).

International Code Set Support
Single character and multibyte character code sets are supported.

EXAMPLES
Rename a file in the current directory:

mv old-filename new-filename

Rename a directory in the current directory:

mv old-dirname new-dirname

Rename a file in the current directory whose name starts with a nonprinting control character or a character that is special to the shell, such as - and * (extra care may be required depending on the situation):

mv ./bad-filename new-filename
mv ./?bad-filename new-filename
mv ./*bad-filename new-filename

Move directory sourcedir and its contents to a new location (targetdir) in the file system (upon completion, a subdirectory named sourcedir resides in directory targetdir):

mv sourcedir targetdir

Move all files and directories (including links) in the current directory to a new location underneath targetdir:

mv * targetdir

Move all files and directories (including links) in sourcedir to a new location underneath targetdir (sourcedir and targetdir are in separate directory paths):

mv sourcedir/* targetdir

WARNINGS
If file1 and new-file exist on different file systems, mv copies the file and deletes the original. In this case the mover becomes the owner and any linking relationship with other files is lost. mv cannot carry hard links across file systems. If file1 is a directory, mv copies the entire directory structure onto the destination file system and deletes the original.

mv cannot be used to perform the following operations:

- Rename either the current working directory or its parent directory using the . or .. notation.

- Rename a directory to a new name identical to the name of a file contained in the same parent directory.

DEPENDENCIES
    NFS
        Access control lists of networked files are summarized (as returned in
        st_mode by stat(2)), but not copied to the new file. When using mv on
        such files, a + is not printed after the mode value when asking for
        permission to overwrite a file.

AUTHOR
        mv was developed by AT&T, the University of California, Berkeley and
        HP.

SEE ALSO
        cp(1), cpio(1), ln(1), rm(1), link(1M), lstat(2), readlink(2),
        stat(2), symlink(2), symlink(4), acl(5).

STANDARDS CONFORMANCE
        mv: SVID2, SVID3, XPG2, XPG3, XPG4, POSIX.2

pwd

pwd - Present working directory name.

```
pwd(1)                                                                    pwd(1)

NAME
     pwd - working directory name

SYNOPSIS

     pwd

DESCRIPTION
     pwd prints the path name of the working (current) directory.

EXTERNAL INFLUENCES
   Environment Variables
     LC_MESSAGES determines the language in which messages are displayed.

     If LC_MESSAGES is not specified in the environment or is set to the
     empty string, the value of LANG is used as a default for each
     unspecified or empty variable.  If LANG is not specified or is set to
     the empty string, a default of "C" (see lang(5)) is used instead of
     LANG.

     If any internationalization variable contains an invalid setting, pwd
     behaves as if all internationalization variables are set to "C".  See
     environ(5).

   International Code Set Support
     Single- and multi-byte character code sets are supported.

DIAGNOSTICS
     Cannot open ..

     Read error in ..
          Possible file system trouble; contact system administrator.

     pwd: cannot access parent directories
          Current directory has been removed (usually by a different
          process).  Use cd command to move to a valid directory (see
          cd(1)).

EXAMPLES
     This command lists the path of the current working directory.  If your
     home directory were /mnt/staff and the command cd camp/nevada were
     executed from the home directory, typing pwd would produce the
     following:

          /mnt/staff/camp/nevada
```

AUTHOR
     pwd was developed by AT&T and HP.

SEE ALSO
     cd(1).

STANDARDS CONFORMANCE
     pwd: SVID2, SVID3, XPG2, XPG3, XPG4, POSIX.2

rm

rm - Remove files or directories.

rm(1)   rm(1)

NAME
     rm - remove files or directories

SYNOPSIS

     rm [-f|-i] [-Rr] file ...

DESCRIPTION
     The rm command removes the entries for one or more files from a
     directory. If an entry was the last link to the file, the file is
     destroyed. Removal of a file requires write and search (execute)
     permission in its directory, but no permissions on the file itself.
     However, if the sticky bit is set on the directory containing the
     file, only the owner of the file, the owner of the directory, or a
     user having appropriate privileges can remove the file.

     If a user does not have write permission for a file to be removed and
     standard input is a terminal, a prompt containing the file name and
     its permissions is printed requesting that the removal of the file be
     confirmed (see Access Control Lists below). A line is then read from
     standard input. If that line begins with y the file is deleted;
     otherwise, the file remains. No questions are asked when the -f
     option is given or if standard input is not a terminal.

     If file is of type directory, and the -f option is not specified, and
     either the permissions of file do not permit writing and standard
     input is a terminal or the -i option is specified, rm writes a prompt
     to standard error and reads a line from standard input. If the
     response does not begin with y, it does nothing more with the current
     file and goes on to any remaining files.

     Options
     rm recognizes the following options:

          -f   Force each file or directory to be removed without prompting
               for confirmation, regardless of the permissions of the
               entry. This option also suppresses diagnostic messages
               regarding nonexistent operands.

               This option does not suppress any diagnostic messages other
               than those regarding nonexistent operands. To suppress all
               error message and interactive prompts, the -f option should
               be used while redirecting standard error output to
               /dev/null.

               This option ignores any previous occurrence of the -i
               option.

          -i   Write a prompt to standard error requesting confirmation
               before removing each entry.

This option ignores any previous occurrence of the -f option.

-R   For each argument that is a directory, this option causes rm to recursively delete the entire contents of that directory before removing the directory itself. When used in conjunction with the -i option, rm asks whether to examine each directory before interactively removing files in that directory and again afterward to confirm removing the directory itself.

The -R option will descend to arbitrary depths in a file hierarchy and will not fail due to path length limitations unless the length of file name, file specified by the user exceeds system limitations.

-r   Equivalent to -R.

Access Control Lists
   If a file has optional ACL entries, rm displays a plus sign (+) after the file's permissions. The permissions shown summarize the file's st_mode value returned by stat() (see stat(2)). See also acl(5).

EXTERNAL INFLUENCES
   Environment Variables
      LANG provides a default value for the internationalization variables that are unset or null. If LANG is unset or null, the default value of "C" (see lang(5)) is used. If any of the internationalization variables contains an invalid setting, rm will behave as if all internationalization variables are set to "C". See environ(5).

      LC_ALL If set to a non-empty string value, overrides the values of all the other internationalization variables.

      LC_CTYPE determines the interpretation of file names as single and/or multi-byte characters, the classification of characters as printable, and the characters matched by character class expressions in regular expressions.

      LC_MESSAGES determines the locale that should be used to affect the format and contents of diagnostic messages written to standard error and informative messages written to standard output.

      NLSPATH determines the location of message catalogues for the processing of LC_MESSAGES.

   International Code Set Support
      Single- and multibyte character code sets are supported.

DIAGNOSTICS
   Generally self-explanatory. Note that the -f option does not suppress all diagnostic messages.

   It is forbidden to remove the file .., in order to avoid the consequences of using a command such as:

        rm -r .*

   If a designated file is a directory, an error comment is printed unless the -R or -r option is used.

EXAMPLES
   Remove files with a prompt for verification:

        rm -i file1 file2

Remove all the files in a directory:

    rm -i mydirectory/*

Note that the previous command removes files only, and does not remove any directories in mydirectory.

Remove a file in the current directory whose name starts with - or * or some other character that is special to the shell:

    rm ./-filename
    rm *filename
    etc.

Remove a file in the current directory whose name starts with some strange (usually nonprinting, invisible) character or perhaps has spaces at the beginning or end of the filename, prompting for confirmation:

    rm -i *filename*

If *filename* is not unique in the directory, enter n when each of the other files is prompted.

A powerful and dangerous command to remove a directory is:

    rm -fR directoryname

or

    rm -Rf directoryname

which removes all files and directories from directoryname without any prompting for verification to remove the files or the directories. This command should only be used when you are absolutely certain that all the files and directories in directoryname as well as directoryname itself are to be removed.

DEPENDENCIES
  NFS
    rm does not display a plus sign (+) to indicate the existence of optional access control list entries when asking for confirmation before removing a networked file.

SEE ALSO
    rmdir(1), unlink(2), acl(5).

STANDARDS CONFORMANCE
    rm: SVID2, SVID3, XPG2, XPG3, XPG4, POSIX.2

rmdir

rmdir - Remove directories.

```
rmdir(1)                                                          rmdir(1)

NAME
     rmdir - remove directories

SYNOPSIS

     rmdir [-f|-i] [-p] dir ...

DESCRIPTION
     rmdir removes the directory entry for each dir operand that refers to
     an empty directory.

     Directories are removed in the order specified.  Consequently, if a
     directory and a subdirectory of that directory are both specified as
     arguments, the subdirectory must be specified before the parent
     directory so that the parent directory will be empty when rmdir tries
     to remove it.  Removal of a directory requires write and search
     (execute) permission in its parent directory, but no permissions on
     the directory itself; but if the sticky bit is set on the parent
     directory, only the owner of the directory, the owner of the parent
     directory, or a user having appropriate privileges can remove the
     directory.

     Options
     rmdir recognizes the following options:

          -f   Force each directory to be removed without prompting for
               confirmation, regardless of the presence of the -i option.
               This option also suppresses diagnostic messages regarding
               non-existent operands.

               This option does not suppress any diagnostic messages other
               than those regarding non-existent operands.  To suppress all
               error message and interactive prompts, the -f option should
               be used while redirecting the standard error output to
               /dev/null.

               This option ignores any previous occurrence of the -i
               option.

          -i   Write a prompt to the standard error output requesting
               confirmation before removing each directory.

               This option ignores any previous occurrence of the -f
               option.

          -p   Path removal.  If, after removing a directory with more than
               one pathname component, the parent directory of that
               directory is now empty, rmdir removes the empty parent
               directory.  This continues until rmdir encounters a non-
               empty parent directory, or until all components of the
```

original pathname have been removed.

When used in conjunction with the -i option, rmdir asks whether to remove each directory component of a path.

EXTERNAL INFLUENCES
    Environment Variables
        LANG provides a default value for the internationalization variables that are unset or null. If LANG is unset or null, the default value of "C" (see lang(5)) is used. If any of the internationalization variables contains an invalid setting, rmdir will behave as if all internationalization variables are set to "C". See environ(5).

        LC_ALL If set to a non-empty string value, overrides the values of all the other internationalization variables.

        LC_CTYPE determines the interpretation of dir names as single and/or multi-byte characters, the classification of characters as printable, and the characters matched by character class expressions in regular expressions.

        LC_MESSAGES determines the locale that should be used to affect the format and contents of diagnostic messages written to standard error and informative messages written to standard output.

        NLSPATH determines the location of message catalogues for the processing of LC_MESSAGES.

    International Code Set Support
        Single- and multi-byte character code sets are supported.

DIAGNOSTICS
        Generally self-explanatory. Note that the -f option does not suppress all diagnostic messages.

EXAMPLES
        To remove directories with a prompt for verification:

                rmdir -i directories

        To remove as much as possible of a path, type:

                rmdir -p component1/component2/dir

SEE ALSO
        rm(1), rmdir(2), stat(2).

STANDARDS CONFORMANCE
        rmdir: SVID2, XPG2, XPG3, XPG4

CHAPTER 17

Viewing Files - Redirection, cat, more, pg, head, and tail Commands

First Things First

Before we can get into any serious work with UNIX commands, we'll cover a few different ways to view files in this chapter. Many of the commands covered in this chapter for viewing files will be used in many chapters throughout the book.

Another topic important to many of the UNIX commands to be covered as well as viewing files is redirection. In this chapter, we'll see some commonly used redirection techniques and then some methonds of viewing files. In fact, the very first viewing command that is covered in this chapter uses redirection, so it's important that you understand the basics of redirection before proceeding further. Here's what we'll cover in this chapter:

- Redirection
- **cat**, **more**, **pg**, **head**, and **tail** commands for viewing files

Redirection

Before we cover viewing files, let's talk about redirection for a minute because I use some redirection in the upcoming section. I cover redirection under shell programming, but for now, I want to give you just a quick introduction to redirection so that we can more effectively cover some of the commands in this chapter.

UNIX is set up such that commands usually take their input from the keyboard, often called *standard input*, and usually send their output to the screen, often called *standard output*. Commands also send error information to the screen. It is not always desirable for input to come from standard input and output and errors to go to standard output. You are given a lot of control to override these defaults. This is called redirection. Table 17-1 shows many common forms of redirection.

As shown in the table, to redirect the output of a command from standard output to a file, you would use ">". This works almost all of the time. If you have an environment variable called **noclobber** set, then redirecting to an existing file does not work (we'll cover environment variables shortly). The **noclobber** does not permit redirection to write over an existing file. If you try to write over an existing file, such as **/tmp/processes** below, you receive a message that the file exists:

man page

ps - 13

```
#  ps  -ef  >  /tmp/processes
/tmp/processes:  File exists
```

You can, however, use a "!" with redirection to force a file to be overwritten. Using ">!" forces a file to be overwritten, and ">>!" will force the output to be appended to the end of an existing file. Examples of these are shown in Table 17-1.

TABLE 17-1   Commonly Used Redirection Forms

Command or Assignment	Example	Description
<	**wc -l < .login**	Standard input redirection: execute **wc** (word count) and list number of lines (**-l**) in **.login**
>	**ps -ef > /tmp/processes**	Standard output redirection: execute **ps** and send output to file **/tmp/processes**
>>	**ps -ef >> /tmp/processes**	Append standard output: execute **ps** and append output to the end of file **/tmp/processes**
>!	**ps -ef >! /tmp/processes**	Append output redirection and override **noclobber**: write over **/tmp/processes**, even if it exists
>>!	**ps -ef >>! /tmp/processes**	Append standard output and override **noclobber**: append to the end of **/tmp/processes**
| (pipe)	**ps | wc -l**	Run **ps** and use the result as input to **wc**
0 - standard input **1** - standard output **2** - standard error	**cat program 2> errors**	**cat** the file **program** to standard output and redirect errors to the file **errors**
	cat program 2>> errors	**cat** the file **program** to standard output and append errors to the file **errors**
	find / -name '*.c' -print > cprograms 2>errors	**find** all files on the system ending in **.c** and place the list of files in **cprograms** in the current working directory and send all errors (file descriptor 2) to the file **errors** in current working directory
	find / -name '*.c' -print > cprograms 2>&1	**find** all files on the system ending in **.c**, place the list of files in **cprograms** in the current working directory, and send all errors (file descriptor 2) to same place as file descriptor 1 (**cprograms**)

Using the symbols shown in Table 17-1, you can redirect from *standard input* and *standard output*. For instance, rather than display the output on the screen, you can send the output to file. We will use some of these redirection forms in upcoming examples.

Viewing Files with cat, more, pg, head, and tail

To begin with, let's look at a long file. In fact, let's look at a file so long that it will not fit on your screen if you were to print out the contents of the file to your screen.

The **cat** command (short for concatenate) does just this; it prints out the file to your screen. If, however, the file is long, then you will only see the end of the file on your screen. Remember the user *denise* from earlier in the book? She had a lot of files in her directory. Let's list the files in her directory and redirect the output to a file called **listing** with the following command:

```
$ ls -a /home/denise > listing
```

When we **cat listing** to the screen, we see only the end of the file, as shown in Figure 17-1. We know that this is the end of the file because I have issued **cat** with the *-n* option which includes line numbers. The line numbers indicate that this is not the beginning of the file.

```
┌─────────────────────────────────────────────────────────────────┐
│ ─                           cat -n example                    ▫ □ │
├─────────────────────────────────────────────────────────────────┤
│      106   rclock.exe                                             │
│      107   rkhelp.exe                                             │
│      108   sb.txt                                                 │
│      109   shellupd.exe                                           │
│      110   smsup2.exe                                             │
│      111   softinit.remotesoftcm                                  │
│      112   srvpr.exe                                              │
│      113   tabnd1.exe                                             │
│      114   target.exe                                             │
│      115   tcp41a.exe                                             │
│      116   tnds2.exe                                              │
│      117   trace.TRC1                                             │
│      118   trace.TRC1.Z.uue                                       │
│      119   upgrade.exe                                            │
│      120   uue.syntax                                             │
│      121   v103.txt                                               │
│      122   whoon                                                  │
│      123   win95app.exe                                           │
│      124   wsdrv1.exe                                             │
│      125   wsos21.exe                                             │
│      126   wsos22.exe                                             │
│      127   wsos23.exe                                             │
│      128   xferp110.zip                                           │
│ $ ▄                                                               │
└─────────────────────────────────────────────────────────────────┘
```

Figure 17-1   **cat -n** Command

Seeing only the end of this file is not what we had in mind. Using **pg** (for page), we see one screen at time, as shown in Figure 17-2:

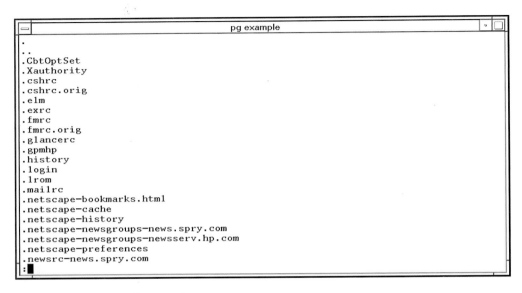

Figure 17-2   **pg** Command

The **more** command produces the same output as **pg,** as shown in Figure 17-3:

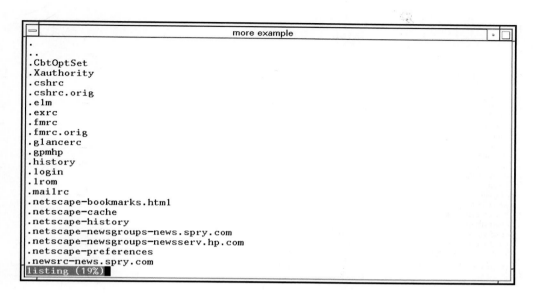

Figure 17-3   **more** Command

This is more like it; now we can scroll on a screen-by-screen basis with both **pg** and **more**. However, sometimes you want to view only the beginning or end of a file. You can use the **head** command to view the beginning of a file and the **tail** command to view the end of a file. The following two examples of **head** and **tail** (see Figures 17-4 and 17-5) show viewing the first 20 lines of **listing** and the last 20 lines of **listing**, respectively:

man page

more - 17

man page

head - 17

man page

tail - 17

man page

pg - 17

```
┌──────────────────────────────────────────────────────────────────────────────┐
│ ▭                              head example                              ▫  ▢  │
├──────────────────────────────────────────────────────────────────────────────┤
│ $ head -20 listing                                                             │
│ .                                                                              │
│ ..                                                                             │
│ .CbtOptSet                                                                     │
│ .Xauthority                                                                    │
│ .cshrc                                                                         │
│ .cshrc.orig                                                                    │
│ .elm                                                                           │
│ .exrc                                                                          │
│ .fmrc                                                                          │
│ .fmrc.orig                                                                     │
│ .glancerc                                                                      │
│ .gpmhp                                                                         │
│ .history                                                                       │
│ .login                                                                         │
│ .lrom                                                                          │
│ .mailrc                                                                        │
│ .netscape-bookmarks.html                                                       │
│ .netscape-cache                                                                │
│ .netscape-history                                                              │
│ .netscape-newsgroups-news.spry.com                                             │
│ $ █                                                                            │
└──────────────────────────────────────────────────────────────────────────────┘
```

Figure 17-4   head Command

```
┌──────────────────────────────────────────────────────────────────────────────┐
│ ▭                              tail example                              ▫  ▢  │
├──────────────────────────────────────────────────────────────────────────────┤
│ $ tail -20 listing                                                             │
│ shellupd.exe                                                                   │
│ smsup2.exe                                                                     │
│ softinit.remotesoftcm                                                          │
│ srvpr.exe                                                                      │
│ tabnd1.exe                                                                     │
│ target.exe                                                                     │
│ tcp41a.exe                                                                     │
│ tnds2.exe                                                                      │
│ trace.TRC1                                                                     │
│ trace.TRC1.Z.uue                                                               │
│ upgrade.exe                                                                    │
│ uue.syntax                                                                     │
│ v103.txt                                                                       │
│ whoon                                                                          │
│ win95app.exe                                                                   │
│ wsdrv1.exe                                                                     │
│ wsos21.exe                                                                     │
│ wsos22.exe                                                                     │
│ wsos23.exe                                                                     │
│ xferp110.zip                                                                   │
│ $ █                                                                            │
└──────────────────────────────────────────────────────────────────────────────┘
```

Figure 17-5   tail Command

The command you use depends on the information you wish to display. My personal preference, whether viewing the contents of a large file or a long listing of files, is to use **more**. I don't have a good reason for this, and all I can say is that we are creatures of habit and I have always used **more**. The following are command summaries for **cat**, **pg**, **more**, **head**, and **tail**. I included some of the most frequently used options associated with these commands. Because none of the commands are difficult to use, I suggest that you try each command and see whether one suits your needs better than the others.

Here are summaries of the **cat, pg** (not available on all UNIX variants,) **more, head,** and **tail** commands.

cat - Display, combine, append, copy, or create files.

Options

-	Used as a substitute for specifying a file name when you want to use the keyboard for standard input.
-n	Line numbers are displayed along with output lines.
-p	Replace multiple consecutive empty lines with only one empty line.
-s	This is silent mode, which suppresses information about nonexistent files.
-u	Output is unbuffered, which means that it is handled character by character.
-v	Print most non-printing characters visibly.

pg - Display all or parts of a file.

Options

-number	The number of lines you wish to display.
-p string	Use *string* to specify a prompt.
-c	Clear the screen before displaying the next page of the file.

| -f | Don't split lines being displayed. |
| -n | A command is issued as soon as a command letter is typed, rather than having to issue a new line character. |

more - Display all or parts of a file one screen at a time.

Options

-c	Clear the screen before displaying the next page of the file.
-d	Display a prompt at the bottom of the screen with brief instructions.
-f	Wrap text to fit the screen and judge page length accordingly.
-n	The number of lines in the display window is set to *n*.
-s	Squeeze multiple consecutive empty lines onto one empty line.

head - Provide only the first few lines of a file.

Options

-c	The output is produced with a specified number of bytes.
-l	The output is produced with a specified number of lines. This is the default.
-n count	The number of bytes or lines is specified by *count*. You can also use -count to specify the number of bytes or lines, which is shown in the example. The default count is 10.

tail - Provide the last few lines of a file.

man page

tail - 17

Options

-bnumber	Specify the number of blocks from the end of the file you wish to begin displaying.
-cnumber	Specify the number of characters from the end of the file you wish to begin displaying.
-nnumber	Specify the number of lines from the end of the file you wish to begin displaying. You can also specify a number or minus sign and number, as shown in the example, to specify the number of lines from the end of file to begin displaying.

Manual Pages for Some Commands Used in Chapter 17

The following are the HP-UX manual pages for many of the commands used in the chapter. Commands often differ among UNIX variants, so you may find differences in the options or other areas for some commands; however, the following manual pages serve as an excellent reference.

cat

cat - Concatenate files.

cat(1)   cat(1)

NAME
     cat - concatenate, copy, and print files

SYNOPSIS

     cat [-benrstuv] file ...

DESCRIPTION
     cat reads each file in sequence and writes it on the standard output.
     Thus:

          cat file

     prints file on the default standard output device;

          cat file1 file2 > file3

     concatenates file1 and file2, and places the result in file3.

     If - is appears as a file argument, cat uses standard input. To
     combine standard input and other files, use a combination of - and
     file arguments.

  Options
     cat recognizes the following options:

          -b   Omit line numbers from blank lines when -n option is
               specified. If this option is specified, the -n option is
               automatically selected.

          -e   Print a $ character at the end of each line (prior to the
               new-line). If this option is specified, the -v option is
               automatically selected.

          -n   Display output lines preceded by line numbers, numbered
               sequentially from 1.

          -r   Replace multiple consecutive empty lines with one empty
               line, so that there is never more than one empty line
               between lines containing characters.

          -s   Silent option. cat suppresses error messages about non-
               existent files, identical input and output, and write
               errors. Normally, input and output files cannot have
               identical names unless the file is a special file.

          -t   Print each tab character as ^I. If this option is
               specified, the -v option is automatically selected.

          -u   Do not buffer output (handle character-by-character).
               Normally, output is buffered.

-v　　Cause non-printing characters (with the exception of tabs,
new-lines and form-feeds) to be printed visibly. Control
characters are printed using the form ^X (Ctrl-X), and the
DEL character (octal 0177) is printed as ^? (see ascii(5)).
Single-byte control characters whose most significant bit is
set, are printed using the form M-^x, where x is the
character specified by the seven low order bits. All other
non-printing characters are printed as M-x, where x is the
character specified by the seven low order bits. This
option is influenced by the LC_CTYPE environment variable
and its corresponding code set.

EXTERNAL INFLUENCES
　　Environment Variables
　　　　LANG provides a default value for the internationalization variables
　　　　that are unset or null. If LANG is unset or null, the default value of
　　　　"C" (see lang(5)) is used. If any of the internationalization
　　　　variables contains an invalid setting, cat will behave as if all
　　　　internationalization variables are set to "C". See environ(5).

　　　　LC_ALL If set to a non-empty string value, overrides the values of all
　　　　the other internationalization variables.

　　　　LC_CTYPE determines the interpretation of text as single and/or
　　　　multi-byte characters, the classification of characters as printable,
　　　　and the characters matched by character class expressions in regular
　　　　expressions.

　　　　LC_MESSAGES determines the locale that should be used to affect the
　　　　format and contents of diagnostic messages written to standard error
　　　　and informative messages written to standard output.

　　　　NLSPATH determines the location of message catalogues for the
　　　　processing of LC_MESSAGES.

　　International Code Set Support
　　　　Single- and multi-byte character code sets are supported.

RETURN VALUE
　　Exit values are:

　　　　0　　　　Successful completion.
　　　　>0　　　Error condition occurred.

EXAMPLES
　　To create a zero-length file, use any of the following:

　　　　cat /dev/null > file
　　　　cp /dev/null file
　　　　touch file

　　The following prints ^I for all the occurrences of tab character in
　　file1

　　　　cat -t file1

　　To suppress error messages about files that do not exist, use:

　　　　cat -s file1 file2 file3 > file

　　If file2 does not exist, the above command concatenates file1 and
　　file3 without reporting the error on file2. The result is the same if
　　-s option is not used, except that cat displays the error message.

To view non-printable characters in file2, use:

        cat -v file2

WARNINGS
    Command formats such as

        cat file1 file2 > file1

    overwrites the data in file1 before the concatenation begins, thus
    destroying the file. Therefore, be careful when using shell special
    characters.

SEE ALSO
    cp(1), more(1), pg(1), pr(1), rmnl(1), ssp(1).

STANDARDS CONFORMANCE
    cat: SVID2, SVID3, XPG2, XPG3, XPG4, POSIX.2

head

man page

head - 17

head - Show first few lines of a file.

```
head(1)                                                           head(1)

NAME
      head - give first few lines

SYNOPSIS

      head [-c|-l] [-n count] [file ...]

      Obsolescent:
      head [-count] [file ...]

DESCRIPTION
      head prints on standard output the first count lines of each of the
      specified files, or of the standard input.  If count is omitted it
      defaults to 10.

      If multiple files are specified, head outputs before each file a line
      of this form:

          ==> file <==

   Options
      -c           The quantity of output is measured in bytes.

      -count       The number of units of output.  This option is provided
                   for backward compatibility (see -n below) and is
                   mutually exclusive of all other options.

      -l           The quantity of output is measured in lines; this is
                   the default.

      -n count     The number of lines (default) or bytes output.  count
                   is an unsigned decimal integer.  If -n (or -count) is
                   not given, the default quantity is 10.  This option
                   provides the same functionality as the -count option,
                   but in a more standard way.  Use of the -n option is
                   recommended where portability between systems is
                   important.

EXTERNAL INFLUENCES
   Environment Variables
      LC_CTYPE determines the interpretation of text within file as single
      and/or multi-byte characters.
```

LC_MESSAGES determines the language in which messages are displayed.

If LC_CTYPE or LC_MESSAGES is not specified in the environment or is set to the empty string, the value of LANG is used as a default for each unspecified or empty variable. If LANG is not specified or is set to the empty string, a default of "C" (see lang(5)) is used instead of LANG.

If any internationalization variable contains an invalid setting, head behaves as if all internationalization variables are set to "C". See environ(5).

International Code Set Support
Single- and multi-byte character code sets are supported.

SEE ALSO
tail(1).

STANDARDS CONFORMANCE
head: SVID3, XPG4, POSIX.2

more

man page

more - 17

more - File-viewing filter.

---

more(1)   more(1)

NAME
     more, page - file perusal filter for crt viewing

SYNOPSIS

     more [-n] [-cdefisuvz] [-n number] [-p command] [-t tagstring] [-x
     tabs] [-W option] [+linenumber] [+/pattern] [name ...]

     page [-n] [-cdefisuvz] [-n number] [-p command] [-t tagstring] [-x
     tabs] [-W option] [+linenumber] [+/pattern] [name ...]

REMARKS:
     pg is preferred in some standards and has some added functionality,
     but does not support character highlighting (see pg(1)).

DESCRIPTION
     more is a filter for examining continuous text, one screenful at a
     time, on a soft-copy terminal. It is quite similar to pg, and is
     retained primarily for backward compatibility. more normally pauses
     after each screenful, printing the filename at the bottom of the
     screen. To display one more line, press <Return>. To display another
     screenful press <Space>. Other possibilities are described later.

     more and page differ only slightly. more scrolls the screen upward as
     it prints the next page. page clears the screen and prints a new
     screenful of text when it prints a new page. Both provide one line of
     overlap between screenfuls.

     name can be a filename or -, specifying standard input. more
     processes file arguments in the order given.

     more supports the Basic Regular Expression syntax (see regexp(5)).

     more recognizes the following command line options:

          -n number   Set the number of lines in the display window to
                         number, a positive decimal integer. The default
                         is one line less than the the number of lines
                         displayed by the terminal; on a screen that
                         displays 24 lines, the default is 23. The -n flag
                         overrides any values obtained from the
                         environment.

          -n   Same as -n number except that the number of lines
                         is set to n.

          -c   Draw each page by beginning at the top of the
                         screen, and erase each line just before drawing on
                         it. This avoids scrolling the screen, making it
                         easier to read while more is writing. This option

	is ignored if the terminal has no clear-to-end-of-line capability.
-d	Prompt user with the message Press space to continue, q to quit, h for help at the end of each screenful. This is useful if more is being used as a filter in some setting, such as a training class, where many users might be unsophisticated.
-e	Exit immediately after writing the last line of the last file in the argument list
-f	Count logical lines, rather than screen lines. That is, long lines are not folded. This option is recommended if nroff output is being piped through ul, since the latter can generate escape sequences. These escape sequences contain characters that would ordinarily occupy screen positions, but which do not print when sent to the terminal as part of an escape sequence. Thus more might assume lines are longer than they really are, and fold lines erroneously.
-i	Perform pattern matching in searches without regard to case.
-s	Squeeze multiple blank lines from the output, producing only one blank line. Especially helpful when viewing nroff output, this option maximizes the useful information present on the screen.
-u	Normally, more handles underlining and bold such as produced by nroff in a manner appropriate to the particular terminal: if the terminal supports underlining or has a highlighting (usually inverse-video) mode, more outputs appropriate escape sequences to enable underlining, else highlighting mode, for underlined information in the source file. If the terminal supports highlighting, more uses that mode information that should be printed in boldface type. The -u option suppresses this processing, as do the "ul" and "os" terminfo flags.
-v	Do not display nonprinting characters graphically; by default, all non-ASCII and control characters (except <Tab>, <Backspace>, and <Return>) are displayed visibly in the form ^X for <Ctrl-x>, or M-x for non-ASCII character x.
-z	Same as not specifying -v, with the exception of displaying <Backspace> as ^H, <Return> as ^M, and <Tab> as ^I.
-p command	Execute the more command initially in the command argument for each file examined. If the command is a positioning command, such as a line number or a regular expression search, sets the current position to represent the final results of the command, without writing any intermediate lines of the file. If the positioning command is unsuccessful, the first line in the file is the current position.
-t tagstring	Write the screenful of the file containing the tag

named by the tagstring argument. The specified
tag appears in the current position. If both -p
and -t options are specified, more processes -t
first; that is, the file containing the tagstring
is selected by -t and then the command is
executed.

-x tabs
Set the tabstops every tabs position. The default
value for the tabs argument is 8.

-W option
Provides optional extensions to the more command.
Currently, the following two options are
supported:

notite
Prevents more from sending the terminal
initialization string before displaying the
file. This argument also prevents more from
sending the terminal de-initialization string
before exiting.

tite
Causes more to send the initialization and
de-initialization strings. This is the
default.

+linenumber
Start listing such that the current position
is set to linenumber.

+/pattern
Start listing such that the current position
is set to the line matching the regular
expression pattern.

The number of lines available per screen is determined by the -n
option, if present or by examining values in the environment. The
actual number of lines written is one less than this number, as the
last line of the screen is used to write a user prompt and user input.

The number of columns available per line is determined by examining
values in the environment. more writes lines containing more
characters than would fit into this number of columns by breaking the
line into one more logical lines where each of these lines but the
last contains the number of characters needed to fill the columns.
The logical lines are written independently of each other; that is,
commands affecting a single line affect them separately.

While determining the number of lines and the number of columns, if
the methods described above do not yield any number then more uses
terminfo descriptor files (see term(4)). If this also fails then the
number of lines is set to 24 and the number of columns to 80.

When standard output is a terminal and -u is not specified, more
treats backspace characters and carriage-return characters specially.

- A character, followed first by a backspace character, then by
  an underscore (_), causes that character to be written as
  underlined text, if the terminal supports that. An underscore,
  followed first by a backspace character, then any character,
  also causes that character to be written as underlined text,
  if the terminal supports that.

- A backspace character that appears between two identical
  printable characters causes the first of those two characters
  to be written as emboldened text, if the terminal type
  supports that, and the second to be discarded. Immediately
  subsequent occurrences of backspaces/character pairs for that

same character is also discarded.

- Other backspace character sequences is written directly to the terminal, which generally causes the character preceding the backspace character to be suppressed in the display.

- A carriage-return character at the end of a line is ignored, rather than being written as a control character.

If the standard output is not a terminal device, more always exits when it reaches end-of-file on the last file in its argument list. Otherwise, for all files but the last, more prompts, with an indication that it has reached the end of file, along with the name of the next file. For the last file specified, or for the standard input if no file is specified, more prompts, indicating end-fo-file, and accept additional commands. If the next command specifies forward scrolling, more will exit. If the -e option is specified, more will exit immediately after writing the last line of the last file.

more uses the environment variable MORE to preset any flags desired. The MORE variable thus sets a string containing flags and arguments, preceded with hyphens and blank-character-separated as on the command line. Any command-line flags or arguments are processed after those in the MORE variable, as if the command line were as follows:

    more $MORE flags arguments

For example, to view files using the -c mode of operation, the shell command sequence

    MORE='-c' ; export MORE or the csh command

    setenv MORE -c

causes all invocations of more, including invocations by programs such as man and msgs, to use this mode. The command sequence that sets up the MORE environment variable is usually placed in the .profile or .cshrc file.

In the following descriptions, the current position refers to two things:

- the position of the current line on the screen

- the line number (in the file) of the current line on the screen

The line on the screen corresponding to the current position is the third line on the screen. If this is not possible (there are fewer than three lines to display or this is the first page of the file, or it is the last page of the file), then the current position is either the first or last line on the screen.

Other sequences that can be typed when more pauses, and their effects, are as follows (i is an optional integer argument, defaulting to 1):

```
i<Return>
ij
i<Ctrl-e>
i<Space>          Scroll forward i lines. The default i for <Space>
                  is one screenful; for j and <Return> it is one
                  line. The entire i lines are written, even if i is
                  more than the screen size. At end-of-file,
                  <Return> causes more to continue with the next
                  file in the list, or exits if the current file is
                  the last file in the list.
```

id i`<Ctrl-d>`	Scroll forward i lines, with a default of one half of the screen size. If i is specified, it becomes the new default for subsequent d and u commands.
iu i`<Ctrl-u>`	Scrolls backward i lines, with a default of one half of the screen size. If i is specified, it becomes the new default for subsequent d and u commands.
ik i`<Ctrl-y>`	Scrolls backward i lines, with a default of one line. The entire i lines are written, even if i is more than the screen size.
iz	Display i more lines and sets the new window (screenful) size to i .
ig	Go to line i in the file, with a default of 1 (beginning of file). Scroll or rewrite the screen so that the line is at the current position. If i is not specified, then more displays the first screenful in the file.
iG	Go to line i in the file, with a default of the end of the file. If i is not specified, scrolls or rewrites screen so that the last line in the file is at the bottom of the screen. If i is specified, scrolls or rewrites the screen so that the line is at the current position.
is	Skip forward i lines, with a default of 1, and write the next screenful beginning at that point. If i would cause the current position to be such that less than one screenful would be written, the last screenful in the file is written.
if i`<Ctrl-f>`	Move forward i lines, with a default of one screenful. At end-of-file, more will continue with the next file in the list, or exit if the current file is the last file in the list.
ib i`<Ctrl-b>`	Move backward i lines, with a default of one screenful. If i is more than the screen size, only the final screenful will be written.
q, Q, :q, :Q, ZZ	Exit from more.
= :f `<Ctrl-g>`	Write the name of the file currently being examined, the number relative to the total number of files there are to examine, the current line number, the current byte number, and the total bytes to write and what percentage of the file precedes the current position. All of these items reference the first byte of the line after the last line written.
v	Invoke an editor to edit the current file being examined. The name of the editor is taken from the

environment variable EDITOR, or default to vi. If
EDITOR represents either vi or ex, the editor is
invoked with options such that the current editor
line is the physical line corresponding to the
current position in more at the time of the
invocation.

When the editor exits, more resumes on the current
file by rewriting the screen with the current line
as the current position.

h   Display a description of all the more commands.

i/[!]expression

Search forward in the file for the i-th line
containing the regular expression expression. The
default value for i is 1. The search starts at the
line following the current position. If the
search is successful, the screen is modified so
that the searched-for line is in the current
position. The null regular expression (/<Return>)
repeats the search using the previous regular
expression. If the character ! is included, the
lines for searching are those that do not contain
expression.

If there are less than i occurrences of
expression, and the input is a file rather than a
pipe, then the position in the file remains
unchanged.

The user's erase and kill characters can be used
to edit the regular expression. Erasing back past
the first column cancels the search command.

i?[!]expression

Same as /, but searches backward in the file for
the i th line containing the regular expression
expression.

in   Repeat the previous search for the i-th line
(default 1) containing the last expression (or not
containing the last expression, if the previous
search was /! or ?!).

iN   Repeat the search for the opposite direction of
the previous search for the i-th line (default 1)
containing the last expression

''   (single quotes) Return to the position from which
the last large movement command was executed (
"large movement" is defined as any movement of
more than a screenful of lines). If no such
movements have been made, return to the beginning
of the file.

!command   Invoke a shell with command. The characters % and
! in command are replaced with the current file
name and the previous shell command, respectively.
If there is no current file name, % is not
expanded. The sequences \% and \! are replaced by
% and ! respectively.

:e [file]
E [file]   Examine a new file. If the file argument is not
specified, the "current" file (see the :n and :p

commands) from the list of files in the command line is re-examined. The filename is subjected to the process of shell word expansions. If file is a # (number sign) character, the previously examined file is re-examined.

i:n   Examine the next file. If i is specified, examines the i-th next file specified in the command line.

i:p   Examine the previous file. If a number i is specified, examines the i-th previous file specified in the command line.

:t tagstring   Go to the supplied tagstring and scroll or rewrite the screen with that line in the current position.

m letter   Mark the current position with the specified letter, where letter represents the name of one of the lower-case letters of the portable character set.

' letter   Return to the position that was previously marked with the specified letter, making that line the current position.

r
<Ctrl-l>   Refresh the screen.

R   Refresh the screen, discarding any buffered input.

The commands take effect immediately; i.e., it is not necessary to press <Return>. Up to the time when the command character itself is given, the line-kill character can be used to cancel the numerical argument being formed.

If the standard output is not a teletype, more is equivalent to cat(1).

more supports the SIGWINCH signal, and redraws the screen in response to window size changes.

EXTERNAL INFLUENCES
    Environment Variables
        COLUMNS   Overrides the system-selected horizontal screen size.

        EDITOR   Used by the v command to select an editor.

        LANG   Provides a default value for the internationalization variables that are unset or null. If LANG is unset or null, the default value of "C" (see lang(5)) is used. If any of the internationalization variables contains an invalid setting, more will behave as if all internationalization variables are set to "C". See environ(5).

        LC_ALL   If set to a non-empty string value, overrides the values of all the other internationalization variables.

        LC_CTYPE   Determines the interpretation of text as single and/or multi-byte characters, the classification of characters as printable, and the characters matched by character class expressions in regular expressions.

LC_MESSAGES   Determines the locale that should be used to affect the format and contents of diagnostic messages written to standard error and informative messages written to standard output.

NLSPATH   Determines the location of message catalogues for the processing of LC_MESSAGES.

LINES   Overrides the system-selected vertical screen size, used as the number of lines in a screenful. The -n option takes precedence over the LINES variable for determining the number of lines in a screenful.

MORE   Determines a string containing options, preceded with hyphens and blank-character-separated as on the command line. Any command-line options are processed after those in the MORE variable. The MORE variable takes precedence over the TERM and LINES variables for determining the number of lines in a screenful.

TERM   Determines the name of the terminal type.

International Code Set Support
Single- and multi-byte character code sets are supported.

EXAMPLES
To view a simple file, use:

```
more filename
```

To preview nroff output, use a command resembling:

```
nroff -mm +2 doc.n | more -s
```

If the file contains tables, use:

```
tbl file | nroff -mm | col | more -s
```

To display file stuff in a fifteen line-window and convert multiple adjacent blank lines into a single blank line:

```
more -s -n 15 stuff
```

To examine each file with its last screenful:

```
more -p G file1 file2
```

To examine each file starting with line 100 in the current position (third line, so line 98 is the first line written):

```
more -p 100g file1 file2
```

To examine the file that contains the tagstring tag with line 30 in the current position:

```
more -t tag -p 30g
```

WARNINGS
    Standard error, file descriptor 2, is normally used for input during
    interactive use and should not be redirected (see Input/Output section
    in the manpage of the shell in use).

FILES
    /usr/share/lib/terminfo/?/*   compiled terminal capability data base

AUTHOR
    more was developed by Mark Nudleman, University of California,
    Berkeley, OSF, and HP.

SEE ALSO
    csh(1), man(1), pg(1), sh(1), term(4), terminfo(4), environ(5),
    lang(5), regexp(5).

STANDARDS CONFORMANCE
    more: XPG4

pg

pg - File-viewing filter.

pg(1)   pg(1)

NAME
     pg - file perusal filter for soft-copy terminals

SYNOPSIS

     pg [-number] [-pstring] [-cefns] [+linenumber] [+/pattern] [file ...]

   Remarks
     pg and more are both used in similar situations (see more(1)). Text
     highlighting features supported by more are not available from pg.
     However, pg has some useful features not provided by more.

DESCRIPTION
     pg is a text file filter that allows the examination of files one
     screenful at a time on a soft-copy terminal. If - is used as a file
     argument, or pg detects NULL arguments in the comand line, the
     standard input is used. Each screenful is followed by a prompt. To
     display a new page, press Return. Other possibilities are enumerated
     below.

     This command is different from other paginators such as more in that
     it can back up for reviewing something that has already passed. The
     method for doing this is explained below.

     In order to determine terminal attributes, pg scans the terminfo data
     base for the terminal type specified by the environment variable TERM
     (see terminfo(4)). If TERM is not defined, terminal type dumb is
     assumed.

   Options
     pg recognizes the following command line options:

          -number   number is an integer specifying the size (in
                         lines) of the window that pg is to use instead of
                         the default (on a terminal containing 24 lines,
                         the default window size is 23).

          -p string   Causes pg to use string as the prompt. If the
                         prompt string contains a %d, the first occurrence
                         of %d in the prompt is replaced by the current
                         page number when the prompt is issued. The
                         default prompt string is a colon (:).

          -c   Home the cursor and clear the screen before
                         displaying each page. This option is ignored if
                         clear_screen is not defined in the terminfo data
                         base for this terminal type.

          -e   Causes pg to not pause at the end of each file.

          -f   Normally, pg splits lines longer than the screen

width, but some sequences of characters in the
text being displayed (such as escape sequences for
underlining) generate undesirable results. The -f
option inhibits pg from splitting lines.

-n   Normally, commands must be terminated by a new-
            line character. This option causes an automatic
            end-of-command as soon as a command letter is
            entered.

-s   Causes pg to print all messages and prompts in
            standout mode (usually inverse video).

+linenumber   Start display at linenumber.

+/pattern/   Start up at the first line containing text that
               matches the regular expression pattern.

pg looks in the environment variable PG to preset any flags desired.
For example, if you prefer to view files using the -c mode of
operation, the Bourne-shell command sequence PG='-c' ; export PG or
the C-shell command setenv PG -c causes all invocations of pg,
including invocations by programs such as man and msgs, to use this
mode. The command sequence to set up the PG environment variable is
normally placed in the user .profile or .cshrc file.

The responses that can be typed when pg pauses can be divided into
three categories: those causing further perusal, those that search,
and those that modify the perusal environment.

Commands that cause further perusal normally take a preceding address,
an optionally signed number indicating the point from which further
text should be displayed. This address is interpreted either in pages
or lines, depending on the command. A signed address specifies a
point relative to the current page or line; an unsigned address
specifies an address relative to the beginning of the file. Each
command has a default address that is used if none is provided.

Perusal commands and their defaults are as follows:

   (+1)<newline> or <blank>
                    Displays one page. The address is specified in
                    pages.

   (+1) l   With a relative address, pg simulates scrolling
                    the screen, forward or backward, the number of
                    lines specified. With an absolute address pg
                    prints a screenful beginning at the specified
                    line.

   (+1) d or ^D   Simulates scrolling a half-screen forward or
                    backward.

The following perusal commands take no address:

   . or ^L   Typing a single period causes the current page of
                    text to be redisplayed.

   $ Displays the last windowful in the file. Use with
                    caution when the input is a pipe.

The following commands are available for searching for text patterns
in the text. The Basic Regular Expression syntax (see regexp(5)) is
supported. Regular expressions must always be terminated by a new-
line character, even if the -n option is specified.

i/pattern/   Search forward for the ith (default i=1) occurrence of pattern. Searching begins immediately after the current page and continues to the end of the current file, without wrap-around.

i^pattern^
i?pattern?   Search backwards for the ith (default i=1) occurrence of pattern. Searching begins immediately before the current page and continues to the beginning of the current file, without wrap-around. The ^ notation is useful for Adds 100 terminals which cannot properly handle the ?.

After searching, pg normally displays the line found at the top of the screen. This can be modified by appending m or b to the search command to leave the line found in the middle or at the bottom of the window from now on. The suffix t can be used to restore the original situation.

pg users can modify the perusal environment with the following commands:

in   Begin perusing the ith next file in the command line. The i is an unsigned number, default value is 1.

ip   Begin perusing the ith previous file in the command line. i is an unsigned number, default is 1.

iw   Display another window of text. If i is present, set the window size to i.

s filename   Save the input in the named file. Only the current file being perused is saved. The white space between the s and filename is optional. This command must always be terminated by a new-line character, even if the -n option is specified.

h   Help by displaying an abbreviated summary of available commands.

q or Q   Quit pg.

!command   command is passed to the shell, whose name is taken from the SHELL environment variable. If this is not available, the default shell is used. This command must always be terminated by a new-line character, even if the -n option is specified.

To cause pg to stop sending output and display the prompt at any time when output is being sent to the terminal, press the quit key (normally Ctrl-\) or the interrupt (break) key. Any one of the above commands can then be entered in the normal manner. Unfortunately, some output is lost when this is done, due to the fact that any characters waiting in the terminal's output queue are flushed when the quit signal occurs.

If the standard output is not a terminal, pg is functionally equivalent to cat (see cat(1)), except that a header is printed before each file if more than one file is specified.

EXTERNAL INFLUENCES

Environment Variables
   LC_COLLATE determines the collating sequence used in evaluating
   regular expressions.

   LC_CTYPE determines the interpretation of text as single and/or
   multi-byte characters, and the characters matched by character class
   expressions in regular expressions.

   LANG determines the language in which messages are displayed.

   If LC_COLLATE or LC_CTYPE is not specified in the environment or is
   set to the empty string, the value of LANG is used as a default for
   each unspecified or empty variable. If LANG is not specified or is
   set to the empty string, a default of "C" (see lang(5)) is used
   instead of LANG. If any internationalization variable contains an
   invalid setting, pg behaves as if all internationalization variables
   are set to "C". See environ(5).

International Code Set Support
   Single- and multi-byte character code sets are supported.

EXAMPLEs
     To use pg when reading system news:

          news | pg -p "(Page %d):"

WARNINGS
     If terminal tabs are not set every eight positions, undesirable
     results may occur.

     When using pg as a filter with another command that changes the
     terminal I/O options (such as crypt(1)), terminal settings may not be
     restored correctly.

     While waiting for terminal input, pg responds to BREAK, DEL, and ^ by
     terminating execution. Between prompts, however, these signals
     interrupt pg's current task and place the user in prompt mode. These
     should be used with caution when input is being read from a pipe,
     because an interrupt is likely to terminate the other commands in the
     pipeline.

     Users of more will find that the z and f commands are available, and
     that the terminal /, ^, or ? can be omitted from the pattern search
     commands.

FILES
     /usr/share/lib/terminfo/?/*   terminal information data base

     /tmp/pg*   temporary file when input is
                                              from a pipe

SEE ALSO
     crypt(1), grep(1), more(1), terminfo(4), environ(5), lang(5),
     regexp(5).

STANDARDS CONFORMANCE
     pg: SVID2, SVID3, XPG2, XPG3

tail

tail - Produce the last part of a file.

```
tail(1)                                                              tail(1)

NAME
     tail - deliver the last part of a file

SYNOPSIS

     tail [-f] [-b number] [file]
     tail [-f] [-c number] [file]
     tail [-f] [-n number] [file]

   Obsolescent:
     tail [+-[number][l|b|c] [-f] [file]

DESCRIPTION
     tail copies the named file to the standard output beginning at a
     designated place.  If no file is named, standard input is used.

   Command Forms
     tail can be used in three forms as indicated above:

          tail -b number...      Copy file starting at number blocks from
                                 end or beginning of file.

          tail -c number...      Copy file starting at number bytes from end
                                 or beginning of file.

          tail -n number...
             or
          tail number...         Copy file starting at number lines from end
                                 or beginning of file.

     tail with no options specified is equivalent to tail -n 10....

   Options and Command-Line Arguments
     tail recognizes the following options and command-line arguments:

          -f               Follow option.  If the input file is a regular
                           file or if file specifies a FIFO, do not terminate
                           after the last line of the input file has been
                           copied, but read and copy further bytes from the
                           input file when they become available (tail enters
                           an endless loop wherein it sleeps for one second
                           then attempts to read and copy further records
                           from the input file).  This is useful when
                           monitoring text being written to a file by another
                           process.  If no file argument is specified and the
                           input is a pipe (FIFO), the -f option is ignored.

          number           Decimal integer indicating quantity of output to
                           be copied, measured in units specified by
                           accompanying option.  If number is preceded by a +
```

character, copy operation starts number units from
beginning of file. If number is preceded by a -
character or the option name, copy operation
starts number units from end of file. If number
is not preceded by a b, c, or n option, -n is
assumed. If both the option and number are not
specified, -n 10 is assumed.

-b number   Copy file beginning number 512-byte blocks from
             end or beginning of file. If number is not
             specified, -b 10 is assumed. See number
             description above.

-c number   Copy file beginning number bytes from end or
             beginning of file. If number is not specified, -c
             10 is assumed. See number description above.

-n number   Copy file beginning number lines from end or
             beginning of file. If number is not specified, -n
             10 is assumed. See number description above.

file   Name of file to be copied. If not specified, the
             standard input is used.

If the -c option is specified, the input file can contain arbitrary
data. Otherwise, the input file should be a text file.

Obsolescent Form
    In the obsolescent form, option letters can be concatenated after the
    number argument to select blocks, bytes, or lines. If this syntax is
    used, +-number must be the first argument given. If number is not
    specified, -10 is assumed. This version is provided for backward
    compatibility only. The forms discussed previously are recommended
    for portability.

EXTERNAL INFLUENCES
    Environment Variables
        LC_CTYPE determines the locale for the interpretation of sequences of
        bytes of text data as characters (e.g., single- versus multibyte
        characters in arguments and input files).

        LC_MESSAGES determines the language in which messages are displayed.

        If LC_CTYPE or LC_MESSAGES is not specified in the environment or is
        set to the empty string, the value of LANG is used as a default for
        each unspecified or empty variable. If LANG is not specified or is
        set to the empty string, a default of "C" (see lang(5)) is used
        instead of LANG.

        If any internationalization variable contains an invalid setting, tail
        behaves as if all internationalization variables are set to "C". See
        environ(5).

    International Code Set Support
        Single- and multi-byte character code sets are supported. However,
        the b and c options can break multi-byte characters and should be used
        with caution in a multi-byte locale environment.

EXAMPLES
    Print the last three lines in file file1 to the standard output, and
    leave tail in ``follow'' mode:

        tail -fn 3 file1
           or
        tail -3 -f file1

Print the last 15 bytes of file logfile followed by any lines that are
appended to logfile after tail is initiated until it is killed:

```
tail -fc15 logfile
   or
tail -f -c 15 logfile
```

Three ways to print an entire file:

```
tail -b +1 file
tail -c +1 file
tail -n +1 file
```

WARNINGS

Tails relative to end-of-file are stored in a 20-Kbyte buffer, and
thus are limited in length. Therefore, be wary of the results when
piping output from other commands into tail.

Various kinds of anomalous behavior may occur with character special
files.

SEE ALSO

dd(1), head(1).

STANDARDS CONFORMANCE

tail: SVID2, SVID3, XPG2, XPG3, XPG4, POSIX.2

CHAPTER 18

UNIX Tools - split, wc, sort, cmp, diff, comm, dircmp, cut, paste, join, and tr

Not All Commands on All UNIX Variants

A variety of commands are covered in this chapter, including:

- **split**, **wc**, **sort**, **cmp**, **diff**, **comm**, **dircmp**, **cut**, **paste**, **join**, and **tr** commands

I cover many useful and enjoyable commands in this chapter. All the commands, however, are not available on all UNIX variants. If a specific command is not available on your system, then you probably have a similar command or can combine more than one command to achieve the desired result.

split

man page

split - 18

Some files are just too long. The file **listing** we earlier looked at may be more easily managed if split into multiple files. We can use the **split** command to make **listing** into files 25 lines long, as shown in Figure 18-1:

```
┌─                              split example                              ─ □
│ $ 11 listing
│ -rw-------    1 denise    users        1430 Dec 19 16:30 listing
│ $
│ $ split -1 25 listing
│ $
│ $ 11 x*
│ -rw-------    1 denise    users         330 Dec 19 16:40 xaa
│ -rw-------    1 denise    users         267 Dec 19 16:40 xab
│ -rw-------    1 denise    users         268 Dec 19 16:40 xac
│ -rw-------    1 denise    users         256 Dec 19 16:40 xad
│ -rw-------    1 denise    users         274 Dec 19 16:40 xae
│ -rw-------    1 denise    users          35 Dec 19 16:40 xaf
│ $ ■
```

Figure 18-1   split Command

Note that the **split** command produced several files from **listing** called **xaa**, **xab**, and so on. The *-l* option is used to specify the number of lines in files produced by **split**.

Here is a summary of the **split** command:

split - Split a file into multiple files.

Options

-l line_count	Split the file into files with line_count lines per file.
-b n	Split the file into files with n bytes per file.

WC

We know that we have split **listing** into separate files of 25 lines each, but how many lines were in **listing** originally? How about the number of words in **listing**? Those of us who get paid by the word for some of the articles we write often want to know. How about the number of characters in a file? The **wc** command can produce a word, line, and character count for you. Figure 18-2 shows issuing the **wc** command with the -*wlc* options, which produce a count of words with the -*w* option, lines with the -*l* option, and characters with the -*c* option.

man page

wc - 18

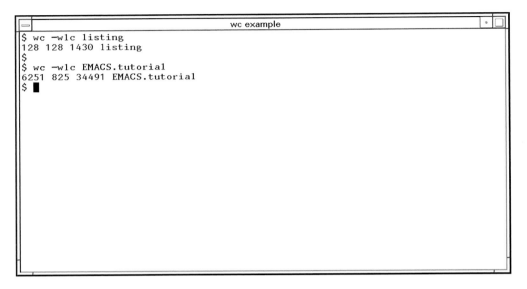

Figure 18-2 **wc** Command

Notice that the number of words and lines produced by **wc** is the same for the file **listing**. The reason is that each line contains exactly one word. When we display the words, lines, and characters with the **wc** command for the text file **EMACS.tutorial**, we can see that the number of words is *6251*, the number of lines is *825*, and the number of characters is *34491*. In a text file, in this case a tutorial, you would expect many more words than lines.

Here is a summary of the **wc** command:

wc - Produce a count of words, lines, and characters.

Options

-l	Print the number of lines in a file.
-w	Print the number of words in a file.
-c	Print the number of characters in a file.

sort

Sometimes the contents of files are not sorted in the way you would like. You can use the **sort** command to sort files with a variety of options.

You may find as you use your UNIX system more and more that your system administrator is riding you about the amount of disk space you are consuming. You can monitor the amount of disk space you are consuming with the **du** command. Figure 18-3 shows creating a file called **disk_space** that lists the amount of disk space consumed by files and directories and shows the first 20 lines of the file:

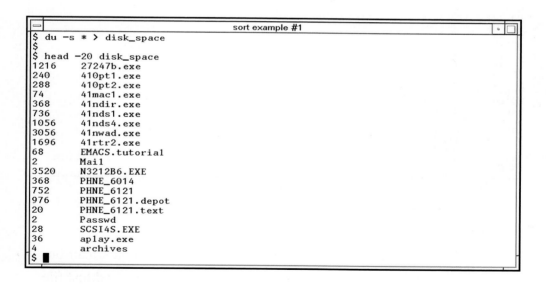

```
                              sort example #1
$ du -s * > disk_space
$
$ head -20 disk_space
1216     27247b.exe
240      410pt1.exe
288      410pt2.exe
74       41mac1.exe
368      41ndir.exe
736      41nds1.exe
1056     41nds4.exe
3056     41nwad.exe
1696     41rtr2.exe
68       EMACS.tutorial
2        Mail
3520     N3212B6.EXE
368      PHNE_6014
752      PHNE_6121
976      PHNE_6121.depot
20       PHNE_6121.text
2        Passwd
28       SCSI4S.EXE
36       aplay.exe
4        archives
$
```

Figure 18-3   **sort** Command Example #1

man page

sort - 18

Notice that the result is sorted alphabetically. In many cases, this is what you want. If the file were not sorted alphabetically, you could use the **sort** command to do so. In this case, we don't care as much about seeing entries in alphabetical order as we do in numeric order, that is, the files and directories that are consuming the most space. Figure 18-4 shows sorting the file **disk_space** numerically with the *-n* option and reversing the order of the sort with the *-r* option so that the biggest numbers appear first. We then specify the output file name with the *-o* option.

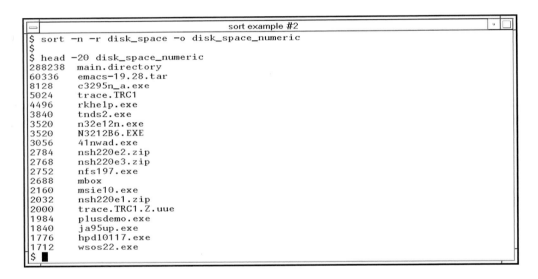

```
                              sort example #2
$ sort -n -r disk_space -o disk_space_numeric
$
$ head -20 disk_space_numeric
288238   main.directory
60336    emacs-19.28.tar
8128     c3295n_a.exe
5024     trace.TRC1
4496     rkhelp.exe
3840     tnds2.exe
3520     n32e12n.exe
3520     N3212B6.EXE
3056     41nwad.exe
2784     nsh220e2.zip
2768     nsh220e3.zip
2752     nfs197.exe
2688     mbox
2160     msie10.exe
2032     nsh220e1.zip
2000     trace.TRC1.Z.uue
1984     plusdemo.exe
1840     ja95up.exe
1776     hpd10117.exe
1712     wsos22.exe
$
```

Figure 18-4   **sort** Command Example #2

What if the items being sorted had many more fields than our two-column disk usage example? Let's go back to the **passwd.test** file for a more complex sort. Let's **cat passwd.test** so we can again see its contents:

```
# cat passwd.test
root:PgYQCkVH65hyQ:0:0:root:/root:/bin/bash
bin:*:1:1:bin:/bin:
daemon:*:2:2:daemon:/sbin:
adm:*:3:4:adm:/var/adm:
lp:*:4:7:lp:/var/spool/lpd:
sync:*:5:0:sync:/sbin:/bin/sync
shutdown:*:6:11:shutdown:/sbin:/sbin/shutdown
halt:*:7:0:halt:/sbin:/sbin/halt
mail:*:8:12:mail:/var/spool/mail:
news:*:9:13:news:/var/spool/news:
uucp:*:10:14:uucp:/var/spool/uucp:
operator:*:11:0:operator:/root:
games:*:12:100:games:/usr/games:
gopher:*:13:30:gopher:/usr/lib/gopher-data:
ftp:*:14:50:FTP User:/home/ftp:
man:*:15:15:Manuals Owner:/:
nobody:*:65534:65534:Nobody:/:/bin/false
col:Wh0yzfAV2qm2Y:100:100:Caldera OpenLinux
                    User:/home/col:/bin/bash
```

man page

cat - 17

man page

sort - 18

Now let's use **sort** to determine which users are in the same group. Fields are separated in **passwd.test** by a colon (:). The fourth field is the group to which a user belongs. For instance, *bin* is in group *1*, *daemon* in group *2*, and so on. To sort by group, we would have to specify three options to the **sort** command. The first is to specify the delimiter (or field separator) of colon (:) using the *-t* option. Next we would have to specify the field on which we wish to sort with the *-k* option. Finally, we want a numeric sort, so use the *-n* option. The following example shows a numeric sort of the **passwd.test** file by the fourth field:

```
# sort -t: -k4 -n passwd.test
halt:*:7:0:halt:/sbin:/sbin/halt
operator:*:11:0:operator:/root:
root:PgYQCkVH65hyQ:0:0:root:/root:/bin/bash
sync:*:5:0:sync:/sbin:/bin/sync
bin:*:1:1:bin:/bin:
```

```
daemon:*:2:2:daemon:/sbin:
adm:*:3:4:adm:/var/adm:
lp:*:4:7:lp:/var/spool/lpd:
shutdown:*:6:11:shutdown:/sbin:/sbin/shutdown
mail:*:8:12:mail:/var/spool/mail:
news:*:9:13:news:/var/spool/news:
uucp:*:10:14:uucp:/var/spool/uucp:
man:*:15:15:Manuals Owner:/:
gopher:*:13:30:gopher:/usr/lib/gopher-data:
ftp:*:14:50:FTP User:/home/ftp:
col:Wh0yzfAV2qm2Y:100:100:Caldera OpenLinux
                 User:/home/col:/bin/bash
games:*:12:100:games:/usr/games:
nobody:*:65534:65534:Nobody:/:/bin/false
```

man page

sort - 18

The following is a summary of the **sort** command.

sort - Sort lines of files (alphabetically by default).

Options

-b	Ignore leading spaces and tabs.
-c	Check whether files are already sorted, and if so, do nothing.
-d	Ignore punctuation and sort in dictionary order.
-f	Ignore the case of entries when sorting.
-i	Ignore non-ASCII characters when sorting.
-ks	Use field s as the field on which to base the sort.
-m	Merge sorted files.
-n	Sort in numeric order.
-o file	Specify the output file name rather than write to standard output.
-r	Reverse the order of the sort by starting with the last letter of the alphabet or with the largest number, as we did in the example.
+n	Skip n fields or columns before sorting.

cmp, diff, and comm

A fact of life is that as you go about editing files, you may occasionally lose track of what changes you have made to which files. You may then need to make comparisons of files. Let's take a look at three such commands, **cmp**, **diff**, and **comm** and see how they compare files.

Let's assume that we have modified a script called **llsum**. The unmodified version of **llsum** was saved as **llsum.orig**. Using the **head** command, we can view the first 20 lines of **llsum** and then the first 20 lines of **llsum.orig**:

```
# head -20 llsum
#
#!/bin/sh
# Displays a truncated long listing (ll) and
# displays size statistics
# of the files in the listing.

ll $* | \
awk ' BEGIN { x=i=0; printf "%-25s%-10s%8s%8s\n",\
                   "FILENAME","OWNER","SIZE","TYPE" }
       $1 ~ /^[-dlps]/  {# line format for normal files
              printf "%-25s%-10s%8d",$9,$3,$5
              x = x + $5
                 i++
                     }
       $1 ~ /^-/ { printf "%8s\n","file" }  # standard file
types
       $1 ~ /^d/ { printf "%8s\n","dir" }
       $1 ~ /^l/ { printf "%8s\n","link" }
       $1 ~ /^p/ { printf "%8s\n","pipe" }
       $1 ~ /^s/ { printf "%8s\n","socket" }
       $1 ~ /^[bc]/ { # line format for device files
                           printf              "%-25s%-
10s%8s%8s\n",$10,$3,"","dev"
                     }
#
# head -20 llsum.orig
#
#!/bin/sh
# Displays a truncated long listing (ll) and
# displays size statistics
# of the files in the listing.

ll $* | \
awk ' BEGIN { x=i=0; printf "%-16s%-10s%8s%8s\n",\
```

```
                          "FILENAME","OWNER","SIZE","TYPE" }
         $1 ~ /^[-dlps]/  {# line format for normal files
              printf "%-16s%-10s%8d",$9,$3,$5
              x = x + $5
                i++
                     }
        $1 ~ /^-/ { printf "%8s\n","file" }  # standard file
types
        $1 ~ /^d/ { printf "%8s\n","dir" }
        $1 ~ /^l/ { printf "%8s\n","link" }
        $1 ~ /^p/ { printf "%8s\n","pipe" }
        $1 ~ /^s/ { printf "%8s\n","socket" }
        $1 ~ /^[bc]/ { # line format for device files
                          printf                    "%-16s%-
10s%8s%8s\n",$10,$3,"","dev"
                     }
```

I'm not sure what changes I made to **llsum.orig** to improve it, so we can first use **cmp** to see whether indeed differences exist between the files.

man page

cmp - 18

```
$
$ cmp llsum llsum.orig
llsum llsum.orig differ: char 154, line 6
$
```

cmp does not report back much information, only that character *154* in the file at line *6* is different in the two files. There may indeed be other differences, but this is all we know about so far.

To get information about all of the differences in the two files, we could use the *-l* option to **cmp**:

```
$ cmp -l llsum llsum.orig
    154   62   61
    155   65   66
    306   62   61
    307   65   66
    675   62   61
    676   65   66
```

This is not all that useful an output, however. W want to see not only the position of the differences, but also the differences themselves.

Now we can use **diff** to describe all the differences in the two files:

man page

diff - 18

```
$ diff llsum llsum.orig
6c6
< awk ' BEGIN { x=i=0; printf "%-25s%-10s%8s%8s\n",\
---
> awk ' BEGIN { x=i=0; printf "%-16s%-10s%8s%8s\n",\
9c9
<             printf "%-25s%-10s%8d",$9,$3,$5
---
>             printf "%-16s%-10s%8d",$9,$3,$5
19c19
<             printf "%-25s%-10s%8s%8s\n",$10,$3,"","dev"
---
>             printf "%-16s%-10s%8s%8s\n",$10,$3,"","dev"
$
```

We now know that lines *6*, *9*, and *25* are different in the two files and these lines are also listed for us. From this listing, we can see that the number *16* in **llsum.orig** was changed to *25* in the newer **llsum** file, and this accounts for all of the differences in the two files. The less than sign (<) precedes lines from the first file, in this case **llsum**. The greater than sign (>) precedes lines from the second file, in this case **llsum.orig**. I made this change, starting the second group of information from character *16* to character *25*, because I wanted the second group of information, produced by **llsum,** to start at column *25*. The second group of information is the *owner,* as shown in the following example:

```
$ llsum
FILENAME                    OWNER          SIZE     TYPE

README                      denise          810     file
backup_files                denise         3408     file
biography                   denise          427     file
cshtest                     denise         1024      dir
gkill                       denise         1855     file
gkill.out                   denise          191     file
hostck                      denise          924     file
ifstat                      denise         1422     file
```

```
ifstat.int              denise           2147    file
ifstat.out              denise            723    file
introdos                denise          54018    file
introux                 denise          52476    file
letter                  denise          23552    file
letter.auto             denise          69632    file
letter.auto.recover     denise          71680    file
letter.backup           denise          23552    file
letter.lck              denise             57    file
letter.recover          denise          69632    file
llsum                   denise           1267    file
llsum.orig              denise           1267    file
llsum.out               denise           1657    file
llsum.tomd.out          denise           1356    file
psg                     denise            670    file
psg.int                 denise            802    file
psg.out                 denise            122    file
sam_adduser             denise           1010    file
tdolan                  denise           1024     dir
trash                   denise           4554    file
trash.out               denise            329    file
typescript              denise           2017    file

The files listed occupy 393605 bytes (0.3754 Mbytes)
Average file size is 13120 bytes

$
```

When we run **llsum.orig**, clearly the second group of information, which is the *owner*, starts at column 16 and not column 32:

```
$ llsum.orig
FILENAME        OWNER          SIZE    TYPE

README          denise          810    file
backup_files    denise         3408    file
biography       denise          427    file
cshtest         denise         1024     dir
gkill           denise         1855    file
gkill.out       denise          191    file
hostck          denise          924    file
ifstat          denise         1422    file
ifstat.int      denise         2147    file
ifstat.out      denise          723    file
introdos        denise        54018    file
introux         denise        52476    file
letter          denise        23552    file
letter.auto     denise        69632    file
```

```
letter.auto.rec    denise       71680     file
letter.backup      denise       23552     file
letter.lck         denise          57     file
letter.recover     denise       69632     file
llsum              denise        1267     file
llsum.orig         denise        1267     file
llsum.out          denise        1657     file
llsum.tomd.out     denise        1356     file
psg                denise         670     file
psg.int            denise         802     file
psg.out            denise         122     file
sam_adduser        denise        1010     file
tdolan             denise        1024      dir
trash              denise        4554     file
trash.out          denise         329     file
typescript         denise        3894     file

The files listed occupy 395482 bytes (0.3772 Mbytes)
Average file size is 13182 bytes


script done on Mon Dec 11 12:59:18

$
```

man page

comm - 18

We can compare two sorted files using **comm** and see the lines that are unique to each file, as well as the lines found in both files. When we compare two files with **comm**, the lines that are unique to the first file appear in the first column, the lines unique to the second file appear in the second column and the lines contained in both files appear in the third column. Let's go back to the **/etc/passwd** file to illustrate this comparison. We'll compare two **/etc/passwd** files, the active **/etc/passwd** file in use and an old **/etc/passwd** file from a backup:

man page

passwd - 5

```
# comm /etc/passwd /etc/passwd.backup
                root:PgYQCkVH65hyQ:0:0:root:/root:/bin/bash
                bin:*:1:1:bin:/bin:
                daemon:*:2:2:daemon:/sbin:
                adm:*:3:4:adm:/var/adm:
                lp:*:4:7:lp:/var/spool/lpd:
                sync:*:5:0:sync:/sbin:/bin/sync
                shutdown:*:6:11:shutdown:/sbin:/sbin/shutdown
                halt:*:7:0:halt:/sbin:/sbin/halt
                mail:*:8:12:mail:/var/spool/mail:
```

```
                    news:*:9:13:news:/var/spool/news:
                    uucp:*:10:14:uucp:/var/spool/uucp:
            operator1:*:12:0:operator:/root:
                    operator:*:11:0:operator:/root:
      games:*:12:100:games:/usr/games:
                    gopher:*:13:30:gopher:/usr/lib/gopher-data:
                    ftp:*:14:50:FTP User:/home/ftp:
                    man:*:15:15:Manuals Owner:/:
                    nobody:*:65534:65534:Nobody:/:/bin/false
                    col:Wh0yzfAV2qm2Y:100:100:Caldera
                    OpenLinux User:/home/col:/bin/bash
```

You can see from this output that the user *games* appears only in the active **/etc/passwd** file, the user *operator1* appears only in the **/etc/passwd.backup** file, and all of the other entries appear in both files.

The following is a summary of the **cmp** and **diff** commands.

man page
cmp - 18

cmp - Compare the contents of two files. The byte position and line number of the first difference between the two files is returned.

man page
diff - 18

Options

    -l   Display the byte position and differing characters for all differences within a file.

    -s   Work silently; that is, only exit codes are returned.

diff - Compares two files and reports differing lines.

Options

    -b   Ignore blanks at the end of a line.

    -i   Ignore case differences.

    -t   Expand tabs in output to spaces.

    -w   Ignore spaces and tabs.

dircmp

Why stop at comparing files? You will probably have many directories in your user area as well. **dircmp** compares two directories and produces information about the contents of directories.

To begin with let's perform a long listing of two directories:

```
$ ls -l krsort.dir.old
total 168
-rwxr-xr-x   1 denise    users       34592 Oct 31 11:27 krsort
-rwxr-xr-x   1 denise    users        3234 Oct 31 11:27 krsort.c
-rwxr-xr-x   1 denise    users       32756 Oct 31 11:27 krsort.dos
-rw-r--r--   1 denise    users        9922 Oct 31 11:27 krsort.q
-rwxr-xr-x   1 denise    users        3085 Oct 31 11:27 krsortorig.c
$
$ ls -l krsort.dir.new
total 168
-rwxr-xr-x   1 denise    users       34592 Oct 31 15:17 krsort
-rwxr-xr-x   1 denise    users       32756 Oct 31 15:17 krsort.dos
-rw-r--r--   1 denise    users        9922 Oct 31 15:17 krsort.q
-rwxr-xr-x   1 denise    users        3234 Oct 31 15:17 krsort.test.c
-rwxr-xr-x   1 denise    users        3085 Oct 31 15:17 krsortorig.c
$
```

From this listing, you can see clearly that one file is unique to each directory. **krsort.c** appears in only the **krsort.dir.old** directory, and **krsort.test.c** appears in only the **krsort.dir.new** directory. Let's now use **dircmp** to inform us of the differences in these two directories:

```
$ dircmp krsort.dir.old krsort.dir.new

krsort.dir.old only and krsort.dir.new only Page 1

./krsort.c          ./krsort.test.c
```

```
Comparison of krsort.dir.old krsort.dir.new Page 1


directory           .
same                ./krsort
same                ./krsort.dos
same                ./krsort.q
same                ./krsortorig.c

$
```

This is a useful output. First, the files that appear in only one directory are listed. Then, the files common to both directories are listed.

man page

dircmp - 18

The following is a summary of the **dircmp** command.

dircmp - Compare directories.

Options

-d   Compare the contents of files with the same name in both directories and produce a report of what must be done to make the files identical.

-s   Suppress information about different files.

cut

There are times when you have an output that has too many fields in it. When we issued the **llsum** command earlier, it produced four fields: *FILENAME*, *OWNER*, *SIZE*, and *TYPE*. What if we want to take this output and look at just the *FILENAME* and *SIZE*. We could modify the **llsum** script, or we could use the **cut** command to eliminate the *OWNER* and *TYPE* fields with the following commands:

man page

cut - 18

```
$ llsum | cut -c 1-25,37-43

FILENAME                 SIZE
README                    810
backup_files             3408
biography                 427
cshtest                  1024
gkill                    1855
gkill.out                 191
hostck                    924
ifstat                   1422
ifstat.int               2147
ifstat.out                723
introdos                54018
introux                 52476
letter                  23552
letter.auto             69632
letter.auto.recover     71680
letter.backup           23552
letter.lck                 57
letter.recover          69632
llsum                    1267
llsum.orig               1267
llsum.out                1657
llsum.tomd.out           1356
psg                       670
psg.int                   802
psg.out                   122
sam_adduser              1010
tdolan                   1024
trash                    4554
trash.out                 329
typescript                 74

The files listed occupy 3 (0.373
Average file size is 1305
$
```

This has produced a list from **llsum**, which is piped to **cut**. Only characters *1* through *25* and *37* through *43* have been extracted. These

man page

grep - 19

characters correspond to the fields we want. At the end of the output are two lines that are only partially printed. We don't want these lines, so we can use **grep -v** to eliminate them and print all other lines. The output of this command is saved to the file **llsum.out** at the end of this output, which we'll use later:

```
$ ./llsum | grep -v "bytes" | cut -c 1-25,37-43

FILENAME                 SIZE
README                    810
backup_files             3408
biography                 427
cshtest                  1024
gkill                    1855
gkill.out                 191
hostck                    924
ifstat                   1422
ifstat.int               2147
ifstat.out                723
introdos                54018
introux                 52476
letter                  23552
letter.auto             69632
letter.auto.recover     71680
letter.backup           23552
letter.lck                 57
letter.recover          69632
llsum                    1267
llsum.orig               1267
llsum.out                1657
llsum.tomd.out           1356
psg                       670
psg.int                   802
psg.out                   122
sam_adduser              1010
tdolan                   1024
trash                    4554
trash.out                 329
typescript               1242

$ llsum | grep -v "bytes" | cut -c 1-25,37-4_3 > llsum.out
$
```

man page

cut - 18

The following is a summary of the **cut** command, with some of the more commonly used options.

cut - Extract specified fields from each line.

Options

-c list   Extract based on character position, as shown in the example.

-f list   Extract based on fields.

-d char   The character following the *d* is the delimiter when using the -f option. The delimiter is the character that separates fields.

man page
paste - 18

paste

Files can be merged together in a variety of ways. If you want to merge files on a line-by-line basis, you can use the **paste** command. The first line in the second file is pasted to the end of the first line in the first file and so on.

man page
cut - 18

Let's use the **cut** command just covered and extract only the permissions field, or characters *1* through *10*, to get only the permissions for files. We'll then save these in the file **ll.out**:

man page
ls - 15

```
$ ls -al | cut -c 1-10

total 798
drwxrwxrwx
drwxrwxrwx
-rwxrwxrwx
-rwxrwxrwx
-rwxrwxrwx
drwxr-xr-x
-rwxrwxrwx
-rw-r--r--
-rwxrwxrwx
-rwxrwxrwx
-rwxr-xr-x
-rw-r--r--
-rw-r--r--
```

```
-rwxrwxrwx
-rw-r--r--
-rw-r--r--
-rw-r--r--
-rw-r--r--
-rw-rw-rw-
-rw-r--r--
-rw-r--r--
-rwxrwxrwx
-rwxr-xr-x
-rw-r--r--
-rw-r--r--
-rwxrwxrwx
-rwxr-xr-x
-rw-r--r--
-rwxrwxrwx
drwxr-xr-x
-rwxrwxrwx
-rw-r--r--
-rw-r--r--
```

man page

ls - 15

```
$ ls -al | cut -c 1-10 > ll.out
$
```

man page

cut - 18

We can now use the **paste** command to paste the permissions saved in the **ll.out** file to the other file-related information in the **llsum.out** file:

man page

paste - 18

```
$ paste llsum.out ll.out
```

FILENAME	SIZE	total 792
README	810	-rwxrwxrwx
backup_files	3408	-rwxrwxrwx
biography	427	-rwxrwxrwx
cshtest	1024	drwxr-xr-x
gkill	1855	-rwxrwxrwx
gkill.out	191	-rw-r--r--
hostck	924	-rwxrwxrwx
ifstat	1422	-rwxrwxrwx
ifstat.int	2147	-rwxr-xr-x
ifstat.out	723	-rw-r--r--
introdos	54018	-rw-r--r--
introux	52476	-rwxrwxrwx
letter	23552	-rw-r--r--
letter.auto	69632	-rw-r--r--
letter.auto.recover	71680	-rw-r--r--
letter.backup	23552	-rw-r--r--
letter.lck	57	-rw-rw-rw-
letter.recover	69632	-rw-r--r--
ll.out	1057	-rw-r--r--
llsum	1267	-rwxrwxrwx
llsum.orig	1267	-rwxr-xr-x
llsum.out	1657	-rw-r--r--

```
llsum.tomd.out             1356          -rw-r--r--
psg                         670          -rwxrwxrwx
psg.int                     802          -rwxr-xr-x
psg.out                     122          -rw-r--r--
sam_adduser                1010          -rwxrwxrwx
tdolan                     1024          drwxr-xr-x
trash                      4554          -rwxrwxrwx
trash.out                   329          -rw-r--r--
typescript                  679          -rw-r--r--

$
```

This has produced a list that includes *FILENAME* and *SIZE* from **llsum.out** and permissions from **ll.out**.

If both files have the same first field, you can use the **join** command to merge the two files:

The following is a summary of the **paste** and **join** commands, with some of the more commonly used options:

man page

join - 18

man page

paste - 18

paste - Merge lines of files.

Options

    -d list   Use *list* as the delimiter between columns. You can use special escape sequences for *list* such as \n for newline and \t for tab.

join - Combine two presorted files that have a common key field.

Options

    -a n   Produce the normal output and also generate a line for each line that can't be joined in 1 or 2.

    -e string   Replace empty fields in output with *string*.

    -t char   Use *char* as the field separator.

tr

man page

tr - 18

man page

ls - 15

tr translates characters. **tr** is ideal for such tasks as changing case. For instance, what if you want to translate all lowercase characters to upper case? The following example shows listing files that have the suffix "zip" and then translates these files into uppercase:

```
$ ls -al *.zip
file1.zip
file2.zip
file3.zip
file4.zip
file5.zip
file6.zip
file7.zip
$ ls -al *.zip | tr "[:lower:]" "[:upper:]"
FILE1.ZIP
FILE2.ZIP
FILE3.ZIP
FILE4.ZIP
FILE5.ZIP
FILE6.ZIP
FILE7.ZIP
$
```

We use brackets in this case because we are translating a class of characters.

The following is a summary of the **tr** command, with some of the more commonly used options.

tr - Translate characters.

Options

-A	Translate on a byte-by-byte basis.
-d	Delete all occurrences of characters specified.
[:class:]	Translate from one character class to another, such as from lowercase class to uppercase class, as shown in the example.

Manual Pages for Some Commands Used in Chapter 18

The following are the HP-UX manual pages for many of the commands used in this chapter. Commands often differ among UNIX variants, so you may find differences in the options or other areas for some commands; however, the following manual pages serve as an excellent reference.

cmp

man page

cmp - 18

cmp - Compare files.

---

cmp(1)   cmp(1)

NAME
     cmp - compare two files

SYNOPSIS

     cmp [-l] [-s] file1 file2

DESCRIPTION
     cmp compares two files (if file1 or file2 is -, the standard input is
     used). Under default options, cmp makes no comment if the files are
     the same; if they differ, it announces the byte and line number at
     which the difference occurred. If one file is an initial subsequence
     of the other, that fact is noted.

     cmp recognizes the following options:

        -l   Print the byte number (decimal) and the differing bytes
                  (octal) for each difference (byte numbering begins at 1
                  rather than 0).

        -s   Print nothing for differing files; return codes only.

EXTERNAL INFLUENCES
   Environment Variables
     LANG determines the language in which messages are displayed. If LANG
     is not specified or is set to the empty string, a default of "C" (see
     lang(5)) is used instead of LANG. If any internationalization
     variable contains an invalid setting, cmp behaves as if all
     internationalization variables are set to "C". See environ(5).

   International Code Set Support
     Single- and multi-byte character code sets are supported.

DIAGNOSTICS
     cmp returns the following exit values:

        0   Files are identical.
        1   Files are not identical.
        2   Inaccessible or missing argument.

     cmp prints the following warning if the comparison succeeds till the
     end of file of file1(file2) is reached.

           cmp: EOF on file1(file2)

SEE ALSO
     comm(1), diff(1).

STANDARDS CONFORMANCE
     cmp: SVID2, SVID3, XPG2, XPG3, XPG4, POSIX.2

comm

comm - Produce three-column output of sorted files.

NAME
     comm - select or reject lines common to two sorted files

SYNOPSIS

     comm [-[123]] file1 file2

DESCRIPTION
     comm reads file1 and file2, which should be ordered in increasing
     collating sequence (see sort(1) and Environment Variables below), and
     produces a three-column output:

          Column 1:   Lines that appear only in file1,
          Column 2:   Lines that appear only in file2,
          Column 3:   Lines that appear in both files.

     If - is used for file1 or file2, the standard input is used.

     Options 1, 2, or 3 suppress printing of the corresponding column.
     Thus comm -12 prints only the lines common to the two files; comm -23
     prints only lines in the first file but not in the second; comm -123
     does nothing useful.

EXTERNAL INFLUENCES
   Environment Variables
     LC_COLLATE determines the collating sequence comm expects from the
     input files.

     LC_MESSAGES determines the language in which messages are displayed.

     If LC_MESSAGES is not specified in the environment or is set to the
     empty string, the value of LANG determines the language in which
     messages are displayed. If LC_COLLATE is not specified in the
     environment or is set to the empty string, the value of LANG is used
     as a default. If LANG is not specified or is set to the empty string,
     a default of ``C'' (see lang(5)) is used instead of LANG. If any
     internationalization variable contains an invalid setting, comm
     behaves as if all internationalization variables are set to ``C''.
     See environ(5).

   International Code Set Support
     Single- and multi-byte character code sets are supported.

EXAMPLES
     The following examples assume that file1 and file2 have been ordered
     in the collating sequence defined by the LC_COLLATE or LANG
     environment variable.

     Print all lines common to file1 and file2 (in other words, print
     column 3):

```
comm -12 file1 file2
```

Print all lines that appear in file1 but not in file2 (in other words, print column 1):

```
comm -23 file1 file2
```

Print all lines that appear in file2 but not in file1 (in other words, print column 2):

```
comm -13 file1 file2
```

SEE ALSO
    cmp(1), diff(1), sdiff(1), sort(1), uniq(1).

STANDARDS CONFORMANCE
    comm: SVID2, SVID3, XPG2, XPG3, XPG4, POSIX.2

cut

cut - Cut selected fields from the lines in a file.

```
cut(1)                                                                    cut(1)

NAME
     cut - cut out (extract) selected fields of each line of a file

SYNOPSIS

     cut -c list [file ...]
     cut -b list [-n] [file ...]
     cut -f list [-d char] [-s] [file ...]

DESCRIPTION
     cut cuts out (extracts) columns from a table or fields from each line
     in a file; in data base parlance, it implements the projection of a
     relation.  Fields as specified by list can be fixed length (defined in
     terms of character or byte position in a line when using the -c or -b
     option), or the length can vary from line to line and be marked with a
     field delimiter character such as the tab character (when using the -f
     option).  cut can be used as a filter; if no files are given, the
     standard input is used.

     When processing single-byte character sets, the -c and -b options are
     equivalent and produce identical results.  When processing multi-byte
     character sets, when the -b and -n options are used together, their
     combined behavior is very similar, but not identical to the -c option.

     Options
     Options are interpreted as follows:

          list           A comma-separated list of integer byte (-b
                         option), character (-c option), or field (-f
                         option) numbers, in increasing order, with
                         optional - to indicate ranges.  For example:


                              1,4,7
                                   Positions 1, 4, and 7.
                              1-3,8
                                   Positions 1 through 3 and 8.
                              -5,10
                                   Positions 1 through 5 and 10.
                              3-   Position 3 through last position.


          -b list        Cut based on a list of bytes.  Each selected byte
                         is output unless the -n option is also specified.

          -c list        Cut based on character positions specified by list
                         (-c 1-72 extracts the first 72 characters of each
                         line).

          -f list        Where list is a list of fields assumed to be
```

separated in the file by a delimiter character
(see -d); for example, -f 1,7 copies the first and
seventh field only. Lines with no field
delimiters will be passed through intact (useful
for table subheadings), unless -s is specified.

-d char   The character following -d is the field delimiter
            (-f option only). Default is tab. Space or other
            characters with special meaning to the shell must
            be quoted. Adjacent field delimiters delimit null
            fields.

-n   Do not split characters. If the high end of a
            range within a list is not the last byte of a
            character, that character is not included in the
            output. However, if the low end of a range within
            a list is not the first byte of a character, the
            entire character is included in the output."

-s   Suppresses lines with no delimiter characters when
            using -f option. Unless -s is specified, lines
            with no delimiters appear in the output without
            alteration.

Hints
    Use grep to extract text from a file based on text pattern recognition
    (using regular expressions). Use paste to merge files line-by-line in
    columnar format. To rearrange columns in a table in a different
    sequence, use cut and paste. See grep(1) and paste(1) for more
    information.

EXTERNAL INFLUENCES
    Environment Variables
        LC_CTYPE determines the interpretation of text as single and/or
        multi-byte characters.

        If LC_CTYPE is not specified in the environment or is set to the empty
        string, the value of LANG is used as a default for each unspecified or
        empty variable. If LANG is not specified or is set to the empty
        string, a default of "C" (see lang(5)) is used instead of LANG. If
        any internationalization variable contains an invalid setting, cut
        behaves as if all internationalization variables are set to "C". See
        environ(5).

    International Code Set Support
        The delimiter specified with the -d argument must be a single-byte
        character. Otherwise, single- and multi-byte character code sets are
        supported.

EXAMPLES
    Password file mapping of user ID to user names:

        cut -d : -f 1,5 /etc/passwd

    Set environment variable name to current login name:

        name=`who am i | cut -f 1 -d " "`

    Convert file source containing lines of arbitrary length into two
    files where file1 contains the first 500 bytes (unless the 500th byte
    is within a multi-byte character), and file2 contains the remainder of
    each line:

        cut -b 1-500 -n source > file1
        cut -b 500- -n source > file2

DIAGNOSTICS

line too long Line length must not exceed LINE_MAX characters or
fields, including the new-line character (see
limits(5).

bad list for b/c/f option
Missing -b, -c, or -f option or incorrectly specified
list. No error occurs if a line has fewer fields than
the list calls for.

no fields   list is empty.

WARNINGS

cut does not expand tabs. Pipe text through expand(1) if tab
expansion is required.

Backspace characters are treated the same as any other character. To
eliminate backspace characters before processing by cut, use the fold
or col command (see fold(1) and col(1)).

AUTHOR

cut was developed by OSF and HP.

SEE ALSO

grep(1), paste(1).

STANDARDS CONFORMANCE

cut: SVID2, SVID3, XPG2, XPG3, XPG4, POSIX.2

diff

diff - File and directory comparison.

```
diff(1)                                                                  diff(1)

NAME
     diff - differential file and directory comparator

SYNOPSIS

     diff [-C n] [-S name] [-lrs] [-bcefhintw] dir1 dir2
     diff [-C n] [-S name] [-bcefhintw] file1 file2
     diff [-D string] [-biw] file1 file2

DESCRIPTION
  Comparing Directories
     If both arguments are directories, diff sorts the contents of the
     directories by name, then runs the regular file diff algorithm
     (described below) on text files that have the same name in each
     directory but are different.  Binary files that differ, common
     subdirectories, and files that appear in only one directory are
     listed.  When comparing directories, the following options are
     recognized:

          -l           Long output format; each text file diff is piped
                       through pr to paginate it (see pr(1)).  Other
                       differences are remembered and summarized after all
                       text file differences are reported.

          -r           Applies diff recursively to common subdirectories
                       encountered.

          -s           diff reports files that are identical but otherwise
                       not mentioned.

          -S name      Starts a directory diff in the middle of the sorted
                       directory, beginning with file name.

  Comparing Files
     When run on regular files, and when comparing text files that differ
     during directory comparison, diff tells what lines must be changed in
     the files to bring them into agreement.  diff usually finds a smallest
     sufficient set of file differences.  However, it can be misled by
     lines containing very few characters or by other situations.  If
     neither file1 nor file2 is a directory, either can be specified as -,
     in which case the standard input is used.  If file1 is a directory, a
     file in that directory whose filename is the same as the filename of
     file2 is used (and vice versa).

     There are several options for output format.  The default output
     format contains lines resembling the following:

          n1 a n3,n4
          n1,n2 d n3
          n1,n2 c n3,n4
```

These lines resemble ed commands to convert file1 into file2. The numbers after the letters pertain to file2. In fact, by exchanging a for d and reading backwards one may ascertain equally how to convert file2 into file1. As in ed, identical pairs where n1=n2 or n3=n4 are abbreviated as a single number.

Following each of these lines come all the lines that are affected in the first file flagged by <, then all the lines that are affected in the second file flagged by >.

Except for -b, -w, -i, or -t which can be given with any of the others, the following options are mutually exclusive:

-e Produce a script of a, c, and d commands for the ed editor suitable for recreating file2 from file1. Extra commands are added to the output when comparing directories with -e, so that the result is a shell script for converting text files common to the two directories from their state in dir1 to their state in dir2 (see sh-bourne(1)

-f Produce a script similar to that of the -e option that is not useful with ed but is more readable by humans.

-n Produce a script similar to that of -e, but in the opposite order, and with a count of changed lines on each insert or delete command. This is the form used by rcsdiff (see rcsdiff(1)).

-c Produce a difference list with 3 lines of context. -c modifies the output format slightly: the output begins with identification of the files involved, followed by their creation dates, then each change separated by a line containing about twelve asterisks (*)s. Lines removed from file1 are marked with -, and lines added to file2 are marked +. Lines that change from one file to the other are marked in both files with with !. Changes that lie within 3 lines of each other in the file are grouped together on output.

-C n Output format similar to -c but with n lines of context.

-h Do a fast, half-hearted job. This option works only when changed stretches are short and well separated, but can be used on files of unlimited length.

-D string
    Create a merged version of file1 and file2 on the standard output, with C preprocessor controls included so that a compilation of the result without defining string is equivalent to compiling file1, while compiling the result with string defined is equivalent to compiling file2.

-b Ignore trailing blanks (spaces and tabs) and treat other strings of blanks as equal.

-w Ignore all whitespace (blanks and tabs). For example, if (a == b) and if(a==b) are treated as equal.

-i Ignores uppercase/lowercase differences. Thus A is treated the same as a.

-t Expand tabs in output lines. Normal or -c output adds one or more characters to the front of each line. Resulting misalignment of indentation in the original

source lines can make the output listing difficult to
interpret. This option preserves original source file
indentation.

EXTERNAL INFLUENCES
  Environment Variables
      LANG determines the locale to use for the locale categories when both
      LC_ALL and the corresponding environment variable (beginning with LC_)
      do not specify a locale. If LANG is not set or is set to the empty
      string, a default of "C" (see lang(5)) is used.

      LC_CTYPE determines the space characters for the diff command, and the
      interpretation of text within file as single- and/or multi-byte
      characters.

      LC_MESSAGES determines the language in which messages are displayed.

      If any internationalization variable contains an invalid setting, diff
      and diffh behave as if all internationalization variables are set to
      "C". See environ(5).

  International Code Set Support
      Single- and multi-byte character code sets are supported with the
      exception that diff and diffh do not recognize multi-byte alternative
      space characters.

RETURN VALUE
      Upon completion, diff returns with one of the following exit values:

          0   No differences were found.

          1   Differences were found.

          >1   An error occurred.

EXAMPLES
      The following command creates a script file script:

          diff -e x1 x2 >script

      w is added to the end of the script in order to save the file:

          echo w >> script

      The script file can then be used to create the file x2 from the file
      x1 using the editor ed in the following manner:

          ed x1 < script

      The following command produces the difference output with 2 lines of
      context information before and after the line that was different:

          diff -C2 x1 x2

      The following command ignores all blanks and tabs and ignores
      uppercase-lowercase differences.

          diff -wi x1 x2

WARNINGS
      Editing scripts produced by the -e or -f option are naive about
      creating lines consisting of a single dot (.).

      When comparing directories with the -b, -w, or -i options specified,
      diff first compares the files in the same manner as cmp, then runs the
      diff algorithm if they are not equal. This may cause a small amount

of spurious output if the files are identical except for insignificant blank strings or uppercase/lowercase differences.

The default algorithm requires memory allocation of roughly six times the size of the file. If sufficient memory is not available for handling large files, the -h option or bdiff can be used (see bdiff(1)).

When run on directories with the -r option, diff recursively descends sub-trees. When comparing deep multi-level directories, more memory may be required than is currently available on the system. The amount of memory required depends on the depth of recursion and the size of the files.

AUTHOR
diff was developed by AT&T, the University of California, Berkeley, and HP.

FILES
/usr/lbin/diffh   used by -h option

SEE ALSO
bdiff(1), cmp(1), comm(1), diff3(1), diffmk(1), dircmp(1), ed(1), more(1), nroff(1), rcsdiff(1), sccsdiff(1), sdiff(1), terminfo(4).

STANDARDS CONFORMANCE
diff: SVID2, SVID3, XPG2, XPG3, XPG4, POSIX.2

dircmp

man page

dircmp - 18

dircmp - Compare directories and produce results.

```
dircmp(1)                                                          dircmp(1)

NAME
     dircmp - directory comparison

SYNOPSIS

     dircmp [-d] [-s] [-wn] dir1 dir2

DESCRIPTION
     dircmp examines dir1 and dir2 and generates various tabulated
     information about the contents of the directories.  Sorted listings of
     files that are unique to each directory are generated for all the
     options.  If no option is entered, a sorted list is output indicating
     whether the filenames common to both directories have the same
     contents.

          -d        Compare the contents of files with the same name in both
                    directories and output a list telling what must be
                    changed in the two files to bring them into agreement.
                    The list format is described in diff(1).

          -s        Suppress messages about identical files.

          -wn       Change the width of the output line to n characters.  The
                    default width is 72.

EXTERNAL INFLUENCES
  Environment Variables
     LC_COLLATE determines the order in which the output is sorted.

     If LC_COLLATE is not specified in the environment or is set to the
     empty string, the value of LANG is used as a default.  If LANG is not
     specified or is set to the empty string, a default of ``C'' (see
     lang(5)) is used instead of LANG.  If any internationalization
     variable contains an invalid setting, dircmp behaves as if all
     internationalization variables are set to ``C'' (see environ(5)).

  International Code Set Support
     Single- and multi-byte character code sets are supported.

EXAMPLES
     Compare the two directories slate and sleet and produce a list of
     changes that would make the directories identical:

          dircmp -d slate sleet

SEE ALSO
     cmp(1), diff(1).

STANDARDS CONFORMANCE
     dircmp: SVID2, SVID3, XPG2, XPG3
```

join

join - Join two relations based on lines in files.

join(1)   join(1)

NAME
      join - relational database operator

SYNOPSIS

      join [options] file1 file2

DESCRIPTION
      join forms, on the standard output, a join of the two relations
      specified by the lines of file1 and file2. If file1 or file2 is -,
      the standard input is used.

      file1 and file2 must be sorted in increasing collating sequence (see
      Environment Variables below) on the fields on which they are to be
      joined; normally the first in each line.

      The output contains one line for each pair of lines in file1 and file2
      that have identical join fields. The output line normally consists of
      the common field followed by the rest of the line from file1, then the
      rest of the line from file2.

      The default input field separators are space, tab, or new-line. In
      this case, multiple separators count as one field separator, and
      leading separators are ignored. The default output field separator is
      a space.

      Some of the below options use the argument n. This argument should be
      a 1 or a 2 referring to either file1 or file2, respectively.

      Options
        -a n   In addition to the normal output, produce a line for each
                        unpairable line in file n, where n is 1 or 2.

        -e s   Replace empty output fields by string s.

        -j m   Join on field m of both files. The argument m must be
                        delimited by space characters. This option and the
                        following two are provided for backward compatibility.
                        Use of the -1 and -2 options (see below) is recommended
                        for portability.

        -j1 m   Join on field m of file1.

        -j2 m   Join on field m of file2.

        -o list   Each output line comprises the fields specified in list,
                        each element of which has the form n.m, where n is a file
                        number and m is a field number. The common field is not
                        printed unless specifically requested.

        -t c   Use character c as a separator (tab character). Every

appearance of c in a line is significant. The character c
is used as the field separator for both input and output.

-v file_number
        Instead of the default output, produce a line only for
        each unpairable line in file_number, where file_number is
        1 or 2.

-1 f   Join on field f of file 1. Fields are numbered starting
        with 1.

-2 f   Join on field f of file 2. Fields are numbered starting
        with 1.

EXTERNAL INFLUENCES
  Environment Variables
    LC_COLLATE determines the collating sequence join expects from input
    files.

    LC_CTYPE determines the alternative blank character as an input field
    separator, and the interpretation of data within files as single
    and/or multi-byte characters. LC_CTYPE also determines whether the
    separator defined through the -t option is a single- or multi-byte
    character.

    If LC_COLLATE or LC_CTYPE is not specified in the environment or is
    set to the empty string, the value of LANG is used as a default for
    each unspecified or empty variable. If LANG is not specified or is
    set to the empty string, a default of ``C'' (see lang(5)) is used
    instead of LANG. If any internationalization variable contains an
    invalid setting, join behaves as if all internationalization variables
    are set to ``C'' (see environ(5)).

  International Code Set Support
    Single- and multi-byte character code sets are supported with the
    exception that multi-byte-character file names are not supported.

EXAMPLES
    The following command line joins the password file and the group file,
    matching on the numeric group ID, and outputting the login name, the
    group name, and the login directory. It is assumed that the files
    have been sorted in the collating sequence defined by the LC_COLLATE
    or LANG environment variable on the group ID fields.

        join -1 4 -2 3 -o 1.1 2.1 1.6 -t: /etc/passwd /etc/group

    The following command produces an output consisting all possible
    combinations of lines that have identical first fields in the two
    sorted files sf1 and sf2, with each line consisting of the first and
    third fields from sorted_file1 and the second and fourth fields from
    sorted_file2:

        join -j1 1 -j2 1 -o 1.1, 2.2, 1.3, 2.4 sorted_file1 sorted_file2

WARNINGS
>   With default field separation, the collating sequence is that of sort
>   -b; with -t, the sequence is that of a plain sort.
>
>   The conventions of join, sort, comm, uniq, and awk are incongruous.
>
>   Numeric filenames may cause conflict when the -o option is used
>   immediately before listing filenames.

AUTHOR
>   join was developed by OSF and HP.

SEE ALSO
>   awk(1), comm(1), sort(1), uniq(1).

STANDARDS CONFORMANCE
>   join: SVID2, SVID3, XPG2, XPG3, XPG4, POSIX.2

paste

paste - Merge lines of files.

---

paste(1)   paste(1)

NAME
     paste - merge same lines of several files or subsequent lines of one
     file

SYNOPSIS
     paste file1 file2 ...
     paste -d list file1 file2 ...
     paste -s [-d list] file1 file2 ...

DESCRIPTION
     In the first two forms, paste concatenates corresponding lines of the
     given input files file1, file2, etc. It treats each file as a column
     or columns in a table and pastes them together horizontally (parallel
     merging). In other words, it is the horizontal counterpart of cat(1)
     which concatenates vertically; i.e., one file after the other. In the
     -s option form above, paste replaces the function of an older command
     with the same name by combining subsequent lines of the input file
     (serial merging). In all cases, lines are glued together with the tab
     character, or with characters from an optionally specified list.
     Output is to standard output, so paste can be used as the start of a
     pipe, or as a filter if - is used instead of a file name.

     paste recognizes the following options and command-line arguments:

          -d   Without this option, the new-line characters of all but
                    the last file (or last line in case of the -s option)
                    are replaced by a tab character. This option allows
                    replacing the tab character by one or more alternate
                    characters (see below).

          list   One or more characters immediately following -d replace
                    the default tab as the line concatenation character.
                    The list is used circularly; i.e., when exhausted, it
                    is reused. In parallel merging (that is, no -s
                    option), the lines from the last file are always
                    terminated with a new-line character, not from the
                    list. The list can contain the special escape
                    sequences: \n (new-line), \t (tab), \\ (backslash), and
                    \0 (empty string, not a null character). Quoting may
                    be necessary if characters have special meaning to the
                    shell. (For example, to get one backslash, use -
                    d"\\\\").

          -s   Merge subsequent lines rather than one from each input
                    file. Use tab for concatenation, unless a list is
                    specified with the -d option. Regardless of the list,
                    the very last character of the file is forced to be a
                    new-line.

          -         Can be used in place of any file name to read a line from the standard input (there is no prompting).

EXTERNAL INFLUENCES
　　Environment Variables
　　　　LC_CTYPE determines the locale for the interpretation of text as
　　　　single- and/or multi-byte characters.

　　　　LC_MESSAGES determines the language in which messages are displayed.

　　　　If LC_CTYPE or LC_MESSAGES is not specified in the environment or is
　　　　set to the empty string, the value of LANG is used as a default for
　　　　each unspecified or empty variable. If LANG is not specified or is
　　　　set to the empty string, a default of "C" (see lang(5)) is used
　　　　instead of LANG.

　　　　If any internationalization variable contains an invalid setting,
　　　　paste behaves as if all internationalization variables are set to "C".
　　　　See environ(5).

　　International Code Set Support
　　　　Single- and multi-byte character code sets are supported.

RETURN VALUE
　　These commands return the following values upon completion:

　　　　0　　Completed successfully.

　　　　>0　An error occurred.

EXAMPLES
　　List directory in one column:

　　　　ls | paste -d" " -

　　List directory in four columns

　　　　ls | paste - - - -

　　Combine pairs of lines into lines

　　　　paste -s -d"\t\n" file

　Notes
　　pr -t -m... works similarly, but creates extra blanks, tabs and new-
　　lines for a nice page layout.

DIAGNOSTICS
　　too many files　　　　　　　Except for the -s option, no more than
　　　　　　　　　　　　　　　　　OPEN_MAX - 3 input files can be specified
　　　　　　　　　　　　　　　　　(see limits(5)).

AUTHOR
　　paste was developed by OSF and HP.

SEE ALSO
　　cut(1), grep(1), pr(1).

STANDARDS CONFORMANCE
　　paste: SVID2, SVID3, XPG2, XPG3, XPG4, POSIX.2

sort

man page

sort - 18

sort - Sort contents of files.

---

sort(1)   sort(1)

NAME
     sort - sort or merge files

SYNOPSIS

     sort [-m] [-o output] [-bdfinruM] [-t char] [-k keydef] [-y [kmem]] [-z
     recsz] [-T dir] [file ...]

     sort [-c] [-AbdfinruM] [-t char] [-k keydef] [-y [kmem]] [-z recsz] [-T
     dir] [file ...]

DESCRIPTION
     sort performs one of the following functions:

     1.   Sorts lines of all the named files together and writes the
          result to the specified output.

     2.   Merges lines of all the named (presorted) files together and
          writes the result to the specified output.

     3.   Checks that a single input file is correctly presorted.

     The standard input is read if - is used as a file name or no input
     files are specified.

     Comparisons are based on one or more sort keys extracted from each
     line of input. By default, there is one sort key, the entire input
     line. Ordering is lexicographic by characters using the collating
     sequence of the current locale. If the locale is not specified or is
     set to the POSIX locale, then ordering is lexicographic by bytes in
     machine-collating sequence. If the locale includes multi-byte
     characters, single-byte characters are machine-collated before multi-
     byte characters.

     Behavior Modification Options
     The following options alter the default behavior:

          -A   Sorts on a byte-by-byte basis using each character's
                    encoded value. On some systems, extended characters
                    will be considered negative values, and so sort
                    before ASCII characters. If you are sorting ASCII
                    characters in a non-C/POSIX locale, this flag
                    performs much faster.

          -c   Check that the single input file is sorted according
                    to the ordering rules. No output is produced; the
                    exit code is set to indicate the result.

          -m   Merge only; the input files are assumed to be already
                    sorted.

-o output   The argument given is the name of an output file to use instead of the standard output. This file can be the same as one of the input files.

-u   Unique: suppress all but one in each set of lines having equal keys. If used with the -c option, check to see that there are no lines with duplicate keys, in addition to checking that the input file is sorted.

-y [kmem]   The amount of main memory used by the sort can have a large impact on its performance. If this option is omitted, sort begins using a system default memory size, and continues to use more space as needed. If this option is presented with a value, kmem, sort starts using that number of kilobytes of memory, unless the administrative minimum or maximum is violated, in which case the corresponding extremum will be used. Thus, -y 0 is guaranteed to start with minimum memory. By convention, -y (with no argument) starts with maximum memory.

-z recsz   The size of the longest line read is recorded in the sort phase so that buffers can be allocated during the merge phase. If the sort phase is omitted via the -c or -m options, a popular system default size will be used. Lines longer than the buffer size will cause sort to terminate abnormally. Supplying the actual number of bytes in the longest line to be merged (or some larger value) will prevent abnormal termination.

-T dir   Use dir as the directory for temporary scratch files rather than the default directory, which is is one of the following, tried in order: the directory as specified in the TMPDIR environment variable; /var/tmp, and finally, /tmp.

Ordering Rule Options
    When ordering options appear before restricted sort key specifications, the ordering rules are applied globally to all sort keys. When attached to a specific sort key (described below), the ordering options override all global ordering options for that key.

    The following options override the default ordering rules:

-d   Quasi-dictionary order: only alphanumeric characters and blanks (spaces and tabs), as defined by LC_CTYPE are significant in comparisons (see environ(5)).

             (XPG4 only.) The behavior is undefined for a sort key to which -i or -n also applies.

-f   Fold letters. Prior to being compared, all lowercase letters are effectively converted into their uppercase equivalents, as defined by LC_CTYPE.

-i   In non-numeric comparisons, ignore all characters which are non-printable, as defined by LC_CTYPE. For the ASCII character set, octal character codes 001 through 037 and 0177 are ignored.

-n   The sort key is restricted to an initial numeric string consisting of optional blanks, an optional minus sign, zero or more digits with optional radix character, and optional thousands separators. The radix and thousands separator characters are defined by LC_NUMERIC. The field is sorted by arithmetic value. An empty (missing) numeric field is treated as arithmetic zero. Leading zeros and plus or minus signs on zeros do not affect the ordering. The -n option implies the -b option (see below).

-r   Reverse the sense of comparisons.

-M   Compare as months. The first several non-blank characters of the field are folded to uppercase and compared with the langinfo(5) items ABMON_1 < ABMON_2 < ... < ABMON_12. An invalid field is treated as being less than ABMON_1 string. For example, American month names are compared such that JAN < FEB < ... < DEC. An invalid field is treated as being less than all months. The -M option implies the -b option (see below).

Field Separator Options
  The treatment of field separators can be altered using the options:

-t char   Use char as the field separator character; char is not considered to be part of a field (although it can be included in a sort key). Each occurrence of char is significant (for example, <char><char> delimits an empty field). If -t is not specified, <blank> characters will be used as default field separators; each maximal sequence of <blank> characters that follows a non-<blank> character is a field separator.

-b   Ignore leading blanks when determining the starting and ending positions of a restricted sort key. If the -b option is specified before the first -k option (+pos1 argument), it is applied to all -k options (+pos1 arguments). Otherwise, the -b option can be attached independently to each -k field_start or field_end option (+pos1 or (-pos2 argument; see below). Note that the -b option is only effective when restricted sort key specifications are given.

Restricted Sort Key
  -k keydef   The keydef argument defines a restricted sort key. The format of this definition is

                 field_start[type][,field_end[type]]

              which defines a key field beginning at field_start and ending at field_end. The characters at positions field_start and field_end are included in the key field, providing that field_end does not precede field_start. A missing field_end means the end of the line. Fields and characters within fields are numbered starting with 1. Note that this is different than the obsolete form of restricted sort keys, where numbering starts at 0. See WARNINGS below.

              Specifying field_start and field_end involves the notion of a field, a minimal sequence of characters followed by a field separator or a new-line. By default, the first blank of a sequence of blanks acts as the field separator. All blanks in a sequence of blanks are considered to be part of the next field; for example, all blanks at the beginning of a line are considered to be part of the first field.

The arguments field_start and field_end each have the
form m.n which are optionally followed by one or more
of the type options b, d, f, i, n, r, or M. These
modifiers have the functionality for this key only,
that their command-line counterparts have for the
entire record.

A field_start position specified by m.n is
interpreted to mean the nth character in the mth
field. A missing n means .1, indicating the first
character of the mth field. If the -b option is in
effect, n is counted from the first non-blank
character in the mth field.

A field_end position specified by m.n is interpreted
to mean the nth character in the mth field. If n is
missing, the mth field ends at the last character of
the field. If the -b option is in effect, n is
counted from the first non-<blank> character in the
mth field.

Multiple -k options are permitted and are significant
in command line order. A maximum of 9 -k options can
be given. If no -k option is specified, a default
sort key of the entire line is used. When there are
multiple sort keys, later keys are compared only
after all earlier keys compare equal. Lines that
otherwise compare equal are ordered with all bytes
significant. If all the specified keys compare
equal, the entire record is used as the final key.

The -k option is intended to replace the obsolete
[+pos1 [+pos2]] notation, using field_start and
field_end respectively. The fully specified [+pos1
[+pos2]] form:

         +w.x-y.z

is equivalent to:

         -k w+1.x+1,y.0 (if z == 0)
         -k w+1.x+1,y+1.z (if z > 0)

Obsolete Restricted Sort Key
    The notation +pos1 -pos2 restricts a sort key to one beginning at pos1
    and ending at pos2. The characters at positions pos1 and pos2 are
    included in the sort key (provided that pos2 does not precede pos1).
    A missing -pos2 means the end of the line.

    Specifying pos1 and pos2 involves the notion of a field, a minimal
    sequence of characters followed by a field separator or a new-line.
    By default, the first blank (space or tab) of a sequence of blanks
    acts as the field separator. All blanks in a sequence of blanks are
    considered to be part of the next field; for example, all blanks at
    the beginning of a line are considered to be part of the first field.

    pos1 and pos2 each have the form m.n optionally followed by one or
    more of the flags bdfinrM. A starting position specified by +m.n is
    interpreted to mean character n+1 in field m+1. A missing .n means
    .0, indicating the first character of field m+1. If the b flag is in
    effect, n is counted from the first non-blank in field m+1; +m.0b
    refers to the first non-blank character in field m+1.

    A last position specified by -m.n is interpreted to mean the nth

character (including separators) after the last character of the m th
field. A missing .n means .0, indicating the last character of the
mth field. If the b flag is in effect, n is counted from the last
leading blank in field m+1; -m.1b refers to the first non-blank in
field m+1.

EXTERNAL INFLUENCES
    Environment Variables
        LC_COLLATE determines the default ordering rules applied to the sort.

        LC_CTYPE determines the locale for interpretation of sequences of
        bytes of text data as characters (e.g., single- verses multibyte
        characters in arguments and input files) and the behavior of character
        classification for the -b, -d, -f, -i, and -n options.

        LC_NUMERIC determines the definition of the radix and thousands
        separator characters for the -n option.

        LC_TIME determines the month names for the -M option.

        LC_MESSAGES determines the language in which messages are displayed.

        LC_ALL determines the locale to use to override the values of all the
        other internationalization variables.

        NLSPATH determines the location of message catalogs for the processing
        of LC_MESSAGES.

        LANG provides a default value for the internationalization variables
        that are unset or null. If LANG is unset or null, the default value of
        "C" (see lang(5)) is used.

        If any of the internationalization variables contains an invalid
        setting, sort behaves as if all internationalization variables are set
        to "C". See environ(5).

    International Code Set Support
        Single- and multi-byte character code sets are supported.

EXAMPLES
    Sort the contents of infile with the second field as the sort key:

        sort -k 2,2 infile

    Sort, in reverse order, the contents of infile1 and infile2, placing
    the output in outfile and using the first two characters of the second
    field as the sort key:

        sort -r -o outfile -k 2.1,2.2 infile1 infile2

    Sort, in reverse order, the contents of infile1 and infile2, using the
    first non-blank character of the fourth field as the sort key:

        sort -r -k 4.1b,4.1b infile1 infile2

    Print the password file (/etc/passwd) sorted by numeric user ID (the
    third colon-separated field):

        sort -t: -k 3n,3 /etc/passwd

    Print the lines of the presorted file infile, suppressing all but the
    first occurrence of lines having the same third field:

        sort -mu -k 3,3 infile

DIAGNOSTICS

sort exits with one of the following values:

0 All input files were output successfully, or -c was specified and the input file was correctly presorted.

1 Under the -c option, the file was not ordered as specified, or if the -c and -u options were both specified, two input lines were found with equal keys. This exit status is not returned if the -c option is not used.

>1 An error occurred such as when one or more input lines are too long.

When the last line of an input file is missing a new-line character, sort appends one, prints a warning message, and continues.

If an error occurs when accessing the tables that contain the collation rules for the specified language, sort prints a warning message and defaults to the POSIX locale.

If a -d, -f, or -i option is specified for a language with multi-byte characters, sort prints a warning message and ignores the option.

WARNINGS

Numbering of fields and characters within fields (-k option) has changed to conform to the POSIX standard. Beginning at HP-UX Release 9.0, the -k option numbers fields and characters within fields, starting with 1. Prior to HP-UX Release 9.0, numbering started at 0.

A field separator specified by the -t option is recognized only if it is a single-byte character.

The character type classification categories alpha, digit, space, and print are not defined for multi-byte characters. For languages with multi-byte characters, all characters are significant in comparisons.

FILES

/var/tmp/stm???
/tmp/stm???

AUTHOR

sort was developed by OSF and HP.

SEE ALSO

comm(1), join(1), uniq(1), collate8(4), environ(5), hpnls(5), lang(5).

STANDARDS CONFORMANCE

sort: SVID2, SVID3, XPG2, XPG3, XPG4, POSIX.2

tr

man page

tr - 18

tr - Substitute selected characters.

```
tr(1)                                                                  tr(1)

NAME
     tr - translate characters

SYNOPSIS

     tr [-Acs] string1 string2

     tr -s [-Ac] string1

     tr -d [-Ac] string1

     tr -ds [-Ac] string1 string1

DESCRIPTION
     tr copies the standard input to the standard output with substitution
     or deletion of selected characters.  Input characters from string1 are
     replaced with the corresponding characters in string2. If necessary,
     string1 and string2 can be quoted to avoid pattern matching by the
     shell.

     tr recognizes the following command line options:

          -A             Translates on a byte-by-byte basis. When this flag
                         is specified tr does not support extended
                         characters.

          -c             Complements the set of characters in string1,
                         which is the set of all characters in the current
                         character set, as defined by the current setting
                         of LC_CTYPE, except for those actually specified
                         in the string1 argument. These characters are
                         placed in the array in ascending collation
                         sequence, as defined by the current setting of
                         LC_COLLATE.

          -d             Deletes all occurrences of input characters or
                         collating elements found in the array specified in
                         string1.

                         If -c and -d are both specified, all characters
                         except those specified by string1 are deleted. The
                         contents of string2 are ignored, unless -s is also
                         specified. Note, however, that the same string
                         cannot be used for both the -d and the -s flags;
                         when both flags are specified, both string1 (used
                         for deletion) and string2 (used for squeezing) are
                         required.

                         If -d is not specified, each input character or
                         collating element found in the array specified by
                         string1 is replaced by the character or collating
```

element in the same relative position specified by string2.

-s   Replaces any character specified in string1 that occurs as a string of two or more repeating characters as a single instance of the character in string2.

If the string2 contains a character class, the argument's array contains all of the characters in that character class. For example:

tr -s '[:space:]'

In a case conversion, however, the string2 array contains only those characters defined as the second characters in each of the toupper or tolower character pairs, as appropriate. For example:

tr -s '[:upper:]' '[:lower:]'

The following abbreviation conventions can be used to introduce ranges of characters, repeated characters or single-character collating elements into the strings:

c1-c2 or   Stands for the range of collating elements c1
[c1-c2]   through c2, inclusive, as defined by the current setting of the LC_COLLATE locale category.

[:class:]or Stands for all the characters belonging to the
[[:class:]] defined character class, as defined by the current setting of LC_CTYPE locale category. The following character class names will be accepted when specified in string1: alnum, alpha, blank, cntrl. digit, graph, lower, print, punct, space, upper, or xdigit, Character classes are expanded in collation order.

When the -d and -s flags are specified together, any of the character class names are accepted in string2; otherwise, only character class names lower or upper are accepted in string2 and then only if the corresponding character class (upper and lower, respectively) is specified in the same relative position in string1. Such a specification is interpreted as a request for case conversion.

When [:lower:] appears in string1 and [:upper:] appears in string2, the arrays contain characters from the toupper mapping in the LC_CTYPE category of the current locale. When [:upper:] appears in string1 and [:lower:] appears in string2, the arrays contain the characters from the tolower mapping in the LC_CTYPE category of the current locale.

[=c=]or   Stands for all the characters or collating
[[=c=]]   elements belonging to the same equivalence class as c, as defined by the current setting of LC_COLLATE locale category. An equivalence class expression is allowed only in string1, or in string2 when it is being used by the combined -d and -s options.

[a*n]   Stands for n repetitions of a. If the first digit
                      of n is 0, n is considered octal; otherwise, n is
                      treated as a decimal value. A zero or missing n
                      is interpreted as large enough to extend string2-
                      based sequence to the length of the string1-based
                      sequence.

The escape character \ can be used as in the shell to remove special
meaning from any character in a string. In addition, \ followed by 1,
2, or 3 octal digits represents the character whose ASCII code is
given by those digits.

An ASCII NUL character in string1 or string2 can be represented only
as an escaped character; i.e. as \000, but is treated like other
characters and translated correctly if so specified. NUL characters
in the input are not stripped out unless the option -d "\000" is
given.

EXTERNAL INFLUENCES
   Environment Variables
      LANG provides a default value for the internationalization variables
      that are unset or null. If LANG is unset or null, the default value of
      "C" (see lang(5)) is used. If any of the internationalization
      variables contains an invalid setting, tr will behave as if all
      internationalization variables are set to "C". See environ(5).

      LC_ALL If set to a non-empty string value, overrides the values of all
      the other internationalization variables.

      LC_CTYPE determines the interpretation of text as single and/or
      multi-byte characters, the classification of characters as printable,
      and the characters matched by character class expressions in regular
      expressions.

      LC_MESSAGES determines the locale that should be used to affect the
      format and contents of diagnostic messages written to standard error
      and informative messages written to standard output.

      NLSPATH determines the location of message catalogues for the
      processing of LC_MESSAGES.

RETURN VALUE
      tr exits with one of the following values:

         0   All input was processed successfully.

         >0   An error occurred.

EXAMPLES
      For the ASCII character set and default collation sequence, create a
      list of all the words in file1, one per line in file2, where a word is
      taken to be a maximal string of alphabetics. Quote the strings to
      protect the special characters from interpretation by the shell (012
      is the ASCII code for a new-line (line feed) character:

            tr -cs "[A-Z][a-z]" "[\012*]" <file1 >file2

      Same as above, but for all character sets and collation sequences:

            tr -cs "[:alpha:]" "[\012*]" <file1 >file2

      Translate all lower case characters in file1 to upper case and write
      the result to standard output.

               tr "[:lower:]" "[:upper:]" <file1

Use an equivalence class to identify accented variants of the base character e in file1, strip them of diacritical marks and write the result to file2:

        tr "[=e=]" "[e*]" <file1 >file2

Translate each digit in file1 to a # (number sign), and write the result to file2.

        tr "0-9" "[#*]" <file1 >file2

The * (asterisk) tells tr to repeat the # (number sign) enough times to make the second string as long as the first one.

AUTHOR
     tr was developed by OSF and HP.

SEE ALSO
     ed(1), sh(1), ascii(5), environ(5), lang(5), regexp(5).

STANDARDS CONFORMANCE
     tr: SVID2, SVID3, XPG2, XPG3, XPG4, POSIX.2

WC

man page

wc - 18

wc - Count words, bytes, and lines.

```
wc(1)                                                                    wc(1)

NAME
     wc - word, line, and byte or character count

SYNOPSIS

     wc [-c|-m] [-lw] [names]

DESCRIPTION
     The wc command counts lines, words, and bytes or characters in the
     named files, or in the standard input if no names are specified.  It
     also keeps a total count for all named files.

     A word is a maximal string of characters delimited by spaces, tabs, or
     new-lines.

     wc recognizes the following command-line options:

          -c        Write to the standard output the number of bytes in
                    each input file.

          -m        Write to the standard output the number of characters
                    in each input file.

          -w        Write to the standard output the number of words in
                    each input file.

          -l        Write to the standard output the number of newline
                    characters in each input file.

     The c and m options are mutually exclusive.  Otherwise, the l, w, and
     c or m options can be used in any combination to specify that a subset
     of lines, words, and bytes or characters are to be reported.

     When any option is specified, wc will report only the information
     requested by the specified options.  If no option is specified, The
     default output is -lwc.

     When names are specified on the command line, they are printed along
     with the counts.

EXTERNAL INFLUENCES
   Environment Variables
     LC_CTYPE determines the range of graphics and space characters, and
     the interpretation of text as single- and/or multi-byte characters.

     LC_MESSAGES determines the language in which messages are displayed.

     If LC_CTYPE or LC_MESSAGES is not specified in the environment or is
     set to the empty string, the value of LANG is used as a default for
     each unspecified or empty variable.  If LANG is not specified or is
     set to the empty string, a default of "C" (see lang(5)) is used
```

instead of LANG.

If any internationalization variable contains an invalid setting, wc
behaves as if all internationalization variables are set to "C". See
environ(5).

International Code Set Support
   Single- and multi-byte character code sets are supported.

WARNINGS
   The wc command counts the number of newlines to determine the line
   count. If a text file has a final line that is not terminated with a
   newline character, the count will be off by one.

Standard Output (XPG4 only)
   By default, the standard output contains an entry for each input file
   of the form:

   "%d %d %d %s\n", <newlines>, <words>, <bytes>, <file>

   If the -m option is specified, the number of characters replaces the
   <bytes> field in this format.

   If any options are specified and the -l option is not specified, the
   number of newlines are not written.

   If any options are specified and the -w option is not specified, the
   number of words are not written.

   If any options are specified and neither -c nor -m is specified, the
   number of bytes or characters are not written.

   If no input file operands are specified, no flie name is written and
   no blank characters preceding the pathname is written.

   If more than one input file operand is specified, an additional line
   is written, of the same format as the other lines, except that the
   word total (in the POSIX Locale) is written instead of a pathname and
   the total of each column is written as appropriate. Such an
   additional line, if any, is written at the end of the input.

Exit Status
   The wc utility shall exit with one of the following values

      0   Successful completion.

      >0   An error occured.

EXAMPLES
   Print the number of words and characters in file1:

      wc -wm file1

   The following is printed when the above command is executed:

      n1 n2   file1

   where n1 is the number of words and n2 is the number of characters in
   file1.

STANDARDS CONFORMANCE
   wc: SVID2, SVID3, XPG2, XPG3, XPG4, POSIX.2

CHAPTER 19

Advanced UNIX Tools - Regular Expressions, sed, awk, and grep

Three Commands

The three commands covered in this chapter, along with regular expressions (pattern matching), are often grouped together. There are even many books available devoted to **awk** and **sed**. In these books, **grep** usually goes along for the ride because **awk** is somewhat derived from **sed** and **grep**. In addition, the use of regular expressions for pattern matching that are used for **awk**, **sed**, and **grep** are similar.

man page

awk - 19

We'll take a look at regular expressions and pattern matching in general, and then cover the three commands in this chapter:

man page

sed - 19

man page

grep - 19

- Regular expressions

- **sed**, **awk**, and **grep** commands

Regular Expression Words-of-Caution

Regular expressions describe patterns for which you are searching. A regular expression usually defines the pattern for which you are searching using wildcards. Since a regular expression defines a pattern you are searching for, the terms "regular expression" and "pattern matching" are often used interchangably.

Let's get down to a couple of words-of-caution immediately:

man page

find - 20

• **Regular expressions are different from file matching patterns used by the shell**. Regular expressions are used by both the shell and many other programs, including those covered in this chapter. The file matching done by the shell and programs such as **find** is different from the regular expressions covered in this chapter.

• **Use single quotes around regular expressions**. The meta-characters used in this chapter must be quoted in order to be passed to the shell as an argument. You will, therefore, see most regular expressions in this chapter quoted.

Expressions Are Strings and Wildcards

man page

vi - 21

When using the programs in this book, such as **grep** and **vi**, you provide a regular expression that the program evaluates. The command will search for the pattern you supply. The pattern could be as simple

as a string or it could wildcards. The wildcards used by many programs are called meta-characters.

man page

awk - 19

Table 19-1 shows a list of meta-characters and the program(s) to
which they apply. Only the programs covered in this book (**awk**, **grep**,
sed, and **vi**) are shown in Table 19-1. These meta-characters may be
used with other programs, such as **ed** and **egrep**, as well, which are
not covered in the book. Table 19-1 describes the meta-characters and
their use.

man page

grep - 19

man page

sed - 19

TABLE 19-1   Meta-Characters and Programs to Which They Apply

Meta-Character	awk	grep	sed	vi	Use
.	Yes	Yes	Yes	Yes	Match any single character.
*	Yes	Yes	Yes	Yes	Match any number of the single character that precedes *.
[...]	Yes	Yes	Yes	Yes	Match any <u>one</u> of the characters in the set [...].
$	Yes	Yes	Yes	Yes	Matches the end of the line.
^	Yes	Yes	Yes	Yes	Matches the beginning of the line.
\	Yes	Yes	Yes	Yes	Escape the special character that follows \.
\{n,m\}	Yes	Yes	No	No	Match a range of occurrences of a single character between n and m.
+	Yes	No	No	No	Match one or more occurrences of the preceding regular expression.
?	Yes	No	No	No	Match zero or one occurrence of the preceding regular expression.

Meta-Character	awk	grep	sed	vi	Use
|	Yes	No	No	No	The preceding <u>or</u> following regular expression can be matched.
()	Yes	No	No	No	Groups regular expressions in a typical parenthesis fashion.
\{ \}	No	No	No	Yes	Match a word's beginning or end.

You may want to refer to this table when regular expressions are used for one of the commands in the table.

sed

vi - 21

sed - 19

Most of the editing performed on UNIX systems is done with **vi**. I have devoted a chapter to **vi** in this book, because of its prominence as a UNIX editor. Many times, we don't have the luxury of invoking **vi** when we need to edit a file. You may be writing a shell program or piping information between processes and need to edit in a non-interactive manner. **sed** can help here. Its name comes from *stream editor,* and it's a tool for filtering text files.

You can specify the name of the file you wish to edit with **sed** or it takes its input from standard input. **sed** reads one line at a time and performs the editing you specify to each line. You can specify specific line numbers for **sed** to edit as well.

sed uses many of the same commands as **ed**. You can view some of the **ed** commands in the **vi** chapter, and I also supply a summary of these at the end of this **sed** section.

You can invoke **sed** in the following two ways:

```
sed [-n][-e] 'command' filename(s)
sed [-n]-f scriptfile filename(s)
```

man page

sed - 19

The first form of **sed** is for issuing commands on the command line. By default, **sed** will display all lines. The *-n* specifies that you want only to print lines that are specified with the **p** command.

If you supply more than one instruction on the command line, then you *-e* is used to inform **sed** that the next argument is an instruction.

The second form allows you to specify one or more scripts containing editing commands.

The following is a summary of the three options that appear in the two different forms of **sed**:

-n	Print only lines that are specified with the **p** command.
-e command	The argument following *-e* is an editing command.
-f filename	The argument following *-f* is a file containing editing commands.

Let's view a couple of simple examples of what you can do with **sed**. These examples use some of the **sed** commands that appear at the end of this section. We'll use a file called **passwd.test**. We'll view this

man page

cat - 17

man page

sed - 19

file with **cat** and then view only lines *16*, *17*, and *18* using the *p* option to **sed**, indicating we want only the specified lines printed:

```
# cat passwd.test
root:PgYQCkVH65hyQ:0:0:root:/root:/bin/bash
bin:*:1:1:bin:/bin:
daemon:*:2:2:daemon:/sbin:
adm:*:3:4:adm:/var/adm:
lp:*:4:7:lp:/var/spool/lpd:
sync:*:5:0:sync:/sbin:/bin/sync
shutdown:*:6:11:shutdown:/sbin:/sbin/shutdown
halt:*:7:0:halt:/sbin:/sbin/halt
mail:*:8:12:mail:/var/spool/mail:
news:*:9:13:news:/var/spool/news:
uucp:*:10:14:uucp:/var/spool/uucp:
operator:*:11:0:operator:/root:
games:*:12:100:games:/usr/games:
gopher:*:13:30:gopher:/usr/lib/gopher-data:
ftp:*:14:50:FTP User:/home/ftp:
man:*:15:15:Manuals Owner:/:
nobody:*:65534:65534:Nobody:/:/bin/false
col:Wh0yzfAV2qm2Y:100:100:Caldera OpenLinux User:/home/col:/bin/bash
#
# sed 16,18p passwd.test
root:PgYQCkVH65hyQ:0:0:root:/root:/bin/bash
bin:*:1:1:bin:/bin:
daemon:*:2:2:daemon:/sbin:
adm:*:3:4:adm:/var/adm:
lp:*:4:7:lp:/var/spool/lpd:
sync:*:5:0:sync:/sbin:/bin/sync
shutdown:*:6:11:shutdown:/sbin:/sbin/shutdown
halt:*:7:0:halt:/sbin:/sbin/halt
mail:*:8:12:mail:/var/spool/mail:
news:*:9:13:news:/var/spool/news:
uucp:*:10:14:uucp:/var/spool/uucp:
operator:*:11:0:operator:/root:
games:*:12:100:games:/usr/games:
gopher:*:13:30:gopher:/usr/lib/gopher-data:
ftp:*:14:50:FTP User:/home/ftp:
man:*:15:15:Manuals Owner:/:
man:*:15:15:Manuals Owner:/:
nobody:*:65534:65534:Nobody:/:/bin/false
nobody:*:65534:65534:Nobody:/:/bin/false
col:Wh0yzfAV2qm2Y:100:100:Caldera OpenLinux User:/home/col:/bin/bash
col:Wh0yzfAV2qm2Y:100:100:Caldera OpenLinux User:/home/col:/bin/bash
#
# sed -n 16,18p passwd.test
man:*:15:15:Manuals Owner:/:
nobody:*:65534:65534:Nobody:/:/bin/false
col:Wh0yzfAV2qm2Y:100:100:Caldera OpenLinux User:/home/col:/bin/bash
```

The first attempt to print only lines *16*, *17*, and *18* results in all of the lines in the file being printed and lines *16, 17,* and *18* being printed twice. The reason is that **sed** reads each line of input and acts on each line. In order to specify the lines on which to act, we used the *-n* switch to suppress all lines from going to standard output. We then specify the lines we want to print and these will indeed go to standard output.

Now that we know how to view lines 16, 17, and 18 of the file, let's again view **passwd.test** and delete those same three lines with *d*:

```
# cat passwd.test
root:PgYQCkVH65hyQ:0:0:root:/root:/bin/bash
bin:*:1:1:bin:/bin:
daemon:*:2:2:daemon:/sbin:
adm:*:3:4:adm:/var/adm:
lp:*:4:7:lp:/var/spool/lpd:
sync:*:5:0:sync:/sbin:/bin/sync
shutdown:*:6:11:shutdown:/sbin:/sbin/shutdown
halt:*:7:0:halt:/sbin:/sbin/halt
mail:*:8:12:mail:/var/spool/mail:
news:*:9:13:news:/var/spool/news:
uucp:*:10:14:uucp:/var/spool/uucp:
operator:*:11:0:operator:/root:
games:*:12:100:games:/usr/games:
gopher:*:13:30:gopher:/usr/lib/gopher-data:
ftp:*:14:50:FTP User:/home/ftp:
man:*:15:15:Manuals Owner:/:
nobody:*:65534:65534:Nobody:/:/bin/false
col:Wh0yzfAV2qm2Y:100:100:Caldera OpenLinux User:/home/col:/bin/bash
#
# sed 16,18d passwd.test
root:PgYQCkVH65hyQ:0:0:root:/root:/bin/bash
bin:*:1:1:bin:/bin:
daemon:*:2:2:daemon:/sbin:
adm:*:3:4:adm:/var/adm:
lp:*:4:7:lp:/var/spool/lpd:
sync:*:5:0:sync:/sbin:/bin/sync
shutdown:*:6:11:shutdown:/sbin:/sbin/shutdown
halt:*:7:0:halt:/sbin:/sbin/halt
mail:*:8:12:mail:/var/spool/mail:
news:*:9:13:news:/var/spool/news:
uucp:*:10:14:uucp:/var/spool/uucp:
operator:*:11:0:operator:/root:
games:*:12:100:games:/usr/games:
gopher:*:13:30:gopher:/usr/lib/gopher-data:
ftp:*:14:50:FTP User:/home/ftp:
```

man page

grep - 19

man page

sed - 19

As with our earlier **grep** example, we enclose any special characters in single quotes to make sure that they are not interfered with and are passed directly to **sed** unmodified and uninterpreted by the shell. In this example, we specify the range of lines to delete, *16* through *18*, and the *d* for delete. We could specify just one line to delete, such as *16*, and not specify an entire range. Because we did not redirect the output as part of the **sed** command line, the result is sent to standard output. The original file remains intact.

We could search for a pattern in a file and delete only those lines containing the pattern. The following example shows searching for *bash* and deleting the lines that contain *bash:*

```
# cat passwd.test
root:PgYQCkVH65hyQ:0:0:root:/root:/bin/bash
bin:*:1:1:bin:/bin:
daemon:*:2:2:daemon:/sbin:
adm:*:3:4:adm:/var/adm:
lp:*:4:7:lp:/var/spool/lpd:
sync:*:5:0:sync:/sbin:/bin/sync
shutdown:*:6:11:shutdown:/sbin:/sbin/shutdown
halt:*:7:0:halt:/sbin:/sbin/halt
mail:*:8:12:mail:/var/spool/mail:
news:*:9:13:news:/var/spool/news:
uucp:*:10:14:uucp:/var/spool/uucp:
operator:*:11:0:operator:/root:
games:*:12:100:games:/usr/games:
gopher:*:13:30:gopher:/usr/lib/gopher-data:
ftp:*:14:50:FTP User:/home/ftp:
man:*:15:15:Manuals Owner:/:
nobody:*:65534:65534:Nobody:/:/bin/false
col:Wh0yzfAV2qm2Y:100:100:Caldera OpenLinux User:/home/col:/bin/bash
#
# sed '/bash/ d' passwd.test
bin:*:1:1:bin:/bin:
daemon:*:2:2:daemon:/sbin:
adm:*:3:4:adm:/var/adm:
lp:*:4:7:lp:/var/spool/lpd:
sync:*:5:0:sync:/sbin:/bin/sync
shutdown:*:6:11:shutdown:/sbin:/sbin/shutdown
halt:*:7:0:halt:/sbin:/sbin/halt
mail:*:8:12:mail:/var/spool/mail:
news:*:9:13:news:/var/spool/news:
uucp:*:10:14:uucp:/var/spool/uucp:
operator:*:11:0:operator:/root:
games:*:12:100:games:/usr/games:
gopher:*:13:30:gopher:/usr/lib/gopher-data:
ftp:*:14:50:FTP User:/home/ftp:
man:*:15:15:Manuals Owner:/:
nobody:*:65534:65534:Nobody:/:/bin/false
```

Both lines containing *bash* were deleted from **passwd.test** (the *root* line and the *col* line).

As I had mentioned earlier, it is a good idea to use single quotes around all regular expressions. In this example, I enclosed in single quotes the pattern for which I was searching and the command to execute.

What if you wanted to delete all lines except those that contain *bash?* You would insert an exclamation mark before the *d* to delete all lines except those that contain *bash,* as shown in the following example:

```
# cat passwd.test
root:PgYQCkVH65hyQ:0:0:root:/root:/bin/bash
bin:*:1:1:bin:/bin:
daemon:*:2:2:daemon:/sbin:
adm:*:3:4:adm:/var/adm:
lp:*:4:7:lp:/var/spool/lpd:
sync:*:5:0:sync:/sbin:/bin/sync
shutdown:*:6:11:shutdown:/sbin:/sbin/shutdown
halt:*:7:0:halt:/sbin:/sbin/halt
mail:*:8:12:mail:/var/spool/mail:
news:*:9:13:news:/var/spool/news:
uucp:*:10:14:uucp:/var/spool/uucp:
operator:*:11:0:operator:/root:
games:*:12:100:games:/usr/games:
gopher:*:13:30:gopher:/usr/lib/gopher-data:
ftp:*:14:50:FTP User:/home/ftp:
man:*:15:15:Manuals Owner:/:
nobody:*:65534:65534:Nobody:/:/bin/false
col:Wh0yzfAV2qm2Y:100:100:Caldera OpenLinux User:/home/col:/bin/bash
#
# sed '/bash/ !d' passwd.test
root:PgYQCkVH65hyQ:0:0:root:/root:/bin/bash
col:Wh0yzfAV2qm2Y:100:100:Caldera OpenLinux User:/home/col:/bin/bash
```

This resulted in all but the two lines containing *bash* to be deleted from **passwd.test**.

Now that we have seen how to display and delete specific lines of the file, let's see how to add three lines to the end of the file:

```
# sed '$a\
> This is a backup of passwd file\
> for viewing purposes only\
> so do not modify' passwd.test
root:PgYQCkVH65hyQ:0:0:root:/root:/bin/bash
bin:*:1:1:bin:/bin:
daemon:*:2:2:daemon:/sbin:
adm:*:3:4:adm:/var/adm:
lp:*:4:7:lp:/var/spool/lpd:
sync:*:5:0:sync:/sbin:/bin/sync
shutdown:*:6:11:shutdown:/sbin:/sbin/shutdown
halt:*:7:0:halt:/sbin:/sbin/halt
mail:*:8:12:mail:/var/spool/mail:
news:*:9:13:news:/var/spool/news:
uucp:*:10:14:uucp:/var/spool/uucp:
operator:*:11:0:operator:/root:
games:*:12:100:games:/usr/games:
gopher:*:13:30:gopher:/usr/lib/gopher-data:
ftp:*:14:50:FTP User:/home/ftp:
man:*:15:15:Manuals Owner:/:
nobody:*:65534:65534:Nobody:/:/bin/false
col:Wh0yzfAV2qm2Y:100:100:Caldera OpenLinux User:/home/col:/bin/bash
This is a backup of passwd file
for viewing purposes only
so do not modify
```

The backslashes (\) are used liberally in this example. Each back-slash represents a new line. We go to the end of the file, as designated by the $, then we add a new line with the backslash, and then add the text we wish and a new line after the text. These lines are great to add to the end of the file, but we really should add them to the beginning of the file. The following example shows this approach:

```
# sed '1i\
> This is a backup passwd file\
> for viewing purposes only\
> so do not modify\
> ' passwd.test
This is a backup passwd file
for viewing purposes only
so do not modify
root:PgYQCkVH65hyQ:0:0:root:/root:/bin/bash
bin:*:1:1:bin:/bin:
daemon:*:2:2:daemon:/sbin:
adm:*:3:4:adm:/var/adm:
lp:*:4:7:lp:/var/spool/lpd:
sync:*:5:0:sync:/sbin:/bin/sync
shutdown:*:6:11:shutdown:/sbin:/sbin/shutdown
halt:*:7:0:halt:/sbin:/sbin/halt
mail:*:8:12:mail:/var/spool/mail:
news:*:9:13:news:/var/spool/news:
uucp:*:10:14:uucp:/var/spool/uucp:
operator:*:11:0:operator:/root:
games:*:12:100:games:/usr/games:
gopher:*:13:30:gopher:/usr/lib/gopher-data:
ftp:*:14:50:FTP User:/home/ftp:
man:*:15:15:Manuals Owner:/:
nobody:*:65534:65534:Nobody:/:/bin/false
col:Wh0yzfAV2qm2Y:100:100:Caldera OpenLinux User:/home/col:/bin/bash
```

man page

sed - 19

First, we run **sed**, specifying that on line one we are going to begin inserting the text shown. We use the single quote immediately following **sed** and use another single quote on the last line when we are done specifying all the information, except for the input file, which is **passwd.test**.

We have only scratched the surface of commands you can use with **sed**. The following **sed** summary includes the commands we have used (*p* for print; *d* for delete; and *a* for add), as well as others that were not part of the examples.

sed - Stream editor.

Commands

a	Append text.
b	Branch to a label.
c	Replace lines with text.
d	Delete the current text buffer.
D	Delete the first line of the current text buffer.
g	Paste overwriting contents of the hold space.
G	Paste the hold space below the address rather than overwriting it.
h	Copy the pattern space into hold space.
H	Append the contents of pattern space into hold space.
i	Insert text.
l	List the contents of the pattern space.
n	Read the next line of input into the pattern space.
N	Append next line of input to pattern space.
p	Print the pattern space.
P	Print from the start of the pattern space up to and including new line.
q	Quit when address is encountered.
r	Read in a file.
s	Substitute patterns.
t	Branch if substitution has been made to the current pattern space.
w	Append the contents of the pattern space to the specified *file*.
x	Interchange the contents of the holding area and pattern space.
y	Translate characters.

awk

man page

awk - 19

man page

grep - 19

man page

cut - 18

man page

paste - 18

awk can pretty much do it all. With **awk**, you can search, modify files, generate reports, and a lot more. **awk** performs these tasks by searching for patterns in lines of input (from standard input or from a file). For each line that matches the specified pattern, it can perform some very complex processing on that line. The code to actually process matching lines of input is a cross between a shell script and a C program.

Data manipulation tasks that would be very complex with combinations of **grep**, **cut,** and **paste** are very easily done with **awk**. Because **awk** is a programming language, it can also perform mathematical operations or check the input very easily (shells don't do math very well). It can even do floating-point math (shells deal only with integers and strings).

The basic form of an **awk** program looks like this:

```
awk '/pattern_to_match/ {prog to run}' input_file_names
```

Notice that the whole program is enclosed in single quotes. If no input file names are specified, **awk** reads from standard input (as from a pipe).

The *pattern_to_match* must appear between the / characters. The pattern is actually a regular expression. Regular expressions were covered earlier in this chapter. Some common regular expression examples are included shortly.

The program to execute is written in **awk** code, which looks something like C. The program is executed whenever a line of input matches the *pattern_to_match*. If */pattern_to_match/* does not precede the program in *{ }*, then the program is executed for every line of input.

awk works with fields of the input lines. Fields are words separated by white space or some other field separator. **awk** uses white space as a field separator by default. You can use the *-F* option to specify the field separator as shown in a later example. The fields in **awk** patterns and programs are referenced with *$*, followed by the field number. For example, the second field of an input line is *$2*. If you are using an **awk** command in your shell programs, the fields (*$1, $2*, etc.) are not confused with the shell script's positional parameters because the **awk** variables are enclosed in single , causing the shell to ignore them.

You really need to see some examples of using **awk** to appreciate its power. The following few examples use a file called **newfiles**, which contains a list of files on a system less than 15 days old. This file is generated as part of a system administration audit program that checks various aspects of a UNIX system. The following shows the contents of **newfiles**:

```
# cat newfiles
PROG>>>>> report of files not older than 14 days by find
the file system is /
-rw-r--r--   1 root        root           567 Dec   7 07:16 ./etc/mnttab
-rw-r--r--   1 root        root         20713 Dec   7 07:18 ./etc/rc.log
-rw-r--r--   1 root        root             0 Dec   7 07:17 ./etc/hpC2400/hparray.map
-rw-r--r--   1 root        root             0 Dec   7 07:17 ./etc/hpC2400/hparray.devs
-rw-r--r--   1 root        root             0 Dec   7 07:17 ./etc/hpC2400/hparray.luns
-rw-r--r--   1 root        root             0 Dec   7 07:17 ./etc/hpC2400/hparray.addr
-r-s------   1 root        root             0 Dec   7 07:17 ./etc/hpC2400/pscan.lock
-r-s------   1 root        root             0 Dec   7 07:17 ./etc/hpC2400/monitor.lock
-rw-r--r--   1 root        root         14299 Dec   7 07:17 ./etc/hpC2400/HPARRAY.INFO
-rw-r--r--   1 bin         bin           8553 Dec   7 07:02 ./etc/shutdownlog
-rw-r--r--   1 root        mail         32768 Dec   7 07:16 ./etc/mail/aliases.db
-rw-r--r--   1 root        mail            33 Dec   7 07:16 ./etc/mail/sendmail.pid
-rw-r--r--   1 root        root            13 Dec   7 07:16 ./etc/opt/dce/boot_time
-rw-r--r--   1 root        root           720 Dec   7 13:34 ./etc/utmp
-rw-r--r--   1 root        root             0 Dec   7 07:16 ./etc/xtab
-rw-r--r--   1 root        root             0 Dec   7 07:18 ./etc/rmtab
-rw-r--r--   1 root        root         40814 Dec   7 07:15 ./etc/rc.log.old
-rw-r--r--   1 root        root          4620 Dec   7 13:34 ./etc/utmpx
-rw-r--r--   1 root        root             9 Dec   7 13:17 ./etc/ntp.drift
-rw-r--r--   1 root        root           616 Dec   7 07:15 ./etc/auto_parms.log
-rw-r--r--   1 root        sys            219 Dec   7 07:00 ./etc/auto_parms.log.old
-rw-rw-rw-   1 root        sys            520 Nov 23 12:37 ./.sw/sessions/swlist.last
-r--r--r--   1 root        informix        76 Dec   7 07:17 ./INFORMIXTMP/.inf.shmPSREP
-r--r--r--   1 root        informix        76 Dec   7 07:18 ./INFORMIXTMP/.inf.shmPSDEV
-rw-------   1 autosys     autosys       4052 Nov 25 14:08 ./home/autosys/.sh_history
-rw-------   1 tsaxs       users         2228 Dec   1 13:15 ./home/tsaxs/.sh_history
-rw-------   1 tsfxo       users         2862 Nov 24 10:08 ./home/tsfxo/.sh_history
PROG>>>>> report of files not older than 14 days by find
the file system is /usr
-rw-rw-rw-   6 opop6       users           21 Dec   7 13:46 ./local/adm/etc/lmonitor.hst
-rw-r--r--   1 tsgjf       users         1093 Dec   7 13:17
./local/flexlm/licenses/license.log
PROG>>>>> report of files not older than 14 days by find
the file system is /opt
-rw-rw-r--   1 bin         bin            200 Dec   7 07:17 ./pred/bin/OPSDBPF
-rw-r--r--   1 root        sys         800028 Dec   7 07:17 ./pred/bin/PSRNLOGD
PROG>>>>> report of files not older than 14 days by find
the file system is /var
-rw-r--r--   1 root        sys          45089 Dec   7 07:16 ./adm/sw/swagentd.log
-rw-rw-rw-   1 root        sys            562 Dec   7 07:16 ./adm/sw/sessions/swlist.last
-rw-rw-r--   1 root        root         12236 Dec   7 07:16 ./adm/ps_data
-rw-r--r--   1 root        root            65 Dec   7 07:17 ./adm/cron/log
-rw-r--r--   1 root        root           162 Dec   7 07:00 ./adm/cron/OLDlog
-r--r--r--   1 root        root        734143 Dec   7 07:16 ./adm/syslog/mail.log
```

```
-rw-r--r--   1 root      root        65743 Dec  7 13:56 ./adm/syslog/syslog.log
-rw-r--r--   1 root      root      4924974 Dec  7 07:02 ./adm/syslog/OLDsyslog.log
-rw-rw-r--   1 adm       adm       2750700 Dec  7 13:52 ./adm/wtmp
-rw-------   1 root      other      145920 Dec  3 14:36 ./adm/btmp
-rw-r--r--   1 lp        lp             33 Dec  7 07:17 ./adm/lp/log
-rw-r--r--   1 lp        lp             67 Dec  7 07:01 ./adm/lp/oldlog
-rw-r--r--   1 root      root         4330 Dec  7 07:18 ./adm/diag/device_table
-rw-r--r--   1 root      root           34 Dec  7 07:18 ./adm/diag/misc_sys_data
-rwxr-xr-x   1 root      root       995368 Nov 22 15:16 ./adm/diag/LOG0190
-rwxr-xr-x   1 root      root       995368 Nov 23 02:05 ./adm/diag/LOG0191
-rwxr-xr-x   1 root      root       453964 Nov 23 07:01 ./adm/diag/LOG0192
-rwxr-xr-x   1 root      root       970448 Nov 23 18:35 ./adm/diag/LOG0193
-rwxr-xr-x   1 root      root       995368 Nov 24 05:24 ./adm/diag/LOG0194
-rwxr-xr-x   1 root      root       995368 Nov 24 16:14 ./adm/diag/LOG0195
-rwxr-xr-x   1 root      root       995368 Nov 25 03:03 ./adm/diag/LOG0196
-rwxr-xr-x   1 root      root       995368 Nov 25 13:52 ./adm/diag/LOG0197
-rwxr-xr-x   1 root      root       995368 Nov 26 00:41 ./adm/diag/LOG0198
-rwxr-xr-x   1 root      root       995368 Nov 26 11:31 ./adm/diag/LOG0199
-rwxr-xr-x   1 root      root       995368 Nov 26 22:20 ./adm/diag/LOG0200
-rwxr-xr-x   1 root      root       995368 Nov 27 09:09 ./adm/diag/LOG0201
-rwxr-xr-x   1 root      root       995368 Nov 27 19:58 ./adm/diag/LOG0202
-rwxr-xr-x   1 root      root       995368 Nov 28 06:48 ./adm/diag/LOG0203
-rwxr-xr-x   1 root      root       995368 Nov 28 17:37 ./adm/diag/LOG0204
-rwxr-xr-x   1 root      root       995368 Nov 29 04:26 ./adm/diag/LOG0205
-rwxr-xr-x   1 root      root       995368 Nov 29 15:16 ./adm/diag/LOG0206
-rwxr-xr-x   1 root      root       995368 Nov 30 02:05 ./adm/diag/LOG0207
-rwxr-xr-x   1 root      root       452020 Nov 30 06:59 ./adm/diag/LOG0208
-rwxr-xr-x   1 root      root       970448 Nov 30 18:35 ./adm/diag/LOG0209
-rwxr-xr-x   1 root      root       995368 Dec  1 05:24 ./adm/diag/LOG0210
-rwxr-xr-x   1 root      root       995368 Dec  1 16:13 ./adm/diag/LOG0211
-rwxr-xr-x   1 root      root       995368 Dec  2 03:03 ./adm/diag/LOG0212
-rwxr-xr-x   1 root      root       995368 Dec  2 13:52 ./adm/diag/LOG0213
-rwxr-xr-x   1 root      root       995368 Dec  3 00:41 ./adm/diag/LOG0214
-rwxr-xr-x   1 root      root       995368 Dec  3 11:31 ./adm/diag/LOG0215
-rwxr-xr-x   1 root      root       995368 Dec  3 22:20 ./adm/diag/LOG0216
-rwxr-xr-x   1 root      root       995368 Dec  4 09:09 ./adm/diag/LOG0217
-rwxr-xr-x   1 root      root       995368 Dec  4 19:58 ./adm/diag/LOG0218
-rwxr-xr-x   1 root      root       995368 Dec  5 06:48 ./adm/diag/LOG0219
-rwxr-xr-x   1 root      root       995368 Dec  5 17:37 ./adm/diag/LOG0220
-rwxr-xr-x   1 root      root       995368 Dec  6 04:26 ./adm/diag/LOG0221
-rwxr-xr-x   1 root      root       995368 Dec  6 15:15 ./adm/diag/LOG0222
-rwxr-xr-x   1 root      root       995368 Dec  7 02:05 ./adm/diag/LOG0223
-rwxr-xr-x   1 root      root       453964 Dec  7 07:00 ./adm/diag/LOG0224
-rwxr-xr-x   1 root      root       543740 Dec  7 13:57 ./adm/diag/LOG0225
-rw-r--r--   1 root      root        19587 Dec  7 07:16 ./adm/ptydaemonlog
-rw-r--r--   1 root      root           52 Dec  7 07:16 ./adm/conslog.opts
-rw-r--r--   1 root      root            0 Dec  7 07:16 ./adm/rpc.statd.log
-rw-r--r--   1 root      root            0 Dec  7 07:16 ./adm/rpc.lockd.log
-rw-r--r--   1 root      root        24250 Dec  7 07:16 ./adm/vtdaemonlog
-rw-------   1 root      root          214 Dec  7 12:07 ./adm/sulog
-rw-------   1 root      root          381 Dec  3 17:34 ./adm/OLDsulog
-rw-r--r--   1 root      sys           145 Dec  7 07:16 ./adm/rbootd.log
-rw-------   1 sysadm    psoft          60 Dec  1 16:59 ./tmp/EAAa09057
-rw-r--r--   1 tsgjf     users           0 Dec  7 13:17 ./tmp/lockHPCUPLANGS
-rw-r--r--   1 tsgjf     users         175 Dec  7 06:40 ./tmp/.flexlm/lmgrd.1507
-rw-r--r--   1 tsgjf     users         175 Dec  7 13:28 ./tmp/.flexlm/lmgrd.1505
-rw-r--r--   1 lp        lp              0 Dec  7 07:17 ./spool/lp/outputq
-rw-rw-rw-   1 lp        lp              4 Dec  7 07:17 ./spool/lp/SCHEDLOCK
-rw-------   1 root      sys             0 Nov 23 07:00
./spool/cron/tmp/croutAAAa01030
-rw-------   1 root      sys             0 Nov 30 07:00
./spool/cron/tmp/croutAAAa01039
-rw-------   1 root      sys             0 Dec  7 07:00
./spool/cron/tmp/croutAAAb01039
-rw-r--r--   1 root      root            4 Dec  7 07:16 ./run/syslog.pid
-rw-r--r--   1 root      root            4 Dec  7 07:16 ./run/gated.pid
-rw-r--r--   1 root      sys           145 Dec  7 07:16 ./run/gated.version
-rw-r--r--   1 root      sys             3 Dec  7 07:16 ./statmon/state
-rw-r--r--   1 root      root        29771 Dec  7 07:16
./opt/dce/config/dce_config.log
-rw-r--r--   1 root      sys            74 Dec  7 07:16
./opt/dce/rpc/local/00404/srvr_socks
-rw-r--r--   1 root      root           72 Dec  7 07:16
./opt/dce/rpc/local/00927/srvr_socks
-rw-r--r--   1 root      root        32768 Dec  7 07:16 ./opt/dce/dced/Ep.db
```

```
-rw-r--r--   1 root       root        32768 Dec   7 07:20 ./opt/dce/dced/Llb.db
-rw-r--r--   1 root       root            0 Nov 30 07:16 ./opt/perf/status.ttd
-rw-r--r--   1 root       root           33 Dec   7 07:17 ./opt/perf/datafiles/RUN
-rwxrwxrwx   1 root       sys       9243180 Dec   7 13:55 ./opt/perf/datafiles/logappl
-rwxrwxrwx   1 root       sys       8697612 Dec   7 13:55 ./opt/perf/datafiles/logdev
-rwxrwxrwx   1 root       sys       9195152 Dec   7 13:55 ./opt/perf/datafiles/logglob
-rwxrwxrwx   1 root       sys         11112 Dec   7 07:17 ./opt/perf/datafiles/logindx
-rwxrwxrwx   1 root       sys       17639080 Dec  7 13:57
./opt/perf/datafiles/logproc
-rwxrwxrwx   1 root       sys          3797 Dec   7 07:17
./opt/perf/datafiles/mikslp.data
-rw-rw-rw-   1 root       sys           105 Nov 30 10:45 ./opt/perf/datafiles/agdb
-rw-r--r--   1 root       root            5 Dec   7 07:17
./opt/perf/datafiles/.perflbd.pid
-rw-rw-rw-   1 root       sys         21176 Dec   7 07:20 ./opt/perf/status.scope
-rw-rw-rw-   1 root       root            5 Nov 30 07:16 ./opt/perf/ttd.pid
-rw-r--r--   1 root       root            0 Dec   7 07:17 ./opt/perf/status.mi
-rw-rw-rw-   1 root       sys          8254 Dec   7 07:17 ./opt/perf/status.perflbd
-rw-rw-rw-   1 root       sys         21507 Dec   7 07:20 ./opt/perf/status.rep_server
-rw-rw-rw-   1 root       sys         24570 Dec   7 07:20 ./opt/perf/status.alarmgen
-rw-rw-rw-   1 root       sys        160956 Dec   6 21:13 ./opt/omni/log/inet.log
-rw-rw-rw-   1 root       sys        158796 Dec   7 07:17 ./sam/log/samlog
-rw-r--r--   1 root       root        64730 Dec   7 07:17 ./sam/boot.config
-rw-rw-rw-   1 root       sys         11906 Nov 24 14:27 ./sam/poe.iout
-rw-rw-rw-   1 root       sys         11906 Nov 23 09:10 ./sam/poe.iout.old
-rw-rw-rw-   1 root       sys            29 Nov 24 14:27 ./sam/poe.dion
```

You can see that this file contains several fields separated by white space. The next example evaluates the third field to determine whether it equals "adm," and if so, the line is printed:

```
# awk '$3 == "adm" {print}' newfiles
-rw-rw-r--   1 adm        adm       2750700 Dec   7 13:52 ./adm/wtmp
```

There is precisely one line that contains exactly "adm" in the third field.

The next example evaluates the third field to determine whether it approximately equals "adm," meaning that the third field has "adm" embedded in it, and if so, the line is printed:

```
# awk '$3 ~ "adm" {print}' newfiles
-rw-rw-r--   1 adm        adm       2750700 Dec   7 13:52 ./adm/wtmp
-rw-------   1 sysadm     psoft          60 Dec   1 16:59 ./tmp/EAAa09057
```

This result prints the line from the last example, which has "adm" in the third field as well as a line that contains "sysadm."

The next example performs the same search as the previous example; however, this time only fields nine and five are printed:

```
# awk '$3 ~ "adm" {print $9, $5}' newfiles
./adm/wtmp 2750700
./tmp/EAAa09057 60
```

This time only the name of the file, field nine, and the size of the file were printed.

The next example evaluates the third field to determine if it does not equal "root," and if so, prints the entire line:

```
# awk '$3 != "root" {print}' newfiles
PROG>>>>> report of files not older than 14 days by find
the file system is /
-rw-r--r--    1 bin        bin          8553 Dec  7 07:02 ./etc/shutdownlog
-rw-------    1 autosys    autosys      4052 Nov 25 14:08 ./home/autosys/.sh_history
-rw-------    1 tsaxs      users        2228 Dec  1 13:15 ./home/tsaxs/.sh_history
-rw-------    1 tsfxo      users        2862 Nov 24 10:08 ./home/tsfxo/.sh_history
PROG>>>>> report of files not older than 14 days by find
the file system is /usr
-rw-rw-rw-    1 opop6      users          21 Dec  7 13:46 ./local/adm/etc/lmonitor.hst
-rw-r--r--    1 tsgjf      users        1093 Dec  7 13:17
./local/flexlm/licenses/license.log
PROG>>>>> report of files not older than 14 days by find
the file system is /opt
-rw-rw-r--    1 bin        bin           200 Dec  7 07:17 ./pred/bin/OPSDBPF
PROG>>>>> report of files not older than 14 days by find
the file system is /var
-rw-rw-r--    1 adm        adm       2750700 Dec  7 13:52 ./adm/wtmp
-rw-r--r--    1 lp         lp             33 Dec  7 07:17 ./adm/lp/log
-rw-r--r--    1 lp         lp             67 Dec  7 07:01 ./adm/lp/oldlog
-rw-------    1 sysadm     psoft          60 Dec  1 16:59 ./tmp/EAAa09057
-rw-r--r--    1 tsgjf      users           0 Dec  7 13:17 ./tmp/lockHPCUPLANGS
-rw-r--r--    1 tsgjf      users         175 Dec  7 06:40 ./tmp/.flexlm/lmgrd.1507
-rw-r--r--    1 tsgjf      users         175 Dec  7 13:28 ./tmp/.flexlm/lmgrd.1505
-rw-r--r--    1 lp         lp              0 Dec  7 07:17 ./spool/lp/outputq
-rw-rw-rw-    1 lp         lp              4 Dec  7 07:17 ./spool/lp/SCHEDLOCK
```

This command results in many lines being printed that do not have "root" in the third field.

newfiles had whitespace to separate the fields. We don't often have this luxury in the UNIX world. The upcoming examples use **passwd.test**, which has a colon(:) as a field separator. **passwd.test** is shown below:

```
# cat passwd.test
root:PgYQCkVH65hyQ:0:0:root:/root:/bin/bash
bin:*:1:1:bin:/bin:
daemon:*:2:2:daemon:/sbin:
adm:*:3:4:adm:/var/adm:
lp:*:4:7:lp:/var/spool/lpd:
sync:*:5:0:sync:/sbin:/bin/sync
shutdown:*:6:11:shutdown:/sbin:/sbin/shutdown
halt:*:7:0:halt:/sbin:/sbin/halt
mail:*:8:12:mail:/var/spool/mail:
```

```
news:*:9:13:news:/var/spool/news:
uucp:*:10:14:uucp:/var/spool/uucp:
operator:*:11:0:operator:/root:
games:*:12:100:games:/usr/games:
gopher:*:13:30:gopher:/usr/lib/gopher-data:
ftp:*:14:50:FTP User:/home/ftp:
man:*:15:15:Manuals Owner:/:
nobody:*:65534:65534:Nobody:/:/bin/false
col:Wh0yzfAV2qm2Y:100:100:Caldera OpenLinux User:/home/col:/bin/bash
```

You can specify the field separator with the *-F* option followed by a separator, which is a colon(:) in **passwd.test**. The following example specifies the field separator and then evaluates the first field to determine whether it equals "root," and if so, prints out the entire line:

```
# awk -F: '$1 == "root" {print}' passwd.test
root:PgYQCkVH65hyQ:0:0:root:/root:/bin/bash
```

The following example specifies the field separator and then evaluates the fourth field to determine whether it equals "0," which means the user is a member of the same group as root, and if so, prints out the entire line:

```
# awk -F: '$4 == "0" {print}' passwd.test
root:PgYQCkVH65hyQ:0:0:root:/root:/bin/bash
sync:*:5:0:sync:/sbin:/bin/sync
halt:*:7:0:halt:/sbin:/sbin/halt
operator:*:11:0:operator:/root:
```

You can perform many types of comparisons besides == using **awk**. The following examples show the use of several comparison operators on our trusty **passwd.test** file. The first example prints all users who are in a group with a value less than *14*:

man page

awk - 19

```
# awk -F: '$4 < 14 {print}' passwd.test
root:PgYQCkVH65hyQ:0:0:root:/root:/bin/bash
bin:*:1:1:bin:/bin:
daemon:*:2:2:daemon:/sbin:
adm:*:3:4:adm:/var/adm:
lp:*:4:7:lp:/var/spool/lpd:
```

```
sync:*:5:0:sync:/sbin:/bin/sync
shutdown:*:6:11:shutdown:/sbin:/sbin/shutdown
halt:*:7:0:halt:/sbin:/sbin/halt
mail:*:8:12:mail:/var/spool/mail:
news:*:9:13:news:/var/spool/news:
operator:*:11:0:operator:/root:
```

The next example prints all users who are in a group with a value less than or equal to *14*:

```
# awk -F: '$4 <= 14 {print}' passwd.test
root:PgYQCkVH65hyQ:0:0:root:/root:/bin/bash
bin:*:1:1:bin:/bin:
daemon:*:2:2:daemon:/sbin:
adm:*:3:4:adm:/var/adm:
lp:*:4:7:lp:/var/spool/lpd:
sync:*:5:0:sync:/sbin:/bin/sync
shutdown:*:6:11:shutdown:/sbin:/sbin/shutdown
halt:*:7:0:halt:/sbin:/sbin/halt
mail:*:8:12:mail:/var/spool/mail:
news:*:9:13:news:/var/spool/news:
uucp:*:10:14:uucp:/var/spool/uucp:
operator:*:11:0:operator:/root:
```

Let's now print all users who are in a group that does not have a value of *14*:

```
# awk -F: '$4 != 14 {print}' passwd.test
root:PgYQCkVH65hyQ:0:0:root:/root:/bin/bash
bin:*:1:1:bin:/bin:
daemon:*:2:2:daemon:/sbin:
adm:*:3:4:adm:/var/adm:
lp:*:4:7:lp:/var/spool/lpd:
sync:*:5:0:sync:/sbin:/bin/sync
shutdown:*:6:11:shutdown:/sbin:/sbin/shutdown
halt:*:7:0:halt:/sbin:/sbin/halt
mail:*:8:12:mail:/var/spool/mail:
news:*:9:13:news:/var/spool/news:
operator:*:11:0:operator:/root:
games:*:12:100:games:/usr/games:
gopher:*:13:30:gopher:/usr/lib/gopher-data:
ftp:*:14:50:FTP User:/home/ftp:
man:*:15:15:Manuals Owner:/:
nobody:*:65534:65534:Nobody:/:/bin/false
col:Wh0yzfAV2qm2Y:100:100:Caldera OpenLinux User:/home/col:/bin/bash
```

Let's now print all users who are in a group with a value greater than or equal to *14*:

```
# awk -F: '$4 >= 14 {print}' passwd.test
uucp:*:10:14:uucp:/var/spool/uucp:
games:*:12:100:games:/usr/games:
gopher:*:13:30:gopher:/usr/lib/gopher-data:
ftp:*:14:50:FTP User:/home/ftp:
man:*:15:15:Manuals Owner:/:
```

```
nobody:*:65534:65534:Nobody:/:/bin/false
col:Wh0yzfAV2qm2Y:100:100:Caldera OpenLinux User:/home/col:/bin/bash
```

The last example shows all users who are in a group with a value greater than 14:

```
# awk -F: '$4 > 14 {print}' passwd.test
games:*:12:100:games:/usr/games:
gopher:*:13:30:gopher:/usr/lib/gopher-data:
ftp:*:14:50:FTP User:/home/ftp:
man:*:15:15:Manuals Owner:/:
nobody:*:65534:65534:Nobody:/:/bin/false
col:Wh0yzfAV2qm2Y:100:100:Caldera OpenLinux User:/home/col:/bin/bash
```

man page

awk - 19

There is much more to **awk** than what I covered in this section. There are additional **awk** examples in the shell programming chapter.

The following table summarizes some of the comparison operators of **awk** covered in this section:

awk - Search a line for a specified pattern and perform operation(s).

Comparison operators:

<	Less than.
<=	Less than or equal to.
==	Equal to.
~	Strings match.
!=	Not equal to.
>=	Greater than or equal to.
>	Greater than.

grep

man page

grep - 19

Here in the information age, we have too much information. We are constantly trying to extract the information we are after from stacks of information. The **grep** command is used to search for text and display it. **grep** stands for General Regular Expression Parser. Let's first look at a few simple searches and display the output with **grep**. Figure 19-1 shows creating a long listing for **/home/denise**, and using **grep**, we search for patterns.

```
                              grep example
$ ls -a /home/denise | grep netscape
.netscape-bookmarks.html
.netscape-cache
.netscape-history
.netscape-newsgroups-news.spry.com
.netscape-newsgroups-newsserv.hp.com
.netscape-preferences
$ ls -a /home/denise | grep -c netscape
6
$ ls -a /home/denise | grep NETSCAPE
$ ls -a /home/denise | grep -i NETSCAPE
.netscape-bookmarks.html
.netscape-cache
.netscape-history
.netscape-newsgroups-news.spry.com
.netscape-newsgroups-newsserv.hp.com
.netscape-preferences
$ ls -a /home/denise | grep -F "netscape
> .c"
.cshrc
.cshrc.orig
.netscape-bookmarks.html
.netscape-cache
.netscape-history
.netscape-newsgroups-news.spry.com
.netscape-newsgroups-newsserv.hp.com
.netscape-preferences
.newsrc-news.spry.com
.newsrc-newsserv.hp.com
$ ▮      __ __
```

Figure 19-1　**grep** Command

First, we search for the pattern *netscape*. This produces a list of files, all of which begin with *.netscape*.

Next we use the *-c* option to create a count for the number of times that *netscape* is found. The result is 6.

Do you think that **grep** is case-sensitive? The next example shows searching for the pattern *NETSCAPE,* and no matching patterns exist.

Using the *-i* option causes **grep** to ignore uppercase and lower case and just search for the pattern, and again, all the original matches are found.

Also, more than one pattern can be searched for. Using the **-F** option, both *netscape* and *.c* are searched for and a longer list of matches are found. Notice that two patterns to search for are enclosed in double quotes and are separated by a new line.

Let's now take a look at a couple more advanced searches using **grep**. We'll use the **passwd.test** file as the basis for our searches because each line in it contains a lot of information. To start, the following is the contents of the **passwd.test** file on a Linux system:

```
# cat passwd.test
root:PgYQCkVH65hyQ:0:0:root:/root:/bin/bash
bin:*:1:1:bin:/bin:
daemon:*:2:2:daemon:/sbin:
adm:*:3:4:adm:/var/adm:
lp:*:4:7:lp:/var/spool/lpd:
sync:*:5:0:sync:/sbin:/bin/sync
shutdown:*:6:11:shutdown:/sbin:/sbin/shutdown
halt:*:7:0:halt:/sbin:/sbin/halt
mail:*:8:12:mail:/var/spool/mail:
news:*:9:13:news:/var/spool/news:
uucp:*:10:14:uucp:/var/spool/uucp:
operator:*:11:0:operator:/root:
games:*:12:100:games:/usr/games:
gopher:*:13:30:gopher:/usr/lib/gopher-data:
ftp:*:14:50:FTP User:/home/ftp:
man:*:15:15:Manuals Owner:/:
nobody:*:65534:65534:Nobody:/:/bin/false
col:Wh0yzfAV2qm2Y:100:100:Caldera OpenLinux
     User:/home/col:/bin/bash
```

We can search for a string in the password file just as we did in the earlier **grep** example. The following example searches for *news* in the **passwd.test** file:

```
# grep news passwd.test
news:*:9:13:news:/var/spool/news:
```

Now let's check to see whether there is a user named *bin* in the **passwd.test** file. In order for a user named *bin* to have an entry in the **passwd.test** file, the user name, in this case *bin*, would be the first entry in the line. Here is the result of searching for this user:

```
# grep bin passwd.test
root:PgYQCkVH65hyQ:0:0:root:/root:/bin/bash
bin:*:1:1:bin:/bin:
daemon:*:2:2:daemon:/sbin:
sync:*:5:0:sync:/sbin:/bin/sync
shutdown:*:6:11:shutdown:/sbin:/sbin/shutdown
halt:*:7:0:halt:/sbin:/sbin/halt
nobody:*:65534:65534:Nobody:/:/bin/false
col:Wh0yzfAV2qm2Y:100:100:Caldera OpenLinux
     User:/home/col:/bin/bash
```

Many lines from **passwd.test** are indeed produced that contain the string *bin*; however, we have to search through these lines in order to find the user *bin,* which is the line in which *bin* is the first string that appears. This is more than we wanted when we initiated our search. We wanted to see a user name *bin* that would appear at the beginning of a line. We can further qualify our search, in this case to limit the search to a string at the beginning of a line, by using pattern matching discussed at the beginning of this chapter (see the Table 19-1.) In this case, we want to search only at the beginning of a line for *bin*, so we'll qualify our search with a caret (^) to restrict the search to only the beginning of the line, as shown in the following example:

```
# grep ^bin passwd.test
bin:*:1:1:bin:/bin:
```

This search results in exactly the information in which we are interested, that is, a line beginning with *bin*. When using special characters, such as the caret(^) in this example, you should enclose the special characters in single quotes ('). Special characters may be interpreted by the shell and cause problems with the arguments we're trying to send to **grep**. Enclosing the search pattern in single quotes will ensures that the search pattern, in this case *^bin,* is passed directly to **grep**. The search pattern in single quotes looks like the following:

man page

grep - 19

```
# grep '^bin' passwd.test
bin:*:1:1:bin:/bin:
```

Because we are going to have to search for this line in the **passwd.test** file after we find it, we may as well print out the line number as well as the line itself by using the *-n* option, as shown in the following example:

```
# grep -n '^bin' passwd.test
2:bin:*:1:1:bin:/bin:
```

The following is a summary of the **grep** command:

grep - Search for text and display results.

Options

-c	Return the number of matches without showing you the text.
-h	Show the text with no reference to file names.
-i	Ignore the case when searching.

-l	Return the names of files containing a match without showing you the text.
-n	Return the line number of the text searched for in a file as well as the text itself.
-v	Return the lines that do not match the text you searched for.
-E	Search for more than one expression (same as **egrep**).
-F	Search for more than one expression (same as **fgrep**).

Manual Pages for Some Commands Used in Chapter 19

The following are the HP-UX manual pages for many of the commands used in the chapter. Commands often differ among UNIX variants, so you may find differences in the options or other areas for some commands; however, the following manual pages serve as an excellent reference.

awk

awk - Pattern-processing language.

```
awk(1)                                                              awk(1)

NAME
     awk - pattern-directed scanning and processing language

SYNOPSIS

     awk [-Ffs] [-v var=value] [program | -f progfile ...] [file ...]

DESCRIPTION
     awk scans each input file for lines that match any of a set of
     patterns specified literally in program or in one or more files
     specified as -f progfile.  With each pattern there can be an
     associated action that is to be performed when a line in a file
     matches the pattern.  Each line is matched against the pattern
     of every pattern-action statement, and the associated action is
     performed for each matched pattern.  The file name - means the
     standard input.  Any file of the form var=value is treated as an
     assignment, not a filename.  An assignment is evaluated at the time it
     would have been opened if it were a filename, unless the -v option is
     used.

     An input line is made up of fields separated by white space, or by
     regular expression FS.  The fields are denoted $1, $2, ...; $0 refers
     to the entire line.

Options
     awk recognizes the following options and arguments:

          -F fs          Specify regular expression used to separate
                         fields.  The default is to recognize space and tab
                         characters, and to discard leading spaces and
                         tabs.  If the -F option is used, leading input
                         field separators are no longer discarded.

          -f progfile    Specify an awk program file.  Up to 100 program
                         files can be specified.  The pattern-action
                         statements in these files are executed in the same
                         order as the files were specified.

          -v var=value   Cause var=value assignment to occur before the
                         BEGIN action (if it exists) is executed.

Statements
     A pattern-action statement has the form:

          pattern { action }

     A missing { action } means print the line; a missing pattern always
     matches.  Pattern-action statements are separated by new-lines or
     semicolons.

     An action is a sequence of statements.  A statement can be one of the
```

following:

```
if(expression) statement [else statement]
while(expression) statement
for(expression;expression;expression) statement
for(var in array) statement
do statement while(expression)
break
continue
{[statement ...]}
expression                      # commonly var=expression
print[expression-list] [> expression]
printf format [, expression-list] [> expression]
return [expression]
next            # skip remaining patterns on this input line.
delete array [expression]       # delete an array element.
exit [expression]       # exit immediately; status is expression.
```

Statements are terminated by semicolons, newlines or right braces. An empty expression-list stands for $0. String constants are quoted ("") , with the usual C escapes recognized within. Expressions take on string or numeric values as appropriate, and are built using the operators +, -, *, /, %, ^ (exponentiation), and concatenation (indicated by a blank). The operators ++, --, +=, -=, *=, /=, %=, ^=, **=, >, >=, <, <=, ==, !=, and ?: are also available in expressions. Variables can be scalars, array elements (denoted x[i]) or fields. Variables are initialized to the null string. Array subscripts can be any string, not necessarily numeric (this allows for a form of associative memory). Multiple subscripts such as [i,j,k] are permitted. The constituents are concatenated, separated by the value of SUBSEP.

The print statement prints its arguments on the standard output (or on a file if >file or >>file is present or on a pipe if |cmd is present), separated by the current output field separator, and terminated by the output record separator. file and cmd can be literal names or parenthesized expressions. Identical string values in different statements denote the same open file. The printf statement formats its expression list according to the format (see printf(3)).

Built-In Functions
The built-in function close(expr) closes the file or pipe expr opened by a print or printf statement or a call to getline with the same string-valued expr. This function returns zero if successful, otherwise, it returns non-zero.

The customary functions exp, log, sqrt, sin, cos, atan2 are built in. Other built-in functions are:

blength[([s])]   Length of its associated argument (in bytes)
                   taken as a string, or of $0 if no argument.

length[([s])]   Length of its associated argument (in characters)
                   taken as a string, or of $0 if no argument.

rand()   Returns a random number between zero and one.

srand([expr])   Sets the seed value for rand, and returns the
                   previous seed value. If no argument is given,
                   the time of day is used as the seed value;
                   otherwise, expr is used.

int(x)   Truncates to an integer value

substr(s, m[, n]) Return the at most n-character substring of s
                   that begins at position m, numbering from 1. If

	n is omitted, the substring is limited by the length of string s.
index(s, t)	Return the position, in characters, numbering from 1, in string s where string t first occurs, or zero if it does not occur at all.
match(s, ere)	Return the position, in characters, numbering from 1, in string s where the extended regular expression ere occurs, or 0 if it does not. The variables RSTART and RLENGTH are set to the position and length of the matched string.
split(s, a[, fs])	Splits the string s into array elements a[1], a[2], ..., a[n], and returns n. The separation is done with the regular expression fs, or with the field separator FS if fs is not given.
sub(ere, repl [, in])	Substitutes repl for the first occurrence of the extended regular expression ere in the string in. If in is not given, $0 is used.
gsub	Same as sub except that all occurrences of the regular expression are replaced; sub and gsub return the number of replacements.
sprintf(fmt, expr, ...)	String resulting from formatting expr ... according to the printf(3S) format fmt
system(cmd)	Executes cmd and returns its exit status
toupper(s)	Converts the argument string s to uppercase and returns the result.
tolower(s)	Converts the argument string s to lowercase and returns the result.

The built-in function getline sets $0 to the next input record from the current input file; getline < file sets $0 to the next record from file. getline x sets variable x instead. Finally, cmd | getline pipes the output of cmd into getline; each call of getline returns the next line of output from cmd. In all cases, getline returns 1 for a successful input, 0 for end of file, and -1 for an error.

Patterns
    Patterns are arbitrary Boolean combinations (with ! || &&) of regular expressions and relational expressions. awk supports Extended Regular Expressions as described in regexp(5). Isolated regular expressions in a pattern apply to the entire line. Regular expressions can also occur in relational expressions, using the operators ~ and !~. /re/ is a constant regular expression; any string (constant or variable) can be used as a regular expression, except in the position of an isolated regular expression in a pattern.

    A pattern can consist of two patterns separated by a comma; in this case, the action is performed for all lines from an occurrence of the first pattern though an occurrence of the second.

    A relational expression is one of the following:

        expression matchop regular-expression
        expression relop expression
        expression in array-name
        (expr,expr,...) in array-name

where a relop is any of the six relational operators in C, and a matchop is either ~ (matches) or !~ (does not match). A conditional is an arithmetic expression, a relational expression, or a Boolean combination of the two.

The special patterns BEGIN and END can be used to capture control before the first input line is read and after the last. BEGIN and END do not combine with other patterns.

Special Characters
The following special escape sequences are recognized by awk in both regular expressions and strings:

Escape	Meaning
\a	alert character
\b	backspace character
\f	form-feed character
\n	new-line character
\r	carriage-return character
\t	tab character
\v	vertical-tab character
\nnn	1- to 3-digit octal value nnn
\xhhh	1- to n-digit hexadecimal number

Variable Names
Variable names with special meanings are:

FS	Input field separator regular expression; a space character by default; also settable by option -Ffs.
NF	The number of fields in the current record.
NR	The ordinal number of the current record from the start of input. Inside a BEGIN action the value is zero. Inside an END action the value is the number of the last record processed.
FNR	The ordinal number of the current record in the current file. Inside a BEGIN action the value is zero. Inside an END action the value is the number of the last record processed in the last file processed.
FILENAME	A pathname of the current input file.
RS	The input record separator; a newline character by default.
OFS	The print statement output field separator; a space character by default.
ORS	The print statement output record separator; a newline character by default.
OFMT	Output format for numbers (default %.6g). If the value of OFMT is not a floating-point format specification, the results are unspecified.
CONVFMT	Internal conversion format for numbers (default %.6g). If the value of CONVFMT is not a floating-point format specification, the results are unspecified.

SUBSEP	The subscript separator string for multi-dimensional arrays; the default value is " 34"
ARGC	The number of elements in the ARGV array.
ARGV	An array of command line arguments, excluding options and the program argument numbered from zero to ARGC-1.
	The arguments in ARGV can be modified or added to; ARGC can be altered. As each input file ends, awk will treat the next non-null element of ARGV, up to the current value of ARGC-1, inclusive, as the name of the next input file. Thus, setting an element of ARGV to null means that it will not be treated as an input file. The name - indicates the standard input. If an argument matches the format of an assignment operand, this argument will be treated as an assignment rather than a file argument.
ENVIRON	Array of environment variables; subscripts are names. For example, if environment variable V=thing, ENVIRON["V"] produces thing.
RSTART	The starting position of the string matched by the match function, numbering from 1. This is always equivalent to the return value of the match function.
RLENGTH	The length of the string matched by the match function.

Functions can be defined (at the position of a pattern-action statement) as follows:

```
function foo(a, b, c) { ...; return x }
```

Parameters are passed by value if scalar, and by reference if array name. Functions can be called recursively. Parameters are local to the function; all other variables are global.

Note that if pattern-action statements are used in an HP-UX command line as an argument to the awk command, the pattern-action statement must be enclosed in single quotes to protect it from the shell. For example, to print lines longer than 72 characters, the pattern-action statement as used in a script (-f progfile command form) is:

```
length > 72
```

The same pattern action statement used as an argument to the awk command is quoted in this manner:

```
awk 'length > 72'
```

EXTERNAL INFLUENCES
   Environment Variables
      LANG   Provides a default value for the internationalization variables that are unset or null. If LANG is unset or null, the default value of "C" (see lang(5)) is used. If any of the internationalization variables contains an invalid setting, awk will behave as if all internationalization variables are set to "C". See environ(5).

LC_ALL   If set to a non-empty string value, overrides the
                        values of all the other internationalization variables.

LC_CTYPE   Determines the interpretation of text as single and/or
                        multi-byte characters, the classification of characters
                        as printable, and the characters matched by character
                        class expressions in regular expressions.

LC_NUMERIC   Determines the radix character used when interpreting
                        numeric input, performing conversion between numeric
                        and string values and formatting numeric output.
                        Regardless of locale, the period character (the
                        decimal-point character of the POSIX locale) is the
                        decimal-point character recognized in processing awk
                        programs (including assignments in command-line
                        arguments).

LC_COLLATE   Determines the locale for the behavior of ranges,
                        equivalence classes and multi-character collating
                        elements within regular expressions.

LC_MESSAGES   Determines the locale that should be used to affect the
                        format and contents of diagnostic messages written to
                        standard error and informative messages written to
                        standard output.

NLSPATH   Determines the location of message catalogues for the
                        processing of LC_MESSAGES.

PATH   Determines the search path when looking for commands
                        executed by system(cmd), or input and output pipes.

In addition, all environment variables will be visible via the awk
variable ENVIRON.

International Code Set Support
    Single- and multi-byte character code sets are supported except that
    variable names must contain only ASCII characters and regular
    expressions must contain only valid characters.

DIAGNOSTICS
    awk supports up to 199 fields ($1, $2, ..., $199) per record.

EXAMPLES
    Print lines longer than 72 characters:

        length > 72

    Print first two fields in opposite order:

        { print $2, $1 }

    Same, with input fields separated by comma and/or blanks and tabs:

        BEGIN { FS = ",[\t]*|[\t]+" }
              { print $2, $1 }

    Add up first column, print sum and average:

              { s += $1 }"
        END   { print "sum is", s, " average is", s/NR }

    Print all lines between start/stop pairs:

        /start/, /stop/

Simulate echo command (see echo(1)):

```
BEGIN   {                          # Simulate echo(1)
        for (i = 1; i < ARGC; i++) printf "%s ", ARGV[i]
        printf "\n"
        exit }
```

AUTHOR
    awk was developed by AT&T, IBM, OSF, and HP.

SEE ALSO
    lex(1), sed(1).
    A. V. Aho, B. W. Kernighan, P. J. Weinberger: The AWK Programming
    Language, Addison-Wesley, 1988.

STANDARDS CONFORMANCE
    awk: SVID2, SVID3, XPG2, XPG3, XPG4, POSIX.2

grep

grep - Command to match a specified pattern.

```
grep(1)                                                          grep(1)

NAME
     grep, egrep, fgrep - search a file for a pattern

SYNOPSIS

    Plain call with pattern
       grep [-E|-F] [-c|-l|-q] [-insvx] pattern [file ...]

    Call with (multiple) -e pattern
       grep [-E|-F] [-c|-l|-q] [-binsvx] -e pattern...  [-e pattern] ...
          [file ...]

    Call with -f file
       grep [-E|-F] [-c|-l|-q] [-insvx] [-f pattern_file] [file ...]

    Obsolescent:
       egrep [-cefilnsv] [expression] [file ...]

       fgrep [-cefilnsvx] [strings] [file ...]

DESCRIPTION
       The grep command searches the input text files (standard input
       default) for lines matching a pattern.  Normally, each line found is
       copied to the standard output.  grep supports the Basic Regular
       Expression syntax (see regexp(5)).  The -E option (egrep) supports
       Extended Regular Expression (ERE) syntax (see regexp(5)).  The -F
       option (fgrep) searches for fixed strings using the fast Boyer-Moore
       string searching algorithm.  The -E and -F options treat newlines
       embedded in the pattern as alternation characters.  A null expression
       or string matches every line.

       The forms egrep and fgrep are maintained for backward compatibility.
       The use of the -E and -F options is recommended for portability.

    Options
               -E               Extended regular expressions.  Each pattern
                                specified is a sequence of one or more EREs.
                                The EREs can be separated by newline
                                characters or given in separate -e expression
                                options.  A pattern matches an input line if
                                any ERE in the sequence matches the contents
                                of the input line without its trailing
                                newline character.  The same functionality is
                                obtained by using egrep.

               -F               Fixed strings.  Each pattern specified is a
                                sequence of one or more strings.  Strings can
                                be separated by newline characters or given
                                in separate -e expression options.  A pattern
                                matches an input line if the line contains
                                any of the strings in the sequence.  The same
```

functionality is obtained by using fgrep.

-b   Each line is preceded by the block number on
                            which it was found. This is useful in
                            locating disk block numbers by context.
                            Block numbers are calculated by dividing by
                            512 the number of bytes that have been read
                            from the file and rounding down the result.

-c   Only a count of matching lines is printed.

-e expression   Same as a simple expression argument, but
                            useful when the expression begins with a
                            hyphen (-). Multiple -e options can be used
                            to specify multiple patterns; an input line
                            is selected if it matches any of the
                            specified patterns.

-f pattern_file   The regular expression (grep and grep -E) or
                            strings list (grep -F) is taken from the
                            pattern_file.

-i   Ignore uppercase/lowercase distinctions
                            during comparisons.

-l   Only the names of files with matching lines
                            are listed (once), separated by newlines. If
                            standard input is searched, a path name of -
                            is listed.

-n   Each line is preceded by its relative line
                            number in the file starting at 1. The line
                            number is reset for each file searched. This
                            option is ignored if -c, -b, -l, or -q is
                            specified.

-q   (Quiet) Do not write anything to the standard
                            output, regardless of matching lines. Exit
                            with zero status upon finding the first
                            matching line. Overrides any options that
                            would produce output.

-s   Error messages produced for nonexistent or
                            unreadable files are suppressed.

-v   All lines but those matching are printed.

-x   (eXact) Matches are recognized only when the
                            entire input line matches the fixed string or
                            regular expression.

In all cases in which output is generated, the file name is output if
there is more than one input file. Care should be taken when using
the characters $, *, [, ^, |, (,), and \ in expression, because they
are also meaningful to the shell. It is safest to enclose the entire
expression argument in single quotes ('...').

EXTERNAL INFLUENCES
Environment Variables
    LANG determines the locale to use for the locale categories when both
    LC_ALL and the corresponding environment variable (beginning with LC_)
    do not specify a locale. If LANG is not specified or is set to the
    empty string, a default of C (see lang(5)) is used.

    LC_ALL determines the locale to use to override any values for locale categories specified by the settings of LANG or any environment variables beginning with LC_.

LC_COLLATE determines the collating sequence used in evaluating regular expressions.

LC_CTYPE determines the interpretation of text as single byte and/or multi-byte characters, the classification of characters as letters, the case information for the -i option, and the characters matched by character class expressions in regular expressions.

LC_MESSAGES determines the language in which messages are displayed.

If any internationalization variable contains an invalid setting, the commands behave as if all internationalization variables are set to C. See environ(5).

International Code Set Support
Single-byte and multi-byte character code sets are supported.

RETURN VALUE
Upon completion, grep returns one of the following values:

    0   One or more matches found.
    1   No match found.
    2   Syntax error or inaccessible file (even if matches were
         found).

EXAMPLES
In the Bourne shell (sh(1)) the following example searches two files, finding all lines containing occurrences of any of four strings:

    grep -F 'if
    then
    else
    fi' file1 file2

Note that the single quotes are necessary to tell grep -F when the strings have ended and the file names have begun.

For the C shell (see csh(1)) the following command can be used:

    grep -F 'if\ then\ else\ fi' file1 file2

To search a file named address containing the following entries:

    Ken   112 Warring St. Apt. A
    Judy   387 Bowditch Apt. 12
    Ann   429 Sixth St.

the command:

    grep Judy address

prints:

    Judy 387 Bowditch Apt. 12

To search a file for lines that contain either a Dec or Nov, use either of the following commands:

    grep -E '[Dd]ec|[Nn]ov' file

    egrep -i 'dec|nov' file

Search all files in the current directory for the string xyz:

```
grep xyz *
```

Search all files in the current directory subtree for the string xyz, and ensure that no error occurs due to file name expansion exceeding system argument list limits:

```
find . -type f -print |xargs grep xyz
```

The previous example does not print the name of files where string xyz appears. To force grep to print file names, add a second argument to the grep command portion of the command line:

```
find . -type f -print |xargs grep xyz /dev/null
```

In this form, the first file name is that produced by find, and the second file name is the null file.

WARNINGS
    (XPG4 only.) If the -q option is specified, the exit status will be zero if an input line is selected, even if an error was detected. Otherwise, default actions will be performed.

SEE ALSO
    sed(1), sh(1), regcomp(3C), environ(5), lang(5), regexp(5).

STANDARDS CONFORMANCE
    grep: SVID2, SVID3, XPG2, XPG3, XPG4, POSIX.2

    egrep: SVID2, SVID3, XPG2, XPG3, XPG4, POSIX.2

    fgrep: SVID2, SVID3, XPG2, XPG3, XPG4, POSIX.2

sed

man page

sed - 19

sed - Stream text editor.

---

sed(1)   sed(1)

NAME
     sed - stream text editor

SYNOPSIS

     sed [-n] script [file ...]

     sed [-n] [-e script] ... [-f script_file] ... [file ...]

DESCRIPTION
     sed copies the named text files (standard input default) to the
     standard output, edited according to a script containing up to 100
     commands. Only complete input lines are processed. Any input text at
     the end of a file that is not terminated by a new-line character is
     ignored.

   Options
     sed recognizes the following options:

          -f script_file
                    Take script from file script_file.

          -e script   Edit according to script. If there is just one -e
                       option and no -f options, the flag -e can be omitted.

          -n   Suppress the default output.

     sed interprets all -escript and -fscript_file arguments in the order
     given. Use caution, if mixing -e and -f options, to avoid
     unpredictable or incorrect results.

   Command Scripts
     A script consists of editor commands, one per line, of the following
     form:

          [address [, address]] function [arguments]

     In normal operation, sed cyclically copies a line of input into a
     pattern space (unless there is something left after a D command),
     applies in sequence all commands whose addresses select that pattern
     space, and, at the end of the script, copies the pattern space to the
     standard output (except under -n) and deletes the pattern space.

     Some of the commands use a hold space to save all or part of the
     pattern space for subsequent retrieval.

   Command Addresses
     An address is either a decimal number that counts input lines
     cumulatively across files, a $ which addresses the last line of input,
     or a context address; that is, a /regular expression/ in the style of

ed(1) modified thus:

- In a context address, the construction \?regular expression?, where ? is any character, is identical to /regular expression/. Note that in the context address \xabc\xdefx, the second x stands for itself, so that the regular expression is abcxdef.

- The escape sequence \n matches a new-line character embedded in the pattern space.

- A period (.) matches any character except the terminal new-line of the pattern space.

- A command line with no addresses selects every pattern space.

- A command line with one address selects each pattern space that matches the address.

- A command line with two addresses selects the inclusive range from the first pattern space that matches the first address through the next pattern space that matches the second (if the second address is a number less than or equal to the line number first selected, only one line is selected). Thereafter the process is repeated, looking again for the first address.

sed supports Basic Regular Expression syntax (see regexp(5)).

Editing commands can also be applied to only non-selected pattern spaces by use of the negation function ! (described below).

Command Functions

In the following list of functions, the maximum number of permissible addresses for each function is indicated in parentheses. Other function elements are interpreted as follows:

text	One or more lines, all but the last of which end with \ to hide the new-line. Backslashes in text are treated like backslashes in the replacement string of an s command, and can be used to protect initial blanks and tabs against the stripping that is done on every script line.
rfile	Must terminate the command line, and must be preceded by exactly one blank.
wfile	Must terminate the command line, and must be preceded by exactly one blank. Each wfile is created before processing begins. There can be at most 10 distinct wfile arguments.

sed recognizes the following functions:

(1)a\
text   Append. Place text on the output before reading next input line.

(2)b label   Branch to the : command bearing label. If no label is specified, branch to the end of the script.

(2)c\
text   Change. Delete the pattern space. With 0 or 1 address or at the end of a 2-address range, place text on the output. Start the next cycle.

(2)d	Delete pattern space and start the next cycle.
(2)D	Delete initial segment of pattern space through first new-line and start the next cycle.
(2)g	Replace contents of the pattern space with contents of the hold space.
(2)G	Append contents of hold space to the pattern space.
(2)h	Replace contents of the hold space with contents of the pattern space.
(2)H	Append the contents of the pattern space to the hold space.
(1)i\ text	Insert. Place text on the standard output.
(2)l	List the pattern space on the standard output in an unambiguous form. Non-printing characters are spelled in three-digit octal number format (with a preceding backslash), and long lines are folded.
(2)n	Copy the pattern space to the standard output if the default output has not been suppressed (by the -n option on the command line or the #n command in the script file). Replace the pattern space with the next line of input.
(2)N	Append the next line of input to the pattern space with an embedded new-line. (The current line number changes.)
(2)p	Print. Copy the pattern space to the standard output.
(2)P	Copy the initial segment of the pattern space through the first new-line to the standard output.
(1)q	Quit. Branch to the end of the script. Do not start a new cycle.
(1)r rfile	Read contents of rfile and place on output before reading the next input line.

(2)s/regular expression/replacement/flags
Substitute replacement string for instances of regular expression in the pattern space. Any character can be used instead of /. For a fuller description see ed(1). flags is zero or more of:

n	n=1-2048 (LINE_MAX). Substitute for just the nth occurrence of regular expression in the pattern space.
g	Global. Substitute for all non-overlapping instances of regular expression rather than just the first one.
p	Print the pattern space if a replacement was made and the default output has been suppressed (by the -n option on the command line or the #n command in the script file).
w wfile	Write. Append the pattern space to wfile if a replacement was made.

(2)t label   Test. Branch to the : command bearing the label if any
substitutions have been made since the most recent reading
of an input line or execution of a t. If label is empty,
branch to the end of the script.

(2)w wfile   Write. Append the pattern space to wfile.

(2)x   Exchange the contents of the pattern and hold spaces.

(2)y/string1/string2/
    Transform. Replace all occurrences of characters in
string1 with the corresponding character in string2. The
lengths of string1 and string2 must be equal.

(2)! function
    Don't. Apply the function (or group, if function is {}
only to lines not selected by the address or addresses.

(0): label   This command does nothing; it bears a label for b and t
commands to branch to.

(1)=   Place the current line number on the standard output as a
line.

(2){   Execute the following commands through a matching } only
when the pattern space is selected. The syntax is:

```
{ cmd1
cmd2
cmd3
 .
 .
 .
}
```

(0)   An empty command is ignored.

(0)#   If a # appears as the first character on the first line of
a script file, that entire line is treated as a comment
with one exception: If the character after the # is an n,
the default output is suppressed. The rest of the line
after #n is also ignored. A script file must contain at
least one non-comment line.

EXTERNAL INFLUENCES
  Environment Variables
    LANG provides a default value for the internationalization variables
that are unset or null. If LANG is unset or null, the default value of
"C" (see lang(5)) is used. If any of the internationalization
variables contains an invalid setting, sed will behave as if all
internationalization variables are set to "C". See environ(5).

    LC_ALL If set to a non-empty string value, overrides the values of all
the other internationalization variables.

    LC_CTYPE determines the interpretation of text as single and/or
multi-byte characters, the classification of characters as printable,
and the characters matched by character class expressions in regular
expressions.

    LC_MESSAGES determines the locale that should be used to affect the
format and contents of diagnostic messages written to standard error
and informative messages written to standard output.

    NLSPATH determines the location of message catalogues for the processing of LC_MESSAGES.

International Code Set Support
Single- and multi-byte character code sets are supported.

EXAMPLES
Make a simple substitution in a file from the command line or from a
shell script, changing abc to xyz:

        sed 's/abc/xyz/' file1 >file1.out

Same as above but use shell or environment variables var1 and var2 in
search and replacement strings:

        sed "s/$var1/$var2/" file1 >file1.out

    or

        sed 's/'$var1'/'$var2'/' file1 >file1.out

Multiple substitutions in a single command:

        sed -e 's/abc/xyz/' -e 's/lmn/rst/' file1

    or

        sed -e 's/abc/xyz/' \
        -e 's/lmn/rst/' \
        file1 >file1.out

WARNINGS
sed limits command scripts to a total of not more than 100 commands.

The hold space is limited to 8192 characters.

sed processes only text files. See the glossary for a definition of
text files and their limitations.

AUTHOR
sed was developed by OSF and HP.

SEE ALSO
awk(1), ed(1), grep(1), environ(5), lang(5), regexp(5).

sed: A Non-Interactive Streaming Editor tutorial in the Text
Processing Users Guide.

STANDARDS CONFORMANCE
sed: SVID2, SVID3, XPG2, XPG3, XPG4, POSIX.2

CHAPTER 20

find Command

find Overview

The **find** command is used to locate files by traversing the UNIX tree structure. You can start from any point on the system, even the root level, and traverse through the entire hierarchy. After finding files, you can also perform actions on them.

man page

find - 20

The general format of the **find** command is as follows:

```
find path operators
```

path is the directory in which **find** will begin a search. *operators* are one or more of the many **find** options you specify. The end of this section contains a list of commonly used operators to **find**. We'll work with several of the most commonly used operators in some of the upcoming examples.

The most common result of **find** is to produce a list of files. You can produce a list of files in the current working directory, specified by a dot (.), and *print* those files, as shown in the following example:

man page

cd - 16

man page

ls - 15

man page

find - 20

```
# cd /home
#
# ls -l
total 3
drwxr-xr-x   3 col      users       1024 Nov  8 14:09 col
drwxr-xr-x   6 root     root        1024 Nov  8 14:08 ftp
drwxr-xr-x   6 root     root        1024 Nov  8 14:08 httpd
#
# find . -print
.
./httpd
./httpd/apache
./httpd/apache/doc
./httpd/apache/doc/manual.ps.gz
./httpd/cgi-bin
./httpd/cgi-bin/HelpIndex
./httpd/cgi-bin/HelpScreen
./httpd/html
./httpd/html/dt
./httpd/html/dt/dt.html
./httpd/html/dt/dt.html.idx
./httpd/html/dt/dt.index
./httpd/html/dt/expert.gif
./httpd/html/dt/hint.gif
./httpd/html/dt/index.gif
./httpd/html/dt/info2.gif
./httpd/html/dt/note.gif
./httpd/html/dt/sysadm.gif
./httpd/html/dt/up.gif
./httpd/html/dt/warning.gif
./httpd/icons
./ftp
./ftp/bin
./ftp/bin/gzip
./ftp/bin/ls
./ftp/bin/tar
./ftp/bin/zcat
./ftp/etc
./ftp/etc/group
./ftp/etc/passwd
./ftp/lib
./ftp/pub
./col
./col/.bashrc
./col/.cshrc
./col/.login
./col/.profile
./col/lg
./col/lg/lg_layouts
./col/lg/lg_layouts/User
./col/lg/lg3_prefs
./col/lg/lg3_soundPref
./col/lg/lg3_startup
```

This **find** operation was performed from the **/home** directory. Notice that there are only three home directories under **/home**, and the **find** command traverses the hierarchy for each of the three home directories. Keep in mind that you probably don't want to perform this

find operation at the root level. You will traverse the entire hierarchy and get a list of every file on the system.

When using **find**, you may discover that you receive a message like the following when a file or directory is encountered for which you do not have adequate permission to traverse:

```
find: /var/spool/cron: Permission denied
```

This is not an ucommon message when running **find**, so don't panic. Users working outside their home directory often encounter this message when running a variety of commands, including **find**.

A typical **find** command will specify the path in which to search for a specific file. In this case, the *expression* is the *name* of the file for which you wish to search, as shown in the following example:

```
# find /home -name ftp
/home/ftp
```

In this example, we search the *path* **/home** looking for the *name* **ftp**.

Finding Files of a Specific Type

You may want to perform a **find** operation to produce a list of files only and not include directories in the operation. The following **find** is similar to what we performed earlier, but this time it produces a list of files only. This is achieved by specifying that we are looking for type *f* for files:

```
# find /home -type f -print
/home/httpd/apache/doc/manual.ps.gz
/home/httpd/cgi-bin/HelpIndex
/home/httpd/cgi-bin/HelpScreen
/home/httpd/html/dt/dt.html
/home/httpd/html/dt/dt.html.idx
/home/httpd/html/dt/dt.index
```

```
/home/httpd/html/dt/expert.gif
/home/httpd/html/dt/hint.gif
/home/httpd/html/dt/index.gif
/home/httpd/html/dt/info2.gif
/home/httpd/html/dt/note.gif
/home/httpd/html/dt/sysadm.gif
/home/httpd/html/dt/up.gif
/home/httpd/html/dt/warning.gif
/home/ftp/bin/gzip
/home/ftp/bin/ls
/home/ftp/bin/tar
/home/ftp/etc/group
/home/ftp/etc/passwd
/home/col/.bashrc
/home/col/.cshrc
/home/col/.login
/home/col/.profile
/home/col/lg/lg_layouts/User
/home/col/lg/lg3_prefs
/home/col/lg/lg3_soundPref
/home/col/lg/lg3_startup
```

You can search for a variety of different *types* such as *f* for a file as shown in the example, *b* for a block special file, *l* for a symbolic link, and so on.

Find Empty Files and Directories

man page

find - 20

A useful test when performing a **find** operation is to locate empty files. The following example searches for all empty files and directories on the system with the *-empty* operator that is available on some UNIX variants, including Linux. This is only a partial output because it's so long:

```
# find / -empty -print
/lost+found
/var/adm/LST/analyse
/var/spool/lpd
/var/spool/news
/var/spool/uucp
/var/spool/mqueue
/var/spool/atjobs/.SEQ
/var/spool/atspool
/var/spool/cron
/var/spool/fax/outgoing/locks
/var/spool/fax/incoming
/var/spool/voice/incoming
/var/spool/voice/messages
/var/spool/rwho
/var/spool/uucppublic
/var/lib/LST/log
/var/lib/LST/analyse
/var/lib/LST/disks
/var/lib/LST/catalog
/var/lib/LST/conflicts
```

```
/var/lib/LST/saved
/var/lib/LST/replaced
/var/lib/LST/deleted
/var/lib/games
/var/local
/var/lock/subsys/inet
/var/lock/subsys/ipx
/var/lock/subsys/syslog
/var/lock/subsys/amd
/var/lock/subsys/cron
/var/lock/subsys/atd
/var/lock/subsys/mta
/var/lock/subsys/rstatd
/var/lock/subsys/httpd
/var/log/httpd/apache/access_log
/var/log/xferlog
/var/log/uucp
/var/log/secure
/var/log/spooler
/var/named
/var/nis
/var/preserve
/var/run/xlaunch
/var/tmp
```

-
-
-

```
/proc/net/snmp
/proc/net/raw
/proc/net/igmp
/proc/net/arp
/proc/net/unix
/proc/cpuinfo
/proc/pci
/proc/version
/proc/kmsg
/proc/meminfo
/proc/uptime
/proc/loadavg
/proc/mdstat
/etc/modules/options
/etc/motd
/etc/exports
/etc/ppp/options
/tmp/LST
/tmp/.XF86Setup235/f51cb27-315ae55/ServerOut-2
/tmp/.XF86Setup246/13617839-11c71c71/ServerOut-2
/tmp/.XF86Setup262/1f2cc0a9-aea314d/ServerOut-2
/tmp/.XF86Setup288/17963ff7-21ca966f/ServerOut-2
/tmp/fsslog
/mnt/floppy
/mnt/cdrom
/usr/doc/html/woven/LDP/install-guide-2.2.2.html/images.idx
/usr/lib/games
/usr/lib/groff/tmac/mm/locale
/usr/lib/groff/tmac/mm/se_locale
/usr/lib/kbd/keytables/patch_tables.orig
/usr/lib/perl5/i386-linux/5.003/auto/GDBM_File/GDBM_File.bs
/usr/lib/perl5/i386-linux/5.003/auto/DB_File/DB_File.bs
/usr/lib/perl5/i386-linux/5.003/auto/Fcntl/Fcntl.bs
/usr/lib/perl5/i386-linux/5.003/auto/FileHandle/FileHandle.bs
/usr/lib/perl5/i386-linux/5.003/auto/NDBM_File/NDBM_File.bs
/usr/lib/perl5/i386-linux/5.003/auto/POSIX/POSIX.bs
/usr/lib/perl5/i386-linux/5.003/auto/SDBM_File/SDBM_File.bs
/usr/lib/perl5/i386-linux/5.003/auto/Safe/Safe.bs
/usr/lib/perl5/i386-linux/5.003/auto/Socket/Socket.bs
/usr/lib/perl5/i386-linux/5.003/auto/Text/ParseWords
/usr/lib/perl5/site_perl/i386-linux
/usr/lib/linuxdoc-sgml/null.sty
/usr/etc
/usr/include/g++
/usr/include/netax25
```

```
/usr/include/netipx
/usr/include/readline
/usr/local/bin
/usr/local/doc
/usr/local/etc
/usr/local/games
/usr/local/info
/usr/local/lib
/usr/local/man/man1
/usr/local/man/man2
/usr/local/man/man3
/usr/local/man/man4
/usr/local/man/man5
/usr/local/man/man6
/usr/local/man/man7
/usr/local/man/man8
/usr/local/man/man9
/usr/local/man/mann
/usr/local/sbin
/usr/local/src
/usr/man/man9
/usr/man/mann
/usr/src/linux-2.0.29/include/linux/modules
/usr/src/linux-2.0.29/modules
/usr/src/redhat/BUILD
/usr/src/redhat/RPMS/i386
/usr/src/redhat/SOURCES
/usr/src/redhat/SPECS
/usr/src/redhat/SRPMS
/usr/X11R6/doc
/usr/X11R6/lib/X11/x11perfcomp
/usr/visix/fss/En_US.8859
/usr/visix/vls/En_US.8859
/usr/openwin/share/src/xview
/auto
/initrd
/home/httpd/icons
/home/ftp/lib
/home/ftp/pub
/opt/bin
/opt/man
/root/lg/lg3_hosts
/amd/nycald1/auto/.vTRASH
#
# ll /auto
total 0
```

man page

find - 20

All the files and directories listed as a result of this **find** operation are empty. The long listing of **/auto** shown as part of the example, confirms this fact. Keep in mind that -*empty* is not available on all UNIX variants.

Finding Files By Name, Size, and Both Name and Size

Let's perform a couple of independent finds and then combine the criteria of the finds. The finds in the following example are performed on a small, desktop system. This allows me to search the entire system for files meeting various criteria. You may be working on a much larger, more elaborate system so use caution when searching the entire system for files. You may slow down other users for a long period of time depending on the number of files on the system both locally and accessible over the network.

First let's find for all files on the system ending in **.c** with the command below:

```
# find / -name *.c -print
/usr/X11R6/include/X11/Xaw/Template.c
/usr/X11R6/include/Xaw3d/Template.c
/usr/X11R6/lib/X11/etc/et4000clock.c
/usr/doc/glibc-2.1.1/examples.threads/ex1.c
/usr/doc/glibc-2.1.1/examples.threads/ex2.c
/usr/doc/glibc-2.1.1/examples.threads/ex3.c
/usr/doc/glibc-2.1.1/examples.threads/ex4.c
/usr/doc/glibc-2.1.1/examples.threads/ex5.c
/usr/doc/glibc-2.1.1/examples.threads/ex6.c



      .
      .
      .


/usr/doc/bind-8.2/notes/db_names.c
/usr/doc/libpng-1.0.3/example.c
/usr/doc/FAQ/html/clone.c
/usr/doc/gnome-libs-devel/devel-docs/gnomeui/gnomeui-scan.c
#
```

You can see from this find that there are many files on the system ending in **.c**. I included only the beginning and end of this search because the entire output would be too long.

I also ran this command and piped the output to **wc**, which showed 1737 files on the system ending in **.c** as shown in the following example:

```
# find / -name *.c | wc
   1737     1737    77044
#
```

man page

find - 20

Now we can search for all files on the system greater than *500,000* characters in size with the **find** command below:

```
# find / -size +500000c -print
/dev/core
/etc/X11/core
/var/lib/rpm/packages.rpm
/var/lib/rpm/fileindex.rpm
/var/lib/dosemu/hdimage.freedos
/var/lib/slocate/slocate.db
/var/lock/samba/SHARE_MEM_FILE
/proc/kcore
/home/ftp/lib/libc-2.1.1.so
/home/test/linux1.xwd
/lib/libc-2.1.1.so
/lib/libdb-2.1.1.so
/lib/libm-2.1.1.so
/root/core

                    .
                    .
                    .

/usr/share/gnome/help/users-guide/C/figs/full.gif
/usr/share/emacs/20.3/etc/DOC-20.3.1
/usr/share/emacs/20.3/leim/quail/ZIRANMA.el
/usr/share/emacs/20.3/leim/quail/ZIRANMA.elc
/usr/share/emacs/20.3/leim/skk/skkdic.el
/usr/share/emacs/20.3/leim/skk/skkdic.elc
/usr/share/emacs/20.3/lisp/loaddefs.el
/usr/share/sounds/card_shuffle.wav
/usr/share/sounds/startup2.wav
/usr/share/guavac/classes.zip
```

man page

wc - 18

I only included the beginning and end of this listing as well since there were many files of size greater than *500,000* characters on the system.

I also ran this command and piped the output to **wc**, which showed *215* files on the system with a size greater than *500,000* characters as shown in the following example:

```
# find / -size +500000c -print | wc
    215     215    6281
#
```

Let's now combine the two commands and see how many of the files on the system ending in **.c** are also greater than *500,000* characters in size:

```
# find / -name *.c -size +500000c -print
/usr/src/drivers/scsi/advansys.c
#
```

Of the 1737 files on the system ending in **.c** and the 215 files greater than *500,000* characters in size, only one file, **advansys.c**, meets both criteria. There is an implied *and* in the previous **find** command. We could have explicitly specified an *and*, however, it is implied in the **find** command. The **find** did indeed result in files that end in **.c** *and* are greater than 500,000 characters. The upcoming **find** uses the *or* operator, which is not implied.

man page

find - 20

What if we wanted to find both files ending in **.c** and **.o** that are greater than *500000* characters in size? We could use the *-o* operator which would "or" the files ending in **.c** and **.o**. The following example shows this **find** operation:

```
find / -size +500000c \(  -name *.c -o -name *.a \) -print
find / -size +500000c \(  -name *.c -o -name *.a \) -print | wc
```

```
# find / -size +500000c \( -name *.c -o -name *.a \) -print
/usr/X11R6/lib/libMagick.a
/usr/X11R6/lib/libX11.a
/usr/lib/bind/lib/libbind.a
/usr/lib/bind/lib/libbind_r.a
/usr/lib/libbfd.a
/usr/lib/libBLT.a
/usr/lib/libstdc++-2-libc6.1-1-2.9.0.a
/usr/lib/libc.a

        .
        .
        .
```

```
/usr/lib/libinn.a
/usr/lib/libtiff.a
/usr/lib/liblinuxconf.a
/usr/lib/libform_g.a
/usr/lib/libncurses_g.a
/usr/lib/python1.5/config/libpython1.5.a
/usr/lib/libpisock.a
/usr/lib/libcustoms.a
/usr/lib/libqt.a
/usr/lib/libst.a
/usr/src/drivers/scsi/advansys.c
#
```

man page

find - 20

The two file extensions for which we are searching are placed in parentheses. A backslash is required before the open and close parentheses because the parentheses have meaning to the shell and we want them to be used only to specify the precedence in our **find** command and not to be used by the shell. The result of this **find** shows that many files ending in **.a** and **.c** meet the criteria of greater than *500,000* characters.

Let's now pipe the output of this commnd to **wc** to see precisely the number of files ending in either **.c** *or* **.o** *and* have a size greater than *500,000* characters:

```
# find / -size +500000c \( -name *.c -o -name *.a \) -print | wc
    39      39     982
#
```

Of the *39* files that meet the criteria, we know that *38* ended in **.a** because our earlier example showed that only one file ending in **.c** met the criteria.

Finding Files By Owner, Type, and Permissions

You can find objects on the system owned by particular users and groups. To find all of the objects owned by user "news" on the system, we would use the following command:

```
# find / -user news -print
/etc/rc.d/rc.news
/etc/news
/etc/news/cleanfeed.conf
/etc/news/actsync.cfg
/etc/news/actsync.ign
/etc/news/control.ctl
/etc/news/cycbuff.conf
/etc/news/distrib.pats
/etc/news/expire.ctl
/etc/news/incoming.conf
/etc/news/inn.conf
/etc/news/innfeed.conf
/etc/news/innreport.conf
/etc/news/innwatch.ctl
/etc/news/moderators
/etc/news/motd.news
/etc/news/news2mail.cf
/etc/news/newsfeeds
/etc/news/nnrp.access
/etc/news/nnrpd.track
/etc/news/nntpsend.ctl
/etc/news/overview.ctl
/etc/news/overview.fmt
/etc/news/passwd.nntp
/etc/news/storage.conf


        .
        .
        .


/usr/man/man8/tally.control.8
/usr/man/man8/tally.unwanted.8
/usr/man/man8/writelog.8
```

Using the *-user* operator we can specify either the name of the user, in this case "news", or the user identification number. The following example shows performing the same **find** operation using the user identification number of "news," in this case "9," instead of the name "news":

man page

find - 20

```
# find / -user 9 -print
/etc/rc.d/rc.news
/etc/news
/etc/news/cleanfeed.conf
/etc/news/actsync.cfg
/etc/news/actsync.ign
/etc/news/control.ctl
/etc/news/cycbuff.conf
/etc/news/distrib.pats
/etc/news/expire.ctl
/etc/news/incoming.conf
/etc/news/inn.conf
/etc/news/innfeed.conf
/etc/news/innreport.conf
/etc/news/innwatch.ctl
/etc/news/moderators
/etc/news/motd.news
/etc/news/news2mail.cf
/etc/news/newsfeeds
/etc/news/nnrp.access
/etc/news/nnrpd.track
/etc/news/nntpsend.ctl
/etc/news/overview.ctl
/etc/news/overview.fmt
/etc/news/passwd.nntp
/etc/news/storage.conf

            .
            .
            .

/usr/man/man8/tally.control.8
/usr/man/man8/tally.unwanted.8
/usr/man/man8/writelog.8
```

man page

find - 20

This **find** operation produced exactly the same results using the name "news" and the user idenfication number "9."

You can search for a variety of different *types* such as *f* for a file, as shown in the example, *b* for a block special file, *l* for a symbolic link, and so on. We could add *type -d* to find only directories belonging "news" as in the following command:

```
# find / -user news -type d -perm 775 -print
/etc/news
/var/lib/news
```

```
/var/log/news
/var/log/news/OLD
/var/spool/news
/var/spool/news/archive
/var/spool/news/articles
/var/spool/news/incoming
/var/spool/news/incoming/bad
/var/spool/news/innfeed
/var/spool/news/outgoing
/var/spool/news/overview
/var/spool/news/uniover
/var/spool/slrnpull
/usr/bin/auth
/usr/bin/control
/usr/bin/filter
/usr/bin/rnews.libexec
```

man page

find - 20

This is another example of using the implied *and* of **find** meaning that the **find** will print items that are both owned by "news" *and* are directories only.

Let's now add a specific permission for the directories to our implied *and*. We'll **find** only objects belonging to "news" that are directories with a permission of 775 in the following example:

```
# find / -user news -type d -perm 775 -print
/etc/news
/var/lib/news
/var/log/news
/var/log/news/OLD
/var/spool/news
/var/spool/news/archive
/var/spool/news/articles
/var/spool/news/incoming
/var/spool/news/incoming/bad
/var/spool/news/innfeed
/var/spool/news/outgoing
/var/spool/news/overview
/var/spool/news/uniover
/var/spool/slrnpull
/usr/bin/auth
/usr/bin/control
/usr/bin/filter
/usr/bin/rnews.libexec
```

We searched for directories belonging to "news" in which both the owner and those in the group have read-write-execute permission, and others having read-execute access. This is a common type of **find** operation for system administrators to perform - looking for files and directories belonging to a specific user and having specific permissions.

Finding Long Unaccessed Files and Running Commands on Found Files

We all have old files on our systems and in our home directories that have not been accessed in a long time. To find files in a home directory that have not been accessed in the last 200 days, you would issue the following command:

```
# find . -atime +200 -print
./hp/.Xdefaults
./hp/.bash_logout
./hp/.bash_profile
./hp/.bashrc
./hp/.kde/share/apps/kfm/desktop
./hp/.kde/share/config/desktop0rc
./hp/.kde/share/config/kcmdisplayrc
./hp/.kde/share/config/kfmrc
./hp/.kde/share/config/kpanelrc
./hp/.kde/share/config/kvtrc
./hp/.kderc
./hp/Desktop/.directory
./hp/Desktop/Printer.kdelnk
./hp/Desktop/Templates/Device.kdelnk
./hp/Desktop/Templates/Ftpurl.kdelnk
./hp/Desktop/Templates/MimeType.kdelnk
./hp/Desktop/Templates/Program.kdelnk
./hp/Desktop/Templates/URL.kdelnk
./hp/Desktop/Templates/WWWUrl.kdelnk
./hp/Desktop/cdrom.kdelnk
./hp/Desktop/floppy.kdelnk
./hp/.screenrc
./hp/.bash_history
./test/.Xdefaults
./test/.bash_logout
./test/.bash_profile
./test/.bashrc
./test/.kde/share/apps/kfm/desktop
./test/.kde/share/config/desktop0rc
./test/.kde/share/config/kcmdisplayrc
```

```
./test/.kde/share/config/kfmrc
./test/.kde/share/config/kpanelrc
./test/.kde/share/config/kvtrc
./test/.kderc
./test/Desktop/.directory
./test/Desktop/Printer.kdelnk
./test/Desktop/Templates/Device.kdelnk
./test/Desktop/Templates/Ftpurl.kdelnk
./test/Desktop/Templates/MimeType.kdelnk
./test/Desktop/Templates/Program.kdelnk
./test/Desktop/Templates/URL.kdelnk
./test/Desktop/Templates/WWWUrl.kdelnk
./test/Desktop/cdrom.kdelnk
./test/Desktop/floppy.kdelnk
./test/.screenrc
./test/linux1.xwd
./test/.bash_history
#
```

Several files were produced as a result of this search. I could run the same command and add to it an **ls -l** command so I could look at additional information on the file with the following command:

man page

ls - 15

```
# find . -atime +200 -exec ls -l {} \;

-rw-r--r--   1 hp        hp         1422 Aug 28   ./hp/.Xdefaults
-rw-r--r--   1 hp        hp           24 Aug 28   ./hp/.bash_logout
-rw-r--r--   1 hp        hp          230 Aug 28   ./hp/.bash_profile
-rw-r--r--   1 hp        hp          124 Aug 28   ./hp/.bashrc
-rw-r--r--   1 hp        hp          260 Aug 28   ./hp/.kde/share/apps/kfm/desktop
-rw-r--r--   1 hp        hp          234 Aug 28   ./hp/.kde/share/config/desktop0rc
-rw-r--r--   1 hp        hp           49 Aug 28   ./hp/.kde/share/config/kcmdisplayrc
-rw-r--r--   1 hp        hp           95 Aug 28   ./hp/.kde/share/config/kfmrc
-rw-r--r--   1 hp        hp          456 Aug 28   ./hp/.kde/share/config/kpanelrc
-rw-r--r--   1 hp        hp          255 Aug 28   ./hp/.kde/share/config/kvtrc
-rw-r--r--   1 hp        hp          966 Aug 28   ./hp/.kderc
-rw-r--r--   1 hp        hp           85 Aug 28   ./hp/Desktop/.directory
-rw-r--r--   1 hp        hp          222 Aug 28   ./hp/Desktop/Printer.kdelnk
-rw-r--r--   1 hp        hp          607 Aug 28   ./hp/Desktop/Templates/Device.kdelnk
-rw-r--r--   1 hp        hp          296 Aug 28   ./hp/Desktop/Templates/Ftpurl.kdelnk
-rw-r--r--   1 hp        hp          324 Aug 28   ./hp/Desktop/Templates/MimeType.kdelnk
-rw-r--r--   1 hp        hp          170 Aug 28   ./hp/Desktop/Templates/Program.kdelnk
-rw-r--r--   1 hp        hp          411 Aug 28   ./hp/Desktop/Templates/URL.kdelnk
-rw-r--r--   1 hp        hp          458 Aug 28   ./hp/Desktop/Templates/WWWUrl.kdelnk
-rw-r--r--   1 hp        hp          376 Aug 28   ./hp/Desktop/cdrom.kdelnk
-rw-r--r--   1 hp        hp          378 Aug 28   ./hp/Desktop/floppy.kdelnk
-rw-rw-r--   1 hp        hp         3505 Aug 28   ./hp/.screenrc
-rw-------   1 hp        hp           34 Aug 28   ./hp/.bash_history
-rw-r--r--   1 test      test       1422 Aug 28   ./test/.Xdefaults
-rw-r--r--   1 test      test         24 Aug 28   ./test/.bash_logout
-rw-r--r--   1 test      test        230 Aug 28   ./test/.bash_profile
-rw-r--r--   1 test      test        124 Aug 28   ./test/.bashrc
-rw-r--r--   1 test      test        260 Aug 28   ./test/.kde/share/apps/kfm/desktop
-rw-r--r--   1 test      test        234 Aug 28   ./test/.kde/share/config/desktop0rc
-rw-r--r--   1 test      test         49 Aug 28   ./test/.kde/share/config/kcmdisplayrc
-rw-r--r--   1 test      test         95 Aug 28   ./test/.kde/share/config/kfmrc
-rw-r--r--   1 test      test        456 Aug 28   ./test/.kde/share/config/kpanelrc
-rw-r--r--   1 test      test        255 Aug 28   ./test/.kde/share/config/kvtrc
-rw-r--r--   1 test      test        966 Aug 28   ./test/.kderc
-rw-r--r--   1 test      test         85 Aug 28   ./test/Desktop/.directory
-rw-r--r--   1 test      test        222 Aug 28   ./test/Desktop/Printer.kdelnk
-rw-r--r--   1 test      test        607 Aug 28   ./test/Desktop/Templates/Device.kdelnk
-rw-r--r--   1 test      test        296 Aug 28   ./test/Desktop/Templates/Ftpurl.kdelnk
-rw-r--r--   1 test      test        324 Aug 28   ./test/Desktop/Templates/MimeType.kdelnk
-rw-r--r--   1 test      test        170 Aug 28   ./test/Desktop/Templates/Program.kdelnk
```

```
-rw-r--r--   1 test      test         411 Aug 28   ./test/Desktop/Templates/URL.kdelnk
-rw-r--r--   1 test      test         458 Aug 28   ./test/Desktop/Templates/WWWUrl.kdelnk
-rw-r--r--   1 test      test         376 Aug 28   ./test/Desktop/cdrom.kdelnk
-rw-r--r--   1 test      test         378 Aug 28   ./test/Desktop/floppy.kdelnk
-rw-rw-r--   1 test      test        3505 Aug 28   ./test/.screenrc
-rwxrwxrwx   1 root      root      614955 Aug 28   ./test/linux1.xwd
-rw-------   1 test      test          13 Aug 28   ./test/.bash_history
#
```

This command produces the same output as the previous example and puts the output of **find** in the place where the curly brackets appear. The **ls -l** will use the filename produced by **find**, which is inside the curly brackets, as an argument. You follow the command with a semicolon so that the shell knows where the command ends, and you must use the backslash as an escape for the semicolon so the **find** command recognizes the semicolon.

Find Summary

This chapter contained many examples of common **find** operations. There are many addtional **find** operators that were not covered. The following is a summary of some of the more commonly used operators of **find**. There is also a manual page at the end of this chapter describing **find** in more detail. Depending on the UNIX variant you are using, the *-print* option may or may not be needed.

find - Search for files.

Commonly used operators or options:

-atime *n*

Find files that were accessed *n* days ago. +*n* finds files accessed greater than *n* days ago and -*n* will find files accessed less than *n* days ago.

-ctime *n*

Find files in which the inode was modified *n* days ago. +*n* finds files in which the inode was modified greater than *n* days ago and -*n* will find files in which the inode modified less than *n* days ago.

-exec *command*

Execute *command.*

-group *name*

Find files belonging to the given group *name* where *name* can also be the group ID number.

-mount

Do not descend directories on other file systems (not available on all UNIX variants.)

-mtime *n*

Find files that were modified *n* days ago. +*n* finds files modified greater than *n* days ago and -*n* will find files modified less than *n* days ago.

-newer *file*

File was modified more recently than *file.*

-name *pattern*

Look for file name of *pattern.*

-ok *command*

Check to see that it is okay to execute *command* before doing so. This is similar to -exec except you are prompted for permission.

-perm *mode*

Find files with the specified access *mode*. You would supply the access *mode* in octal.

-print

Print the current file name to standard output.

-type t

File has a type of *t*, such as *d* for directory and *f* for file.

-size *n*

Find files with a size of *n* blocks. A block is usually 512 bytes. Using +*n* will find files greater than *n* blocks, *nc* will find files *n* characters in size and +*nc* will find files greater than *n* characters in size.

-user *uname*

File is owned by *uname*.

Multiple Criteria:

-a to and two operators (operator1 -a operator2)

-o to or two operators (operator1 -o operator2)

! to specify the operator not be matched (!operator)

\(expression)\ to specify that this this expression be evaluated before others to specify preference.

Manual Pages for find Command Used in Chapter 20

The following is the HP-UX manual page for the **find** command. Commands often differ among UNIX variants, so you may find differences in the options or other areas for this command; however, the following manual pages serve as an excellent reference.

find

find - Find the files on system by recursively searching through the hierarchy.

NAME
     find - find files

SYNOPSIS

     find pathname_list [expression]

DESCRIPTION
     The find command recursively descends the directory hierarchy for each
     path name in pathname_list (that is, one or more path names) seeking
     files that match a Boolean expression written in the primaries given
     below. By default, find does not follow symbolic links.

     The Boolean expression is evaluated using short-circuit evaluation.
     This means that whenever the result of a Boolean operation (AND or OR)
     is known from evaluating the left-hand argument, the right-hand
     argument is not evaluated.

     In the descriptions of the primaries, the argument n represents a
     decimal integer; +n means more than n, -n means less than n, and n
     means exactly n.

     The following primaries are recognized:

     -depth   A position-independent term which causes
                              descent of the directory hierarchy to be done
                              so that all entries in a directory are acted
                              on before the directory itself. This can be
                              useful when find is used with cpio(1) to
                              transfer files that are contained in
                              directories without write permission. It is
                              also useful when using cpio(1) and the
                              modification dates of directories must be
                              preserved. Always true.

     -follow   A position-independent term which causes find
                              to follow symbolic links. Always true.

     -fsonly FStype   A position-independent term which causes find
                              to stop descending any directory whose file
                              system is not of the type specified by
                              FStype, where FStype is one of cdfs, hfs, or
                              nfs, representing the CDFS, HFS, or NFS file
                              system type, respectively.

                              In this context, mount points inherit the
                              FStype of their parent directory. This means
                              that when -fsonly hfs has been specified and
                              find encounters an NFS mount point that is
                              mounted on an HFS file system, the mount
                              point will be visited but entries below that

mount point will not. It is important to note that when -fsonly nfs has been specified, any HFS file systems that are beneath the mount point of an NFS file system are not traversed. Always true.

-xdev A position-independent term that causes find to avoid crossing any file system mount points that exist below starting points enumerated in pathname_list. The mount point itself is visited, but entries below the mount point are not. Always true.

-mountstop Identical to -xdev. This primary is provided for backward compatibility only. -xdev is preferred over -mountstop.

-name file True if file matches the last component of the current file name. The matching is performed according to Pattern Matching Notation (see regexp(5)).

-path file Same as -name except the full path (as would be output by -print) is used instead of just the base name. Note that / characters are not treated as a special case. For example, */.profile matches ./home/fred/.profile.

-perm [-]mode In this primary, the argument mode is used to represent file mode bits. The argument is identical in format to the mode operand as described in chmod(1), with the exception that the first character must not be the - operator. When using the symbolic form of mode, the starting template is assumed to have all file mode bits cleared.

If the leading minus is omitted, this primary is true when the file permission bits exactly match the value of mode. Bits associated with the symbolic attributes s (set-user-ID, set-group-ID) and t (sticky bit) are ignored when the minus is omitted.

If mode is preceded by a minus, this primary is true if all of the bits that are set in mode are also set in the file permission bits. In this case, the bits associated with the symbolic attributes s and t are significant.

-fstype FStype True if the file system to which the file belongs is of type FStype, where FStype is one of cdfs, hfs, or nfs, corresponding to the CDFS, HFS, or NFS file system type, respectively.

-type c True if the type of the file is c, where c is one of:

f	Regular file
d	Directory
b	Block special file
c	Character special file
p	FIFO (named pipe)
l	Symbolic link

s	Socket
n	Network special file
M	Mount point

-links n

True if the file has n links.

-user uname

True if the file belongs to the user uname. If uname is numeric and does not appear as a login name in the /etc/passwd file, it is taken as a user ID. The uname operand can be preceded by a + or - to modify the comparison operation as described previously.

-group gname

True if the file belongs to the group gname. If gname is numeric and does not appear in the /etc/group file, it is taken as a group ID. The gname operand can be preceded by a + or - to modify the comparison operation as described previously.

-nouser

True if the file belongs to a user ID that is not listed in the password database. See passwd(4).

-nogroup

True if the file belongs to a group ID that is not listed in the group database. See group(4).

-size n[c]

True if the file is n blocks long. If n is followed by a c, the size is in bytes.

-atime n

True if the file has been accessed in n days. The access time of directories in pathname_list is changed by find itself.

-mtime n

True if the file has been modified in n days.

-ctime n

True if the file inode has been changed in n days.

-newer file

True if the current file has been modified more recently than the argument file.

-newer[tv1[tv2]] file

True if the indicated time value (tv1) of the current file is newer than the indicated time value (tv2) of file. The time values tv1 and tv2 are each selected from the set of characters:

a	The time the file was last accessed
c	The time the inode of the file was last modified
m	The time the file was last modified

If the tv2 character is omitted, it defaults to m. Note that the -newer option is equivalent to -newermm.

Syntax examples;

```
-newera file
-newermc file
```

-inum n   True if the file serial number (inode number) is n. Note that file serial numbers are unique only within a given file system. Therefore, matching file serial numbers does not guarantee that the referenced files are the same unless you restrict the search to a single file system.

-linkedto path   True if the file is the same physical file as the file specified by path (i.e., linked to path). This primary is similar to -inum, but correctly detects when a file is hard-linked to path, even when multiple file systems are searched.

-print   Causes the current path name to be printed. Always true.

-exec cmd   True if the executed cmd returns a zero value as exit status. The end of cmd must be punctuated by a semicolon (semicolon is special to the shell and must be escaped). Any command argument {} is replaced by the current path name.

-ok cmd   Same as -exec except that the generated command line is printed with a question mark first, and is executed only if the user responds by typing y.

-cpio device   Write the current file on device in cpio(4) format (5120-byte records). The use of -cpio implies -depth. Always true.

-ncpio   Same as -cpio but adds the -c option to cpio. The use of -ncpio implies -depth. Always true.

-prune   If the current entry is a directory, cause find to skip that directory. This can be useful to avoid walking certain directories, or to avoid recursive loops when using cpio -p. Note, however, that -prune is useless if the -depth option has also been given. See the description of -only and the EXAMPLES section, below, for more information. Always true.

-only   This is a positive-logic version of -prune. A -prune is performed after every directory, unless -only is successfully evaluated for that directory. As an example, the following three commands are equivalent:

```
find . -fsonly hfs -print
find . -print -fstype hfs -only
find . -print ! -fstype hfs -prune
```

Note, however, that -only is useless if the -depth option has also been given. Always true.

(expression)   True if the parenthesized expression is true. The spaces are required. Parentheses are

special to the shell and must be escaped, as
in \(and \).

Primaries can be combined by using the following operators (in order
of decreasing precedence):

! expression	Logical NOT operator. True if expression is not true.
expression [-a] expression	Logical AND operator. True if both of the expressions are true.
expression -o expression	Logical OR operator. True if either or both of the expressions are true.

If expression is omitted, or if none of -print, -ok, -exec, -cpio, or
-ncpio is specified, -print is assumed.

Access Control Lists
   The -acl primary enables the user to search for access control list
   entries. It is true if the file's access control list matches an
   access control list pattern or contains optional access control list
   entries (see acl(5)). It has three forms:

-acl aclpatt	Match all files whose access control list includes all (zero or more) pattern entries specified by the aclpatt pattern.
-acl =aclpatt	Match a file only if its access control list includes all (zero or more) pattern entries specified by the aclpatt pattern, and every entry in its access control list is matched by at least one pattern entry specified in the aclpatt pattern.
-acl opt	Match all files containing optional access control list entries.

The aclpatt string can be given as an operator or short form pattern;
see acl(5).

By default, -acl is true for files whose access control lists include
all the (zero or more) access control list patterns in aclpatt. A
file's access control list can also contain unmatched entries.

If aclpatt begins with =, the remainder of the string must match all
entries in a file's access control list.

The aclpatt string (by default, or the part following =) can be either
an access control list or an access control list pattern. However, if
it is an access control list, aclpatt must include at least the three
base entries ((user.%, mode), (%.group, mode), and (%.%, mode)).

As a special case, if aclpatt is the word opt, the primary is true for
files with access control list entries.

EXTERNAL INFLUENCES
   Environment Variables
      If an internationalization variable is not specified or is null, it
      defaults to the value of LANG.

      If LANG is not specified or is null, it defaults to C (see lang(5)).

      If LC_ALL is set to a nonempty string value, it overrides the values
      of all the other internationalization variables.

If any internationalization variable contains an invalid setting, all
internationalization variables default to C (see environ(5)).

LC_CTYPE determines the interpretation of text as single and/or
multibyte characters, the classification of characters as printable,
and the characters matched by character class expressions in regular
expressions.

LC_MESSAGES determines the locale that should be used to affect the
format and contents of diagnostic messages written to standard error
and informative messages written to standard output.

NLSPATH determines the location of message catalogues for the
processing of LC_MESSAGES.

International Code Set Support
    Single- and multibyte character code sets are supported.

EXAMPLES
    Search the two directories /example and /new/example for files
    containing the string Where are you and print the names of the files:

        find /example /new/example -exec grep -l 'Where are you' {} \;

    Remove all files named a.out or *.o that have not been accessed for a
    week:

        find / \(-name a.out -o -name '*.o' \) -atime +7 -exec rm {} \;

        Note that the spaces delimiting the escaped parentheses are
        required.

    Print the names of all files on this machine. Avoid walking nfs
    directories while still printing the nfs mount points:

        find / -fsonly hfs -print

    Copy the entire file system to a disk mounted on /Disk, avoiding the
    recursive copy problem. Both commands are equivalent (note the use of
    -path instead of -name):

        cd /; find . ! -path ./Disk -only -print | cpio -pdxm /Disk

        cd /; find . -path ./Disk -prune -o -print | cpio -pdxm /Disk

    Copy the root disk to a disk mounted on /Disk, skipping all mounted
    file systems below /. Note that -xdev does not cause / to be skipped,
    even though it is a mount point. This is because / is the starting
    point and -xdev only affects entries below starting points.

        cd /; find . -xdev -print | cpio -pdm /Disk

    Change permissions on all regular files in a directory subtree to mode
    444, and permissions on all directories to 555:

        find <pathname> -type f -print | xargs chmod 444
        find <pathname> -type d -print | xargs chmod 555

        Note that output from find was piped to xargs(1) instead of using
        the -exec primary. This is because when a large number of files
        or directories is to be processed by a single command, the -exec
        primary spawns a separate process for each file or directory,
        whereas xargs collects file names or directory names into
        multiple arguments to a single chmod command, resulting in fewer
        processes and greater system efficiency.

Access Control List Examples

Find all files not owned by user karl that have access control lists
with at least one entry associated with karl, and one entry for no
specific user in group bin with the read bit on and the write bit off:

    find / ! -user karl -acl 'karl.*, %.bin+r-w' -print

Find all files that have a read bit set in any access control list
entry:

    find / -acl '*.*+r' -print

Find all files that have the write bit unset and execute bit set in
every access control list entry:

    find / -acl '=*.*-w+x' -print

Find all files that have optional access control list entries:

    find / -acl opt -print

DEPENDENCIES

NFS

The -acl primary is always false for NFS files.

WARNINGS

Because of interoperability goals, cpio does not support archiving
files larger than 2GB or files that have user/group IDs larger than
60,000 (60K). Files with user/group IDs greater than 60K are archived
and restored under the user/group ID of the current process.

AUTHOR

find was developed by AT&T and HP.

FILES

/etc/group	Group names
/etc/mnttab	Mount points
/etc/passwd	User names

SEE ALSO

chacl(1), chmod(1), cpio(1), sh(1), test(1), xargs(1), mknod(2),
stat(2), cpio(4), fs(4), group(4), passwd(4), acl(5), environ(5),
lang(5), regexp(5).

STANDARDS CONFORMANCE

find: SVID2, SVID3, XPG2, XPG3, XPG4, POSIX.2

CHAPTER 21

The vi Editor

The vi Editor

In this chapter, we'll cover the following topics:

- Regular expressions
- **vi**

Many UNIX users have a Graphical User Interface (GUI) through which they access their UNIX system. The Common Desktop Environment (CDE) is the most commonly used GUI on UNIX systems. It is based on the X Windows System and Motif, which together provide an advanced windowing environment. A chapter in this book is devoted to CDE. Most UNIX GUIs provide a graphical editor. Despite the fact that these graphical editors are a standard part of most GUIs, the visual editor, **vi**, still remains the most popular UNIX editor. With many fine graphics-based editors as a standard part of most UNIX GUIs and a plethora of editors available as part of personal computer windowing environments, why am I covering **vi**? The

man page

vi - 21

answer is two-fold. First, not everyone using a UNIX system has access to a graphics display and may therefore need to know and use **vi**. Because **vi** comes with most UNIX-based systems and is a powerful editor, many new UNIX users end up using and liking it. Second, **vi** has traditionally been thought of as *the* UNIX editor. Few UNIX users have not used **vi**. This fact does not mean that it is everyone's primary editor; however, virtually all UNIX users have had some experience with **vi**.

Also, a line editor called **ed** comes with many UNIX systems. It is now seldom used because **vi** is a screen editor. Also available is an enhanced version of **ed** called **ex**. **vi** is much more widely used than either of the line editors, so I'll cover only **vi** in this chapter.

I'll cover the *basics* of using **vi** in this chapter. You can experiment with what is covered here, and if you really like it, you can investigate some of the more advanced features of **vi**. A quick reference card summarizing all the **vi** commands covered in this chapter is included with this book.

The following table is a list of tables in this chapter that summarize some of the more commonly used **vi** commands by function:

Table Number	vi Function
Expr	Regular Expressions
Introduction	Modes and Notations in **vi**
1	Starting a **vi** Session
2	Cursor Control Commands in **vi**
3	Adding Text in **vi**
4	Deleting Text in **vi**
5	Changing Text in **vi**
6	Search and Replace in **vi**
7	Copying in **vi**
8	Undo in **vi**

Table Number	vi Function
9	Saving Text and Exiting **vi**
10	Options in **vi**
11	Status in **vi**
12	Positioning and Marking in **vi**
13	Joining Lines in **vi**
14	Cursor Placement and Adjusting Screen in **vi**
15	Shell Escape Commands in **vi**
16	Macros and Abbreviations in **vi**
17	Indenting Text in **vi**
18	Shell Filters in **vi**
19	Pattern Matching in **vi**

Regular Expression Words-of-Caution

Regular expressions describe patterns for which you are searching. The regular expression usually defines the pattern for which you are searching using wildcards. Since a regular expression defines a pattern you are searching for, the terms "regular expression" and "pattern matching" are often used interchangably.

Let's get down to a couple of words-of-caution immediately:

> • **Regular expressions are different from file-matching patterns used by the shell**. Regular expressions are used by both the shell and many programs, including those covered in this chapter. The file matching

done by the shell and programs such as **find** are different from the regular expressions covered in this chapter.

• **Use single quotes around regular expressions**. The meta-characters used in this chapter must be quoted in order to be passed to the shell as an argument. You will, therefore, see most regular expressions in this chapter quoted.

Expressions Are Strings and Wildcards

man page

grep - 19

man page

vi - 21

When using the programs in this book, such as **grep** and **vi**, you provide a regular expression that the program evaluates. The command will search for the pattern you supply. The pattern could be as simple as a string or it could include wildcards. The wildcards used by many programs are called meta-characters.

man page

awk - 19

man page

sed - 19

Table 21-1 shows a list of meta-characters and the program(s) to which they apply. Only the programs covered in this book (**awk**, **grep**, **sed**, and **vi**) are shown in Table 21-Expr. These meta-characters may be used with other programs, such as **ed** and **egrep**, as well, which are not covered in the book. Table 21-Expr describes the meta-characters and their use.

TABLE 21-Expr Meta-Characters and Programs to Which They Apply

Meta-Character	awk	grep	sed	vi	Use
.	Yes	Yes	Yes	Yes	Match any single character.
*	Yes	Yes	Yes	Yes	Match any number of the single character that precedes *.
[...]	Yes	Yes	Yes	Yes	Match any <u>one</u> of the characters in the set [...].
$	Yes	Yes	Yes	Yes	Matches the end of the line.
^	Yes	Yes	Yes	Yes	Matches the beginning of the line.
\	Yes	Yes	Yes	Yes	Escape the special character that follows \.
\{n,m\}	Yes	Yes	No	No	Match a range of occurrences of a single character between n and m.
+	Yes	No	No	No	Match one or more occurrences of the preceding regular expression.
?	Yes	No	No	No	Match zero or one occurrence of the preceding regular expression.
		Yes	No	No	No	The preceding <u>or</u> following regular expression can be matched.
()	Yes	No	No	No	Groups regular expressions in a typical parenthesis fashion.
\{ \}	No	No	No	Yes	Match a word's beginning or end.

You may want to refer to this table when regular expressions are used for one of the commands in the table.

Modes and Notations

We're first going to cover some of the fundamentals of the operation of **vi** called modes, and then go over some of the notations used in the tables in this chapter.

A feature of **vi** that often confuses new users is that it has modes. When you are in *command mode*, everything you type is interpreted as a command. In *command mode*, you can specify such actions as the location to which you want the cursor to move. When you are in *input mode*, everything you type is information to be added to the file. *Command mode* is the default when you start **vi**. You can move into *command mode* from *input mode* at any time by pressing the *escape* key. You move into *insert mode* from *command mode* by typing one of the *input mode* commands covered shortly.

vi commands don't really have a standard form. For this reason, I cover common notations. Table 21-Introduction summarizes modes and commands in **vi**:

TABLE 21- Introduction Modes and Notations in **vi**

Mode or Notation	Description
Command Mode	You are issuing commands such as moving the cursor or deleting text, rather than inserting or changing text when in command mode. You can switch to insert mode by issuing an insert mode command such as **i** for insert or **a** for add text.

Mode or Notation	Description
Insert Mode	You are in insert mode when changing or inserting more than one character of text. You can switch to command mode by pressing the *escape* key.
: (colon commands)	Commands that start with a **:** are completed by pressing the *return* key.
control (**^**) commands	When a command uses the *control* (**^**) key, you press and hold down the *control* key and then press the next key that is part of the command. For instance, **^g** means press and hold *control* and then **g** to get the status on the file you are editing.
file for the name of a file	Many commands require you to specify the name of a file. For instance, in the command **vi** *file,* you would substitute the name of the file you wish to edit for *file.*
char for the name of a character	Many commands require you to specify a single character. For instance, in the command **f***char,* you would substitute the character you wish to search for in place of *char.*
cursor_command for a cursor movement command	Many commands require you to specify a cursor command to execute. For instance, in the command **d***cursor_command,* you would substitute for *cursor_command* the command you wish to execute.
string for a character string	Many commands require you to specify a character string. For instance, in the command **/***string,* you would substitute for *string* the character string for which you wish to search.

Starting a vi Session

Let's jump right in and edit a file. For most of the examples in this chapter, I perform various **vi** commands and capture the results in an

man page

vi - 21

X Window. The best way to learn any topic is by example. I not only provide many examples, but I also capture each example in an X Window so that you can see the results of each command. From the command line, we type **vi** and the name of the file we wish to edit, in this case **wisdom**:

```
$ vi wisdom
```

We are then editing the file **wisdom** as shown in Figure 21-1. **wisdom** contains a passage from <u>Tao Te Ching</u> or "Book of the Way." We use this file throughout this chapter.

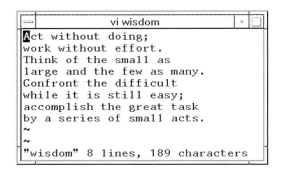

Figure 21-1   Editing the File **wisdom**

The bottom line in Figure 21-1 is the message line in **vi**. After invoking **vi,** the message line indicates the name of the file, the number of lines, and the number of characters in the file. Different messages appear on the message line, depending on the command you issue, as we see in upcoming examples. If a tilde appears on any lines in the file, as it does in the two lines above the message line in **wisdom**, it means that not enough lines exist to fill up the screen. The cursor is the dark box that appears at line 1 in Figure 21-1.

We can specify several file names, and after saving the first file move on to the second file by entering **:n**, and continue going through the list of files in this way. Or we can specify a file and position the cursor on the last line in the file. The default is for the cursor to appear over the first character in the file, as shown in Figure 21-1.

Table 21-1 shows some of the ways we can start a **vi** session:

TABLE 21-1 Starting a **vi** Session

Command	Description
vi *file*	Edit *file*.
vi -r *file*	Edit last saved version of *file* after a crash.
vi -R *file*	Edit *file* in read-only mode.
vi + *n file*	Edit *file* and place cursor at line *n*.
vi + *file*	Edit *file* and place cursor on last line.
vi *file1 file2 file3 ...*	Edit *file1* through *file3*, and after saving changes in *file1*, you can move to *file2* by entering **:n**.
vi +/string file	Edit *file* and place cursor at the beginning of the line containing *string*.

Figure 21-2 shows editing wisdom and placing the cursor at line 5 with the command **vi +5 wisdom**:

man page

vi - 21

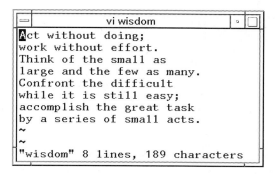

Figure 21-2 Editing the File **wisdom** and Placing Cursor at Line 5 with **vi +5 wisdom**

Figure 21-3 shows editing **wisdom** and placing the cursor at the last line of the file with the command **vi + wisdom**.

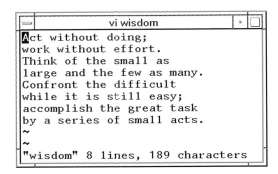

Figure 21-3 Editing the File **wisdom** and Placing Cursor at Last Line with **vi + wisdom**

Figure 21-4 shows editing wisdom and placing the cursor at the line containing *task* with **vi +/task wisdom**.

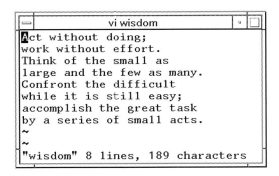

Figure 21-4 Editing the File **wisdom** and Placing Cursor at Line Containing *task* with **vi +/task wisdom**

Cursor Control Commands

man page

vi - 21

A key skill to develop in **vi** is getting the cursor to the desired position. You do this in *command mode*. You have a variety of ways to move the cursor around the screen. Table 21-2 summarizes some of the more commonly used cursor movements:

TABLE 21-2 Cursor Control Commands In **vi**

Command	Cursor Movement
h or **^h**	Move left one character.
j or **^j** or **^n**	Move down one line.
k or **^p**	Move up one line.
l or **space**	Move right one character.
G	Go to the last line of the file.
*n***G**	Go to line number *n*.
G$	Go to the last character in the file.
1G	Go to the first line in the file.
w	Go to the beginning of the next word.
W	Go to the beginning of next word, ignore punctuation.
b	Go to the beginning of the previous word.
B	Go to the start of previous word, ignore punctuation.
L	Go to the last line of the screen.
M	Go to the middle line of the screen.
H	Go to the first line of the screen.
e	Move to the end of the next word.
E	Move to the end of the next word, ignore punctuation.
(	Go to the beginning of the sentence.

TABLE 21-2 Cursor Control Commands In **vi**

Command	Cursor Movement
)	Go to the end of the sentence.
{	Go to the beginning of the paragraph.
}	Go to the beginning of the next paragraph.
0 or |	Go to the first column in the current line.
n|	Go to column *n* in the current line.
^ (caret)	Go to the first non-blank character in the current line.
$	Go to the last character in the current line.
+ or *return*	Go to the first character in the next line.
-	Go to the first non-blank character in the previous line.

man page

vi - 21

I know that the fact that you have to remember these commands in order to get the cursor to the desired position may seem a little strange at first, but this is the way **vi** works. Let's use **wisdom** to show how some of these cursor movements work. Figures 21-5 and 21-6 show some cursor movements. Like all of the upcoming figures, Figures 21-5 and 21-6 show **wisdom** before a command is entered on the left and the result after the command is entered on the right. The command issued appears in the middle. Some of the commands in upcoming figures use the *enter* and *escape* keys.

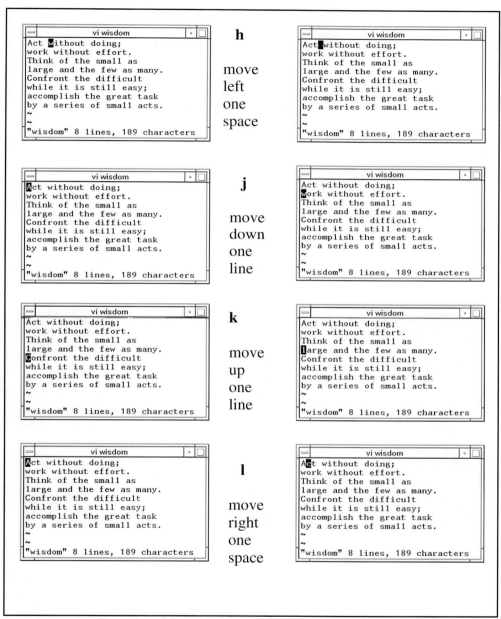

Figure 21-5 Examples of Cursor Movement in **vi** (**h**, **j**, **k**, and **l**)

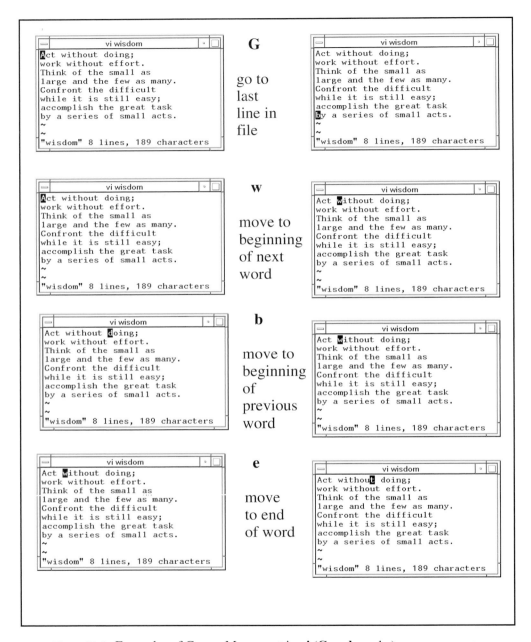

Figure 21-6 Examples of Cursor Movement in **vi** (**G**, **w**, **b**, and **e**)

Adding Text in vi

Now that we know how to move around the cursor, let's do something with it. You need to first learn about cursor movement, because the commands for adding text take place relative to the position of the cursor. Table 21-3 summarizes some commands for adding text:

TABLE 21-3 Adding Text In **vi**

Command	Insertion Action
a	Append new text after the cursor.
A	Append new text after the end of the current line.
i	Insert new text before the cursor.
I	Insert new text before the beginning of the current line.
o	Open a line below the current line and insert.
O	Open a line above the current line and insert.
:r *file*	Read *file* and insert after the current line.
:n r *file*	Read *file* and insert after line *n*.
escape	Get back to command mode.
^v *char*	Ignore special meaning of *char* when inserting. This is for inserting special characters.

Let's now look at some examples of adding text into **wisdom** in Figure 21-7:

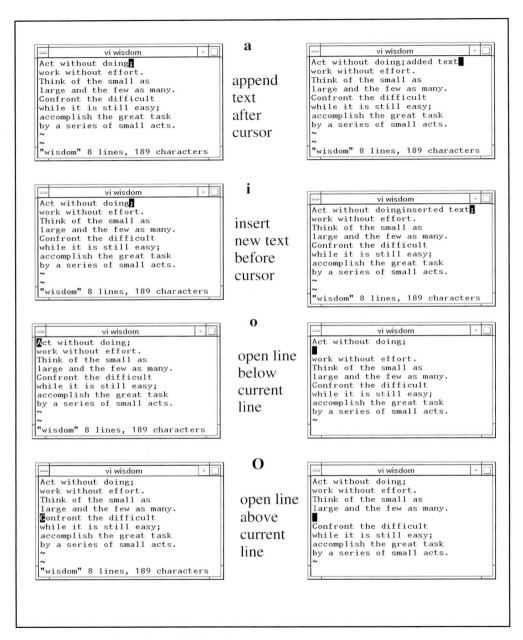

Figure 21-7 Examples of Adding Text in **vi**

Deleting Text in vi

We also need to learn about cursor movement before learning how to delete text, because the commands for deleting text take place relative to the position of the cursor. Table 21-4 summarizes some commands for deleting text:

TABLE 21-4 Deleting Text In **vi**

Command	Deletion Action
x	Delete the character at the cursor. You can also put a number in front of x to specify the number of characters to delete.
*n*x	Delete *n* characters beginning with the current.
X	Delete the previous character. You can also put a number in front of X to specify the number of previous characters to delete.
*n*X	Delete previous *n* characters.
dw	Delete to the beginning of the next word.
*n*dw	Delete the next *n* words beginning with the current.
dG	Delete lines to the end of the file.
dd	Delete the entire line.
*n*dd	Delete *n* lines beginning with the current.
db	Delete the previous word.
*n*db	Delete the previous *n* words beginning with the current.
:*n*,*m*d	Deletes lines *n* through *m*.

TABLE 21-4 Deleting Text In **vi**

Command	Deletion Action
D or **d$**	Delete from the cursor to the end of the line.
d*cursor_command*	Delete text to the *cursor_command*. **dG** would delete from the current line to the end of the file.
^h or *backspace*	While inserting, delete the previous character.
^w	While inserting, delete the previous word.

Let's now look at some examples of deleting text from **wisdom** in Figures 21-8 and 21-9:

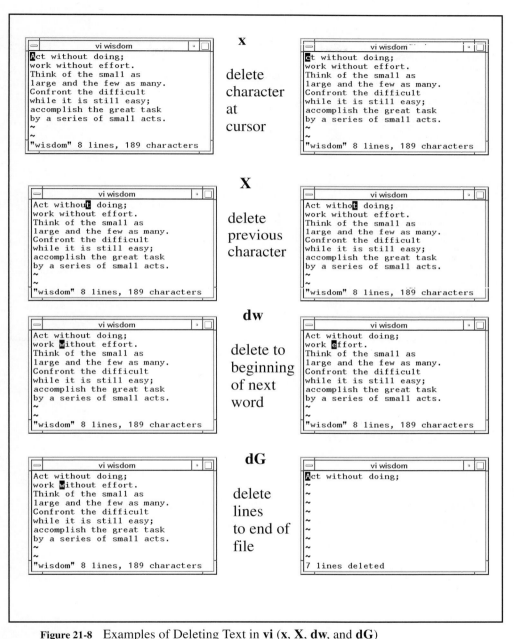

Figure 21-8 Examples of Deleting Text in **vi** (**x**, **X**, **dw**, and **dG**)

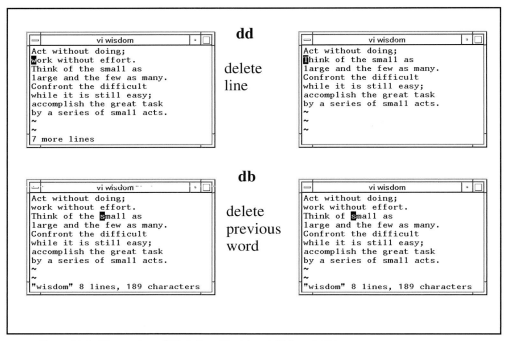

Figure 21-9 Examples of Deleting Text in **vi** (**dd** and **db**)

Changing Text in vi

man page

vi - 21

Okay, you've added text and deleted text, and now you want to change text. **vi** isn't so bad so far, is it? Table 21-5 summarizes some commands for changing text:

TABLE 21-5 Changing Text In **vi**

Command (Preceding these commands with a number repeats the commands any number of times.)	**Replacement Action**
r_char_	Replace the current character with _char._
R_text escape_	Replace the current characters with _text_ until _escape_ is entered.
s_text escape_	Substitute _text_ for the current character.
S or **cc**_text escape_	Substitute _text_ for the entire line.
cw_text escape_	Change the current word to _text._
C_text escape_	Change the rest of the current line to _text._
cG _escape_	Change to the end of the file.
c_cursor_cmd_ **text** _escape_	Change to _text_ from the current position to _cursor_cmd._

Let's now look at some examples of replacing text from **wisdom** in Figures 21-10 and 21-11:

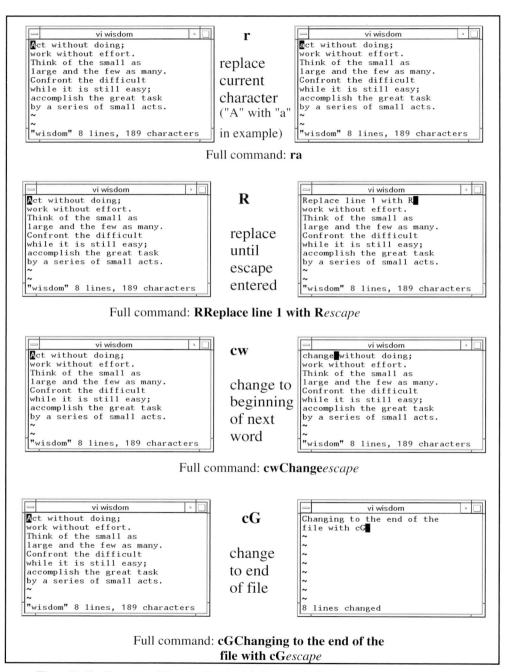

Figure 21-10   Examples of Changing Text in **vi** (**r**, **R**, **cw**, and **cG**)

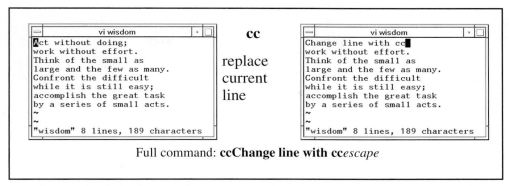

Full command: **ccChange line with cc**_escape_

Figure 21-11   Example of Changing Text in **vi** with **cc**

Search and Replace in vi

man page

vi - 21

You have a lot of search and replace functionality in **vi**. Table 21-6 summarizes some of the more common search-and-replace functionality in **vi**:

TABLE 21-6 Search And Replace In **vi**

Command	Search and Replace Action
/text	Search for **text** going forward into the file.
?text	Search for **text** going backward into the file.
n	Repeat the search in the same direction as the original search.
N	Repeat the search in the opposite direction as the original search.
ftext	Search for text going forward in the current line.
Ftext	Search for text going backward in the current line.

TABLE 21-6 Search And Replace In **vi**

Command	Search and Replace Action
t*text*	Search for *text* going forward in the current line and stop at the character before *text*.
T*text*	Search for *text* going backward in the current line to character after *text*.
:set ic	Ignore case when searching.
:set noic	Make searching case-sensitive.
:s/*oldtext***/***newtext***/**	Substitute *newtext* for *oldtext*.
:*m***,***n***s/***oldtext***/***newtext***/**	Substitute *newtext* for *oldtext* in lines *m* through *n*.
&	Repeat the last **:s** command.
:g/*text1***/s/***text2***/***text3*	Find line containing *text1*, replace *text2* with *text3*.
:g/*text***/***command*	Run *command* on all lines that contain *text*.
:v/*text***/***command*	Run *command* on all lines that do not contain *text*.

Let's now look at some examples of searching and replacing text in **wisdom** in Figure 21-12:

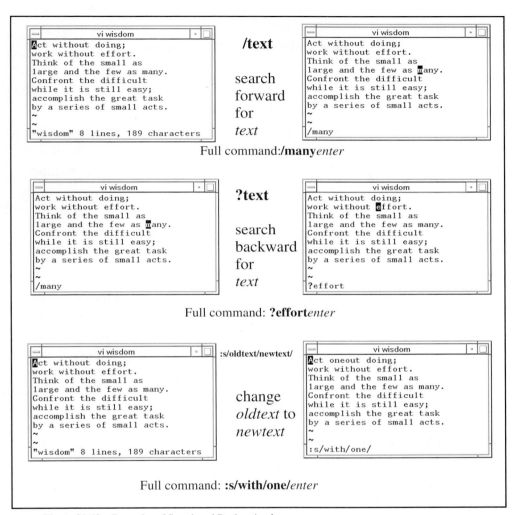

Figure 21-12 Examples of Search and Replace in **vi**

You can perform advanced searches with **:g** and **:v**. You can find and display all the lines in a file containing **while** with the following command:

```
:g/while/p
```

The **/p** in this command line is the print command used with the **ex** editor. You could find all the lines in the file that contain *while* and delete those lines with the following command:

```
:g/while/d
```

You can also specify the specific line numbers for which you want the search to take place. The following command finds all the lines between 10 and 20 that contain *while* and prints the line number on which they appear:

```
:10,20g/while/nu
```

:g runs a command on the lines that contain the text for which we are searching, and **:v** runs a command on the lines that do not contain the specified text. The following three commands act on the lines that do not contain *while*, in the same way that the previous three act on the lines that do contain *while*:

```
:v/while/p
```

```
:v/while/d
```

```
:10,20v/while/nu
```

The first command prints lines that do not contain *while*. The second command deletes the lines on which *while* does not appear. The third command prints the line number between *10* and *20* on which *while* does not appear.

Copying Text in vi

man page

vi - 21

You can copy text in **vi**. Some commands for copying are shown in Table 21-7:

TABLE 21-7 Copying In **vi**

Command	Copy Action
yy	Yank the current line.
nyy	Yank **n** lines.
p (lower case)	Put the yanked text after the cursor.
p (upper case)	Put the yanked text before the cursor.
*"(a-z)n***yy**	Copy *n* lines into the buffer named in parentheses. Omit *n* for the current line.
*"(a-z)n***dd**	Delete *n* lines into the buffer named in parentheses. Omit *n* for the current line.
*"(a-z)***p**	Put lines named in the buffer in parentheses after current line.
*"(a-z)***P**	Put lines named in the buffer in parentheses before the current line.

Let's now look at some examples of copying text in **wisdom** in Figure 21-13:

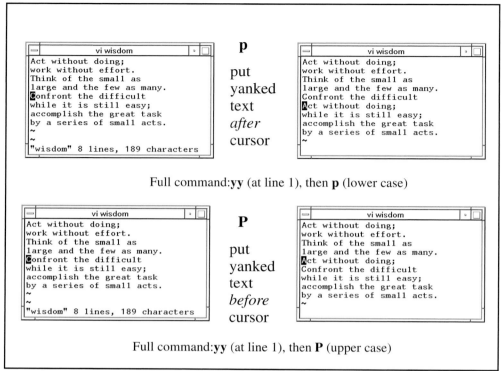

Figure 21-13   Copying in vi

Undo and Repeat in vi

man page

vi - 21

You can easily undo and repeat changes in **vi** with the commands shown in Table 21-8:

TABLE 21-8 Unso In **vi**

Command	Undo Action
u	Undo the last change.
U	Undo all changes to the current line.
. (period)	Repeat the last change.
, (comma)	Repeat, in reverse direction, last **f**, **F**, **t**, or **T** search command.
; (semi-colon)	Repeat last **f**, **F**, **t**, or **T** search command.
"*n***p**	Retrieve the last *n*th delete (a limited number of deletes are in the buffer, usually nine).
n	Repeat last **/** or **?** search command.
N	Repeat, in reverse direction, last **/** or **?** search command.

Save Text and Exit vi

man page

vi - 21

You have a number of different ways to save files and exit **vi**, some of which are summarized in Table 21-9:

TABLE 21-9 Saving Text and Exiting **vi**

Command	Save and/or Quit Action
:w	Save the file but don't exit **vi**.
:w *file*	Save changes in *file* but don't quit **vi**.
:wq or **ZZ** or **:x**	Save the file and quit **vi**.

TABLE 21-9 Saving Text and Exiting **vi**

Command	Save and/or Quit Action
:q!	Quit **vi** without saving the file.
:e!	Re-edit the file, discarding changes since the last write.

Options in vi

man page

vi - 21

There are many options you can set and unset in **vi**. To set an option, you type **:set** *option*. To unset an option, you type **:set no***option*. Table 21-10 summarizes some of the more commonly used options:

TABLE 21-10 Options In **vi**

Option	Action
:set all	Print all options.
:set no*option*	Turn off *option*.
:set nu	Prefix lines with line number.
:set showmode	Show whether input or replace mode.
:set noic	Ignore case when searching.
:set list	Show tabs (^l) and end of line ($).
:set ts=8	Set tab stops for text input.
:set window=*n*	Set number of lines in a text window to *n*.

Let's now prefix lines with line numbers and show input or replace mode in Figure 21-14:

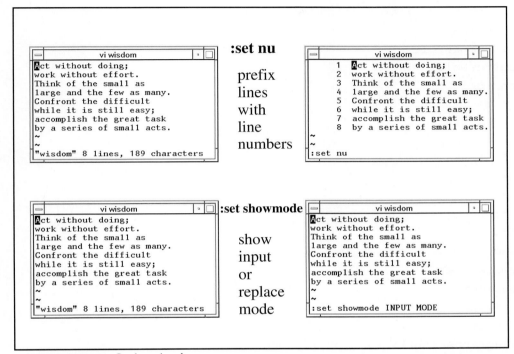

Figure 21-14   Options in **vi**

Many additional options are available beyond those in Table 21-10. The following is a list of options produced on a UNIX system from the **:set all** command. You should issue this command when in **vi** to see the options available to you:

man page

vi - 21

`:set all`

noautoindent

autoprint

noautowrite

nobeautify

directory=/var/tmp

nodoubleescape

noedcompatible

noerrorbells

noexrc

flash

hardtabs=8

noignorecase

keyboardedit

nokeyboardedit!

nolisp

nolist

magic

mesg

nomodelines

nonumber

nonovice

nooptimize

paragraphs=IPLPPPQPP LIpplpipnpbp

prompt

noreadonly

redraw

remap

report=5

scroll=11

sections=NHSHH HUuhsh+c

shell=/sbin/sh

shiftwidth=8

noshowmatch

noshowmode

noslowopen

tabstop=8

```
taglength=0
tags=tags /usr/lib/tags
tagstack
term=hp
noterse
timeout
timeoutlen=500
ttytype=hp
warn
window=23
wrapscan
wrapmargin=0
nowriteany
noshowmatch
noshowmode
```

Many of the options are preceded by a "no," indicating that the option is not set. You may want to list your options with **:set all** and then experiment with the options of interest to you to see the effect they will have on your **vi** session.

man page

vi - 21

Status in vi

You can obtain a lot of useful status information with some simple commands in **vi**. You can display the current line number, number of lines in the file, file name, and other status information with the commands shown in Table 21-11:

TABLE 21-11 Status In **vi**

Option	Action
:.=	Print the current line number.
:=	Print the number of lines in the file.
^g	Show the file name, current line number, total lines in the file, and percent of file location.
:l	Use the letter "l" to display various special characters such as tab and newline.

Section Positioning and Placing Marks in Text

man page

vi - 21

You can define sections of text to which you can move as well as mark text with characters and move to those marks. Table 21-12 summarizes positioning and marking in **vi**:

TABLE 21-12 Positioning and Marking In **vi**

Option	Action
{	Insert { in first column to define section.
[[	Go back to beginning of section.
]]	Forward to beginning of next section.
m(*a-z*)	Mark current position with a letter such as **mz** for mark *z*.
'(*a-z*)	Move cursor to specified mark such as '**z** for move to *z*.

Joining Lines in vi

man page

vi - 21

You can join one or more lines in **vi** using the commands shown in Table 21-13:

TABLE 21-13 Joining Lines In **vi**

Option	Action
J	Join the next line to the end of the current line.
*n*J	Join the next *n* lines.

Cursor Placement and Adjusting the Screen

You can place the cursor anywhere in your file and adjust the screen in a variety of ways using the commands shown in Table 21-14:

TABLE 21-14 Cursor Placement and Adjusting the Screen In **vi**

Option	Action
H	Move cursor to top line of the screen.
*n*H	Move cursor to *n* line from the top of the screen.

TABLE 21-14 Cursor Placement and Adjusting the Screen In **vi**

Option	Action
M	Move cursor to the middle of the screen.
L	Move cursor to the bottom line of the screen.
*n***L**	Move cursor to line *n* from the bottom of the screen.
^e (control-e)	Move screen up one line.
^y	Move screen down one line.
^u	Move screen up one-half page.
^d	Move screen down one-half page.
^b	Move screen up one page.
^f	Move screen down one page.
^l (letter l)	Redraw screen.
z - *return*	Make current line the top of screen.
*n***z** - *return*	Make *n* line the top of screen.
z.	Make current line the middle line.
*n***z.**	Make line *n* the middle line on screen.
z-	Make current line the bottom line.
*n***z-**	Make line *n* the bottom line on screen.

Shell Escape Commands

man page

vi - 21

You can run a UNIX command without exiting **vi** by using shell escape commands. You could do something as simple as start a sub-shell with the **:sh** command. You could also run a command outside the file you are editing without exiting **vi**. Table 21-15 describes shell escape commands:

TABLE 21-15 Shell Escape Commands In **vi**

Option	Action
:! *command*	Execute shell command *command* such as **:! ls**.
:!!	Execute last shell command.
:r! *command*	Read and insert output from *command*, such as **:r! ls** to run **ls** and read contents.
:w !*command*	Send currently edited file to *command* as standard input and execute *command*, such as **:w ! grep all**.
:cd *directory*	Change the current working directory to *directory*.
:sh	Start a sub-shell and use **^d** (control-d) to return to **vi**.
:so *file*	Read and execute commands in the shell program *file*.

An example of using **:w** would be to send the file **wisdom** as standard input to **grep,** looking for all lines that contain *all*, as in the following example:

man page

grep - 19

```
:w ! grep all
Think of the small as
by a series of small acts.
```

You can issue the **:so** command to read and execute the commands in a file. Issuing the following command when in **vi** would run the commands in the file **file_with_commands**:

```
:so file_with_commands
```

This file contains the following two commands:

```
:set nu
:g/all/p
```

When we issue the earlier **:so** command, line numbers are shown with the **:set nu** command and the following lines containing *all* are printed:

```
Think of the small as
by a series of small acts.
```

Macros and Abbreviations

man page

vi - 21

You are not limited to issuing individual **vi** commands. You can define strings of **vi** commands and define a key corresponding to this string that you can recall. When defining the keys for your macros, you can't use the following: **K V g q v * =** and function keys. There are also control keys you can't use, so stay away from control keys in general. Table 21-16 shows macros and abbreviations.

TABLE 21-16 Macros and Abbreviations In **vi**

Option	Action
:map *key command_seq*	Define *key* to run *command_seq*, such as **:map e ea** to append text whenever you use **e** to move to the end of a word.
:map	Display all defined macros on the status line.
:umap *key*	Remove the macro for *key*.

TABLE 21-16 Macros and Abbreviations In **vi**

Option	Action
:ab *string1 string2*	Define an abbreviation such that when *string1* is inserted, replace it with *string2*. When inserting text type *string1*, press *escape* key and *string2* will be inserted.
:ab	Display all abbreviations.
:cd *directory*	Change the current working directory to *directory*.
:una *string*	Unabbreviate *string*.
	Avoid control keys, symbols, and don't use characters: **K V g q v * =** and function keys.

An example of using the **map** command would be to automatically add text when you move to the end, as shown with the following **map** command:

```
:map e ea
```

This command maps **e** to **ea**. When you go to the end of the next word with **e**, you are also placed in insert mode with **a** so that you can append new text immediately after the end of the word.

You can also abbreviate long sequences with **ab**. For instance, you could abbreviate *system administration* with *sa* with the following command:

```
:ab sa system administration
```

Now, whenever you insert text, type *sa* and then press the *escape* key to complete the insert; the string *system administration* appears. *sa* is an abbreviation for *system administration*.

Indenting Text

You can indent text in a variety of different ways. Table 21-17 shows some of the more commonly used indenting commands:

TABLE 21-17 Indenting Text In **vi**

Option	Action
^i (control i) or *tab*	While inserting text, insert on shift width. Shift width can be defined.
:set ai	Turn on auto-indentation.
:set sw=*n*	Set shift width to *n* characters.
n<<	Shift *n* lines left by one shift width.
n>>	Shift *n* lines right by one shift width. For example, **3>>** shifts the next three lines right by one shift width.

Before you adjust the shift width, you may want to issue **:set all** in order to see the current number of characters to which the shift width is set. It is usually eight characters by default. To set shift width to 16 characters, issue the following command:

:set sw=16

You can then shift over the next three lines to the right by 16 characters each, with the following command:

3>>

The next three lines are then shifted right by 16 characters.

Shell Filters

You can send information from the file you are editing to a command and then replace the original text with the output of the command. Table 21-18 shows a shell filter:

TABLE 21-18 Shell Filters In **vi**

Option	Action
!*cursor_command command*	Send text from the current position to that described by *cursor_command* to the shell *command*. For example, use **!} grep admin** to take text from the current position to the end of the paragraph, run this text through **grep** looking for the word *admin*, and replace existing text with the output of **grep**.

Pattern Matching

Pattern matching allows you to find patterns within the file you are editing. You can then perform functions such as changing what you have found in some way. Table 21-19 shows some of the most common pattern-matching commands:

TABLE 21-19 Pattern Matching In **vi**

Option	Action
^ (caret)	Match the beginning of the line. To search for **Think** at only the beginning of the line, you would use: **/^Think** You can use this in combination with **$**, which matches to the end of the line, to delete all blank lines with: **:g/^$/d.**
$	Match end of line. To match **last.** only when it is followed by a newline character, you would use: **/last.$**
.	Match any single character.
\<	Match beginning of word.
\>	Match end of word.
[*string*]	Match any single character in *string*. To find **mp**, **mP**, **Mp**, or **MP**, use: **/[mM][pP]** Change all occurrences of **input** or **Input** to **INPUT** with: **:%s/[Ii]nput/INPUT/g**
[^*string*]	Match any character not in *string*.
[*a-p*]	Match any character between *a* and *p*.
*****	Match zero or more occurrences of previous character in expression.
****	Escape meaning of next character. To search for [, use the following: **\[**
****	Escape the \ character.

You may find pattern matching a little confusing when you first start to use it, so I'll go through several simple examples to get you started. Keep in mind that many of the pattern-matching techniques described here also work outside **vi** in your shell.

Matching a Set

We'll begin with the *square bracket operator*. To match any of the single characters *m, f,* or *p*, you would use the following:

```
/[mfp]
```

A common pattern to match would be a word with the first letter in the word, either uppercase or lowercase. To match *input* or *Input*, you would use the following:

```
/[Ii]nput
```

After you match either *Input* or *input*, you could then change it to *INPUT* with the following command:

```
:%s/[Ii]nput/INPUT/g
```

You can use sequences of expressions to search for more than one character, as shown in the following example:

```
/[mM][pP]
```

This sequence will match *mp, mP, Mp,* or *MP*. You are, in effect, searching for any of the four two-character strings.

Matching a Range

You can also use the square bracket operator to match single characters within a range. To find an occurrence of any digit in a file, you could use either of the two following square bracket searches:

`/[0123456789]`

or

`/[0-9]`

The hyphen denotes a range within the square bracket. To find any character, either uppercase or lowercase, you could use the following:

`/[a-zA-Z]`

To search for characters that normally have a special meaning, such as [, you can ignore, or escape, the special meaning by preceding the special character with a \ (backslash). To search for [in **vi**, for instance, you would use the following sequence:

`/\[`

This search finds the first occurrence of [.

Beginning and End of Line Search

You can specify that you wish your pattern match to take place at only the beginning or end of a line. To specify a beginning of the line pattern match, use the ^ (caret) preceding your desired pattern, as shown in the following example:

```
/^Think
```

This matches *Think* only when it appears at the beginning of a line.

To specify an end-of-the-line pattern match, use a **$** (dollar sign) following your desired pattern, as shown in the following example:

```
/last.$
```

This matches *last.* only when it is followed by a newline.

Manual Pages for vi Command Used in Chapter 21

The following section contains copies of the manual pages for **vi**.

vi

vi - Run visual editor.

vi(1)   vi(1)

NAME
     vi, view, vedit - screen-oriented (visual) text editor

SYNOPSIS

     vi [-] [-l] [-r] [-R] [-t tag] [-v] [-V] [-wsize] [-x] [+command] [file
     ...]

   XPG4 Synopsis
     vi [-rR] [-c command] [-t tag] [-w size] [file ...]

   Obsolescent Options
     vi [-rR] [+command] [-t tag] [-w size] [file ...]

     view [-] [-l] [-r] [-R] [-t tag] [-v] [-V] [-wsize] [-x] [+command]
     [file ...]

     vedit [-] [-r] [-R] [-l] [-t tag] [-v] [-V] [-wsize] [-x] [+command]
     [file ...]

   Remarks
     The program names ex, edit, vi, view, and vedit are separate
     personalities of the same program. This manual entry describes the
     behavior of the vi/view/vedit personality.

DESCRIPTION
     The vi (visual) program is a display-oriented text editor that is
     based on the underlying ex line editor (see ex(1)). It is possible to
     switch back and forth between the two and to execute ex commands from
     within vi. The line-editor commands and the editor options are
     described in ex(1). Only the visual mode commands are described here.

     The view program is identical to vi except that the readonly editor
     option is set (see ex(1)).

     The vedit program is somewhat friendlier for beginners and casual
     users. The report editor option is set to 1, and the nomagic, novice,
     and showmode editor options are set.

     In vi, the terminal screen acts as a window into a memory copy of the
     file being edited. Changes made to the file copy are reflected in the
     screen display. The position of the cursor on the screen indicates
     the position within the file copy.

     The environment variable TERM must specify a terminal type that is
     defined in the terminfo database (see terminfo(4)). Otherwise, a
     message is displayed and the line-editor is invoked.

     As with ex, editor initialization scripts can be placed in the
     environment variable EXINIT, or in the file .exrc in the current or
     home directory.

Options and Arguments
vi recognizes the following command-line options and arguments:

- Suppress all interactive-user feedback. This is useful when editor commands are taken from scripts.

-l Set the lisp editor option (see ex(1)). Provides indents appropriate for lisp code. The (,), {, }, [[, and]] commands in vi are modified to function with lisp source code.

-r Recover the specified files after an editor or system crash. If no file is specified, a list of all saved files is printed. You must be the owner of the saved file in order to recover it (superuser cannot recover files owned by other users).

-R Set the readonly editor option to prevent overwriting a file inadvertently (see ex(1)).

-t tag Execute the tag tag command to load and position a predefined file. See the tag command and the tags editor option in ex(1).

-v Invoke visual mode (vi). Useful with ex, it has no effect on vi.

-V Set verbose mode. Editor commands are displayed as they are executed when input from a .exrc file or a source file (see the source command in ex(1)).

-wsize Set the value of the window editor option to size. If size is omitted, it defaults to 3.

-x Set encryption mode. You are prompted for a key to allow for the creation or editing of an encrypted file (see the crypt command in ex(1)).

-c command (XPG4 only.)

+command (Obsolescent) Begin editing by executing the specified ex command-mode commands. As with the normal ex command-line entries, the command option-argument can consist of multiple ex commands separated by vertical-line commands (|). The use of commands that enter input mode in this manner produces undefined results.

file Specify the file or files to be edited. If more than one file is specified, they are processed in the order given. If the -r option is also specified, the files are read from the recovery area.

(XPG4 only.) If both the -t tag and -c command (or the obsolescent +command) options are given, the -t tag will be processed first, that is, the file containing the tag is selected by -t and then the command is executed.

When invoked, vi is in command mode. input mode is initiated by several commands used to insert or change text.

In input mode, ESC (escape) is used to leave input mode; however, two consecutive ESC characters are required to leave input mode if the doubleescape editor option is set (see ex(1)).

In command mode, ESC is used to cancel a partial command; the terminal bell sounds if the editor is not in input mode and there is no partially entered command.

WARNING: ESC completes a "bottom line" command (see below).

The last (bottom) line of the screen is used to echo the input for search commands (/ and ?), ex commands (:), and system commands (!). It is also used to report errors or print other messages.

The receipt of SIGINT during text input or during the input of a command on the bottom line terminates the input (or cancels the command) and returns the editor to command mode. During command mode, SIGINT causes the bell to be sounded. In general the bell indicates an error (such as an unrecognized key).

Lines displayed on the screen containing only a ~ indicate that the last line above them is the last line of the file (the ~ lines are past the end of the file). Terminals with limited local intelligence might display lines on the screen marked with an @. These indicate space on the screen not corresponding to lines in the file. (These lines can be removed by entering a ^R, forcing the editor to retype the screen without these holes.)

If the system crashes or vi aborts due to an internal error or unexpected signal, vi attempts to preserve the buffer if any unwritten changes were made. Use the -r command line option to retrieve the saved changes.

The vi text editor supports the SIGWINCH signal, and redraws the screen in response to window-size changes.

Command Summary

Most commands accept a preceding number as an argument, either to give a size or position (for display or movement commands), or as a repeat count (for commands that change text). For simplicity, this optional argument is referred to as count when its effect is described.

The following operators can be followed by a movement command to specify an extent of text to be affected: c, d, y, <, >, !, and =. The region specified begins at the current cursor position and ends just prior to the cursor position indicated by the move. If the command operates on lines only, all the lines that fall partly or wholly within this region are affected. Otherwise the exact marked region is affected.

In the following description, control characters are indicated in the form ^X, which represents Ctrl-X. Whitespace is defined to be the characters space, tab, and alternative space. Alternative space is the first character of the ALT_PUNCT item described in langinfo(5) for the language specified by the LANG environment variable (see environ(5)).

Unless otherwise specified, the commands are interpreted in command mode and have no special effect in input mode.

    ^B   Scroll backward to display the previous window of text. A preceding count specifies the number of windows to go back. Two lines of overlap are kept if possible.

    ^D   Scroll forward a half-window of text. A preceding count gives the number of (logical) lines to scroll, and is remembered for future ^D and ^U commands.

    ^D   (input mode) Backs up over the indentation provided by autoindent or ^T to the next multiple of

shiftwidth spaces. Whitespace inserted by ^T at
other than the beginning of a line cannot be backed
over using ^D. A preceding ^ removes all indentation
for the current and subsequent input lines of the
current input mode until new indentation is
established by inserting leading whitespace, either
by direct input or by using ^T.

^E   Scroll forward one line, leaving the cursor where it
is if possible.

^F   Scroll forward to display the window of text
following the current one. A preceding count
specifies the number of windows to advance. Two
lines of overlap are kept if possible.

(XPG4 only.) The current line is displayed and the
cursor is moved to the first nonblank character of
the current line or the first character if the line
is a blank line.

^G   Print the current file name and other information,
including the number of lines and the current
position (equivalent to the ex command f).

^H   Move one space to the left (stops at the left
margin). A preceding count specifies the number of
spaces to back up. (Same as h).

^H   (input mode) Move the cursor left to the previous
input character without erasing it from the screen.
The character is deleted from the saved text.

^J   Move the cursor down one line in the same column, if
possible. A preceding count specifies the number of
lines to move down. (Same as ^N and j).

^L   Clear and redraw the screen. Use when the screen is
scrambled for any reason.

^M   Move to the first nonwhitespace character in the next
line. A preceding count specifies the number of
lines to advance.

^N   Same as ^J and j.

^P   Move the cursor up one line in the same column. A
preceding count specifies the number of lines to move
up (same as k).

^R   Redraw the current screen, eliminating the false
lines marked with @ (which do not correspond to
actual lines in the file).

^T   Pop the tag stack. See the pop command in ex(1).

^T   (input mode) Insert shiftwidth whitespace. If at the
beginning of the line, this inserted space can only
be backed over using ^D.

^U   Scroll up a half-window of text. A preceding count
gives the number of (logical) lines to scroll, and is
remembered for future ^D and ^U commands.

^V   In input mode, ^V quotes the next character to permit
the insertion of special characters (including ESC)

into the file.

^W   In input mode, ^W backs up one word; the deleted
            characters remain on the display.

^Y   Scroll backward one line, leaving the cursor where it
            is, if possible.

^[Cancel a partially formed command; ^[sounds the bell
            if there is no partially formed command.

            In input mode, ^[terminates input mode. However,
            two consecutive ESC characters are required to
            terminate input mode if the doubleescape editor
            option is set (see ex(1)).

            When entering a command on the bottom line of the
            screen (ex command line or search pattern with \ or
            ?), terminate input and execute command.

            On many terminals, ^[can be entered by pressing the
            ESC or ESCAPE key.

^\   Exit vi and enter ex command mode. If in input mode,
            terminate the input first.

^]   Take the word at or after the cursor as a tag and
            execute the tagMbobC editor command (see ex(1)).

^^   Return to the previous file (equivalent to :ex #).

space   Move one space to the right (stops at the end of the
            line). A preceding count specifies the number of
            spaces to go forward (same as l).

erase   Erase, where erase is the user-designated erase
            character (see stty(1)). Same as ^H.

kill   Kill, where kill is the user-designated kill
            character (see stty(1)). In input mode, kill backs
            up to the beginning of the current input line without
            erasing the line from the screen display.

susp   Suspend the editor session and return to the calling
            shell, where susp is the user-designated process-
            control suspend character (see stty(1)). See ex(1)
            for more information on the suspend editor command.

!   An operator that passes specified lines from the
            buffer as standard input to the specified system
            command, and replaces those lines with the standard
            output from the command. The ! is followed by a
            movement command specifying the lines to be passed
            (lines from the current position to the end of the
            movement) and then the command (terminated as usual
            by a return). A preceding count is passed on to the
            movement command after !.

            Doubling ! and preceding it by count causes that
            many lines, starting with the current line, to be
            passed.

"   Use to precede a named buffer specification. There
            are named buffers 1 through 9 in which the editor
            places deleted text. The named buffers a through z

are available to the user for saving deleted or
yanked text; see also y, below.

$ Move to the end of the current line. A preceding
count specifies the number of lines to advance (for
example, 2$ causes the cursor to advance to the end
of the next line).

% Move to the parenthesis or brace that matches the
parenthesis or brace at the current cursor position.

& Same as the ex command & (that is, & repeats the
previous substitute command).

' When followed by a ', vi returns to the previous
context, placing the cursor at the beginning of the
line. (The previous context is set whenever a
nonrelative move is made.) When followed by a letter
a-z, returns to the line marked with that letter (see
the m command), at the first nonwhitespace character
in the line.

When used with an operator such as d to specify an
extent of text, the operation takes place over
complete lines (see also `).

` When followed by a `, vi returns to the previous
context, placing the cursor at the character position
marked (the previous context is set whenever a
nonrelative move is made). When followed by a letter
a z, returns to the line marked with that letter (see
the m command), at the character position marked.

When used with an operator such as d to specify an
extent of text, the operation takes place from the
exact marked place to the current position within the
line (see also ').

[[Back up to the previous section boundary. A section
is defined by the value of the sections option.
Lines that start with a form feed (^L) or { also stop
[[.

If the option lisp is set, the cursor stops at each (
at the beginning of a line.

]] Move forward to a section boundary (see [[).

^ Move to the first nonwhitespace position on the
current line.

(Move backward to the beginning of a sentence. A
sentence ends at a ., !, or ? followed by either the
end of a line or by two spaces. Any number of
closing),], ", and ' characters can appear between
the ., !, or ? and the spaces or end of line. If a
count is specified, the cursor moves back the
specified number of sentences.

If the lisp option is set, the cursor moves to the
beginning of a lisp s-expression. Sentences also
begin at paragraph and section boundaries (see { and
[[).

) Move forward to the beginning of a sentence. If a

count is specified, the cursor advances the specified
number of sentences (see ().

{   Move back to the beginning of the preceding
paragraph. A paragraph is defined by the value of
the paragraphs option. A completely empty line and a
section boundary (see [[above) are also interpreted
as the beginning of a paragraph. If a count is
specified, the cursor moves backward the specified
number of paragraphs.

}   Move forward to the beginning of the next paragraph.
If a count is specified, the cursor advances the
specified number of paragraphs (see {).

| Requires a preceding count; the cursor moves to the
specified column of the current line (if possible).

+   Move to the first nonwhitespace character in the next
line. If a count is specified, the cursor advances
the specified number of lines (same as ^M).

,   The comma (,) performs the reverse action of the last
f, F, t, or T command issued, by searching in the
opposite direction on the current line. If a count
is specified, the cursor repeats the search the
specified number of times.

-       The hyphen character (-) moves the cursor to the
first nonwhitespace character in the previous line.
If a count is specified, the cursor moves back the
specified number of times.

_   The underscore character (_) moves the cursor to the
first nonwhitespace character in the current line.
If a count is specified, the cursor advances the
specified number of lines, with the current line
being counted as the first line; no count or a count
of 1 specifies the current line.

.   Repeat the last command that changed the buffer. If
a count is specified, the command is repeated the
specified number of times.

/   Read a string from the last line on the screen,
interpret it as a regular expression, and scan
forward for the next occurrence of a matching string.
The search begins when the user types a carriage
return to terminate the pattern; the search can be
terminated by sending SIGINT (or the user-designated
interrupt character).

When used with an operator to specify an extent of
text, the defined region begins with the current
cursor position and ends at the beginning of the
matched string. Entire lines can be specified by
giving an offset from the matched line (by using a
closing / followed by a +n or -n).

0   Move to the first character on the current line (the
0 is not interpreted as a command when preceded by a
nonzero digit).

:   The colon character (:) begins an ex command. The :
and the entered command are echoed on the bottom

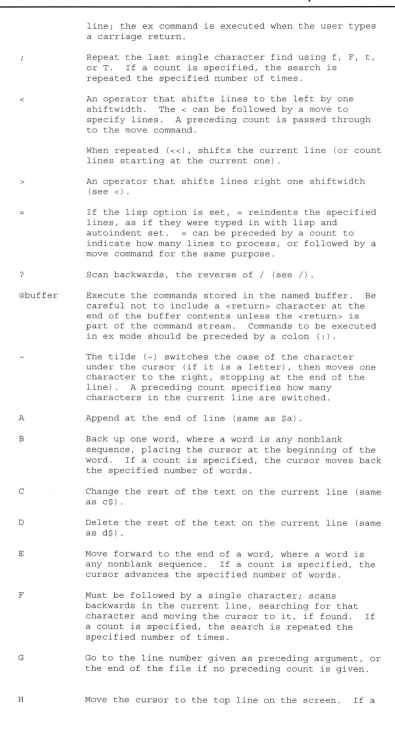

line; the ex command is executed when the user types
a carriage return.

;   Repeat the last single character find using f, F, t,
         or T. If a count is specified, the search is
         repeated the specified number of times.

<   An operator that shifts lines to the left by one
         shiftwidth. The < can be followed by a move to
         specify lines. A preceding count is passed through
         to the move command.

         When repeated (<<), shifts the current line (or count
         lines starting at the current one).

>   An operator that shifts lines right one shiftwidth
         (see <).

=   If the lisp option is set, = reindents the specified
         lines, as if they were typed in with lisp and
         autoindent set. = can be preceded by a count to
         indicate how many lines to process, or followed by a
         move command for the same purpose.

?   Scan backwards, the reverse of / (see /).

@buffer Execute the commands stored in the named buffer. Be
         careful not to include a <return> character at the
         end of the buffer contents unless the <return> is
         part of the command stream. Commands to be executed
         in ex mode should be preceded by a colon (:).

~   The tilde (~) switches the case of the character
         under the cursor (if it is a letter), then moves one
         character to the right, stopping at the end of the
         line). A preceding count specifies how many
         characters in the current line are switched.

A   Append at the end of line (same as $a).

B   Back up one word, where a word is any nonblank
         sequence, placing the cursor at the beginning of the
         word. If a count is specified, the cursor moves back
         the specified number of words.

C   Change the rest of the text on the current line (same
         as c$).

D   Delete the rest of the text on the current line (same
         as d$).

E   Move forward to the end of a word, where a word is
         any nonblank sequence. If a count is specified, the
         cursor advances the specified number of words.

F   Must be followed by a single character; scans
         backwards in the current line, searching for that
         character and moving the cursor to it, if found. If
         a count is specified, the search is repeated the
         specified number of times.

G   Go to the line number given as preceding argument, or
         the end of the file if no preceding count is given.

H   Move the cursor to the top line on the screen. If a

count is given, the cursor moves to count number of
lines from the top of the screen. The cursor is
placed on the first nonwhitespace character on the
line. If used as the target of an operator, entire
lines are affected.

I   Insert at the beginning of a line (same as ^ followed
by i).

J   Join the current line with the next one, supplying
appropriate whitespace: one space between words, two
spaces after a period, and no spaces at all if the
first character of the next line is a closing
parenthesis ()). A preceding count causes the
specified number of lines to be joined, instead of
just two.

L   Move the cursor to the first nonwhitespace character
of the last line on the screen. If a count is given,
the cursor moves to count number of lines from the
bottom of the screen. When used with an operator,
entire lines are affected.

M   Move the cursor to the middle line on the screen, at
the first nonwhitespace position on the line.

N   Scan for the next match of the last pattern given to
/ or ?, but in the opposite direction; this is the
reverse of n.

O   Open a new line above the current line and enter
input mode.

P   Put back (replace) the last deleted or yanked text
before/above the cursor. Entire lines of text are
returned above the cursor if entire lines were
deleted or yanked. Otherwise, the text is inserted
just before the cursor.

         (XPG4 only.) In this case, the cursor is moved to
last column position of the inserted characters.

         If P is preceded by a named buffer specification (x),
the contents of that buffer are retrieved instead.

Q   Exit vi and enter ex command mode.

R   Replace characters on the screen with characters
entered, until the input is terminated with ESC.

S   Change entire lines (same as cc). A preceding count
changes the specified number of lines.

T   Must be followed by a single character; scan
backwards in the current line for that character,
and, if found, place the cursor just after that
character. A count is equivalent to repeating the
search the specified number of times.

U   Restore the current line to its state before the
cursor was last moved to it.

         (XPG4 only.) The cursor position is set to the column
position 1 or to the position indicated by the
previous line if the autoindent is set.

W
Move forward to the beginning of a word in the current line, where a word is a sequence of nonblank characters. If the current position is at the beginning of a word, the current position is within a bigword or the character at that position cannot be a part of a bigword, the current position shall move to the first character of the next bigword. If no subsequent bigword exists on the current line, the current position shall move to the first character of the first bigword on the first following line that contains the bigword. For this command, an empty or blank line is considered to contain exactly one bigword. The current line is set to the line containing the bigword selected and the current position is set to the first character of the bigword selected. A preceding count specifies the number of words to advance.

X
Delete the character before the cursor. A preceding count repeats the effect, but only characters on the current line are deleted.

Y
Place (yank) a copy of the current line into the unnamed buffer (same as yy). If a count is specified, count lines are copied to the buffer. If the Y is preceded by a buffer name, the lines are copied to the named buffer.

ZZ
Exit the editor, writing out the buffer if it was changed since the last write (same as the ex command x). Note that if the last write was to a different file and no changes have occurred since, the editor exits without writing out the buffer.

a
Enter input mode, appending the entered text after the current cursor position. A preceding count causes the inserted text to be replicated the specified number of times, but only if the inserted text is all on one line.

b
Back up to the previous beginning of a word in the current line. A word is a sequence of alphanumerics or a sequence of special characters. A preceding count repeats the effect.

c
Must be followed by a movement command. Delete the specified region of text, and enter input mode to replace deleted text with new text. If more than part of a single line is affected, the deleted text is saved in the numeric buffers. If only part of the current line is affected, the last character deleted is marked with a $. A preceding count passes that value through to the move command. If the command is cc, the entire current line is changed.

d
Must be followed by a movement command. Delete the specified region of text. If more than part of a line is affected, the text is saved in the numeric buffers. A preceding count passes that value through to the move command. If the command is dd, the entire current line is deleted.

e
Move forward to the end of the next word, defined as for b. A preceding count repeats the effect.

f
Must be followed by a single character; scan the rest

of the current line for that character, and moves the cursor to it if found. A preceding count repeats the action that many times.

h	Move the cursor one character to the left (same as ^H). A preceding count repeats the effect.
i	Enter input mode, inserting the entered text before the cursor (see a).
j	Move the cursor one line down in the same column (same as ^J and ^N).
k	Move the cursor one line up (same as ^P).
l	Move the cursor one character to the right (same as \<space\>).
mx	Mark the current position of the cursor. x is a lowercase letter, a-z, that is used with the ` and ' commands to refer to the marked line or line position.
n	Repeat the last / or ? scanning commands.
o	Open a line below the current line and enter input mode; otherwise like O.
p	Put text after/below the cursor; otherwise like P.
r	Must be followed by a single character; the character under the cursor is replaced by the specified one. (The new character can be a new-line.) If r is preceded by a count, count characters are replaced by the specified character.
s	Delete the single character under the cursor and enter input mode; the entered text replaces the deleted character. A preceding count specifies how many characters on the current line are changed. The last character being changed is marked with a $, as for c.
t	Must be followed by a single character; scan the remainder of the line for that character. The cursor moves to the column prior to the character if the character is found. A preceding count is equivalent to repeating the search count times.
u	Reverse the last change made to the current buffer. If repeated, u alternates between these two states; thus is its own inverse. When used after an insertion of text on more than one line, the lines are saved in the numerically named buffers.
w	Move forward to the beginning of the next word (where word is defined as in b). A preceding count specifies how many words the cursor advances.
x	Delete the single character under the cursor. When x is preceded by a count, x deletes the specified number of characters forward from the cursor position, but only on the current line.
y	Must be followed by a movement command; the specified text is copied (yanked) into the unnamed temporary

buffer. If preceded by a named buffer specification,
"x, the text is placed in that buffer also. If the
command is yy, the entire current line is yanked.

z   Redraw the screen with the current line placed as
                  specified by the following options: z<return>
                  specifies the top of the screen, z. the center of
                  the screen, and z- the bottom of the screen. The
                  commands z^ and z+ are similar to ^B and ^F,
                  respectively. However, z^ and z+ do not attempt to
                  maintain two lines of overlap. A count after the z
                  and before the following character to specifies the
                  number of lines displayed in the redrawn screen. A
                  count before the z gives the number of the line to
                  use as the reference line instead of the default
                  current line.

Keyboard Editing Keys
    At initialization, the editor automatically maps some terminal
    keyboard editing keys to equivalent visual mode commands. These
    mappings are only established for keys that are listed in the
    following table and defined in the terminfo(4) database as valid for
    the current terminal (as specified by the TERM environment variable).

    Both command and input mode mappings are created (see the map command
    in ex(1)). With the exception of the insertchar keys, which simply
    toggle input mode on and off, the input mode mappings exit input mode,
    perform the same action as the command mode mapping, and then reenter
    input mode.

    On certain terminals, the character sequence sent by a keyboard
    editing key, which is then mapped to a visual mode command, can be the
    same character sequence a user might enter to perform another command
    or set of commands. This is most likely to happen with the input mode
    mappings; therefore, on these terminals, the input mode mappings are
    disabled by default. Users can override the disabling and enabling of
    both the command and input mode keyboard editing key mappings by
    setting the keyboardedit and keyboardedit! editor options as
    appropriate (see ex(1)). The timeout, timeoutlen, and doubleescape
    editor options are alternative methods of addressing this problem.

terminfo entry	command mode map	input mode map	map name	description
key_ic	i	^[	inschar	insert char
key_eic	i	^[	inschar	end insert char
key_up	k	^[ka	up	arrow up
key_down	j	^[ja	down	arrow down
key_left	h	^[ha	left	arrow left
key_right	l	^[la	right	arrow right
key_home	H	^[Ha	home	arrow home
key_il	o^[	^[o^[a	insline	insert line
key_dl	dd	^[dda	delline	delete line
key_clear	^L	^[^La	clear	clear screen
key_eol	d$	^[d$a	clreol	clear line
key_sf	^E	^[^Ea	scrollf	scroll down
key_dc	x	^[xa	delchar	delete char
key_npage	^F	^[^Fa	npage	next page
key_ppage	^B	^[^Ba	ppage	previous page
key_sr	^Y	^[^Ya	sr	scroll up
key_eos	dG	^[dGa	clreos	clear to end of screen

EXTERNAL INFLUENCES
     Support for international codes and environment variables are as
     follows:

Environment Variables
     UNIX95 specifies using the XPG4 behaviour for this command.

     COLUMNS overrides the system-selected horizontal screen size.

     LINES overrides the system-selected vertical screen size, used as the
     number of lines in a screenful and the vertical screen size in visual
     mode.

     SHELL is a variable that shall be interpreted as the preferred
     command-line interpreter for use in !, shell, read, and other commands
     with an operand of the form !string. For the shell command the
     program shall be invoked with the two arguments -c and string.   If
     this variable is null or not set, the sh utility shall be used.

     TERM is a variable that shall be interpreted as the name of the
     terminal type. If this variable is unset or null, an unspecified
     default terminal type shall be used.

     PATH determines the search path for the shell command specified in the
     editor commands, shell, read, and write. EXINIT determines a list of
     ex commands that will be executed on editor startup, before reading
     the first file. The list can contain multiple commands by separating
     them using a vertical line (|) character.

     HOME determines a pathname of a directory that will be searched for an
     editor startup file named .exrc.

     LC_ALL This variable shall determine the locale to be used to override
     any values for locale categories specified by the setting of LANG or
     any environment variables beginning with LC_.

     LC_MESSAGES determines the locale that should be used to affect the
     format and contents of diagnostic messages written to standard error
     and informative messages written to standard output.

     LC_COLLATE determines the collating sequence used in evaluating
     regular expressions and in processing the tags file. LC_CTYPE
     determines the interpretation of text as single and/or multi-byte
     characters, the classification of characters as uppercase or lowercase
     letters, the shifting of letters between uppercase and lowercase, and
     the characters matched by character class expressions in regular
     expressions.

     LANG determines the language in which messages are displayed.

     LANGOPTS specifies options determining how text for right-to-left
     languages is stored in input and output files. See environ(5).

     If LC_COLLATE or LC_CTYPE is not specified in the environment or is
     set to the empty string, the value of LANG is used as a default for
     each unspecified or empty variable. If LANG is not specified or is
     set to the empty string, a default of "C" (see lang(5)) is used
     instead of LANG. If any internationalization variable contains an
     invalid setting, the editor behaves as if all internationalization
     variables are set to "C". See environ(5).

International Code Set Support
     Single- and multi-byte character code sets are supported.

WARNINGS
     See also the WARNINGS section in ex(1).

Program Limits
    vi places the following limits on files being edited:

Maximum Line Length
    LINE_MAX characters (defined in <limits.h>), including 2-3 bytes
    for overhead. Thus, if the value specified for LINE_MAX is 2048,
    a line length up to 2044 characters should cause no problem.

    If you load a file that contain lines longer than the specified
    limit, the lines are truncated to the stated maximum length.
    Saving the file will write the truncated version over the
    original file, thus overwriting the original lines completely.

    Attempting to create lines longer than the allowable maximum for
    the editor produces a line too long error message.

Maximum File Size
    The maximum file length of 234,239 lines is silently enforced.

Other limits:

    - 256 characters per global command list.

    - 128 characters in a file name in vi or ex open mode. On
      short-file-name HP-UX systems, the maximum file name length is
      14 characters.

    - 128 characters in a previous insert/delete buffer.

    - 100 characters in a shell-escape command.

    - 63 characters in a string-valued option (:set command).

    - 30 characters in a program tag name.

    - 32 or fewer macros defined by map command.

    - 512 or fewer characters total in combined map macros.

AUTHOR
    vi was developed by the University of California, Berkeley. The 16-
    bit extensions to vi are based in part on software of the Toshiba
    Corporation.

SEE ALSO
    ctags(1), ed(1), ex(1), stty(1), write(1), terminfo(4), environ(5),
    lang(5), regexp(5).

    The Ultimate Guide to the vi and ex Text Editors,
        Benjamin/Cummings Publishing Company, Inc., ISBN 0-8053-4460-8,
        HP part number 97005-90015.

STANDARDS CONFORMANCE
    vi: SVID2, SVID3, XPG2, XPG3, XPG4

CHAPTER 22

Introduction to the KornShell, C Shell, and Bash

Different Shells

HP-UX, like all UNIX variants, allows you to select among different shells. A lot of material is available on the POSIX shell, which is the default HP-UX shell in most cases. There is less information available on the other widely used shells so I have decided to cover them in this chapter. The shell is important to you as a system administrator and user because it is your window into the system. I decided to include the KornShell and C shell in this chapter because so many new HP-UX users and system administrators use them as their shells even though the POSIX shell is the default on most systems. I included Bash because it is widely used in Open Source enviornments and many Open Source GNU tools are available for HP-UX 11i. The upcoming sections cover these three shells. The KornShell section also covers some important topics related to shells such as *File Name Expansion, Redirection, Background Jobs,* and *umask and Permissions.* Some of these topics have been covered in other chapters of the book, but these topics are closely related to your shell, so I decided to include them here as well.

Introduction to KornShell

man page

ksh - 22

Most UNIX variants allow you to select among several shells. Because of its versatility and ease of use, many system administrators configure the KornShell for new users. The KornShell was derived from the Bourne Shell and has much of the same functionality of the Bourne Shell. **ksh** is the program you run on most UNIX systems, including HP-UX, that supplies KornShell functionality. It is also often referred to as the K shell. I use **ksh** throughout this chapter. You can use the **ksh** in the following three ways:

- Interactively type commands on the command line.

- Group commonly executed sets of commands into command files that you canexecute by typing the name of the file.

- Create KornShell programs using the structured programming techniques of the shell.

These three techniques are listed in the order in which you'll probably use them. First, you log in and use interactive commands. Then you group together commonly used commands and execute them with a single command. Finally, you may want to create sophisticated shell scripts.

For this reason, I describe these aspects of the KornShell in the order in which they are listed. The command file and programming aspects of the KornShell are covered as part of the Shell Programming Chapter 23.

The examples in this chapter are performed on a variety of different systems, not just HP-UX. This is because many system administrators use **ksh** on several different UNIX variants. You would probably find both your user setup and the operation of the KornShell on other systems similar to what is covered in this chapter. Much of the setup of any shell is performed by the system administrator, so you will surely find differences in your KornShell setup compared with what is shown in this chapter. In general, however, the operation of the KornShell is similar from one system to another.

Startup Files

The first activity you perform after you log into the system is to issue commands at the prompt. A command you may want to issue immediately is **ls -al**. Here is what I see on my system after executing this command, producing a long listing of all files:

man page

ls - 15

```
martyp $ ls -al
total 22
drwxr-xr-x    2 martyp    staff          512 Mar 15 11:37 .
drwxrwxr-x    4 root      sys            512 Mar  4 09:24 ..
-rw-r--r--    1 martyp    staff          124 Mar 15 11:36 .cshrc
-rw-r--r--    1 martyp    staff          562 Mar  4 09:24 .profile
-rw-------    1 martyp    staff         7056 Apr  6 07:24 .sh_history
martyp $
```

man page

ksh - 22

This produces a short list of files. Some of these files, such as **.profile** and **.cshrc**, are startup files for **ksh** and the C shell, respectively. Upon logging in to a system, you normally execute system startup files for your shell and then execute any local startup files that you have in your home directory. In this case, I have a minimal **ksh** startup file in my home directory - only a **.profile** that has very little in it. Virtually all the startup activity for this user comes from the system profile, usually **/etc/profile.** You can usually read **/etc/profile**, so you can see what your system administrator has set up for you and other users. You can then modify your local **.profile** to include a variety of functionality. Your local **.profile** is usually run at login, immediately after the system **/etc/profile**.

After running all the startup scripts associated with your **ksh** login, your environment is set up for you. Although our local **.profile** didn't do much other than set up our prompt, a lot of setup took place with the system files that were run.

Another file you have is called the *Environment* file. This file name is defined by the environment variable **ENV**. This file is usually **.kshrc** in your home directory. Using the environment file, you can define which options, aliases, and other information will be passed to subprocesses. By default, your existing environment variables are passed to subprocesses. You can use the environment file to pass other information along as well.

You should take a look at your **ksh** startup files, including **/etc/ profile**, **.profile**, and **.kshrc**.

We'll discuss much of the specific **ksh** functionality provided for you as part of your startup programs in the upcoming sections.

The History File, .sh_history

ksh keeps a history list of the commands you have issued. If you wish to reissue a command or view a command you earlier issued, you can use the history list. By default, **.sh_history** in your home directory is used as a history file. When your system administrator creates your **ksh** home directory, this file is probably present and used as your default history file.

By default, most systems save the 128 most recently executed commands. You can specify any number of commands to be included in the history list. The following line sets the history list to 200:

```
HISTSIZE=200
```

Most users make this entry in their home **.profile**. After you have added this line to your **.profile**, the history list is set to *200*.

Recalling from the History List

You can view the most recent commands issued, along with their corresponding line numbers, with the **history** command as shown in the following example:

```
martyp $ history
116      history 128
117      history 128 | more
118      history 200
119      alias
120      history 1
121      inv
122      env
123      env | more
124      history 1
125      more .profile
126      env | grep HIS
127      exit
128      env
129      env | grep HIS
130      more .profile
131      history
martyp $
```

Notice in this example that command number *127* is the **exit**, or command to log out, from the last session. Command number *128* is the **env** command I issued immediately upon establishing the next session.

We can also print the history list without line numbers using the *-n* option as shown in the following example:

```
martyp $ history -n
         history 128 | more
         history 200
         alias
         history 1
         inv
         env
         env | more
         history 1
         more .profile
         env | grep HIS
         exit
         env
         env | grep HIS
         more .profile
         history
```

```
        history -n
martyp $
```

To produce a complete list of commands in the history list, we issue the following command:

```
martyp $ history 0
5       env
6       more .profile
7       set
8       env | grep CDP
9       env | grep cdp
10      echo $SHELLL
11      echo $SHELL
12      more .profile
13      ll
14      ls -al /etc/profile
15      more /etc/profile
16      more /etc/profile | grep PS
17      exhoecE
18      ECHO
19      echo $ENV
20      env | more
21      echo $ENV
22      env | more
23      env | grep ENV
24      env | grep env
25      more /usr/bin/env
26      ls -al
27      more /etc/.kshrc
28      find / -name .kshrc
29      more /etc/passwd
30      more /etc/passwd | grep /home
31      ll /home/oracle
32      ls -al /home/oracle
33      ll /home
34      ls -al /home
35      ls -al /home/ptc-nfs
36      ls -al /home/ptc-nfs | more
37      ls -al /root
38      cd /root/users
39      ls -al
40      ls -al verasu
41      ls -al rodtsu
42       cd rodtsu
43      more .kshrc
44      more .env
45      ls
46      ls -l
47      ls -a
```

```
48      more .kshrc
49      cd ..
50      ls -al
51      ls -al | more
52      exit
53      ls -al
54      more .sh*
55      history
56      env | grep his
57      env | grep HIS
58      env | grep IS
59      env | more
60       env | grep FC
61      env | grep EDI
62      history
63      echo $HISTIZE
64      echo $HISTSIZE
65      env | more
66      ls -al
67      history 128
68      history
69      history 1 104
70      exit
71      alias
72      more /etc/profile | grep alias
73      ll
74      la -al
75      ls -al
76      more .profile
77      ls -al
78      more .cshrc
79      alias ll="ls -al"
80      aliase
81      alias
82      ll
83      exit
84      alias
85      alias
86      history
87      fc -l
88      man fc
89      man fc
90      man fc
91      alias
92      ps
93      ps -ef
94      ps -efl
95      ps
96      ls -alF
97      ls -al
98      alias ls="ls -al"
99      alias
```

```
100      ls
101      alias
102      unalias ls
103      ls
104      ls -al
105      alias
106      history
107      alias
108      unalias history
109      history
110      fc -l
111      history
112      alias hisotry="fc -l"
113      history
114      alias history="fc -l"
115      history
116      history 128
117      history 128 | more
118      history 200
119      alias
120      history 1
121      inv
122      env
123      env | more
124      history 1
125      more .profile
126      env | grep HIS
127      exit
128      env
129      env | grep HIS
130      more .profile
131      history
132      history 0
martyp $
```

history 0 prints from the very first command, zero, to the present command. Because only 128 commands are saved by default, the first few oldest commands, zero through four, dropped off the history list. This means that we really started at command number five when we requested to start the list from command number zero.

To produce a list from command *100* to the present command, we issue the following:

```
martyp $ history 100
100      ls
101      alias
```

```
102      unalias ls
103      ls
104      ls -al
105      alias
106      history
107      alias
108      unalias history
109      history
110      fc -l
111      history
112      alias hisotry="fc -l"
113      history
114      alias history="fc -l"
115      history
116      history 128
117      history 128 | more
118      history 200
119      alias
120      history 1
121      inv
122      env
123      env | more
124      history 1
125      more .profile
126      env | grep HIS
127      exit
128      env
129      env | grep HIS
130      more .profile
131      history
132      history 0
133      history
134      history -n
135      history 100
martyp $
```

To list the current command and the *20* commands preceding it, we issue the following:

```
martyp $ history -20
116      history 128
117      history 128 | more
118      history 200
119      alias
120      history 1
121      inv
122      env
```

```
123     env | more
124     history 1
125     more .profile
126     env | grep HIS
127     exit
128     env
129     env | grep HIS
130     more .profile
131     history
132     history 0
133     history
134     history -n
135     history 100
136     history -20
martyp $
```

The *-20* goes back from the current command a full 20 commands. In this case, **history** is using the current command as the default place to begin producing the list. You can list the last 20 commands *preceding* the current command by specifying the range *-1 -20* as shown in the following example:

```
martyp $ history -1 -20
136     history -20
135     history 100
134     history -n
133     history
132     history 0
131     history
130     more .profile
129     env | grep HIS
128     env
127     exit
126     env | grep HIS
125     more .profile
124     history 1
123     env | more
122     env
121     inv
120     history 1
119     alias
118     history 200
117     history 128 | more
martyp $
```

Notice in this example that the current command, **history -1 -20**, is not shown in the list because the *-1* starts the list with the preceding command. This is effectively producing a range of commands to list.

You can also reverse the order of the last 20 commands by specifying *-20* first and then the *-1* as shown in the following example:

```
martyp $ history -20 -1
118      history 200
119      alias
120      history 1
121      inv
122      env
123      env | more
124      history 1
125      more .profile
126      env | grep HIS
127      exit
128      env
129      env | grep HIS
130      more .profile
131      history
132      history 0
133      history
134      history -n
135      history 100
136      history -20
137      history -1 -20
martyp $
```

You can also produce a list from the last time a command was issued to the current command. The following example shows producing a list from the last **fc** command to the current command:

```
martyp $ history fc
110      fc -l
111      history
112      alias hisotry="fc -l"
113      history
114      alias history="fc -l"
115      history
116      history 128
117      history 128 | more
118      history 200
119      alias
```

```
120      history 1
121      inv
122      env
123      env | more
124      history 1
125      more .profile
126      env | grep HIS
127      exit
128      env
129      env | grep HIS
130      more .profile
131      history
132      history 0
133      history
134      history -n
135      history 100
136      history -20
137      history -1 -20
138      history -20 -1
139      history
140      history grep
141      history env
142      history
143      history fc
martyp $
```

You can also reverse this list using the *-r* option as shown in the following example:

```
martyp $ history -r fc
144      history -r fc
143      history fc
142      history
141      history env
140      history grep
139      history
138      history -20 -1
137      history -1 -20
136      history -20
135      history 100
134      history -n
133      history
132      history 0
131      history
130      more .profile
129      env | grep HIS
128      env
127      exit
126      env | grep HIS
```

```
125      more .profile
124      history 1
123      env | more
122      env
121      inv
120      history 1
119      alias
118      history 200
117      history 128 | more
116      history 128
115      history
114      alias history="fc -l"
113      history
112      alias hisotry="fc -l"
111      history
110      fc -l
martyp $
```

Having access to this history list is a great feature of the Korn-Shell. You can view all the commands you have issued, including your typing errors, in any format you wish. In the next section, we start using the commands in the history list by recalling them.

Re-executing Commands with r

You can reissue a command with the **r** command. To reissue the last command, you simply type **r**. In the following example, I issue the command **history 5** to view the last five commands from the history list. I then type **r** to reissue the last command, and again the last five commands are listed:

```
martyp $ history -5
301      whoami
302      pwd
303      more /etc/passwd
304       ps -efl
305      cat .profile
306      history -5
martyp $ r
history -5
```

```
302      pwd
303      more /etc/passwd
304       ps -efl
305      cat .profile
306      history -5
307      history -5
martyp $
```

You can reissue a specific command number by typing **r**, a space, and the number of the command you wish to reissue. In the following example, I issue the **history** command number 302:

```
martyp $ history
294      history -5
295      whoami
296      pwd
297      more /etc/passwd
298      ps -efl
299      cat /etc/profile
300      history 5
301      whoami
302      pwd
303      more /etc/passwd
304       ps -efl
305      cat .profile
306      history -5
307      history -5
308      history -5
309      history
martyp $ r 302
pwd
/home/martyp
martyp $
```

You can also give the name of the command you wish to reissue. Let's say that you want to reissue the last **fc** command. You would simply give the letter "f" along with the **r** command, and the last command that started with *f* would be reissued as shown in the following example:

```
martyp $ history
308      history -5
309      history
310      pwd
311      whoami
312      pwd
313      cat /etc/profile
314      ls
315      fc -l
316      env
317      who
318      cat /etc/passwd
319      ls -al
320      history
321      more .profile
322      set
323      history
martyp $ r f
fc -l
309      history
310      pwd
311      whoami
312      pwd
313      cat /etc/profile
314      ls
315      fc -l
316      env
317      who
318      cat /etc/passwd
319      ls -al
320      history
321      more .profile
322      set
323      history
324      fc -l
martyp $
```

man page

vi - 21

You can also perform some substitution with the **r** command. If you issued the **vi** command earlier and want to rerun **vi** but specify a different file name to edit, you can substitute a new file name. The following example shows reissuing an earlier **vi** command, except now we'll replace the original filename we edited, **.profile**, with the new filename we want to edit, **.kshrc**. In this example, we'll first run the **history** command, then reissue the **vi** command to edit **.kshrc**, and then we'll run the command again to see our revised **vi** command:

```
martyp $ history
316     env
317     who
318     cat /etc/passwd
319     ls -al
320     history
321     more .profile
322     set
323     history
324     fc -l
325     vi .profile
326     set
327     ls -al
328     env
329     who
330     more /etc/passwd | grep marty
331     history
martyp $ r vi .profile=.kshrc
martyp $ history
318     cat /etc/passwd
319     ls -al
320     history
321     more .profile
322     set
323     history
324     fc -l
325     vi .profile
326     set
327     ls -al
328     env
329     who
330     more /etc/passwd | grep marty
331     history
332     vi .kshrc
333     history
martyp $
```

This command substitutes **.kshrc** for **.profile** on the command line.

man page

vi - 21

This leads us to more advanced command-line editing. You may want to recall a command earlier issued and edit the command line using **vi** editor commands. The next section covers command-line editing.

Fetching Commands Using vi Directives

man page

vi - 21

You can edit entries in your history list with either the **vi** or **emacs** editor. I will cover the **vi** editor in this chapter, because it is the most widely used on UNIX systems. You can, however, perform all the same functions shown in this chapter with the **emacs** editor.

You edit the history list using **vi** the same way you edit a file using **vi**. You press the *escape* key and use standard **vi** keys for moving up and down, left and right, inserting deleting, and changing text. In this section, I cover fetching a command from the history list using **vi** commands and then I cover editing the command after you have restored it to the command line. After the command has been edited to your liking, you press *enter* to execute the command and place it at the very bottom of the command list.

Your editor is normally set in either your local **.profile** or **/etc/profile**. You can view these files to see what editor has been set for you by your system administrator. When I issue the **env** and **set** commands on my system, both report *EDITOR=vi*. This corresponds with my **/etc/profile** which has the editor set to **vi**.

Let's first take a look at fetching some previously issued commands using **vi**. The examples in this section use **vi** functionality that is described in both the **vi** chapter and on the **vi** quick reference card. The **k**, **j**, **G**, and search commands in this section operate in the same manner on the command line as they would if you were using **vi** to edit a file.

Pressing the *escape* key and a command allows you to perform various functions in the **ksh**. The following example shows producing the history list and issuing *escape* **k** to recall the previous command:

man page

ksh - 22

```
martyp $ history
125     man fc
126     set | more
127      exit
128     history
129     k
130     env | more
```

```
131      set | more
132      more .profile
133      more .profile | grep rof
134      more .profile | grep vi
135      more /etc/profile | grep vi
136      set |grep edit
137      set | grep vi
138      env | grep vi
139      history
140      who
martyp $ history
```

man page

ksh - 22

Issuing *escape* **k** recalled the last command issued, in this case the **who** command at line 140. Each time you press **k**, the preceding **ksh** command is fetched. This is the same as pressing *escape* and the - (hyphen) key. You can specify the number of commands you wish to go back in the history list with *escape n***k**, where *n* is the number of commands you want to go back in the history list. The following example shows issuing *escape* **5k** to fetch the fifth command back in the history list:

```
martyp $ history
125      man fc
126      set | more
127       exit
128      history
129      k
130      env | more
131      set | more
132      more .profile
133      more .profile | grep rof
134      more .profile | grep vi
135      more /etc/profile | grep vi
136      set |grep edit
137      set | grep vi
138      env | grep vi
139      history
140      who
martyp $ set |grep edit
```

man page

grep - 19

Issuing *escape* **5k** fetched the fifth command back in the history list at line *136*. This is the same as having issued *escape* **5-**.

You can also move forward in the history list, using **j** in the same way we used **k** to move back in the history list. Let's issue *escape* **5k** to move back five commands in the history list to line *136*, and then we can use *escape* **3j** to move forward three commands to line *139*, as shown in the following example:

```
martyp $ history
125     man fc
126     set | more
127      exit
128     history
129     k
130     env | more
131     set | more
132     more .profile
133     more .profile | grep rof
134     more .profile | grep vi
135     more /etc/profile | grep vi
136     set |grep edit
137     set | grep vi
138     env | grep vi
139     history
140     history
martyp $ who
```

Issuing *escape* **3j** moved us forward to line *139*, which is the same as having issued *escape* **3-**.

We can also go back to the oldest command in the history list with *escape* **G**. You can go back to a specific command number from the history list with *escape* *n***G**, where *n* is a specific command number from the history file. The following example shows issuing *escape* **126G** to go back to line *126* from the history list:

```
martyp $ history
125     man fc
126     set | more
127      exit
128     history
129     k
130     env | more
131     set | more
132     more .profile
133     more .profile | grep rof
134     more .profile | grep vi
135     more /etc/profile | grep vi
```

```
136      set |grep edit
137      set | grep vi
138      env | grep vi
139      history
140      who
martyp $ set | more
```

You can also recall lines from the history list based on searches. If, for instance, you want to recall the most recently issued command from the history list that has in it **profile**, you would issue **/profile**, which is the slash character followed by **profile**, to get the result shown in the following example:

```
martyp $ history
125      man fc
126      set | more
127       exit
128      history
129      k
130      env | more
131      set | more
132      more .profile
133      more .profile | grep rof
134      more .profile | grep vi
135      more /etc/profile | grep vi
136      set |grep edit
137      set | grep vi
138      env | grep vi
139      history
140      who
martyp $ more /etc/profile | grep vi
```

Searching for the most recent occurrence of **profile** produces line *135*. Many of the other searches in **vi** work at the command line. The **vi** chapter and **vi** quick reference card have more searching commands that you may want to try at the command line.

Editing on the Command Line Using vi Directives

After you have "fetched" the command you wish to edit or you have entered a command that needs editing, you can use your **vi** directives to make modifications on the command line.

The **ksh** puts you in input mode immediately upon fetching a command from the history list. This approach is the converse of the **vi** program that you use to edit files, which puts you in control mode by default. After you have fetched a command from the history list, you must press *escape* in order to move into control mode when using **vi** in **ksh**.

man page

ksh - 22

Let's now perform some simple modifications to commands we have fetched from the history list. We recall line number 286 from the history list with the sequence *escape* **286G**. After recalling this command, we insert *cat* at the beginning of the command with **i cat**. **i** is for insert text to the left of the current cursor position. The following example shows the result of both the fetch of line *286* and inserting **cat**:

man page

cat - 17

```
martyp $ history
285      history
286      more /etc/profile | grep vi
287      who
288      whoami
289      who
290      ls -al
291      alias
292      pwd
293      ls -al /home
294      cat .profile
295      history
296      vi .profile
297      cat /etc/passwd
298      cat /etc/passwd | grep donna
299      pwd
300      history
martyp $ cat more /etc/profile | grep vi
```

You can see that **i cat** inserted *cat* at the very beginning of the line.

We can again recall line *286* and use **A** to append text to the very end of the line, as shown in the following example:

```
martyp $ history
285     history
286     more /etc/profile | grep vi
287     who
288     whoami
289     who
290     ls -al
291     alias
292     pwd
293     ls -al /home
294     cat .profile
295     history
296     vi .profile
297     cat /etc/passwd
298     cat /etc/passwd | grep donna
299     pwd
300     history
martyp $ more /etc/profile | grep vieditor
```

man page

more - 17

man page

grep - 19

In this example, we used the squence **A editor** to insert the word *editor* at the very end of the command line we had recalled.

We can recall this line and change *more* at the beginning of the line to *cat* by issuing the sequence **cw cat**, as shown in the following example:

```
martyp $ history
285     history
286     more /etc/profile | grep vi
287     who
288     whoami
289     who
290     ls -al
291     alias
292     pwd
293     ls -al /home
294     cat .profile
295     history
296     vi .profile
```

```
297      cat /etc/passwd
298      cat /etc/passwd | grep donna
299      pwd
300      history
martyp $ cat /etc/profile | grep vi
```

man page

cat - 17

This changes *more* to *cat* on the command line.

To delete the word *more* without replacing it, we fetch line 286 and issue **dw**, as shown in the following example:

man page

grep - 19

```
martyp $ history
285      history
286      more /etc/profile | grep vi
287      who
288      whoami
289      who
290      ls -al
291      alias
292      pwd
293      ls -al /home
294      cat .profile
295      history
296      vi .profile
297      cat /etc/passwd
298      cat /etc/passwd | grep donna
299      pwd
300      history
martyp $   /etc/profile | grep vi
```

If we are unhappy with the most recent command issued, we can undo the command by issuing **u**, which undoes the **dw** we used to remove *more* on the command line, as shown in the following example:

```
martyp $ history
285      history
286      more /etc/profile | grep vi
287      who
288      whoami
289      who
290      ls -al
291      alias
```

```
292     pwd
293     ls -al /home
294     cat .profile
295     history
296     vi .profile
297     cat /etc/passwd
298     cat /etc/passwd | grep donna
299     pwd
300     history
martyp $ more /etc/profile | grep vi
```

man page

more - 17

man page

grep - 19

man page

vi - 21

Issuing **u** puts back the *more* that we had removed with **dw**.

You may want to try using both of the **vi** commands I have covered here, as well as other commands to add, delete, change, search and replace, copy, and undo at the command line.

Aliases in KornShell

An alias is a name that you select for a frequently used command or series of commands. Many aliases are predefined for you.

The **alias** command, without any arguments, lists all aliases. This list includes both preset aliases as well as those you have set. The following command shows the preset aliases on the system on which I am working:

```
martyp $ alias
autoload='typeset -fu'
command='command '
functions='typeset -f'
history='fc -l'
hyper1=HHLIC='/opt/local/bristol/hyperhelp/licenses/hpptc1;export HHLIC'
hyper36=HHLIC='/opt/local/bristol/hyperhelp/licenses/hpptc36;export HHLIC'
hyper83=HHLIC='/opt/local/bristol/hyperhelp/licenses/hpptc83;export HHLIC'
hyper95=HHLIC='/opt/local/bristol/hyperhelp/licenses/hpptc95;export HHLIC'
integer='typeset -i'
local=typeset
nohup='nohup '
r='fc -e -'
stop='kill -STOP'
suspend='kill -STOP $$'
martyp $
```

Many preset aliases are shown as a result of typing the **alias** command without any options.

Many of these aliases are related to somewhat advanced use of the KornShell, such as job control. Others are useful to you right away. The *history* alias, for instance, lists the commands in the **.sh_history** file and precedes each entry by a line number. The *r* alias allows you to re-run the the last command that appears in the history list.

You are not limited to using only preset aliases. You can set your own aliases. The following example shows setting an alias, producing a list of aliases to see whether indeed our new alias has been set, and then running our alias:

```
martyp $ alias ls="ls -al"
martyp $ alias
autoload='typeset -fu'
command='command '
functions='typeset -f'
history='fc -l'
hyper1=HHLIC='/opt/local/bristol/hyperhelp/licenses/hpptc1;export HHLIC'
hyper36=HHLIC='/opt/local/bristol/hyperhelp/licenses/hpptc36;export HHLIC'
hyper83=HHLIC='/opt/local/bristol/hyperhelp/licenses/hpptc83;export HHLIC'
hyper95=HHLIC='/opt/local/bristol/hyperhelp/licenses/hpptc95;export HHLIC'
integer='typeset -i'
local=typeset
ls='ls -al'
nohup='nohup '
r='fc -e -'
stop='kill -STOP'
suspend='kill -STOP $$'
martyp $ ls
total 26
drwxr-xr-x   2 martyp    staff          512 Mar 15 11:37 .
drwxrwxr-x   4 root      sys            512 Mar  4 09:24 ..
-rw-r--r--   1 martyp    staff          124 Mar 15 11:36 .cshrc
-rw-r--r--   1 martyp    staff          562 Mar  4 09:24 .profile
-rw-------   1 martyp    staff         9058 Apr 10 06:58 .sh_history
martyp $
```

man page

ls - 15

The first command set an alias that executes **ls -al** whenever we type **ls**. I issued the **alias** command to see whether indeed the new alias would appear in the list of aliases. It appears right after *local* and right before *nohup* in the alphabetical list of aliases. The final command shows running **ls**, which produces the same listing that you would receive from running the **ls -al** command.

You don't have to keep an alias for the duration of your session after having set it. If you don't like an alias, you can use the **unalias** command to remove an alias.

To see **unalias** work, let's again produce a list of aliases, use **unalias** to unset the *history* alias, run the *history* command to see whether indeed it has been removed, and then run the **fc -l** command to which the *history* alias was mapped:

```
martyp $ alias
autoload='typeset -fu'
command='command '
functions='typeset -f'
history='fc -l'
hyper1=HHLIC='/opt/local/bristol/hyperhelp/licenses/hpptc1;export HHLIC'
hyper36=HHLIC='/opt/local/bristol/hyperhelp/licenses/hpptc36;export HHLIC'
hyper83=HHLIC='/opt/local/bristol/hyperhelp/licenses/hpptc83;export HHLIC'
hyper95=HHLIC='/opt/local/bristol/hyperhelp/licenses/hpptc95;export HHLIC'
integer='typeset -i'
local=typeset
nohup='nohup '
r='fc -e -'
stop='kill -STOP'
suspend='kill -STOP $$'
martyp $ unalias history
martyp $ history
ksh: history:  not found
martyp $ fc -l
131     ps
132     ls -alF
133     ls -al
134     alias ls="ls -al"
135     alias
136     ls
137     alias
138     unalias ls
139     ls
140     ls -al
141     alias
142     history
143     alias
144     unalias history
145     history
146     fc -l
martyp $
```

man page

ksh - 22

When we **unalias** *history* and then run *history,* **ksh** is unable to find it and produces the message *history: not found.* When we run **fc -l**, a list of the most recently issued commands with their corresponding numbers is produced. This makes it clear that when you run the *history* alias, you are actually running the **fc -l** command.

Command and Path Completion

man page

ksh - 22

ksh sometimes knows what you're thinking. You can type part of a command or pathname and **ksh** can complete the remainder for you. You can type part of a command or pathname and press the *escape* key to complete the command. If, for instance, you wish to issue the **uname** command to view the current system run level but can't remember the full command, you can type "un" and *escape,* followed by the "=" key, and the command is completed for you. In the following example, we'll change to the **/sbin** directory, list its contents, and then type **un***escape***=**:

man page

cd - 16

```
martyp $ cd /sbin
martyp $ ls -al
total 11704
drwxrwxr-x   2 root     sys          512 Nov 27 14:55 .
drwxr-xr-x  31 root     root        1024 Apr 19 03:24 ..
-r-xr-xr-x   1 bin      bin       200356 Sep  1  1998 autopush
lrwxrwxrwx   1 root     root          21 Nov 27 14:55 bpgetfile -> ../usr/sbin/e
-r-xr-xr-x   1 bin      bin       470436 Sep  1  1998 dhcpagent
-r-xr-xr-x   1 bin      bin       433064 Sep  1  1998 dhcpinfo
-r-xr-xr-x   1 bin      bin       253664 Sep  1  1998 fdisk
-r-xr-xr-x   1 bin      bin       762816 Sep  1  1998 hostconfig
-r-xr-xr-x   1 bin      bin       535900 Sep  1  1998 ifconfig
-r-xr-xr-x   1 root     sys       516484 Sep  1  1998 init
-r-xr-xr-x   2 bin      root      257444 Sep  1  1998 jsh
-r-xr-xr-x   1 bin      bin       224596 Sep  1  1998 mount
-r-xr-xr-x   1 root     sys         6935 Jan  1  1970 mountall
-rwxr--r--   3 root     sys         2689 Jan  1  1970 rc0
-rwxr--r--   1 root     sys         2905 Jan  1  1970 rc1
-rwxr--r--   1 root     sys         2491 Jan  1  1970 rc2
-rwxr--r--   1 root     sys         1948 Jan  1  1970 rc3
-rwxr--r--   3 root     sys         2689 Jan  1  1970 rc5
-rwxr--r--   3 root     sys         2689 Jan  1  1970 rc6
-rwxr--r--   1 root     sys         9412 Jan  1  1970 rcS
-r-xr-xr-x   2 bin      root      257444 Sep  1  1998 sh
-r-xr-xr-x   1 bin      bin       195300 Sep  1  1998 soconfig
lrwxrwxrwx   1 root     root          13 Nov 27 14:40 su -> ../usr/bin/su
-r-xr-xr-x   1 root     sys       473808 Sep  1  1998 su.static
-r-xr-xr-x   1 root     bin       288544 Sep  1  1998 sulogin
-rwxr--r--   1 root     sys         3138 Jan  1  1970 swapadd
-r-xr-xr-x   1 bin      bin        29736 Sep  1  1998 sync
-r-xr-xr-x   1 root     sys       435004 Sep  1  1998 uadmin
-r-xr-xr-x   1 bin      bin       213408 Sep  1  1998 umount
-r-xr-xr-x   1 root     sys         3292 Jan  1  1970 umountall
-r-xr-xr-x   1 bin      bin       193152 Sep  1  1998 uname
martyp $ un                                        ;typed unescape=
1) uname
martyp $ un
```

ksh determined that the only command that starts with "un" is **uname**. The **uname** command was listed and *un* was again put at the command prompt for me. You can't see the *escape***=** I typed after the first "un," so I made a comment to the side showing the full command.

Rather than list all files starting with "un," you can replace the current word with all files that match by typing **un**escape*, as shown in the following example:

man page

cd - 16

man page

ls - 15

```
martyp $ cd /sbin
martyp $ ls -al
total 11704
drwxrwxr-x   2 root     sys          512 Nov 27 14:55 .
drwxr-xr-x  31 root     root        1024 Apr 19 03:24 ..
-r-xr-xr-x   1 bin      bin       200356 Sep  1  1998 autopush
lrwxrwxrwx   1 root     root          21 Nov 27 14:55 bpgetfile -> ../usr/sbin/e
-r-xr-xr-x   1 bin      bin       470436 Sep  1  1998 dhcpagent
-r-xr-xr-x   1 bin      bin       433064 Sep  1  1998 dhcpinfo
-r-xr-xr-x   1 bin      bin       253664 Sep  1  1998 fdisk
-r-xr-xr-x   1 bin      bin       762816 Sep  1  1998 hostconfig
-r-xr-xr-x   1 bin      bin       535900 Sep  1  1998 ifconfig
-r-xr-xr-x   1 root     sys       516484 Sep  1  1998 init
-r-xr-xr-x   2 bin      root      257444 Sep  1  1998 jsh
-r-xr-xr-x   1 bin      bin       224596 Sep  1  1998 mount
-r-xr-xr-x   1 root     sys         6935 Jan  1  1970 mountall
-rwxr--r--   3 root     sys         2689 Jan  1  1970 rc0
-rwxr--r--   1 root     sys         2905 Jan  1  1970 rc1
-rwxr--r--   1 root     sys         2491 Jan  1  1970 rc2
-rwxr--r--   1 root     sys         1948 Jan  1  1970 rc3
-rwxr--r--   3 root     sys         2689 Jan  1  1970 rc5
-rwxr--r--   3 root     sys         2689 Jan  1  1970 rc6
-rwxr--r--   1 root     sys         9412 Jan  1  1970 rcS
-r-xr-xr-x   2 bin      root      257444 Sep  1  1998 sh
-r-xr-xr-x   1 bin      bin       195300 Sep  1  1998 soconfig
lrwxrwxrwx   1 root     root          13 Nov 27 14:40 su -> ../usr/bin/su
-r-xr-xr-x   1 root     sys       473808 Sep  1  1998 su.static
-r-xr-xr-x   1 root     bin       288544 Sep  1  1998 sulogin
-rwxr--r--   1 root     sys         3138 Jan  1  1970 swapadd
-r-xr-xr-x   1 bin      bin        29736 Sep  1  1998 sync
-r-xr-xr-x   1 root     sys       435004 Sep  1  1998 uadmin
-r-xr-xr-x   1 bin      bin       213408 Sep  1  1998 umount
-r-xr-xr-x   1 root     sys         3292 Jan  1  1970 umountall
-r-xr-xr-x   1 bin      bin       193152 Sep  1  1998 uname
martyp $ uname                                         ;typed unescape*
```

You can see in this example that **uname** is replaced right at the prompt with the only command that matched **un**escape*.

The next example shows using **um**escape= to get a list of all files that start with "um," then using **um**escape* to get all files matched to "um," and finally using **um**escape\ to replace the current word with the first file name that starts with "um":

```
martyp $ ls -al
total 11704
drwxrwxr-x   2 root     sys          512 Nov 27 14:55 .
drwxr-xr-x  31 root     root        1024 Apr 19 03:24 ..
-r-xr-xr-x   1 bin      bin       200356 Sep  1  1998 autopush
lrwxrwxrwx   1 root     root          21 Nov 27 14:55 bpgetfile -> ../usr/sbin/e
-r-xr-xr-x   1 bin      bin       470436 Sep  1  1998 dhcpagent
-r-xr-xr-x   1 bin      bin       433064 Sep  1  1998 dhcpinfo
-r-xr-xr-x   1 bin      bin       253664 Sep  1  1998 fdisk
-r-xr-xr-x   1 bin      bin       762816 Sep  1  1998 hostconfig
```

```
-r-xr-xr-x   1 bin    bin     535900 Sep  1  1998 ifconfig
-r-xr-xr-x   1 root   sys     516484 Sep  1  1998 init
-r-xr-xr-x   2 bin    root    257444 Sep  1  1998 jsh
-r-xr-xr-x   1 bin    bin     224596 Sep  1  1998 mount
-r-xr-xr-x   1 root   sys       6935 Jan  1  1970 mountall
-rwxr--r--   3 root   sys       2689 Jan  1  1970 rc0
-rwxr--r--   1 root   sys       2905 Jan  1  1970 rc1
-rwxr--r--   1 root   sys       2491 Jan  1  1970 rc2
-rwxr--r--   1 root   sys       1948 Jan  1  1970 rc3
-rwxr--r--   3 root   sys       2689 Jan  1  1970 rc5
-rwxr--r--   3 root   sys       2689 Jan  1  1970 rc6
-rwxr--r--   1 root   sys       9412 Jan  1  1970 rcS
-r-xr-xr-x   2 bin    root    257444 Sep  1  1998 sh
-r-xr-xr-x   1 bin    bin     195300 Sep  1  1998 soconfig
lrwxrwxrwx   1 root   root        13 Nov 27 14:40 su -> ../usr/bin/su
-r-xr-xr-x   1 root   sys     473808 Sep  1  1998 su.static
-r-xr-xr-x   1 root   bin     288544 Sep  1  1998 sulogin
-rwxr--r--   1 root   sys       3138 Jan  1  1970 swapadd
-r-xr-xr-x   1 bin    bin      29736 Sep  1  1998 sync
-r-xr-xr-x   1 root   sys     435004 Sep  1  1998 uadmin
-r-xr-xr-x   1 bin    bin     213408 Sep  1  1998 umount
-r-xr-xr-x   1 root   sys       3292 Jan  1  1970 umountall
-r-xr-xr-x   1 bin    bin     193152 Sep  1  1998 uname
martyp $ um                              ;typed umescape=
1) umount
2) umountall
martyp $ umount umountall                ;typed umescape*
martyp $ umount                          ;typed umescape\
```

Let's now work with a command and arguments that will be file names. What if the characters you type are not unique, as they were with "un" in the **/sbin** directory? If the command or pathname is not unique, then **ksh** shows you the options for completing the command. The following example shows typing **ls r***escape***=** to get a list of commands that start with "r":

ksh - 22

ls - 15

```
martyp $ ls -al
total 11704
drwxrwxr-x    2 root   sys        512 Nov 27 14:55 .
drwxr-xr-x   31 root   root      1024 Apr 19 03:24 ..
-r-xr-xr-x    1 bin    bin     200356 Sep  1  1998 autopush
lrwxrwxrwx    1 root   root        21 Nov 27 14:55 bpgetfile -> ../usr/sbin/e
-r-xr-xr-x    1 bin    bin     470436 Sep  1  1998 dhcpagent
-r-xr-xr-x    1 bin    bin     433064 Sep  1  1998 dhcpinfo
-r-xr-xr-x    1 bin    bin     253664 Sep  1  1998 fdisk
-r-xr-xr-x    1 bin    bin     762816 Sep  1  1998 hostconfig
-r-xr-xr-x    1 bin    bin     535900 Sep  1  1998 ifconfig
-r-xr-xr-x    1 root   sys     516484 Sep  1  1998 init
-r-xr-xr-x    2 bin    root    257444 Sep  1  1998 jsh
-r-xr-xr-x    1 bin    bin     224596 Sep  1  1998 mount
-r-xr-xr-x    1 root   sys       6935 Jan  1  1970 mountall
-rwxr--r--    3 root   sys       2689 Jan  1  1970 rc0
-rwxr--r--    1 root   sys       2905 Jan  1  1970 rc1
-rwxr--r--    1 root   sys       2491 Jan  1  1970 rc2
-rwxr--r--    1 root   sys       1948 Jan  1  1970 rc3
-rwxr--r--    3 root   sys       2689 Jan  1  1970 rc5
-rwxr--r--    3 root   sys       2689 Jan  1  1970 rc6
-rwxr--r--    1 root   sys       9412 Jan  1  1970 rcS
-r-xr-xr-x    2 bin    root    257444 Sep  1  1998 sh
-r-xr-xr-x    1 bin    bin     195300 Sep  1  1998 soconfig
lrwxrwxrwx    1 root   root        13 Nov 27 14:40 su -> ../usr/bin/su
-r-xr-xr-x    1 root   sys     473808 Sep  1  1998 su.static
-r-xr-xr-x    1 root   bin     288544 Sep  1  1998 sulogin
-rwxr--r--    1 root   sys       3138 Jan  1  1970 swapadd
```

man page

ls - 15

```
-r-xr-xr-x    1 bin     bin      29736 Sep  1  1998 sync
-r-xr-xr-x    1 root    sys     435004 Sep  1  1998 uadmin
-r-xr-xr-x    1 bin     bin     213408 Sep  1  1998 umount
-r-xr-xr-x    1 root    sys       3292 Jan  1  1970 umountall
-r-xr-xr-x    1 bin     bin     193152 Sep  1  1998 uname
martyp $ ls r                                ;typed ls rescape=
1) rc0
2) rc1
3) rc2
4) rc3
5) rc5
6) rc6
7) rcS
martyp $ ls r
```

man page

ksh - 22

You can see from this example that typing **ls -r***escape=* produced a list of seven files. Again, the **ls r** was placed for me at the next prompt. You can use the information left for you at the next prompt to perform additional **ksh** file name expansion. Let's again perform our **ls r***escape=,* which produces the list of seven files beginning with *r.* Our next prompt will have **ls r** waiting for us, and this time we'll type *escape**, which will produce a list of all seven files for us on the line:

```
martyp $ ls -al
total 11704
drwxrwxr-x    2 root    sys        512 Nov 27 14:55 .
drwxr-xr-x   31 root    root      1024 Apr 19 03:24 ..
-r-xr-xr-x    1 bin     bin     200356 Sep  1  1998 autopush
lrwxrwxrwx    1 root    root        21 Nov 27 14:55 bpgetfile -> ../usr/sbin/e
-r-xr-xr-x    1 bin     bin     470436 Sep  1  1998 dhcpagent
-r-xr-xr-x    1 bin     bin     433064 Sep  1  1998 dhcpinfo
-r-xr-xr-x    1 bin     bin     253664 Sep  1  1998 fdisk
-r-xr-xr-x    1 bin     bin     762816 Sep  1  1998 hostconfig
-r-xr-xr-x    1 bin     bin     535900 Sep  1  1998 ifconfig
-r-xr-xr-x    1 root    sys     516484 Sep  1  1998 init
-r-xr-xr-x    2 bin     root    257444 Sep  1  1998 jsh
-r-xr-xr-x    1 bin     bin     224596 Sep  1  1998 mount
-r-xr-xr-x    1 root    sys       6935 Jan  1  1970 mountall
-rwxr--r--    3 root    sys       2689 Jan  1  1970 rc0
-rwxr--r--    1 root    sys       2905 Jan  1  1970 rc1
-rwxr--r--    1 root    sys       2491 Jan  1  1970 rc2
-rwxr--r--    1 root    sys       1948 Jan  1  1970 rc3
-rwxr--r--    3 root    sys       2689 Jan  1  1970 rc5
-rwxr--r--    3 root    sys       2689 Jan  1  1970 rc6
-rwxr--r--    1 root    sys       9412 Jan  1  1970 rcS
-r-xr-xr-x    2 bin     root    257444 Sep  1  1998 sh
-r-xr-xr-x    1 bin     bin     195300 Sep  1  1998 soconfig
lrwxrwxrwx    1 root    root        13 Nov 27 14:40 su -> ../usr/bin/su
-r-xr-xr-x    1 root    sys     473808 Sep  1  1998 su.static
-r-xr-xr-x    1 root    bin     288544 Sep  1  1998 sulogin
-rwxr--r--    1 root    sys       3138 Jan  1  1970 swapadd
-r-xr-xr-x    1 bin     bin      29736 Sep  1  1998 sync
-r-xr-xr-x    1 root    sys     435004 Sep  1  1998 uadmin
-r-xr-xr-x    1 bin     bin     213408 Sep  1  1998 umount
-r-xr-xr-x    1 root    sys       3292 Jan  1  1970 umountall
-r-xr-xr-x    1 bin     bin     193152 Sep  1  1998 uname
martyp $ ls r                                ;typed ls rescape=
1) rc0
2) rc1
3) rc2
4) rc3
5) rc5
```

```
6) rc6
7) rcS
martyp $ ls rc0 rc1 rc2 rc3 rc5 rc6 rcS
                                    ;typed escape* to get seven files
```

escape* listed all seven files beginning with *r* and placed them on the command line.

In the next example we'll issue both the *escape=* and *escape**. We'll then type **ls** *escape_* (underscore), which puts the last word of the last command in the line, which is *rcS*:

ls - 15

```
martyp $ ls -al
total 11704
drwxrwxr-x    2 root    sys         512 Nov 27 14:55 .
drwxr-xr-x   31 root    root       1024 Apr 19 03:24 ..
-r-xr-xr-x    1 bin     bin      200356 Sep  1  1998 autopush
lrwxrwxrwx    1 root    root         21 Nov 27 14:55 bpgetfile -> ../usr/sbin/e
-r-xr-xr-x    1 bin     bin      470436 Sep  1  1998 dhcpagent
-r-xr-xr-x    1 bin     bin      433064 Sep  1  1998 dhcpinfo
-r-xr-xr-x    1 bin     bin      253664 Sep  1  1998 fdisk
-r-xr-xr-x    1 bin     bin      762816 Sep  1  1998 hostconfig
-r-xr-xr-x    1 bin     bin      535900 Sep  1  1998 ifconfig
-r-xr-xr-x    1 root    sys      516484 Sep  1  1998 init
-r-xr-xr-x    2 bin     root     257444 Sep  1  1998 jsh
-r-xr-xr-x    1 bin     bin      224596 Sep  1  1998 mount
-r-xr-xr-x    1 root    sys        6935 Jan  1  1970 mountall
-rwxr--r--    3 root    sys        2689 Jan  1  1970 rc0
-rwxr--r--    1 root    sys        2905 Jan  1  1970 rc1
-rwxr--r--    1 root    sys        2491 Jan  1  1970 rc2
-rwxr--r--    1 root    sys        1948 Jan  1  1970 rc3
-rwxr--r--    3 root    sys        2689 Jan  1  1970 rc5
-rwxr--r--    3 root    sys        2689 Jan  1  1970 rc6
-rwxr--r--    1 root    sys        9412 Jan  1  1970 rcS
-r-xr-xr-x    2 bin     root     257444 Sep  1  1998 sh
-r-xr-xr-x    1 bin     bin      195300 Sep  1  1998 soconfig
lrwxrwxrwx    1 root    root         13 Nov 27 14:40 su -> ../usr/bin/su
-r-xr-xr-x    1 root    sys      473808 Sep  1  1998 su.static
-r-xr-xr-x    1 root    bin      288544 Sep  1  1998 sulogin
-rwxr--r--    1 root    sys        3138 Jan  1  1970 swapadd
-r-xr-xr-x    1 bin     bin       29736 Sep  1  1998 sync
-r-xr-xr-x    1 root    sys      435004 Sep  1  1998 uadmin
-r-xr-xr-x    1 bin     bin      213408 Sep  1  1998 umount
-r-xr-xr-x    1 root    sys        3292 Jan  1  1970 umountall
-r-xr-xr-x    1 bin     bin      193152 Sep  1  1998 uname
martyp $ ls r                         ;typed ls rescape=
1) rc0
2) rc1
3) rc2
4) rc3
5) rc5
6) rc6
7) rcS
martyp $ ls rc0 rc1 rc2 rc3 rc5 rc6 rcS   ;typed escape* to get seven files
rc0  rc1  rc2  rc3  rc5  rc6  rcS
martyp $ ls  rcS                      ;typed lsescape_ to get last word
rcS
martyp $
```

Now that we've seen how to get the last of the words to appear on the command line with *escape_*, how about the third word of the last command? You can specify the third word by typing *escape3_* or substitute for the "3" for any of the words on the last command line. The following example shows listing the third word of the last command:

man page

Is - 15

```
martyp $ ls -al
total 11704
drwxrwxr-x    2 root     sys          512 Nov 27 14:55 .
drwxr-xr-x   31 root     root        1024 Apr 19 03:24 ..
-r-xr-xr-x    1 bin      bin       200356 Sep  1  1998 autopush
lrwxrwxrwx    1 root     root          21 Nov 27 14:55 bpgetfile -> ../usr/sbin/e
-r-xr-xr-x    1 bin      bin       470436 Sep  1  1998 dhcpagent
-r-xr-xr-x    1 bin      bin       433064 Sep  1  1998 dhcpinfo
-r-xr-xr-x    1 bin      bin       253664 Sep  1  1998 fdisk
-r-xr-xr-x    1 bin      bin       762816 Sep  1  1998 hostconfig
-r-xr-xr-x    1 bin      bin       535900 Sep  1  1998 ifconfig
-r-xr-xr-x    1 root     sys       516484 Sep  1  1998 init
-r-xr-xr-x    2 bin      root      257444 Sep  1  1998 jsh
-r-xr-xr-x    1 bin      bin       224596 Sep  1  1998 mount
-r-xr-xr-x    1 root     sys         6935 Jan  1  1970 mountall
-rwxr--r--    3 root     sys         2689 Jan  1  1970 rc0
-rwxr--r--    1 root     sys         2905 Jan  1  1970 rc1
-rwxr--r--    1 root     sys         2491 Jan  1  1970 rc2
-rwxr--r--    1 root     sys         1948 Jan  1  1970 rc3
-rwxr--r--    3 root     sys         2689 Jan  1  1970 rc5
-rwxr--r--    3 root     sys         2689 Jan  1  1970 rc6
-rwxr--r--    1 root     sys         9412 Jan  1  1970 rcS
-r-xr-xr-x    2 bin      root      257444 Sep  1  1998 sh
-r-xr-xr-x    1 bin      bin       195300 Sep  1  1998 soconfig
lrwxrwxrwx    1 root     root          13 Nov 27 14:40 su -> ../usr/bin/su
-r-xr-xr-x    1 root     sys       473808 Sep  1  1998 su.static
-r-xr-xr-x    1 root     bin       288544 Sep  1  1998 sulogin
-rwxr--r--    1 root     sys         3138 Jan  1  1970 swapadd
-r-xr-xr-x    1 bin      bin        29736 Sep  1  1998 sync
-r-xr-xr-x    1 root     sys       435004 Sep  1  1998 uadmin
-r-xr-xr-x    1 bin      bin       213408 Sep  1  1998 umount
-r-xr-xr-x    1 root     sys         3292 Jan  1  1970 umountall
-r-xr-xr-x    1 bin      bin       193152 Sep  1  1998 uname
martyp $ ls r                          ;typed ls rescape=
1) rc0
2) rc1
3) rc2
4) rc3
5) rc5
6) rc6
7) rcS
martyp $ ls rc0 rc1 rc2 rc3 rc5 rc6 rcS       ;typed escape* to get seven files
rc0  rc1  rc2  rc3  rc5  rc6  rcS
martyp $ ls  rc1                       ;typed lsescape3_ to get third word
```

Because the previous command included the **ls** command, the third word is not **rc2** but **rc1**, because **ls** was the first entry in the previous command.

The Table 22-1 summarizes the command and path completion used in the previous examples:

TABLE 22-1 Command and Path Completion in **ksh**

Word or Command (type *escape* before each)	Result
word*escape*=	Displays a numbered list of file names beginning with **word**.
word*escape**	Replaces **word** with all files matched.
word*escape*\	Replaces **word** with the first file name that starts with **word**.
command word*escape*=	Displays a numbered list of file names beginning with **word**.
command word*escape**	Replaces **word** with all files matched.
command word*escape*_	Inserts the last word of the last command at the cursor position.
command word*escape*_3	Inserts the third word of the last command at the cursor position.

File Name Expansion

man page

ksh - 22

In your general activities working with **ksh**, you have to perform a lot of file-name-related work, including crafting shell scripts that deal with file names. An overview of file name expansion is useful to ensure that you're comfortable with this topic before you start writing shell scripts.

Table 22-2 lists some common filename expansion and pattern matching commands:

TABLE 22-2 File Name Expansion and Pattern Matching

Character(s)	Example	Description
*	1) **ls *.c**	Match zero or more characters
?	2) **ls conf.?**	Match any single character
[list]	3) **ls conf.[co]**	Match any character in list
[lower-upper]	4) **ls libdd.9873[5-6].sl**	Match any character in range
str{str1,str2,str3,...}	5) **ls ux*.{700,300}**	Expand str with contents of { }
~	6) **ls -a ~**	Home directory
~username	7) **ls -a ~gene**	Home directory of username

The following are more detailed descriptions of the examples shown in Table 22-2:

1. To list all files in a directory that end in ".c," you could do the following:

$ **ls *.c**
        conf. SAM.c conf.c

2. To find all the files in a directory named "conf" with an extension of one character, you could do the following:

$ **ls conf.?**
        conf.c conf.o conf.1

3. To list all the files in a directory named "conf" with only the extension "c" or "o," you could do the following:

$ **ls conf.{co}**
        conf.c conf.o

4. To list files with similar names but with a specific field that covers a range, you could do the following:

$ **ls libdd9873[5-6].sl**
    libdd98735.sl libdd98736.sl

man page

ls - 15

5. To list files that start with "ux" and have the extension "300" or "700," you could do the following:

$ **ls ux*.{700,300}**
    uxbootlf.700 uxinstfs.300

6. To list the files in your home directory, you could use ~:

$ **ls -a ~**
  .   .cshrc.org .login   .shrc.org
  ..   .exrc   .login.org   .cshrc
 .history

7. To list the files in the home directory of a user, you can do the following:

```
$   ls -a ~gene
              .             .history      splinedat    under.des
              ..            .login        trail.txt    xtra.part
         .chsrc         .login.org    ESP-File
         .cshrc.org  .profile      Mail
         .exrc          .shrc.org     opt
```

man page

ksh - 22

Many of these techniques are useful when working with **ksh** and writing shell scripts, so you want to become familiar with file name expansion.

Redirection (I/O Redirection)

UNIX is set up such that commands usually take their input from the keyboard, often called standard input, and usually send output to the screen, often called standard output. Commands also send error information to the screen. You do not always want input to come from standard input and output and errors to go to standard output. You are given a lot of control to override these defaults. This is called redirection. Table 22-3 shows many common forms of redirection.

As shown in Table 22-3, to redirect the output of a command from standard output to a file, you use ">". This works almost all of the time. If you have an environment variable called **noclobber** set, then redirecting to an existing file does not work (we'll cover environment variables shortly). The **noclobber** does not permit redirection to write over an existing file. If you try to write over an existing file, such as **/tmp/processes** below, you receive a message that the file exists:

man page

ps - 13

```
#  ps  -ef  > /tmp/processes
/tmp/processes:  File exists
```

You can, however, use a "!" with redirection to force a file to be overwritten. Using ">!" forces a file to be overwritten, and ">>!" forces the output to be appended to the end of an existing file. Examples of these are shown in Table 22-3.

TABLE 22-3 Commonly Used Redirection Forms

Command or Assignment	Example	Description
<	**wc -l < .login**	Standard input redirection: execute **wc** (word count) and list number of lines (**-l**) in **.login**
>	**ps -ef > /tmp/processes**	Standard output redirection: execute **ps** and send output to file **/tmp/processes**

Command or Assignment	Example	Description
>>	**ps -ef >> /tmp/processes**	Append standard output: execute **ps** and append output to the end of file **/tmp/processes**
>!	**ps -ef >! /tmp/processes**	Standard output redirection and override **noclobber**: write over **/tmp/processes** even if it exists
>>!	**ps -ef >>! /tmp/processes**	Append standard output and override **noclobber**: append to the end of **/tmp/processes**
| (pipe)	**ps | wc -l**	Run **ps** and use the result as input to **wc**
0 - standard input		
1 - standard output		
2 - standard error	**cat program 2> errors**	**cat** the file **program** to standard output and redirect errors to the file **errors**
	cat program 2>> errors	**cat** the file **program** to standard output and append errors to the file **errors**
	find / -name '*.c' -print > cprograms 2>errors	**find** all files on the system ending in **.c**, place the list of files in **cprograms** in the current working directory, and send all errors (file descriptor 2) to the file **errors** in current working directory
	find / -name '*.c' -print > cprograms 2>&1	**find** all files on the system ending in **.c**, place the list of files in **cprograms** in the current working directory, and send all errors (file descriptor 2) to same place as file descriptor 1 (**cprograms**)

Environment Variables

An environment variable is a name associated with a string. The name is the variable and the string is its value. Environment variables are also available to sub-shells or processes spawned by the shell. In most cases, you see environment variables capitalized, which is the convention on most systems.

When you issue a command on the system, you usually enter a relative pathname, not an absolute pathname. The command you issue is found because the *PATH* variable points to the location of directories where commands are located. Without this *PATH* variable, you would have to type the absolute pathname of every command you issue. When you issue a command, the shell searches the directories listed in the *PATH* variable in the order in which they are listed. A good way to see many of the environment variables you have set is with the **env** command as shown below:

```
martyp $ env
_=/usr/bin/env
MANPATH=:/opt/local/ptc/sysadmin/scripts:/opt/local/ptc/man:/
opt/local/altrasofn
_INIT_UTS_RELEASE=5.7
HZ=100
_INIT_UTS_MACHINE=sun4m
EPC=true
PATH=/usr/bin:/usr/ucb:/etc:.
WEB_SERVER=sioux.rose.hp.com
_INIT_UTS_VERSION=Generic
MODEL=SPARCstation-10
OS_REV=5.7
EDITOR=vi
_INIT_RUN_NPREV=0
CLASSPATH=.:/usr/java/lib:
LOGNAME=martyp
_INIT_UTS_NODENAME=sunsys
_INIT_UTS_ISA=sparc
MAIL=/var/mail/martyp
ERASE=^H
OS=solaris
PS1=$PWD
$LOGNAME $TOKEN
_INIT_PREV_LEVEL=S
HOST=sunsys
TESTEXPERT_HOME=/opt/local/svn/te33
TA_HOME=/opt/local/platinum/solaris2/testadvise
MA_HOME=/opt/local/platinum/solaris2/memadvise
CL_LICENSE_FILE=/opt/local/CenterLine/configs/license.dat
SHELL=/bin/ksh
PROFILE_DIR=/opt/local/ptc/sysadmin/profile.d
OSTYPE=solaris2
HOME=/home/martyp
_INIT_UTS_SYSNAME=SunOS
TERM=vt100
LD_LIBRARY_PATH=:/opt/local/parasoft/lib.solaris
MWHOME=/opt/local/mainsoft/mainwin/mw
FMHOME=/opt/local/adobe/frame
PWD=/home/martyp
TZ=US/Pacific
_INIT_RUN_LEVEL=3
```

```
CLEARCASE_BLD_UMASK=02
_INIT_UTS_PLATFORM=SUNW,SPARCstation-10
martyp $
```

As you can see, other environment variables in addition to *PATH* make working on your UNIX system easier. You may want to issue other commmands related to **ksh** variables. Table 22-4 summarizes some **ksh**-related variable commands you may want to issue on your system.

man page

ksh - 6

TABLE 22-4   **ksh**-Related Variable Commands

Command	Description
env	Lists all environment variables (exported). These variables are normally uppercase and passed to child processes.
set	Prints all local and exported set variables.
set -o	Lists all built-in variables that are set to *on* or *off*.
typeset	Displays all variables and associated attributes, functions, and integers.
typeset +	Displays only the names of variables.

You may want to try all these commands on your system to see what variables have been set for you.

If you want to know the value of a specific environment variable, you could use the **echo** command to see its value, as shown below for the environment variable *HOME*:

```
martyp $ echo $HOME
/home/martyp
```

Similarly, to view the operating system type on this specific computer, you could issue the following command:

```
martyp $ echo $OSTYPE
solaris2
```

The "$" preceding the environment variable name specifies that the value of the variable be sent to standard output. In this case, the value of the environment variable *HOME* is **/home/martyp**, which means that the current user has a home directory of **/home/martyp**.

man page

ksh - 22

You can define your own environment variables in **ksh** with the following syntax:

```
export NAME=value
```

Many users like to customize the **ksh** prompts. Most systems provide four **ksh** prompts by default. You can normally modify the first two prompts. The first, called **PS1**, is the primary prompt. The second, called **PS2**, appears after you have partially typed a command and pressed *enter.* **PS1** is normally set to a *$* and **PS2** to *>,* by default.

The following example sets **PS1** to our home directory, a space, the current history number, a space, and dollar sign:

man page

pwd - 16

```
PS1="`pwd` ! $ "
```

We'll leave the default for **PS2** as *>.* The following sequence shows issuing a command at our new **PS1** prompt and the default **PS2** prompt:

```
/home/martyp 187 $ print "This is new PS1
> but default PS2"
This is new PS1
but default PS2
/home/martyp 188 $
```

This example shows the new **PS1**, including the history entry incrementing from *187* to *188*, and the default **PS2** when the incomplete **print** command was issued.

You can also append to the end of an existing variable with the following format:

```
export NAME="$NAME:appended_information"
```

To add **/home/martyp/programs** to the existing *PATH* environment variable, for instance, you issue the following command:

```
export PATH="$PATH:/home/martyp/programs"
```

This appends the path **/home/martyp/programs** to the environment variable *PATH*.

A great deal of flexibility is available when working with **ksh**. You should view all your variables and update those that make your job easier. Some customization, such as updating **PS1** and your **PATH**, can also make your job easier.

Background Jobs and Job Control

When you run a command, as we have done so far in many examples, you don't get back the prompt until the command has completed. These commands have been run in the foreground. Some commands can take a long time to complete, in which case, you'll be waiting a long time for the prompt to return. As an alternative to waiting for the prompt to return, you can run the command in the background, meaning that it is running behind the scenes while you perform other work. Because UNIX is multi-tasking it is happy to run many commands in the background and still provide you with a prompt to issue yet more commands.

In order to run a command in the background, you simply add an ampersand (&) to the end of the command line. When you follow your command with an ampersand, the command is run in the background and the prompt is immediately returned.

Let's now run some commands on our Solaris system. We'll first run a command to find all of the files in **/usr** that end in ".c," which takes some time to complete. We'll preface the **find** string with the **time** command so that we know how long the command takes to complete:

man page

find - 20

```
martyp $ time find /usr -name *.c
              .
              .
              .
/usr/demo/link_audit/src/dumpbind.c
/usr/demo/link_audit/src/env.c
/usr/demo/link_audit/src/hash.c
/usr/demo/link_audit/src/perfcnt.c
/usr/demo/link_audit/src/symbindrep.c
/usr/demo/link_audit/src/truss.c
/usr/demo/link_audit/src/who.c
find: cannot read dir /usr/aset: Permission denied

real    1m21.04s
user    0m1.51s
sys     0m12.67s
```

This commad took roughly one minute and 21 seconds to complete. Because it was run in the foreground we were unable to issue any other commands while it was running, because we had to wait for the prompt to return.

An alternative to running the command in the foreground is to issue the command followed by an ampersand, in which case the job runs in the background and the prompt returns immediately, as shown in the following example:

```
martyp $ time find /usr -name *.c > cprogs 2>&1 &
[3]      16279
martyp $
real    2m10.20s
user    0m1.31s
sys     0m8.62s
```

The result of running this command in the background produces a job number in brackets and the process id, or PID, as the second number. All the outputs of this command, including errors, are written to the file **cprogs**. The prompt was immediately returned after we issued the command, and after it completed, the output of **time** was sent to the screen. We could have begun issuing additional commands immediately after issuing the command in the background.

You have control over both foreground jobs and background jobs. To suspend a foreground job, you type the "control" and "z" keys simultaneously, as shown in the following example:

man page

find - 20

```
martyp $ find /usr -name *.c
/usr/openwin/share/include/X11/Xaw/Template.c
/usr/openwin/share/src/dig_samples/DnD/main.c
/usr/openwin/share/src/dig_samples/DnD/owner.c
/usr/openwin/share/src/dig_samples/DnD/requestor.c
/usr/openwin/share/src/dig_samples/Tooltalk/olit_tt.c
/usr/openwin/share/src/dig_samples/Tooltalk/
tt_callbacks.c
/usr/openwin/share/src/dig_samples/Tooltalk/tt_code.c
/usr/openwin/share/src/dig_samples/ce1/ce_map1.c
/usr/openwin/share/src/dig_samples/ce2/ce_simple.c
/usr/openwin/share/src/dig_samples/dnd_olit/olitdnd.c
/usr/openwin/share/src/dig_samples/dnd_xview1/
xview_dnd.c
/usr/openwin/share/src/dig_samples/dnd_xview2/
xview_dnd2.c
/usr/openwin/share/src/dig_samples/selection_olit/
olit_sel.c
/usr/openwin/share/src/dig_samples/tooltalk_simple/tt-
send.c
/usr/openwin/share/src/olit/oldials/oldials.c
/usr/openwin/share/src/olit/olitbook/ch10/draw.c
^Z[3] + Stopped (SIGTSTP)          find /usr -name *.c
```

After *ctrl-z* is pressed, the **find** command is interrupted at the point at which you type *ctrl-z*. The command is suspended at this point, and you are shown the job number, in this case "3," and its status is listed as "Stopped". This command has only been suspended; it is not gone forever. You can start this process in the foreground with **fg**, or run it in the background with **bg**. Using **bg** runs the command as if you had followed it with an "&". It is started from the point at which you interrupted it. You do not have to supply a job number when you issue the **fg** or **bg** command, because the default is to perform the specified operation on the last job, which in this case is job number *3*.

Notice that in this example we have stopped job number *3*. This means that there are other jobs running with a lower job numbers. You can use the **jobs** command to get a list of all jobs and their status. You can then control the jobs by issuing commands such as **fg** followed by a "%" and the job number to run the command in the foreground, or a **bg** followed by a "%" and the job number to run the command in the background. If you wish to terminate a job altogether, you can issue the **kill** command followed by a "%" and the job number.

In the process of creating the examples in this section, I have started and suspended many jobs. The following example shows listing all jobs with the **jobs** command, killing jobs *1* and *2* with **kill**, and running job 3 in the background:

```
martyp $ jobs
[3]  + Stopped (SIGTSTP)  find /usr -name *.c
[2]  - Running            time find / -name gnu* > gnu 2>&1 &
[1]    Running              time find / -name *.c > cprogs
2>&1 &
martyp $ kill %1
[1]    Terminated           time find / -name *.c > cprogs
2>&1 &
martyp $ kill %2
[2]  - Terminated          time find / -name gnu* > gnu 2>&1 &
martyp $ bg %3
[3]       find /usr -name *.c&
martyp $
```

Notice that an ampersand was added to job *3* when we requested that it be run in the background. Killing jobs 1 and 2 and running job 3 in the background returns the prompt so that you can perform additional work.

umask and Permissions

An additional topic to cover related to **ksh** is file permissions and the way they relate to **umask**. This is important because you may write shell programs, and the permissions control the access that others will have to these programs. **umask** is used to specify permission settings for new files and directories.

Let's start with an example of a long listing of a file. We'll use **ls -l** in the following examples:

```
sys1 1: ls -l script1
-rwxr-xr-x  1  marty  users  120 Jul 26 10:20 script1
```

The access rights for this file are defined by the position of read (r), write (w), and execute (x) when the **ls -l** command is issued. Figure 22-1 shows the three groups of three access rights for this file:

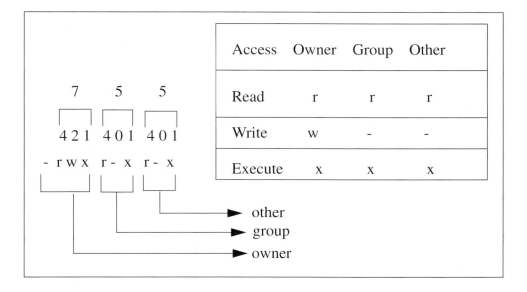

Figure 22-1 Example of File Permissions

The owner of this file has read, write, and execute permissions on the file. The group to which the user belongs has read and execute permissions, and others also have read and execute permissions. The permissions on this file can be specified by the octal sum of each field, which is 755.

man page

umask - 22

What happens if you craft a new shell script or any new file? What permission settings exist? You want to execute the shell script, so you need execute permission for the file. You can use **umask** to define the defaults for all your new files and directories.

By default, most systems start with a permission of 777 for directories and 666 for files. These mean that everyone has complete access to all directories you create and everyone has read and write access to all files you create. These defaults are modified with the value of **umask**.

You can view your **umask** in the following two ways:

```
martyp $ umask
002
martyp $ umask -S
u=rwx,g=rwx,o=rx
martyp $
```

The first example displays the octal value of **umask**, which we'll cover shortly, and the second example shows the symbolic value of **umask**.

The **umask** is used to *disable* access. You start with a **umask** and use the fields to disable some level of access. The **umask** command uses three octal fields. The fields are the sum of the access codes for user, group, and other as shown in Figure 22-2:

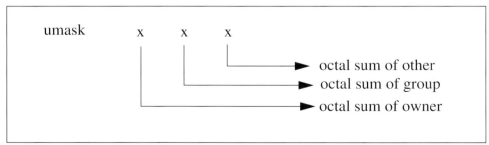

Figure 22-2   umask Fields

The *complement* of the umask field is "*anded*" with the default setting to change the **umask**. You can set **umask** by specifying its value. In our earlier example we viewed **umask** two different ways. To set the **umask**, you simply issue **umask** and the desired value. Setting **umask** to *022*, for example, removes write permissions of directories for "group" and "other," as shown in Figure 22-3:

man page

umask - 22

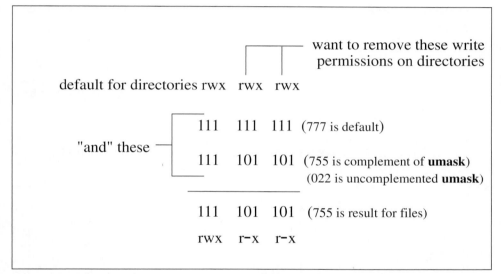

Figure 22-3 **umask** Example

umask 022 changes the directory permissions to 755 in this example.

Similarly, a **umask** of *022* changes the default permission of 666 for files to 644, which would be read-only for group and other.

Change File Permissions with chmod

The **chmod** command is used to change the permissions on a file. Irrespective of what takes place with **umask** as just described, you can change a file's permissions at any time with **chmod**. You need to be the owner of the file or superuser to change a file's permissions with **chmod** in most cases. Let's start our discussion of **chmod** with the listing of the file **sort**:

```
$ ls -l sort
-rwxr-x--x   1 marty      users      120 Jul 26 10:20 sort
```

Figure 22-4 shows a breakdown of the permissions on **sort**:

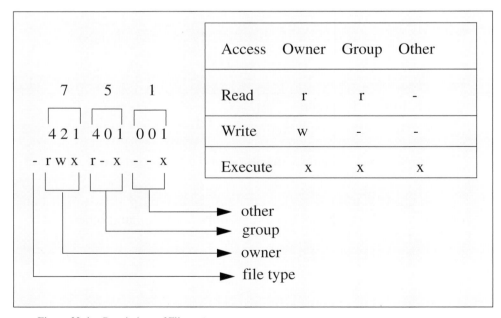

Figure 22-4   Permissions of File **sort**

man page

chmod - 16

You have very little control over the type of file defined. You do, however, have a great deal of control over the permissions of this file if it belongs to you. The **chmod** command is used to change the permissions on a file or directory. If you are the owner of the file, you can have a field day changing the permissions on the file.

Two means exist by which you can change the permissions: symbolic and numeric. I focus first on the numeric mode, because the numbers involved are easy to manage, and I sometimes find new UNIX users get hung up on the meanings of some of the symbols. I'll then cover the symbols and include the symbol meanings in the **chmod** summary.

First of all, what do I mean by numbers? Looking at the numbers for **sort**, we see permissions of 751: 7 for *owner* (hundred's position), 5 for *group* (ten's position), and 1 for *other* (one's position). Figure 22-5 helps with the meanings of the positions:

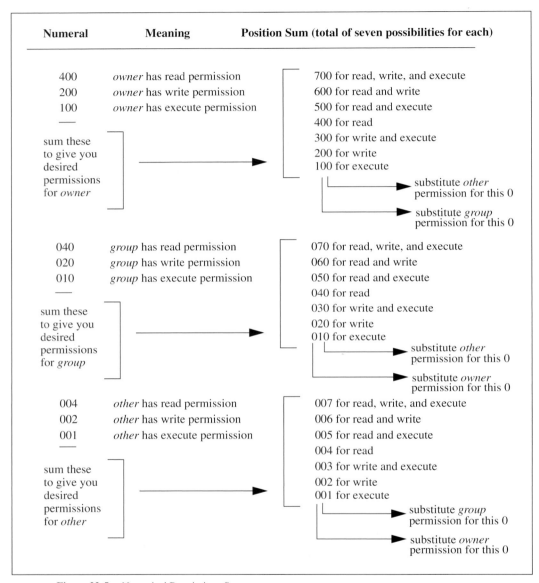

Figure 22-5   Numerical Permissions Summary

Selecting the desired permissions for *owner*, *group*, and *other*, you use the **chmod** command to assign those permissions to a file or directory. Some of these permission possibilities are infrequently used, such as execute only, because you usually need to have read access to a file in order to execute it; however, I included all possibilities in figure 22-5 for completeness. In addition to the permission mode bits shown in Figure 22-5, there are also miscellaneous mode bits, which you don't need to be concerned with at this time.

If you decide that you would like to add write permission of the file **sort** for *group*, and remove all permissions for *other*, you would simply execute the **chmod** command with the appropriate numeric value. The following set of commands first list the existing permissions for **sort**, next change the permissions on **sort**, and finally list the new permissions on **sort**:

man page

chmod - 16

```
$ ls -l sort
-rwxr-x--x   1 marty      users      120 Jul 26 10:20 sort

$ chmod 770 sort

$ ls -l sort
-rwxrwx---   1 marty      users      120 Jul 26 10:20 sort
```

man page

ls - 15

The same set of commands to change the permissions using the symbolic mode would be:

```
$ ls -l sort
-rwxr-x--x   1 marty      users      120 Jul 26 10:20 sort

$ chmod g+w,o-x sort

$ ls -l sort
-rwxrwx---   1 marty      users      120 Jul 26 10:20 sort
```

In symbolic mode, you issue the **chmod** command and specify who will be affected by the change [user (u), group (g), other (o), or all (a)], the operation you wish to perform [add (+), delete (-), or replace (=)], and the permission you wish to specify [read (r), write (w), or execute (x)]. In the previous example using symbolic mode, write (w) permission is being added (+) for *group* (g), and execute (x) permission is being removed (-) for *other* (o).

man page

chmod- 16

The following is a summary of some of the more commonly used symbols of **chmod**:

chmod - Change permissions of specified files using the following symbolic mode list.

Symbol of who is affected:

u	User is affected.
g	Group is affected.
o	Other is affected.
a	All users are affected.

Operation to perform:

+	Add permission.
-	Remove permission.
=	Replace permission.

Permission specified:

r	Read permission.
w	Write permission.
x	Execute permission.
u	Copy user permissions.
g	Copy group permissions.
o	Copy other permissions.

Introduction to the C Shell

The C shell is similar to other shells in that it provides a user interface to UNIX. You can use the C shell in the following three ways:

- Interactively type commands on the command line.
- Group commonly executed sets of commands into command files that you can execute by typing the name of the file.
- Create C shell programs using the structured programming techniques of the C shell.

These three techniques are listed in the order in which you'll probably use them. First, you log in and use interactive commands. Then you group together commonly used commands and execute them with a single command. Finally, you may want to create sophisticated shell scripts.

In this chapter, I cover login and interactive commands and a lot of useful ways to use the C shell.

Most of the examples in this chapter are from Solaris and HP-UX systems. You probably will find both your user setup and the operation of the C shell on other systems similar to what is covered in this chapter. Much of the setup of any shell is performed by the system administrator, so you will surely find differences in your C shell setup compared with what is shown in this chapter. In general, however, the operation of the C shell is similar from one system to another.

Issuing Commands

man page

ls - 15

The first activity you perform after you log in to the system is to issue commands at the prompt. A command you may want to issue immediately is **ls -al**. Here is what I see on my system after executing this:

```
sys1 7: ls -al
total 10
drwxr-x---    2 martyp2     users         96 May   5 09:34 .
drwxr-xr-x   10 root        root        1024 May   5 10:38 ..
-rw-r--r--    1 martyp2     users        814 May   5 09:34 .cshrc
-rw-r--r--    1 martyp2     users        347 May   5 09:34 .exrc
-rw-r--r--    1 martyp2     users        341 May   5 09:34 .login
-rw-r--r--    1 martyp2     users        446 May   5 09:34 .profile
sys1 8:
```

The C shell prompt consists of system name (sys1) followed by the command number and a colon. I cover the prompt shortly.

ls -al shows two files related to the C shell in this user area:

.cshrc and **.login**

Figure 22-6 shows the contents of **.cshrc**:

```
# Default user .cshrc file (/usr/bin/csh initialization).

# Usage:  Copy this file to a user's home directory and edit it to
# customize it to taste.  It is run by csh each time it starts up.

# Set up default command search path:
#
# (For security, this default is a minimal set.)

      set path=( $path )

# Set up C shell environment:

      if ( $?prompt ) then          # shell is interactive.
         set history=20             # previous commands to remember.
         set savehist=20            # number to save across sessions.
         set system=`hostname`      # name of this system.
         set prompt = "$system \!: " # command prompt.

         # Sample alias:

         alias     status  '(date; bdf)'

         # More sample aliases:

         alias     d      dirs
         alias     pd     pushd
         alias     pd2    pushd +2
         alias     po     popd
         alias     m      more
      endif
```

Figure 22-6　Sample **.cshrc**

Figure 22-7 shows the contents of **.login**:

```
# @(#) $Revision: 72.3 $


# Default user .login file ( /usr/bin/csh initialization )

# Set up the default search paths:
set path=( $path )

#set up the terminal
eval `tset -s -Q -m ':?hp' `
stty erase "^H" kill "^U" intr "^C" eof "^D" susp "^Z" hupcl ixon ixoff
tostop
tabs

# Set up shell environment:
set noclobber
set history=20
```

Figure 22-7 Sample **.login**

The .cshrc File

The sequence of events after login varies from one UNIX system to another. On many systems, the **.cshrc** is first read and executed by the C shell. You can modify the **.cshrc** file to specify the command-line prompt you wish to use, initialize the history list, and define aliases. The upcoming sections describe the way the **.cshrc** file shown in Figure 22-6 defines these. Let's first take a quick look at the **.login** file in the next section.

The .login File

On many UNIX systems, the **.login** file is read after the **.cshrc** file. There are only two issues related to setup present in the example shown. The first is the **tset** command, which sets the *TERM* environment variable. The **eval** preceding **tset** means that the C shell executes **tset** and its arguments without creating a child process. This allows **tset** to set environment variables in the current shell instead of a sub-shell, which would be useless. The **stty** command is used to set terminal I/O options. The two **set** commands are used to define shell variables, which I describe shortly. The **noclobber** does not permit redirection to write over an existing file. If you try to write over an existing file, such as **/tmp/processes** below, you receive a message that the file exists:

man page

ps - 13

```
sys1 1:  ps  -ef  > /tmp/processes
/tmp/processes:  File exists
```

The ">" means to take the output of **ps** and rather than write it to your screen, write it to **/tmp/processes**. The file **/tmp/processes** will not be written over, however, with the output of **ps -ef** because **/tmp/processes** already exists and an environment variable called **noclobber** has been set. If **noclobber** is set, then redirecting output to this file will not take place. This is a useful technique for preventing existing files from being accidently overwritten. There are many forms of redirection that you'll find useful. Redirection is covered later in this chapter.

Initialize History List in .cshrc

The C shell can keep a history list of the commands you have issued. If you wish to reissue a command or view a command you earlier issued, you can use the history list.

The commands issued are referred to by number, so you want to have a number appear at the command prompt. The following line in **.cshrc** provides a number following the system name:

```
set prompt = "$system \!: "

sys1 1:
```

We get into shell and environment variables shortly, but for now it is sufficient to know that **$system** corresponds to system name "sys1."

You can specify the number of previously issued commands you want to save and view when you issue the **history** command. The following line in **.cshrc** sets the history list to 20:

```
set history = 20
```

The last 20 commands issued are displayed when you issue the **history** command.

The *savehist* variable allows you to save a specified number of history commands after logout. By default, when you log out, the history list is cleared. This variable has a value of 20, so that upon the next login there will be 20 commands from the previous session will be saved.

Command-Line History

You can view the history list a variety of different ways. Let's first view the last 20 commands by simply issuing the **history** command:

```
sys1 23: history
    4 whoami
    5 pwd
    6 find / -name login -print &
    7 hostname
    8 who
    9 more /etc/passwd
   10 history
   11 history 5
   12 echo $PATH
   13 more .login
   14 cat .login
   15 exit
   16 exit
   17 history -h
   18 pwd
   19 whoami
   20 cd /tmp
   21 cat database.log
   22 cd
   23 history
sys1 24:
```

We can also print the history list without line numbers, as shown in the following example:

```
sys1 24: history -h
pwd
find / -name login -print &
hostname
who
more /etc/passwd
history
history 5
echo $PATH
more .login
cat .login
exit
```

```
exit
history -h
pwd
whoami
cd /tmp
cat database.log
cd
history
history -h
sys1 25:
```

Next, let's print the history list in reverse order:

```
sys1 25: history -r
    25 history -r
    24 history -h
    23 history
    22 cd
    21 cat database.log
    20 cd /tmp
    19 whoami
    18 pwd
    17 history -h
    16 exit
    15 exit
    14 cat .login
    13 more .login
    12 echo $PATH
    11 history 5
    10 history
     9 more /etc/passwd
     8 who
     7 hostname
     6 find / -name login -print &
sys1 26:
```

We can also select the number of events we want to print from the history list. The following example prints only the last ten commands from the history list:

```
sys1 26: history 10
    17 history -h
    18 pwd
```

```
   19  whoami
   20  cd /tmp
   21  cat database.log
   22  cd
   23  history
   24  history -h
   25  history -r
   26  history 10
sys1 27:
```

You can see that you have a variety of ways to produce a list of commands previously issued. Table 22-5 summarizes the commands issued in this section:

TABLE 22-5 Command-Line History

Command	Description	Example
history	The history list is produced with each command numbered.	**history**
history -h	The history list is produced without line numbers.	**history -h**
history -r	The history list is produced in reverse order with each command numbered.	**history -r**
history *n*	The last *n* commands from the history list are produced with each command numbered.	**history 10**

Re-Executing Commands from the History List

You can re-execute commands from the history list using a variety of techniques. We'll re-execute commands from the history list using the most common techniques.

You can repeat the last command with **!!**, the second command with **!2**, and the last command that started with "c" with **!c**. Let's issue the **history** command to get a list of the last 20 commands and then re-execute some of them:

```
sys1 27: history
     8 who
     9 more /etc/passwd
    10 history
    11 history 5
    12 echo $PATH
    13 more .login
    14 cat .login
    15 exit
    16 exit
    17 history -h
    18 pwd
    19 whoami
    20 cd /tmp
    21 cat database.log
    22 cd
    23 history
    24 history -h
    25 history -r
    26 history 10
    27 history
sys1 28:
```

Let's first reissue the last command with **!!**:

```
sys1 28: !!
history
     9 more /etc/passwd
    10 history
    11 history 5
    12 echo $PATH
    13 more .login
    14 cat .login
    15 exit
    16 exit
    17 history -h
    18 pwd
    19 whoami
    20 cd /tmp
    21 cat database.log
    22 cd
    23 history
    24 history -h
    25 history -r
    26 history 10
```

```
        27 history
        28 history
sys1 29:
```

Let's now reissue the 19th command with **!19**:

```
sys1 29: !19
whoami
martyp2
sys1 30:
```

Let's now reissue the last command beginning with "p" with **!p**:

```
sys1 30: !p
pwd
/home/martyp2
sys1 31:
```

Table 22-6 includes some of the more commonly used history list recall commands:

TABLE 22-6   Recalling from History List

Command	Description	Example
!N	Issue command **N**	**!2**
!!	Issue last command	**!!**
!-N	Issue **Nth** command from last command issued	**!-N**
!str	Issue last command starting with **str**	**!c**
!?str?	Issue last command that had **str** anyplace in command line	**!?cat?**
!{str}str2	Append **str2** to last command with **str1**	**!{cd} /tmp**
^str1^str2^	Substitute **str2** for **str1** in last command	**^cat^more^**

Aliases in .cshrc

An alias is a name that you select for a frequently used command or series of commands. Many aliases are predefined for you.

You can use the **.cshrc** file as a place where your aliases are stored and read every time you log in. You can also define aliases at the command-line prompt, but these are cleared when you log out.

The **alias** command, without any arguments, lists all aliases. This list includes both preset aliases as well as those you have set. The following **alias** command shows all preset aliases on the system on which I am working:

```
sys1 7: alias
d        dirs
m        more
pd       pushd
pd2      (pushd +2)
po       popd
status   (date; bdf)
sys1 8:
```

You are not restricted to using only the preset aliases. To create your own alias, you first issue the **alias** command, the name of the alias, and then the command or commands that are executed when the alias is executed.

Let's now create a few simple aliases. The first creates an alias of "h" for the **history** command:

```
sys1 1: alias h history
sys1 2: h
        history
```

Every time you type **h**, the history command is executed.

The following example creates an alias of a command that contains spaces, so the command is surrounded by single quotes:

```
alias ls='ls -al'
alias
ls
```

man page

ls - 15

The first command creates an alias for "ls" that executes the **ls -al** command. We then issued the **alias** command to see whether indeed the new alias appears in the list of aliases. Then we run **ls** to see whether **ls -al** is run.

You don't have to keep an alias for the duration of your session after having set it. If you don't like an alias, you can use the **unalias** command to remove an alias.

To see **unalias** work, let's again produce a list of aliases, use **unalias** to unset the **h** alias, and run the **h** command to see if indeed it has been removed:

```
unalias h
h
```

When we issued **unalias** to remove the **h** alias and then try to run *h,* we were told that **h** is not found.

```
sys1 3:alias procs 'echo "Number of processes are: \c";
ps -ef | wc -l'
                        # single quote on outside
                        # double quote on inside
```

man page

ps - 13

When you run **procs**, you see the following:

```
sys1 4: procs
Number of processes are: 44
```

man page

wc - 18

A lot of quoting takes place in this command line. To understand what is taking place on this line, consult Table 22-7 for help.

TABLE 22-7 Shell Quoting

Character(s)	Description
'cmd'	Single quote means to take the string character literally
"str"	Double quote means to allow command and variable substitution
\c	Escape character that prevents everything following it from printing, including new line
`str`	Grave means to execute command and substitute output

Applying Table 22-7 to the earlier **procs** alias, we can see what comprises this alias. The alias begins with a single quote, which means execute the command(s) within the single quotes. The first command is the **echo** command, which uses double quotes to specify the characters to **echo**. Embedded in the double quotes is the escape character \c, which prevents a new line from being printed. The semicolons separate commands. **ps** is then run to produce a list of processes, and the output is piped (|) to word count (**wc**) which produces a count of the number of lines. There are actually 43 processes running, because an extra line consisting of the **ps** headings is reported by **wc**.

man page

ps - 13

man page

wc - 18

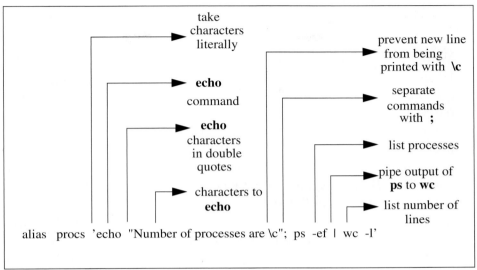

Figure 22-8 Quoting Example

As you can see in Figure 22-8, some of the quoting becomes tricky. An understanding of quoting is important if you wish to modify and reuse existing shell scripts or craft your own.

Introduction to Bash

With many developers using the Open Source development tools in HP-UX 11i, there is a lot of interest in Bash. Bash is widely used, although not required, when using GNU tools. In addition, the Linux-based UNIX operating systems I have used configure Bash as the default shell. Bash is covered in this section on a Linux system, however, the features of Bash covered exist on HP-UX as well. Bash possesses many of the fine features of other shells, and in fact derives its name from **B**ourne **A**gain **SH**ell, which is a dead giveaway that it possesses at least some of the features of the Bourne shell. Bash is similar to other shells in that it provides a user interface to UNIX. You can use the Bash shell in the following three ways:

- Interactively type commands on the command line.

- Group commonly executed sets of commands into command files that you can execute by typing the name of the file.

- Create Bash shell programs using the structured programming techniques of the shell.

These three techniques are listed in the order in which you'll probably use them. First, you log in and use interactive commands. Then you group together commonly used commands and execute them with a single command. Finally, you may want to create sophisticated shell scripts.

For this reason, I'll describe these aspects of the Bash shell in the order in which they are listed. The command file and programming aspects of the Bash shell are covered as part of the "Shell Programming" chapter. Bash is very similar to the KornShell, which is the shell used in the shell programming chapter. You can, therefore, use the shell programming chapter as an introduction to programming with Bash as well. Keep in mind, however, that differences always occur when programming with one shell vs. another.

Issuing Commands

The first activity you perform after you log into the system is to issue commands at the prompt. A command you may want to issue immediately is **ls -al**. Here is what I see on my system after executing this command to check my present working directory and producing a long listing of all files when logged in as root:

man page

pwd - 16

```
# pwd
# ls -al
total 46
drwxr-xr-x    5 root     root            1024 Nov 26 19:40 .
drwxr-xr-x   20 root     root            1024 Nov  8 20:10 ..
-rw-r--r--    1 root     root             964 Nov 26 19:40 .bash_history
-rw-r--r--    1 root     root             674 Feb  5  1997 .bashrc
-rw-r--r--    1 root     root             602 Feb  5  1997 .cshrc
-rw-r--r--    1 root     root           14815 Nov  8 20:09 .fvwmrc.menus.prep
-rw-r--r--    1 root     root             116 Feb  5  1997 .login
-rw-r--r--    1 root     root             234 Feb  5  1997 .profile
drwxr-xr-x    2 root     root            1024 Nov  8 14:10 .seyon
-rw-r--r--    1 root     root            4276 Nov  8 20:09 XF86Config
-r--r--r--    1 root     root           13875 Nov  8 20:05 XF86Config.bak
drwxrwxrwx    2 root     root            1024 Nov 26 19:40 book
drwxr-xr-x    5 root     root            1024 Nov 14 18:12 lg
-rw-r--r--    1 root     root               0 Nov 26 19:40 typescript
#
```

man page

ls - 15

Among the files produced in the long listing of all files is a Bash startup file called **.bashrc**. The following shows the contents of the **.bashrc** file:

man page

cat - 17

```
# cat .bashrc
# ~/.bashrc --
#   The individual per-interactive-shell startup file for bash

. /etc/profile

# try solve this tedious 'Backspace vs. Delete' problem...
if [ -z "$TERM" ]; then
  echo ".bashrc: TERM empty: this shouldn't happen!" 1>&2
  echo "    Please contact 'support@lst.de'" 1>&2
else
  case $TERM in
  linux*)
    stty erase '^?'
    ;;
  *)
    stty erase '^H'
    ;;
  esac
fi

# general environment settings
#export GROFF_TYPESETTER=latin1
```

```
#export LC_CTYPE=iso-8859-1
export LESSCHARSET=latin1
#export METAMAIL_PAGER=less

HISTSIZE=100

alias which='type -path'
alias h=history
alias j="jobs -l"
alias l="ls -Fax"
alias ll="ls -Alg"
alias pd=pushd
alias z=suspend

#
```

The **bashrc** file has some interesting contents are in the **.bashrc** file. Among them is a value for *HISTSIZE*, which we'll get into shortly, and a set of aliases. These aliases are "shortcuts" for long commands. When I issue the **ll** command, for instance, I am really issuing the **ls -Alg** command.

I may execute both the local **.profile** shown in the earlier long listing as well as **/etc/profile**. **/etc/profile** usually performs setup for all users who log into the system. The following is a listing of **/etc/profile**:

```
# cat /etc/profile
# /etc/profile
# System wide environment and startup programs
# Functions and aliases go in $HOME/.bashrc

PATH="/bin:/usr/bin:/opt/bin:/usr/X11R6/bin:/usr/openwin/bin:/usr/TeX/bin:/usr/
local/bin"

umask 022

if [ `id -gn` = `id -un` ] && [ `id -u` != 0 ]; then
  umask 002
fi

if [ -z "$UID" ]; then
  UID=`id -u`
fi

if [ "$UID" = 0 ]; then
  PATH=/sbin:/usr/sbin:$PATH
else
  PATH=$PATH:
fi
USER=`id -un`
LOGNAME=$USER

export PATH USER LOGNAME

HOSTNAME=`/bin/hostname`
MAIL="/var/spool/mail/$USER"

export HOSTNAME MAIL
```

```
if [ -n "$BASH_VERSION" ]; then
  # (aliases now in $HOME/.bashrc, resp. /etc/skel/.bashrc)
  export PS1="[\u@\h \W]\\$ "
  export HISTSIZE=100
fi

#
```

We'll also cover some of the contents of **/etc/profile**.

Initializing the History List in .bashrc

The Bash shell can keep a history list of the commands you have issued. If you wish to reissue a command or view a command you earlier issued, you can use the history list.

You can specify any number of commands to be included in the history list. The following line in **.bashrc** sets the history list to 100:

```
set history = 100
```

One hundred commands will be saved in the history list. When you log, out the last 100 commands you have issued are stored in the history list. The next time you log in you can view these 100 commands; however, as you issue commands, the oldest commands fall off the history list. This fact is shown in the following example:

```
# history
    2  more history
    3   ll
    4  cd ..
    5  pwd
    6  cd ..
    7  ll
    8  cd ..
```

```
 9  ll
10  ll log
11  cd log
12  more *
13  l
14  ll
15  cd /
16  ll
17  cd
18  XF86Setup
19  XF86Setup
20  startx
21  ll
22  pwd
23  ll
24  ll /
25  XF86Setup
26  ll
27  startx
28  find / -name XF86Config*
29  cp /usr/X11R6/lib/X11/XF86Config.eg .
30  ll
31  XF86Setup
32  XF86Setup
33  startx
34  ll
35  mv XF86Config.eg XF86Config
36  XF86Setup
37  startx
38  shutdown -h now
39  man ls
40  man ll
41  man ls
42  man file
43  lsr
44  man chmod
45  man chmod
46  shutdown -h now
47  pwd
48  ls -l
49  pwd
50  ls -a
51  ls -al
52  pwd
53  ls -al
54  more .profile
55  more .bashrc
56
57  alias
58  ll
59  pwd
60  script
```

```
 61   script
 62   scrit
 63   script
 64   more .bashrc
 65   more .bashrc
 66   ll
 67   more .profile
 68   ll
 69   more .bashrc | grep P
 70   more .profile | grep P
 71   env
 72   more /.profile
 73   more /etc/profile
 74   more /etc/profile | grep PS
 75   find / -name *profile* -print
 76   more .bashrc
 77    more .bashrc
 78   ll /etc/profi*
 79   cp /etc/profile /etc/profile.orig
 80   vi /etc/profile
 81   exit
 82   cp /etc/profile.orig /etc/profile
 83   history
 84
 85   exit
 86   history
 87   history
 88      ll
 89      ll
 90   history
 91   ll /etc/profi*
 92   ll /etc/profi*
 93    more .bashrc
 94     history
 95   ll
 96   cd /root
 97   ll
 98   history | more
 99    history | more
100     exit
101   history
```

Notice in this example that command number *100* is the **exit**, or command to log out, from the last session. Command number *101* is the **history** command I issued immediately upon establishing the next session.

Recalling from the History List

All these commands (**cp, more, find, ll**) are in the history list with their corresponding numbers. You can repeat the last command with **!!**, the 89th command with **!89**, and the last command that started with "m" with **!m**, all of which are shown in the following example:

```
# !!
history
    3   ll
    4   cd ..
    5   pwd
    6   cd ..
    7   ll
    8   cd ..
    9   ll
   10   ll log
   11   cd log
   12   more *
   13   l
   14   ll
   15   cd /
   16   ll
   17   cd
   18   XF86Setup
   19   XF86Setup
   20   startx
   21   ll
   22   pwd
   23   ll
   24   ll /
   25   XF86Setup
   26   ll
   27   startx
   28   find / -name XF86Config*
   29   cp /usr/X11R6/lib/X11/XF86Config.eg .
   30   ll
   31   XF86Setup
   32   XF86Setup
   33   startx
   34   ll
   35   mv XF86Config.eg XF86Config
   36   XF86Setup
   37   startx
   38   shutdown -h now
   39   man ls
   40   man ll
   41   man ls
   42   man file
   43   lsr
   44   man chmod
   45   man chmod
   46   shutdown -h now
   47   pwd
   48   ls -l
   49   pwd
   50   ls -a
   51   ls -al
   52   pwd
   53   ls -al
   54   more .profile
   55   more .bashrc
   56
   57   alias
   58   ll
```

```
  59  pwd
  60  script
  61  script
  62  scrit
  63  script
  64  more .bashrc
  65  more .bashrc
  66  ll
  67  more .profile
  68  ll
  69  more .bashrc | grep P
  70  more .profile | grep P
  71  env
  72  more /.profile
  73  more /etc/profile
  74  more /etc/profile | grep PS
  75  find / -name *profile* -print
  76  more .bashrc
  77   more .bashrc
  78  ll /etc/profi*
  79  cp /etc/profile /etc/profile.orig
  80  vi /etc/profile
  81  exit
  82  cp /etc/profile.orig /etc/profile
  83  history
  84
  85  exit
  86  history
  87  history
  88   ll
  89   ll
  90  history
  91  ll /etc/profi*
  92  ll /etc/profi*
  93   more .bashrc
  94    history
  95  ll
  96  cd /root
  97  ll
  98  history | more
  99   history | more
 100    exit
 101  history
 102  history
# !89
  ll
total 44
-rw-r--r--   1 root      root           956 Nov 26 19:33 .bash_history
-rw-r--r--   1 root      root           674 Feb  5  1997 .bashrc
-rw-r--r--   1 root      root           602 Feb  5  1997 .cshrc
-rw-r--r--   1 root      root         14815 Nov  8 20:09 .fvwmrc.menus.prep
-rw-r--r--   1 root      root           116 Feb  5  1997 .login
-rw-r--r--   1 root      root           234 Feb  5  1997 .profile
drwxr-xr-x   2 root      root          1024 Nov  8 14:10 .seyon
-rw-r--r--   1 root      root          4276 Nov  8 20:09 XF86Config
-r--r--r--   1 root      root         13875 Nov  8 20:05 XF86Config.bak
drwxrwxrwx   2 root      root          1024 Nov 13 21:25 book
drwxr-xr-x   5 root      root          1024 Nov 14 18:12 lg
-rw-r--r--   1 root      root             0 Nov 26 19:36 typescript
# !m
more .bashrc
# ~/.bashrc --
#   The individual per-interactive-shell startup file for bash

. /etc/profile

# try solve this tedious 'Backspace vs. Delete' problem...
if [ -z "$TERM" ]; then
  echo ".bashrc: TERM empty: this shouldn't happen!" 1>&2
  echo "   Please contact 'support@lst.de'" 1>&2
else
  case $TERM in
  linux*)
    stty erase '^?'
    ;;
```

```
    *)
       stty erase '^H'
       ;;
    esac
  fi

  # general environment settings
  #export GROFF_TYPESETTER=latin1
  #export LC_CTYPE=iso-8859-1
  [7m--More--(70%)[m
  export LESSCHARSET=latin1
  #export METAMAIL_PAGER=less

  HISTSIZE=100

  alias which='type -path'
  alias h=history
  alias j="jobs -l"
  alias l="ls -Fax"
  alias ll="ls -Alg"
  alias pd=pushd
  alias z=suspend

  [root@nycald1 /root]#
  Script done on Thu Nov 26 19:39:51 1998
```

Table 22-8 includes some of the more commonly used history
list recall commands:

TABLE 22-8   Recalling from the History List

Command	Description	Example
!*N*	Issue command **N**	**!2**
!!	Issue last command	**!!**
!-*N*	Issue **Nth** command from last command issued	**!-N**
!*str*	Issue last command starting with **str**	**!c**
!?*str*?	Issue last command that had **str** anyplace in command line	**!?cat?**
!{*str1*}*str2*	Append **str2** to last command with **str1**	**!{cd} /tmp**
^*str1*^*str2*^	Substitute **str2** for **str1** in last command	**^cat^more^**

Editing on the Command Line

Using the history list is a great way of viewing and reissuing commands. Bash also supports command-line editing. You can use the up arrow key to move back one command in the history list. When you press the up arrow key, the last command from the history list appears on the command line. Every time you press the up arrow key, you move back one more command in the history list. When a command appears on the command line, you can press the "Enter" key to issue the command. You can modify the command by using the left and right arrow keys to move to a point in the command line and type additional information, or use the "backspace" and "delete" keys to remove information from the command line.

Aliases in .bashrc

An alias is a name that you select for a frequently used command or series of commands. You can use the **.bashrc** file as a place where your aliases are stored and read every time you log in. In the earlier **.bashrc** file, seven aliases were already set up. You can add additional aliases in the **.bashrc** file or define aliases at the command-line prompt, but these will be cleared when you log out.

Here is a list of the aliases that are already set up for us in the **.bashrc** file and an example of running the aliases **l** and **ll**:

```
# alias
alias h='history'
alias j='jobs -l'
alias l='ls -Fax'
alias ll='ls -Alg'
alias pd='pushd'
alias which='type -path'
alias z='suspend'
```

```
#
# 1
./                      ../                    .bash_history          .bashrc
.cshrc                  .fvwmrc.menus.prep     .login                 .profile
.seyon/                 XF86Config             XF86Config.bak         book/
lg/                     typescript
#
# ll
total 44
-rw-r--r--    1 root        root              970 Nov 26 21:35 .bash_history
-rw-r--r--    1 root        root              674 Feb  5  1997 .bashrc
-rw-r--r--    1 root        root              602 Feb  5  1997 .cshrc
-rw-r--r--    1 root        root            14815 Nov  8 20:09 .fvwmrc.menus.prep
-rw-r--r--    1 root        root              116 Feb  5  1997 .login
-rw-r--r--    1 root        root              234 Feb  5  1997 .profile
drwxr-xr-x    2 root        root             1024 Nov  8 14:10 .seyon
-rw-r--r--    1 root        root             4276 Nov  8 20:09 XF86Config
-r--r--r--    1 root        root            13875 Nov  8 20:05 XF86Config.bak
drwxrwxrwx    2 root        root             1024 Nov 26 19:41 book
drwxr-xr-x    5 root        root             1024 Nov 14 18:12 lg
-rw-r--r--    1 root        root                0 Nov 26 21:35 typescript
#
```

man page

ps - 13

man page

wc - 18

These are all very useful indeed, but let's now set up our own alias. Suppose that we want to know how many processes are running on the system. We'll create an alias called "procs" that does this for us. The **ps** command produces a list of processes. We'll issue **ps** and pipe (|) this output to **wc** with the "l" option to tell us how many lines are present. The pipe (|) directs the output of **ps** to be used as the input to **wc**. The **ps** command produces a list of processes, and **wc -l** gives us a count of the number of lines. Therefore, we'll know the total number of processes running. The following example first shows the output of **ps**, then our **alias** command, and finally the output produced by the **alias** command:

```
# ps
  PID TTY STAT   TIME COMMAND
  188   2 S     0:00 /sbin/getty tty2 VC linux
  189   3 S     0:00 /sbin/getty tty3 VC linux
  190   4 S     0:00 /sbin/getty tty4 VC linux
  191   5 S     0:00 /sbin/getty tty5 VC linux
  192   6 S     0:00 /sbin/getty tty6 VC linux
  619   1 S     0:00 login root
  620   1 S     0:00 -bash
  642   1 S     0:00 script
  643   1 S     0:00 script
  644  p0 S     0:00 bash -i
  656  p0 R     0:00 ps
#
# alias procs='echo "Number of processes are: ";ps | wc -l'
#
```

```
# procs
Number of processes are: 11
#
```

This alias works great. All we have to type is "procs" to see the number of processes running on our system.

A lot of quoting takes place in this command line. To understand what is taking place on this line, consult Table 22-9:

Table 22-9   Shell Quoting

Character(s)	Description
'cmd'	Single quote means to take the string character literally
"str"	Double quote means allow command and variable substitution
\c	Escape character prevents everything following it from printing, including new line
`str`	Grave means to execute command and substitute output

Applying Table 22-9 to the earlier **procs** alias, we can see what comprises this alias. The alias begins with a single quote, which means execute the command(s) within the single quotes. The first command is **echo**, which uses double quotes to specify the characters to **echo**. We could have added the escape character **\c**, which would have prevented a new line from being printed. The semicolons separate commands. **ps** is then run to produce a list of processes, and the output is piped (|) to word count (**wc**), which produces a count of the number of lines, as shown in Figure 22-9:

man page

ps - 13

man page

wc - 18

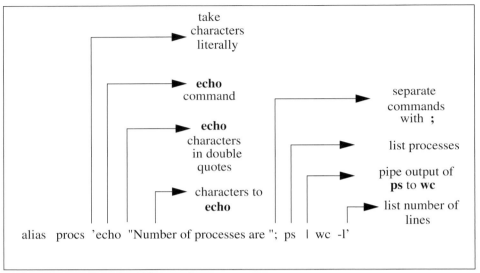

Figure 22-9 Quoting Example

As you can see in Figure 22-9, some of the quoting becomes tricky. An understanding of quoting is important if you wish to modify and reuse existing shell scripts or craft your own.

Command and Path Completion

Bash sometimes knows what you're thinking. You can type part of a command or pathname, and Bash can complete the remainder for you. You can type part of a command or pathname and use the "tab" key to complete the command. If, for instance, you wish to issue the **run-level** command to view the current system run level, but can't remember the full command, you can type "run" and press the tab key and the command is completed for you as shown in the following example:

```
# run<tab key>level
N 3
```

Bash determined that the only command that starts with "run" is **runlevel** and completed the command.

As long as you issue the command or pathname to the extent that it is unique, then Bash completes it for you. If the command or pathname is not unique, then Bash shows you the options for completing the command. The following example shows typing "ru" and two tabs to get a list of commands that start with "ru":

```
# ru<tab key><tab key>
runlevel   rusers
```

You can see from this example that typing "ru" produced two possible commands - **runlevel** and **rusers**.

This great completion also works for path names. If you change directory to "/b," you get the following result:

```
# cd /b<tab key><tab key>
bin   boot
```

man page

cd - 16

Because two directories at the root level begin with "b," Bash could not determine which of the two you wanted and listed both.

Manual Pages for Some Commands Used in Chapter 22

The following are the HP-UX manual pages for many of the commands used in this chapter. Commands often differ among UNIX variants, so you may find differences in the options or other areas for some commands; however, the following manual pages serve as an excellent reference.

kill

kill - Send signal to a process.

kill(1)   kill(1)

NAME
     kill - send a signal to a process; terminate a process

SYNOPSIS

     kill [-s signame] pid ...

     kill [-s signum] pid ...

     kill -l

   Obsolescent Versions:
     kill -signame pid ...

     kill -signum pid ...

DESCRIPTION
     The kill command sends a signal to each process specified by a pid
     process identifier. The default signal is SIGTERM, which normally
     terminates processes that do not trap or ignore the signal.

     pid is a process identifier, an unsigned or negative integer that can
     be one of the following:

          > 0 The number of a process.

          = 0 All processes, except special system processes, whose
               process group ID is equal to the process group ID of the
               sender.

          =-1 All processes, except special system processes, if the user
               has appropriate privileges. Otherwise, all processes,
               except special system processes, whose real or effective
               user ID is the same as the user ID of the sending process.

          <-1 All processes, except special system processes, whose
               process group ID is equal to the absolute value of pid and
               whose real or effective user ID is the same as the user of
               the sending process.

     Process numbers can be found with the ps command (see ps(1)) and with
     the built-in jobs command available in some shells.

   Options
     kill recognizes the following options:

          -l   (ell)   List all values of signame supported by the
                             implementation. No signals are sent with this
                             option. The symbolic names of the signals

(without the SIG prefix) are written to
standard output, separated by spaces and
newlines.

-s signame	Send the specified signal name. The default is SIGTERM, number 15. signame can be specified in upper- and/or lowercase, with or without the SIG prefix. These values can be obtained by using the -l option. The symbolic name SIGNULL represents signal value zero. See "Signal Names and Numbers" below.
-s signum	Send the specified decimal signal number. The default is 15, SIGTERM. See "Signal Names and Numbers" below.
-signame	(Obsolescent.) Equivalent to -s signame.
-signum	(Obsolescent.) Equivalent to -s signum.

Signal Names and Numbers
   The following table describes a few of the more common signals that
   can be useful from a terminal. For a complete list and a full
   description, see the header file <signal.h> and the manual entry
   signal(5).

signum	signame	Name	Description
0	SIGNULL	Null	Check access to pid
1	SIGHUP	Hangup	Terminate; can be trapped
2	SIGINT	Interrupt	Terminate; can be trapped
3	SIGQUIT	Quit	Terminate with core dump; can be trapped
9	SIGKILL	Kill	Forced termination; cannot be trapped
15	SIGTERM	Terminate	Terminate; can be trapped
24	SIGSTOP	Stop	Pause the process; cannot be trapped
25	SIGTSTP	Terminal stop	Pause the process; can be trapped
26	SIGCONT	Continue	Run a stopped process

SIGNULL (0), the null signal, invokes error checking but no signal is
actually sent. This can be used to test the validity or existence of
pid.

SIGTERM (15), the (default) terminate signal, can be trapped by the
receiving process, allowing the receiver to execute an orderly
shutdown or to ignore the signal entirely. For orderly operations,
this is the perferred choice.

SIGKILL (9), the kill signal, forces a process to terminate
immediately. Since SIGKILL cannot be trapped or ignored, it is useful
for terminating a process that does not respond to SIGTERM.

The receiving process must belong to the user of the sending process,
unless the user has appropriate privileges.

As a single special case, the continue signal SIGCONT can be sent to
any process that is a member of the same session as the sending
process.

RETURN VALUE
   Upon completion, kill returns with one of the following values:

0	At least one matching process was found for each pid operand, and the specified signal was successfully processed for at least one matching process.

>0   An error occurred.

EXAMPLES

The command:

kill 6135

signals process number 6135 to terminate. This gives the process an opportunity to exit gracefully (removing temporary files, etc.).

The following equivalent commands:

kill -s SIGKILL 6135
kill -s KILL 6135
kill -s 9 6135
kill -SIGKILL 6135
kill -KILL 6135
kill -9 6135

terminate process number 6135 abruptly by sending a SIGKILL signal to the process. This tells the kernel to remove the process immediately.

WARNINGS

If a process hangs during some operation (such as I/O) so that it is never scheduled, it cannot die until it is allowed to run. Thus, such a process may never go away after the kill. Similarly, defunct processes (see ps(1)) may have already finished executing, but remain on the system until their parent reaps them (see wait(2)). Using kill to send signals to them has no effect.

Some non-HP-UX implementations provide kill only as a shell built-in command.

DEPENDENCIES

This manual entry describes the external command /usr/bin/kill and the built-in kill command of the POSIX shell (see sh-posix(1)). Other shells, such as C and Korn (see csh(1) and ksh(1) respectively), also provide kill as a built-in command. The syntax for and output from these built-ins may be different.

SEE ALSO

csh(1), ksh(1), ps(1), sh(1), sh-bourne(1), sh-posix(1), kill(2), wait(2), signal(5).

STANDARDS CONFORMANCE

kill: SVID2, SVID3, XPG2, XPG3, XPG4, POSIX.2

ksh

ksh - Command programming language.

```
ksh(1)                                                              ksh(1)

NAME
     ksh, rksh - shell, the standard/restricted command programming
     language

SYNOPSIS

     ksh [+aefhikmnoprstuvx] [+o option] ...  [-c string] [arg ...]
     rksh [+aefhikmnoprstuvx] [+o option] ...  [-c string] [arg ...]

DESCRIPTION
     ksh is a command programming language that executes commands read from
     a terminal or a file.  rksh is a restricted version of the command
     interpreter ksh, used to set up login names and execution environments
     whose capabilities are more controlled than those of the standard
     shell.  See Invoking ksh and Special Commands sections later in this
     entry for details about command line options and arguments,
     particularly the set command.

     Definitions
     metacharacter   One of the following characters:

                     ;   &   (   )   |   <   >   new-line   space   tab

     blank           A tab or space character.

     identifier      A sequence of letters, digits, or underscores starting
                     with a letter or underscore.  Identifiers are used as
                     names for functions and named parameters.

     word            A sequence of characters separated by one or more non-
                     quoted metacharacters .

     command         A sequence of characters in the syntax of the shell
                     language.  The shell reads each command and carries out
                     the desired action, either directly or by invoking
                     separate utilities.

     special command
                     A command that is carried out by the shell without
                     creating a separate process.  Often called ``built-in
                     commands''.  Except for documented side effects, most
                     special commands can be implemented as separate
                     utilities.

     #               The # character is interpreted as the beginning of a
                     comment.  See Quoting below.

     Commands
     A simple-command is a sequence of blank-separated words that can be
     preceded by a parameter assignment list.  (See Environment below).
     The first word specifies the name of the command to be executed.
```

Except as specified below, the remaining words are passed as arguments to the invoked command. The command name is passed as argument 0 (see exec(2)). The value of a simple-command is its exit status if it terminates normally, or (octal) 200+status if it terminates abnormally (see signal(5) for a list of status values).

A pipeline is a sequence of one or more commands separated by |. The standard output of each command except the last is connected by a pipe (see pipe(2)) to the standard input of the next command. Each command is run as a separate process; the shell waits for the last command to terminate. The exit status of a pipeline is the exit status of the last command in the pipeline.

A list is a sequence of one or more pipelines separated by ;, &, &&, or ||, and optionally terminated by ;, &, or |&. Of these five symbols, ;, &, and |& have equal precedence. && and || have a higher but also equal precedence. A semicolon (;) causes sequential execution of the preceding pipeline; an ampersand (&) causes asynchronous execution of the preceding pipeline (that is, the shell does not wait for that pipeline to finish). The symbol |& causes asynchronous execution of the preceding command or pipeline with a two-way pipe established to the parent shell (known as a co-process). The standard input and output of the spawned command can be written to and read from by the parent shell using the -p option of the special commands read and print described later. The symbol && (||) causes the list following it to be executed only if the preceding pipeline returns a zero (non-zero) value. An arbitrary number of new-lines can appear in a list, instead of semicolons, to delimit commands.

A command is either a simple-command or one of the following. Unless otherwise stated, the value returned by a command is that of the last simple-command executed in the command.

for identifier [in word ...] do list done
> Each time for is executed, identifier is set to the next word taken from the in word list. If in word ... is omitted, for executes the do list once for each positional parameter set (see Parameter Substitution below). Execution ends when there are no more words in the list.

select identifier [in word...] do list done
> A select command prints on standard error (file descriptor 2), the set of words, each preceded by a number. If in word ... is omitted, the positional parameters are used instead (see Parameter Substitution below). The PS3 prompt is printed and a line is read from the standard input. If this line consists of the number of one of the listed words, the value of the parameter identifier is set to the word corresponding to this number. If this line is empty, the selection list is printed again. Otherwise the value of the parameter identifier is set to null. The contents of the line read from standard input is saved in the parameter REPLY. The list is executed for each selection until a break or end-of-file (eof) is encountered.

case word in [[(] pattern [|pattern] ...) list ;;] ... esac
> A case command executes the list associated with the first pattern that matches word. The form of the patterns is identical to that used for file name generation (see File Name Generation below).

if list then list [elif list then list] ... [else list]fi
> The list following if is executed and, if it returns a

zero exit status, the list following the first then is executed. Otherwise, the list following elif is executed and, if its value is zero, the list following the next then is executed. Failing that, the else list is executed. If no else list or then list is executed, if returns a zero exit status.

while list do list done

until list do list done
> A while command repeatedly executes the while list, and if the exit status of the last command in the list is zero, executes the do list; otherwise the loop terminates. If no commands in the do list are executed, while returns a zero exit status; until can be used in place of while to negate the loop termination test.

(list)
> Execute list in a separate environment. If two adjacent open parentheses are needed for nesting, a space must be inserted to avoid arithmetic evaluation as described below.

{ list;}
> Execute list, but not in a separate environment. Note that { is a keyword and requires a trailing blank to be recognized.

[[expression]]
> Evaluates expression and returns a zero exit status when expression is true. See Conditional Expressions below, for a description of expression. Note that [[and]] are keywords and require blanks between them and expression.

function identifier {list;}

identifier () {list;}
> Define a function referred to by identifier. The body of the function is the list of commands between { and } (see Functions below).

time pipeline   pipeline is executed and the elapsed time, user time, and system time are printed on standard error.

The following keywords are recognized only as the first word of a command and when not quoted:

    if then else elif fi case esac for while until do done { }
    function select time [[ ]]

Comments
A word beginning with # causes that word and all subsequent characters up to a new-line to be ignored.

Aliasing
The first word of each command is replaced by the text of an alias, if an alias for this word has been defined. An alias name consists of any number of characters excluding metacharacters, quoting characters, file expansion characters, parameter and command substitution characters, and =. The replacement string can contain any valid shell script, including the metacharacters listed above. The first word of each command in the replaced text, other than any that are in the process of being replaced, is tested for additional aliases. If the last character of the alias value is a blank, the word following the alias is also checked for alias substitution. Aliases can be used to redefine special built-in commands, but cannot be used to redefine the

keywords listed above. Aliases can be created, listed, and exported
with the alias command and can be removed with the unalias command.
Exported aliases remain in effect for subshells but must be
reinitialized for separate invocations of the shell (see Invoking ksh
below).

Aliasing is performed when scripts are read, not while they are
executed. Therefore, for it to take effect, alias must be executed
before the command referring to the alias is read.

Aliases are frequently used as a shorthand for full path names. An
option to the aliasing facility allows the value of the alias to be
automatically set to the full path name of the corresponding command.
These aliases are called tracked aliases. The value of a tracked
alias is defined the first time the identifier is read and becomes
undefined each time the PATH variable is reset. These aliases remain
tracked so that the next reference redefines the value. Several
tracked aliases are compiled into the shell. The -h option of the set
command converts each command name that is an identifier into a
tracked alias.

The following exported aliases are compiled into the shell but can be
unset or redefined:

```
autoload='typeset -fu'
false='let 0'
functions='typeset -f'
hash='alias -t -'
history='fc -l'
integer='typeset -i'
nohup='nohup '
r='fc -e -'
stop='kill -STOP'
suspend='kill -STOP $$'
true=':'
type='whence -v'
```

Tilde Substitution
  After alias substitution is performed, each word is checked to see if
  it begins with an unquoted ~. If it does, the word up to a / is
  checked to see if it matches a user name in the /etc/passwd file. If
  a match is found, the ~ and the matched login name are replaced by the
  login directory of the matched user. This is called a tilde
  substitution. If no match is found, the original text is left
  unchanged. A ~, alone or before a /, is replaced by the value of the
  HOME parameter. A ~ followed by a + or - is replaced by the value of
  the parameter PWD and OLDPWD, respectively. In addition, tilde
  substitution is attempted when the value of a parameter assignment
  begins with a ~.

Command Substitution
  The standard output from a command enclosed in parenthesis preceded by
  a dollar sign ($(command)) or a pair of back single quotes (accent
  grave) (`command`) can be used as part or all of a word; trailing
  new-lines are removed. In the second (archaic) form, the string
  between the quotes is processed for special quoting characters before
  the command is executed (see Quoting below). The command substitution
  $(cat file) can be replaced by the equivalent but faster $(<file).
  Command substitution of most special commands (built-ins) that do not
  perform I/O redirection are carried out without creating a separate
  process. However, command substitution of a function creates a
  separate process to execute the function and all commands (built-in or
  otherwise) in that function.

  An arithmetic expression enclosed in double parenthesis preceded by a
  dollar sign ($((expression))) is replaced by the value of the

arithmetic expression within the double parenthesis (see Arithmetic Evaluation below for a description of arithmetic expressions).

Parameter Substitution

A parameter is an identifier, one or more digits, or any of the characters *, @, #, ?, -, $, and !. A named parameter (a parameter denoted by an identifier) has a value and zero or more attributes. Named parameters can be assigned values and attributes by using the typeset special command. Attributes supported by ksh are described later with the typeset special command. Exported parameters pass values and attributes to the environment.

The shell supports a limited one-dimensional array facility. An element of an array parameter is referenced by a subscript. A subscript is denoted by a [followed by an arithmetic expression (see Arithmetic Evaluation below) followed by a]. To assign values to an array, use set -A name value .... The value of all subscripts must be in the range of 0 through 1023. Arrays need not be declared. Any reference to a named parameter with a valid subscript is legal and an array is created if necessary. Referencing an array without a subscript is equivalent to referencing the first element.

The value of a named parameter can also be assigned by writing:

        name=value [name=value] ...

If the -i integer attribute is set for name, the value is subject to arithmetic evaluation as described below.

Positional parameters, parameters denoted by a number, can be assigned values with the set special command. Parameter $0 is set from argument zero when the shell is invoked.

The character $ is used to introduce substitutable parameters.

${parameter}	Substitute the value of the parameter, if any. Braces are required when parameter is followed by a letter, digit, or underscore that should not be interpreted as part of its name or when a named parameter is subscripted. If parameter is one or more digits, it is a positional parameter. A positional parameter of more than one digit must be enclosed in braces. If parameter is * or @ all the positional parameters, starting with $1, are substituted (separated by a field separator character). If an array identifier with subscript * or @ is used, the value for each element is substituted (separated by a field separator character). The shell reads all the characters from ${ to the matching } as part of the same word even if it contains braces or metacharacters.
${#parameter}	If parameter is * or @, the number of positional parameters is substituted. Otherwise, the length of the value of the parameter is substituted.
${#identifier[*]}	Substitute the number of elements in the array identifier.
${parameter:-word}	If parameter is set and is non-null, substitute its value; otherwise substitute word.

${parameter:=word}   If parameter is not set or is null, set it to
                       word; then substitute the value of the
                       parameter. Positional parameters cannot be
                       assigned in this way.

${parameter:?word}   If parameter is set and is non-null,
                       substitute its value; otherwise, print word
                       and exit from the shell. If word is omitted,
                       a standard message is printed.

${parameter:+word}   If parameter is set and is non-null,
                       substitute word; otherwise substitute
                       nothing.

${parameter#pattern}

${parameter##pattern}
                       If the shell pattern matches the beginning of
                       the value of parameter, the value of this
                       substitution is the value of the parameter
                       with the matched portion deleted; otherwise
                       the value of this parameter is substituted.
                       In the former case, the smallest matching
                       pattern is deleted; in the latter case, the
                       largest matching pattern is deleted.

${parameter%pattern}

${parameter%%pattern}
                       If the shell pattern matches the end of the
                       value of parameter, the value of parameter
                       with the matched part is deleted; otherwise
                       substitute the value of parameter. In the
                       former, the smallest matching pattern is
                       deleted; in the latter, the largest matching
                       pattern is deleted.

In the above, word is not evaluated unless it is used as the
substituted string. Thus, in the following example, pwd is
executed only if d is not set or is null:

echo ${d:-$(pwd)}

If the colon (:) is omitted from the above expressions, the shell
only checks to determine whether or not parameter is set.

The following parameters are set automatically by the shell:

    #   The number of positional parameters in decimal.
    -              Options supplied to the shell on invocation or by
                   the set command.
    ?   The decimal value returned by the last executed
                   command.
    $ The process number of this shell.
    _   Initially, the value of _ is an absolute pathname
                   of the shell or script being executed as passed in
                   the environment. Subsequently it is assigned the
                   last argument of the previous command. This
                   parameter is not set for commands which are
                   asynchronous. This parameter is also used to hold
                   the name of the matching MAIL file when checking
                   for mail.
    !   The process number of the last background command
                   invoked.
    COLUMNS   If this variable is set, its value is used to
                   define the width of the edit window for the shell

	edit modes and for printing select lists. In a windowed environment, if the shell detects that the window size has changed, the shell updates the value of COLUMNS.
ERRNO	The value of errno as set by the most recently failed system call. This value is system dependent and is intended for debugging purposes.
LINENO	The line number of the current line within the script or function being executed.
LINES	If this variable is set, the value is used to determine the column length for printing select lists. select lists print vertically until about two-thirds of LINES lines are filled. In a windowed environment, if the shell detects that the window size has changed, the shell updates the value of LINES.
OLDPWD	The previous working directory set by the cd command.
OPTARG	The value of the last option argument processed by the getopts special command.
OPTIND	The index of the last option argument processed by the getopts special command.
PPID	The process number of the parent of the shell.
PWD	The present working directory set by the cd command.
RANDOM	Each time this parameter is evaluated, a random integer, uniformly distributed between 0 and 32767, is generated. The sequence of random numbers can be initialized by assigning a numeric value to RANDOM.
REPLY	This parameter is set by the select statement and by the read special command when no arguments are supplied.
SECONDS	Each time this parameter is referenced, the number of seconds since shell invocation is returned. If this parameter is assigned a value, the value returned upon reference is the value that was assigned plus the number of seconds since the assignment.

The following parameters are used by the shell:

CDPATH	The search path for the cd command.
EDITOR	If the value of this variable ends in emacs, gmacs, or vi and the VISUAL variable is not set, the corresponding option is turned on (see set in Special Commands below).
ENV	If this parameter is set, parameter substitution is performed on the value to generate the path name of the script to be executed when the shell is invoked (see Invoking ksh below). This file is typically used for alias and function definitions.
FCEDIT	The default editor name for the fc command.
FPATH	The search path for function definitions. This path is searched when a function with the -u attribute is referenced and when a command is not found. If an executable file is found, then it is read and executed in the current environment.
IFS	Internal field separators, normally space, tab, and new-line that are used to separate command words resulting from command or parameter substitution, and for separating words with the special command read. The first character of the IFS parameter is used to separate arguments for

	the "$*" substitution (see Quoting below).
HISTFILE	If this parameter is set when the shell is invoked, its value is the path name of the file that is used to store the command history. The default value is $HOME/.sh_history. If the user has appropriate privileges and no HISTFILE is given, then no history file is used (see Command Re-entry below).
HISTSIZE	If this parameter is set when the shell is invoked, the number of previously entered commands accessible to this shell will be greater than or equal to this number. The default is 128.
HOME	The default argument (home directory) for the cd command.
MAIL	If this parameter is set to the name of a mail file and the MAILPATH parameter is not set, the shell informs the user of arrival of mail in the specified file.
MAILCHECK	This variable specifies how often (in seconds) the shell checks for changes in the modification time of any of the files specified by the MAILPATH or MAIL parameters. The default value is 600 seconds. When the time has elapsed the shell checks before issuing the next prompt.
MAILPATH	A list of file names separated by colons (:). If this parameter is set, the shell informs the user of any modifications to the specified files that have occurred within the last MAILCHECK seconds. Each file name can be followed by a ? and a message to be printed, in which case the message undergoes parameter and command substitution with the parameter $_ defined as the name of the changed file. The default message is you have mail in $_.
PATH	The search path for commands (see Execution below). The user cannot change PATH if executing rksh (except in the .profile file).
PS1	The value of this parameter is expanded for parameter substitution, to define the primary prompt string which, by default, is $ followed by a space character. The character ! in the primary prompt string is replaced by the command number (see Command Re-entry below). To include a ! in the prompt, use !!.
PS2	Secondary prompt string, by default > followed by a space character.
PS3	Selection prompt string used within a select loop, by default #? followed by a space character.
PS4	The value of this variable is expanded for parameter substitution and precedes each line of an execution trace. If PS4 is unset, the execution trace prompt is + followed by a space character.
SHELL	The path name of the shell is kept in the environment. When invoked, the shell is restricted if the value of this variable contains an r in the basename.
TMOUT	If set to a value greater than zero, the shell terminates if a command is not entered within the prescribed number of seconds after issuing the PS1 prompt.
VISUAL	Invokes the corresponding option when the value of this variable ends in emacs, gmacs, or vi (see set in Special Commands below).

The shell gives default values to PATH, PS1, PS2, MAILCHECK, TMOUT,

and IFS. HOME, SHELL, ENV, and MAIL are never set automatically by
the shell (although HOME, SHELL, and MAIL are set by login(1)).

Blank Interpretation
After parameter and command substitution, the results of substitution
are scanned for field separator characters (found in IFS), and split
into distinct arguments where such characters are found. ksh retains
explicit null arguments (or '') but removes implicit null arguments
(those resulting from parameters that have no values).

File Name Generation
Following substitution, each command word is processed as a pattern
for file name expansion unless the -f option has been set. The form
of the patterns is the Pattern Matching Notation defined by regexp(5).
The word is replaced with sorted file names matching the pattern. If
no file name is found that matches the pattern, the word is left
unchanged.

In addition to the notation described in regexp(5), ksh recognizes
composite patterns made up of one or more pattern lists separated from
each other with a |. Composite patterns can be formed with one or
more of the following:

?(pattern-list)	Optionally matches any one of the given patterns.
*(pattern-list)	Matches zero or more occurrences of the given patterns.
+(pattern-list)	Matches one or more occurrences of the given patterns.
@(pattern-list)	Matches exactly one of the given patterns.
!(pattern-list)	Matches anything, except one of the given patterns.

Quoting
Each of the metacharacters listed above (See Definitions above) has a
special meaning to the shell and causes termination of a word unless
quoted. A character can be quoted (i.e., made to stand for itself) by
preceding it with a \. The pair \new-line is ignored. All characters
enclosed between a pair of single quote marks (''), are quoted. A
single quote cannot appear within single quotes. Inside double quote
marks (""), parameter and command substitution occurs and \ quotes the
characters \, `, ", and $. $* and $@ have identical meanings when not
quoted or when used as a parameter assignment value or as a file name.
However, when used as a command argument, "$*" is equivalent to
"$1d$2d...", where d is the first character of the IFS parameter,
whereas "$@" is equivalent to "$1" "$2" .... Inside back single quote
(accent grave) marks (``) \ quotes the characters \, `, and $. If the
back single quotes occur within double quotes, \ also quotes the
character ".

The special meaning of keywords or aliases can be removed by quoting
any character of the keyword. The recognition of function names or
special command names listed below cannot be altered by quoting them.

Arithmetic Evaluation
The ability to perform integer arithmetic is provided with the special
command let. Evaluations are performed using long arithmetic.
Constants take the form [base#]n, where base is a decimal number
between two and thirty-six representing the arithmetic base and n is a
number in that base. If base is omitted, base 10 is used.

An arithmetic expression uses the same syntax, precedence, and

associativity of expression of the C language. All the integral
operators, other than ++, --, ?:, and , are supported. Variables can
be referenced by name within an arithmetic expression without using
the parameter substitution syntax. When a variable is referenced, its
value is evaluated as an arithmetic expression.

An internal integer representation of a variable can be specified with
the -i option of the typeset special command. Arithmetic evaluation
is performed on the value of each assignment to a variable with the -i
attribute. If you do not specify an arithmetic base, the first
assignment to the variable determines the arithmetic base. This base
is used when parameter substitution occurs.

Since many of the arithmetic operators require quoting, an alternative
form of the let command is provided. For any command beginning with
((, all characters until the matching)) are treated as a quoted
expression. More precisely, ((...)) is equivalent to let "...".

Prompting
  When used interactively, the shell prompts with the value of PS1
  before reading a command. If at any time a new-line is typed and
  further input is needed to complete a command, the secondary prompt
  (the value of PS2) is issued.

Conditional Expressions.
  A conditional expression is used with the [[compound command to test
  attributes of files and to compare strings. Word splitting and file
  name generation are not performed on the words between [[and]].
  Each expression can be constructed from one or more of the following
  unary or binary expressions:

-a file	True if file exists.
-b file	True if file exists and is a block special file.
-c file	True if file exists and is a character special file.
-d file	True if file exists and is a directory.
-f file	True if file exists and is an ordinary file.
-g file	True if file exists and is has its setgid bit set.
-h file	True if file exists and is a a symbolic link.
-k file	True if file exists and is has its sticky bit set.
-n string	True if length of string is non-zero.
-o option	True if option named option is on.
-p file	True if file exists and is a fifo special file or a pipe.
-r file	True if file exists and is readable by current process.
-s file	True if file exists and has size greater than zero.
-t fildes	True if file descriptor number fildes is open and associated with a terminal device.
-u file	True if file exists and is has its setuid bit set.
-w file	True if file exists and is writable by current process.
-x file	True if file exists and is executable by current process. If file exists and is a directory, the current process has permission to search in the directory.
-z string	True if length of string is zero.
-H file	True if file exists and is a hidden directory (see cdf(4)).

`-L file`	True if file exists and is a symbolic link.
`-O file`	True if file exists and is owned by the effective user ID of this process.
`-G file`	True if file exists and its group matches the effective group ID of this process.
`-S file`	True if file exists and is a socket.
`file1 -nt file2`	True if file1 exists and is newer than file2.
`file1 -ot file2`	True if file1 exists and is older than file2.
`file1 -ef file2`	True if file1 and file2 exist and refer to the same file.
`string = pattern`	True if string matches pattern.
`string != pattern`	True if string does not match pattern.
`string1 < string2`	True if string1 comes before string2 based on ASCII value of their characters.
`string1 > string2`	True if string1 comes after string2 based on ASCII value of their characters.
`exp1 -eq exp2`	True if exp1 is equal to exp2.
`exp1 -ne exp2`	True if exp1 is not equal to exp2.
`exp1 -lt exp2`	True if exp1 is less than exp2.
`exp1 -gt exp2`	True if exp1 is greater than exp2.
`exp1 -le exp2`	True if exp1 is less than or equal to exp2.
`exp1 -ge exp2`	True if exp1 is greater than or equal to exp2.

A compound expression can be constructed from these primitives by using any of the following, listed in decreasing order of precedence.

`(expression)`	True, if expression is true. Used to group expressions.
`! expression`	True if expression is false.
`expression1 && expression2`	True, if expression1 and expression2 are both true.
`expression1 || expression2`	True, if either expression1 or expression2 is true.

Input/Output

Before a command is executed, its input and output can be redirected using a special notation interpreted by the shell. The following can appear anywhere in a simple-command or can precede or follow a command and are not passed on to the invoked command. Command and parameter substitution occurs before word or digit is used, except as noted below. File name generation occurs only if the pattern matches a single file and blank interpretation is not performed.

`<word`	Use file word as standard input (file descriptor 0).
`>word`	Use file word as standard output (file descriptor 1). If the file does not exist, it is created. If the file exists, and the noclobber option is on, an error occurs; otherwise, the file is truncated to zero length.
`>|word`	Sames as >, except that it overrides the noclobber option.
`>>word`	Use file word as standard output. If the file exists, output is appended to it (by first searching for the end-of-file); otherwise, the file is created.

<>word   Open file word for reading and writing as standard
                            input. If the file does not exist it is created.

<<[-]word   The shell input is read up to a line that matches
                            word, or to an end-of-file. No parameter
                            substitution, command substitution, or file name
                            generation is performed on word. The resulting
                            document, called a here-document, becomes the
                            standard input. If any character of word is
                            quoted, no interpretation is placed upon the
                            characters of the document. Otherwise, parameter
                            and command substitution occurs, \new-line is
                            ignored, and \ must be used to quote the
                            characters \, $, `, and the first character of
                            word. If - is appended to <<, all leading tabs
                            are stripped from word and from the document.

<&digit   The standard input is duplicated from file
                            descriptor digit (see dup(2)).

>&digit   The standard output is duplicated to file
                            descriptor digit (see dup(2)).

<&-   The standard input is closed.

>&-   The standard output is closed.

<&p   The input from the co-process is moved to standard
                            input.

>&p   The output to the co-process is moved to standard
                            output.

If one of the above is preceded by a digit, the file descriptor number
cited is that specified by the digit (instead of the default 0 or 1).
For example:

     ... 2>&1

means file descriptor 2 is to be opened for writing as a duplicate of
file descriptor 1.

Redirection order is significant because the shell evaluates
redirections referencing file descriptors in terms of the currently
open file associated with the specified file descriptor at the time of
evaluation. For example:

     ... 1>fname 2>&1

first assigns file descriptor 1 (standard output) to file fname, then
assigns file descriptor 2 (standard error) to the file assigned to
file descriptor 1; i.e., fname. On the other hand, if the order of
redirection is reversed as follows:

     ... 2>&1 1>fname

file descriptor 2 is assigned to the current standard output (user
terminal unless a different assignment is inherited). File descriptor
1 is then reassigned to file fname without changing the assignment of
file descriptor 2.

The input and output of a co-process can be moved to a numbered file
descriptor allowing other commands to write to them and read from them
using the above redirection operators. If the input of the current
co-process is moved to a numbered file descriptor, another co-process

can be started.

If a command is followed by & and job control is inactive, the default standard input for the command is the empty file /dev/null. Otherwise, the environment for the execution of a command contains the file descriptors of the invoking shell as modified by input/output specifications.

Environment
The environment (see environ(5)) is a list of name-value pairs passed to an executed program much like a normal argument list. The names must be identifiers and the values are character strings. The shell interacts with the environment in several ways. When invoked, the shell scans the environment and creates a parameter for each name found, gives it the corresponding value, and marks it export. Executed commands inherit the environment. If the user modifies the values of these parameters or creates new ones by using the export or typeset -x commands, the values become part of the environment. The environment seen by any executed command is thus composed of any name-value pairs originally inherited by the shell whose values can be modified by the current shell, plus any additions which must be noted in export or typeset -x commands.

The environment for any simple-command or function can be augmented by prefixing it with one or more parameter assignments. A parameter assignment argument takes the form identifier=value. For example,

    TERM=450 cmd args

and

    (export TERM; TERM=450; cmd args)

are equivalent (as far as the above execution of cmd is concerned except for special commands listed below that are preceded by a dagger).

If the -k option is set, all parameter assignment arguments are placed in the environment, even if they occur after the command name. The following echo statement prints a=b c. After the -k option is set, the second echo statement prints only c:

    echo a=b c
    set -k
    echo a=b c

This feature is intended for use with scripts written for early versions of the shell, and its use in new scripts is strongly discouraged. It is likely to disappear someday.

Functions
The function keyword (described in the Commands section above) is used to define shell functions. Shell functions are read and stored internally. Alias names are resolved when the function is read. Functions are executed like commands, with the arguments passed as positional parameters (see Execution below).

Functions execute in the same process as the caller except that command substitution of a function creates a new process. Functions share all files and present working directory with the caller. Traps caught by the caller are reset to their default action inside the function. If a function does not catch or specifically ignore a trap condition, the function terminates and the condition is passed on to the caller. A trap on EXIT set inside a function is executed after the function completes in the environment of the caller. Ordinarily, variables are shared between the calling program and the function.

However, the typeset special command used within a function defines local variables whose scope includes the current function and all functions it calls.

The special command return is used to return from function calls. Errors within functions return control to the caller.

Function identifiers can be listed with the +f option of the typeset special command. Function identifiers and the associated text of the functions can be listed with the -f option. Functions can be undefined with the -f option of the unset special command.

Ordinarily, functions are unset when the shell executes a shell script. The -xf option of the typeset command allows a function to be exported to scripts that are executed without reinvoking the shell. Functions that must be defined across separate invocations of the shell should be placed in the ENV file.

Jobs

If the monitor option of the set command is turned on, an interactive shell associates a job with each pipeline. It keeps a table of current jobs, printed by the jobs command, and assigns them small integer numbers. When a job is started asynchronously with &, the shell prints a line resembling:

    [1] 1234

indicating that job number 1 was started asynchronously and had one (top-level) process whose process ID was 1234.

If you are running a job and want to do something else, type the suspend character (usually ^Z (Ctrl-Z)) to send a STOP signal to the current job. The shell then indicates that the job has been `Stopped', and prints another prompt. The state of this job can be manipulated by using the bg command to put it in the background, running other commands (while it is stopped or running in the background), and eventually restarting or returning the job to the foreground by using the fg command. A ^Z takes effect immediately and resembles an interrupt, since pending output and unread input are discarded when ^Z is typed.

A job run in the background stops if it tries to read from the terminal. Background jobs normally are allowed to produce output, but can be disabled by giving the stty tostop command. If the user sets this tty option, background jobs stop when trying to produce output.

There are several ways to refer to jobs in the shell. A job can be referred to by the process ID of any process in the job or by one of the following:

%number	The job with the given number.
%string	Any job whose command line begins with string.
%?string	Any job whose command line contains string.
%%	Current job.
%+	Equivalent to %%.
%-	Previous job.

The shell learns immediately when a process changes state. It informs the user when a job is blocked and prevented from further progress, but only just before it prints a prompt.

When the monitor mode is on, each background job that completes triggers any trap set for CHLD.

Attempting to leave the shell while jobs are running or stopped produces the warning, You have stopped (running) jobs. Use the jobs command to identify them. An immediate attempt to exit again terminates the stopped jobs; the shell does not produce a warning the second time.

Signals

The INT and QUIT signals for an invoked command are ignored if the command is followed by & and the monitor option is off. Otherwise, signals have the values inherited by the shell from its parent, with the exception of signal 11 (but see also the trap command below).

Execution

Substitutions are made each time a command is executed. If the command name matches one of the Special Commands listed below, it is executed within the current shell process. Next, ksh checks the command name to determine whether it matches one of the user-defined functions. If it does, ksh saves the positional parameters and then sets them to the arguments of the function call. The positional parameter 0 is set to the function name. When the function completes or issues a return, ksh restores the positional parameter list and executes any trap set on EXIT within the function. The value of a function is the value of the last command executed. A function is executed in the current shell process. If a command name is not a special command or a user-defined function, ksh creates a process and attempts to execute the command using exec (see exec(2)).

The shell parameter PATH defines the search path for the directory containing the command. Alternative directory names are separated by a colon (:). The default path is /usr/bin: (specifying /usr/bin and the current directory in that order). Note that the current directory is specified by a null path name which can appear immediately after the equals sign, between colon delimiters, or at the end of the path list. The search path is not used if the command name contains a /. Otherwise, each directory in the path is searched for an executable file. If the file has execute permissions but is not a directory or an executable object code file, it is assumed to be a script file, which is a file of data for an interpreter. If the first two characters of the script file are #!, exec (see exec(2)) expects an interpreter path name to follow. exec then attempts to execute the specified interpreter as a separate process to read the entire script file. If a call to exec fails, /usr/bin/ksh is spawned to interpret the script file. All non-exported aliases, functions, and named parameters are removed in this case. If the shell command file does not have read permission, or if the setuid and/or setgid bits are set on the file, the shell executes an agent to set up the permissions and execute the shell with the shell command file passed down as an open file. A parenthesized command is also executed in a sub-shell without removing non-exported quantities.

Command Re-entry

The text of the last HISTSIZE (default 128) commands entered from a terminal device is saved in a history file. The file $HOME/.sh_history is used if the HISTFILE variable is not set or writable. A shell can access the commands of all interactive shells that use the same named HISTFILE. The special command fc is used to list or edit a portion of this file. The portion of the file to be edited or listed can be selected by number or by giving the first character or characters of the command. A single command or range of

commands can be specified. If no editor program is specified as an
argument to fc, the value of the FCEDIT parameter is used. If FCEDIT
is not defined, /usr/bin/ed is used. The edited command is printed
and re-executed upon leaving the editor. The editor name - is used to
skip the editing phase and to re-execute the command. In this case a
substitution parameter of the form old=new can be used to modify the
command before execution. For example, if r is aliased to fc -e -,
typing r bad=good c re-executes the most recent command that starts
with the letter c and replaces the first occurrence of the string bad
with the string good.

umask

umask - Display or set creation mask.

```
umask(1)                                                              umask(1)

NAME
      umask - set or display the file mode creation mask

SYNOPSIS

    Set Mask:
     umask mask

    Display Mask:
     umask [-S]

DESCRIPTION
      The umask command sets the value of the file mode creation mask or
      displays the current one.  The mask affects the initial value of the
      file mode (permission) bits for subsequently created files.

   Setting the File Mode Creation Mask
      The umask mask command sets a new file mode creation mask for the
      current shell execution environment.  mask can be a symbolic or
      numeric (obsolescent) value.

      A symbolic mask provides a flexible way of modifying the mask
      permission bits individually or as a group.  A numeric mask specifies
      all the permission bits at one time.

      When a mask is specified, no output is written to standard output.

      Symbolic Mask Value

      A symbolic mask replaces or modifies the current file mode creation
      mask.  It is specified as specified as a comma-separated list of
      operations in the following format.  Whitespace is not permitted.

          [who][operator][permissions][,...]

      The fields can have the following values:

          who            One or more of the following letters:


                              u    Modify permissions for user (owner).
                              g    Modify permissions for group.
                              o    Modify permissions for others.

                         Or:


                              a    Modify permissions for all (a = ugo).


          operator       One of the following symbols:
```

```
                              +     Add permissions to the existing mask for
                                    who.
                              -     Delete permissions from the existing
                                    mask for who.
                              =     Replace the existing mask for who with
                                    permissions.


           permissions    One or more of the following letters:


                              r     The read permission.
                              w     The write permission.
                              x     The execute/search permission.
```

If one or two of the fields are omitted, the following table applies:

Format Entered	Effect	Input	Equals
who	Delete current permissions for who	g	g=
operator	No action	-	(none)
permissions	Equal to: a+permissions	rw	a+rw
who=	Delete current permissions for who	u=	u=
who+	No action	u+	(none)
who-	No action	u-	(none)
whopermissions	Equal to: who=permissions	ux	u=x
operatorpermissions	Equal to: aoperatorpermissions	-rw	a-rw

Numeric Mask Value (Obsolescent)

A numeric mask replaces the current file mode creation mask. It is
specified as an unsigned octal integer, constructed from the logical
OR (sum) of the following mode bits (leading zeros can be omitted):

```
           0400  ( a=rwx,u-r)  Read by owner
           0200  ( a=rwx,u-w)  Write by owner
           0100  ( a=rwx,u-x)  Execute (search in directory) by owner
           0040  ( a=rwx,g-r)  Read by group
           0020  ( a=rwx,g-w)  Write by group
           0010  ( a=rwx,g-x)  Execute/search by group
           0004  ( a=rwx,o-r)  Read by others
           0002  ( a=rwx,o-w)  Write by others
           0001  ( a=rwx,o-x)  Execute/search by others
```

Displaying the Current Mask Value

To display the current file mode creation mask value, use one of the
commands:

```
           umask -S      Print the current file mode creation mask in a
                         symbolic format:

                             u=[r][w][x],g=[r][w][x],o=[r][w][x]

                         The characters r (read), w (write), and x
                         (execute/search) represent the bits that are clear
                         in the mask for u (user/owner), g (group), and o
                         (other).  All other bits are set.

           umask         Print the current file mode creation mask as an
                         octal value.

                         The zero bits in the numeric value correspond to
                         the displayed r, w, and x permission characters in
```

the symbolic value. The one bits in the numeric
value correspond to the missing permission
characters in the symbolic value.

Depending on implementation, the display consists
of one to four octal digits; the first digit is
always zero (see DEPENDENCIES). The rightmost
three digits (leading zeros implied as needed)
represent the bits that are set or clear in the
mask.

Both forms produce output that can be used as the mask argument to set
the mask in a subsequent umask command.

General Operation
When a new file is created (see creat(2)), each bit that is set in the
file mode creation mask causes the corresponding permission bit in the
the file mode to be cleared (disabled). Conversely, bits that are
clear in the mask allow the corresponding file mode bits to be enabled
in newly created files.

For example, the mask u=rwx,g=rx,o=rx (022) disables group and other
write permissions. As a result, files normally created with a file
mode shown by the ls -l command as -rwxrwxrwx (777) become mode -
rwxr-xr-x (755); while files created with file mode -rw-rw-rw- (666)
become mode -rw-r--r-- (644).

Note that the file creation mode mask does not affect the set-user-id,
set-group-id, or "sticky" bits.

The file creation mode mask is also used by the chmod command (see
chmod(1)).

Since umask affects the current shell execution environment, it is
generally provided as a shell regular built-in (see DEPENDENCIES.

If umask is called in a subshell or separate utility execution
environment, such as one of the following:

        (umask 002)
        nohup umask ...
        find . -exec umask ...

it does not affect the file mode creation mask of the calling
environment.

The default mask is u=rwx,g=rwx,o=rwx (000).

RETURN VALUE
umask exits with one of the following values:

        0   The file mode creation mask was successfully changed or no
             mask operand was supplied.

        >0   An error occurred.

EXAMPLES
In these examples, each line show an alternate way of accomplishing
the same task.

Set the umask value to produce read and write permissions for the
file's owner and read permissions for all others (ls -l displays -rw-
r--r-- on newly created files):

        umask u=rwx,g=rx,o=rx   symbolic mode

```
     umask a=rx,u+w          symbolic mode
     umask 022               numeric mode
```

Set the umask value to produce read, and write permissions for the
file's owner, read-only for others users in the same group, and no
access to others (-rw-r-----):

```
     umask a-rwx,u+rw,g+r     symbolic mode
     umask 137               numeric mode
```

Set the umask value to deny read, write, and execute permissions to
everyone (----------):

```
     umask a=                symbolic mode
     umask 777               numeric mode
```

Add the write permission to the current mask for everyone (there is no
equivalent numeric mode):

```
     umask a+w               symbolic mode
```

WARNINGS
     If you set a mask that prevents read or write access for the user
     (owner), many programs, such as editors, that create temporary files
     will fail because they cannot access the file data.

DEPENDENCIES
     The umask command is implemented both as a separate executable file
     (/usr/bin/umask) and as built-in shell commands.

  POSIX Shell and Separate File
     All features are supported (see sh-posix(1). The numeric mask display
     uses a minimum of two digits.

  Korn Shell
     The -S option is not supported in the Korn shell built-in command (see
     ksh(1). The numeric mask display uses a minimum of two digits.

  C Shell
     The -S option and symbolic mask values are not supported in the C
     shell built-in command (see csh(1). The numeric mask display uses a
     minimum of one digit.

  Bourne Shell
     The -S option and symbolic mask values are not supported in the Bourne
     shell built-in command (see sh-bourne(1). The numeric mask display
     always consists of four digits.

SEE ALSO
     chmod(1), csh(1), ksh(1), sh-posix(1), sh(1), chmod(2), creat(2),
     umask(2).

STANDARDS CONFORMANCE
     umask: SVID2, SVID3, XPG2, XPG3, XPG4, POSIX.2

CHAPTER 23

Introduction to Shell Programming

Shell Programming

There is much more to a shell than meets the eye. The shell can do much more than the command-line interpreter everyone is used to using. UNIX shells actually provide a powerful interpretive programming language as well.

In this chapter, we'll cover **ksh** shell programming. I chose **ksh** because most **ksh** programming techniques work with the Bourne shell as well. There is a follow-on to **ksh** programming at the end of the chapter for **csh** because the **csh** employs some different programming techniques than the **ksh**.

We'll cover the most important **ksh** programming techniques. The climax of this chapter is a fairly sophisticated shell program to remove files and place them in a directory, rather than just permanently removing files from the system with **rm**. This program employs all the shell programming techiques covered in the chapter. This shell program, called **trash**, with some minor modifications, can be run in the Bourne shell as well.

The shell is one of the most powerful and veratile features on any UNIX system. If you can't find the right command to accomplish a task, you can probably build it quite easily using a shell script.

The best way to learn shell programming is by example. There are many examples given in this chapter. Some serve no purpose other than to demonstrate the current topic. Most, however, are useful tools or parts of tools that you can easily expand and adapt into your environment. The examples provide easy-to-understand prompts and output messages. Most examples show what is needed to provide the functionality we are after. They do not do a great deal of error checking. From my experience, however, it only takes a few minutes to get a shell program to do what you want; it can take hours to handle every situation and every error condition. Therefore, these programs are not very dressed up (maybe a sport coat versus a tuxedo). I'm giving you what you need to know to build some useful tools for your environment. I hope that you will have enough knowledge and interest by the time we get to the end of this chapter to learn and do more.

Most of the examples in this chapter were performed on a Solaris system; however, shells are nearly identical going from one system to another, so you should be able to get the programs in this chapter running on your system quickly.

Steps to Create Shell Programs

When you craft a shell program, there are some initial steps you want to perform so that you have consistency among all of your programs. The following is a list of some important concepts to employ with your shell programs:

1. **Names of shell programs and their output** - You should give your shell programs and their output a meaningful name. If you call your shell programs *script1, script2,* and so on, these will not have any meaning for you and other potential users of the programs. If your shell program finds files of a particular

type, then you can name the program *filefind* or some other descriptive name. Do the same with the output of shell programs. Don't call the output of a shell program *output1* if there is some descriptive name you can give it such as *filefind.out*. Also avoid naming shell programs and their output names that already exist. You may use commands such as **read** and **test**, so you may create confusion and conflicts if you were to give your program and their output the same names. The first shell program in this chapter shows today's date. If we were to name the program **date**, we would actually run the system **date** command as opposed to our shell program **date**. The reason is that in most cases, the system **date** command would be found before our shell program **date** file.

2. **Repository for shell programs** - If you plan to produce numerous shell programs, you may want to place them in a directory. You can have a directory in your home directory called **bin** or **shellprogs**, in which all programs are located. You can then update your path to include the directory name where your shell programs are located.

3. **Specify shell to execute program** - The very first line of the program specifies the shell to be used to execute the program. The path of the shell is preceeded by **#!**, which is a "magic number" that indicates that the path of the shell is about to follow. The shell programs in this chapter use the **ksh** path.

4. **Formatting of shell programs** - Do not underestimate the importance of proper formatting to enhance the readability of shell programs. You should indent areas of the program to indicate that commands are part of a group. Indenting only three or four spaces is fine for groups of commands. You may also want to set autoindent in **vi** so that the next line starts at the same point as the previous line (try **:set ai** in **vi** to see how this technique works). You can break up long lines by placing a \ (backslash) at the end of one line and continue the command on the next line.

5. **Comments** - Include detailed comments in your shell program. You can write paragraphs of comments to describe what

an upcoming section of your program will accomplish. These will help you understand your program when you look at it months or years after having originally created it as well as help others understand the program. No limit exists on the amout of comments you can include. Start comment lines with a # (pound sign).

6. **Make the shell program executable** - The **chmod** command covered in the previous chapters introducing various shells is used to make your program executable.

Following the previous list of recommendations will make creating and using shell programs more efficient. Now we need to cover the types of shell programs.

A shell program is simply a file containing a set of commands you wish to execute sequentially. The file needs to be set with execute permissions so that you can execute it just by typing the name of the script.

There are two basic forms of shell programs exist:

1. **Simple command files** - When you have a command line or set of command lines that you use over and over, you can use one simple command to execute them all.

2. **Structured programs** - The shell provides much more than the ability to "batch" together a series of commands. It has many of the features that any higher-level programming language contains:

   • Variables for storing data

   • Decision-making controls (the **if** and **case** commands)

   • Looping abilities (the **for** and **while** loops)

   • Function calls for modularity

Given these two basic forms you can build everything from simple command replacements to much larger and more complex data manipulation and system administration tools.

ksh Programming

I have created a directory in my home directory called **shellprogs** to serve as a repository for my shell programs. In order to execute these programs without having to specify an absolute path, I have updated my path in **.profile** to include the following line:

```
export PATH=${PATH}:~shellprogs
```

This adds **/home/martyp/shellprogs** to my path assuming colon is the delimiter, which is usually the case. After updating **.profile** you can log out and log in to update your path. You can issue the command below to confirm that your path has indeed been updated to include the directory in which you keep your shell programs:

```
martyp $ echo $PATH
/usr/bin:/usr/ucb:/etc:.:/home/martyp/shellprogs
martyp $
```

Let's now go to the **shellprogs** directory and type a simple command file called **today**:

```
#!/bin/ksh
# This is a simple command file to display today's date.
echo "Today's date is"
date +%x
```

Before we look at each line in the program, let's run it to see the output:

man page

ls - 15

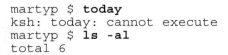
```
martyp $ today
ksh: today: cannot execute
martyp $ ls -al
total 6
```

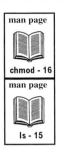

man page

chmod - 16

man page

ls - 15

```
drwxrwxr-x    2 martyp      staff        512 May 21 09:53 .
drwxrwx---    4 martyp      staff        512 May 21 09:25 ..
-rw-rw-r--    1 martyp      staff        100 May 21 09:54 today
martyp $ chmod +x today
martyp $ ls -al
total 6
drwxrwxr-x    2 martyp      staff        512 May 21 09:53 .
drwxrwx---    4 martyp      staff        512 May 21 09:25 ..
-rwxrwxr-x    1 martyp      staff        100 May 21 09:54 today
martyp $ today
Today's date is
05/21/99
martyp $
```

We could not execute **today** because the file was created without execute permissions, which we confirm by performing a long listing. We then add execute permission to the file with **chmod +x**, which is confirmed with the next long listing. We are then able to execute **today** and view its results.

man page

umask - 22

The **umask** discussion in each of the earlier shell chapters describes the defaults for new files. Almost invariably, new files are created without execute permission; therefore, you will have to update the permissions on the file to include execute.

Let's now walk through this simple shell program and analyze each line.

```
#!/bin/ksh
```

man page

ksh -22

The first line specifies that the **ksh** will be used. If you are using Bash, C shell, or any other shell, you would specify its location in this manner. Some systems have multiple versions of shells running on them. It may be that a shell has been updated since the last release and some users may want to maintain the old version of the shell. For this reason, you want to be sure that the absolute path you specify is indeed that of the shell you wish to use. Note that the **#!** must be the very first two characters in the file.

Normally, when you run a shell program, the system tries to execute commands using the same shell you are using for your interactive command lines. If we don't include this line, someone running a shell other than the **ksh** might have unexpected results when trying to run one of our programs.

man page

ksh - 22

As a good practice, you should include **#!shellname** as the first line of every shell program you write.

Let's now view the next line of our program:

```
# This is a simple command file to display today's date.
```

These are comments. Everything after a # in a command line is considered a comment (**#!** on the first line is the one very big exception). Keep in mind my early remarks about including comments liberally. It is a great pleasure to share a well commented shell program with a friend, knowing that you have adequately documented the program with comments.

Here is the next command:

```
echo "Today's date is"
```

The **echo** command generates prompts and messages in shell programs. See the **echo** manual entry to see all the options available with **echo** for formatting your output. We commonly enclose the string to be displayed in double quotes. In this case, we did because we needed to let the shell know that the apostrophe was part of the string and not a single quote that needs a match.

Next is the last command in our program:

```
date +%x
```

This executes the **date** command. There are indeed many options to the **date** command, some of which are not intuitive. In this case, we use one of the simplest forms of the command, which simply produces today's date.

Let's cover one more example of a command file that you may find useful. This program informs you of the present working directory and then produces a long listing of the files in the directory. The following is a listing of the shell program **myll**:

```
#!/bin/ksh
# This is a simple shell program that displays the current
# directory name before a long file listing (ll) of that
# directory.
# The script name is myll
echo "Long listing of directory:"
pwd
echo
ll -l
```

man page

ls - 15

This program uses **ll**; you may need to use **ls -al**. The following is what **myll** looks like when it runs:

```
martyp $ myll
Long listing of directory:
/home/martyp/shellprogs

total 4
-rwxrwxr-x    1 martyp    staff      220 May 24 05:28 myll
-rwxrwxr-x    1 martyp    staff      100 May 21 09:54 today
martyp $
```

This name of the present working directory is **/home/martyp/ shellprogs**. A long listing of the contents of this directory shows the two programs we have covered so far in this chapter.

Before we can produce more complex shell programs, we need to learn more about some of the programming features built into the shell. Let's start with shell variables.

Shell Variables

A shell variable is similar to a variable in any programming language. A variable is simply a name you give to a storage location. Unlike most languages, however, you never have to declare or initialize your variables; you just use them.

Shell variables can have just about any name that starts with a letter (uppercase or lowercase). To avoid confusion with special shell characters (like file name generation characters), keep the names simple and use just letters, numbers, and underscore (_).

To assign values to shell variables, you simply type the following:

```
name=value
```

Note that there are no spaces before and after the = character.

Here are some examples of setting shell variables from the command line. These examples work correctly:

```
$ myname=ralph
$ HerName=mary
```

This one does not work because of the space after "his":

```
$ his name=norton
his: not found
```

The shell assumes that "his" is a command and tries to execute it. The rest of the line is ignored.

This example contains an illegal character (+) in the name:

```
$ one+one=two
one+one=two: not found
```

A variable must start with a letter. A common mistake is to give a variable a name that makes perfect sense to you but does not start with a letter. The following example uses a variable that starts with a number:

```
$ 3word=hi
3word=hi: not found
```

The "3" causes a "not found" to be produced when we attempt to assign this variable.

Now that we can store values in our variables, we need to know how to use those values. The dollar sign ($) is used to get the value of a variable. Any time the shell sees a $ in the command line, it assumes that the characters immediately following it are a variable name. It replaces the *$variable* with its value. Here are some simple examples using variables at the command line:

```
$ myname=ralph
$ echo myname
myname
$ echo $myname
ralph
$ echo $abc123
```

In the first **echo** command, there is no $, so the shell ignores **myname**, and **echo** gets **myname** as an argument to be echoed. In the second **echo**, however, the shell sees the $, looks up the value of **myname,** and puts it on the command line. Now **echo** sees **ralph** as its argument (not **myname** or **$myname**). The final **echo** statement is similar, except that we have not given a value to **abc123** so the shell assumes that it has no value and replaces **$abc123** with nothing. Therefore, echo has no arguments and echos a blank line.

There may be times when you want to concatenate variables and strings. This is very easy to do in the shell:

```
$ myname=ralph
$ echo "My name is $myname"
My name is ralph
```

There may be times when the shell can become confused if the variable name is not easily identified in the command line:

```
$ string=dobeedobee
$ echo "$stringdoo"
```

We wanted to display "dobeedobee," but the shell thought the variable name was stringdoo, which had no value. To accomplish this we can use curly braces around the variable name to separate it from surrounding characters:

```
$ echo "${string}doo"
dobeedobeedoo
```

You can set variables in shell programs in the same way, but you might also like to do things such as save the output of a command in a variable so that we can use it later. You may want to ask users a question and read their response into a variable so that you can examine it.

Command Substitution

Command substitution allows us to save the output from a command (**stdout**) into a shell variable. To demonstrate this, let's take another look at how our "today" example can be done using command substitution.

```
#!/bin/ksh
d=`date +%x`
echo "Today's date is $d"
```

The back quotes (') around the **date** command tell the shell to execute date and place its output on the command line. The output will then be assigned to the variable **d**. We'll name this updated script **today1** and run it:

```
$ today1
Today's date is 05/24/00
```

We could also have done this task without using the variable **d**. We could have just included the **date** command in the echo string, as shown in the **today2** script shown in the following example:

```
#!/bin/ksh
echo "Today's date is 'date +%x'"
```

When we run this program, we see exactly the same output as we did with **today1**:

```
$ today2
Today's date is 05/24/00
```

We'll use shell variables and command substitution extensively in some of the upcoming examples. Let's now cover reading user input.

Reading User Input

The most common way to get information from the user is to prompt him or her and then read the response. The **echo** command is most commonly used to display the prompt; then the **read** command is used to read a line of input from the user (standard input). Words from the input line can be assigned to one or several shell variables.

Here is an example with comments to show you how **read** can be used:

```
#!/bin/ksh
# program: readtest
echo "Please enter your name: \c"     # the \c leaves cursor on
                                       # this line.

read name       # I have no $ because we are doing an assignment
                # of whatever the user enters into name.

echo "Hello, $name"

echo "Please enter your two favorite colors: \c"

read color1 color2        # first word goes into color1
                          # remainder of line goes into color2

echo "You entered $color2 and $color1"
```

If we ran this program, it would look something like this:

```
$ readtest
Please enter your name: gerry
Hello, gerry
Please enter your two favorite colors: blue green
You entered green and blue
$
```

Notice how the **read** command assigned the two words entered for colors into the two respective color variables. If the user entered fewer words than the **read** command was expecting, the remaining variables are set to null. If the user enters too many words, all extra words entered are assigned into the last variable. This technique is how you can get a whole line of input into one variable. Here's an example of what happens whn you enter more than two colors:

```
$ readtest
Please enter your name: gerry
Hello, gerry
Please enter your two favorite colors: chartreuse orchid
blue You entered orchid blue and chartreuse
$
```

The program took the last two colors entered and assigned them to *color2*. For this reason, you have to be careful of what a user may enter with the read command and how you map that information to variables.

You may have a built-in variable used with **read** called *REPLY.* With *REPLY,* a line of input is assigned to the variable *REPLY.* I tend not to use this often because I don't like to leave anything to chance. I normally explicitly name a variable to which input is assigned. The following example shows the listing and running of **readtest1**, which includes a line that contains only the **read** command, the response of which is assigned to *REPLY*:

man page

cat - 17

```
martyp $cat readtest1

#!/bin/ksh
# program: readtest
echo "Please enter your name: \c"        # the \c leaves cursor on
                                         # this line.

read name       # I have no $ because we are doing an assignment
                # of whatever the user enters into name.

echo "Hello, $name"

echo "Please enter your two favorite colors: \c"

read color1 color2        # first word entered goes into color1
                          # remainder of line goes into color2

echo "You entered $color2 and $color1"
echo "Where are you from?"
read                                      # read response into $REPLY
echo "I'm sure $REPLY is great"


martyp $ readtest1
Please enter your name: MARTY
Hello, MARTY
Please enter your two favorite colors: RED BLUE
You entered BLUE and RED
Where are you from?
MANY DIFFERENT PLACES
I'm sure MANY DIFFERENT PLACES is great
martyp $
```

You can see in this example that the response I typed of "MANY DIFFERENT PLACES" was indeed read into *REPLY.*

Although **echo** is used throughout this chapter, you may also see **print** used to display lines on the screen.

Arguments to Shell Programs

Shell programs can have command-line arguments just like any regular command. Command-line arguments that you use when you invoke your shell program are stored in a special set of variables. These are called the positional parameters.

The first ten words on the command line are directly accessible in the shell program using the special variables **$0-$9**. This is how they work:

$0	The command name
$1	The first argument
$2	The second argument
$3	.
	.
	.
$9	The ninth argument

If you are not sure how many command line arguments you may get when your program is run, there are two other variables that can help:

$#	The number of command-line arguments
$*	A space-separated list of all the command-line arguments (which does not include the command name)

The variable **$*** is commonly used with the **for** loop (soon to be explained) to process shell script command lines with any number of arguments.

Let's now take the **myll** we worked with earlier and modify it to produce a long listing of the directory that we specify when we run the program. Figure 23-1 shows the modified **myll**:

```
#!/bin/ksh
# This is a simple shell program that takes one command line
# argument (a directory name) and then displays the full pathname
# of that directory before doing a long file listing (ll) on
# it.
#
# The script name is myll
cd $1
echo "Long listing of the `pwd` directory:"
echo
ls -l
```

Figure 23-1 **myll** Shell Program

If we run **myll** with a directory name, the script changes directory, echoes the message containing the full path name (notice the command substitution), and then executes the **ls -l** command.

Note that the **cd** in the **myll** program will change only the working directory of the script; it does not affect the working directory of the shell from which we run **myll**.

```
martyp $ myll /tmp
Long listing of the /tmp directory:

total 2384
-rw-------    1 root     sys        265228 Feb 22 15:21 dtdbcache_:0
-rw-r--r--    1 root     sys         70829 Feb 23 10:44 g
-rw-r--r--    1 root     sys         13642 Feb 23 10:48 i
-rw-rw-rw-    1 root     root        14071 May 24 06:10 license_log
-rwxr-xr-x    1 chrisb   users         317 Apr 20 17:38 ls
-rw-rw-r--    1 root     sys          4441 Mar 25 14:37 mwaps7454
-rw-rw-rw-    1 anne     users        4341 May 20 13:56 ps23974
-rw-r--r--    1 rodt     users        4218 Apr 14 11:17 ps3358
-rw-r--r--    1 rodt     users        4763 Feb 24 07:23 ps6465
-rw-rw-r--    1 root     sys          4446 Mar 25 14:31 ps7036
-rw-rw-r--    1 root     sys          4442 Mar 25 14:35 ps7138
-rw-rw-r--    1 root     sys          4446 Mar 25 14:35 ps7215
-rw-rw-r--    1 root     sys          4498 Mar 25 14:36 ps7342
```

```
-rw-rw-r--   1 root     sys          4446 Mar 25 14:38 ps7622
-rw-rw-r--   1 root     sys          4615 Mar 25 15:30 ps7812
-rw-rw-r--   1 root     sys          5728 Feb 18 11:09 ps_data
-rw-r--r--   1 root     sys             0 Apr 26 10:50 sh20890.1
-rw-r--r--   1 root     sys             0 Apr 26 10:50 sh20891.1
-rw-r--r--   1 root     sys             0 Apr 26 10:51 sh20978.1
-rw-r--r--   1 root     sys             0 Apr 26 10:51 sh20979.1
-rw-r--r--   1 chrisb   users        5325 Mar 26 13:42 sman_9664
-rw-rw-r--   1 root     sys        295996 Mar  1 10:15 ups_data
drwx------   2 root     other          69 Mar  9 11:37 whatis.11526
drwx------   2 root     other          69 Mar  9 11:37 whatis.11686
drwx------   2 root     other          69 Mar  9 11:38 whatis.11853
drwx------   2 root     other          69 Mar  9 11:38 whatis.12014
-rw-r--r--   1 root     sys        354221 Feb 23 10:49 x
-rw-r--r--   1 chrisb   users           0 Feb 23 14:39 xx
martyp $
```

In this case, we could give **myll** no argument and it would still work properly. If we don't provide any command-line arguments, then **$1** will be null, so nothing goes on the command line after **cd**. This will make **cd** take us to our home directory and perform the **ll** there.

man page

cd - 16

If we provide more than one argument, only the first is used and any others are ignored.

If we use a command-line argument, it *must* be a directory name; otherwise, the **cd** command fails and the script terminates with a "bad directory" error message. Later I will show how to test for valid directory names and file names so that you can work around potential errors.

A more complex example can be used to build new versions of the **ps** command. Below are two examples that use command line arguments and command substitution to help you with your process management.

man page

ps - 13

The **psg** shell program in Figure 23-2 is handy for searching through what is typically a long process status listing to find only cer-

grep - 19

tain commands or user processes. These examples use **grep**. **grep** finds all lines that contain the pattern for which you are searching.

```
#!/usr/bin/sh
# Program name: psg
# Usage: psg some_pattern
#
# This program searches through a process status (ps -ef)
# listing for a pattern given as the first command-line
# argument.
procs=`ps -ef`                         # Get the process listing
head=`echo "$procs" | line`            # Take off the first line (the
                                       # headings)
echo "$head"                           # Write out the headings
echo "$procs" | grep -i $1 | grep -v $0 # Write out lines
        # containing $1 but not this program's command line

# Note that $procs MUST be quoted or the newlines in the ps
# -ef listing will be turned into spaces when echoed. $head
# must also be quoted to preserve any extra white space.
```

Figure 23-2 **psg** Shell Program

Here's what **psg** looks like when it runs. In this example, we want to look at all the Korn shells running on the system.

```
martyp $ psg ksh
    UID    PID  PPID  C    STIME TTY      TIME CMD
   root   2954  2936  0  Feb 22 ?        0:01 /bin/ksh /usr/dt/bin/Xsession
   root   3002  2999  0  Feb 22 pts/2    0:01 -ksh -c       unset DT;      DISPLg
   root   3067     1  0  Feb 22 ?        0:00 /bin/ksh /usr/dt/bin/sdtvolcheckm
  jnola  11516 11514  0   May 11 pts/3   0:01 -ksh
 martyp  29291 29289  0 09:30:04 pts/4   0:02 -ksh
```

ps - 13

This program also works to find the terminal, process ID, parent process ID, start date, and any other information from **ps**.

As a user, you may start processes that you wish to stop. You may, for instance, start an application that does not come up on your display. You can identify the process with **psg** and then use the next program to stop the process, provided that you have the rights to stop the process.

The **gkill** shell program in Figure 23-3 searches through a **ps -ef** listing for a pattern (just like **psg**); then it kills all listed processes. The examples use the **cut** command, which allows you to specify a range of columns to retain.

man page

cut - 18

```
#!/usr/bin/sh
# Program name: gkill
# Usage: gkill some_pattern
# This program will find all processes that contain the
# pattern specified as the first command line argument then
# kills those processes.
# get the process listing
procs=`ps -ef`
echo "The following processes will be killed:"
# Here we list the processes to kill. We don't kill this
# process
echo "$procs" | grep -i $1 | grep -v $0
# Allow the user a chance to cancel.
echo "\nPress Return to continue Ctrl-C to exit"
# If the user presses Ctrl-C the program will exit.
# Otherwise this read waits for the next return character and
# continue.
read junk
# find the pattern and cut out the pid field
pids=`echo "$procs" | grep -i $1 | grep -v $0 | cut -c9-15`
# kill the processes
kill $pids
```

Figure 23-3 **gkill** Shell Program

If we don't provide any command-line arguments, **grep** issues an error and the program continues. In the next section, we will learn how to check if **$1** is set and how to gracefully clean up if it's not.

man page

grep - 19

Let's now start a process in the background, use the **psg** program to identify the process number, and then use **gkill** to stop the process:

man page

find - 20

```
martyp $ find / -name .c > cprogs 2>&1 &
[1]     29683
martyp $ psg find
     UID   PID  PPID  C    STIME TTY        TIME CMD
   martyp 29683 29579  7 13:54:19 pts/4     0:02 find / -name .c
martyp $ gkill 29683
The following processes will be killed:
   martyp 29683 29579 10 13:54:19 pts/4     0:03 find / -name .c

Press Return to continue Ctrl-C to exit

martyp $
```

man page

find - 20

man page

kill - 22

When we start the **find** command, we are given its process number. To be sure we don't **kill** the wrong process, I checked for all of the **find** programs running with **psg**. When I was sure of the process number to **kill**, I used **psg** to **kill** the process.

Although the shell programs in this section were simple, they employed many important shell programming techniques. Let's now move to testing and branching, which are some of the most powerful aspects of shell programming.

Testing and Branching

Decision-making is one of the shell's most powerful features. You have two ways to check conditions and branch to a piece of code that can handle that condition.

For example, you may want to ask the user a question and then check whether the answer was yes or no. You may also want to check whether a file exists before you operate on it. In either case, you can use the **if** command to accomplish the task. Here are a few shell script segments that explain each part of the **if** command:

```
echo "Continue? \c"
read ans
if [ "$ans" = "n" ]
then
      echo "Goodbye"
      exit
fi
```

The **echo** and **read** provide a prompt and response, as usual. The **if** statement executes the next command, and if it succeeds, it executes any commands between the **then** and the **fi** (**if** spelled backwards).

Note that the \c in the **echo** command suppresses the new line that **echo** normally generates. This action leaves the cursor on the line immediately after the "Continue? " prompt. This is commonly used when prompting for user input.

The **test** command is the most common command to use with the **if** command. The ["$ans" = "n"] is the **test** command. It performs many types of file, string, and numeric logical tests, and if the condition is true, the test succeeds.

The syntax of the **test** command requires spaces around the [ ] or you will get a syntax error when the program runs. Also notice the double quotes around the response variable **$ans**. These are a strange anomaly with the **test** command. If the user presses only [[RETURN]] at the prompt without typing any other character, the value of **$ans** will be null. If we didn't have the quote marks around **$ans** in the **test** command, it would look like this when the value of **$ans** was substituted into the **test** command:

```
[ = "n" ]
```

This generates a "test: argument expected" error when you run the program. This is a very common mistake, and if you ever get this error, you should look for variables in your **test** commands with null values.

There is another form of the **if** command that is very common. It allows you to do one thing if a condition is met or do something else if not:

```
if [    ]          # if some condition is true
then
                   # do something
else
                   # otherwise do this
fi
```

There are many conditions that the **test** command can test. Table 23-1 shows some of the more common conditions for which you can test.

TABLE 23-1   **test** Command Conditions

String tests:

["$a" == "string"]	True if $a is equal to "string"
["$a" != "string"]	True if $a is NOT equal to "string"
[-z "$a"]	True if $a is null (zero characters)
[-n "$a"]	True if $a is NOT null

Numeric tests:

[$x -eq 1]	True if $x is equal to 1
[$x -ne 1]	True if $x is NOT equal to 1
[$x -lt 1]	True if $x is less than 1
[$x -gt 1]	True if $x is greater than 1
[$x -le 1]	True if $x is less than or equal to 1
[$x -ge 1]	True if $x is greater than or equal to 1

File tests:

[-d $file]	True if $file is a directory
[-f $file]	True if $file is a file
[-s $file]	True if $file is a file with > 0 bytes
[-r $file]	True if $file is readable
[-w $file]	True if $file is writable
[-x $file]	True if $file is executable

Tests can be combined using -*a* to logically "AND" the tests together, -*o* to logically "OR" two tests, and *!* to "negate" a test. For example, this test statement is true only if the **$interactive** variable is set to true or **$file** is a directory:

```
[ "$interactive" = "TRUE" -o -d $file ]
```

This will be used in some of the upcoming example programs.

Here is a useful extension to the **gkill** program earlier shown. It checks to see that we have exactly one command-line argument before the program will attempt to do the processing. It uses a numeric test and the *$#* variable, which represents the number of command-line arguments. It should be inserted before any other lines of code in the **gkill** example given above:

```
# If we don't have exactly one command-line argument,
# write an error and exit.
if [ $# -ne 1 ]
then
      echo "Usage: $0 pattern"
      echo "Some pattern matching the processes to kill""
      echo "must be specified"
      exit 1 # Exit 1 terminates the program and tells the
             # calling shell that we had an error.
fi
```

Some other possible extensions to the **gkill** program might be to:

man page

kill - 22

- Allow the user to specify a signal to use with the **kill** command. For example:

  `gkill -9 ralph`

  would find all of ralph's processes and then kill them with **kill -9**.

- Make sure that a valid message is printed if we can't find any processes to kill using the specified pattern.

This same type of command-line check is easily applied to the **psg** program to make sure you that have exactly one argument representing the pattern for which to search.

When you are reading user input, you may want to check if the user entered a value at all. If not, you would provide a reasonable default value. This is easily done with a variable modifier.

This example reads an answer ("ans") from the user and then checks its value using an **if** command:

```
echo "Do you really want to remove all of your files? \c"
read ans
if [ ${ans:-n} == y ]
then
    rm -rf *
fi
```

The **${ans:-n}** statement checks the value of **$ans**. If there is a value in **$ans,** use it in the command line. If the user simply pressed [[RETURN]] at the prompt, **$ans** will be null. In this case, **${ans:-n}** will evaluate to *n* when we do the comparison. Basically, in one small statement it says, "if the user did not provide an answer, assume they meant *n*."

There is another modifier that is often used:

```
${var:=default}
```

It returns the value of **var** if it is set; it returns the default if **var** is not set, and it will also assign the default as the value of **var** for future use.

Making Decisions with the case Statement

The **case** statement is another way to make decisions and test conditions in shell programs. It is most commonly used to check for certain patterns in command-line arguments. For example, if you wanted to determine whether the first command-line argument is an option (starts with a -), the **case** statement is the easiest way to do so. The **case** statement is also used to respond to different user input (such as asking the user to select a choice from a menu).

The **case** statement is probably one of the most complicated shell commands because of its syntax:

```
case pattern_to_match in
        pattern1)   cmdA
                    cmdB
                ;;
        pattern2)  cmdC
                ;;
              ...
        *)  cmdZ
                ;;
esac
```

pattern_to_match is usually a shell variable that you are testing (like a command-line argument or a user response). If *pattern_to_match* matches *pattern1*, then commands *cmdA* and *cmdB* are executed. The **;;** separates this pattern's command list from the next pattern. In all cases, when **;;** is reached, the program jumps to the **esac** (**case** spelled backwards).

If *pattern_to_match* matches *pattern2*, then *cmdC* is executed and we jump to **esac**, the end of the **case** statement.

The * is provided so that if *pattern_to_match* did not match anything else, it will execute *cmdZ*. It's important to have a default action to handle the case where the user types an invalid entry.

For more robust pattern matching, any file name generation characters (*, [ ], ?) can be used to do special pattern matches. There is also a very useful way to check for multiple patterns in one line using the | symbol, which means logical "OR". Here's an example:

```
echo "Do you want to continue? (y/n) \c"
read ans
case $ans in
        y|Y) echo "Continuing"
             ...
           ;;
        n|N) echo "Done, Goodbye"
             exit
           ;;
        *) echo "Invalid input"
           ;;
esac
```

Here is another example where we are testing to see whether *$1* (the first command-line argument) is a valid option (a character we recognize that begins with a -):

```
case $1 in
        -l | -d) # Perform a listing
                echo "All files in $HOME:\n"
                ll -R $HOME | more
                ;;
        -i) # -i means set to an interactive flag to true
            interactive="TRUE"
                ;;
        *)  # Invalid input
            echo "$0: $1 is an invalid option"
            exit 1
            ;;
esac
```

A **case** statement is used in another example later in this chapter.

Looping

There are many times when you want to perform an action repeatedly. In the shell, there are two ways to do this:

1. The **for** loop takes a list of items and performs the commands in the loop once for each item in the list.

2. The **while** loop executes some commands (usually the **test** command) if that command executes successfully. (If the test condition is true, then the commands in the loop are executed, and the command is again executed to see whether we should loop again.)

The basic format of the **for** loop is:

```
for var in list_of_items
do
        cmdA
        cmdB
        cmdC
done
```

When the loop starts, the variable **var** has its value set to the first word in the *list_of_items* through which to loop. Then the three commands between the **do** and the **done** statements are executed. After the program reaches the **done** statement, it goes back to the top of the loop and assigns **var** to the next item in the list, executes the commands, and so on. The last time through the loop, the program continues with the next executable statement after the **done** statement.

The *list_of_items* can be any list of words separated by white space. You can type the words or use variables or command substitution to build the list. For example, let's say that we want to copy a new **.kshrc** file into the home directory of several users. A **for** loop is the easiest way to do so:

```
for name in ralph norton alice edith archie
do
        echo $name
        cp /tmp/.kshrc.new /users/$name/.kshrc
done
```

This example can be extended to copy certain files to several machines using the **rcp** command and verify that they got there using the **remsh** command:

```
for host in neptune jupiter mars earth sun
do
        echo $host
        rcp /etc/passwd /etc/hosts $host:/etc
        rcp /.profile $host:/.profile
        remsh $host ll /etc/passwd /etc/hosts /.profile
done
```

You can also process lists of files in the current directory using command substitution to generate the *list_of_items*:

```
for file in `ls`
do
     if [ -r $file ]
     then
            echo "$file is readable
     fi
done
```

Note that **for file in** * would have done the same thing.

man page

cat - 17

If you have a large list of things you would like to loop through and you don't want to type them on the command line, you can enter them in a file instead. Then, using the **cat** command and command substitution, you can generate the *list_of_items*:

```
for i in `cat important_files`
do
    # do something with each of the files listed in the
    # important_files file.
done
```

The **for** loop, however, is most commonly used to process the list of command line arguments (**$***):

```
for name in $*
do
    if [ ! -f $name -a ! -d $name ]
    then
      echo "$name is not a valid file or directory name"
    else
      # do something with the file or directory
    fi
done
```

The upcoming **trash** program contains a **for** loop that processes command-line arguments in a similar way.

The while Loop

The **while** loop has the following format:

```
while cmd1
do
        cmdA
        cmdB
        cmdC
done
```

cmd1 is executed first. If it executes successfully, then the commands between the **do** and the **done** statements are executed. **cmd1** is then executed again; if successful, the commands in the loop are executed again, and so on. When **cmd1** fails, the program jumps past the **done** statement and resumes execution with the next executable statement.

Most of the time, the command executed in place of **cmd1** is the **test** command. You can then perform logical tests as described in the **if** section. If the test succeeds (is true), the commands in the loop are executed and the script tests the condition again. The **while** loop is useful if you have a fixed number of times you want the loop to run or if you want something to happen until some condition is met.

Let's now take a look at an example of using **while**. We'll run the **netstat** command once every 30 seconds a total of ten times, looking for the output of our primary LAN interface. In the case of the Solaris system on which we are running, this will be *le0*. Keep in mind that your primary LAN interface may have a different name, almost surely if you are not using a Solaris system. Let's first take a look at our short program.

man page

netstat - 12

This program displays the primary LAN interface (*le0*) statistics, which may be *lan0* or some other name depending on the UNIX variant you are using, using **netstat** ten times, once every 30 seconds:

```
#!/bin/ksh
i=1
while [ $i -le 10 ]
do
        print $i
        netstat -i | grep le0
        sleep 30
        let i=i+1
done
```

We increment *i* in a very simple fashion by adding one to it each time through the loop. We evaluate the value of *i* every time through the loop to determine whether it is less than or equal to (*le*) ten. If so, we run **netstat -i**.

Before we run this program, called **net1**, let's run the **netstat -i** command to view its output, and then run **net1**. Please keep in mind that the **netstat** command varies greatly among UNIX variants, so your output may look much different.

```
martyp $ netstat -i
Name  Mtu   Net/Dest    Address      Ipkts      Ierrs  Opkts     Oerrs  Collis  Queue
lo0   8232  loopback    localhost    18927030   0      18927030  0      0          0
le0   1500  sunsys      sunsys       310417964  0      17193381  52064  7573173
sunsys:/home/martyp/shellprogs
martyp $ net1
1
le0   1500  sunsys      sunsys          310418018 0       17193388 52064 7573173
2
le0   1500  sunsys      sunsys          310418738 0       17193395 52064 7573173
3
le0   1500  sunsys      sunsys          310419579 0       17193401 52064 7573173
4
le0   1500  sunsys      sunsys          310420295 0       17193405 52064 7573173
5
le0   1500  sunsys      sunsys          310421099 0       17193446 52064 7573173
6
le0   1500  sunsys      sunsys          310421786 0       17193455 52064 7573173
7
le0   1500  sunsys      sunsys          310422425 0       17193462 52064 7573173
8
le0   1500  sunsys      sunsys          310423089 0       17193467 52064 7573173
9
le0   1500  sunsys      sunsys          310423749 0       17193471 52064 7573173
10
le0   1500  sunsys      sunsys          310424507 0       17193478 52064 7573173
sunsys:/home/martyp/shellprogs
martyp $
```

net1 produces just the output we want for *le0* every 30 seconds on our system, called *sunsys*. We also print out the value of *i* each time through the loop just so that we can see that we are incrementing it properly.

On HP-UX 11i systems the **netstat** command was modified to provide less information. The **lanadmin** command can be used to supply detailed information on *collisions* and *errors*. The following script runs **lanscan** to automatically produce a list of network interface cards on an 11i system and then produces a **lanadmin** output for each card.

```
#!/bin/sh
#@(#) $Header: $
#@(#) Description: Script to create network stats output with lanadmin
#@(#) $Source:  $
#@(#) $Locker: $
#@(#) $Log:  $
#@(#)
#  INPUT:
#  OUTPUT:
#  FILES ACCESSED:
```

```
#   NOTES:
#   AUTHOR:
#   REVISION HISTORY:
# Setup path
PATH=/bin:/usr/bin:/usr/sbin/:/usr/local/bin/;export PATH
#
# Determine OS Revision level
# run lanscan to determine network cards
#
OS_VERSION=$(uname -r | awk -F. '{print $2}')
if [ $OS_VERSION -lt 10 ]
then
   COMMAND1=/bin/landiag
else
   COMMAND1=/usr/sbin/lanadmin
fi
if [ -x $COMMAND1 ]
then
   COMMAND2=/usr/sbin/lanscan
   if [ -x  $COMMAND2 ]
   then
     if [ $OS_VERSION -lt 10 ]
     then
       for CARD in `ls -1 /dev/lan* | awk -F "/" '{print $3}'`
       do
         echo ""


$COMMAND1 -t <<- EOF 2> /dev/null | egrep "="
lan
name $CARD
display

quit
EOF
       done
#
# use field 3 of lanscan output to obtain card instance used for ppa below
#
     else
         for NMID in `$COMMAND2 | grep 0x | awk '{print $3}'`
         do
           echo ""


$COMMAND1 -t <<- EOF 2> /dev/null | egrep "="
lan
ppa $NMID
display

quit
EOF
         done
     fi
   else
     print
     print
     print "The command \"$COMMAND2\" is not executable"
     print "No data from \"$COMMAND1\" will be collected"
     print
     print
   fi
else
     print
     print
     print "The command \"$COMMAND1\" is not executable"
     print
   print
fi
```

Field three of **lanscan** is used to provide the *ppa* information to **lanadmin** as the card instance for which a **lanadmin** output will be produced. The following is the **lanscan** output and result of running the script on a system with five network cards that are *ppa 0* through *1*:

```
# lanscan

Hardware Station         Crd Hdw   Net-Interface  NM  MAC     HP-DLPI DLPI
Path     Address         In# State NamePPA         ID  Type    Support Mjr#
0/0/0/0     0x001083FEDCB7 0  UP    lan0 snap0     1   ETHER   Yes     119
0/4/0/0/4/0 0x001083F72ED0 1  UP    lan1 snap1     2   ETHER   Yes     119
0/4/0/0/5/0 0x001083F72E9B 2  UP    lan2 snap2     3   ETHER   Yes     119
0/4/0/0/6/0 0x001083F77E22 3  UP    lan3 snap3     4   ETHER   Yes     119
0/4/0/0/7/0 0x001083F71E59 4  UP    lan4 snap4     5   ETHER   Yes     119


# networkscript.sh

PPA Number                          = 0
Description                         = lan0 Hewlett-Packard 10/100 TX Half-Duplex  TT = 1500
Type (value)                        = ethernet-csmacd(6)
MTU Size                            = 1500
Speed                               = 10000000
Station Address                     = 0x1083fedcb7
Administration Status (value)       = up(1)
Operation Status (value)            = down(2)
Last Change                         = 10440
Inbound Octets                      = 0
Inbound Unicast Packets             = 0
Inbound Non-Unicast Packets         = 0
Inbound Discards                    = 0
Inbound Errors                      = 0
Inbound Unknown Protocols           = 0
Outbound Octets                     = 820
Outbound Unicast Packets            = 20
Outbound Non-Unicast Packets        = 0
Outbound Discards                   = 0
Outbound Errors                     = 0
Outbound Queue Length               = 0
Specific                            = 655367
Index                               = 1
Alignment Errors                    = 0
FCS Errors                          = 0
Single Collision Frames             = 0
Multiple Collision Frames           = 0
Deferred Transmissions              = 0
Late Collisions                     = 0
Excessive Collisions                = 0
Internal MAC Transmit Errors        = 0
Carrier Sense Errors                = 0
Frames Too Long                     = 0
Internal MAC Receive Errors         = 0

PPA Number                          = 1
Description                         = lan1 Hewlett-Packard 10/100 TX Full-Duplex  TT = 1500
Type (value)                        = ethernet-csmacd(6)
MTU Size                            = 1500
Speed                               = 100000000
Station Address                     = 0x1083f72ed0
Administration Status (value)       = up(1)
Operation Status (value)            = up(1)
Last Change                         = 11018
```

```
Inbound Octets                        = 2778542151
Inbound Unicast Packets               = 10008640
Inbound Non-Unicast Packets           = 14480929
Inbound Discards                      = 0
Inbound Errors                        = 0
Inbound Unknown Protocols             = 12443000
Outbound Octets                       = 3811379313
Outbound Unicast Packets              = 18378160
Outbound Non-Unicast Packets          = 50019
Outbound Discards                     = 0
Outbound Errors                       = 0
Outbound Queue Length                 = 0
Specific                              = 655367
Index                                 = 2
Alignment Errors                      = 0
FCS Errors                            = 0
Single Collision Frames               = 0
Multiple Collision Frames             = 0
Deferred Transmissions                = 0
Late Collisions                       = 0
Excessive Collisions                  = 0
Internal MAC Transmit Errors          = 0
Carrier Sense Errors                  = 0
Frames Too Long                       = 0
Internal MAC Receive Errors           = 0

PPA Number                            = 2
Description                           = lan2 Hewlett-Packard 10/100 TX Full-Duplex  TT = 1500
Type (value)                          = ethernet-csmacd(6)
MTU Size                              = 1500
Speed                                 = 100000000
Station Address                       = 0x1083f72e9b
Administration Status (value)         = up(1)
Operation Status (value)              = up(1)
Last Change                           = 12223
Inbound Octets                        = 1053052283
Inbound Unicast Packets               = 660
Inbound Non-Unicast Packets           = 14478087
Inbound Discards                      = 0
Inbound Errors                        = 0
Inbound Unknown Protocols             = 12442909
Outbound Octets                       = 5802138
Outbound Unicast Packets              = 43576
Outbound Non-Unicast Packets          = 43065
Outbound Discards                     = 0
Outbound Errors                       = 0
Outbound Queue Length                 = 0
Specific                              = 655367
Index                                 = 3
Alignment Errors                      = 0
FCS Errors                            = 0
Single Collision Frames               = 0
Multiple Collision Frames             = 0
Deferred Transmissions                = 0
Late Collisions                       = 0
Excessive Collisions                  = 0
Internal MAC Transmit Errors          = 0
Carrier Sense Errors                  = 0
Frames Too Long                       = 0
Internal MAC Receive Errors           = 0

PPA Number                            = 3
Description                           = lan3 Hewlett-Packard 10/100 TX Full-Duplex  TT = 1500
Type (value)                          = ethernet-csmacd(6)
MTU Size                              = 1500
Speed                                 = 100000000
Station Address                       = 0x1083f77e22
Administration Status (value)         = up(1)
Operation Status (value)              = up(1)
Last Change                           = 13428
Inbound Octets                        = 943616591
Inbound Unicast Packets               = 9064639
Inbound Non-Unicast Packets           = 765175
Inbound Discards                      = 0
Inbound Errors                        = 0
```

```
Inbound Unknown Protocols       = 39
Outbound Octets                 = 6454687
Outbound Unicast Packets        = 58769
Outbound Non-Unicast Packets    = 43040
Outbound Discards               = 0
Outbound Errors                 = 0
Outbound Queue Length           = 0
Specific                        = 655367
Index                           = 4
Alignment Errors                = 0
FCS Errors                      = 0
Single Collision Frames         = 0
Multiple Collision Frames       = 0
Deferred Transmissions          = 0
Late Collisions                 = 0
Excessive Collisions            = 0
Internal MAC Transmit Errors    = 0
Carrier Sense Errors            = 0
Frames Too Long                 = 0
Internal MAC Receive Errors     = 0

PPA Number                      = 4
Description                     = lan4 Hewlett-Packard 10/100 TX Full-Duplex  TT = 1500
Type (value)                    = ethernet-csmacd(6)
MTU Size                        = 1500
Speed                           = 100000000
Station Address                 = 0x1083f71e59
Administration Status (value)   = up(1)
Operation Status (value)        = up(1)
Last Change                     = 14633
Inbound Octets                  = 249984023
Inbound Unicast Packets         = 2628160
Inbound Non-Unicast Packets     = 765196
Inbound Discards                = 0
Inbound Errors                  = 0
Inbound Unknown Protocols       = 49
Outbound Octets                 = 3886863362
Outbound Unicast Packets        = 10894938
Outbound Non-Unicast Packets    = 425625
Outbound Discards               = 0
Outbound Errors                 = 0
Outbound Queue Length           = 0
Specific                        = 655367
Index                           = 5
Alignment Errors                = 0
FCS Errors                      = 0
Single Collision Frames         = 0
Multiple Collision Frames       = 0
Deferred Transmissions          = 0
Late Collisions                 = 0
Excessive Collisions            = 0
Internal MAC Transmit Errors    = 0
Carrier Sense Errors            = 0
Frames Too Long                 = 0
Internal MAC Receive Errors     = 0
```

Immediately before **lanscan** is run our script prints the *ppa* number so that we know the network interface card for which the **lanscan** output is produced.

For all five network cards in our example there are no collisions or errors, as shown near the end of each **lanadmin** output, however, these fields are produced by **lanadmin**.

The **while** loop can also be used to process command-line arguments one at a time, using the number of command-line arguments and the **shift** command:

```
while [ $# -ne 0 ]
do
    case $1 in
    -*) # $1 must be an option because it starts with -
        # Add it to the list of options:
        opts="$opts $1"
        ;;
     *) # $1 must be an argument. Add it to the list of
        # command-line arguments:
        args="$args $1"
        ;;
    esac
    shift
done
```

The **shift** command shifts the remaining arguments in **$*** to the left by one position and decrements **$#**. What was the first argument (**$1**) is now gone forever; what was in **$2** is now in **$1**, etc. In the process of shifting command-line arguments, **$#** is also decremented to accurately reflect the number of arguments left in **$***.

You may want some commands to run until the user stops the program or until some stop condition is met. An infinite **while** loop is the best way to do so. For example, let's say that we are prompting users for some input and we will continue to prompt them until they give us valid input:

```
while true
do
    # prompt users and get their response
    echo "Enter yes or no: \c"
    read ans

    # Check whether the response is valid
    if [ "$ans" == "yes" -o "$ans" == "no" ]
    then
    # If it is valid, stop the looping
    break
  else
    # Otherwise print an error message and try it again
    # from the top of the loop
    echo "Invalid input, try again!\n"
```

```
    fi
done
# Now that we have valid input, we can process the user's
# request
    .
    .
    .
```

true is a special command that always executes successfully. The loop does not terminate unless the user stops the program by killing it or until a **break** command is executed in the loop. The **break** command will stop the loop.

Shell Functions

As you write shell programs, you will notice that there are certain sets of commands appear in many places within a program. For example, several times in a script, you may check user input and issue an appropriate message if input is invalid. It can be tedious to type the same lines of code in your program numerous times. It can be a nuisance if you later want to change these lines.

Instead, you can you can put these commands into a shell function. Functions look and act like a new command that can be used inside the script. Here's an example of a basic shell function:

```
# This is a function that may be called from anywhere
within
# the program. It displays a standard usage error message
# and then exits the program.

print_usage()
{
    echo "Usage:"
    echo "To trash files: $0 [-i] files_to_trash..."
    echo "Display trashed files: $0 -d"
    echo "Remove all trashed files: $0 -rm"
    echo "Print this message: $0 -help"
    exit 1
}
```

print_usage is now a new command in your shell program. You can use it anywhere in this script.

Shell functions also have their own set of positional parameters (**$1-$9**, **$#**, and **$***), so you can pass them arguments just like any other command. The only nuance is that **$0** represents the name of the shell program, not the name of the function.

Earlier, we talked about arguments. When you type the name of the shell script, you can supply arguments that are saved in the variables **$1** through **$9**. The first ten words on the command line are directly accessible in the shell program using the special variables **$0-$9**. The following shows how they work:

$0	The command name
$1	The first argument
$2	The second argument
$3	.
	.
	.
$9	The ninth argument

If you are not sure how many command-line arguments you may get when your program is run, there are two other variables that can help:

$#	The number of command-line arguments
$*	A space-separated list of all of the command line arguments (which does *not* include the command name).

The variable **$*** is commonly used with a **for** loop to process shell script command lines with any number of arguments.

Figure 23-4 is a fairly complex program that exercises all the concepts we have covered so far. It is a **trash** program that removes files from their original locations. Instead of removing them permanently, it places them in a trash can in your home directory. This is a fairly robust program, but I'm sure that you can think of many extensions as you read through it.

```
#!/bin/ksh
# for Bourne use /bin/sh
# Program name: trash
# Usage:
#  To trash files:    trash [-i] file_names_to_trash ...
#  Display trashed files:    trash -d
#  Remove all trashed files: trash -rm
#  Print a help message:    trash -help
# This program takes any number of directory or file name
# arguments. If the argument is a file it will be removed
# from its current place in the file system and placed in the
# user's trash directory ($HOME/.trash). If the argument is a
# directory name the program will ask if the user really
# wants to trash the whole directory.
#
# This program also takes an -i (interactive) option. Like
# the rm command, if the -i is the first argument on the
# command line, the program stops and asks if each file
# named in the remaining arguments should be trashed.
#
# The -d (display) option shows the contents of the
# user's trashed files.
#
# The -help option displays a usage message for the user.
```

Figure 23-4   **trash** Shell Program

```
# The -rm (remove) option interactively
# asks the user if each file or directory in the trash
# directory should be removed permanently.
#
# The -h, -d and -rm options may not be used with
# any other command line arguments.

# Possible extensions:
# - Enhance the -rm option to remove a list of files
# from the trash directory from the command line.
# - Create a program to be run by cron once nightly to empty
# everyone's trash directory.

# This is a function that may be called from anywhere within
# the program. It displays a standard usage error message
# then exits the program.
print_usage()
{
  echo "Usage:"
  echo "To trash files: $0 [-i] file_names_to_trash ..."
  echo "Display trashed files:    $0 -d"
  echo "Remove all trashed files: $0 -rm"
  echo "Print this message:       $0 -help"
exit 1
}
# Make sure we have at least one command-line argument before
# we start.
if [ $# -lt 1 ]
then
     print_usage
fi

# If this flag is true then we need to do interactive
# processing.
interactive="FALSE"

# This is the name of the trash can.
trash_dir="$HOME/.trash"

# Make sure the trash directory exists before we go any
# further.
if [ ! -d $trash_dir ]
then
     mkdir $trash_dir
fi
# Sort out the command-line arguments.
case $1 in
   -help) # Print a help message.
      print_usage
      ;;
```

Figure 23-4   **trash** Shell Program (Continued)

```
-d | -rm) # a -d or -rm were given
        # If it was not the only command-line argument
        # then display a usage message and then exit.
        if [ $# -ne 1 ]
        then
            print_usage
        fi

        # Otherwise do the task requested.
        if [ $1 == "-d" ]
        then
            echo "The contents of $trash_dir:\n"
            ls -l -R $trash_dir | more
        else
            # remove all files from the trash directory
            rm -rf $trash_dir/*
            # get any dotfiles too
            rm -rf $trash_dir/.[!.]*
        fi

        # Now we can exit successfully.
        exit 0
        ;;
-i) # If the first argument is -i ask about each file as it
        # is processed.
        interactive="TRUE"
        # Take -i off the command line so we know that the
        # rest of the arguments are file or directory names.
        shift
        ;;
-*) # Check for an option we don't understand.
        echo "$1 is not a recognized option."
        print_usage
        ;;
    esac

# Just for fun we'll keep a count of the files that were
# trashed.
count=0

for file in $*
do
    # First make sure the file or directory to be renamed exists.
    # If it doesn't, add it to a list of bad files to be written
    # out later. Otherwise process it.
    if [ ! -f $file -a ! -d $file ]
    then
        bad_files="$bad_files $file"
    else
    # If we are in interactive mode ask for confirmation
    # on each file. Otherwise ask about directories.
```

Figure 23-4 **trash** Shell Program (Continued)

```
if [ "$interactive" = "TRUE" -o -d $file ]
then
    # Ask the user for confirmation (default answer is no).
    if [ -d $file ]
    then
       echo "Do you want to trash the dir $file ? (y/n) n\b\c"
    else
       echo "Do you really want to trash $file ? (y/n) n\b\c"
    fi
    read doit

    # If the user answered y then do the move.
    # Otherwise print a message that the file was not touched.
    if [ "${doit:-n}" = y ]
    then
        mv -i $file $trash_dir
        echo "$file was trashed to $trash_dir"
        let count=count+1
    # for Bourne use: count=`expr $count + 1`
    else
        echo "$file was not trashed"
    fi
  else # We are not in interactive mode, so just do it.
      mv -i $file $trash_dir
      let count=count+1
   #for Bourne use: count=`expr  $count + 1`
  fi
fi
done
echo "$0: trashed $count item(s)"
if [ -n "$bad_files" ]
then
    echo "The following name(s) do not exist and \c"
    echo "could not be trashed:"
    echo "$bad_files"
fi
exit 0
```

Figure 23-4 **trash** Shell Program (Continued)

Let's now run the **trash** program. The following example shows issuing just the program named **trash**, the next example shows issuing **trash -help**, the next example shows issuing **trash -i junk** to interactively remove the file **junk**, and the last example shows issuing **trash -d** to display files that have been removed with **trash** and are in the **/home/martyp/trash** directory:

```
martyp $ trash
Usage:
To trash files: trash [-i] file_names_to_trash ...
Display trashed files:    trash -d
Remove all trashed files: trash -rm
Print this message:       trash -help
martyp $ trash -help
Usage:
To trash files: trash [-i] file_names_to_trash ...
Display trashed files:    trash -d
Remove all trashed files: trash -rm
Print this message:       trash -help
martyp $ trash -i junk
Do you really want to trash junk ? (y/n) y
mv: overwrite /home/martyp/.trash/junk (yes/no)? yes
junk was trashed to /home/martyp/.trash
trash: trashed 1 item(s)
martyp $ trash -d
The contents of /home/martyp/.trash:

/home/martyp/.trash:
total 1364
-rw-------    1 martyp    staff       684808 May 30 05:31 core
-rwxrwxr-x    1 martyp    staff          631 May 30 06:45 file1
-rwxrwxr-x    1 martyp    staff           45 May 31 06:04 junk
martyp $
```

Notice that when we removed the file **junk**, **trash** asked us whether we wanted to overwrite a file by the same name that had been earlier removed with **trash** and placed in the **/home/martyp/trash** directory.

This program employs every concept we have covered in this shell programming chapter so far. You may want to take a close look at this program so that you can use these techniques in the programs you craft. I have also included comments for the lines that need to be changed to make this program work in the Bourne shell. The Korn-Shell and Bourne shell are very similar, so you can use most of the same techniques when writing programs for these two shells.

awk in Shell Programs

man page

awk - 19

awk is a very powerful symbolic programming language and data manipulation tool.

man page

grep - 19

Simply stated, **awk** searches for patterns in lines of input (from standard input or from a file). For each line that matches the specified pattern, it can perform some very complex processing on that line. The code to actually process matching lines of input is a cross between a shell script and a C program.

man page

cut - 18

Data manipulation tasks that would be very complex with combinations of **grep**, **cut,** and **paste** are very easily done with **awk**. Because **awk** is a programming language, it can also perform mathematical operations or check the input very easily, a task that is normally difficult with shells. It can even perform floating-point math.

man page

paste - 18

The basic form of an **awk** program looks like this:

```
awk '/pattern_to_match/ { program to run }' input_file_names
```

Notice that the whole program is enclosed in single quotes. If no input file names are specified, **awk** reads from standard input (as from a pipe).

The *pattern_to_match* must appear between the **/** (slash) characters. The pattern is actually called a regular expression. Some common regular expression examples are shown shortly.

The program to execute is written in **awk** code, which looks something like C. The program is executed whenever a line of input matches the *pattern_to_match*. If */pattern_to_match/* does not precede the program in **{ }**, then the program is executed for every line of input.

awk works with fields of the input lines. Fields are words separated by white space. The fields in **awk** patterns and programs are referenced with **$**, followed by the field number. For example, the second field of an input line is **$2**. If you are using an **awk** command in your shell programs, the fields (**$1**, **$2**, etc.) are not confused with the shell script's positional parameters, because the **awk** variables are enclosed in single quotes and the shell ignores them.

But I don't want to just talk about it. Let's take a look at some examples.

This simple example lists just the terminals that are active on your system in which the terminal name is the second field of a **who** listing:

```
who | awk '{ print $2 }'
```

Here is an example of running **who** and then running this one-line command:

```
martyp $ who
thomfsu     console        Feb 22 15:21   (:0)
martyp    pts/3          May 31 06:03  (atlm0216.atl.hp.com)
martyp $ who  | awk '{print $2}'
console
pts/3
martyp $
```

This output shows only the active terminals on the system.

Note that **cut** could have done this also, but you would have had to know exactly which columns the terminal name occupied in the **who** output, as shown below:

```
martyp $ who
thomfsu     console       Feb 22 15:21     (:0)
martyp           pts/3                  May  31  06:03
(atlm0216.atl.hp.com)
martyp $ who | cut -c12-20
console
pts/3
martyp $
```

If the user or terminal name is longer than normal in any line, this command does not work. The **awk** example will work because it looks at fields, not columns.

Some trivia to wow your friends with at your next cocktail party: **awk** is the first letter of the last names of its authors - Alfred Aho, Peter Weinberger, and Brian Kernighan.

man page

awk - 19

An HP-UX Logical Volume Manager Shell Program

In a section of Chapter 8 covering "Adding Disks," I provided an example of the HP-UX steps required to manually add a volume group consisting of five primary disks and five alternate disks. This manual procedure was done for one of ten volume groups. The remaining nine volume groups would have to be added using the same manual procedure, changing the names of the disks and volume groups as part of the manual procedure. Since manually performing these steps is highly error-prone, this is an ideal procedure to automate with a shell program.

To begin automating this procedure, let's take a look at the file that contains the physical disks to be used for the primary and alternate paths on the XP 256. The XP 256 is an advanced storage device that has in it the capability to failover to an alternate controller should the primary controller fail. The same sets of disks are connected to the primary and alternate controller but the disks are given two different sets of device files. One set is for the disks when connected to the primary controller and the second set is for the same disks when connected to the alternate controllers. This is the same concept that you may have encountered if you are a ServiceGuard user. There is a set of disks connected through two different paths, so you must define the disks with different names depending on whether they are connected through the primary or alternate path. The following is a listing of the file **pri** containing the primary disks in groups of five:

```
c9t0d0  c9t0d1  c9t0d2  c8t0d0  c8t0d1
c7t0d0  c7t0d1  c7t0d2  c10t0d0  c10t0d1
c9t0d3  c9t0d4  c9t0d5  c8t0d3  c8t0d4
c7t0d3  c7t0d4  c7t0d5  c10t0d3  c10t0d4
c9t0d6  c9t0d7  c9t1d0  c8t0d6  c8t0d7
c7t0d6  c7t0d7  c7t1d0  c10t0d6  c10t0d7
c9t1d1  c9t1d2  c9t1d3  c8t1d1  c8t1d2
c7t1d1  c7t1d2  c7t1d3  c10t1d1  c10t1d2
c9t1d4  c9t1d5  c9t1d6  c8t1d4  c8t1d5
c7t1d4  c7t1d5  c7t1d6  c10t1d4  c10t1d5
```

Notice that in this listing the disks have been grouped in fives. Each group of five disks will constitute a volume group. There are a total of 10 groups of five disks that will be placed in volume groups *vgu01* through *vgu10*.

There will also be an alternate group of five disks. The alternate disks will be used in the event of a disk controller failover as described earlier. The following is a listing of the file **alt**, containing a list of alternate disks in groups of five:

```
c8t8d0   c8t8d1   c8t8d2   c9t8d0   c9t8d1
c10t8d0  c10t8d1  c10t8d2  c7t8d0   c7t8d1
c8t8d3   c8t8d4   c8t8d5   c9t8d3   c9t8d4
c10t8d3  c10t8d4  c10t8d5  c7t8d3   c7t8d4
c8t8d6   c8t8d7   c8t9d0   c9t8d6   c9t8d7
c10t8d6  c10t8d7  c10t9d0  c7t8d6   c7t8d7
c8t9d1   c8t9d2   c8t9d3   c9t9d1   c9t9d2
c10t9d1  c10t9d2  c10t9d3  c7t9d1   c7t9d2
c8t9d4   c8t9d5   c8t9d6   c9t9d4   c9t9d5
c10t9d4  c10t9d5  c10t9d6  c7t9d4   c7t9d5
```

There are a total of 10 groups of alternate disks shown in this listing that will also be part of the volume groups *vgu01* through *vgu10*. Using these primary and alternate disks that have been setup on the

XP 256, we'll setup the appropriate volumes on the host system. In this example the host system is a V-Class system.

Let's now cover the steps to manually create one of these volume groups. First, we'll create a physical volume for each of the disks in the volume group with the **pvcreate** command. Next we'll create a directory for the volume group with **mkdir**, then create a device special file for the volume group within the directory with **mknod**. This will setup the directory and special file required for the first of the 10 volume groups. Next, we'll create the volume group in which the five primary disks will be contained using **vgcreate**. We'll specify the first disk when we create the volume group and then include the other disks in the volume group with **vgextend**. Then we will extend the volume group with **vgextend** to include the five alternate disks. The final step is to create a single logical volume for the entire volume group. You might want to create several logical volumes within a volume group but in our example, we need only one logical volume that consumes the entire capacity of the volume group, which is 8755 physical extents. The following procedure is the list of manual steps to create the first volume group, which we'll then automate with a shell program:

man page "pv" - 8

man page mkdir - 16

man page "vg" - 8

```
# pvcreate /dev/rdsk/c9t0d0      # run for each of the 5 pri disks


# mkdir /dev/vgu01               # make dir for first vol group


# mknod /dev/vgu01/group -c 64 0x01000
                                 # create special file with major
                                   and minor numbers shown

# vgcreate /dev/vgu01 /dev/dsk/c9t0d0
                                 # Place first disk in volume group


# vgextend /dev/vgu01 /dev/dsk/c9t0d1
                                 # extend volume with remaining four
                                   primary disks disks


# vgextend /dev/vgu01 /dev/dsk/c8t8d0
                                 # extend volume group to include five
                                   alternte disks

# lvcreate -l 8755 /dev/vgu01    # creates lvol1 (lvol1 by default)
                                   that consumes all 8755 extents
```

We completed the procedure for only one disk and there are nine additional disks in this volume group. In addition, there are another nine volume groups for which this procedure must be completed. That is a total of an additional 99 disks for which various commands must be run. There is a lot of room for error with that much typing involved, so this is an ideal process to automate.

Since there are a primary set of disks and an alternate set of disks, we'll write a short program to automate each procedure. The following program performs all of the steps required to create a physical volume for each disk, create a volume group, and include the primary disks in it:

```ksh
#!/bin/ksh
set -x              ;set tracing on

  vgnum=$1          ;first item on each line is the volume group no.
  shift             ;shift to get to first disk

  for i in $*       ;run pvcreate for every disk name in first line
  do
    pvcreate /dev/rdsk/$i
  done

  reada             ;pause program to view what has been run

  mkdir /dev/vgu$vgnum                         ;mkdir for volume group
  mknod /dev/vgu$vgnum/group c 0x$(vgnum)0000  ;mknod for volume group
  vgcreate /dev/vgu$vgnum /dev/dsk/$1          ;vgcreate 1st disk in vg

  shift             ;shift over to second disk

  for i in $*       ;extend volume group to include remaining four disks
  do
    vgextend /dev/vgu$vgnum /dev/dsk/$i
  done

  lvcreate -l 8755 /dev/vgu$vgnum   ;create single log vol for entire vg
```

I use *set -x* in this file to turn on execution tracing. I always do this when first debugging a shell program so you can see the lines in the shell program as they are executed. The line being executed will appear with a "+" in front of it, followed by the what you would normally see when the program is run. The *read a* is a way of pausing the program to wait for input so I can review what has been run to that point of the program.

In order for this program to run, we have to slightly modify the file containing the primary disk devices and add the volume group number to the beginning of each line. In addition I decided to call the program from the file that has the primary disks in it and operate on one line of disks at a time. The following listing shows the updated file containing the name of the shell program in the previous listing (**vg.sh**) followed by the volume group number and then the list of five primary disks names for each volume group:

```
#vg.sh 01 c9t0d0 c9t0d1 c9t0d2 c8t0d0 c8t0d1
#read a
#vg.sh 02 c7t0d0 c7t0d1 c7t0d2 c10t0d0 c10t0d1
#read a
#vg.sh 03 c9t0d3 c9t0d4 c9t0d5 c8t0d3 c8t0d4
#read a
#vg.sh 04 c7t0d3 c7t0d4 c7t0d5 c10t0d3 c10t0d4
#read a
#vg.sh 05 c9t0d6 c9t0d7 c9t1d0 c8t0d6 c8t0d7
#read a
#vg.sh 06 c7t0d6 c7t0d7 c7t1d0 c10t0d6 c10t0d7
#read a
#vg.sh 07 c9t1d1 c9t1d2 c9t1d3 c8t1d1 c8t1d2
#read a
#vg.sh 08 c7t1d1 c7t1d2 c7t1d3 c10t1d1 c10t1d2
#read a
#vg.sh 09 c9t1d4 c9t1d5 c9t1d6 c8t1d4 c8t1d5
#read a
#vg.sh 10 c7t1d4 c7t1d5 c7t1d6 c10t1d4 c10t1d5
```

The *read a* between lines of this file will pause and wait for you to enter a *Return* before the next line will be executed. I did this in case I decided to run several lines and I wanted to check the results between the execution of lines.

We can now uncomment the first line of the file and type the file name **pri** and it will call **vg.sh** and run the program (you have to give appropriate permissions to the files and make sure both **vg.sh** and **pri** are executable). I like to run such files one line at a time and check the volume groups as they are created. The script is written to run one line at a time, but is easily modifyable to run all 10 lines.

We need to do much less work with the alternate disk names. The physical volumes have already been created, and the volume group and single logical volume already setup in **vg.sh**. We'll create another script called **vga.sh**, "a" for alternate, in which we'll extend the volume group to include the alternte name for each disk. This script is shown in the listing below:

```
#!/bin/ksh
set -x              ;set tracing on

  vgnum=$1          ;first item on each line is the volume group number
  shift             ;shift to get to first disk

  for i in $*       ;extend vol group to include all five disks on line

     vgextend /dev/vgu$vgnum /dev/dsk/$i

  done
```

This script performs only the task of extending the volume group *vgnum* to include all five disks that appear on the line. Much like the file **pri** the file **alt** will call the script **vga.alt** as shown in the following listing:

```
#vga.sh 01 c8t8d0   c8t8d1   c8t8d2   c9t8d0 c9t8d1
#vga.sh 02 c10t8d0  c10t8d1  c10t8d2  c7t8d0 c7t8d1
#vga.sh 03 c8t8d3   c8t8d4   c8t8d5   c9t8d3 c9t8d4
#vga.sh 04 c10t8d3  c10t8d4  c10t8d5  c7t8d3 c7t8d4
#vga.sh 05 c8t8d6   c8t8d7   c8t9d0   c9t8d6 c9t8d7
#vga.sh 06 c10t8d6  c10t8d7  c10t9d0  c7t8d6 c7t8d7
#vga.sh 07 c8t9d1   c8t9d2   c8t9d3   c9t9d1 c9t9d2
#vga.sh 08 c10t9d1  c10t9d2  c10t9d3  c7t9d1 c7t9d2
```

```
#vga.sh 09 c8t9d4   c8t9d5   c8t9d6   c9t9d4  c9t9d5
#vga.sh 10 c10t9d4 c10t9d5 c10t9d6 c7t9d4 c7t9d5
```

You would uncomment the line for which you want to run the script. Again, you could run all ten lines but I like to check what has taken place after each line has been run. You could add the *read a* between lines of this file if you wanted to run several lines and have a pause between them to check the results.

These two scripts automate a lot of typing. There are 100 disks for which commands must be run as well as other Logical Volume Manager commands. This is the type of HP-UX system administration task that is ideally suited for shell programming.

I completed the steps that had to be run for the additional disks to complete the work such as the **vgcreate** for the addtional four disks and the **vgextend** for additional nine disk devices. I included only the first disk in the examples so you could see the initial steps that had to be taken.

We don't have to setup any RAID levels within the primary or alternate volume because this is being done internally to the XP 256.

The following **vgdisplay** listing shows the disks we setup for volume group *vgu01* with both the groups of five primary and alternate disks:

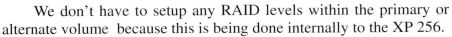

```
# vgdisplay /dev/vgu01 -v
```

```
VG Name                  /dev/vgu01
VG Write Access          read/write
VG Status                available
Max LV                   255
Cur LV                   1
Open LV                  1
Max PV                   16
Cur PV                   5
Act PV                   5
Max PE per PV            1751
VGDA                     10
PE Size (Mbytes)         4
Total PE                 8755
Alloc PE                 8755
Free PE                  0
Total PVG                0
Total Spare PVs          0
```

```
Total Spare PVs in use        0

    --- Logical volumes ---
    LV Name                   /dev/vgu01/lvol1
    LV Status                 available/syncd
    LV Size (Mbytes)          35020
    Current LE                8755
    Allocated PE              8755
    Used PV                   5


    --- Physical volumes ---
    PV Name                   /dev/dsk/c9t0d0
    PV Name                   /dev/dsk/c8t8d0Alternate Link
    PV Status                 available
    Total PE                  1751
    Free PE                   0

    PV Name                   /dev/dsk/c9t0d1
    PV Name                   /dev/dsk/c8t8d1Alternate Link
    PV Status                 available
    Total PE                  1751
    Free PE                   0

    PV Name                   /dev/dsk/c9t0d2
    PV Name                   /dev/dsk/c8t8d2Alternate Link
    PV Status                 available
    Total PE                  1751
    Free PE                   0

    PV Name                   /dev/dsk/c8t0d0
    PV Name                   /dev/dsk/c9t8d0Alternate Link
    PV Status                 available
    Total PE                  1751
    Free PE                   0

    PV Name                   /dev/dsk/c8t0d1
    PV Name                   /dev/dsk/c9t8d1Alternate Link
    PV Status                 available
    Total PE                  1751
    Free PE                   0
```

There are some points of interest to cover in this **vgdisplay**. The first is that there is a primary and alternate path to the same disk as we had defined them earlier. For instance, the first disk in the volume group has a primary path name of *c9t0d0* and an alterate path name of *c8t8d0*. Next, both the volume group *vgu01* and the only logical volume in it *lvol1* consist of a total of 8755 PE or physical extents (the size of a volume group is PE x PE size or 8755 x 4MB in our case.)

We should also check one logical volume on *vgu01* called *lvol1*. We can check the parameters of this logical volume with the **lvdisplay** command as shown in the following example:

```
# lvdisplay -v /dev/vgu01/l*

--- Logical volumes ---
LV Name                      /dev/vgu01/lvol1
VG Name                      /dev/vgu01
LV Permission                read/write
LV Status                    available/syncd
Mirror copies                0
Consistency Recovery         MWC
Schedule                     parallel
LV Size (Mbytes)             35020
Current LE                   8755
Allocated PE                 8755
Stripes                      0
Stripe Size (Kbytes)         0
Bad block                    on
Allocation                   strict
IO Timeout (Seconds)         default

    --- Distribution of logical volume ---
    PV Name           LE on PV   PE on PV
    /dev/dsk/c9t0d0   1751       1751
    /dev/dsk/c9t0d1   1751       1751
    /dev/dsk/c9t0d2   1751       1751
    /dev/dsk/c8t0d0   1751       1751
    /dev/dsk/c8t0d1   1751       1751

    --- Logical extents ---
    LE     PV1                 PE1     Status 1
    00000  /dev/dsk/c9t0d0     00000   current
    00001  /dev/dsk/c9t0d0     00001   current
    00002  /dev/dsk/c9t0d0     00002   current
    00003  /dev/dsk/c9t0d0     00003   current
    00004  /dev/dsk/c9t0d0     00004   current
    00005  /dev/dsk/c9t0d0     00005   current
    00006  /dev/dsk/c9t0d0     00006   current
    00007  /dev/dsk/c9t0d0     00007   current
    00008  /dev/dsk/c9t0d0     00008   current
    00009  /dev/dsk/c9t0d0     00009   current
    00010  /dev/dsk/c9t0d0     00010   current
    00011  /dev/dsk/c9t0d0     00011   current
    00012  /dev/dsk/c9t0d0     00012   current
    00013  /dev/dsk/c9t0d0     00013   current
    00014  /dev/dsk/c9t0d0     00014   current
    00015  /dev/dsk/c9t0d0     00015   current
    00016  /dev/dsk/c9t0d0     00016   current
    00017  /dev/dsk/c9t0d0     00017   current
    00018  /dev/dsk/c9t0d0     00018   current
    00019  /dev/dsk/c9t0d0     00019   current
    00020  /dev/dsk/c9t0d0     00020   current
```

```
00021 /dev/dsk/c9t0d0        00021 current
00022 /dev/dsk/c9t0d0        00022 current
00023 /dev/dsk/c9t0d0        00023 current
00024 /dev/dsk/c9t0d0        00024 current
00025 /dev/dsk/c9t0d0        00025 current
00026 /dev/dsk/c9t0d0        00026 current
00027 /dev/dsk/c9t0d0        00027 current
00028 /dev/dsk/c9t0d0        00028 current
00029 /dev/dsk/c9t0d0        00029 current
00030 /dev/dsk/c9t0d0        00030 current
00031 /dev/dsk/c9t0d0        00031 current
00032 /dev/dsk/c9t0d0        00032 current
                  .
                  .
                  .
08733 /dev/dsk/c8t0d1        01729 current
08734 /dev/dsk/c8t0d1        01730 current
08735 /dev/dsk/c8t0d1        01731 current
08736 /dev/dsk/c8t0d1        01732 current
08737 /dev/dsk/c8t0d1        01733 current
08738 /dev/dsk/c8t0d1        01734 current
08739 /dev/dsk/c8t0d1        01735 current
08740 /dev/dsk/c8t0d1        01736 current
08741 /dev/dsk/c8t0d1        01737 current
08742 /dev/dsk/c8t0d1        01738 current
08743 /dev/dsk/c8t0d1        01739 current
08744 /dev/dsk/c8t0d1        01740 current
08745 /dev/dsk/c8t0d1        01741 current
08746 /dev/dsk/c8t0d1        01742 current
08747 /dev/dsk/c8t0d1        01743 current
08748 /dev/dsk/c8t0d1        01744 current
08749 /dev/dsk/c8t0d1        01745 current
08750 /dev/dsk/c8t0d1        01746 current
08751 /dev/dsk/c8t0d1        01747 current
08752 /dev/dsk/c8t0d1        01748 current
08753 /dev/dsk/c8t0d1        01749 current
08754 /dev/dsk/c8t0d1        01750 current
```

This listing has been abbreviated where the three dots are shown. Only the beginning of the first disk and end of the last disk are shown. The **lvdisplay** does indeed show the five primary disks of which the logical volume is comprised.

The final step is to place a file system on the logical volume we have setup in *vgu00*. This is a task for which SAM is ideally suited. I completed this procedure using SAM in Chapter 8, so you can refer to it if you want to see the SAM screen shots.

The next section is a short introduction to C shell programming.

C Shell Programming

Although shell programming techniques apply to all shells, generally speaking, there are some differences exist between the C shell and the KornShell. If you are using the C shell, I want you to get off to a quick start, so I'll cover the basics of C shell programming in this section. I'll cover each shell programming technique briefly and use basic examples to help reinforce each technique. In all of the following shell programs, any line beginning with a "#" is a comment. This is true except for the very first line of a shell program in which the shell the script is written for is executed. In all of the following programs, the C shell is executed with **#!/bin/csh**, which is the path of the C shell on the Solaris system used in the examples.

Command Substitution

The shell variables earlier covered can be used to save the output from a command. You can then use these variables when issuing other commands. The following shell program executes the **date** command and saves the results in the variable **d**. The variable **d** is then used within the **echo** command in the program **cdate**:

```
#!/bin/csh
# program "today" that provides the date
set d=`date +%x`
echo "Today's date is $d"
```

When we run **cdate**, the following is produced:

```
martyp $ cdate
Today's date is 06/01/00
martyp $
```

The "+%x" in the above example produces the current date. Command substitution of this type is used in several upcoming shell scripts.

Reading User Input

Two common methods help you read user input to shell programs. The first is to prompt the user for information, and the second is to provide arguments to shell programs.

To begin, I'll cover prompting a user for information. A character, word, or sentence can be read into a variable. The following example first shows prompting the user for a word, and then a sentence:

```
#!/bin/csh
echo "Please enter your name:"
set name = $<
echo "hello, $name"
echo "Please enter your favorite quote:"
set quote = $<
echo "Your favorite quote is:"
echo $quote
```

Here is an example of running this program:

```
martyp $ userinput
Please enter your name:
Marty
hello, Marty
Please enter your favorite quote:
Creating is the essence of life.
Your favorite quote is:
Creating is the essence of life.
martyp $
```

Using this technique, you can prompt a user for information in a shell program. This technique is used in an upcoming program.

You can also enter command line arguments. When you type the name of the shell script, you can supply arguments that are saved in the variables **$1** through **$9**. The first ten words on the command line are directly accessible in the shell program using the special variables **$0-$9**. This is how they work:

$0	The command name
$1	The first argument
$2	The second argument
$3	.
	.
	.
$9	The ninth argument

If you are not sure how many command-line arguments you may get when your program is run, there are two other variables that can help:

$#	The number of command-line arguments
$*	A space-separated list of all the command-line arguments (which does *not* include the command name)

The variable **$*** is commonly used with the **for** loop (soon to be explained) to process shell script command lines with any number of arguments.

The following script changes to the specified directory (**$1**) and searches for the specified pattern (**$2**) in the specified file (**$3**):

```
#!/bin/csh
# search
# Usage: search directory pattern file
echo " "
cd $1                  # change to search dir and
grep -n "$2" $3        # search for $2 in $3
echo " "               # print line
endif
```

grep is used to search a file for a pattern and print the line in which the pattern was found. **awk**, which was earlier covered, can be used to pick out a specific field within a line.

Here is an example of the **search** program:

```
martyp $ search /home/martyp/shellprogs awk ifstat

12:# as one command so it can be easily piped to awk.
18:awk 'BEGIN { printf "%10s%10s%10s%10s%10s\n", "ipkts",
38:' # End of the awk program.

martyp $
```

In this example, we run **search** in the directory **/home/martyp/ shellprogs**, looking for the pattern **awk** in the file **ifstat**. The result of this search produces three lines in the file **ifstat**, in which **awk** appears. These are lines number 12, 18, and 38.

In the next section, we'll expand this program somewhat to include testing and branching.

Testing and Branching

There are many kinds of decision-making your shell programs can perform. **if** provides the flexibility to make decisions and take the appropriate action. Let's expand the **search** script to verify that three arguments have been provided:

```
#!/bin/csh
# search
# Usage: search directory pattern files

if ($#argv != 3) then              # if < 3 args provided

        echo "Usage: search directory pattern files"
                                # then print Usage
else
```

```
            echo " "                 # else print line and
            cd $1                    # change to search dir
            grep -n "$2" $3          # search for $2 in $3
            echo " "                 # print line
endif
```

This program is called **search1**. We run this program using the same arguments as we did with the **search** program; however, **search1** is enhanced to provide a *usage* message if we don't provide arguments when we run it. The following example shows running **search1**:

```
martyp $ search1
Usage: search directory pattern files
martyp $ search1 /home/martyp/shellprogs awk llsum

12:# drwxrwxrwx 2  gerry  aec  24  Mar 21 18:25    awk_ex
15:# awk field numbers:
18:awk ' BEGIN { x=i=0; printf "%-16s%-10s%8s%8s\n", \

martyp $
```

On the first attempt to run **search1**, we provided no arguments. The program checked to see whether we provided fewer than three arguments and produced the *Usage* message, because it found fewer than three arguments. Upon seeing the *Usage* message, it became clear how to use the program and we provided the required three arguments on the next attempt to run the program. In this example, we run **search1** in the directory **/home/martyp/shellprogs**, looking for the pattern **awk** in the file **llsum**. The result of this search produces three lines in the file **llsum**, in which **awk** appears. These are lines number 12, 15, and 18.

man page

awk - 19

Here are four commonly used forms of **if**:

1)   if (expression) command

2)   if (expression) then
                              command(s)

endif

3)   if (expression) then
                                command(s)
                        else
                                command(s)
                endif

4)   if (expression) then
                                command(s)
                        [else if expression) then
                                command(s)]

                                .
                                .
                                .

                        [else
                                command(s)]
                endif

There are many operators that can be used in the C shell to compare integer values, such as the < used in the previous example. Here is a list of operators:

>	greater than
<	less than
>=	greater than or equal to
<=	less than or equal to
==	equal to
!=	not equal to

Looping

The C shell supports a number of techniques to support looping, including:

1) The **foreach** loop, which takes a list of items and performs the commands in the loop once for each item in the list.

2) The **while** loop, which executes a command (such as the **test** command) if the command executes successfully.

The format of the **foreach** loop is

foreach name (list)
           command(s)
end

The following example uses a **foreach** loop to test whether or not the systems in the **/etc/hosts** file are connected to the local host.

```
#!/bin/csh
#Program name: csh_hostck

#This program will test connectivity to all other hosts in
#your network listed in your /etc/hosts file.

# It uses the awk command to get the names from the hosts file
#and the ping command to check connectivity.

#Note that we use /bin/echo because csh echo doesn't support
#escape chars like \t or \c which are used in the
#foreach loop.

#Any line in /etc/hosts that starts with a number represents
#a host entry. Anything else is a comment or a blank line.

#Find all lines in /etc/hosts that start with a number and
#print the second field (the hostname).

set hosts=`awk '/^[1-9]/ { print $2 }' /etc/hosts`
                   # grave on outside, single quote on inside

     /bin/echo "Remote host connection status:"

foreach sys ($hosts)
     /bin/echo "$sys - \c"
                    # send one 64 byte packet and look for
                    # the"is alive" message in
                    # the output that indicates success.
                    # messages vary between UNIX variants.
```

```
    ping $sys 64 1 | grep "is alive" > /dev/null
    if ( $status == 0 ) then
            echo "OK"
    else
            echo "DID NOT RESPOND"
    endif
end
```

man page

awk - 19

The crazy-looking line with **awk** is used to obtain the name of remote hosts from the **/etc/hosts** file. The **foreach** loop takes all of the items in the list, the hosts in this case, and checks the status of each.

The **hosts** file on this system has three entries: the localhost, the LAN interface, and a DNS system. When we run the program in the following example, we expect to see a result for the testing of all three entries:

```
martyp $ csh_hostck
Remote host connection status:
localhost - OK
sunsys - OK
dnssrv1 - OK
martyp $
```

man page

ping - 12

All three entries in the **hosts** file have been evaluated with **ping** and produce a status of *OK*. When hardcoding information into scripts, such as the path of **ping** and the result you get from the **ping** command, please keep in mind that these may vary among different UNIX variants. One of the reasons you want to liberally comment your shell programs is to make them easy to modify under such circumstances.

You could use the **while** loop to execute commands for some number of iterations. The **while** loop is in the following format:

while (expression)
        command(s)
end

man page

netstat - 12

The following program, called **netcheck**, runs **netstat** at the desired interval, and prints out the heading once and the status of *le0* nine times:

```
#!/bin/csh
# program to run netstat at every specified interval
# Usage: netcheck interval

set limit=9                 # set limit on number times
                            # to run netstat

echo " "
netstat -i | grep Name      # print netstat line with head-
ings
set count=0
while ($count<$limit)       # if limit hasn't reached
                            # limit run netstat
        netstat -i | grep le0
        sleep $1            # sleep for interval
                            # specified on command line
        @ count++           # increment limit
end
echo "count has reached $limit, run netcheck again to see
le0 status"
```

Here is an example run of the **netcheck** program:

```
martyp $ netcheck 3

Name Mtu  Net/Dest   Address      Ipkts      Ierrs Opkts     Oerrs Collis Queue
le0  1500 sunsys     sunsys       314374989  0     17252200  52135 7580906
le0  1500 sunsys     sunsys       314375038  0     17252203  52135 7580906
le0  1500 sunsys     sunsys       314375114  0     17252206  52135 7580906
le0  1500 sunsys     sunsys       314375185  0     17252209  52135 7580906
le0  1500 sunsys     sunsys       314375257  0     17252212  52135 7580906
le0  1500 sunsys     sunsys       314375332  0     17252215  52135 7580906
le0  1500 sunsys     sunsys       314375444  0     17252218  52135 7580906
le0  1500 sunsys     sunsys       314375508  0     17252221  52135 7580906
le0  1500 sunsys     sunsys       314375588  0     17252224  52135 7580906
count has reached 9, run netcheck again to see le0 status
martyp $
```

man page

netstat - 12

The output of **netcheck** produces nine **netstat** outputs at the three-second interval we had specified. Keep in mind that you may have to modify such information as the name of the LAN interface when you use this program on your system.

This program increments the expression with the following:

@ count++

If the expression is true, then the command(s) will execute. The @count++ is an assignment operator in the form of:

@ variable_name operator expression

In this case, the variable is first assigned with "=" and is later auto incremented (++). There are a number of operations that can be performed on the variable, as described in Table 23-2:

TABLE 23-2 Assignment Operators

Operation	Symbol	Example with count = 100	Result
store value	=	@count=100	100
auto increment	++	@count++	101
auto decrement	--	@count--	99
add value	+=	@count+=50	150
subtract value	-=	@count-=50	50
multiply by value	*=	@count*=2	200
divide by value	/=	@count/2	50

There are also comparison operators, such as the "<" used in the example, as well as arithmetic, bitwise, and logical operators. As you craft more and more shell scripts, you will want to use all these operators.

There are a set of test conditions related to files that are useful when writing shell scripts that use files. Using the format **- operator filename**, you can use the tests in Table 23-3.

TABLE 23-3   Operator File Name Tests

Operator	Meaning
r	read access
w	write access
x	execute access
o	ownership
z	zero length
f	file, not a directory
d	directory, not a file

The following program, called **filetest,** uses these operators to test the file **.profile**. Because **.profile** is not executable, of zero length, or a directory, I would expect **filetest** to find these false.

Here is a long listing of **.profile**:

man page

ls - 15

```
martyp $ ls -al .profile
-rw-r--r--   1 martyp   staff        594 May 21 09:29 ../.profile
martyp $
```

Here is a listing of the shell script **filetest**:

```
#!/bin/csh
#  Program to test file $1

if (-e $1) then
```

```
                    echo "$1 exists"
                    else
                    echo "$1 does not exist"
endif

if (-z $1) then
                    echo "$1 is zero length"
                    else
                    echo "$1 is not zero length"
endif

if (-f $1) then
                    echo "$1 is a file"
                    else
                    echo "$1 is not a file"
endif

if (-d $1) then
                    echo "$1 is a directory"
                    else
                    echo "$1 is not a directory"
endif

if (-o $1) then
                    echo "you own $1 "
                    else
                    echo "you don't own $1 "
endif

if (-r $1) then
                    echo "$1 is readable"
                    else
                    echo "$1 is not readable"
endif

if (-w $1) then
                    echo "$1 is writable"
                    else
                    echo "$1 is not writable"
endif

if (-x $1) then
                    echo "$1 is executable"
                    else
                    echo "$1 is not executable"
endif
```

This is a somewhat extreme example of testing a file; however, I wanted to include many of the file tests.

Here is the output of **filetest** using **.profile** as input:

```
martyp $ filetest /home/martyp/.profile
/home/martyp/.profile exists
/home/martyp/.profile is not zero length
/home/martyp/.profile is a file
/home/martyp/.profile is not a directory
you own /home/martyp/.profile
/home/martyp/.profile is readable
/home/martyp/.profile is writable
/home/martyp/.profile is not executable
martyp $
```

The result of having run **filetest** on **.profile** produces the file test results that we expect.

The next section covers a way of making decisions with **switch**.

Decision Making with switch

You can use **switch** to make decisions within a shell program. You can use **switch** to test command-line arguments or interactive input to shell programs as shown in the upcoming example. If, for example, you wanted to create a menu in a shell program and you needed to determine which option a user selected when running this shell program, you can use **switch**.

The syntax of **switch** looks like the following:

```
switch (pattern_to_match)

case pattern1
            commands
            breaksw

case pattern2
            commands
```

```
                            breaksw

            case pattern 3
                        commands
                        breaksw

            default
                        commands
                        breaksw
        endsw
```

pattern_to_match is the user input that you are testing, and if it is equal to *pattern1*, then the commands under *pattern1* are executed. If *pattern_to_match* and *pattern2* are the same, then the commands under *pattern2* will be executed, and so on. If no match occurs between *pattern_to_match* and one of the case statement patterns, then the default is executed. The following program allows you to pick from between two scripts on its menu. These are the two shell programs we crafted earlier in this chapter. You can expand this script to include as many of your programs as you wish. This example uses **switch**:

```
#!/bin/csh
# Program pickscript to run some of
# the C shell scripts we've created
# Usage: pickscript
echo " ------------------------------------------"
echo "                  Sys Admin Menu            "
echo "------------------------------------------"
echo " "
echo " 1            netcheck for network interface "
echo " "
echo " 2            hostck to check connection     "
echo "                 to hosts in /etc/hosts      "
echo "                                             "
echo " ------------------------------------------"
echo " "
echo " Please enter your selection -> \c"

set pick = $<      # read input which is number of script
echo " "
switch ($pick)     # and assign to variable pick

            case 1          # if 1 was selected execute this
            $HOME/cshscripts/netcheck 5
            breaksw
```

```
                     case 2          # if 2 was selected, execute this
                     $HOME/cshscripts/hostck
                     breaksw

                     default
                     echo "Please select 1 or 2 next time"
                     breaksw

          endsw
```

This program allows us to select from between two scripts to run. Let's take a look at an example of running this program:

```
martyp $ pickscript
------------------------------------------------
                    Sys Admin Menu
------------------------------------------------

   1            netcheck for network interface

   2            hostck to check connection
                 to hosts in /etc/hosts

      ------------------------------------------------

 Please enter your selection
1

Name  Mtu  Net/Dest    Address        Ipkts    Ierrs Opkts  Oerrs Collis Queue
le0   1500 sunsys      sunsys         314996747 0    17261251 52135 7580952
le0   1500 sunsys      sunsys         314996862 0    17261256 52135 7580952
le0   1500 sunsys      sunsys         314997189 0    17261266 52135 7580952
le0   1500 sunsys      sunsys         314997319 0    17261269 52135 7580952
le0   1500 sunsys      sunsys         314997420 0    17261272 52135 7580952
le0   1500 sunsys      sunsys         314997630 0    17261275 52135 7580952
le0   1500 sunsys      sunsys         314997774 0    17261278 52135 7580952
le0   1500 sunsys      sunsys         314997904 0    17261281 52135 7580952
le0   1500 sunsys      sunsys         314998020 0    17261284 52135 7580952
count has reached 9, run netcheck again to see lan0 status
martyp $
```

We selected option *1* when we ran **pickscript**. You can use this program as the basis for running the many shell programs you may write.

Debugging C Shell Programs

When you begin C shell programming, you'll probably make a lot of simple syntax-related errors. Using the *-n* option to **csh**, you can have the C shell check the syntax of your program without executing it. I also use the *-v* option to produce a verbose output. This can sometimes lead to too much information, so I start with *-v* and if there is too much feedback results, I eliminate it.

The following example is the earlier **search1** program, which includes a check that three arguments have been provided. When checking to see that **$#argv** is equal to 3, I left off the right parenthesis. Here is the listing of the program and a syntax check showing the error:

man page

cat - 17

```
martyp $ cat search1
#!/bin/csh
# search
# Usage: search directory pattern files

if ($#argv !3 3 then                # if < 3 args provided

        echo "Usage: search directory pattern files"
                                     # then print Usage
else
        echo " "                     # else print line and
        cd $1                        # change to search dir
        grep -n "$2" $3              # search for $2 in $3
        echo " "                     # print line
endif

martyp $ csh -nv search1
if ( $#argv != 3 then
Too many ('s
martyp $
```

The **csh -nv** has performed a syntax check with verbose output. First, the line in question is printed and then an error message that tells you what is wrong with the line. In this case, it is clear that I have left off a right parenthesis.

After fixing the problem, I can run the program with the *-x*, which causes all commands to be echoed immediately before execution. The following example shows a run of the **search** program:

```
martyp $ csh -xv search1 shellprogs grep csh_hostck

if ( $#argv != 3 ) then
if ( 3 != 3 ) then

echo " "
echo

cd $1
cd /home/martyp/shellprogs
grep -n "$2" $3
grep -n grep csh_hostck
25:     /usr/sbin/ping $sys 64 1 | grep "is alive" > /dev/
null
echo " "
echo

endif
endif
martyp $
```

You can follow what is taking place on a line-by-line basis. The line beginning with 25 is the line in the file **csh_hostck** that has **grep** in it, that is, the output you would have received if the program had been run without the *-xv* options.

man page

grep - 19

I would recommend performing the syntax check (*-n*) with a new shell program, and then echo all commands with the *-x* option only if you get unexpected results when you run the program. The debugging options will surely help you at some point when you run into problems with the shell programs you craft.

How Long Does It Take?

You can use the **time** command to see a report of the amount of time your shell program takes to run. The output of **time** is different for many UNIX variants. You may want to view the manual page for **time** to see what output you can expect. A typical output of **time** when in **csh** is shown in Figure 23-5:

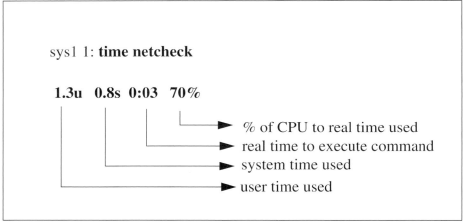

Figure 23-5 **time** Example (different among UNIX variants)

Because some of the scripts you write may consume a substantial amount of system resources, you may want to consider investigating some of the job-control capabilities of the C shell. The simplest job control you can use is to run scripts in the background so that the priority of the script is low. By issuing the script name followed by the **&** (ampersand), you will run the script in the background. If you run several scripts in the background, you can get the status of these by issuing the **jobs** command. This is a more advanced C shell topic, but depending on the level of complexity of scripts you write, you may want to look into job control.

Manual Pages for Some Commands Used in Chapter 23

There are no manual pages included for this chapter. The manual pages for commands used in this chapter appear in other chapters, including:

ksh - Chapter 22

grep, **awk**, **sed**, and other tools - Chapter 19

CHAPTER 24

CIFS/9000 and Samba

CIFS/9000 Overview

CIFS/9000 Server is an HP product based on Samba that provides file and print services to CIFS clients. The server is an HP 9000 and the clients are usually Windows-based systems, however, the client could also be an HP 9000 or any system running CIFS client software. CIFS/9000 Client is used to access file and print services on a CIFS server. To an HP-UX user running CIFS/9000 Client software, the shares on CIFS/9000 Server look like UNIX filesystems whether they are on a UNIX server or a Windows server. The server could be an HP 9000 running CIFS/9000 Server, a Windows-based system, or any system running CIFS as a server. In this chapter, I'll cover only CIFS/9000 Server being accessed by a Windows-based system since that is the use for which most HP 9000 users will deploy CIFS/9000.

CIFS stands for Common Internet File System, which is a Windows specification for remote file access. CIFS is a remote access protocol based largely on Server Message Block (SMB) that has long been used as the native file-sharing protocol on Windows-based systems. CIFS is a remote file access protocol that sits on top of the host file system(s). As mentioned earlier there is both a CIFS Server, for which I'll use and HP 9000 system in this chapter, as well a CIFS Client, for which I'll use a Windows-based system in this chapter. We'll setup CIFS/9000 server such that an HP-UX file system can be mounted on a Windows-based system.

CIFS/9000 Server is based on Samba open source software. For that reason, the second half of this chapter is from one of my other books covering Samba running on a Linux system. The HP 9000 setup of CIFS/9000 Server covered in the first half of this chapter is very similar to the Samba setup on a Linux system covered in the second half of this chapter.

My goal in the first half of this chapter is to give an overview of the setup of CIFS/9000 and demonstrate a subset of its functionality. We'll focus on the file server functionality only. We'll set up shares on the CIFS/9000 server system that will appear as a drive letters and icons on a Windows system.

CIFS/9000 Server provides this file-sharing functionality using Server Message Block (SMB) protocol as described earlier. SMB runs on top of TCP/IP. In our example in this chapter, both the Windows system and CIFS/9000 Server system are running TCP/IP and SMB. These provide all of the technology that is required to establish file sharing between the two systems.

Chapter 26 covers the Network File System (NFS) running on a Windows system and accessing files on a UNIX system. This functionality is similar to that which we'll cover with CIFS/9000 in this chapter. In addition to the file-sharing capability, CIFS/9000 also provides printer sharing and additional user access control capability. We won't focus on these capabilities in this chapter, however, CIFS/9000 does indeed provide some advanced functionality in these areas.

At the time of this writing, CIFS/9000 contains the functinality just mentioned, including: file-sharing; printer sharing; and advanced user access control of files. There are many advancements taking place with Samba that will be incorporated into CIFS/9000 and other software provided under the GNU Public License (GPL) as free software. Because the software is free, many individuals have access to it and spend time enhancing the software. For this reason, you may find that additional functionality is included in CIFS/9000 in the future.

Installing CIFS/9000

CIFS/9000 is loaded from CD-ROM like any other HP application. Figure 24-1 shows the **swintall** screen with the two CIFS/9000 components that are part of the parent bundle. As shown in the figure, you receive both the source code and the compiled version of CIFS/9000 Server as one bundled product. The same would be true of the CIFS/9000 Client software. The source code is included because CIFS/9000 Server is based on Samba Open Source software for which source code is freely available.

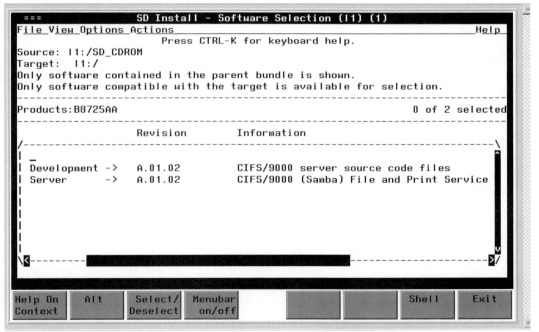

Figure 24-1 Installing CIFS/9000 Server with **swinstall**

After having installed both components of the parent bundle shown in Figure 24-1, we have all of the software present on our system to configure CIFS/9000 Server. Although I don't plan on modifying the source code, I may view it at some point, so I loaded it as well.

Let's next change directory to **/opt** (for optional software) and see what directories have been created in the following listing:

```
# cd /opt
# ls -l
total 10
dr-xr-xr-x    6 bin       bin            96 Jul 11 19:27 audio
dr-xr-xr-x   10 bin       bin          1024 Jul 11 19:27 dce
dr-xr-xr-x    4 bin       bin          1024 Jul 11 19:44 dcelocal
dr-xr-xr-x    3 bin       bin            96 Jul 11 19:25 fc
dr-xr-xr-x    3 bin       bin            96 Jul 11 19:18 fcms
dr-xr-xr-x    4 bin       bin            96 Jul 11 19:44 graphics
drwxr-xr-x    5 root      sys            96 Jul 11 19:29 hparray
dr-xr-xr-x    4 bin       bin            96 Jul 11 19:27 ifor
dr-xr-xr-x   16 bin       bin          1024 Jul 12 13:10 ignite
dr-xr-xr-x    3 bin       bin            96 Jul 11 19:26 image
drwxr-xr-x    2 root      root           96 Jul 11 19:14 lost+found
dr-xr-xr-x    7 bin       bin            96 Jul 11 19:25 nettladm
drwxr-xr-x    2 root      sys          1024 Jul 11 22:57 networkdocs
dr-xr-xr-x    7 bin       bin            96 Jul 11 19:27 pd
drwxr-xr-x    8 root      users        1024 Jul 18 11:53 samba
drwxr-xr-x    3 root      users          96 Jul 18 11:53 samba_src
dr-xr-xr-x    5 bin       bin            96 Jul 11 19:25 upgrade
dr-xr-xr-x    4 bin       bin            96 Jul 11 19:27 video
drwxr-xr-x    3 root      sys            96 Jul 12 13:10 webadmin
#
```

This listing shows that there are both the **samba** and **samba_src** directories that we loaded in **/opt**. The CIFS/9000 product with which we'll be working is loaded in the **samba** directory, so let's change to it and then see what files and directories are present under **/opt/samba** and **/opt/samba/bin**:

```
# ls -l /opt/samba
total 44
-rwxr-xr-x    1 root      users        17982 Jul  7  1999 COPYING
drwxr-xr-x    4 root      users           96 Jul 18 11:53 HA
-rwxr-xr-x    1 root      users          772 Jan 10  2000 README
drwxr-xr-x    2 root      users         1024 Jul 18 11:53 bin
drwxr-xr-x    7 root      users         1024 Jul 18 11:53 docs
drwxr-xr-x    6 root      users           96 Jul 18 11:53 man
drwxr-xr-x    2 root      users         1024 Jul 18 11:53 script
drwxr-xr-x    6 root      users           96 Jul 18 11:53 swat
```

```
# ls -l /opt/samba/bin
total 13588
-rwxr-xr-x   1 root      users         1708 Apr 20 17:38 addtosmbpass
-rwxr-xr-x   1 root      users          446 Apr 20 17:38 convert_smbpasswd
-rwxr-xr-x   1 root      users       292124 Apr 20 17:38 make_printerdef
-rwxr-xr-x   1 root      users       292115 Apr 20 17:38 make_smbcodepage
-rwxr-xr-x   1 root      users       579513 Apr 20 17:38 nmbd
-rwxr-xr-x   1 root      users       402933 Apr 20 17:38 nmblookup
-rwxr-xr-x   1 root      users       752117 Apr 20 17:38 rpcclient
-rwxr-xr-x   1 root      users        12988 Apr 20 17:38 samba_setup
-rwxr-xr-x   1 root      users       476863 Apr 20 17:38 smbclient
-rwxr-xr-x   1 root      users      1302921 Apr 20 17:38 smbd
-rwxr-xr-x   1 root      users       707074 Apr 20 17:38 smbpasswd
-rwxr-xr-x   1 root      users       402929 Apr 20 17:38 smbspool
-rwxr-xr-x   1 root      users       324986 Apr 20 17:38 smbstatus
-rwxr-xr-x   1 root      users         4862 Apr 20 17:38 smbtar
-rwxr-xr-x   1 root      users         1860 Apr 20 17:38 startsmb
-rwxr-xr-x   1 root      users         2340 Apr 20 17:38 stopsmb
-rwxr-xr-x   1 root      users       789251 Apr 20 17:38 swat
-rwxr-xr-x   1 root      users       288012 Apr 20 17:38 testparm
-rwxr-xr-x   1 root      users       312629 Apr 20 17:38 testprns
# export PATH=$PATH:/opt/samba/bin
#
```

There are some files in **/opt/samba/bin** of interest. Let's take a look at one of these used to configure CIFS/9000 in the upcoming section.

Configuring CIFS/9000

Among the executables that appear in the **/opt/samba/bin** directory is **samba_setup**. When you run this program, it performs some of the initial CIFS/9000 setup, including the name of the domain or workgroup and selecting the authentication to be used. Authentication gets a little tricky because you have a few options. The Samba part of this chapter covers some of the authentication issues. Let's now run **samba_setup**:

```
# samba_setup

This is a utility to help you configure your HP-UX system as
a SAMBA server.  This should only be run once after the initial
installation of SAMBA.
Do you wish to continue with the configuration?
(Y or N)?  : y

Proceeding with samba_setup...


You now must choose what level of authentication you
would like this SAMBA server to use:
1) domain
2) server
3) user
4) share
5) CANCEL
#? 3

You have chosen user level authentication
Is this correct?
(Y or N)?  : y

Enter the name you wish the SAMBA server to be known as (the
netbios name), or just hit enter if you want to keep the default
server name (l1):


Enter the name of the domain or workgroup that
you want this SAMBA server to be a part of: users

Configuring SAMBA server with user level authentication...

Your SAMBA server should now be ready to start.

You may wish to put /opt/samba/bin in the PATH for root
so that you don't have to type the fully qualified path
name for the SAMBA utilities and commands.
#
```

The minimal configuration we completed, along with information related to the Samba configuration, is in **/etc/opt/samba/
smb.conf**, which is shown in the following listing:

```
# cat /etc/opt/samba/smb.conf
# This is the main Samba configuration file. You should read the
# smb.conf(5) manual page in order to understand the options listed
# here. Samba has a huge number of configurable options (perhaps too
# many!) most of which are not shown in this example
#
# Any line which starts with a ; (semi-colon) or a # (hash)
# is a comment and is ignored. In this example we will use a #
# for commentry and a ; for parts of the config file that you
# may wish to enable
#
# NOTE: Whenever you modify this file you should run the command
"testparm"
# to check that you have not many any basic syntactic errors.
#
#========================
Global Settings
========================
[global]
   netbios name = l1

# workgroup = NT-Domain-Name or Workgroup-Name, eg: REDHAT4
   workgroup = users

# server string is the equivalent of the NT Description field
   server string = Samba Server

# this tells Samba to use a separate log file for each machine
# that connects
   log file = /var/opt/samba/log.%m

# Put a capping on the size of the log files (in Kb).
   max log size = 1000

# Security mode. Most people will want user level security. See
# security_level.txt for details.
   security = user
# Use password server option only with security = server or domain
   password server = *

# You may wish to use password encryption. Please read
# ENCRYPTION.txt, Win95.txt and WinNT.txt in the Samba documenta-
tion.
# Do not enable this option unless you have read those documents
  encrypt passwords = no

# Most people will find that this option gives better performance.
# See speed.txt and the manual pages for details
   socket options = TCP_NODELAY

# Browser Control Options:
# set local master to no if you don't want Samba to become a master
# browser on your network. Otherwise the normal election rules apply
   local master = no

   read only = no
   preserve case = yes
   short preserve case = no
```

```
    dos filetime resolution = yes
    syslog = 0

#============================                    Share           Definitions
============================
[homes]
    comment = Home Directories
    browseable = no

# This one is useful for people to share files
[tmp]
    path = /tmp

#
```

You can modify this file directory to make changes for your environment.

In order to run CIFS/9000, we need to start the Samba server. This is done manually with the **startsmb** program as shown in the following listing:

```
# /opt/samba/bin/startsmb
Samba started successfully; process ids: smbd: 25363, nmbd: 25361
# ps -ef | grep samba
    root 25363     1   0 12:10:45 ?           0:00 /opt/samba/bin/smbd -D
    root 25361     1   0 12:10:45 ?           0:00 /opt/samba/bin/nmbd -D
#
```

man page

ps - 13

We have successfully started the Samba server with **startsmb** as confirmed by the Samba daemons shown in the **ps** output. We want to start Samba every time our system boots, so we can modify the **/etc/rc.config.d/samba** file and change the value of *RUN_SAMBA* to *1* as shown in the following listing:

```
# pwd
/etc/rc.config.d
# cat samba
#
# (c) Copyright Hewlett-Packard Company 1999
#
# This program is free software; you can redistribute it and/or mod-
ify
# it under the terms of the GNU General Public License as published by
```

```
# the Free Software Foundation; either version 2 of the License, or
(at
# your option) any later version.
#
# This program is distributed in the hope that it will be useful, but
# WITHOUT ANY WARRANTY; without even the implied warranty of
# MERCHANTABILITY or FITNESS FOR A PARTICULAR PURPOSE.  See GNU Gen-
eral
# Public License for more details.
#
# You should have received a copy of the GNU General Public License
# along with this program; if not, write to the Free Software
# Foundation, Inc., 675 Mass Ave, Cambridge, MA 02139, USA.
#
# samba configuration: set RUN_SAMBA to a non-zero value to
# initiate the SAMBA server at run level 2.
#
# Installed at /etc/rc.config.d/samba
#

RUN_SAMBA=1
#
```

man page

"sw" - 2

Up to this point, we have loaded CIFS/9000 using **swinstall**, performed some minimal configuration, and started Samba. The entire process has taken only minutes and we're ready to use CIFS/9000.

Now that we have loaded Samba and performed the initial configuration, we'll move to our Windows system and access an HP-UX file system on the Windows system as if it were local.

Map a Network Drive

Although we haven't done much work, we're now ready to map a network drive on our Windows system to an HP-UX file system.

Let's map the root file system on our CIFS/9000 server to **F:** on our Windows system as shown in Figure 24-2:

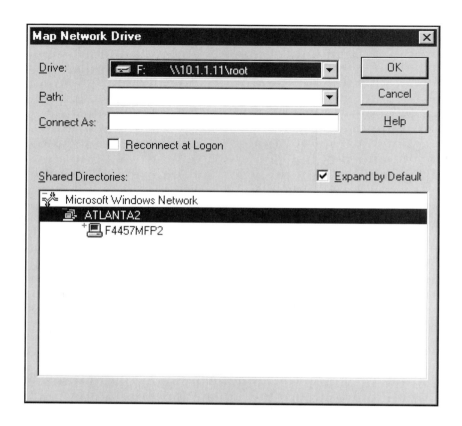

Figure 24-2 Map Root FileSystem on CIFS/9000 Server to **F:**

We now have access to the root filesystem on our CIFS/9000
server (10.1.1.11), as though it were local to our Windows system.

Figure 24-3 shows accessing **F:**, which is root on our CIFS/9000 Server, to view the files and directories:

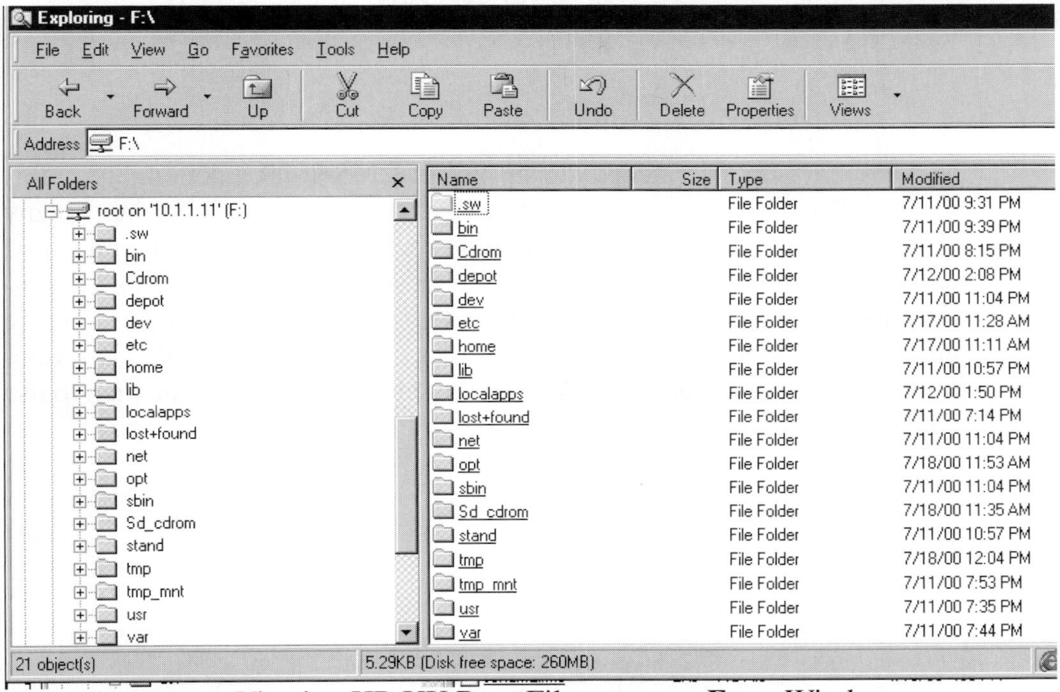

Figure 24-3 Viewing HP-UX Root Filesystem as **F:** on Windows

We can also use the **net view** command on our Windows system to see both the root filesystem on our CIFS/9000 server that we have mapped to **F:** as well as **tmp**, which was in **smb.conf** but was not mapped to a drive letter, as shown in the following listing:

```
C:\> net view \\10.1.1.11

Shared resources at \\10.1.1.11

Samba Server
```

```
Share name      Type      Used as      Comment
-------------------------------------------------
root            Disk      F:           Home Directories
tmp             Disk

The command completed successfully.

C:\>
```

We have only scratched the surface of CIFS/9000 functionality in this section. The subjects of user authentication, printing, ACLs, and many other topics were not covered. The next section covering Samba on Linux includes some additional sections of interest, such as the Web-based configuration tool for Samba called SWAT, that you may want to review. There are some documents on *docs.hp.com* that contain more detailed information on CIFS/9000 that you'll want to download and print if you plan to use CIFS/9000 in your environment.

Samba Overview

Samba is an application that allows a UNIX host to act as a file server for Windows systems. The Windows systems can access UNIX file-systems and printers using their native Windows networking.

Our goal in this chapter is to give an overview of the setup of Samba and demonstrate a subset of its functionality. We'll focus on the file server functionality only. We'll set up shares on a remote UNIX system that will appear as a drive letters and icons on a Windows system. Because Samba comes with the Red Hat Linux software used throughout this book, we'll set up and run Samba on a Linux system. Samba is available for most UNIX variants.

Samba provides its file-sharing functionality using Server Message Block (SMB) protocol. SMB runs on top of TCP/IP. In our example in this chapter, both the Windows system and UNIX system are running TCP/IP and SMB. These provide all of the technology that is required to establish file sharing between the two systems.

Chapter 26 covered Network File System (NFS) running on a Windows system and accessing files on a UNIX system. This functionality is similar to that which we'll cover with Samba in this section. In addition to the file-sharing capability, Samba also provides printer sharing and addtional user access control capability. We won't focus on these capabilities in this chapter, however, Samba does indeed provide some advanced functionality in these areas.

At the time of this writing Samba contains the functionality just mentioned file-sharing, printer sharing, and advanced user access control of files. There are many advancements taking place with Samba and other software provided under GNU Public License (GPL) as free software. Because the software is free, many individuals have access to it and spend time enhancing the software. For this reason, you may find that additional functionality is included in Samba and other such software. There are many enhancements planned for Samba, including an administration tool and other advancements that were not available at the time this chapter was written. There is more information about obtaining Samba and other free software at the end of this chapter.

Setup

Because Samba is supplied on the Red Hat Linux CD-ROM, we'll walk through a simple Samba setup using Red Hat Linux. When installing Red Hat Linux, you can select the software packages you wish to load, as you can on most all UNIX variants. If you did not load Samba at the time you originally loaded the operating system, you can use the *Gnome RPM* tool or **rpm** from the command line to load Samba or any other software. These tools were briefly discussed in the System Administration chapter.

Using *Linuxconf,* we'll perform some simple tasks to set up Samba. Figure 24-4 shows the *Linuxconf* window *Disk Shares* under *Samba file server* with the three disk shares we'll be using in this example:

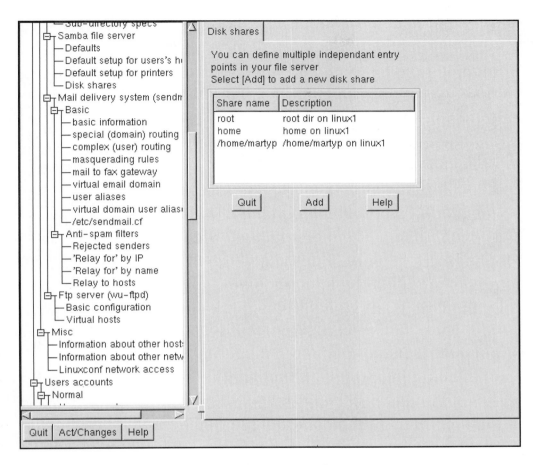

Figure 24-4 Share Information in *Linuxconf*

There are three share names on our Linux system that we will make available to other systems running SMB. Figure 24-5 shows more detailed information about the middle share called *home*:

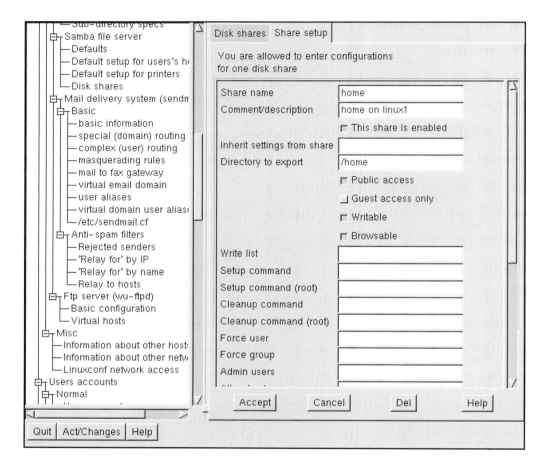

Figure 24-5 **/home** Share Information in *Linuxconf*

This share is for the **/home** directory on *linux1*. Note the four selections related to permissions in the figure. We have granted *Public access*, *Writable*, and *Browsable* rights on this share. We have not restricted it to *Guest only access*. On this share, we have been unrestrictive with respect to the rights granted it. You'll want to consider these rights carefully on your system as you go about assigning these rights. Keep in mind that we're not using any user authentication in our examples, in order to keep them simple. In practice, however, you'll want to make sure that you assign appropriate rights to the shares.

With three shares having been assigned, we'll use *Linuxconf* to start *smb*. We'll do so by enabling *smb* in *Control service activity,* as shown in Figure 24-6:

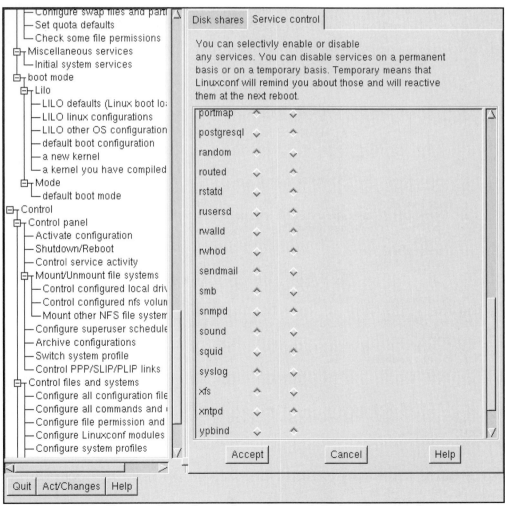

Figure 24-6 Start *smb* in *Control service activity* in *Linuxconf*

smb has been enabled so that the service will start when the system boots.

Before we begin using *smb*, let's perform a couple of quick checks on the work we have performed with *Linuxconf*. We could have accomplished manually everything we have done with *Linuxconf*.

The first check is to view the file **/etc/smb.conf**. This is the file that contains all our SMB configuration information. For now, let's go right to the "Share Definitions" section to confirm that the three shares we configured in *Linuxconf* have proper entries in **/etc/smb.conf**:

```
#=============== Share Definitions =========================
[homes]
    comment = Home Directories
    browseable = no
    writable = yes

# Un-comment the following and create the netlogon directory for
Domain Logons
; [netlogon]
;    comment = Network Logon Service
;    path = /home/netlogon
;    guest ok = yes
;    writable = no
;    share modes = no


# Un-comment the following to provide a specific roving profile
share
# the default is to use the user's home directory
;[Profiles]
;     path = /home/profiles
;     browseable = no
;     guest ok = yes


# NOTE: If you have a BSD-style print system there is no need to
# specifically define each individual printer
[printers]
    comment = All Printers
    path = /var/spool/samba
    browseable = no
# Set public = yes to allow user 'guest account' to print
    guest ok = no
    writable = no
    printable = yes
```

```
[root]
    comment = root dir on linux1
    available = yes
    path = /
    public = yes
    guest only = no
    writable = yes
    browseable = yes
    only user = no
[home]
    comment = home on linux1
    available = yes
    path = /home
    public = yes
    guest only = no
    writable = yes
    browseable = yes
    only user = no
[/home/martyp]
    comment = /home/martyp on linux1
    available = yes
    path = /home/martyp
    public = yes
    guest only = no
    writable = yes
    browseable = yes
    only user = no
```

There are indeed entries in **/etc/smb.conf** for the three shares we configured in *Linuxconf* with the permissions we set up. These are shown near the end of the listing. Next we'll run a Samba utilitiy called **testparm**. This utility will check our **/etc/smb.conf** file for errors. This utility produces a very long output which I won't include here, but you'll want to run this and check for any warnings or errors it produces.

For our **/etc/smb.conf** file, **testparm** produced only one warning that appeared at the very beginning of the file, which is shown in the following listing:

```
# testparm smb.conf

Load smb config files from /etc/smb.conf
Processing section "[homes]"
Processing section "[printers]"
Processing section "[root]"
```

```
Processing section "[home]"
Processing section "[/home/martyp]"
Loaded services file OK.
WARNING: You have some share names that are longer than 8 chars
These may give errors while browsing or may not be accessible
to some older clients
Press enter to see a dump of your service definitions
```

●

●

●

testparm produced the warning for a long share name and also included a list of our three shares, which looked to be in order. We won't address the long share name warning because the Windows system used in the example can handle the long name. If, however, we were on a DOS system, there would be a problem with this name. We'll see shortly how these potential name incompatibilities are addressed by Linux.

The next check we want to perform is to see that the daemon for Samba, called **smbd**, is indeed running, as shown in the following listing:

ps - 13

```
# ps -efl | grep smbd

140 S root     490    1 0 60   0   -  553 do_sel Sep28 ?        00:00:00 [smbd]
140 S root    1493  490 0 60   0   -  896 do_sel Sep29 ?        00:00:00 smbd -D
000 S root    1976 1951 0 70   0   -  288 pipe_r 09:09 pts/1    00:00:00 grep smbd
```

This **ps** output shows that **smbd** is running. Next let's check that the *netbios-ssn* service is running in the "LISTEN" state as shown in the following example:

netstat - 12

grep - 19

```
# netstat -a | grep netbios

tcp     0      0 linux1:netbios-ssn     f4457mfp2:1047      ESTABLISHED
tcp     0      0 *:netbios-ssn          *:*                 LISTEN
udp     0      0 linux1:netbios-dgm     *:*
udp     0      0 linux1:netbios-ns      *:*
udp     0      0 *:netbios-dgm          *:*
udp     0      0 *:netbios-ns           *:*
```

The output of this listing shows that *netbios* is running. There is an "ESTABLISHED" connection shown which you won't see until you have created a connection to your Samba server. I had already established this connection as I prepared the examples in this chapter.

We can also use the Samba client to access files on the Windows system from our Linux system. Although we won't cover this capability, mostly because the Linux system will normally act as a file server and not the other way around, there is a utility called **smbclient** that provides a lot of useful information. Let's now get the overall status of the Samba setup with the **smbclient** utility, as shown in the following listing:

```
# smbclient -L linux1

Added interface ip=192.168.1.1 bcast=192.168.1.255 nmask=255.255.255.0

Domain=[MYGROUP] OS=[Unix] Server=[Samba 2.0.3]

                Sharename      Type      Comment
                ---------      ----      -------
                root           Disk      root dir on linux1
                home           Disk      home on linux1
                /home/martyp   Disk      /home/martyp on linux1
                IPC$           IPC       IPC Service (Samba Server)
                lp             Printer

                Server                   Comment
                ---------                -------
                LINUX1                   Samba Server

                Workgroup                Master
                ---------                -------
                ATLANTA2                 F4457MFP2
                MYGROUP                  LINUX1
```

This utility produces a useful summary of the Samba setup, including the three shares we set up, the Samba server for our example, and other useful information.

We could continue to test Samba on the server, but the listings we viewed give every indication that Samba is running. Let's now move to the Windows client and use *explorer* to access the shares we made available on our Samba server.

Using Shares

Using *Explorer,* we'll now map a network drive. We'll map **/root** on the Samba server *linux1* to drive **E:** on the Windows system as shown in Figure 24-7:

Figure 24-7   Map Drive **E:** to **/root**

We could have mapped this network drive at the command line on the PC using **net use E:\\192.168.1.1\root**. After having successfully mapped **E:** to **/** on *linux1* using *Explorer,* we can access this directory on our Windows system as shown in Figure 24-8:

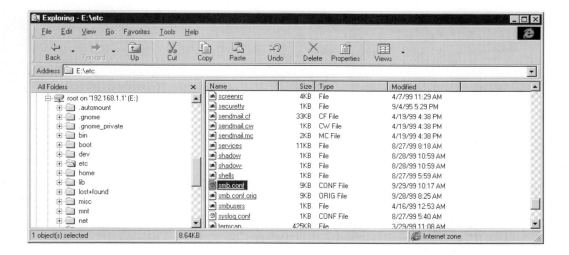

Figure 24-8   View **E:\etc** on Windows System

In Figure 24-8, we have changed to the **/etc** directory on *linux1* and have selected the **smb.conf** file. You can see from this example that **/** on *linux1* is fully accessable on the Windows system. We have access to all three shares on *linux1*, as the following listing shows on the Windows system:

```
c: net view \\192.168.1.1

Shared resources at \\192.168.1.1

Samba Server

Share name    Type          Used as   Comment

-------------------------------------------------------------
/home/martyp   Disk          G:        /home/martyp on linux1
home           Disk          F:          home on linux1
lp             Print
root           Disk          E:          root dir on linux1
The command completed successfully.
```

This listing shows that all three of the *linux1* shares are now available on the Windows system. We have not configured any printer sharing, which is also included as part of Samba functionality, so there is no reference to any printers.

Additional Samba Topics

Samba Web Configuration Tool (SWAT)

SWAT is a Web-based administration tool for Samba. It is easy to configure and provides a simple interface for most Samba configuration tasks. On our Red Hat Linux system, the following steps had to be performed to get SWAT running. If you have a different UNIX variant, then your steps will be different.

Confirm that the following line exists in **/etc/services**:

```
swat            901/tcp
```

Next, uncomment the following line in **/etc/inetd.conf**. This line was already in the file as part of the Linux operating system load:

```
swat stream tcp nowait.400 root /usr/sbin/swat swat
```

Kill the **inetd** process by first finding its Process ID (PID) and then issuing the **kill** command for that PID:

man page

ps - 13

```
# ps -ef | grep inetd
# kill -1 PID of inetd
```

man page

grep - 19

Now we can run SWAT from a browser interface, in this case Netscape, by specifying the IP address of the Samba server and the port number *901*:

man page

kill - 22

```
# netscape http://192.168.1.1:901
```

The browser requests a user name and password when SWAT is invoked to ensure that only users with sufficient rights can make modifications to the Samba configuration in SWAT.

Figure 24-9 shows the SWAT interface. It includes links for *HOME, GLOBALS, SHARES, PRINTERS, STATUS, VIEW,* and *PASSWORD*.

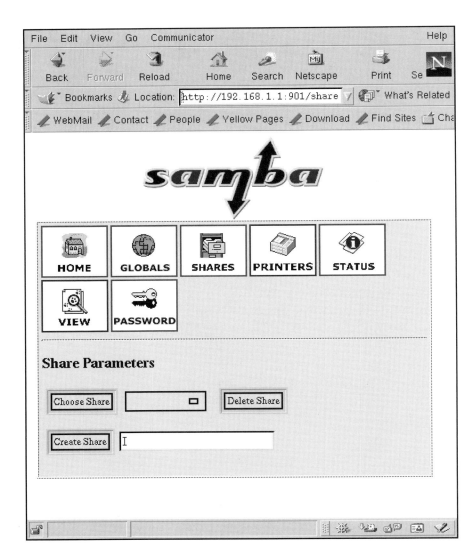

Figure 24-9 SWAT with *SHARES* Selected

The three shares we had earlier conifgured are available in SWAT by selecting *SHARES* from Figure 24-9. SWAT is a good interface for Samba configuration, but there is no substitute for knowing some of the manual processes we experienced earlier in the chapter.

For changes to take effect that are made with SWAT, we had to restart **smbd** with the following command:

```
# /etc/rc.d/init.d/smb restart
```

There is great documentation on the Linux system describing SWAT and all of its capabilities. Figure 24-10 shows the *HOME* page for SWAT with documentation on many of the topics we have covered in this chapter.

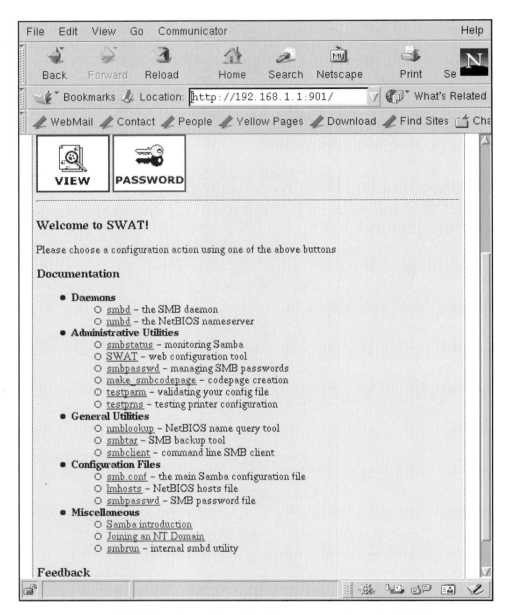

Figure 24-10   SWAT *HOME* Showing Documentation Available

There is also extensive online documentation for all Samba-related software at *www.samba.org*.

Log Files

Like most UNIX applications, Samba provides extensive logging. The **smb.conf** file contains a section that allows you to specify the level of Samba logging you wish to take place. The short section below shows that you can have separate log files for each Windows machine that connects, and you can specify the maximum size of the log file:

```
# this tells Samba to use a separate log file for each machine
# that connects
    log file = /var/log/samba/log.%m

# Put a capping on the size of the log files (in Kb).
    max log size = 50
```

The directory **/var/log/samba** contains a variety of Samba log files, including the log file for the Windows system used in our examples in this chapter, called *f4457mfp2,* as shown in the following listing:

man page

ls - 15

```
# ls -l /var/log/samba

total 14
-rw-r--r--    1 root     root         1915 Sep 30 09:29 log.f4457mfp2
-rw-r--r--    1 root     root          213 Sep 29 10:14 log.linux1
-rw-r--r--    1 root     root            0 Sep 29 04:02 log.nmb
-rw-r--r--    1 root     root         8234 Sep 28 12:25 log.nmb.1
-rw-r--r--    1 root     root         2015 Sep 28 12:19 log.smb
-rw-r--r--    1 root     root            0 Oct  1 11:17 smbconf3.txt
```

File Name Mangling

Among the many Windows and UNIX incompatibilities that exist are file names. Depending on the version of Windows you are using, there may be extensive file name incompatibilities with UNIX. Figure 24-11 is an *Explorer* window with the file **gnome_private** selected, which is on the Linux server. On our Windows NT system, this file name looks fine. However, also in this figure is a *Properties* window showing that the DOS name for this file would change dramatically if we were on a DOS system.

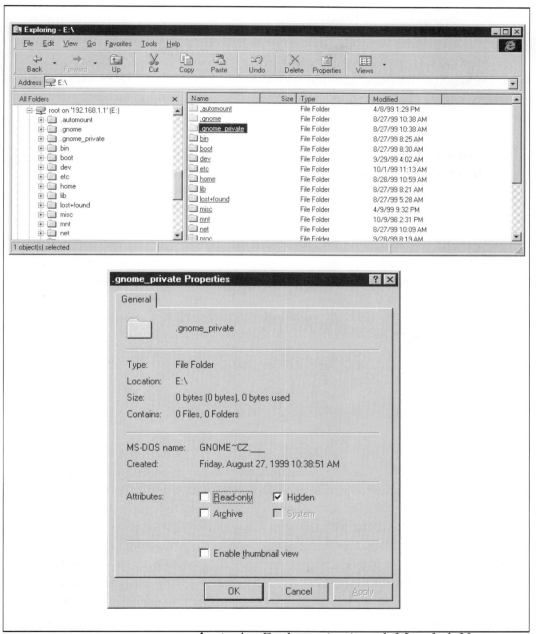

Figure 24-11 **.gnome_private** in *Explorer* (top) and Mangled Name (bottom)

In the case of my Windows system, there is no problem handling the file name **.gnome_private** as it appears on the Linux system. In the case of a DOS system, however, there would be extensive "mangling" of the file name that would have to take place. DOS uses only 8.3 file names, or those with eight characters and a three-character extension.

Samba mangles files that start with a dot, such as the one in this example, by removing the leading dot, printing the first five characters and then a tilde, and then applying a hash algorithm to the original filename to come up with the last two characters. This results in a total of eight characters for the filename. All the characters are uppercase.

If the file does not begin with a dot, then the file name will be generated in the same way as described in the previous paragraph. The extension consists of the first three characters to the right of the dot converted to uppercase. This results in a total of eight characters for the filename and three for the extension.

In our example, the filename **.gnome_private** would be given a DOS name of **GNOME~CZ**. You have some control over mangling in the **smb.conf** file.

User Issues

I have avoided making a serious user-related configuration in this chapter in the interest of keeping the examples simple. You will probably not have this luxury unless you are in an environment where you are the only user on both the Windows and UNIX systems.

Users and groups have always been an important part of every UNIX system. Users and groups were not as important in the Windows world until more recently. This change results in some Windows environments in which there is not a complete user and group policy in place which could be used by Samba.

Samba takes into account both an environment in which you have set up Windows users and groups and one in which you may not have worked out all the issues related to Windows users and groups.

User-level authentication in Samba is set up in such a way that a client can use a given service if they supply the correct user name and password. Share-level authentication takes place by granting access based on the rights of the "guest account" on the UNIX system. This is true unless a client used a user name and password in this or a previous session. Needless to say, there is a lot to consider with user authentication.

The **smb.conf** file has an entry in which you can specify the security as "user" or "share," as shown in the following lines:

```
security = user

security = share
```

man page

passwd - 5

Most systems employ user-level security. When this is done users are checked against their names in the **passwd** file and access is granted accordingly.

There are many additional issues related to user authentication that you'll want to investigate if you set up Samba. The documentation supplied with Samba as part of Red Hat Linux is excellent, and the background information on the Web sites listed later in this chapter is informative as well.

Samba Utilities and Programs

We have used several Samba utilities and programs in this chapter. The following list gives a description of the most often used Samba-related commands. There are manual pages for all these, which are part of most Samba installations.

- **smbd** - This is the daemon that provides file and print services to SMB clients, such as the Windows system used in our examples throughout this chapter.

- **nmbd** - This is the daemon that provides NetBIOS name server capability and browsing.

- **smbclient** - A program that gives the server access to remotely mounted SMB shares on other servers.

- **testparm** - A test program for **/etc/smb.conf**.

- **smbstatus** - Program that displays status information about current Samba connections.

- **smbpasswd** - Program used to change a user's SMB password on the local machine.

- **smbrun** - Program that runs shell commands for **smbd**.

- **smbtar** - Program to back up SMB shares directly to a UNIX tape drive.

- **smbmount** - Used to mount an SMB file system.

- **smbumount** - Used to unmount an SMB file system.

The online manual pages for these and other Samba-related commands provide more detail. Even in a simple setup such as the one performed in this chapter, you will want to run some of these programs.

Obtaining Samba

In the examples used throughout this chapter, we set up Samba on a Linux system that had Samba installed on it as part of the Red Hat Linux CD-ROM. If Samba does not come on the CD-ROM provided with your UNIX variant or if you wish to be sure that you're loading the very latest Samba, then you can obtain Samba from the Web.

www.samba.org is the place to start. From this Web site, you can select a "download site" in your country. You can also select "Web sites" on *www.samba.org* that provide a wealth of information on

Samba, including the GNU General Public License mentioned earlier in the chapter.

There is extensive documentation on Samba-related Web sites, including detailed descriptions of the programs that I listed earlier and used in this chapter.

If you decide to download Samba, you'll probably be given an option of loading a precompiled Samba on your system or building and compiling Samba yourself. The choice you make depends on a lot of factors. If you have a good, reliable Samba distribution, as we did in this chapter when working with Red Hat Linux, then working with a precompiled Samba may be best. If you're interested in learning more about how Samba works and is configured, and want the very latest and greatest version, then download the source and compile it yourself.

Even if you have a great prepackaged Samba, as we did in this chapter, it is still worth visiting the Samba-related Web sites to view the extensive documentation available.

CHAPTER 25

The X Window System

X Window System Background

X Windows is a *network*-based windowing environment, not a system-based windowing environment. For this reason, it is ideal for giving you a window into your UNIX system from your Windows system.

X Windows is an industry standard for supporting windowed user interfaces across a computer network. Because it is an industry standard, many companies offer X server products for operating systems such as Windows (we'll get into the "server" and "client" terminology of X Windows shortly). X Windows is not just a windowing system on your computer but a windowing system across the network.

X Windows is independent of the hardware or operating system on which it runs. All it needs is a server and a client. The server and client may be two different systems or the same system; that detail doesn't matter. The server is a program that provides input/output devices such as your display, keyboard, and mouse. The client is the program that takes commands from the server such as an application.

The client and server roles are much different from those we normally associate with these terms. The X Windows server is on your

local system (in this chapter, it is on your Windows system), and the X
Windows client is the application that communicates with the server
(in this chapter, it will be the UNIX system running a program such as
a System Administration Tool). We normally think of the small desktop system as the client and the larger, more powerful system as the
server. With X Windows, however, it is the system that controls X
Windows that is the server, and the system that responds to the commands is the client. I often refer to a powerful client as the "host," in
order to minimize confusion over this distinction.

In X Windows, the software that manages a single screen, keyboard, and mouse is known as an X server. A client is an application
that displays on the X server. The X client sends requests to the X
server, such as a request for information. The X server accepts
requests from multiple X clients and returns information and errors to
the X client.

Sitting on one of the Windows systems on a network, you could
open an X Window into several UNIX hosts. You could therefore
have one window open to *UNIX_System1*, another window open to
UNIX_System2, and so on.

The X server performs the following functions:

• Displays drawing requests on the screen.

• Replies to information requests.

• Reports an error associated with a request.

• Manages the keyboard, mouse, and display.

• Creates, maps, and removes windows.

The X client performs the following functions:

• Sends requests to the server.

• Receives events and errors from the server.

X Server Software

There are many fine X Server products on the market. I loaded *Exceed 6* (what I'll call *Exceed*) from Hummingbird Communications Ltd. on my system for demonstrating how X Windows can be used in a Windows and UNIX environment. I will use *Exceed* in the examples in this chapter. Figure 25-1 shows the full menu structure from having loaded Hummingbird's X Windows product *Exceed:*

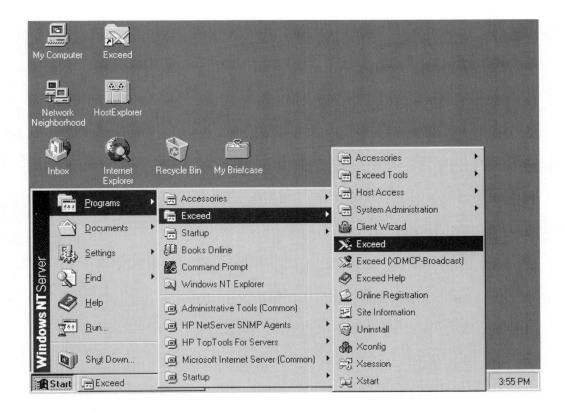

Figure 25-1 The *Programs-Exceed* Menu

Selecting the Exceed icon from the very top of Figure 25-1 produces a group of Exceed icons that is an alternative to accessing items from the menu of Figure 25-1. Figure 25-2 shows the icon group:

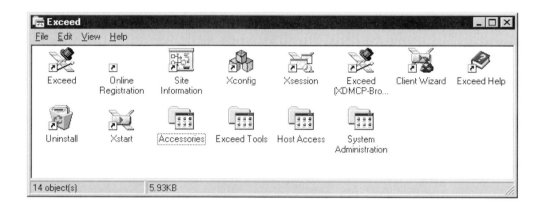

Figure 25-2 The *Exceed* Group

The *Exceed* menu pick from Figure 25-1 allows you to establish an X Windows connection between your Windows system and UNIX system. You can specify the host to which you want to connect, the UNIX system in this case, the user you want to be connected as on the host, and the command to run on the UNIX system. Figure 25-3 shows the *Xstart* window:

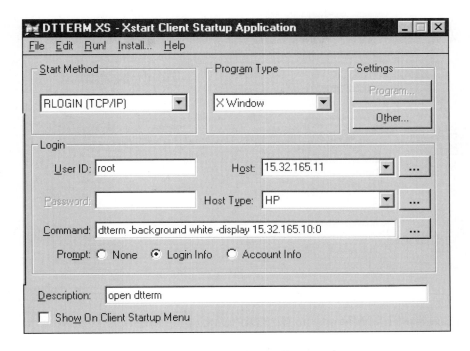

Figure 25-3 Establishing an X Windows Connection

The window in Figure 25-3 is labeled "DTTERM.XS." After you set up the *Xstart* window with the information you want, you can save the configuration. In this case, I am issuing the **dtterm** command, so I saved the window under this name. The system type can be most any system running X Windows. I used an HP-UX system in the upcoming examples, so the *Host Type* is *HP*. The complete **dtterm** command used will run on most UNIX systems running the Common Desktop Environment and is shown below:

dtterm -background white -display 15.32.165.10:0

Selecting *Run!* from the window in Figure 25-3 brings up the window in Figure 25-4, from which you can issue the *Password* and make other changes:

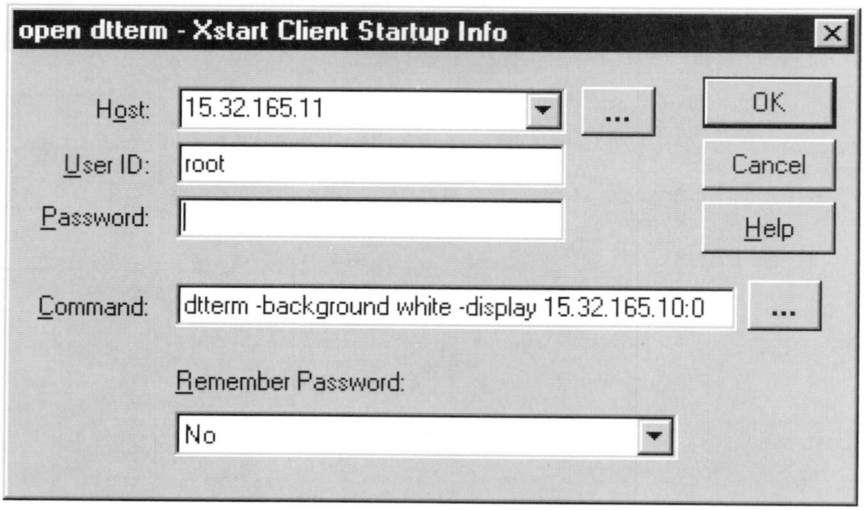

open dtterm - Xstart Client Startup Info   ☒

Host: 15.32.165.11   ▼   ...   OK

User ID: root   Cancel

Password: | Help

Command: dtterm -background white -display 15.32.165.10:0   ...

Remember Password:

No   ▼

Figure 25-4 Establishing an X Windows Connection

This command starts a **dtterm** window, which is a standard window program on UNIX with a white background, and displays the window on the system at the IP address *15.32.165.11*. The IP address in this case is the Windows system on which you are issuing the command, which is the X Windows server. The ":0" indicates that the first display on the Windows system will be used for **dtterm**, because in the X Windows world, you can have several displays on a system. The system on which the command runs is *15.32.165.10*. This is the UNIX system that acts as the X Windows client.

Although you are typing this information on your Windows system, this command is being transferred to the UNIX system you specified in the *Xstart* box. This transfer will have the same result as typing the **dtterm** command shown on the UNIX system directly.

When you type your password and click *OK*, a **dtterm** window appears on your Windows system that is a window into your UNIX system. Figure 25-5 shows the **dtterm** window open on the Windows system.

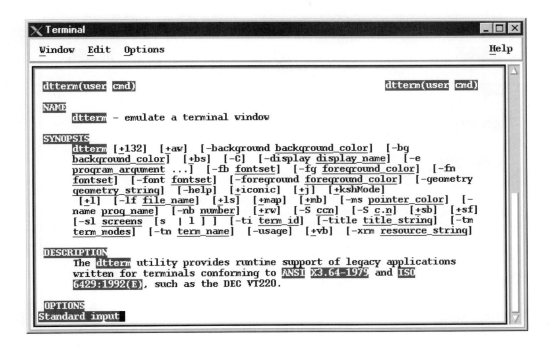

Figure 25-5 **dtterm** Running on UNIX and Displayed on Windows

Figure 25-5 is a **dtterm** window displayed on the Windows system, but running on the UNIX system. The window currently has open the HP-UX manual page for **dtterm**. You can issue any commands in this **dtterm** window that you could issue if you were sitting on the UNIX system directly. Keep in mind, though, that your access to the UNIX system is based on the rights of the user you specified in the *Xstart* window.

You can use *Xstart* to run any program for which you have appropriate permissions on the UNIX system. Figure 25-6 shows an

xterm window that is displayed on the Windows system, but is running on the UNIX system:

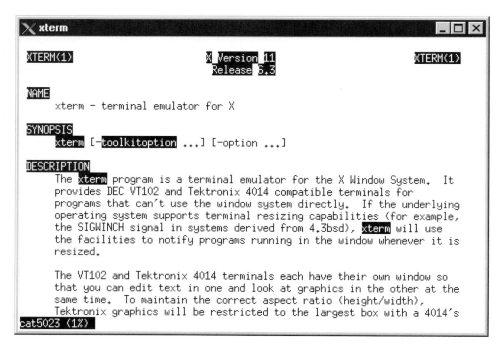

Figure 25-6 **xterm** Running on UNIX and Displayed on Windows

You are by no means limited to running only terminal windows such as **dtterm** and **xterm** under X Windows in this environment. You can invoke your commonly used applications or perform system management functions as well. Figure 25-7 shows the System Administration Manager (SAM), which is the primary system administration tool on HP-UX, running on the UNIX system and displayed on the Windows system with *Kernel Configuration* selected:

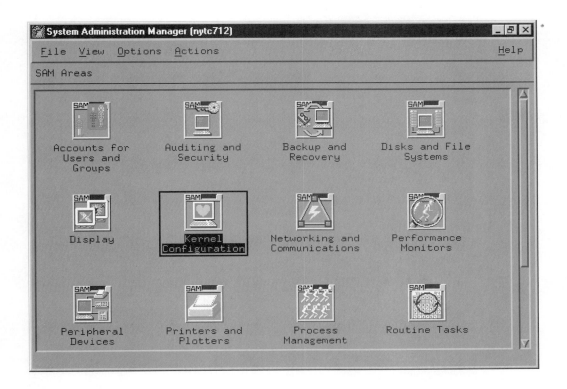

Figure 25-7 SAM Running on HP-UX and Displayed on Windows

You have no reason, however, to limit your use of *Exceed* to opening single windows or single applications. *Exceed* can also be used to run the Common Desktop Environment (CDE) used on most UNIX operating systems. CDE is a windowing environment that allows you to open several "desktops," which results in many windows.

By modifying a few parameters in *Exceed*, you can specify that the entire CDE environment run on your Windows system. CDE allows you to have multiple workspaces in with which you can organize the functional tasks you are performing. Figure 25-8 shows CDE running on our Windows system with the first of the workspaces selected called *program:*

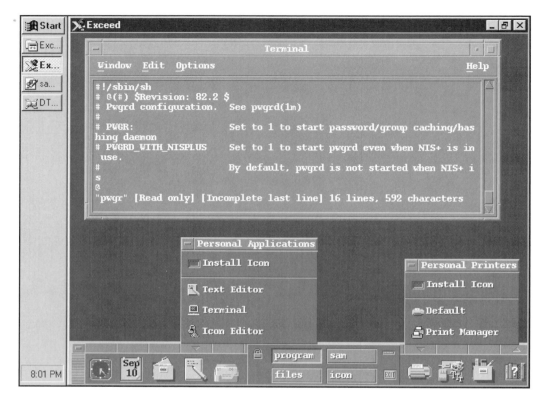

Figure 25-8 CDE *program* Workspace

program is the first of the four workspaces shown on the bottom middle of Figure 25-8. There are three other workspaces for this user that we will view labeled *sam, files,* and *icon*.

Figure 25-9 shows the *sam* workspace, in which we have invoked the System Administration Manager:

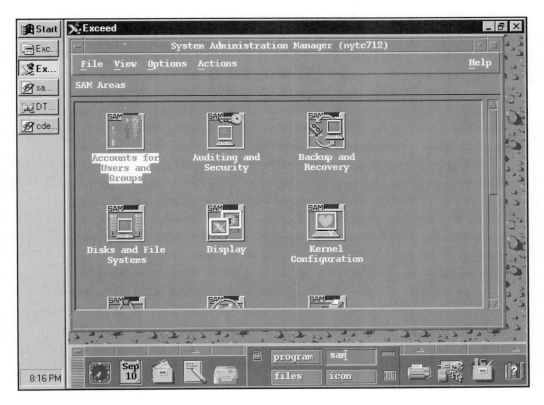

Figure 25-9 CDE *sam* Workspace

Figure 25-10 shows the *files* workspace, in which we have invoked the CDE *File Manager*:

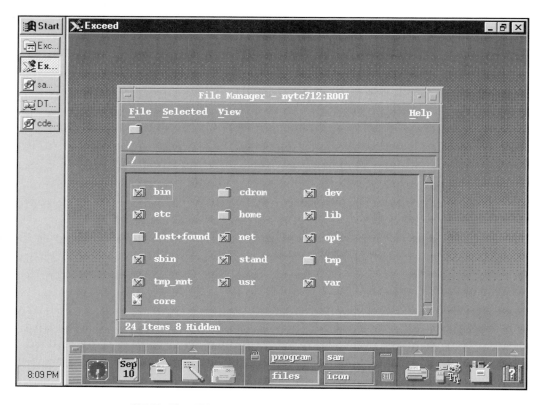

Figure 25-10 CDE *files* Workspace

Figure 25-11 shows the *icon* workspace, in which we have invoked the *Icon Editor*:

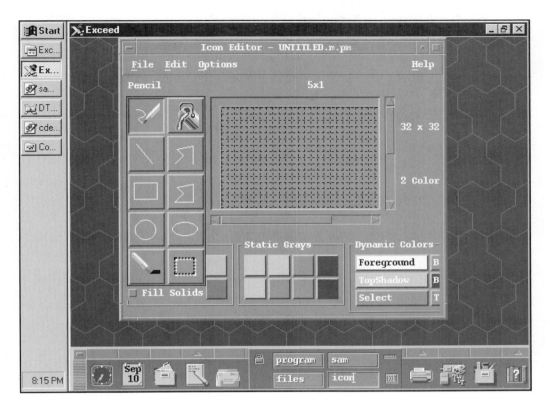

Figure 25-11 CDE *icon* Workspace

This technique, using X Windows on the Windows system to display applications running on the UNIX system, is powerful in this heterogeneous environment. It is also inexpensive and simple to install. You have a choice using *Exceed* to either open individual UNIX windows while working on your Windows system or run the entire Common Desktop Environment from your Windows system. I find that users who spend a majority of their time working on the UNIX system, such as UNIX developers, like to run the entire Common Desktop Environment on their Windows system. Users who spend a majority of time on their Windows systems and need only occasional access to UNIX usually open a **dtterm** or **xterm** window from the Windows system. *Exceed* gives you the flexibility to access UNIX from Windows using either technique.

We can also take this interoperability one step further by introducing data sharing into this mixed environment. Just as X Windows on UNIX and the Windows user interface are not compatible, the ways in which data is shared in UNIX and Windows environments are different. Chapter 16 covers a way in which data sharing between UNIX and Windows takes place.

CHAPTER 26

Networking - UNIX and Windows Interoperability

NFS and X Windows

This chapter and Chapter 24 combine to provide background on some useful interoperability. In this chapter, I use a networking product on the Windows system that provides transparent access to the data on the UNIX system using Network File System (NFS). In Chapter 24, I covered Windows and UNIX interoperability by running an X server program on a Windows system, providing graphical access to a UNIX system. Using the X Window System (X Windows), you have a graphical means of connecting a Windows system to a UNIX system, and using NFS, you have a way of easily sharing data between these two systems. These two technologies, X Windows and NFS, provide the foundation for a variety of other useful interoperability between the two operating systems.

Although I provided TCP/IP background earlier in the book, I am going to include it again here so that you don't have to flip back and forth if you have to review TCP/IP.

TCP/IP Networking Background

You can see the seven layers of network functionality in the ISO/OSI model shown in Figure 26-1. I'll cover these layers at a cursory level, so that you have some background into this networking model. The top layers are the ones that you spend time working with, because they are closest to the functionality to which you can relate. The bottom layers are, however, also important to understand at some level, so that you can perform any configuration necessary to improve the network performance of your system and have a major impact on the overall performance of your system.

Layer Number	Layer Name	Data Form	Comments
7	Application		User applications here.
6	Presentation		Applications prepared.
5	Session		Applications prepared.
4	Transport	Packet	Port-to-port transportation handled by TCP.
3	Network	Datagram	Internet Protocol (IP) handles routing by going directly to the destination or default router.
2	Link	Frame	Data encapsulated in Ethernet or IEEE 802.3 with source and destination addresses.
1	Physical		Physical connection between systems. Usually thinnet or twisted pair.

Figure 26-1 ISO/OSI Network Layer Functions

I'll start reviewing Figure 26-1 at the bottom, with layer 1, and describe each of the four bottom layers. This model is the International Standards Organization Open Systems Interconnection (ISO/OSI) model. It is helpful to visualize the way in which networking layers interact.

Physical Layer

The beginning is the physical interconnect between the systems on your network. Without the **physical layer**, you can't communicate between systems, and all the great functionality you would like to implement will not be possible. The physical layer converts the data you would like to transmit to the analog signals that travel along the wire (I'll assume for now that whatever physical layer you have in place uses wires). The information traveling into a network interface is taken off the wire and prepared for use by the next layer.

Link Layer

In order to connect to other systems local to your system, you use the link layer that is able to establish a connection to all the other systems on your local segment. This is the layer where you have either IEEE 802.3 or Ethernet. These are "encapsulation" methods, named so because your data is put in one of these two forms (either IEEE 802.3 or Ethernet). Data is transferred at the link layer in frames (just another name for data), with the source and destination addresses and some other information attached. You might think that because there are two different encapsulation methods they must be much different. This conclusion, however, is not the case. IEEE 802.3 and Ethernet are nearly identical. So with the bottom two layers, you have a physical connection between your systems and data that is encapsulated into one of two formats with a source and destination address attached. Figure 26-2 lists the components of an *Ethernet* encapsulation and includes comments about IEEE802.3 encapsulation where appropriate.

destination address	6 bytes	address to which data is sent
source address	6 bytes	address from which data is sent
type	2 bytes	the "length count" in 802.3
data	46-1500 bytes	38-1492 bytes for 802.3
crc	4 bytes	checksum to detect errors

Figure 26-2 Ethernet Encapsulation

One interesting item to note is the difference in the maximum data size between IEEE 802.3 and Ethernet of 1492 and 1500 bytes, respectively. This is the Maximum Transfer Unit (MTU). The data in Ethernet is called a *frame* (the re-encapsulation of data at the next layer up is called a *datagram* in IP, and encapsulation at two levels up is called a *packet* for TCP.)

Keep in mind that Ethernet and IEEE 802.3 can run on the same physical connection, but there are indeed differences between the two encapsulation methods.

Network Layer

Next we work up to the third layer, which is the network layer. This layer is synonymous with the Internet Protocol (IP). Data at this layer is called a *datagram*. This is the layer that handles the routing of data around the network. Data that gets routed with IP sometimes encounters an error of some type, which is reported back to the source system with an Internet Control Message Protocol (ICMP) message.

Unfortunately, the information that IP uses does not conveniently fit inside an Ethernet frame, so you end up with fragmented data. This is really re-encapsulation of the data, so you end up with a lot of inefficiency as you work your way up the layers.

IP handles routing in a simple fashion. If data is sent to a destination connected directly to your system, then the data is sent directly to that system. If, on the other hand, the destination is not connected directly to your system, the data is sent to the default router. The default router, sometimes called a gateway, then has the responsibility to handle getting the data to its destination.

Transport Layer

This layer can be viewed as one level up from the network layer, because it communicates with *ports*. TCP is the most common protocol found at this level, and it forms packets that are sent from port to port. These ports are used by network programs such as **telnet**, **rlogin**, **ftp**, and so on. You can see that these programs, associated with ports, are at the highest level I have covered while analyzing the layer diagram.

Internet Protocol (IP) Addressing

The Internet Protocol address (IP address) is a class "A," "B," or "C" address (class "D" and "E" addresses exist that I will not cover). A class "A" network supports many more nodes per network than a class "B" or "C" network. IP addresses consist of four fields. The purpose of breaking down the IP address into four fields is to define a node (or host) address and a network address. Figure 26-3 summarizes the relationships between the classes and addresses.

Address Class	Networks	Nodes per Network	Bits Defining Network	Bits Defining Nodes per Network
A	a few	the most	8 bits	24 bits
B	many	many	16 bits	16 bits
C	the most	a few	24 bits	8 bits
Reserved	-	-	-	-

Figure 26-3 Comparison of Internet Protocol (IP) Addresses

These bit patterns are significant in that the number of bits defines the ranges of networks and nodes in each class. For instance, a class A address uses 8 bits to define networks, and a class C address uses 24 bits to define networks. A class A address therefore supports fewer networks than a class C address. A class A address, however, supports many more nodes per network than a class C address. Taking these relationships one step further, we can now view the specific parameters associated with these address classes in Figure 26-4.

Figure 26-4 Address Classes

Address Class	Networks Supported	Nodes per Network	Address Range		
A	127	16777215	0.0.0.1	-	127.255.255.254
B	16383	65535	128.0.0.1	-	191.255.255.254
C	2097157	255	192.0.0.1	-	223.255.254.254
Reserved	-	-	224.0.0.0	-	255.255.255.255
Looking at the 32-bit address in binary form, you can see how to determine the class of an address:					

Figure 26-4   Address Classes (Continued)

Class "A"

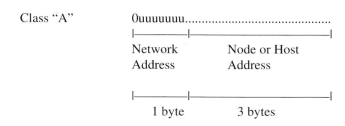

net.host.host.host

A class "A" address has the first bit set to 0. You can see how so many nodes per network can be supported with all the bits devoted to the node or host address. The first bit of a class A address is 0, and the remaining 7 bits of the network portion are used to define the network. There are then a total of 3 bytes devoted to defining the nodes within a network.

Class "B"

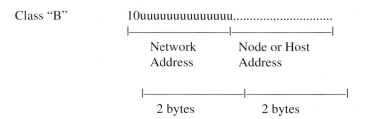

net.net.host.host

A class "B" address has the first bit set to a 1 and the second bit to a 0. There are more networks supported here than with a class A address, but fewer nodes per network. With a class B address, there are 2 bytes devoted to the network portion of the address and 2 bytes are devoted to the node portion of the address.

Figure 26-4 Address Classes (Continued)

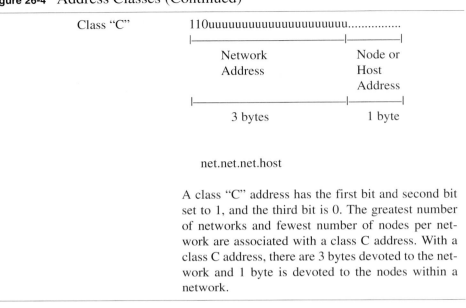

net.net.net.host

A class "C" address has the first bit and second bit set to 1, and the third bit is 0. The greatest number of networks and fewest number of nodes per network are associated with a class C address. With a class C address, there are 3 bytes devoted to the network and 1 byte is devoted to the nodes within a network.

Every interface on your network must have a unique IP address. Systems that have two network interfaces must have two unique IP addresses. I will cover some networking commands in Windows in an upcoming chapter.

NFS Background

I am not going to limit the discussion and examples in this chapter to NFS. There are other services used to share files that are also useful, such as File Transfer Protocol (FTP), which I'll show examples of as well. Because NFS is so widely used in the UNIX user community, it is one of my goals to expose you to how NFS can be used in a Windows and UNIX environment.

NFS allows you to mount disks on remote systems so that they appear as though they are local to your system. Similarly, NFS allows remote systems to mount your local disk so that it looks as though it is local to the remote system.

NFS, like X Windows, has a unique set of terminology. Here are definitions of some of the more important NFS terms:

Node   A computer system that is attached to or is part of a computer network.

Client   A node that requests data or services from other nodes (servers).

Server   A node that provides data or services to other nodes (clients) on the network.

File System   A disk partition or logical volume, or in the case of a workstation, this might be the entire disk.

Export   To make a file system available for mounting on remote nodes using NFS.

Mount   To access a remote file system using NFS.

Mount Point   The name of a directory on which the NFS file system is mounted.

Import   To mount a remote file system.

Before any data can be shared using NFS, the UNIX system must be set up with exported file systems. The **/etc/exports** file is often used on UNIX to define what file systems are exported.

This file has in it the directories exported and options such as "ro" for read-only and "anon," which handles requests from anonymous users. If "anon" is equal to *65535*, then anonymous users are denied access.

The following is an example **/etc/exports** file in which **/opt/app1** is exported to everyone but anonymous users, and **/opt/app1** is exported only to the system named *system2*:

```
/opt/app1    -anon=65534
/opt/app2    -access=system2
```

You may need to run a program such as **exportfs -a** on your UNIX system if you add a file system to export.

Although we are going to focus on exporting UNIX file systems to be mounted by Windows systems in this chapter, I can think of no reason that we could not do the converse as well. Windows file systems can be mounted on a UNIX system just as UNIX file systems are mounted in Windows. Remote file systems to be mounted locally on a UNIX system are often put in **/etc/fstab**. Here is an example of an entry in **/etc/fstab** of a remote file system that is mounted locally. The remote directory **/opt/app3** on *system2* is mounted locally under **/opt/opt3**:

```
system2:/opt/app3   /opt/app3   nfs   rw,suid   0   0
```

man page

showmount - 11

You can use the **showmount** command available on many UNIX systems to show all remote systems (clients) that have mounted a local file system. **showmount** is useful for determining the file systems that are most often mounted by clients with NFS. The output of **showmount** is particularly easy to read because it lists the host name and the directory that was mounted by the client. You have the three following options to the **showmount** command:

man page

showmount
- 11

-a prints output in the format "name:directory," as shown above.

-d lists all the local directories that have been remotely mounted by clients.

-e prints a list of exported file systems.

Using Windows and UNIX Networking

I use the *NFS Maestro* product from Hummingbird Communications Ltd. on Windows to demonstrate the networking interoperability in this chapter.

You would typically run your NFS client, such as *NFS Maestro*, on your Windows system in order to mount file systems on a UNIX system. This setup means that all your Windows clients would run *NFS Maestro*. Depending on the number of Windows systems you have, you may find loading an NFS client on each and every system to be a daunting task. Hummingbird Communications has an alternative. Rather than loading the NFS client on each system, you can use a Windows system to act as a gateway between your Windows systems and your UNIX systems. *NFS Maestro Gateway* bridges your Windows network to your UNIX network. All Windows clients go through the *NFS Maestro Gateway* system in order to perform NFS access to the UNIX systems, thereby simplifying the installation and administration of NFS on Windows.

NFS Maestro Gateway bridges your Microsoft Server Message Block (SMB) network to your UNIX network by acting as a proxy. It forwards SMB requests from a Windows client to a UNIX NFS server and vice versa.

The performance of using a dedicated *NFS Maestro* client is superior to that of using *NFS Maestro Gateway*. Like many system administration topics, there is a trade-off that takes place between simplicity and performance. In this chapter I'll cover using a dedicated *NFS Maestro* client to access file systems on a UNIX server.

Figure 26-5 shows the menu for the Maestro product after I installed it.

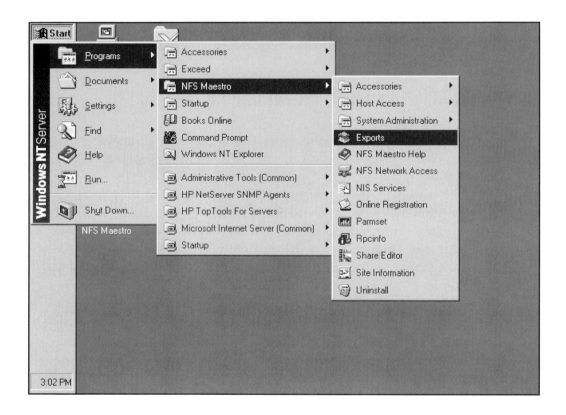

Figure 26-5 Hummingbird Maestro Menu in Windows

As you can see in Figure 26-5, there is much more than NFS functionality is part of *NFS Maestro*. I will cover some additional functionality later in this chapter; however, my specific objectives are to cover the most important Windows and UNIX interoperability topics related to networking.

The NFS icons can also be accessed as part of a group from the *NFS Maestro* icon as shown in Figure 26-6.

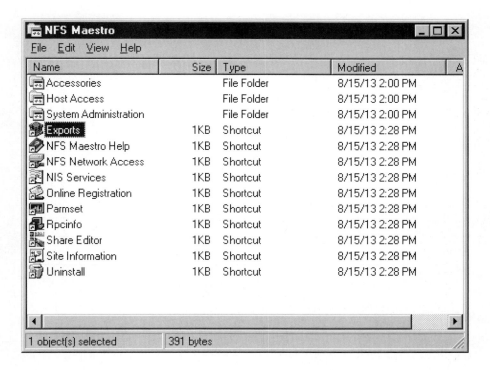

Figure 26-6 *NFS* Group

Before we use NFS with our Windows and UNIX systems, let's first see what file systems we have available to us.

Using the Common Desktop Environment (CDE) on our Windows system from Chapter 15, we can sit at the Windows system and work on the UNIX system. Figure 26-7 shows the Common Desktop Environment with a *Terminal* window open:

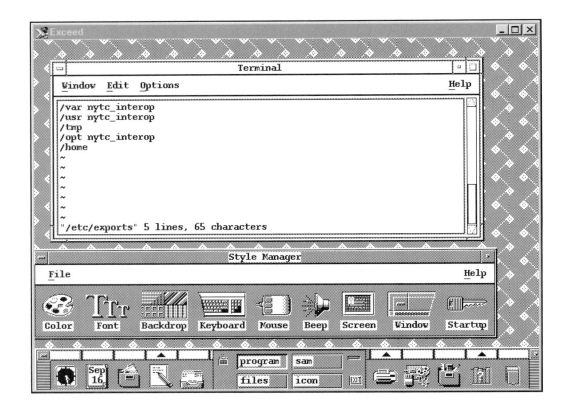

Figure 26-7 Common Desktop Environment on UNIX with **/etc/ exports** Shown

There are several file systems exported on this UNIX system. Some, such as **/home** and **/tmp,** have no restrictions on them; others do have restrictions. We don't, however, have to open a *Terminal* window in order to see this file. We can use the *NFS Maestro* menu pick *Exports* to bring up the window shown in Figure 26-8:

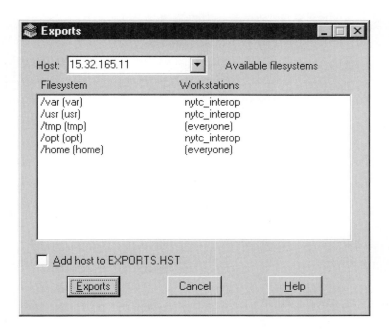

Figure 25-8 *Exports* Window Showing Exported File Systems

You can use the IP address, as shown in Figure 26-8, or the host name to specify the host on which you wish to view the exported file systems. You can see that this window takes the **/etc/exports** file and clarifies some of the entries. The entries that have no restrictions now have an "(everyone)" associated with them, and only system *nytc_interop* may mount the other file systems.

Now we can specify one or more of these exported file systems on the UNIX system that we wish to mount on the Windows system. Using the *NFS Network Access* selection from the *NFS Maestro* menu, we can specify one of these file systems to mount. Figure 26-9 shows mounting **/home/hp** on the UNIX system on the **F:** drive of the Windows system. Note that we are UNIX user *hp* when we mount this file system.

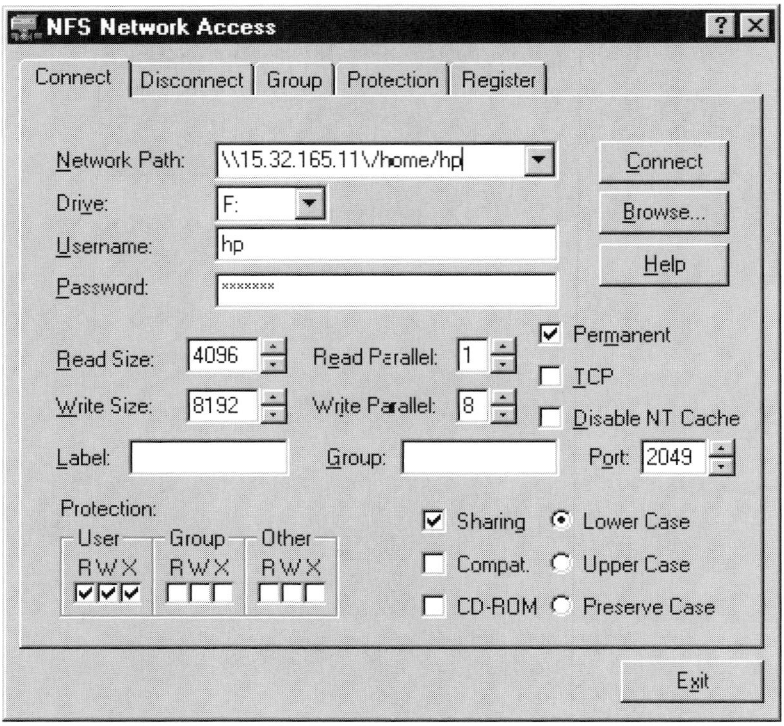

Figure 26-9 *NFS Network Access* Window Mounting **/home/hp** as **F:**

After you click the *Connect* button on the window, you have **/home/hp** mounted as **F:**. The means by which you specify the system and file system you wish to mount with NFS Maestro is two slashes preceding the IP address or system name, another slash following the IP address or system name, and then the name of the file system you wish to mount. Note that the forward slash is part of the file system name. I used the IP address of the system. To view all the mounted file systems on the Windows system, you can invoke Windows *Explorer*.

Figure 26-10 shows several file systems mounted in an *Explorer* window, including **/home/hp** on **F:**.

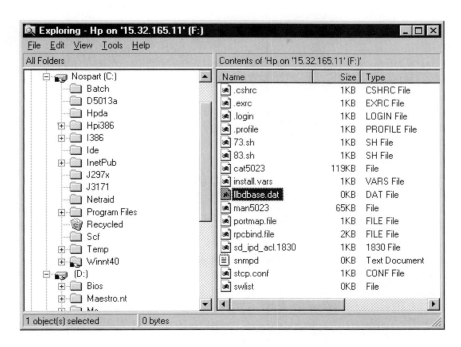

Figure 26-10   Windows *Explorer* Showing **/home/hp** as **F:**

This window shows **/home/hp** on drive **F:**. On the right side of the window is a listing of files in **/home/hp** on the UNIX system. These files are now fully accessible on the Windows system (provided that the appropriate access rights have been provided). You may need to adjust the *Explorer* to *Show all files* in order to see the hidden UNIX files. You can now manipulate these UNIX files in *Explorer* on the Windows system just as if they were local to the system. This is a powerful concept - to go beyond the barrier of only the Windows file system to freely manipulate UNIX files.

The permissions of these NFS mounted files are not shown in the *Explorer* window. We can select specific files and view their properties. Figure 26-11 shows viewing the **.cshrc** file:

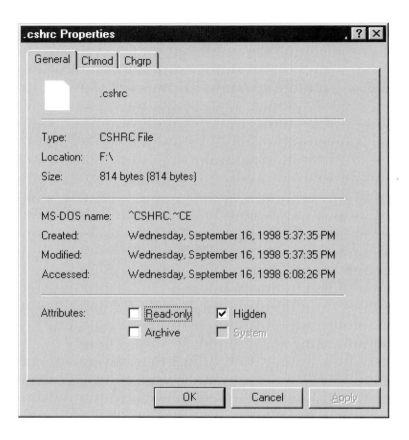

Figure 26-11 Viewing the Properties of **.cshrc**

The **.cshrc** file is *Hidden* and is not *Read-only*, meaning that we can manipulate this file.

Next let's view the properties of **install.vars** as shown in Figure 26-12.

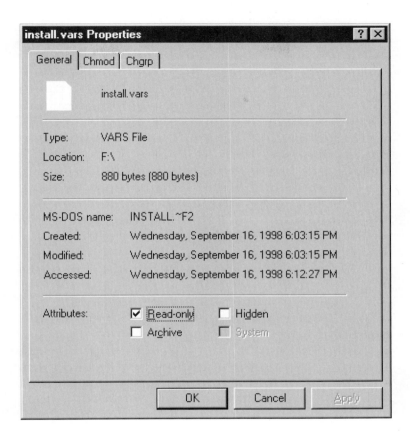

Figure 26-12　Viewing the Properties of **install.vars**

install.vars is *Read-only* because this file is owned by *root* on the UNIX system and not by user *hp,* which is the UNIX user under which we mounted **/home/hp**.

We are unable to *Chmod*, or modify the permissions on this file, because it is owned by root and we have mounted **/home/hp** as the user *hp,* as shown in Figure 26-13:

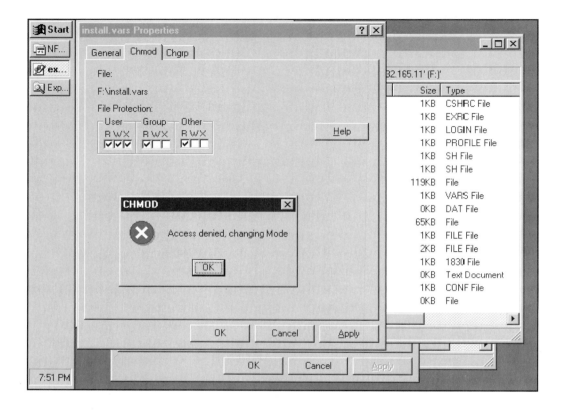

Figure 26-13   Failed Attempt to Change Permissions of **install.vars**

This error indicates that we are prevented from changing the permissions on **install.vars**.

An example of how you might go about using *Explorer* is to copy a Windows NT directory to UNIX. Figure 26-14 shows two *Explorer* windows. The top window has an **nfs** directory on the Windows system, which is being copied to a directory of the same name on the UNIX system in the bottom window. As the copy from the Windows system to the UNIX system takes place, a status window appears, which shows the name of the file within the **nfs** directory (**exp2.bmp**) being copied.

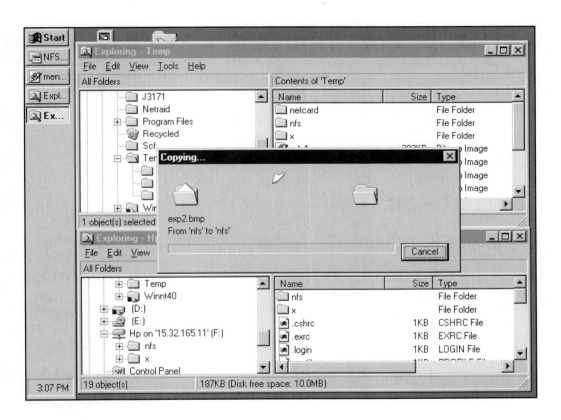

Figure 26-14 Copying a Windows NT Directory to UNIX Using *Explorer*

This copy from Windows to UNIX using *Explorer* demonstrates the ease with which files can be shared between these two operating systems.

File Transfer Protocol (FTP)

man page

ftp - 12

I started this chapter covering NFS on Windows and UNIX for interoperability, because NFS is the predominant means of sharing files in the UNIX world. NFS is used almost universally to share data among networked UNIX systems. NFS allows you to share data in real time, meaning that you can work on a UNIX file while sitting at your Windows system. This approach is file sharing. You can also copy data between your Windows and UNIX systems using FTP. This approach is not file sharing; however, the FTP functionality of *NFS Maestro* makes it easy to transfer files between Windows and UNIX.

Figure 26-15 shows the dialog box that you would use to establish a connection to a UNIX system from Windows:

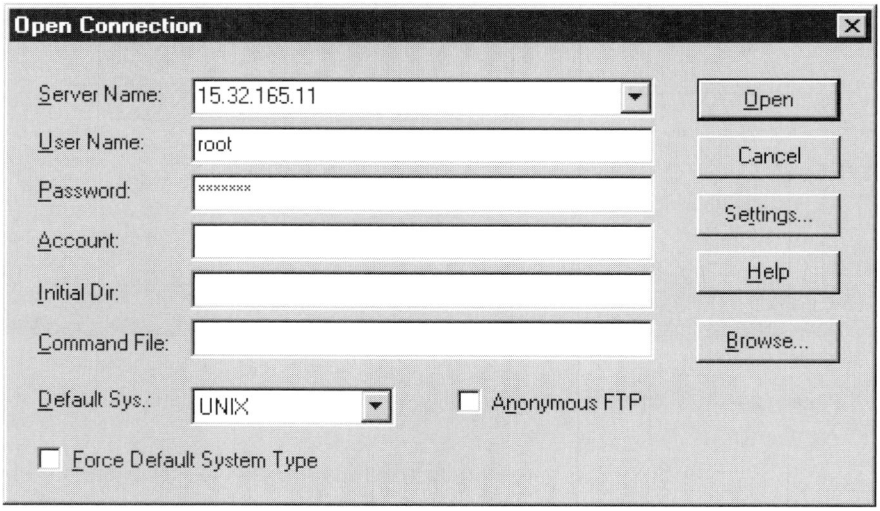

Figure 26-15   Establishing a Connection to UNIX from Windows

After having established the connection, a window appears in which you can traverse the UNIX file systems while working at your Windows system. Figure 26-16 shows viewing the **/home/hp** directory on a UNIX system through the *FTP* window.

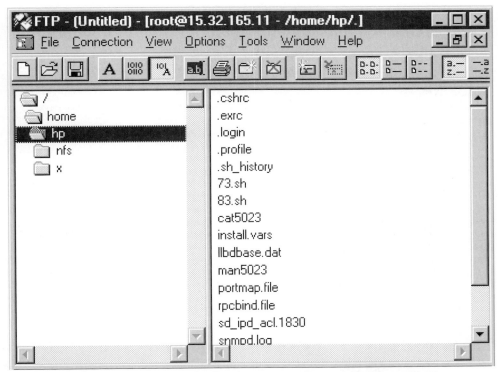

Figure 26-16   Viewing the **/home/hp** Directory Using the *FTP* Window

You can also copy files graphically using FTP. You can open two *FTP* windows and copy files and directories from one system to the other. Figure 26-17 shows copying the directory **c:\temp\x** on the Windows system to **/home/hp/x** on the UNIX system. This was performed using the icons in the two windows. The **x** directory did not exist on the UNIX system and was created as part of the copy. As the copy from the Windows system to the UNIX system takes place, a status window appears, which shows the name of the file within the **x** directory (**xmenu2.bmp**) being copied.

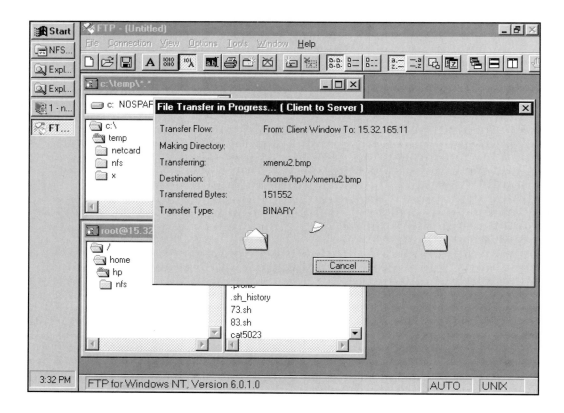

Figure 26-17   Using FTP to Copy a Directory from Windows to UNIX

There are a variety of options you can select when running FTP. Notice in Figure 26-17 that the "Transfer Type:" is *binary*. This is one of the options I selected prior to initiating the transfer.

Although this functionality is not as extensive as the file sharing of NFS, it is widely used to copy files from system to system and therefore can play a role in Windows and UNIX interoperability.

I used icons to specify the information to be copied in this example. You could also have used the FTP command. The following is an overview of FTP, including an example of running it from the command line and a command summary.

man page

ftp - 12

File Transfer Protocol (FTP) Transfer a file, or multiple files, from one system to another, such as Windows to UNIX. The following example shows copying the file **/tmp/krsort.c** from *system2* (remote host) to the local directory on *system1* (local host):

	comments
$ ftp system2	Issue ftp command
Connected to system2.	
system2 FTP server (Version 16.2) ready.	
Name (system2:root): root	Log in to system2
Password required for root.	
Password:	Enter password
User root logged in.	
Remote system type is UNIX.	
Using binary mode to transfer files.	
ftp> **cd /tmp**	**cd** to **/tmp** on system2
CWD command successful	
ftp> **get krsort.c**	Get **krsort.c** file
PORT command successful	
Opening BINARY mode data connection for **krsort.c**	
Transfer complete.	
2896 bytes received in 0.08 seconds	
ftp> **bye**	Exit ftp
Goodbye.	
$	

man page

ftp - 12

In this example, both systems are running UNIX; however, the commands you issue through **FTP** are operating-system-independent. The **cd** for change directory and **get** commands used above work for any operating system on which **FTP** is running. If you become familiar with just a few **FTP** commands, you may find that transferring information in a heterogeneous networking environment is not difficult.

Because **FTP** is so widely used, I describe some of the more commonly used **FTP** commands:

ftp - File Transfer Protocol for copying files across a network.

The following list includes some commonly used **ftp** commands. This list is not complete.

ascii   Set the type of file transferred to ASCII. This means that you will be transferring an ASCII file from one system to another. This is the default, so you don't have to set it.

Example: **ascii**

binary   Set the type of file transferred to binary. This means that you'll be transferring a binary file from one system to another. If, for instance, you want to have a directory on your UNIX system that will hold applications that you will copy to non-UNIX systems, then you will want to use binary transfer.

Example: **binary**

cd   Change to the specified directory on the remote host.

Example: **cd /tmp**

dir   List the contents of a directory on the remote system to the screen or to a file on the local system if you specify a local file name.

get   Copy the specified remote file to the specified local file. If you don't specify a local file name, then the remote file name is used.

lcd   Change to the specified directory on the local host.

Example: **lcd /tmp**

ls   List the contents of a directory on the remote system to the screen or to a file on the local system if you specify a local file name.

mget   Copy multiple files from the remote host to the local host.

Example: **mget *.c**

put   Copy the specified local file to the specified remote file. If you don't specify a remote file name, then the local file name is used.

Example: **put test.c**

mput   Copy multiple files from the local host to the remote host.

Example: **mput *.c**

system   Show the type of operating system running on the remote host.

Example: **system**

           bye/quit   Close the connection to the remote host.

                      Example: **bye**

Other **FTP** commands exist in addition to those I have covered here.

Other Connection Topics

man page

telnet - 12

There are other means by which you can connect to a UNIX system. Two popular techniques for connecting to other systems are FTP, which was just covered, and TELNET. NFS Maestro supplies the capability for both of these. I could sit at the Windows system using TEL-NET with a window open on the UNIX system and issue commands.

Figure 26-18 shows the *HostExplorer* window, which is used to specify the characteristics of your TELNET session:

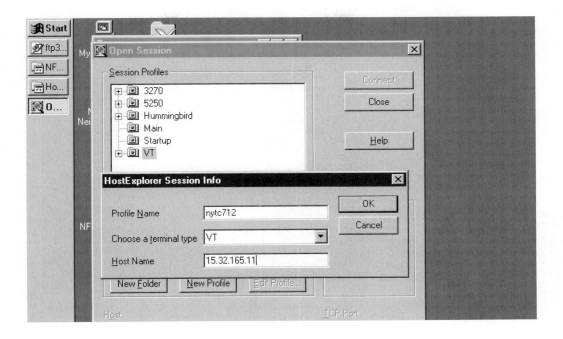

Figure 26-18 Specifying Characteristics of a *HostExplorer* Session

I selected *VT* in the *HostExplorer* window and was able to log in to the UNIX system, as shown in Figure 26-19:

```
1 - hp (15.32.165.11)
File  Edit  Transfer  Fonts  Options  Macro  View  Window  Help

$ ll -a
total 398
drwxr-xr-x    3 hp      users      1024 Sep 16 18:25 .
drwxr-xr-x    4 root    root         96 Sep 16 17:37 ..
-rw-r--r--    1 hp      users       814 Sep 16 17:37 .cshrc
-rw-r--r--    1 hp      users       347 Sep 16 17:37 .exrc
-rw-r--r--    1 hp      users       341 Sep 16 17:37 .login
-rw-r--r--    1 hp      users       446 Sep 16 17:37 .profile
-rw-------    1 hp      users        14 Sep 16 18:25 .sh_history
-rw-r--r--    1 root    sys          23 Sep 16 18:03 73.sh
-rw-r--r--    1 root    sys          23 Sep 16 18:03 83.sh
-rw-rw-rw-    1 root    sys      120922 Sep 16 18:03 cat5023
-rw-r--r--    1 root    sys         880 Sep 16 18:03 install.vars
-r--r--r--    1 root    sys           0 Sep 16 18:03 llbdbase.dat
-rw-rw-rw-    1 root    sys       66113 Sep 16 18:03 man5023
drwx------    2 hp      users      1024 Sep 16 18:17 nfs
-rw-------    1 root    sys         484 Sep 16 18:03 portmap.file
-rw-------    1 root    sys        1692 Sep 16 18:03 rpcbind.file
-rw-r--r--    1 root    sys          74 Sep 16 18:03 sd_ipd_acl.183
-rwxrwxrwx    1 root    sys           0 Sep 16 18:03 snmpd.log
-rw-r--r--    1 root    sys          60 Sep 16 18:03 stcp.conf
-rw-r--r--    1 root    sys           0 Sep 16 18:03 swlist
$
```

Figure 26-19   *telnet* Window

In this window, we can issue UNIX commands just as if we were sitting at a terminal connected directly to the UNIX system. This window shows **/home/hp**, including the **nfs** directory copied earlier, and permissions, owner, and group of all files and directories.

telnet is widely used in heterogenous environments. With X Windows, you get graphical functionality that is not part of *telnet*.

man page

rpcinfo - 12

The protocols running on the UNIX system are assigned to ports. We can view these ports, protocols, and associated information using the **rpcinfo** command on the UNIX system as shown in Figure 26-20:

Figure 26-20 **rpcinfo** Command on UNIX

There is a lot of information in this window in which we are interested related to NFS. We do not, however, have to establish a *telnet* session with the UNIX system and issue **rpcinfo** to see this information. The *Rpcinfo* menu pick under *Maestro* will query the UNIX host and list the services it is running. Figure 26-21 shows this window:

man page

rpcinfo - 12

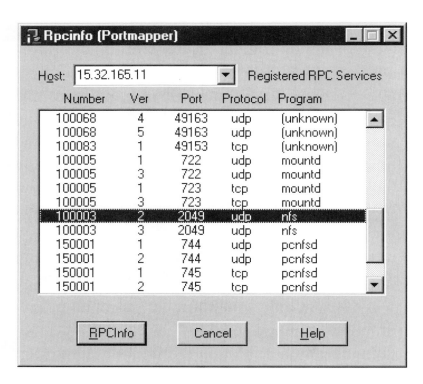

Figure 25-21   *Rpcinfo* Window on Windows

RPC stands for Remote Procedure Call. There are a variety of programs for which there is RPC-related information. Several programs are required to achieve Windows and UNIX interoperability.

The first number shown is the program number. There are widely accepted RPC numbers for various programs. For NFS, the program number is *100003*. The next number is the version of the protocol. In this case, NFS is version *2*. The next number is the port. The port number is used by both the client, which is the Windows system in our case, and the server, which is the UNIX system in our case, to communicate using NFS. The next field is the protocol used, which is usually *UDP* or *TCP.* The final field is the program name.

In the case of NFS, I had to ensure that *NFS, portmapper, mountd,* and *pcnfsd* were running on my UNIX system before I could use the *NFS Maestro NFS* product.

Rpcinfo is a useful tool for viewing all the information on the host to which your Windows system will connect.

CHAPTER 27

Advanced Server for UNIX

Windows Functionality on UNIX

To this point, we have been discussing moving UNIX functionality such as X Windows and NFS onto Windows in order to achieve interoperability. Why not do the converse? Having some Windows functionality on UNIX would certainly be helpful in some cases. UNIX resources such as printers and disks could then be shared with several Windows systems on the network.

Advanced Server for UNIX® is an AT&T product that serves as the basis for many products that bring Windows functionality to UNIX. Advanced Server for UNIX Systems is the result of a joint development agreement between AT&T and Microsoft Corporation. It provides Windows functionality that facilitates Windows and UNIX interoperability. With Advanced Server for UNIX, a UNIX system can act as a Primary or Backup Domain Controller (PDC or BDC), a file server, a print server, or any other Windows functional component. Most major UNIX vendors have a product that is based on Advanced Server for UNIX. This chapter will use the HP-UX implementation of Advanced Server for UNIX called Advanced Server/9000. Other implementations of Advanced Server for UNIX are similar, so you can use the examples in this chapter as a basis of understanding for other such implementations.

This chapter makes use of some of the **net** commands of Windows, especially the **net share** command. When I am working on the UNIX system (*dloaner*) in this chapter, I use the command line including some **net** commands. When I am working on the Windows system (*hpsystem1*) in this chapter, I will use graphical Windows functionality, which is preferable to issuing commands on the command line. I use both the command line and graphical methods so that you can see the difference in the two approaches. You may want to explore some of these **net** commands described in the "Command Line" chapter and using the online help of your Windows system as you progress through this chapter. Here is a list of some widely used **net** commands and a brief explanation of each:

net accounts   Used to maintain the user accounts database.

net computer   Used to add or delete computers from the domain database.

net config server

Displays or changes settings for a server service on which the command is executed.

net config workstation

Displays or changes settings for the workstation service on which the command is executed.

net continue   Reactivates a Windows service that has been suspended with the **net pause** command.

net file	Used for network file manipulation, such as listing ID numbers, closing a shared file, removing file locks, and so on.
net group	Used to add, display, or modify global groups on servers.
net help	Displays a listing of help options for any net command.
net helpmsg	Displays explanations of Windows network messages such as errors, warnings, and alerts.
net localgroup	Used to modify local groups on computers.
net name	Used to add or delete a "messaging name" at a computer, which is the name to which messages are sent.
net print	Used to list print jobs and shared queues.
net send	Sends messages to other users, computers, and "messaging names" on the network.
net session	Used to list or disconnect sessions between the computer and other computers on the network.

net share   Shares a server's resources with other computers on the network.

net start   Used to start services such as *server*.

net statistics   Displays the statistics log for the local Workstation or Server service.

net stop   Used to stop services such as *server*.

net time   Synchronizes the computer's clock with another computer on the domain.

net use   Displays, connects, or disconnects a computer with shared resources.

net user   Creates or modifies user accounts.

net view   Lists resources being shared on a computer.

Installing Advanced Server/9000 on UNIX

You can easily install and configure Advanced Server/9000 on your UNIX system. Advanced Server/9000 is installed using Software Distributor on your HP-UX system, just as you would load any other software. After installing Advanced Server/9000, you must run the configuration script called **asu_inst**. The following text shows running **asu_inst** to configure the UNIX system *dloaner* to be a Backup Domain Controller (BDC) for the Windows system *hpsystem1*:

```
# /opt/asu/lanman/bin/asu_inst

This request script will prompt you for information which is necessary
to install and configure your Advanced Server for UNIX Systems.


There are two installation modes:


Express Setup - the installation scripts use default settings so
installation is quick and easy.  You may change these settings
after installation completes.  The server is installed as a
primary domain controller in its own domain.

Custom Setup - this mode allows you to specify the settings at the
beginning of installation.  If you select this mode, you must
specify the server's name, the domain it will participate in,
and the role in that domain.

NOTE: The installation requires a password for the administrative account.
A default password of 'password' will be used, although you may elect to
be prompted for a different password at the end of the installation.

If you are installing many servers it is strongly recommended that you use
the default password for all installations.  Be sure to change these
passwords after determining that your network is operating correctly.

Do you want Express Setup [y/n]? y

Advanced Server for UNIX provides a NETLOGON service which simplifies the
administration of multiple servers. A single user accounts database can be
shared by multiple servers grouped together into an administrative
collection called a domain. Within a domain, each server has a designated
role. A single server, called the primary domain controller, manages all
changes to the user accounts database and automatically distributes those
changes to other servers, called backup domain controllers, within the same
domain. You may now supply a server name (the name which this server
will be known on the network), the role that this server will perform
in that domain (primary or backup), and a domain name.


Enter the name of the server
or press Enter to select 'dloaner':

Each server must be given a role in a domain.  The possible roles are:

primary domain controller:
    Administration server. Distributes user accounts information
            to backup domain controllers. Validates network logon requests.
    There can be only one primary domain controller per domain.

backup domain controller:
            Receives user account information from the primary domain
            controller. Validates network logon requests and can be promoted
    to primary if the primary domain controller is not accessible.


Enter role (primary or backup): backup
```

This installation will configure the server as a backup domain controller.
You will be prompted to enter the name of the primary domain controller,
and an administrative account name on the primary along with its password.
In order for this installation to complete successfully, the primary domain
controller must be running and connected to the network.

Enter the name of the primary domain controller (eg, abc_asu): hpsystem1

Confirm choices for server dloaner:
                                role   : backup
                                primary: hpsystem1
Is this correct [y/n]? y
_&a0y0C_J
Enter the name of an administrative account on the primary
domain controller 'hpsystem1' or press Enter to select 'administrator':

This procedure requires the password for the administrative account on
'hpsystem1'. If the password is the default ('password') created
during installation, you will not need to be prompted for a password.
If you have changed the password, you should allow this program to prompt
for a password after the files have been installed.

Do you want to use the default password [y/n]? y

Advanced Server/9000
Copyright (c) 1988, 1991-1996 AT&T and Microsoft
Copyright (c) 1992-1996 Hewlett-Packard
All rights reserved

Adding Advanced Server for UNIX Systems administrative users and groups
Add
Comment <Advanced Server account>
Home Dir </opt/asu/lanman>
UID <100>
GID <99>
Shell </sbin/false>
Name <lanman>
pw_name: lanman
pw_passwd: *
pw_uid: 100
pw_gid: 99
pw_age: ?
pw_comment:
pw_gecos: Advanced Server account
pw_dir: /opt/asu/lanman
pw_shell: /sbin/false
enter addusr
pw_name = lanman
pw_passwd = *
pw_uid = 100
pw_gid = 99
pw_gecos = Advanced Server account
pw_dir = /opt/asu/lanman
pw_shell = /sbin/false
enter_quiet_zone()
exit_quiet_zone()
exiting addusr, error = 0
Add
Comment <Advanced Server Administrator>
Home Dir </var/opt/asu/lanman/lmxadmin>
GID <99>
Name <lmxadmin>
pw_name: lmxadmin
pw_passwd: *
pw_uid: 0

```
pw_gid: 99
pw_age: ?
pw_comment:
pw_gecos: Advanced Server Administrator
pw_dir: /var/opt/asu/lanman/lmxadmin
pw_shell:
enter addusr
pw_name = lmxadmin
pw_passwd = *
pw_uid = 0
pw_gid = 99
pw_gecos = Advanced Server Administrator
pw_dir = /var/opt/asu/lanman/lmxadmin
pw_shell =
enter_quiet_zone()
exit_quiet_zone()
exiting addusr, error = 0
Add
Comment <Advanced Server GUEST Login>
Shell </sbin/false>
GID <99>
Name <lmxguest>
pw_name: lmxguest
pw_passwd: *
pw_uid: 0
pw_gid: 99
pw_age: ?
pw_comment:
pw_gecos: Advanced Server GUEST Login
pw_dir:
pw_shell: /sbin/false
enter addusr
pw_name = lmxguest
pw_passwd = *
pw_uid = 0
pw_gid = 99
pw_gecos = Advanced Server GUEST Login
pw_dir = /usr/lmxguest
pw_shell = /sbin/false
enter_quiet_zone()
exit_quiet_zone()
exiting addusr, error = 0
Add
Comment <Advanced Server World Login>
Shell </sbin/false>
GID <99>
Name <lmworld>
pw_name: lmworld
pw_passwd: *
pw_uid: 0
pw_gid: 99
pw_age: ?
pw_comment:
pw_gecos: Advanced Server World Login
pw_dir:
pw_shell: /sbin/false
enter addusr
pw_name = lmworld
pw_passwd = *
pw_uid = 0
pw_gid = 99
pw_gecos = Advanced Server World Login
pw_dir = /usr/lmworld
pw_shell = /sbin/false
enter_quiet_zone()
exit_quiet_zone()
```

```
exiting addusr, error = 0

Creating Directory: /home/lanman
Setting owner, group, and permissions for installed files....

Enter the password for administrator on hpsystem1:
Re-enter password:

Contacting the server 'hpsystem1' ... Success

Creating Advanced Server for UNIX Systems accounts database.

Starting the Advanced Server for UNIX Systems...

The Advanced Server for UNIX Systems is now operational.
#
```

After the installation and configuration are complete, you have **netdemon** running, which is an essential component of Advanced Server/9000, as shown in the following **ps** command:

man page

ps - 13

```
# ps -ef | grep netdemon
    root  1100    1  0 10:18:38 ?           0:00 /opt/lmu/netbios/bin/netde-
mon
    #
```

In addition to **netdemon**, NetBIOS must also be running.

Advanced Server/9000 starts several processes on your UNIX system in addition to **netdemon**. You can also verify that the Advanced Server/9000 server is running by viewing its processes with the **ps** command:

```
# ps -ef | grep lm
    root  3285    1     0 10:37:19 ?        0:00 lmx.dmn
    root  3200    1     0 10:36:57 ?        0:00 lmx.ctrl
    root  3262  3200    0 10:37:07 ?        0:00 lmx.srv -s 1
    root  3295    1     0 10:37:20 ?        0:00 lmx.sched
    root  3289    1     0 10:37:19 ?        0:00 lmx.browser
    root  1100    1     0 10:18:38 ?        0:00 /opt/lmu/netbios/bin/netdemon
    #
```

Many process are shown here, such as *lmx.dmn,* which is the daemon; *lmx.ctrl,* which is the control process; *lmx.sched,* which is the scheduler; *lmx.browser* which is the browser; and *lmx.srv,* which is a client session. If Advanced Server/9000 is not running, you would use the **net start server** command to start the server. Similarly, you would stop the server with **net stop server**.

In addition, you have several users and groups that have been created on your UNIX system to facilitate using Advanced Server/9000 with your Windows systems. The new users are shown in the upcoming **/etc/passwd** file, and the new groups are shown in the upcoming **/etc/group** file:

man page

cat - 17

```
# cat /etc/passwd
root:jThTuY9OhNxGY:0:3::/:/sbin/sh
daemon:*:1:5::/:/sbin/sh
bin:*:2:2::/usr/bin:/sbin/sh
sys:*:3:3::/:
adm:*:4:4::/var/adm:/sbin/sh
uucp:*:5:3::/var/spool/uucppublic:/usr/lbin/uucp/uucico
lp:*:9:7::/var/spool/lp:/sbin/sh
nuucp:*:11:11::/var/spool/uucppublic:/usr/lbin/uucp/uucico
hpdb:*:27:1:ALLBASE:/:/sbin/sh
nobody:*:-2:-2147483648::/:
lanman:*:100:99:Advanced Server account:/opt/asu/lanman:/sbin/false
lmxadmin:*:202:99:Advanced Server Administrator:/var/opt/asu/lanman/lmxadmin:
lmxguest:*:203:99:Advanced Server GUEST Login:/usr/lmxguest:/sbin/false
lmworld:*:204:99:Advanced Server World Login:/usr/lmworld:/sbin/false
# cat /etc/group
root::0:root
other::1:root,hpdb
bin::2:root,bin
sys::3:root,uucp
adm::4:root,adm
daemon::5:root,daemon
mail::6:root
lp::7:root,lp
tty::10:
nuucp::11:nuucp
users::20:root
nogroup:*:-2:
DOS----::99:lanman
DOS-a--::98:lanman
DOS--s-::97:lanman
DOS---h::96:lanman
DOS-as-::95:lanman
DOS-a-h::94:lanman
DOS--sh::93:lanman
DOS-ash::92:lanman
#
```

In addition to the UNIX system modifications that have automatically taken place, the Windows Primary Domain Controller (PDC) now recognizes the UNIX system as the backup domain controller. Figure 27-1 shows a screen shot from the Windows system *hpsystem1*, which is the primary domain controller. The screen shot shows *dloaner* acting as the backup domain controller and the default shared directories on the UNIX system *dloaner.* The share properties for one of the shares, **C:\opt\asu\lanman**, are also shown.

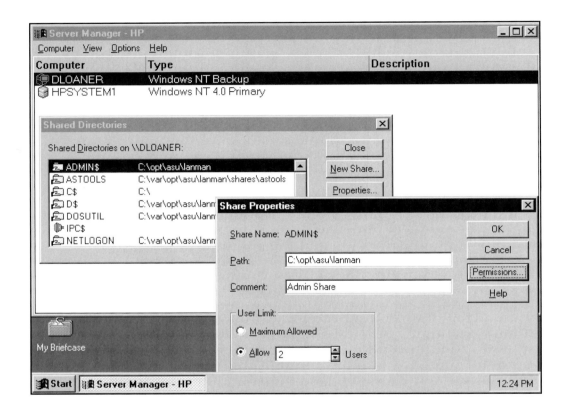

Figure 27-1 Default Shares after Loading and Configuring Advanced Server/9000

These shares can also be viewed on the command line of the UNIX system using the *net* command, as shown in the following output:

```
# /opt/asu/lanman/bin/net share

Sharename      Resource                          Remark
---------------------------------------------------------------------------
ADMIN$         C:\OPT\ASU\LANMAN                 Admin Share
IPC$                                             IPC Share
C$             C:\                               Root Share
D$             C:\VAR\OPT\ASU\LANMAN\SHARES      SystemRoot Share
ASTOOLS        C:\VAR\OPT\ASU\LANMAN\SHARES...   Advanced Server Tools
DOSUTIL        C:\VAR\OPT\ASU\LANMAN\SHARES...   DOS Utilities
NETLOGON       C:\VAR\OPT\ASU\LANMAN\SHARES...   Logon Scripts Directory
PATCHES        C:\VAR\OPT\ASU\LANMAN\SHARES...   Client Patches
PRINTLOG       C:\VAR\OPT\ASU\LANMAN\SHARES...   LP printer messages
USERS          C:\HOME\LANMAN                    Users Directory
The command completed successfully.
#
```

These are the default shares that have been set up by Advanced Server/9000. Those followed by a $ are hidden shares used only for administrative purposes. When you run *Windows Explorer,* you don't see these hidden directories.

You can set up additional shares, such as the printer and disk we will set up in the upcoming sections, *"Sharing a Printer"* and *"Sharing a File System,"* respectively.

Sharing a Printer

In addition to the default sharing that takes place with Advanced Server/9000, there may be additional resources you may want to share between Windows and UNIX systems.

For example you may have a printer used in your UNIX environment to which you want Windows systems to have access. The following commands show adding a shared printer and viewing it in UNIX.

The first command is **lpstat** on UNIX, which shows the status of the existing printer *laser*:

man page

lpstat - 10

```
# lpstat -t
scheduler is running
system default destination: laser
device for laser: /dev/c2t0d0_lp
laser accepting requests since Feb 11 17:23
printer laser is idle.  enabled since Feb 11 17:23
fence priority : 0
no entries
#
```

Next we run the **net** command and specify the printer *laser* as a shared printer device:

```
# /opt/asu/lanman/bin/net net share laser=laser /print
laser was successfully shared
```

To see the configuration of the printer, we can issue the **net print** command as shown below:

```
# net print laser /options
Printing options for LASER

Status               Queue Active
Remark
Print Devices        laser
Driver               HP-UX LM/X Print Manager
Separator file
Priority             5
Print after          12:00 AM
Print until          12:00 AM
Print processor
Parameters           COPIES=1 EJECT=AUTO BANNER=YES
The command completed successfully.
#
```

After printing a text file from the Windows system onto the device *laser* connected to the UNIX system running Advanced Server/9000, I received a bunch of unintelligible information on the printed sheet. The Advanced Server/9000 printer was not configured *raw*. I issued the following command to make the printer *raw*:

```
# net print laser /parms:types=-oraw
The command completed successfully.
```

The new configuration, with the *TYPES=-oraw*, is shown in the following output. This device successfully printed from the Windows system to the UNIX system running Advanced Server/9000 to which *laser* is connected:

```
# net print laser /options
Printing options for LASER

Status              Queue Active
Remark
Print Devices       laser
Driver              HP-UX LM/X Print Manager
Separator file
Priority            5
Print after         12:00 AM
Print until         12:00 AM
Print processor
Parameters          COPIES=1 TYPES=-oraw EJECT=AUTO BANNER=YES
The command completed successfully.
#
```

We can now view all the shared devices with the **net** command:

```
# /opt/asu/lanman/bin/net share

Sharename    Resource                        Remark
-------------------------------------------------------------------------
ADMIN$       C:\OPT\ASU\LANMAN               Admin Share
IPC$                                         IPC Share
C$           C:\                             Root Share
D$           C:\VAR\OPT\ASU\LANMAN\SHARES    SystemRoot Share
ASTOOLS      C:\VAR\OPT\ASU\LANMAN\SHARES... Advanced Server Tools
DOSUTIL      C:\VAR\OPT\ASU\LANMAN\SHARES... DOS Utilities
NETLOGON     C:\VAR\OPT\ASU\LANMAN\SHARES... Logon Scripts Directory
PATCHES      C:\VAR\OPT\ASU\LANMAN\SHARES... Client Patches
PRINTLOG     C:\VAR\OPT\ASU\LANMAN\SHARES... LP printer messages
USERS        C:\HOME\LANMAN                  Users Directory
LASER        laser                           Spooled
The command completed successfully.
#
```

The last item in this listing is the printer *laser* that was added with the **net** command. All the previous commands were issued on the UNIX system running Advanced Server/9000. We can now view the shared devices of *dloaner* on the Windows system using *Explorer* to confirm that the printer *laser* is a shared device, as shown in Figure 27-2.

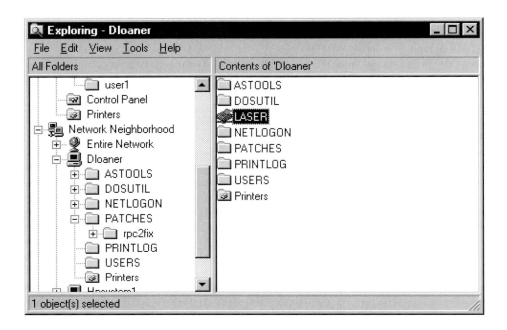

Figure 27-2 Windows *Explorer* Showing Printer *Laser*

The details of this shared printer can be viewed in *Printers* under *Control Panel*.

Sharing a File System

With the printer having been added, the shares that are now set up on the UNIX system running Advanced Server/9000 look like the following:

```
# /opt/asu/lanman/bin/net share

Sharename      Resource                          Remark
--------------------------------------------------------------------------------
ADMIN$         C:\OPT\ASU\LANMAN                 Admin Share
IPC$                                             IPC Share
C$             C:\                               Root Share
D$             C:\VAR\OPT\ASU\LANMAN\SHARES      SystemRoot Share
ASTOOLS        C:\VAR\OPT\ASU\LANMAN\SHARES...   Advanced Server Tools
DOSUTIL        C:\VAR\OPT\ASU\LANMAN\SHARES...   DOS Utilities
NETLOGON       C:\VAR\OPT\ASU\LANMAN\SHARES...   Logon Scripts Directory
PATCHES        C:\VAR\OPT\ASU\LANMAN\SHARES...   Client Patches
PRINTLOG       C:\VAR\OPT\ASU\LANMAN\SHARES...   LP printer messages
USERS          C:\HOME\LANMAN                    Users Directory
LASER          laser                             Spooled
The command completed successfully.
#
```

The shares shown include the printer that was added. We could now issue the **net share** command and add a UNIX file system to be shared. To share the **/home** directory on the UNIX system *dloaner,* we would issue the following command:

```
# /opt/asu/lanman/bin/net share home=c:/home
home was shared successfully
```

Note that the UNIX notation for the directory was issued with the slash (/) rather than the backslash (\), as you would on a Windows system. We can now view the shares on *dloaner*, including the new *HOME* share, with the **net** command:

```
# /opt/asu/lanman/bin/net share

Sharename      Resource                          Remark
--------------------------------------------------------------------------------
ADMIN$         C:\OPT\ASU\LANMAN                 Admin Share
IPC$                                             IPC Share
C$             C:\                               Root Share
D$             C:\VAR\OPT\ASU\LANMAN\SHARES      SystemRoot Share
ASTOOLS        C:\VAR\OPT\ASU\LANMAN\SHARES...   Advanced Server Tools
DOSUTIL        C:\VAR\OPT\ASU\LANMAN\SHARES...   DOS Utilities
HOME           C:\HOME
NETLOGON       C:\VAR\OPT\ASU\LANMAN\SHARES...   Logon Scripts Directory
PATCHES        C:\VAR\OPT\ASU\LANMAN\SHARES...   Client Patches
PRINTLOG       C:\VAR\OPT\ASU\LANMAN\SHARES...   LP printer messages
USERS          C:\HOME\LANMAN                    Users Directory
LASER          laser                             Spooled
The command completed successfully.
#
```

You could now view this share on the Windows system and map it to a drive, as shown in Figure 27-3.

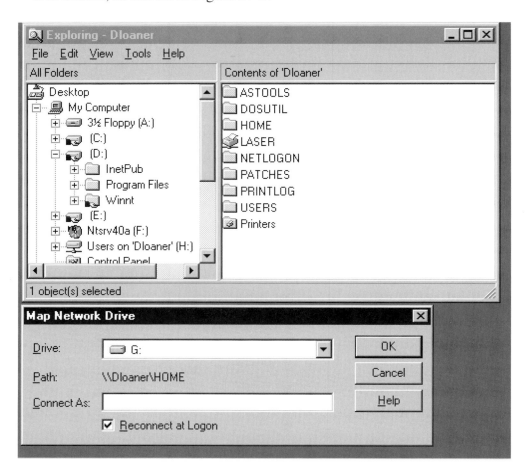

Figure 27-3 Windows *Explorer* Showing New Share *HOME*

I covered only a small subset of Advanced Server/9000 functionality in this chapter. I covered using a UNIX system running Advanced Server/9000 as a backup domain controller, sharing a UNIX-connected printer with a Windows network, and sharing a UNIX-connected disk with a Windows network. These are some of the more common uses for Advanced Server/9000. Nearly everything you can do with a Windows system can be done with Advanced Server/9000, so don't limit yourself to only the functionality covered in this chapter.

CHAPTER 28

The Windows Command Line: NET Commands, POSIX Utilities, and Others

Introduction for UNIX System Administrators

UNIX system administration is performed mostly from the command line. There are very good system administration interfaces through which many routine system administration tasks can be performed; however, the command line is still used before any graphical tool for most UNIX system administrators. The converse is true for Windows. With Windows, most system administration functions are performed with "point and click." There are, however, many functions you can perform from the command line in Windows. In this UNIX and Windows interoperability chapter, I will cover the Windows command line in general and a group of POSIX utilities that give you UNIX functionality in Windows in particular.

I'll begin with Windows "NET" commands, which are system administration commands for Windows. I'll then cover the POSIX commands you can run at the Windows command line that give you UNIX functionality in Windows, such as **grep**, **ls**, and so on. I'll finally cover some additional Windows commands you can issue to perform such tasks as backup and running a command at a specific time.

The POSIX commands are what really constitute the UNIX and Windows portion of this chapter. I think, however, that covering the other Windows commands gives UNIX system administrators an idea of the type of Windows system administration commands available.

The Windows Command Line

The whole Windows operating system is based on performing system administration tasks through the graphical user interface. Why, then, would I include a chapter on the command line? Well, many of us have used operating systems for which the lion's share of system administration work takes place at the command line - and old habits die hard.

The purpose of this chapter is to demonstrate some useful commands that are issued at the command line. You can then decide whether using such commands is helpful to the administration of your Windows server or whether you wish to use only the graphical user interface of Windows.

NET Commands

This section describes some of the **net** commands of Windows. Here is a list of some widely used **net** commands and a brief explanation of each:

net accounts	Used to maintain the user accounts database.
net computer	Used to add or delete computers from the domain database.

net config server

> Displays or changes settings for a server ser-
> vice on which the command is executed.

net config workstation

> Displays or changes settings for the worksta-
> tion service on which the command is executed.

net continue   Reactivates a Windows service that has been
                     suspended with the **net pause** command.

net file   Used for network file manipulation, such as
                     listing ID numbers, closing a shared file,
                     removing file locks, and so on.

net group   Used to add, display, or modify global
                     groups on servers.

net help   Displays a listing of help options for any *net*
                     command.

net helpmsg   Displays explanations of Windows network
                     messages, such as errors, warnings, and
                     alerts.

net localgroup   Used to modify local groups on computers.

net name	Used to add or delete a "messaging name" at a computer, which is the name to which messages are sent.
net print	Used to list print jobs and shared queues.
net send	Sends messages to other users, computers, and "messaging names" on the network.
net session	Used to list or disconnect sessions between the computer and other computers on the network.
net share	Shares a server's resources with other computers on the network.
net start	Used to start services such as *server*.
net statistics	Displays the statistics log for the local Workstation or Server service.
net stop	Used to stop services such as *server*.
net time	Synchronizes the computer's clock with another computer on the domain.
net use	Displays, connects, or disconnects a computer with shared resources.

net user   Creates or modifies user accounts.

net view   Lists resources being shared on a computer.

The following are brief descriptions of some of the NET commands and examples of using them.

Many of the descriptions include command summaries that were obtained by typing the command name followed by **/?**. For instance, to get a command summary for the **NET ACCOUNTS** command, you would type the following:

```
C:\ NET ACCOUNTS /?
```


You can also get detailed help information by typing **HELP** and the command name, as shown in the following example:

```
C:\ HELP NET ACCOUNTS
```

NET ACCOUNTS

NET ACCOUNTS - Maintains user account database.

The following is a summary of the **NET ACCOUNTS** command:

```
C:\ NET ACCOUNTS /?
NET ACCOUNTS [/FORCELOGOFF:{minutes | NO}] [/MINPWLEN:length]
             [/MAXPWAGE:{days | UNLIMITED}] [/MINPWAGE:days]
             [/UNIQUEPW:number] [/DOMAIN]
NET ACCOUNTS [/SYNC]
```

Some commonly used options follow:

/DOMAIN	Perform the specified action on the domain controller rather than the current computer.
/FORCELOGOFF	Line numbers are displayed, along with output lines.
/MINPWLEN:length	Specify the minimum number of characters for a password with *length*.
/MAXPWAGE:days	Specify the maximum number of *days* a password is valid, or use the *unlimited* option to specify no limit on password validity.
/MINPWAGE:days	Specify the minimum number of *days* that must pass before a user

is permitted to change their password.

/UNIQUEPW:number · A user password must be unique for the number of changes specified by *number.*

/SYNCH · Synchronize the account database.

The following example shows **NET ACCOUNTS** with no options specified:

```
C:\ NET ACCOUNTS
Force user logoff how long after time expires?:     Never
Minimum password age (days):                        0
Maximum password age (days):                        42
Minimum password length:                            0
Length of password history maintained:              None
Lockout threshold:                                  Never
Lockout duration (minutes):                         30
Lockout observation window (minutes):               30
Computer role:                                      BACKUP
Primary Domain controller for workstation domain:   \\NISDEV
The command completed successfully.
```

We'll now issue **NET ACCOUNTS** with the *MINPWLEN* option to change the minimum password length to five characters:

```
C:\ NET ACCOUNTS /MINPWLEN:5

The request will be processed at the primary domain controller for domain
NSDNIS

The command completed successfully.
```

Reissuing **NET ACCOUNTS** with no options reflects the new minimum password length:

```
C:\ NET ACCOUNTS

Force user logoff how long after time expires?:    Never
Minimum password age (days):                        0
Maximum password age (days):                        42
Minimum password length:                            5
Length of password history maintained:              None
Lockout threshold:                                  Never
Lockout duration (minutes):                         30
Lockout observation window (minutes):               30
Computer role:                                      BACKUP
Primary Domain controller for workstation domain:   \\NISDEV
The command completed successfully.
```

NET COMPUTER

NET COMPUTER - Adds or deletes computers from the domain database.

The following is a summary of the **NET COMPUTER** command:

```
C:\ NET COMPUTER /?
NET COMPUTER  \\computername {/ADD | /DEL}
```

Some commonly used options follow:

\\computername	Name of the computer to be added or deleted.
/ADD	Add the computer.
/DEL	Delete the computer.

The following example shows adding a computer using the */ADD* option:

```
C:\ NET COMPUTER \\SYSTEM2 /ADD
The request will be processed at the primary domain controller for domain
NSDNIS.

The command completed successfully.
```

NET CONFIG SERVER

NET CONFIG SERVER - As a member of Administrator's group, you can change the settings for a service.

The following is a summary of the **NET CONFIG SERVER** command:

```
C:\ NET CONFIG SERVER /?

NET CONFIG SERVER  [/AUTODISCONNECT:time]
                   [/SRVCOMMENT:"text"]
                   [/HIDDEN:{YES | NO}]
```

Some commonly used options follow:

/AUTODISCONNECT:time	Use *time* to specify the number of minutes that pass before an inactive account is disconnected.

/SRVCOMMENT:"text"

/HIDDEN:{YES|NO}

NET CONTINUE

NET CONTINUE - Reactivates a Windows service that had been suspended with **NET PAUSE**.

The following is a summary of the **NET CONTINUE** command:

```
C:\ NET CONTINUE /?
NET CONTINUE service
```

You can pause and continue many Windows services with the **NET PAUSE** and **NET CONTINUE** commands, respectively. The following example shows using the **NET PAUSE** command to pause the **NET LOGON** service and then restart it with the **NET CONTINUE** command.

Figure 28-1 is the *Services* dialog box from a system, showing some of the services running on a system:

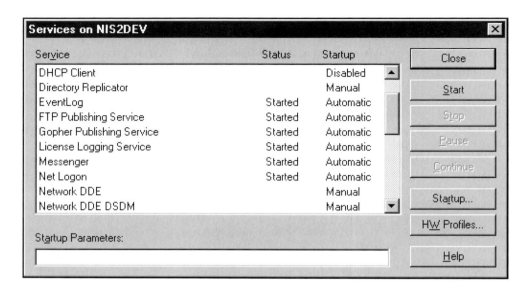

Figure 28-1 *Service* Dialog Box with Net Logon Started

We'll now use the **NET PAUSE** command to pause the *Net Logon* service:

```
C:\NET PAUSE NTLOGON
The Net Logon service was paused successfully.
```

Figure 28-2 is the *Services* dialog box again, showing that the *Net Logon* service has indeed been paused:

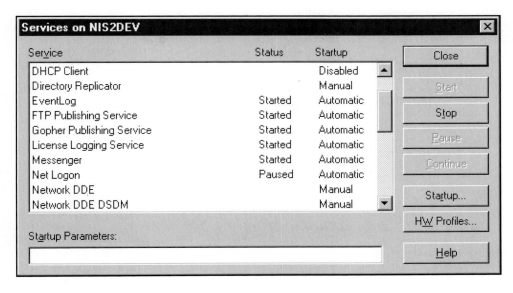

Figure 28-2 *Service* Dialog Box with Net Logon Paused

We can now resume the *Net Logon* service with the following **NET CONTINUE** command:

```
C:\NET CONTINUE NTLOGON
The Net Logon service was continued successfully.
```

NET FILE

NET FILE - This command lists and closes open files.

The following is a summary of the **NET FILE** command:

```
C:\ NET FILE /?

NET FILE  [id [/CLOSE]]
```

Some commonly used options follow:

id	Specify the identification number of the file you wish to view.
id /CLOSE	Close the file specified by the *id* number.

The following example shows issuing the **NET FILE** command with no options:

```
C:\ NET FILE

ID         Path                                   User name           # Locks

-----------------------------------------------------------------------------
97         C:\tif_map_proj\sql                    leung_k             0
147        \PIPE\samr                             administrator       0
148        \PIPE\lsarpc                           administrator       0
The command completed successfully.
```

This output shows the open files on the server. You can close one of these shared files or remove locks from the file.

NET GROUP

NET GROUP - This command displays and allows you to manipulate groups on a server. Without specifying any option, this command lists groups.

The following is a summary of the **NET GROUP** command:

```
C:\ NET GROUP /?

NET GROUP [groupname [/COMMENT:"text"]] [DOMAIN]
          groupname {/ADD [/COMMENT:"text"] | /DELETE} [/DOMAIN]
          groupname username [...] {/ADD | /DELETE} [/DOMAIN]
```

Some commonly used options follow:

/ADD	Add a group to a domain or a *username* to a group.
/DELETE	Delete a group from a domain or a *username* from a group.
groupname	Specify the *groupname* for the operation. With no options, the users who are part of the group are displayed. You can also use the *ADD* or *DELETE* options with the *groupname* to specify a *username* to add to the group.
/COMMENT:"text"	Add this comment to the *groupname*.
/DOMAIN	The operation will be performed on the primary domain control-

	ler. This option is the default for Windows server systems.
username	This user will be added or removed from the group. Any number of users can be specified.

The following example shows issuing the **NET GROUP** command to add the group *hp consultants*:

```
C:/ NET GROUP "hp consultants" /ADD

The request will be processed at the primary domain controller for domain
NSDNIS.

The command completed successfully.
```

Next we add the user *marty* to the group *hp consultants* on the local system:

```
C:\ NET GROUP "hp consultants" marty /ADD

The request will be processed at the primary domain controller for domain
NSDNIS.

The command completed successfully.
```

Next we add a comment to *hp consultants*:

```
C:\ NET GROUP "hp consultants" /COMMENT:"Group For HP Consultants"

The request will be processed at the primary domain controller for domain
NSDNIS.

The command completed successfully.
```

We can now view our handiwork by looking at the information we have added associated with the group *hp consultants*:

```
C:\ NET GROUP "hp consultants"

Group name        hp consultants
Comment           Group For HP Consultants

Members

-------------------------------------------------------------------------
marty
The command completed successfully.
```

This output confirms that we have created the group *hp consultants*, that *marty* is a member of this group, and that our comment has indeed been associated with the group.

NET HELP

NET HELP - Use this command to get help on any of the NET commands.

A commonly used option follows:

NET HELP command | more   This provides information about
                                      the *command* you specify.

The following example shows issuing the **NET HELP** command
to get a list of commands for which help is available:

```
C:\ NET HELP

The syntax of this command is:

NET HELP command
    -or-
NET command /HELP

   Commands available are:

   NET ACCOUNTS              NET HELP              NET SHARE
   NET COMPUTER             NET HELPMSG           NET START
   NET CONFIG               NET LOCALGROUP        NET STATISTICS
   NET CONFIG SERVER        NET NAME              NET STOP
   NET CONFIG WORKSTATION   NET PAUSE             NET TIME
   NET CONTINUE             NET PRINT             NET USE
   NET FILE                 NET SEND              NET USER
   NET GROUP                NET SESSION           NET VIEW

   NET HELP SERVICES lists the network services you can start.
   NET HELP SYNTAX explains how to read NET HELP syntax lines.
   NET HELP command | MORE displays Help one screen at a time.
```

The following example shows issuing the **NET HELP** command
to get information about the **NET GROUP** command:

```
C:\ NET HELP NET GROUP

The syntax of this command is:

NET GROUP [groupname [/COMMENT:"text"]] [/DOMAIN]
          groupname {/ADD [/COMMENT:"text"] | /DELETE} [/DOMAIN]
          groupname username [...] {/ADD | /DELETE} [/DOMAIN]

NET GROUP adds, displays, or modifies global groups on servers. Used
without parameters, it displays the groupnames on the server.
```

```
        groupname           Is the name of the group to add, expand, or delete.
                            Supply only a groupname to view a list of users
                            in a group.
        /COMMENT:"text"     Adds a comment for a new or existing group.
                            The comment can have as many as 48 characters. Enclose
                            the text in quotation marks.
        /DOMAIN             Performs the operation on the primary domain controller
                            of the current domain. Otherwise, the operation is
                            performed on the local computer.
                            This parameter applies only to Windows
                            Workstation computers that are members of
                            a Windows Server domain. By default,
                            Windows Server computers perform
                            operations on the primary domain controller.
        username[ ...]      Lists one or more usernames to add to or remove from
                            a group. Separate multiple username entries with a space.
        /ADD                Adds a group, or adds a username to a group.
        /DELETE             Removes a group, or removes a username from a group.

        NET HELP command | MORE displays Help one screen at a time.
```

NET HELPMSG

NET HELPMSG - Gets information on four-digit network message codes. Use only the four digits to get information on the code.

The following is the format of the **NET HELPMSG** command:

NET HELPMSG message#	Provides information about the four-digit *messagenumber* you specify.

The following command shows issuing the **NET GROUP** command to add a group to a system. After issuing this command, an error number is provided.

```
C:\ NET GROUP "hp consultants" /ADD

The group already exists.

More help is available by typing NET HELPMSG 2233.
```

We can now use the **NET HELPMSG** command to get information about the specific four-digit code:

```
C:\ NET HELPMSG 2223

The group already exists.

EXPLANATION

You tried to create a group with a group name that already exists.

ACTION

Use a different group name for the new group. To display
a list of group names established on the server, type:

              NET GROUP
```

NET LOCALGROUP

NET LOCALGROUP - This command displays and allows you to manipulate groups on a computer. Without specifying any option, this command lists groups.

The following is a summary of the **NET LOCALGROUP** command:

```
C:\ NET LOCALGROUP /?
NET LOCALGROUP [groupname [/COMMENT:"text"]] [DOMAIN]
               groupname {/ADD [/COMMENT:"text"] | /DELETE} [/DOMAIN]
               groupname name [...] {/ADD | /DELETE} [/DOMAIN]
```

Some commonly used options follow:

/ADD	Add a group to a domain or a *username* to a group.
/DELETE	Delete a group from a domain or a *username* from a group.
groupname	Specify the *groupname* for the operation. With no options, the users who are part of the local group are displayed. You can also use the *ADD* or *DELETE* options with the *groupname* to specify a *username* to add to the group.
/COMMENT:"text"	Add this comment to the *groupname*.

/DOMAIN

The operation will be performed on the primary domain controller. If this option is not used, the operation will take place on the local computer. This is the default for Windows server systems.

name

This is the user name(s) or group name(s) to be added or removed from the group. Any number can be specified.

NET NAME

NET NAME - This command adds or deletes a messaging name from a computer. This command is not to be confused with **NET USER,** which adds or deletes user accounts on a system.

The following is a summary of the **NET NAME** command:

```
C:\ NET NAME /?

NET NAME [name [/ADD | DELETE]]
```

Some commonly used options follow:

name	Name to add or delete.
/ADD	Adds a name to the computer.
/DELETE	Deletes a name from the computer.

NET PAUSE

NET PAUSE - Suspends a Windows service.

The following is a summary of the **NET PAUSE** command:

```
C:\ NET PAUSE /?
NET PAUSE service
```

You can pause and continue many Windows services with the **NET PAUSE** and **NET CONTINUE** commands, respectively. The following example shows using the **NET PAUSE** command to pause the **NET LOGON** service and then to restart it with the **NET CONTINUE** command.

Figure 28-3 shows the *Services* dialog box from a system, showing some of the services running on a system:

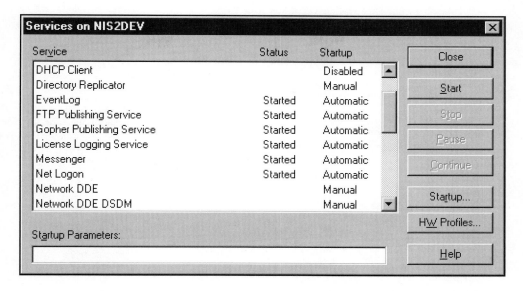

Figure 28-3 *Service* Dialog Box with Net Logon Started

We now use the **NET PAUSE** command to pause the *Net Logon* service:

```
C:\NET PAUSE NTLOGON
The Net Logon service was paused successfully.
```

Figure 28-4 is again the *Services* dialog box, this time showing that the *Net Logon* service has indeed been paused:

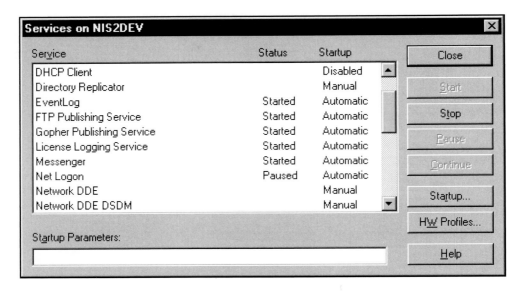

Figure 28-4 *Service* Dialog Box with Net Logon Paused

We can now continue the *Net Logon* service with the following
NET CONTINUE command:

```
C:\NET CONTINUE NTLOGON

The Net Logon service was continued successfully.
```

NET PRINT

NET PRINT - This command lists print jobs and shared queues.

The following is a command summary of the **NET PRINT** command:

```
C:\ NET PRINT /?

NET PRINT \\computername\sharename
          [\\computername] job# [/HOLD | /RELEASE | /DELETE]
```

Some commonly used options follow:

\\computername	The *computername* sharing the print queues.
sharename	The print queue *sharename*.
job#	The unique number assigned to a print job.
/HOLD	The job is assigned a status of *HOLD*, which means that it will not be printed until it is released or deleted.
/RELEASE	Releases a print job so that it can be printed.
/DELETE	Deletes a print job from the print queue.

NET SEND

NET SEND - Sends messages to other users, computers, or messaging names on the network.

The following is a summary of the **NET SEND** command.

```
C:\ NET SEND /?

NET SEND {name | * | /DOMAIN[:name] | /USERS} message
```

Some commonly used options follow:

name	The user name, computer name, or messaging name to which the message is to be sent. Use quotation marks if there are blank characters in the name.
*	Use * to send a message to all users within your group rather than an individual name.
/DOMAIN[:domainname]	Use /DOMAIN to send a message to all users in the /DOMAIN. You can also specify a *domainname* to which you want the message sent.
message	This is the text message you want sent.

The following example shows issuing the **NET SEND** command to send a message to a specific user:

```
NET SEND marty Our NetServer LXr has arrived for installation.
```

Figure 28-5 shows the alert box that appears on the screen of the computer on which *marty* is working.

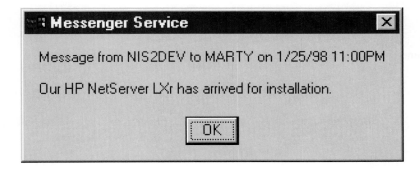

Figure 28-5 Alert Box Produced from the **NET SEND** Command

NET SESSION

NET SESSION - Views or disconnects sessions between computers.

The following is a summary of the **NET SESSION** command.

```
C:\ NET SESSION /?
NET SESSION [\\computername] [/DELETE]
```

Some commonly used options follow:

\\computername	Lists session-related information for *computername*.
/DELETE	Terminates a session between the local computer and *computername*, closing open files. Without a *computername*, all sessions are ended.

NET SHARE

NET SHARE - This command is used to list information about existing shares or to share a server's resources with other network users. The command lists information about existing shares if you don't specify any options.

The following is a summary of the **NET SHARE** command.

```
C:\ NET SHARE /?
NET SHARE sharename
         sharename=drive:path [USERS:number | /UNLIMITED]
                   [REMARK:"text"]
         sharename [/USERS:number | /UNLIMITED]
                   [/REMARK:"text"]
         {sharename | devicename | drive:path} /DELETE
```

Some commonly used options follow:

sharename	Network name of the shared resource. Using the *sharename* only displays information about the share.
devicename	Used to specify printers to be shared with *sharename*. Use LP1-LPT9 as a *devicename*.
drive:path	Use this option to specify that a specific drive and path for a directory are to be shared.
/USERS:number	Use this option to specify the maximum number of users that can simultaneously access a shared resource.

/UNLIMITED	An unlimited number of users may simultaneously access a shared resource.
/REMARK:"text"	Associates a remark with the specified shared resource.
/DELETE	Sharing is deleted for the specified resource.

Let's now use **NET SHARE** to set up a new share on a system. To begin, let's look at the existing shares using the **NET SHARE** command with no options:

```
D:\ NET SHARE


Share name    Resource                        Remark

-------------------------------------------------------------------------
ADMIN$        D:\WINNT                        Remote Admin
IPC$                                          Remote IPC
C$            C:\                             Default share
print$        D:\WINNT\system32\spool\drivers Printer Drivers
D$            D:\                             Default share
E$            E:\                             Default share
net_share     C:\net_share
NETLOGON      D:\WINNT\system32\Repl\Import\S Logon server share
HPLaserJ5     LPT1:                  Spooled  HP LaserJet 5MP
The command completed successfully.
```

Now we can set up a share of the **c:\measureware** directory with a *sharename* of *measure* and a maximum number of five users:

```
C:\ NET SHARE measure=c:\measureware /users:5

measure was shared successfully
```

Issuing the NET SHARE command shows that the share named "measureware" has been established:

```
C:\ NET SHARE

Share name    Resource                            Remark

-------------------------------------------------------------------------
D$            D:\                                 Default share
ADMIN$        D:\WINNT                      ·     Remote Admin
IPC$                                              Remote IPC
C$            C:\                                 Default share
print$        D:\WINNT\system32\spool\drivers Printer Drivers
E$            E:\                                 Default share
measure       c:\measureware
net_share     C:\net_share
NETLOGON      D:\WINNT\system32\Repl\Import\S Logon server share
HPLaserJ5     LPT1:                     Spooled   HP LaserJet 5MP
The command completed successfully.
```

NET START

NET START - This command starts services that have been stopped using the **NET STOP** command or that have not been started. Issue **NET START** without options to see a list of currently running services.

The following is a summary of the **NET START** command:

```
C:\ NET START /?

NET START [service]
```

The following example shows issuing the **NET START** command without any options to list currently running services:

```
C:/ NET START

These Windows services are started:

   Alerter
   Computer Browser
   EventLog
   FTP Publishing Service
   Gateway Service for NetWare
   Gopher Publishing Service
   License Logging Service
   MeasureWare Agent
   MeasureWare Transaction Manager
   Messenger
   Net Logon
   NT LM Security Support Provider
   OracleServiceTMI
   OracleStartTMI
   OracleTNSListener
   Plug and Play
   Remote Procedure Call (RPC) Locator
   Remote Procedure Call (RPC) Service
   Schedule
   Server
   Spooler
   STP/A - TCP/IP Page Server (TMI)
   TCP/IP NetBIOS Helper
   UPS
   Workstation
   World Wide Web Publishing Service

The command completed successfully.
```

There are many services listed in the example that are not native to Windows. For instance, MeasureWare (HP performance tools) and Oracle services. These can be started and stopped with the **NET START** and **NET STOP** commands, respectively.

NET STATISTICS

NET STATISTICS - Use this command to display the statistics log for a service. Issue **NET STATISTICS** without options to display statistics for all services.

The following is a summary of the **NET STATISTICS** command:

```
C:\ NET STATISTICS /?

NET STATISTICS [WORKSTATION | SERVER]
```

Some commonly used options follow:

SERVER	Displays server service statistics.
WORKSTATION	Displays workstation service statistics.

The following example shows issuing the **NET STATISTICS** command with no options:

```
C:\ NET STATISTICS
Server Statistics for \\NISDEV

Statistics since 1/21/98 8:49 AM

Sessions accepted                      3
Sessions timed-out                     32
Sessions errored-out                   32

Kilobytes sent                         165941
Kilobytes received                     33118

Mean response time (msec)              0

System errors                          0
Permission violations                  2
Password violations                    0

Files accessed                         12787
Communication devices accessed         0
```

```
    Print jobs spooled              0

    Times buffers exhausted

     Big buffers                    0
     Request buffers                0

    The command completed successfully.
```

NET STOP

NET STOP - This command stops a service that was started using the **NET START** command.

The following is a summary of the **NET STOP** command:

```
C:\ NET STOP /?
NET STOP service
```

One option to the **NET STOP** command is:

service

The name of a service that can be stopped.

NET TIME

NET TIME - This command is used to display the time for a computer or to synchronize the clock of one computer with the clock of another computer.

The following is a summary of the **NET TIME** command.

```
C:\ NET TIME /?

NET TIME [\\computername | /DOMAIN[:domainname]] [/SET]
```

Some commonly used options follow:

\\computername	The computer with which you want to synchronize the time or of which you want to display the time.
/DOMAIN[:domainname]	The domain name with which you want to synchronize the time.
/SET	Sets the computer's time with the time on the specified computer or domain.

NET USE

NET USE - Lists the connections of a computer, or establishes or removes shared resources. Without options, this command lists the connections of a computer.

The following is a summary of the **NET USE** command:

```
C:\ NET USE /?
NET USE [devicename | *] [//computername\sharename[/volume] [password | *]]
        [/USER:[domainname\]username]
        [[/DELETE] | [/PERSISTENT:{YES | NO}]]
NET USE [devicename | *] [password | *]] [/HOME]
NET USE [PERSISTENT:{YES | NO}]
```

Some commonly used options follow:

devicename	Specifies a name to be connected or disconnected. The possibilities include such names as drives and printers.
//computername	This is the name of the computer that controls the shared resource.
/sharename	The network name of the shared device.
password	The password that is required to get access to the shared resource.
*	Produces a password prompt for the user attempting to use the shared resource.

/USER	Specifies a different user name for the connection.
domainname	A different domain from the current domain is used.
username	Specifies a user logon name.
/HOME	Connects a user to their home directory.
/DELETE	Cancels a network connection and removes it from the list of persistent connections.
/PERSISTENT {yes | no}	Specifying *yes* means that the connections are re-established at the next logon. Specifying *no* does not save the connection for future logons.

The following example shows issuing the **NET USE** command with no options:

```
C:\ NET USE

New connections will be remembered.

Status      Local    Remote                     Network

-------------------------------------------------------------------------------
OK          P:       \\DEVSYS\Disk_C            Microsoft Windows Network
The command completed successfully.
```

The directory *Disk_C* on remote system *DEVSYS* is viewed under **P:** on the local system.

NET USER

NET USER - This command creates and modifies accounts on computers. This can also be used without options to list accounts.

The following is a summary of the **NET USER** command:

```
C:\ NET USER /?
NET USER [username [password | *] [options]] [/DOMAIN]
         username {password | *} /ADD [options] [/DOMAIN]
         username [/DELETE] [/DOMAIN]
```

Some commonly used options follow:

/ADD	Adds a user account.
/DELETE	Removes a user account.
username	The name of the account to manipulate. You can add, delete, modify, or view the account.
password	Assigns or changes the password of a user account.
*	Displays the password prompt.
/DOMAIN	The action is to be performed on the primary domain controller.

additional options

You have many additional options such as expiration date, of the account, path of the users logon profile, and many others.

The following example shows issuing the **NET USER** command with no options:

```
C:\ NET USER

User accounts for \\NIS2DEV

-------------------------------------------------------------------------------
Administrator            arleo_j               burgos_c
Guest                    IUSR_NIS2DEV          IUSR_NISDEV
johnt                    leung_k               marty
mckenna_b
The command completed successfully.
```

Using the second form of the command shown earlier, we can add a new user to the system:

```
C:\ NET USER amyp * /ADD

Type a password for the user:

Retype the password to confirm:

The request will be processed at the primary domain controller for domain DEV.

The command completed successfully.
```

The asterisk in the **NET USER** command means that we want to be prompted for the password for the new user *amyp*.

NET VIEW

NET VIEW - This command lists the resources being shared on a computer. You can use this command without options to display a list of computers on the domain.

The following is a summary of the **NET VIEW** command:

```
C:\ NET VIEW /?
NET VIEW [\\computername | /DOMAIN[:domainname]]
NET VIEW /NETWORK:NW [\\computername]
```

Some commonly used options follow:

//computername	Specifies the name of the computer for which you want to view shared resources.
/DOMAIN:domainname	Specifies the name of the domain for which you wish to view shared resources.
/NETWORK:NW	Displays NetWare servers on the network.

The following example shows issuing the **NET VIEW** command with no options, producing a list of computers in the current domain:

```
C:\ NET VIEW

Server Name          Remark

-----------------------------------------------------------------------------
\\NIS2DEV
\\NISDEV
The command completed successfully.
```

The following example shows issuing the **NET VIEW** command while specifying the *DOMAIN* to be viewed:

```
C:\ NET VIEW /DOMAIN:nisdomain

Server Name              Remark

-----------------------------------------------------------------------
\\HPSYSTEM1
\\KITTY
\\NIS
The command completed successfully.
```

The following example shows issuing the **NET VIEW** command while specifying a specific *computername* in the current domain to view:

```
C:\ NET VIEW \\nisdev

Shared resources at \\hpsystem1

Share name   Type        Used as  Comment

-----------------------------------------------------------------------
HPLaserJ5    Print                HP LaserJet 5MP
measure      Disk
net_share    Disk
NETLOGON     Disk                 Logon server share
The command completed successfully.
```

POSIX Utilities

The Microsoft Windows NT Server *Resource Kit* (referred to as *Resource Kit* throughout this chapter) has on it several POSIX utilities that UNIX system administrators find useful when using Windows. The *Resource Kit* in general is a fantastic system administration resource. Although I will focus on only POSIX utilities in this book, the *Resource Kit* has in it a wealth of information. The *Resource Kit* is

man page

cat - 17

man page

chmod - 16

man page

find - 20

man page

ls - 15

man page

mv - 16

available from Microsoft Press, Redmond, WA. The POSIX utilities include such useful commands as **cat, chmod, find, ls, mv,** and others. The commands that are available on the *Resource Kit* vary somewhat from architecture to architecture. In this chapter, I focus on only the "I386" utilities and not the utilities for other architectures.

The *Resource Kit* has on it the file **POSIX.WRI**, which describes the POSIX utilities in detail. In this chapter, I'll just provide a brief overview of the utilities and examples of using some of the utilities. Most UNIX system administrators are familiar with these utilities in UNIX but may find differences in the options to these utilities when using the *Resource Kit* version.

I have made every effort to limit the number of "add-on" products to Windows and UNIX covered in this book. The *Resource Kit*, however, is so useful to Windows system administrators that not covering at least some part of it, such as the POSIX utilities, would leave a void in the discussion of Windows system administration. You can find out more information about the *Resource Kit* on the Microsoft Web site. You can buy it at many computer, electronic, and book stores. Be sure to buy the *Resource Kit* for the version of Windows you are running. There is also a *Resource Kit* for both the Server and Workstation versions of Windows. I used the Server *Resource Kit* for the POSIX commands covered in this chapter.

Both the source code and executables for the POSIX utilities are on the *Resource Kit*. The following is a listing of the POSIX executables for I386 on the *Resource Kit* CD-ROM. I used the POSIX utility **ls -l** to produce this listing:

```
F:\I386\GNU\POSIX> ls -l

-rwxrwxrwx   1 Everyone Everyone   101748 Sep  6 12:39 CAT.EXE
-rwxrwxrwx   1 Everyone Everyone   116188 Sep  6 12:39 CHMOD.EXE
-rwxrwxrwx   1 Everyone Everyone   110920 Sep  6 12:39 CHOWN.EXE
-rwxrwxrwx   1 Everyone Everyone   111208 Sep  6 12:39 CP.EXE
-rwxrwxrwx   1 Everyone Everyone   173580 Sep  6 12:39 FIND.EXE
-rwxrwxrwx   1 Everyone Everyone   144256 Sep  6 12:39 GREP.EXE
-rwxrwxrwx   1 Everyone Everyone    90960 Sep  6 12:39 LN.EXE
-rwxrwxrwx   1 Everyone Everyone   128532 Sep  6 12:39 LS.EXE
-rwxrwxrwx   1 Everyone Everyone    88984 Sep  6 12:39 MKDIR.EXE
-rwxrwxrwx   1 Everyone Everyone    99096 Sep  6 12:39 MV.EXE
-rwxrwxrwx   1 Everyone Everyone   114564 Sep  6 12:39 RM.EXE
-rwxrwxrwx   1 Everyone Everyone    85004 Sep  6 12:39 RMDIR.EXE
-rwxrwxrwx   1 Everyone Everyone   362528 Sep  6 12:39 SH.EXE
-rwxrwxrwx   1 Everyone Everyone    91244 Sep  6 12:39 TOUCH.EXE
-rwxrwxrwx   1 Everyone Everyone   287628 Sep  6 12:39 VI.EXE
-rwxrwxrwx   1 Everyone Everyone    95392 Sep  6 12:39 WC.EXE
```

The directory in which these utilities are located is the **F:** drive, which is my CD-ROM, in **I386\GNU\POSIX**, which is the I386 version of these utilities. The following are command summaries of the POSIX utilities. A brief description of some of the utilities as well as some of the more commonly used options to the utilities are included. In some cases, you also have an example of having run the utility. The **POSIX.WRI** file on the *Resource Kit* provides an exhaustive description of each utility.

cat

man page

cat - 17

cat - Display, combine, append, copy, or create files.

Some commonly used options follow:

-n   Line numbers are displayed, along with output lines.

-u   Output is unbuffered, which means that it is handled character-by-character.

-v   Prints most nonprinting characters visibly.

The following example shows using the **-n** option with **cat**:

```
D:\WINNT\system> cat -n setup.inf

 1   [setup]
 2       help = setup.hlp
 3
 4   ;   Place any programs here that should be run at the end of setup.
 5   ;   These apps will be run in order of their appearance here.
 6   [run]
 7
 8   [dialog]
 9       caption   = "Windows Setup"
10       exit      = "Exit Windows Setup"
11       title     = "Installing Windows 3.1"
12       options   = "In addition to installing Windows 3.1, you can:"
13       printwait = "Please wait while Setup configures your printer(s)..."

                        .
                        .
                        .

20   [data]
```

```
21   ; Disk space required
22   ; <type of setup>= <Full install space>, <Min install space>
23
24      upd2x386full = 10000000,6144000 ; 10.0 Mb, 6.144 Mb
25      upd2x286full = 9000000,6144000  ;  9.0 Mb, 6.144 Mb
26      upd3x386full = 5500000,5000000  ;  5.5 Mb, 5.0 Mb
27      upd3x286full = 5500000,5000000  ;  5.5 Mb, 5.0 Mb
28
29      new386full   = 10000000,6144000 ; 10.0 Mb, 6.144 Mb
30      new286full   = 9000000,6144000  ;  9.0 Mb, 6.144 Mb
31
32      netadmin    = 16000000          ; 16.0 Mb
33      netadminupd = 16000000          ; 16.0 Mb
34      upd2x386net = 300000            ;  .3 Mb
35      upd3x386net = 300000            ;  .3 Mb
36      upd2x286net = 300000            ;  .3 Mb
37      upd3x286net = 300000            ;  .3 Mb
38      new386net   = 300000,300000     ;  .3 Mb,  .3 Mb
39      new286net   = 300000,300000     ;  .3 Mb,  .3 Mb
40
41
42
43   ; Defaults used in setting up and names of a few files
44      startup   = WIN.COM
```

chmod

man page

chmod - 16

chmod - Changes permissions of specified files using symbolic or absolute (sometimes called numeric) modes. Symbolic mode is described below.

Symbol of who is affected:

u	User is affected.
g	Group is affected.
o	Other is affected.
a	All users are affected.

Operation to perform:

+	Add permission.
-	Remove permission.
=	Replace permission.

Permission specified:

r	Read permission.
w	Write permission.
x	Execute permission.
u	Copy user permissions.
g	Copy group permissions.
o	Copy other permissions.

The following example uses both modes. Using absolute or numeric mode, the permissions on the file **cat1.exe** are changed from 666 to 777. Using symbolic mode, the execute permissions are then removed for all users:

```
D:\> ls -l cat1.exe

-rw-rw-rw-    1 Administ Administ     71323 Feb 20 11:34 cat1.exe

D:\> chmod 777 cat1.exe

D:\> ls -l cat1.exe
```

```
-rwxrwxrwx    1 Administ Administ     71323 Feb 20 11:34 cat1.exe

D:\> chmod a-x cat1.exe

D:\> ls -l cat1.exe

-rw-rw-rw-    1 Administ Administ     71323 Feb 20 11:34 cat1.exe
```

cp

man page

cp - 16

cp - Copies files and directories.

Some commonly used options follow:

-i   Interactive copy whereby you are prompted to confirm whether or not you wish to overwrite an existing file.

-f   Forces existing files to be overwritten by files being copied if a conflict occurs in file names.

-p   Preserves permissions when copying.

-R   Copies recursively which includes subtrees.

The following example shows using the **cp** command to copy **cat1.exe** to **cat2.exe,** and then a listing of all files beginning with **cat** is produced:

man page

ls - 15

```
D:\> cp cat1.exe cat2.exe

D:\> ls -l cat*

-rw-rw-rw-    1 Administ Administ      71323 Feb 20 11:34 cat1.exe
-rw-rw-rw-    1 Administ Administ      71323 Feb 20 11:47 cat2.exe
```

find

find - Recursively descends a directory structure looking for the file(s) listed.

man page

find - 20

Some commonly used options follow:

-f   Specifies a file hierarchy for **find** to traverse.

-s   When symbolic links are encountered, the file refer-
            enced by the link and not the link itself will be used.

-x   Doesn't descend into directories that have a device
            number different from that of the file from which the
            descent began.

-print   Prints pathname to standard output.

-size n   True if the file's size is n.

grep

man page

grep - 19

grep - Searches for text and displays result.

The following example shows using **grep** to find the expression "shell" everywhere it appears inside the file **setup.inf**:

```
D:\> grep shell setup.inf

[shell]
00000000="shell versions below 3.01",,unsupported_net
00030100="shell versions below 3.21",,novell301
00032100="shell versions 3.21 and above",,novell321
00032600="shell versions 3.26 and above",,novell326
    #win.shell, 0:
    #win.shell, 0:
[win.shell]
    shell.dll
    system.ini, Boot,    "oldshell"        ,"shell"
```

ls

ls - Lists the contents of a directory.

Some commonly used options:

-a	List all entries.
-c	Use time file was last modified for producing order in which files are listed.
-d	List only the directory name, not its contents.
-g	Include the group in the output.
-i	Print the inode number in the first column of the report.
-q	Nonprinting characters are represented by a "?".
-r	Reverse the order in which files are printed.
-s	Show the size in blocks instead of bytes.
-t	List in order of time saved with most recent first.
-u	Use time of last access instead of last modification for determining order in which files are printed.
-A	Same as -a, except current and parent directories aren't listed.
-C	Multicolumn output produced.
-F	Directory followed by a "/", executable by an "*", symbolic link by an "@".
-L	List file or directory to which link points.
-R	Recursively list subdirectories.

I include several examples on the next few pages.

man page

ls - 15

```
D:\> ls -a

Blue Monday 16.bmp
Blue Monday.bmp
Coffee Bean 16.bmp
Coffee Bean.bmp
Config
Cursors
FORMS
FeatherTexture.bmp
Fiddle Head.bmp
Fonts
Furry Dog 16.bmp
Furry Dog.bmp
Geometrix.bmp
Gone Fishing.bmp
Greenstone.bmp
Hazy Autumn 16.bmp
Help
Hiking Boot.bmp
Leaf Fossils 16.bmp
Leather 16.bmp
Maple Trails.bmp
Media
NETLOGON.CHG
NOTEPAD.EXE
Petroglyph 16.bmp
Prairie Wind.bmp
Profiles
REGEDIT.EXE
Rhododendron.bmp
River Sumida.bmp
Santa Fe Stucco.bmp
Seaside 16.bmp
Seaside.bmp
ShellNew
Snakeskin.bmp
Soap Bubbles.bmp
Solstice.bmp
Swimming Pool.bmp
TASKMAN.EXE
TEMP
Upstream 16.bmp
WIN.INI
WINFILE.INI
WINHELP.EXE
Zapotec 16.bmp
Zapotec.bmp
_DEFAULT.PIF
black16.scr
clock.avi
control.ini
explorer.exe
inetsrv.mif
inf
lanma256.bmp
lanmannt.bmp
network.wri
poledit.exe
printer.wri
repair
setup.old
setuplog.txt
system
system.ini
system32
vmmreg32.dll
welcome.exe
winhlp32.exe
```

```
D:\> ls -l

-rwxrwxrwx   1 Administ NETWORK      8310 Aug  9  1996 Blue Monday 16.bmp
-rwxrwxrwx   1 Administ NETWORK     37940 Aug  9  1996 Blue Monday.bmp
-rwxrwxrwx   1 Administ NETWORK      8312 Aug  9  1996 Coffee Bean 16.bmp
-rwxrwxrwx   1 Administ NETWORK     17062 Aug  9  1996 Coffee Bean.bmp
drwx---rwx   1 Administ Administ        0 Feb 10 10:39 Config
drwx---rwx   1 Administ Administ        0 Feb 10 16:22 Cursors
drwxrwxrwx   1 Administ NETWORK         0 Feb 10 16:23 FORMS
-rwxrwxrwx   1 Administ NETWORK     16730 Aug  9  1996 FeatherTexture.bmp
-rwxrwxrwx   1 Administ NETWORK     65922 Aug  9  1996 Fiddle Head.bmp
drwx---rwx   1 Administ Administ     8192 Feb 10 10:39 Fonts
-rwxrwxrwx   1 Administ NETWORK     18552 Aug  9  1996 Furry Dog 16.bmp
-rwxrwxrwx   1 Administ NETWORK     37940 Aug  9  1996 Furry Dog.bmp
-rwxrwxrwx   1 Administ NETWORK      4328 Aug  9  1996 Geometrix.bmp
-rwxrwxrwx   1 Administ NETWORK     17336 Aug  9  1996 Gone Fishing.bmp
-rwxrwxrwx   1 Administ NETWORK     26582 Aug  9  1996 Greenstone.bmp
-rwxrwxrwx   1 Administ NETWORK     32888 Aug  9  1996 Hazy Autumn 16.bmp
drwx---rwx   1 Administ Administ        0 Feb 19 15:10 Help
-rwxrwxrwx   1 Administ NETWORK     37854 Aug  9  1996 Hiking Boot.bmp
-rwxrwxrwx   1 Administ NETWORK     12920 Aug  9  1996 Leaf Fossils 16.bmp
-rwxrwxrwx   1 Administ NETWORK      6392 Aug  9  1996 Leather 16.bmp
-rwxrwxrwx   1 Administ NETWORK     26566 Aug  9  1996 Maple Trails.bmp
drwx---rwx   1 Administ Administ        0 Feb 10 16:23 Media
-rwxrwxrwx   1 Administ NETWORK     65536 Feb 11 10:35 NETLOGON.CHG
-rwxrwxrwx   1 Administ NETWORK     45328 Aug  8  1996 NOTEPAD.EXE
-rwxrwxrwx   1 Administ NETWORK     16504 Aug  9  1996 Petroglyph 16.bmp
-rwxrwxrwx   1 Administ NETWORK     65954 Aug  9  1996 Prairie Wind.bmp
drwxrwxrwx   1 Administ NETWORK      4096 Feb 10 16:32 Profiles
-rwxrwxr-x   1 Administ NETWORK     71952 Aug  8  1996 REGEDIT.EXE
-rwxrwxrwx   1 Administ NETWORK     17362 Aug  9  1996 Rhododendron.bmp
-rwxrwxrwx   1 Administ NETWORK     26208 Aug  9  1996 River Sumida.bmp
-rwxrwxrwx   1 Administ NETWORK     65832 Aug  9  1996 Santa Fe Stucco.bmp
-rwxrwxrwx   1 Administ NETWORK      8312 Aug  9  1996 Seaside 16.bmp
-rwxrwxr-x   1 Administ NETWORK     17334 Aug  9  1996 Seaside.bmp
drwxrwxrwx   1 Administ NETWORK         0 Feb 10 16:22 ShellNew
-rwxrwxrwx   1 Administ NETWORK     10292 Aug  9  1996 Snakeskin.bmp
-rwxrwxrwx   1 Administ NETWORK     65978 Aug  9  1996 Soap Bubbles.bmp
-rwxrwxr-x   1 Administ NETWORK     17334 Aug  9  1996 Solstice.bmp
-rwxrwxrwx   1 Administ NETWORK     26202 Aug  9  1996 Swimming Pool.bmp
-rwxrwxrwx   1 Administ NETWORK     32016 Aug  8  1996 TASKMAN.EXE
drwxrwxrwx   1 Administ NETWORK         0 Feb 20 09:59 TEMP
-rwxrwxrwx   1 Administ NETWORK     32888 Aug  9  1996 Upstream 16.bmp
-rwxrwxrwx   1 Administ NETWORK       239 Feb 10 16:23 WIN.INI
-rwxrwxr-x   1 Administ NETWORK         3 Aug  8  1996 WINFILE.INI
-rwxrwxr-x   1 Administ NETWORK    256192 Aug  8  1996 WINHELP.EXE
-rwxrwxrwx   1 Administ NETWORK      8312 Aug  9  1996 Zapotec 16.bmp
-rwxrwxr-x   1 Administ NETWORK      9522 Aug  9  1996 Zapotec.bmp
-rwxrwxr-x   1 Administ NETWORK       707 Aug  8  1996 _DEFAULT.PIF
-rwx---r-x   1 Administ Administ      5328 Aug  8  1996 black16.scr
-rwx---r-x   1 Administ Administ     82944 Aug  8  1996 clock.avi
-rwxrwxrwx   1 Administ NETWORK         0 Feb 10 11:18 control.ini
-rwx---r-x   1 Administ Administ    234256 Aug  8  1996 explorer.exe
-rwxrwxrwx   1 Administ NETWORK      1628 Feb 10 11:20 inetsrv.mif
drwx---rwx   1 Administ Administ     47104 Feb 10 10:56 inf
-rwx---r-x   1 Administ Administ    157044 Aug  8  1996 lanma256.bmp
-rwx---r-x   1 Administ Administ    157044 Aug  8  1996 lanmannt.bmp
-rwx---r-x   1 Administ Administ     67328 Aug  8  1996 network.wri
-rwx---r-x   1 Administ Administ    123152 Aug  8  1996 poledit.exe
-rwx---r-x   1 Administ Administ     34816 Aug  8  1996 printer.wri
drwx---rwx   1 Administ Administ        0 Feb 10 16:24 repair
-rwxrwxrwx   1 Administ NETWORK      2499 Feb 10 16:23 setup.old
-rwxrwxrwx   1 Administ NETWORK       138 Feb 10 16:22 setuplog.txt
drwx---rwx   1 Administ Administ     4096 Feb 20 10:07 system
-rwx---r-x   1 Administ Administ       219 Aug  8  1996 system.ini
drwx---rwx   1 Administ Administ    167936 Feb 20 09:50 system32
-rwx---r-x   1 Administ Administ     24336 Aug  8  1996 vmmreg32.dll
-rwx---r-x   1 Administ Administ     22288 Aug  8  1996 welcome.exe
-rwx---r-x   1 Administ Administ    310032 Aug  8  1996 winhlp32.exe
```

man page

ls - 15

```
D:\> ls -C
```

```
Blue Monday 16.bmpGreenstone.bmpRhododendron.bmpWINFILE.INI      poledit.exe
Blue Monday.bmp Hazy Autumn 16.bmpRiver Sumida.bmpWINHELP.EXE    printer.wri
Coffee Bean 16.bmpHelp         Santa Fe Stucco.bmpZapotec 16.bmprepair
Coffee Bean.bmp Hiking Boot.bmp Seaside 16.bmp  Zapotec.bmp      setup.old
Config          Leaf Fossils 16.bmpSeaside.bmp  _DEFAULT.PIF     setuplog.txt
Cursors         Leather 16.bmp  ShellNew         black16.scr      system
FORMS           Maple Trails.bmpSnakeskin.bmp   clock.avi        system.ini
FeatherTexture.bmpMedia         Soap Bubbles.bmpcontrol.ini      system32
Fiddle Head.bmp NETLOGON.CHG    Solstice.bmp     explorer.exe     vmmreg32.dll
Fonts           NOTEPAD.EXE     Swimming Pool.bmpinetsrv.mif     welcome.exe
Furry Dog 16.bmpPetroglyph 16.bmpTASKMAN.EXE    inf              winhlp32.exe
Furry Dog.bmp   Prairie Wind.bmpTEMP             lanma256.bmp
Geometrix.bmp   Profiles        Upstream 16.bmp lanmannt.bmp
Gone Fishing.bmpREGEDIT.EXE     WIN.INI          network.wri
```

mkdir

mkdir - Creates specified directories.

man page

mkdir - 16

The following is a commonly used option:

-p   Creates intermediate directories to achieve the full path. If you want to create several layers of directories down, use **-p**.

mv

mv - Renames files and directories.

Some commonly used options follow:

-i   Interactive move whereby you are prompted to confirm whether or not you wish to overwrite an existing file.

-f   Forces existing files to be overwritten by files being moved if a conflict occurs in file names.

rm

rm - Removes files and directories.

man page

rm - 16

Some commonly used options follow:

-d   Removes directories as well as other file types.

-i   Interactive remove whereby you are prompted to con-
            firm whether or not you wish to remove an existing
            file.

-f   Forces files to be removed.

-r (-R)   Recursively removes the contents of the directory and
           then the directory itself.

touch

touch - Changes the modification and/or last access times of a file, or creates a file.

Some commonly used options:

-c   Does not create a specified file if it does not exist.

-f   Forces a touch of a file, regardless of permissions.

The following example creates **file1** with **touch**:

man page

ls - 15

```
D:\> ls -l file1
ls:file1: No such file or directory

D:\> touch file1

D:\> ls -l file1

-rw-rw-rw-   1 Administ Administ        0 Feb 20 11:45 file1
```

WC

wc - Produces a count of words, lines, and characters.

man page

wc - 18

Some commonly used options follow:

-l   Prints the number of lines in a file.

-w   Prints the number of words in a file.

-c   Prints the number of characters in a file.

The first example lists the contents of a directory and pipes the output to **wc**. The second example provides **wc** information about the file **system.ini**.

```
D:\> ls

CAT.EXE
CHMOD.EXE
CHOWN.EXE
CP.EXE
FIND.EXE
GREP.EXE
LN.EXE
LS.EXE
MKDIR.EXE
MV.EXE
RM.EXE
RMDIR.EXE
SH.EXE
TOUCH.EXE
VI.EXE
WC.EXE

D:\> ls | wc -wlc
      16      16      132

D:\> wc -wlc system.ini
      13      17      219 system.ini
```

Additional Commands

There are many additional commands in Windows that can be issued at the command line. I will present some of these commands in an informal manner.

Networking Commands

You have access to many useful networking commands on the command line in Windows. Some of the commands not covered here that you may want to look into include the following:

- **lpr**

- **route**

- **finger**

- **rexec**

- **ftp**

- **telnet** (opens a *telnet* window in the Windows environment)

- **hostname**

- **lpq**

- **tracert**

- **rcp**

- **rsh**

- **tftp**

You can find out more about these commands by typing the command name and **/?** at the command prompt, such as **telnet /?**. In the upcoming sections, I cover some additional commands that I often use.

arp

arp is used to display and edit the Address Resolution Protocol (arp) cache, which maps IP addresses to physical hardware addresses. The cache has in it one or more addresses of recently accessed systems. The following example shows issuing the **arp** command on a Windows system at address *113* and the address of the system most recently accessed at *111*, with its physical hardware address shown.

```
d: arp -a

Interface: 159.260.112.113 on Interface 2
    Internet Address        Physical Address       Type
    159.260.112.111         08-00-09-f0-bc-40      dynamic
```

There are several options to the **arp** command that you can view by issuing the **arp /?** command.

ipconfig

ipconfig is used to display the current networking interface parameters. The following example shows issuing the **ipconfig** command on a Windows system at address 113 with the **/all** option set, which shows all information related to the networking interface:

```
d: ipconfig /all
```

```
Windows IP Configuration

            Host Name . . . . . . . . . : hpsystem1
            DNS Servers . . . . . . . . :
            Node Type . . . . . . . . . : Broadcast
            NetBIOS Scope ID. . . . . . :
            IP Routing Enabled. . . . . : No
            WINS Proxy Enabled. . . . . : No
            NetBIOS Resolution Uses DNS : No

Ethernet adapter Hpddnd31:

            Description . . . . . . . . : HP DeskDirect
                                          10/100 LAN Adapter
            Physical Address. . . . . . : 08-00-09-D9-
9A-8A
            DHCP Enabled. . . . . . . . : No
            IP Address. . . . . . . . . : 159.260.112.113
            Subnet Mask . . . . . . . . : 255.255.255.0
            Default Gateway . . . . . . : 159.260.112.250
```

There are several options to the **ipconfig** command that you can view by issuing the **ipconfig /?** command.

netstat

man page

netstat - 12

netstat provides network protocol statistics. The following **netstat** example uses the **-e** and **-s** options, which show Ethernet statistics and statistics for various protocols, respectively. The Ethernet statistics associated with the **-e** option are under "Interface Statistics" and end with "IP Statistics":

```
d: netstat -e -s
```

```
Interface Statistics
```

	Received	Sent
Bytes	3182007276	2446436
Unicast packets	11046	9604
Non-unicast packets	21827982	7932

```
Discards                               0                      0
Errors                                 0                      1
Unknown protocols               4946670
```

IP Statistics

```
   Packets Received                        = 20489869
   Received Header Errors                  = 133441
   Received Address Errors                 = 28222
   Datagrams Forwarded                     = 0
   Unknown Protocols Received              = 0
   Received Packets Discarded              = 0
   Received Packets Delivered              = 20328206
   Output Requests                         = 12004
   Routing Discards                        = 0
   Discarded Output Packets                = 0
   Output Packet No Route                  = 0
   Reassembly Required                     = 0
   Reassembly Successful                   = 0
   Reassembly Failures                     = 0
   Datagrams Successfully Fragmented       = 0
   Datagrams Failing Fragmentation         = 0
   Fragments Created                       = 0
```

ICMP Statistics

```
                            Received       Sent
   Messages                 3702           23
   Errors                   0              0
   Destination Unreachable  4              5
   Time Exceeded            0              0
   Parameter Problems       0              0
   Source Quenchs           0              0
   Redirects                3680           0
   Echos                    5              13
   Echo Replies             13             5
   Timestamps               0              0
   Timestamp Replies        0              0
   Address Masks            0              0
   Address Mask Replies     0              0
```

TCP Statistics

```
   Active Opens                        = 27
   Passive Opens                       = 8
   Failed Connection Attempts          = 1
   Reset Connections                   = 15
   Current Connections                 = 2
   Segments Received                   = 1888
   Segments Sent                       = 1854
   Segments Retransmitted              = 3
```

```
UDP Statistics

    Datagrams Received    = 607489
    No Ports              = 19718827
    Receive Errors        = 0
    Datagrams Sent        = 10124
```

There are several options to the **netstat** command that you can view by issuing the **netstat /?** command. If you wish to see the changes in the value of statistics, you can specify an interval after which the statistics will again be displayed.

ping

ping is used to determine whether or not a host is reachable on the network. **ping** causes an echo request that sends packets that are returned by the destination host you specify. There are several options to the **ping** command you can specify. The following example uses the **-n** option to specify the number of times you want to send the packets, and **-l** specifies the length of packets for which the maximum of *8192* is used:

```
d: ping -n 9 -l 8192 system2

Pinging system2 [159.260.112.111] with 8192 bytes of da-
ta:

Reply from 159.260.112.111: bytes=8192 time=20ms TTL=255
Reply from 159.260.112.111: bytes=8192 time=20ms TTL=255
Reply from 159.260.112.111: bytes=8192 time=21ms TTL=255
Reply from 159.260.112.111: bytes=8192 time=20ms TTL=255
Reply from 159.260.112.111: bytes=8192 time=10ms TTL=255
Reply from 159.260.112.111: bytes=8192 time=30ms TTL=255
Reply from 159.260.112.111: bytes=8192 time=30ms TTL=255
Reply from 159.260.112.111: bytes=8192 time=20ms TTL=255
Reply from 159.260.112.111: bytes=8192 time=20ms TTL=255
```

There are several additional options to the **ping** command that you can view by issuing the **ping /?** command.

Permissions with cacls

You can view and change permissions of files from the command line with **cacls**. Figure 28-6 shows the help screen for the **cacls** command.

```
Command Prompt                                                    _ □ ×
D:\>help cacls
Displays or modifies access control lists (ACLs) of files

CACLS filename [/T] [/E] [/C] [/G user:perm] [/R user [...]]
               [/P user:perm [...]] [/D user [...]]
   filename     Displays ACLs.
   /T           Changes ACLs of specified files in
                the current directory and all subdirectories.
   /E           Edit ACL instead of replacing it.
   /C           Continue on access denied errors.
   /G user:perm Grant specified user access rights.
                Perm can be: R  Read
                             C  Change (write)
                             F  Full control
   /R user      Revoke specified user's access rights (only valid with /E).
   /P user:perm Replace specified user's access rights.
                Perm can be: N  None
                             R  Read
                             C  Change (write)
                             F  Full control
   /D user      Deny specified user access.
Wildcards can be used to specify more that one file in a command.
You can specify more than one user in a command.

D:\>
```

Figure 28-6   **cacls** Help Screen

cacls is used to display and modify the access control lists of files. You can see in Figure 28-6 that you have four different types of access rights for files that were described in detail earlier. The following list shows the abbreviations for access rights that are associated with the **cacls** command:

N	None
R	Read
C	Change
F	Full Control

Figure 28-7 shows using both **cacls** and the *File Permissions* window to view the existing permissions for **D:\WINNT\REGE-DIT.EXE**. This is one of the most important files on the system that was used in an earlier chapter to view and modify Registry information on the system. This is a file that you want to carefully manage access rights to, in order to avoid any operating system mishaps.

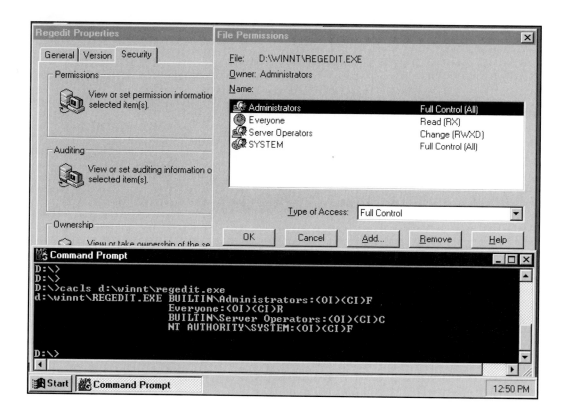

Figure 28-7   D:\WINNT\REGEDIT.EXE Permissions

Notice that *Server Operators* do indeed have *Change* rights to this file. You can, of course, modify the permissions on this or any file on the system. The *File Permissions* window and the output of the

cacls command are in different formats; however, they contain the same information.

Command-Line Backup

An alternative to using the graphical tools to initiate backups is to use the command line. Using the **NTBACKUP** command, you can initiate backups at the command line or build batch files using this command. You can combine the **NTBACKUP** command with the **AT** command to schedule backups. Provided that the *SCHEDULE* service is started, you can specify the time for which a job will be scheduled. Let's take a closer look at these two commands to see how they may be combined to schedule backups.

NTBACKUP

NTBACKUP - This command is used to initiate backups at the command line.

The following is a summary of the **NTBACKUP** command:

```
C:\ NTBACUKP /?
NTBACKUP operation path [/a][/v][/r][/d"text"][/b][/hc:{on | off}]
                      [/t{option}][/l"filename"][/e][/TAPE:{n}]
```

Some commonly used options follow:

operation	The *operation* to perform, such as *backup*.
path	The directories you wish to back up.
/a	Append this backup to those on the tape rather than replacing the contents of the tape with the current job.
/b	Include the local registry in the backup.
/d"text"	Description of the backup set is defined by the text in quotation marks.
/e	The backup log will contain only exceptions rather than the full backup log.

/hc:{on |off}	Specify whether or not to use hardware compression for the backup. You can use this option only if you don't use the /a option.
/L"filename"	The file name to be used for the backup log.
/r	Restricted access to the tape will be used. You can use this option only if you don't use the /A option.
/t option	Specify the type of backup, such as normal, copy, incremental, differential, or daily.
/tape:{n}	Specify the tape drive to be used if indeed the server has more than one tape drive.
/v	Verify the operation.

To back up the **oracle** directory with a *normal* backup, recording exceptions only in the log file, performing tape verification, and including a description of "oracle backup," you would issue the following command.

```
C:\ NTBACKUP backup d:/oracle /e /v /t normal /d "oracle backup"
```

AT

AT - This command is used to schedule jobs.

The following is a summary of the **AT** command:

```
C:\ AT /?

AT [//computername] [id] [/DELETE] | /DELETE [/YES]]

AT [//computername] time [/INTERACTIVE][/EVERY:date[,...]  |  [/NEXT:date[,...]]
"command"
```

Some commonly used options follow:

//computername	Computer on which the command will execute.
id	The identification number assigned to a scheduled command.
/DELETE	Cancel a scheduled command. You can use an id to cancel jobs associated with that *id* or cancel all scheduled commands.
/YES	Reply *YES* as confirmation of canceled jobs.
time	The *time* at which the job should be scheduled, in 24-hour format.
/INTERACTIVE	The job will run interactively rather than in the background.

/EVERY:date[,...]	Repeating jobs are scheduled with *dates* (Monday, Tuesday, and so on) or a day of the month (1-31).
/NEXT:date[,...]	Use this option to schedule a job the next time *date* occurs. Specify one or more dates (Monday, Tuesday, and so on) or a day of the month (1-31).
"command"	The *command* to be executed.

We can now combine the previous **NTBACKUP** command with **AT,** to perform a scheduled backup. By placing the previous **NTBACKUP** command in the file **backup,** we can issue the following command:

```
C:\ AT 03:00 /every:Monday,Tuesday,Wednesday,Thursday,Friday "backup"
```

CHAPTER 29

Services for UNIX (SFU)

Introduction to SFU

Microsoft Services for UNIX (SFU) provides interoperability between UNIX and Windows in many essential areas. Microsoft has packaged several widely used third-party interoperability products in SFU. Such important UNIX and Windows interoperability functions as NFS, Telnet, and UNIX utilities are part of SFU. Figure 29-1 shows these functions as menu picks that are displayed when SFU is loaded on a Windows system. We'll go through the most important functional areas of SFU in the upcoming sections, starting with NFS.

Using the Network File System (NFS) Functionality of SFU

With the NFS functionality of SFU, you would typically run your NFS client, such as the one included with SFU, on your Windows system in order to mount file systems on a UNIX system.

The NFS client of SFU bridges your Microsoft Server Message Block (SMB) network to your UNIX network by acting as a proxy. It forwards SMB requests from a Windows client to a UNIX NFS server, and vice versa. I always concentrate on the *client* aspect of NFS running on Windows, because UNIX systems are usually bigger, more centralized systems to which Windows users want to get access. Therefore, Windows users usually mount UNIX directories on their Windows systems and not vice versa.

This situation is not necessarily the case. With SFU, you can also set up your Windows system as an NFS Server. Figure 29-1 shows the menu structure of SFU after it has been installed. The *Server for NFS* menu pick is selected.

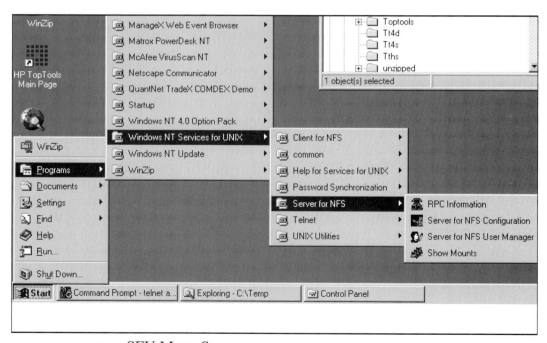

Figure 29-1   SFU Menu Structure

To begin, we'll focus on the *Client for NFS* option, because this is very commonly used in mixed Windows and UNIX environments, and we'll then come back to the *Server for NFS* option later in the chapter.

Under *Client for NFS Configuration* are the following six categories of information to enter related to NFS:

Authentication
Mount Options
File Access
Filenames
Configured NFS LANs
Symbolic Links

Let's walk through each of these, beginning with *Authentication,* shown in Figure 29-2.

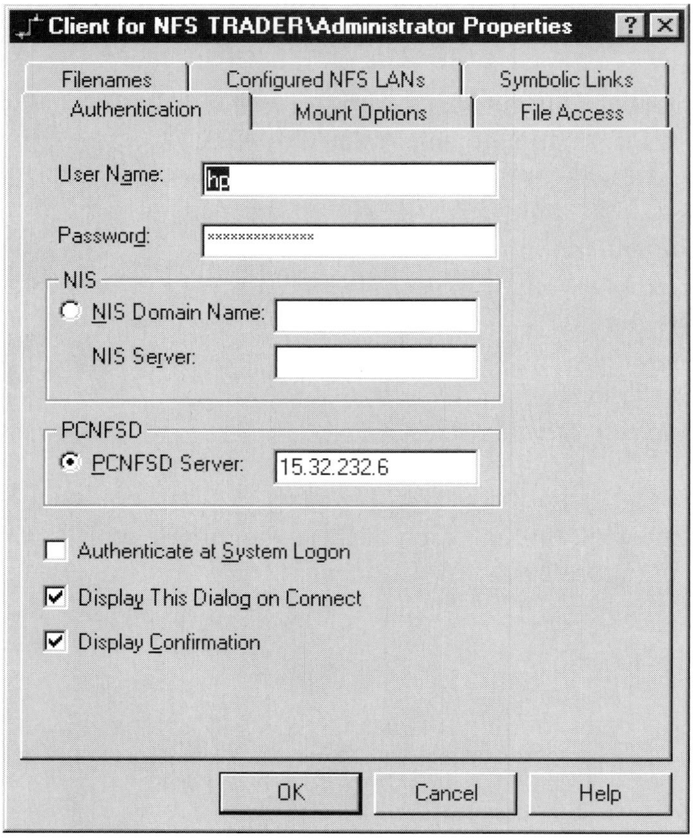

Figure 29-2 SFU *Authentication*

Authentication requires us to add some basic information about our connection to the NFS server. The *User Name* and *Password* are those we use to connect to the NFS Server. These should be set up on the server in advance of attempting to make a connection to the server. You also have the option to use NIS, which won't be part of this example. The server to which you are making an NFS connection must be running the PC NFS daemon. You can check to see whether your server is running this daemon. Figure 29-3 shows checking for **pcnfsd** on the NFS server:

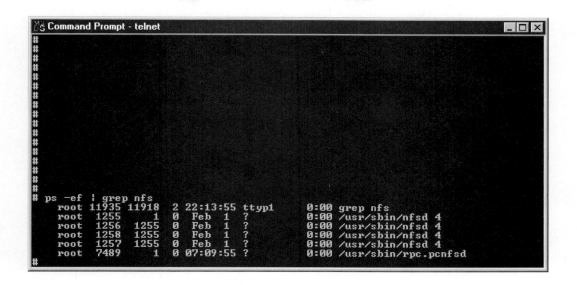

```
# 
# 
# 
# 
# 
# 
# 
# 
# 
# 
# 
# 
# 
# 
# 
# 
# 
# ps -ef | grep nfs
    root 11935 11918 2 22:13:55 ttyp1    0:00 grep nfs
    root  1255     1  0  Feb  1  ?       0:00 /usr/sbin/nfsd 4
    root  1256  1255  0  Feb  1  ?       0:00 /usr/sbin/nfsd 4
    root  1258  1255  0  Feb  1  ?       0:00 /usr/sbin/nfsd 4
    root  1257  1255  0  Feb  1  ?       0:00 /usr/sbin/nfsd 4
    root  7489     1  0 07:09:55  ?      0:00 /usr/sbin/rpc.pcnfsd
# 
```

Figure 29-3 Checking for **pcnfsd** on a UNIX System

The last entry, using **ps**, shows that **pcnfsd** is indeed running on our NFS server.

With the *User Name, Password,* and *PCNFSD Server* specified, we can move on to *Configured NFS LANs*. Figure 29-4 shows that I have configured two LANs on which I want to use NFS:

man page

ps - 13

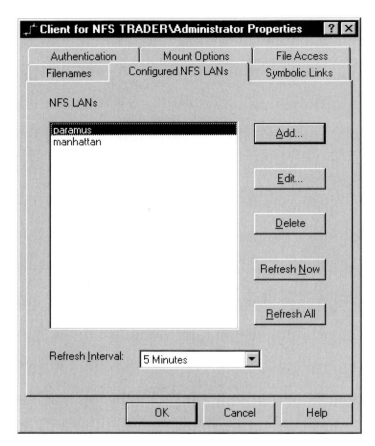

Figure 29-4 SFU *Configured NFS LANs*

You can *Edit...* these LANs to include such information as the *Broadcast Address,* as shown in Figure 29-5:

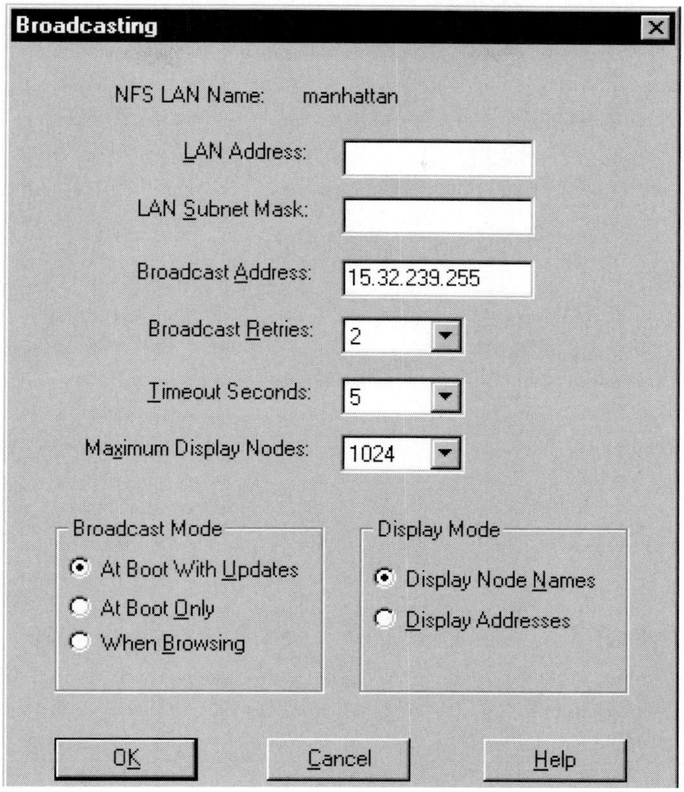

Figure 29-5 Edit a Specific LAN

Next you have options for the way symbolic links will be handled when you establish a client NFS connection. Symbolic links are a way of mapping a file or directory to an existing file or directory. If you select *Resolve Symbolic Links,* then you will be shown the actual path name to which the link is set. The options available for *Symbolic Links* are shown in Figure 29-6:

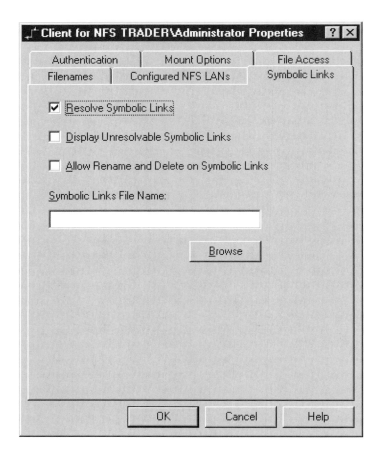

Figure 29-6 SFU *Client for NFS*

I typically like to resolve symbolic links, but don't care to manipulate existing links or display those that cannot be resolved.

There are somewhat different conventions used in file naming
on Windows and UNIX. SFU gives you several options related to
Filenames as shown in Figure 29-7.

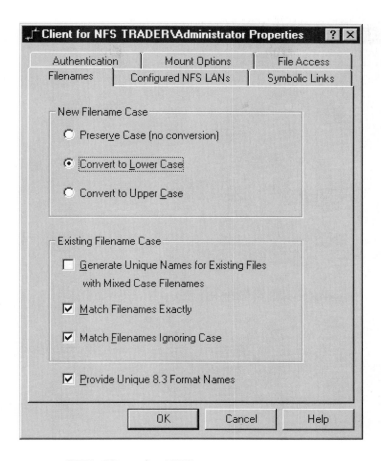

Figure 29-7 SFU *Client for NFS*

I like all new file names to be lowercase. This seems to result in the minimum amount of confusion when working with multiple operating systems. I also like to work with existing file names exactly as they exist, as indicated by the options I have chosen in Figure 29-7.

There are many mount options that you have when working with NFS. Figure 29-8 shows the *Mount Options* window:

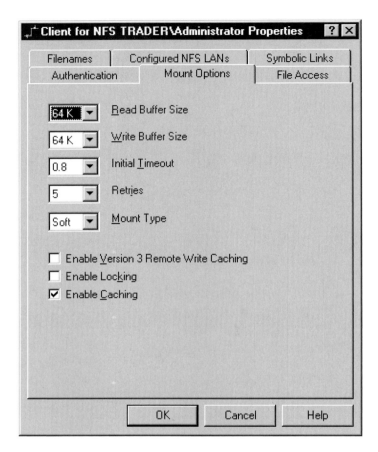

Figure 29-8 SFU *Mount Options*

We are using the default *Read Buffer Size* of 64,000 bytes. I like
to keep this number large, because it is the data part of the packet used
during NFS reads. In general, bigger is better. The same is true of the
Write Buffer Size. The *Initial_Timeout* specifies the amount of time to
wait for a response from the server before a retry. *Retries* specifies the
number of times you'll attempt to access the server before dropping
the operation altogether. I also use a *Mount Type* of *Soft,* as opposed to
Hard, and I check *Enable Caching.*

File Access allows you to specify privileges for users establishing NFS mounts. These are the privileges you're accustomed to seeing when working with files as shown in Figure 29-9.

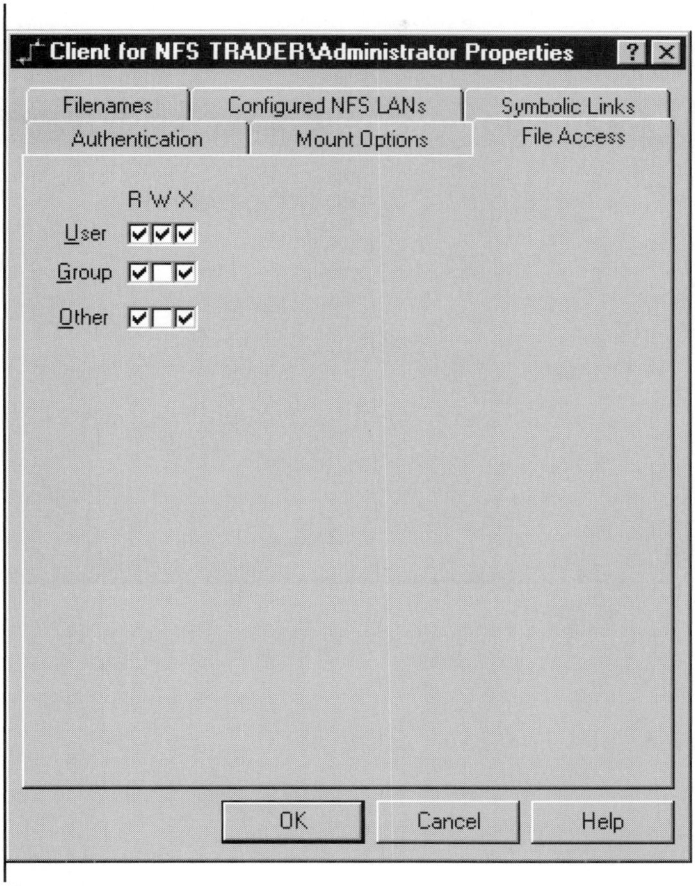

Figure 29-9 SFU *File Access*

By default, *User* will have unlimited access to files, and those in the *Group* and *Other* will have read (*R*) and execute (*X*) access only. These are common privilege assignments.

We can easily establish our NFS connection by selecting *OK* from the *Authentication* window shown in Figure 29-2. A box appears asking you to confirm the user name and other information, such as that shown in Figure 29-10.

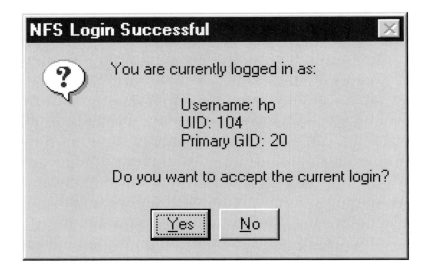

Figure 29-10 NFS *Login Successful*

The *Username*, *UID*, and *Primary GID* correspond to those on the UNIX NFS server. If we view the **passwd** file on the UNIX NFS server system and look for our user *hp*, we'll see the following entry:

```
hp:EkyXw/N.EwFNw:104:20::/home/hp:/sbin/sh
```

The information in this **passwd** entry corresponds to that shown in our *NFS Login* window.

After login takes place, we can view the file systems exported on the UNIX NFS server using *Explorer* on our Windows system. Figure 29-11 shows the *manhattan* LAN with a specific system selected:

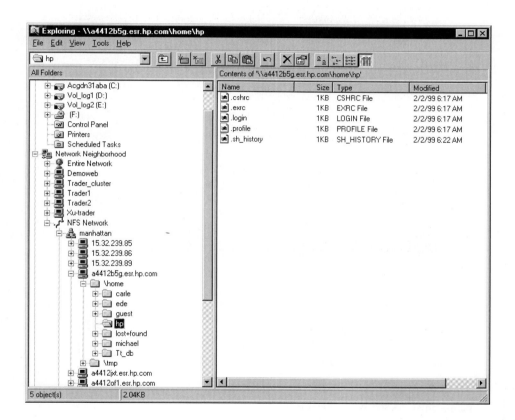

Figure 29-11 Viewing the NFS Mounted File System

\home\hp is selected, and the right *Explorer* window shows the files in the **\home\hp** directory. We have permission to manipulate the files in the **hp** directory. We can check this by selecting a file, such as

.cshrc, and viewing its properties. Figure 29-12 shows the *Properties* window.

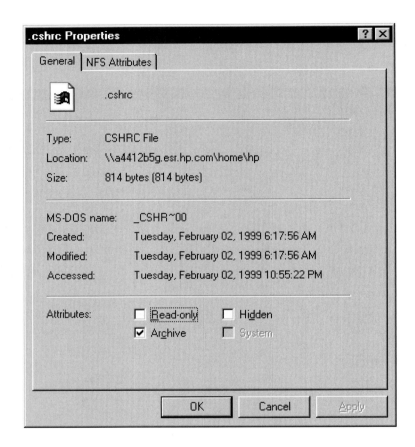

Figure 29-12   SFU *Properties*

The *Read-only* box in this window is not checked; therefore, we have full access to this file.

Telnet Client

There is also a Telnet client loaded as part of SFU. Selecting *Telnet - Telnet Client* from the SFU menu produces the Telnet window shown in Figure 29-13.

man page

telnet - 12

```
Telnet Client                                                    _ □ ×
# ls -al  /home/hp
total 12
drwxr-xr-x    2 hp       users          96 Feb  2 07:17 .
drwxr-xr-x    9 root     root         1024 Feb  2 07:17 ..
-rw-r--r--    1 hp       sys           814 Feb  2 07:17 .cshrc
-rw-r--r--    1 hp       sys           347 Feb  2 07:17 .exrc
-rw-r--r--    1 hp       sys           341 Feb  2 07:17 .login
-rw-r--r--    1 hp       users         446 Feb  2 07:17 .profile
-rw-------    1 hp       sys           144 Feb  2 07:22 .sh_history
#
#
#
#
#
#
#
#
#
#
#
#
#
```

Figure 29-13 SFU *Telnet Client*

I have created a long listing of the contents of **/home/hp** in this Telnet window.

Telnet Server

man page

telnet - 12

There is also a Telnet server loaded as part of SFU. This means you can connect from a UNIX system, or any other system with a Telnet client, to a Windows NT system with the SFU Telnet server. Figure 29-14 shows accessing the Windows Telnet server from a UNIX system:

```
Command Prompt - telnet a4412b5g                                    _ □ ×
*=================================================================
Welcome to Microsoft Telnet Server.
*=================================================================
C:\>dir sfu
 Volume in drive C is ACGDN31ABA
 Volume Serial Number is 3E28-1006

 Directory of C:\sfu

02/02/99   05:12p       <DIR>          .
02/02/99   05:12p       <DIR>          ..
02/02/99   05:12p       <DIR>          common
02/02/99   05:12p       <DIR>          Telnet
02/02/99   05:12p       <DIR>          Shell
02/02/99   05:12p       <DIR>          DiskAccess
02/02/99   05:12p       <DIR>          help
02/09/99   06:08p       <DIR>          DiskShare
02/09/99   06:08p       <DIR>          PswdSync
               9 File(s)               0 bytes
                         586,285,056 bytes free

C:\>
```

Figure 29-14   SFU *Telnet Server*

In Figure 29-14, I have initiated a Telnet session from my UNIX system to my Windows system. After receiving the welcome information from the Microsoft Telnet server, I can issue commands, such as the **dir** shown, exactly as I would from the prompt if I were working directly on the Windows system.

The Telnet server functionality of SFU gives some direct access from UNIX to Windows, which is a big help in mixed environments.

This functionality is further enhanced by many UNIX utilities that you can run on the Windows system through this Telnet connection or on the Windows system directly. The next section, "UNIX Utilities," covers these utilities.

UNIX Utilities

One highly desirable capability of SFU is a UNIX Command Shell invoked with *Unix Utilities - Unix Command Shell*. Figure 29-15 shows a window open with the UNIX utilities listed.

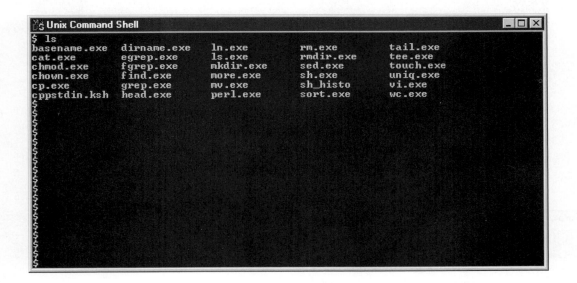

Figure 29-15 SFU UNIX Utilities Listed

The utilities listed in Figure 29-15 work in SFU just the way they work in UNIX. You also have access to these UNIX utilities through a

man page

pwd - 16

Telnet session that you can establish from another system. To give you an idea how these utilities work, let's issue a few commands, as shown in Figure 29-16.

```
Unix Command Shell                                              _ □ ✕
$ pwd
C:/SFU/Shell
$ cd /
$ pwd
C:/
$ ls
AUTOEXEC.ADT                      Multimedia Files
AUTOEXEC.BAT                      NT4SP3
Acrobat3                          NTOPTION
BOOT.BAK                          Program Files
COMMAND.COM                       SETUP
CONFIG.SYS                        SFU
DMI                               TT4D
FIRSTBOO.TXT                      TT4S
HP_INFO                           TTHS
I386                              Temp
IE401SP1                          Toptools
Inetpub                           WINNT
Internet Explorer 4.01 SP1 Setup  boot.ini
LAN                               pagefile.sys
MOUSE                             webhelp
MktData                                        .
$
$
$
$ _
```

Figure 29-16 SFU Example of Using Some UNIX Utilities

man page

cd - 16

man page

ls - 15

This window shows that when we invoke *Unix Utilities,* we are in the **C:/SFU/Shell** directory on our Windows system. We change directory to **C:** by issuing **cd /**, as we would on a UNIX system. **pwd** confirms that we are at the **C:** level. We then issue an **ls** to see the files in **C:**.

Let's issue two more of the *Unix Utilities* to get a better feel for how these utilities perform in Windows, as shown in Figure 29-17:

```
 ₃5 Unix Command Shell                                              _ □ ×
$ ls │ grep -i s
CONFIG.SYS
FIRSTBOO.TXT
IE401SP1
Internet Explorer 4.01 SP1 Setup
MOUSE
Multimedia Files
NT4SP3
Program Files
SETUP
SFU
TT4S
TTHS
Toptools
pagefile.sys
$ ls │ grep -i s │ wc
      14      20     166
$
$
$
$
$
$
$
$
$
```

Figure 29-17   SFU Example of Using Some UNIX Utilities

man page

ls -15

man page

grep - 19

In this window, we issued an **ls** and a **grep** command that ignored case (-*i*) and searched for *s*. Files that contained both upper- and lowercase *s* were listed. We then piped this same output to **wc** to get a word count.

NFS Server

Not only can a Windows system act as an NFS client, but it can also act as an NFS server with SFU. A system running NFS can mount a file system exported on a Windows system.

Under *Server for NFS Configuration,* you can configure all aspects of your NFS server setup. The defaults for most categories of configuration are fine for initial testing, which we'll perform here. You may want to later perform additional configuration to tune your NFS server.

For our example, I've created one *Share Name,* as shown in Figure 29-18.

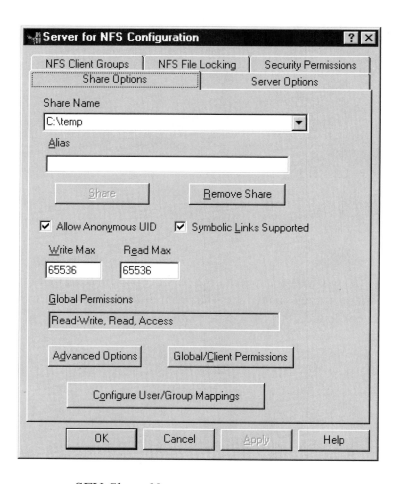

Figure 29-18 SFU *Share Name*

By selecting **Server for NFS Configuration** from the menu and then *Share Options,* I entered the *Share Name* **C:\tem**p shown in Figure 29-18.

We can view *Mount Information* to see what file systems we have exported, as shown in Figure 29-19.

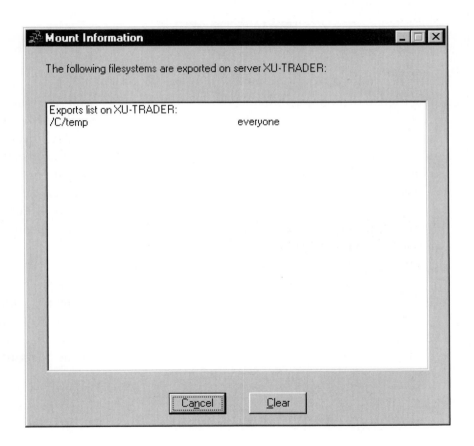

Figure 29-19 SFU *Mount Information*

Our file system of **C:\temp** is indeed in the exported list with no restrictions on who may access it.

With this *Share Name* having been established, we can use the defaults for all other categories of NFS server configuration and mount **C:\temp** on a UNIX system. To mount **C:\temp**, you would issue the following command on your UNIX system:

man page

mount - 8

```
# mount 19.32.23.112:C:\temp /ntmount
```

This command will work on most UNIX systems. We have first specified the mount command, which you would normally issue as root. Next is the name of the Windows system that has the file system we wish to mount on it; in this case, I have used the IP address rather than the system name. The system name, or IP address, is followed by a colon (:). Next is the name of the file system we wish to mount as it appears on the Windows system, in this case **C:\temp**. Last is the name of the directory on the UNIX system under which we'll mount **C:\temp**, in this case **/ntmount**. You can also add a variety of different options with the **mount** command, but we'll use all defaults in our example.

Let's now check to see whether indeed the NFS mount we specified has been established on the UNIX system. The following example shows issuing the **bdf** command (which is somewhat similar to the **df** command covered earlier in this book) on the UNIX system to see whether the mount has been established, then a **cd** to the **ntmount** directory, and finally an **ls** of the files in this directory:

man page

bdf - 8

man page

cd - 16

```
# bdf
Filesystem             kbytes      used     avail %used Mounted on
/dev/vg00/lvol3        151552     53165     92162   37% /
/dev/vg00/lvol1         47829     14324     28722   33% /stand
/dev/vg00/lvol8        163840     87595     71039   55% /var
/dev/vg00/lvol7        339968    314984     23189   93% /usr
/dev/vg00/lvol6        102400     62284     37607   62% /tmp
/dev/vg00/lvol5       1048576    656649    367439   64% /opt
```

```
/dev/vg00/lvol4        69632    32448     34850   48%  /home
/dev/vgCE/lvpatch    1024000     1357    958732    0%  /ce/patches
/dev/vgCE/lvfw        512000     1294    478856    0%  /ce/firmware
/dev/vgCE/cetmp       512000   419166     87028   83%  /ce/ce-tmp
19.32.23.112:temp    2096160  1523360    572800   73%  /ntmount
# cd /ntmount
# ls
_istmp0.dir         test.html          ~df8ec8.tmp        ~dfd65e.tmp
_istmp1.dir         tt2.exe            ~df8ee7.tmp        ~dfd65f.tmp
_istmp2.dir         tt3.exe            ~dfa393.tmp        ~dfd660.tmp
ie401sp1.exe        ttdemo.zip         ~dfa394.tmp        ~dfd66b.tmp
ie4setup.exe        ttwiz(1).exe       ~dfa3a3.tmp        ~dfd66c.tmp
jack.log            wbemcore.exe       ~dfa3a4.tmp        ~dfe649.tmp
jack1.log           winzip70.exe       ~dfb2a.tmp         ~dfe64a.tmp
jack2.log           ~df7e2f.tmp        ~dfb39.tmp         ~dfe64b.tmp
mmc14.tmp           ~df7e40.tmp        ~dfb3a.tmp         ~dfe64c.tmp
mmcaaa7.tmp         ~df7e41.tmp        ~dfd63c.tmp        ~dfe659.tmp
mmcaaad.tmp         ~df7e42.tmp        ~dfd63d.tmp        ~dfe65a.tmp
mmcaab1.tmp         ~df7e4f.tmp        ~dfd64c.tmp        ~dfe65b.tmp
nph-ntfinal.exe     ~df7e50.tmp        ~dfd64d.tmp        ~dfe65c.tmp
ntagt33e.exe        ~df7e51.tmp        ~dfd64e.tmp        ~dfe65d.tmp
ntoption.exe        ~df7e52.tmp        ~dfd64f.tmp        ~dfe669.tmp
sfu                 ~df7e53.tmp        ~dfd65b.tmp
sfu1                ~df8e99.tmp        ~dfd65c.tmp
temp.log            ~df8ea9.tmp        ~dfd65d.tmp
```

man page

cd -16

man page

ls - 15

After issuing this command, we see **/ntmount** as one of the file systems mounted on the UNIX system. At this point, I changed to a user other than root, because it is inadvisable in general for root to be manipulating files on an NFS mounted file system. I changed to user *hp*. We will next change directory to **/ntmount** and view its contents that correspond to those under **C:\temp** on the Windows system. Issuing a long listing, we see the files with ownership of *hp*:

```
$ ll
total 5710
drwxrwxrwx    2 hp        users             64 Feb   9 17:58 _istmp0.dir
drwxrwxrwx    3 hp        users             96 Feb   2 10:18 _istmp1.dir
drwxrwxrwx    2 hp        users             64 Feb   2 10:19 _istmp2.dir
-rwxrwxrwx    1 hp        users       24227193 Feb   1 19:50 ie401sp1.exe
-rwxrwxrwx    1 hp        users         443160 Jan 10 10:21 ie4setup.exe
-rwxrwxrwx    1 hp        users            218 Feb 10  1999 jack.log
-rwxrwxrwx    1 hp        users            218 Feb 10  1999 jack1.log
-rwxrwxrwx    1 hp        users            218 Feb 10  1999 jack2.log
-rwxrwxrwx    1 hp        users          60416 Feb   2 15:26 mmc14.tmp
-rwxrwxrwx    1 hp        users         102400 Feb   9 09:24 mmcaaa7.tmp
-rwxrwxrwx    1 hp        users         102400 Feb   9 12:40 mmcaaad.tmp
-rwxrwxrwx    1 hp        users         102400 Feb   9 12:40 mmcaab1.tmp
-rwxrwxrwx    1 hp        users         464200 Feb   1 19:33 nph-ntfinal.exe
-rwxrwxrwx    1 hp        users        5514240 Feb   1 17:43 ntagt33e.exe
-rwxrwxrwx    1 hp        users       38940572 Feb   1 20:07 ntoption.exe
drwxrwxrwx   20 hp        users            640 Feb   3 09:58 sfu
drwxrwxrwx    5 hp        users            160 Feb 10  1999 sfu1
-rwxrwxrwx    1 hp        users            218 Feb   2 11:34 temp.log
```

```
-rwxrwxrwx   1 hp        users            35 Feb  1 19:48 test.html
-rwxrwxrwx   1 hp        users       7046429 Feb  1 20:19 tt2.exe
-rwxrwxrwx   1 hp        users       5758110 Feb  1 20:21 tt3.exe
-rwxrwxrwx   1 hp        users       3232301 Feb  3 15:18 ttdemo.zip
-rwxrwxrwx   1 hp        users       1086772 Feb  1 16:53 ttwiz(1).exe
-rwxrwxrwx   1 hp        users       3456925 Feb  1 19:55 wbemcore.exe
-rwxrwxrwx   1 hp        users        943949 Feb  3 15:51 winzip70.exe
-rwxrwxrwx   1 hp        users          4096 Feb  2 15:26 ~df7e2f.tmp
-rwxrwxrwx   1 hp        users          3584 Feb  2 15:26 ~df7e40.tmp
-rwxrwxrwx   1 hp        users          3584 Feb  2 15:26 ~df7e41.tmp
-rwxrwxrwx   1 hp        users          3584 Feb  2 15:26 ~df7e42.tmp
-rwxrwxrwx   1 hp        users          3072 Feb  2 15:26 ~df7e4f.tmp
-rwxrwxrwx   1 hp        users          3072 Feb  2 15:26 ~df7e50.tmp
-rwxrwxrwx   1 hp        users          3584 Feb  2 15:26 ~df7e51.tmp
-rwxrwxrwx   1 hp        users          3584 Feb  2 15:26 ~df7e52.tmp
-rwxrwxrwx   1 hp        users          3584 Feb  2 15:26 ~df7e53.tmp
-rwxrwxrwx   1 hp        users          9728 Feb  9 09:24 ~df8e99.tmp
-rwxrwxrwx   1 hp        users          3072 Feb  9 09:24 ~df8ea9.tmp
-rwxrwxrwx   1 hp        users          5120 Feb  9 09:24 ~df8ec8.tmp
-rwxrwxrwx   1 hp        users          3584 Feb  9 09:24 ~df8ee7.tmp
-rwxrwxrwx   1 hp        users          6144 Feb  2 15:26 ~dfa393.tmp
-rwxrwxrwx   1 hp        users          9728 Feb  2 15:26 ~dfa394.tmp
-rwxrwxrwx   1 hp        users          3072 Feb  2 15:26 ~dfa3a3.tmp
-rwxrwxrwx   1 hp        users          5120 Feb  2 15:26 ~dfa3a4.tmp
-rwxrwxrwx   1 hp        users          3072 Feb  9 09:24 ~dfb2a.tmp
-rwxrwxrwx   1 hp        users          3072 Feb  9 09:24 ~dfb39.tmp
-rwxrwxrwx   1 hp        users          3072 Feb  9 09:24 ~dfb3a.tmp
-rwxrwxrwx   1 hp        users          4608 Feb  9 09:24 ~dfd63c.tmp
-rwxrwxrwx   1 hp        users         16384 Feb  9 09:24 ~dfd63d.tmp
-rwxrwxrwx   1 hp        users          4608 Feb  9 09:24 ~dfd64c.tmp
-rwxrwxrwx   1 hp        users          3072 Feb  9 09:24 ~dfd64d.tmp
-rwxrwxrwx   1 hp        users          3072 Feb  9 09:24 ~dfd64e.tmp
-rwxrwxrwx   1 hp        users          3072 Feb  9 09:24 ~dfd64f.tmp
-rwxrwxrwx   1 hp        users          3072 Feb  9 09:24 ~dfd65b.tmp
-rwxrwxrwx   1 hp        users          3072 Feb  9 09:24 ~dfd65c.tmp
-rwxrwxrwx   1 hp        users          3072 Feb  9 09:24 ~dfd65d.tmp
-rwxrwxrwx   1 hp        users          3072 Feb  9 09:24 ~dfd65e.tmp
-rwxrwxrwx   1 hp        users          3072 Feb  9 09:24 ~dfd65f.tmp
-rwxrwxrwx   1 hp        users          8192 Feb  9 09:24 ~dfd660.tmp
-rwxrwxrwx   1 hp        users          4608 Feb  9 09:24 ~dfd66b.tmp
-rwxrwxrwx   1 hp        users          3072 Feb  9 09:24 ~dfd66c.tmp
-rwxrwxrwx   1 hp        users          4096 Feb  9 09:24 ~dfe649.tmp
-rwxrwxrwx   1 hp        users          3584 Feb  9 09:24 ~dfe64a.tmp
-rwxrwxrwx   1 hp        users          3584 Feb  9 09:24 ~dfe64b.tmp
-rwxrwxrwx   1 hp        users          3584 Feb  9 09:24 ~dfe64c.tmp
-rwxrwxrwx   1 hp        users          3584 Feb  9 09:24 ~dfe659.tmp
-rwxrwxrwx   1 hp        users          3072 Feb  9 09:24 ~dfe65a.tmp
-rwxrwxrwx   1 hp        users          3072 Feb  9 09:24 ~dfe65b.tmp
-rwxrwxrwx   1 hp        users          3584 Feb  9 09:24 ~dfe65c.tmp
-rwxrwxrwx   1 hp        users          3584 Feb  9 09:24 ~dfe65d.tmp
-rwxrwxrwx   1 hp        users          3584 Feb  9 09:24 ~dfe669.tmp
$
```

We do indeed see that user *hp* and the corresponding group of *users* are part of this long listing.

The NFS Server setup we have performed in this section can be combined with the NFS Client setup performed earlier to allow the Windows file system to be exported as part of the NFS Server and imported as part of the NFS Client. The extent to which you use NFS as part of your file-sharing strategy depends on the makeup of your environment. Because NFS is available on most all UNIX variants, you may find that using NFS on Windows makes sense for your environment. If you expect heavy NFS use in a mixed Windows and

UNIX environment, you may want to start small, with a few key directories shared using NFS, and test its performance to make sure that it is adequate for your users. As you can see from the previous examples, NFS on Windows can greatly enhance the overall file sharing in your mixed Windows and UNIX environment.

Password Synchronization

SFU synchronizes Windows passwords to UNIX. I didn't include an example of this synchronization. There is an encrypted file sent from Windows to UNIX containing password information. The file should be set to read-only for root. There is also a daemon that is required to implement the password synchronization. After the setup is complete, user passwords on UNIX will be synchronized with those on Windows.

Appendix A

Virtual Partitions Background

Partition Background

The two partition types supported on HP 9000 systems running HP-UX 11i are hard and virtual partitions. At the time of this writing, hard partitions are available on Superdome systems and consist primarily of hardware components that are combined to form the hard partition. Virtual partitions are available on many HP 9000 systems and are meant to be created, modified, and deleted on-the-fly.

This appendix consists mostly of information on virtual partitions from a white paper produced by HP entitled *hp virtual partitions*. This white paper is on the CD-ROM in its original form. I've taken the information from this white paper and reformatted it with permission from HP because it contains so much useful background information on virtual partitions.

Virtual Partitions (vPars)

For effective partitioning, it's necessary to isolate operating environments such that multiple applications can coexist on the same server or cluster, while assuring complete privacy. In addition, it's often necessary to dynamically create, modify, or even delete the isolated operating environments on a running server without interrupting non-related partitions. To meet this need, HP has developed HP Virtual Partitions - a unique technology that provides application (including name space) and operating systems isolation that runs on single server nodes or nPartitions (hard partitions on Superdome). Available for L-Class, N-Class, and Superdome server nodes, these virtual partitions can be dynamically created using software commands. Each partition runs its own image of the HP-UX 11i operating system (or later) and can host its own applications in a fully isolated environment. Within each virtual partition, up to 64 resource partitions can be created and utilized using solutions such as Process Resource Manager and HP-UX Workload Manager.

HP Virtual Partitions is a powerful, flexible tool that makes it possible to run multiple workloads-each with their unique OS configuration requirements-on the same server at the same time. It's also extremely well suited for making more effective use of underutilized server nodes. Additionally, HP Virtual Partitions are ideal for testing new or enhanced products in a production environment without the need to duplicate the entire environment. Figure A-1 is an example of a single N-Class server running four vPars:

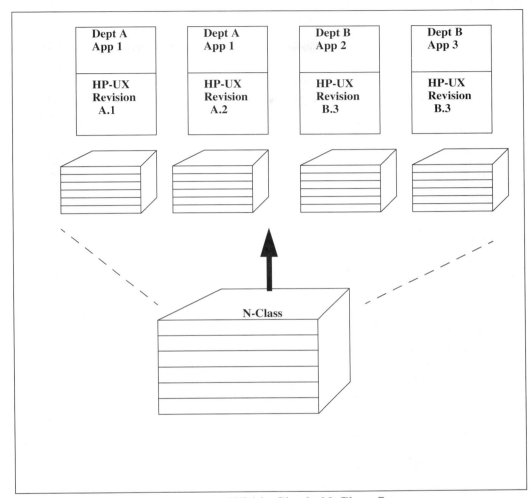

Figure A-1 Virtual Partitions Within Single N-Class Server

vPar Features

Many users of Enterprise-class systems find utilization rates rarely above 50%. These characteristics are attributable to a variety of reasons, but much is dependent upon servers being dedicated to a single application, which rarely fully utilizes the system.

vPars allow an administrator to allocate a subset of the system resources to each partition. Now each partition can run separate instances of the operating system with different OS versions, applications, or users. In general, a vPar will own a specified amount of memory or one or more ranges of physical memory, a specified pool of CPUs, and a set of I/O cards in the server.

Many users deploy multiple servers for reasons other than additional CPU capacity. For example, ISPs deploy small Web servers for customers that need to manage their own content. The reason for this hype of the deployment is to maintain customer data isolation in addition to improving performance. vPars can provide a means for isolating one set of users from another.

vPars allow greater flexibility in configuring servers. For example, many businesses have applications that are cyclic in nature such as payroll, end-of-month billing, etc. Many times, the cycles for the applications are not aligned. Normally, servers need to be configured to handle peak loads. This can lead to poor utilization as discussed above. With vPars, applications can be allocated to a larger percentage of the system resources during the peak usage times and utilize less resources during off-peak times. This frees up hardware resources that can be assigned to other vPars, where the applications may be experiencing a high demand for these resources.

In addition to reconfiguration to cover peak loads, many times operating system adoption rates are slowed because all parts of all solutions that run on the server must be available and qualified before a server can be upgraded. vPars provide a way to do rolling OS and software upgrades on a given server. With vPars, the server can be partitioned into multiple operating system revisions. Applications available on the new OS release can take advantage of the new features. Those applications not yet available on the new OS can be executed on the same system, but run on an older version of the OS.

vPars can be used to set up isolated partitions as test environments. This could be for new revisions of current applications or for the deployment of new applications. vPars allow testing on the exact deployment environment. This improves the quality of the test without replicating the cost of the deployment environment.

In traditional server environments, all CPUs within a server run the same OS instance and one or more applications. Application and OS failures may affect the entire system. For this reason, running fine-grained vPars can limit the impact of application or OS failures on overall application availability. For improved single system availability, vPars allows you to run one application per partition. When a software failure does occur in one of the partitions, the application of that particular partition may be lost, but the rest of the applications on the other partitions continue to run. In fact, even if the OS panics in one of the partitions, applications running on the other vPars are not affected.

One of the inherent problems in a single system is the difficulty in expanding CPU resources when the demands of the application or multiple applications exceed the server's configuration. Usually the system would need to be shut down and additional CPUs added. With vPars, a large server could have CPUs dynamically moved from one vPar to another without bringing the entire system down. This would allow resources to be moved to vPars with the greatest demands, or they could be removed from vPars when they are no longer required.

Here is a bullet list of some significant vPar features:

- Core functionality is available for free with every HP-UX 11i release.
- Support for HP 9000 L-Class, N-Class, and SuperDome (including nPartitions)
- Support of multiple HP-UX instances (HP-UX 11i and later)
- Different virtual partitions can run different versions of HP-UX
- Single CPU granularity (virtual partition may contain single CPU)
    L-Class-recommended up to 2 virtual partitions (max. 4)
    N-Class-recommended up to 4 virtual partitions (max. 8)
    Superdome-recommended up to 32 virtual partitions (max. 64)

- Dynamic reassignment of CPUs across virtual partitions
- Software fault isolation (application, including name space, and OS isolation)
- Individual reconfiguration and reboot are supported in vPars. - virtual partitions don't affect each other.
- Command line interface (in future via GUI)
- Single toggle console
- Compatible with PRM, HP-UX WLM, ServiceControl Manager, and MC/ServiceGuard

vPars Operational Overview

To understand how vPars work, it is best to compare it to a generic HP-UX server. Figure A-2 shows a 4-way HP-UX server. Without vPars, the entire server would be controlled by a single instance of HP-UX. All of the resources (CPU, Memory, and Disk) would be dedicated to the applications running in this single instance. The software stack for this server would look like the one in Figure A-3.

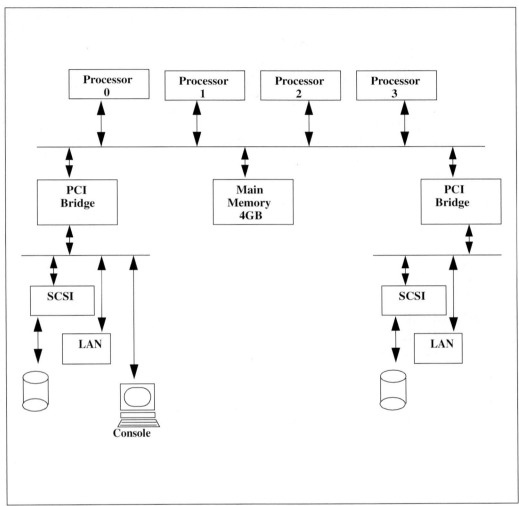

Figure A-2   Generic HP-UX Server Block Diagram

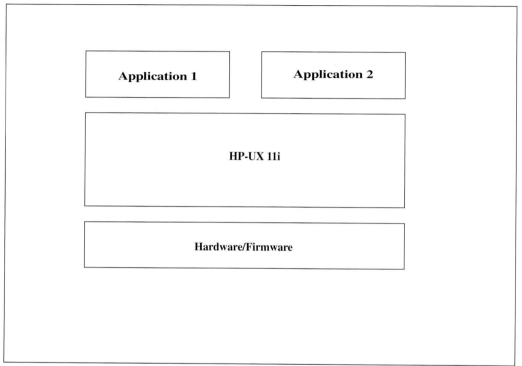

Figure A-3   Generic HP-UX Server Software Stack

Using vPars, the server in Figure A-3 can be broken into two partitions, each with a subset of the hardware (Figure A-4). Each vPar has its own boot disk, at least one CPU, one LAN connection, and enough memory to run HP-UX and the applications that are intended to be hosted on this vPar. Since each vPar can run its own copy of HP-UX (potentially at different release versions or patch levels), each is completely isolated from software errors, system panics, etc. A software stack for two vPars is shown in Figure A-5.

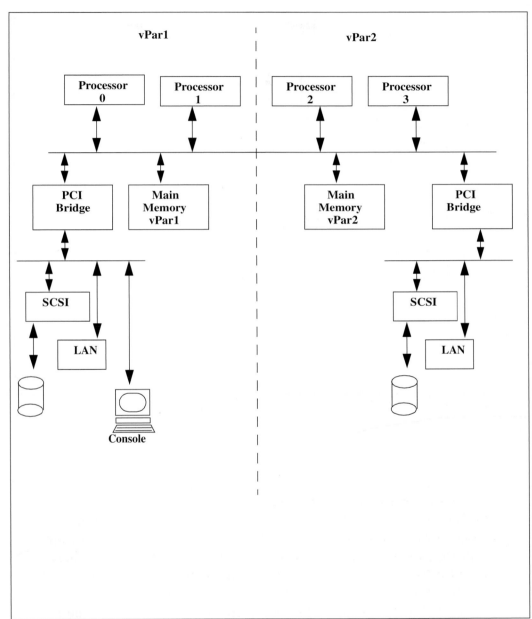

Figure A-4 Generic HP-UX Server Block Diagram with Two vPars

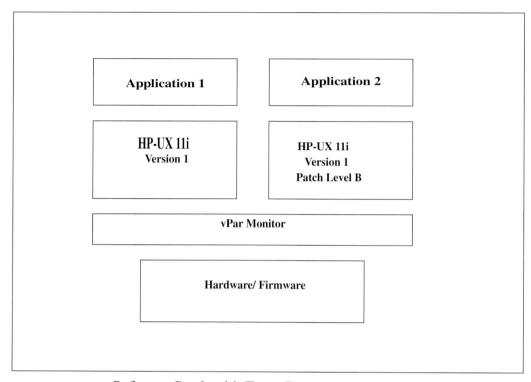

Figure A-5   Software Stack with Two vPars

Notice that there is an additional layer of software in the vPar software stack, the Virtual Partition Monitor (vPar Monitor). The vPar Monitor manages the partitioning of the resources and creates the illusion for each instance of HP-UX that it is on a standalone system with only the resources that have been dedicated to that vPar. Each instance of HP-UX is completely unaware of the additional hardware in the system. The individual instances of HP-UX have complete ownership of the hardware resources they've been assigned to. The monitor is not involved in accessing I/O hardware or physical memory once it has transferred ownership of the hardware to a vPar.

The Virtual Partition Monitor, or vPar Monitor, manages resources, loads kernels, and emulates global platform resources to create the illusion that each individual vPar is a complete HP-UX system. At the heart of the monitor is the partition database that tracks what resources are associated with which vPar. When the vPar Monitor is running, the master copy of this database is kept in the monitor. All changes to the partition database are preserved across system reboots.

In a system running without vPars, the HP-UX kernel is booted directly by the secondary loader from the Initial System Loader (ISL) prompt using a command like:

```
ISL>hpux /stand/vmunix
```

If vPars are used, the vPar Monitor is booted from ISL instead of HP-UX. The monitor will then load the individual vPars. In a system with vPars, this initial load command would look like:

```
ISL>hpux /stand/vpmon
```

The monitor code is loaded from the file **/stand/vpmon** on the system boot device in the same way as a normal HP-UX kernel would be loaded from the file **/stand/vmunix**. The monitor loads the partition database from **/stand/vpdb** and internally creates each vPar according to the resources allocated to each one in the database. If there are no command-line options, the monitor is booted in interactive mode with a command-line interface. Once the vPars are up and running, the vPar Monitor is infrequently invoked. The monitor is invoked only when HP-UX makes calls to the firmware, when the OS is shutting down, or when vPars management commands are executed.

Commands to create and manage the virtual partitions will be listed shortly.

Hardware and Software Support for vPars

The first release of vPars will be supported on L-Class and N-Class Servers running HP-UX 11i. SuperDome partitions will be supported shortly after first release. Plans to support other operating systems on an IA-64 platform such as Windows or Linux are under investigation.

The recommended number of vPars for HP 9000 servers is up to 2 vPars on an L-Class, up to 4 vPars on an N-Class, and up to 32 vPars on a SuperDome (a maximum of up to 4, 8, and 64, respectively). vPars are also supported within nPartitions of SuperDome consisting of multiple cells. Each cell can support up to two vPars. CPUs are not shared or time-sliced between vPars. A vPar can be configured to have just one CPU. HP Virtual Partitions also provides operational flexibility by allowing you to reassign CPUs from one partition to another-without having to reboot the affected partitions.

Memory allocation for vPars is done by specifying either the amount of memory or one or more physical memory ranges. Under no circumstances is sharing of physical memory allowed between multiple vPars. Each vPar will require a minimal amount of memory for booting HP-UX and running the applications.

Dynamic re-assignment of physical pages among vPars without rebooting is being investigated, but will not be supported at first release.

The first release of vPars requires that each Local PCI Bus Adapter (top-level PCI bus) is assigned to, at most, one vPar. Therefore, the Local Bus Adapters (LBAs) and interface cards attached to those LBAs may not be shared among vPars. Sharing of LBAs and interface cards will be investigated for future releases of vPars.

The system console on a standalone (non-partitioned) server serves two distinct and unique purposes. First, the system console is used to monitor and interact with the Guardian Service Processor (GSP) and Initial System Loader (ISL). Additionally, the system console is used to monitor and interact with HP-UX, particularly when the system is in single-user mode or when networking or terminal services are unavailable. With vPars, the system console continues to be used for interacting with GSP and ISL. However, each vPar may designate a separate serial port to be used for its vPar console for monitoring and interacting with HP-UX. Alternatively, a vPar may elect to use a "virtual console." When configured to use a virtual console, the vPar uses the system console in a multiplexed fashion. When the system console is multiplexed among several vPars, a system administrator with access to the system console may open a console session on any of those vPars.

Managing vPars

There are a set of commands for creating and managing vPars. The definitions of the vPars are stored as a binary file on one or more of the vPar boot disks. The default location is **/stand/vpdb** on the disk that the monitor image was loaded from-usually the system boot device. Changes made to the partition database are synchronized with the monitor and preserved across reboots. The commands can be issued from any of the active vPars, provided appropriate user permission is granted.

There are a number of vPar commands available to the system administrator. These commands can be executed from any active vPar. A summary follows:

vpcreate - create a vPar, with or without resources

vpdestroy - destroy a vPar, where the partition definition is removed and all resources associated with the given vPar are reclaimed by monitor.

vpadd - add resources to an existing vPar

vpremove - remove resources from an existing vPar

vpmodify - modifies attributes of an existing vPar (such as changing the boot device)

vpboot - start a vPar

vpreset - stop a vPar

vpdisplay - display one or more vPar definitions, including resources and attributes associated with each defined vPar

vpstatus - check status (up or down) of one or more vPars

At first release, all vPar commands will need to be performed via a command line interface from an active vPar. The next release of vPars will have support for both SAM (System Administrator Manager) and SCM (ServiceControl Manager). Both these tools will help system administrators adopt vPars and ease both management and monitoring of vPar environments.

vPars and Security

Each virtual partition functions like a standalone server and thus is administrated via the root user like any other HP-UX server. vPar commands to modify vPars are performed by root. A root user on any vPar can run vPar commands for its vPar or any other vPar on the system. With this in mind, certain security features have been incorporated into the vPars implementation to alleviate potential security problems. A summary of these features follows:

- Protection against applications in one vPar intentionally or accidentally stomping on or reading another vPar's memory.

- Resources (such as CPU or Memory) cannot be accessed simultaneously by two vPars. Resources must first be removed from one vPar, then added to another.

- Non-root users cannot create, modify, or destroy vPars.

- A resource must be available before it can be added to a vPar

- Two vPar commands can run simultaneously from two different vPars, but all access to the monitor will be serialized.

- The monitor ensures that the partition database is synchronized with the monitor's internal state.

vPars and System Isolation

In traditional server environments, all CPUs within a server run a single OS instance and one or more applications. Application and OS failures may affect the entire system. With HP Virtual Partitions, however, the software stack contains the vPar Monitor between the hardware/firmware level and the OS, allowing each partition to support a different instance of HP-UX 11i (or later), with each instance capable of being at a different version and patch level.

Consequently, if any virtual partition crashes, only that particular virtual partition is affected-providing complete software isolation. This isolation of OS at the version and patch level also enables rolling OS and application upgrades.

There are shared hardware components on a system or Super-Dome hardware partition whose failure could bring down the entire server or hard partition, including all the vPars. Virtual Partitions are not necessarily isolated from the failure of a hardware resource that is bound to another vPar. Increased isolation of some hardware failures to a single vPar is being considered for a future release.

A high-availability system configuration requires at least two paths from each vPar to any critical device. Special care needs to be taken when designing the highest availability within a vPar environment. MC/ServiceGuard can be used to improve application availability.

vPars and iCOD, ServiceGuard, and Others

Instant Capacity on Demand (iCOD) is an option available on many HP 9000 servers. This allows a fully populated CPU configuration for the server, but only a subset of CPUs have to be activiated initially. Additional CPUs can be "turned on" via a command-line interface.

Together, iCOD and vPars offer unique configuration opportunities for system administrators on HP 9000 servers. At the first release, coexistence of both iCOD and vPars on a single server will not be supported; however, support is planned for a future release.

MC/ServiceGuard will be supported on vPars. However, because of the various vPar configurations on HP 9000 servers and Superdome hardware partitions, careful design criteria will need to be adhered to. By the first release of vPars, the MC/ServiceGuard Support Organization will supply recommended guidelines for using vPars in mission critical implementations.

HP's resource partitioning solutions - Process Resource Manager (PRM) and HP-UX WorkLoad Manager (WLM) - enable dynamic and goal-based resource management respectively. These solutions allow one to distribute system resources among different workloads on a single system or a single OS instance. HP PRM and HP-UX WLM are compatible with vPars, providing an additional degree of flexibility and control within a virtual partition.

vPar Example

Let's now take a look at the way in three vPars can be implemented on an N-Class system (Figure A-6).

Our example uses an 8-way N-Class server. We want to partition the system such that the three following vPars are setup:

vPar Number	0	1	2
vPar Name	Bergen	Oslo	Trondheim
Bound CPU Hardware Paths	33, 37	41, 45	105, 109
Physical Memory Ranges	0x01000000 (112 MB) 0x40000000 (512 MB)	0x08000000 (128 MB) 0x60000000 (1024 MB)	0x10000000 (128 MB) 0xA0000000 (1024 MB)
I/O Hardware Paths	0/0/* 0/4/*	0/8/* 1/10/*	0/5/* 1/4/*
Special Devices	Boot: 0/0/2/0.6.0 Console: 0/0/4/0 LAN: 0/0/0/0	Boot: 0/8/0/0.5.0 Console: Virtual LAN: 1/10/0/0/4/0	Boot: 1/4/0/0.5.0 Console: Virtual LAN: 0/5/0/0/4/0
Kernel Image	/stand/vmunix	/stand/vmunix	/stand/vmunix

Figure A-6 vPar Definition for 8-Way N-Class Example

"Bergen" will own the entire core I/O and therefore will use the built-in disk at 0/0/2/0.6.0 as its boot device and the built-in LAN at *0/0/0/0*. "Oslo" will have a SCSI card installed in slot #4 (hardware path *0/8/0/0*) for its boot disk and a network adapter card installed in slot #9 (hardware path *1/10/0/0*). "Trondheim" will have a SCSI card installed in slot #9 (hardware path *1/4/0/0*) for its boot disk and a network adapter in slot #1 (hardware path *0/5/0/0*).

Using the normal HP-UX installation procedures covered in Chapter 2 we install a copy of HP-UX 11i and vPar product patches on one of the boot disks. Any of the disk formats supported by HP-UX may be used.

Next, we create the vPar database. Since the primary boot path for the system corresponds to *Bergen's* boot disk, we will create the partition database there. With the system booted on *Bergen's* boot disk, we execute the following commands to create **/stand/vpdb**:

```
# vpcreate Bergen -C -P 33 -P 37 -M 0x01000000:112MB\
-M 0x40000000:512MB -i 0/0/* -i 0/4/* -i 0/0/2/0.6.0:boot\
-i 0/0/4/0:console -k /stand/vmunix -A auto:on


# vpcreate Oslo -C -P 41 -P 45 -M 0x08000000:128MB\
-M 0x60000000: 1024MB -i 0/8/* -i 1/10/* -i 0/8/0/0.5.0:boot\
-k /stand/vmunix -A auto:on


# vpcreate Trondheim -C -P 105 -P 109 -M 0x10000000:128MB\
-M 0xA0000000:1024MB -i 0/5/* -i 1/4/* -i 0/4//0/0.5.0:boot\
-k /stand/vmunix -A auto:on
```

The following are descriptions of the options used in the previous commands for *Bergen*:

-C (Create database file if it doesn't exist)

-P 33-P 37 (Add processors at hardware paths 33 and 37)

-M 0x01000000:112MB (Physical memory range, base:size)

-i 0/0/* (Add I/O device at specific hardware path)

-i 0/0/2/0.6.0:boot (boot device for vPar)

-i 0/0/4/0:console (console device for vPar)

-k /stand/vmunix (kernel image to boot)

-A auto:on (autoboot attribute set to on)

After having completed these steps, we reboot the system to the vPar Monitor. This is done by rebooting *Bergen* and interrupting the boot process at the ISL as described in Chapter 1. At the ISL prompt, instead of launching **/stand/vmunix**, we launch **/stand/vpmon** and have **vpmon** launch *Bergen*:

```
ISL>hpux /stand/vpmon loadvp Bergen
```

The secondary loader (**hpux**) will locate, load, and launch the vPar monitor (**vpmon**), which will then locate, load, and launch *Bergen's* kernel (**vmunix**).

Now we have to install the remaining vPars. From *Bergen's* command line, we boot the remaining vPars from the Ignite/UX install media with the following commands.

```
# vpboot oslo -I- <IgniteServer>
# vpboot trondheim -I <IgniteServer>
```

The procedure just covered results in the three vPars defined in Figure A-6.

Booting the vPar Monitor is very similar to booting HP-UX. Instead of specifying **/stand/vmunix** on the command line or in the **AUTO** file, **/stand/vpmon** is specified.

To launch *Oslo* from the ISL prompt, the following command can be used:

```
ISL> hpux /stand/vpmon loadvp Oslo
```

To launch all vPars from the ISL command line, use the *-all* option to the **loadvp** command:

```
ISL> hpux /stand/vpmon loadvp -all
```

Migrating CPUs Between Running vPars

Migrating CPUs among running vPars is supported in the first release of vPars. A vPar must be brought down before changing other resources such as memory.

In terms of CPU migration, the first release implements the concept of "bound" and "floating" CPUs. This is required since HP-UX does not currently have the capability of reassigning I/O interrupts dynamically between CPUs. CPUs that have I/O interrupts assigned to them are called "bound" CPUs because they are bound to a given vPar. CPUs not bound to any vPar are called "floating" CPUs and can be temporarily assigned to a vPar via **vpadd**.

Notice that in defining *Bergen*, *Oslo,* and *Trondheim,* we allocated two CPUs to each as bound CPUs. Since it is an 8-way system, there are two CPUs left that are floating. As long as the configuration of a vPar is not marked as static (via the *static* attribute for the **vpcreate** or **vpmodify** commands), the floating CPUs can be added or removed to a vPar without rebooting.

To add a floating CPU to *Oslo*:

```
# vpadd Oslo -p 1
```

The *-p* option is used to specify that a single CPU is to be added, but the monitor chooses which CPU to use. Conversely, to remove a CPU from *Oslo*:

```
# vpremove Oslo -p 1
```

The commands will return an error if there are no more CPUs to add or remove. The **top** (manual page *1m*) command or GlancePlus/UX can be used to see which CPUs are active in a vPar.

Viewing vPar Resources

vpdisplay shows all resources associated with a vPar. With the *-a* option, **vpdisplay** lists the resources for all defined vPars. Here's what the output looks like for *Bergen, Oslo,* and *Trondheim*:

```
# vpdisplay -a
VP: Bergen Attributes: AUTOBOOT Bound CPU: 33 Bound CPU: 37
Memory range: Base:0x01000000 (112MB) Memory range:
Base:0x40000000 (512MB) I/O: 0.0.* I/O: 0.4.* I/O:
0.0.2.0.6.0 BOOT I/O: 0.0.4.0 CONSOLE Kernel Image: /stand/
vmunix
VP: Oslo Attributes: AUTOBOOT Bound CPU: 41 Bound CPU: 45 Mem-
ory range: Base:0x08000000 (128MB) Memory range:
Base:0x60000000 (1024MB) I/O: 0.8.* I/O: 1.10.* I/O:
0.8.0.0.5.0 BOOT Kernel Image: /stand/vmunix
VP: Trondheim Attributes: AUTOBOOT Bound CPU: 105 Bound CPU:
109 Memory range: Base:0x10000000 (128MB) Memory range:
Base:0xA0000000 (1024MB) I/O: 0.5.* I/O: 1.4.* I/O:
1.4.0.0.5.0 BOOT Kernel Image: /stand/vmunix
```

vPar Status

The **vpstatus** command is used to determine the state of other vPars. With no arguments, **vpstatus** indicates whether the current system is running in a vPar or not. To determine the state of all vPars, the *-a* option is used. The status of a specific vPar can be obtained by specifying it on the command line. **vpstatus** reports the following states: *up, down, hung,* and *crashing*. "up" means that the monitor has launched it and has not detected a crash or hang. "hung" means that the vPar has stopped issuing heartbeats to the monitor. "crashing" means that the vPar has notified the monitor that it is going down ungracefully (panic or reset). "down" means that its resources have been returned to the monitor and the vPar is ready to be booted.

```
# vpstatus -a
0 Bergen : up
1 Oslo : up
2 Trondheim : down
```

Resetting a vPar

Just as it is occasionally necessary to issue a hard reset or TOC command (soft reset) for an HP-UX system, it is occasionally necessary to reset a vPar that is hung.

To issue a hard reset on a system, the administrator types a *CNTL-B* at the console to connect to a service processor and then types the command **rs** to initiate the hard reset. This still works with vPars, but it resets the entire system, including the monitor. Using **vpreset**, a vPar can be sent an emulated hard reset as follows:

```
# vpreset Bergen -h
```

The *-h* causes an emulation of a hard reset. It also has the side-effect of overriding the current autoboot setting for that vPar; therefore, the vPar must be manually restarted via vpboot.

To issue a soft reset (TOC) on a system, a **tc** command is sent to the service processor instead of an **rs**. A soft reset allows HP-UX to attempt to capture some state and potentially create a crash dump. If a *TOC* is issued on a system with vPars, a system soft reset is initiated and no vPar state is captured. A vPar can be soft reset using **vpreset** without the *-h* option. As with a *TOC* on a non-vPar system, HP-UX gets a chance to capture state and save a crash dump. That vPar then either shuts down or reboots according to the setting of the autoboot attribute for that vPar.

Other vPars are unaffected when a vPar is reset.

Instant Capacity on Demand (iCOD)

When you order iCOD, you'll receive a server with up to the full complement of processors (four for the L-Class, eight for the N-Class, 32 for the V-Class, and 16, 32, or 64 for SuperDome depending on your model). You can get a server fully loaded with CPUs, yet you pay only for the processors you plan to use on day one—there is no charge for the extra CPUs. When your needs change and you require more processing power, you can instantly activate the needed processors with a simple HP-UX command.

In the future, HP intends to expand the program to include other server components (such as memory and I/O). In addition, COD programs are being looked at for storage su-systems and HyperPlex (clusters). Long term, HP will move to a complete "utility-based" pricing model for our servers and storage infrastructure.

vPar URLs

The following list of references provides useful background information on related products and topics:

vPar Product Information
http://www.hp.com/go/servicecontrol

vPar User's Guide
http://docs.hp.com/hpux/

Instant Capacity on Demand (iCOD)
http://www.hp.com/go/icod

Appendix B

NFS Performance Assessment

HP-UX 10.X/11.0/11i NFS Performance Assessment

The following document is intended to help narrow the scope of an HP- UX 10.X/11.0/11i NFS performance problem down to a specific HP-UX OS subsystem, such as the TCP/IP ARPA transport, local NFS processes, remote NFS server, link interface, external network, etc. These steps can also be used with HP-UX 11.0/11i NFS over TCP. Many of the steps listed below are typically done during a live dial-up support event by HP.

Some of the steps are intended to gather pertinent data and interpret that data, and others are simply meant to gather data for later analysis by HP. The entire document is intended to educate the reader on the issues and scope of assessing an NFS performance problem.

Defining Performance Measures

The first step in assessing any performance problem is to understand the performance measurements being taken. Typically performance issues are first noted in the use of real applications as opposed to pure performance tests. In that case, care needs to be taken in understanding what the real application is doing in detail in order to understand all the OS and network resources being utilized.

A common performance slowdown scenario encountered is when NFS copy times of large amounts of data would intermittently get quite long. Times for a 'good' copy and a 'slow' copy were noted. When the nature of the copy was investigated it was revealed that the 'copy' was actually a retrieval of many different files from many different servers on the network. This greatly broadens the list of potential causes for poor performance. For this reason, it is necessary to simplify the performance testing as much as possible to address/eliminate as many variables as possible. By defining a test that evaluates each component separately, the performance issue can be narrowed to a specific source/subsystem more quickly.

The following subsystems/areas are involved in any NFS client/ server interaction and we should try to assess the health of each subsystem separately:

• HP-UX local file system resources

• HP-UX local memory management

• HP-UX local client automount/map configurations

• HP-UX local NFS related RPC daemons

• HP-UX TCP/IP "ARPA" transport stack

• HP-UX Interface link. 10/100BaseT typically

• External network switches/routers/interconnect devices

• External NFS servers

• Name resolution services, either local or remote; DNS/NIS in general.

• Application-specific resources such as file locks and other IPC mechanisms.

As you can see finding root cause for an observed NFS performance issue can entail quite a lot of detailed investigation into many different subsystems. The remainder of this document is intended to narrow down a performance issue (as much as possible) into one of these areas.

HP-UX Local File System Resources

This is primarily an issue for NFS servers. There are many components to consider that can have an impact on performance. Let's cover the most important in the following list:

Review kernel tunables that affect the size of name cache and inode cache such as *ninode* and *ncsize*. Tools such as GlancePlus can report on the DNLC (Dynamic Name Lookup Cache) hit/miss rates and can be used to tune these values.

Review the directory structure layout. Thousands of files at one directory level for example, will drastically affect performance for NFS requests using/ accessing files in that directory.

File system fragmentation can be a problem. This causes slow access times (*open( )* and *close( )* system calls) for local non-NFS usage as well.

Local File system type can have a big impact on performance. HFS has better write performance that JFS due to the journaling mechanism inherent in the JFS file system. The tradeoff:, however, is buffer cache problems with HFS filesystems. See "HP-UX local memory management" below.

File system usage and management should be considered. Don't let filesystems constantly be 100% full.

Use of symbolic links, particularly if the link points back to an automounter managed path name can have an affect on performance. The use of symbolic links causes extra NFS requests for lookups involving these files. In some cases, it can cause delays while the real path of a file is resolved by the server or client.

HP-UX Local Memory Management

This is an issue on both the HP-UX NFS client and server sides. Things to check/consider that can affect performance are shown below:

The maximum size of the buffer cache on an HPUX NFS client should be 10% of main memory, or ~300Mbytes, which ever is least. Excessive buffer cache size causes poor performance due to the overhead of buffer cache management involving NFS, particularly if HFS filesystems are in use for the local filesystem.

The same 10% or 300MB guideline holds true for an NFS Server using HFS disks. However, most NFS Servers use VxFS filesystems, which do not have these same buffer cache issues. Size the buffer cache with VxFS filesystems to whatever size will maximize HP-UX VxFS Performance (e.g., 50% or larger).

The above values are rules of thumb but are widely used with great success in a wide range of systems from workstations to high-end large servers. Tools such as **vmstat** and GlancePlus can be used to monitor the pagein and pageout rates as well as the buffer cache hit rates.

It is assumed that memory utilization in general is well below 100% and peaks to 100% infrequently. Many tools exist to monitor memory usage, such as **vmstat**, **top**, and GlancePlus.

When data is read repeatedly in multiple performance test runs, much of the file data will actually be found to be still present and valid in local buffer cache. During such tests, an unmount and remount of the NFS server file system is required to ensure consistent results from test run to test run. This is a common cause of inconsistent NFS performance measurements.

HP-UX Local Automount and Map Configurations

If the automounter is used extensively in the environment, you will need to pay attention to the options specified in the maps for various servers. Things to consider that can affect client NFS performance:

Read/write size is specified. This is a consideration when the network topology MTU size and IP fragmentation through a router are concerns. By tuning the read/write size, accommodations can be made for network topology limitations. For example, if an NFS server on FDDI with a 4K MTU is causing a router to perform IP fragmentation, the client could request a read/write size of less than 1460 bytes to ensure all replies from the server will not need to be fragmented. The trade-off is more requests to transfer the total amount of data read or written.

Attribute caching, which is generally a good thing to have (it is enabled by default), can greatly affect performance test results due to the hidden use of the cache from test run to test run. To be sure an apples-to-apples comparison is being made, disabling attribute caching can be done temporarily.

Synchronous vs. Asynchronous Writes

NFS Version 2 vs. Version 3 is specified. The NFS V3 protocol has many performance-related improvements over the V2 protocol and can greatly affect system -to system performance results if the systems are not using the same protocol. Not all servers and clients support both V2 and V3.

Replicated Server lists should be careful to ensure that all servers are correct, i.e., they exist, are up, and have the labeled mount point exported.

Automounter environment variables (the *-D* command-line option for auto-mount) are correct and reflect options/paths that truly exist on the servers.

The timeout value for unused file systems (default is 5 minutes) should be made sufficiently large to avoid unnecessary mounting and unmounting. The appropriate value depends on the NFS client's usage patterns for the mounted file systems. If using AutoFS indirect maps, the OS will attempt to unmount the NFS file system when the timeout value expires. When this is done, the buffer cache for the automounted file system is cleared, even if the filesystem is busy. This can cause performance issues should large programs be referenced over the AutoFS indirect map mount point, even when using CacheFS.

HP-UX Local NFS-Related Daemons

This section gets rather involved, but we will start with the client side RPC daemons and discuss what tasks they perform and what to do when a task seems to be delayed or involved in a performance issue. Then we will look at the NFS server-side daemons and what can contribute to performance issues for those processes, and how to measure and observe their activities.

NFS client processes are (in no particular order):

• automount/automountd

• biod

• rpc.lockd and rpc.statd

• rpcbind (11.X/11i) or portmap (10.X)

• autofs_proc AutoFS kernal process

NFS server side daemons are:

• nfsd

• rpc.mountd

• rpc.pcnfsd (if so configured)

• rpc.lockd and rpc.statd

• rpcbind (11.X/11i) or portmap (10.X)

• nfskd NFS Server kernal process (11.X/11i)

Let's now take a closer look at the items in the bullet list beginning with the NFS client side first:

automount/automountd - This is a client side process that is configured to monitor access to certain defined directories which it manages and (based on the automount maps) mount a file system with certain options under that mount point. This all happens transparently to the user accessing the automount managed path. This process is a single threaded process and can be affected by delays in some of the common tasks it performs. Name resolution problems can delay automount from processing requests in a timely fashion. For instance, if automount maps point back to local mounts on the same system, there is interaction with the local rpc.mountd daemon. A common problem is a non-responsive rpc.mountd daemon on another NFS server that automount is trying to access. To determine exactly what automount is spending it's time doing, you can enable debug logging to the default log file under **/var/adm/automount.log**. To do this, send a **kill -17** signal to the automount process. It will start verbose debug logging to the log file until another **kill -17** is sent to it. The resulting output can then be read to determine exactly what the process is doing. In some cases the output may not be incredibly meaningful with HP assistance, but the output is non-the-less important.

If the automount process appears to be hung, under no circumstances should you send it a hard kill (as in a **kill -9**), as this will leave certain kernel structures in place which will require a reboot to clear. The man page on automount talks about this explicitly.

A point to remember: once an NFS server is mounted, the automounter's job is done. Any performance issues from that point forward should not involve automounter.

biod - This is the client-side kernel process that handles process requests over an NFS mount point. Each biod is single threaded on HP-UX 10.20/11.X, and thus having the correct number of them configured for the client is important. By default, four biod's are started for an NFS client. Depending on the number of different processes running using NFS, the number of different NFS servers accessed, and the response times from the NFS servers, the number of biods can be increased. Often 8 to 16 are used. A process writing large files to an NFS Server can monopolize biods under some circumstances. We have seen cases where running 0 biods improved point-to-point performance when only using a single NFS read/write process on the system. To observe what these biods are doing, you can use a number of tools to track the NFS client requests. The most obvious is 'nfsstat -c' which dumps to NFS client statistics for the system. The types of calls and events it reports are all tasks performed by the biods and the supporting kernel NFS code.

An example of how to use these statistics to roughly locate the source of poor performance would be as follows:

```
hp10cux2$ nfsstat -c


Client rpc:
calls       badcalls    retrans     badxid      timeout     wait        newcred
1081        0           0           10          8           10          0

Client nfs:
calls       badcalls    nclget      nclsleep
1074        0           1074        0
null        getattr     setattr     root        lookup      readlink    read
0   0%      240 22%     0   0%      0   0%      636 59%     0   0%      34  3%
wrcache     write       create      remove      rename      link        symlink
0   0%      0   0%      0   0%      1   0%      0   0%      0   0%      0   0%
mkdir       rmdir       readdir     statfs
0   0%      0   0%      160 14%     3   0%
```

For the above statistics the items of note are the number of retransmissions, timeouts, and badxids. The following is a description of some of the entries:

calls - The total number of RPC calls made.

badcalls - The total number of calls rejected by the RPC layer.

retrans - The number of times a call had to be retransmitted due to a timeout while waiting for a reply from the server.

badxid - The number of times a reply from a server was received which did not correspond to any outstanding call.

timeout - The number of times a call timed out while waiting for a reply from the server.

wait - The number of times a call had to wait because no client handle was available.

newcred - The number of times authentication information had to be refreshed.

Since the number of badxids received is roughly the same as the timeouts, this indicates that the NFS server involved is simply late or slow in responding, perhaps due to load. The late reply will be seen as a transaction ID which is no longer valid. The read/write sizes and timeout values can be altered in the mount options to accomodate this on a per server basis.

If the retransmit/timeout rates are an order of magnitude larger than the badxid count, it would indicate that the replies were simply dropped/lost somewhere in transit to or from the server. To isolate where in the path the packets are being dropped, a network trace using the client (nettl tracing in HP's case), server, or an external analyzer is needed. Some switches/routers keep statistics on packet loss on a per port basis as well.

The **nfsstat -m** command can be used to show per-mount performance statistics to help isolate which servers are slow in responding. A slow or unresponsive NFS Server can degrade overall HP-UX NFS client performance. A slow or unresponsive server with have consis-

tent response times of 100msec or greater in **nfsstat -m** output. This
output looks like the following:

```
hp10cux2$ nfsstat -m
mnt from hp10cux6:/tmp (Addr 15.24.46.26)
                Flags:   hard,int, read size=8192, write size=8192,  count = 4
        Lookups:  srtt=  7 ( 17ms), dev=  4 ( 20ms), cur=  2 (40ms)
                Reads:    srtt=  7 ( 17ms), dev=  3 ( 15ms), cur=  2 (40ms)
                All:      srtt=  7 ( 17ms), dev=  4 ( 20ms), cur=  2 (40ms)

slowmnt from slowserv:/export (Addr 15.24.100.41)
                Flags:   hard,int, read size=8192, write size=8192,  count = 4
        Lookups:  srtt=  7 ( 400ms), dev=  4 ( 60ms), cur=  2 (540ms)
                Reads:    srtt=  7 ( 380ms), dev=  3 ( 15ms), cur=  2 (360ms)
                All:      srtt=  7 ( 400ms), dev=  4 ( 55ms), cur=  2 (410ms)
```

Here you can see the NFS server called "slowmnt" is running 10x
slower than the NFS server called "hp10cux6". Repeat the **nfsstat -m**
to see if the pattern continues, or if the issue is transient or temporary.

rpc.statd and rpc.lockd - The man page for these two RPC daemons describes their basic purpose, but what follows is a detailed
description. Suffice it to say that sending a SIGUSR2 (**kill -17**) signal
to the processes enables debug logging output for interpretation by HP
or other brave souls.

As for performance, the biggest contributor in this area is application-level contention for file locks.

Details of how **rpc.lockd** and **rpc.statd** are implemented step by
step follows:

1. a user process issues a lock system call

2. when the kernel resolves the file name to an rnode, it contacts the
local (client) lock daemon.

3. the lock daemon contacts its local status daemon to request monitoring.

4. the status daemon returns to the lock daemon.

5. the client lock daemon queries the server portmap for the server lock daemon's port number.

6. the server portmap replies with the server lock daemon's port number.

7. the client lock daemon sends a lock request to the server lock daemon.

8. the server lock daemon contacts its status daemon to request client monitoring.

9. the status daemon replies to the lock daemon.

10. the server lock daemon contacts its kernel for the lock.

11. the kernel replies with the lock result.

12. the server lock daemon queries the client portmap for the client lock daemon port number.

13. the client portmap replies with the client lock daemon's port number.

14. the server lock daemon replies to the client lock daemon with the results of the lock request.

15. the client lock daemon returns to the kernel.

16. the kernel returns the system call to the calling process.

17. In the event of a server crash, upon recovery, the server status daemon will notify the client status daemon that locks were lost and must be reclaimed. The client will reissue a request for any locks held before the crash by repeating Steps 5 through 14.

Not all of these details can be captured in **nettl** since some of the steps are handled within system calls and not on the network. However, details that can assist in debugging NFS file-locking problems can be captured using the lockd and statd logging facilities. In releases 10.X/11.X of HP-UX this logging can be invoked by sending the SIGUSR2 signal to the daemon (e.g. **kill -17**).

rpcbind (11.X/11i) or **portmap** (10.X) - This process manages the registration and mapping of RPC program numbers to UDP/TCP port numbers. The information it provides is used by local and remote RPC's to communicate with the registered RPCs on the system. For performance issues, it is important to know that the port numbers currently used by clients are correct and consistent with the registered ports currently in use on the system. For example, the UDP port number used to communicate with the rpc.mountd on an NFS server is obtained by querying the portmap process on that server. As a supporting piece of information, the current port assignments for the RPC programs on a system are obtained via **rpcinfo -p localhost** and likewise the same information from any system can be obtained via **rpcinfo -p**. This same utility can be used to test the health of any registered RPC program by sending it a NULL procedure request, which simply tests to see if the RPC server process is responding. Typical usage is:

`/usr/sbin/rpcinfo` [-n portnum] -u host program [version]

for a UDP query and

`/usr/sbin/rpcinfo` [-n portnum] -t host program [version]

for a TCP query.

The value of this usage of **rpcinfo** is to monitor an RPC process and/or ID an RPC process that is non-responsive on the local system or a remote system. This makes it possible to create scripts to monitor the health of the processes used in NFS server environments. In fact, it is common in MC/ServiceGuard environments to use the MC/ServiceGuard NFS Toolkit monitoring script, which uses **rpcinfo**.

autofs_proc AutoFS kernal process - This process is used by the AutoFS filesystem to perform kernal tasks in user space code. Kernel helper processes have a PPID of 0 and are not killable.

The NFS server side daemons not yet covered are:

nfsd - There can be any number of these daemon processes running on a server. The nfsd daemons are the ones which receive the client NFS requests and service those requests. Each is single threaded and handles one request at a time. The default number of them on an HP system is four. The nfsstat command reports the server side statistics via **nfsstat -s**. The rpcinfo command can be used to send them a NULL procedure request (**rpcinfo - u localhost 100003**) to see if they are responding. The client side **nfsstat -m** output is a better measure of exactly how responsive this server is being.

Information on what these processes are doing can be found by using nettl tracing, nettl logging, and repeated use of the **nfsstat** command. For reference, nettl tracing is the HP network tracing facility that allows tracing network traffic at many different layers, including UDP, TCP, IP, LINK etc. The **nettl** subsystem also allows for logging facilities for use by some kernel subsystems like NFS. By default, there is no nettl tracing enabled and only ERROR and DISASTER level nettl are logging enabled. The command to enable **nettl** tracing is:

```
nettl -tn pduin pduout -e all -tm 90000 -s 1024 -f raw
```

To stop tracing, use the following:

```
nettl -tf -e all
```

This will create one or two output files containing raw, unformatted trace data for all kernel subsystems that support tracing. It can, on a busy server, fail to keep up with the traffic rate and often must be used to trace only specific subsystems such as ns_ls_ip which is the IP transport layer. The **nettl -ss** command will show all subsystems and the man page provides other usage options. An example of tracing only at the IP layer would be:

```
nettl -tn pduin pduout -e ns_ls_ip -tm 90000 -s 1024 -f raw
```

To format the traces, use **netfmt -n -lN -f raw.TRC0** (or raw.TRC1 depending on which of the two possible output files you want to format..TRC0 will always contain the most recent data and the .TRC1 file is the file the older data is wrapped to.)

To increase **nettl** logging for any subsystem (again enter **nettl -ss** to list all subsystems), use:

```
nettl -l i w e d -e ns_ls_nfs
```

This will enable the Informative level as well as the Warning level of the NFS subsystem.

The **nettl** log output goes into a file called **/var/adm/nettl.LOG00** or **.LOG01** for later formatting using the **netfmt** command, as in **netfmt -f /var/adm/nettl.LOG00**.

Interpretation of nettl traces for NFS performance purposes usually involves formatting the trace and looking for duplicate transaction IDs in the requests going out or the replies coming back. Sometimes, the purpose of the trace is to observe what types of requests a process is making, to whom, and what the requests/replies look like..ie replies indicating the request failed, etc. This phase of the data analysis can be very time consuming, so care should be taken to capture as tight a sample of data surrounding a problem as possible.

The raw nettl trace can be formatted using filters to extract specific UDP/TCP/IP port numbers as well as RPC call direction and time.see the netfmt man pages for details.

In a situation where the nfsds are all *busy/hung/non-responsive*, it will be useful to see what the kernel stack trace is for the processes to see what they are stuck/sleeping on. The tool for doing this is known as q4 and is found in **/usr/contrib/bin**. The HP Response Center can assist in usage of the tool if the problem has been narrowed down to hung nfsds. An option for gathering the q4 data live is to take a memory dump (TOC the system) and these same tools can be used to analyze the dump.

rpc.mountd - This server side daemon is responsible for processing mount requests from NFS clients, including requests from the local system. It is a single threaded process and handles mount requests in a serial fashion. If an NFS server is being reported as *not responding,* it may be due to delays in the mounting process. In that case, you could do the following to determine if the rpc.mountd daemon is alive and well on the server in question:

```
rpcinfo -p | grep mountd /* see if rpc.mountd is registered */
rpcinfo -u mountd /* rpc.mountd is ok via UDP */
rpcinfo -t mountd /* rpc.mountd is ok via TCP */
kill -17 /* enable debug logging */
```

Attempt mount or simulate work load :

```
kill -17 /* disables debug logging */
```

view the **/var/adm/rpc.mountd.log** file for debug output.

If the **rpc.mountd** process is running (**ps -elf** shows a running rpc.mountd process) but the above rpcinfo commands get no reply, the q4 utility can again be used to try to determine if the process is sleeping in kernel code, and if so, where. Also, a **nettl** trace at the IP layer could be gathered to see if there is any traffic to/from the ports that **rpcinfo -p** shows the NFS server **rpc.mountd** using. This trace can be gathered on the NFS client or server side (assuming the NFS server is HP).

In an environment that makes extensive use of automount, you will have to refer to the automount maps in some cases to determine which server(s) the mount request is going to.

nfskd - NFS Server kernal process (11.X/11i) This process is used to by the NFS Server subsystem to perform kernal tasks in user space code. Kernel helper processes have a PPID of 0 and are not killable.

HP-UX TCP/IP ARPA Transport Stack

The ARPA transport stack provides the UDP/TCP/IP delivery for the NFS-related traffic. There are a number of different tools and methods by which the health of this subsystem can be determined. For purposes of NFS performance, the goal is to determine if the transport itself is a contributing factor in a performance problem. To do this, we can eliminate the NFS layer by simply testing for delivery or packet loss problems using non-NFS protocols. If there is a packet delivery problem between an NFS client and server, the problem would affect any IP protocol, not just NFS over UDP. Some tests to perform:

- Start by noting current ARPA transport statistics:

```
netstat -s > netstats.baseline /* netstat reports all kinds
of TCP/UDP/IP/ICMP stats */
```

- Perform an FTP 'put' from the local system to a remote FTP server file of **/dev/null**:

```
ftp> put ./largefile /dev/null
```

- Perform an FTP 'get' from another FTP server to the local /dev/null

```
ftp> get largefile /dev/null
```

The use of **/dev/null** avoids the file system commit time that can affect the throughput times.

Once some of these tests are run, the **netstat -s** output can be re-gathered to get a delta on the various statistics. Of most concern would be the TCP retransmissions, and completely duplicate packets. These statistics steadily increasing would indicate packet loss (any IP protocol packet loss, not just TCP) in the network topology. Packet loss like this would show up as NFS timeouts and retransmissions and badxids in the **nfsstat -c** output.

Other tools exist to measure transport throughput time for UDP and TCP as well. A well known tool is netperf, and a simpler contributed tool is ttcp (for Test TCP). Both are designed to measure raw transfer rates, and in the UDP case, packet loss. In evaluating the UDP statistics (most current NFS implementations use UDP) as reported by netstat -p UDP , there are a few items of interest to note. Since most of the NFS related daemons listen on UDP sockets, the socket overflow statistic can be an indicator that the local system deamon is unable keep up with the rate of inbound traffic destined for that UDP port. Unfortunately, the statistic does not tell you which UDP had the overflow condition. On 11.0, the Streams based transport stack will send an ICMP SourceQuench message in response to a socket overflow, and thus through nettl tracing you can determine when and on which UDP sockets the overflow occurred. If the socket involved is the 2049 UDP port, this is the well-known port for NFS and could be an indication that the NFS server is overloaded.more nfsd's may help, but an overall review of the system's performance would be in order.

Another **netstat -p** UDP output statistic is the UDP checksum error. If UDP checksum errors are occurring, it indicates that another IP level device in the network (perhaps a router doing IP fragmentation) is not correctly fragmenting or passing on the UDP datagrams.

The goal for this phase of investigation is to determine if the network throughput problem is affecting any and all IP traffic or is it only affecting NFS traffic. If there appears to be a network throughput issue, it may still be inside the HP system (the interface link itself) but external analyzers may be needed to further isolate the root cause. The suggested methods listed in the previous section can be used to gather traces of the transport traffic.

HP-UX Interface Links

There is one more HP subsystem that handles NFS traffic to consider and that is the network interface card itself. Again, at this level problems do not seek out and afflict the NFS protocol alone, but rather would affect any and all network traffic. The commands used to check the state of the interface link can vary based on the interface type (FDDI, Gigabit, 10/100bt, etc.), but there are common utilities that apply to all links that can be queried first.

The **lanadmin** utility can be used to look at various link states and statistics. Lanadmin reports the following types of statsistics:

```
LAN INTERFACE STATUS DISPLAY
Network Management ID                    = 5

Description                              lan0Hewlett-PackardLANnterface
Hw Rev 0
Type (value)                            = ethernet-csmacd(6)
MTU Size                                = 1500
Speed                                  = 10000000
Station Address                         = 0x8000962d46e<
Administration Status (value)                = Ip(1)
Operation Status (value)                = up(1)
Last Change                             = 4240
Inbound Octets                          = 1367077289
Inbound Unicast Packets                 = 2229272<
Inbound Non-Unicast Packets             = 11441297
Inbound Discards                        = 0
inbound Errors                          = 0
Inbound Unknown Protocols               = 2038323
Outbound Octets                         = 231493601
Outbound Unicast Packets                = 2102972
Outbound Non-Unicast Packets            = 990
Outbound Discards                       = 0
Outbound Errors                         = 0
Outbound Queue Length                   = 0

Specific                                = 655367

Alignment Errors                        = 0
FCS Errors                              = 0
Single Collision Frames                 = 4754
Multiple Collision Frames               = 6944
Deferred Transmissions                  = 40830
```

```
Late Collisions                    = 0
Excessive Collisions               = 0
Internal MAC Transmit Errors       = 0
Carrier Sense Errors               = 0
Frames Too Long                    = 0
Internal MAC Receive Errors        = 0
```

The specific link-type considerations such as speed and duplex settings should be verified to be consistent and correct with the network switch equipment attached.

External Network Switches, Routers, and Interconnect Devices

If the performance/packet loss problem appears to be outside the HP system, the various Network management tools used to support the interconnect devices will need to be used. Most equipment will report similar per-port statistics to those listed by **lanadmin** in the previous section. Again, external analyzers are sometimes required to provide the definitive view of the traffic pattern and to isolate a device that is losing packets.

Also of concern in this area is the routing (if NFS client server traffic is between subnets) taken by packets through the network. Routing tables on the NFS client/server need to be checked to make sure the path the traffic is taking through the network is well understood. Utilities such as **traceroute**, **ping -o**, and other network management tools can help map out the traffic pattern in a routed topology.

On the HP system side, the **netstat -rn** command will dump the HP routing tables.

External NFS Servers

The obvious issue here is that the poor NFS performance seen on a client may be due to a non-responsive NFS server(s) elsewhere in the network. The **nfsstat -m** command can be used to check response times on a per-mount basis, but other indications of the non-responsive server can be found on the console output as well as the **/var/adm/syslog/syslog.log** file. It should be noted that the non-responsive NFS server could already be mounted, or the NFS client might be in the process of trying to mount the server. Both would result in similar syslog.log messages.

Name Resolution - NIS and DNS in General

Many of the NFS daemon processes make use of libc calls, which will rely on the NIS/DNS facilities in use on the system. Seemingly poor response from rpc.mountd for example, may be due to the fact that (since it is single threaded) it is hung, waiting for a reply from an NIS/DNS hostname query. If the various debug log files for the NFS daemons indicate hostname/user authentication activity, you may want to verifiy that the name service NIS/DNS facilities are working correctly.

Application-Specific Resource Contention

This area of performance consideration requires an in-depth knowledge of the application using NFS. File locking issues at an application level need to be considered as well as IPC mechanisms. Application-level logging is the best level at which to understand what the processes are doing. The fact that they are accessing files over an NFS mount point may not have anything to do with the resource contention. By using a test scenario that does not include the application itself, many of these application variables can be eliminated.

In Conclusion

There are many factors affecting NFS Performance. These include the Network link layer and switches, the reliability of TCP/IP datagram delivery, the ability of NFS client and server processes to effectively process NFS requests, and applications utilizing NFS resources. NFS performance assessment requires scientific, step-by-step analysis of all these factors, from which solutions may be found.

INDEX

A

Absolute path names, 1108-1111

Accounts for users and groups (in SAM), 563-572

Adding a periperhal, 237-240
    lsdev, 238
    mksf, 238-240

Adding disks, 401-415
  shell program to automate adding disks, 404-407

Adding file system, 411-414

Adding groups and users (in SAM), 563-572

Adding users and groups (in SAM), 563-572

Advanced Server for UNIX ASU, 1645-1662

Agent (Vantagepoint, 761-773)

aio_listio_max, 132

aio_max_ops, 133

aio_physmem_pct, 133

aio_prio_delta_max, 134

acctresume, 135

acctsuspend, 135

Aliases in shell, 140401406

allocate_fs_swapmap, 136

alwaysdump, 137

Amount of available memory, 242-246

Analyzer (Vantagepoint), 761-773

arp, 863-864
    (as part of Secure Web Console setup), 27

Arguments to shell programs, 1501-1503

ARPA (Networking, 805)
  ARPA, 820-823

ASU, 1645-1662

Auditing (system), 991-1050
  disk and file system, 1008-1010
  examples, 1016-1049
  kernel, 1011-1012
  logical volume manager, 1004-1006
  networking, 1012-1015
  performance, 1006-1008
  printer, 1012
  security, 1001-1003
   system configuration repository, 991-997

Auditing and security, 573-577

awk, 1264-1271, 1278-1284

B

Background jobs and job control, 1421-1424

Backup, 289-358
  cpio, 298-303, 317-322
  dump, 313-315
  dd, 311-312, 323-325
  fbackup, 304-310, 326-335
  frecover, 304-310, 336-342
  restore, 313-315
  tar, 292-297, 343-348
  vxdump, 313-315, 349-352
  vxrestore, 313-315, 353-338

S

HP's world-class education and training offers hands on education solutions including:

- Linux
- HP-UX System and Network Administration
- Advanced HP-UX System Administration
- IT Service Management using advanced Internet technologies
- Microsoft Windows NT/2000
- Internet/Intranet
- MPE/iX
- Database Administration
- Software Development

HP's new IT Professional Certification program provides rigorous technical qualification for specific IT job roles including HP-UX System Administration, Network Management, Unix/NT Servers and Applications Management, and IT Service Management.

become hp certified

http://education.hp.com

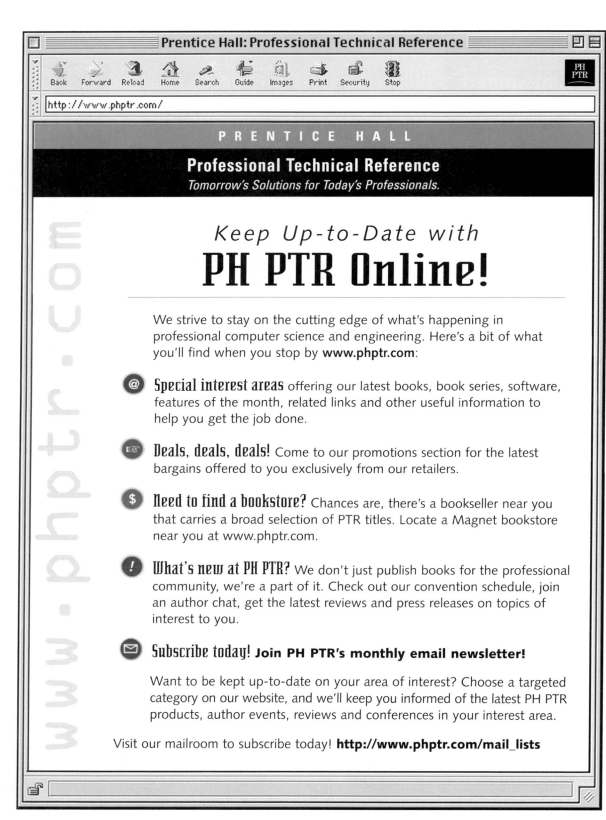

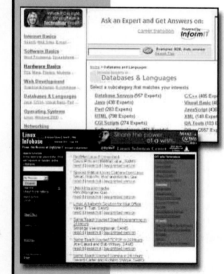

LICENSE AGREEMENT AND LIMITED WARRANTY